SOUTHERN INDIA

THE HOSPITAL SHIP "MADRAS."

Photo by [illegible], Madras.

SOUTHERN INDIA

ITS HISTORY, PEOPLE, COMMERCE, AND INDUSTRIAL RESOURCES

COMPILED BY

SOMERSET PLAYNE

ASSISTED BY

J. W. BOND

EDITED BY

ARNOLD WRIGHT

GYAN

Published by

Gyan Publishing House
5, Ansari Road
Daryaganj, New Delhi-110002
Phone: 011-47034999, 9811692060
E-mail: books@gyanbooks.com

Distribution Network
gyanbooks.com
India, USA, Canada, UK, Australia, France

ISBN : 978-81-212-4053-6 (PB)
First Published, London, 1914-1915

2nd Impression 2020

Printed at: Gyan Press, Delhi.

Southern India
Edited: Arnold Wright

SOUTHERN INDIA

Its History, People, Commerce, and Industrial Resources

COMPILED BY

SOMERSET PLAYNE, F.R.G.S.

ASSISTED BY J. W. BOND

EDITED BY ARNOLD WRIGHT

THE FOREIGN AND COLONIAL COMPILING AND PUBLISHING CO.

27 PILGRIM STREET, LONDON, E.C.

1914–1915

PREFACE

IN submitting this work to the public the compiler deems it desirable to offer a brief explanation of the aims which he has kept in view in carrying through the enterprise. Inspired with the belief that there was an opening for publications dealing in an exhaustive and attractive way with the outlying portions of the Empire, which owing to their marvellous development in recent years present an extraordinary field for literary and pictorial treatment, he formed plans for the production of such a series. He turned his attention in succession to British East Africa and Uganda, the Cape, and the Orange Free State, compiling for each territory a comprehensive book designed on lines suited to modern needs. The unqualified success which attended these ventures in countries in which agriculture was the most important interest led him by a natural stage of development in his plans to New Zealand, whose magnificent natural resources and splendid enterprise place her in the forefront of the agricultural lands, not merely of the Empire, but of the world. As events proved, no happier choice of a subject for literary treatment could have been made. On the one hand there was a wealth of material which ensured immediate success for the venture on its literary and artistic side: on the other there existed in a pronounced form that spirit of friendliness to the projected pictorial and descriptive survey of the Dominion without which the compiler's operations could not have been carried through with advantage to himself or to the interests of New Zealand. The book on publication met with a most flattering reception, and may be said to have found a place amongst the standard literature of the Dominions.

From New Zealand to India is a far cry, but the compiler, when his work was completed in the Dominion, without hesitation directed his steps to the great Eastern possession of the Crown, believing that the features of his books which had met with favour in the regions which had been the scene of the colonizing efforts of the British people would have an equal attraction in India where, though the conditions of life are vitally different, the same spirit of progress animates the commercial community, and infuses new life into the older civilization of the sub-Continent. Landing at Madras, the earliest seat of British power in India, he and his staff at the close of 1913 commenced their labours upon the present work. They met with the greatest kindness and encouragement from all sections of the community, and received assistance from individual officials and others in positions of authority which was of the highest value.

PREFACE

Unfortunately the early prospect that offered of a speedy and successful issue for the venture was placed completely beyond realization by the Great War which burst upon Europe and the world in August 1914. That tremendous catactysm changed the whole face of life in India as elsewhere, and for a time paralysed ordinary business operations. Only when the notorious "Emden" had ceased from troubling, and seaborne commerce took its accustomed course, were normal conditions restored. Since then there has been a healthy reaction which has given to India an enviable pre-eminence for commercial activity amongst the countries under the sway of the Allies. But so far as the present publication is concerned the war has been the source of much delay and many difficulties. Only the kindly co-operation and goodwill of friends have, in fact, made it possible to carry through the programme which was originally sketched. In some particulars, notably in the absence of uniformity in the spelling of names of places and persons, the exact reader may find occasion for criticism, but it is hoped that in these matters allowance will be made for the heavy difficulties which were in the path of the compiler and his staff, in the customs and usages of a community which practises a delightful variety in the rendering in English of Indian names, and which is tenacious of its right to spell as it pleases.

The work in its broad outlines, it may be hoped, may be left to speak for itself. It fills a position apart from the general run of publications relative to India. While it embodies material of a character commonly associated with the admirable works issued from time to time under official auspices, it also embraces literary and popular features not found in those productions, and has, besides, an immense amount of information relative to the purely commercial aspects of life, which are not touched either in the official works or in the ordinary travellers books about India. Moreover, the pages are illustrated by a wealth of photographic material, absolutely without precedent in any literary undertaking dealing with the Indian Empire. These features, literary, utilitarian, and artistic, it is believed from the experience gained elsewhere, and from the cordial reception everywhere given in Southern India to the venture, will ensure for it a friendly welcome from the Indian public, and ultimately a recognized place in the bibliography of the Great Dependency.

CONTENTS

CONTENTS

SOUTHERN INDIA

ITS HISTORY, PEOPLE, COMMERCE, AND INDUSTRIAL RESOURCES

EARLY HISTORY

By ARNOLD WRIGHT

CHAPTER I

Introductory—Southern India in ancient times—The Dravidian kingdoms—The Aryan conquest—The Andhra dynasty—Rival kingdoms—Mahommedan invasion—The rise of the Vizayanagar dynasty—The Bahmani kingdom established—The Mahommedan chiefs of the Deccan—Occupation of Vizayanagar and its subsequent destruction by Mahommedans—Aurungzebe establishes his power in the South.

IN speaking of India, those who are unacquainted with the country are apt to regard it as a self-contained and unified territorial area like France or Spain or Italy. Actually it is more a continent than a country—a continent in which there are even wider differences of race, language, and religion, to say nothing of physical characteristics, than are to be found in Europe itself. British rule has done much in various ways to secure uniformity and to create a true feeling of solidarity amongst India's myriad peoples, but the sense of division remains an insuperable bar to centralizing tendencies be they political, administrative, economic, or social. "East is East, and West is West" is as true when applied to India as it is in the wider meaning given to it by Mr. Kipling. And it may, perhaps, be still more emphatically said of our great Eastern Empire that "North is North, and South is South," for a great gulf separates these geographical divisions. In race and language they are for the most part widely removed from each other, and the respective aptitudes of the population supply contrasts which are as striking as those which differentiate the inhabitants of Northern Europe from their congeners of the Mediterranean littoral.

Southern India derives not a few of its present-day peculiarities from the conditions of the remote past. The successive waves of conquest which swept over India drove before them the aboriginal tribes who inhabited the land before the dawn of history. Many of them found refuge in the wild and hilly region of the South, where they still eke out a hard existence, a pathetic monument of racial tenacity. One of the earliest of the non-Aryan groups of invaders, the Dravidians, firmly settling themselves on the land, gave to Southern India the languages—Telugu, Kanarese, Tamil, and Malayalam—spoken there to-day. They also brought with them the rudiments of civilization and forms of government and customs which, though uncouth and imperfect in modern eyes, were yet far in advance of the tribal organizations they supplanted.

Several powerful kingdoms in course of time grew up in Southern India under Dravidian influence. In the edicts of Asoka (250 B.C.) mention is made of States ruled by the Pandyas, Cholas, and Chuas, and we also catch instructive glimpses of the opulent Dravidian regime in ancient Sanskrit writings. A virile race, the Dravidians maintained their individuality in the face of the pressure of Aryan civilization. Nevertheless, in time the all-conquering people from the North deposed the native dynasties and gave a line of Aryan kings to the then existing Tamil States. Dr. R. G. Bhandarkar, an expert authority on Oriental history, places the period of the establishment of this Aryan ascendancy at between the seventh and the fourth centuries B.C. Under it Southern India flourished in a marked degree. As far back as the fifth century B.C. a great trade was carried on between its ports and Western Asia, and some centuries later, when the Romans entered into commercial relations with India, they found a regular trade being carried on between the Persian Gulf on the one side and Ceylon on the other. Coins of the Andhra dynasty, which flourished between

200 B.C. and A.D. 250, afford testimony to the importance of the maritime interests of these early South Indian States. In one of them appears the device of a two-masted ship, evidently of great size, a symbol, no doubt, of the wide-reaching activities of the country.

Amongst the Southern India States mentioned in the "Ramayana" are the Andhras of the Godavery and the Krishna, the Pandyas of Madura, the Cholas of Tanjore, and the Keralas or Cheras of the West Coast. Especially conspicuous amongst these early Aryan kingdoms was the Andhra dynasty of the Satavahanas, which dates from about two centuries before the Christian era. These kings ruled the whole of the middle of India from sea to sea, and their territory southwards extended as far as the limits of the Tamil kingdoms. Many fine monuments, notably the famous Amravati Stupe, attest the splendour of their period. The dynasty declined in power early in the Christian era, and gave place to new rulers, the principal of whom were the Rashtrakutas, the Guptas, and the Chalukyas and the Pallawas. At the end of the eighth century the Rashtrakutas had asserted their sovereignty over most of the Kanarese speaking districts; but two centuries later they in turn were supplanted by the Chalukyas, who, with the aid of a Malwa king, recovered the territory that had been taken from them at an earlier period, and added to this important areas which they had not hitherto controlled. Another turn in the wheel of destiny brought, in the twelfth century, the Cholas to the front as the leading power of the South. Their domination was not absolute, for in the South was the powerful Pandyan kingdom of Madura, in the North the Warangal Ganpatis held the Telugu country previously ruled by the Eastern Chalukyas, while the Yadavas governed all the territory formerly held by the Western Chalukyas, as well as the Konkan and part of Mysore, and the Deccan was a bone of contention between the Deogiri Yadavas and the Hoysalas.

At the close of the thirteenth century the Mahommedans appeared in Southern India to contest with the existing Hindu dynasties the title to supremacy. The first invasion, which took place in 1294, under the direction of Ala-ud-din Khilji, nephew of Jabal-ud-din, Emperor of Delhi, though attended by some vicissitudes, resulted in the complete submission of Ramachandra, the Yadava king, and the cession of Ellichpur and its territories. Not content with the measure of control given him under this settlement, Ala-ud-din, after he had become emperor in 1307, sent Malik Kafur against Ramachandra, alleging as an excuse for this new act of aggression the non-payment of tribute. Deogiri, the capital, was occupied, and Ramachandra was sent a prisoner to Delhi. He was afterwards released and sent back to his territory. But the days of Hindu ascendancy were numbered, and though he did not live to see the transformation completed, only a few years elapsed before the whole of the Deccan had passed under the government

BRONZE FIGURE OF NATESA OR NATARAJA, THE DANCING SIVA.

of the Mahommedans. The conquest would have been extended much farther had it not been for the action of the Hindus, who, to meet the common danger, united their forces under the leadership of two brothers, men of proved ability. These princes, Harihara and Bukka by name, so cleverly directed the fortunes of their race at this critical period that they built up on the ruins of the old Hindu dynasties a new kingdom. It had as its capital a great city called Vizayanagar, a centre of commercial wealth and intellectual activity, and in its day the most famous Hindu centre in India. In vain the Mahommedans attempted to destroy this upstart power. They not only failed in this, but were compelled to relinquish most of their conquests in the Deccan owing to the valour and energy with which the Vizayanagar kings, aided by their celebrated minister, Madhavacharya, prosecuted their military operations against them. The Mahommedan strength at this juncture was seriously weakened by dissensions culminating in a revolt of the local authorities against Delhi and the establishment in 1347 at Gulburga of what was subsequently to be known as the Bahmani dynasty. Rallying under their new banner the Mahommedans again became a power in the South. Even when in 1481 the Bahmani dynasty disappeared and gave place to seven separate kingdoms created by the most powerful chiefs of the Deccan, the aggressive force of Mahommedanism was not materially weakened. There was rather from this period a fresh development of activity radiating from the separate centres at which the chiefs had established themselves, which were Bijapur, Bidar, Berar, Ahmednagar, and Golconda. The Mahommedans found a formidable opponent in the Vizayanagar king, Krishnadera, who ascended the throne in 1509. A strong, self-reliant, and enlightened ruler, Krishnadera organized the forces of his State with consummate skill, and built up a military power of exceptional magnitude. Nunez, the Portuguese historian, places the size of the Vizayanagar army at this period at seven hundred thousand, and though this is possibly an exaggeration, the force must have been of great strength, for we find it inflicting a crushing defeat upon Adil Shah, one of the strongest of the Deccan chiefs, and seizing Raichore. Unfortunately for Vizayanagar, the virile brain which accomplished these things was taken from it in 1529 or 1530, and the power of the State devolved upon a weak and tyrannical prince, ill-fitted by temperament or training for the stern work of resisting Mahommedan aggression.

The Deccan chiefs were not slow to take advantage of the opportunity which the degenerate new regime supplied for the execution of their design. Joining forces they, in January 1565, marched against the Hindu army and inflicted upon it a crushing defeat at a place north of the Tangabhadra. Rama Raya, the Hindu king, was slain with a vast number of his followers, and his capital was afterwards occupied and so completely destroyed that it disappeared from the list of Indian cities. Driven out of their old home, the representatives of the Vizayanagar dynasty took refuge first at Pemikonda and afterwards at Chandragiri, where they continued to exercise a shadowy authority

1. NUNDY DROOG.
From "Views in the Mysore Country." Published in 1794.

2. RYACOTTAH.
From "Views in the Mysore Country." Published in 1794.

3. HOOLIOOR DROOG.

4. RAMGHERRY.
From "Views in the Mysore Country." Published in 1794.

over the Hindu population for the best part of a century.. Their power, feebly asserted by their deputies, who were sometimes styled Governors and at other times dignified with the title of Viceroy, was ultimately usurped by their representatives, who set up independent principalities. These self-created chiefs included the Naiks of Madura, the Wodojars of Mysore, and the numerous Poligars who, in the later British era, constituted a Hindu aristocracy.

The downfall of Hindu power would have been more complete but for the weakness which developed amongst the Mahommedans as soon as Vizayanagar had been destroyed. At variance amongst themselves, the Deccan chiefs were unable to drive home their conquest of the Hindu capital by a Southern advance. It was not until a good many years afterwards, when the Mahommedan kingdoms of Bijapur and Golconda had attained to some eminence in the hierarchy of Indian States, that a fresh aggressive move was made in this quarter. The kings of these principalities then extended the boundaries of their possessions into the Carnatic proper (or Balaghat) and into the region below the Ghats. Their further progress was arrested by the action of the Mogul Emperor, Aurungzebe, who in 1687 brought them under the subjection of his government. The deposed King of Golconda now gave place to a Nawab of the Carnatic, with his capital at Arcot, under a scheme which made him subject to the Nizam of the Deccan at Hyderabad. Bijapur, which had been won largely with the assistance of Mahratta generals, was given an ill-defined status, and ultimately fell under Mahratta domination. Afterwards, in 1761, when Mysore was captured by Hyder Ali, there was a revival of Mahommedan influence in circumstances which appeared for a time to foreshadow a marked change in the balance of power in Southern India. But the defeat of that clever ruler's son and successor by the British, in circumstances hereafter to be related, disposed once and for all of the dream of Mahommedan ascendancy in Southern India.

CHAPTER II

European influence introduced—The Portuguese at Goa—The English at Surat and on the Coromandel coast—English factories at Masulipatam and Armagaon—Francis Day obtains grant for a factory at Madrasapatam—Importance of the grant—Cogan and Day occupy the new territory—Construction of Fort St. George commenced—Censure of the directors—Cogan's reply—Committee of inquiry into the occupation—Cogan exonerated—Cogan's career after quitting India.

LONG before the final overthrow of the great Hindu State of Vizayanagar the influence of Europeans had begun to permeate Southern India. First in the field were the Portuguese, who having firmly seated themselves at Goa, on the western coast of India, entered into close relations with many of the powers in the interior, and notably with the Hindu representatives of the State of Vizayanagar. For a great number of years they had a close monopoly of the advantages, commercial and political, which attached to the exposition of the strange new principles of the West, and especially to those which pertained to the military art. They made the best of their opportunities, and secured a firm lodgment in most of the native Courts, to the infinite profit of their trade. For the best part of a century they held their privileged position unchallenged, and then they had to face the inevitable competition of formidable rivals. The first blow was struck on the west coast, when the English representatives of the East India Company, landing first at Surat in 1611, opened up communications with the Mogul power with the view of securing a permanent foothold in the country. Though attended with many checks and disappointments, this enterprise was in due time attended with success, and under a more or less precarious tenure a factory was established at Surat. Trade here was subjected to many and serious disadvantages arising out of the hostility of the Portuguese, and the despotic and capricious policy of the Mogul authority. But enough experience was obtained by the representatives of the Company to enable them to realize to the fullest extent the splendid character of the field that India offered to English enterprise. One lesson which they early imbibed was that if a due amount of success was to be achieved, openings for trade must be sought at other places than Surat. Western India was highly important as the centre on which the great trade routes from the Red Sea and the Persian Gulf converged, but experience soon taught them that it was not by any means the only sphere of commercial influence worth the working. Their education in the advantages of Indian trade openings was hastened by the action of the Dutch in Java and the Malay Archipelago, where, in spite of a definite agreement between the two races, the Dutch had oppressed the English and finally driven them altogether from that particular sphere of commercial activity. Harassed by their implacable rivals, the Company's forlorn representatives sought a refuge at Masulipatam in 1620, but were speedily ejected from here, as they had been a short time previously from Bantam by the Dutch. Undeterred by this rebuff, the Company's agents two years later made a second effort to obtain a lodgment on the Coromandel coast, and this time were successful. A connection was established with the local traders, whose products from the looms of Southern India—the muslins and the calicoes and the rest—were already greatly prized in the home markets. So encouraging were the results of the first few years' business at Masulipatam that the directors were induced in 1625 to give their assent to the establishment of a second factory at Armagaon, farther up the East Coast. The original intention was to make the new post subordinate to the older one, but in 1628, owing to the intolerable oppression of the native authorities, represented by the minions of the King of Golconda, it was decided to close the Masulipatam establishment and concentrate attention on Armagaon. In keeping with its position as a head settlement, the place was fortified, and quarters were erected for a large staff of factors and agents. But it was not long before it was discovered that the site was ill-chosen for the purpose for which it was intended, and in 1632 a *farman* to trade having been obtained from the King of Golconda, which seemed to promise better treatment, there was a fresh flitting to Masulipatam.

Still the position on the East Coast was not regarded as satisfactory. At Masulipatam the English were in too close proximity to the Dutch to be either pleasant or profitable. Moreover, the exactions of the local officials, though not so gross as in earlier days, were sufficiently irksome to make a change of venue for the factory desirable. The Company's agents by this time were quite familiar with the coast and had a pretty shrewd idea that they might find elsewhere a site which would not be open to the objections which were associated with the existing factory. In 1637 Francis Day, who at or about this time was chief at Armagaon, conducted a little mission on his own account to see if he could not discover a better position. He turned his attention to the coast line near Pollechere, the

1. EAST VIEW OF BANGALORE, WITH THE CYPRUS GARDEN, FROM A PAGODA.
From "Picturesque Scenery in the Kingdom of Mysore." Edited by Edward Orme. Published in 1804.

2. OOTRAY DROOG.
From "Views in the Mysore Country." Published in 1794.

3. NORTH VIEW OF SEWANDROOG.
Showing the attack in December 1791. From "Twelve Views in the Kingdom of Mysore." Published in 1804.

4. EAST VIEW OF SHOLE GHURRY, FROM THE CAMP AT ARNEE.
From "Picturesque Scenery in the Kingdom of Mysore." Edited by Edward Orme. Published in 1804.

modern Pondicherry, where he had been led, probably by past experience, to look for the kind of opening he sought. The native authority hereabouts was vested in one of the representatives of the Vizayanagar prince, a certain Naik named Damarla Venkatadri Venkatappa, or Venkatapati, who ruled the coast from Pulicat to the Portuguese settlement of San Thome. Communications appear to have been opened up with this worthy, but with what result is not clear from the records. Probably Day was merely feeling his way and made no definite proposals. At all events he had no authority to enter into negotiations on this occasion. The formal opening for such came in 1639, when he was instructed by Thomas Ivie, who had just arrived from Bantam, to sail down the coast and attempt to secure a site for a permanent settlement.

Keen official and shrewd business man as he was, Day, we may be sure, undertook the duty imposed on him with alacrity. He steered a direct course for a little town—more properly speaking, village—called Madrasapatam, situated three miles north of San Thome. On arrival at his destination he promptly got into touch with the Naik Damarla, from whom with little difficulty he obtained a grant of territory with trading privileges and authority to form a settlement and build a fort. With this valuable concession in his wallet he returned in all haste to Masulipatam. His ardour was somewhat damped on arrival here by the discovery that Ivie's credentials as agent were disputed by a newcomer named Thomas Morley Cogan, who had been appointed direct from home in ignorance of Ivie's selection by the Bantam Presidency, and who had arrived overland from Surat to take up his duties. After an awkward interval of doubt and controversy, it was decided by the majority of the factors in the settlement that Cogan, having been selected by the chief authority, must rule. This decision does not appear to have been taken with any reference to the action in regard to the new settlement, and from the fact that the grant went forward to Surat and was approved by them, we may take it that the policy of forming a new *point d'appui* on the coast was generally accepted by those on the spot who understood the urgent necessity for a change.

Day had certainly, if his colleagues had only known it, achieved great things on that mission of his to the sandy wastes of the squalid village of Madrasapatam. He had acquired nothing less than the title-deeds of a territory which was the germ of an Empire, for this plot of ground, carefully defined in the Naik's grant, was the first land that the Company held in full sovereignty in India. The site of what was afterwards to be the splendid city of Madras, it was the true beginning of that Imperial India of which not merely Britons, but all English-speaking people the wide world over, are so justly proud. Day probably had no conception of the magnitude of his triumph. His horizon was bounded by his ledgers, and his aspirations at the highest were to establish a position convenient for trade and reasonably secure from the irritating aggressiveness of domineering native officials and the machinations of jealous competitors. The practice of thinking Imperially was to come later, when on the spot which he secured for British posterity Clive first formed in his mind those splendid schemes of conquest which afterwards found fruition on the historic field of Plassy. Nevertheless, Day, with all the necessary limitations of his environment, must have had a soul which rose above the mere routine of the trading factory. He had studied Dutch methods at close quarters, and probably clearly perceived that successful commerce in the India of this period must go hand in hand with the might of the strong right arm. Realizing this, he made the independent effort he did to force the sluggish hand of authority by paving the way for the Naik's grant. Without knowing it, he was in the truest sense of the term an Empire builder, for to him belongs the chief credit of well and truly laying the corner-stone of British India.

The creation of the new settlement at Madraspatam was attended with difficulties which might have discouraged less resolute and far-seeing men than Day and his chief associate in the enterprise proved themselves. In the first place the authorities at Surat were chary of giving their authority for the necessary transfer of the establishment from Armagaon. They appear to have shrunk from the responsibility of sanctioning a move which necessarily involved considerable expense and the outcome of which seemed to them doubtful. They temporized so long that Cogan and Day took the matter into their own hands and occupied the newly assigned territory. It was while the arrangements for transfer were in actual progress, in February 1640, that the definite orders for that proceeding from President Fremlen and the Council at Surat were received. Armed with this authority the enterprising factors hastened the work of evacuation at Armagaon. A few days later the entire staff of the factory embarked in the *Eagle* and the *Unity*, two of the Company's ships then in port, and sailed for Madrasapatam, which they reached on February 20, 1640. Their enthusiasm was somewhat chilled when they arrived at their destination by the discovery that the Naik's engagement embodied in the grant of territory to build a fort did not in his view cover any greater obligation than that of erecting a stockade. For the Company's purposes a stockade was of little value: only a strongly built masonry fort could be effective protection against such outside aggression as the little force of English traders might expect to encounter. Not to be thus foiled of their purpose by this unlooked-for check, Cogan and Day decided to erect permanent works on their own responsibility. This course was taken without loss of time, and a commencement was made with the erection of a solid structure at a point on the surf bank of sand which lay between the Elembore River and the sea, three-quarters of a mile north of the outlet and just south of the town or village of Madrasapatam. Good progress was made with the work in the earliest months of the occupation, but fourteen years elapsed before the design was completed.

While the work of building the fort was in its earliest stage, a cyclone broke over the new settlement and caused the total loss of the two vessels in the roadstead, besides doing other damage. This calamity only temporarily damped the ardour of the Englishmen, and they proceeded with their preparations with such energy that before long quite a considerable community had grown up about the fort, the settlers including a good many Portuguese of pure and mixed blood, and a substantial body of native artisans, chiefly weavers, from Masulipatam and elsewhere.

As a beginning the results achieved reflected the highest credit on the pioneers, but the expenses had been necessarily heavy, and the directors, when they heard of what had been done, were enraged at the action of their servants in committing them to such an extent. They sent out with the ship *Hopewell*, which arrived at Madrasapatam in 1642, a furious letter, in which they severely censured Cogan for establishing the new settlement and for the losses sustained in the wreck of the Company's ships. Day at this juncture was in Surat, on his way to England, and it remained for Cogan to bear the full brunt of the Company's anger. He did not sit down meekly under the unjustifiable castigation which had been administered from home. In his reply, which is dated September 1642, he wrote with strong feeling: "When wee doe, as that wee doe often, fall into consideration how much your worships are displeased with us for proceeding on this worke, it even breaks some of our hearts. 'Tis now too late to wish it undone and yet wee may not but tell you that if soe be your worships will follow this coast trade (or rather the Karnatt) this place may prove as good as the best; but all things must have its growth and time." The writer went on to say that the natives were not to be trusted, and that the Company must have on the coast a place to retire to under its own command. This was not alone their opinion, but was the opinion of their Presidents at Bantam and Surat. "Then from Surat 'twas said" (the letter proceeds), "Build when you build no such mocke fort as was Armagaon. The Dutch saw the necessitie of it 30 years since which made them proceed from Pullicatt to their unreasonable expense in moneys besides loss of men ere brought to perfection. But wee beseeche you, if these people build us a forte and pay the garrison in what securitie is your estate and our lives? Surely in none at all for it is farr more freedome to live without a forte than within, unless the forte be at its own devotion. But this forte of yours if your worships did butt follow this trade as it might be followed, or that you had but two or three small vessels to voyage in to and to draw trade hither, all your charges would be borne with advantage. But if your worships are resolved absolutely to leave this trade of Karnatt, advise us, and you shall not be a pice loser for what work is done and moneys disbursed, which being so, and that your worships conclude of one of the two ways wee hope to heare of noe more of the forte."

A very sensible and, indeed, unanswerable rejoinder. Security and freedom were the essence of successful trading in the East at this period, and the desiderata were only to be obtained by the Company having a *pied-à-terre* of its own free from outside interference. The lesson was one which the directors at home were loth to learn, and they would probably never have learned it had it not been for men like Cogan and Day, who forced their hands at critical moments.

The Surat Council in principle supported Cogan and Day in their action in occupying Madrasapatam, though they "blamed their indiscretion or negligence that would not better understand the Naique." In regard to the situation as it existed in 1641 when they wrote they had no fear. They had found the Naik and his people "faire conditioned and indifferent honest," and while that chief remained and they had the sea open to furnish them with food they had no fear of what any one could do against them. Some time later, when Cogan went to England, he took with him a letter from the Presidency, in which the earlier arguments were reinforced. In this communication it was intimated that Mr. Francis Day "was the first projecture and contriver of that forte or castle in Madrasapatam, which another with a greate deal of discontent, laboure, and paines hath now brought to some good pass, being a place of securitie on that coast as the onelie place of secured saiftie with that title of honour (Castle) that ever our nation enjoyed in East India and therefore in our opinion to be highly esteemed." They were sure that if their worships continued the Indian trade, in a few years the place "will not onelie quitt its owne charge but allsoe produce benefitt and put moneys into your purses by bringing a trade thither, raiseing a custom there, paying of duties by the inhabitants neere adjoyning, and being replenyshd with merchants, weavers, etc."

When he was actually confronted by the directors Cogan made an able defence. He pointed out that the Company's agents in India must necessarily be given a very wide discretion, and that in fact the Company had often enjoined them to settle in India "all disputes and differences," so that the authorities at home should not be troubled with them. He showed very clearly by facts which he cited that the responsibility for the construction of the fort was shared by his colleagues at Surat, and that in any event against the cost of the works on the fort—then estimated at 9,250 pagodas—might be set the expenditure which would have been necessary to repair the ruinous fort at Armagaon if Madras had not been occupied.

After what appear to have been protracted proceedings, the committee in a declaration dated May 13, 1645, exonerated Cogan. They stated that the building of the fort was a very indiscreet action when the Company's stock was so small, yet they realized that if the stock were large the settlement might be "very commodious and advantageous for them." Should, however, it not come up to expectations, "it can" (they said) "bee charged upon noe man more justly then on Mr. Day." Undoubtedly to Day belongs the chief honour of securing the first secure foothold in India for English power. He, daring greatly, as the records show, accepted responsibility at the right moment and clinched a bargain which might never have been made but for his strength of purpose. It is unfortunate, having regard to the importance of his services as an Empire builder, that little is known of his later career. After administering the affairs of the new settlement for four years he retired to England, where, amid the turmoil of the Civil War, he disappeared from public view.

Cogan's Indian career was apparently closed with the termination of the inquiry, at which he assisted. With his modest competence he settled down to the leisured life of a private gentleman at Greenwich, until the great constitutional struggle brought him into prominence. Fighting on the side of the King he gained unenviable distinction as a foe of the Commonwealth and had to fly the country. He returned in a few years, and was in such good odour in 1657 that he was created a Baronet of Ulster, the title of knighthood having previously been conferred upon him between 1640 and 1645 by King Charles. Cogan left two daughters, one of whom married Christopher Musgrave, the head of the well-known family seated at Eden Hall, Cumberland. As has been seen, Cogan played a very conspicuous part in the acquisition of Madras, and deserves to share with Day the credit which attaches to that venture. Until the researches of Mr. William Foster and Mr. H. A. Love laid bare the whole of the transactions in connection with the business, little justice had been done to his memory.

CHAPTER III

Early days of the new settlement—New grant from Raja Sir Ranja of Vizayanagar—The King of Golconda confirms the grant—Terrible famine in Southern India—Life in Madras—The first chaplain—Political controversies—Nawab of the Carnatic threatens Madras—Sir Edward Winter's administration—His far-seeing policy—George Foxcroft sent out to supersede Winter—Winter forcibly seizes the government—The causes of the revolt—Winter justifies his usurpation—Company sends out Clavell to re-establish their authority—Winter declines to recognize his credentials—Expedition to Madras to depose Winter—The submission of the rebels—Sir William Langhorne institutes an inquiry into the revolt—Winter's later career—George Foxcroft the first Governor of Fort St. George.

MADRASAPATAM, or, as we may now call it, Madras, in its earliest days had the usual struggling existence of a European settlement in the East. The fort by the shore was slowly rearing its head amid the sand. Landwards was growing up a straggling bazaar, ministering to the wants of the rapidly increasing native population, which had been attracted by the prospect of lucrative work offered by the Company's agents. At a distance, looking jealously on at the new experiment of the English, were the Dutch, who could not tolerate the idea that their hated rivals should have a factory anywhere in the East in any region in which they traded. Nearer home, at San Thomé, were the Portuguese, outwardly friendly, but ready to seize every opening that offered of reducing the influence of the newcomers. Looming in the background was a native difficulty of menacing proportions, which promised to undermine the already precarious basis upon which the settlement was founded. The worst trouble, almost needless to say, was the last named. It arose through one of those sudden changes in native authority which are so characteristic of Indian history. Through the machinations of the Dutch, Naik Damarla Venkatappa, from whom the grant of the site of the settlement was obtained, was disgraced by his master, Rajah Sir Ranja, the phantom king of the phantom kingdom of Vizayanagar, and conferred on a man named Millai, otherwise Chenna Chetti, a native merchant who had acted for the Dutch. Not without reason the English factors at Madras were gravely distrustful of Millai. He was obviously a creature of the Dutch, and the Dutch at this time were all powerful on the East Coast. As the Bantam President, writing home about this period, remarked, they had driven the Portuguese out of nearly all their strongholds, and had reduced the Danes to an equally helpless position. There therefore practically only remained the English as effective competitors of the Hollanders, and, observed the Bantam functionary pitifully, " 'Tis very probable wee may be in the same predicament in a short time, being so far removed and estranged from our masters and your good opinions that all that goes from hence meets with disrespects and scorne."

Gloomy as the outlook was, the settlement, thanks to the exercise of judicious diplomacy on the part of the Company's servants, escaped the threatened storm. The difficulty, indeed, was turned to advantage, for in the place of the grant of the Naik, whose authoritativeness was questionable, the Company received, in October or November 1645, from Rajah Sir Ranja a new grant empowering the Company to administer justice, and assigning new territory on the borders of the settlement in the shape of "the Jacall ground." The concession was as timely as it was acceptable. Two years later the last vestige of Vizayanagar sovereignty was swept away by the King of Golconda, who occupied the Carnatic and all the territory of the ancient Hindu State as far as the coast. Accepting the accomplished fact with their usual ductility, the Company's agents sought and obtained from the new overlord the confirmation of their grant. Thus within seven years of the making of the original concession, the English power was firmly seated on the East Coast, in spite of intrigues which at one time appeared likely to destroy it in this quarter.

Ere the political cloud had completely dispersed, a formidable new source of anxiety arose in the occurrence of a terrible famine which devastated the whole of the districts by the East Coast, and brought the European settlements to the verge of ruin. How fearful the havoc wrought was may be gathered from the records. In a letter to Surat the Madras factors wrote: "Wee are now driven to that pass that wee are forced to goe to lowance of rice and are not able to subsist longer than 5 or 8 days. Our wants are such that wee are ashamed to make it known." It was mentioned that in Madras in five months there had died 4,000 persons, in Pulicatt 15,000, and as many at San Thomé. "So that," continued the communication, "there is not above one-third of the weavers, printers and workers livinge of what were formerly which causeth cloth in these parts to bee 15 per cent. dearer than formerly and little or none at all to be procured." The timely arrival of a cargo of rice relieved the necessities of the factors and their people, but the unfortunate natives in the districts continued for a long time to suffer. Indeed, for generations afterwards memories of this frightful time lingered in the country.

Life in Madras for the Englishmen at this period must have been hard to support even without the suffering which famine brought in its train. Apart from the monotonous round of duty associated with the Company's trading operations, there was little to occupy the activities of the young Englishmen stranded on this none too attractive part of the Coromandel coast. Movements were strictly circumscribed by the unsettled condition of the adjacent districts. The refinements and luxuries and the congenial companionship which to-day help the Briton to bear his exile and even enjoy it were unknown. There was merely a dull dead-level of existence, which was only sustained by the thought that some day the worker might, by his private trading, amass sufficient money to retire to Europe to spend his later days in ease and affluence. In the circumstances it is not surprising that the moral tone of the little English community at Madras left much to be desired. The directors at home, aware of this fact, in 1646 sent out to the new settlement the Rev. W. Isaacson to act as chaplain. He was selected for his sacred office by reason of the fact that he was "of a very civil and fair deportment," and one likely "to work a reformation in that disordered place." Apparently the expectations entertained of his influence were not altogether realized, for we read in a record written some time after his arrival at his post that he was of "too mylde a disposition to work upon such rugged natures" as those of "these debast soldiers composing the garrison." However, he deserves to be held in remembrance as the first of a long line of worthy ministers of religion who filled the Madras Chaplaincy.

Apart from the direct statement quoted in the previous paragraph, there is ample evidence in the records to show that life proceeded anything but smoothly in the infant settlement. The controversies of the Civil War then raging at home appear to have been transferred to Madras, and given an additional zest to the mutual bickerings of the inhabitants. The fact that the military commander, a Captain Martin, was a Royalist, and did not strive to conceal his political prepossessions, was a source of keen dissatisfaction to his brother officials, most of whom were probably supporters of the Parliament, as their superiors at home were. It was complained of Martin that "he bitterly inveyed in the yeares of 1651 and 1652 against Independents, Presbiterians, Protestants and Papists though comonly with this conclusion that if there were any true religion in the world 'twas that of the Papists." He also "inveyed against Governor Cromwell in this manner, how that before these warres beganne hee was a pore cowardly fellow and would take a cuff on the eare from any man: that he frequented punch houses with the soldiers and indulged in gaming." This scandal about the Protector was reinforced by piquant comments on local officials. One —the Accountant—was designated "in a derogating and degrading manner" "the sonne of a Tayler's threade," and the Agent was styled "the sonne of a greazed butcher."

Captain Martin, not to be outdone in this battle of slander, brought against his critics a batch of accusations of a formidable character. Referring to the principal of them he said: "And for the said Leigh his life and conversation hee is one that hath been knowne to bee druncke neare upon a month togither and hath drawne others of the Company's servants to accompany him in his druncknesse insomuch as it is verily believed that Mr. Wm. Gurney and Mr. James Moore were thereby brought into such diseases as helped them forward to their last ends. For it was Mr. Leigh's custome to bee druncke by nyne of the clock in the forenoone and he goes into the Tancke where he falls asleepe . . . and hath been soe usually overtaken at the public service of God whilst the minister was at prayers that the said Leigh tourned Clarke (out of the zealousness of his religion) and cryes Amen, Amen, Amen, Amen, Amen, until hee fall asleepe and soe remayned after all the company were risen from their devotion."

The unfortunate Leigh who is here so mercilessly gibbeted lost his life by drowning at sea in 1656, and we hear no more of these squabbles. Bitter as the feeling was amongst the expatriated Englishmen, they were speedily made to sink their differences in the face of a menace which for a time threatened the existence of the settlement, in the shape of an attack by Mir Jumlah, the Nawab of the Carnatic. The Nawab's hostility had been excited by the action of the Madras factors in seizing a junk of 500 tons burden belonging to the Nawab which was anchored off San Thomé. The capture was made in retaliation for acts of aggression on the part of the Nawab's agents. It was an ill-advised step, because the vessel was empty at the time and there was nothing to set off against the trouble which was swiftly brought upon the settlement by the seizure. The Nawab, enraged at the insolence of the Englishmen, descended upon Madras with a large force. For a time things looked critical, but eventually a composition was made with Mir Jumlah by which the junk was returned to him, and the Englishmen were left in undisturbed possession of the fort and town on payment of an annual sum of 380 pagodas in lieu of half the customs to which the Nawab, as the inheritor of the rights of the Vizayanagar chief, deemed himself to be entitled to. By this arrangement the original grant was confirmed and a new era was opened up in which the Company and the Mahommedan authorities were brought into relationship. Before this stage in the history of Madras was reached—in September 1655—the settlement had been reduced to an Agency.

1. EMBARKING AT MADRAS, 1837. **2. LANDING AT MADRAS, 1837.**

In 1662 the chief direction of the Company's affairs at Madras devolved upon Sir Edward Winter, an able official who contributed one of the strangest and most interesting chapters in the history of the settlement. Winter brought to his work a strong resolution and a capacity far above that of the ordinary official of the period. Under his skilled guidance the fort was strengthened and an impetus was given to public works. It was during his term of office that the first Anglican place of worship in Madras was built. The edifice which he caused to be erected was described by Daniel Hewart, who visited Madras in the period 1670-8 as "prettily built of wood and inside so beautiful that it is a pleasure to peep into it." "I do not know that anywhere in the whole of India I have seen a finer," enthusiastically adds the traveller. Another of Winter's services was the provision of a hospital. The urgent need for such an institution may be gathered from a contemporary record, which depicts the hard fate of the members of the garrison under the harsh regime which then obtained. The men, we are told, were held strictly to their duty "soe that the fresh souldiers which came forth this year taking up their habitation in the bleake wind in the hall fell sick. Four of them are dead: about tenne remain at this time very sick and complain (and it seems not without reason) that the wages are not sufficient to supply them now in this time of their sickness. Soe that rather than to see Englishmen dropp away like dogges in that manner for want of Christian charity towards them we have thought it very convenient that they might have a house on purpose for them and people to look after them and to see that nothing comes in to them, neither of meate nor drinke but what the doctor alloweth."

If Winter had stopped at efforts to improve the material well-being of the community, his name would probably have gone down to obscurity like those of other administrators of the period who were content to efface themselves, if need be, at the behest of superior authority. But he was of a masterful disposition and did not submit tamely to the bonds imposed by a directorate which was oftentimes ill-informed and prejudiced. He had been sent out at an important stage in the Company's history. Charles II, on coming to the throne at the Restoration, had granted a new Charter which conferred new and extended powers, including the right of their chief agents "to judge all persons belonging to the said Governor and Company or that should live under them, in all causes, whether civil or criminal, according to the laws of the kingdom and to execute judgment accordingly." The cessation of hostilities with the Dutch, which had sadly hampered trade on the Coromandel Coast, as elsewhere in India, was a further incentive to development. Wielding authority as President of Fort St. George and the chief Agent on the East Coast, Winter had embarked upon a bold and far-reaching policy designed to give solidity to the Company's hold on the trade of this part of India. Instead of effecting retrenchments, as he was expected to do, he inaugurated measures which involved considerable additional expenditure. In his dispatches home he advocated a still more ambitious programme based on the idea that if the Company were to be successful they must, like their great rivals the Dutch, be in the possession of large capital and have at their command a strong naval force. The directors, who were still staggering under the heavy load of debt inherited from the troublous period of the Civil Wars, took fright at the proposals. They not only failed to appreciate the necessity for the measures put forward, but they distrusted the good faith of their Agent. As the situation appeared to them to call for urgent measures, they decided upon the drastic course of superseding the daring innovator. The man chosen to supplant Winter was a certain George Foxcroft, who appears to have held Puritanical and anti-monarchical views, and to have been otherwise unsuited to preside over the destinies of a community whose leanings were overwhelmingly Royalist.

Foxcroft was accompanied to Madras by his brother Nathaniel, an equally sturdy upholder of principles which ran counter to those of the majority. Landing at Madras in June, the pair speedily made themselves obnoxious to their colleagues, whose prejudices doubtless took a keener edge because of the injustice which they considered had been done to Winter by his deposition. Quarrels speedily developed in the necessarily close intimacy of the fort. Umbrage was taken at the frankness of the Foxcrofts, who aired their political opinions with irritating freedom, and on one occasion went the length of expounding the view that no king had any right to his throne except might, and that a man's interest came before that of the sovereign. The heat engendered by these controversies might have evaporated if Winter had been disposed to accept his dismissal; but though he was at first ready to submit, his feelings were so worked upon by the indiscretions of the Foxcrofts that he made up his mind to stay and challenge the edict from home which deprived him of his authority. He was probably induced to take this course by the knowledge that he could rely upon the support of the bulk of the Company's servants in the settlement, and especially those who formed the military element. However that may have been, the *coup d'état* involved in the forcible removal from power of the new President was easily accomplished.

A lively description of the episode, which is given in Mr. C. R. Wilson's "The Early Annals of the English in Bengal," brings vividly before us the scene which was enacted on Saturday, September 16, 1665, as the culminating stage of the plot against Foxcroft. "At the time of morning prayer just as the Agent was going to Church, he learnt that the soldiers were in arms against him. Drawing his rapier, the only weapon ordinarily worn in the fort, he hurried down the stairs which led from his rooms to the quadrangle below, followed by Samebrooke and Dawes (two members of his Council). At the foot of the stairs the Agent beheld an ominous sight. There stood the whole garrison fully armed. Their swords were drawn; their pistols cocked; at their head was Captain Chuseman (the captain of the garrison). On the men seeing Foxcroft and his friends the cry arose, 'For the King! For the King! Knock them down! Fire!' The Agent advanced to ask for an explanation, but Chuseman answered by discharging his pistol and rushing at him with his sword. He closed with the Agent and flung him to the ground.

"This was the signal for the rest to fire. . . . The result of the volley was that no one was mortally wounded except Dawes, who had halted on the stairs. Samebrooke, who rushed forward to help the fallen Agent, escaped unhurt; but closing with Chuseman he was set on by the soldiers and knocked down. Nathaniel Foxcroft, a brisk man in a broil, contrived to get his pistols from his room on the ground floor; yet he was seized before he could do any execution.

"In a few minutes the affray was over. George Foxcroft was clapped up in a rubbish hole and Sir Edward Winter resumed the Government of Fort St. George. On the 19th September he made a solemn declaration that he had accepted the office of Chief Director in consequence of the exigencies of the Company's affairs and upon the unanimous request of the

Company's factors, servants, and officers, until it should be ordered otherwise either by the plurality of the Council or by the Court."

Such was the revolution with which Madras signalized its earliest existence as a Presidency. The *coup d'état* is so amazing as to be almost incomprehensible to our modern understandings, nurtured as they are in the traditions of a Civil Service which is first and last and all the time loyal. It can only be understood if we bear in mind the insecure tenure of the Company's existence and the character of the times in which the events just narrated took place. On the one hand was a commercial organization entering upon a new phase of an apparently precarious existence under the ægis of one of the most unreliable of monarchs ; on the other, beneath the surface of social life were the smouldering fires of one of the most momentous internecine conflicts ever waged in Europe. The two influences acted and reacted on the position of the English in India. The Puritanical element, which had long had sway in the Company's Councils both at home and in India, was not the more tolerable to the Royalist element when the change of sentiment in the homeland had ousted it from power. Rather it was that the old narrowness and rigidity of principles acted on the mind of the anti-Puritans as an irritant, and bred a spirit of quarrelsomeness which welcomed any opening that offered for the repudiation of the hated doctrines of the Republicans. So when the pugnacious Foxcrofts with their levelling doctrines burst into the little Royalist world at Fort St. George, they fell easy victims to a conspiracy which was directed not only to the maintenance in power of a popular official, but to the vindication of a political faith tenaciously and even truculently held.

When Winter had firmly established his position, he bethought himself of justifying his conduct to the home authorities. He did so in an able document in which, after a reference to the traitorous conduct of the Foxcrofts and the necessity which it had imposed upon him of taking vigorous action, he enlarged upon the position of the Company on the Coromandel Coast and upon the necessity of maintaining it with the aid of armed cruisers. While deferring to their instructors as to the withdrawal of the out agencies, he drew a graphic picture of the loss of prestige that would flow from such procedure. Besides forwarding this communication to the directors, Winter addressed letters to the King, to the Archbishop of Canterbury, and to the King's officer in command at Bombay, giving his version of the events. At the same time Foxcroft, on his own behalf from his place of captivity, addressed to Masulipatam a long letter reciting his misfortunes and asking for assistance.

As soon as the news of the revolution reached England measures were taken to assert the Company's outraged authority. To this end the King, on the application of the directors, sent out a special agent, Clavell by name, charged with the duty of restoring the *status quo*. Clavell reached India in 1667, but only to find that he had made a useless journey. Aided and abetted by the Royalist Governor of Bombay, who had a fine contempt for Puritans, Winter declined to recognize Clavell's authority. He affected to regard him as an impostor and denounced his credentials as gross forgeries. Neither the King's Government nor the Company could afford to permit so gross a defiance of direct commands. It was consequently decided to send out under a Royal Commission a powerful force to reduce the rebel Government of Madras by force if necessary. On May 21, 1668, a portion of the special squadron of five vessels anchored off Madras. Two officials who went off from shore to greet the visitors were promptly made prisoners. Subsequently a demand was sent ashore in the King's name for the rendition of the fort. Winter declined to accede unless his personal safety was guaranteed and a promise was given to respect property. These terms, after some discussion, were conceded, and on August 22nd troops were landed from the ships and took formal possession of the fort.

Foxcroft's release from captivity was not followed, as might have been anticipated, by his immediate restoration to power. In common with Winter he remained a resident at the fort while the Commission which had come out in the ships sought to get at the truth of the business. Sir William Langhorne, the head of this Commission, who took over the Agency, did his best to disentangle the facts from the mass of prejudice and ill-will with which the settlement was seething ; but the task proved too difficult for him, and at the end of eighteen months he felt impelled to refer the matter home. The issue, as far as it was affected by the rivalry of Winter and the Foxcrofts, was simplified by the death, on October 26, 1669, of Nathaniel Foxcroft. George Foxcroft remained at Madras officiating as Agent until 1672, when he returned to England. Winter went home in the same year, not in any sense as a culprit, but as an ordinary passenger. He had apparently outlived the resentment which his conduct in the first instance excited in the minds of the authorities in England. Probably he had also established a powerful Court influence which acted as an effectual safeguard against anything in the nature of punishment. Whether that was the case or not, Winter's treason had in it an element which appealed to the sympathies of influential people in England. Added to dislike of men of the Foxcroft type was a strong and growing feeling in favour of the bold policy advocated by Winter. So this startling episode in the early life of Madras fades away, leaving no more trace behind than any of the innumerable "regrettable incidents" of which the record of English life in India in these days largely consisted.

Winter died in the odour of Court favour in England, and was buried in Battersea Church. Over his monument in the sacred building appear certain lines which are worthy of reproduction, as they give an interesting picture of the man as he appeared to his friends. This is his epitaph :—

Alone, unarm'd a Tygre he opprest,
And crusht to death the monster of a beast,
Twice twenty Moors he overthrew
Singly on foot, some wounded, some he slew;
Dispers'd the rest ; what more cou'd Sampson do ?
True to his friends, a terror to his foes,
Here now in peace his honour'd bones repose.

Before we quit this exciting period in Madras history it is worth noting that George Foxcroft was the first official of the Company who held the title of Governor of Fort St. George. An interesting fact, brought out very clearly in "Vestiges of Old Madras," is that the distinction was conferred owing to a murder. A slave girl in the house of a certain Mrs. Ascantia Dawes came to a violent end, and suspicion pointed to the mistress as the perpetrator of the crime. In doubt as to their powers, the Agent and Council sought instructions from England. The Court held that under Charles II's Charter of 1661 they had authority to make their Agent at Fort St. George Governor with judicial powers, and this course they took in order to ensure in the future the due administration of justice in such cases as that of the unfortunate slave girl.

CHAPTER IV

Appearance of the French on the Coromandel Coast—François Martin founds Pondicherry—Augmentation of the garrison of Fort St. George—European adventurers in Southern India—Mahratta raids in Southern India—Education system established in Madras—Streynsham Master's administration—Municipal machinery created at Madras—Growth of Madras—Job Charnock and the English factors from Bengal take refuge in Fort St. George—A turning-point in the history of the English in India.

Up to the time of Winter's *coup d'état*, the English had had to contend mainly with Dutch rivalry in the competition for the Indian trade, but before he had finally disappeared from the scene a new and powerful antagonist appeared on the Coromandel Coast in the French. In pursuance of a grandiose scheme for the conquest of the Eastern markets, which was favoured by Louis XIV, the French in 1672 sent a considerable force to San Thomé, which they captured without much difficulty. Their presence on the coast excited the animosity of the Dutch, who, forming an alliance with the King of Golconda, blockaded the fort and starved it into capitulation on August 24, 1674. Afterwards the place was handed over by the Dutch to the Mahommedan authority, and the fortifications were demolished. Thwarted in this direction, the French, under François Martin, in January, 1676, effected a lodgment at a point farther south, where the famous settlement of Pondicherry was founded, a lasting monument to the spacious age of French enterprise in India.

Alarmed at the growing aggressiveness of the French, the English authorities at Madras caused the garrison to be considerably augmented. In 1673 the military force consisted of 241 English infantry and 14 artillery, in addition to 163 Portuguese militia. For the first time the troops were put in uniform, not only "for the handsome representation of them in their exercise, but for the greater awe to the adversary besides the encouragement to themselves." It is probable that the occupation of Bombay by King's troops, which a few years earlier had brought a large body of uniformed soldiers to India, had suggested the desirability of a regular equipment for the Company's fighting men. But no doubt a powerful incentive to military display was supplied by the growth of European influence in Southern India. Apart from the forces maintained by the rival companies on the coast, the interior swarmed with adventurers, who thronged the native Courts, and in various capacities, chiefly in their armies, served the ruling princes. The King of Golconda had quite a European retinue drawn from every European nation that had relations with the East at this juncture. They were, for the most part, a dissolute, swashbuckling crew, who did little credit to the countries of their birth. An interesting picture of them is supplied in the "Storia do Mogor," the entertaining work written by the Venetian Manucci, who, after a long term of service at the Golconda Court, settled down to the life of a private citizen in Madras and died there in 1708. One story which Manucci tells is the following:

"When the sixth King of Gulkandah, Sultan Abdulla Kutab Shah, was on the throne (1611-72) he had serving in his artillery men of four European nations. As these great rulers delight in acquainting themselves with persons' characters through the actions they perform, he tried an experiment. He sent word for the slaughter of a stag and it was divided into joints. He then ordered the distribution of pieces, one to each nation. The Englishman, without waiting until they handed it to him, laid hold on the biggest piece there was and carried it off. From this the King said this nation loves to take things at its own risk. The Dutchman held out a hand humbly and accepted the share offered to him. From this it was inferred that this nation is one of merchants who through their humility have become rich. The Portuguese refused his portion, telling his servant he might take it. At this the King said that this nation was over proud, and would rather die of hunger than abandon its dignity. The Frenchman, without waiting for orders, laid hold of his sword, struck it into two pieces, and swelling his chest marched off. Judging from this, the King said that this nation was a valorous one, most generous and fond of living. He ordered the Frenchman to be appointed captain over his artillery."[1]

The condition of India at this period was such as to afford abundant scope for the activity of military adventurers of all races. The Mogul power was tottering under the disintegrating influences of internecine warfare. In the South the Mahommedan domination was weakened by domestic strife, and by the incapacity of high officials who failed to grasp the truth that a happy and contented people is the best defence of a State. Over all was the sinister shadow of the Mahratta menace with its fell manifestations of rapine and destruction. The redoubtable Sivaji, now in the full tide of his career as a guerilla leader, was sweeping through the land like a merciless torrent. In 1677 his hordes had penetrated to the South almost as far as Madras, and we catch a glimpse of his activities in the records of Fort St. George, where we have set forth an application made by him to the English authorities for a supply of engineers to assist him in the campaign he was then conducting. We are told that the Agent made him a "civil excuse," because, says the cautious official, "it is wholly unfit for us to meddle in it, there being many factors consequent thereon, as well of encreasing his power as of rendering both Golcondah and the Moghull our enemys, all these parts being spread with his spies and himself and army having come near this way."

War's alarms did not prevent the English officials at Madras from prosecuting the work of sound administration in the infant settlement. It was in this year which saw Sivaji ravaging the districts in the vicinity of Fort St. George that the foundations were laid of the splendid education system of which Madras is so justly proud. The beginning was made with the importation of Ralph Orde as a schoolmaster on a salary of £50 a year. Orde was brought out with the main purpose of teaching the children of the Company's servants "to read English and to write and cypher." With a generous recognition of the responsibilities of the Company it was stipulated that "if any of the other natives as Portuguez, the Gentues or others, will send their children to school," they should be taught, as the children of the Company's servants were, gratis. Thus a system of free education was established at a very early period in the history of Madras as an English possession.

After George Fox's departure in 1672 Sir William Langhorne had directed affairs at Fort St. George as chief official. When he retired in 1678 he gave place to Streynsham Master, an able official who is best known to the present generation from his "Diary," which was published a few years ago amongst the valuable volumes of Indian Records which have

[1] "Storia do Mogor, 1655–1708." Indian Text Series, vol. xiv. p. 94.

1. SOUTH-EAST VIEW OF THE ROCK OF TRICHINOPOLY.

From "A Brief History of Ancient and Modern India," Edited by Edward Orme. Published in 1804.

2. KISTNAGHURRY.

From "Picturesque Scenery in the Kingdom of Mysore."

3. THE LAKE OF MOOTY TALLAOW, NEAR SERINGAPATAM.

From "Twelve Views of Places in the Kingdom of Mysore." Published in 1804.

1. A VIEW FROM THE KING'S BARRACKS, FORT ST. GEORGE.
From "A Brief History of Ancient and Modern India." Edited by Edward Orme. Published in 1804.

2. FORT SQUARE, FROM THE SOUTH SIDE OF THE PARADE, FORT ST. GEORGE.
From "A Brief History of Ancient and Modern India."

3. A VIEW IN THE NORTH STREET OF FORT ST. GEORGE.
From "A Brief History of Ancient and Modern India."

issued from the press. Master, who was a scion of an old Kentish family, first went out to India in 1656, at the age of sixteen. He was a man of considerable attainments, and before going to Madras had made quite a mark at Surat, notably by his gallant defence of the factory there when it was attacked by Sivaji in 1670. Master, before actively taking up his duties at Fort St. George, proceeded on a tour of the Company's establishments in the Bay of Bengal. The fruits of his observations recorded in his famous "Diary" give a minute and valuable account of the condition of the English settlements in this part of India. His views on the points to which he directed his special attention are shrewd and well informed, and the whole composition is that of a man of singular breadth of outlook and business capacity. But amongst his other qualities was an independence of mind which ill-accorded with the somewhat servile traditions of the Company's service of his day. The consequence was that when he had been only three years in his new post at Madras he was superseded by the directors. In the letter in which he received his dismissal, reference was made to his "scornfull excuse" for the "unmannerly passages" in his earlier communications "wherein you say you crave our parden for your plainnesse and conclude that you usually wrote as you ought with obsequiousnesse, in which you betray your own weaknesse, first in supposing that we cannot judge between plainnesse and insolence, and, secondly, in running yourself upon the same rock on which your predecessor split, which if our Agent had been as well versed in history as he is in the vain ostentatious pomp of India he would never have been guilty of." Finally, Master was told that no indifferent man could read his letters without wondering at his "intollerable presumption and indiscretion."

Master, on returning to England in 1682, became involved in litigation with the Company, with the consequence that he was compelled in 1691 to make a payment to his old masters of £1,200. But he had his revenge later when on the formation of the new East India Company he became Chairman of the Board of Directors. He died in 1724 at the advanced age of 85.

Master was succeeded in the Governorship by William Gyfford, an old servant of the Company, who had previously lived some years in the settlement. He in turn was replaced in 1687 by Elihu Yale, the founder of the famous American University. It was during Yale's Governorship that the first municipal constitution was conferred upon Madras. Under a charter prepared in 1687 by the Company under the powers conferred upon it by its own charter a Corporation was established from the 29th of September, 1688, consisting of a Mayor, 12 Aldermen, and 60 or more burgesses. As in English municipalities, the mayoralty was an annual office, but the aldermanic bench was constituted on lines suited to the needs of an Indian settlement. It was provided that while vacancies should be filled by election from the list of burgesses, three of the Aldermen should always be covenanted servants of the Company. In consonance with this stipulation, the first batch of Aldermen included three members of Council. Supporting them were a representative body of influential citizens, including a French merchant, two Portuguese merchants, two Jewish merchants, and two native merchants. The burgesses were selected on similarly broad principles. Nor were the framers of the Constitution unmindful of what was due to the dignity of this new body. Robes of scarlet serge were ordained for the Mayor and Aldermen, and white silk gowns for the burgesses, while it was provided that the Mayor and Aldermen might "enjoy the honour and privilege of wearing Rundelloes and have Kettysols (Umbrellas) borne over them and may ride on horseback in the same order as is used by the Lord Mayor and Aldermen of London, having their horses decently furnished with saddles and bridles and other trimmings after one form and manner." The launching of the new constitution was marked with fitting pomp. First the Charter was read in the presence of the principal inhabitants, who had been summoned for the occasion in the Council Chamber in the Fort. Afterwards the Company went to "a handsome dinner," and "about three in the evening the whole Corporation marcht in their severall robes with the maces before the Mayor to the Town Hall," where some preliminary business was done. Nothing hardly could have been more auspicious than the inauguration of the era of local government, but before many months had passed away a change had come over the scene. First an acrimonious dispute broke out between the Mayor (Nathaniel Higginson) and the Governor in reference to the application of certain taxes to municipal purposes. Subsequently the directors expressed strong disapproval of the fact that no fewer than eight of the Aldermen were Englishmen. With a catholicity of spirit which did them credit they expressed the view that the board should "consist of the heads of the severall foreign castes, viz. one Armenian, one or two Hebrews, one or two Portuguese, one or two Gentues (Hindoos) and one Moor (Mahommedan)." A more serious complaint against the Corporation was that they had done nothing to justify their existence. Though definitely instructed to erect a Town Hall, several years elapsed before they took any practical step towards the prosecution of the work. Their trouble no doubt was the one which beset the Israelites in Egypt—the lack of straw for their bricks. The withdrawal of the taxation allotted to them in the first instance had left them with a barren exchequer, and they were not disposed to take personal risks in connection with what was a plain public obligation. Eventually this particular difficulty was overcome by the borrowing of money, with the assent of the Company, and the Town Hall was built. But in the troublous years which followed, the Corporation receded more and more into the background, until it became a mere shadow.

Madras by the end of the seventeenth century had become an imposing city of 400,000 inhabitants. Its growth had been uninterrupted, and in the last decades of the century phenomenal. In the seven years between 1674 and 1681 the number of inhabitants quadrupled, and between 1681 and 1691 the increase was twofold. Up to that period no European settlement in the East had made such a rapid advance. Madras's pre-eminence on the East Coast at this juncture was absolute. It drew to itself the bulk of the trade of this part of Southern India, and a substantial portion of that of the Bay of Bengal, and, as was indicated by Streynsham Master's missions, it wielded an undisputed political influence over this Eastern sphere of the Company's operations in India. An event which emphasized its importance was the descent upon the settlement in 1689 of the entire establishment of the English factories in Bengal, with Job Charnock at their head. The Englishmen, driven from pillar to post by the Mogul authorities and unwisely handled by Captain Heath, a special envoy the Company had sent out to strengthen their position in Bengal, had been compelled to take refuge at Fort St. George to avoid attack and probable annihilation at the hands of the Mahommedan power. After remaining some months in the secure haven that Madras then afforded, Charnock and his associates returned to the Hooghly and there and then laid the foundations of Calcutta in 1690. This was the turning-point in the history of the English relations with Bengal and, indeed, with the whole of Eastern India. As the years went by the centre of political influence gravitated more and more northwards, until finally, in the second half of the eighteenth century, Madras was deposed from its position of supremacy by Calcutta. Another development which was directed from Madras in the closing years of the seventeenth century, and which was the beginning of a notable extension of the Company's influence, was the foundation of the settlement of Bencoolen on the west coast of Sumatra. Bencoolen had a melancholy history—a record of failure which made its name a byword in the Company's annals. But its occupation constitutes a conspicuous landmark in the history of British power in the East, since it was the starting-point of that new India that is comprehended in the British Malaya of to-day.

CHAPTER V

Aurungzebe's expedition to Southern India—Thomas Pitt becomes Governor of Madras—Daud Khan, Nawab of the Carnatic, visits Madras—A second visit—Pitt effects a composition with Daud Khan—Blockade of Madras—Further arrangement with Daud Khan—Pitt's statesmanship—His personal characteristics—Prosperity of Madras—New charter—A judicial system established—Decline of trade.

TOWARDS the end of the seventeenth century a great change came over the fortunes of Southern India. Intent on crushing the irritating power of the Mahrattas, the Emperor Aurungzebe in 1686 led an army southwards, with Bijapur and Golconda as its principal objectives. After reducing these territories and adding them to the Mogul Empire, Aurungzebe directed his operations against the Mahrattas. He took Sivaji's son Sambhaji prisoner and put him to death in 1689, but he could make no real headway against the elusive tactics of the Mahrattas, who, when defeated in one centre, reappeared often in greater strength in another.

Madras had its full share of the anxieties consequent upon the changes in the political position in Southern India. Several years passed, however, before there was any direct menace to the position of the English at Madras. When the storm broke the chief direction of the Company's affairs was in the hands of one of the ablest men who figured in the list of the Company's administrators in these early days. The Governor of the period was Thomas Pitt, the ancestor of two of the greatest statesmen to whom the destinies of Britain were ever entrusted. Thomas Pitt was one of the class of adventurers who in the last half of the seventeenth century swarmed in India. His early career in the East had been associated with irregular trading operations at the expense of the Company's monopoly. He was, indeed, *par excellence*, an interloper—one of that hated body whose operations were the subject of so many wrathful comments and vituperative edicts which from time to time went out to India from the directors. More than once he had incurred legal penalties for his infringements of the Company's charter, but gifted with an indomitable resolution and an assurance which was proof against all attempts to suppress him, he had serenely prosecuted his profitable operations in the Bay of Bengal. At length the Company, making a virtue of necessity, took the bold and, as it proved, successful step of attaching Pitt to their interest by conferring upon him the office of Governor of Fort St. George.

Pitt, landing at Madras on July 7, 1698, took over charge from Nathaniel Higginson, who had succeeded Yale in 1692. He speedily had an opportunity of showing his statesmanship. In the year after his arrival he received an intimation from Nawab Zulfikar Khan, the Emperor's representative in the Deccan, that Daud Khan, his (the Nawab's) deputy, would pay a visit to Madras. Pitt, whose wide experience of Mogul ways taught him to be cautious, took immediate measures to place the settlement in a state of defence. He, however, affected to welcome the proposed visit and made arrangements for the envoy's reception with fitting state. Daud Khan, arriving on April 2, 1699, spent two days at Madras at a house placed at his disposal. The relations between the visitor and his hosts were outwardly friendly, but there was an undercurrent of suspicion which prevented any real *rapprochement* between the two. In the beginning of 1701 Daud Khan, having in the meantime been appointed Nawab of the Carnatic, appeared at Arcot with a considerable force. The first direct notice the authorities at Madras had of his presence in their vicinity was the receipt of a request that they would send him "sundry sort of liquors." Pitt, understanding that he had to meet a scarcely veiled demand for blackmail, sent Manucci, the Venetian who, as previously stated, had taken up his residence at Madras, to the Nawab's camp with a number of presents, including the strong drink specifically mentioned. Daud Khan scornfully rejected the gifts as inadequate, sending back word by Manucci that if greater generosity was not shown he would appoint a Governor for Blacktown and develop San Thomé at the expense of Madras. Pitt disregarded his threat for a time, but when Daud Khan in the following July appeared at San Thomé with a force of 10,000 men, he deemed it advisable to send two of the members of his Council to the Nawab's camp with a fresh assortment of presents, with the object of conciliating him. The Nawab, however, still continued obdurate. He had set his heart on squeezing the Company for a substantial sum, and was not to be put off with the customary offerings. Pitt, perceiving that trouble was brewing, strengthened the garrison by landing men from three ships in the roads and by increasing his Portuguese and native levies. This resolute attitude brought the Nawab to his senses. He now consented to receive the presents, and gave further evidence of his friendliness by inviting himself to dinner in the fort. Pitt accepted his overtures with every show of alacrity. On the day of the Nawab's visit he caused the streets to be lined with troops, and in company with an imposing retinue went to the outskirts of the town to meet the self-invited guest and escort him into the fort. When the Council House was reached Pitt "set by the Nawab two glasses of rich cordiall waters and bade him welcome," while a salute of 21 guns was fired in his honour. The banquet, which was prepared under the direction of a Persian, consisted of 600 dishes, great and small, of which, we are told in the records, the Nawab and all with him ate very heartily. After the repast "dancing wenches" entertained the guests until the evening, when the whole party returned to San Thomé. Daud Khan was so pleased with his visit that before leaving he expressed a desire to extend his experiences of the English by a visit to one of the Company's ships on the following day. The necessary arrangements were consequently made for his embarkation from Triplicane, "but," says the veracious chronicle, "he being very drunk over night was not in a condition to go and deferred it until to-morrow morning." The breakfast prepared for his consumption was, however, sent to San Thomé, and apparently he was not so bad as not to be able to enjoy it, for we are told "he accepted it very kindly." A few days later the Nawab quitted the district, much to the relief of his unwilling hosts, but the English had by no means seen the last of him. In six months' time he was back again at San Thomé with a large force, which he employed in instituting a strict blockade of the fort. He justified his action by a reference to an Imperial Order, dated November 16, 1701, interdicting trade with Europeans on the ground that they had failed to prevent piracies committed on ships sailing under the Moslem flag. Pitt immediately took steps to meet the threatened aggression. An appeal to the Danes for help was responded to by the dispatch of a vessel from Tranquebar to Madras with provisions. The Dutch were also invited to assist, but they excused themselves on what seemed inadequate grounds. The truth, no doubt, was that there was no desire on the part of the Hollanders to make things smoother for their rivals than they could help. About the middle of March, when the blockade had been in progress some weeks, Daud Khan intimated that his retirement might be purchased by the payment of Rs. 30,000. Pitt, recognizing that he was in a somewhat difficult position, accepted the principle of a fine, and ultimately managed to buy off his importunate friend by the payment of Rs. 25,000. All now went well for a time. Daud Khan had other matters to engage his attention, and he left Madras in peace. In November 1706, however, he again bethought himself of the flourishing settlement on the coast, and of the good cheer which offered there. Presenting himself at Fort St. George with a force of 2,500 men, he comported himself in characteristic fashion. "During his stay here," Pitt wrote home to the directors, "he has drunk very hard and is seldom in humour, grumbling very much at the small amount of our present." The last glimpse we get of him in the records is in a letter to Pitt where he asks for 1,000 bottles of liquor, a modest request which was partially responded to by the dispatch of 250 bottles.

In the whole of this intercourse with the bibulous Nawab Pitt showed himself a consummate statesman. By his combination of tact and firmness he kept the Mahommedan forces at arm's length, and at small expense saved Madras from hostilities which, if they had matured, might have resulted disastrously to the settlement, having regard to the inadequacy of the forces at his disposal for defence. Pitt's unerring knowledge of Oriental character, gained in long years of experience in India, no doubt stood him in good stead in this anxious period of his Governorship. The iron hand in the velvet glove he realized was the great need of the then situation in India. Writing home in 1703 in reference to the Mogul officials he said: "You will see they have a great mind to quarrel with us again, and it is most certain that the Moors will never let your trade run on quietly, as formerly, till they are well beaten. Besides, your having suffered your servants to be treated after that most ignominious manner at Surat for many years past has encouraged them to attempt the like in all your settlements, and I hear in Bengal that they *chawbuck* Englishmen in their public *darbars*, which formerly they never presumed to do, and the *junkaneers* all over the country are very insolent; only those within our reach I keep in pretty good order by now and then giving them a pretty good banging."

Throughout his career at Madras Pitt kept steadily before him the necessity of maintaining relations with the Mogul power with dignity and firmness. He never missed an opportunity of extending influence at the Mogul Court on this basis. When the great struggle for the succession took place on the deposition of Aurungzebe, Pitt enormously strengthened the position of the Company by entering into relations with influential adherents of Shah Alum, and conspicuously with Zain-ud-Din Khan, Lord High Steward of the Household. This junctionary in 1708 sent a letter to Fort St. George "professing great kindness and tendering his service in any affair." The communication was received by Pitt and his colleagues with appropriately friendly tokens. They sent to the Lord High Steward's lady, who happened to be residing at San Thomé, a suitable present, and they wrote asking the confirmation of privileges granted by Aurungzebe. Correspondence followed, and the most cordial relations were established. Pitt, seeing his opportunity, prepared a sumptuous present for the Emperor, which he designed should be presented to him at Golconda on the occasion of his visit there in 1709. But before the scheme could be carried out the directors deprived Pitt of his office, and the opening for consolidating British power was missed.

In the fullest sense of the term Pitt maintained the dignity of his office. His outgoings and incomings were marked by considerable pomp. No one knew better than he that outward display was an essential feature of any European establishment which aspired to power in the India of that day. In his personal relations with his colleagues he was probably more feared than respected. His enemies accused him of avarice and meanness and set many stories about to illustrate this phase of his character. The best known of these has reference to the acquisition of the famous diamond which Pitt acquired by purchase for a modest sum from a native dealer, and the sale of which at an enormous figure laid the foundation of his fortune. According to his calumniators, Pitt stole the diamond. Pope, who had no love for Pitt or his class, gave point to the allegations in the famous lines:

Asleep and naked as an Indian lay,
An honest factor stole a gem away;
He pledged it to the knight: the knight had wit,
So kept the diamond and the rogue was bit.

Pitt undoubtedly was what in familiar phrase is styled "close," but he had his attractive side, as his letters show. We read of him taking a kindly interest in humble connections, conducting experiments in gardening, and generally leading the life of a man who looked upon the world with kindly eyes. "It was his general force of character," writes Yule, "his fidelity to the cause of his employers (in spite of his master fault of keenness in money making), his decision in dealing with difficulties, that won his reputation. He was always ready; always cool in action, however bitter in language; he always saw what to do and did it." It is no disrespect to his many eminent successors to say that Thomas Pitt was one of the greatest Governors of Madras.

Madras was left by Pitt in a condition of prosperity it had never previously known. It was mentioned in one of the official letters of the period that in 1710 there were 50 ships at one time in the roads and above 200 small craft, while the revenues of the settlement aggregated 70,000 pagodas per annum. The growing importance of the place suggested to the authorities at home the advisability of overhauling the administrative arrangements. As a consequence of their deliberations a new charter, dated September 24, 1726, was obtained from George I, and was put into operation about the middle of the following year. Under this instrument an entirely new municipal body was created, at the head of which was a Mayor and nine Aldermen. The Mayor and the Aldermen were constituted a Court of Record, authorized to try all civil suits, an appeal to lie to the Governor and Council, whose decision was to be final in cases of judgments up to 1,000 pagodas. Where judgments involved a larger sum the appeal might be to the King in Council. Further powers of the charter were that the Governor and five senior members of Council were to be Justices of the Peace of the town of Madras, that the junior member of Council at the outset was to be nominated Sheriff of Fort St. George on the understanding that there should be thereafter an annual election to the office, that the Governor and five senior members of Council should be a Court of Record and Commissioners of Oyer and Terminer and General Jaol Delivery for trying all offences, except high treason, committed within the town or any of the Company's factories or within 10 English miles of the same. The formal introduction of the charter took place on August 17, 1727, with great ceremony. On September 12th following it was decided that the Justices of the Peace should be also Justices of the Choultry to decide small causes up to 20 pagodas. Some months later this arrangement for the trial of petty actions was supplanted by the establishment of a Sheriff's Court, where cases could be tried with a right of appeal to the Mayor's Court in certain circumstances. The directors, however, declined to sanction the alteration, and in the end there was a reversion to the original scheme of Justices of the Peace sitting at the Choultry.

Between 1730 and 1735, when Thomas Pitt's cousin, George Murton Pitt, was Governor, the trade of Madras underwent a serious decline. So marked was the deterioration that the directors in 1732 "despaired of ever seeing Madras retrieve its ancient glory of sending several thousand bales of calico in a season, which was the constant practice for so many years." The cause of the falling off was to a large extent the unsettled condition of Southern India owing to the ravages of the Mahrattas. An attempt was made by the founding, in 1736, of Chintadripetta, and the establishment there of 230 families to retrieve the situation. But the political conditions of the time were such as to prevent any substantial change. What emphasized the disability under which the settlement was labouring for the directors was the need they found themselves in to strengthen the garrison so as to guard against possible attacks from outside. In 1735 they sent out as reinforcements no fewer than 600 Europeans, under the command of Major Charles Knipe, an able and experienced officer with a record of thirty years' service at home and abroad. This addition to the Company's forces may be regarded as the beginning of the formation of that little Grand Army which, in the next few decades, was to win for itself fame and for the British nation the possession of India.

CHAPTER VI

French rivalry—War between Great Britain and France—Dupleix makes a demonstration against Madras—Withdrawal of the British fleet—Subsequent attack and capture of Fort St. George by de la Bourdonnais—Dupleix repudiates the conditions granted by de la Bourdonnais—De la Bourdonnais withdraws from the coast—His later career—The Nawab of the Carnatic attacks the French at Madras—Defeat of the Nawab's army—Dupleix decides to make the conquest of Madras permanent—Consternation of the English—Flight to Fort St. David—Clive assists in the defence of the fort—Clive's military qualities—The Rev. Francis Fordyce and Clive—Admiral Boscawen arrives off the coast—Assists in the attack on Pondicherry—Reoccupation of Madras by the British.

UP to the end of the seventeenth century and even beyond the main rivalry in the East amongst the European nations had been between the English and the Dutch. The eighteenth century had not long dawned before a new and formidable antagonist of the English appeared on the scene in the guise of a body of French adventurers—able, brave, and versatile—who were prepared to contest with them for the great prize of ascendancy in Southern India. In its earliest stages the conflict between the representatives of the two races took the form of commercial and political intrigue and counter-intrigue, but when in 1744 war broke out between Great Britain and France, a more serious aspect was given to affairs. The pen, hitherto mainly used, now gave place to the sword, and on both sides there was the making of history by men who afterwards won a place in the everlasting Halls of Fame.

As soon as the news of the declaration of war reached Madras, Nicholas Morse, the then Governor, in conjunction with his Council, took active steps to cause a close observation to be kept upon the French at Pondicherry. Dupleix, who was the Governor at the time, sent a proposal that the two nations should preserve peace eastward of the Cape by mutual agreement, but Morse demurred to this on the ground that he had no authority to enter into any such arrangement. Meanwhile, there had been sent out secretly from home, under Commodore Curtis Barnett, a squadron consisting of two sixty-gun ships, one fifty, and one twenty, with besides a number of small vessels acquired by capture. The force reached Fort St. David on July 22, 1745, and went on to Madras on August 30th following. Dupleix at first appears to have been intimidated by the imposing squadron the British had at their disposal, but in January 1746 he thought the conditions sufficiently favourable to justify a demonstration against Madras. The French squadron which was sent out was, however, quick to discover that Commodore Barnett was not to be caught napping, and it beat a hasty retreat. All would have gone well for the British, probably, had not they, on April 29th following, the misfortune to lose this capable sailor. His successor, Captain Edward Peyton, lacked his qualities of leadership, and was not at all the man to handle such a crisis as that which now confronted the authorities at Madras. The danger for them was that the French had brought up from the Isles of France and Bourbon a powerful fleet commanded by de la Bourdonnais, consisting of nine ships manned by 3,300 men. When this imposing force reached the Coromandel Coast at the end of May 1746, it was met off Negapatam by the British squadron and an engagement ensued. The fighting continued until dark, when Peyton decided, in view of the leaky condition of his ship, the *Medway*, to sail for Trincomalee. This he did, practically leaving Madras undefended from the sea for the time being. Dupleix was for taking advantage of the opening, but de la Bourdonnais held to the opinion that until the British squadron had been disposed of an attack would be dangerous. Some dissensions which arose between the two leaders on this question

1. GRAND MOSQUE AT SERINGAPATAM.
3. SERINGAPATAM.
From "Views in the Mysore Country." Published in 1794.

2. SKETCH OF THE SOUTH WORKS OF SERINGAPATAM.
4. SERINGAPATAM.
From "Picturesque Scenery in the Kingdom of Mysore." Edited by Edward Orme. Published in 1804.

of strategy were cut short by the return of the British ships to the coast. As Peyton showed no disposition to attack, an experimental demonstration was made against Madras by some ships under M. de la Porte Barre. The French squadron entered the Madras Roads and fired on the Company's ship, the *Princess Mary*, which was lying there at anchor. The raid was an entire success, as it was well calculated to be, seeing that Peyton at the time it was made was in full flight from the coast which he had been sent to protect.

The fate of Madras was practically sealed by the withdrawal of the squadron. On September 3rd the French fleet appeared off Madras prepared to attack the position with all the available force then at hand. It was formidable enough to create a very real sense of alarm amongst the British. The garrison was utterly inadequate to resist an assault by the large disciplined force which the French had at their disposal. The supreme military command had in the May previous, owing to the death of Major Knipe, devolved upon Major Stringer Lawrence, a name which was afterwards to be inscribed on the roll of the founders of the British Indian Empire, and with such a commander there was a full guarantee that the best use would be made of both men and material. But the positions to be defended were extensive, and no skill in leadership could altogether compensate for the inadequacy of fighting units.

De la Bourdonnais' first move was to land a detachment of 600 men at Trevembore, a few miles south of San Thomé, and march them along the shore under cover of the guns of the fleet. When the invading force reached a position about one mile south of the fort, an entrenched camp was formed and a battery of five mortars was installed on the beach at the south end of the river bar. At midnight the same day (September 3rd) a free merchant of Madras, named Barnewall, who had married Dupleix's daughter, presented himself at the French headquarters at Triplicane with a verbal request from Morse that the ladies of the station should be allowed to leave. De la Bourdonnais agreed to permit Mrs. Morse and Mrs. Barnewall, with a female companion to be selected by each, to leave. But the offer was declined, the ladies to whom the privilege was extended preferring to remain and share with the others in the dangers of the siege. Subsequently all the women and children were removed to St. Andrew's Church for safety, one end of the building being appropriated to their use, while the rest of the edifice was allotted to the surgeons for the treatment of the wounded. The next day the French completed the landing of the attacking force, which consisted of 1,000 Europeans and 800 native soldiers. After reconnoitring the position, de la Bourdonnais decided to make his attack from the west, and moved his camp to Chintadripetta in order more effectively to superintend the operations. On September 5th the French advanced as far as the Company's garden, and there established, under cover of the house, a battery of ten mortars. A sally made from the fort in the direction of the now partly deserted camp was easily repulsed. Two days later the French guns opened fire on the fort. The bombardment, which was continued for two days, produced a panic amongst the civil population. The situation eventually became so bad that the authorities decided to seek an accommodation with the enemy.

At an early hour on the 9th a deputation, consisting of Mr. William Monson, the second member of Council, accompanied by Mr. John Hallyburton, lately chief of Madipollam, waited on de la Bourdonnais. In reply to their request for information as to terms, the French commander stated that the possession of the place must be the basis of negotiation. The envoys demurred to this, representing that they had simply come to offer ransom, and stating that if this proposal was rejected the garrison would fight to the last. De la Bourdonnais dilated on the futility of resistance, and drew attention to a breaching battery of eighteen 24-pound guns which he had ready. He said: "Gentlemen, you'll give up your town and all within it, and I promise you, upon my honour, to put you in possession of it again upon paying the ransom" After some further conversation, Monson and Hallyburton returned to confer with the Governor. Meanwhile, the bombardment was resumed and was continued throughout the night. The following morning Monson and Hallyburton again presented themselves at the French camp and intimated that they were prepared to deliver up the fort provided the right to ransom the place was admitted De la Bourdonnais readily assented to this condition, and the capitulation signed by the Governor was then handed to him. The terms upon which the position was surrendered were that the British garrison and the inhabitants should be prisoners of war, but that the members of Council and others of superior rank should be released on parole and be permitted "to go and come wherever they please, even into Europe, provided they shall not carry arms against France." In order to facilitate the ransom of the town the Governor and his Council should cease to be prisoners of war immediately they entered into negotiations with M. de la Bourdonnais. Meanwhile the garrison were to be conducted to Fort St. David, prisoners of war pending the ransom of the place.

When all the preliminaries had been settled, the French troops marched across the island to the western gate of the White Town, where they were received by Governor Morse, who presented his sword to the French commander. Thereafter the troops marched into the fort and the pulling down of the British flag and the hoisting of the white lilies of France put the seal on one of the most remarkable conquests that the French ever won in India.

After the French had comfortably settled themselves in their new quarters, the knotty question of the ransom was discussed. A serious difficulty soon presented itself. While de la Bourdonnais was in favour of the ultimate return of the place to its British owners, and had, as we have seen, definitely pledged himself to that course, Dupleix wanted to have the absolute disposal of the place in order that he might turn it over to the Nawab, whose powerful support he would thereby gain in the prosecution of the splendid schemes of aggrandisement for the French which he had in view. De la Bourdonnais stuck honourably to his bargain, and fixing 1,100,000 pagodas as the amount of the ransom, provisionally agreed to the terms of a treaty embodying the essential conditions relating to the ransom. Before the treaty was actually signed, Dupleix sent two members of his Council to Madras, nominally to assist in the work of treaty making, but actually to enforce his views as to the retention of the town. When he discovered, as he soon did, that de la Bourdonnais was not to be influenced in this fashion, he dispatched a special mission to Madras consisting of Major-General de Bury and MM. Bruyère and Paradis, charged with the duty of deposing de la Bourdonnais. The French commander was no more intimidated by the new mission than he was influenced by the earlier one. When

Dupleix's declaration removing him from the chief authority was read out in the full Council, he stated that he recognized no authority superior to his own. Afterwards, to give emphasis to his declaration of independence, he embarked the Pondicherry troops and arrested the three Councillors who had been sent practically to supersede him. Having done this he sent to Dupleix to inquire whether he would assent to the treaty if the evacuation were deferred until January. Eventually Dupleix agreed to this compromise, and additional articles having been inserted in the draft treaty to bring it into harmony with the new conditions, the compact was finally ratified. Before the signatures were affixed (on October 10th), a terrible storm, which occurred on the night of October 2nd, worked great havoc with the French fleet, and de la Bourdonnais, fearing possibly an attack from a British force, which would have been fatal in his then condition, decided to leave the coast. Having made over the command of Madras to d'Esprémćnil, one of Dupleix's leading councillors, he set sail on October 12th for the Isle of France.

To complete the story of de la Bourdonnais' career, it may be said that he arrived safely at Mauritius, but soon quitted the island again for Europe, travelling from the Cape in a Dutch vessel. On the way up the English Channel this ship had to put into Falmouth owing to stress of weather. While on shore there de la Bourdonnais was recognized by a British naval officer and arrested. Afterwards he was released on parole and allowed to return to France; but, to use a homely simile, it was a case of "jumping out of the frying-pan into the fire," for he was arrested on arrival in Paris and cast into the Bastille to answer various charges which had been brought against him by his enemies. For three years he was detained a prisoner, and when he was ultimately given his freedom he was a broken man. He died in 1753.

The French were not permitted long to enjoy unchallenged the important conquest they had made. Dupleix's anxiety to prevent the conclusion of a treaty which would allow of the return of the place to the British had arisen to a large extent from fear of a native attack. Quite early in the operations against the English, he had received from the Nawab a note threatening to drive the French from Pondicherry if they did not forbear from attacking Madras. This was followed early in September by another communication couched in even more menacing language. As the French made no response to the Nawab's demands, that dignitary sent a considerable force and laid siege to Madras. The Frenchmen made a spirited defence, and in a sally on October 22nd routed a considerable part of the Mahommedan besiegers, capturing their camp. Meanwhile, Dupleix forwarded from Pondicherry a reinforcement of 400 men. This body, arriving at the bank of the Adyar, found the Nawab's army of 10,000 men prepared to dispute its passage. In spite of the formidable odds against them, the Frenchmen crossed the river and fell upon the

LORD CLIVE.

Nawab's army, which broke under the onslaught and fled in disorder. Paradis, who was in charge of the French force, now resumed his march to Madras, where he was naturally received with great rejoicing.

Dupleix having thus made himself master of the situation, decided to annul the treaty of ransom and make the conquest of Madras a permanent one. As Barthlémy declined to be a party to such a gross act of bad faith, he was superseded by Paradis, whose antagonism to de la Bourdonnais made him a pliant tool in the work of upsetting the settlement. Acting on instructions from Pondicherry, Paradis on October 30th publicly and formally announced that the treaty was void and that Madras was the property of the French East India Company, to be held for the King of France.

Consternation seized the English at this flagrant act of dishonour. Feeling that they were absolved from their parole by the repudiation of the treaty, Clive and a number of the military officers fled to Fort St. David, there to await the turn of the tide which they felt could not be very distant. Morse and several of the leading civil officials proceeded to Pondicherry, where they were well received by Dupleix.

At Fort St. David the little band of Britons from Madras maintained an unequal but for the most part successful war against the French. They repulsed several land attacks, the most important of which was delivered on March 1 and 2, 1747, when the patriots were severely tried, being, in fact, only saved from disaster by the timely arrival of a British squadron of eight ships from Bombay with substantial reinforcements. These operations will be ever memorable for affording an opening for the militarv career of Clive. A reference to him in the records indicates that from the first his singular genius for military affairs was recognized. "Mr. Robert Clive," the entry runs, "having served as a Volunteer in the late engagement and requesting to be entertained as ensign, the same is granted him and a commission ordered to be drawn out accordingly." Another entry said: "Mr. Robert Clive, Writer in the service, being of a martial disposition, and having acted as a Volunteer in our late engagement, we have granted him an Ensign's Commission upon his application for the same." From home in due course came approval of the action taken in regard to Clive. "Be sure," wrote the directors, "to encourage Ensign Clive in his martial pursuits. According to his merit any improvement he shall make therein shall be duly regarded by us." It was not often that talent was thus early recognized in the service of the Company. The history of the great enterprise, indeed, affords only too many melancholy examples of stupidity in dealing with men of exceptional ability.

Clive's promotion rapidly followed his entrance into the military state. As early as January 1749 we find him raised to the position of Quartermaster, an office which at the time must have called for the exercise of exceptional qualities. He had not very long discharged his new duties before he became involved in a personal quarrel of a particularly irritating kind with the chaplain, the Rev. Francis Fordyce, who had recently come to St. David from Bencoolen with a character for quarrelsomeness which he abundantly sustained. The episode is fully related in a deposition made by Clive at a subsequent period when the matter came up for official investigation. Clive said : "That being at dinner with Messrs. Dalton and Worth on or about the 16th day of February at Bandipollam, they told him Mr. Fordyce had said to a gentleman in public company that he was a scoundrel and a coward, and that he had shook his cane over him in the presence of Mr. Levy Moses. Mr. Clive further says that some time before this he had been informed by Captain Cope that Mr. Fordyce did in conversation with him threaten to break every bone in his skin ; and he says that these repeated abuses so irritated him that he could not forbear on meeting Mr. Fordyce in Cuddalore to reproach him with his behaviour, which he told him was so injurious he could bear it no longer, and thereupon struck him two or three times with his cane ; which at last Mr. Fordyce returned and then closed in with him, but that they were presently parted by Captain Lucas who happened to be by."

Clive went on to say that he was not the only person who had been abused and calumniated by Mr. Fordyce, for he had "aspersed the character of Mr. Joseph Fowke, by saying that he was a dark and designing villain, that he would slit his nose the first time he met him, and that he had knocked him under the table at the Governours." Other examples of the militant cleric's violence were cited, and the relation was closed with the statement that Mr. Fordyce "was generally detested and shunned both at St. Helena and on the West Coast of Africa on account of his meddling disposition, which made him obnoxious to every one."

Right was so strongly on Clive's side that the Council summarily dismissed Fordyce and dispatched him to England In their report on the subject to the authorities at home the Council spoke of Clive as one "who is generally esteemed, a very quiet person and no ways guilty of disturbances."

The work ahead was of too stern a description for personal squabbles of this character to find much scope. At the end of July 1748 Admiral Boscawen, the well-known naval commander, arrived off the coast with a strong fleet consisting of ten vessels, of which six were ships of the line. With characteristic energy he prepared to deal with the foe which had inflicted such loss upon the British on the coast. In conjunction with the military forces at St. David, commanded by Major Stringer Lawrence, he delivered an attack on Pondicherry in the early days of August. The operation was entered upon under unhappy circumstances. At the very outset Major Lawrence was taken prisoner, while a second prominent member of the land force, Mr. Hallyburton, was shot dead by one of his own sepoys, who entertained a grudge against him. Boscawen, notwithstanding these discouragements, persisted with the siege, and possibly might have achieved some result if the season had been earlier. As matters stood he was compelled by the approach of the monsoon in October to raise the siege and quit the coast. The rebuff was of the less consequence because even before the hostilities at Pondicherry had been entered upon the political status of the Coromandel coast, so far as it affected the British settlements, had been decided by the treaty of Aix la Chapelle, the preliminary stages of which were concluded on April 19, 1748. Under this instrument Madras was restored to the British, and all the officials detained in French hands were set at liberty.

The formal reoccupation by the British took place on August 21, 1749, amid the great rejoicings of the native inhabitants "who," according to the official chronicler, "thronged there in great numbers immediately on hoisting the English flag, though all the art the French made use of could not induce them to return while they were in possession." Following upon the reoccupation of Madras came the acquisition of San Thomé, over which the British flag was hoisted on October 11, 1749, by Boscawen, who had been prompted to take the action by the news that came to hand of Dupleix's designs upon the place. In other respects the British power was promptly reasserted, so that by the end of the year the whole machinery of administration along the coast was in full swing again. But it was not until April 6, 1752, that the Presidency was transferred from Fort St. David to Madras.

CHAPTER VII

British and French rivalry in the Carnatic—Clive conducts an expedition to Arcot—The battles of Arnee and Conjeveram—Capitulation of the French at the Jambukrishna Pagoda on the island of Srirangam—Defeat of a British force at Gingee by the French—Major Stringer Lawrence avenges the defeat—Clive captures Covelong and Chingleput—Clive's marriage—Conclusion of peace with the French—Clive reduces the pirate stronghold of Angria at Gheriah—Capture of Calcutta by Suraj-ud-Dowlah—Clive fights the battle of Plassy—Renewal of the war with France—Lally occupies Cuddalore and besieges Fort St. David—The fort occupied and destroyed—Attack on Madras—Admiral Pocock's squadron relieves the garrison—Defeat of the French under Conflans by the British—Salabut Jung renounces the French alliance—Admiral Pocock defeats the French fleet under D'Ache—Colonel Eyre Coote defeats the French at Wandewash—Downfall of French power in India.

WHILE the British and French were fighting out their quarrel along the coast a mightier issue was rapidly ripening in the Carnatic—the issue, that is, of the future paramountcy of India. In a few years a number of important changes had occurred in the dynastic condition of India. In April 1748 Mahomed Shah, the Emperor, had expired, and his death was followed two months later by that of Nizam-ul-Mulk, formerly known as Chin Kilick Khan. The demise of the latter led to the appearance of rival claimants for the vacant office of Nizam in the persons of Nasir Jang, Nizam-ul-Mulk's son, and a grandson named Muzaffar Jang. The British upheld the pretensions of the former, while the latter's cause was espoused by the French. This game of cross-purposes was extended to the Carnatic, where, under similar conditions of rivalry, the British and the French identified themselves with the interests of opposing parties. The British nominee was Nawab Anwar-ud-din, while the French pinned their faith to the dynasty of Dost Ali and Safdar Ali. It happened that at this period the last representative of the ancient regime was a prisoner in the hands of the Mahrattas. Dupleix astutely paid the ransom of the Nawab, and having obtained his release induced him to join in a movement the French were making in conjunction with Muzaffar Jang's forces against Nawab Anwar-ud-din. Battle was joined at Ambur, in August 1749, with the result that Nawab Anwar-ud-din was slain, his eldest son, Mahfuz Khan, made prisoner, and Chanda Sahib appointed Nawab of the Carnatic. The ultimate outcome of these occurrences was that a good part of Southern India was divided into two hostile camps, Muzaffar Jang and Chanda Sahib being on one side supported by the French, while on the other were Nasir Jang and Mahomed Ali, upheld, after a somewhat feeble fashion, by the English. In March 1750 Mahomed Ali left Trichinopoly to join hands with Nasir Jang at Valdore, a place fifteen miles south-west of Pondicherry. The junction was effected, but whatever advantages might have accrued from it were materially lessened by the withdrawal of the British forces up to that time operating with the native army. A failure to pay the contingent was deemed by the authorities at Fort St. David a good and sufficient reason for this defection. But they speedily had evidence of the ill-effects of leaving their *protégés* to their own devices. Bussy, the French commander, realizing that he had a clear road, now entered upon a vigorous campaign. He achieved a notable victory at Gingee, and in other ways greatly advanced the prestige of the French arms. Before the year was out French influence was predominant throughout the Carnatic. On the death of Nasir Jang in December, Muzaffar Jang had become Nizam, and when he, in turn, was removed a month later, the French put in his place Salabat Jang, brother of Nasir Jang. Meanwhile, Mahomed Ali was being besieged in Trichinopoly in circumstances which appeared to offer small hope of his success. The British authorities, surveying the situation, came to the conclusion that their duty was to intervene with a view of securing, if possible, the relief of Mahommed Ali. This they deemed could be best effected by an attack on Arcot, the almost inevitable effect of which must be to raise the siege of Trichinopoly.

For this important work the Madras Council had at the time no more experienced officer than Clive, but as we have seen, the official mind had already recognized the high military qualities that the young ensign possessed, and there was the injunction from home to employ him to justify the selection. If any misgivings were ever entertained as to the wisdom of the appointment, they were entirely dispelled by the manner in which Clive executed his mission. The story has been made classical by Macaulay, though there is reason to think that he allowed his passion for literary effect to get the better of him in some of the picturesque details, notably in that famous story of the sepoys giving their rice to their European comrades and themselves subsisting on the water in which the grain was boiled. Still, even divested of all its pretty embroidery, the account of the enterprise supplies thrilling reading. Marching out of Fort St. George on August 26, 1751, with a force of 200 Europeans and 300 Sepoys, with eight officers, half of whom were civil servants, Clive entered Arcot on September 1st. For some days he was unopposed, but gradually the enemy under Chanda Sahib drew its toils around him, and on September 23rd the little British force was closely besieged in the fort. For fifty days Clive held the position against overwhelming odds, repulsing a determined attempt to storm the walls. Ultimately relief was sent from Madras in the shape of a force under Captain Kilpatrick. Clive soon took the offensive, and in brilliant engagements at Arnee and Conjeveram showed that he was a force to be reckoned with in the clash of arms then proceeding in Southern India.

1. A VIEW OF PART OF SAN THOMÉ STREET, FORT ST. GEORGE.
From "A Brief History of Ancient and Modern India." Published in 1804.

2. A VIEW OF MOUNT ST. THOMAS, NEAR MADRAS.
From "Picturesque Scenery in the Kingdom of Mysore." Edited by Edward Orme. Published in 1804.

On Major Stringer Lawrence's return to India on March 14, 1752, with the rank of Commander-in-Chief in India, the conduct of the campaign naturally devolved upon him, but he had Clive as his right-hand man, and the young ensign's shrewd judgment and cool courage no doubt largely ministered to the successes which were ultimately achieved. These were neither few nor unimportant. The most conspicuous of them was the defeat of the French and the capitulation, on June 13, 1752, of the forces under Law at the Jambukrishna Pagoda on the island of Srirangam on the Cauvery. On this occasion 35 officers, 785 European soldiers, and 2,000 Sepoys laid down their arms, and the British took possession of 41 pieces of cannon and an immense store of ammunition. This was one of the heaviest blows that the French power had up to this date received in India, and though, before twelve months were out, the genius of Dupleix had to a considerable extent retrieved the disaster, the distinct turn of the tide in the direction of British supremacy may be said to date from this memorable June day in 1752.

The actual course of events may be briefly stated. While Lawrence and Clive were both away in Madras recuperating after the fatigues of the campaign, the British force which had occupied Trichinopoly evacuated that place and marched against Gingee, then in French occupation. Stoutly resisted by the garrison and taken in rear by a force sent out from Pondicherry by Dupleix, they were badly beaten and retired in disorder. On news of the disaster reaching Madras, Major Stringer Lawrence, though ill at the time, proceeded immediately by sea to Fort St. David, promptly organized the force that was there and marched out against the French. Issue was joined on September 6, 1752, when after a stubbornly contested fight he won a great victory over the enemy. Kerjean, the French commander, with 15 of his officers and about 100 men were taken prisoners, and a good many were killed and wounded. The loss on the British side was 1 officer killed, 4 wounded, and 70 men killed and wounded. This signal victory was followed by the capture by the British of the Forts of Covelong and Chingleput, two posts of some importance in the then conditions of warfare.

Clive's name is conspicuously associated with this brilliant page in the history of the British in Southern India. He marched against them with an insignificant force, the European portion of which consisted of 200 raw recruits, "the sweepings of the English jails, and so little disciplined that, on a shot from the Fort of Covelong killing one of them, all the rest ran away." Nevertheless, says Malleson, in his "The French in India," "even upon this rabble Clive exercised an influence so magical; he won their respect to such an extent by his own contempt of danger and personal daring, his failing health notwithstanding, that at their head and by their means he reduced Covelong, defeated a force of 700 Sepoys and 40 Europeans sent by Dupleix to relieve it, and then, marching on Chingleput, the strongest place next to Gingee in that part of the country, forced the French garrison of 40 Europeans and 500 Sepoys to evacuate it."

With a promptitude which did credit to their sense of the value of good leading, the Company sent out to India a generous appreciation of the services of both Lawrence and Clive. It was stated in this rescript that it was to the young soldier's "courage and conduct that the late favourable turn in affairs" was greatly owing, and he was assured that the directors had "a just sense of his services." Material tokens of the official goodwill were afterwards forthcoming in the shape of swords of honour for the two commanders, of the value of £750 and £500 respectively.

Clive married in Madras on February 18, 1752, and went to England shortly afterwards on a well-earned holiday. The fame of his achievements had preceded him, and he met with a most flattering reception from the Government authorities of the period. It was probably not a little to the interest excited by his visit that was due the dispatch in 1754 to Madras of a naval squadron of six ships under Admiral Charles Watson, with a regiment of foot under the command of Colonel John Adlercon, and a detachment of Royal Artillery commanded by Captain-Lieutenant William Hislop. Greatly impressed with this display of force, M. Godehen, who had succeeded Dupleix in the command of the French settlements, hastened to propose a suspension of arms. As the British at the time had well established their prestige, they were not unwilling to accept the proposal, which they did in formal terms on October 11th.

Meanwhile, throughout India at this juncture there was an ominous gathering of clouds which boded ill for the British. Clive's return to India in November 1755, in the circumstances was well timed. On arriving in Bombay he found congenial employment ready to hand in the rooting out of a nest of pirates which had long been a thorn in the side of the local administration. Clive did the work with characteristic dispatch and completeness. After a two days' bombardment, the stronghold of the pirate chief, Angria, at Gheriah, was stormed, and the entire garrison put to the sword. Proceeding afterwards to Madras the gallant young commander took his seat as second of Council on May 25th, and was preparing to settle down to the humdrum existence of Deputy-Governor of Fort St. David, when the startling news was received of the capture of Calcutta by Suraj-ud-Dowlah, with the concomitant Black Hole tragedy. The sensation caused was naturally great, for the blow was the greatest that had been delivered at the British power in India since it had secured a firm foothold in the country. An expedition was promptly organized to reassert British power in Bengal, the presence of Admiral Watson's squadron in port affording a valuable support for the measures which were undertaken. As Lawrence was too enfeebled to take command of the troops, there was an idea of giving the control over to Colonel Adlercon, but happily for Clive's reputation, happily for the British power in India, the brilliant young hero of Arcot was selected for the position. How he acquitted himself of his task, and on the historic field of Plassy laid firmly the foundations of the edifice of British India as it exists to-day, is a matter of history and one which lies beyond the scope of this narrative.

Our interest centres in the struggle between the British and the French, which entered upon a new phase in Southern India in 1757 owing to the outbreak of war between Great Britain and France. While Clive in Bengal seized Chandernagore, the French promptly made themselves master of the Coromandel coast from Vizagapatam to Masulipatam. A fleet of eleven vessels with a substantial land force under Lally, which arrived from France at the end of April 1758, seemed to offer a prospect of further successes—a prospect which deepened when an engagement between the British fleets off the coast produced no decisive result.

While the sea engagement was proceeding Lally attacked Cuddalore, and at the close of a few days' fighting occupied the fort. The members of the garrison were permitted to retire to Fort St. David, but the French, vigorously pursuing their campaign, on May 8th laid siege to the fort with a formidable force composed of 3,500 European troops. Messages had been sent from Madras directing Major Potier, the commander, to hold on at all costs, but owing to the demoralization of the garrison this worthy deemed that the position was untenable and surrendered it on June 1st. Lally, who had no men to spare for an occupation of the place, and was intent on bigger game, razed the fortifications and destroyed the principal buildings. With the completion of the work of destruction the history of Fort St. David ended, for the site was never afterwards reoccupied by the Company.

Quitting Fort St. David, Lally directed his attention to Tanjore, but his plans missed fire badly and he was fain compelled to attempt to retrieve his reputation by an attack on Madras. He arrived off that place on December 12, 1758, with an army which consisted of 3,000 Europeans, 500 native cavalry, and 3,000 Sepoys. Against this formidable force the British were only able to muster for the entire duties of the defence of the fort and town 1,758 Europeans, 2,200 Sepoys, and 200 horse. There was, however, a body of troops at Chingleput under Captain Achilles Preston, and Major Cailland had an additional force at Tanjore which was useful for acting on the enemy's lines of communications. What, however, the British lacked in numbers they probably made up in leading. The then Governor of Madras, George Pigott (afterwards Lord Pigott), was a man of great administrative ability and sound judgment, and Stringer Lawrence, who was in military command, was a host in himself. The early period of the French occupation of the environs of the fort was consumed in plundering Black Town, which they did very thoroughly. But a vigorous sally by a British force of 600 men under Colonel Draper, on December 14th, gave them more legitimate employment. At the outset the British carried all before them, and one of their leaders, Brigadier-General Count d'Estaing, was taken prisoner, but the French, rallying spiritedly, made a heavy counter attack which drove back Colonel Draper's force to Madras in confusion. Fortunately the advantage thus secured was not followed up by the French, or Madras would probably have fallen a second time to the invader. As things were the British loss was sufficiently heavy, the casualties amounting to one-third of the entire force. Lally had some difficulty in getting up his guns, but on the second day of the New Year he had two batteries in position, and with these he commenced a bombardment which lasted almost without interruption for forty-two days. By this time a breach had been effected in the walls and the way had otherwise been prepared for an assault which Lally made up his mind to deliver. Before, however, he could complete his plans he had the mortification of seeing, on February 16th, a powerful British squadron of six ships under Admiral Pocock enter the roads.

The arrival of this timely reinforcement was the death-blow to his plans. Destroying most of his stores, and dispatching to Pondicherry as many of his wounded as he could get away, he retired, Malleson says, "full of rage and mortification by way of San Thomé to Conjeveram. Thus failed the great enterprise on which Lally had set his heart—to which he had devoted every energy of body and mind." The British, however, only held the position at great cost. Their casualties during the siege amounted to 29 officers killed and dangerously wounded, 581 Europeans, and 762 Sepoys killed, wounded, or deserted.

After this rebuff to Lally the great struggle between the British and the French entered upon its final stage. Responding to a call for help made by Rajah Anunderas, of Chicacole, who had driven the French out of Vizagapatam, Clive, then in supreme military authority in Bengal, sent by sea on October 12, 1758, a force consisting of 500 Europeans and 2,000 Sepoys with eighteen guns. This body, landing at Vizagapatam on October 20th, moved out against the French General, Conflans, who had established himself at Rajamundez. An easy victory was gained by the British, who, after driving their adversaries out of their position, marched onwards to Rajamundez, which they occupied on December 10th. Conflans retired on Masulipatam, in the meantime calling to his aid the French garrisons at various points. Undeterred by the knowledge that the French had received heavy reinforcements in this way, and that in addition a powerful native force of 15,000 horse and 20,000 foot had taken the field intent on his destruction, Forde followed up Conflans and besieged him in Masulipatam. As the year advanced his position became precarious, but with the spirit of indomitable courage which animated so many of the British officers of this period, he determined not to be turned from his purpose by the difficulties which stood so ominously in his path. On the night of April 7, 1759, he gathered his troops and assaulted the position of the enemy. Though the odds against them were tremendous, the assailants carried everything before them, and when morning dawned Conflans was a prisoner and his army was disarmed. The results of this victory were far-reaching. Under its immediate influence Salabut Jang concluded a treaty with Forde, whereby he renounced the French alliance, agreed never to allow a French contingent in the Deccan, and ceded to the British territories yielding an annual revenue of four lakhs of rupees. The compact practically sealed the fate of the French in India, but there remained yet a notable series of conflicts before the Gallic spirit of enterprise in India flickered out.

Lally, retreating from Madras, as we have seen, took up a position at Conjeveram. After a period he proceeded alone to Arcot to arrange for the provisioning of the army, leaving the command in the hands of de Soupire. He had not been long away when a British force, commanded by Major Brereton, successor to Lawrence in the military command, appeared in the vicinity. By skilful manœuvring Brereton compelled de Soupire to retire to Arcot, and while he was away the British force attacked and occupied Conjeveram. Lally, in spite of illness, strove manfully against the adverse influences that were overwhelming him with disaster, and even gained some minor successes, but his troops were mutinous and his resources indifferent, while repeated defeats had weakened the once powerful hold that the French had on the native forces. A ray of hope shone out in September when a strong French squadron, under Count d'Aché, appeared off the coast prepared to re-establish French *prestige*. This fleet, consisting of eleven ships of large size, was in gun power and manning superior to the British fleet, also of eleven ships, under Admiral Pocock, then on the station, and a contest seemed to offer a promise of a French victory. But when the issue was joined on September 10th, off Fort St. David, the British, after a hot cannonade, compelled the French fleet to retire with considerable loss. D'Aché himself was wounded in the course of the action, and seems to have been left with little stomach for further fighting when his battered vessels dropped anchor off Pondicherry. He hurriedly landed the stores he had brought out, and in spite of all the protests of Lally, sailed for Europe, never to return. His defection, if such it can be called, was the more serious as the British at this juncture had received a substantial military reinforcement, consisting of 300 men under the command of Colonel Eyre Coote, a name which was thenceforward to occupy a high place in the annals of British India. Before Coote could join forces with Brereton, the latter had moved out of his cantonments with a body of 2,000 Europeans to attack the French at Wandewash. His enterprise, though well conceived and attended with some success at the outset, had ended in disaster. It remained for Colonel Eyre Coote to retrieve the situation, which he did in the famous battle of Wandewash, fought on January 22, 1760, by which the French were decisively defeated, Bussy being taken prisoner and the French forces dispersed. Though the numbers employed in the battle were small, Malleson classes it among the decisive battles of the world, for, he says, "it dealt a fatal and decisive blow to French domination in India. It shattered to the ground the mighty fabric which Martin, Dumas, and Dupleix had contributed to erect; it dissipated all the hopes of Lally; it sealed the fate of Pondicherry." After the fight the French strongholds one after another fell into the hands of the British. Pondicherry, which had been taken in January 1761, was restored to France by the Peace of Paris in 1763, but from this time forward Britain wielded a supremacy in Southern India which was unchallenged by any European Power.

CHAPTER VIII

Hostilities between the British and Hyder Ali—Hyder Ali threatens Madras—Conclusion of peace—Warren Hastings assumes the government of Madras—Great change in the status of the British in India—Lord Pigott arrives in Madras as Governor—His disagreements with his Council—Lord Pigott deposed by the majority and made prisoner—Death of Lord Pigott—Mr. Whitehill sent out by the directors to re-establish the government of Lord Pigott—Unsuccessful indictment of the majority for causing Lord Pigott's death—Their subsequent trial and punishment in England.

THOUGH a formidable rival had been disposed of in the defeat of the French, the British power in Madras was still far from being consolidated. It held its own on the coast by virtue of the British command of the sea, but in the interior there were native combinations which threatened the peace of the settlement and at times even menaced its existence. The Nizam of Hyderabad was joined in the north by the Mahrattas against the Nawab of the Carnatic and Hyder Ali, the ruler of Mysore, in the south. In the first instance the Nizam assisted Hyder Ali in attacking the Carnatic, whose interests the British were at the time defending, but after the campaign the prince made peace with the Company, thereby setting a seal to the treaty concluded in the previous year, by which the British were confirmed in the grant made by the Mogul to Clive of the Northern Circars, with the exception of Guntoor, which passed under the control of Hyderabad.

Hostilities soon broke out afresh between the Company and Hyder Ali. For some time the campaign proceeded without much progress being made on the British side, mainly owing to the inept policy of the Madras Council, which interfered with the military plans to such an extent as to render effective work impossible.

At the beginning of 1769, when the operations had continued some time, Hyder Ali expressed a desire for peace. His overtures were not rejected, but the Governor, Charles Bourchier, while keeping Hyder Ali engaged in discussion, took the hostile and somewhat deceitful course of directing Colonel Smith, who was in charge of the Company's military interests, to threaten the enemy's force. Hyder Ali rose to the situation. He affected to be intimidated by the British move, and caused the bulk of his army to fall back on Cuddalore. When the strategic movement had properly developed, he put himself at the head of 6,000 cavalry and made a forced march on Madras. His arrival there created a somewhat painful sensation amongst the Company's officials. They now realized that they would have to concede to force what they were hitherto not prepared to yield to persuasion. After brief negotiations they concluded with Hyder Ali a treaty for an offensive and defensive alliance and for the mutual restitution of conquests.

Within a few months after this none too creditable episode in Madras history, the administration was strengthened by the arrival in the settlement of Warren Hastings, who shares with Clive the honour of founding British power in India on a settled basis. Hastings joined the Council in 1769 and remained until the month of February 1772. He left no great mark upon the administration, but the records show that he took a very lively interest in the development of the settlement. One of his proposals was the construction of a pier. He thought that the surf at Madras was not more formidable than that at Margate, where the historic "jetty" then existed, and he invited his brother-in-law, Woodman, to obtain the opinion of Smeaton or some other expert authority upon the feasibility of a scheme which he outlined. A prompt response was made to the request, and Hastings was furnished from home with designs supplemented by the plans of Ramsgate pier, which the surveyor of that town had furnished to Woodman. But the project never materialized in Hastings's time, partly, no doubt, owing to his transfer to Bengal, where far more important questions than the provision of a pier to save wet feet at Madras awaited him.

Hastings's departure from Madras marked the close of an epoch in British Indian history. The Company was no longer a trading body existing on the sufferance of capricious native rulers. It had become a great ruling authority already strong enough to dictate its will to a considerable part of India. The change was formally marked by the passage of the Regulating Act of 1773, by which Parliamentary control was established over the Company and a supreme authority was created in Bengal, with Hastings as its head with the title of Governor-General. Under this enactment Madras, which had been practically independent in common with Bombay and Bencoolen, dropped into a subordinate position.

Following closely upon Hastings's period of service in Madras came a remarkable episode in the life of the community, which created great stir at the time not only in India but in Europe. At the end of 1775 there arrived at Madras Lord Pigott, the hero of the episode described in a previous chapter, who had been sent out by the directors to supersede the Governor, Mr. Alexander Wynch. The latter had got into bad odour at home by assisting in the conquest of Tanjore, the deposition of the Rajah, and the transfer of the rule of

1. THE NORTH ENTRANCE INTO THE FORT OF BANGALORE. 2. GENERAL VIEW OF BANGALORE.

From "Picturesque Scenery in the Kingdom of Mysore." Edited by Edward Orme. Published in 1804.

3. NORTH ENTRANCE TO TIPU'S PALACE, BANGALORE.

From "Picturesque Scenery in the Kingdom of Mysore."

4. NORTH FRONT OF TIPU'S PALACE, BANGALORE.

From "Picturesque Scenery in the Kingdom of Mysore."

the State to the Nawab of the Carnatic. Stern disapproval was expressed of this action, and Lord Pigott carried with him specific instructions to reverse the policy of his predecessor and restore Tanjore to the Rajah. It may be supposed that an envoy of this description was not one likely to be received with effusion in a community constituted as was that of Madras, where most of the members of the service were bound to each other by the closest ties. The new Governor had only been in office a few weeks before the most serious differences developed. Trouble arose at the outset over the terms in which the rendition of Tanjore should be made. Pigott thought that loans made to the Nawab for the support of his troops and for advances made to the inhabitants for cultivation were matters of private concern. This view was opposed by an important section of the Council, who held that the amount involved was a legitimate public charge, which should be set against the Tanjore revenues. On a division it was found that five were for Pigott's view and seven against. The majority gave effect to their view by further resolving that the Nawab was entitled to the Government share of the next crop in Tanjore. Enraged at this opposition, Lord Pigott reported to the directors that the majority had repudiated his proceedings in connection with Tanjore.

Shortly afterwards a new source of difference arose on the question of the appointment of an official to the Tanjore command. A proposal was made that Colonel Stuart should be selected, but Pigott moved that a Council should be be set up with Mr. Russell as chief. The Governor's suggestion was set aside, and the Council was moved by one of its members, Mackay, to consider the question of the instructions to be given to Stuart. On Pigott declining to put this motion, the members of the Council recorded their views separately. It was found that a majority approved the instructions, but in spite of this Pigott resolutely refused to sign them. This was followed by a new move on the part of the majority, who prepared a minute condemning the Governor's conduct as "unconstitutional and illegal." Pigott, however, stood resolutely to his guns, declaring that no resolution of the majority could be valid without his concurrence, and urging further that the power of veto was vested in himself. The next step of the majority was to draft an order to the secretary to issue the instructions. The document was in process of signature when Lord Pigott seized it and intimated his intention not to allow the matter to proceed further without a reference to England. Immediately afterwards he drew from his pocket a paper from which he read as follows :

"I charge George Stratton and Henry Brooke, Esquires, of being guilty of an act subversive of the authority of Government and tending to introduce anarchy in the signing (an) order to the Secretary to give instructions to Colonel Stuart which has not been approved and passed by the President of Council." When he had thus unburdened himself Lord Pigott gave effect to his words by moving the suspension of Messrs. Stratton and Brooke, the prime movers in the business of which he complained. Four members, Mackay, Jourdan, Palmer, and Floyer, voted against the motion ; three others, Stone, Dalrymple, and Russell, pronounced in its favour. The President's vote as a member made the voting equal. Consequently it remained for him to give his casting vote to carry the motion, and, needless to say, he did not hesitate to record it. A strong protest now came from the majority, who indignantly inveighed against "the unexampled outrage offered to the constitution," and the arbitrary behaviour shown to two of their number "by an illegal attempt to suspend them in order by a trick to gain a majority."

No further development of consequence took place until three days later (August 23rd), when Lord Pigott at a specially convened meeting of the Council suspended Floyer, Palmer, Jourdan, and Mackay, and caused to be placed under arrest Sir Robert Fletcher, an officer of some notoriety, who had come out from England in the previous October as provisional Commander-in-Chief. At the same time Lord Pigott nominated Colonel Stuart for the chief command. In taking this strong action Lord Pigott had doubtless relied on the strength which his position gave him, but he had reckoned without the spirit of *camaraderie* which drew the military to the side of the majority, who were fighting, as they regarded, for private rights against corporate greed.

When the majority realized that Lord Pigott's intention was to crush them with the weight of his official status, they decided upon the strong measure of placing him under arrest and assuming supreme control. The *coup d'état* was carried out without unnecessary loss of time. Acting under their directions Colonel Stuart caused Lord Pigott to be arrested. The circumstances of this extraordinary episode were related by Lord Pigott subsequently in the following words : "Between seven and eight o'clock at night (August 24th) I went from the Government house with Colonel Stuart to my chaise. On the island between the two bridges I saw Lieutenant-Colonel Edington, the Adjutant-General, come running across the road from the southern side towards the chaise. Supposing he wanted to speak to us, I reined in the horses ; and when Edington got near their heads he waved his naked sword and cried *Seapoys*, whereupon a party of Seapoys came from behind the trees on the other side, and Captain Lysanght, with a pistol in his hand, came up to the chaise from that side and said to me, 'You are my prisoner,' or words to that effect ; and then Colonel Stuart seized hold of my arm, and said, 'Go, sir,' or 'Go out, sir,' and an orderly sergeant drove away the orderly servant who was behind the chaise with my sword. I was then conducted by Captain Lysanght to Mr. Benfield's post-chaise ; Captain Lysanght opened the chaise door, and an orderly sergeant came out of it. I was told to get into it and Captain Lysanght came in also, keeping the pistol in his hand, and there was an orderly sergeant behind the chaise. As we passed the Seapoy General at the Company's Garden house, Captain Lysanght said, 'My Lord, you must on no account call out,' or words to that effect. When we had arrived near to the Long Tank, about three miles from town, he told me that he was carrying me to the Mount to deliver me into charge of Major Horne, and that he acted under Colonel Stuart's orders. About this time he let down the blinds of the chaise. I expressed my fears for the safety of the people in the town, to which Captain Lysanght replied he believed Colonel Stuart had taken every necessary precaution on that head." On arrival at Major Horne's bungalow Lord Pigott was informed that it was intended to remove him to Chingleput for detention pending instructions from home. The intimation was very badly received by the Governor. According to Lieutenant-Colonel Edington, who was entrusted with the duty of carrying out the orders of the majority, when he heard what his destination was "he threw his arms about Major Horne, claimed his protection, repeating his former resolution of not stirring alone from thence alive. He then addressed himself to the centries and soldiers to the following purpose: I am your lawful Governor appointed by the Court of directors, and none but they have a power to take from me my Commission. Those who have attempted to do it and all concerned are rebels, damned rascals who I will hang every one. I have been forty years in the Company's service; once taken prisoner. I defended Madras when laid siege to by the French and obliged them to raise it, for which I received the thanks of my King and country as well as of the Honourable Company; at the same time created a peer of Ireland. And a great deal to the above effect, adding: You are my soldiers; you are four hundred brave fellows and I will march at your head against all the forces along the Coast, and concluded with the most opprobrious language against the present Governor (Mr. Stratton) and Council. And that Lieutenant-Colonel Edington, pointing to him, was one of the villains or rascals who had made him prisoner." At this interesting juncture Messrs. Monckton, Dalrymple, and Lathom appeared on the scene, "the two former using such gross and abusive expressions, particularly Mr. Monckton, against the Governor (Mr. Stratton) and the other gentlemen of the Council . . . as Lieutenant-Colonel Edington never heard gentlemen make use of before."

Considering that the time had come for action, Edington addressed the guard, telling them what his instructions were and asking whether they were prepared to obey his orders. As no response was made to his inquiry he repeated it, and the officer in charge of the detachment then replied that he would obey Major Horne's commands. Major Horne, on being appealed to by Edington, declared that he could answer for the troops with his life. Apparently his confidence was not so great as to allow the matter to be put to the test, for when the Major and Edington had had a little private conference, the latter came to the conclusion to suspend the execution of the Council's orders until he had heard further from them.

Lord Pigott's incarceration becoming known, there was naturally much excitement in the settlement. While the general sentiment of the community seems to have been on the side of the majority, there was a powerful minority who strongly disapproved of the course adopted and resolutely declined to recognize the new Government. Sir Edward Hughes, the commander of the naval squadron on the station, hearing of the Governor's arrest, hastened to Major Horne's bungalow to ascertain from Lord Pigott's own lips what had occurred. As a result of the interview he sent in a demand to the majority that Major Horne should be given an order to furnish a safe conduct to Lord Pigott to his (the Admiral's) ship. Hughes was asked whether he would be responsible for the tranquillity of the Company's settlements if his request were complied with. This reply was accepted by the Admiral as being tantamount to a refusal, and he wrote expressing regret and telling the majority that they must take upon themselves all the ill consequences of their action. Lord Pigott's friends, finding that this means of escape for him was not open, considered the advisability of applying to the local Mayor's Court for a writ of *Habeas Corpus*. They, however, reluctantly abandoned the idea on the advice of Judge Lemaistre, of the Calcutta Supreme Court, who considered that the powers of this tribunal did not extend to the granting of such writs.

Lord Pigott remained a prisoner until May 11, 1777, when he expired, after an illness of a few weeks, from a gastric attack brought on by exposure to the sun while gardening at the Mount. Through the influence of his friends an inquest was held on the body, and evidence was given tending to show that the deceased's death was due to his confinement. It says a good deal for the skill with which the jury was empanelled as well as for the spirit abroad in the station at the time, that a verdict of wilful murder was returned against Stratton and his associates in the majority, including Fletcher, Edington, Stuart, and Horne.

Meanwhile news of the *coup d'état* had reached England, and had created there the sensation that it was calculated to do. The directors took a very severe view of the action of the majority, which they regarded as subversive of legal authority. They peremptorily directed that Lord Pigott should be freed and restored to the full exercise of his powers pending his return to England, and suspended the members of the majority Government and their associates, directing that they should not be permitted to ship for home in the same boat as Lord Pigott. With a clear perception of the real cause of the upheaval the directors issued definite instructions that in future no Governor or member of Council "shall be directly or indirectly . . . concerned in, or have any dealings or transactions . . . in money or in goods of any kind whatsoever for his or their use, benefit, profit, or advantage, with the princes and natives of the country."

The dispatch was entrusted to Mr. Whitehill, who had been named as one of seven officials selected to constitute the new administration. Instead of taking the usual passage by sea, Mr. Whitehill travelled overland *via* Suez and reached Madras in what was then probably the record time of 79 days after quitting London. Arriving at Fort St. George on August 31st, Whitehill was confronted with the somewhat startling situation created by the death of Lord Pigott. Stratton's Government having submitted at once to the fiat of the directors, Whitehill proceeded to give effect to the verdict of the coroner's jury by causing proceedings to be instituted against the majority in the Court of Quarter Sessions. On the second day of the sitting of the Court, October 1, 1777, the justices were so impressed with the extraordinarily intricate character of the legal questions involved that they decided to seek the advice of the High Court of Bengal. When the reply to their interrogations was forthcoming, it was, as might be expected, against the prosecution. The judges of the Supreme Court (Impey, Chambers, Lemaistre, and Hyde) held that there was no legally appointed coroner in Madras, and that if there had been the materials of the inquest were insufficient for an indictment for either murder or manslaughter.

Though Stratton and his associates escaped from the toils of the enemy in Madras, they were not so fortunate so far as their machinations at home were concerned. As the result of a motion brought forward in the House of Commons in 1779 by Admiral Pigott, Stratton, Brooke, Floyer, and Mackay were placed on their trial for misdemeanour, and ultimately convicted and fined £1,000 each. This was the rather tame ending of a sensational episode, but no doubt there were influences at work to save the majority from the full consequences of their acts.

SOUTHERN INDIA

CHAPTER IX

Sir Horace Rumbold's administration—Fresh outbreak of war between Great Britain and France—Capture of Pondicherry—Rumbold's mistaken policy in dealing with the Nizam of Hyderabad—Trouble with Hyder Ali—Rumbold charged with oppression and corruption—He defeats the accusation—Hyder Ali's descent into the Carnatic—Colonel Baillie's force annihilated at Conjeveram—Sir Eyre Coote sent to retrieve the disaster—Second battle of Wandewash—Conclusion of peace—Death of Hyder Ali—Tipu Sultan commences hostilities against the British—His subsequent defeat—Humiliating terms forced upon him—Renewal of the war—Capture of Seringapatam by the British and death of Tipu Sultan—The Mysore settlement—Territorial changes—Consolidation of British power in Southern India—Terrible famine.

Sir Horace Rumbold was sent out to fill Lord Pigott's place at Madras. His name is one which historically is closely associated with British development in Southern India. This was rather because of his defects than his virtues, for he was of the class of unscrupulous Anglo-Indian Nabobs who in this period made such an unfavourable impression on Society in England, into which their great wealth, often ill-gotten, introduced them. Rumbold's emoluments as Governor were fixed at the handsome amount of 40,000 pagodas per annum, while each of the members of his Council received 16,000 pagodas per annum. In providing these large salaries, which contrasted strikingly with the miserable emoluments previously assigned, the directors, no doubt, wished to strike at the root of the private trade which had produced such disastrous consequences in the recent administration. But Madras was very well able to pay liberally for the services of its officials at this juncture. The revenue of the Presidency had in recent years grown enormously, and stood at just under 30 lakhs of pagodas in the estimates for the financial year 1778-9.

Within a few weeks of the installation of the new Government, war broke out afresh between Great Britain and France, and again the two races were brought into collision in Southern India. Pondicherry, as the chief, and, indeed, practically only seat of French power in the Peninsula, was the inevitable object of British attack. On receipt of orders from home a well-equipped expedition was organized under the command of Sir Hector Munro, who had arrived in India with Rumbold, and, on September 18th, after a brisk sea fight, in which the British squadron under Sir Edward Vernon drove off a superior French fleet, the attack on the settlement was commenced. When the bombardment had continued for a month, and an assault had become practicable, the French commander, M. Bellecombe, surrendered. Afterwards M. Bellecombe and the French garrison were permitted to leave India for France, and the fortifications of Pondicherry, by the advice of Sir Eyre Coote, who landed from England in December, were demolished. Meanwhile, Sir Horace Rumbold was soon speeding home with the dispatch announcing the capitulation. The news excited great enthusiasm in England, and the public cordially acquiesced in the honours conferred in connection with the achievement by the King, these including a baronetcy for Rumbold and a knighthood for Munro.

The fair promise held out for Rumbold's tenure of power by the well-planned Pondicherry expedition was not realized. The Governor, indeed, managed in quite extraordinary fashion to disturb the delicately adjusted balance of power in Southern India. His most serious offence was his treatment of the Nizam of Hyderabad, whose friendship was indispensable to the maintenance of our position. At an earlier period, as has been seen, the Madras Government agreed to hold the Northern Circars as from the Nizam, in spite of the fact that the Company had obtained an absolute grant of them from the Emperor. Rumbold upset this arrangement by inducing Basalat Jang, the Nizam's brother, who had been granted a lease of Guntoor, to allow of its transfer to Nawab Walajah. What was, perhaps, more serious as an indication of policy, he announced his intention of withdrawing the Nizam's subsidy on the ground that it had been improperly granted. His action was strenuously opposed by Mr. John Holland, the Resident at the Nizam's Court, and Warren Hastings put a veto on the proposals. Rumbold, however, declined to recognize the authority of the Supreme Government in the matter, and went the length of suspending Holland for his temerity in appealing against his decrees. While the echoes of this controversy were resounding through the halls of East India House, Rumbold found himself involved in serious trouble with Hyder Ali of Mysore, who was incensed at the failure of the Madras Government to fulfil some of the provisions of the treaty of 1769, and who, moreover, objected strongly to the Company's then recent occupation of Mahé, which place he regarded as being under his protection.

Sickness, either real or diplomatic, at this critical moment compelled Rumbold to return to England in April 1780. On his arrival home he had to face charges of oppression and corruption formulated in a Bill of Pains and Penalties introduced in the House of Commons. The story that went about at the time that Rumbold had started his career in life as a waiter at White's lent piquancy to the proceedings, but the ex-Governor, whatever his origin, was a clever intriguer, and he had no difficulty in spiking the guns of his enemies with the aid of a Parliamentary wire-puller named Rigby, who managed to get the Bill talked out. Rumbold lived down the charges against him, built himself a lordly country seat at Woodhall Park, Hertfordshire, and entering Parliament became a prominent figure in English public life until his death in 1791.

In the interregnum which followed Rumbold's departure, while Whitehill was temporarily discharging the duties of Governor, Hyder Ali made his famous descent into the Carnatic. Gathering his forces about him, after making a composition with the Mahommedan and Mahratta powers, he swept through the country like a devastating torrent. Burke has given a moving picture of the terrible destruction he wrought in one of the best-known passages of his speech on the Nabob of Arcot's debts.

Taken by surprise by the sudden irruption, the Government hesitated as to the course they should pursue. Their indecision was productive of lamentable consequences. A British force under Colonel Baillie, while marching from Guntoor to effect a junction with troops sent out from Madras under Sir Hector Munro, was attacked by Hyder Ali at Conjeveram and annihilated. This destruction of Baillie's force, which took place on December 10, 1780, was one of the most notable disasters that overtook British arms in India at that period. The envelopment of the little British force was quickly effected. In vain the gallant troops endeavoured to escape from the toils woven around them. Hyder had made his dispositions so well that escape was practically impossible. Still, the men, though decimated by fire, declined to surrender. At length, seeing that further resistance was hopeless, Baillie directed a flag of truce to be raised. The enemy promptly rushed in, intent on massacring the gallant remnant of the force, now only about 300, but the

1. A VIEW OF THE ROYAL ARTILLERY ENCAMPMENT, CONJEVERAM.

From "Picturesque Scenery in the Kingdom of Mysore." Edited by Edward Orme. Published in 1804.

2. GATEWAY AT VELLORE. 3. BORTH AND PART OF THE EAST FACE OF AASEERGHUR.

French officers with Hyder befriended them and they were saved to grace a Seringapatam triumph. In the fighting 70 officers out of 86 were killed, and the losses amongst the rank and file were also abnormally heavy. Nor was this the entire tale of the disaster. Munro, finding how things had gone with Baillie, made a hasty retreat upon Madras, casting his heavy guns into the great tank at Conjeveram to expedite his movements.

Matters had now become critical, and an urgent appeal was made to Calcutta for assistance. Promptly responding to the call, Hastings sent to the Southern Presidency a considerable body of reinforcements under the command of Sir Eyre Coote. The gallant old warrior was not able to take the field until the new year had been ushered in, but once he got into action he speedily put a different complexion upon the situation. After capturing Carangooly he marched to Wandewash, and by a curious stroke of fate relieved the British force in occupation of that place on the anniversary of his victory there twenty-one years previously. The campaign after this languished. Coote was old and war-worn, and his military arrangements lacked the vigour which had once characterized them. For three years the campaign continued, and then an unsatisfactory peace was concluded very much on the basis of the former arrangement, under which there was a mutual restitution of conquests.

In 1782, during the height of the military operations, Hyder Ali died, and the succession devolved upon his son, Tipu Sultan. This prince had few of the strong qualities of his predecessor, but he had to the full his tenacious hatred of the British, and he had not been long on the throne before he was giving unmistakable evidence of his bellicose intentions. In 1788 he came into collision with the Company by an unprovoked raid upon Tanjore, which was in alliance with the British. The prince's attitude was so threatening that it was deemed necessary to read him a severe lesson. Taking the field in person, Lord Cornwallis, who at the time was Governor-General, conducted a campaign against Tipu in which the Nizam and the Mahrattas participated on the British side. Two years' vigorous fighting, however, were required to bring Tipu to his senses, and it was not until a British army was under the walls of Seringapatam, his capital, closely besieging it, that he agreed to peace. The terms imposed were onerous. Tipu had to cede to the Allies half his territories, and to pay an indemnity of three crores and thirty lakhs of rupees. The British share in the spoils of victory included the country round Dindigul and the districts of Salem and Malabar.

Tipu, mortified at his loss of territory, nurtured a deadly hatred of the British, which only awaited a suitable opportunity of venting itself. This opportunity appeared to come when, under Napoleon, French ambitions in the East received a new and potent impulse. The wily Sultan got into communication with the French Governor of the Isle of France, and through him received promises of assistance from France in any war of aggression he might wage against the British. Lord Mornington, who had just been appointed Governor-General, landing at Madras early in 1798, and receiving reports of the state of affairs in Mysore from Colonel Wellesley, decided to leave no time for these schemes to develop, but to attack Tipu. Under his directions an imposing force was, towards the end of the year, assembled at Vellore, consisting of 20,000 trained troops of the Madras army. An arrangement was also made for the co-operation of 6,000 of the Company's troops from Bombay, and for the presence of a contingent of 10,000 from Hyderabad composed of the Nizam's army and the subsidiary force. A body of Mahratta horse gave further strength to the British expedition.

TIPU SULTAN.
From a portrait at the India Office.

After a successful march through the enemy's territory the British appeared before Seringapatam in the early days of April and promptly invested it. General Harris, the ancestor of two noblemen who later made most popular Indian Governors, was in supreme command of the operations as Commander-in-Chief of the Presidency. It was a fortunate circumstance that he had as one of his chief lieutenants General David Baird, who twenty years earlier, on the occasion of the defeat of Baillie's force, had been taken prisoner and had spent a long period of captivity in the town. His intimate local knowledge, besides being of exceptional value in the drawing up of a plan of campaign, marked him out as the natural leader of the attack at close quarters, with which the operations would culminate. Taking his place at the head of the storming column on May 4th, Baird led the troops to a brilliant though hard-fought victory. In the fighting Tipu was slain, and with him many of the principal nobles of the State. So decisive was the victory that the whole country surrendered without further opposition.

With Tipu's death ended the Mahommedan dynasty. After the war the British placed on the vacant throne a representative of the Hindu dynasty which had reigned prior to Hyder Ali's usurpation in 1761. Tipu's territories were divided amongst the victorious Allies, the British share including Kanara, Coimbatore, and Wynaad.

Following upon the Mysore settlement came other important territorial arrangements. In 1799 the Company obtained control of the State of Tanjore, whose Raja, under the arrangement making the change, was granted an annual payment. A year later the Nizam, in consideration of the maintenance of a subsidiary force in his State, relinquished to the British all the territory he had received in the wars with Mysore. These "ceded districts" included the present district of Bellary, Anantapur, Cuddapah, and part of Kurnool. Still later, in 1801, the Nawab of the Carnatic having been proved guilty of treasonable correspondence with Tipu, was compelled to resign the government of his country to the Company, under an arrangement which permitted him to retain his titular dignity and to live in the enjoyment of a handsome income. In the person of the Prince of Arcot, the first native nobleman of Madras, we have the modern representative of the Mahommedan rulers of the Carnatic. These acquisitions gave substantial form to the Company's possessions in Southern India. The Madras Presidency, from a mere administrative expression, became a splendid reality. The British flag now floated in undisputed power from the Northern Circars to Cape Comorin, with the exception of part of the Kurnool district, a few minor native States, and the insignificant foreign settlements of Pondicherry and Tranquebar.

Though the British power in Southern India was strengthened by a gradual process of aggrandizement, forced by the stern logic of a situation in which French rivalry combined with native arrogance and duplicity offered challenges which could not be ignored, the credit for the final rounding off process almost entirely belongs to Lord Wellesley. Within a twelve month after landing in Calcutta, as Marshman points out, he extinguished the French party and influence at Hyderabad, and made all the Nizam's resources subservient to British interests; he annihilated the Kingdom of Mysore, and he established the Company's authority in the South on so firm a basis that it has never since been seriously contested. That he dared to act in defiance of instructions in some instances is his greater glory. In writing to Pitt in reference to his policy, he said, "I suppose you will either hang me or honour me magnificently for my deeds. In either case I shall be gratified; for an English gallows is better than an Indian throne." History records that in this case at least it was honour and not contumely that the Empire-builder received.

Prior to the final crushing of the Mahommedan power in Mysore during the administration of Lord Macartney (1781-5), Madras was visited by one of those terrible famines which have given the Southern Presidency such unenviable pre-eminence. Though mainly due to the failure of the monsoon, the scarcity was seriously aggravated by Hyder Ali's terrible ravages. People in the Presidency capital strove nobly to mitigate the horrors of the visitation, but their best efforts only touched the fringe of a problem of the greatest magnitude—the feeding of millions. A British officer writing home in 1782 says that "the complicated scene of horror was such as to benumb every humanized faculty of the soul. In the Black Town," he goes on to say, "so great was the mortality that the dead bodies were too numerous to be carried off by the utmost exertion, and the putrid exhalations which arose from those numberless emaciated victims of famine strewed in every quarter of the settlement became dangerous and distressing." Not until the beginning of 1784, on the conclusion of peace with Mysore, was the rigour of the visitation stayed.

SIR DAVID BAIRD DISCOVERING THE BODY OF TIPU SAIB.

CHAPTER X

The mutiny of Vellore—Court-martial on the prisoners—Lord Minto's decision as to the punishment of the guilty—Disaffection amongst the European officers of the Madras army—General Macdowall's violent manifesto—Sir George Barlow suspends Major Boles, the Deputy Adjutant-General, for issuing the manifesto—Officers protest against the Governor's action—Four of the objectors suspended—Open mutiny of officers—Sir George Barlow's firmness—Submission of the malcontents—Lord Minto deals with the situation—Recall of Sir George Barlow—The Nawab of Arcot's claims—Land settlement of Madras—Sir Thomas Munro's association with the measure—His career as Governor—His character and attainments—The affairs of the Mysore State—Lord William Bentinck's settlement—The Nabobs of the Carnatic—Lord Harris's minute—The last of the nabobs.

THE new century was not very old before an episode in Madras startled the British in India and caused a feeling of consternation at home which largely modified the favourable impression which the successful consolidation of British interests in the Peninsula had created. This was the affair known in history as "the Mutiny of Vellore." The event occurred on July 10, 1806. On the morning of that day the sepoy force of 1,500, which included a large proportion of Mysore Mahommedans, rose on the small European garrison of 370. Having secured the main guard and the powder-magazine, they attacked the troops in barracks.

Taken at a disadvantage, the European soldiers were readily shot down ere they could retaliate. Before long no fewer than 82 of them had been killed and 91 wounded. The mutineers, fired by their cheap triumph, next turned their attentions to the officers, and subsequently massacred 13 of them. So completely did the British power now appear to be wiped out that the rebels had the audacity to hoist the ensign of the deposed house of Mysore in token of the change of situation. But their triumph was short lived. Colonel Gillespie, who was in garrison at Arcot, eight miles away, on getting news of the mutiny, proceeded without a moment's delay with a detachment of the 19th Dragoons to Vellore. With his galloper guns he blew open the door of the fort and then wreaked condign vengeance on the rebels. Before the attack was stayed as many as between three and four hundred had been killed. Afterwards the remnants of the European force were collected, and careful dispositions made against a renewal of the disturbances. A court of inquiry which was held into the mutiny made it perfectly clear that though the intrigues of the deposed Mysore prince were the immediate cause of the outbreak, the disaffection had its real origin in a number of recently introduced army regulations which ran counter to the prejudices of the native troops. When the facts had been elucidated, Lord William Bentinck, in whose Governor-Generalship the regulations had been drafted, was recalled, and Lord Minto was sent out charged with the special duty of undoing the mischief that had been worked. The new Governor-General, as it happened, arrived at Madras at the moment when the court-martial was deciding the cases of the mutineers. Seventeen of the ringleaders had already been executed, and there were six hundred other convicted prisoners whose fate was hanging in the balance. The Supreme Government had ordered their transportation beyond the seas as a lesson to others, but Lord William Bentinck before leaving had left on record a minute advising a milder course. As the situation had become completely peaceful once more, Lord Minto, especially in view of the feeling in England, considered that the lenient policy advocated by his predecessor might be followed. His decision, therefore, was that the mutineers should be granted a pardon, but he directed that they should be dismissed the Company's service and declared incapable of ever re-entering it. The clemency shown was not misplaced. The Madras army from this time forward was a pattern of discipline. It even withstood the shock of the great mutiny of 1857, which shattered the Bengal army and caused British power in the North to rock to its foundations.

Ere the echoes of the Vellore Mutiny died away, Madras was the scene of another military mutiny—this time of the officers of the European garrison. The cause of this outbreak was the action of the Court of Directors in enforcing military retrenchments upon the Madras Government. Economy at the expense of a military caste is always a dangerous line of policy in a country in which the military power is powerful, and at Madras at this time the natural feeling of dissatisfaction at the use of the pruning-knife upon cherished and valuable privileges was heightened by personal prejudices of a marked character. The anger at the issue of the edict of reform centred upon Colonel Munro, the Quartermaster-General, who had made remarks in his report which were considered to reflect upon the character of the officers. A demand was made to General Macdowall, the Commander-in-Chief, that he should be put upon his trial by court-martial. General Macdowall weakly conceded to the clamour of the mess-room to the extent of placing him under arrest. Colonel Munro appealed to the Governor in Council, under whose authority he had acted, with the result that he was as promptly released as he had been made prisoner. The intervention of the superior civil authority occasioned an extraordinary outbreak on the part of General Macdowall. He denounced the action taken in interference of his authority, and stated that nothing but his approaching departure for Europe prevented him from putting Colonel Munro upon his trial for disrespect to the Commander-in-Chief and contempt for the military power in resorting to the Governor in Council in defiance of the judgment of the head of the army. Colonel Munro was also bitterly attacked personally.

General Macdowall's violent manifestoes elicited an equally heated reply from Sir George Barlow, the Governor. Not content with verbal protests, Barlow took the extreme course of deposing General Macdowall from office, although he was then on board ship ready to leave for England, and in the natural order of things would have relinquished his office in a few hours. What was an even more arbitrary exercise of power was the suspension of Major Boles, the Deputy Adjutant-General who had signed the Commander-in-Chief's order. The Major urged with irresistible force that he was only carrying out the orders of a superior officer—orders that he perforce was compelled to obey. The Governor was too irate to listen to reason, and the officer continued under arrest. As might have been expected, this ill-considered policy speedily had the effect of enraging the already greatly irritated military community. The officers all over the Presidency took up his case, and memorials were forwarded from every station commending his conduct and severely reprobating the proceedings taken against him. On May 1, 1810, when the agitation had been in progress for some time—at a time when its violence had spent itself—Sir George Barlow took the inept course of suspending four officers of high rank and removing eight others from their commands on the ground that they had taken an active part in the movement. The almost immediate effect of the measures was to elicit from a hundred and fifty officers of the Jaulna and Hyderabad Divisions a defiant memorial demanding the release of the officers "to prevent the horrors of civil war and the ultimate loss of a large portion of the British possessions in India and the dreadful blow it would inflict on the mother-country." The open mutiny of the Company's European regiment at Masulipatam served to emphasize the gravity of the position.

Nothing hardly could have been more unsatisfactory than Sir George Barlow's policy up to this point; but the coming of the crisis appeared to brace him up to a proper height of executive ability. Instead of weakly yielding to the mutineers, as many men would have done in the face of the terrible difficulties of the position, he boldly rallied to his side all the forces of law and order that he could command. These were neither few nor unimportant. Besides the King's regiments at Madras, and the garrisons of Bengal, Bombay, and Ceylon, he had behind him the entire weight of the official community as well as the best elements in the merchant ranks, where, naturally, there was no desire for an upheaval such as the military hot-heads contemplated. The native army was a more dubious quantity, but, as events proved, the sepoys, save in one instance

—the garrison of Seringapatam, where disaffected regiments were fired upon by the King's troops and 150 killed—remained true to their allegiance.

Sir George Barlow's firmness had the effect that firmness usually has where a rising against authority is concerned. The officers of the Hyderabad Brigade, on looking over the precipice upon the edge of which they stood, promptly came to the conclusion that the perils were too great to be faced. Their submission, conveyed in a penitent letter addressed to Lord Minto, the Viceroy, on August 11th, settled the fate of the movement. The Jaulna Brigade, which was actually two marches on the road to Madras intent upon the deposition of the Government, hastily retraced its steps and its officers made their peace. Five days later the European regiment at Masulipatam followed suit, and when a little later the rebels in the Seringapatam garrison surrendered, the crisis was at an end. Lord Minto, who had been brought from Calcutta by the astonishing news of the defection of the European officers, proceeded to deal with the situation. In a minute couched in firm yet conciliatory language, while announcing his intention to mete out punishment to those who had incurred blame, he spoke of his anxiety for the welfare of the Madras Army and besought the assistance of all patriotic individuals to that end. Following upon the publication of this order came the issuing of a general amnesty to all but 21 officers, four of whom were cashiered and one acquitted, while the remainder were given the alternative of dismissal. The punishment was lenient enough in view of the gravity of the offence, and even at that the wind was tempered to the shorn lamb, for after an interval all the officers without exception were restored to the service. By an historic act of justice the real penalty fell upon Sir George Barlow, who, after prolonged debates at the India House, was recalled.

This was the last serious trouble that was ever experienced amongst the European troops in India. It originated in executive incompetence and lack of tact, but a predisposing cause unquestionably was the demoralization consequent upon the easily earned wealth of the adventurers who, from Clive downwards, in the previous half-century had shaken the pagoda-tree with such fruitful results to themselves. The character of the age is reflected in another episode which greatly fluttered the official dovecotes of the India of that day. This was the proceedings relative to the historic settlement of the Nawab of Arcot's claims. A Commission appointed by Parliament investigated the claims, which amounted to the huge sum of 30 crores of rupees. Many of the claims were deemed to be fraudulent, but they had sufficient vitality to allow of a good deal of speculation in them, and this had gone on to a very large extent. After the Commission, which was composed of Bengal civil servants because of their impartiality, had commenced its sittings, the question of the validity of a bond put in by a certain native, Reddy Rao, who held the appointment of accountant to the Commission, was raised by a native named Papia. Its

1. N.W. VIEW OF THE DOLPHIN'S NOSE, AT VIZAGAPATAM.
From an old print.

2. SKETCH OF THE PEER MUSJED AND HILL NEAR THE DOLPHIN'S NOSE AT VIZAGAPATAM.
From an old print.

validity was upheld by the Commissioners, and a prosecution was ordered against Papia's witnesses for perjury. On his side Papia charged Reddy Rao with forgery, and that worthy having been brought before a magistrate was committed for trial. Sir George Barlow now intervened by directing the Advocate-General to defend Reddy Rao. This act of partiality created a most unfavourable impression, which was deepened when the Governor ordered that the magistrate who had convicted Reddy Rao should be dismissed and expelled from the country Mr. Parry, a merchant, who had dared to oppose the Commissioners. The criminal proceedings against Reddy Rao resulted in his conviction on the charge of forgery, but the jury recommended him to mercy. In consequence of this recommendation the prisoner was pardoned, but before the formal documents reached India he had committed suicide by swallowing poison. After his death it was discovered that he was deeply implicated in the criminality associated with the Carnatic bonds, and that the particular bond in regard to which he was convicted was what it was represented by Papia to be—a fraud. Barlow's implication in this and other administrative scandals gave to his period of power an unenviable distinction. It was said of it, not without justification, that it was "a season of unprecedented private misery and unexampled peril and alarm."

In the early years of the nineteenth century was concluded the much controverted settlement of the Madras Presidency. The work was carried out under the direction of Sir Thomas Munro, an able and conscientious official who had had long experience in administrative work in India, notably in the Ceded Districts, but whose early career had been spent in the field as an officer under the command of Sir Hector Munro and Sir Eyre Coote. Munro's settlement was based on the principle that the Government was the absolute owner of the land and that it had the right to impose its own terms upon those who cultivated. Acting on this assumption, which was held by his critics to bear very unfavourably and even unjustly on established private interests, he imposed a rent or tax which was to be paid annually by the cultivators or *ryots*. The settlement, it was provided, should be made from year to year with each *ryot*, and should be equal to one-third of the produce. Munro received cordial support for his scheme from Lord William Bentinck, the then Governor, but he had to contend with a large amount of opposition from officials in Madras and also from the authorities in Bengal. There were, unquestionably, features of the scheme which in working proved highly oppressive. As a consequence, when Munro quitted the Ceded Districts where the principles of settlement were worked out, the *ryotwari* system was abandoned in favour of a system first of triennial and subsequently of decennial leases, under which the revenue of an entire village was farmed to the principal *ryot*, or in the event of his refusal to an outsider. The new methods in practise proved even worse than the old, and after an eight year's trial they were abandoned and Munro had the satisfaction of seeing his system re-established, not again to be deposed.

FORT DEFIANCE AND THE LANDSCAPE NEAR IT, NEAR MADURA.
From an old drawing at the India Office.

Munro's connection with Madras did not terminate with this important contribution to the building up of the British Government in India. After some years of useful work in London as the guide, philosopher, and friend of the Court of Directors, he, in the autumn of 1814, returned to Madras as the head of a special Commission, bringing with him, as his newly wedded bride, the beautiful Miss Campbell of Ayrshire, whose portrait by Sir Thomas Lawrence is one of the art treasures of Government House, Madras. The mission which took Munro to India at this juncture was the reorganization of the judicial and police systems on modern lines. His work proved a difficult one owing to the objections of local officials, but by tact and perseverance he at length contrived to win approval for a series of regulations involving organic changes in the two departments of the administration with which his work dealt. The most important feature of the changes was the transference of the superintendence of the police and the functions of the magistrate of the district to the collector, the employment of village officials in the discharge of police duties, the conferment upon head men of villages of powers of hearing and determining petty suits, the extension of the powers of native judges, and the legalization of a system of village and district panchayats, or courts of arbitration.

Munro's reputation was so greatly enchanced by the work in connection with the Commission that when, in 1819, the Governorship of Madras fell vacant on the retirement of Mr. Elliot, he was offered the post. For seven years he discharged the duties, achieving fresh distinction by his statesmanlike direction of the affairs of the Southern Presidency, at a period when the important conquests of the previous two decades were being consolidated. His vast and intimate experience of India stood him in good stead in the work which he found to his hand. Frequent tours made throughout the Presidency brought him into the closest touch with the people, and his numerous minutes on subjects of administrative interest which came up for discussion showed a profundity of knowledge of Indian conditions which gave them a high value in the official literature of that day. It was during his Governorship that the first Burmah war occurred, and the event brought into relief his high qualities as an organizer of victory, for it was largely to the prompt and efficient aid that he sent from Madras to the scene of hostilities that the success of the campaign was due. While he was in the zenith of his fame as an administrator, on July 6, 1827, he was mortally stricken with cholera, to the great grief of the native community, by whom he was affectionately regarded as a veritable Father of the People. The fine equestrian statue by Chantrey, which stands on the road from Fort St. George to Government House, is a silent reminder to the inhabitants of Madras of to-day of one whose strong virtues and solid qualities contributed in no slight degree to the foundation of the present prosperity of Madras.

In England Sir Thomas Munro's death was greatly regretted. He was one of the few Anglo-Indians of that time whose name was familiarly known and whose services were appreciated in the home Government circle. Canning, who was responsible for his appointment to the Governorship of Madras, in a speech in Parliament stated of him that "Europe never produced a more accomplished statesman, nor India, fertile as it was in heroes, a more skilful soldier."

The affairs of the Mysore State were a subject of serious anxiety to the administration in the later years of Sir Thomas Munro's Governorship. Sir Thomas Munro had never favoured the arrangement which the Supreme Government made. His view was that the revival of the old dynasty was a mistake, as there was no attachment towards the family among the natives, for it had long been despised and forgotten. If he could have had his way he would have divided the Mysore territory between the Company and the Nizam. But the dispatch in which he set forth his views arrived too late to prevent the elevation of the boy prince of the Vizayanagar family to the throne, though Lord Wellesley in the official documents of the time was so far influenced as to declare that "the territories thus placed under the nominal sovereignty of the Raja of Mysore constituted substantially an integral portion of our own dominions"—language which found formal expression in the treaty of cession in which the prince's powers were narrowed to an extreme and the right of British supervision and interference was carefully preserved.

At the outset all went well with the new regime in Mysore. Poornea, the famous Brahmin minister of Hyder and Tipu, sagaciously conducted the administration under the able oversight of Sir Barry Close, Webbe, and Colonel Wilks, a trio of officers of high character and experience. They managed so well that when the time came in 1811 for the young Raja to assume the government of the State on attaining his majority there was a surplus of two crores of rupees in the treasury. As has often happened in Oriental States, the prince speedily fell a victim to the bad influences that are never absent at an Indian Court when youth is at the prow and there is an overflowing exchequer. Dismissing the faithful Poornea, he entered into a career of extravagance which resulted, in a comparatively short space of time, in the transformation of the State from a contented and prosperous territory into a land of misrule. In vain the British authorities warned the prince of the certain results of his folly. He steadily ignored all representations, persisting, with a sublime disregard for the future, in his policy, in which prodigality of expenditure and oppressiveness of administration went hand in hand. At length, in 1830, the inhabitants of the State, no longer able to bear the burden put upon them, rose in rebellion. The movement, strengthened by assistance from the Southern Mahratta country, became in a short time so formidable that the British, in the interest of the peace of the Company's territories, were compelled to intervene. This they did effectually by marching a large British force into Mysore and establishing a military control of the country. The inhabitants welcomed the intervention, which they rightly regarded as saving them from the action of a cruel tyranny and guaranteeing their future under settled conditions.

Lord William Bentinck, the Governor-General, upon whom devolved the duty of arranging the new conditions under which Mysore should be ruled, decided that the entire administration should be taken over by the British, with the proviso that the Raja should receive the amount stipulated in the treaty—a lakh of star pagodas and a fifth of the net revenue. The prince protested against the action taken, and pleaded that at least the administration should be carried on in his name. Subsequently, in consequence of the report of a Commission of inquiry into the rebellion, the findings of which went to show that in some cases the charges of oppression had been exaggerated, Lord William Bentinck sought to revise the settlement by proposing a scheme by which the Company would take over a portion of the State sufficient for the payment of the subsidy provided in the treaty and hand the remainder over to the Raja. But the Court of Directors, who had strongly supported the original arrangement, were in no mood to relinquish any of the advantages that it carried with it, and the settlement was soon afterwards confirmed by the Ministry.

MAUSOLEUM AT COLAR.
From an old print at the India Office.

SOUTHERN INDIA

Lord Dalhousie's memorable administration of the Government of India touched Madras in one interesting particular. It was during the official career of this great pro-Consul that the last vestiges of power and position of the once all-powerful Nabobs of the Carnatic were extinguished. The position for a long time previously had become an anomalous one. When, at the time of the capture of Seringapatam, the British authorities found that the then Nabob had been treacherously negotiating with Tipu against them, they declared all treaties between the British Government and him null and void, and also intimated that they regarded the title of his family to the *musnud* extinct. Later, as an act of generosity and not as a right, the British Government agreed to pay the Nabob an allowance of 213,421 pagodas a year out of the revenues of the Carnatic. Blessed with this substantial income the Nabob settled down in residence at the Chepauk Palace, where he received royal salutes and other hollow marks of his departed state. Dying in 1819 in anything but the odour of sanctity, this Nabob was succeeded by his son, who in turn was followed in 1825 by his son. The latter, when he attained to the position, was an infant, and spent his early years under the guidance of British officials. It was his death without succession that gave rise to the question of the continuance of the Nabobship. The prince's uncle, Azim Jah, failing a direct heir, put in a claim to the title and allowances. The question was taken up by the Madras Government, and the then Governor, Lord Harris, prepared an elaborate minute, in which he set out the considerations which, in his view, should govern the matter. His opinion, briefly, was that the Nabobship was an anachronism and should be abolished. He recommended, however, that a handsome allowance should be made to Azim Jah, and that financial arrangements should be entered into for liquidation of the very large debts that he then owed. Lord Dalhousie fully supported Lord Harris's proposal, holding that the treaty of 1801 was a purely personal settlement concluded between the Company on the one part and the Nabob Azim-ud-Dowlah on the other, without any mention of heirs or successors. Azim Jah strove to secure a relaxation of the condition that he should be the last of the Nabobs, but the home authorities declined to be influenced in the direction of a mitigation of this proviso, and they caused it to be officially declared that the title and dignity of Nabob and all the advantages annexed to it by the Treaty of 1801 were at an end.

CHAPTER XI

An era of progress—Tribal disturbances—Human sacrifice—Scheme of land revenue settlement—Results—Inam Commission—Scheme for dealing with inams introduced—Construction of railways—Establishment of Public Works Department—The planting industry—Coffee and tea cultivation—Agricultural Department established—Government cinchona cultivation—The Forest Department created—Famine in Southern India—The Great Famine of 1876-8—Recent famine administration—Conclusion.

As the nineteenth century advanced Southern India settled down to an existence in which, with the growth of British power, the arts of Peace had a steadily increasing range. The elimination of foreign European influence, on the one hand, and the settlement of the limits of the native-ruled territory on the other, gave stability to the position and paved the way for an era of commercial development. Remote from the distant areas in the North where on bloody battlefields the power of Britain was being consolidated, the Madras Presidency pursued its tranquil course. Its closest association with the conflict that still went on for ascendancy, was in the period of the Burmese campaigns of 1824 and 1852, when it furnished large contingents of troops to aid in the assertion of British power. The Madras sepoy in many hard-fought contests showed that he had lost none of the prowess which had gained him renown in the campaigns under Clive and Coote, and the Presidency added to his value by sending him into the field admirably equipped and with an abundance of stores drawn from its rich natural resources. A few years after the close of the second Burmese campaigns, when the great Mutiny shook British power to its foundations, the Madras Army stood firm, and of all India the southern region was least affected by the upheaval. The *Pax Britannica* would have been absolutely complete in the Madras Presidency during the nineteenth century but for sporadic disturbances arising out of the turbulence of certain of the racial elements within its borders. At one time and another the Nairs have been restive, and there have been repeated outbreaks amongst the Moplahs, a fanatical tribe in whom is a large infusion of Arab blood, occupying a district on the west coast. Trouble, too, has come from the wild tribes inhabiting the hills of Ganjam and Vizagapatam, and in Rumpa, on the northern frontier, more than once, and conspicuously in 1879, the authorities have had to take serious measures to stamp out unrest. The problem of maintaining the peace amongst the wild, untutored hill people has been complicated by the existence of tribal customs which, though of immemorial usage and stoutly adhered to, could not be tolerated under British rule. Strange as it may seem to the Western understanding, amongst the Khonds, one of the largest of the tribes of the hill region referred to, human sacrifice was, until a comparatively recent period, extensively practised under the name of ***Meriah***. On the extent of the evil being brought to the notice of the authorities, a special agency was established to cope with it, and the practice has now been suppressed. The advance of civilization, the extension of railways, the diffusion of education, and the widening of the avenues of employment have, however, probably done as much as the direct action of Government to produce an improvement in respect of these degrading usages.

Steady as was the progress made after the downfall of Tipu and the consolidation of British power in the annexed territory, a good deal was wanting in the conditions under which the administration was conducted. In 1855 less than a fifth of the area of the Presidency was cultivated, while more than half of the area recorded as arable was waste. Though population had largely increased and there had been uninterrupted peace, there had in all these years been no material increase of revenue or extension of cultivation. The incidence of assessment was everywhere very unequal, while a succession of years of low prices had had the practical effect of raising rates which it was admitted were already too high. It was calculated that on the average the Government at that time took as its share 50 per cent. of the gross in wet, and 35 per cent. in dry; while to give the ryot any real proprietary interest in the land and to induce an extension of cultivation, from 25 to 30 per cent. of the gross was, it was thought, the utmost the Government should claim. The Presidency of Madras was also the only province in India in which no regular survey had been instituted. The early surveys, even the best of them, were defective. There were no maps, district, talook, or village, and no permanent boundaries; and the records of the survey, such as they were, had been but imperfectly preserved. These early surveys, moreover, extended to only a few districts of the Presidency, and there were districts in which the sole records of the area liable to assessment were the unchecked entries in the curnum's accounts. On these and such-like considerations Government determined in 1855 that a general revision should be made of the assessments of the Presidency, founded on what seemed the only right basis of a land revenue settlement, an accurate survey, and a more or less exact classification of soils. Following upon this the Revenue Settlement Department was constituted in 1858, with Mr. Newill as the first director. A scheme of operations was outlined estimated to cost 76½ lakhs, spread over a period of fifteen or twenty years. The result was expected to be an immediate loss of revenue, but, as events proved, this was more than recouped by extension of cultivation. The settlement of the whole of the Trichinopoly, Kistna, Godavery, Nellore, and Salem districts, and of parts of South Arcot, Kurnool, Cuddapah, and Tinnevelly, was completed by 1874, the area settled by the department in these fifteen years aggregating 27,892 square miles, and the cost incurred, including demarcation, amounting to Rs.42,84,775. The cost of settlement proper was Rs.24,06,733, or 83 rupees per square mile.

The department continued to be administered under a separate head till the latter part of 1879, when in consequence of the financial exigencies of the Empire the appointment of director was abolished and the strength of the department reduced by about half. The department under these altered conditions was administered by a member of the Board of Revenue. This arrangement lasted until the end of 1882, when the appointment of director was revived and conjoined with that of the newly constituted Directorate of Agriculture.

Arising out of the question of the land settlement and intimately associated with it was the establishment during the Government of Lord Harris in November 1858 of the Inam Commission for the purpose of regulating land under the peculiar form of tenure known as inam. It should be explained that an inam means ordinarily a gift by a superior to an inferior, and that in the connection now being dealt with the term is applied to the grant by the State of the permanent right in one case to occupy land without paying rent to the State, and in another case to collect Government assessment on land. Grants of this kind were numerous in the Hindu period, and the Mahommedan rulers of Southern India continued the system. The British also at the outset made inam grants, but the evils flowing from a system which tended permanently to alienate land from taxation came in course of time to be recognized, and in 1822, and again in 1829, the Court of Directors of the East India Company directed that grants of land should be restricted to special cases. Subsequently active measures were taken to suppress the system, and great dissatisfaction was caused in consequence among the inam holders, who, not without some

CAGE IN WHICH CAPT. P. ANSTRUTHER, OF THE MADRAS ARTILLERY, WAS KEPT WHILE A PRISONER IN THE HANDS OF THE CHINESE, DURING THE FIRST CHINA WAR IN 1840.

Photo by J. F. Peters.

reason, regarded the official regulations as striking at their rights.

It fell to Sir Charles Trevelyan, Lord Harris's successor in the governorship, to devise a scheme for dealing with the inams. In a minute dated May 13, 1859, he propounded certain rules by which the principles enunciated by the Board of Directors were to be applied. The basis of his proposals was that when it should be proved that land had for fifty years been in the possession of a person, or those through whom he claimed, without the payment of land tax, such length of possession should be held to be good title to that land as inam, whatever might have been the origin of the possession. When the title to an inam based on length of possession was once established, it was then to be open to the holder to proceed as follows: In the case of an inam held for personal benefit he could either retain the inam according to his actual tenure subject to the liability of lapse and without the power of alienation; or he could enfranchise it by payment of a moderately substantial annual quit rent, or a single fixed commutation sum equal to so many years' purchase of the quit rent. With regard to service, those that were attached to services still required were to be continued intact; but where the services were such that they could not be made available for any useful public purpose, the holder was to be compulsorily enfranchised. As regards lands forming endowments of temples and mosques held in remuneration for services to be rendered therein, these were to be confirmed on their existing tenures, and to be resumable only when the object for which they were held had ceased to exist. The work of the Inam Commission was conducted on these principles until 1869 when the bulk of the work had been completed, and under the pressing necessity of reducing expenditure the department was dissolved, the work remaining to be done being entrusted to a member of the Board of Revenue. Subsequently the control of inam affairs was entrusted to the Director of Revenue Settlement and Agriculture.

The middle of the last century was a period fruitful for the development of the Presidency. Two events stand out very prominently in association with the commercial interests. These are the commencement of the construction of railways on the 9th of June, 1853, by the turning of the first sod of the railway from Madras to Menil, the pioneer section of the Madras Railway Company's system, and the creation in 1858 of a Public Works Department. Both these events had a marked influence on the Presidency's trade, the simultaneous construction of railways and the driving of roads through the interior acting as a healthy stimulus to commercial and trading operations.

Agriculture also witnessed some striking developments in the Madras Presidency in this mid-nineteenth century period. It was then that the great planting industry came into existence. Coffee plants introduced as a curiosity into Wynaad some eighty years since led to the regular cultivation of the plant on commercial lines. A plantation established by Mr. Glasson on a hill at Manantoddy in 1840 gave the lead, and soon quite a considerable amount of capital was embarked in the industry. But the land taken up for the purpose was unsuitable, and in consequence of the inevitable failures the industry was transferred to South Wynaad. Here again the first ventures were not fortunate, but the industry increased nevertheless, and in 1862 there were 9,932 acres under cultivation, an acreage which by 1868 had increased more than threefold. As the pioneer planters were British, so, to a large extent, was the development of the industry in European hands. In the early seventies, planting operations in the Nilgiris were extensively entered upon, with the result that in the course of a few years a very large amount of land had been taken up to the advantage of the district, whose prosperity may be said to date from this period. Owing to the ravages of disease and other causes, the coffee industry has at different times been subjected to serious vicissitudes, but thanks to the tenacity and skill of the planters and to the faith of capitalists in the future of the enterprise, the industry now occupies a position of stability which offers every promise of permanence.

Tea cultivation was introduced later than coffee cultivation, although successful experiments were conducted with the plant in the Nilgiris as far back as the year 1835. It was not until about 1865 that the acreage under tea was at all considerable, and many years after that elapsed before the industry attained to a position of real importance. In recent years, however, tea planting in Southern India has made enormous strides and bids fair in time to rival coffee as an element in the prosperity of the Madras Presidency.

Owing to the growth in importance of the agricultural industry, the Government in the latter part of 1882 established an Agricultural Department, and placed it in charge of the Director of Revenue Settlement. The department is entrusted with the general supervision of agricultural interests throughout the Presidency, and as the years have gone by has become an increasingly valuable adjunct of the administration.

Apart from the work of planters who have operated on commercial lines, the Madras Presidency has taken a leading part in the development of tropical agriculture. A notable phase of the earlier official activity in this direction was the establishment of Government cinchona plantations on the Nilgiri Hills. The first instalment of plants was taken from South America to Ootacamund by Mr. Clements R. Markham in 1860, but owing to their bad condition the experiment was not a success. A later supply received in the following year from England and Java proved more satisfactory. Under the able superintendence of Mr. McIvor, a former superintendent of the Government Gardens at Ootacamund, vigorous plantations were quickly established, and when that gentleman died in 1876 the venture was an assured success. In 1867 more than two million plants were to be found in the Government plantations, which then covered an area of 677 acres. It was not until 1871 that the first results of what had been a very expensive operation for the Government were secured. In that year 7,294 lb. of dry bark was sent for sale to England, where it realized £763, the price averaging 2s. 6½d. A second consignment of 23,646 lb. made in the spring of 1873 sold at an average price of 3s. 2¼d. and realized £3,144. Shipments were made in successive years until 1880, by which time the shipments had mounted to 567,800 lb. and the amount received in connection with the sales, £131,080. The sales in subsequent years were so good that by 1884 the entire outlay on the plantations (which then stood at £208,174) had been more than recouped. In more recent times the results have been less favourable financially owing to the heavy drop in the price of quinine.

Madras is a land of magnificent forests and the conservation of its timber resources is a highly important consideration alike from a commercial and a sociological point of view. It was, however, not until 1847 that any really effective steps were taken to protect the forests in a systematic way. In that year, consequent upon a representation from the Executive Engineer of Malabar as to the injury that was being done by the extraction of teak-trees for the Bombay market, a special officer was appointed to explore, conserve, and work the Government forests. In 1856 a further advance was made by the appointment of Dr. Cleghorn with more extensive powers as Conservator of Forests of the whole Presidency. For some years the department did good work, the Conservator acting under the direct authority of the Government. But in 1872-3 the mistake was made of reducing the authority of the head of the department by making him a simple inspector charged with the duty of giving advice to Collectors of districts. It was not until 1883, after a report made by Dr. Brandis, Inspector-General of Forests to the Government of India, that the department was fully organized. Accepting the principal recommendations made by Dr. Brandis, the Madras Government thoroughly overhauled its Forest Department and passed a Forest Act on lines which the larger experience of India had shown to be necessary for the effective protection of forests.

Famine is a gaunt spectre which has ever haunted the British administrator in the Madras Presidency since the responsibility for the Government rested on British shoulders. Owing to the meteorological conditions of Southern India the greater part of the Presidency is peculiarly liable to failures of the crops. Historical records show that under native rule as under our own the population was at times grievously afflicted by famine. Of the visitation in 1633 already referred to, the East India Company's agents at Masulipatam wrote to the authorities at home that "the living were eating up the dead, and men durst scarcely travel in the country for fear they should be killed and eaten." At irregular intervals there were famines more or less severe throughout the early period of British rule. One very disastrous visitation occurred in 1832-4, when Guntur, Nellore, Masulipatam, Cuddapah, Bellary, and North Arcot were ravaged. The mortality was frightful. Of 500,000 inhabitants of the old Guntur district, no fewer than 150,000 perished, and this in spite of the fact that 52 lakhs of rupees were spent on relief. But even this calamity pales into insignificance before "the great famine" of 1876-8, which made a waste of the Deccan districts, Nellore, Chingleput, North Arcot, Salem, Coimbatore, and Tinnevelly.

According to an official writer in the "Madras Manual of the Administration," this great famine of 1876-8 was in respect of the area and population affected and the duration and intensity of the distress the most important calamity of its kind experienced in British India since the beginning of the century. The failure of the summer rains of 1876 extended over about half of the Presidency, the distress being most intense in the same tract as that lying above the Eastern Ghauts which suffered in the earlier famines of 1833 and 1854. Altogether the drought affected an area of about 200,000 square miles, occupied by a population of 36 millions. The area of the Madras Presidency seriously affected was estimated at 74,000 square miles, and the population inhabiting it at 16,000,000 persons. No districts entirely escaped between the Kistna River and Cape Comorin, but the distress was most severe in the tract immediately south of the Tongabudra, including the districts of Bellary, Kurnool, Cuddapah, and Nellore, and farther south in North Arcot and Salem. Mysore was also seriously affected. The measures taken for the relief of the famine were severely criticized at the time, and no doubt they in many respects left much to be desired. The vast size of the calamity, however, made the adoption of effective measures difficult. At the outset the Government were confronted with almost insuperable difficulties in transporting grain to the famine-stricken districts. The railways and roads were altogether inadequate to bear the tremendous strain that was involved in the feeding from outside sources of a population about half that of England. Nevertheless, between August 1876 and November 1877, 724,339 tons of grain were distributed in the interior, the freight of which alone involved an expenditure of Rs.55,36,590. This remarkable importation had, there can be no doubt, a wide-reaching influence in alleviating the distress, but in spite of it the mortality was appalling. In some areas half the population was swept away. When the magnitude of the catastrophe was realized in England, a great movement was initiated at the London Mansion House for the relief of distress. Sympathy was widespread, and eventually the Lord Mayor's Fund reached the splendid total of £820,000, an amount which at the time was a record in the history of British charity. The funds were administered through the agency of local committees at Madras, and they did much to reduce the sum total of misery by distributing seed grain and providing ploughs and cattle and other permanent necessaries for cultivators who would otherwise have had no means of livelihood after the famine. Government relief operations were finally brought to a close in October 1878. The total expenditure involved by the famine reached the enormous sum of 815½ lakhs.

Since the great famine there have been a number of visitations, happily of less severity. The worst of the series was the famine of 1896-7, when 86 lakhs were spent on relief works, and the remissions of revenue amounted to 24 lakhs. In the treatment of these calamities an enormous advance was made by the Government, and the mortality was light compared with that of the earlier famine. So marked has been the progress in methods of famine administration and so great has been the improvement in means of communication in the Presidency that a reproduction of the horrors of the years 1876-8 is exceedingly improbable.

Madras in recent times has been ruled by a succession of able and public-spirited Governors who have done their best to carry forward the great traditions of British rule in India. Though the policy pursued by them has occasionally led to controversy, there has been maintained an unvarying standard of devotion to duty and exalted purpose which has served to strengthen the foundations of

1. BOMBARDMENT OF MADRAS, SEPTEMBER 22, 1914. PREMISES OF THE MADRAS SAILING CLUB.
Photo by R. V. Solomon.

2. BOMBARDMENT OF MADRAS, SEPTEMBER 22, 1914. THE OIL TANKS ABLAZE.

3. THE BOMBARDMENT OF MADRAS, SEPTEMBER 22, 1914. ONE OF THE OIL TANKS.
Photo by R. V. Solomon.

government and ensure the uninterrupted progress of the Presidency on the lines of peaceful development which have been followed since the Great Famine. Not until the Great War cast its sinister shadow over India, in common with the rest of the Empire, did any serious influence arise to interrupt the steady advance of Southern India in commercial prosperity. Then for a time, owing to the operations of the German cruiser *Emden,* which ravaged shipping in the Bay of Bengal and bombarded Madras, the outlook was clouded ; but with the destruction of the notorious raider the prospect again improved, and as these words are penned a new era appears to be opening, offering promise of settled conditions which will permit the resumption in undiminished force of the movement which has so happily marked the history of Southern India in the last few decades. The injury done by the titanic conflict to this portion of the Empire is likely to be unimportant. To some extent the country may actually profit by the influences of the war. The great increase in the consumption of tea, for example, can scarcely fail to act as a stimulus to that important planting industry. But whether the economic results be favourable or unfavourable, the sense of oneness with the Empire which the war has brought to India must remain a source of inspiration to rulers, and to the governed an influence which will make for the further advancement of the Great Dependency in all that tends to its welfare.

VIEW OF MADRAS AT THE BEGINNING OF THE EIGHTEENTH CENTURY

NAYAR GIRLS, UPPER CLASS.

Photo by Nicholas & Co.

NATIVE RACES

By C. HAYAVADANA RAO

SOUTHERN India has been for many centuries peopled by a variety of races. These races have, by constant miscegenation, become intermixed so much that it has been found difficult, even after some years of patient scientific research, to differentiate them. Their study, though of engrossing interest is beset with many difficulties. Foremost among these is the paucity of material from which general deductions may be drawn. Though earnest workers in the field of South Indian ethnology have been by no means rare, especially during the past decade or two, yet they have been far too few considering the field they have had to cover. Valuable as their researches have been, they cannot be said to have either exhausted the ground or given the final quietus to the many debatable questions that their investigations have raised. The material, even such as it is, has a value of its own. It has, for instance, enabled us to dispel much of the doubt and uncertainty that once prevailed as regards the origins of the races which have contributed to make up the present population of South India. This population is as heterogenous as may well be imagined. It is made up of racial types which have since prehistoric times become superimposed one over the other. The work of unravelling this tangled web has been one of immense difficulty, but it has, to a certain extent, been successfully tackled. The earliest races of which any traces have been found are connected with the prehistoric remains of the Madras Presidency and the associated States of Travancore and Cochin and the Provinces of Mysore and Coorg. These remains are closely connected with the old sites, both residential and sepulchral, which are found scattered throughout the length and breadth of the Peninsula. A prehistoric survey on scientific lines of Southern India is still a desideratum, and what such a survey could accomplish may be imagined from the fact that these sites have been studied only in the most casual way by a handful of itinerating officials, with other and more pressing duties of their own. The Indian Archæological Department has in recent years wisely conserved these sites, but their systematic survey has still to be undertaken. Such a survey, if accomplished, would furnish, as Mr. R. Bruce Foote, F.G.S., pointed out long ago, much larger data than yet exist as to the distribution over the southernmost districts of the Peninsula of the Palæolithic people whose remains in the shape of chipped stone implements have been found embedded in Pleistocene deposits in so many localities in the Carnatic and Deccan plateau. It would also help very much to bridge over the hiatus in time which now appears to exist between the era of those very rude people and that of the Neolithic tribes which followed them in the same country. Such work would also incidentally help to find the evidence as to the quarter from which the Dravidian tribes entered the Peninsula, still a problem of great ethnological interest. Then again, such a survey would enable us to answer the very interesting question: Were the first Dravidian immigrants who settled in Southern India in a Neolithic stage of culture? or, Must the polished people be considered as pre-Dravidian? If, as Bruce Foote suggests, the question be answered in the latter way, a fresh immigration must be postulated by which the true Dravidians reached their present country. If the answer affirms the former proposition, the idea of a further immigration may be dispensed with, for the early iron people appear to be the direct descendants of the Neolithic tribes and the ancestors of the present inhabitants.[1] The evidence thus far gathered supports the latter inference. It also indicates that Southern India had at least three ages of culture. First, the Palæolithic Age, to which belong the earliest known remains of human industry, represented by implements prepared by chipping only, to an edge or point, stones of suitable size and great hardness. The tools which were used for such chipping were other stones of convenient shape. Only a few implements of this age have been discovered. So far the discoveries have come mainly from the districts round Madras, viz. Chingelput, North Arcot, and Nellore, and a few from Bellary and the Nizam's Dominions. Though the collection is numerically small, it contains some choice specimens of several types of the chipped implements which have been figured by Mr. Bruce Foote in his catalogue. Of these may be mentioned the following: the oval implements, the circular form, the axe-shaped ones, the spear-head type, and lastly, the flake knife. The very rude people who made these implements were succeeded in their country, long after them, by a set of inhabitants who belonged to the next stage of cultuıe, the Neolithic. These are represented by implements and weapons, in much greater variety of form and material, made by chipping and subsequently grinding and polishing suitably hard and tough stones. The art of making pottery and of drilling stone and other hard materials had been discovered, but the tools used in preparing implements, both warlike and industrial, were still predominantly stone ones. High-class specimens of this age are very few. This is due not so much to the want of sites connected with the people of this age, but to the want of careful exploration of the country. The Southern Deccan is particularly rich in them, and the specimens now housed in the Madras Museum have come mainly from the Shevaroy Hills, in the Salem District, Peacock Hill in the Bellary District, and Sirvanur, in the District of Trichinopoly. On the summit of Peacock Hill Mr. Bruce Foote found many evidences of the former settlements of Neolithic man, in the shape of terraces riveted with rough stone walls, near which were great accumulations of pottery, bones of bovine animals, tanks made by damning streams, and shallow troughs hollowed out in the rocks, which were apparently used for crushing corn. He also discovered stone celts in all stages of manufacture, chipped, ground, and polished, and flakes struck off them during the process of fabrication.

After the Neolithic tribes came the iron people. These were probably the direct descendants of the Neolithic tribes and are the ancestors of the present Dravidian tribes of the South. In the age to which these people belonged stone implements were almost entirely displaced by iron ones, the art of iron-smelting having been discovered, and the use of iron implements having, from the intrinsic superiority and the far greater facility of their manufacture, spread very rapidly. Wheel-made pottery had also come into general use, and many other metals, besides iron, had begun to be worked. The arts generally now made great advance. The discoveries belonging to this age cover a wide field and come from many distant parts of Southern India. In fact, so far as Southern India is concerned, it may be stated generally that remains of this age may be found in almost any tract of country. They are usually connected with prehistoric burial-grounds, such as stone circles, cairns, cromlechs, barrows, and cistvaens. Among the places where these have been traced—and even opened up in certain cases—are the following: Nilgiris, Travancore, Malabar, Cochin, Tinnevelly, Madura, Palni Hills, Coimbatore, Salem, North Arcot, South Arcot, Chingelput, Bangalore, Coorg, Anantapur, Bellary, and Kurnool. Most of these have been opened either by district officers, missionaries, railway engineers, or officers connected with the Geological or Survey of India Departments. Several of these have done very useful work, though in some instances of an amateur kind, and the little that we know of the prehistoric peoples of the south is largely due to their disinterested labours. Amongst the most systematic of these workers was Mr. J. W. Breeks, who was Commissioner of the Nilgiris in the sixties of last century. The results of his researches were posthumously published by his widow, in 1871, under the title of "Primitive Tribes of the Nilgiris," together with excellent plates. This work is still a standard authority on the prehistoric remains of the Nilgiris and of the tribes living on them now. The Breeks's collection is now preserved in the Madras Museum, and it is, as Mr. Bruce Foote rightly observes, the gem of the prehistoric series in it. The bulk of this series consists of pottery, amongst which are many unique forms, quite unlike anything as yet known from other parts of Southern India. Much of our present knowledge of this age—the iron age—is based on a study of this series, and of the remains found in other parts of Southern India by other officers as detailed above. What follows is but a bare outline of the study as made by Mr. Bruce Foote, whose knowledge of this subject was quite unrivalled in this part of India. Among the most striking objects of the pottery series are tall jars, many-storied cylinders of varying diameters, with round or conical vases, fashioned to rest upon pottery ring-stands or to be struck into soft soil like the amphoræ of classical times. These jars were surmounted by domed lids, sometimes infitting, but mostly projecting over the edges of the jars they covered. On these lids stood or sat figures of the most varied kind, of men or animals, much more rarely of inanimate objects, but all modelled in the rudest or most grotesque style imaginable. Rude and ugly as these figures are, yet those representing men and women are of supreme interest because of the light they throw upon the stage of civilization to which their makers had attained; they tell us of the fashion

[1] R. Bruce Foote's "Prehistoric Antiquities" (1901), vii.

1, 2, 3, 4. NAYAR GIRLS. 5. RURAL NAYAR.

Photos by Nicholas & Co.

of the garments they wore; the ornaments with which they were adorned; and the arms or implements they used or carried. Many figures of their domestic animals, especially their buffaloes and sheep, are decorated with garlands and bells, and show much ornamentation. The decoration of buffalo horns seems to have engaged their particular attention, judging from the many specimens unearthed. Among the domestic animals they possessed or were acquainted with, were the following: buffalo, cow, sheep, horse or pony, camel, elephant, dog "cock-tailed," pig (?), and goat. They appear to have also known some of the wild animals, and among these were the leopard, sambur, doe, and bustard, but they probably were not ignorant concerning the tiger, bear, bison, jungle-fowl, monkey, snakes, cobra and hamadryas. They might also have known many more, but probably they took too little interest in them for the potters to represent them, or, what is more likely, they for some superstitious reason or other avoided them. At any rate there are many animals not represented by the iron age potters which ordinarily one might have expected them to figure. Thus, with the sole exception of the peacock, none of the birds which are so prominent in later Hindu mythological sculptures occur among the clay figurines. There are no hawks, eagles, vultures, parrots, swans, tortoises or fish, all of which are so frequently met with in Hindu sculpture.

Among the arms borne by these people were short-handled axes, swords, daggers, and maces, but of spears there is no positive evidence. The same is the case with the bow and the arrow, though the existence of both at a somewhat later age, if not then, is amply proved by the finding of many iron arrow-heads on graves. From the figurines the inference has been drawn that the people of this age wore very scanty clothing, as on their bodies no clothes are shown except waist-cloths worn quite narrow. This is in marked contrast with the habits of the people of the times represented on the Sanchi Tope. "There can be no doubt," says Mr. Bruce Foote, "that the costumes of the people represented by the figurines are much more archaic than those of the Sanchi Tope people which were worn more than two thousand years ago, and that fact of itself throws back the age of the figurines themselves possibly many centuries, and gives great probability to the assumption that the art of iron smelting and working became known in India fully three thousand years ago, if not more. If so, the antiquity of the neolithic remains, both implements and sites, may be regarded as in many cases very much higher." Men and women appear to have worn head-dresses of various shapes, mostly peaked caps, with the peaked summit hanging more or less in a forward position. Necklaces, with or without pendants, are common; so too are elaborate belts worn both in front and behind. Garlands are also equally common, and these hang down on the breast and the back. Bracelets, armlets, and anklets are also to be seen on many figures, and some of the first-named were apparently elaborately made, and if designed in metal must have been heavy. On several figures are markings which, Mr. Bruce Foote thinks, "may be regarded as painting or more probably tattooing." The men wore their beards clipped rather short, but they were apparently of thick growth. Many curious types of domestic or other articles which they used have been unearthed. Among these may be mentioned *lotahs*—one, a prototype of the present-day *lotah*, and the other specially remarkable for its conical protuberances, "mamelons," or "paps," shown on one side, which recall similar decoration in parts of the owl-faced terra-cotta vases discovered by Schliemann in his fourth city of Ilios; tail-necked, many-ringed or storied round-bottomed *chatties*; vessels of unique patterns, some brightly ornamented and elaborately finished; many types of bowls; different kinds of vases, one of these, rather low in shape, is peculiar to Travancore; libation cups and seed boxes used in sowing grain and other small seeds. Writing of the tall vases found in many places, Mr. Bruce Foote remarks: "There is in some of the South Indian antique pottery, especially the tall vases, a certain resemblance to Egyptian, Greek, and Etruscan ceramic vases, and some unquestionably show forms of elegance and beauty, but they fall short chiefly in respect of good proportion or finish of the classical forms. The two principal points of difference are the almost entire absence in the Indian types of handles and spouts, which the Western types show in such great variety of forms and exceeding elegance. One reason for this absence of those pleasing accessories may probably be found in the originally inferior quality of the clay used, in the insufficient preparation it underwent, and very largely in the altogether insufficient firing to which the pottery was generally subjected. This necessarily resulted in the production of a ware greatly deficient in tenacity and strength, so that tall and delicately looped handles were an impossibility, and therefore were not attempted by the Indian potters of early days."

These old folk buried the relics of their dead in sepulchral urns, and it is from a study of these that we know anything at all about them. These urns are buried in stone circles, cromlechs, and mounds widely scattered over the country. The Buddhist *chaityas* were probably a later development of these prehistoric memorials raised for the dead, while the *sculptured* cromlech and cistvaens found on the Nilgiris probably belong to a later date. However this may be, in the true prehistoric grave the funeral urns are now found low down in the grave. These are usually low, flattish[1] vessels with or without covers, and they have been known to contain a few burnt bones with fine black or brown mould, in which are found small gold ornaments, bronze and iron rings, beads of glass or agate, or small cowries with perforated backs. In other vessels of this flattened type in Nilgiri graves, Mr. Breeks discovered the beautiful bronze vases and bowls which, as Mr. Bruce Foote justly remarks, form the gems of the whole collection.[2] The most remarkable of these is very handsome and classical in shape and form. The foot is detached, the sides have two bands of flutings, and inside and out the lotus pattern is most beautifully worked. Remarking on this and the other vessels, Mr. Bruce Foote says: "The bronze vessels are so elegant in shape in many cases that it is difficult to believe that they were produced in India, for they present much more resemblance to Græco-Egyptian art works." With these bronze vessels were also found various weapons and domestic implements, spears, javelins, arrow-heads, razors, sickles, shears, and tweezers. Those made of iron were found completely oxidized, while some made of bronze were better preserved, but none of these is now to be found in the Breeks collection.

Here we may well take leave of prehistoric man and his culture, but there are one or two interesting questions which might well be considered at this stage. Has Palæolithic man any representatives still left in Southern India? Or, to vary the question, Can any of the existing

[1] Bruce Foote, l.c., fig. 595, Plate V.
[2] Ibid., Plates X to XV.

1. A DANCING GIRL.
Photo by Nicholas & Co.

2. DANCING GIRL (GESTURES INDICATE DIFFERENT SENTIMENTS).

3. A MADURA VILLAGE BELLE.

4. A GANJAM WOMAN.
Photo by Van der Lowen.

5. A VILLAGE GIRL OF THE SOUTH.

6. DANCING GIRL.
Photo by Nicholas & Co.

South Indian tribes be traced to him? This is a tempting question, but there are hardly any materials to answer it directly. The prehistoric remains hitherto unearthed have yielded few skeletons to show aright the type to which prehistoric man belonged. Even where these remains have been found it is difficult to assign them to a definite period. Parts of human skulls traced by Mr. Rea have been assigned to the Iron Age.[1] The erection of stone circles and cromlechs is still practised by some of the primitive tribes of Southern India, so that the age of such erections is in many cases highly doubtful. Genuine prehistoric sites have not so far yielded human skeletons, and this has largely stood in the way of the determination of this particularly interesting point. But there are certain considerations that might lead us to infer that some at least of the wilder tribes whom we meet with in the impenetrable jungles and hills of Southern India may be racially traced to Primitive man of Palæolithic times. If the Dravidian of to-day is the descendant of the Neolithic man of prehistoric times, there is at least the possibility that the pre-Dravidian, represented by the jungle and hill tribes just mentioned above, is the descendant of the Palæolithic man. Recent research has led to the general conclusion that the non-Aryan population of Southern India is made up of at least two different racial stocks, which have been called pre-Dravidian, or Arche-Dravidian and Dravidian. If, as is believed, the Dravidian represents Neolithic man, is it not possible, at least, that the pre-Dravidian represents in part even Palæolithic man? In culture, wherever the pre-Dravidian has not been altered to any extent by modern influences,[2] he remains about as primitive as his forbear of prehistoric times. Even where he has changed, the changes he has undergone are, it might be conceded, commensurate with the ages which have elapsed since the days of Palæolithic man in Southern India.

That is the trend of the reasoning to-day, made possible by the researches of the last twenty years or so, although even certain older writers have maintained this theory of identity. Perhaps Dalton, in his "Ethnology of Bengal," was the first to speculate on this point. Speaking of the Vindhyan hill-men, whom he knew intimately, he said that "here we still find specimens of the lowest type of humanity; creatures who might justly be regarded as the unimproved descendants of the manufacturers of the stone implements found in the Damodar coal-fields. These are the true aborigines, the *Asuras*, from whom a considerable proportion of the black pigment is derived which has darkened the skins of a large section of the [Indian] population." Dr. Keane[1] adopting this theory, goes on to suggest that India was first peopled by woolly headed Negritos from Malaysia, who "could easily have moved through Tenasserim and Arakan round the Bay of Bengal to the Himalayan slopes, where they have left traces of their former presence, and whence they gradually spread over the Peninsula, most probably in early Palæolithic times." He traces their existence from the Himalayan slopes to the southern uplands of Travancore, Cochin, Coorg, and Mysore. From an examination of the more backward amongst their present-day descendants—e.g. the Koravas of the Madras Presidency and the Jaungs of Orissa—he infers that they must have been not only dark, but also short in stature, in fact, so short as to be styled pygmies. In support of this theory may be adduced the tradition which extensively prevails in Southern India that the cromlechs and dolmens mark the burial-sites of a race of pygmies who at one time formed the general population of the land. They are variously termed *Moriar Mane, Pandu Kuzhi* (from a supposed connection with Pandavas, or dating from Pandava, i.e. very ancient times), and *Mandu* or *Mandavar Kuzhi* (i.e. the pits of the dead). However called, they are in most localities believed to be the burial-sites of a pygmy race, and in certain others as even the dwelling-places of the same race. The idea that the cromlechs and dolmens—in most cases diminutive structures—could possibly have been the abodes of men at any time, may itself be taken as significant of the belief in a pygmy race that has so far proved itself persistent in Southern India. The evidence of the Hindu Epic "Ramayana" may also be incidentally referred to in this connection. This epic has been taken to represent events that occurred between, say, the fourteenth and tenth centuries B.C. Whether this is so or not, there can be no question that the tribes referred to in it as living in Southern India had long since passed out of the minds of the men who belonged to the time of Valmiki. The "Ramayana" describes India south of the Vindhyas as one interminable forest, inhabited by barbarous aborigines, who are described as veritable monkeys and bears of various kinds. Though to their physical appearance a bestial description is given, so far as mental and moral considerations go, they are given the attributes of sentient human beings. They are described as persons endowed with likes and dislikes; with passion and vigour; with kingdoms to lose and kingdoms to gain; with domestic quarrels and internecine warfare; with even a code of morals which put to shame their Aryan neighbours in the north. They scheme for foreign aid, they form alliances, they know the use of weapons of warfare, they improvise armies, they are capable of marching long distances, and they are possessed of engineering skill sufficient to help in the bridging of rivers. Withal they are described as possessed of physical characteristics reminding a civilized race of the monkey and the bear, and as addicted to habits of life revolting to the Aryans. A possible inference is that the indigenous race of the South was of a physically repellent type, highly prognathous and strongly reminding civilized people of a type akin to the monkey and the bear, and their habits of life were probably on a par with their low culture. This tradition of their physical uncouth-

A NAYAR GIRL (UPPER CLASS).
Photo by Nicholas & Co.

[1] Bruce Foote, l.c., p. 130.

[2] For a graphic description of the manner in which primitive tribes have been affected by contact with civilized neighbours, see Mr. E. Thurston's "Tribes and Castes of Southern India," I, Introduction, pp. xiv to xviii.

[1] Dr. Keane's Introduction to Mr. L. K. Anantha Krishna Iyer's "Cochin Tribes and Castes," I, pp. xx and xxv.

ness and low culture appears to have survived to a very late period. Even with the distance of time, poets with imaginative faculties highly developed, in describing the successful adventures of eponymous Aryan heroes, described their opponents and allies in the South, not as a race of pygmies with prognathous faces, hairy bodies, savage habits, and enveloped in dresses so strange to the eye as to show a tail, but as veritable monkeys and bears though endowed with every human attribute in the mental plane. This latter description was rendered necessary because the legends on which undoubtedly the main story of the epic was based made it apparently plain that, but for such frank admission, Rama's exploits would be rendered impossible and the epic lose its very basis. That this belief in a pygmy race, strikingly prognathous in the face, short in stature, and endowed with a tail at the back of the body, survived to late Buddhist times is rendered possible by a remarkable stone panel forming part of the far-famed Sanchi *Stupa*.[1] Sir Herbert Risley was the first to draw public attention to this rather neglected panel.[2] This shows the higher and lower physical types of the days of the epic as conceived by the people of Buddhist times. Under trees with conventional foliage and fruit, three women, diminutive in size, and attired in tight clothing without skirts, kneel in prayer before a small shrine or altar. In the foreground, the leader of a procession of monkeys—short in size, highly prognathous in face, and with tails at the backs—bears in both hands a bowl of liquid and stoops to offer it at the shrine. His solemn look and the strangely adoring look of his following seem intended to portray reverence, devotion, and humility. In the background four stately figures, two men and two women of tall stature and regular features, clothed in flowing robes and wearing elaborate turbans, look on with folded hands in what seems apparent approval of this remarkable act of worship. From the racial point of view, this carving would, as Sir Herbert rightly remarks, "belong to the same order of ideas as the story in the 'Ramayana' of the army of apes who assisted Rama in the invasion of Ceylon. It shows us the higher race on friendly terms with the lower, but keenly conscious of the essential difference of type, and taking no active part in the ceremony, at which they appear as sympathetic but patronizing spectators." Here we see physically depicted the two types, and the apish appearance of the lower type is insisted on. The question whether their type is rightly conceived or described need not detain us long. For the incidents with which they are connected—so far as the "Ramayana" is concerned—took place, say, some fourteen centuries before Christ, and Valmiki's picture of the times, though based on the earliest recensions and kept alive by the professional reciters, was a highly coloured one, and possibly included ideas more of his own times about peoples and their manners of olden days than anything else. Ideas about physical bearing are likely to last long in the memories of people, more especially in India, where physical types strikingly different from each other have always been in evidence. And as regards the tail, it may be pointed out that it probably referred to a peculiarity in the mode of the dressing of the lower class people, whom the earliest Aryans came into contact with in the South of India. Thus the traveller's marvellous tale about the "tailed men" of the Nicobars has been explained on this basis. They have been found, in fact, to owe their origin to the tail-like method of wearing the loin-cloth,[1] a kind of custom that still obtains among certain classes in Southern India on ceremonial occasions. In later days, when the conception of their physical type corresponded more and more with that of the monkey, the Aryans described them as actually endowed not only with apish physical characteristics in the face, but also generally in the body. This made the identification of the earliest people of South India with monkeys all but complete, though they had still the attributes of thinking people left to them. The inference seems irresistible that the monkey and bear tribes described to us in the "Ramayana" were really human beings; that they belonged to a low physical type. Still, they had attained to the elements of civilization which allowed of their being ruled by kings and princes, their possessing a code of morals, and a mode of warfare that was by no means despicable, and their seeking alliances with their Aryan neighbours to settle their own internecine wars. Possibly, as in Europe,[2] so in India during the Palæolithic times, different human varieties (representing the monkey and the bear) were already existent in it; and that though in their physical characters they were in some respects more animal-like than some of the Indians of to-day, they were hardly more so than certain of the lower physical types to be met with to-day in Africa and Australia. Though undoubtedly human in all respects, probably where they differed from the Indian of the present, they approximated to the lower physical type, which is still in existence.

NAYAR GIRL WITH NECK ORNAMENTS AND UMBRELLA.

Photo by Nicholas & Co.

Not long ago excavations conducted by Mr. Rea, Superintendent of Archæology in Madras, at an extensive prehistoric burial-ground at Adittanallur, in Tinnevelly, the southernmost district of the Madras Presidency, brought to light an excellent series of iron implements, bronzes, pottery utensils, and large burial-urns of the type which is traditionally believed to have been made for the reception of the corpses of a race of pygmies.[3] Many of these urns contained human bones and skulls, some of which are of

[1] In the State of Bhopal, in Central India.

[2] Risley's "People of India," pp. 4–5. He has reproduced a part of the panel on the cover of his book.

[1] E. H. Man, *Journ. Anth. Inst.*, XV, p. 442.

[2] A. C. Haddon, "Hist. of Anthropology," p. 72.

[3] Annual Report, Archæological Survey of India Southern Circle, 1902–3.

immense interest, since they exhibit unmistakable prognathism—i.e. projection of the lower jaw—a character which, according to Mr. Edgar Thurston, occasionally occurs in existing man in Southern India. Two of the skulls found at Adittanallur are now preserved in the Madras Museum, and they are conspicuously prognathous. Though Mr. Thurston is unable to subscribe to the general prognathism of the Dravidian tribes of Southern India or of the jungle people, he admits the existence of examples thereof.[1] This survival of prognathism in the existing type has to be traced to the influence of a prognathous ancestor. Writing of the Adittanallur burial-site, Mons. L. Lapicque, who recently visited Southern India, says :—

" J'ai rapporté un specimen des urnes funéraires, avec une collection assez complète du mobilier funéraire. J'ai rapporté aussi un crâne en assez bon état, et parfaitement déterminable. Il est hyperdolichocéphale, et s'accorde avec la série que le service d'archeologie de Madras a déjà réunie. Je pense que la race d'Adichanallour appartient aux pré-Dravidiens."

Six of the most perfect skulls from Adittanallur measured by Mr. Thurston yielded the following results :—

Cephalic Index.

66, 66·5, 67·8, 67·8, 77·1, and 78.

Compare with this the results obtained by measuring forty each of the most numerous of the Tamil castes of Southern India to-day :—

Caste.	Cephalic Index below 70.
Palli	64·4 to 69·6
Paraiyan.........	64·8 to 69·5
Vallala	67·9 to 69·6

This shows how the hyperdolichocephalic type survives in the dolichocephalic inhabitants of the south.

Though this reasoning may sound plausible enough, it is far more safe to treat the question as an open one. In the absence of any undoubted Palæolithic skulls to judge from, it seems right that generalizations are not indulged in. Even in Europe, where Palæolithic man has received particular attention, it has not been possible to say whether any of the existing European races could be traced to the several human varieties which existed in Palæolithic times. Duckworth, who has carefully examined the morphological characters of the Neanderthal, Spy, and Krapina remains, states as his opinion that "the individuals thus characterized are associated in a group specially distinct from the modern Hominidæ to which the

GANJAM DANCING GIRLS.

Photo by Van der Lowen.

name Homo primogenius of Homo neanderthalensis has been applied."[1] The time, therefore, has not yet arrived for saying whether any of the existing primitive tribes of Southern India are racially traceable to Palæolithic man. We want more definite evidence, in the shape of undoubted Palæolithic skulls and skeletons, before we can pronounce any opinion on this point. For this, an organized prehistoric survey is necessary, and until this is accomplished, questions of this kind are best left untouched.

It is now fairly established that some at least of the forest and hill tribes of Southern India represent, racially, a population that is distinct from the Dravidians who form its main bulk, speaking popularly of the rest of the non-Aryan population of Southern India. At one time, when our knowledge of the racial origins of the people of the South was not as great or as good as now, it was held—notably by Dr. Caldwell, for instance—that the jungle and hill tribes and the servile castes of the South were a section of the Dravidians who had been driven to the hills or were rendered servile by the rest of their own people. This theory finds very little support, if any at all, nowadays. Opinion favours the view that some at least of these tribes and castes belong to a race of people, who, for want of a better name, have been called the pre-Dravidian race. These include the Kurumbars, the Sholagars, the Irulans, the Chenchus, the Yenadis, the Kadirs, the Kanikars, the Malai Vedans, the Paniyans, the Paliyans, the Vedans, the Bedars, and many others that may be mentioned. The Bedars have in the Kanarese districts attained to a high position in the social scale, but this is largely due to their having been in the wars of the eighteenth century engaged as soldiers in Haidar's armies, and later, in the irregular hordes kept by a number of *palaigars* in Madras, Mysore, and the Southern Mahratta country. The Vedans of the Tamil country belong essentially to the same stock, and in some instances the Vedans, who live by the hase, as their name would indicate, are still to be met with in the recesses of the thickest forests in Southern India. Some of them have been engaged as forest servants by the Government, and in this capacity their services have been, on occasions, highly appreciated. Some of them are excellent shots, and as guides to *shikaris* they occupy a very high place in the estimation of European sportsmen in the South. To the same stock, probably, must be traced the Veddahs—a really corrupted form of the Tamil Vedar and the Kanarese Bedar, both meaning " hunter "—of the island of Ceylon. These are so very like in appearance to the many jungle tribes of Southern India, that when Mr. Edgar Thurston, of the Madras Museum, saw a number of photographs of Veddahs, brought by Dr. and Mrs. Seligmann, he made the remark that he should not have known them from photographs of Indian jungle tribes."[1] Dr. and Mrs. Seligmann themselves state their views of the Veddahs in fairly definite terms. They write : " We regard them as part of the same race as the so-called Dravidian tribes of Southern India." Dr. Haddon also considers[2] that this jungle tribe of Ceylon should be classed with the Kurumbas, Irulahs, and some other jungle tribes of the Deccan as pre-Dravidians. This point may be taken as fairly settled, though it is still a somewhat disputed one, and the question still remains as to what branch of the hominidæ should we ascribe these kindred jungle tribes of South

[1] Mr. Edgar Thurston's "Tribes and Castes of Southern India," I, Introduction, p. xxvi, Plate I.

[1] W. L. H. Duckworth, "Morphology and Anthropology" (1904), pp. 520–42; cf. also "Man" (1902), p. 186.

[1] Seligmann, "The Veddahs," 1911, p. 416, f.n. 1.

[2] "Races of Man," pp. 7 and 13

India and Ceylon? This is a point that has given rise to much discussion, but is not yet satisfactorily settled. Much confusion has arisen in the discussion of this subject by the loose manner in which the term "Dravidian" has been used—a kind of usage which still lurks, it must be added, in the works of even recent writers. The term was first brought into use by Dr. Caldwell, who applied it to all who spoke the Dravidian languages, and to all of whom he ascribed a common racial origin. He replaced the term "Tamulic" of Bunsen and previous writers by the new term "Dravidian," to which he gave a racial significance. At the same time he reserved the terms "Tamil" and "Tamulic" for the language of that name. The latter term itself was originally applied to the tribes and castes of the South because of the fact that Tamil was the best known of the languages at the time to first speculators in Indian Ethnology. The term "Dravidian" is only another form of "Tamil," and it survives in that form in the name of a Tamil settlement in the heart of the Telugu country, Dimili (more properly Dramila or Dravida), near Vizagapatam. It is convenient to reserve the term "Dravidian" to those people who are racially distinct from the Aryans on the one side and the pre-Dravidians, whom we are just discussing, on the other. It may be that the term has not tended to clarification of ideas in the confused tangle of Indian ethnology. But it is right to point out that it has the merit of being a term which includes, according to popular usage, a great deal more than its root meaning would have us believe. It has also the additional advantage of designating racially the bulk of the South Indian population inhabiting a tract of country known from time immemorial as Dravida. Those who object to it are apt to forget the vast field which a single term has to cover, and in any case they will first have to suggest an equally good, if not a more suitable one, in its place, before it can be discarded. If the term is reserved to describe those people who neither belong to the pre-Dravidian race, now represented by the jungle tribes, nor to the Aryan element which later found shelter among them, a distinct step will have been gained in the study of Indian ethnology. The difficulty engendered by this indiscriminate use of the term "Dravidian" by the earlier writers will be apparent when we consider the divergent views which have been put forth to explain the origins of the jungle tribes we have been discussing above. One set of writers maintained that they are the representatives of a submerged Negrito element which in early days found its way into Southern India. De Quatrefages was among the first to suggest this theory; he believed in the widespread dissemination of the Negrito race, and as time went on this theory gained weight with many writers. He says: "All the so-called Dravidian population, and many others known by different names, indicate, by their physical characters, the presence of a black ethnological element. Documents of all sorts, photographs and skulls, testify that this element is almost completely Negrito." Flower and Lydekker, referring to the Dravidians, say that "in Southern India they are largely mixed up with a negro element." Topinard speaks of the remnants of the black race as being shut up in the mountains of Central India, and in the South as under the name of the Yenadis, Maravars, Kurumbas, Veddas, and others. Sir George Campbell says: "I take as a great division of tribes and castes the black aboriginal tribes of the interior hills and jungles. There can, I suppose, be no duobt they are the remnants of a race which occupied India before the Hindus. They are evidently the remains of an element the greater portion of which has been absorbed by, or amalgamated with, the modern Indian race." And regarding the pre-Dravidian race as a race of Negritos, he says that "among some of the inferior tribes of the south the remains of the thick lips, the very black skin, and other features may still be traced; but, colour perhaps excepted, the aboriginal features are probably gradually wearing away." This theory, which had met with silent opposition in certain quarters, including that of Sir William Turner, the great craniologist, was restated with vigour not long ago by Dr. Keane.[1] His argument is best stated in his own words. After premising that "all the prehistoric movements must, in fact, be assumed to have set in from the north southwards, so that the whole of the peninsula was occupied during the Stone Ages by successive streams of primitive people descending from the Himalayan and Vindhyan slopes to the extremity of the mainland," he says: "The first arrivals were undoubtedly the Negrito, whom I have called the 'submerged element,' because they now form the substratum, have nowhere preserved their racial or social independence, have even lost their original Negrito speech, and are now everywhere *merged* in the surrounding Kolarian and Dravidian populations.[2] Whence came this black element, the presence of which I hope here to place beyond reasonable doubt? Herr Fehlinger thinks they reached India partly from Africa and partly from Australasia ('Naturwiss Wochenschr,' 1904, iii). But I cannot believe there are two black strains in India. One satisfies all the conditions, and that one can scarcely have come either from Africa, which is barred by the Indian Ocean, or from Australia, which is shut off by the Eastern Archipelago. Moreover, both Africans and Australians are mostly tall (5 ft. 8 in. to 5 ft. 10 in.), whereas the Dravidians and Kolarians, amongst whom black is conspicuous, are nearly all undersized—the Koravas, 5 ft. 3 in., and many Korava women real dwarfs (about 4 ft. 9 in.), together with the Jaungs, still shorter, under 5 ft., women 4 ft. 8 in. (Dalton). The inference is that in India the dark autochthons were pygmies apparently allied to the Ætas of the Philippines, and to the Samangs and Sakais still surviving in the Malay Peninsula. From Malaysia these woolly headed Negritos could easily have moved through Tenasserim and Arakan, round the Bay of Bengal to the

"THE MORNING STRETCH."

Photo by Nicholas & Co.

[1] See Keane's Introduction to Mr. L. K. Anantha Krishna Iyer's "Cochin Tribes and Castes," I, xx to xxix.

[2] Dr. Keane, contesting Sir Herbert Risley's theory of the identity of Kolarians with Dravidians, holds that they belong to different racial stocks, and speak radically different languages. L.c., xx to xxix.

Himalayan slopes, where they have left traces of their former presence, and whence they gradually spread over the Peninsula, most probably in early Palæolithic times. Their *spoor* may everywhere be followed from the Negroid flat-faced, curly haired Kocch of Assam 'with the thick, protuberant lips of the Negro,' to the swarthy and irregular-featured Nepalese *Hayas*, thence to the numerous *Santals* of Chota Nagpur 'with a cast of countenance almost approaching the Negro type, and to the neighbouring Bhumiyas with 'coarse, Negro-like features and frizzly hair,' and the diminutive Juang jungle-folk with depressed nasal bone, dilated nostrils, large mouth, very thick lips, and black, frizzled hair. The kindred *Dhangars, Khonds,* and *Gonds* of the Vindhyan range 'show to this day features more closely resembling the *lower Negro type* than any I have met with amongst the tribes of Bengal.' Thus speaks Dalton, who knew these Vindhyan hill-men well, and who adds that here we still find specimens of the lowest type of humanity, creatures who might justly be regarded as the unimproved descendants of the manufacturers of the stone implements found in the Damodar coal-fields. These are the true aborigines, the Asuras, from whom a considerable proportion of the black pigment is derived which has darkened the skins of a large section of the [Indian] population. Equally unmistakable evidences of the underlying Negroid element are presented by the low-caste hill-men of the Southern uplands. Some years ago Drs. F. Jagor and G. Koerbin collected a great body of anthropological data from more than two hundred and fifty of these aborigines, representing as many as fifty-four tribes from almost every part of the Madras Presidency. Since then the list has been supplemented by the researches of Mr. E. Thurston, of Mr. Nanjundayya for Mysore, and of Mr. (Anantha Krishna) Iyer for Cochin. We are now, therefore, in a position to speak with confidence of the general physical characteristics of these jungle people. . . . It will suffice to say that Negroid contacts and influences are almost everywhere betrayed in the black colour, crisp or frizzly hair, broad nose, thick lips, low stature, very long arms, and other marked Negro traits of these aborigines. Thus, the *Veddahs* of Travancore are described as all but black, with hair very black, wavy, and crisp, and similar characters are attributed to the *Paraiyans* of the Wynaad, the *Kadars* and *Malasars* of Coimbatore and Cochin, the *Kurumbas* and *Imlas* of the Nilgiris, the *Malayalis*, the *Pallis, Shanars,* and *Katumaratis* of the Salem District, the *Vellalas* of Madura, and above all, to the *Paniyans* of 'pronounced negro features.'" Dr. Keane adduces the evidence derived from numerous recent photographs, which also reveal, according to him, "Negroid traits in a very striking manner. Such are the Kadar men, several of the Malayan, and Eravallen women, and the Izhuva and Thandapulaya groups [in Cochin]." He then adds: "Now comes the question: how have the present Dravidian and Kolarian low castes acquired these Negroid characters which could not have been brought from beyond the Hindu Kush or the Himalayas, where the indigenous populations have always been either white, regular-featured Aryans of Caucasic type, or else yellow, lank-haired Mongols? The inference seems obvious that these Dravidians and Kolarians are a blend in diverse proportions of Asiatic intruders with the true black indigenes of the Peninsula. In other words, they acquired their Negroid characters by secular interminglings with Negrito aborigines." If this be so, how did the original aborigines lose their language? Dr. Keane thinks that they dropped it as they got absorbed by the Kolarians and Dravidians. Here is his theory in full: "Beyond the Vindhyan range they [the Kolarians,who, according to him, came from the north-east, and the Dravidians, who came from the north-west] have nearly everywhere absorbed or replaced both the Negrito substratum and the Kolarian indigenes. Hence it is that at present all the natives of the southern uplands—Mysore, Coorg, Cochin, and Travancore—speak various forms of the Dravidian tongue. Here again Mr. [Anantha Krishna] Iyer unconsciously supplies some particulars of great ethnical value. Thus we learn that the Nattu Malayans speak a mixed Tamil-Malayan dialect with such a peculiar pronunciation as to be quite unintelligible to the more cultured Dravidians of the plains. In fact, their command of articulate speech is so weak that the defect is made up by gestures! The Nayadis also speak Malayalam, but pronounce it so badly that strangers 'cannot easily comprehend their speech,' and the same is true of the Pulayans, if not of all the jungle people without exception. All this finds its counterpart among the descendants of the plantation negroes, whose mother-tongues have for many generations been English, French, Spanish, or Portuguese, yet they still continue to mispronounce or speak these languages barbarously. The phenomenon is explained by the Russian explorer, Miklukho Maclay, who rightly attributes the absolute impossibility of our imitating certain utterances in some of the New Guinea languages to 'fundamental differences in the anatomical structure of the larynx and the whole muscular system of the organs of speech in the two races' (European and Papuan). But anatomical differences imply racial differences, and thus we again see that the Cochin and other low-caste aborigines now speaking broken Dravidian dialects were not originally Dravidians, but, as above stated, a blend in diverse proportion of superimposed Negrito, Kolarian, and Dravidian racial strata."

Such is the theory of Dr. Keane in nearly his own words. While he is definite in his views, and goes as far as one could in the line of argumentation which he puts forward, there are writers who are inclined to be a great deal more cautious in their inferences. They are content to leave matters in a more fluid state, and they are impressed with the difficulty of evolving anything like a reasonable theory out of the conflicting data available. While Dr. Keane finds unmistakable traces of a submerged Negrito element in the South Indian population, Mons. Louis Lapicque, whom I have already quoted, finds no evidence in it of a race to be compared, for instance, to the Negritos of the Andamans. He says in a passage which deserves to be quoted :—

"Dans les montagnes des Nilghirris et d'Ane'male, situées au cœur de la contree dravidienne, on a signalé depuis longtemps des petits sauvages crepus, qu'on a même pensè pouvoir, sur des documents insuffisants, identifier avec les negritos. En réalité, il n'existe pas dans ces montagnes, ni probablement nulle part dans l'Inde, un témoin de la race primitive comparable, comme pureté, aux Andamanais ni même aux autres Negritos. Ce que l'on trouve la, c'est simplement, mais c'est fort précieux, une population métisse qui continue au delà du Paria la série générale de l'Inde. Au bord de la forêt vierge ou dans les collines partiellement defrichées, il y a des castes demi-Parias, demi-sauvages. La hiérachie sociale les classe

1. TIYA WOMAN. 2. TODA GIRL. 3. CHERUMA GIRL. 4. TIYA WOMAN.

au-dessous du Paria ; on peut même trouver des groupes ou les faces nègres, nettement dessinè, est tout à fait prédominant. Ehbien, dans ces groupes, les chevelures sont en generale frisées, et on en observe quelques-unes qu'on peut même appeler crépuses. On a donc le moyen de prolonger par l'imagination la série des castes indiennes jusq'au type primitif que était (nous n'avons plus qu'un pas a faire pour le reconstruire), un *Nègre*. . . . Nous sommes arrivés à reconstituer les traits nègres d'un type disparu en prolongeant une série graduée de métis. Par la même méthode nous pouvons déterminer théoriquement la forme du crâne de ce type. Avec une assez grande certitude, je crois pouvoir affirmer, après de nombreuses mesures systématiques, que le nègre primitif de l'Inde était sousdolichocéphale avec un indice voisin de 75 ou 76. Sa taille, plus difficile à préciser, car les conditions de vie modifient ce caractère, devait être petite, plus haute pourtant que celle des Andamanais. Quant au nom qu'il convient de lui attribuer, la discussion des faits sociaux et linguistiques sur lesquels est fondée la notion de dravidien permet d'établir que ce nègre était antérieur aux dravidiens ; il faut donc l'appeler *Pré-dravidien*, ou, si nous voulons lui donner un nom qui ne soit pas relatif à une autre population, on peut l'appeler *Nègre Paria*."

Mons. Lapicque has been rather widely followed by a number of recent writers. Mr. Thurston [1] whose knowledge of South Indian jungle tribes is unique, and Dr. A. C. Haddon [2] incline to favour the term "pre-Dravidian." Mr. Thurston styles them the modern representatives of the Dayus who are referred to in the Hindu sacred writings and traditions as black-skinned, noseless, unholy savages. According to recent nomenclature, these pre-Dravidians are said to belong to the group of melanous dolichocephalic cymotrichi or dark-skinned narrow-headed people with wavy, or curly (not woolly) hair, who are further differentiated from many of the Dravidian classes—Tamil, Telugu, Canarese, and others, by shortness of stature and broad (platyrhine) noses.[1] That the primitive inhabitant of South India was dolichocephalic or subdolichocephalic is amply proved by the researches of Mr. Thurston among the jungle tribes of the Tamil, Telugu, and Malayalam tracts. The following table of cephalic indices published by him strikingly illustrates the point :—

[1] "Tribes and Castes of Southern India" (1909) I, Intro., p. lv ; also in "India and the Durbar" (1911), pp. 215–16.

[2] "Races of Man," pp. 7 and 13.

Jungle Tribe.	Average.	Maximum.	Minimum.
Kadir	72·9	80·0	69·1
Irula	73·1	78·6	68·4
Kanikar	73·4	78·9	69·1
Mala Vedan ...	73·4	80·9	68·8
Panaiyan ...	74·0	81·1	69·4
Chenchu ...	74·3	80·5	64·3
Sholaga	74·9	79·3	67·8
Paliyan	75·7	79·1	72·9
Irula (Nilgiris) ...	75·8	80·9	70·8
Kurumba ...	76·5	83·3	71·8

Mr. Thurston traces not only this peculiarity in the shape of the head of the jungle tribes of Southern India to-day to the lasting influence of a dolichocephalic or sub-dolichocephalic pre-Dravidian element in it, but also to the high nasal index

[1] "India and the Durbar," p. 215.

of the jungle tribes of the present day, and even of many of the inhabitants of Southern India to the same source.

The following two tables of nasal indices, one relating to various South Indian jungle tribes, and the other to individuals belonging to many different castes and tribes of South India, all of dark colour, short of stature, and with nasal index exceeding 90, indicate the position put forward by him :—

NASAL INDEX OF JUNGLE TRIBES.

Tribe.	Nasal Index.		
	Average.	Maximum.	Minimum.
Paniyan	95·1	108·6	72·9
Kadir	89·8	115·4	72·9
Kurumba ...	86·1	111·1	70·8
Sholaga	85·1	107·7	72·8
Mala Vedan ...	84·9	102·6	71·1
Irula (Nilgiris) ...	84·9	100·0	72·3
Kanikar	84·6	105·0	72·3
Chenchu	81·9	95·7	68·1

NASAL INDEX OF A MIXED COLLECTION OF INDIVIDUALS.

Caste or Tribe of Individual.	Nasal Index.
Vokkaliga	90·7
Moger	90·7
Saiyid Muhammedan ...	90·9
Kammalan	90·9
Chakkiliyan	90·9
Vellala	91·6
Karga Vellala... ...	92·7
Pattar Brahm... ...	92·9
Odde	93·0
Smarth Brahman ...	95·1
Palli	95·1
Pallan	100·0
Bestha	100·0
Mukkuvan	100·0
Agasa	100·0
Tamil Paraiyan ...	105·0

Both Mr. Thurston and Dr. Haddon agree in thinking that the pre-Dravidians are ethnically related to the Veddas of Ceylon, and the Sakais of the Malay Peninsula. Mr. Thurston sums up his theory very briefly in one of his recent contributions. "There are," he says, "strong grounds for the belief that the pre-Dravidians are ethnically related to the Veddas of Ceylon, the Toalas of the Celebes, the Batin of Sumatra, the Sakais of the Malay Peninsula, and possibly to the Australians. Much literature has been devoted to the theory of the connection between the 'Dravidians' and the Australians, partly on the strength of certain characters which the Dravidian and Australian languages have in common, and the use by certain Dravidian castes (Kallan and Maravan) of a carved ivory or wooden throwing-stick called *valia tadi*, which is supposed to bear a resemblance to the Australian boomerang. Huxley even went so far as to say that an ordinary coolie, such as one can see among the sailors of any East India vessel in the London Docks, would, if stripped, pass very well for an Australian, although the skull and the lower jaw are generally less coarse. According to Wallace, the Indo-Malayan Archipelago, comprising the islands of Borneo, Java, and Sumatra, was formerly connected by Malacca with the Asiatic Continent, while the Austro-Malayan Archipelago, comprising Celebes, the Moluccas, etc., was directly connected with Australia. An important ethnographic fact is that the method of tree-climbing by means of bamboo-pegs resorted to by the Dayaks of Borneo, as given by Wallace, might have been written on the Anamalai hills of Southern India, and would apply equally well in every detail to the pre-Dravidian Kadirs, who inhabit that mountain range. Still further affinities between these people and the inhabitants of the Malay Archipelago are illustrated by the practice of chipping the incisor teeth, and the wearing by adult females of a bamboo hair-comb, the design on which bears a striking resemblance to that on the combs worn by some Malay tribes."[1] This theory receives support from, or is rather partially based on, the investigations of writers who have worked among the Sakais on the one hand and the Australians on the other. Writing of the racial affinities of the Sakais, Skeat and Blagden write: "An alternative theory comes to us on the high authority of Virchow, who puts it forward, however, in a somewhat tentative manner. It consists in regarding the Sakai as an outlying branch of a racial group formed by the Vedda (of Ceylon), Tamil, Kurumba, and Australian races. . . . Of these the height is variable, but in all four of the races compared, it is certainly greater than that of the Negrito races. The skin colour, again, it is true, agrees to a remarkable degree, but the general hair character appears to be uniformly long, black, and wavy, and the skull-index, on the other hand, appears to indicate consistently a dolichocephalic or long-shaped head."[2]

[1] "India and the Durbar," pp. 215–16. The argument is set out in a much more elaborate form in the "Castes and Tribes of Southern India," I, pp. xxi–xxiv.

[2] "Pagan Races of the Malay Peninsula" (1906).

Referring to the Sakais they remark: "In evidence of their striking resemblance to the Veddas it is perhaps worth remarking that one of the brothers Sarasin, who had lived among the Veddas and knew them very well, when shown a photograph of a typical Sakai, at first supposed it to be a Vedda." Commenting on this passage, Mr. Thurston writes: "For myself, when I first saw the photographs of Sakais published by Skeat and Blagden it was difficult to realize that I was not looking at pictures of Kadirs, Paniyans, Kurumbas, or other jungle folk of Southern India."[1] Then, again, writing of the racial affinities of the Australians, Professor R. Semon says: "We must, without hesitation, presume that the ancestors of the Australians stood, at the time of their immigration to the continent, on a lower rung of culture than their living representatives of to-day. Whence and in what manner the immigration took place, it is difficult to determine. In the neighbouring quarter of the globe there lives no race which is closely related to the Australians. Their nearest neighbours, the Papuans of New Guinea, the Malays of Sunda Islands, and the Maoris of New Zealand, stand in no close relationship to them. On the other hand we find, farther away, among the Dravidian aborigines of India, types which remind us forcibly of the Australians in their anthropological characters." Huxley, in the words already quoted, here goes a little too far in his accentuation of the similarity of type. We are, however, undoubtedly confronted with a number of characters—skull formation, features, wavy curled hair—in common between the Australians and Dravidians, which gain in importance from the fact that by the researches of Norris, Bleek, and Caldwell, a number of points of resemblance between the Australian and Dravidian languages have been discovered, and this despite the fact that the homes of the two races are so far apart, and that a number of races are wedged in between these, whose languages have no relationship whatever to either the Dravidian or Australian. There is much that speaks in favour of the view that the Australians and the Dravidians sprang from a common main branch of the human race. According to the laborious researches of Paul and Fritz Sarasin, the Veddas of Ceylon, whom one might call pre-Dravidians, would represent an off-

[1] "Tribes and Castes of Southern India," I, Introd., pp. v–xxiii.

shoot from this main stem. When they branched off, they stood on a very low rung of development, and seem to have made hardly any progress worth mentioning." In this passage the terms "Dravidian aborigines," "Dravidians," and "pre-Dravidians" are used in a rather loose manner, and one is not quite clear as to whom Professor Semon is really writing of. It would appear that following the earlier writers who used the term "Dravidian" to represent the "pre-Dravidian" as well as the "Dravidians," he uses the one as synonymous with the other in one place, while he reserves the title of "pre-Dravidian" for the Veddas. At the same time, it seems apparent he is thinking of Dravidians proper when he speaks of the language of Dravidians, and calls in the help of linguistic analogy to decide in his favour. The same confusion is to be traced in the writings of certain other recent writers. This shows how necessary it is to use the term "Dravidian" in its more restricted sense of designating the more advanced castes and tribes of Southern India speaking the languages that have been grouped under the head of "Dravidian." If the language of the Dravidians proper was also the language of the pre-Dravidians, Professor Semon and those who have followed him may have some justification for their use of terms in the manner they have done. But it is almost a case of begging the question when we assume that their languages were identical. It is true that all speak the same languages now, having regard to the linguistic areas in which they live, but have they done so from primeval times? If not, can it make for scientific accuracy if this terminological inexactitude is perpetuated indefinitely? It may perhaps be conceded that certain at least of the jungle tribes of Southern India have much in common with the Veddas of Ceylon, the Sakais, and other tribes of the Malay Peninsula, and with the Australian aborigines. But it is a question if the Dravidian proper did not find his way into Australia as well in later times. If he did, the existence of the boomerang in Australia and the resemblances which have been traced between the Dravidian and Australian languages is easily explained. This aspect of the question will be further referred to later on in this treatise. It may suffice here for the present to note that such a migration in primeval times is rendered probable when we remember that otherwise it is difficult to explain the observed similarities in language and social system in the Dravidians proper and the Australians. That Australia was open on the north and north-west to primitive migration both from India and Papuasia seems to be admitted by those who have considered the question in any detail. "That such migrations took place," writes Dr. A. H. Keane,[1] "scarcely admits of any doubt, and the Rev. John Mathew[2] concludes that the Australian continent was first occupied by a homogenous branch of the Papuan race, either from New Guinea or Malaysia, and that these first arrivals, to be regarded as true aborigines, passed into Tasmania, which at that time probably formed continuous land with Australia. Thus the now extinct Tasmanians would represent the primitive type, which, in Australia became modified, but not effaced, by crossing with later immigrants, chiefly from India. These are identified, as they have been by other ethnologists, with the Dravidians, and the writer remarks that although the Australians are still in a state of savagery, and the Dravidians of India have been for many ages a people civilized in a great measure, and possessed of literature, the two peoples are affiliated by deeply-marked characteristics in their social system, as shown by the boomerang, which, unless locally evolved, must have been introduced from India. But the variations in the physical characters of the natives appear to be too great to be accounted for by a single graft, hence Malays also are introduced from the Eastern Archipelago, which would explain both the straight hair in many districts, and a number of pure Malay words in several of the native languages." The evidence of geology appears to support this view. "It is highly probable," writes Mr. W. T. Blandford, in his "Manual of Geology of India," that the metamorphic area of Eastern Burma was land in the Tertiary period, and that the other tertiary deposits of Assam, Burma, and the Malay Islands were formed in a deep gulf or around and amongst an archipelago, like that now existing farther to the south-east. . . . Some peculiarities of the recent fauna indicate a connection between the Malay Islands, Southern India, and Africa, in early Tertiary times ; and a land area may have extended to the south of India at this period." That migration from India was possible in primeval times may be inferred to some extent by the fact that migration has long been going on from the eastern sea-board of India to Burma and the French Indies on the one side, and the Straits Settlements on the other. In the former, inscriptions and architectural remains attest to Indian emigration within historical times, while in the latter—in Java and Sumatra in particular

FISHER GIRLS, MALABAR.

Photo by Nicholas & Co.

[1] "Ethnology," 1896.

[2] Pro. R. Soc., N.S. Wales, xxiii, part iii.

—Hindu influence was at one time so predominant, both in religion and arts, that volumes have been devoted to them by Dutch writers. Apparently Kalinga kings and people occupied the islands in the fifth and sixth centuries of the Christian era, if not earlier. Inscriptions found in Java specifically name Kalinga in India as the region from which the Hindu colonists emigrated. "Kalinga" was in popular Javanese corrupted into "Kling," a name by which all people of India, irrespective of race or creed, are still known to the Javanese and others. Kalinga was in ancient times the name given to a kingdom on the east coast of India, which had its capital at Vengi or Vegi, in the modern Kistna district. Even now emigration to the Straits Settlements from the districts of South Arcot and Tanjore is a well-recognized fact, and often exceeds fifty thousand persons in a year.

THE VILLAGE CRIER.
Photo by Nicholas & Co.

In what stage of culture were the pre-Dravidians at the time they first came in contact with the Dravidians proper? That is a question more easy to put than to answer. Tradition supports the view that some at least of the tribes forming them had attained to something like a civilized life. The "Ramayana" gives us vivid pictures of the life led by the savage kings of the south, and if it is to be taken to enshrine the tradition current in India of a bygone age, it must be taken to render possible at least the view that the present condition of the pre-Dravidians is not to be conclusively taken against certain at least of their progenitors having enjoyed the elements of a civilized life. The best example of to-day of the pre-Dravidian race of Southern India are the Kadirs of the Anamalai hills, the Paniyans of Malabar and the south-east Wynaad, the Kurumbas of the Nilgiris, the Solagars of Coimbatore, the Yeruvas of Coorg, the Kurumbas and Irulas of Mysore, and the primitive tribes of Cochin. These do not by any means show any remarkable aptitude for progress, nor is there anything in their present position to show that they at any time attained to anything higher in the social scale. But it would be ignoring much in the shape of evidence if we place too much reliance on this argument. Sections of particular tribes have been known to have acquired social and even political distinction both here and elsewhere, and current tradition supports the view that sections of these tribes might have at one time secured some such distinction in Southern India long before the Dravidians came amidst them. The Kurubas who probably represent the civilized among the Kurumba tribe apparently had risen to a fairly respectable social and political eminence at one time. Even now the Kurumbas are much feared on the Nilgiris, where they are still found in their primitive state. The Bedars—who represent the civilized section of the Vedans of the South—are a highly civilized tribe, and many of the Palaigars of the Ceded Districts of the eighteenth century, belonged to this caste. Among the Veddas of Ceylon the same thing seems to have occurred—a civilized section being much in advance of their savage brethren, yet lurking in the forests.[1] Many quaint survivals of the independent position which several of these primitive tribes and now despised castes at one time enjoyed are still to be met with throughout the length and breadth of Southern India. At Melkota and Belur in Mysore, the Holeyars (i.e. Paraiyans) have the right of entering the temple on three days of the year, especially set apart for them. In the great festival of Siva at Tiruvalur, in Tanjore, the headman of the Paraiyans is mounted on an elephant with the image of the presiding deity, and carries his *chouri* (whisks). In Madras and at Vizagapatam, the Brahmans had to go through the form of asking the consent of the lowest castes to their marriages, though the custom has now died out.[2] Dr. Caldwell notes the fact that in Madras when a *tali* (marriage symbol) is tied round the back of the idol in the name of the entire community, a Paraiyan is chosen to represent the people as the goddess's bridegroom. To these, perhaps, might be added the fact that the lower village officers, the *Vettiyan*, the *talaiari*, the *dandasi*, and the *toti*, are, in the majority of South Indian villages, of the Paraiyan caste ; secondly, the custom which prevails in some parts of making a Paraiyan walk along the boundaries of a field with a pot of water on his head when there is any dispute about their exact position.[3] Further, it may be noted that at the death of a casteman the most important person is the Paraiyan, who is always called to the house immediately a death takes place. He, first of all, must bathe for the dead, the people of the house furnishing the necessary soap-nut and hot water. Then he must be furnished with a new cloth and a good meal, after which he precedes the funeral procession to the burning-ground. On the arrival of the corpse the Paraiyan must intercede with the goddess Kali on behalf of the dead man, to throw open the doors which bar the passage of the departed spirit in its flight to the other world. He then pronounces a number of

[1] Seligmann's "Veddas," page 27. Seligmann, however, takes a different view.

[2] "Indian Antiquary," Vol. III, p. 191.

[3] "Madras Census Report," 1891, p. 245; also Rice's "Mysore and Coorg," I, 313.

mantras (chants) over the dead body, after which the burning takes place. This is even more apparent in the case of the Kanarese Holeyans (the Paraiyans of the Kanarese country). The Kulavadi, who is unhesitatingly admitted to be the *de jure* owner of the village, is entitled to receive, and actually does receive, a certain burial-fee—or, as it is forcibly put, "they buy from him the ground for [burying] the dead [*nelahaga*]." [1] The jungle Kurumbas play a leading part at the seed-sowing ceremony of the Badagas of the Nilgiris. The Badaga priest puts some grain into the cloth of a Kurumba, and yoking the bullocks to the plough, makes three furrows in the soil. The Kurumba, removing his turban, places it on the ground. He then kneels between the furrows and scatters the grain on the soil. So much are the Kurumbas on the Nilgiris respected that every Badaga family pays annual tax of four annas to them, and if, perchance, a Kurumba comes to a Badaga village, a subscription is raised as an inducement to him to take his departure.[2] The Kurumba is as much feared as a mountebank as the true owner of all land on the Nilgiris. That the Kurumba and and allied tribes were acquainted from very early times with the working of gold, diamond, and other mines in Southern India seems admitted on all hands. At Nilambur, in south-east Wynaad (Nilgiris) the mines were worked by Kurumba slaves, who were subjected to horrible cruelties if the gold they found was deficient in quantity.[3] There were, it is said, in 1830, some 100,000 slaves in Malabar engaged in this work; they were bought and sold like cattle, the value of a man being from Rs. 5 to Rs. 20.[4] Mr. Brough Smyth, the Australian mining expert who visited the Wynaad gold-mines and reported on them in 1879-80, gives an account of the Kurumba workings. He says that they indicate three different degrees of knowledge in the miner's art: they consisted of (1) quarrying on the outcrops of veins; (2) vertical shafts; (3) adits; (4) vertical shafts with adits; (5) shafts on underlie. Among these the most remarkable are the vertical shafts: they are even when in solid quartz sometimes 70 ft. in depth, with smooth and perfectly plumb sides. What the tools were which enabled the miners to produce such work in hard, dense quartz, no one appears able to suggest. The fragments of stone obtained from these various mines were pounded with hand-mullers, the pounding-places being still seen, and the pounded stone was then, it is believed, washed in a wooden dish and treated with mercury.[1] Similarly at all other gold and diamond mines, it is the pre-Dravidians who are spoken of as having first worked them. Indeed, Mr. Ball, who has specially written on this point, remarks: "There is one point in reference to the discovery of diamonds about which much might be written. In the majority of cases they belong to the aboriginal tribes, and were probably chiefly of the Dravidian family, the trade being hereditary. There is nothing to connect the earliest workings distinctly with Aryan influence; in fact, the Sambalpur localities were in the country of the Sabaras or Savaras, which may perhaps have been in the Saubira of the [Pauranic] list. The Panna mines were formerly, and still are, worked chiefly by Gonds or Kols, and the miners in Southern India, though some of them are simply described as low outcasts, all probably came from the same family. It may, of course, be said in answer to this that mining and washing would naturally fall to the lot of helot races, but in some of the localities it is doubtful whether the Aryans ever held paramount power." [1] It is possible that the pre-Dravidians were already acquainted with the methods of working mines, and that they were utilized in later times in this work by both Dravidians and Aryans.

Now we come to the Dravidians proper. As already pointed out, much confusion in thought and writing has crept in by the loose use of the term "Dravidian." If we restrict the term "pre-Dravidian" to the race that is now represented by the jungle tribes and servile castes of Southern India, we shall have gained a distinct step forward in Indian ethnological terminology. We can, in that case, reserve the term "Dravidian" to the castes and tribes which, broadly speaking, are fairly advanced in the social scale, and are speaking either one or the other of the Dravidian languages or dialects. This term "Dravidian" it would be best to reserve to the generality of the South India people who are neither "pre-Dravidian" nor Aryan, using the latter term in its usually accepted sense. Who were these Dravidians, and how did they reach Southern India? There are different theories held on these interesting questions, and all that can be attempted here is but a brief summary of them. The earlier speculators in Indian ethnological discussions were mostly philologists, who

BRAHMINS PERFORMING MORNING ABLUTIONS.

Photo by Nicholas & Co.

[1] Rice, loc. cit., I, 313.

[2] Thurston, loc. cit., I, 87.

[3] Collector Sheffield's Report to Madras Government, 1831, quoted by V. Ball in "Geology of India," III, 181.

[4] Mr. F. H. Barber's evidence before Lords' Committee on East India Affairs, 1830. Ibid., 181.

[1] Brough Smyth's report summarized by V. Ball in "Geology of India," III, 183.

[1] V. Ball, loc. cit., III, 3.

based their classification of races on language. By observing a certain number of common characteristic features of a number of languages, they concluded that the races who spoke these languages should belong to the same family. Though this principle of classification of races has been very generally discredited, it has unfortunately left some relics of its former strength in many different places, and among these India must be counted as one. These philologists observed many characteristics common to Turanian languages, among which they brought in the Dravidian group, and from them they inferred—as was usual in their days—the racial identity of the various people speaking them. Thus were the Dravidians traced to the Turanian family. The theory was developed in its completest form by Max Müller and Bunsen [1] and widely followed until very recently by most writers on Indian history.[2] According to Max Müller and Bunsen, there were Turanian migrations towards the north and the south. One migration to the north settled on the rivers Meikong, Menam, the Irrawaddy, and the Brahmaputra, and formed the Tai tribes, while one to the south followed the courses of the Amur and the Lena, and founded the Tangusic tribes. A second migration to the south, finding the country occupied, pushed on to the islands and the sea and laid the foundation of the Malay tribes; while a second to the north is supposed to have originated the numerous Mongol tribes and to have pressed westward along the chain of the Altai Mountains. Still a third to the north produced the Turkish peoples, even as far west as the Ural Mountains and the frontier of Europe. A third to the south is believed to have advanced towards Tibet and India, and in later times they have poured its hordes through the Himalayas and to have formed the original native population of India. The last Turanian wanderers to the south were, according to this theory, the forefathers of the Tamils and allied peoples, and the last to the north were the ancestors of the Finns and of the Basques in Spain, as well as of the Samoieds in Siberia. All these moving streams of people, it should be remembered, flowed from the mountain plateaus of Central Asia long before the historic period.

A TODA.

This theory is, however, open to criticism. The only evidence of these Turanian migrations lies in the structure of a number of languages, but no tradition, song, monument, or historical record has preserved any mention of these primeval wanderings of the first races of Turanian men and women. The theory rests solely upon the morphological classification of languages. The upholders of the theory believe that this classification may be used as a test of race, inasmuch as, according to them, all those who speak isolating languages belong to one racial stock, those who speak inflexional languages to another, those who speak agglutinative languages to still another, and so on. The argument, however, fails when applied to the agglutinative languages, the very ones upon which the theory in question rests, for the speakers of these belong to different racial stocks. If Dr. Keane's view be correct, the whole theory is untenable. He says [1] that isolating, inflexional, and polysynthetic families of languages are all derived from separate agglutinative types. "The true test of agglutination," he says, "is the power of the particles to become detached and shift their places in the combined form. . . . A vast number of languages are of this agglutinating order, from which all the others have emerged in diverse directions. . . . From that stage language developed according to its different initial tendencies in various directions towards complete decomposition . . . as in the particle languages of the Malayo-Polynesian group; polysynthesis, as in most of the American groups; and synthesis, as in the inflecting Aryan-Semitic and Hametic groups. . . . And if it is objected that some languages have never got beyond the agglutinating state, the answer is that some animals have never got beyond the classes of fish or reptiles." This theory of the evolution of speech has been objected to by the upholders of the old, but now exploded, theory of root origin. Thus Sayce speaks of the "magical frontier between flexion and agglutination," which can never be "cleared, since to pass from agglutination to inflexion is to revolutionize the whole system of thought and language, and the basis on which it rests, and break with the past psychological history and tendencies of speech." But, as Jespersen [2] says: "Revolutions do take place in the world of languages, even if they take more time than it takes the French to change their constitutions. If a thousand years suffice to change a type of speech like that of King Alfred into the totally different one of Queen Victoria, then the much longer period which palæontologists and zoologists accord to mankind on this earth could work still greater wonders. Sayce stands with regard to these three or four types of speech in much the same attitude which naturalists held with regard to the notion of 'species' before Darwin came."

Dr. Caldwell, one of the supporters of the North-West Passage theory, is strongly against the Southern Dravidians being classed, in regard to their physical characteristics, with the Turanians or Mongolians.[3] He thinks that there is no difference between the heads or features

[1] Max Müller's "Turanian Researches" included in Bunsen's "Outlines of Universal History," p. 237.

[2] The late Sir William Wilson Hunter in his "Indian Empire" says: "The Dravidians seem, generally speaking, to have found their way into the Punjaub by the north-west passes. They now inhabit the southern part of the three-sided tableland as far down as Cape Comorin, the southernmost point of India. . . . The Dravidians then rushed forward in a mighty body to the south." The term "Turanian" is derived from Turan, the barbarous countries "outside" or beyond Iran and the Aryans. Max Müller says: "'Tura' refers to the 'swiftness' of the horse, thus describing the nomadic races in contradistinction to the 'agricultural' Indo-Aryans." See "Science of Language," p. 238. The Turanian physical type is described by Mr. J. R. Logan. Of late the term "Mongolian" has taken the place of "Turanian," and that physical type is described by Keane in his "Ethnology," pp. 228 and 297.

[1] "Ethnology," pp. 209, 211, 213.

[2] "Progress in Language," p. 132, quoted by Keane in his "Ethnology," pp. 209–10.

[3] Fergusson, curiously enough, attributes a Southern origin to them, but yet calls them Turanians. "History of India and Eastern Architecture," p. 11.

of the Dravidians and those of the Brahmans, and says that the varieties of feature or physiognomy and colour are so minute and unimportant that, in the absence of any class difference in the shape of the head, they are consistent with the supposition of oneness of blood, and may safely be referred to local, social, and individual causes of difference—the caste system, the prohibition of intermarriages and social intercourse, and the absence of common bonds of sympathy. The Dravidian type of head, he says, will even bear to be directly compared with the European. Even among the lower classes of Dravidians, the Mongolian smoothness of skin, scantiness of hair, flatness of face, and the peculiar monotonous olive hue of the Mongolian complexion are never met with. As regards other elements of the Mongolian type, it is chiefly, if not solely, among the lower classes that they are seen, and they do not constitute the class-type of any caste whatever. They are, Dr. Caldwell says, exceptional instances, which scarcely at all affect the general rule. He adds: "I have no doubt that similar exceptional instances could easily be pointed out among the lower classes of our own race." On the whole, he is inclined to believe in the Caucasian physical type of the Dravidians. To prove the general correctness of his reasoning he points to the physical type of Todas, who are so distinctly Caucasic in the opinion of many persons, that they have been regarded as Celts, Romans, or Jews, and of all Dravidian tribes they have been most thoroughly guarded by their secluded position from Brahmanical influences. Instead of being more Mongol-like than the Aryanized Dravidians, they are distinctly Caucasic. Sir George Campbell is of the same opinion, but he and Dr. Caldwell, though they believe in the Caucasic type of the Dravidians, do not assign satisfactory reasons for their belief. The North-West Passage theory is their stumbling-block. The fact seems to be that Caucasic human type, having evolved itself in the northern regions of Africa, successively spread over Northern Africa, Southern India and Australia through the existing Indo-African-Austral continent, northwards to Iberia, and thence to West and Central Europe. The first migrating groups seem to have been of a low type, and to one of these must be traced, through their existing Indo-African continent, the peopling of Southern India by a melanochroid Caucasian type during the late Pliocene and early Pleistocene times. That such was probably the case is proved not only by the fact that the Dravidian now presents a melanochroid Caucasic physical type, but also by the fact that the Australians retain certain Caucasian physical characteristics which could only be explained by a migration of Indian melanochroid Caucasians into Australia when the Indo-African-Austral continent existed, and when Australia was accessible on the north and north-west sides to migrations from both India and Papuasia. Leading ethnologists are strongly of opinion that there is a marked resemblance between the physical type of the Drávidians and that of the Australians.

Flower and Lydekker bring under Caucasian melanochroid the Dravidians and Veddas of Ceylon, and in regard to Australia say that it might have been "originally peopled with frizzly-haired Melanesians, but a strong infusion of some other race, probably a low form of Caucasian melanchroi, such as that which still inhabits the interior of the southern part of India, has spread throughout the land from the north-west and produced a modification of the physical characters, especially of the hair."[1] Mr. Crooke says that the Dravidians represent an emigration from the African continent; and Professor Semon says that "the features of the Australians, with all their ugliness and coarseness, frequently remind one of Caucasian features." De Quatrefages[2] recognizes the existence of Caucasian, Negro, and Mongol elements in Australia; and, lastly, Giglioli goes so far as to speak of an Aryan element in Australia.

Again, zoology, geology, and botany are one in declaring that South India was in early times peopled from the south and not by the north-west passes of India. Peschel suggested that the primeval home of man was a continent now sunk below the surface of the Indian Ocean, which extended along the south of Asia as it is at present, and towards the west as far as Madagascar and the south-east shores of Africa; and towards the east as far as Further India and the Straits of Sunda. To this hypothetical continent he gave the name of Lemuria, from the mammals of that name which were characteristic of it. Though the Lemurian hypothesis, as at first propounded and for the purpose it was originally intended to serve, has been rightly rejected by Wallace,[1] yet this categorical denial of an Indo-African-Austral continent in pre-Tertiary times has not been accepted. It has been pointed out that he has not fully stated the facts, and that the actual distribution of certain genera of birds, fish, reptiles, and land mollusca is strongly suggestive of dry land having formerly extended from Southern India to Madagascar.[2] This view has been confirmed by the investigations of the Indian Geological Survey. Mr. Oldham says that at the close of the Jurassic period the land connection with Africa was still maintained, and also in the Cretaceous period, the close of which witnessed the great outburst of volcanic activities which buried the whole of Western India deep in lava and ashes, contemporaneously with the great series of earth movements which resulted in the elevation of the Himalayas and the extra-Peninsular ranges generally. In the Tertiary era we find no further evidence of land connection with Africa. At an early period the west coast was approximately in its present position, and it is probable that at the close of the Cretaceous and at the commencement of the Eocene period the Indo-African continent was finally broken up, and all but the remnants in India and South Africa sunk beneath the sea.[3] A third objection to the Turanian and North-West Passage hypothesis is that they make the physical type of the Dravidian to be Mongolian. Mr. Hodgson, who is followed by later writers, says that in the Tamilian form there is less height, less symmetry, more dumpiness of flesh than the Aryan; in the face a kind of lozenge colour caused by the large cheek-bones; less perpendicularity in the features in the front, occasioned not so much by defect of forehead and chin as by excess of jaws and mouth; a larger proportion of face to head, and less roundness in the latter; a broader, flatter face, with features less symmetrical but perhaps more expressive, at least, of individuality; a shorter, wider nose, often clubbed at the end and furnished with round nostrils; eyes less round and less fully opened and not evenly crossing the face by their line of aperture; ears larger; lips thicker; beard deficient; colour brunette, as in the Aryan type,

[1] "Mammals, Living and Existing," p. 748.

[2] "Races Humaines," Vol. L, p. 335.

[1] "Island Life," p. 488.

[2] "Proceedings of the Geological Society of London, 1890." W. T. Blandford's Presidential Address, p. 88.

[3] See on the whole subject "A Manual of the Geology of India," by R. D. Oldham, pp. 210–11, 248, 493–4.

but darker on the whole.[1] It may be remarked that this description does not apply to the Dravidians, whether civilized or uncivilized, of Southern India. As Dr. Caldwell says: "Many of these physical characteristics which Mr. Hodgson attributes to the Tamilians may undoubtedly be observed in the sub-Himalayan tribes of Nepal and Assam, and in a smaller degree in the Santals and Kols, but in these, too, it has been pointed out by eminent Indian and foreign ethnologists that the Dravidian type prevails.[2] The inexpediency of using as a general appellation so definite a term as Tamilian appears from the error into which Mr. Hodgson has fallen of attributing the same or similar physical characteristics to the Dravidians or Tamilians of Southern India as to his northern 'Tamilian' tribes, though they differ from these almost as much as do the Brahmans themselves. On the whole, it seems that Mr. Hodgson and others of his school, persuaded by similarities of lingual characteristics in the so-called Turanian group of languages, were led to believe in a similarity of physical type among the different members of that group."

NAYARS.

Photo by Nicholas & Co.

Though this view has something to be said for it, it has not by any means been uniformly accepted. Sir William Turner, the eminent craniologist, has not accepted that part of the theory which finds similarities between the Dravidians and the Australians.[1] He finds the difference between the skulls of the two peoples too radical to admit of their origins being identical. He says that "by a careful comparison of Australian and Dravidian crania there ought not to be much difficulty in distinguishing one from the other. The comparative study of the characters of the two series of crania has not led me to the conclusion that they can be adduced in support of the theory of the unity of the two people." It is a question if the term "Dravidian" is used here in the strict sense of defining a person who is neither a pre-Dravidian nor an Aryan. There is evidence in the writings of Sir William himself to show that he is actually thinking of pre-Dravidians while he is writing of the Dravidians. Sir Herbert Risley follows him so far as to say that his is "the last word of scientific authority." But Sir Herbert's own theory is somewhat complicated. He denies that the Dravidians ever came through the north-west passes of India, and suggests that they are "the earliest inhabitants of India of whom we have any knowledge." He also agrees with Sir William Turner in the view that no direct evidence of either a past or a present Negrito population in India has yet been obtained. This naturally leads him to a novel classification, based primarily on anthropometric grounds, of the Dravidians, a term which, according to him, would include both pre Dravidians and Dravidians. While to Mr. Thurston, for instance, the Paniyans of Malabar and the south-east Wynaad are typical of the pre-Dravidian tribes of Southern India;[1] to Sir Herbert Risley the selfsame Paniyans are one of the "two most characteristic representatives of the Dravidian type in all India between the valley of the Ganges and the Island of Ceylon"; the other being the Santals. The Santals, according to Dr. Keane, are not Dravidian at all, but a tribe belonging to the Kolarians. Where such fundamental differences in views exist it is best to be a little more explicit. In denying a trans-Himalayan origin to the Dravidians, Sir Herbert Risley says that he combats the view of Sir William Wilson Hunter that the Dravidians and Kolarians belonged to one racial stock, and that they entered by the north-west and north-east passes of India and came into conflict later on the Vindhyas, from whence the Dravidians marched down to the south. This theory, as already stated above, is based partially on the writings of Max Müller and Bunsen. Sir Herbert in rejecting it says:[2] "The bases of this theory is obscure.

[1] *Journal of the Asiatic Society of Bengal*, 1849. Even Mr. Keane seems to countenance this. See "Ethnology," Homo Mongolicus.

[2] Risley, Reclus, Hunter, and others.

[1] "Contributions to the Craniology of the People of the Empire of India," Part II. "The Aborigines of Chota Nagpur and of the Central Provinces; the people of Orissa, Veddahs, and Negritos, 1900," see "Transactions of the Royal Society of Edinburgh," Vol. XXXIV, Part III (No. 28); Vol. XL, Part I (No. 6).

[1] "India and the Durbar," p. 216.

[2] "People of India," pp. 46–7.

Its account of the Dravidians seems to rest upon a supposed affinity between the Brahui dialect of Baluchistan and the languages of Southern India; while the hypothesis of the north-eastern origin of the Kolarians and Dravidians is purely linguistic, and does not correspond to any differences of physical type. Secondly, it is extremely improbable that a large body of very black and conspicuously long-headed types should have come from the one region of the earth which is peopled exclusively by races with broad heads and yellow complexions. With this we may dismiss the theory which assigns a trans-Himalayan origin to the Dravidians. Taking them as we find them now, it may safely be said that their present geographical distribution, the marked uniformity of physical characters among the more primitive members of the group, their animistic religion, their distinctive languages, their stone monuments, and their retention of a primitive system of totemism justify us in regarding them as the earliest inhabitants of whom we have any knowledge." That, it may be said in one word, evades the whole point at issue. The question is, where did the Dravidians come from? Sir Herbert Risley leaves the question where it was before he tackled it; he does not appear to suggest that they are autochthonous: rather he would seem anxious to leave the question open for the time being. Then as to his classification of the Dravidians. He divides the Dravidians of India into four main groups: the Scytho-Dravidian, the Aryo-Dravidian, the Mongolo-Dravidian, and the Dravidian, each of whom he thus describes:[1] (1) The Scytho-Dravidian type of Western India, comprising the Maratha Brahmans, the Kunbis, and the Coorgs; probably formed by a mixture of Scythian and Dravidian elements, the former predominating in the higher groups, the latter in the lower. The head is broad; complexion fair; hair on face rather scanty; stature medium; nose moderately fine and not conspicuously long. (2) The Aryo-Dravidian type, found in the United Provinces of Agra and Oudh, in parts of Rajputana, in Bihar, and Ceylon, and represented in its upper strata by the Hindustani Brahman and in its lower by the Chamar. It is probably the result of intermixture, in varying proportions, of the Indo-Aryan and Dravidian types, the former element predominating in the lower groups and the latter in the higher. The head form is long with a tendency to medium; the complexion varies from lightish brown to black; the nose ranges from medium to broad, being always broader than among the Indo-Aryans; the stature is lower than in the latter group, and is usually below the average. (3) The Mongolo-Dravidian type of Lower Bengal and Orissa, comprising the Bengalese Brahmans and Kayasths, the Mahommedans of Eastern Bengal, and other groups peculiar to this part of India. Probably this is a blend of the higher groups. The head is broad; complexion dark; hair on face usually plentiful; stature medium; and nose medium with a tendency to breadth. (4) The Dravidian type, extending from Ceylon to the Valley of the Ganges, and pervading the whole of Madras, Hyderabad, the Central Provinces, most of Central India, and Chota Nagpur. Its most characteristic representatives are the Paniyans of the South Indian hills and the Santals of Chota Nagpur. Probably the original type of the population of India, now modified to a varied extent by the admixture of Aryan, Scythian, and Mongoloid elements. In typical specimens the stature is short, or below mean; the complexion very dark; hair plentiful, with an occasional tendency to curl; eyes dark; head long; nose very broad, sometimes depressed at the root, but not so as to make the face appear flat.

DWARF FAKIR.

The classification of Sir Herbert has been vigorously assailed from two sides. Dr. Haddon thinks that it is vitiated by the introduction of the Scythian element into the discussion, an element of whose racial origins scarcely anything definite is known.[1] Then Dr. Keane has attacked it as unsatisfactory because it does not, according to him, take into consideration

[1] Loc. cit., pp. 32–3.

[1] "Races of Man."

all the known facts. He protests[1] against the confused lumping together, as he calls it, of many primitive peoples as Dravidians or Munda-Dravidians, or Aryo-Dravidians, or Indo-Dravidians, or Scytho-Dravidians, or by other equally unintelligible and misguiding complex terms. "Surely," he says, "groups needing to be thus expressed by compound terms must be assumed to represent still earlier crossings, which, modern researches have confirmed this view by maintaining a relationship between the Kolarian and the Dravidian languages (Report, p. 2789; see also Sir Herbert's "The People of India," 1908). Thus, as anthropometry claims to prove that there is no distinct *physical* Kolarian type, so philology is called in to prove that there is no distinct *linguistic* Kolarian type, so that Kolarian cannot be a stock language, but must be belonging to a linguistic family which has no connection whatever with the Dravidian family. He also argues that the Dravidians and Kolarians are radically distinct both in language and race, and that there is nothing in common between them. His argument is too long to quote here, but it lays bare the contradictory character of the reasoning adopted by Sir Herbert and his coadjutors and the admissions they themselves make as to the

1. IRULA MAN. 2. IRULA GIRL. 3. YOUNG IRULA GIRL.

Photos by Nicholas & Co.

however, no attempt is here made to determine." He then proceeds: "Then, in their Census Reports, Sir Herbert Risley and his fellow-worker, Mr. E. A. Gait, denounce the time-honoured term Kolarian (revived by Sir George Campbell), as altogether fantastic, and relegate the Kolarians themselves, with the 'Lost Ten Tribes,' to cloudland. Deceived by the remarkably uniform results of his own anthropometric studies, Sir Herbert claims to have disproved the existence of a distinct Kolarian race, the 'so-called Kolarians' being simply members of the great Dravidian family, and related to the Dravidian stock tongue. In the report the proscribed Kolarian is replaced by Max Müller's *Munda*, this being one of the chief members of the group, and thus is formed the hypothetical 'Dravido-Munda-family,' which looms largely in the pages of the report, where the two component terms are treated as related branches of one stock language. Such are the main current views, which, although they have received the seal of official authority, are radically wrong; and they have, in fact, once more reduced Indian ethnology to an almost hopeless state of chaos." He goes on to remark that the Kolarians are quite a distinct people, and speak dialects essential dissimilarity of the Dravidian and Kolarian languages, and ends with comparing a typical language from each family (Tamil representing the Dravidian and Santali the Kolarian), and demonstrates the utterly unscientific character of the reasoning adopted. Dr. Keane concludes by saying: "I have gone into these details at the risk of wearying the reader in order to show once for all how absolutely unrelated are the Kolarian and Dravidian forms of speech. Thus is at the same time established the radical difference of the two races who are called 'Dravidians' in the census report." Wherefrom did these two races reach India? Dr. Keane says that "as the

[1] Anantha Krishna Iyer's "Castes and Tribes of Cochin," I, Introduction, xx–xxi and xxvii–xxix.

Kolarians reached India from the north or the north-east, so the Dravidians came almost certainly from the north-west, where they appear to have left behind them the belated Brahuis [1] of Baluchistan. Beyond the Vindhyan range they have nearly everywhere absorbed or replaced both the Negrito substratum and the Kolarian indigenes. Hence it is that at present all the natives of the southern uplands—Mysore, Coorg, Cochin, and Travancore—speak various forms of the Dravidian mother-tongue." Sir Herbert Risley himself is hardly satisfied with his own classification, and among the limitations he places upon them is one that deserves to be quoted. "It may be said," he states, "that the names assigned to the types beg the highly speculative question of the elements which have contributed to their formation. The criticism is unanswerable. One can but admit its truth, and plead by way of justification that we must have some distinctive names for our types; that names based solely on physical characters are no better than bundles of formulæ, and that if hypotheses of origin are worth constructing at all one should nót shrink from expressing them in their most telling form." The only answer to this argument is that the names are not "in their telling form," and one feels that he is nowhere nearer the origins of the races after having got to the end of Sir Herbert's classification than he was before he took it into serious consideration. It does seem that Sir Herbert has not thoroughly assimilated well-known facts, and so has been unable to get to the root of the matter. Dr. Keane himself, it will thus be observed, is a believer in the theory which holds that the Dravidians came through the north-west passes of India from across Central Asia. He, of all recent writers, is the only one who stands for this theory, though it is difficult to say on what grounds he bases it.

1. BATHING IN A TEMPLE TANK, KUMBAKONAM. 2. "HOME, SWEET HOME." 3. NATIVE HUTS.

Photo by Nicholas & Co.

The conflicting theories indicate the extremely difficult character of the Dravidian problem. If future research is to settle it in anything like a satisfactory manner, attention must primarily be directed at least to four important points: (1) Defining the term "pre-Dravidian" in a strict manner, and scientifically tracing the affiliation of the tribes or castes which should be grouped under that head; (2) defining likewise the term "Dravidian" and fixing its exact connotation, more especially pointing out how far the term, used in a racial sense, can be held to be coterminous in its significance with the term as used in its linguistic sense; (3) defining aright how far the descriptions of the earlier authorities of the racial affinities of the South Indian people should be taken as applicable to "pre-Dravidians" and how far to "Dravidians"; and (4) defining how far the Dravidians have absorbed and supplanted the pre-Dravidians.

It would be interesting to know how far the Dravidians were advanced when they came in contact with the first stream of Indo-Aryan immigrants, who apparently came in small numbers. It is, in fact, admitted by most writers that the

[1] Sir Herbert Risley takes the opposite view. See his "People of India," pp. 12 and 49. At p. 49 he says: "The present speakers of Brahui are certainly not Dravidian by race." The latest writer on Brahuis is Mr. Denys Bray, I.C.S. His views will be found in the Baluchistan Census Report, 1911, "The Brahui Language," Part I.

introduction of Aryan culture into the south of India was the result, not of conquest, but of a peaceful and gradual process of colonization. It is difficult to say exactly when the first immigrants began to settle in it. The south—Dakshinapatha—was during the earliest times forbidden ground to the Aryans, and to it were assigned slowly wandering saints and kings who had been banished from their own kingdoms in the north. At any rate, such a suggestion is made possible by the Ramayana itself, which represents Rama as being invited by the same Agasthaya to overthrow Ravana, the leader of the giant race—possibly representing the indigenes of the south and Ceylon, both being closely connected in history and religion from time immemorial. Tamil tradition suggests that Agasthaya was the first to lead an Aryan colony into the south of India; in fact, to the southernmost part of India, the Pothiya Hills, near Cape Comorin. The Aiteraya Brahmana gives the names of certain degraded barbarous tribes—among them being the Andhras—and it may be inferred from this that part at least of the eastern seaboard of South India was known to the Aryans. The writings of Baudhayana, the earliest Sutra writer who, according to Bulher,[1] probably lived and taught in the fifth century B.C., indicate that Aryan culture, during his time, extended so far south as Kalinga, the eastern seaboard stretching from Orissa to the Kistna. It is clear from his writings that Southern India had not only been colonized by immigrants from the north, but also had in it several flourishing kingdoms, which were the seats of distinct schools of learning and law. Baudhayana himself was probably an old settler in the south, for although he professes high regard for Aryavarta (or the Gangetic valley), he takes great care to mention peculiar local customs and laws, such as eating in the company of uninitiated persons and one's wife, the use of stale food, and marrying the daughter of a maternal uncle or paternal aunt. Dr. Bülher thinks that he lived, taught, and founded his school in the Andhra country between the Godavari and the Kistna Rivers. By linguistic arguments he shows that Baudhayana cannot have written later than the third century B.C., and adduces grounds for assigning him to a date as early as the fifth century B.C. This is, roughly speaking, the period in which Greece came into relationship with India. Pythagoras, who lived in the sixth century B.C., seems to have owed something to India; Herodotus writes of it in his history; and Megasthenes, who was ambassador at the Court of Chandragupta, the grandfather of Asoka, in the fourth century B.C., directly refers to Southern India. Describing the establishment of a Pandyan kingdom in the south, he says: "Herakles begat a daughter in India whom he called Pandaia. To her he assigned that portion of India which lies towards the south and extends to the sea, while he distributed the people subject to her rule into three hundred and sixty-five villages, giving orders that one village should each day bring to the treasury the royal tribute, so that the queen might always have the assistance of the men whose turn it was to pay tribute in coercing those who for the time being were defaulters in their payments."[1] This account is to a certain extent confirmed both by Pliny and the early Tamil poets. According to them a certain princess, Sindha Devi, of the race of the Pandus, then reigning at Mathura, on the banks of the Jumna, led a colony of the Aryans and founded Dakshina (or Southern) Madura on the banks of the Vaigai. She is said to have married a Tamil chieftain, and her descendants called themselves Panchavans and Kaurians after the famous Pandavas and Kauravas of the north. The traditional stories told about the founding of the modern city of Madura appear to countenance this very old legend. Meanwhile Buddhism has been founded—Buddha was born about 557 B.C.—and was slowly spreading to the south of India and Ceylon. The latter, though separated by sea, has always been geographically and historically an appendage of India, and at some remote period was doubtless even coterminous with the mainland. Buddhism spread to both countries probably simultaneously. At any rate, Ceylonese tradition assigns the Aryan occupation of this island to one Vizaya, a Buddhist prince, whom it sets down to the middle of the sixth century B.C. Making allowance for the anxiety of priests to make the occupation of Ceylon correspond with the supposed date of the birth of Buddha, it may fairly well be supposed that Ceylon was in Aryan occupation in the fifth century B.C. Asoka (272-18 B.C.) made Buddhism his State religion, and ruled practically over the whole of India, excepting the southernmost part of the Peninsula. He made the first real attempt to preach Buddhism in the south, and tradition says that his son and daughter preached in Ceylon as well. Two of his rock edicts, the second and the thirteenth, refer to the independent kingdoms in the south—the Kalinga, Chola, Pandya, and Kerala—and to Ceylon. In the second edict Asoka mentions the curative arrangements he ordered for both man and beast in all his dominions as well as among his neighbours, among whom figure in the south the Cholas, the Pandyas, and the Keralas. He caused wells to be dug and trees to be planted along the roadsides. The thirteenth edict details the circumstances under which Kalinga, a part of Southern India, was conquered by him, and the remorse he felt for the loss of life which had occurred. At least three of his edicts have been found in Southern India—two in the Ganjam district and one in Mysore. Brahmi inscriptions, which probably belong to 250 B.C. or thereabouts, have been found in different parts of Southern India, but their true significance is still unknown. They show, however, that the south was, even prior to Asoka's time, in constant communication with the north; otherwise the introduction of the script in which these inscriptions are cut out cannot be satisfactorily explained. However this may be, it seems certain that by the time of Asoka, Aryans had consolidated their position in widely different parts of the south. They appear, from all accounts, to have impressed the indigenous kings with their superior abilities, and in time they came to occupy important positions at their courts, and developed their languages, and eventually made them even follow their religious, moral, and legal codes, in so far as their assimilation was possible. Early Tamil poets describe their influence at the palaces of the kings of the south, their literary powers, and the sacrificial fires they caused to be raised to proclaim their greatness. When Buddhism and Jainism spread to the south this influence was to a certain extent counteracted, but it was not without a long and tough fight that the representatives of Aryan culture yielded their power. With the opening up of the country fresh streams of settlers from the north poured down, some at the instance of kings, some in search of fields and pastures new, and some probably driven by famine or pestilence, or even political disturbances in the north. The earlier Pallava grants have taught us that

[1] "Dharma Sastra," Introduction.

[1] McCrindle's "Ancient India," p. 158.

that Brahmans were already in enjoyment of court favour in the fourth and fifth centuries A.D. Mr. Rice says:[1] "Traditions whose authenticity there seems no reason to doubt are preserved of the introduction in the third and fourth centuries A.D. of Brahmans, the progenitors of the Haiga or Havika Brahmans, of the Nagar country, from Ahichehtra in Panchala or Rohilkhand, by one of the Kadamba kings." This king seems to have been one Mayura Varma, who is, in the Sahyadri Kanda, said to have introduced Brahman colonists from the north and granted them sixty-four villages below the Ghauts."[2] Sir George Campbell describes these Brahmans as a very fair race, with large eyes and aquiline noses, which would seem to show that they came from little intermixed northern sources. "It may fairly be assumed," writes Sir Harold Stuart, "that Brahmans were already in the fourth century settled in the Chalukya and Pallava countries."[3] Already well settled and strong even in their influence, fresh immigration should have helped the Brahmans, the sole repositories of Aryan culture in the south, and they soon combated the Buddhist and Jain faiths, and eventually threw them overboard. This was followed by fresh immigration into the south, and the new arrivals seem to have settled in great numbers on the banks of the Godavari and Kistna, the nearest eligible sites in their southward course, and thence gradually in later times they spread farther south. Between the seventh and ninth centuries what remained of Buddhism and Jainism received its last deathblow at the hands of the Saivite saints and the Vaishnavite Alwars, followed by the successful tours and preaching of Kumarilla Bhatta and Sankaracharya. This rendered Brahmanism practically supreme in Southern India. The twelfth century saw the birth of the great Vaishnavite reformer, Ramanuja, who tried to weave the indigenous population into the Brahmanic system. All recent immigrations date subsequently to the Mahommedan conquest at the end of the twelfth century, and the movements from the north to the southern portions of the Peninsula are later than the capture of Warrangal and the annihilation of the Telingana monarchy by the foundation of the Hindu Empire of Vizayanagar on the Tungabhadra in the early part of the fourteenth century, which held at bay the Mahommedans for more than two hundred and fifty years.

This rapid summary of the occupation of the south by people from the north possessing or professing Aryan culture, shows its essentially peaceful character. Here there was nothing in the nature of a military conquest of a type with which we are so familiar in other parts of the world. There is no tradition of Kshatriya princes from the north leading expeditions to the south and conquering it from the indigenous rulers and making settlements in it. In fact, the tradition is all the other way. It points to the peaceful settlement from time to time, occasionally at the request of the indigenous kings themselves, and sometimes induced by circumstances in their original homes, of individuals or families of Brahmins. "The Three Thousand of Tillai" (Tillai Muvayarathar), "The Six Thousand Niyogis" (Aruvelu Niyogis) of the East Coast; "The Eight Thousand" (Ashtasahasram) of the extreme south; "The Northeners" (Vadamas) as opposed to "Southerners," i.e. those already settled; "The Northern Northerners" (Vada desa Vadamal) as opposed to "Northerners of the south," i.e. Northeners long settled in the southern country; "The Northerners" (Vadagalais) as opposed to the "Southerners" (Thenkalais, earlier settlers); "Those from the north" (Badagunadu) as opposed to those from the western country; "The Desathas," and many other similar Brahmanical divisions and subdivisions, all resident at present in Southern India, indicate the very quiet manner in which the south has from time immemorial been occupied by Brahman settlers from the north or north-west. These Brahmans, the sole repositories, as I have remarked, of what passed for Aryan culture in India, doubtless followed their own social and religious institutions. It is unnecessary to describe elaborately what these institutions are, but the most prominent among them, differentiating them as a class from the resident local racial types—the Dravidians and pre-Dravidians—may be stated. Even long anterior to their advent into India the Aryans had evolved the family based upon the patriarchal model, and they retained no traces of Totemism or of Hetairism, of families being reckoned on the mother's side, or of inheritance through females. In India itself, they, in later times, socially developed the caste system, and, in the sphere of religion, the philosophical speculations known as the Upanishads, which directly led to the rise of Buddhism and Jainism in the land, with the result that while the caste system tried to mould society into a rigid, compact whole, these new religious tendencies helped to democratize it, and to narrow the gulf of differences between the Aryan and the non-Aryan. Whatever the effect of these new tendencies, the older customs, the older thoughts, and the older social and religious institutions have clung to the non-Aryans as much as to the Aryans, and these help us to trace their racial origins to a certain extent. In family institutions, in religion, and in marital and other rites, the Aryan differs, or differed until recently, radically from the Dravidian of the south. The Brahmanization of the non-Aryan has long been in process, and despite the apparent levelling down of differences and the moulding of social institutions on the Brahmanic model, the differences still existing show that the intermingling, though it has gone on for many a century now, has not affected the cardinal points. These we will consider under certain heads presently. Before we do this we would do well to consider one or two topics of preliminary interest. How far have the Brahmans—who are perhaps the sole representatives of the old Indo-Aryans in the south of India—been affected in their physical type? In the true Aryan form there is height, symmetry, lightness, and flexibility, an oval contour of face, with ample forehead and moderate jaws and mouth, a round chin, perpendicular with the forehead, a regular set of distinct and fine features; a well-raised and unexpanded nose, and well-sized and freely opened eye, running directly across the face, no want of eyebrows, eyelash, or beard, and, lastly, a clear brunette complexion, often not darker than that of Southern Europeans. Now it is obvious that this description cannot be applied to all those who call themselves Brahmans in Southern India. While a great many come fairly near to it, it is an undoubted fact that large numbers are as far from it as can well be imagined. There are, for instance, in Southern India, Brahmans who are as black as many tribes of negroes, and again, vast numbers of Dravidians proper have shown a tendency to approximate to the Aryan type. These two facts show that secular interminglings have had their effect on the physical type of both races. The influence of geographical position, of climate, of diet, and of circumstances of

1 "Mysore inscriptions," p. xxxvii.
2 "Mysore and Coorg," I, 313–14.
3 "Madras Census Report," 1891, p. 260.

birth, cannot altogether answer the change that is perceivable in the two types. Contact metamorphosis is before one's eyes changing large masses of people still untouched by outside influences. This shows the effect of such metamorphosis for ages past. The earliest settlers were probably stray persons, and in their case it seems permissible to presume that secular intermingling was something of a necessity. That such interminglings should have occurred might be inferred as much from what is happening to-day in many parts of India as from the writings of Brahman legists. In Malabar we see to-day a semi-legalized system of intermingling between the Aryan and the Dravidian. In fact, in Malabar, marriage among the Namputiri Brahmans—the Brahmans of the locality, described by Mr. Faucett as the "truest Aryans in South India"—is entirely restricted to the eldest son, the other brothers entering into polyandrous relations with Nayar women. In the Agency tracts of the east coast districts such intermingling is still of common occurrence, and the determination of parentage there is practically on lines sketched out in Manu's well-known Code of laws. The tenth chapter of that Code, which probably dates in its present form from about the second century A.D., indicates possibly an attempt on the part of systematizers of Indian law to explain existing facts. Whether the theory of the origin of castes as set out in it is true or false, there can be no question that at the time the systematizers started their work, the four primary castes were already well recognized, and the intermingling between them was also an admitted fact. The necessity, therefore, for determining the parentage of children born as the result of such intermingling, was apparently felt to be a necessity, and Manu set down what must, as a matter of custom, have been followed among the people at the time. Law, as conceived by Manu and other Hindu legists, is based largely on custom, and there is much in Manu himself which is not understandable except with reference to existing beliefs and customs. It seems undoubted that, at least to a certain extent, law in India has proved stationary because it was primarily based on custom, and on custom, too, that was conceived to be unchangeable. It has been remarked by a great authority that Manu stated as law what the Brahmans thought ought to be law, but which, as a matter of fact, was nothing of the kind. There may be an element of truth in this criticism of Manu, but it is largely vitiated by the ignorance it betrays of its true character. Manu's laws are primarily based on custom as existing, or existent until recently, and in most cases they merely set down as law what was mere usage in large tracts of the country. Here and there attempts at generalizations may be observed, but these are easily detected. Attempts to benefit the Brahmans as a class may be observed, but it is a question if the Brahman had not by then come to be regarded with extreme reverence and respect to deserve the special concessions which he seeks for himself. However this may be, it is necessary to note that Manu's idea of the evolution of castes, as the result of the crossing of the four traditional castes and of the crossings of the resultant crosses, seems to be based on conditions of life actually existing at the time. It is necessary to separate his theory of the origin of caste, which may be based on the fanciful picture portrayed by the Purusha Sukta (Rig Veda X), from the attempt made by him to evolve general rules to govern the conditions which he actually finds in his own time. Intermingling had become common, and questions affecting status, paternity, inheritance, and other matters seem to have risen up for consideration. Careful attention had to be given to the framing of rules to deal effectively with such subjects without causing any violent departure from the social or legal procedure. Individual cases must have been decided upon particular lines, and these must have led to the issue of general rules which should have had the sanction of usage in large areas. When the turn for the legist and the systematizer came, he apparently took cognizance of these, trying to explain away differences, and evolving rules out of existing usage which, while they admitted no actual change in the old laws, in effect made law conform to established custom. A close consideration of Manu's chapter x ought to make this intelligible even to the casual reader: (1) He finds it necessary to prescribe rules to regulate marriages between men and women of different castes, and to determine the status of the children of such unions. These could not have been set down to meet imaginary or hypothetical cases, but they should, on the other hand, have been found sufficient to meet a real situation which had come to exist in society; (2) Manu bases these rules on certain fixed principles which still govern such unions in India. (3) These rules are so closely reasoned out that they appear to be evolved from actual usage existent at the time. (4) Manu gives certain names to resultant crosses and prescribes occupations for them. These have come down to our times, which shows that his scheme of castes is not a picture evolved from the imagination of priests. (5) Some of the rules laid down by Manu are only intelligible from the point of view of society of the time of which he was writing; for example, according to him, eating with men of another caste or eating food prepared by men of another caste does not seem to entail degradation, as each of these does in most parts of India to-day. In Malabar, which had been shut up for ages by its peculiar physical conditions, Brahmans do eat with other castes even to this day (under certain restrictions) without losing caste. But it is an exception of the kind that proves the rule. Society has, since Manu's days, grown more conservative in this matter. (6) Manu's scheme of castes shows that the industrial arts had not developed then, for we find few or no castes set down to them. This seems to indicate that Manu was rigidly limited by the actual conditions existing at the time in Indian society. (7) Manu himself seems to admit a falling off among the twice-born (i.e. Brahman, Kshatriya, and Vaisya) classes from their lofty social position when, in his zeal for systematization, he tries to trace the origins of tribal or natural groups, such as the Malla, the Licchivi, the Nata, the Karana, the Dravida, to degraded members of twice-born men who he stigmatizes as Vratyas. He practically records here that secular interminglings between members of the twice-born castes and the non-Aryan races were by no means rare. So far as Brahmans are concerned he even goes a step farther, and signifies the classes of Brahmans whom he considers degraded and as unfit to be treated as Brahmans on ceremonial occasions.[1] These include physicians, temple-priests, sellers of meat, shopkeepers, actors, singers, cow-herds, oilmen, keepers of gambling houses, sellers of spices, makers of bows and arrows, trainers of elephants, oxen, horses, or camels, astrologers, bird-fanciers, fencing masters, architects, breeders of sporting dogs, falconers, cultivators, shepherds, and carriers of dead bodies. So far as Southern India is concerned this is by no

[1] George Bulher's "Laws of Manu," III, 151–66.

means a fanciful list, for instances of Brahmans following, or who until recently followed, most, if not all, of these different occupations can be easily quoted. These are considered low even now in the Brahman social scale, and it would be interesting to know whether their degradation was due solely to their falling away from their traditional function as priests or to other causes as well. It is possible that their looked down upon, with the result that certain crosses were altogether ostracized from society and allowed to live only in the most abject manner imaginable. In fact, Manu's whole scheme of castes recognizes intermingling of races as a necessary evil, and goes to reduce its consequences within what is conceived to be certain legitimate limits. Thus, while Manu recognizes it to be just that men of but formed a distinct caste by themselves and went by a new name. Thus, according to Manu, the son of a Brahman by a Vaisya woman is an Ambastha (the Ambatta of Southern India), to whom is allotted the art of healing; while the son of a Brahman by a Sudra woman is a Nishda, who should live by fishing, and so on. In the converse case, where the woman belongs to the higher caste and

1. THEATRICAL TROUPE.
Photo by W. H. Reed.

2. DANCING GIRLS, SALLURAPETTA.
Photo by K. Vincent Solomon.

3. PERFORMING BULLOCK.

4. DANCING GIRLS (SINGING POSE).
Photo by Nicholas & Co.

degradation was due as much to the omission of priestly duties as to the commission of prohibited acts on their part.

These considerations enable us to picture to ourselves to some extent the mental attitude of the Aryan law-givers towards the non-Aryans. This attitude was one which was shaped by the actual results brought about by contact between the races occupying the Peninsula. We infer from Manu that secular intermingling had reached a stage in his time which forced attention to the subject; that some kinds of interminglings were regarded by society in his time as inevitable; and that some other kinds were the three higher castes may marry women of any of the classes below them, he considers it improper for the women of the three higher castes to marry men below them in status. The one kind of union he terms *anuloma* (in the right order), and the other he terms *pratiloma* (in the wrong order). As regards the children born of unions in the right order, that is, in cases where men married in the caste next in order of precedence to themselves, the offspring took the woman's rank and no new caste was formed. In cases where the mother came from castes lower down in the social scale, her children belonged neither to her group nor to their father's, the man to the lower, the children are degraded and cast out of society. Perhaps the true origins of certain at least of the servile castes of Southern India are to be traced to these crosses. A word of caution needs to be added here. Manu nowhere suggests that intermingling between the races was anything more than casual. It might be that it was even common, but this does not mean that Aryan society was so far demoralized as to regard intermingling as the rule. The very idea that rigid rules were wanted to regulate results of this intermingling shows that it was becoming rapidly common, and if not checked, would lead to consequences which might endanger society. Society, possibly, was in a state of flux yet, but that it was quickly changing Manu himself bears ample testimony in his laws.

Recent anthropometric researches seem to lend some support to the view that secular intermingling has been going on for ages past in Southern India. In writing of the nasal index of the Dravidian and comparing it with that of the Aryan, Mr. Thurston, in his "Tribes and Castes of Southern India," states that there "is obviously far less connection between the Brahman minimum and the Paraiyan maximum average, and the frequent occurrences of high nasal indices, resulting from short, broad noses, in many classes has to be accounted for." In explaining this phenomenon he says that the Brahmanizing of the non-Aryans has been going on for a long time, and then quotes from Sir Harold Stuart's Report on the Madras Census of 1891, which records what it calls the "general belief" that the Brahmans of the south are not "pure Aryans but are a mixed Aryan and Dravidian race." He next cites popular traditions current in different parts of South India where wholesale conversions of non-Brahmans into Brahmans have occurred, and he seeks support for these traditions from the fact that high-class Brahmans do not care to recognize the Brahminhood of these spurious Brahmans. He then sums up his deduction in the remark: "Between a Brahman of high culture with fair complexion, and long, narrow nose on the one hand, and a less highly civilized Brahman with dark skin and short, broad nose on the other, there is a vast difference, which can only be reasonably explained on the assumption of racial admixture; and it is no insult to the higher members of the Brahman community to trace in their more lowly brethren the result of crossing with a dark-skinned and broad-nosed race of short stature." This may have been indeed so, even though it may be deemed unnecessary to give any credence to the stories of wholesale conversions.

Despite the fact that this intermingling has been going on for ages past, the tendency has been for those representing Aryan culture to keep to themselves in social and religious matters. The gradual process of Brahmanization of the non-Aryans in India has affected, only to a superficial extent, the customs and habits of the Dravidians of the south. It is true that the Dravidian is gradually coming to adopt the beliefs and notions of the Aryan in social and religious matters, but the fundamental positions assumed by the two in regard to them remain unaltered to a large extent. These merit some slight consideration here, as they are likely to show the exact nature of the struggle that is daily going on in Southern India between competing customs and beliefs for supremacy. This part of the subject may be considered under the heads of (1) Marriage, (2) Family Institutions, and (3) Religion.

First, as to marriage: The Brahman marriage system requires that every girl should be married before puberty, it prohibits the re-marriage of widows, and allows a dissolution of marriage only on the ground of adultery of the wife. But the case is different with the Dravidians. Though the existence of absolute promiscuity without rule or restraint, even among inferior races, who according to strict evolutionary ideas must be regarded as survivals, has been denied, a conjugal form very near to it has been admitted. This is the collective marriage of clan to clan. No relic of it exists among the Dravidians, though the very thing itself exists among certain Australians, who are, according to some, a cross between the Dravidians and the Papuans. Other varieties of marriage are more common among the Dravidians, and may be classed under the general heads of polygamy, polyandry, and monogamy. Since the first exists among both Aryans and Dravidians we have little concern with it. Polyandry was unknown to the Indo-Aryans, and traces of its existence are found among the various Dravidian tribes. It has come into existence in the infanticide of girls, among the Todas of the Nilgiri Hills. The sale of girls was contrived to put down this, and men, in order to lighten the expense of purchase, were content to have one wife in common. It is quite certain that it exists among the Todas, though occasionally they deny it, and also among certain castes of South Malabar, Cochin, and Travancore. Among the Kallans of Madura marriage depends entirely upon consanguinity, and is irrespective altogether of the wishes of either of the parties concerned or their parents. That this tribe was originally polyandrous seems inferable, one of the customs of the western Kallans being specially curious. It constantly happens that a woman is the wife of ten, eight, six, or two husbands, who are held to be fathers jointly and severally of any children which she may bear. And still more curiously, when they grow up they for some unknown reason invariably style themselves the children not of ten, eight, or six fathers, as the case may be, but of eight and two, or six and two, or four and two fathers. That polyandry also existed among the Karakat Vellalans appears evident from the fact that wives are accustomed to grant the last favour to their husband's relations, though adultery outside the caste entails expulsion therefrom. Again, fraternal polyandry exists among the Pantas of Vizagapatam, Kistna, Nellore, and South Arcot. The Kannuavan class of Reddis of Coimbatore seem to retain a custom of the same kind, as the wife may bestow favours on paramours without hindrance, provided they be of the same caste with her. The Malas retain a relic of clan marriage. If the wife divorces her husband and re-marries, her second husband must pay a fine—not to the previous husband, but to the caste. A similar custom, but in a different form, is found amongst the Paniyans. Before a marriage can be performed the consent of four *kuttans* of the three classes of Paniyan elders is necessary. Among the Koya or Kois, a tribe of Godavari and Jaipur, the bride is carried off by force, usually with the connivance of the village headman, and it is said that some do not object to run away with the wife of another. Among the Chenchus of Nellore and Kurnool the marriage ceremony is of a very peculiar kind. The couple run away one night from their houses and return next day as husband and wife. Re-marriage of widows is allowed, but the second husband must be the brother of the first. But it is noteworthy that among the Paraiyans no trace of polyandry is found. The Peddapantas of Cuddapah, Nellore, Kurnool, and North Arcot, the Gaudas of Ganjam, Vizagapatam, and the Agency Tracts do not use the *tali*, which answers to the European wedding-ring and the Brahman *mangalyam* among other Dravidian tribes. Among the Tottiyans of Madura, Tinnevelly, Coimbatore, and Salem adultery is no crime when committed within the family circle; nay, newly married wives are even compelled to cohabit with their husband's nearest relations, although a *liaison* with an outsider involves expulsion from caste. Among the Anuppans of Madura, Tinnevelly, and Coimbatore adultery is no crime if committed with the class before the husband comes of age. This is not without its significance. Comparative study of contemporary primitive communities has made it clear that in polyandrous countries in particular, and in that confused state of primitive families in which men live either in a freedom almost bordering on promiscuity or in groups half-polyandrous or polygamous, there is no actual widowhood, or state of being a widow, for woman. The disappearance of one of the men with whom a woman has lived in intimate relations makes no great change in her position. Under a polygamous *régime* it is quite otherwise, for then the wives are private property. Their master has nearly always bought them, and their subjection is very great. Therefore at the death of their master they are treated exactly like chattels; they follow the fate of the goods and pass into the hands of the heir, who can keep or sell them.[1] Widow re-marriage is allowed among all classes. Free sexual unions are common even in the present day among such castes as the Badagas, the Nayars, and the Tiyyans of Malabar, the Bants and Villavans of Canara, the Maravans, the Kallans, the Pallans, the Vannans, the Shanars, the Paraiyans, the Chakkliyans of the Tamil district, and the Khonds and Savaras of the northern hill tracts, besides a host of smaller castes and tribes throughout the Presidency. But, as Sir Harold Stuart observes, where Brahmanical customs have had great influence there exist not only endless marriage ceremonies but also great difficulties in the way of obtaining a divorce, as among the greater number of Telugu castes. We must not, however, be misled by this. Among the generality of the classes not only does free sexual union exist, but no great difficulty is experienced in obtaining a divorce. Either party is free to terminate the marriage tie at will, or for the very slightest reasons. Generally the reimbursement of the marriage expenses or the payment of some small fixed fee is necessary, but in some cases even this restraint—if we may so term it—on divorce does not exist. The degree of formality varies from the mere return or taking away of the *tali*, to a written decision by a *Panchayat* (Council of Five Caste Elders), or meeting of householders, while among some of the west coast castes it is doubtful if any formality at all is required. These statements might induce one to generalize. But we must guard ourselves against such a temptation, for it has been well pointed out that "we must not believe, with certain sociologists, that polyandry has ever been a universal and necessary matrimonial stage. The enormous consumption of men necessitated by a savage or barbarous life has often given an impulse to polygamy. It is only in certain societies, where female infanticide has exceeded all measure, or in certain islands or regions with little or no population, where conquerors badly off for wives came to settle, that polyandry has become general and enduring. It is surely an exceptional form of marriage."[1] Yet, as is observed by Sir Harold Stuart, this much seems to be certain of the Dravidian tribes. In the beginning the marriage tie was certainly very loose; at a later stage it developed into polyandry, though even this may not have been universal or extensively practised; at a still later stage, as the free divorce shows, it developed into monandry."[2]

[1] Letourneau's "Evolution of Marriage," p. 266.

PARIAHS, MADRAS.

Next, as to Dravidian family institutions: while the matriarchate seems to have been almost universal among the Dravidians, it was unknown to the immigrant Aryans even in their primeval seat.[1] From the very earliest times speculation has been rife as to the origin of human societies. Even Sir H. Maine's graphic exposition of it,[2] based as it is upon the comparative method, is not free from doubt or objection. According to him, human societies have always and everywhere started with the family—that is, the patriarchal family—mainly composed of the father, the mother or mothers, and the children. From this first family, grouped submissively round the despotic father, similar families are supposed to have sprung, which by union constituted in time tribes, societies, and states. Dravidian India, if put in the witness-box, would seem to falsify this. The truly primitive stock is no other than the clan; that is, a small consanguineous group on which the kinship is still very much confused. The father is not seen to be the principal personage, nor has he as yet any recognized social existence. "Within the primitive social limit, the familiar clan," says Professor Letourneau, "every one was consanguine, but in a confused way; the wives had several husbands and the husbands several wives; the degrees of kinship were not individual, but applied to classes of individuals. At this period of social development it was difficult to distinguish as yet the real from the possible, and fictitious from real consanguinity."[3] In many Tamil districts of the Presidency of Madras, more especially in Malabar, custom still designates as brothers the children of either two brothers or two sisters, but the children of the brother and of the sister are only looked upon as cousins-german. Again, in Malabar certain families never make any partition, and thus preserve the custom of the ancient family clan. From this consanguineous clan the first to become detached seems to be the maternal family, based on uterine filiation, the only possible filiation capable of proof. Instances of this among the Dravidians are not wanting. It is well known that among the Nayars the reign of the matriarchate is pre-eminent; also the exogamous limit within which one may marry indicates maternal filiation. In South Malabar for both males and females it is the circle of one's own *tarawad*, that is, all members tracing descent from a common female ancestor in the female line only. The

[1] Letourneau's "Evolution of Marriage," pp. 76–7.

[2] On the whole subject see "Madras Census Report for 1891," chap. x (*et passim*).

[1] Dr. Schrader's "Prehistoric Antiquities of the Aryan Peoples."

[2] "Ancient Law and Early History Institutions."

[3] See Letourneau's "Evolution of Marriage."

limit is even wider in North Malabar, the stronghold of conservatism. There it includes all the members of the same *illam*, which consists of several *tarawads* with community of interest and even pollution.[1] Intermarriage between two persons having the same *tarawad* name is not allowed, even though it is quite impossible to trace descent to a common ancestor for the identity of descent. A relic no doubt of this seems to be the custom, prevalent in other parts of the Presidency, of not marrying a woman of the same name. Again, every image of the Deity worshipped by the Dravidians is invariably found to be a goddess who is worshipped as mother. "Divine motherhood," says Robertson Smith, "like the kinship of men and gods in general, was to the heathen Semites a physical fact, and the development of the corresponding cults and myths laid more stress on the physical than on the ethical side of maternity, and gave prominence to sexual ideas which were never edifying and often repulsive. Specially was this the case when the change in the law of kinship deprived the mother of her old pre-eminence in the family, and transferred to the father the greater part of her authority and dignity."[2] So, then, in the transition from maternal filiation to paternal filiation, these passionate goddesses gave a religious sanction to sexual licence, and almost every one of them has "even demanded of the daughters of her worshippers a shameful sacrifice of their chastity, before they were permitted to bind themselves for the rest of their lives to that conjugal fidelity which their goddesses despised." Thus prostitution became a religious duty, as it is amongst the Kaikolans even to this day, and worship became orgiastic and extremely licentious, as it is amongst the Khonds, Tiyyans, and certain Malabar lower castes. Phallic worship, which from certain passages in the Rig Veda[3] seems to have been widely prevalent amongst the Dravidians, signified the transition from maternal to paternal filiation. Again, phallic worship has been identified with serpent worship, which is prevalent in all parts of South India, particularly in Malabar and South Canara.

Lastly, the religion of the Dravidians seems to differ fundamentally from the Brahmanical religion. Devil worship, it has been remarked,[4] was quite unknown to the Aryans, but, as Dr. Caldwell says, the beginnings of Dravidian religious ideas must be traced to a belief in spirits and the fear of the evils which they inflict. With morality this religion has little or no connection, and its doctrine of immortality consists almost entirely in the representation that the earthly life is continued elsewhere, while of the doctrine that men will receive hereafter according to what they have done, only the first beginnings are to be traced in it.[1] There is no priesthood attached to it, and those who act as priests do not belong to any hereditary or exclusive class. At ordinary times the head of the family, or sometimes that of the community, officiates. Almost all Dravidian tribes worship devils, side by side with Brahmanical deities, but this worship is found in its most conspicuous form in South Canara, Malabar, Tinnevelly, and Travancore—that is to say, wherever the Dravidian population has been least touched by the Aryan immigrant minority. Connected with this is the ancestor-worship found among the Todas, Kurumbars, Khonds, and others, originating in the belief that if the soul of the departed is not, at certain fixed times, properly attended to, it will do harm. With this the priest comes into existence, and his most solemn duty is to slay the victims whose blood is required to quench the thirst of the deities. Sacrifice is the most fundamental doctrine of religion, and the demons of South India were satisfied with nothing less than that of a living animal. That human sacrifice was originally practised cannot be doubted.[1] And *sati* itself—which, by the way, is not an Aryan rite, and for which there is no authority in the Rig Veda[2]—seems to have been borrowed from the Dravidians. Though the Aryan and Dravidian have been as the poles asunder in regard to fundamental conceptions, a consideration of the effects of their intermingling in South India will show how their differences are wearing away, steadily though slowly. England, like India, has been the meeting ground of many races, but the practical fusion of the races who invaded England has added to its strength rather than weakened it. But the Aryan conquest of South India was more social and religious than ethnical. In India the Aryans were brought into contact with an ethnically different race, and the caste system seems to have originated in the ethnical differences between the invaders and the occupants. Mr. Sherring observes that "caste owes . . . its origin to the Brahman. . . . It is his invention." It is, indeed, true that the peculiarities of the Indian caste system afford occasion for the entertainment of the most divergent views as to its influence on Hindu progress. While some, like Comte, have extolled it to the skies, others, like Sir Henry Maine, have condemned it as the "most disastrous and blighting of human institutions." The truth seems to lie between these extreme views. In the earliest stages there was progress in spite of caste; possibly it even aided progress by specialization of the social functions, but after Hindu society had reached a certain stage of progress all the good it did was to keep it at that stage to prevent it from going to pieces. Caste has held together the heterogeneous elements of Hindu society, but at the same time has kept them permanently distinct, thus preventing that fusion which in other countries, like England, has produced more or less homogeneous nations. But as to its origin there ought certainly to be no mistake. In a sense it came into existence even

CUSTARD-APPLE SELLER.

Photo by Nicholas & Co.

[1] Logan's "Malabar Manual," pp. 117–18.

[2] "Religion of the Semites."

[3] VII, 21, 5; and X, 99, 3.

[4] "Manual of the Administration of the Madras Presidency," p. 71, note 24.

[1] "Madras Census Report for 1891," p. 60.

[1] "Manual of the Administration of the Madras Presidency," p. 71.

[2] See Professor Wilson's "Essays," Vol. III "Essay on Human Sacrifices." The passage that is usually quoted from the Rig Veda is there shown to be spurious.

before the Brahman proper had come into existence. It undoubtedly has an ethnic basis. As Sir Herbert Risley says, "In India alone were the Aryans brought into close contact with an unequivocally black race. The sense of differences of colour, which, for all our talk of common humanity, still plays a great and, politically, often an inconvenient part in the history of the world, finds forcible expression in the Vedic descriptions of the people whom the Aryans found in possession of the plains of India. In a well-known passage the god Indra is praised for having protected the Aryan colour, and the word meaning colour (*varna*) is used down to the present day as the equivalent of caste, more especially with reference to the castes believed to be of Aryan descent." But when and how did the great religious and social movement described by Sir Alfred Lyall [1] as "the gradual Brahmanizing of the aboriginal non-Aryan or casteless tribes" of South India take place? The earliest Tamil grammar extant, which was composed by Tholkappiyan, a Brahman of the Bharadwaja Gotra, in the first or second century B.C.,[2] when describing the Dravidian classes of society, tries to bring the Dravidian tribes into the fold of the caste system. The Brahman heads the poll; then come the kings who are pure Dravidians, classed as Kshatriyas; thirdly the traders, classed as Vaisya; and lastly the Vellalas are singled out and told that their only calling is the cultivation of the soil, thereby possibly implying that they must be classed as Sudras.[3] The combined effect of the Jain and Buddhist religions on the primitive religion of the south was feeble in the extreme. Though in individual cases, as notably in the case of Tiruvalluvar, who, though born a Paraiyan, was in religious belief a Jain, it might have weaned away persons from the older beliefs and customs; it left large masses of people still devoted to their gods and goddesses. Socially it is possible that the more democratic spirit of these religions led to the betterment of non-Aryan people generally. But there is reason to believe that these exchanged their creeds not as individual converts did, from a sense of conviction, but as a matter of necessity in certain cases, or in certain others as a matter of expediency. The *Vihara* or the *basti* in these cases took the place of the old temple, and there was possibly not much more to disturb the older conditions of life. If the present is any guide to the past it should have been in those days what it actually is in these. Many centuries of Brahmanic supremacy have not yet completely absorbed the older beliefs and superstitions, the older religions and customs, and the older modes of looking at things. If anything, the tendency in the Buddhist days was to leave things alone. Unlike Brahmanism, Buddhism never succeeded in absorbing older beliefs and ideals. When Buddhism and Jainism declined under the cumulative effects of internal decay and external pressure, the people who until then were either Buddhists or Jains passed under the new Brahmanic yoke without anybody knowing anything about it. Indeed, if the stories chronicled in the Saivite and Vaishnavite religious books of the south are to be believed—and they appear to be based on historical events in the last resort—the non-Aryans themselves seem to have actively helped in winning the country back to Brahmanism. The doctrines of the equality of the sexes and the equality of man, and the respect for animal life which these religions inculcated, were absorbed by the new Brahmanism that came into existence in the south. Both Saivism and Vaishnavism preach these doctrines, and Brahmanism as proclaimed by Sankara, Ramanuja, and Madhva in the south counts these among its fundamental tenets. It is useless to speculate on the question as to what would have been the present condition of the South Indian peoples if Buddhism and Jainism had not been extirpated from among them. The best elements in them have been absorbed by the new Brahmanism, and its effect on them has been of a mixed kind. Caste, which had to some extent at least been broken into by them, got a further lease of life. Indeed, it may be said that its ramifications now knew no bounds. The physical conditions of the country helped its vigorous growth in the south. Southern India, unlike Northern, presents barriers at every step, so that even without caste people are strangers to each other. On plateaus or hilltops, surrounded by fever-breeding marshes, racial and tribal distinctions are more easily preserved intact than on plains open to the influences of every incoming race. Northern India, being the fighting ground of many alien races, soon lost its individuality, racially and politically, but Southern India, secure from alien influences, developed before very long a civilization and history of its own, more or less untouched by outsiders until the advent of the British. Thus it is that we find Southern India much more distinctively Hindu than the Northern or Western; much more conservative than either in religion and manners; and a much more powerful stronghold of caste than either. In Southern India the Aryans have ever been in the minority, the main bulk of the population being Dravidian, so that when the temporary check on caste introduced by the Jain and Buddhist schismatics was withdrawn, its formation went forward with a bound, as it were. Differences therefore in custom between peoples living in the Pandya, Chola, Kerala, Chera, and Kalinga countries varied indefinitely, and these were, in time, increased rather than diminished by the religious differences which were developed by the Saivite teachers and the Vaishnavite saints and the religious and social reformers who followed them in later times. The period during which all this took place may be roughly placed between the eighth and fourteenth centuries, at the commencement of which Southern India, for the first time in its history, passed under the sway of a centralized monarchy—the kingdom of Vijayanagar. Putting it very briefly, it

A FORTUNE-TELLER.

Photo by Van der Lowen.

[1] "Asiatic Studies," p. 102.

[2] *Madras Review*, Vol. III, p. 394.

[3] *Ibid.*

may be said that the beginning of the eighth century saw the non-Aryan Vaishnava Alwars and Siva teachers fight their intellectual and religious battles; the end of the same century witnessed the birth of Sankara; the eleventh produced Ramanuja and the twelfth Madhva, by which time all the Dravidian classes, from the highest to the lowest, were brought under the caste system, and were so profoundly influenced by it that the right and left hand faction disputes came into existence.

The development of the caste system showed itself in certain directions which may be briefly set down. First, it led to a revival of learning in the south. The social and religious upheaval caused by the defeat of the schismatics and the reassertion of Brahmanic supremacy was followed by a desire for popular literature, in which Brahmans took the leading part. This revival of learning, which commenced about the beginning of the eleventh century, ultimately led to the translation of the Indo-Aryan epic poems into the principal Dravidian languages. In the Telugu country the translation of the Sanskrit "Mahabharata" into Telugu was commenced in the first quarter of that century, and completed about the middle of the fourteenth, and the translation of the "Ramayana" into Telugu was commenced about the twelfth century and completed about the fourteenth. Though the Tamil country possessed a translation of the "Mahabharata" by the eleventh century, yet that century saw the popularization of the Puranas and the production of a Tamil grammar. The beginning of the next century saw the translation into Tamil of the "Ramayana." In the Kannada country versions of the epic stories were published during the tenth and succeeding two centuries, but regular translations began to be made only in the sixteenth century, which, with the preceeding century, saw the publication of Malayalam translations; though these versions of the "Ramayana" seem to have been current even during the fourteenth century. The principal translator on the west coast was an oilmonger, the story of whose persecution by the Brahmans indicates the feeling with which the latter viewed the situation.

Then there is reason to believe that the new creed gave an impetus to architecture. This took two forms: religious and secular. Secular examples have been lost to us through a variety of causes; e.g. change of capital, destruction wrought by enemy kings, destruction through natural causes, such as floods and overflowing of the sea, and through decay. It is possible, too, that the earlier secular buildings—those of a time later than the fourteenth century A.D. have survived up to the present time, including the famous Tirumal Nayak's palace, the Tamakan palace at Madura, the palaces in the old Gingee fortress, and elsewhere—were of wood. It was in the south, first of all, that they developed a taste for buildings in stone, and it is possible that this change was due as much to the Dravidian builders as to the excellent material which South India offered to them. The gradual elevation in the social scale of the artisan castes generally, perhaps, indicates the process of Aryanization which they have undergone. The country before very long, i.e. within the period ranging from the eighth to the fourteenth century, was dotted all over with large and small temples built of stone, or cut out of solid rock. The most famous examples of the latter type are to be seen at Mahabalipuram, or the Seven Pagodas, which date from the eighth century A.D. Any village in South India affords an example of the former. The famous Tanjore temple and the equally distinguished one at Madura belong to this epoch; on the east coast the celebrated temple of Simhachalam may be set down to this time, and on the Mysore side the principal temples at Halebid belong to this period. In later times, when the country passed under the sovereignty of the Vijayanagar kings, these gave a fresh impetus to temple, secular, and military architecture. Several of the more important temples were rebuilt or enlarged very considerably by them. Their incredible wealth also helped them to construct afresh or remodel the old forts in the country, and their military prowess brought under their sway the whole country from the River Tungabhadra to Cape Comorin. People in the south had a foretaste of Moslem oppression and cruelty in Malik Kafur's invasion of A.D. 1312, and they were apparently willing to show a united front to the Moslems of the north by coming under the newly erected monarchy of the Vijayanagar kings (A.D. 1314-1565). These kings kept in check the Mahommedans for more than two hundred years, and saved Southern India from misrule during that period. Incidentally, they proved to be great patrons of literature, and the renaissance that Telugu literature enjoyed during the last half century of this dynasty's existence was as much the result of Brahman as of Dravidian effort.

The continued existence of a highly centralized Government, the proximity of an alien enemy (the Moslem), and the close living together of rival faiths and beliefs in the same land, led besides to the growth of the spirit of toleration in South India. Jains were either in an absolute minority or out of court favour; Buddhism had been absorbed or banished out of the land; and there were none left for persecution to work on. This helped to conserve the energies of the people for work in useful directions. Arts and industries flourished; architecture came into prominence; trade and commerce, both inland and overland, made rapid progress; more money flowed into the country and afforded opportunities to kings amassing colossal riches for spending on public and private charities. In all this Dravidians contributed as much, if not more than, the Brahmans. The kings themselves were Dravidians, but that they depended on Brahmans for first securing the allegiance of millions of inhabitants in the south, and, secondly, maintaining it through two centuries or more, can hardly be doubted. The empire itself was founded under Brahman inspiration, if not auspices, and its first acts were directed to pacify the religious wounds inflicted on the people by the Moslem invaders by re-opening temples, restoring worship in them, and repairing them even in certain cases. These causes and many others besides, brought the Brahman and the Dravidian closer and closer together, to the mutual advantage of both. One effect—a direct one, be it said—of all this was to hasten the process of Brahmanization, which had been retarded to a slight extent by the Jain and Buddhist propaganda.

As to the processes of absorption, they are probably the same as those described by Sir Herbert Risley in speaking of the Bengal tribes and castes. The leading men of an aboriginal tribe, having somehow got on in the world, and become independent landed proprietors, managed to enrol themselves in one of the leading castes. They usually set up as Rajputs, their first step being to start with a Brahman priest, who invented for them a mythical ancestor, supplied them with a family miracle connected with the locality where their tribe was settled, and discovered that they belonged to some hitherto unheard-of clan of the great Rajput community. Thus the tribal name was lost in the caste, and with it the possibility of accurately differentiating them from Hindus of pure blood and of assigning them to any particular non-Aryan tribe. Again, a number of aborigines would embrace the tenets of a Hindu religious sect, thus losing their tribal name and becoming Vaishnavas and Saivites. Once again, a whole tribe would enrol themselves in the ranks of Hinduism under the style of a new caste, which, though claiming an origin of remote antiquity, is readily distinguishable by its name from the standard and recognized castes, as in the case of the Nayakers, who claim to be Kshatriyas. In some cases a whole tribe, or section of a tribe, would become gradually converted to Hinduism without abandoning their tribal designation; as in the case of the Todas and Kotas of the Nilgiri Hills.[1]

The above facts elucidate the *religious* aspect of the Aryan immigration into South India, and they prominently point to the fact that the great Aryan contribution to South India is the substitution of the Saivism and Vaishnavism in place of its old animism, shamanism, serpent, and phallic worship.[2] Rudra of the Rig Veda absorbed into himself, in his horrible form, the non-Aryan gods and devils, and became pre-eminently the god of destruction. In his peaceable form he became the husband of passionate Dravidian goddesses, who were all merged into one being under the name of Sati, the "good and faithful wife." Vaishnavism, with its highly philosophic conception of God, dealt the death-blow to vulgar animism and superstitious shamanism, and inevitably led to the slow but sure development of self-reverence, self-knowledge, and self-control on the part of its believers. Vishnu being regarded as pre-eminently a god of protecting love, Vaishnavism could not but be opposed to bloody sacrifices. Like Saivism, it also absorbed non-Aryan goddesses, and like it adopted non-Aryan forms of theology and worship, only trying hard to improve them as is shown by its vain attempts to convert the dancing girl attached to Hindu temples (a relic of the old religious prostitution) into a nun and servant of God. The greater part of all that is good and beautiful in the literature of the Dravidian language can be easily seen to be the result of the inspiration possessed by Saivism and Vaishnavism, and even Dr. Caldwell admits that "the Dravidians appear to have been indebted for the higher arts of life and a considerable portion of their literary culture" to Brahmanical colonists of early times. In fact, all over India vernacular literature appears to have had a purely religious origin. Such is the elevating influence of a higher form of religion on the development of higher social conditions from comparatively low ones.

[1] Risley, "Tribes and Castes of Bengal," Introduction, pp. xv–xvii.

[2] On this subject see an interesting lecture on "The Function of Religion in Social Evolution," by Professor M. Rangacharya, M.A.

By far the most important *social* effect of the advent of the Aryans was the introduction of agriculture and the establishment of village communities in South India. Dr. Schrader[1] is of opinion that the Indo-Aryans possessed a rudimentary knowledge of agriculture even in their primeval state. The Rig Veda makes it certain that they were extremely well acquainted with it when they settled on the Indus, and that the word "Arya" is the one word which distinguishes them as a class from the aborigines. Such knowledge of agriculture as the Dravidians had, or when they began to practise it themselves before they came in contact with the Aryans is uncertain, but it was probably on the extensive system, as that would fit most easily with their other modes of obtaining subsistence. They were not so ignorant of tillage as not to practise it at all. Primitive agriculture is perfectly consistent with a very migratory life. Some migratory tribes at the present day, as, for instance, the Kaffirs of South Africa, diversify the monotony of their life by occasionally growing a crop. But with the advent of the Aryans the system of "intensive" cultivation was introduced, and this is what is meant when it is said that agriculture was introduced among the Dravidians by the immigrant Aryans, an event which is placed by Dr. Caldwell about 750 B.C., but as already pointed out, the Aitareya Brahmana makes it probable that it was about the ninth century B.C. Along with it also, perhaps, the village community system was introduced into South India by the Aryans. The clearing of the primeval forests and the extension of civilization was, as we have seen, one of the chief functions of the Dravidian tribes under the guidance of the immigrant Aryans.[2] Each new clearance gradually grew into a village; in the first instance the village was probably formed by a group of colonists who cultivated the lands in their collective capacity for their common benefit, but in course of time it comprised a community of independent householders, each of whom had his own family, his own homestead, consisting of one separate parcel of arable land, and a common right to the neighbouring pastures. The multiplication of families by the inclusion of Dravidians was followed by new clearings, and thus the deep forest was brought more and more under the subjection of man, and cultivation advanced with the inclusion of more Dravidians into the communal group. This settlement into village communities is not possible when the method of extensive cultivation prevails, for the people would have no permanent houses, their dwellings only being roughly put together to serve as temporary shelters. But with the introduction of the intensive method such a settlement is rendered very easy, and the actual moment of settlement is only a question of over-population. A very remarkable passage in the Rig Veda[1] makes it highly probable that the Indo-Aryans themselves in their primeval states were only acquainted with *extensive* cultivation, but that by the time they first crossed the Indus they began to practise the *intensive* method, a fact which rendered easy their settlement into village communities, which in later times grew into kingdoms, as in the Gangetic valley. It is hardly possible to over-estimate the importance of the change from one system of cultivation to the other. As Dr. Cunningham observes,[2] "so long as a tribe is migratory they cannot accumulate any store of wealth, such as they must have if they are to set themselves energetically to make the most of the resources of the particular place where they dwell. So soon as they have any opportunities of storing they may begin to look forward to a more distant future, not merely to next harvest; and they may begin to expend their toil on improvements which will be of value for many years to come. The wandering shepherd is able by migration to shirk the difficulties of overcoming nature; while wealth in the form of herds is not susceptible of *indefinite* increase; scarcity of fodder limits it, and the chances of disease and droughts render this sort of wealth liable to total destruction from

[1] "Prehistoric Antiquities of the Aryan Peoples." Translated by F. B. Jevons.

[2] "Colonization of Indraprastha." Wheeler's "History of India," Vol. I, also Mackenzie MSS.

[1] X, 101.

[2] "Growth of English Industry and Commerce," Vol. I, p. 34.

changes in the seasons. There are many natural barriers to the increase of pastoral riches, but the man with a settled store has entered on a mode of life in which there are infinite possibilities of progress; he may obtain and lay up not one sort of wealth only, but wealth of different kinds, and thus possibilities of trade will arise. Then again his store of wealth enables him to look far ahead and engage in work which will ultimately prove most useful, even though it yields no immediate return, and he may set himself to acquire skill in various directions. The step from located stores to fixed houses is comparatively easy; and when once a tribe has settled in permanent habitations, the prospect of steady progress, without assignable limit, in numbers, in national wealth, and in culture, really lies open before them." Hence the usual presumption th.t the organization of village communities in India is pre-Aryan and is the result of the higher practical capacity of the Dravidians, seems to be untenable.

Thus, while the effect of the Aryan advent upon the Dravidians seems to have been all in their favour, the effect of their non-fusion owing to their ethnic differences seem to have been wholly detrimental to the general progress of the society which may now be called Hindu, and whose religion may now well be termed Hinduism. Hinduism is a socio-religious institution; it is a social organization resting upon caste, with its roots deep in ethnical elements, and with a superstructure regulated by a system of division based upon the occupations of the people and modified by geographical position. It is also a religious confederacy representing the coalition of the Brahmanical Vedic faith with the Dravidian rites and Buddhist beliefs.[1] Not only did the caste system originate in ethnic differences, but the peculiarly strong religious trait of the Indo-Aryan, which he has imparted to all non-Aryans who have come in contact with him, must also be traced to the same source. An Indian writer rightly observes: "This religious temperament has been the blessing as well as the curse of the Hindu."[1] He says: "If his spirituality has made him bear the ills of life with fortitude and equanimity it has also contributed to intensify those ills. If owing to his spirituality he is happy even in starvation, his devotion to his religion and scrupulous regard for its injunctions in social matters have brought this state of chronic starvation upon himself. If for centuries his country has been depleted by foreigners; if to-day he is a helpless spectator of the ruin of the arts and manufactures of his country, it is not a little owing to the sway of religion over him in matters which should not be governed by religion at all. The caste system is in the main answerable for the absence of public spirit and patriotism among the Hindus. Organized resistance was offered to early invasions, but only by the fighting castes, who were patriotic more for the honour of their race and their class than from a love of their countrymen generally. There was scarcely any sympathy between them and the teeming millions who composed the

1. HEAD OF A MAHOMMEDAN. 2. MAHOMMEDAN WOMAN SOLICITING ALMS.

[1] Compare Sir William Wilson Hunter's "Indian Empire," p. 241.

[1] Bose's "History of Hindu Civilization during British Rule," Vol. I, Introduction.

lower castes. At the time of the Mahommedan conquest India was well populated, and had the Hindus been permeated with a sense of nationality and of patriotism, it would not have been possible for the Mahommedans to have established their empire in India." When they did offer a national opposition it was when the Puritan Aurangzebe touched their religious susceptibilities, and the secret of British rule lies not so much in its military strength or in the benefits it is supposed to confer, as in the caste system, in the general indifference of the people to anything which is not connected with their religion, and in the disposition fostered by a spiritual civilization.

But is there no hope of a fusion of the various castes that divide the Empire? Of immediate ethnic fusion there is not the least possibility, nor could it well be accomplished under the existing conditions of Hindu society. The ground must be ploughed, the soil must be fertilized; some of the seeds may fall on barren ground, some may be picked up by the birds of the air; thorns may choke others; while only a few may fall on fertile soil. The firstfruits may in all probability be scanty, but the steady, persistent, and judicious application of labour will yield a hundredfold, a thousandfold, and even ten-thousandfold. Even so it is with the work of welding the various disjointed elements composing the Hindu peoples into one nation. English education is the greatest solvent of Hindu society, and it is, further, also its salvation. It has created new aims and aspirations in the peoples of India, and the famous minute of Macaulay marks the dawn of a new epoch in the history of India—it gave birth to modern India, it has made possible a "united" India. It has created an intellectual sympathy unknown in former times, and it has brought the political bond, which holds the Hindus together in modern times, as a nation, to the forefront. It is the leaven of Hindu society. It is breaking the protective spirit [1] of Hinduism in social matters, so long the greatest impediment in ethnical fusion. English education is to Hindu society what the Reformation was to England. "The Reformation," says Bishop Westcott, "was the affirmation . . . of individuality. . . . Individuality is not the sum of life, but it is an essential part of life in every region of our nature and our work for the part and for the whole. It is true, though it is not the whole truth, that we must live and die alone with God."

One of the most important effects of English education in India is the growth of individualism. An invariable concomitant of this individualism in its early stages is the growth of selfishness, and selfishness in the joint Hindu family means its break-up. However much we may feel for the gradual disruption of the venerable joint Hindu home, yet the fact must be faced that, if Hindu society is to progress at all, the *customary* basis upon which the Hindu joint family rests must yield place to a more stable basis, namely, that self-controlling freedom which is the result of the growth of knowledge and self-reliance, which enables men to impose of their own free will restraints on their own actions. But the time during which "the old order changeth, yielding place to new," the time during which the new collectivism based upon self-disciplined individuality displaces the old collectivism based upon instinct, in short, the transition stage between mediæval and modern India, may be (and it is so in fact) a difficult one to pass through. No transition stage, however, is a bed of roses. Individualism must be pruned of its roughness, of its barrenness, and of its selfishness, before it can work out India's salvation. The process of growth which is to be sure is always slow. The best natures often want to shorten this long process in their desire to achieve in a decade the work of a century, but this temptation has to be resisted.[1] If it is not the results will be disastrous. As Professor Marshall writes: "Projects for great and sudden changes are now, as ever, foredoomed to failure and to cause reaction. We are still unable to move safely if we move so fast that our new plans of life altogether outrun our instincts. It is true that human nature can be modified; new ideals, new opportunities, and new methods of action may, as history shows, alter it very much, even in a few generations. This change in human nature has perhaps never covered so wide an area and moved so quickly as in the present generation. But still it is a growth, and therefore gradual; and changes of our social organization must wait on it, and must therefore be gradual too. But though they wait on it they may always keep a little in advance of it, promoting the growth of our higher social nature by giving it always some new and higher work to do, some practical ideal towards which we strive. Thus, step by step, we may attain to an order of social life in which the common good overrules individual caprice even more than it did in the early ages before the sway of individualism began. Unselfishness then will be the offspring of deliberate will, though aided by instinct; individual freedom will then develop itself in collective freedom —a happy contrast to the older order of life in which individual slavery by custom caused collective slavery and stagnation, broken only by the caprice of despotism or the caprice of revolution." Congresses and conferences and recent Acts of the Legislature are to be regarded as the signs of the rise of this individualistic spirit, which, let us hope, in time will create a new India, which, to the glory of all Englishmen justly proud of their august mission to this historic soil, shall surely shine forth the brightest jewel in England's Crown.

[1] "Social Aspects of Christianity," p. 121.

[1] See on this theme an excellent address delivered by the late Hon. Mr. Justice M. G. Ranade at a meeting of the Sixth National Social Conference. Report. Appendix, pp. 20, 21.

SOUTHERN INDIA

THE SYRIAN CHRISTIANS OF MALANKARA (TRAVANCORE AND COCHIN)

By P. JOHN MATHEW

THE Syrian Christians of Malabar are the descendants of the earlier Christians of the whole world. When the now civilized nations were immersed in utter ignorance and worshipping idols, the colony of Malabar Christians were worshipping the true God in churches built by them. Even when the ancient Britons were worshipping the idols Odin and Thor, this band of Christians had their churches and a form of worship on the lines of the creed which they hold to-day.

There are many historians who have written an account of this ancient Church, but some of them differ from the truth. There are those who say that St. Thomas the Apostle came to Malankara (Travancore and Cochin); others say that a man named Thomas came to preach the Gospel of Christ at a later date, but every writer admits that this Christian Church was established here long before the Gospel was preached in Europe.

It is admitted even by the Brahmins that St. Thomas visited India and converted some of the people in the villages, and it can be clearly proved from the high status which the Christians in Malabar hold among their high-caste Hindu neighbours that they were at one time of the same status as the Brahmins.

All the Syrian Christians and their neighbours, the high-caste Hindus, firmly believe that the Apostle St. Thomas landed at Cranganoor in A.D. 52; that he established churches at Niranam, Quilon, Chayil, Chockamangalam, Maliancara, Kottakave, and Palur, but only one remains to-day, that is, Niranam. The Apostle after preaching in Travancore and Cochin went to Mylapore, and a tradition has been widely held from early times, and is accepted as true by many writers of repute, that he suffered a martyr's death at that place.

The Christian Church on the Malabar coast, whether it was founded by St. Thomas or at a later date, existed through long centuries, and was in full vigour when the Portuguese came to Calicut in 1498. Adherents were forcibly compelled by the power of the Portuguese to submit for a time to Rome, but they escaped from submission to the Roman yoke when the Dutch drove the Portuguese away, and ever since that date the Church has held its pristine purity of doctrine and ritual.

The first historical fact on record is that one of the bishops present at the Council of Nicea in the year 325 signed the decrees of the Council as John, Bishop of Persia and Great India. This clearly proves that the Apostle had consecrated bishops in Malabar before he left these shores, but the argument that Great India may be the India west of the Indus is out of the question, as there were no Christians there then, nor are there even now. A few decades after the coming of the Apostle a merchant named Thomas of Cana, who had trade connections with this coast, became acquainted with this Church, and in the year 345 he brought from Syria, Bagdad, and Jerusalem about four hundred families and landed them at Cranganoor, among them being a bishop named Joseph and some priests. After this immigration this ancient Church seems to have been placed in a better position. Cheruman Perumal, the then ruler of Cranganoor, conferred many privileges on Thomas of Cana, one of which was a gift of some copper plates dated 348. These old plates were taken away by the Portuguese, and are believed to be in the Vatican in Rome, while there are other similar ones still in the possession of the Syrian Christians.

Day, in his "Land of the Perumal" (p. 215), speaks of a bishop named Frumentius, with episcopal authority in South India about 365. In the sixth century the Alexandrian traveller, Cosmas Inidcoplesustes, visited Malabar, and he says that "in Male" (meaning Malabar) "there are Christians, and in Kallina (Quilon) there is a bishop." There are four documents to show the antiquity of the Syrian Church, namely, two copper plates and two inscriptions on stone slabs. These stones can be seen in the Valipally Church at Kottayam, to which place they are said to have been brought from a very old building near Cranganoor. The stones are carved and inscriptions appear above and below the cross. There is a similar cross in the church at St. Thomas's Mount, near Madras, and the inscriptions and carvings on it are the same. The letters on the older stone at Kottayam and on the stone at the Mount are said to have been inscribed about the middle of the seventh century. Translations of the inscriptions on these stones have differed very considerably from each other. Dr. Burnell's translation runs as follows: "In persecution by the cross was the suffering of this One who is the God above and true Christ; God above and guide ever pure." Dr. E. W. West gives the following: "What freed the true Messiah the forgiving the upbraiding from hardship. The crucifixion from the tree and the anguish of this." Dr. Haugh, of Munich, translates: "He that believes in the Messiah and in God in the height and also in the Holy Ghost is in the grace of Him who suffered the pain of the cross."

Above the cross of the Valipally Church is half of the Pahlave inscription of the older stone, "The Messiah and God in the height and the Holy Ghost." While below the cross is a Syriac version of Galatians vi. 14, "Let me not glory except in the cross of our Lord Jesus Christ." The copper plate grants are in the old Seminary at Kottayam, and one of these is said by Dr. Burnell to be a grant in the year 774 by King Veera Ragavachakravarthy to Eravy Korattan of Cranganoor, making over to him the village of Manigramam, and investing him with the rank of a Prabhu. It is in old Nanammonam Tamil letters, with some Grantha ones intermingled. The second document is on five sheets of copper fastened by a ring; of the ten pages of copper thus furnished seven are written in Tamil and two in Pahlave and Arabic with Kufic characters, while the four signatures are in Hebrew.

It is clearly proved from these inscriptions on stone and copper that the Christians at that time built and owned churches and held a very high position in the country. The one missing copper plate which contained the grants was deposited by Mar Jacob, about 1530, with the Portuguese in the factory at Cochin, and it was found there by Colonel Macaulay in 1806. The following extract is interesting in connection with the remark of John de Marignoli that "the Christians had charge of the public weighing, the brokerage, and customs of all that might be measured by the para, weighed by the balance, stretched by the line, and of all that might be counted or carried."

The history of this ancient Church for a considerable number of years is almost a blank, but the fact remains that it prospered without the interference of any foreigners during that period.

Documentary evidence is, however, forthcoming to the effect that in 1504 the Syrian Christians in India wrote to the Nestorian Patriarch of Babylon to send some bishops (Assemen, iii. 588), and on the arrival of the latter in the year 1504 they wrote the following report: "There are here about thirty thousand families, common in faith with us, and they pray God for your prosperity now that they have commenced to build more churches."

The Portuguese, who arrived on the Malabar coast during the visits of Vasco da Gama early in the sixteenth century, began to persecute the Syrian Christians, many of them being either deported or drowned in the sea, but when Dutch authority became supreme in the year 1663 the Churches again enjoyed their former freedom, and they went so far as to exact an oath from their clergy that no allegiance should be paid to the King of Portugal.

When the English took the place of the Dutch the Syrian Christians attracted their attention, and in 1806 Dr. Buchanan of Calcutta visited the Syrians, and during a tour among them he saw Archdeacon Mar Thomas, who discussed with him the possibility of a union between his flock and the Church of England. When Dr. Buchanan returned to Europe he published in 1811 his "Christian Researches in India," a book which first brought to the knowledge of the British public the existence of Syrian Christians in India.

Trouble arose soon between two branches of the Syrians and Europeans missionaries in connection with the ordination of students and with regard to the ownership of Church property and as to the auditing of accounts.

Three arbitrators were appointed, and the property was divided between the Syrian Christians, the Church Missionary, and the London Missionary Societies. The Metropolitan did not submit personally to this arbitration, and he asserted that the endowments were made for the education of the Syrian Christians, and consequently could not be given to the Missionary Societies. He wrote to the Madras Government about the injustice of this decision, but as the Resident was helping the missionaries, the Madras Government decided that the arbitration was final. Appeal was then made to the Court of Directors of the East India Company, who replied that the arbitration was irregular and that the dispute ought to be settled by a Civil Court, but before this decision was made known the property was made over to the Church Missionary Society by the Resident. The Society being in possession (and the Resident being all-powerful in a Native State), refused to hand over the property, therefore the Syrian Metropolitan took no further steps.

After the separation a strong party, who were influenced by the teaching of the missionaries, sent a young Syrian Christian youth, named Mathew, to Antioch. In 1841 he arrived at Mardin, the seat of the Patriarch, where he was ordained as priest and subsequently as bishop, when he was sent back to Travancore with authority as Metropolitan of Malankara. Bishop Mathew returned to Travancore in 1843, under the name of Mar Athanasius, and claimed his bishopric.

There were many disputes about this date, chiefly as to the line of succession of the Patriarchs and as to the position and power of Mar Athanasius. These disputes reached the Travancore Durbar, who appointed a committee to report upon the credentials, with the result that the claims of Mar Athanasius were recognized. The Travancore Durbar, upon receiving the report, placed that cleric in office, handing over to him the Seminary and all property belonging to the community. In 1849 the Patriarch sent over a bishop named Stephanus, but on his arrival dissensions arose among the Syrian Christians, and the Resident hearing of them, ordered him to leave the shores. The latter, however, appealed against the order of the Resident to the Court of Directors in London, and in 1857 an order was received forbidding interference and stating that the disputes of the Syrian Christians must be settled by themselves. In 1863 the Travancore Government issued a notification informing the public that they were at liberty to follow Mar Cyril, Secretary of the former Patriarch, on condition that they must build churches for themselves, and leave the followers of Mar Athanasius in sole possession of the existing places of worship. By this proclamation Mar Athanasius became the possessor of all the churches and seminaries, together with the endowments, and he remained in undisputed possession until 1868, when, in order to strengthen his position, he consecrated his cousin Thomas, appointing him as his coadjutor and successor. Athanasius died in 1877, and he was quietly succeeded by his cousin, Mar Thomas, but in the meantime Mar Cyril sent one Joseph to Antioch, and the Patriarch consecrated him. Joseph landed in Travancore in 1866, taking the name of Mar Dionysius, and in 1869 he applied to the Madras Government to interfere on his behalf. This request was refused, and he was asked to file a suit. In 1872 the Patriarch, Ignatius XXXIII, vexed to find the loss of an important portion of his Patriarchate, left Antioch in 1874 to visit London, where he interviewed the Archbishop of Canterbury and other influential personages. Eventually the Secretary of State issued orders forbidding any interference with the Syrians. In March 1874 the Travancore Government issued a proclamation that the Durbar abstained from any interference with the Syrian Church, and that claims to appointments or to property must be tried in the courts of law. Consequently Mar Dionysius filed a suit in the Alleppey Zilla court for the recovery of the Seminary at Kottayam and of other properties belonging to the Syrian Churches. This suit was pending for ten years, and in 1889 the final verdict was pronounced, although two widely different judgments were given in the High Court. The European judge said that, after the breach of the Syrians with Rome in 1665, this ancient Church obtained episcopal orders from the Patriarch of Antioch, but remained autonomous, with the custom that each Metran consecrated his successor, and that the consent of the Patriarch was not required for the regular consecration and for the due succession of prelates. He therefore decided against Mar Dionysius in favour of Mar Thomas Athanasius. But the two Hindu judges dissented from this decision, and said that the Syrian Church was under the Jacobite Patriarch of Antioch, and he was the only authority competent to consecrate prelates in the Syrian Church in Travancore, that Mar Dionysius was properly ordained by this authority, and that he was accepted at a meeting in 1876 by a majority of the community. On the above grounds they decided in favour of the Jacobite party to be in possession of the Seminary and of all other property pertaining to it. The Secretary of State also filed an interpleader suit to determine which party was entitled to receive the interest of the three thousand star pagodas, and this also was decided in favour of Mar Dionysius. When this action was pending in the law courts, and when an immense sum of money was being spent by both parties, there was a proposal from the leaders for a compromise. At that time Mr. P. John, the author's father, and one of the first officers who entered the British service, was the chief adviser of Mar Athanasius, and recommended the latter to decline to make any arrangement, saying that it was better to lose all the property and remain as an entirely separate body.

The Reformed Syrians have nearly 154 churches and a population of 100,000 families. The Jacobites also have the same number of churches and schools, but on account of the dissensions in their midst by the excommunication of the Metran, and owing to the legal suits in regard to the possession of these churches and schools, their progress has been retarded, while the Mar Thoma, or the Reformed Syrian Christians, are progressing rapidly. In 1893 Mar Thoma Athanasius died, and he was succeeded by his brother, Titus Mar Thoma, a very pious man, during whose time much progress was made. Titus Mar Thoma died in 1905, and he consecrated his nephew, who is the present Metropolitan. Recently Patriarch Abdulla came to him and excommunicated the successor of Mar Dionysius and consecrated other Metrans. Again an interpleader suit has been filed by the Secretary of State to determine which party is entitled to the interest of the 1808 investment. The Seminary Church, Cheriapally, and all others of importance are closed for worship, and the half a dozen Metrans are going about from place to place. But the reformed party, who acted upon the valuable advice of Mr. P. John, are enjoying perfect peace and harmony, and though they were deprived of all the old churches, they have built new ones and schools, and are progressing in the primitive purity of the original church. They have a Seminary at Tiruvalla, a High School at Kottayam, and another (for girls) at Tiruvalla.

1. BOILING OF SACRED MILK, KOTAGIRI DISTRICT.

Whichever side of the pot boils over first, that side of the land will be most fertile and prosperous.

Photo by Mrs. A. Moore.

2 AND 3. BADAGA FIRE FEAST.

This feast generally takes place on the Monday following the February full moon. Those who intend to walk through the fire arrive the night before, and bathe next day. The fire is lighted by a Udaya priest, who afterwards offers to it a coconut, some plantains, and sprinkles holy water on it, and after burning camphor and incense, leads the procession through it.

Photo by Mrs. A. Moore.

BABY AFLOAT ON A VICTORIA REGIA LEAF.

Photo by Nicholas & Co.

FLORA

BY P. F. FYSON B.A., F.L.S., PROFESSOR OF BOTANY, PRESIDENCY COLLEGE, MADRAS

AS South India lies entirely within the tropics, the northern limit of our area being at about the 16th parallel, and Cape Comorin, at the extreme south, just on the 4th, it might be thought that the uniformity of climate, general in the tropics, would induce a similar uniformity in the flora.

On the contrary, the vegetation is more varied than probably that of any other area of equal size which does not come within the range of the Himalayas or the Andes. The factors which chiefly determine the vegetation of a district, long connected as ours has been with a great continent, are rainfall, temperature, soil, and the requirements of man. The last is usually neglected in discussions on botanical distribution, but with an old and thickly populated district it is of considerable importance, for man, by his clearing of forest land for crops, and continual destruction of the smaller trees for firewood and as fodder for his cattle, has changed the face of the country even in historically recent times. Of the natural factors we have every variety, with extremes as great almost as are to be found in any country, and it is the extremes that tell. Not the average rainfall, but the weeks of incessant rain, such as occur on the mountains of Malabar during the south-west monsoon, or the months of drought which dry the soil so completely both in the north and in the south of our area: not the average temperature, whether it be 65° or 75°, but the fierce heat of the sun in May and the cold, dry winds which blow over mountain-tops: these kill the ill-adapted or delicate plant, and so determine the character of the vegetation. And where could we look for greater extremes of soil than the loose sand of the coastal fringe that is dry in an hour after days of incessant rain, and the black cotton soil which holds its moisture like a sponge not very far below the surface after weeks of drought; the rocks and stones of the smaller hills which dot the whole plain, and the great mud-flats at the mouths of our rivers?

If we take the country from east to west we have (1) the coastal fringe of sandy shore and numerous backwaters, broken by mud-flats at the mouths of rivers; (2) the Coromandel, a strip of low land, from 20 to 1,500 ft. above sea-level, and varying in breadth from 20 to 150 miles; (3) the central plateau of Mysore, rising to 3,000 or 4,000 ft. in the south and west, where it is bounded by (4) the Western Ghauts, and flanked on the north-east by (5) the hilly district of the Eastern Ghauts; (6) the Highlands of the Nilgiris and Travancore ranges; and (7) the Malabar coast. Each of these seven areas has its own distinctive vegetation.

As one approaches Madras by sea one is struck by the entire absence of any

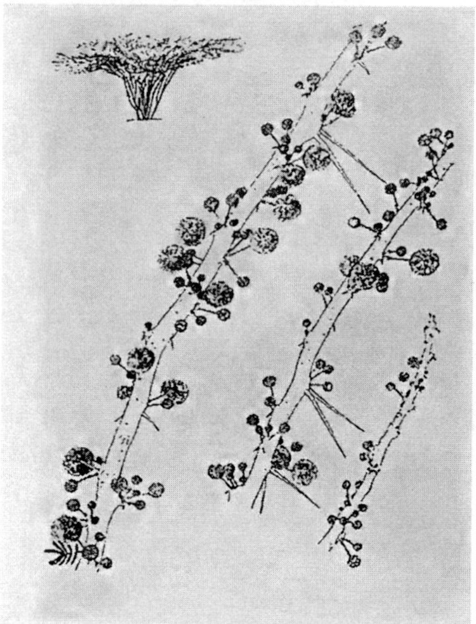

ACACIA PLANIFRONS.

R. Natesan, del.

cliff, there being only a low, sandy shore with Coconut Palms and the larch-like Casuarina behind. A nearer view shows sand-dunes great and small, sparsely covered with the Goat's-foot Convolvulus (*Ipomœa per-capræ*), with small leaves on its long-trailing stems; the creeping Hawks'-bit (*Launea pinnatefida*), showing a row of small tufted leaves, which are connected underground; and the small Sandgrass (*Cyperus arenaria*); or densely clothed by the Great Spiny Sword-grass (*Spinifex squarrosus*), impassable except to the well-protected foot. In places on the coast are long stretches of a thorny dwarf Date (*Phœnix acaulis*). Here and there are clumps of the Screw Pine (*Pandanus*), which is no relation of the Pines, but is certainly screwed. A little distance from the actual beach are the yellow-flowered Portia (*Thespesia populnea*), called also, but erroneously, the Tulip-tree, Casuarina, and Coconut, all of which have been planted. Casuarina, like Eucalyptus, is one of Australia's gifts to the world. It will grow everywhere in the poorest soil, and, like Eucalyptus on the hills, makes excellent firewood. At the mouths of rivers, of the smallest or of the largest, the muddy or less sandy banks are lined with Mangroves, a group of trees not all botanically related, but alike in being adapted to these particular situations. Some grow up out of the water on numerous stick-like roots, which are unaffected by the ebb and flow of the tide, or the rush of a river in flood, as a single stem might be. Round the base of others one sees root-suckers growing up out of the soil like a miniature forest. These suckers are internally spongy, like a lung, and are specially developed to carry air to the lower water-logged roots. With most of the Mangroves the fruit has a single seed, which germinates while still on the tree, and throws out a club-shaped root 5 to 7 in. in length, which, when at last it falls, immediately anchors the young plant in the soft mud. Both these groups, the vegetation of the sands and that of the mud-flats, are found nowhere else except on the seashore, and only on the shores of tropical countries. They are therefore worth the attention of the visitor.

The Coromandel, a strip of plain between the eastern shore and the central plateau, presents to the traveller by rail a continuous succession of small fields of paddy, cholam, and other crops, surrounded by rows of Palmyra Palms or groups of Coconuts; while here and there are stretches of low scrub, euphemistically labelled "Reserve Forest"; and scattered everywhere are rocky hills of every size from 50 to 250 ft. in height. On these wild nature offers no inducements to the explorer, whether by foot or on horseback, unless he be a botanist. Nearly every bush and climber is beset with sharp spines or curved prickles, which pull threads out of the strongest cloth, and harass one at every step; while the rough, stony ground makes riding difficult. The commonest trees one sees from the train are the Bābool (*Acacia arabica*), with small feathery leaves, small fluffy balls of bright yellow flowers, and long grey pods, curiously like a row of buttons or flat beads joined edge to edge. Low on the ground is a spiny shrub (*Carisa carundas*), with white, star-like flowers, which can be seen in blossom nearly all the year round. Prominent among the trees lining the roads is the Tamarind, whose shade by day is denser perhaps than that of any other tree, yet it allows the light of the full moon to stream through. Its fruit, like small, badly-made sausages, has an acid pulp, which is universally used for cleaning brass cooking-pots. Another is the Banyan (*Ficus bengalensis*), perhaps the most interesting and characteristic tree of India, because of the roots which grow down from the branches and ultimately form stout pillars round the main trunk. Its fruit is a small scarlet fig, eagerly devoured by crows and squirrels, and useful also in the cooking-pot. Own brother to the Banyan is the Peepul (*Ficus religiosa*), with heart-shaped. long-pointed leaves which tremble in the breeze like an aspen. Round large trees there is usually a built-up platform of earth or masonry bearing a shrine. Butterworth in "Some Madras Trees" records a trunk of 34 ft. in girth, and there is a fine specimen in the Agri-Horticultural Society's gardens in Madras. The Rāin-tree (*Pithecolobium dulce*), planted now so much because of its rapid growth, is an imported Mimosa with large mauve flower-heads.

Of the many common trees which one meets everywhere mention must be made of the Cashew (*Anacardium occidentale*), which grows a nut at the end of its pear-shaped fruit. The latter is too astringent for European taste, but the kernel of the nut is very commonly served with after-dinner dessert. Belonging to the same

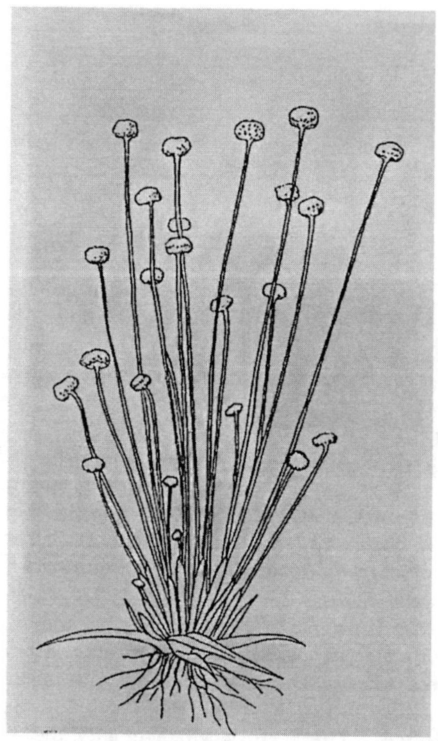

ERIOCAULON QUINQUANGULARE.

family, but with a fruit that has under cultivation lost its astringency, is the Mango (*Mangifera indica*). This is usually a medium-sized, spreading, but not tall tree, and occurs in almost every

1. VANDA ROXBURGHII.
R. Natesan, del.

2. MILLINGTONIA HORTENSIS.
R. Natesan, del.

3. PLUMERIA ALBA.

4. CASSIA AURICULATA.
D. R. Fyson, del.

5. LEPIDAGATHIS CRISTATA.

6. BAUHINIA PURPUREA.
R. Natesan, del.

good-sized garden, and also in plantations, locally known as *topes*. The fruit ripens during the hot weather, but a fool made of the unripe fruits at Christmas-time is an agreeable delicacy. And here it may be said, in opposition to the universal belief in the abundance of fruits in tropical countries, that we are not really well off in this respect. Near Bangalore introduced apples and strawberries do fairly well, but the native fruits—if we except the orange and the banana—are as a rule astringent or poor in flavour. The best are, perhaps, the Custard-apple (*Anona*) and Guava, but the latter consists mostly of hard seeds, and only the thick rind is eaten. Of the banana, however (locally known always as a plantain), we have certainly an excellent variety, and oranges can be had nearly all the year round. The really fine tropical fruits, such as the Mangosteen, do not thrive well here.

Most visitors come out in the cool weather—between October and January—and at that time the evenings are scented with the beautiful Indian Cork (*Millingtonia hortensis*), a tall, handsome tree, with long white tubular flowers hanging in untidy clusters. Shortly after this appears the Bastard Silk-cotton tree (*Bombax malabaricum*), a fine tree with massive prickly trunk and nearly flat flowers, 2 to 3 in. across, which, seen from below in bright sunlight against the blue sky, are of the most beautiful transparent pink. They appear before the leaves, and this is the case also with many other trees. Another striking characteristic of many of our commonest trees is the quickness with which the old leaves are changed for new. For two or three days there will be a constant rustle of falling leaves, and by the end of a week the tree will be clothed again in fresh foliage. Indeed, one may often see one side of a tree with new leaves while the other side has still its old ones.

Another leafless flower is the Indian Torch (*Erythrina indica*), which, though a tree, belongs to the Bean tribe. It has very large red flowers, in a double row, sloping backwards and facing upwards along horizontal spikes. The combination of unopened buds at the point, the rich vermilion of the opened flowers in the middle, and the dark withered remains, or young pods, behind, is marvellously reminiscent of a blazing torch in the wind. A truly royal flower is that of *Lagerstroemia flos-reginæ*. The flowers of this tree stand in strong, erect spikes, and measure 2 to 3 in. across, and have delicately crumpled mauve blossoms. An own brother to this—*Lagerstroemia indica*—is a small bush grown in many gardens throughout India.

A curious small tree which flowers also at this time is the Prickly Broom (*Parkinsonia aculeata*), an American importation. Each leaf is represented by a tuft of narrow, green, tape-like pinnas, along the edge of which are set the small oval leaflets, and along with each bunch of four pinnas is a stout thorn. The flowers are yellow, thin as tissue paper, and delicately suffused with brown. Last of the cold-weather flowering trees is the Flame-tree (*Spathodea campanulata*), a native of tropical Africa, which does very well here, and is conspicuous in Madras and other towns. Above the crown of dark-green foliage are groups of large, orange-coloured flowers. The buds contain water, which, on being pressed, can be squirted a considerable distance.

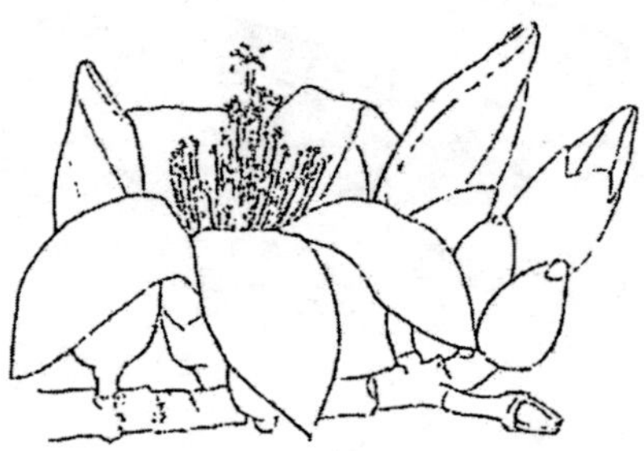

FLOWER OF BOMBAX MALABARICUM.

R. Natesan, del.

Such are the most conspicuous, perhaps, of our cold-weather flowering trees. But there are many others, with smaller or less noticeable flowers, among which space permits us to mention only the Neem (*Melia azadrlachta*), whose leaves are useful in keeping insects out of one's clothes, and from whose fruit the best watch-makers' oil is expressed. But beautiful as are so many of these flowering trees they do not approach for mere splendour of colour the trees of the hot-weather months. The season begins in April with the magnificent *Peltophorum ferrugineum*, which was brought originally from the Straits, and is one of the largest of our Coromandel trees. It comes out in spikes of flat golden-yellow flowers, suffused with brown. This is followed by the Pagoda-tree or Temple flower, and Frangapani (*Plumeria acutifolia* and *P. alba*) with extraordinarily thick, smooth branches ending in tufts of white, trumpet-shaped flowers, with most delicious fragrance. These are still in flower when the Gold-mohur or Ghui-mohur (*Poinciana regia*) spread its scarlet sheets across one's view. Many people call this the "Flame of the Forest," but it is not a forest tree, and it is not of a true flame colour, being too red. Its country of origin is unknown, but it seems to have been cultivated for centuries in China under the name "Peacock's Eye"—a curiously fanciful name for a flower which has no trace of blue in it! But there can be no doubt of its beauty. Whether in the early days when, without leaves to detract from its colour, the flowers show in richest scarlet across the blue sky, or later, when the fresh green of the new leaves serves only to enhance the red of the blossoms, it must be pronounced one of the most gorgeous trees of the world. At this time appears also the Indian Laburnum (*Cassia fistula*), with its festoons of yellow flowers, measuring a couple of inches across. And in May there flowers, too, a characteristic tree of tropical coasts, *Calophyllum inophyllum*, the whiteness of whose delicately scented flowers is enhanced by their dead-white stalks and by the deep green of glossy leaves. The round green fruits, about the size of the core of a golf-ball, may be found nearly all the year round.

Among the universally cultivated garden shrubs, mention must be made of *Ixora coccinea* and other species of the genus, with bunches of scarlet or white flowers, consisting of a long, slender tube, ending in four narrow or triangular petals, which in bud are twisted together. Another useful genus is Hibiscus, with many hybrids and cultivated varieties, which are often here called Shoe-flower—a curious misnomer—and *Bauhinia*, called, because of its divided leaves, after the twin brothers Bauhin.

In July, and again in December, after the rains, many of our smaller shrubs come into blossom, and a host of small flowers strew the ground. Mauve and lilac-coloured bells of *Ruellia prostrata*, spikes of small, two-lipped, purple-spotted flowers of *Justicia procumbens*; tiny scarlet pea-flowers of *Indigofera enneaphylla*; deep-blue *Evolvulus alsinoides*, which, though belonging to the convolvulus family, is in general appearance very like the English Speedwell; yellow groundsel-like flower heads of *Vicoa auriculata*, and curiously spider-like spreading *Lepidagathis cristata*, which has earned its name for seeming to feed on mere stones. In our hedgerows appear many varieties of *Jasminum*, with their familiar starry flowers ; a strangely disagreeable smelling Passion Flower, *P. fœtida,* several varieties of the Convolvulus family,

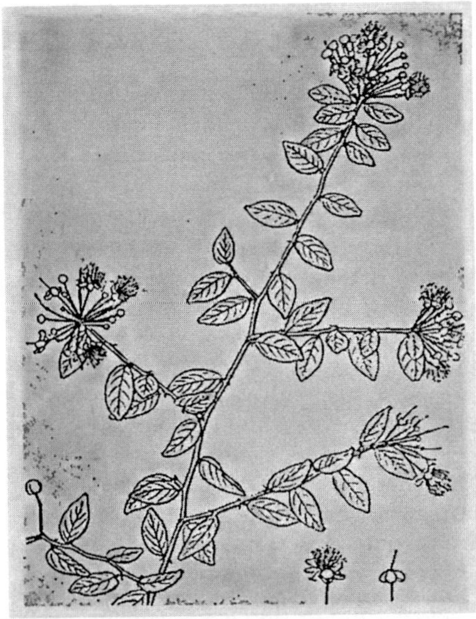

CAPPARIS SEPIARIA.

mostly species of *Ipomœa* (a genus of the tropics, very similar to *Convolvulus*), and, especially in the drier and rockier parts, thorny climbers such as *Toddalia aculeata,* a member of the orange family, and several species of *Capparis* and its allies. On open wastes are bushes of *Cassia auriculata,* which, in the luxuriance of its yellow blossoms reminds one of broom ; and in standing or slowly running water, *Neptunia oleracea,* floating by means of soft, spongy outgrowths of the stems, carries up above the water its beautiful yellow spikes, of which the lowest flowers have long, narrow staminodes. The damp ground to the side sparkles with a white flowered *Striga,* the grey-headed Hatpin-flower (*Eriocaulon quinquangulare*), and many other small plants. Of orchids there are but few, and in gardens it is difficult to grow any of the more ornamental kinds, except *Vanda roxburghi,* which flourishes well on trees in Madras.

These are but a few of the beautiful plants of this district, which, as is usually the case with comparatively dry and poor stony soil, abounds in brilliantly coloured flowers of all kinds. None of them, however, form sheets of colour, as do the bluebells, daffodils, and gentians of temperate climates. Botanically, the district is of African affinity, its flora bearing more resemblance to that of eastern tropical Africa than to the countries on the east of India.

In the extreme south the climate is drier and hotter, and similar to that of Egypt, and the curiously flat-topped *Acacia planifrous* forms cedar-like tiers of foliage on the rocky hill-sides. Its nearest ally, and one exactly like it in the flat top, occurs only on the dry lands of Africa. Another link is the almost leafless *Caparis aphylla,* which occurs also in Egypt and Arabia.

The Palmyra, or toddy-palm, cultivated throughout this district, is to be seen in the south in greatest numbers. It will be recognized at once by its very black trunk and tuft of stiff leaves, which are fringed or cut like the fingers of the hand, and folded fan-wise. The other common palms, the Coconut, Date, and Areca, or Betel-nut, have leaves divided finely, like

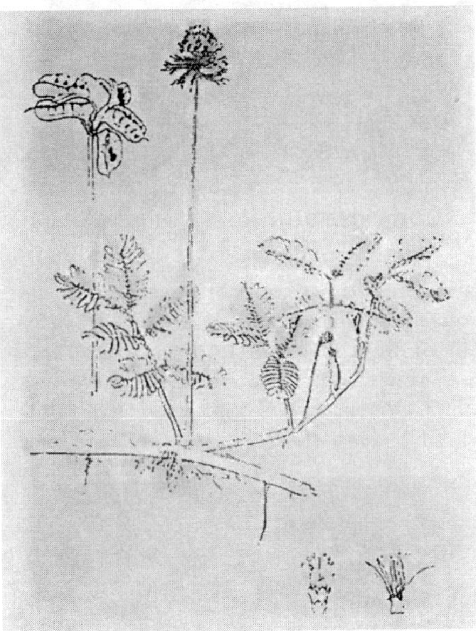

NEPTUNIA OLERACEA.

D. R. Fyson, del.

a feather. And here it may be said that the characteristic feature of palms is their undivided trunk, ending in a crown of leaves. Most palms never branch, or only in consequence of some injury.

The Palmyra is one of the most valuable of tropical plants, almost every part, the trunk, fruit, leaves, and the fibres round the leaf-stalks, being made use of in various ways. But the chief reason for its cultivation, and the origin of its name of toddy-palm, is the sweet, fermentable liquid which is drawn from the young flower-stalks. These are cut off short and made to drip into small earthenware vessels, *chatties,* in which the liquid collects. This is also practised with the coconut-palm, especially near towns. The wild Date (*Phœnix sylvestus*), with shorter, straighter stems than the coconut, and large, round heads of gracefully drooping leaves, has hard, quite inedible fruits, but it also yields a toddy. In this case the stem itself is notched near the crown, and this often causes the trunks to have sudden and irregular bends.

To the north of the Coromandel, and on the northern limits of our area, lies the broken, hilly country of the Eastern Ghauts, the only part in Southern India with deciduous forest. The railway journey from Guntakul traverses this region, and to any one who has time during the early months of the year, the journey is well worth making ; for, apart from the beauty of the scenery, with its deep ravines and rocky crags, many of the trees are then out in full beauty. Chief amongst them may be mentioned the true Silk-cotton (*Eriodendron anfractuosum*), with its rigidly horizontal branches, and the Bastard Silk-cotton (*Bombax malabaricum*), both of which are found also in the Coromandel ; the true "Flame of the Forest" (*Butea frondosa*), spreading through the forest like sheets of flame ; the noble Teak (*Tectona grandis*), with its broad leaves and small flowers, together with other valuable timber trees, such as the Ebony (*Diospyrus ebenum*). In some places the bare rock

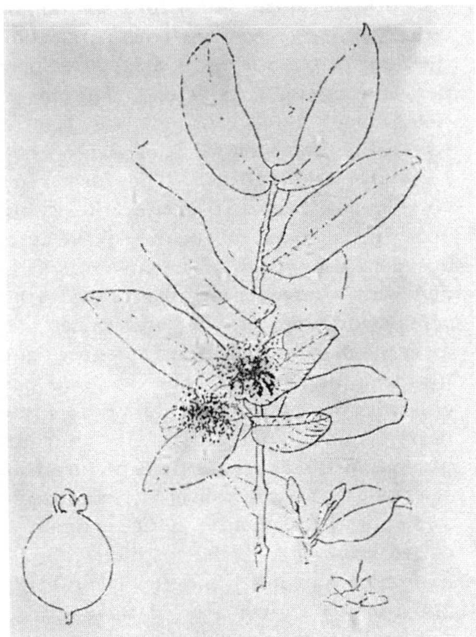

GUAVA FLOWER AND FRUIT.

D. R. Fyson, del.

becomes very hot under the noonday sun, and the vegetation consists largely of leafless *Euphorbias,* with stems and branches as thin as a lead pencil, or a couple of inches in thickness and much twisted and thorny, in cactus fashion.

To the west of this region we pass into the black cotton soil, the character and colour of which has been the subject of numerous investigations. In summer the surface is cracked and broken almost to a powder, and the wind that blows over it feels like a blast from a furnace. But in its depths it still retains water from the previous rains, and it seems peculiarly adapted for Indian cotton. Of wild plants the chief are the Babool (*Acacia arabica*), *Parkinsonia, Cassia auriculata, Jatropha,* and species of *Capparis* and *Zizyphus,* closely allied to those mentioned before. Hedges of the thin leafless *Euphorbia tirucalli* are common about the villages, as are the neem, toddy-palm, and orange. Botanically this district is nearly related to the Coromandel, though the peculiar condition of its soil makes the flora, in detail, distinctive.

On entering the Mysore plateau we find a vegetation similar to that of the plains. To the north is undulating grassland with stretches of small scrub, and here and there nothing but a dwarf date. To the west, as the Western Ghauts are approached, the country has the appearance of open park-land. Dotted about are clumps of small trees; on the slopes of the valleys are dense forests or plantations of coffee or fruit-trees, and along the floor of the valleys one sees tier upon tier of irrigated rice-fields. This, at an elevation of 3,000 ft. above the level of the sea, is the country of the planter, both European and Indian. The former devotes himself almost entirely to coffee, and grows some of the finest flavoured beans in the world. The latter is satisfied with a mixed crop of rice and other cereals, oranges, citrons, and spices such as cardamom, in addition to coffee; and, nearer Bangalore, he achieves some success with European fruits, such as strawberry, apple, and pear. For a coffee plantation the finest portions of forest are selected, where the soil is rich and deep; and one occasionally notices upon an estate remnants of the original jungle—giants, perhaps, of some 200 ft. in height and of 50 ft. girth around their spreading base. For where in temperate climes the bole of a tree is as a rule fairly circular down to the ground, and hardly wider at the base than a few feet higher up, in the luxuriant tropical forest the stem is usually strengthened at the base by buttress-like extensions, which add enormously to its girth. Such a buttress may project several feet from the main part of the trunk, and yet be but a few inches in thickness.

To the north the country slopes down to an elevation of only 1,500 ft., and passes into the great cotton belt. In its forests are seen some of the most valuable of South Indian timbers. Of these the Satin-wood (*Chloroxylon swietenia*), Tun (*Cedreta toona*), and universally cultivated Neem (*Melia azadirachta*) are near relations of Mahogany. Others are the Indian Red Sandal-wood (*Pterocarpus santalinus*), and Rosewood or Blackwood (*Dalbergia latifolia*). The cultivation and exploiting of Sandal-wood (*Santalium album*) is a very important source of revenue to the Mysore Government.

ALOE AMERICANA IN FLOWER.
Photo by P. F. F.

TREE FERNS AT COONOOR.

Throughout this elevated plateau the Mango, Figs of various kinds, Indian Laburnum, Tamarind, and other trees mentioned before are everywhere met with, and thrive even better than on the plains.

Malabar, the country between the outer slopes of the Western Ghauts and the sea, is quite a narrow strip, and differs from the rest of Southern India in its peculiarly humid climate and excessive rainfall. Here at sea-level flourishes the coconut palm in a luxuriance unapproached on the east coast, and a boat journey down the lagoons which run behind the shore is a unique experience. Here also are cultivated the areca-nut palm, pepper-vine, and other spices, and the slopes of the mountains are clothed in a dense forest, which stretches almost continuously for hundreds of miles northwards from Cape Comorin. As we enter this country we leave behind the low, thorny scrub of the eastern plains, with their Acacias, Cactus-like Euphorbias, and other desert and dry-land plants of African affinity, and plunge into a flora allied to that of the Malay regions. Here grow many useful timber trees (insufficiently exploited only because of the difficulties of transport), and palms of various kinds, notably Sago (*Arenga saccharifera*) and the giant *Corypha umbraculifera,* one of the largest of all, each single leaf of which will make a covering for a cart. The trunk is a couple of feet or more in thickness, and rears its crown from 50 to 80 ft. in height. Once only in its lifetime does this palm flower, and then it throws up above its crown of leaves a huge, much-branched spike, 30 ft. in height, bearing innumerable flowers. For a couple of years this may remain, shedding hundreds of seeds; then the whole gigantic palm dies, and gradually disappears. Among the smaller plants Orchids, Balsams, and Strobilanths are abundant, the last-named having the same habitat as the *Corypha* and *Aloe* in flowering but once in its life. On the rocks of the river-beds grow several species of the curious tropical water-plant, *Podostemon,* which have no stem or leaves, but only flattened roots, by which they glue themselves to the stones, like lichens, loving best those places where the current flows swiftest. The flowers are minute, and open when the water runs low, but one of the species actually sets its seeds under water without opening the flower. The tops of the range are covered in many places with grass running up to 8 or 10 ft. in height, and difficult to penetrate.

The highest peaks of the Western Ghauts, and the highest of India south of the Himalayas and Khasi Hills, are the Nilgiri and Pulney ranges, and the less frequently visited Anamalais, which are usually approached from the eastern side. These run up to 8,500 ft., and have an undulating plateau at about 7,000 ft. As we climb the Nilgiris by rail or road from Mettupalaiyam the prevailing thorny scrub of the plains soon gives way to groves of the slender Areca Palm, and the air is scented with the heavy perfumes of the foot-hills. Here we see the last of the Banyan and Tamarind, and presently the Plantain, or Banana, also disappears, their place being taken by the Jak and the Bamboo. At 3,000 ft. these bamboos, looking for all the world like monster ferns, die out, and one enters a thin forest of mixed character. Rubber and oranges are cultivated with more or less success, and at a higher elevation one sees coffee and tea plantations. The trees are connected by numerous creepers, whose thin stems, hanging from branch to branch, make penetration difficult. On reaching the edge of the plateau, at an altitude of about 5,000 ft., the cool breeze, chilly in comparison with the stuffiness of the moist valleys, prepares the traveller for a change of vegetation. And it comes with startling rapidity. On all sides he now finds reminders of familiar plants of Europe and North America; at first few, then as he passes across to the higher parts near Ootacamund, at 7,000 ft., more and more numerous, until he feels he is again in a country possessed of temperate climate. Here grow many of the familiar field and wayside flowers of England: Rose, Bramble, Clematis, Barberry, St. John's Wort, Gentian, Violet, Buttercup, Orchids, and many others; not of the same species, certainly, but obviously nearly all allied, and of the same genus. But in addition to these there are many plants which occur elsewhere only on tropical mountains, and conspicuous among them is *Strobilanthes kunthianus*, which flowers in such masses every ten or twelve years as to clothe the hill-sides with a bright blue colour. Some suppose that the name Nilgiri, or Neilgherry (blue mountains), was originally given on this account. There are several other Strobilanthes, mostly growing in the small woods, or *sholas*, and they share the same peculiarity of flowering only once every few years and of dying after the seed has ripened. Another conspicuous tropical and chiefly Indian genus is *Osbeckia*, with deep purple petals on a very roughly hairy calyx. America is represented by a *Gaultheria*, every part of which is strongly scented with oil of winter-green. With the Australian flora there are several links, notably in the Sticky-seeds (*Pittosporum*), of which we have two native species: and round all our hill stations the introduced Blue Gum, Blackwood (*Melanoxylon*), and Wattles (*Acacia*) are very conspicuous. But the native trees and the smaller elements of the woods belong mainly to tropical mountains. And when the flora of the plateau is analysed it is found that about half the wild genera are such as grow on tropical mountains, whether of Asia, Africa, or America. A good instance of this is the Giant Lobelia (*Lobelia excelsa*),

1. CALOTROPIS GIGANTEA. 2. HELICHRYSUM BUDDLEOIDES. *Photo by P. F. F.* 3. GOLD MOHR (POINCIANA REGIA). *Photo by P. F. F.*

which has spikes running up to 6 or 7 ft., and seems, at first sight, an impossible relative of our delicate blue-flowered garden Lobelias. Others of the same type, however, are on the mountains of tropical Asia, Africa, especially Abyssinia, and the Sandwich Islands. To find a similar vegetation one must go to the highlands of Ceylon, or to the Khasi Hills, 1,500 miles away in a direct line. These mountain-tops are, indeed, like islands in a vast ocean, and, botanically, are as completely isolated from each other and from other regions of like climate as, say, are the islands of the Pacific in regard to their human inhabitants. Hardly a plant which is seen here can be grown on the plains or on the Mysore plateau, or even on the western mountain ranges to the north of us.

Reviewing the flora as a whole, we may say that it is essentially tropical, but made up of four main elements of by no means equal importance: African, Malayan, tropical highland, and temperate. Though there is, of course, some mixing, especially on the borders of several districts, these correspond roughly to the plains and the Mysore plateau, the sea beach all round and the Malabar strip, and the higher mountain-tops. We have examples of the evergreen and deciduous forest, thorn-scrub and swamp, seashore and mountain vegetation. We have no Pines, Oaks, Beeches, or other common trees of Europe, only one Conifer, and one or two species of the ancient order of Cycads, remnants of which are scattered over all the warmer parts of the world.

To any one who is familiar with the wild flowers of England or any other temperate climate, there is much of intense interest. Not a single familiar genus, hardly even a family, except the larger and cosmopolitan ones, will he find on the South Indian plains. But instead he will be introduced to their tropical cousins, by whom they are represented, as, for instance, Ranunculaceæ by Anonaceæ, Cruciferæ by Capparidiæ, Hypericum by Guttiferæ, Umbeliferæ by Araliaceæ, Caprifoliaceæ by Rubiaceæ, Scropulariaceæ by Acanthaceæ. And when we consider the great variety of the flora, a sample of the greater variety of that of all India, we shall not be surprised that this continent has been the training ground of some of the world's greatest floristic botanists.

SUNSET ON THE ADYAR.

Photo by Nicholas.

FINANCE

By W. B. HUNTER, Bank of Madras

FINANCE, except to the student of economics, is a subject of small interest, and to the student a financial treatise unsupported by complete statistics is of no value. Space will not permit of finance in Southern India being treated in detail here, and the object aimed at is therefore not to add to the knowledge of the student, but rather to give the general reader an outline of how the financial wheel revolves.

Southern India comprises the Presidency of Madras and the Native States of Mysore, Travancore, Cochin, and Puducottah, but a complete understanding of the finance of Southern India cannot be arrived at without reference to the finance of the Government of India. Taking the figures of the financial year 1913-14, the total revenue of the Government of India may be put down at roughly £85,000,000, part of which is derived from sources wholly assigned to the Imperial Government, such as Customs, £7,500,000; salt, £3,500,000; opium, £1,500,000; and profit on railways, £17,500,000; against which, on the expenditure side, a sum of £7,250,000 appears for interest on capital expenditure. The revenue of the Presidency of Madras for the same year amounted to, roughly, £5,000,000, after paying to the Government of India the whole of the revenue derived from Customs, salt, and profit on railways, together with £4,000,000—half the revenue derived from land revenue, stamp, excise, and assessed taxes. It will thus be seen that the Government of India's finances in prosperous times get the whole benefit of increases in some of the most important sources of revenue, and half the benefit of increases in four-fifths of the sources of revenue of the Provincial Government. It thus happens that frequently while the Provincial Governments are doing little more than making their budgets balance, the Government of India enjoys large surpluses. These latter are not, as a rule, utilized in reducing taxation, as they cannot safely be counted on as permanent. They are therefore treated more in the way of windfalls, and distributed for special purposes. A portion goes in the reduction of unproductive debt. Loans are not necessarily paid off, but capital expenditure on railways and irrigation is met in part out of revenue, which automatically reduces the amount of loans not represented by capital expenditure on reproductive works. In this manner the unproductive debt of the Government of India has been reduced to quite an insignificant figure: out of a total debt of £274,000,000 only £12,125,000 represent debt not covered by reproductive works. Then again, large grants are given to the Provincial Governments for non-recurring capital expenditure, and in this way in recent years Southern India has come in for considerable windfalls for education, sanitation, and similar purposes. Nor does the Government of India restrict its special contributions to Provincial Governments, but when times are prosperous large grants are sometimes given to such bodies as Port Trusts, Municipalities, and City Improvement Trusts. Though Southern India cannot rejoice in having received all she could comfortably spend on urgent projects, nevertheless she cannot complain of having been entirely left out in the cold.

The Provincial Governments have no borrowing powers, and in consequence their budgets seldom show an item of interest, unless it is on the receipt side. All borrowing for productive works, such as railways and irrigation, is undertaken by the Imperial Government. Important projects, after approval by the Government of India, are placed on the Imperial programme, but a place there does not mean that the work will be undertaken in the near future, as the last on the programme may be the first to be constructed, and vice versa. In consequence the Provincial Governments have to be constantly on the watch and insistent on their needs, or their projects, however necessary and promising they may be, are likely to be overlooked. In recent years Southern India has not been well favoured, but signs are not wanting that the needs of the Presidency are now to be more favourably considered.

The system of Imperial borrowing for local works has no doubt some advantages, but it is hoped the time will soon arrive when Presidency Governments will be given power to encourage their own capitalists to subscribe to the issue of local loans. Indirectly they already have this power, as will be explained shortly. What is required is a forward policy with an extension of borrowing powers, and it is pleasing to be able to record that it is evident that the local Government is fully alive to this, and is embarking on several important railway and harbour construction schemes.

The general scheme of local Government finance having now been outlined, the finances of Municipalities and Local Boards will be touched upon. It has been mentioned that although local Governments have no direct borrowing powers, indirectly they have. This power is derived through the Local Authorities' Loans Act, which enabled municipal bodies and district boards, with the sanction of the local Government, to raise loans on the security of their revenues, but, with the exception of the Madras Corporation, local bodies have not attempted to raise funds in this manner to any appreciable extent. The reason for this is not far to seek—at least so far as municipalities are concerned. In the first place, capital in Southern India is not over-plentiful, and, owing largely to ancient customs and laws of inheritance, whereby wives and daughters cannot be beneficiaries under a will, nor inherit any portion of the family property, whether real or otherwise, savings to a considerable extent is expended in jewels for the ladies of the household, by which means alone they can be provided for. Secondly, there are few municipalities whose revenues and credit are sufficiently strong to enable them to float loans in the open market, and even the larger ones do not raise funds in this manner, and will never attempt it so long as the local Governments pursue their present policy. For as the Imperial Government out of its surpluses makes grants to local Governments and large public bodies, so do the local Governments make advances to smaller municipalities, lending the balance required for any particular work at 4 per cent. No municipality will attempt to float a public loan at 5 per cent., the lowest rate at which they could borrow in the open market, when, by waiting their turn, they can get the money from Government at 4 per cent.

Even the Corporation of Madras, with a revenue approaching £200,000, is unable to float loans in the open market to cover all its requirements, and it has to look to the Imperial Government for grants and to the local Government for advances and loans. Out of the total debt of £650,000, about one-third represents loans from Government. Here, again, it is largely a matter of rates, as if it cannot borrow in the open market at 4 per cent. it naturally applies to the Government.

To turn now to the other important local bodies—the District Boards. One of their principal spheres of action is the upkeep and construction of ways of communication. In recent years many of them have imposed upon themselves a special tax to form a fund to build railways, and in many instances the accumulation of this tax has reached a considerable figure, but it is obvious that to collect out of the income of a small cess sufficient capital to construct even a short line means many years of weary waiting. To obviate this arrangements are now being made to float loans bearing 4½ per cent. interest, and it is probable that in the near future many much-needed railways will be under construction. A better security than these railway loans would be hard to find, for the cess alone will in most cases cover the whole interest and go far towards creating a sinking fund, leaving out of consideration the annual profit of the lines, which in most cases will bring in from 4 to 5 per cent. as soon as they are opened.

In Southern India there is only one Port Trust, namely, that of Madras, and the authorities have in recent years been pursuing a forward policy, and, for its size, the harbour is now one of the most up to date in India. Financially it is in a sound position, but the Trust so far has had no occasion to come to the open market for loans, all capital requirements having been provided for by loans and grants from the Imperial and local Governments.

With regard to the finances of the Native States of Southern India, all that need be mentioned here is the fact that they are in a flourishing condition. They have good cash balances and invested reserves. Three of them have built good railways out of surplus revenues, and are now building others, while the remaining State is about to build one out of its reserve funds. Only one State has any debt, and that is covered many times over by capital expenditure on reproductive work.

There remains for consideration the general financing of trade. The total seaborne foreign trade of Southern India amounts to about £30,000,000, of which about £12,000,000 represent the value of imports and £18,000,000 the value of exports. The capital for this trade, and for that trade of the inland portions of the country, is provided for by the Bank of Madras (the Presidency bank), the branches of three large English exchange banks, and one French exchange bank. In addition, a large amount of trade is financed by the Natta-Cotta Chetties, a large, wealthy, and influential class of hereditary bankers and commercial men, and also by the *shroffs*, the private Indian bankers of Northern India. There are also a few small joint-stock banks under Indian management, and in recent years Co-operative Credit Societies have been doing good work, and, with careful management, should have a great future before them.

The whole system of finance in India, however, requires reorganization, as, in the relations between the Secretary of State in London and the Imperial Government, between the Imperial and local Governments, between all three and the banks, and even between the banks themselves, there is a lamentable loss of power due to lack of co-operation and co-ordination. At a time when there have been large balances in the hands of the Secretary of State which with great difficulty found employment in London at low rates of interest, considerable amounts locked up in boxes in the reserve treasuries in India have been lying idle, earning no interest, unnecessarily large coin reserves in paper currency have been held, and during this period there has been a bank-rate in India of 8 per cent., and sound proposals have had to be refused. The remedy would appear to be the formation of a Central Bank by the amalgamation of the three Presidency Banks of Bengal, Bombay, and Madras. Such a bank, with the whole resources of the Government of India under its control, and the paper currency under its management, would be an important factor in international finance, and it could extend facilities throughout the whole of India, which in many important centres are at the present day entirely lacking.

THE BANK OF MADRAS.

1. The Bank of Madras. 2. Interior.

THE CHARTERED BANK OF INDIA, AUSTRALIA, AND CHINA.

1. THE CHARTERED BANK OF INDIA, AUSTRALIA, AND CHINA, MADRAS. 2. BANKING HALL.

THE BANK OF MADRAS

The statements and balance-sheets issued from time to time by the directors of the Bank of Madras show that steady progress has been made since its establishment on July 1, 1843, when it was incorporated by charter under Act IX of that year.

The Bank has its head office in Madras and it has branches in the following towns: Alleppey, Bangalore, Bimlipatam, Calicut, Cocanada, Cochin, Coimbatore, Colombo (Ceylon), Guntur, Mangalore, Masulipatam, Negapatam, Ootacamund, Tellicherry, and Tuticorin. In addition to its ordinary banking business it conducts the general banking business of the Government, and it also manages the Public Debt at Madras.

The original capital was Rs. 30,00,000 divided into 3,000 shares of Rs. 1,000 each. The Government held shares in the Bank until 1876, when the Presidency Banks' Act (Act XI) was passed. This Act provided for the Bank taking over at a premium the Government holding; the capital was at the same time fixed at Rs. 50,00,000, with power to increase to Rs. 1,20,00,000, and the denomination of the shares was changed to Rs. 500. The capital has since been twice increased, in 1899 by Rs. 10,00,000, and in 1912 by Rs. 15,00,000, bringing it up to its present figure of Rs. 75,00,000. On both occasions the new shares were issued at a premium of Rs. 500, and this premium was added to the reserve fund. In 1876 (when the Government parted with its shares) the reserve fund stood at Rs. 4,31,250. Large sums have since been added to this fund out of profits, and these amounts, together with the premium on the new shares, have brought the reserve fund up to its present figure of Rs. 74,00,000—a sum practically equal to the Bank's capital.

Under the original charter the bank had the power to issue currency notes, but this privilege was withdrawn by Act XIX of 1861 which vested the monopoly of paper currency in the Government. The Government Treasury was, however, then transferred to the Bank, and the management of the Public Debt at Madras followed in 1867.

During the first ten years of the Bank's working, the dividends averaged 6·29 per cent. For the ten years 1854 to 1863 the average had risen to 8·07 per cent., and, with the exception of a slight setback for the period 1874 to 1883, when the average was 7·40 per cent., the average had risen steadily to 12 per cent. for the five years ended December 31st last.

A pension and gratuity fund for the officers' staff was formed in 1878, and a similar fund for the subordinates in 1889. These funds were amalgamated in 1907. To this fund employees contribute 5 per cent. of their salaries, and the Bank contributes an equivalent amount, and further subsidizes the fund from time to time as occasion requires.

Detailed statements of the Bank's business need not be given here, but a comparison may be made between the years 1893 and 1913 in order to show the growth which has taken place during that period.

Twenty years ago the capital was Rs. 50,00,000; the amount is now Rs. 75,00,000; the reserve fund figures are Rs. 14,50,000 and Rs. 74,00,000 respectively; and the percentage of dividend and bonus has increased from Rs. 9 to Rs. 12. In this period the deposits of the Bank have increased from Rs. 3,28,00,000 to Rs. 8,92,00,000, and trade investments from Rs. 2,06,00,000 to Rs. 6,90,00,000.

The head office is a handsome brick and stone building; it is airy and bright in appearance, and it has exceptionally fine quarters for a number of resident officials.

The directors are: The Honourable Mr. A. D. Jackson, President; Sir Hugh Fraser, Vice-President; Messrs. Gordon Fraser, W. O. David, A. J. Leech, H. P. M. Rae, and C. B. Simpson.

THE CHARTERED BANK OF INDIA, AUSTRALIA, AND CHINA

This bank occupies one of the most desirable business sites in Madras, as it is situated at the corner of the Esplanade and Armenian Street, a position which is the centre of the offices of the leading mercantile firms, is immediately opposite the High Court, and is within 300 yards of the Beach station, the city terminus of the South Indian Railway system. The handsome building—the interior of which resembles a church in appearance—was erected in 1871, but the company did not open it as a branch establishment until the year 1900.

Exchange and general banking business is transacted at the head office in London, and at the following agencies and branches, namely: Amritsar, Bangkok, Batavia, Calcutta, Canton, Cebu, Colombo, Delhi, Foochow, Hankow, Hong Kong, Ilo-ilo, Ipoh, Karachi, Klang, Kobe, Kuala Lumpur, Madras, Malacca, Manila, Medan, New York, Penang, Puket, Rangoon, Saigon, Seremban, Shanghai, Singapore, Sourabaya, Taiping, Tientsin, and Yokohama.

One of the beneficial results of the federation of the Australian States was the impetus which was given to commercial enterprise between that continent and the Far East, and the directors of the bank, alert with regard to the interests of shareholders, forthwith arranged facilities of a special character for the transaction of business. Correspondents have been appointed at all the principal business centres throughout the world where there is not a separate branch or agency. The bank was incorporated by Royal Charter in 1853, with head offices at 38 Bishopsgate, London, E.C.

The following particulars are extracted from the annual report of the directors, and from the balance-sheet for the year ending 31st December, 1913, which were presented at the sixtieth ordinary general meeting of shareholders on the 18th March, 1914.

An exceedingly satisfactory statement of accounts showed that, after providing for bad and doubtful debts, a net profit of £483,253 11s. 9d., inclusive of £132,569 10s. 9d. brought forward from the previous year, had been made. An interim dividend at the rate of 14 per cent. and a bonus to the staff had absorbed £108,000, and out of the amount then available for distribution the directors proposed to pay a final dividend of 14 per cent., together with a bonus of 12s. a share; to add £100,000 to the reserve fund; to increase the officers' superannuation fund by £10,000; to write off the premises account a sum of £25,000; and to carry forward a balance of £120,253 11s. 9d.

The capital of the company is £1,200,000, made up of 60,000 fully paid shares of £20 each; the reserve fund stands at £1,800,000, and the reserve liability of shareholders is £1,200,000. The Court of Directors consists of Sir Montagu Cornish Turner (Chairman), Sir Henry S. Sunningham, K.C.I.E., Mr. Thomas Cutherbertson, Sir Alfred Dent, K.C.M.G., Mr. William Henry Melville Goschen, the Right Hon. Lord George Hamilton, G.C.S.I., Mr. William Foot Mitchell, and Mr. Lewis Alexander Wallace. The managers are Messrs.

THE NATIONAL BANK OF INDIA, LTD.

New Premises in course of erection for the National Bank of India, Ltd., Madras.

T. H. Whitehead and T. Fraser, while Mr. W. E. Preston is sub-manager.

The bankers of the company are: The Bank of England, the London City and Midland Bank, Ltd., the London County and Westminster Bank, Ltd., the National Provincial Bank of England, Ltd., and the National Bank of Scotland, Ltd.

THE NATIONAL BANK OF INDIA, LTD.

This bank was originally established in Calcutta on the 29th September, 1863, as the "Calcutta City Banking Corporation, Ltd.," the name being altered to the National Bank of India, Ltd., on the 2nd March, 1864. A branch was opened at Madras in the year 1877, and there are now others at Bombay, Karachi, Amritsar, Lahore, Cawnpore, Delhi, Chittagong, Tuticorin, and Cochin, in India; at Colombo, Kandy, and Newera Eliya in Ceylon; at Rangoon and Mandalay in Burma; at Aden and Steamer Point, Aden, in Arabia; at Zanzibar, Mombasa, Nairobi, Entebbe, Kampala, Nakuru, Kisurner, and Jinja, in Africa. Interest is allowed at the rate of £2 per cent. per annum on the daily balances of current deposit accounts up to Rs. 1,00,000, but no interest is allowed on total credits of less than Rs. 1,000. Fixed deposits are received upon favourable terms, which may be ascertained on application at any of the offices. General banking business connected with India and England is conducted; interest, dividends, salaries, and pensions are collected; and the safe custody of valuable documents is undertaken. Indian Government securities, stocks, and shares are purchased or sold, and bills payable in Europe, Africa, America, Australia, India, Burma, and Ceylon, are negotiated or collected. Drafts are granted at the exchange of the day on the bank's London office, 26 Bishopsgate Street, E.C., and on its branches and agencies, and, when required, the first of exchange will be forwarded direct to the payee, free of charge. The bankers of the company in Great Britain are the Bank of England, the National Provincial Bank of England, Ltd., and the National Bank of Scotland, Ltd. The premises in which the business of the bank is now carried on in Madras, on the North Beach Road, are being vacated (1915) in favour of a very fine double-storied new building situated in the same road and within a stone's-throw of the High Court of Justice. The main portion of the structure is built of well-made bricks and stone; it has a frontage of 150 ft., a depth of 130 ft., and a height of 60 ft., and it is ornamented with beautifully designed domes, which tower up to 94 ft., while the whole of the front is of locally obtained granite. Upon entering the building, customers will be ushered into a spacious and handsomely furnished banking hall, and on either hand will be found equally well-fitted rooms for the manager and other principal officials The upper story is surrounded by a gallery, and the interior will contain apartments for assistants, together with dining and other rooms.

The ninety-fifth report of the directors (together with a statement of accounts to the 31st December, 1914) was submitted to the shareholders at the annual meeting in London on the 23rd March, 1915, and notwithstanding the crippling effect upon commerce caused by the European War, the very satisfactory position of the bank

BANQUE DE L'INDO-CHINE.

1. Front View of new Building in course of Construction. 2. Side View. 3. The Bank. 4. Private Residence—"Le Petit Banque."

was shown by the fact that the net profits for the previous year, after providing for bad and doubtful debts, amounted to £347,995 13s. 4d., inclusive of a balance brought forward of £78,625 2s. An *ad interim* dividend, at the rate of 12 per cent. per annum, free of income tax, and amounting to £60,000, had been paid for the half-year ending on the 30th June, 1914, and the directors then recommended a further dividend at the rate of 16 per cent. per annum, and a bonus of 2 per cent., making 16 per cent. for the whole year. They further proposed to add £75,000 to the Reserve Fund, raising it to £1,175,000; to write off £10,000 from the House Property Account, and to place £10,000 to the Officers' Pension Fund, leaving a balance of £92,995 13s. 4d. to be carried forward. The amount of the subscribed capital is £2,000,000, of which the sum of £1,000,000 has been paid up by 1,231 shareholders.

The Board of Directors consists of Mr. Robert Campbell, chairman; Mr. Robert Williamson, deputy chairman; and Mr. A. V. Dunlop-Best, Sir John P. Hewett, G.C.S.I., C.I.E., Messrs. Robert Miller, Alfred Simson, J. N. Stuart, and J. A. Toomey. The manager in Madras is Mr. W. Ross Munro.

BANQUE DE L'INDO-CHINE

This limited liability banking company was incorporated in France by charter according to decrees passed respectively on the 21st of January, 1875, the 20th of February, 1888, and the 16th of May, 1900. The head office is in Paris, at No. 15 bis Rue Lafitte, and is under the management of MM. Stanislaus Simon, managing director, and R. Thion de la Chaume, director. The bank has branches in Indo-China and the Far East, and also in French colonies in Asia and elsewhere. Those in French territory are at Djibutil, in French Somaliland; Pondicherry, in India; Saigon, Pnom Penh, and Battambang, in Cochin China and Cambodia; Haiphong, Tourane, and Hanoi, in Tonking and Annam; Noumea, in New Caledonia; Papeete, in Tahiti; while those in the Straits and China are Singapore, in the Straits Settlements; Bangkok, in Siam; Mongtze, in Yunnan; and at Hongkong, Canton, Shanghai, Hankow, Tientsin, and Peking. The Pondicherry branch is one of the oldest, having been established in 1876 by MM. Gauthier and Stanislaus Simon. A large building of very fine architectural design is now in course of construction, and the directors hope to remove to the new premises in the early part of 1915.

The bank has an important note issue in the French colonies in which its agencies are entrusted with State and Government business.

Elsewhere, but chiefly in China, it is one of the principal exchange banks in the Far East, competing keenly with other institutions such as the Hongkong and Shanghai Banking Corporation, the Chartered Bank of India, Australia, and China; the Russo-Asiatic Bank, the Deutsch Asiatic Bank, and the Netherlands Trading Society. The Banque de l'Indo-Chine was one of the five banks of the well-known Consortium in Peking (where it represents French interests) which financed China before and after the recent revolution in that country.

The business of the Bank of India is limited to French territory, where it has during the last few years financed most of the export trade. It has sub-agencies for this purpose around Pondicherry, in Valavanur, and Tindivanam, and on the coast at Cuddalore, Porto Novo, and Negapatam. The exports consist principally of ground nuts, which are consigned to Marseilles, and occasionally to Trieste, Nantes, and Dunkirk. In order to provide storage for nuts prior to shipment the bank has constructed several large buildings, which are now known as Chamber of Commerce godowns; but with the view of facilitating warehousing, it is realized that further accommodation will be necessary in the near future.

The latest financial statement of the bank issued to the shareholders on May 13, 1914, showed that the total note issue amounted to 90,000,000 francs (about £3,750,000). The capital of the company was 48,000,000 francs (£1,920,000), and the reserves reached a sum of 45,000,000 francs (£1,800,000).

1. CHALKING THE DOORSTEPS.

2. PAINTED COTTON HANGING.
Pattern from Kalahasti. Used for decorating temple cars.

3. EXAMPLE OF FINE WEAVING.
Gold thread and silk.

ARTS AND CRAFTS

By W. S. HADAWAY, School of Arts, Madras.

AN account of the artistic activities of Southern India to be at all adequate must necessarily treat of the temple and its appurtenances as the objects of greatest importance. Not only does the temple dominate by its size every landscape in which it occurs, but its importance in the life of the people is greater than that of any other single institution. Almost all of the best of the art of Southern India has some religious significance, whether it be connected actually with a temple, or with domestic architecture or utensils, or the life of the people generally.

It is all art with a purpose, from the *kolam*, a decorative arrangement of white powder, drawn in lines on the ground in front of a doorway, and renewed daily, as an attraction to good spirits to enter the doorway, to the elaborate and highly-wrought temple architecture which forms a fitting place for the abode of the gods. The sole exceptions, perhaps, to this rule that South Indian art is solely hieratic may be found in a few articles of personal jewellery and in some of the paintings of the Tanjore School, which confined itself at first to portraiture of the rajahs and Court attendants of the Mahratta kings, but this is of a later date than the truly indigenous art of the country.

The Hindu temple consists in its simplest form of a rectangular walled enclosure, with a gate, or *gopuram*, in the centre of each wall, facing north, south, east, and west. This walled enclosure may be elaborated, as at the great Vishnu temple at Srirangam, near Trichinopoly, which has seven enclosing walls and fifteen *gopurams*, the outside walls measuring about 3,000 by 2,500 ft. . The evolution of the temple has been, more frequently than not, that some shrine of not very great architectural pretensions has acquired a deep religious importance, and various buildings have been erected around it, each perhaps larger and more elaborate than the previous ones, until finally a magnificent wall and huge gateways enclose the whole. The result, architecturally, from the Western point of view, is more often than not very disappointing.

Among the larger temples only one, that of Tanjore, is built with one architectural feature leading to another of greater importance, and finally culminating in the shrine of *Vimana* itself. It is, perhaps, for this reason that, apart from other interesting features, this temple is considered by many Europeans to be the most generally pleasing of any in Southern India.

SOUTHERN INDIA

The age, the construction, and the style of temple architecture have been very fully discussed in a great variety of publications and guide-books, and it is perhaps unnecessary to enter into these details again. Mention may be made, however, of certain examples as conspicuous in some detail from the artistic point of view, and, beginning with the oldest examples, among the most interesting temples are the rock-cut "raths" at Seven Pagodas, about 35 miles south of Madras. This well-known group of small temples and other works of art, bas-reliefs, and carved caves, is hewn out of solid monoliths—an easy and straightforward method of "building" with no thought of transport to worry the artisans. Considered artistically, the separate buildings and reliefs are much simpler and infinitely more grand in manner than later work, and single figures here and there are worthy of the closest study. Scattered as they are they can only be considered individually, except for the group of five together, which are evidently carved from either a protruding ridge of rock or from a line of separate boulders. The artisans who fashioned these marvellous works simply carved where the stone was found available, and there is no architectural whole or any group effect to be got. The raths themselves vary in size, the largest being about 50 ft. by 25 ft., while the largest of the bas-reliefs, called "Arjuna's Penance"—which is carved in the face of two great rocks—measures 96 ft. by 43 ft.

At several places in the Presidency many other old rock-cut temples are to be found, notably the one at Kalugumalai, in the Tinnevelly district, which has much beautiful detail. Even earlier than the rock temples at Mahabalipuram (Seven Pagodas) are the remains of the Buddhist Stupa, near Dharanikota, in the Guntur district, known as the Amaravati Stupa. The best of these sculptures have been removed and placed either in the British or the Madras Museums. In most of the great temples still in use both early and late architectural detail may be found.

As with the cathedrals of Europe, so these temples have been started in a small way in many instances, and by additions at different periods have finally assumed the size and proportions that we now see. The work still progresses in some places, especially where Nattukottai Chettys are numerous, as in the country around Madura. Here may still be seen important building operations being carried out in almost exactly the same way that the great cathedral builders of Europe employed—that is, without previously drawn architectural plans, elevations, and estimates, but with a master builder in charge of the work, and developing it and elaborating as the building progresses: the only way in which a living architecture is possible. Just because the old hereditary systems are still in constant and practical daily use among Hindus, their buildings are still living and vital things, instinct with life, and still in the vast process of evolution.

Nearly all of the large and important temples are easily accessible, and though in a short account only the more prominent features of the separate ones can be mentioned, to those who are sufficiently interested in the subject almost any single example will provide enough of detail to occupy one's close attention for a considerable time.

The great temples are to be found chiefly to the south or south-west of Madras, the nearest of importance being at Conjeeveram, which boasts of several important examples. The most conspicuous is the Siva temple, though the smaller one, dedicated to Vishnu, at Little Conjeeveram, has some wonderful carving in its hundred-pillared *mantapam.* Besides these two Hindu temples, at a small village called Tiruparattikundram, near by, is an interesting Jain temple well worthy of a visit. Mention should be made of the temple at Tiruvannamalai, where the group enclosed within the walls, situated at the foot of a great hill, is most picturesque; and the small shrine, dedicated to Ganesa, is perhaps the finest of the buildings within the enclosure. Directly north of Tiruvannamalai, and to the west of Madras, the temple of Vellore Fort is famous for its magnificent carving, the detail of which is unsurpassed by that of any other in South India. Near the coast, and about 159 miles south of Madras, is the town of Chidambaram, which contains a very typical large temple, the premises covering an enclosure of about 40 acres. Within the walls are a great variety of buildings, including the hall of a thousand columns, an enclosed tank, the coach-house for the vehicles of the gods, and temples to Lakshmi, Vishnu, Siva, and Parvati, in addition to colossal figures of Nandi (Siva's bull), resting-places for pilgrims, and *mantapams,* while a tank with an adjacent *gopuram* are, together, a very beautiful group. There is a Siva temple at Tiruvallur which exhibits most of the defects of architectural arrangement which have called forth the ire of various European critics, while at Tanjore the only example of a large temple in which the shrine is the most important building, as mentioned above, is to be found. Before reaching Tanjore the many temples of Kumbakonam will prove of considerable interest, though none are particularly fine examples.

Tanjore is the one town which is perhaps more visited by sightseers than any other in the whole of Southern India, but the temple is neither of great beauty, nor is it at all typical of the style as a whole. To one side of the principal *vimana* is a small but most delicately worked shrine, dedicated to Subrahmania, and this alone is, from the artistic point of view, one of the greatest treasures to be found among examples of decorative architecture in Southern India.

Westward from Tanjore is Trichinopoly with its dominating temple on the great rock, but there is little of architectural interest in it, although the construction and the utilization of the rock as a site are remarkable.

A few miles from Trichinopoly, on an island in the Cauvery, is Srirangam, with its huge enclosures, containing a very fair-sized town in its outer precincts. The decorative details of the various temple buildings are inferior to those of Chidambaram, Vellore, or Madura, but the smaller Siva temple, half a mile or so to the east, is architecturally finer than the great Vishnu temple. West of Trichinopoly and not far from Coimbatore is an important temple at Peroor, while southward, at Madura, Tinnevelly, and Rameswaram, are also fine examples of architecture. The tank at Madura is an interesting and beautiful example of this detail of temple architecture, and the building just outside the temple, known as Tirumal Naik's choultry, contains remarkable specimens of carved supporting columns.

Rameswaram temple, situated on the island of the same name, a part of the connecting link of islands between India and Ceylon, called Adam's Bridge, is in many ways the most remarkable of any of the South Indian temples. The great corridors, which extend to about 4,000 ft., are its most striking feature, and the largest single one, of 690 ft., is unequalled in size and effect by any other building in the world. Even the nave of St. Peter's in Rome is but 600 ft. from the

1. PRINTED COTTON CURTAIN.
Pattern from Masulipatam.

2. CARPET.
An old pattern of silk carpet made at Ayyampet.

3. RAJAH SIVAJI OF TANJORE, WITH TWO COURTIERS.
An example of the Tanjore School of Painting, size 30 in. by 24 in.

4. ORNAMENTS WORN BY SYRIAN CHRISTIANS IN COCHIN STATE.

5. SOUTH INDIAN SILVER JEWELLERY.

1. CAST METAL ENDS FOR A "KAVADI" (YOKE).

2. AN ELEPHANT AND GROUP OF FIGURES BUILT OF BRICKS, TERRA-COTTA, AND STUCCO.

3. A FESTIVAL CAR.
Photo by Nicholas & Co.

4. REPRESENTATION IN MARBLE OF A "STUPA," OR "DAGOBA."
From the ruined Buddhist *stupa* at Amaravati, Gunter district, and believed to actually represent that *stupa*.

door to the apse, and a much greater effect of distance is obtained at Rameswaram on account of its roof being comparatively lower.

Hindu architecture of religious and secular character is a very complicated and extraordinary combination of well-established artistic canons, very little of which is as yet understood properly by Western people. Even the great stone temples strike one as of buildings not far removed from construction in wood, but that is partly because arches as supporting features find no place among Hindu architectural canons. The true stone arch, with its inevitable outward thrust, is to the Hindu builder a thing never at rest, "an arch never sleeps" being their manner of expressing its restlessness.

Copper images are enclosed within the temple shrines, and many of these are of great beauty. Europeans are seldom privileged to see these figures of deities, except when the image is taken in procession, and at that time it is so decorated with jewels and flowers that it is quite impossible to see its intrinsic beauty. From photographs, and from the few fine examples which have been found buried and thence found their way into public or private collections, a slight idea can be formed of the great artistic worth of some of the finer examples, and it may be added that nearly every temple can boast of a few at least of these statuettes, although the most venerated one will frequently be found to be artistically quite worthless.

Considerable study has been devoted to these images by artists and critics during the last few years, but as yet only the fringe of the subject has been touched; and no part of India is so rich in fine figures as the Madras Presidency, although without a large number of illustrations it would be impossible to give anything like an adequate idea of them.

The principal gods represented are Siva and Vishnu; their wives, Parvati, Lakshmi, and Bhudevi; while Siva's first son, Ganesa, is also very commonly found. Vishnu as Krishna and some of the Tamil saints are favourite subjects, but the list of names alone would only serve to confuse. When we consider that Siva alone is credited with 1,008 names, and that he is known by a different one in almost every place in which he has "appeared," some idea of the complexity of the Hindu iconographic art may be formed.

Siva, as he appeared as a dancing god, is commonly called "Nataraja" or "Natesa," and this figure offers a fine subject for the maker of his image. In the Government Museum at Madras there are two very fine examples of this appearance, but both of these have been written about and illustrated perhaps more than any other single example of South India art. Very similar in pose, though somewhat different in artistic conception from the Museum examples, is the one illustrated on p. 17. In this will be seen the delicacy and almost spider-like quality of the figure of the deity, posed, as is usual, dancing on the body of an *Asura*, or evil spirit; and the waving hair from which Siva's wife, Ganga, emerges, contributes much to the composition as a whole, its fine and delicate lines contrasting well with the mass of the head and body. The other illustration (Fig. 5 on p. 111) will help to show some of the variety of figures to be found in a single temple. In the top row the second and fourth figures are of Krishna, the centre one of Ganesa, while those at the ends represent two saints. In the lower row the second and third figures give an excellent example of the Hindu ideal for a figure of a goddess, the hips and breasts full and prominent, and the waist small. It may be noticed also that all limbs of the figure are smooth and tapering, without showing decided muscular development or accentuation of the bones and joints; another example of conformity with the Hindu canons of beauty.

It would be easy to multiply examples of fine images, and at the same time to show something of the extent to which art has developed in Madras, but without an account of other activities in what are usually, though erroneously, termed "minor arts," no adequate idea of the subject as a whole could be formed.

Next in importance to the temples among objects of Hindu architecture are the finer examples of secular buildings, and these are practically limited to dwellings, as, for instance, the palace or the less pretentious house. We find no great civil buildings, for all activities connected with the business of a city or a town took place in either the temple or the palace of a ruling rajah. The older remains of large palaces are but four in number, and all, though varying much in individual detail, show in some way—generally by the employment of arches—a picturesque mixture of Mussalman and Hindu architectural styles. The palace at Madura (now the judge's court) is the largest and most complete of any existing example, and its fine colonnades are massive and impressive, though outwardly it has no architectural beauty whatever. The Tanjore Palace, in some of its details reminiscent of Madura, has only an occasional part here and there whi h is worthy

1. BOX FOR CARRYING JEWELS AND BETEL.
Made of red lacquered wood and ornamented with brass

2. AN ELABORATE CAST BRASS LAMP.

of mention. The Chandragiri Palace alone has any pretensions to architectural beauty outwardly, and here we find an attempt—fairly successful—to realize in a single building a united whole. The scattered details now remaining of the Vizayanagar Palace buildings are interesting and picturesque in their mixture of Saracenic cusped arches and Hindu roofing, but we cannot form an adequate idea of their unity as originally constructed.

The finest examples of South Indian artistic activity in domestic buildings is undoubtedly to be found in the few, now fast disappearing, old houses in some of the larger towns; but here again, outwardly, they may have no claim to our attention. The old Hindu house is planned in a most practical manner, considering the life and customs of its occupants.

In town houses a *pial*, or raised verandah, which is approached by a few steps from the ground, is found in the front, and at each end of the *pial*, or at each side of the doorway, are raised seats, which are generally sufficient in length for a person to lie down upon, while the verandah roof is supported by a series of wooden pillars and rafters which are often most elaborately and beautifully carved. This open verandah forms a convenient place for visitors or attendants who, from caste or other reasons, are not admitted into the house itself. The entrance doorway, particularly the framing posts and lintel, are, even in quite unpretentious houses, most wonderfully carved, the lintel generally having a figure of Lakshmi with her attendant elephants, or a *lingam* worked into the design. The door shutters, as a rule, are massive, and ornamented with great brass bosses, and often with fine carvings also, but in many houses the carved doorway may be the sole attempt at decorative detail to be found.

Passing through the doorway of a well-built house, a short passage, with a room on either side, leads into an open courtyard, generally uncovered, and admitting light and air. This is paved and drained, and surrounded by pillars with carved shafts and capitals, and the ceiling beams and doorways leading from the surrounding colonnade may be ornamental in an elaborate manner. The house has one upper story, and a colonnade similar to that on the ground floor surrounds the courtyard below, and this also has elaborately carved pillars, capitals, and beams—in fact, the entire decoration of the inside of the building is confined to the constructional work alone. Sufficient ornamentation is given to the walls by carved doorways, and niches here and there for a lamp are fashioned in the thickness of the wall brickwork.

Beyond the first courtyard there may be others in good-sized houses, and perhaps a small enclosed garden, while a well is found in the majority of the yards. The rooms used by the occupants are small, and generally contain no furniture beyond, perhaps, a fine chest or cots for sleeping purposes The Hindu, unless he be much modernized and affected by Western civilization, does not require tables, chairs, cupboards, or any of the usual furniture of Western houses. A sleeping-mat, or perhaps a cot, a chest of some sort, and cooking utensils comprise the necessary furniture. Occasionally very beautifully worked three-legged stools used in marriage ceremonies may be found, and huge brass lamps, with accommodation for as many as two hundred wicks, are used. If one understands the lack of decoration in the houses of Hindu people so far as walls and furniture are concerned, it is easier to comprehend the very great elaboration of the articles and utensils of every-day use, such as jewellery, wearing apparel, caskets, metal lamps, and trays, and the infinite variety of pots and vessels used in household worship. In houses with no furniture and no patterned walls, objects of great elaboration of detail, in which there are frequently no undecorated spaces whatever, are not out of place, while the same object as a part of the furnishing of a Western house might quite rightly be condemned as over-decorated. It is only fair to judge of Indian wares as being made for the real and genuine use of Indian people in their proper surroundings.

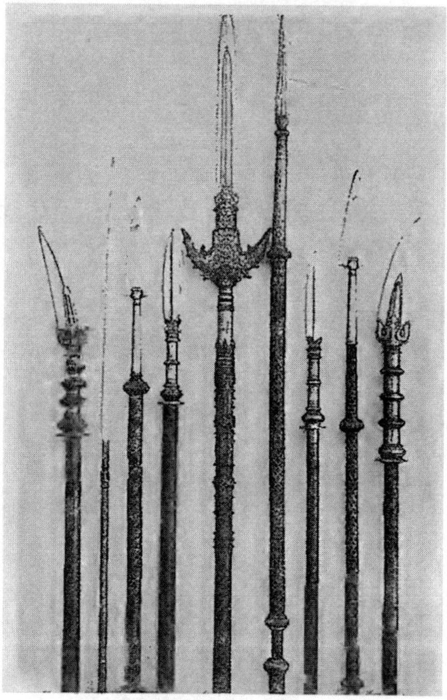

GROUP OF WEAPONS.
Showing elaborate steel and copper work.

The term "minor arts" is a useful and convenient manner of expressing such applied arts as those which go to the fashioning of an article of jewellery, but it is a misnomer, for a small casket, a necklace, or almost any decorated object may be just as truly a "work of art" as a picture or a statue. The separation of the arts into "applied" and "fine" is also wrong, for here again the meaning is obscure.

Architecture is generally regarded as a "fine" art, but there could be no more misleading term used with such an application, architecture being a combination of many arts, such as sculpture and carving applied to the decoration, in addition to the planning and construction of a building. The result may be "fine art" or it may not; but it certainly is the greatest effort of applied art. The only sensible distinction which it seems possible to make is to separate picture-painting and sculpture (not definitely intended for any special place, use, or purpose) from those same arts which are definitely used to bring about an end in the decoration of a certain object or to be used in a specific manner. Considered in this light there is nothing to be found in South Indian art which is other than applied, with the single exception of the smaller paintings of the Tanjore School, which are to be seen as wall decorations in various houses and palaces. All the South Indian sculptural art is definitely designed for beautifying purposes, as in the masses of carvings which cover temple buildings or in the copper images which are made to be worshipped.

This somewhat lengthy explanation is necessary in the present account, for it would be useless to look for or to expect to find any examples of "art for art's sake," as in the best hereditary art of South India such work is not to be found. An object which is made for no particular purpose except to proclaim itself as a beautiful thing—a thing to give pleasure

1. SVAMI AND AMMAN, THUYAGARAJA TEMPLE, TIRUVOTTIYUR.
2. BRONZE IMAGES OF SUBRAHMANIA, WITH VALLIAMMAN AND DEVAYANI, TIRUVOTTIYUR.
3. TREASURE-TROVE CASE-IDOL OF KALINHIMARDHANA OF SRI KRISHNA, KATTU EDAYAR.
4. SHANMUKHA IMAGE.
5. GROUP OF CAST COPPER FIGURES.

merely by its intrinsic beauty alone—is not understood.

Of the greatest importance next to building and architecture, the art of weaving may claim attention, but nowadays, with the changing fashion in women's clothing, many foreign influences have been brought to bear on the patterns employed. While the form of a woman's cloth (which is merely one long strip of 7 or 8 yards in length by little more than a yard in width) has not changed, the patterns used to decorate its ends and borders are new, in the best cloths generally borrowed from the arts of the north of India. All the more elaborate woven cloths of gold thread and silk aim more or less to imitate the cloths which come from Benares, and it is only in common cloths or in old examples that indigenous South Indian woven patterns are to be found. Some of these are of remarkable beauty, both in colour and arrangement of warp and woof threads.

Carpet weaving as an industry is now almost lifeless, but even in quite recent times most charming specimens of both silk and wool were made in patterns which borrowed nothing from northern examples. The silk carpet from Ayyampet, shown in the illustration on p. 105, is a very characteristic example.

In the domain of metal work the South Indian artisan is not to be surpassed by any other workman in the world, either in clever manipulation or in the proper use of the metal itself, casting being a very favourite and much-used process. In jewellery and silver work, too, much of the work may on superficial examination appear somewhat barbaric to Western eyes. There is very beautiful work to be found both among old and modern examples.

Of lacquer work, applied to objects such as trays and shields, boxes and cots, there are two distinct varieties practised in the Presidency. The "Kurnool" lacquer is produced by first building up the pattern with gesso, and it is then gilded and coloured and finally covered with lac in solution, like a thick varnish. The Malabar lacquer work is done by another and better process. The object to be decorated is first coated with a ground colour, generally pure vermilion, though yellow is sometimes used, and the pattern, which consists of lines and scrolls, is painted on, the surface being then gently heated and a flake of carefully purified lacquer placed upon it. This is again heated and rubbed until smooth with a bit of palm leaf, and the result is a fine permanent shiny surface, capable of withstanding much wear.

It is quite impossible to give an adequate idea of all South Indian arts in a limited space, and no mention has yet been made of various other artistic industries, such as the carving of sandalwood and ivory, ornamented arms, and various other works. We can only say that for a people, the great majority of whom depend upon agriculture for a living, there is an astonishing variety of decorative arts practised, but the best examples are seldom found easily, and consequently the usual criticism of them is both ill-considered and unfair, and, withal, generally prejudiced and wrong.

There is much that is really great in South Indian art.

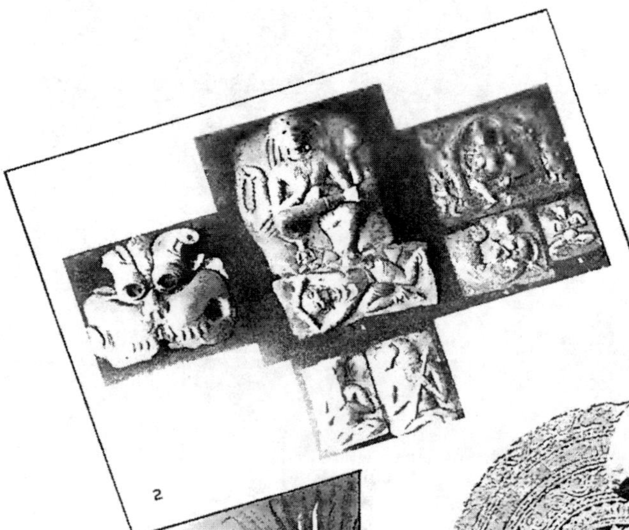

2

1

1. ORNAMENTAL SANDSTONE, HAMPI. 3. WOODEN CAR, NALLUR.

2. GOLD-PLATED COPPER PANELS FROM THE SRISAILAM TEMPLE, KURNOOL DISTRICT.

Presented to the temple in A.D. 1513 by Krishna Rajah, King of Vijayanagar.

RIPON BUILDINGS, MADRAS, BUILT BY P. LOGANATHA MUDALIAR.

Photo by Willie Burke.

THE CITY OF MADRAS AND ENVIRONS

THE city of Madras is an enigma to the stranger; on the landward side it is unpretentious, but when one approaches it from the sea the eye roams over extensive dock accommodation, behind which are warehouses and offices of the leading mercantile firms, the headquarters of institutions, the Supreme Court, Fort St. George, the Law College, and the fine building belonging to the Y.M.C.A., while in the far distance the golden-tipped domes of native temples and shrines are distinctly visible.

Madras is the capital of the Presidency of the same name, and it stretches along the Coromandel Coast for about nine miles, extending nearly three and a half miles inland, and the population was 518,660 at the census of 1911. It is almost perfectly flat, the highest portion being not more than about 25 ft. above sea-level. The absence of a system of proper sanitation is a crying evil, and unprintable words would be necessary to set forth a tithe of the justifiable grumblings of the inhabitants. Lakhs of rupees have been spent by the city fathers in providing a luxurious official home for themselves, but a hundredth part of that expenditure is grudged for the abolition of those death-dealing open drains which may be seen on each side of many of the principal thoroughfares. No wonder that there are periodical outbreaks of cholera, dysentery, and typhoid fever, and no wonder that many visitors describe the town as a place to leave—not to live in.

The native name of Madras is Chennapatnam, which was bestowed upon it by Darmala Venkadri in 1639, in memory of his father, Chennapatnam, at the time when he disposed of the site upon which the city now stands to Mr. Francis Day, the then chief of the settlement of Armagaon, of the East India Company, on the Coromandel Coast.

The climate cannot be said to be particularly unhealthy for Europeans who are careful and moderate in food and drink, but, as in the case of many other oriental cities, epidemics of cholera and small-pox still claim their toll. The mean temperature in the shade ranges between 77° and 92° F., while the extremes are about 65° in winter and 110° F. in June.

The earliest authentic account of municipal government mentions the appointment of watchmen and the imposition of a tax for scavenging purposes in the year 1678. The mayor and corporation assumed control of finance and public works in 1688, and regulations have been promulgated from time to time for the better administration of affairs. Municipal Acts were passed in 1856, 1865, 1867, 1871, 1878, 1884, and 1904, and it is under Act III of 1904 that the city is now governed.

The Corporation of Madras consists of a salaried President and of thirty-six honorary Commissioners, who are ap-

1. GOVERNMENT HOUSE, GUINDY. 2. MADRAS CLUB. 3. THE DOVE COT, MADRAS CLUB.

pointed as follows: Twenty are returned at divisional elections; three are selected by the Madras Chamber of Commerce and by the Madras Trades' Association respectively, and one each by the Harbour Trust and the railway authorities.

The annual income of the city from taxation is rather more than 17 lakhs of rupees, and this represents a yearly charge of Rs.3.5.9 for each individual. It cannot be said that this rate is excessive, and it is idle to suggest that it is sufficient for the upkeep of a city which is 27 square miles in extent.

Many of the streets are exceedingly narrow; a large percentage have no footpaths; several have no other artificial light than that which is given by shops; while very few are lighted by electricity. The refuse accumulators which one sees at intervals in the streets are admirable breeding places for the germs of every fatal disease, and the filth which is allowed to remain in the streets is quite capable of producing an epidemic which might reduce the population by 40 to 50 per cent.

The Presidency of Fort St. George is the official designation of the Madras Presidency, and some particulars should be given here concerning the fortress from which the name has been derived. The fort is situated on the beach, within five minutes' walk from the General Post Office and other public buildings. It consisted, in 1639, of a factory and other premises, which were surrounded by a wall with a few bastions and batteries, but it was very considerably strengthened between the years 1670 and 1680, owing to the presence of the French in the neighbourhood, and on account of the encroachments of the sea. These precautions were not taken a moment too soon, as Dawood Khan blockaded it for three months in the year 1720. The fort was subsequently captured by the French under Labourdonnais, but when the English regained possession in 1743, they engaged some 4,000 labourers to enlarge and strengthen the fortifications, with the result that when the French forces returned in 1758 they found the place strong enough to resist their attacks. Further additions were made after this siege, and about thirty years later the fort was completed. It now (1914) has barrack accommodation for a large number of troops, and it is the headquarters of the Madras Artillery Volunteers (the Governor's Bodyguard), of the Madras Volunteer Guards, and of the 1st Madras and Southern Mahratta Railway Rifles, a detachment of the 86th Infantry, the 67th, 68th, 69th, and 70th Half Corps, A.T. bullocks, and one troop 31st Mule Corps. Within the walls are some of the Government offices—the Council Chamber and Secretariat being among the number—and the Arsenal, which contains a large number of trophies of the wars in which the original Madras Army was engaged.

2

1. THE LAW COURTS, MADRAS.   2. THE LAW COURTS FROM THE Y.M.C.A. BUILDING.

Mount Road is the Regent Street of Madras, and in this neighbourhood there are some remarkably fine buildings, such as Government House, the stores of Messrs. Spencer & Co., Ltd., Whiteway, Laidlaw & Co., Ltd., Wrenn, Bennett & Co., Ltd., W. E. Smith & Co., Ltd., Addison & Co., Ltd., Oakes & Co., Ltd., and Misquith & Co., together with St. George's Cathedral and a number of educational and printing establishments. Extending along the sea front from Fort St. George to San Thomé, is the Marina, which is frequently resorted to on account of the never-failing breezes which are such a valuable asset to this part of the city.

There are a number of open spaces for the recreation of the people, and the majority of the houses occupied by Europeans stand in extensive compounds, or grounds. It was owing to the air of spaciousness that is thus given that the name of "The City of Magnificent Distances" came to be given to Madras. The People's Park, which owes its origin to Sir Charles Trevelyan, a former Governor of the Presidency, contains nearly 120 acres of land, and it is situated in the geographical centre of the city. On the northern boundary are the Moore Market, the Central Station, the new Municipal Buildings, and the Victoria Public Hall, while in other portions of the Park are a zoological and ornithological collection, five lakes, a band-stand, and reserves for football, tennis, and other games.

Robinson Park has a fine botanical garden, which is divided into plots for the various orders of plants, and there is an island at the north-eastern extremity upon which there is a large fernery, presented by the late A. Armoogam Mudaliar in the year 1886. The Agri-Horticultural Society's gardens at Teynampet are stocked with many rare tropical plants and Australian trees, and members of the Society have the privilege of obtaining a certain number of plants without further cost than the amount of their annual subscription.

CHEPAUK PALACE, MADRAS.

The first of the many notable buildings for religious purposes to receive consideration is the Cathedral Church of St. George. It was designed by Major de Haviland, of the Engineers, and it was built in the classic style in the year 1816. Entrances to the nave are through porches supported on massive Ionic pillars; the nave is 100 ft. in length, 27 ft. in width, and about 33 ft. in height; and the original cost of the structure was Rs. 206,842. Some very fine monuments are worthy of inspection: they include one of Bishop Heber; one of the Right Rev. Daniel Corrie, LL.D., first Bishop of Madras; another of Major Broadfoot, C.B., who was one of the Jellalabad garrison; a very imposing statue (by Flaxman) is erected to the memory of James Stephen Lushington, B.C.S.; the figure of Faith holding a cross is dedicated to the Ven. John Mousley, D.D., the first Archdeacon of Madras; and a finely erected monument in memory of John Mack, surgeon, is represented by Hygeia, goddess of health, offering milk to a serpent.

St. Mary's Church, situated within the ramparts of Fort St. George, is an extremely interesting structure, as it was opened as long ago as the year 1680, and it is historically associated with many events of importance in India. The old tombstones deserve particular notice: some of them were removed in 1760 from an old graveyard which was on the site of the present Law College, in China Bazaar Road, while others were taken from the old Capuchin Church of St. Andrew, which was destroyed in 1749, when Madras was handed back to the French after the peace of Aix-la-Chapelle. The statues and monuments inside the building should not be overlooked, particularly those of Lord Pigot, Lord Hobart, Sir Barry Close, George Gilbert Keble, Sir Henry Ward, and of the celebrated missionary, Frederic Christian Schwarz.

One's pulses are stirred when attention is directed to the regimental colours which adorn the walls and pillars, and a thrill is experienced when the eyes fall upon the untarnished colours, hanging near the pulpit, which belonged to the old 102nd Madras Fusiliers (now the Dublin Fusiliers), when it is remembered that they were carried through the second Burmese War in 1852 and in the Indian Mutiny in 1857-8.

There is special interest attaching to the San Thomé Cathedral, about four miles distant from Madras. Southern Indian traditions—supported to some extent by Dr. Medlycott's work on "India and the Apostle St. Thomas"—assert that this Apostle was the founder of the Christian Church in India; that he preached and eventually lived at Mylapore; that he was martyred on the hill known as St. Thomas's Mount in A.D. 68, and that he was buried on the spot where the San Thomé Cathedral now stands. These early Christians suffered great persecutions at a later date, but they succeeded in building a place of worship to replace the one which had been swept away by the sea, and this was in constant use until it fell into ruins. A Portuguese Commission visited the spot in 1523, and another chapel was erected on the site which was identified as the grave of the Apostle. The present Cathedral was built in 1896 by the Rev. Henry da Silva, who was the first to assume the title of Bishop of Mylapore. The Roman Catholic Cathedral in Armenian Street, which is known by the name of the Church of St. Mary of Angels, was built in 1775; but the Capuchin Mission, of which the cathedral is the result, was founded in 1642 by Father Ephraim, who acted with the sanction of Pope Urban VIII.

St. Andrew's (Church of Scotland) is a splendid edifice in the Poonamallee Road, immediately opposite the Egmore railway station. Fifteen years after the commencement of the nineteenth century it was publicly notified in Madras that the East India Company wished to build a Scotch Church for the benefit of their Caledonian employees. The proposal was warmly supported by the general assembly of the Church of Scotland, and the Rev. Dr. Allan was sent out with authority to form a congregation. Services were at once commenced, and eventually the present site—the finest in Madras—was secured for the building. The foundation-stone was laid by Dr. Allan on April 6, 1818, and it was his privilege to conduct the dedication service on the 29th of February, 1821. The church has been described as "perhaps the noblest Christian edifice in Hindustan," and this praise is deserved, as "for stateliness and general lightness of effect St. Andrew's is probably unsurpassed by any building of the same size." The cost of construction was about £20,000, and the land upon which the church is built (7 acres in extent) was purchased for 4,000 "pagodas." The value of a "pagoda" was 4s. 8d. in English money.

Other public and private buildings which are worthy of inspection include Government House, which is situated in an extensive deer park lying between the Cooum River, the Marina, and the Mount and Wallajah Roads. It is a noble building, and its surroundings of well-grown trees make it a charming sylvan retreat, while it is within a short distance from the chief railway stations and from the principal business houses of the city. The banqueting-hall is in a detached building, 80 ft. in length and 60 ft. in width, and it is used for state functions of all kinds. One of the most attractive features of the mansion is the number of fine oil-paintings of persons whose lives were bound up with the advancement of the social and political status of the peoples of India.

The majority of the past Governors are represented on canvas in this gallery; and among the most interesting portraits are those of George III, Queen Charlotte, Major-General Sir Thomas Munro, Bart. (Governor of Madras from 1820 to 1827), Lord Hobart, who held the same office from 1872 to 1875, of Lord Harris, of Lord Mornington, who became Marquis Wellesley, of Lady Munro, and of General Wellesley, who is better known as the Iron Duke. A fine statue of his late Majesty King Edward VII has been erected opposite to the entrance gates to the Governor's residence. It may be observed here that, when the hot weather commences, the King's representative removes to Ootacamund, where the temperature is somewhat lower.

The noble equestrian statue of Sir Thomas Munro stands about half-way between Government House and Fort St. George; it is the work of Chantrey, and it was erected by public subscription at a cost of about Rs. 1,80,000. Other memorials of a similar character have been erected to the memory of her late Majesty Queen Victoria, General Neill, the Rev. Dr. Miller, C.I.E., and of Lord Cornwallis, who conquered Tipu Sultan at Seringapatam.

The Marina, a splendid road for driving or motoring, stretches for a distance of about five miles along the sea front, and it is beautified by several imposing structures. These include the Chepauk Palace, Moorish in style of architecture, which is occupied by several Government departments, and which formerly formed part of the Palace of the Nawabs of the Carnatic; the Aquarium, containing a small but most interesting collection of the weirdest denizens of the deep; and the Senate House of the Madras University, which cost nearly three lakhs of rupees. The new Municipal Offices (called Ripon Buildings), are at the south-west corner of the People's Park, and they form a most imposing pile from whatever direction they are viewed. Their total length is 252 ft., the width is about 125 ft., and a central tower, 132 ft. in height, contains a clock (with four dials, 8 ft. in diameter), which rings the Westminster chimes every hour.

All the rooms are light and airy, and every provision has been made for the comfort and convenience of the large staff of assistants who are housed there. The ground floor contains sixteen rooms, which are occupied by the Revenue Department; the first floor has twenty-two apartments wherein the President of the Corporation, and the employees of the General and Health Departments carry out their duties; while the second story has accommodation for the Council Chamber and for the offices of the Works Department.

The foundation-stone was laid in December 1909 by the late Earl of Minto, the Viceroy at that time, and the opening ceremony took place amid a flourish of trumpets on the 26th of November, 1913, when the present Viceroy, Baron Hardinge of Penshurst, unlocked the doors in the presence of a large and fashionable gathering. Some furnishings and fittings have still to be added, so that the total cost will be upwards of seven lakhs of rupees.

VIEW OF GEORGETOWN, MADRAS, FROM THE LIGHTHOUSE.

Photo by Nicholas & Co.

Two particularly handsome buildings are the High Court of Justice and the Law College, which are situated near to the junction of the Marina with the China Bazaar Road. The decorative portion of

1. CHINA BAZAAR ROAD, MADRAS. 2. BAZAAR SCENE, MADRAS. 3. THE MARINA, MADRAS.

Photo by Nicholas & Co.

the structures is exceedingly chaste, exceptional care having been bestowed upon the ornamental tiling, wood-carving, and the stained glass windows. The new lighthouse is located in the main tower of the High Court, and it was formally handed over by the Public Works Department to the Port Authorities on the 25th of July, 1893. There is a single white light, which is 166 ft. above sea-level, and it gives a flash of two seconds, an eclipse of three seconds, then flash two seconds, and eclipse 23 seconds ; and its luminous range is about 19 marine miles.

The Government Museum is a handsome building situated in the Pantheon Road, and it has a most interesting collection of exhibits illustrating the natural history, and the arts and industries, as well as the antiquities of Southern India. The vivarium section contains indigenous snakes and birds, while the fauna, the flora, and the specimens of mineralogy and archæology are thoroughly representative in character. Galleries, devoted mainly to relics of other days, contain a very fine selection of arms from the Tanjore armoury and from the arsenal in Fort St. George. Visitors should make a special point of seeing the Public Library, which is attached to the Museum. The interior is most beautifully decorated with wood carvings, and large numbers of new published books are added to the shelves each year.

There was a widespread feeling in the Presidency of Madras on the occasion of the Jubilee of her late Majesty Queen Victoria, that some fitting and permanent memorial should be created in order to commemorate her beneficent reign of fifty years, and it was at this juncture that the Government was considering the best means of re-awakening public interest in almost forgotten industrial enterprises. An interchange of ideas followed, and it was decided that the fund which had already been subscribed should be devoted to the spread of technical education. The foundation-stone of the Victoria Technical Institute and Memorial Hall was laid by H.R.H. the Prince of Wales, on the 26th of January, 1906, and about three years were occupied in construction. A handbook published by the Council of the Institute says that : " Mr. Henry Irwin, C.I.E., the Council's architect, has adopted the architecture of the Mogul period, and the general character follows that of the buildings erected by the Mogul emperors at Fatehpur-Sikri, Agra, and Delhi. The entire building is faced with beautiful pink sandstone from the Tada quarries, in many places sculptured in intricate patterns of oriental design, the front portion of the hall being in this respect especially richly decorated. The ornamentation of the interior is in the same style, carried out in white polished plaster, for which Madras is celebrated. The floor is of marble, laid out in geometric patterns."

The Young Men's Christian Association of Madras was instituted on the 18th of January, 1890, being incorporated under Act XXI of 1860, and it occupies a commanding position on the Esplanade, immediately opposite the Law College. It is the only public building in Madras which has been constructed entirely of stone ; and, to show that the institution is a " live " one, it may be observed that the activities of the Association include departments for physical culture, education, religious and social work, and other subjects of interest to men of all ages.

There are upwards of twenty clubs in

Madras, membership to which is open to all classes of society, and among the principal institutions of this class are the following: The Madras Club, famous in the ranks of Indian clubs, the Adyar and Boating Clubs, at Adyar, the Gymkhana Club, the Madras Hunt and Racing Clubs, and the Cosmopolitan Club, situated on Mount Road.

In the middle of the nineteenth century the city of Madras was relatively of more importance as an industrial centre than it is to-day, but after the East India Company ceased to carry on business the trade passed into the hands of Europeans, who, however, failed to meet with the success which their efforts deserved. It was suggested in a Government Census and Trade Report (1912) that the reasons for this failure might be summarized as follows: (1) The natural poverty of the country and the lack of raw materials as a basis for manufacturing operations. (2) The indigenous industries were of a very primitive type, and entirely in the hands of uneducated artisans. (3) The non-official European community was drawn more from the commercial than from the manufacturing classes, and their natural inclination was rather to finance agriculture and develop trade than to risk their capital in industrial work of which they had but little practical knowledge. (4) The limited market for specialized manufactures due to the poverty of the people and the want of facilities for transport. The report further states that during recent years only three new industries have been introduced to take the places of those which have died a natural death. These are (1) the manufacture of aluminium utensils, now carried on by the Indian Aluminium Company; (2) the manufacture of leather by the chrome tanning process, conducted by the Chrome Leather Company, Ltd.; and (3) the manufacture of glass, chiefly soda-water bottles, by the Madras Glass Works.

The principal industries which are still in existence (1914) are cigar and cigarette factories, tobacco-curing works, cotton and oil mills, printing presses, shoe, boot, and sandal making, cotton spinning and weaving, aerated-water factories, carriage building, carpentering and joinery, and skin and hide tanning. The majority of these have not developed to any great extent, but there are indications that a time of increased prosperity is at hand. The improvement in the engineering trades is probably due to the extended use of motor machinery. A considerable expansion, too, has taken place in the output of weaving and spinning mills, and a very marked advance has been made in the output of aerated-water factories. An immense amount of money has been invested in connection with the latter industry by enlarging buildings, by the installation of up-to-date machinery, and by the erection of modern plant for the effective purification of the water.

If industrial concerns are not numerous, however, there is no lack of wholesale and retail businesses of all kinds, ranging from the "Gamages" and the "Whiteleys" of the Mount Road, to the small rabbit-hutch affairs in Georgetown, which by courtesy are designated shops. Some of the huge establishments in the neighbourhood of Government House are vast distributing-centres of a heterogeneous selection of merchandise, and the proprietors of many of these houses are even prepared to construct a railway or make a cigarette, to finance a syndicate or cater for a banquet, to furnish a house or sup-

1. VICTORIA TECHNICAL INSTITUTE, MADRAS (THE MAIN HALL).
2. INTERIOR CONNEMARA PUBLIC LIBRARY, MADRAS, SHOWING STATUE OF LORD CORNWALLIS.

ply a packet of pins, to print a visiting-card or to clothe a woman in the latest creation of Paquin or Worth, and, in short, to execute an order for almost anything which may be advertised in the innumerable sale catalogues of the present day. The bazaars, particularly in the densely populated district of Georgetown, present a marvellous scene of business life in its most primitive aspects. Shops which have any pretensions to respectable size, such as chemists, ironmongers, boot and shoe dealers, or silk and linen merchants, are well stocked with goods of first-class quality, but there are thousands of smaller places in which one sees such a miscellaneous assortment of articles, many of which appear to the passer-by to be of little value, that the visitor asks the question, "How do these people live?" He might, as a matter of fact, address this query to a score of different people, and he would be likely to receive as many different answers, but the general effect of the replies would be that all had, in some way or another, solved the problem of securing a living for themselves and their dependents. But how deceptive are appearances very frequently! There is untold wealth in many of these dens—for that is what they really are—as transactions are continually occurring in which diamonds, rubies, pearls, and other precious stones (worth a king's ransom) are changing hands. It is quite a common occurrence in the bazaars for a person to be offered articles for sale at fully 100 or 150 per cent. more than their actual value, and he is unfortunate if he does not complete his purchases at a third or a fourth of the prices originally demanded.

The anthropologist will be intensely interested in the study of the cross-legged owner sitting among his wares, and he will find still more to appeal to his imagination when he directs his attention to the throng of people in the streets. Here are unkempt, half-clad coolies, both male and female; yonder may be seen the flowing robes of Brahmans, Mahommedans, and others; and again there is a vision of women clothed in *saris* of gorgeous colours, predominant among which are orange, scarlet, blue, and sea and olive greens. The scene is a busy one; streams of human beings are passing up and down from daylight to about eight o'clock in the evening, when the streets become as silent as a graveyard.

Reference should be made here to a few of the other streets and roads, some of which are important thoroughfares. Armenian Street, in Georgetown, runs north and south, in a line parallel with the sea beach and not more than 300 yards distant from it. It contains a considerable number of warehouses and offices belonging to leading merchants. China Bazaar Road is perhaps the busiest native quarter of the city. At the lower end, starting from the Beach Road, are the High Court and Law College, and some banks and insurance offices. Further to the westward is the Flower Bazaar Police Station and Pachiayappa's Indian College and high school, and after these there is an almost interminable succession of shops of Hindu merchants and traders, who are busy from morn till night dealing in all kinds of produce and goods. Elphinstone Bridge Road, in Mylapore, is remembered as being the headquarters of the Theosophical Society. The majority of the banks are situated on the North Beach Road, and here also is the General Post Office, the Customs House, and the head-

1. THE MYLAPORE FESTIVAL CAR.

2. A MOSQUE AT TRIPLICANE.

1. ST. GEORGE'S CATHEDRAL, MADRAS. 2. INTERIOR, ST. GEORGE'S CATHEDRAL.

3. INTERIOR, ST. MARY'S CHURCH, FORT ST. GEORGE. 4. ST. MARY'S CHURCH, FORT ST. GEORGE.

Photos by Nicholas & Co.

quarters of the City Police. The eastern portion of the Poonamallee High Road is narrow, and is lined on the north side for a considerable distance by Hindu shops and dwellings, which are an eyesore to everybody. On approaching the Tramway Company's power station at Egmore, the road widens gradually, and a few hundred yards farther one sees large and well-appointed residences standing in compounds varying from two to ten acres in extent, one of the most important of these buildings being the extensive hostel and premises belonging to the Y.W.C.A. Pantheon Road, also in Egmore, has on the north side the Victoria Technical Institute and Museum, the Connemara Library, and the Government Maternity Hospital and Dispensary, while on the opposite side are several extremely fine dwelling-houses which are almost lost in their well-wooded grounds. Popham's Broadway is the most important business thoroughfare in Georgetown, and it contains a large number of hardware, drug, and other stores, in addition to ironfoundries, wood depots, and masons' yards.

ST. ANDREW'S KIRK, MADRAS.

Photo by Nicholas & Co.

The question of education has received very considerable support during recent years, and a large number of colleges and schools in Madras are affiliated with the Presidency University. The Presidency College, Chepauk, was established in 1841, under the name of the High School of the Madras University. It is affiliated with the University in the Intermediate course, and in several branches of the B.A. Pass and Honours courses. This institution has a long list of professors, whose lectures and demonstrations are given in history, chemistry, botany, geology, zoology, mathematics, physics, and in the English, Sanskrit, Malayalam, Arabic, Persian, Hindustani, Telugu, Tamil, and Kanarese languages. Passing over the colleges for medical, veterinary, and engineering students, reference may be made to the Presidency Training School for mistresses; the School of Arts in Poonamallee Road; the Madras Law College, affiliated in 1892; the Madras Christian College, founded in 1837 by the first missionary of the Church of Scotland in Madras; the Doveton Protestant College, Vepery; St. Mary's European High School; St. Gabriel's High School; the Government Hobart Training School for Mahommedan school mistresses; Pachiayappa's College; the Madras School of Music; and a number of other primary and secondary schools.

The means of communication between the various portions of the city and between the latter and the suburbs are fairly satisfactory as regards variety, but a good deal more in the way of comfort might reasonably be expected.

The South Indian Railway Company, Ltd., have six stations in Madras, namely, Beach, Fort, Park, Egmore, Chetput, and Kodambakam. Egmore stands first in importance, as the majority of the visitors to the capital city alight there; the Beach Station is alongside the harbour, and is therefore especially convenient for passengers arriving or embarking by steamers; the Fort Station almost adjoins the Supreme Court and Law College buildings; while the remaining three provide excellent service for the southern and western suburbs.

Electric tramway cars run at frequent intervals to nearly every part of the city; there is a ten-minute service between Egmore Station and the Custom House on Beach Road, passing through the busiest commercial centres; while branch lines convey passengers to Royapuram, Chintadripet, Mount Road, Royapettah, San Thomé, Triplicane, Pursewaukam, Washermanpet, Mylapore, and other suburban areas.

Motor-cars may be obtained in the city during the day or night at any of the garages which have been opened. Victorias, landaus, and cabs of the "growler" type are not yet taken off the streets, and it is noticeable that there are still a considerable number of persons who are old-fashioned enough to prefer a vehicle drawn by horses. Rickshas are probably patronized more than any other means of conveyance, and the legal charges for the hire of them are reasonable.

A VIEW IN THE ARCHÆOLOGICAL SECTION, MADRAS MUSEUM.

The construction of an artificial harbour at Madras is referred to at considerable length in a special article on page 130,

1. MOHURRUM FESTIVAL, MADRAS.

Photo by Nicholas & Co.

2. ESPLANADE, MADRAS.

1. MOWBRAY ROAD, MADRAS.

2. ST. THOMAS' MOUNT.

3. HENDERSON'S BRIDGE, MADRAS.

but some reference should be made here to the imports and exports. The sea-borne trade of the port has shown a substantial improvement during the last few years, and the percentage of this increase is about equally divided between the foreign and the coasting shipments. The increase in the foreign trade is shown by larger receipts of cotton goods, metals, raw cotton, machinery, kerosene oil, and other sundries, while the increased exports covered practically every branch of merchandise. The statistics of the coasting trade show that the exports of country produce have advanced at the rate of about 15 or 20 per cent. in recent years. The principal items in the list of exports are cotton, seeds, leather, grain, coffee, tea, and pulse, while the chief imports consist of manufactured cotton goods. Considerably more than half of the commerce of the Presidency is done with the British Empire, and 40 per cent. at least of the sea-borne trade passes through the port of Madras.

The environs of Madras are not rich in beauty of scenery, as there is an entire absence of hills to break the monotony of the plains, but what is lacking in this respect is amply atoned for by the historical associations attached to many of the surrounding towns and villages.

It will be convenient in the first place to notice one or two places which are served by the South Indian Railway system. Saidapet, which has a population of more than 7,000 inhabitants, is eight miles distant from Egmore station, and it is the headquarters of the Collector of the Chingleput district.. The principal industries are dyeing and weaving, sufficient cloth being made to supply local requirements. A Government experimental farm and a bacteriological laboratory are situated here, and the town has come to be regarded as an educational centre since a Teachers' College was established. The next stopping-place is Guindy, which has the finest racecourse in Southern India. The country residence of the Governor of the Presidency is an exceedingly fine structure, and it is prettily situated in the centre of an extensive park. The King Institute of bacteriological investigations and for the preparation of vaccine is near to the station. Eleven miles from Madras is St. Thomas's Mount, which is a cantonment town, and the headquarters of the artillery of the Presidency, as well as the station of a brigade of field artillery. There are several handsome buildings here, among them being the Garrison Church, which is dedicated to St. Thomas, and which is said to be an exact copy of the historic church of St. Clement Danes, in the Strand, London. Near to the summit of the mount is an old Roman Catholic Church called the "Expectation of the Blessed Virgin," which now belongs to the Armenian community. The building was erected in the early part of the sixteenth century, and the historian or the archæologist will find food for reflection in a curiously carved stone cross which is to be seen behind the altar. This relic is considered by many reliable authorities to date from about A.D. 800, and a translation of the inscription upon the stone is as follows: "Who believes in the Messiah and in God above, and in the Holy Ghost, is in favour with Him who bore the Cross."

Lying to the west of Georgetown is Vepery, where is situated the Madras Veterinary College. Matriculated students are admitted to a course which extends over three years. Adyar, lying to the

BAND PERFORMANCE AT THE MARINA, MADRAS.

extreme south of the city, contains some of the handsomest private residences in the Presidency. . It has a fine river, upon which is the boathouse of the Madras Boating Club. Egmore, Chetput, Numgumbaukam, and Teynampet, are inhabited almost entirely by Europeans, and it is in these areas that the most beautiful buildings of the city are situated.

THE THEOSOPHICAL SOCIETY

THE Theosophical Society was founded in New York, U.S.A., on November 17, 1875, by Helena Petrovna Blavatsky and Colonel Henry Steele Olcott. The former was a Russian woman of noble birth and extraordinary psychic powers, the latter a United States officer, who fought on the side of the North in the Civil War, and received the thanks of the Government for the ability, integrity, and courage with which he purified and organized the American War Office. The remarkable phenomena shown by Mme. Blavatsky in her immediate circle attracted strong interest, and the philosophy she expounded fascinated the thoughtful students she drew round her and formed into a Society. Colonel Olcott was made president for life, and held that office from November 1875 to February 1907, when he died in the headquarters of the Society, at Adyar, Madras, India.

The objects of the Society, slightly modified in wording from time to time, were fixed finally by the memorandum of association, when the Society was legally incorporated, on April 3, 1905, thirty years after its foundation. They are :

1. To form a nucleus of the Universal Brotherhood of Humanity, without distinction of race, creed, sex, caste, or colour.

2. To encourage the study of Comparative Religion, Philosophy, and Science.

3. To investigate unexplained laws of Nature and the powers latent in man.

Men and women of all religions become members of the Society, none leaving his religion in order to join it, and its members leaven the religions to which they belong with a spirit of liberality and tolerance. Persons of all religions meet on a footing of equality, to teach and to learn, and thus form a peace-making influence among rival creeds. Racial distinctions are ignored in its meetings, and mutual courtesy is observed in all social relations. All offices in the Society are open alike to men and women.

The two founders left the United States in 1878, committing the care of the Society there to their colleague, William E. Judge and, after a brief visit to England *en route*, they established their headquarters in Bombay in 1879. They visited Simla in 1881, and won the sympathy of Mr. A. O. Hume, a high Indian civilian, and of Mr. A. P. Sinnett, editor of the *Pioneer*, then the leading journal in India, and the latter gentleman wrote and published "The Occult World" and "Esoteric Buddhism," books which gave currency to theosophic teachings in the Western world. Mme. Blavatsky's first book, "Isis Unveiled," preceded them in time, being published in 1877, but, while containing an extraordinary mass of information, it gave no coherent exposition of doctrine.

In 1882 Mme. Blavatsky and Colonel Olcott, with the help of a few friends, purchased at Adyar, a suburb of Madras, a small estate of 27 acres, with a bungalow upon it, and there established finally the headquarters of the Theosophical Society, which then had fifty-two lodges, nearly all in India and Ceylon, due to the indefatigable work of the two founders.

In 1884 the missionary proceedings against H. P. Blavatsky occurred, and though a most respectable committee investigated the allegations made against her and acquitted her entirely of fraud, the partial report of Mr. Hodgson, adopted by the Psychical Research Society, blackened her good name, and she is still regarded as fraudulent by the ignorant. Her phenomena are now generally recognized as within psychic power—so much has knowledge advanced—but she suffered the fate of the pioneer and was branded as charlatan. Her work has, however, triumphed, and thousands recognize that they owe to her the philosophy that has illuminated their lives. Her extraordinary knowledge has on many points been justified by the advance of science, and as years pass on the clouds made by the allegations of her accusers are gradually passing away. Her statue in the large hall at Adyar stands as a monument of the Society's gratitude, and, in 1907, that of her colleague, Colonel Olcott, was placed beside it. She passed away in 1891 in London.

Under the ceaseless work of Colonel Olcott the Society steadily expanded, and its influence spread over the civilized world. He was a great builder, and the headquarters became by his hands the fine building it now is. With the exception of a small extension of the library and the verandahs overlooking the river, it remains as he left it. The library was one of his most cherished achievements, and it was he who appointed its present scholarly director, who has so raised it in the opinion of European Orientalists.

When the president-founder, Colonel Olcott, passed away in 1907, he nominated Mrs. Annie Besant as his successor, and his nomination was confirmed by the vote of the Society. During the seven years of her presidency there has been a great expansion of the Society in membership, wealth, and influence.

The headquarters estate now comprises nearly 300 acres, and many buildings have been erected on it for the accommodation of students who flock to it from all parts of the world. There are about sixty white students of different nationalities, and forty Indians, some permanently in residence, working for the Society, the majority coming for either one or two years, and returning to their own countries to carry on theosophical work better equipped than before they went to Adyar.

There is a printing-press employing over a hundred men and boys, and a large publishing house, particulars of which are given on page 126.

The headquarters has also its own bakery and dairy, its steam-laundry, its electric installation, its stores—all conducing to the comfort of the inhabitants —and the whole estate is being brought under cultivation with a view to making it self-supporting.

Adyar is a centre to which are attached 23 national societies, 9 lodges in several countries not yet fully organized, nearly 1,000 lodges in all, with over 23,000 active members. It is the centre also of educational and social activities of a philanthropic character, and once a year there is held a General Convention, to which is reported the work done all over the world.

THE THEOSOPHICAL SOCIETY'S INSTITUTIONS

THE PUBLISHING HOUSE.—Within the Theosophical compound at Adyar is carried on the large publishing business which is the chief method of making Theosophy known to the entire world. The Theosophical Publishing House, once familiar under the title of the *Theosophist* Office, is the chief publisher of Theosophical literature, and the business has grown extensively during the last few years. The output of literature has increased so enormously that the modest premises in which the work was carried on had to be extended two years ago, and an entirely new and palatial set of offices has just been completed. The printing work is also done on the premises by means of a private press owned by the Publishing House.

The Publishing House is not "run for profit." Apart from the number of books turned out yearly, there are several permanent activities which show the propaganda trend of the institution. Every month four magazines are issued: the *Theosophist*, which is the official organ of the President of the Society, has been in existence for thirty-five years. The *Adyar Bulletin*, just entered upon its seventh year, has developed from a journal for the non-sectionalized countries into a Theosophical journal for East and West. In 1913 was started the *Young Citizen*, a magazine designed to instil healthy and patriotic principles into the minds of boys and girls, planting in them seeds in early life such as will later blossom into the flower of good citizenship. The latest activity is the new journal of national reform, entitled the *Commonweal*. It was started in January 1914, and its object is to unite India with England in mutual sympathy and love. It studies the problem of the two countries from an unbiassed point of view. It seeks to remove the disabilities placed on Indians by the British Colonies, and to give to the Indian the same rights and privileges as are extended any other citizen of the British Empire. In short, it stands for Imperialism in the broad sense of that word, and it is a strong advocate of the Federation of Nations.

The Theosophical Publishing House is governed by ideals. All the important work is done by Theosophists, who give their services voluntarily to the great work, and they labour with a willingness and zeal that gold could not buy. But all of them have not the best experience of trained workers, so that much credit is due on account of the work turned out by the Publishing House, which compares most favourably with that of the best firms in India.

A GENERAL VIEW FROM THE RIVER.

This office is a living embodiment of the first object of the Theosophical Society. It makes no distinction of caste, creed, race, sex, or colour. The enthusiasm for the work buries all differences, and a wonderful unity obtains.

HEADQUARTERS COMPOUND. — The situation of the headquarters of the Theosophical Society is a most advantageous one, being in close proximity to the centre of the town of Madras —the distance is only eight miles; it is yet far enough away to possess all the charms of unadulterated country life.

THE THEOSOPHICAL SOCIETY.

1. THE STAFF. 2. THE FOUNDERS OF THE SOCIETY. 3. IN THE LIBRARY. 4. LEADBETTER CHAMBERS.

The actual spot, in a village community incorrectly called Adyar, is one of the most picturesque to be found in all the environs of the Southern Indian metropolis, for it is bordered on one side by the charming Adyar, a little river studded with tiny, verdant islands, and held within romantic and beautiful banks, whereas at another side it is flanked by the grand Bay of Bengal, exhibiting its ever-changing, never exhausted charms, and set off by a strip of most delightful dunes and shore. Thus the estate has Nature for its neighbour on two sides, and Humanity, in the form of typical and interesting little villages of fishermen and tillers of the soil, on the other two.

The estate has grown with the years. Colonel Olcott and Madame H. P. Blavatsky, the founders of the Society, first settled definitely at Adyar in the year 1882, and purchased a small bungalow with grounds to the extent of 27 acres, on the Adyar. Very soon, with the growth of the Theosophical Movement, the accommodation on the estate proved insufficient ; and Colonel Olcott, an American, endowed with energy and foresight, began building, extending, and modifying, with the result that at his death the original modest bungalow had been transformed into a fairly imposing pile of buildings. After his death, Mrs. Annie Besant became President, and with her accession to that office the expansion became still more rapid. Four large and one small contiguous estates were bought, new buildings were erected, and now the headquarters comprises an area of slightly under 300 acres, and holds seven large bungalows, one gigantic ferro-concrete building, capable of housing, in so many separate flats, 28 students, a number of offices and public buildings, and an ever-growing number of private residences.

Ever since Mrs. Besant's accession to the Presidency, special endeavours have been made to utilize part of the grounds for agricultural purposes ; another part is reserved for flower-gardens and for the laying out of a park. Most of the grounds were already well wooded when acquired, containing many beautiful trees —amongst the latter an enormous banyan, one of the finest and largest in India, is the pride of the Adyar inhabitants. The agricultural activities of the Society are mainly directed in such lines as may serve as useful examples for Indian cultivators, or which may benefit them directly. So a large experiment is being made with the cultivation of a variety of spineless cactus, with a view of testing its usefulness as cattle food. A native variety of the plant was discovered by the agricultural estate superintendent, who collected several thousand cuttings of it and planted these out over several acres of the estate. These cuttings have done very well, and if the hopes which are entertained do not prove vain, important results may follow from the experiments to the benefit of the Indian cattle raisers and the agriculturist. A second experiment is being made with the introduction of first-class Australian oranges, which, if they prove suitable for cultivation in the South Indian climate, may become an important source of revenue to Indian fruit-growers. Other considerable plantations are those of coco-nuts, mangoes, bananas, papayas, casuarina-trees, rice, betel-leaves, and kitchen vegetables, all of which, it is hoped, will contribute in time some financial return to the Society, thereby decreasing the working expenses of headquarters, and tending towards making it self-supporting and financially independent of the resources of the Society as such. A visit to the grounds of the headquarters is, because of these circumstances, quite interesting, and fully repays the trouble spent on it. Of course, as the years go by and the Theosophical Society, together with its headquarters, goes on progressing as it has done in the past, the headquarters' ground will become more and more completely laid out and beautified, and there is no exaggeration in expressing the confident expectation that it will in the future become one of the recognized beauty spots of Madras, renowned amongst its inhabitants and unfailingly to be visited by all who happen to pass through the town, both tourists and visitors.

THE ADYAR LIBRARY.—Amongst the many departments to be found at the headquarters of the Theosophical Society at Adyar, one of the most important, and certainly the most interesting for the visitor, is the Adyar Library. In one of the earliest programmes of action published by the Society, the formation of a library was mentioned, but, apart from some preliminary endeavours in this direction, only in 1886 was the ideal definitely realized. On December 29th of that year, on the occasion of the eleventh annual Convention of the Society, the Library was opened by Colonel Olcott, the Founder and the first President of the Theosophical Society. The event was celebrated with due ceremonial, and from a contemporary report we quote the following description :—

" In opening the proceedings, Colonel Olcott, President-Founder, said that the programme of the ceremony of the opening of the Oriental Library was intended to be of an eclectic character, and to show that the Theosophical Society was not founded in the interests of any one sect or any race. A Pandit from Mysore next invoked Ganapati, the god of occult learning, and Sarasvati, the goddess of knowledge, after which a few boys of the Triplicane Sanskrit School sang some verses in Sanskrit. Two Parsi priests then offered a prayer ; and this was followed by the recital of verses in the Pali language by two Buddhist priests, who had come from Ceylon to take part in the ceremony. A Mahommedan maulvi from Hyderabad recited a prayer from the Koran, and prayed for the long life and prosperity of Her Most Gracious Majesty, the Queen-Empress. A recitation of Sanskrit shlokas by Hindu boys was next given, and Sanskrit poems were read, specially composed for the occasion by pandits in different parts of India. Then Colonel Olcott gave his inaugural address."

From the moment the Library was born it proved a most vital entity, growing rapidly and developing in a marvellous manner. From the very beginning special attention was paid to the collection of Sanskrit manuscripts, the repositories of India's intellect and wisdom. Now, after an existence of twenty-seven years the Library can boast of one of the finest and richest—if not the finest and richest—collection of such manuscripts both on paper and on palm leaf, written in a variety of Indian characters, in the whole world. The total of these works has reached the colossal number of about 13,000 units, embracing about 6,000 different works. Besides these manuscripts in the ancient Indian Sanskrit, the library has also collected a few thousand manuscripts in the living Indian vernaculars. For some time to come these collections will constitute the most precious portion of the library.

But there are also other books of note. There is an important collection of Japanese and Chinese Buddhist works, comprising a complete Chinese Tripitaka (the Buddhist holy books) printed in Japan, collected by the late Colonel Olcott during his travels in that country.

THE THEOSOPHICAL SOCIETY.

1. A Palm Grove. 2. Banyan Tree 3. A View from the Roof.
4. A Clump of Cactus Plants 5. Orange Plantations.

Then there are the 333 bulky volumes of the Tibetan Kandjur and Tandjur, which are the Buddhist scriptures in their Tibetan form, and also some other valuable Tibetan works. Again there is a gigantic Chinese encyclopædia in 1,600 volumes, containing about eight times the reading matter of the latest edition of the "Encyclopædia Britannica." Thousands of other printed volumes in Oriental languages supplement the manuscripts, and altogether the Sanskrit portion of the Oriental section of the library is not only among the best to be found in Indian libraries, but it contains many items not to be found at all anywhere else in India.

The Western section of the Library specializes chiefly in about four directions. First there is the division of alphabetical reference works, dictionaries, encyclopædias and similar productions. A very considerable amount of these works systematically collected, enables the student to find a ready answer to almost any question arising during his studies. A second division is that which is formed by specifically Theosophical literature, books as well as periodicals, and here the library is, of course, *facile princeps* before any other.

Then there is the division of comparative religion, philosophy, mysticism, occultism, and similar subjects. A considerable amount of material has been gathered together under this heading. The division of academical and special magazines connected with Oriental studies is also very comprehensive, and enables serious study to be carried on in the library.

In short, the library, entirely supported by the private means of the Society, has, after a quarter of a century's existence, reached a stage where it has become an efficient instrument for research.

The library has also commenced the formation of a museum of works of art, curios, and objects illustrating religious beliefs and practices. Though this collection is as yet still in an embryonic stage it promises to develop as rapidly as the older book department, and high hopes may be legitimately entertained for its future.

A few years ago the library began issuing scholarly publications dealing with Sanskrit philology and Indian philosophy. An ambitious undertaking is the publication of (about 100) minor *Upanishads* together with their translation into English. The complete undertaking will comprise about 15 volumes. The Director of the library, Dr. F. O. Schrader, is the editor and translator. The first volume has already appeared. Several volumes of other works have either appeared, or are in the press, in preparation, or projected.

So the Theosophical Society has created in the Adyar Library a valuable centre for the intellectual side of its manifold activities. The library is improving rapidly, and will certainly not fail soon to attract still wider attention in the world of scholars than it has done hitherto. Its ambition is to become a leading institution amongst those ministering to mental activity in India, and it will not be content until it is recognized as such, not only in India, but throughout the whole world. Seeing what it has already achieved within one quarter of a century, under adverse circumstances and great difficulties, with slender means and little support, it may be confidently expected that another quarter of a century will see its development and emancipation into a first-class storehouse of knowledge, a powerful aid to learning, a true temple of wisdom and intellectual activity.

MADRAS HARBOUR

THE greater portion of the east and west coast of India is singularly devoid of physical conditions which lend themselves naturally to the protection of shipping from wind and waves, and to the economical provision of accommodation for the handling of export and import merchandise. There are a few places where estuaries formed by rivers entering the ocean afford some slight security, but the principal feature is a long stretch of low-lying sand, upon which the rolling surf frequently breaks with stupendous force.

Experts advised that it would be useless to expend money in the building of a sea-wall with the idea of sheltering vessels from the prevailing high winds, but it was claimed that it would be possible to construct works which would enclose an extensive area of smooth water in which cargo could be shipped or landed by means of lighters. There are probably not ten days in a year when boats built in the European style could negotiate the wild breakers on the unsheltered shore with any hope of safety, so that masters of trading ships were compelled to avail themselves of the native-made *masulah*, or surf boat, for the transport of cargo between ship and shore. These may be described as consisting of planks roughly sawn from trees and laced together with strong twine, and without ribs or keel, but this flexible method of construction has the advantage that boats so built are able to carry their two or three tons of cargo over the mountains of surf which threaten, but rarely accomplish, their destruction. They were, and where still in use, as at Pondicherry, are manned by a crew of six or eight men and boys, who navigate them with rude kinds of paddles.

This is the state of affairs which had been in existence from time immemorial until the early sixties, when a screw pile pier was constructed. It was 42 ft. in width, and 17 ft. and 12 ft. above low and high-water level respectively, and as it projected for a distance of 1,100 ft. there was a possibility of landing goods in tolerably fine weather, although during the greater part of the year the work was most precarious.

The rich products of India, including spices, cotton, silks, hides, seeds, perfumes, and precious and other stones have been eagerly sought after by merchants of other countries, who visited these shores in their dhows, which were practically identical with those which may be seen to-day making voyages from Suez and Aden to Bombay and other Indian ports. Old established trading firms in Madras were severely handicapped by the unsatisfactory manner in which cargo had to be dealt with, and the sister ports of Bombay and Calcutta made the most of their opportunities. The Madras Chamber of Commerce gave careful consideration to the question of providing an artificial harbour, and a letter was addressed to the Government, with the result that the Committee, which was formed on the 28th August, 1868, submitted a report in January 1869, with recommendations on the following points, namely, (1) the open roadstead, (2) delay in loading and unloading cargo owing to the use of *masulah* boats, (3) cost of landing and shipping cargo, and extortion of boatmen, and (4) damage of goods.

The investigations of the Committee were thoroughly carried out, and they eventually recommended that a detached breakwater should be constructed, and they further suggested that a request should be made to the Secretary of State that an experienced marine and harbour engineer should be appointed to advise on the matter. The choice fell upon Mr. G. Robertson, who at that time was engaged in reporting upon Indian harbours, and this official supported the scheme propounded by the Committee.

This was in the year 1871, but at this juncture the late Mr. W. Parkes, M.Inst. C.E., obtained information of Mr. Robertson's plans, and he claimed that an enclosed harbour would be more effective than an isolated breakwater. After Mr. Parkes had visited Madras, his proposals, which were estimated to cost £505,000, were approved by the Presidency Government, and the Secretary of State for India in Council sanctioned the construction of the works in 1875; but an actual beginning was not made until two years later.

Plans were adopted for two breakwaters 1,000 yards apart, and running seawards for a distance of about 1,000 yards, and finally curving towards each other, thus leaving an opening of 515 ft. between the pier heads. The foundation-stone of the new system was laid in 1875 by H.R.H. the Prince of Wales (the late King Edward VII) and a commencement was at once made with the north arm.

During the four years from 1877-81 the work proceeded smoothly, interrupted, however, by a condemnatory report in 1879 by Sir Andrew Clarke, R.E., Member of the Viceroy's Council for Public Works, who denounced the scheme on political, financial, nautical, commercial, and engineering grounds, and recommended a design by which the harbour would be detached from the shore, its accommodation increased, its defensive power improved, and egress and ingress facilitated. This fresh proposal was not acceptable to the Imperial Government, so the work, as originally planned by Mr. Parkes, was continued. On the 12th November, 1881, a severe cyclonic disturbance damaged a considerable portion of the works which were nearing completion, and this catastrophe was attributed to the inadequate height of the structure as then designed. Two valuable reports upon the disaster and its probable cause were prepared, and the principal points arrived at were: (*a*) "that wave action caused disturbance at a considerably greater depth than any previously recorded in Europe, and (*b*) that the excessively destructive wave action experienced was unaccompanied by wind of any great force, and that it must therefore be ascribed to a very severe local action somewhere out at sea of which the winds did not, while the waves did, reach Madras.

The main feature of the advice of the experts, however, was that the breakwaters should be strengthened and increased in height, and that a new entrance on the north-east side with a protecting arm should replace the eastern projection. This question was placed before the Home authorities by the Madras and Indian Governments, but the harbour was completed according to the original plan—that is, with a 515 foot eastern entrance—in 1895. The "hoary and insoluble enigma," as it was termed by Lord Curzon, of making Madras harbour a smooth-water enclosure, was continually under discussion, and in 1902 the matter was referred by the Secretary of State to a strong committee composed of Admiral Sir George Nares, Assoc.Inst.C.E., Sir Charles A. Hartley, M.Inst.C.E., and Mr. (afterwards Sir) William Matthews, a former President of the Institute of Civil Engineers. Definite proposals were submitted in the following year, and sanction was then obtained for the construction of a north-eastern entrance and for the closing of the eastern one. The carrying out of the work was entrusted to the superintendence of Mr. F. J. Wilson, M.Inst.C.E., who at the time was chief engineer under the Madras Harbour Trust Board.

It was in the year 1904 that Sir Francis J. E. Spring, K.C.I.E., M.A.I., M.Inst. C.E., who had served for 33½ years with the Indian Government, and who had recently retired from the Secretaryship of the Madras Government's Railway Department, became permanent chairman of the Port Trust, but two years later he added to the chairmanship the office of chief engineer, in succession to Mr. Wilson. A full account of the improvements effected in the remodelling and equipment of the harbour will be found in a most valuable and interesting paper which was submitted on the 16th of April, 1912, to a meeting of the members of the Institution of Civil Engineers by Sir Francis Spring.

The following particulars of the carrying out of the improvements in question have been obtained from Sir Francis Spring's pamphlet, and the kindness of the author in providing a copy is gratefully recognized.

The remodelling consisted of three separate portions, namely, the construction of the new sheltering arm or breakwater; secondly, of the opening out of the new north-eastern entrance; and, thirdly, of the closing of the old eastern entrance.

On the advice of their engineer the Port Trust Authorities adopted a vigorous policy and a comprehensive scheme of improvements was carried out simultaneously with the remodelling of the form of the harbour.

The proposals included (*a*) a radical re-arrangement of the lines and sidings in the Harbour Trust's yard; (*b*) improvements for the handling of coal; (*c*) improved cranes; (*d*) an export pier equipped with cranes; (*e*) a pier for dutiable imports; (*f*) a shed of an area of 1¾ acres for dutiable imports; (*g*) a 7-acre basin for lighters and small craft drawing under 12 ft. of water; (*h*) a slipway for hauling up vessels up to 500 tons burden; (*i*) jetties, cranes, sidings, and other facilities for the timber trade; (*j*) space and sidings for minerals and rough cargo near the boat basin and south arm; (*k*) improved arrangements, pier, waiting, and other rooms for use of passengers; (*l*) wharves and other arrangements for improving the landing of iron; (*m*) extensive arrangements, including hydraulic cranes, for the landing and dispatching or stacking of coal, (*n*) a pier for non-dutiable imports; and (*o*) sheds for non-dutiable goods, whether imports or exports.

A marked increase of trade accompanied the progress of the works, and statistics show that there has been a steady increase in the tonnage of vessels entering Madras.

The north sheltering breakwater is 36 ft. in breadth, and its height above the rubble base is from 43 ft. to 50 ft., and it has been constructed on the sloping slice-work principle which was used in the formation of the earlier breakwaters.

The new north-east entrance was opened in September 1909. The first vessel to pass through the new opening was the British India Steam Navigation

MADRAS PORT TRUST.

1. S.S. "Nevassa" Embarking Passengers at South Quay, Madras Harbour. 2. Shipping Cargo, Madras. 3. Dutiable Import Pier, Madras Harbour.

Company's *Tara*, which made the passage on the 19th of December, 1909, in the presence of H.E. the Viceroy of India.

It was then possible to close the original entrance, and this work occupied a little longer than six months, a most creditable performance considering the many difficulties which had to be encountered. As the old entrance had shoaled up with sand at the rate of 15 ft. in twenty-six years, of which 10 ft. occurred in the last ten years of that period, and as an enormous quantity of sand had been sucked by waves and blown by winds into the harbour, the Port Trust in 1904 had purchased the 900-ton hopper suction dredger *Madras* from Messrs. Simons & Co., of Renfrew. Excellent results have been obtained from this dredger, and now, with the alteration of the form of the harbour, all anxiety has been removed on the score of sand silting up at the entrance and of shoals forming inside it. This vessel dredged 1,400,000 tons in five years, working 1,030 days with an average of 1,360 tons a day at 4s. 9d. a ton.

Further excellent work of a similar character was performed by the bucket-hopper dredger *Triton*, which was used principally for deepening berths for coaling and in the preparation of a sea-bed for ships using the steel wharf.

In the papers referred to Sir Francis Spring gave a very complete account of the internal equipment of the harbour for the speedier handling of traffic, and, although much of this was of too scientific a character for this sketch, some particulars may be given.

Until the year 1905 the port possessed very inferior accommodation for the discharge of cargo, and the first practical addition, in this year, was a 4½-in. screw-pile jetty for exports, which was equipped with eight hand cranes, served by a tramway of 2-ft. gauge.

A 6-in. screw-pile pier, equipped with fourteen 1-ton hydraulic cranes, was added subsequently. The yard for imports of iron in the boat basin is served by five small 6-in. screw-pile jetties, each having a 3-ton hydraulic crane. The timber pond has six similar jetties, each of which has a 3-ton hand crane. The mind of the ordinary layman will be deeply impressed when he reflects upon the inadequate wharfage of early days and when he now realizes what has been accomplished. The length of wharves and piers which were in use early in 1912 was 3,200 ft., and there were 51 hydraulic, 9 steam, and 20 hand cranes, at which from fifty to sixty lighters could be worked simultaneously. Much progress has been made since then, and ultimately, by the end of 1916, there will be a line of masonry ship quays, 3,000 ft. in length, which will extend along the whole of the east side of the harbour from north to south, furnishing accommodation for six steamers, in addition to the three quays for steamers already available.

Behind the piers, wharves, and cranes about 250,000 square feet of new steel shedding have been provided, and these have ample facilities for the sorting and delivery of cargo. Timber can be floated from the sides of ships into a two-acre basin at all tides, and there are cranes, lorries, and railway sidings for its removal.

One of the features of the works, which is of vast importance to the revenue of the Presidency, is the ample provision which has been made for the Government Customs service, and the new sheds are available for appraising values, for opening and closing of packages, and for the preparation of all documents connected therewith. Strong-rooms have been built for the deposit of bullion and for the storage of exciseable liquors. All the sheds and piers are lighted by electricity, and the loading or discharge of cargo can be carried on throughout the night whenever the necessity arises.

Madras Harbour is admirably situated as regards railway communication with the interior; the systems of the Madras and Southern Mahratta, and of the South Indian Railways converge at the port, and further, the majority of the large business houses of the exporting and importing merchants are within a stone's-throw of both railway trucks and wharves. Wagons belonging to each of these companies run over all the lines within the harbour area, and goods can be booked to any station in India from one or other of the two railway offices within the yard.

An abundant supply of labour has always been obtainable, and with the exception of the erecting and plate-laying gangs, who come from Surat and the Punjab respectively, all the hands were secured locally, the rates varying from 6d. to 1s. a day of eight hours. Carpenters, stonemasons, and other craftsmen are paid from 1s. to 2s. a day, according to their capabilities, while leading men received 25 to 50 per cent. more.

As an indication of the growth of trade at the port, it may be observed that the export and the import foreign and coasting trade averaged Rs. 40,27,94,648 for the five years ending between 1908 and 1909, while the period for 1911 to 1912 gave Rs. 51,88,13,974. The figures for the latest period are not yet available, but interim statistics show that a very large increase would be the result of the year's working.

The Port Trust Board, and Sir Francis Spring in particular, is to be congratulated upon its forward policy, and merchants and traders are satisfied that the Board is doing all in its power to ensure cheap freights with Europe, to provide ample accommodation at deep water wharves, to give as much shelter as possible to vessels discharging or shipping cargo, and to offer special advantages in the speedy handling of imports and exports.

ADDISON & CO., LTD.

If there is one special feature which stands out more prominently than any other in connection with the very extensive establishment of Messrs. Addison & Co., Ltd., of Mount Road, Madras, it is that, in each branch, everything in the way of stock or in the management is thoroughly up to date in every respect. The business was founded in 1873 by a Mr. Hawkins, who opened a small printing works, which, however, gave promise of considerable development. Mr. Tom Luker, the present head of the company, purchased the concern in 1886; a stationery department was added two years later; while, in 1892, the proprietor was practically the pioneer in Madras in the cycle industry. Motor-cars were taken up by the firm in 1904, when only one vehicle of this character had previously been seen in Madras. Early in 1906 Mr. Tom Luker was joined by his two elder sons, Messrs. W. H. and A. T. Luker. The business under their joint management has continued to increase rapidly, and the sound of building has seldom been absent since. Only the best types of motor cycles are stocked by the company, such as "Triumphs," "Humbers," "P. & M.," "Sunbeams," and others, and more than six hundred of the first name have been disposed of since 1910. About a dozen cars by leading builders are usually kept in stock, and the accessories in the store-rooms for either car or cycle are of the most modern and complete description. A special feature is made of cutting gear-wheels, and of ordinary

ADDISON & CO., LTD.

1. General View of Showrooms on Mount Road. To the left the Stationery and Fancy Goods Department; in centre Motor Cycles and Lamps; on the right the new Motor-car Showroom now being built (1915).
2. Stationery, Watches, Clocks, and Fancy Goods Showroom.
3. Main Printing Machine-room of Addison Press.
4. Motor Garage: Machine Shops on left, Erecting and Running Shop in centre.

engineering work in fixing up or repairing motors.

In 1909 the firm installed the first complete Harvey Frost vulcanizing plant in Madras for repairing motor tyres. This has been added to considerably, and complete retreading and other work now undertaken.

The works now cover an area of 60,000 square feet, and about 600 hands are employed, exclusive of the European motor experts and departmental managers. In 1909 a new two-storied building, measuring 120 ft. by 42 ft., was erected as a showroom for cars and cycles, for petrol, lamps, Michelin tyres, and all other necessary fittings and appliances. This showroom has proved inadequate, and another big motor-car showroom is being erected adjoining it. This will have a handsome frontage, and should be an addition to the architectural features of Mount Road.

Messrs. Addison & Co., Ltd., have very large dealings in fountain pens, watches and clocks, and in all kinds of fancy goods, while card indexes and office furniture of a stylish character are supplied to Government and other buildings.

Another important branch of the firm's business is surveying instruments and engineers' and drawing office requisites. A large stock of Stanley's, Cooke's, and other leading makers' goods is kept, as well as artists' materials and mathematical instruments.

The printing plant of to-day is very different from that which was in use when Mr. Hawkins commenced business about forty years ago; everything is now of the latest design, and the whole of the machinery is driven by electricity. Engraving on steel dies and on copperplates is very finely executed by competent assistants. A complete lithographic plant turns out coloured labels, almanacs, plans, etc., in a style that compares well with London work. Calendars in as many as fourteen colours have been produced.

Branch establishments have been opened at Ootacamund and Bangalore, and agents have been appointed in about twenty-six important towns in the Presidency.

The firm was registered on November 26, 1914, as a private limited liability company, but the ownership and management remained in the same hands as heretofore. The present directors are Mr. Tom Luker, who personally supervises all buying in England; and his sons, Messrs. W. H. & A. T. Luker, who are joint managing directors in Madras. Messrs. Addison & Co., Ltd., are usually described as being letterpress and lithographic printers, bookbinders, manufacturing stationers, engravers, fancy goods merchants, cycle and motor agents and repairers and general engineers.

BEST & CO., LTD.

One of the leading mercantile houses in Southern India is that of Messrs. Best & Co., Ltd., of North Beach, Madras, who are general merchants, importers and exporters, and agents for a large number of important companies and firms. The founders were Messrs. A. V. Dunlop Best and John McLintock, who entered into partnership in 1879 under the title of Best & Co., taking over and continuing the business connection of Messrs. Aspinwall & Co., who had been established in the city for the previous ten years. Mr. Robert J. Black and Mr. Charles Slater were admitted as partners six years later, and Mr. Vaughan G. Lynn and Mr. Gordon Fraser were admitted into partnership in 1900 and 1909 respectively. In 1911 the firm was registered under the Indian Companies Act of 1882. Mr. Gordon Fraser is managing director in Madras, and the managers are Messrs. W. W. Paul and T. M. Ross.

A very large quantity of produce, such as groundnut kernels and other oil seeds and produce, is exported annually, and large consignments of hides and skins are shipped from Southern India to Europe by this company. Dealers purchase the hides and skins in the various bazaars throughout the Presidency, and they subsequently forward them to the company's warehouses in Madras, where they are sorted, valued, and paid for according to current rates.

The imports consist principally of Manchester piece goods, for which there is a demand from wholesale merchants.

The premises of the company are situated opposite the Beach railway-station and facing the harbour.

Branches of the company have been established at Pondicherry and Secunderabad, and it has agents in all towns of any importance throughout the Madras Presidency and the native States of Southern India. Agencies are held by the company for the P. & O. Steam Navigation Co., Ltd., the Bucknall Steamship Lines, Ltd. (American and Indian line), the Anchor Line, the Societa Veneziana di Navigation a Vapore, the Ellerman Lines, Ltd ("Hall" and "City"), the Asiatic Petroleum Company of India, Ltd., the Anglo-Saxon Oil Co., Ltd., the Anglo-French Textile Co., Ltd., the Hyderabad (Deccan) Co., Ltd., the Barrakur Coal Co., Ltd., the Mysore Gold Mining Co., Ltd., the Oorgaum Gold Mining Company of India, Ltd., the Champion Reef Gold Mining Company of India, Ltd., the Nundydroog Co., Ltd., the Kolar Mines Power Station, Ltd., the Balaghat Gold Mining Co., Ltd., the North Anantapur Gold Mines, Ltd., the Jibutil Gold Mines of Anantapur, Ltd., Hutti (Nizam's) Gold Mines, Ltd., the Kolar Gold Fields Electricity Department, the British Westinghouse Electric and Manufacturing Co., Ltd., Sir W. G. Armstrong, Whitworth & Co., Ltd., Merryweather and Sons, Ltd., Brown, Lennox & Co., Ltd., Sanderson Bros. and Newbould, Ltd., D. H. and G. Haggie, Joseph Dee and Sons, the Hongkong Rope Manufacturing Co., Ltd., the Jeyes' Sanitary Compounds Co., Ltd., Booth's Lion Brand Cement, E. Gaudart & Co. (St. Elizabeth Iron Works, Pondicherry), the Unbreakable Pully and Mill Gearing Co., Ltd., the Barrett Manufacturing Company, Petters, Ltd., Corbett Williams and Son, Ltd., the Associated Manufacturing Company, Thomas Henshelwood & Co., Ltd., Birkmyre Brothers, and Nobel's Explosives Co., Ltd.

BINNY & CO., LTD.

One of the oldest businesses in Madras is that of the well-known firm of Messrs. Binny & Co., Ltd., of Armenian Street, in Georgetown. It was established in or about the year 1790 by Mr. John Binny (who was the captain of a sailing ship) as a general, clearing, and forwarding agency. From the old records we find that another brother, also a sea captain, established a firm of the same name in Calcutta, and that after the two brothers had retired from a seafaring life they continued to run two ships (called the *Success Galley* and the *Surprise Galley*) between Calcutta and Madras. The original premises were situated in Fort St. George, but the business increased by leaps and bounds, and the present extensive buildings were occupied in 1812. The removal to Armenian Street synchronized with an enormous expansion of the firm's interests.

Messrs. Binny & Co., Ltd., are perhaps the largest general merchants in the City of Madras, and they have a banking establishment for the furtherance of

BEST & CO., LTD.

1. OFFICE BUILDINGS. 2. S.S. "CITY OF POONA" (CITY LINE).

BEST & CO., LTD.

1. Explosives Magazine. 2. Oil Installation.

BINNY & CO., LTD. (THE BUCKINGHAM MILLS).

1. East Block, Buckingham Mills. 2. Spinning-room. 3. Warehouse.

business transactions with their many clients. As agents of the British India Steam Navigation Co., Ltd., Messrs. Binny & Co. have acquired a flotilla of boats, and they now handle a very considerable proportion of the imports of Madras. For this purpose they maintain steam and petrol launches, and a fleet of some 35 barges and 30 lighters which have a carrying capacity of about 2,500 tons. The firm are landing agents to the Madras Port Trust, and immigrants from the Straits and Rangoon are transferred to the shore from steamers which do not go alongside the various wharves at the harbour. The employees consist of 400 bargemen and about the same number of stevedores. As a fleet of cargo boats of this size requires to be continually kept in repair, Messrs. Binny & Co. have at the south end of the boat basin a large yard with a slipway, where even their 100-ton barges can be hauled up for periodical inspection. To cope with the increasing difficulty of carting goods from exporters' godowns to the harbour, the firm has recently established a transport service, in which not only the oxen of the country, but steam and petrol lorries of the latest construction are in constant use.

Amongst the varied interests with which this firm is associated are the cotton and wool industry, spinning and weaving, the growing of coffee, and the importing of all kinds of merchandise, together with the agency of Fire, Life, Accident, and other Insurance Companies, and for mercantile, manufacturing, and other firms.

The Buckingham Mill Company, Ltd., of which the firm are secretaries and treasurers, was started in 1877 as a spinning factory only, with a capital of Rs. 500,000, for the working of 16,400 spindles, and employment was found for about 600 operatives, but weaving was introduced in 1890. The capital is now Rs. 14,00,000, and the mill contains 40,000 spindles and 1,100 looms, and more than 5,000 workpeople are employed.

The Carnatic Mill Co., Ltd., for which the firm are secretaries, was founded in 1882 for spinning and weaving, with a capital of Rs. 700,000. There were 16,572 spindles, 129 looms, and 700 operatives, but the capital is now Rs. 10,00,000, and the mill contains 35,000 spindles and 1,050 looms, and about 5,000 hands are in constant employment.

These two mills are three miles distant from the city offices of the firm, but they are within the limits of the municipal area. The mills were started to supply local needs, but with the rise of the Swadeshi movement a market has been secured throughout India and Burma for the sale of their products, which primarily consist of dyed cloth, sheetings, bleach twills, and other similar materials. A large export trade is done with the Straits Settlements, China, and Australia, while customers in the West Indies are served through London and Manchester buyers.

The development of the company's cotton interests has involved the erection of ginning and cotton press factories up-country, in order that the mills may be supplied with raw material.

In addition to the Buckingham and Carnatic Mills, the firm are also the agents, secretaries, and treasurers to the Bangalore Woollen and Cotton Silk Mills Co., Ltd., at Bangalore. This company was started in 1884 (with a capital of Rs. 4,00,000) to take over the business of the Bangalore Woollen Mills and to add thereto the manufacture of cotton yarn and goods. The agency was placed in Messrs. Binny & Co.'s hands in 1886, since which time the mills have more than doubled in size.

The chief products are cotton yarn army blankets, Jhools, and cotton and woollen hosiery, and the weaving of cotton goods is now to be undertaken. The capital is now Rs. 12,00,000, of which the sum of Rs. 10,00,000 is paid up, and there are 19,000 cotton spindles, 1,800 woollen mule spindles, 48 woollen looms, and 100 heads of hosiery machinery, while employment is found for about 1,300 operatives. The mill was originally driven by steam-power, but when electrical energy became available by the supply generated at the Cauvery, a contract was entered into with the Mysore Government, and the machinery is now driven entirely by electricity.

The whole of the output of the mills finds a market in India and Burmah, most of the cotton yarn finding a ready sale locally ; while the company has for many years held most of the important Government contracts for army blankets and Jhools.

Messrs. Binny & Co., Ltd., commenced the cultivation of coffee in Mysore in the early fifties, and they now have about 3,500 acres under this crop. The bean is cured at Mangalore and at Tellicherry, and consignments are shipped from the latter place direct to London. Between 500 tons and 700 tons are exported during a favourable season, and about 1,500 hands are employed on the plantations.

Among the many mercantile and other agencies under the supervision of the firm are: the Madras Electric Supply Corporation of India, Ltd., the Tadpatri Cotton Press Company, Ltd., the Jammalamadugu Press Company, Ltd., the Tirupur Press Company, Ltd., the Standard Life Assurance Company, the Norwich and London Accident Insurance Association, the British and Foreign Marine Insurance Company, Ltd., the Royal Exchange Assurance, the Atlas Assurance Company, Ltd., the Norwich Union Fire Insurance Society, Ltd., the Phœnix Assurance Company, Ltd., the China Fire Insurance Company, Ltd., the Manchester Fire Insurance Company, Ltd., the Netherlands-India Sea and Fire Insurance Co., Ltd., the Palatine Insurance Company, Ltd., the Scottish Union and National Insurance Company, Ltd., the Triton Insurance Company, Ltd., of Calcutta, and Millars Jarrah Timber and Trading Company.

The registered offices of the company are at No. 9 Throgmorton Avenue, London, E.

THE BOMBAY COMPANY, LTD. (DYMES & CO., LTD.)

The Bombay Company, Ltd., which has its head office at Bombay, with branches at Karachi and Calcutta, opened a branch at Madras in 1907, and it acquired the old-established business of Dymes & Co., Ltd., in 1913. The principal trades carried on by the two firms are the exporting of cotton, groundnuts, jute, coir, yarn, and palmyra fibre, together with the importing of cotton piece goods and yarn, sugar, metals, and camphor, while there is also a very large import of teak into Madras and coast ports from the Bombay-Burmah Trading Corporation, Burma and Siam, whose agency is held by the Bombay Company, Ltd.

The firm has cotton presses and ginning factories at Tuticorin, Kadambur, Satur, Virudupati, Dindigul, Prodatore, Timmancherla, Bellary, Adoni, and Raichur, and numerous up-country agencies have been opened for the purchase of cotton, jute, and other goods

Among the agencies held by the firm are those of the Bombay-Burma Trading Corporation, Ltd., the Vishnu

BINNY & CO., LTD. (THE CARNATIC MILLS).

1. Packing Room. 2. General View. 3. Winding Room. 4. Mixing Room.

BINNY & CO., LTD.

1. BINNY AND CO.'S OFFICES. 2. B.I.S.N. CO.'S S.S. "EKMA." 3. A STEAMER AT THE WHARF.

Cotton Mill, Ltd., the Pacific Mail Steamship Company, the Nippon Yusen Kaisha, the Royal, the Imperial, the Eastern, the North China, and the World Marine Insurance Companies, the Trussed Concrete Steel Company, of Detroit, U.S.A., and the Paraffin Paint Company, of San Francisco, U.S.A.

The Madras premises were formerly occupied by the Bank of Madras, and they consist of a fine two-storied building (with an extensive frontage on three streets) in addition to a large number of godowns. The staff employed at Madras and at the up-country agencies and factories comprise about 16 Europeans and several hundred natives.

A. C. BULLMORE'S ARTHURSTON POULTRY FARM.

1. A Corner of the Showroom. 2 and 3. Portions of the Farm.

A. C. BULLMORE

The rearing of poultry may be a success or a dismal failure, according to the manner in which it is undertaken, and to the experience, the energy, and the patience of those who engage in it. It is only in recent years that this matter has received the attention which it deserves, and it has now been conclusively proved that the industry can be made a pleasant and profitable vocation. Farmers and others were at one time wont to keep a number of nondescript fowls, the birds were permitted to mate in a haphazard fashion without the slightest thought being given to their suitability, and the result was that the supply of eggs was wholly insufficient to meet the cost of food. Mr. Arthur C. Bullmore, the owner of the "Arthurston" Poultry Farm, in Mount Road, Madras, is undoubtedly the leading breeder in India of pure strains of fowls, and he is the originator of the celebrated "Arthurston" White Orpingtons and White Leghorns. He commenced business about the year 1900 by importing pens of each of these breeds from some of the principal yards in England, such as Messrs. Whitaker and Toothill, of Leeds, Messrs. W. Cook and Sons and Mr. W. H. Cook, who have runs in the county of Kent, and Mr. J. H. Blackwood, of Somersetshire. In establishing the "Arthurston" strains, Mr. Bullmore secured the best birds from the most skilled breeders in England and Australia. Some from the latter country were obtained from the "Range Poultry Farm" in Queensland, while a pen which was purchased from Mr. Edward Cam, of Preston, England, was closely related to birds which hold the record for the whole world in egg-laying competitions. Mr. Bullmore's fowls are kept under ideal conditions, and particular attention is given to cleanliness and sanitation. The hatching of chickens takes place by both natural and artificial means, some six or seven incubators, each capable of holding 100 eggs, being fully employed during the season. The young birds are reared in "brooders" in batches of from 30 to 40, and they are automatically fed and watered. There is no indiscriminate breeding at "Arthurston," as a most careful selection is made of cockerels and pullets for mating purposes. Fully grown birds as well as chicks have been sent to customers in all parts of India, even as far northwards as Baluchistan, and to Burma, Ceylon, the Straits Settlements, and to Perim Island in the Red Sea, while a consignment of more than 40 head was recently despatched to Java. Hundreds of testi-

DYMES & CO., LTD. (THE BOMBAY CO., LTD.).

1. MADRAS PREMISES. 2. DINDIGUL FACTORY. 3. FACTORY, KADAMBUR. 4. BUNGALOW, KADAMBUR.

monials have been received by Mr. Bullmore, which speak in terms of the highest praise of birds or of settings of eggs which have been purchased from this farm. More than 65 prizes have been gained by Arthurston birds at exhibitions in India, Burma, Penang, and Ceylon. Some of the latest successes include: At Simla in October 1913 first honours were gained for cocks and hens, and for the best country-bred hen, together with the Lieutenant-Governor's cup for the best bird in the show; at Bangalore in 1913 the awards were one gold medal, three silver cups, and three certificates of merit; at Madras in 1914 a silver cup for the best birds in the show was won by Mr. Bullmore's entry; at Ootacamund in May 1914 White Leghorns secured first, second, and third prizes, White Orpingtons were placed first and second, a silver medal for the best imported bird of any "light" variety, a silver cup for the best hen bred by exhibitor, a silver shield for the best Leghorn, and a silver shield for the best hen exhibited by a member of the South Indian Poultry Association. Few poultry owners bestow such attention upon the preparation of birds for exhibition purposes as Mr. Bullmore. He has a training-room in which there are specially fitted coops which are placed upon tables, the surroundings being similar to the arrangements of an ordinary show. Mr. Bullmore is a chemist by profession, and after making a life-long study of poultry ailments he has published a most valuable manual in which various diseases are described and the necessary treatment explained. In addition, he manufactures and supplies all kinds of appliances such as incubators, cellular egg boxes, egg testers, feeding and water-troughs, and trap-nests. He has, naturally, made a careful trial of the principal incubators in the market, and he is satisfied that those made by William Lea are particularly suitable for the Indian climate. Mr. Bullmore is sole agent for these machines in India, Burma, and Ceylon. He is a member of the White Orpington and White Leghorn Clubs of England and America, a member of the Utility Club, England, of the Ceylon Poultry Club, and of the South India Poultry Association. Mr. Bullmore has recently published a revised and enlarged edition of his manual on "Poultry," and this book, which is specially intended for Indian poultry breeders, is full of valuable information as to selection, breeding, management, and exhibiting of fowls, and a careful study of it shows that the author has a remarkably sound knowledge of the industry in which he is engaged. Visitors are always welcomed at Arthurston, and not a single person who has had the pleasure of seeing the magnificent birds in their well-appointed runs and coops has gone away disappointed.

THE CHROME LEATHER COMPANY

The largest tanners and manufacturers of leather goods in Southern India is the claim made by The Chrome Leather Company of Madras with respect to the very extensive commercial enterprises carried on by them. Their business has risen, phoenix-like, from the ashes of past failure, and to-day it occupies a position which many might envy.

The founder, Mr. G. A. Chambers, commenced his business career in the leather trade in London at the age of sixteen; ten years later (1894) he arrived in Madras, and for the following eight years was solely interested in the leather export trade, first as assistant, next as manager. In 1903 he started business on his own account; and has been continuously successful in the hide and skin export trade, a circumstance which has enabled him to pioneer the chrome leather industry in Madras.

For some years prior to commencing business on his own account, Mr. Chambers had been greatly interested in the subject of the development of chrome tanning in this country. He, in the first place, sought to interest leading Madras firms in the industry; he then endeavoured, but without success, to obtain Government assistance, but, eventually (late in 1903), he rented a small tannery at Pallavaram, about 12 miles distant from Madras, and on his own account commenced chrome tanning on a small scale. Later on a combination of interests was effected with Messrs. Simpson & Co., of Madras, who had for some time previously been finishing moroccos and other leathers for use in their carriage furnishing business, and a separate concern was then started under the name of Brown & Co., tanners and leather finishers. A tannery was rented at Tondiarpet, a suburb of Madras, and work was carried on there, but the financial results of the venture were unsatisfactory and eventually it was decided to close it down.

Mr. Chambers was, however, still strongly of the opinion that, given expert management, success might yet be achieved; he accordingly purchased the assets of Brown & Co., and decided to continue the effort on his own account under his firm's name of Chambers & Co., and the business was so carried on until January 1912; when a change was made, new interests being admitted into the export branch of the business, which was continued as Chambers & Co., while the tanning and manufacturing business was carried on solely by Mr. Chambers under the name of The Chrome Leather Company.

It was at first intended to form the latter concern into a limited company, but this idea was given up, as it was thought it would be better to do so when the business had become established and results were such as to justify asking for public support.

After taking over the business from Messrs. Brown & Co., Mr. Chambers in the first place brought out from England an expert tanner and leather finisher (who is still in charge of the tannery), and since then there has been continuous development, except for a very serious set-back and heavy financial loss about three years back, caused by an outbreak of malaria at Tondiarpet, when, labour being practically unobtainable, it was decided to remove the works entirely to a healthier situation. After considerable difficulty, a site of about 25 acres of land was secured at Pallavaram, at a good elevation, with excellent water, and here, two years since, the erection of the new tannery and works was commenced.

The great improvement in the quality of the bark and chrome tanned leathers, produced under the more favourable conditions, has naturally resulted in a continually increasing demand; enlargements to the tannery are being made in all directions, and it is hoped to have same completed early in 1916. Work is at present found for about 400 tannery employees, most of whom are provided with free quarters. A new leather goods factory is also in course of erection on a site adjoining the tannery as the steadily increasing business has caused a demand for more labour than can be accommodated at the present factory at Lecot's Buildings in Georgetown. For the same reason arrangements have been made so that in future the retail trade will be carried on in newly erected premises on the Mount Road facing Niel's statue and near the Madras Club. Here a staff

THE CHROME LEATHER COMPANY.

1. LIME PITS—UNHAIRING SKINS. 2. TANNING DRUMS. 3. TANNING PITS. 4. SETTING-OUT TABLES. 5. BAND KNIFE SPLITTING. 6. FINISHING MACHINES.

of about 100 will be constantly employed in the production of hand-made footwear, for which the excellent wearing qualities have secured a retail mail order footwear trade, larger, we believe, than that of any other single concern in India.

The productions of the company are so varied that they are best summed up in the words, "Any leather (bark or chrome tanned) or any leather article." They find a ready market over a very wide area, embracing South and East Africa, Abyssinia, Aden, the Persian Gulf, Mauritius, India, Burma, Ceylon, and many parts of the Far East.

Leathers for industrial uses, such as cotton ginning washers, picking bands, laces, belting, etc., are produced in considerable quantities, and an even larger trade is assured as the merits of the company's productions become more widely known.

THE CROMPTON ENGINEERING COMPANY.

1. Main Generating Station. 2. Laying Underground Mains.

THE CROMPTON ENGINEERING COMPANY

There is no other firm in Southern India which has been entrusted with such important electrical schemes as the Crompton Engineering Company, of 7 Armenian Street, Madras, who represent the well-known firm of Messrs. Crompton & Co., Ltd., who established their business connections in the city in 1890.

The present concern was originally founded by Colonel Crompton, and it was formed into a limited liability company in 1888. The head office is at Salisbury House, London Wall, London, E.C., with works at Chelmsford, Essex, and branch offices at Glasgow, Newcastle-on-Tyne, Manchester, Birmingham, Bristol, Sydney, Calcutta, Shanghai, and other important centres.

Messrs. Crompton & Co., Ltd., some time ago entered into an important contract with the Madras Electric Supply Corporation for a huge scheme for the supply of electricity within the limits of the city of Madras, and the power-stations were completed and the supply was successfully initiated in 1910.

Messrs. Crompton & Co., Ltd., are specialists in the manufacture of alternating and direct-current dynamos and motors, switchboards, arc lamps, ceiling fans, instruments, and other electrical appliances, and the name of "Crompton" is synonymous with excellence of manufacture. The Crompton Engineering Company are sole agents for Crompton & Co., Ltd., in Southern India, and they hold large stocks of their manufactures in their extensive godowns in McLean Street. They are also agents for the Leeds Fireclay Company, Engleberts oils, Henley's cables, and Dick, Kerr & Co.'s Britannia metallic filament lamps.

As electrical engineers and contractors the Crompton Engineering Company have attained an impregnable position, and they are always prepared to submit schemes for and to undertake the installation of electric light and power in Rajah's palaces, private houses, business premises, mills, factories, harbours, mines, colleges, and other public and private institutions.

H. M. GIBSON & CO.

That densely populated section of the city of Madras known as Georgetown is the centre of keen commercial activities, and new enterprises are constantly coming into existence side by side with establishments whose doors have been open for a century or longer. One of the recent additions is the firm of Messrs. H. M. Gibson & Co., who are conducting a thriving business as dealers in tanned hides and skins and as seed and general produce merchants. The founder —Mr. H. M. Gibson—commenced operations in 1911, and he has a thoroughly practical acquaintance with every detail of the undertaking. No fewer than from 50 to 60 hands are permanently employed, but a considerable amount of extra work is done by contract.

Tanned hides and skins from all over the Presidency are purchased locally through the native dealer or middleman acting for the tanner, and they are then submitted to the process of sorting and pressing before they are baled for export to the United Kingdom or to the United States of America. More than 2,500 bales of tanned hides (kips) were shipped by this firm during the year 1912, but the rapid expansion of business during the following twelve months showed conclusively that these figures had been greatly exceeded.

Messrs. Gibson & Co. have agencies in London, Liverpool, Hamburg, and Australia, and business relations have been commenced with Japan, while they are, further, representatives of the Employers' Liability Assurance Corporation, Ltd.

H. M. GIBSON & CO.

1. Sorting Hides. 2. Baling Hides.

GORDON, WOODROFFE & CO.

It is a most gratifying feature of the commercial activities of the Presidency that the value of its exports and imports show a steady yet very decided increase when a comparison is made between the figures for 1912 and those of four or five years previously. The annual value of the imports of the foreign trade for the five years ending in 1904 was Rs. 10,04,31,332, while the figures for 1912 were Rs. 12,11,53,338, showing an increase of 7 per cent. The exports during the same periods were Rs. 17,24,38,845 and Rs. 23,52,88,715, or an increase of 8 per cent. These figures do not include the value of government stores nor of the very considerable coastal trade, which shows an improvement to the tune of 23 per cent., owing to larger shipments of earthnut seeds to Bengal and of earthnut oil to Burma. The greatly improved position of many classes of produce in foreign exports in 1912 was mainly due to heavier consignments of rice, paddy, copra, seeds, tanned hides, and skins, and coir manufactures.

The majority of the Madras merchants have had a share in this expansion of business, and the reputable firm of Gordon, Woodroffe & Co. has, through its various branches and by manifold agencies, contributed largely to this satisfactory state of affairs.

The city of Madras was selected by the founders of the firm for the commencement of operations about the year 1868, and it is noteworthy that the original premises—to which additions and improvements have been made from time to time—are occupied by the partners of to-day. The latter consist of Mr. G. W. P. Woodroffe, Mr. W. A. Wigzam, Sir Hugh Stein Fraser, and Mr.

J. F. Simpson. The principal imports consist of piece goods, yarns, kerosene oil, metals, and sugar, while the exports include seeds, hides, skins, and general produce. Branches of the business have been established at Bimlipatam, Vizagapatam, Coconada, Pondicherry, and Cuddalore, and consignments of produce are exported direct from these stores to England and other countries.

A factory equipped with the necessary machinery for cutting, drying, and baling Palmyra fibre has been started at Colachel, and several hundred natives are employed in the works, the management of which is in the hands of a capable European. The output of the factory—which, by the way, is composed almost wholly of native sheds—is exported in large quantities to London, Liverpool, Rotterdam, Antwerp, Havre, Hamburg, and New York, and it is used principally for the making of brushes.

The principal city offices of the company are situated on the South Beach Road, but the commercial staff occupies a part of the building, which is entirely separate from that in which the employees who are engaged in shipping and other agency work are located.

Messrs. Gordon, Woodroffe & Co. are agents for three popular steamship companies, namely: The Clan Line, which dispatches two ships a month from Glasgow, Manchester, and Liverpool, with two or three which make the voyage to England monthly according to the quantity of cargo; the Hansa Line, running three steamers a month from Antwerp, one or two from Middlesbrough, and two from New York; and the Well Line, which sends a monthly vessel from Middlesbrough and London.

Agencies for important marine insurance companies include the following: The Transatlantic Marine Insurance Co., Ltd., the Union Insurance Society of Canton, Ltd., the Yangtsze Insurance Association, Ltd., the Canton Insurance Office, Ltd. Among the five offices represented by the firm are the Feuer Assuranz Compagnie Von 1877, the Yorkshire Fire Insurance Corporation, and Union Assurance Society, Ltd., while life policies are obtained from the City of Glasgow Life Assurance Company and the Scottish Imperial Insurance Company. The National Explosives Company, whose magazines are situated only a few miles from Madras, have placed their interests in the hands of this firm, and the latter are, further, connected in the management of tea and coffee estates in Shevaroy and Nilgiris.

It will be readily understood that the wages sheets are somewhat formidable documents, and no fewer than 16 Europeans are employed in the offices in Madras and the various branches.

Messrs. Gordon & Co. are, further, consular agents for the Government of Norway, and their London offices are situated at No. 1 East India Avenue, E.C.

DR. W. H. HALLER

Madras is stated in some guide-books to be a healthy city for Europeans as well as natives, but the large number of practising physicians and surgeons leaves one without doubt that, after all, there are germs to be attacked, fevers to be checked, and general bodily weaknesses and diseases to be overcome.

Dr. W. H. Haller (whose father was a member of the German Cabinet and emigrated to India during a period of political troubles, died in Singapore in 1853) received a portion of his early education at the Government Normal School at Madras, but straitened circumstances subsequently compelled him to rely upon his own personal efforts up to the age of 18, when he entered the Military Medical Department. He had a successful course there, and soon after entered upon a temporary appointment under the Colonial Government in the Straits Settlements. During this period, which extended to four years, the Malayan war broke out, and young Haller was given the medical charge of the expedition, which consisted of a detachment of British troops and Asiatic irregulars.

After returning to Malacca Dr. Haller assumed charge of the duties of the colonial surgeon from Major J. T. Orton, in addition to his other regular duties to the British troops of the station. With a view of obtaining further surgical knowledge, Dr. Haller returned to Madras, where he had the privilege of acting as personal assistant to the senior surgeon of the General Hospital. He spent some five years in that institution, with the exception of about eight months, when he assumed temporary charge as medical officer of the Indian Government steamer, *Patrick Stuart*, during the Afghan rising. When the Burmese war occurred Dr. Haller spent three months in the base hospital at Rangoon. As the severe strain of these campaigns began to have a serious effect upon his health he was permitted to retire with the grant of a small annuity.

Dr. Haller now established himself as a private practitioner in Madras, and he also opened a surgery and pharmacy with the view of supplying his patients with the purest drugs at moderate prices; and as the question of the provision of pure drinking water had become one of paramount importance, he opened an aerated water factory, which is conducted under the most favourable sanitary conditions.

It was about this time that the agent of the "Fellows" Manufacturing Company of New York visited Madras for the purpose of procuring an agent for the sale of their preparations, and he was so struck with the evident success of Dr. Haller's enterprises that the latter's establishment was at once selected as the depôt for supplying drugs to all parts of Southern India. For twenty years this agency has been carried on very successfully in spite of keen competition and of inferior imitations.

Dr. Haller is, further, the representative in the Madras Presidency of Messrs. Parke Davis & Co., of Detroit, U.S.A., and this branch of his business has increased at a remarkable rate during the last few years.

It is a well-known fact that the drugs sent out by these companies are prepared in accordance with the most recent discoveries and improvements in medical science, backed up by up-to-date knowledge in chemical research as well as in clinical medicine, and that they do not deteriorate even after the lapse of a considerable time.

The important firm of Messrs. Oppenheimer & Co., of Queen Victoria Street, London, then offered their agency for the Presidency to the subject of this sketch, and for fifteen years there has been a rapid development in the amount of business which has been transacted. These drugs are prepared with great accuracy by a thoroughly efficient chemical staff, in newly constructed laboratories which are fitted with all modern appliances.

Agencies are also held for specially prepared remedies such as Doan's liver, kidney, and dinner pills, and the Waterbury Company's (of New York) cod-liver oil preparation, all of which are well known throughout the world, and the steadily increasing sales in Madras are evidence of their popularity.

It is only natural that, with so wide an experience, Dr. Haller should have prepared certain medicines which have

GORDON, WOODROFFE & CO.

1. The Offices. 2. S.S. "Clan Macbeth." 3. S.S. "Clan Matheson."

DR. W. H. HALLER.

1. View of the Building. 2. Group of Employees. 3. Dr. Haller.

become household words throughout the Presidency, and reference may be made here to some of them.

His "fever pills" are said to be a certain and rapid cure for malaria, cutting short the course of the disease in about twenty-four hours, and purchasers of them are found in almost every tropical country in the world; the troublesome affliction of asthma, it is alleged, can be completely removed by the use of an asthma liquid or by pills; while the most remarkable success has attended the use of his whooping cough specific, which invariably shortens the duration of the complaint from three months to a couple of weeks. "Hallodeen," or the Indian remedy for dyspepsia, affords considerable relief from this distressing ailment, a permanent cure being effected in many instances.

Haller's special tonic increases the appetite, promotes digestion, and strengthens the action of the liver, and hundreds can bear testimony to the beneficial results which have followed its use.

The spacious and well-stocked premises are situated in Popham's Broadway, and the doctor has a large staff of thoroughly efficient and fully qualified assistants to deal with the very large practice which has been so firmly established, and which extends to all parts of India.

But perhaps the most important feature of Dr. Haller's work at the present time is the success which has followed his treatment of leprosy. Using an indigenous oil in a method of his own, the most happy results have followed, and many remarkable cures have been effected. He has also been most successful in treating tuberculosis, as well as those two greatly dreaded tropical diseases, namely white skin and elephantiasis.

THE HOTEL D'ANGELIS.
THE PARISIAN GARDEN.

THE HOTEL D'ANGELIS

Any discomfort which may be experienced in travelling—especially in a tropical country like Southern India—is very greatly minimized by the satisfaction with which one looks forward to the enjoyment of complete rest in a well-appointed residential hotel where excellent accommodation, coupled with efficient service, may confidently be expected. If one were to rely merely upon the advertisements of proprietors every hotel in the Presidency ought to be like Caesar's wife—above suspicion, but it is a well-known fact that such is not the case. No greater compliment can be paid to a manager than is given when visitors return to a place where they have proved by experience that "cleanliness of rooms, excellent cuisine, courteous servants," or, "leading hotel in the district," are not simply figures of speech. An enviable reputation has been gained by Messrs. G. d'Angelis & Son for the conduct of their establishments in Madras and Ootacamund.

Mr. Giacomo d'Angelis, the head of the firm, was in early life apprenticed to a confectioner in France. In the year 1880 he opened a small shop in Madras, where, by dint of hard work coupled with sound, practical experience, he soon made a name for himself as a restaurateur and general caterer, but he was continually contemplating the construction of a high-class hotel. He subsequently purchased the site upon which the present business is conducted, and the new building was opened in the year 1908.

The hotel occupies a central position in the European quarter of Mount Road, the leading thoroughfare in the city. It is near to Government House and the Madras Club, and within a few minutes' drive from the Central and Egmore railway stations.

A very fine reception-room is noticed on entering the building, whence visitors are transferred to the upper floors by an electric lift, which is a unique feature in Madras hotels. Too great praise cannot be given for the excellence of the sanitary arrangements, as each sleeping apartment is provided with a bath and toilet-room, in which there is an unlimited supply of hot and cold water.

All the ceilings are fitted with embossed steel, which is not only a preventive against undesirable insects, but is also a practical safeguard against fire. Wide passages and verandahs ensure the circulation of an abundance of fresh air, but additional comfort is derived from electric fans, which are to be found in every room. Every inch of flooring is covered with Minton tiles, the utmost cleanliness being thus ensured.

There is a very handsome dining-hall on the first floor, in which more than one hundred guests can be accommodated with meals at separate tables, and adjoining this are several private dining-rooms and a banqueting hall, which will seat sixty persons. The drawing-room is designed after a Swiss *chalet*, and decorators and furnishers have vied with each other in producing a cosy retreat amid most delightfully artistic surroundings.

Billiard players have the choice of three excellent tables, which have been fitted up by J. W. Roberts, of Madras, in a spacious hall measuring 80 feet in length and 30 feet in width, and there are comfortable reading and writing-rooms for ladies and gentlemen. No fewer than four verandahs overlook a charming Parisian garden, which is not equalled in South India for its wealth of shady trees and palms, and here one may be served with light refreshments while listening to the captivating strains of a first-class band of music.

Messrs. d'Angelis & Son are renowned for the excellence of their English, French, and Italian cuisine, and their lengthy experience in catering is a guarantee that the most fastidious customers cannot find fault. An indispensable adjunct to the culinary department, of a large hotel in the East has been provided in the shape of a refrigerating and ice-making plant, and there are, in addition, cool chambers for preserving meat, butter, and other provisions.

A motor-bus is sent to meet the principal trains and steamers, and this vehicle is available for parties desiring to visit places of interest in the neighbourhood.

Not the least important recommendation of this hotel is the fact that the proprietors take an active interest in securing all possible comforts and attention for their visitors, although an expert European manager has direct control over the small army of servants.

THE INDIAN ALUMINIUM COMPANY, LTD.

In 1898 the working of aluminium was introduced into India in the metal work department of the Madras School of Arts, and in 1900 the Indian Aluminium Company was started by Mr. Eardley Norton, then practising as a barrister in Madras, with a view of following up and developing the pioneer work undertaken by the Madras Government. For a time the company and the aluminium department worked in conjunction to open up a market in India, and they met with such success that in 1903 it was considered that the time had arrived when private enterprise could be left to carry on the business unaided; and this opinion was endorsed by the directors of the Indian Aluminium Company, who entered into an agreement with the Madras Government to take over the whole business developed at the School of Arts. The nominal capital of the company was increased to ten lakhs of rupees, and a sufficient number of shares were subscribed to finance the transfer and provide for further developments. The first workshops of the company were on the Mount Road and were rented from the Anjuman, but they soon proved inadequate and, some time before the transfer, the site now occupied by the existing factory was acquired.

In the early days of aluminium working in Madras very little machinery was used, and the number of skilled metal workers who found employment was large, but it was soon found that the primitive methods of the handworkers were inadequate, and gradually machine processes of working were introduced, until at the present time the workshops of the company are probably as complete as any in the world in regard to their equipment. The motive power is supplied by three large gas engines working on suction gas, and the energy is distributed to the various branches of the factory by electricity. The bulk of the work turned out by the company is accomplished by drawing and spinning processes, but no insignificant amount of hand work is still done, and probably in this factory to a greater degree than anywhere else may be found the old craftsman working alongside and in collaboration with modern machine processes.

At first the market for aluminium goods in India was mainly confined to Europeans and the native troops. It was only very slowly that the new metal found its way into the bazaar, but that it has finally done so there is evidence in the fact that the imports of raw metal into India were valued last year at over 25 lakhs of rupees. Its advantages and its limitations are now well known, prejudice against its use is gradually weakening, and there is little doubt that it has found a permanent sphere of utility in meeting some of the domestic requirements of the people of India. So far no attempt has been made to manufacture the raw metal in India, and it is doubtful if ever the conditions essential to success will be realized, and the company is still dependent on Europe for both sheet and ingot metal. The premises, however, are conveniently situated in Madras to develop business in the Farther East, and the exports of aluminium hollow-ware from that city are steadily increasing both in volume and value. The enterprise of the directors has met with deserved success, and as evidence of this it may be mentioned that the average dividend of the last six years has been $12\frac{2}{3}$ per cent.

R. MACLURE

The family druggist is as indispensable an institution as the household physician, and, unless the former has a large variety of pure drugs and is fully qualified to dispense them, all the skill of the medical practitioner is completely nullified. The sole proprietor of this establishment is Mr. R. Maclure Savege, who arrived in India in 1892, and commenced business in Mount Road, Madras, a couple of years later. He is a member of the Pharmaceutical Society of Great Britain, is Vice-President of the Pharmaceutical Society of India, and he is the representative of the Trades Association in the Madras Legislative Council. A large quantity of reli-

THE INDIAN ALUMINIUM COMPANY, LTD.

1. SPINNING SHOP. 2. POWER HOUSE. 3 DRAWING PRESSES.

able chemicals and drugs is kept in stock, and these are imported from England, with the exception of a few tinctures made from spirits which are manufactured on the premises. A special feature is the making up of prescriptions, and no fewer than five assistants and six dispensers are in constant employment, while a large native staff is also kept. Surgical instruments and appliances, together with chemical apparatus and hospital requisites are also obtained from the most distinguished manufacturers in Europe. An aerated water factory has been opened

R. MACLURE.
FRONT VIEW.

and this is an important adjunct of the main business. The premises are substantially constructed of brick, and are situated in the best part of Mount Road, which is the principal thoroughfare in the city.

MADRAS AUTOMOBILES, LTD.

Mechanically propelled vehicles of all descriptions have completely changed the methods of transport in the past few decades. Motor-lorries now convey merchandise from warehouse to railway or port, and the horse-bus and the hansom-cab may be seen at the London Museum. Motor-ploughs and other agricultural implements and machinery have captured the work of farmers, sailing boats have been superseded by launches, and, indeed, it would be a difficult matter to find any branch of commercial enterprise which has not been invaded by the motor engineer. It follows that an enormous industry has sprung into existence, which finds employment for hundreds and thousands of skilled workmen in factories, repair shops, and in sale agencies.

THE MADRAS AUTOMOBILES, LIMITED, was founded by the present managing directors, Mr. F. Robinson Ward (who has had sixteen years' experience in London, Paris, and India as an engineer and motor engineer), and Mr. T. R. Frost (who has been connected with the motor business in Madras since the arrival of the first car many years ago). Their showrooms, situated in the Mount Road, are built on a site covering two acres, and their workshops are within a short distance and occupy a three-storied brick building which has a floor area of 12,000 square feet.

The repair department is the largest of its kind in Southern India, and it is the only one in the city which is under the direct control and supervision of the company's managing directors. It is equipped with the most modern machinery and tools, which are electrically driven, and importing, as they do, the highest grade steel and other necessary materials, the company can assure thoroughly satisfactory repairs.

Various types of motor-cars and motor-cycles are kept in stock or imported to order, and the company have supplied cars to the State of Travancore, the Madras and Southern Mahratta Railway, the Commissioner of Police, the Kala Azar Commission, the Corporation of Madras, and many other influential purchasers.

The company holds the sole agency for the celebrated Austin and Vauxhall English cars, and the Overland American cars, also for Premier cycle-cars and motor-cycles, and a large number of different patterns are always in stock. The company are also the managing agents for Southern India for the celebrated Clincher tyres made by the North British Rubber Company, and the Bellamy solid band tyres.

Accessories and fittings of every description are kept in stock, and immediate personal attention of one of the directors is given at any time during the day or night. An hydraulic press has been specially imported for fitting solid band tyres to the wheels of motor-lorries and omnibuses of any size. In addition to this the company are the managing agents for another company, TRANSPORTS LIMITED, which is devoted entirely to the exploitation of heavy vehicles, and is doing useful missionary work in the districts in this class of car. A highly trained and thoroughly efficient staff of mechanics is maintained, so that the most accurate work in the smallest detail may always be relied upon.

McDOWELL & CO., LTD.

There are certain vital principles which are essential to the progress of any commercial undertaking, and right in the forefront of these are thoroughly up-to-date business qualifications on the part of a proprietor, and a reputation for a consistent standard of quality as regards stock in trade, together with such careful supervision of every detail of work that it will be next to impossible to have any inferior goods placed upon the market. The name of McDowell & Co., Ltd., stands for these and for many other commendable features, and this business house is one of the oldest and most respected concerns in Southern India.

It was established in 1825 by a Dr. McDowell (great-grandfather of Mr. F. E. Hooper, the present managing director), who, after taking his pension from "John" Company, started in business as a wine merchant. The venture proved extremely successful and resulted in the acquisition of many valuable agencies,

MADRAS AUTOMOBILES, LTD.

1. Exterior of Showroom 2. Interior of Showroom. 3. Exterior of Works,

including those of Bisquit Dubouché & Co., of Jarnac, for brandy; Feuerheerd Brothers, Oporto and Jerez, for ports and sherries; George Younger & Sons, the well-known Scotch brewers, and many others, while in late years the firm has undertaken the representation of Messrs. Lipton, Ltd., Van Houtens, Ltd., and other large manufacturing firms and distillers.

The firm has several large godowns for the storage of wines and spirits which they import from Europe, while the blending and bottling of wines and spirits, for which the firm is justly famous, is also carried out on their premises; the utmost cleanliness is preserved in all departments.

It was about the year 1880 that McDowell & Co., Ltd., at the instigation of the late Mr. A. M. Hooper—who was then senior partner—realized the possibilities of the cigar industry in India, and manufacturing operations were commenced at Trichinopoly, which was the first town in Southern India to cater for smokers. The method of curing the indigenous leaf was exceedingly crude at that time, and the firm recognized the fact that, in order to attain a leading position in the cigar world, it would be necessary to obtain higher quality and greater variety of the raw material, and to make use of expert knowledge in the most important work of blending different tobaccos. Messrs. McDowell & Co., Ltd., have more than realized their expectations, and their name on the box of cigars is a guarantee that the quality of the contents cannot be excelled.

Mr. A. M. Hooper threw the full weight of his business capacity and energy into the production of superior goods, and as an increased demand was the natural consequence of his forward policy, it became necessary to make arrangements for greater accommodation. A factory on modern lines was, therefore, opened on the premises of the firm on the Second Line Beach in Madras, and the offices, factories, store, and other rooms occupy an area of more than two acres in extent. To start the enterprise in Madras forty "rollers" and their families were sent from Trichinopoly, and results have proved that the efforts of the firm to meet the largely increasing number of their customers have been amply justified. The number of hands employed now runs into some hundreds.

Up to the year 1900 Indian and Sumatra tobacco alone had been made use of in the factory, but realizing that the public taste was setting towards a higher quality, the firm were the pioneers in the introduction and blending of the finest imported leaf with the Indian tobacco; the blending being entrusted to an expert from Germany, who, by the way, is still employed by the firm.

No expense has been spared in bringing from Europe, when necessary, assistants of long experience in the cigar and tobacco trade, who have been specially employed in making and maintaining the style and finish of cigars and cigarettes as near perfection as possible.

The factory is fitted with the latest and most approved machinery from Europe for the packing and boxing of cigars. Cigars in upwards of 50 sizes and shapes, and in qualities to suit all pockets, are made by the firm, and as a consequence of the extensive care bestowed upon their production, the firm's clients are to be met with in every country of the civilized world. Some of the brands may be referred to here, but nothing else than a personal trial can give an adequate idea of their choice, flavour, and aroma.

In Indians, "The Bahadur" cigar was popular as far back as the year 1880, but its reputation is greatly enhanced today. Among blended cigars the "Light of Asia" and "Bouquet" brands were produced in 1902, and on account of the excellent blending of Indian and foreign tobacco, they are prime favourites in every club and regimental mess in India. The "Pearl of Kashmere," "Lotus Lily," "Reverie," and "Mohini" are, to quote the firm's catalogue, "the summit of the cigar-maker's art," and are far and away the finest cigars turned out of any factory in India. Packed in boxes of 50, they cannot fail to tempt the most fastidious smoker.

The "La Nadar" is a delightful small cigar of sweet nutty flavour, and the firm claims that all the above blended brands are superior to the imported article from Holland—the so-called Dutch Havana—the majority of which contain no Havana tobacco at all. Other favourites which may be mentioned are "Bahadur Reeds," "Queen Empress," "Princessas" and "Specials," but a word in passing of Havanas must suffice. The price-list says: "These two fine cigars, 'Primero Regiales' and 'Primero Aquilas,' are made by the firm from the finest imported tobacco; they are introduced to fill the demand for a really high-class cigar at a moderate price for an after-dinner smoke; they are wrapped in silver foil to keep them in proper condition, and are very highly recommended."

The Madras factory will accommodate 600 hands, and from 75,000 to 100,000 hand-made cigars can be turned out in one day.

The South African war of 1899-1902 tested the resources of the firm very considerably, and an additional factory was established at Trichinopoly, where 1,000 hands were employed in making the famous "Bahadur" cigars. The British troops were clamorous, and it is stated that, during hostilities, no fewer than 16 millions of cigars—which placed end to end would cover a distance of just upon a thousand miles—were shipped to South Africa, and that fully 100,000 were made daily in Trichinopoly alone.

About the year 1904 Messrs. McDowell & Co., Ltd., introduced thoroughly modern cigarette machinery, and as many as 500,000 cigarettes can be turned out by them in a day.

Large stocks of tobacco are kept in six stores; upwards of 1,200 bales of Indian leaf are kept for cigars, and 500 for cigarettes, while the foreign supply reaches about 200 bales. Several brands of cheap cigarettes for the million are made, and the most indigent smoker can scarcely object to the firm's present prices of Rs. 1-8 per 1,000 upwards in packets of five or ten, and Rs. 1-4 packed in boxes of 100. Notwithstanding these low prices the tobacco and the paper are of the purest description. The machinery which makes them is driven by a Hornsby Stockport oil-engine.

One floor of the main premises, 140 ft. in length, is devoted to the manufacture and packing of cigars, and there are separate rooms for branding, labelling, and wrapping the boxes, for storage, and for other purposes. New brands of cigars of various sizes and shapes are constantly being put upon the market, but precautions are taken to ensure the use of only the very best leaf, and great care is taken that no consignment shall leave the warehouse which is not absolutely sound in quality and perfect in condition.

Numerous diplomas, medals, and other awards of merit have been obtained on various occasions in India, and also at the Franco-British, the South African Industrial and Arts, and the Empire of India exhibitions. As an instance of the up-to-date methods employed by Messrs. McDowell & Co., Ltd., it may be said that a small printing-press has been

McDOWELL & CO., LTD.

1. The Buildings. 2. Exterior of Brewery. 3. Chilling Machine at the Brewery.

McDOWELL & CO., LTD.

1. In the Cigar Factory. 2. Packing Department. 3. Sorting Cigars.

erected for the firm's requirements in printing stationery and in binding.

The firm are owners of several godowns, where they have nearly always a stock of 1,000 casks of Johnson's Elephant brand cement, for which they are sole agents in the Madras Presidency. Other branches in this hive of industry include the importation and sale of Lipton's teas, coffees, and stores, and of Van Houten's cocoa.

Agencies are held for Messrs. Van Oppen & Co., carriers, Messrs. Carter, Paterson & Co., carriers, of London, for the Messageries Nationales Forwarding Agency, the Mead Cycle Company, of Liverpool, the Gresham Life Assurance Company, the Swiss National Insurance Company, Basle, the Reliance Marine Insurance Company, of Liverpool, the Federal Marine Insurance Company, of Zurich, the Aachen and Munich Fire Insurance Company, of Aix-la-Chapelle, and the Madras B.B.B. Brewery Co., Ltd. The company have branches in Coorg and other places.

The present managing director is Mr. F. E. Hooper, who has been with the firm seventeen years, and who is ably supported by the managers of the various departments, and by his assistants, Messrs. F. Pinnock, F. Cross, W. G. Penn-Simkins, J. Hermans, and F. W. Mansfield. The Bombay branch is managed by Mr. F. Pinnock, and the London agents are Messrs. Lancelot Dent & Co., of 24 St. Martin's Lane, Cannon Street, E.C.

THE MADRAS B.B.B. BREWERY CO., LTD.

There are not many cities of the same size as Madras which, up to quite a recent date, did not possess a brewery for the manufacture of beer; ale, and stout, and yet this busy, dusty, thirst-producing town had no such industry as brewing until the year 1913, when the Madras B.B.B. Brewery Co., Ltd.—which is an offshoot of the British Beer Breweries, Ltd., of London—was established. The managing agents are Messrs. McDowell & Co., Ltd., of Second Line Beach, Madras, and they have given the same unremitting attention to this venture as to the manufacture of their famous cigars and cigarettes, which have justly earned for themselves an enviable reputation in nearly every civilized country in the world.

The first and the most important consideration in brewing is an abundant supply of pure water, and this was only obtained after fourteen months' diligent search. No fewer than 14 bores were sunk before the spring which is now in use was found. A well 18 ft. in diameter was built, which gives 6,000 gallons of water an hour. This water has been tested by the Government analyst, and it has been certified to be absolutely pure.

The buildings were constructed in accordance with plans designed by Messrs. George Adlam & Sons, of Bristol, England, who supplied the up-to-date brewing plant, and they have been erected in such a manner that enlargements can be carried out and additional plant accommodated without difficulty at any time.

The company has acquired the sole rights for the Madras Presidency for the use of S.T. yeast (Saccharomyces Thermantitonum), which differs from the English type in that it is heat-resisting and impervious to the extreme heat of the summer months on the plains of India. Imported yeast, on the other hand, cannot survive for long a temperature of 75° F., and it rapidly dies in the hot weather months. A fully qualified English brewer and chemist is employed as chief brewer, and some 40 hands are regularly engaged at the brewery.

Exceedingly good examples of India pale ale and light dinner ale are brewed especially for the Indian climate, from the finest Scotch malt and Kent hops. Pilsener, a beautiful light beer, is made from Bavarian hops and Bohemian malt, and it has all the pleasurable characteristics of the imported article ; while a fine double stout of genuine London type is also the product of British malt and hops only.

There is an excellent market in Madras and in the surrounding districts, as the nearest competing brewery is over 200 miles distant.

The management of affairs at the brewery is in the capable hands of Mr. W. R. Prosser, a brewer and brewing chemist of considerable experience, and though the concern only lately started (May 1913), progress has been so satisfactory and such an encouraging reception accorded to its beers that the future of the company should be a bright one.

THE MADRAS STABLE COMPANY

The title at the head of these notes gives a very imperfect idea of the variety and of the extent of the business operations which are carried on under that name by Rajah Venugopal Bahadur, at 17 Mount Road, Madras, and at other places. The primary objects of the company were the importation of, and the dealing in, horses, principally of a class suitable for light harness and saddle work, and a large hacking and livery-stable business has been established, notwithstanding the fact that other methods of locomotion are now finding favour. A carriage factory has been opened, and the proprietor employs a number of skilled workmen in the construction of vehicles of all descriptions, for letting on hire or for sale to private individuals. A shoeing-forge and a veterinary infirmary are indispensable adjuncts of an establishment of this character, and these branches are managed by exceedingly capable officials. A sale by auction of horses, cattle, poultry, carriages, and harness is held weekly in the large yard at Mount Road, while a similar sale of household furniture and other effects takes place at least once in each month. A special feature is made of the breaking-in and training of horses for riding and driving purposes, and the expert manner in which this work is performed reflects the highest credit upon all concerned.

The present century was, however, ushered in to the accompaniment of the hooting of the horns of motor-cars and cycles, to the smell of petrol, to discussions on hill-climbing, to wailings over punctures, to the anathemas of tradesmen whose goods were spoiled by clouds of dust, and to the curses of pedestrians who had—and still have—their vigilance and courage taxed to the utmost in dodging the man in the goggles. The advent of the motor resulted in the immediate removal of a very large number of horses from the roads ; the one-time popular hansom-cabs, landaus, and victorias were replaced by Ford, Daimler, Wolseley, Napier, Humber, de Dion, and other cars ; many carriage-houses were turned into garages, and the very mangers from which high-class steeds were wont to feed have become receptacles for screw-keys, carbide, damaged tyres, and the remains of lamps and other accessories of the petrol-driven machines. Nevertheless, livery-stable keepers and others had to accept the inevitable, and the Madras Stable Company—which is nothing if not up to date—moved with the times by opening extensive motor and engineering works. Sole agencies are held by the company for the Clement-Talbot, All-days, Sizaire, American Maxwell, and Commer and Peugeot cars, and the Madras works are fitted with thoroughly modern machinery, which is driven by electricity.

The headquarter premises in Madras are very extensive, as stabling accommodation can be found for no fewer than 700 horses, in addition to necessary space for motor-cars belonging to the company and to their numerous clients.

The hiring-out of cars in Madras has assumed large proportions, but branches have been formed in Bangalore, Trichinopoly, Puddukottah, and Kodaikanal, in each of which towns a rapidly increasing motor service has been inaugurated. A special service has been organized between Kodaikanal and the railway-station at Kodaikanal Road, where there is a gradient of 1 in 16 in the course of a distance of about 40 miles, while other cars are running between Trichinopoly and Puddukottah, which are 48 miles distant. There are 10 cars on these two systems, and each of them has a seating capacity of 36 passengers.

All kinds of repairs are undertaken by competent workmen, who are employed under the supervision of four highly salaried, fully qualified motor engineers, who have been imported direct from England; while Mr. Nurse, the ubiquitous and very able manager, is keenly alive to the interests of the many clients of the company.

THE INDIAN SIEGWART BEAM COMPANY, LTD.

It is a notorious fact that India is conservative to the core in all that pertains to its commercial, agricultural, or industrial life; but there is distinct evidence that the natives are not averse to changing their traditional methods in favour of new ones when the value of the improved system has been clearly demonstrated. Better crops have been raised when the land has been more scientifically cultivated, linen and woollen goods of superior quality have been produced by the use of modern machinery, and in the construction of buildings there has been a remarkable advance in the way of substituting non-inflammable materials in place of the old-fashioned timber baulks and beams, which have been the cause of innumerable fires and of the loss of thousands of lives.

The Siegwart Beam Company was formed in Madras in 1910, with the object of manufacturing reinforced concrete beams under licence from the International Siegwart Beam Co., Ltd., of Lucerne, Switzerland; and the managers have had an up-hill battle in fighting against unbridled prejudice and determined opposition before they could convince contractors of the immense superiority of the new patent. Prejudices have more force than Acts of Parliament, as the mind of a man concentrates itself upon the "things that be," and an innovation is looked upon with suspicion, if not with absolute distrust; but an old adage says that "the proof of the pudding is in the eating," and as soon as it had been demonstrated that concrete was immeasurably safer than wood in the construction of buildings there was an appreciable recognition of the strenuous efforts which had been put forth at very great expense by the promotors of the company in introducing the improved beam.

In the first place, the beams are hollow, and are therefore proof against fire and the transmission of sound; secondly, they can be placed in position in a remarkably short space of time; and, thirdly, the work known in the building trade as "centering" is entirely unnecessary.

The factory is situated in Mount Road, and it is fitted with excellent electrically driven machinery, which has been imported from Switzerland. Contracts have been completed successfully with the Government Maternity and Ophthalmic Hospitals, the King Institute of Preventive Medicine at Guindy, the Madras Waterworks Pumping Station, the new Government Stationery Offices at Madras, and for the dwelling-houses of the senior officials of the Guaranteed State Railways of the Nizam of Hyderabad and of the Madras and Southern Mahratta Railway Company.

Several buildings which are now in the course of construction in Madras are to be fitted with these beams, and negotiations, which it is believed will end successfully, are now on foot for supplying a considerable quantity in connection with the building of the new capital city of Delhi. These beams are rapidly superseding timber, and inquiries concerning them are now being received from merchants, builders, and others in Calcutta, Bombay, and Rangoon. They can be made to suit the requirements of purchasers—that is, of any strength and of any length up to a clear span of 20 feet. About 50 hands have been constantly employed up to the present time, but the continued growth of the business will necessitate the engagement of a much larger staff.

The company holds the sole agency in the Madras Presidency for the Ideal Concrete Machinery Company of America, who are the makers and owners of the Ideal hollow-block machinery, some of which has been forwarded to the Puddukottah Durbar, to be used in the building of a new palace. Patent rights for the beams are held throughout India and Burma by the Siegwart Company, of whom the Rajah Venugopal Bahadur is the chairman.

No small praise for the success of the company is due to the energy and perseverance of Mr. W. H. Nurse, the managing director.

The registered cable address is "Siegwart."

MASSEY & CO., LTD.

The "Napier" Engineering and Foundry Works belonging to Messrs. Massey & Co., Ltd., are situated in Cochrane's Basin Road, and within a comparatively short distance from the Central Station in the city of Madras. Long before one reaches the premises, attention is attracted by the thuds of steam hammers as they descend with the force of an avalanche; one notices the clanging of chains, the strokes on the blacksmith's anvil, or sees the flames and smoke belching forth from huge furnaces. And, after passing through the gates and entering this hive of industry, the visitor is conducted through a number of buildings, including engine and boiler-rooms, pattern sheds, smiths' shop, casting and other sheds, and in all of these are seen scores of blackened workmen who are busily engaged in manufacturing all kinds of machinery, bridges, rails, beams, gates, and a host of other sundries. Messrs. Massey & Co. hold mercantile agencies for Hornsby oil and gas engines, Rees "Roturbo" pumps; the Gandy Belt Company, Ltd., Barnard's rice-hullers, broad flanged beams, and lock woven mesh for reinforced concrete.

The directors of the company are Messrs. A. W. Rosling, W. G. Gibson, and H. E. Harris, A.M.I.Mech.E. The

THE MADRAS STABLE COMPANY AND INDIAN SIEGWART BEAM COMPANY.

1. Exterior of Stables. 2. Exterior of Motor Department. 3. Indian Siegwart Beam Stores. 4. Indian Siegwart Beam Factory.

secretary is Mr. F. G. Warbrook, A.M.I. Mech.E., and the assistants are Messrs. F. S. Harris and W. Simmons.

THE MERCANTILE BANK OF INDIA

About the middle of the nineteenth century a banking establishment was opened in Madras on the First Line Beach Road, under the name of the Chartered Mercantile Bank of India, London, and China; but a reconstruction took place in 1893, when the name was changed to the Mercantile Bank of India, Ltd. The head offices are at 40 Threadneedle Street, London, E.C.; branches have been opened at Bombay, Karachi, Calcutta, Howrah, Rangoon, Delhi, Colombo, Kandy, Galle, Singapore, Kuala Lumpur, Kota Bharu, Penang, Hongkong, and Shanghai. The London agents are the Bank of England and the London Joint Stock Bank, Ltd. Current deposit accounts are opened, and interest is allowed at the rate of £2 per cent. per annum on daily balances of Rs. 1,000 and upwards. Fixed deposit accounts are received for one year at £4 per centum per annum, and for shorter periods at rates which may be had on application. Approved bills of exchange are purchased, and drafts are sold on the London offices, upon all branches, and on the Bank's agents in Scotland, Ireland, Australia, Africa, Paris, and other places, and these are forwarded to payees, free of charge, at current rates of exchange.

Government securities are bought and sold, dividends are collected, securities are kept in strong-rooms on behalf of clients, and all kinds of general banking business is undertaken.

Three European and about 60 natives are employed, under the management of Mr. H. L. Padday.

OAKES & CO., LTD.

There are many cities and towns in the Presidency of Madras in which there are commercial stores and handsome buildings which will compare very favourably with others to be seen in any part of India. They are substantial structures of high-class architectural merit and their internal furnishings and fittings are most luxurious. Perhaps the majority of these have sprung from very unpretentious beginnings, but the indomitable courage and perseverance of the founders caused the business to expand to such an extent that subsequent owners have been compelled to rebuild or provide additional accommodation in order that they might be able to compete successfully with other merchants.

One of the most commodious stores in the City of Madras is that situated on the Mount Road belonging to Messrs. Oakes & Co., Ltd. The business was established in the year 1843 in premises in Pop-

MASSEY & CO., LTD.
INTERIOR OF FITTING SHOP.

OAKES & CO., LTD.

1. The Cigar Factory. 2. Cigar Factory—Interior. 3. The Head Office. 4 and 5 The Motor Garage.

ham's Broadway, known as the Exchange Hall, the name of the firm being Messrs. Oakes, Partridge & Co. Fortune smiled upon the partners, but they deserved it, as they had become known throughout Southern India for the prompt manner in which they supplied customers with goods of first-class quality at reasonable prices. As general merchants they held a large and varied assortment of all kinds of hard and soft goods, wines and spirits, and they were representatives of a number of insurance and shipping companies. The trade returns of each year largely exceeded those of the previous twelve months, and after about half a century of unexampled progress it was found that the magnitude of the business demanded a larger building and additional assistants in order to deal with it satisfactorily. In the year 1895 a limited liability company was formed, and more commodious premises were secured immediately opposite Government House. The stores in Popham's Broadway were, however, retained as a branch establishment for the hardware and engineering departments.

The head offices of the company—of which the Hon. J. O. Robinson is chairman—are at No. 200 Mount Road, Madras; their representatives in London are Messrs. Spencer & Co., Ltd., 57-8 Broad Street Avenue, E.C., and agencies have been established in various parts of the world.

Enlargement of the newly-obtained stores became necessary after a few years' trading, and one may now spend hours visiting the various showrooms, which are crammed with merchandise of first-class quality only, and then the time would have been far too short to see one-half of the tremendous stock of goods on floors, shelves, racks, or in cabinets.

If any one wishes to become a householder he has only to call at the company's offices, and their estate agency branch will at once secure for him a mansion or a cottage; they will furnish it from garret to cellar, not omitting even the knick-knacks and articles of *vertu* which go such a long way towards making a residence at once homely and attractive. Messrs. Oakes & Co., Ltd., do not undertake to provide wife or housekeeper, but they are prepared to supply every article of clothing which one or the other might require, whether it be dresses for the ballroom, aprons for the kitchen, hats for church, or caps for motoring. The dressmaking and millinery departments are under the management of highly qualified ladies who have the supervision of a number of competent assistants. The branch in which gentlemen are more particularly interested is equally well stocked, and it would indeed be difficult to specify anything in the shape of clothing, travelling requisites, or sporting goods with which they could not be supplied. A few years ago a motor-car and cycle department was established at No. 199 Mount Road, and the company have already disposed of a large number of machines to purchasers in all parts of India. A special feature is made of the adjoining workshops, in which repairs are promptly effected by a large staff of efficient mechanics. Motor tyres, tubes, and accessories of every description are always kept on hand.

The firm are purveyors to H.E. the Governor, Lord Pentland, and, briefly, they are Mess agents, wine and spirit merchants, manufacturers of aerated water and cigars, fodder and grain merchants, auctioneers and estate agents, and dealers in oilman's stores, arms and ammunition, hardware, ironmongery, oils, paints, varnishes, corrugated iron, and cement.

The company are agents for Messrs. George Wheatley & Co., Ltd., of London, Liverpool, and Paris; the Royal Fire and Life Insurance Co., Ltd., of Liverpool; Messrs. Davies, Turner & Co., of London and New York; Messrs. Staveley & Co., of London and Liverpool; Messrs. Pickfords, Ltd., of London; and the American Express Company, of London, Liverpool, and New York.

The cable and telegraphic address of the company is "Oakes, Madras."

OAKES & CO., LTD. (CIGAR FACTORY)

"He who doth not smoke hath either known no great griefs or refuseth himself the softest consolation next that which comes from Heaven." Lord Lytton voiced the feelings of millions of human beings when he wrote those words, and one has only to glance at the world's tobacco bill for a single year to realize to what extent the solacing influence of pipe or cigar is enjoyed. There are, and always will be, cavillers who protest against huge sums of money being expended in smoke, but the remarkably large industry which is carried on in thousands of factories is not likely to be seriously affected by those objectors.

Messrs. Oakes & Co., Ltd., of Madras, established a factory for the manufacture of cigars in the year 1892, and their present works are situated near Guindy Station, on the South Indian Railway, and about 6 miles distant from their head offices in the city. The best Indian tobacco for cigars is grown in the district of Madura, and the curing of the leaf, which is commenced by the planters, is completed by Messrs. Oakes & Co. by the system known as "natural sweating." The first process is damping, which takes place in an afternoon, and on the following morning the leaves are taken from the racks upon which they have been dried during the night and are transferred to the stripping-room, where a number of boys remove the "mid-ribs," after which they are successively dried, blended, and stored ready for use. Then a visit is paid to a room in which are about one hundred men and boys, who are the real makers of the cigar. The employees sit at tables and work in pairs, being known respectively as bunch-makers and rollers. The former takes a quantity of tobacco, and after pressing it roughly into shape he puts around it a binder, which is a strong and sound leaf. This bunch is passed to his colleague, who examines it, works it into proper form, and then puts on the wrapper, or covering leaf. The latter is placed upon the roller's table, upon which it is held closely by suction while it is being cut to the required size and shape. All the cigars which pass through the hands of these men or boys are inspected by a foreman, who returns faulty ones to be re-made.

There is a strong prejudice among smokers against having two or three shades of brown cigars in a box, hence special care is taken at Guindy to sort them in order that there may be uniformity of colour. This work is performed by boys of about seventeen years of age, who subsequently pack them in boxes, which are made under contract on the premises. The drying-room, in which there is a suction-fan, may be seen next, after which there is the labelling-room, where the white edging paper is put on the boxes, and where the company's labels, printed on their own machine, are affixed. The company have a very large sale for their goods throughout the whole of India, and they are also frequent exporters to England, Australia, South Africa, and New Zealand.

Messrs. Oakes & Co. received special appointments as manufacturers of cigars to the Right Hon. Baron Curzon of Kedleston, P.C., and the Right Hon. the Earl of Minto, P.C., Viceroys of India;

PARRY & CO.

1. The Madras Offices. 2. Samalkot Refinery. 3. Distillery, Samalkot.

H.E. Sir Arthur Lawley, G.C.I.E., Governor of Madras, the Right Hon. Lord Lamington, P.C., and H.E. Sir George Sydenham Clarke, Governor of Bombay.

Medals and awards have been received at numerous exhibitions for the high-class quality of the cigars, the following being some of the honours gained : gold medals at the Brewers' Exhibition, Newcastle, England, in 1899, at Cape Town in 1905, and at Lahore in 1909; silver medals at the Calcutta International Exhibition in 1883-4, and at the Paris Exposition in 1900; a bronze medal and diploma at the Colonial and Indian Exhibition in 1886; a bronze medal and first order of merit at the Centennial Exhibition at Melbourne in 1888; and first order of merit at the New Zealand and South Seas Exhibition held at Dunedin in 1889-90.

More than thirty different brands of cigars are made in the factory, and all of these are guaranteed to be absolutely free from opium in any shape or form. The principal brands are Gymkhanas, Empires, Beresfords, Supers, Orientals, and Anglo-Indians.

Supers have been made by the company for more than twenty years, and they were the first Havana-shaped cigars, covered with Sumatra leaf, to be made in India.

Messrs. Oakes & Co., Ltd., issue a most comprehensive and well-illustrated price-list, in which will be found a copy of their private telegraphic code prepared to facilitate the execution of orders from customers who reside at some distance from Madras.

The principal portion of the factory was formerly the residence of the collector of the Chingleput Division of the Presidency, and it stands in about 9 acres of ground.

PARRY & CO.

The founder of this firm was Mr. Thomas Parry, third son of Mr. Edward Parry, of Leighton Hall, Welshpool, who was born in 1768, and came out to Madras at the age of twenty. Shortly after his arrival he accepted a post under the official "Accountant" of Madras, and he remained in association with the authorities for about four years, being at one time private secretary to General Medows, the Governor of Madras, from 1790 to 1792.

In the latter of these years he started business as a shipper of produce to England, partly on his own account and partly in partnership with others. In 1814 he withdrew from this enterprise and again took up official employment, but his name was retained in the title of the firm, and in 1818 he rejoined it.

In 1824 he and a nephew of his, aged only ten, were attacked by cholera while travelling between Porto Novo and Cuddalore, and died on August 24th in that year. They were buried in Christ Church, at Old Town, Cuddalore, in the pavement of which edifice there is a stone to their memory, and a tablet to Parry was also erected in St. George's Cathedral, Madras, and on it inscribed a lengthy eulogy of his good qualities.

Ancient histories of Southern India speak of "Parry's Corner," which was purchased in 1775 for ten thousand "star pagodas," and it is represented to-day by the very extensive range of buildings which are situated at the corner of the Esplanade and of the First Line Beach Road, in the city of Madras. Title deeds which are now in the office of the firm of Parry & Co. show that the property was transferred to Thomas Parry in 1803.

The business was carried on under the name of Thomas Parry & Co. until the year 1829, when the title of Parry, Dare & Co. was adopted. This style was continued for ten years, when the firm again became known as Parry & Co., but there are natives in the Madras Presidency who still speak of "Dare House" when referring to this establishment. There are several very large godowns on the ground floor, and the offices—which are above them—are full of interest, as they contain a series of oil-paintings and photographs of the partners who have been connected with the business from its foundation.

Undoubtedly the finest commercial site in Madras is that upon which these premises stand; it is near to the principal banks and the General Post Office; it is immediately opposite to the Beach railway-station, which is the junction of the South Indian Railways with the Madras and Southern Mahratta Railway Company; and the new wharf and shed accommodation constructed by the Port Trust is within five minutes' walk of the office.

The firm are engaged in a very large way of business as general merchants and bankers, and they are managing agents for several important industrial concerns, as well as agents for a number of life, fire, and marine insurance companies. The partners are Messrs. A. J. Yorke, A. D. Jackson, J. C. Armstrong, and A. F. Buchanan, and branches have been established at Cuddalore, Trichinopoly, Calicut, Tinnevelly, Bangalore, Erode, Ranipet, Tuticorin, Tellicherry, Tanjore, Madura, Panrutti, Porto Novo, Nellikuppam, Cochin, Kulasekarapatnam, Palghat, and at Calcutta.

One of the managing agencies of the firm is that of the East India Distilleries and Sugar Factories, Ltd., whose principal works are at Nellikuppam. Sugar is manufactured there partly from jaggery, which is a product of the palmyrah-tree, and partly from sugar-cane, a considerable quantity of which is grown by the company itself and by the *ryots* living within 10 miles or so of the factory. There is also a large distillery at Nellikuppam, said to be the finest in India, in which arrack is manufactured. Another industry in connection with the Nellikuppam Distillery is the collection of the carbonic acid gas which is generated in the early processes of spirit manufacture. This gas is liquified under great pressure, and packed in steel cylinders for sale to soda-water manufacturers all over India and Burma. In addition to the above, the company is now turning its attention to the manufacture of confectionery at Nellikuppam. A second sugar factory has been opened at Kulasekarapatnam, which is about 35 miles distant by sea from Tuticorin, or by motor-car from Tinnevelly respectively, and sugar is made here from juice and jaggery obtained from palmyrah-trees which abound in the neighbourhood.

The firm are managers, too, of the Presidency Manure Works, Ltd., at Ranipet, where large quantities of bones are crushed by up-to-date machinery, and where chemical fertilizers are prepared. The greater portion of the output of this factory is required to meet an increasing local demand, but a considerable quantity is exported. Fertilizers, it may be noted, are used extensively by planters in the districts of Mysore, the Nilgiris, and in the Wynaad district of Malabar. The Government Department of Agriculture has, in a praiseworthy manner, established experimental agricultural stations where demonstrations are given of the relative values of different kinds of manures, and the *ryots* have taken a keen interest in the subject since it has been proved to them that heavier crops can be obtained by the judicious use of these helps to a scientific cultivation of the land.

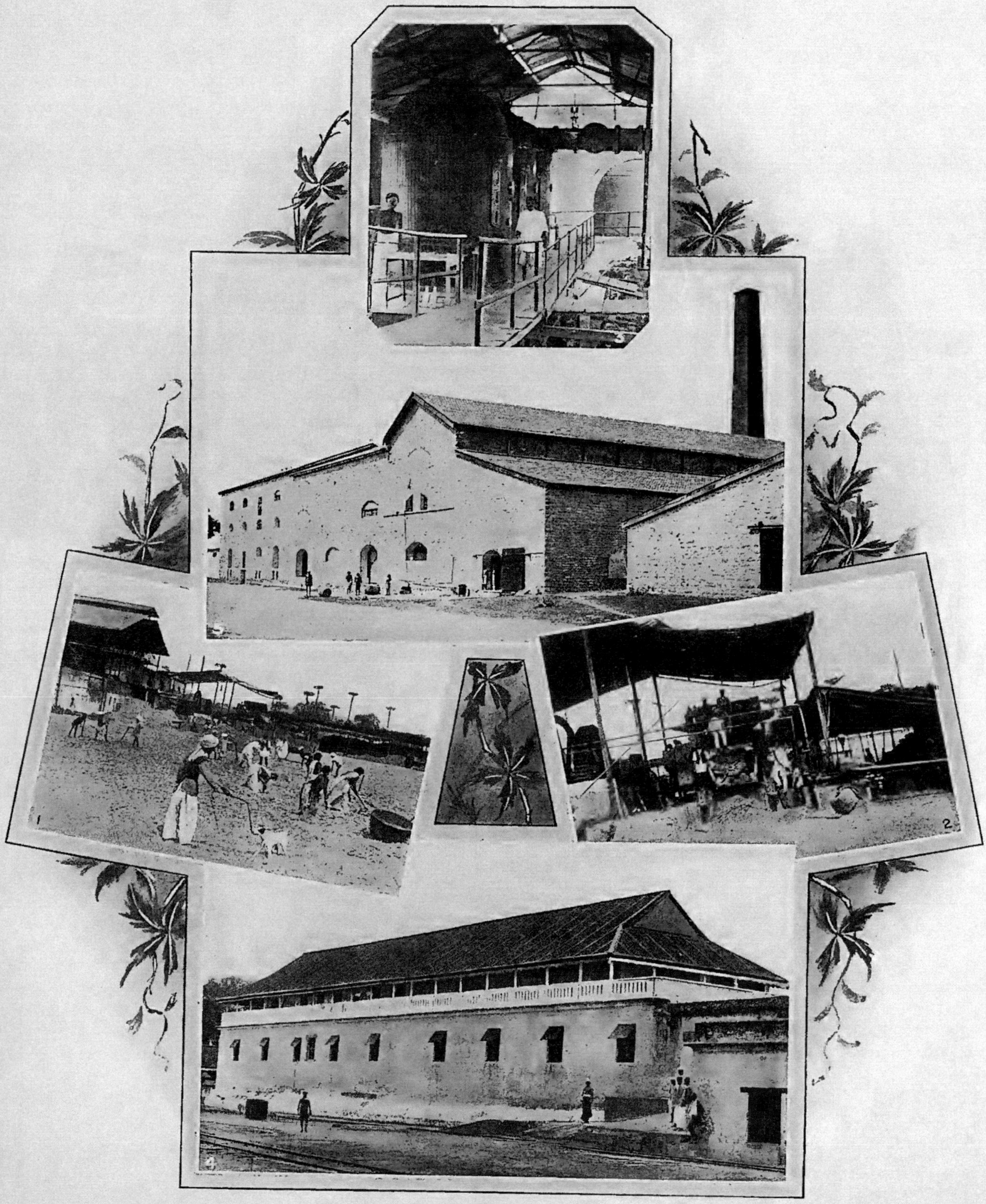

PARRY & CO.

1. ANAKAPALLE CANE MILL. 2. ANOTHER VIEW, ANAKAPALLE CANE MILL. 3. ANAKAPALLE, TRIPLE EFFECT. 4. CUDDALORE BRANCH. 5. FACTORY AT RANIPET.

PARRY & CO.

1. View of No. 2 Cane Mill from No. 2 Bungalow, Nellikuppam. 2. Cane Mill looking from front of the Five-range Boilers. 3 Another View of No. 2 Cane Mill. 4. Steam Ploughing Tackle at work, Nellikuppam. 5. Interior View of Confectionery Plant, Nellikuppam. 6. Side View, from the Jaggery Godowns Plant, Nellikuppam.

The firm also manages the New Malabar Timber Yards and Saw Mills, Ltd., at Kallai, near Calicut, and timber which is obtained from the surrounding hills is sawn into scantlings, railway sleepers, and planks suitable for the use of carpenters and joiners.

Messrs. Parry & Co. are also managing agents of the Deccan Sugar and Abkari Co., Ltd., whose works are situated about 9 miles distant from Coconada. The factory of the latter company can only be worked for about six months of the year, owing to the local supply of jaggery being limited, but the distillation of spirit goes on throughout the whole of the twelve months. The works are adjacent to a line of railway, and one of the Godaveri canals, both of which are available for transport. A plant for crushing cane has been erected at a branch named Anakapalle, which is the centre of a large area devoted to this crop, and additional supplies of refining material will thus become available. The manufacture of sulphuric acid at Ranipet is another industry in which the firm are largely interested, and a pottery has been started, in which jars are made for conveying the acid to all parts of India.

Mercantile agencies in the hands of Messrs. Parry & Co are: The British India Steam Navigation Co., Ltd., at Cuddalore, and the Aermotor Company, of Chicago: and they are agents at Madras for the Natal Direct Line of Steamers, the Alliance Life Assurance Co., Ltd., the English Scottish Law Life Assurance Corporation, the General Accident Assurance Corporation, Ltd., the Merchants' Marine Insurance Company, the Ocean Marine Insurance Company, the Royal Exchange Fire, Life, Accident & Marine Assurance Company, the Sun Fire Insurance Company, the New Zealand Insurance Company (Fire & Marine), the North British & Mercantile Insurance Company, the Ruberoid Co., Ltd., Messrs. Brunner, Mond & Co., Ltd., and the North Western Cyanide Co., Ltd.

JOHN W. ROBERTS & CO.

The senior partner in this firm is a son of the world-renowned John Roberts, who for a considerable time was champion billiard-player in England. His early days were spent in mastering the details connected with the manufacture of billiard tables at his father's factory at Home, but he subsequently removed to Durban, and later to Cape Town in South Africa. Further experience was gained in these places, and he then commenced business on his own account in Madras as a manufacturer of billiard and bagatelle tables, an ivory turner, and art furnisher. Indian mahogany and North Wales slates are used in the construction of the tables, and all carving and turning work is executed on the firm's premises in Mount Road.

Mr. C. N. Lumb is now a partner, and he devotes the greater part of his attention to the rubber department.

SIEMENS BROTHERS' DYNAMO WORKS, LTD.

INTERIOR OF WORKSHOP.

SIEMENS BROTHERS' DYNAMO WORKS, LTD.

Messrs. Siemens Brothers' Dynamo Works, Ltd., of Caxton House, Westminster, London, have a branch in Madras, from which all contracts are undertaken for the Madras Presidency,

Hyderabad, and Ceylon, as well as the native States. A number of large contracts for electrical work in South India have been placed in the hands of Messrs. Siemens Brothers' Dynamo Works, Ltd., with success. The firm employs a staff of European erecting engineers, and have a workshop in Patter's Road.

SHAW, WALLACE & CO.

The head office of this firm is at Calcutta, but branches have been established at Bombay, Colombo, Karachi, Mormugar, Cochin, Tuticorin, Coconada, and at Madras, where business has been carried on for a considerable number of years. Manchester piece-goods, yarns, metals, cement, paper, and numerous other sundries are regularly imported from Europe and elsewhere, while the exports handled by the firm include general produce, skins, hides, and cotton. Timber for general purposes is imported from Burmah, Java, and the Straits Settlements, while larger quantities of railway sleepers are imported from Australia and Java.

Business is done in flour, which is imported from Karachi, Bombay, and Calcutta, and the mills at this last-named place are managed from the firm's Calcutta office. Coal is imported from the several collieries managed by the Calcutta house, and important railway contracts are undertaken.

Shalimar paint, which is manufactured at Calcutta, is a growing business, and previously to this company entering the field the demand for paints was met by supplies imported from Great Britain and the Continent. These paints now hold an important position, as the company have made it their business to turn out these and kindred productions, which are popular, both as regards price and quality.

The Burmah Oil Co., Ltd., is represented by this firm at Madras, and subagencies are to be found in all the principal towns of the Presidency. Extensive tin-making factories have been erected at Madras and at the chief coast ports. The Burmah Oil Company send cargoes of kerosene-oil regularly from Rangoon to Madras, Coconada, Tuticorin, and Cochin, at which places oil is stored in immense tanks. The up-country markets are fed by the dispatch of oil from the place above mentioned, both bulk and packed supplies being sent in tins, which are made at Madras and at coast port installations.

Regular supplies are made of all grades of lubricating, motor, and batching oils, greases, candles, and wax, and the company meet a large part of the petrol demand of the Presidency.

The Anglo-Persian Oil Company is also represented by this firm, and it holds important Admiralty contracts for liquid fuel. Supplies of this fuel, received direct from Persia, are held at Madras, Coconada, Tuticorin, and Cochin, from which centres the surrounding districts are fed.

Other important agencies are held, including the Queensland Fire Marine Insurance Co., Ltd., the Sun Life Assurance Company, of Canada, the National Roofing Company, of America, the Shalimar Paint, Colour, and Varnish Co., Ltd., the South-West Timber Hewers Co-operative Society, the Nederlandsch Indische Houthankap Maatschappij, Java, Messrs. Holman Brothers & Co., Ltd., Messrs. Kirchner & Co., and the Parsons Trading Co., Ltd.

The members of the firm are Messrs. C. W. Wallace, H. S. Ashton, C. Greenway, A. C. Hue, E. A. Chettle (London), J. B. Lloyd, R. C. Caw, G. Kingsley, K. Campbell, W. D. Braithwaite (Calcutta), and E. Comber, of Bombay. The firm's London correspondents are Messrs. R. G. Shaw & Co., of Winchester House, Old Broad Street, E.C., who have other offices at Dundee. European assistants are employed at each branch, and the number of these at the Madras office averages about 10. Some idea of the extent of the firm's undertakings may be gathered from the fact that about 170 Indian clerks are constantly employed.

SIMPSON & CO.

The name of "Simpson" appearing upon carriages, motor-cars, or billiard-tables is a guarantee of excellence of workmanship and of durability of service, and it is the hall-mark of quality for which intending purchasers will look anxiously. The firm was established in 1840 by the late Mr. Simpson, and, after various changes, the business has, since the year 1908, been the exclusive property of Mr. George Underhill Cuddon. This gentleman arrived in India from England in 1891, joining Messrs. Simpson & Co. as an assistant at that time, when the venture had assumed extensive proportions. Mr. Cuddon was not long in passing to the managership; he subsequently became a partner, and, finally, he assumed the position of sole proprietor.

The works and showrooms are situated in one of the best positions in Mount Road, the leading thoroughfare of Madras, and they cover an area of several acres. A large new showroom for motor-cars has been constructed recently, and it is most ornate in character. It is a double-storied building of green and white stone, quarried near Madras, and it has a frontage of 90 ft. upon the main road. Plate-glass windows, 18 ft. in length, a special kind of door, shutters, and sun-blinds have been imported from England. The floor is laid in Italian marble, and the inside pillars are of very chaste designs. Immediately behind this building there is a large plot of land, upon which a garage for the storage of cars is about to be erected.

Visitors, as well as probable purchasers, are always courteously received by the proprietor or his manager, and an inspection of the works will reveal some hundreds of skilled natives, comprising draughtsmen, carpenters, smiths, fitters, moulders, turners, drillers, wheelers, designers, engravers, gilders, polishers, spring and lamp makers, workers in glass and metal, and others who are constantly employed on the premises.

Each department is under the direct superintendence of European assistants, who have had experience in the best houses in the Old Country, and the carriages and cars which are now being sent from the works will compare favourably in point of quality, finish, and price with any others in the world.

All carriages are constructed from selected Indian timbers, which, after lengthy trials, have been found to stand the varied climatic conditions of the East better than those which have been imported from other countries. It is not, however, the bodies alone of the vehicles which are built at the works, as the finest silk laces are made on native looms, and door-handles, springs, lamps, locks, hinges, silver-plating, and other accessories are produced in their respective departments.

It would occupy far too much space to enumerate a tithe of the handsome carriages and carts for which Messrs. Simpson & Co. are famous, but they range in variety from silver state-coaches,

SHAW, WALLACE & CO.

1. EXTERIOR OF OFFICE. 2. INTERIOR OF OFFICE. 3. BURMAH OIL COMPANY'S TANKS. 4. BURMAH OIL COMPANY'S TINNING SHEDS.

designed and upholstered expressly for Royal Durbars and State functions, to the bamboo muster-cart or the Simla ricksha, intended for use in the hills. Sandwiched in between these are Oriental drags, State *howdahs,* Stanhope, Brighton Mail, and other phaetons ; victorias, landaus, broughams, and buggies.

The motor department is under the direct supervision of an engineer from England, who has had great experience in all the details of this branch. Messrs. Simpson & Co., who were among the first to recognize the reality of the then approaching motor industry, constructed workshops and imported and installed up-to-date machinery ; and the medals, cups, and diplomas which have been awarded to them in open competitions are sufficient evidence of the high reputation achieved by the firm.

A large number of cars of the newest designs are always kept in stock, but the firm import any make of chassis to the order of customers, fitting bodies to suit Oriental conditions. Cars are supplied with electric light, writing-tables, cabinets, luncheon sets, baggage-grids, and baskets of every description ; a large stock of accessories is kept on hand constantly, and every class of repairs or rebuilding is carried out by skilled motor mechanics.

A brief reference should be made here to the impetus which was given to this firm's business by the holding of the Coronation Durbar at Delhi towards the end of the year 1911. Beautiful carriages, in addition to some State vehicles, were supplied to the States of Hyderabad, Kolhapur, Jodhpur, Kashmir, Udaipur, Radhanpur, Rajgarh, Panna, and many others, while repairs were undertaken for patrons in Cashmere, Kathiawar, and Central and Southern Indian States. With regard to motors, particular mention should be made of two bodies constructed of indigenous timber combined with aluminium for the panels which were fitted to a 40-h.p. Rolls-Royce and a 60-h.p. Napier chassis respectively, to the order of H.H. the Maharajah of Ulwar ; and it must be a source of great satisfaction to the firm to know that in obtaining these orders they had to compete with firms in London, Paris, and Calcutta.

Agencies are held for the Darracq, Wolseley, Napier, the Hotchkis, and the Rolls-Royce chassis. Several charming landaulette and touring bodies were attached to these, and more than 50 of the Darracq type were in evidence at the Durbar, no fewer than 45 of which were for official use by the Government of India.

Branches and agencies have been established at Secunderabad, Ootacamund, Bombay, Rangoon, Colombo, Penang, and Singapore, while on the walls of the proprietors' office hang special warrants of appointment to H.I.M. King George V, to his late Majesty King Edward VII, to their Highnesses the Nizam of Hyderabad and the Maharajahs of Mysore, Travancore, Vizianagram, and Udaipur. Patronage has been given to the firm by the Gaekwar of Baroda, the Maharajahs of Gwalior, Kashmir, Jeypore, Dholpur, and other States ; by the Sultan of Johore, the Begum of Bhopal, the Jam Sahib of Jamnagar, together with many other rajahs and chiefs.

Gold medals and diplomas were obtained at the Great Exhibition in London in 1851, at the Indian and Colonial Exhibition in 1886, at Kathiawar in 1893, at Madras in 1903, at Bombay in 1904, and at Allahabad at a more recent date.

The billiard department is under first-rate management, and as only very dry timber is used the essential foundation of a good and true table is assured. English materials, such as slates, cushions, cloth, and ivory, are imported direct from the manufacturers ; the Madrassi workmen design elaborate carvings, and thus the firm is able to place upon the market a table which is second to none in India.

One cannot wonder at the expansion of this establishment, as purchasers can always rely upon the soundness of all materials, upon the marvellously clever workmanship displayed, and lastly, but by no means of small importance, they realize that the charges are fair and reasonable.

There is, however, the personal element which has been a potent factor in development, and much of the success is due to the energy and practical knowledge of the proprietor himself and to the confidence—born of experience—which exists between Mr. Cuddon and his patrons on the one hand, and his workmen on the other. When he joined the firm carriage fittings, such as lamps and leather for upholstering, were imported, but local industries have been supported, with the result that these and other accessories are manufactured on the premises.

W. E. SMITH & CO., LTD.

The palatial structure on the Mount Road, Madras, known as Kardyl Buildings, and belonging to Messrs. W. E. Smith & Co., Ltd., is one of the most imposing commercial houses in the city, and the extensive business which is carried on by the firm as wholesale and manufacturing druggists, ophthalmic opticians, dealers in surgical, dental, and veterinary instruments, and makers of aerated waters, places them in the van of the many notable professional men in the Presidency.

Mr. W. E. Smith commenced business in 1868, but the premises, which are now one of the sights of the city, are more than ten times the size of those which were occupied originally. A limited company was formed in 1904, and the present directors are Mr. Walter Donald Smith (chairman and managing director), Mr. Wilfred Fraser Smith, Mr. J. O. Robinson, and Mr. E. Steiner. The registered offices are in Kardyl Buildings, and there are other establishments at Hunter's Road, Vepery, and Esplanade Road, Georgetown (both in Madras), and in Church Buildings, Ootacamund. The London offices are at 52 Leadenhall Street, E.C., while agencies have been opened at Paris and New York, and in the West Indies, Cuba, Mexico, and Australia.

It will be understood that, with such an extensive business, very large stocks of chemicals and drugs have to be kept, and it follows that the frequent importations which are necessary to maintain the supply render it impossible that any but the freshest goods are stored. The shops and warehouses contain an unlimited assortment of patent medicines, proprietary goods, perfumery, toilet soaps, medical, nursery, and sick-room requisites, disinfectants, surgical, veterinary, and optical instruments and appliances, physical apparatus, and other sundries.

Messrs. W. E. Smith & Co., Ltd., publish a very complete catalogue and price-list annually, and this is especially convenient for their innumerable up-country customers who forward their orders by post.

The list of surgical instruments contains illustrations and descriptions of the most modern appliances, as any new or improved goods are obtained from the London establishment as soon as they are placed on the market. A special feature is made of accident emergency cases which contain instructions in "first aid

SIMPSON & CO.

1. Cuddan Building—Simpson and Co.'s Showroom. 2. Entrance to Workshop. 3. A Corner of the Paint Shop.

W. E. SMITH & CO., LTD.

1. "KARDYL" BUILDINGS (THE HEAD OFFICE AND LABORATORIES). 2. THE VEPERY BRANCH.

W. E. SMITH & CO., LTD.

1. Esplanade Branch, Georgetown, Madras. 2. The Branch at Ootacamund.

to the injured," in addition to a supply of bandages, forceps, liniment, oil, and other necessaries, and these have been found to be invaluable in railway and other calamities, in factories, and elsewhere.

The optical department has not a rival in India; the newest and most approved instruments are used in testing the sight, and the most complicated defects are treated by scientific methods which have been acquired by special training and by a careful study of the human eye. Dark and other rooms have been specially fitted up for this important branch, and it is believed that no other company or firm in India makes a practice of testing the sight with the ophthalmoscope and the retinascope. The department is under most efficient management, and it is replete with every description of lenses, the finest Brazilian pebbles and optical glass, gold and solid nickel English-made spectacles, neutral-tinted eye-preservers, field, marine, and opera-glasses and microscopes, together with reading and magnifying-glasses.

None but fully qualified chemists and certified compounders are employed in the dispensing branch, which is under the personal superintendence of the managing director, and this work is carried on in a portion of the premises where the assistants are entirely free from interruptions of any kind. Physicians' prescriptions are prepared accurately, and the finest drugs which can be procured are used.

Quite a formidable array of proprietary preparations of the company is given in the price-list, and these include medicines, lotions, powders, pills, hair dyes, tonics, and tinctures, which have earned a great reputation. All of these articles bear the patented trade-mark of the company.

Messrs. W. E. Smith & Co., Ltd., hold agencies for Messrs. Burroughs, Wellcome & Co.'s "Tabloid" products, and for the specialities of Messrs. Parke Davis & Co., of Detroit, U.S.A., and they are sole proprietors of the "Kardyl" brand of borax soaps, which are said to be antiseptic, non-poisonous, non-corrosive, and non-irritating, and which are as valuable in the nursery as they are for domestic purposes. More than 2,400 cases of these soaps are sold annually.

On entering the premises of this company one cannot help admiring the beautiful showroom, which is 60 ft. in length and 40 ft. in width. Iron castings and wedgwood tiles are prominent features in its construction, and nearly all of the ornate and costly fittings have been imported from the noted firm of Messrs. Drew & Co., of London. The chemist's shop has six fixed and three hanging lights of 100 and 250 candle-power respectively, while the gallery has four lamps of 50 candle-power.

Other parts of the building are occupied by medical men and surgeon dentists. Completely equipped school laboratories have been provided, and most comfortable quarters are found for assistants, who, with 50 clerks, are nearly 200 in number.

Messrs. W. E. Smith & Co., Ltd., have for many years past been engaged in the manufacture of various kinds of aerated waters, and their products are certainly unexcelled by those of any other make in India.

The absolute purity of the water used is guaranteed by the Berkefield system of filtration. The supply is drawn from the Red Hills tank, which is about 10 miles distant from Madras. A pamphlet issued by the company says: "The water contains suspended matter which is removed by elaborate reservoirs and filters erected on our premises on a scale that enables us to use the processes of sedimentation, precipitation, and subsequent filtration so as to secure complete purification."

Similar vigilance has been exercised over the apparatus employed, and every part of the plant with which the water comes into contact is thoroughly up to date from a scientific and hygienic point of view. An improved bottling machine (by Messrs. Barnet, Foster & Co.) is in use, and as many as 4,000 dozens of bottles can be filled daily.

Electricity as well as steam is used for motive purposes, and a small tramway has been constructed for the conveyance of full bottles to the store-room. All bottles are washed in sterilized water in order to ensure perfect cleanliness, and excellent racks have been fixed upon the walls, upon which every single bottle is thoroughly dried.

The soda-water stock is maintained at about 1,000 dozens, while the room for sweetened drinks will hold about the same quantity.

Dr. F. W. Andrews, of the pathological department, St. Bartholomew's Hospital, London, who made an analysis of soda-water manufactured by this company, says: "The soda-water from a bacteriological point of view is pure and good." Lieutenant S. R. Christopher, M.D., Superintendent of the King Institute of Preventive Medicine at Guindy, near Madras, gave a certificate, of which the following is a copy: "I have made bacteriological examinations of the samples of soda-water forwarded by you, and have encountered in each case an extremely high degree of bacterial purity, amounting, in instances where the bottles had been kept some days unopened, to an entire absence of organisms in one cubic centimetre of the sample."

The same high standard of purity has been attained in the manufacture of other beverages, such as kola, gingerade, orange ale, and many others, and the extremely large annual consumption of these drinks is evidence of their popularity.

Much more space might be occupied in speaking of the pre-eminent position occupied by this company, but perhaps the soundest proof may be obtained from the annual reports of the directors and from balance-sheets which have been published.

The ninth ordinary general meeting of shareholders was held on December 30, 1913, and a brief reference may be made to the statement which was then submitted by the directors. The profit for the year ending October 31, 1913, after deducting management and working expenses, was Rs. 1,01,075, but Rs. 5,458 were written off for depreciation on buildings, on machinery, on electric installation, and on furniture and fixtures, thus leaving Rs. 95,617, together with the balance of Rs. 16,191 brought forward from the previous year available for dividend.

An interim dividend of 5 per cent. had been paid in April 1913, and the directors recommended payment of a further dividend at the same rate. After the preference and ordinary shareholders had been paid, there remained a balance to the credit of the profit and loss account of Rs. 11,104 to be carried forward to the following year. For several years past a dividend of not less than 10 per cent. has been declared.

Messrs. W. E. Smith & Co., Ltd., were chemists and druggists by appointment to H.E. the Right Hon. the Earl of Elgin and Kincardine, P.C., Viceroy of India, and they have, further, had the patronage of all the Governors of Madras since about the year 1880.

They are local agents for the Phoenix

Assurance Co., Ltd., which is the oldest institution in the world transacting life business only, and whose total assets exceed 24 crores.

Mr. W. Donald Smith held the important office of Sheriff of Madras during the years 1907 and 1908.

SMITH, STOCKING & CO.

The active partners in this firm—Messrs. W. Smith and R. Stocking—had more than twenty years' practical experience in all branches of a dispensing chemist's and druggist's business before they opened their well-stocked establishment on the Esplanade in Madras in April 1913. A special feature is made of the dispensing of medicines, and medical practitioners rely upon their prescriptions receiving the personal attention of highly qualified men. The premises are splendidly situated on the Esplanade, immediately opposite the High Court of Justice and the Law College, and they consist of a well-lighted shop, dispensary, offices, and store-rooms. The internal fittings are elaborately constructed, and the shelves and showcases contain a large assortment of up-to-date surgical and nursing instruments, drugs of first-class quality, perfumes, and other toilet requisites. A soda-water factory is now being constructed in order to meet the great demand for this popular beverage, and the buildings, the machinery, and the ingredients to be used will be of such a character that the most stringent requirements in hygienic science will be fully met.

SMITH, STOCKING & CO

1. A Front View of the Premises. 2. A Portion of the Showroom.

THE SOUTH INDIAN EXPORT COMPANY, LTD.

This company was formed about the year 1898, when it absorbed the business interests in Southern India of Messrs. DeClermont and Donner (who had been established in Madras for thirty years previously), as general merchants and importers and exporters of all kinds of merchandise.

The present directors are Messrs. R. C. Donner, E. C. Donner, P. E. DeClermont, and G. R. Speyer, while the managing director in the city is Mr. R. S. F. Simson.

The Madras offices are at No. 4 Maclean Street, but the registered headquarters of the firm are at 27 St. Thomas's Street, London, E.C., where the representatives are Messrs. DeClermont & Donner.

The original business of the firm was the export of tanned hides and skins to the English and American markets, and this business has been developed successfully until it now assumes large proportions. Many years ago, however, the firm undertook import business, and while the imports vary considerably in character, the largest tonnage is that of Bengal coal, which ranges between 100,000 and 200,000 tons annually. The bulk of this coal is carried to Madras by steamers and delivered to the railway companies, large mills, and factories. The company also do practically all the bunkering business in Madras, as they hold most of the important contracts with shipping companies all over the world. Owing to the greatly improved harbour facilities and to their experience in the work, the company is able to give a much greater measure of dispatch to bunkering steamers than was possible a few years

THE SOUTH INDIAN EXPORT COMPANY, LTD.

1. SS. "Belle of France" Discharging Coal. 2. SS. "Good Hope." 3. Office Premises—4 Maclean Street, Madras.

ago. Moreover, besides doing a very large business in general imports for the local merchants, the company also makes a special feature of supplying Government and railway departments with certain stores of an engineering character, such as cement, roofing material, hydraulic and water-works appliances.

The Tata Iron and Steel Co., Ltd., is now well-known throughout India for its steel and iron materials, which have met with universal approval, their steel beams and bails being guaranteed to comply with the British standard specification Their agency is in the hands of the S.I.E Co., Ltd., who are also agents for Messrs F. W. Heilgers & Co., Calcutta, a firm which controls many large Jheriah and Raniganj Collieries, the Kinnison Jute Mills, the Titaghur Paper Mills, which are the largest and most successful paper mills in India, and they also represent the Law Union and Rock Fire and Life Insurance Company in the Madras Presidency.

THE SOUTH INDIAN INDUSTRIALS, LTD.

The South Indian Industrials, Ltd., are owners of the Madras Portland Cement Works, the Bangalore Brick and Tile Works, the Reliance Engineering Works, the Chittivalsah Jute Mills, the Goribidnur Sugar Refinery, and the Tiruvalur Rice Mills. These industries were founded by the late firm of Messrs. Arbuthnot & Co., of Madras, who subsequently formed a joint-stock company, styled "Arbuthnot's Industrials, Ltd." It was not long after the formation of this company that there occurred one of the most appalling financial wrecks that has ever been known in the East, and the majority of the shares in the concern were purchased by Messrs. H. A. R. H. Fakir Mahomed Sait and Hajee Ismail Sait. The title was then changed to the "South Indian Industrials, Ltd.," and the management devolved upon the directors, namely, Messrs. Hajee Ismail Sait & Sons and Fakir Mahomed Sait & Sons. During the early part of the year 1914, Messrs. Fakir Mahomed Sait & Sons purchased the interests of their co-directors, and they have now sole control of the works of the company.

The only Portland Cement Works in India at the present time are those belonging to the Industrials, Ltd., which are situated in Basin Bridge Road, in Madras. The average monthly output is from 500 to 600 tons, and the consignments are shipped to all the principal ports in the Presidency. The machinery of the works is thoroughly up to date in every respect, and the electric power is derived from the Madras city service.

A speciality is made of the manufacture of cement pipes, varying in size from 4 to 24 in., which are supplied in large quantities to the Madras Government, principally for irrigation purposes. The cement is known by the name of "Engine" brand, and the company pride themselves on giving "one quality only and that the best." Europeans fill the positions of manager and of chemist, and about 400 hands are constantly employed.

The City Brick and Tile Works at Bangalore are well known throughout the Presidency, and the quality and variety of the manufactures will be understood from the fact that no fewer than seven gold and silver medals have been recently awarded to their exhibits at various shows. The machinery is driven by steam power, and the products of the works are sent to every part of Southern India. A very concise pamphlet and price list is published by the company, and particulars are given with regard to all kinds of bricks, roofing, flooring, ceiling, and ridge tiles, chimney pots, flue-covers, boiler sealings, and fire-clay. A European manager supervises from 200 to 300 hands. The telegraphic address is "Brick-Bangalore."

The Reliance Engineering Works, situated in Basin Bridge Road, Madras, is equipped with modern machinery for manufacturing and repairing, and the motive power is obtained from the city electrical installation. The company are makers of iron roofs, godowns, bungalows, cranes, and ornamental and other castings, and they are contractors for the supply of plant for railways, mills, and factories, for portable and stationary steam and oil-engines, boilers, steel girders, and of mining and agricultural machinery. Electrical appliances are obtained from leading manufacturers, and complete installations are undertaken. A contract has been completed for supplying the new waterworks of the Corporation of Madras with an elevated iron tank, which is the second largest in India, as it has a capacity of a million and a half gallons. The number of employees varies according to the extent of the works on hand, but from 200 to 400 are usually required. The foundry is under the supervision of European managers.

The only jute mills in South India are those which are owned by this company, and which are known by the name of Chittivalsah Jute Mills, 3 miles distant from Bimlipatam, a seaport on the north-east coast of the Madras Presidency. The factory contains 156 looms, and it is most conveniently situated, as jute is grown in the neighbourhood in sufficient quantity to keep the mills at work throughout the whole year. All the machinery—which is driven by steam—has been imported from England, and a thorough trial is always made of any improved appliances which may be placed upon the market. The locally grown crop gives an average annual yield of about 40,000 candies. The manager and his assistant are Europeans, and they have control of about 1,200 employees. The mills form one of the most valuable assets of the Industrials Company.

The Tiruvalur Rice Mills, in the district of Tanjore, and a few miles distant from Negapatam, are the largest of their kind in Southern India, and they are worked in conjunction with a smaller mill situated near to the village of Nidamangalam. Paddy is grown extensively in this district, and the annual output of the two mills respectively is about 200,000 and 40,000 bags, each of 195 lb. in weight. The milling of rice in Tanjore has grown very rapidly in recent years, and the directors of the Industrials Company, unable to cope with the demands made upon them, have just completed the construction of two new factories at Tiruvalur.

The head office of the South Indian Industrials, Ltd., is at Oriental Buildings, Armenian Street, Madras, and the general manager is Mr. Ian Scott Mackenzie.

SPENCER & CO., LTD.

Those who are able, either from personal experience or from a study of commercial records, to make a comparison between the old-fashioned yet steady manner in which a limited amount of business was transacted fifty years ago, and the torpedo-like rush of present-day buying and selling, must be struck with amazement at the enormous changes which have taken place. The little "general" store at the corner has been enlarged on two or three occasions, perhaps, but owing to continued expansion of trade it has at last been compelled to give way to the princely building in which an army of assistants is employed. Railways have been pushed into the interior of various

SPENCER & CO., LTD.

1. Durrant and Spencer's Building. 2. The Head Office Building. 3. Hotel Spencer.

Photos Nos. 1 and 2 Copyright by Weile & Klein, Madras.

countries ; shipping companies have provided more favourable accommodation for the transport of all classes of goods, and harbour authorities have made more suitable arrangements for facilitating the import and export of produce. These, and other circumstances, have tended to a most astounding increase in the volume of the world's trade, and at the same time they have been the cause of the establishment of many firms and companies whose departments have a greater range even than that particular one which boasts of being able to supply anything from a needle to an anchor.

There are many companies in India which have been in existence for considerably more than fifty years, but it is doubtful if any one of them in the Presidency can show a more consistent and steady development than that of Messrs. Spencer & Co., Ltd., whose head offices are in the city of Madras. The enormous commercial turnover which is now associated with the palatial buildings in Mount Road, and with various branch establishments, is the outcome of an unpretentious little business which was opened in Madras in the year 1863 by Mr. Charles Durrant. The latter was joined in partnership by Mr. J. W. Spencer, and the new firm began as auctioneers and wine and general merchants in a building which stood upon the site now occupied by the Hotel d'Angelis. A number of changes in the *personnel* of the firm took place prior to the year 1897, when a limited liability company was formed. It may be mentioned that Mr. Durrant commenced in 1863 with a capital of Rs. 25,000, while the amount paid up by the shareholders of the present company is no less than 40 lakhs of rupees.

A stroll through an almost interminable succession of finely fitted and ornamented rooms in the Mount Road establishment reveals such a remarkable assortment of all kinds of goods that one is bewildered at the quantity and variety, but the following are some of the departments which are so attractive to visitors from all parts of Southern India : oilman stores and provisions, silver and electro-plate, watches and clocks, cutlery, ironmongery and turnery, china and glassware, harness and saddlery, boots and shoes, portmanteaus and travelling requisites, field-glasses and magic-lanterns, gramophones, lamps, games and bicycles, fancy goods, photographic requisites, artists' materials, perfumery and toilet preparations, tobaccos and stationery.

Messrs. Spencer & Co., Ltd., are manufacturers of high-class cigars, which are entirely hand-made from the most carefully selected Havana and Indian leaf, and are rolled with scrupulous care by skilled workmen. Some of the most famous brands are Gold Mohur Special, Catamarans, Todas, Beaconsfields, Puros, Coronas, and Doreto Bouquets. The majority of these are packed in boxes of 50, at prices varying from Rs. 3 to Rs. 10 per 100.

It is claimed by the company that they have for many years held the premier position in the Presidency of Madras for the superior quality of their wines and spirits, and as they are refreshment-room contractors to the Madras and Southern Mahratta and South India Railway systems, and to the Guaranteed State Railway of H.H. the Nizam of Hyderabad, the favourable terms under which they purchase large stocks in bulk and bottle enable them to supply their retail customers at extremely moderate rates.

Well-appointed restaurant cars are attached to mail trains, and the company provide breakfasts, luncheons, and dinners at a moderate cost. Refreshment-rooms at stations are numerous, and the requirements of all classes of passengers from the modest soda-water to the most sumptuous dinner, are promptly attended to. Branches and depôts have been opened at Calcutta, Bombay, Karachi, Bangalore, Secunderabad, Kolar, Ootacamund, Coimbatore, Coonoor, Trichinoply, Waltair, Coconada, Quilon, Madura, Cochin, Pollibetta, Calicut, Mandapam, and other centres. The firm issued a recent Christmas number of their interesting publication called *Spencer's News*, and in it they referred to the fact that the area covered by their branches, refreshment-rooms, depôts, and other stores was not less than 260,000 square miles, and that it extended from Bombay on the west coast to Calcutta on the east, and as far as Tuticorin in the south.

The managing directors are Messrs. J. O. Robinson and J. H. Thonger, in Madras, and Messrs. E. F. Oakshott, P. G. Oakshott, and A. W. D. Oakes, who are resident in London.

The company are proprietors of the following hotels, namely, the "Connemara" and "Spencer's" in Madras, and the "West End" at Bangalore, and they also manage Brind's Hotel in Madras and the Cubbon Hotel in Bangalore.

The Connemara Hotel is a comparatively new building of excellent design and workmanship, and is ideally situated in extensive grounds in one of the most attractive parts of Commander-in-Chiefs' Road, which abuts upon the best portion of Mount Road, in Madras. Electric lights and fans are in every room, and the comfort of families who reside *en suite*, or of visitors who are passing through Madras, is ensured by strict personal supervision on the part of the proprietors. The dining-room is separate from the main structure, and it is particularly airy and well lighted. There are 41 rooms altogether, and each one has a really charming view of tropical trees and plants which abound in the neighbourhood.

Spencer's Hotel in Mount Road is a favourite residence for gentlemen who are engaged professionally or commercially in the "west end" of the city, but owing to its very name it is an attraction to visitors from other parts of the Presidency to whom the name "Spencer" is an everyday word. This house, too, is of recent construction, and no expense has been spared in providing unexcelled accommodation in its 35 rooms, which have been furnished and decorated in a truly artistic style. Electric lights and fans have been fixed upon each floor, and a rigid supervision of the attendants is a feature which is reflected in the comforts and perfect service which are obtained.

THE "BEEHIVE" FOUNDRY

The "Beehive" iron foundry and engineering works belonging to Messrs. Oakes & Co., Ltd., situated at 93 Popham's Broadway, Madras, were established in the year 1843, and the name is certainly not inappropriate, as the activity which prevails in a hive of bees is not excelled by the industry which is manifested by the large staff of employees of this company. During that portion of the year when business is generally quiet, no fewer than from 500 to 600 workmen are engaged, but there is order and regularity in all branches, each of which is under the supervision of a European foreman.

The company have successfully carried out contracts of some magnitude for the railway authorities, for shipping companies, and for many of the leading merchants and builders throughout the Madras Presidency. Considerable extensions have been made to the foundry during recent years in order to meet the increasing demand for structural steel and iron work, and a staff of competent engineers and draughtsmen is kept for the preparation of designs and of estimates of cost.

The company specialize in the construction of steel roof principals, girders, stanchions, oil and water tanks, pulleys, shafting, bridges, sluice-gates, aerial tramways, rubber-washing mills, vacuum dryers, hot-air drying plant, hay or goods sheds, fireproof doors, spiral and straight staircases, sanitary carts, crab winches

tribute to the company that they were in September 1914 entrusted with the necessary iron, steel, and brass work in connection with the fitting up of the hospital ship *Madras*.

Steam power for driving the machinery was used throughout the foundry until the close of the year 1914, when a modern system of electricity was substituted.

The telegraphic and cable address is "Bonami, Madras."

of a number of steam cotton presses and ginning plants throughout the country, and they hold agencies for the Austrian Lloyd Steam Navigation Company, La Compagnie des Messageries Maritime, the German-Australian Line, and the Spanish and Italian mail steamers. Messrs. Volkart have recently been employing about 80 Europeans together with a large number of Indian labourers.

WALKER & CO.

1. Discharging Coal. 2. Sorting Timber.

ballast road rollers, garden seats, and expanded metal.

The store-rooms are always stocked with a large variety of goods such as engineers' tools, builders' and furnishers' brass, sanitary appliances and fittings, agricultural machinery, corn and grain crushers, chaff-cutters, engines and boilers of all kinds, pumping machinery, rolled steam beams, mild steel, doors and window-sashes in teakwood, flooring and ceiling boards, joists, scantlings, and a general assortment of engineers' and contractors' requisites. A number of expert shipwrights are employed to carry out repairs to vessels, and it is no mean

VOLKART BROTHERS

This firm was established at Winterthur in Switzerland, in the year 1881, and although retaining their head office in that town, they opened offices and stores in Armenian Street, in the city of Madras, about seven years later, and that step was succeeded by the formation of branches at Bombay and Karachi. Messrs. Volkart Brothers are general merchants, importers of steel, iron of all descriptions—chiefly, however, in bar and sheet form—as well as being exporters of all kinds of Indian manufactured goods and produce, with cotton and cotton goods as a special feature. The firm are owners

WALKER & CO.

The city of Madras is fortunate in possessing quite a large number of general merchants of repute, and the name of Walker & Co., of Second Line Beach, occupies a prominent position in the list of those firms who have been successful in the upbuilding of the commercial interests of the third largest city in the Indian Empire. Mr. George Walker—the founder—commenced business in the year 1850 as an East India merchant. The principal exports of the firm are tanned skins and hides. A large quantity of teak wood is imported from Rangoon; coal is brought from Calcutta,

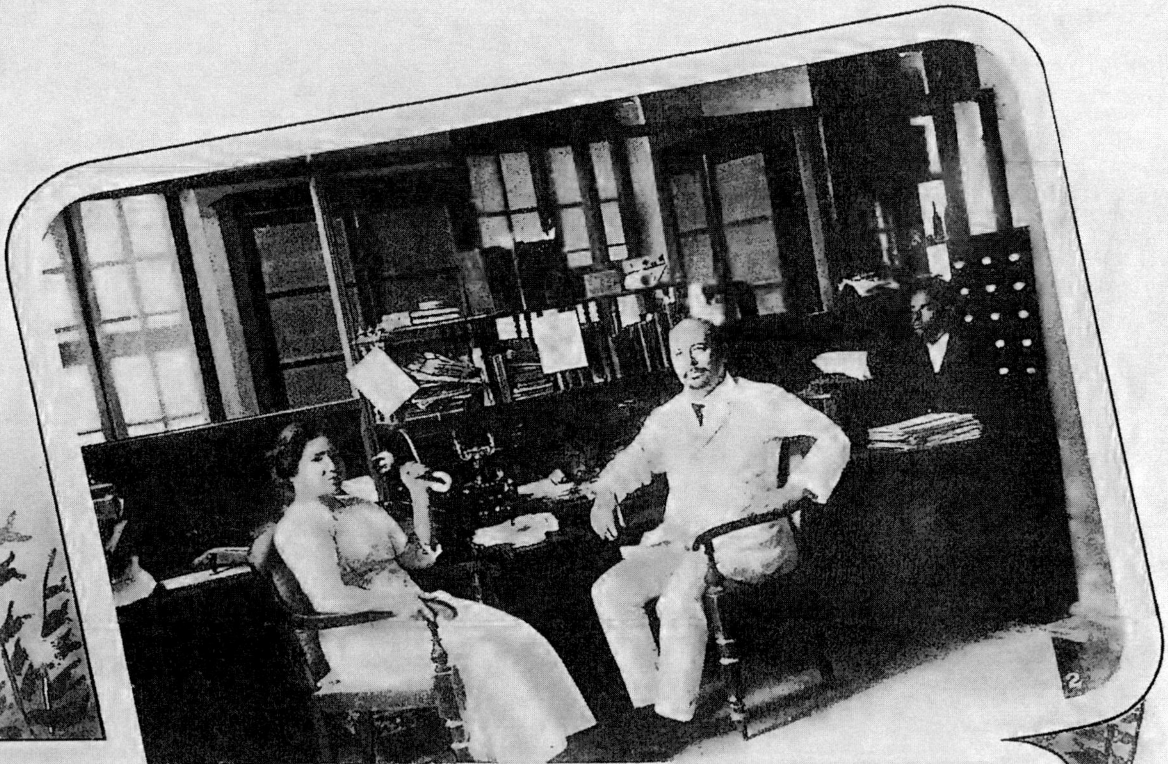

J. W. WILSON & CO., LTD.

1. "VIMO" BUILDINGS. 2. MANAGING DIRECTOR'S OFFICE.

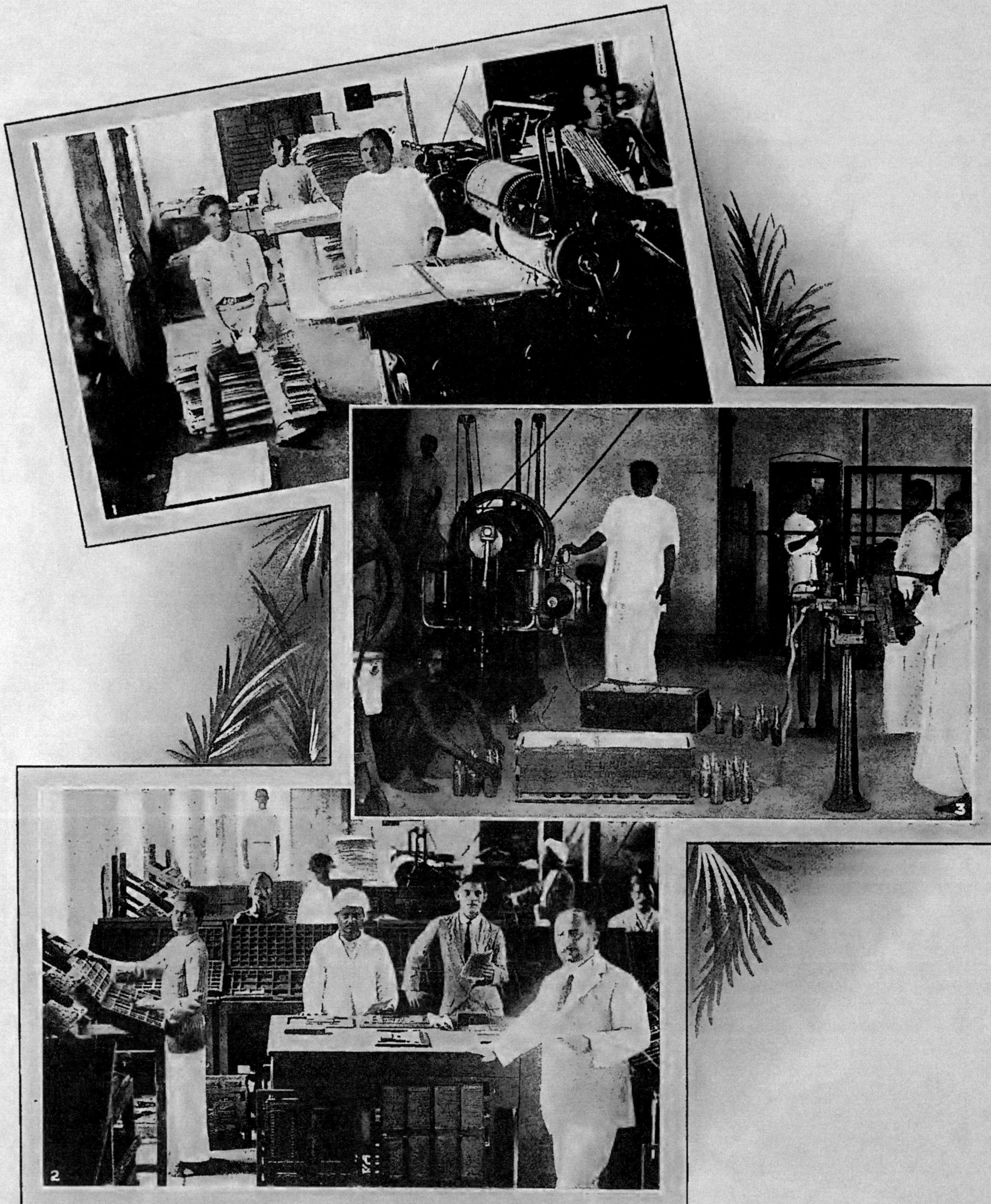

J. W. WILSON & CO., LTD.

1. Machine Room. 2. Composing Room (Press Department). 3. Aerated Water Factory.

and piece goods are obtained from Manchester.

Messrs. Walker hold several important agencies, which include those of the Orient Royal Mail Steam Navigation Company, the Bibby Line of steamers, the Phoenix Assurance Co., Ltd. (Fire), the North British and Mercantile Insurance Co., Ltd. (Life), the Scottish Amicable Life Assurance Company, the State Fire Assurance Co., Ltd., the Southern Mahratta Spinning and Weaving Co., Ltd., James Buchanan & Co., Ltd., H. R. Mansfield and Mansfield Brothers (pipe, tile, and sanitary-ware manufacturers), and Andrew Yule & Co., of Calcutta.

The present partners are J. L. Walker (Europe), F. E. L. Worke (Consular Agent for France), G. K. Walker (Madras), and G. H. Daye (Europe).

The head office in London is carried on under the style of Walker, Munsie & Co., of 1 and 2 Great Winchester Street, E.C.

J. W. WILSON & CO., LTD.

A very modest looking little shop was opened about a quarter of a century ago when Mr. J. W. Wilson commenced business as a chemist and druggist, but customers were attracted by the personality of the proprietor as well as by the purity of the chemicals which he used. Further than that, he made a special feature of the study of ailments common to India, and he expended both time and money in investigating the causes of the diseases and in making practical tests of remedies which he prepared. Thus it was that the business began to grow, that further accommodation became necessary, and that the staff of assistants had to be increased in number from time to time. Remedy after remedy was discovered and placed upon the market, but the most important of all was the one registered as "Vimo," which is one of the most famous medicines in the East, being a food tonic of exceptionally high recuperative character. A few years ago a private limited liability company was formed, and every employee—European, Anglo-Indian, and Indian alike—is a shareholder, and therefore possesses more than a nominal connection with this well-known house. A fully qualified medical staff still carries on investigations on the lines originally laid down by Mr. Wilson, and sufferers in this vast continent, in Burma, Ceylon, Aden, and the East generally are reaping the benefits of the painstaking work and skill of the founder and of those who have been associated with him. The company, naturally, have a very large number of correspondents who are in need of medicines or advice, but the mass of letters is promptly dealt with by an efficient staff who treat, in the strictest confidence, all matters placed before them. Every bottle of medicine bears the impress of a royalty paid portrait stamp, together with the signature of the proprietor.

Messrs. J. W. Wilson & Co., Ltd., hold a larger stock of drugs and chemicals than any other firm of manufacturing chemists in the Presidency of Madras, and have a splendid selection of imported goods which are purchased from the leading establishments in England, France, and America. These include perfumery, soaps and toilet requisites, patent medicines, medical, nursery, and sick-room requisites and surgical appliances.

An aerated-water factory has been opened recently, and it would be impossible for greater care to be taken to ensure absolute purity. The water is carefully precipitated, filtered, and distilled by thoroughly modern machinery and plant, and the company are therefore able to give a guarantee as to the quality of their preparations. "Wilson's Artistic Press" is the title of the branch which supplies labels and other printed matter for the other departments, and this is under the management of Mr. William Wilson. Electric power is in use in the water factory and in the printing works, and the same force is generated for lights and fans throughout the buildings.

The present structure is a handsome red brick building forming three sides of a square, and it contains drug stores, shop, offices, and private dwelling apartments, in addition to the factory and press-rooms. It has a frontage of 365 ft upon one of the principal roads in Madras. The firm holds thousands of testimonials from customers residing in all parts of India, Burma, and Ceylon.

The managing director is Mr. J. W. Wilson, and his European assistants are Messrs. J. W. A. Wilson, W. Wilson, L. Wilson, V. Wilson, A. N. Wilson, C. L. C. Wilson, and F. Wilson.

ALFRED YOUNG & CO., LTD.

The business carried on by this firm (which, by the way, has recently been converted into a private limited company) consists of the exporting of tanned hides and skins, the importing of piece goods and sundries and general commission agency. Dealing in hides and skins does not consist merely in buying in the cheapest markets and selling in the dearest, as any one who proposes to be conversant with the whole business must have expert knowledge of the two most important processes of sorting and classification. Messrs. Young & Co. are recognized as experts in these matters, and the hides which pass through their hands are placed in one of the following divisions, namely, prime Bangalores, ordinary Bangalores, prime Hyderabads, Mutwadas, Pallaverams, Belgaums, Amburs, Vizagapatams, and Coconadas. Skins are tanned at Trichinopoly, Dindigul, Coimbatore, Madras, and other places in the Presidency.

The head offices of the company are at Lancaster House, 29 Rood Street, in the city of Manchester.

FLYING FOXES.

FAUNA

By H. H. F. M. TYLER

THE aim of this article is to give some account of the principal game animals which the sportsman may hope to meet with in the jungles of Southern India. Within this area is to be found a large variety of wild life, from the elephant down to the tiny mouse-deer In fact, with the exception of the hog-deer, the rhinoceros, and the lion, every species of big game which is found anywhere in the continent of India, excluding, of course, those peculiar to the great hill ranges of the north, may be met with in greater or less numbers in the Southern Provinces. One species, the Nilgiri ibex, is found nowhere outside the Madras Presidency. The physical features of the country, and the conditions under which game may be pursued are as varied as the game itself.

On the upper plateaus of the Western Ghauts, a country of rolling downs and dense evergreen forest, the conditions as regards scenery and climate are as near perfect as can be found anywhere; while in the moist and fever-haunted jungles at the base of the hills it is truly in the sweat of his brow that the sportsman earns his trophy.

In some parts the sportsman may step from the train into the midst of the jungle, where he will hear frequent reports from the gangs of railway coolies of tigers being seen crossing the line. Ice may be purchased daily from passing trains, and the daily paper, with the latest Reuter's telegrams, is received a few hours after it has been published in the headquarters of the Presidency.

In other parts a week of strenuous marching will be required to bring the sportsman to his ground, and he may find himself in a country where men and women alike go practically naked, and where, almost within the memory of the present generation, the practice of human sacrifice was being indulged in.

Or, again, the sportsman who to-day is sweltering in the overpowering heat of the jungles at the foot of the Nilgiris, may to-morrow, by the aid of train or motor, be pursuing the sambhur or the ibex in one of the most perfect climates in the world at a height of 6,000 to 8,000 ft., a quick change which can be possible in few other parts of the world.

Among rarer species mention may first be made of the Buffalo (*Bos bubalus*). This animal, whose wide-spread horns form one of the finest trophies which can fall to the sportsman's rifle, is found in sadly diminished numbers only in the eastern part of the Vizagapatam district and the tract of country which borders on the Central Provinces. Within comparatively recent years the buffalo was found in these tracts in herds of large size, but now principally owing to the operations of Indian skin-hunters, it has been practically exterminated in parts where it formerly used to roam. The buffalo is the progenitor of the domestic Indian buffaloes, from which it differs materially only in size. A wild bull will stand upwards of 15 hands at the shoulder, with horns that give a measurement of between 8 and 9 ft., measured sportsman fashion from tip to tip across the forehead. The buffalo is found both in heavy grass jungle and in the more open sal forest. He delights in swamps and is fond of wallowing. Unlike the bison, he keeps to the level country, and does not as a rule ascend hills. The buffalo is by nature extremely bold. Single bulls are sometimes a great nuisance to the villagers, mingling and interbreeding with village cattle, and sometimes refusing to be driven away. The buffalo is more prone to charge than perhaps any other Indian animal except the rhinoceros, and this fact makes his pursuit very exciting.

1. RAT SNAKE CAUGHT IN TENNIS-NET AT BELUR. 2. MANTIS (STICK INSECT). 3 AND 5. CHAMELEONS. 4. PRAYING MANTIS.

The following account of a successful buffalo hunt may be quoted:-

We had followed the trail but a mile or so, when instead of going straight away the tracks began to twist and turn. Presently we came to a place where the bull had evidently stood for some time facing the back trail, as if to see whether he was being pursued. This was just at the edge of a patch of young saplings about 3 or 4 ft. in height, forming a thick cover among the parent stems. The shikari declared that the bull would be found inside this cover, and this, indeed, seemed not unlikely, but it was not so easy to decide what to do next. The cover was too thick and green to have been burned, as had been all the more open jungle, and the dry grass and fallen leaves would make tracking very difficult, and render it quite impossible to move without making a certain amount of noise. As we were still discussing what to do, my attention was attracted by a slight movement far down a vista of trees, and with the glasses I was able to make out the black tips of the bull's horns appearing about a foot or two above the dense undergrowth. There are swinging to and fro with the regularity of a pendulum, and it was clear that the bull was keeping a sharp look out on all sides. It would clearly require the greatest caution to approach, and the jungle was too thick to offer much hope of a shot except at fairly close range. I decided that the best chance of success lay in entering the thicket alone, and was about to make the attempt when low voices were heard approaching, and we saw the syce and the dog boy coming along the trail, so engrossed in deciphering it that for some seconds they failed to observe our frantic gesticulations. I saw the pendulum swing of the great horns grow more rapid; the bull's suspicions were being aroused, and I expected to see him once more dash off in alarm. At length our signals were observed, and after waiting for a few minutes to allow the bull's suspicions to be lulled into a fatal security, I started on the final stalk. The bull was only 200 or 300 yards away, but each yard seemed a furlong. Crouching low among the undergrowth, I could no longer see the horn tips, and it seemed too much to hope that I should still find the bull in the same position as when I started. After what seemed ages, I ventured to raise myself behind the sheltering stem of a tree, and there at last was the mighty bull. He had lain down since I entered the cover, his back towards the wind—no need to keep a look-out that side, his keen scent would warn him of danger from that direction—while the great horns still maintained the regularity of the pendulum swing as the bull glanced this way and that. The very regularity of the swing of that mighty head made the last part of the stalk comparatively easy. Waiting till the bull turned his head away, I crouched forward a few yards, only to freeze into immobility behind a tree as he turned again in my direction. Thus at last I found myself but 30 paces from the bull. Once more the great head swung round, gazing right at the trunk behind which I crouched. Would he never turn away his head? Surely he had scented danger, and I should see that mighty form upraised, and perhaps even have to stand a charge when he found himself so close to his enemy. But no! Again the bull's head swung away, and now the whole brawny neck was exposed. Quickly the heavy rifle came to my shoulder, a yellow flame of cordite spurted from the muzzle, and the bull rolled over on his side, kicking and struggling in his death agony."

In the same localities as the buffalo is found the Barasingha, or Swamp Deer (*Cervus duvauceli*), but it is now extremely rare, and few sportsmen of the present day have been fortunate enough to obtain a specimen within the Madras Presidency.

Another rare animal is the so-called Nilgiri Ibex (*Hemitragus hylocrius*). This wild goat, which is found nowhere outside the Madras Presidency, inhabits the higher ranges of the Western Ghauts. Its northern limit is the Nilgiri Plateau, and from thence it is found in suitable localities southwards as far as the neighbourhood of Cape Comorin. It is not generally found below an elevation of 4,000 ft. Its usual haunts are on the grassy slopes among the crags and precipices of the edge of the plateau. The ibex as a rule keeps to the open and rarely enters the forest. Where undisturbed they may be found feeding on the grassy hills on the upper plateaus, but where much hunted they keep almost entirely to the precipitous faces of the hills. A buck ibex will stand about 40 in. at the shoulder, and the old animals have a clearly marked saddle of grizzled white, whence they are known as saddle-backs. The average horn measurement is about 14 in., and anything over 15 in. is rare. The magnificent scenery amid which the ibex is found lends a peculiar fascination to the pursuit of this most wary animal.

A FINE COLLECTION OF TROPHIES SHOT IN SOUTH- INDIA BY MESSRS. G. & E. HADFIELD.

The following account of them by "Hawkeye" cannot be improved upon:—

"It is a pleasant sight to watch a herd of ibex when undisturbed, the kids frisking here and there on pinnacles or ledges of rocks and beetling cliffs, where there seems scarcely safe foothold for anything much larger than a grasshopper or a fly, the old mothers looking calmly on or grazing steadily while the day is young, cropping the soft moss or tender herbs and sweet short grass springing from the crevices of the craggy precipices in rich abundance.

"Then, again, to see the caution observed in taking up their resting or abiding places for the day, where they may be warmed by the sun, listening to the roar of many waters, and figuratively, we may say, chewing the cud of contentment, and giving themselves up to the full enjoyment of their nomadic life and its romantic haunts. Usually before reposing one of the herd, generally an old doe, may be observed intently gazing below, apparently scanning every spot in the range of her vision, sometimes for half an hour or more before she is satisfied that 'all is well'; strange to say, seldom or never looking up to the rocks above. Then, being satisfied on the one side, she observes the same process on the other, eventually calmly lying down, contented with the precaution she has taken that all is safe. Her post as sentinel is generally a prominent one, on the edge and corner perhaps of some ledge, to be well sheltered from the wind and warmed by the sun, along which the rest of the herd dispose themselves as inclined, fully trusting in the watchful guardian whose manœuvres I have been describing. Should the sentinel be joined by another, or her kid come and lie down by her, they invariably place themselves back to back, or in such a manner that they can keep a look-out on either side. A solitary male goes through all this by himself, and wonderfully careful he is, but when with the herd he reposes in security, leaving it to the females to take precautions for their mutual safety."

The Elephant (*Elephas maximus*) is now found practically only in the Western Ghauts and adjacent hills. In comparatively recent times it was found also in the east of the Presidency; the last elephant is said to have been killed on the Javadi Hills some forty or fifty years ago, while a few are still found in the forests of the Ganjam district on the borders of Orissa. The elephant is now found most commonly in Travancore, on the Anamalai Hills, along the slopes of the Western Ghauts in Malabar and South Canara, on the slopes of the Nilgiris, in the North Coimbatore Hills and the adjacent ranges in Mysore, and also in Coorg. They ascend to the summits of the Anaimalai or Elephant Hills, and have been seen on Anaimudi, the highest peak in Southern India, the elevation of which is close on 9,000 ft. They also frequent the low country at the foot of the hills, their wanderings depending largely on the season and on climatic conditions.

The elephant is generally protected in British territory. Only proclaimed rogues may be shot, but leave may occasionally be obtained to shoot one in Native States or on private land. In Mysore elephants are caught in keddahs, elsewhere throughout the area they are trapped in pits. Elephants have become numerous in places, but within the last six or seven years nearly seven hundred are known to have been captured in Mysore, Coorg, Malabar, Wynaad, and the Anamalais, and their numbers have been considerably reduced.

In some localities immunity from pursuit has made them very bold, and they do a considerable amount of damage by devouring the crops of the villagers, and refuse to be frightened away by the shouts of the watchers who are on guard to protect the fields from the ravages of wild beasts. Solitary tuskers are most troublesome in this respect, the herds being more timid. As a rule the elephant is inoffensive as far as human beings are concerned, but a rogue elephant will frequently terrorize a whole countryside, chasing any one whom it sees and killing any one whom it can catch. There is perhaps no sport which is quite so dangerous as the pursuit of the rogue elephant. His keenness of scent makes it a matter of difficulty to approach him unobserved, while the thickness of the jungle which he usually inhabits gives the sportsman but a poor chance of escape if he should fail to floor him.

The following account of the death of a rogue elephant gives a good idea of the dangers to be overcome:—

"The tracks led us at first through bamboo forest, and then we got into terrible country, which consisted of a series of low hills and deep ravines. The undergrowth of thorns and shrubs was bad enough, but in addition the whole place was chock-full of a sort of reed with long leaves about an inch or so broad. The elephants had, of course, knocked these down in their passage, so going downhill was one long slide and going up beggars description. To add to the difficulties the thorned cane grew everywhere. The reeds were 8 to 10 ft. high on the lower slopes, and taller still in the ravines. On the tops of the hills the undergrowth was only up to our knees. We twisted and turned in all directions, and several times came to places where the elephants had rested. After passing one of these the scent became red-hot, and a pig suddenly grunting put the Korachas into the 'On your marks, gentlemen,' position. Not long after this, at about noon, we heard the elephants feeding in front, and I and one Koracha crept forward. The elephants were in a deep nullah, hidden

TIGER SHOT BY H. H. F. M. TYLER IN HYDERABAD.

1. HERD OF WILD ELEPHANTS IN THE MYSORE FORESTS.
2. WILD ELEPHANTS IN A SMALL ENCLOSURE BEFORE BEING HOBBLED.
3. THE WILD ELEPHANT AT HOME, MYSORE FORESTS.

Photos by Felix Wecksler.

among the reeds and cane. The sides were, for a wonder, clear of reeds, but were covered with a mixed tangle of thorn bushes and saplings. From our side the further bank was visible, but only in one place was there a space sufficiently open for us to see even an elephant. We could only get within 30 yards, and at that distance could see the tops of the reeds shake as the elephants fed on them. The wind seemed steady in the right direction. We watched from behind a huge tree trunk, and the Koracha showed me by signs that he thought the elephants would move towards us. A quarter of an hour thus passed; then suddenly one of the elephants trumpeted, and a tremendous crashing in the reeds ensued. The Koracha bolted away to the side of the ravine. One of the elephants went away to the side and the other crossed the open space mentioned above and stood with its head hidden and body perfectly exposed. I had been looking in the wrong direction, so did not notice whether this elephant was the tusker or no. Consequently I did nothing, but the Koracha, pointing frantically and calling as I then imagined (though, needless to say, he knows not a word of English), 'That is the one,' I took careful aim just behind the shoulder and fired. The elephant moved a yard and then stood still again. Thereupon I fired the left barrel and the brute rolled into the ravine. There was a tremendous crashing noise for a few minutes, and then all was quiet. After a wait I started to climb down to investigate, but gave up the idea on a frenzied protest from the Koracha. He signed that we should clear out, and as it was only wise to give the elephant time to die, I agreed. We had walked 20 yards parallel with the ravine and a few yards from the top when we heard the elephant following us along the bottom. The reeds appeared to me to be only 4 or 5 ft. high, so I concluded the elephant's death struggles were causing it to move down the slope. Thinking another shot would be advisable, I approached to within a distance of 15 yards, the Koracha protesting, but following all the same. The elephant was moving about, and suddenly its head appeared in the normal position. This surprised me greatly, as I still imagined it to be on its side, as it was till then invisible. I fired at the head and it was withdrawn. In a few minutes the trunk appeared, pointed in our direction, and wagging about like a leech. A trumpet, and the elephant came out of the reeds full speed. I had been absolutely deceived as to the depth of the ravine and the height of the reeds: the latter approached 20 ft. The Koracha was off like a shot, and shouted frantically to me to follow. I knew that escape by running was impossible for me in that tangle of thorns and trees, so stood still and trusted to Providence to be able to stop the brute. It got 5 yards out of the reeds, and was then 8 or 10 yards from me. At that point the bank was not far from perpendicular, and the ground being soft and slippery the elephant was temporarily checked. Taking advantage of this I fired, but it had not the desired effect. I see now that I misjudged the position of the head, and put the bullet into the hard bone at the top. I did not dare try and load my right barrel, but thought my best chance was to wait until the elephant was right on me and then fire in his face and try to escape past him in the confusion. Just as this flashed across my mind the elephant turned a bit to the side and exposed the side of

ADVENTURES TOLD BY THE CAMERA.

his head. I immediately fired my second cartridge, and to my relief the elephant fell back into the ravine. Apparently the shot had finished him, for he lay like a log for two or three minutes. The Koracha and I commenced mutual congratulations in dumb show, and were carrying on an excited conversation without being able to understand a word the other said, when the elephant returned to life and started to rise. The Koracha disappeared like magic, and I opened a steady fire on the brute's head. After three ineffectual shots I began to wonder if the orderly was right when he said that the bullets would not penetrate the skin. The elephant recovered rapidly, and if the fourth shot had not floored him I should certainly have retired in confusion This time the brute fell right back into the reeds and lay completely hidden. The noise of his breathing showed that one of the body shots had pierced his lungs, and I imagine that a solid nickel bullet through the lungs has no immediate effect on a large animal, though it must eventually kill it. I now went back to camp, a distance of 3 or 4 miles, and on returning after having some food, found the elephant stone dead.

"The tusks of this elephant measured 5 ft. 9 in. and 5 ft. 11 in. respectively, and weighed 127 lb. the pair."

1. TIGER SHOT BY G. HADFIELD. 2. SHOT BY J. H. WAPSHARE, ON JUNE 28, 1891.
3. RECORD BISON, 46 IN.; SHOT BY GORDON HADFIELD. 4. PANTHER (7 FT. 9 IN.) SHOT BY GORDON HADFIELD.

We come next to the Bison (*Bos gaurus*), the largest of all existing bovines. This magnificent animal is found over a considerable area in Southern India. Its favourite haunts are the forests of the Western Ghauts, where it is found at all elevations. Bison are also found in outlying hill ranges, the Palnis, the North Coimbatore Hills, Mysore, and the Wynaad; on the east of the Presidency a few herds still roam the Javadi Hills, while farther north they may be found in considerable numbers in Godavari and Vizagapatam districts. The best heads are obtained on the Western Ghauts. On the east the average horn measurement is rather smaller. The bison is seldom found far from the neighbourhood of hills, and is most commonly met with at an elevation of between 2,000 and 5,000 ft. Shy and retiring, the bison retires before the approach of man, and in the Northern Circars is rapidly disappearing, owing to the opening up of the country and the increase of cultivation, from many places where a few years ago it was found in large numbers. Bison are subject to epidemics of rinderpest and foot-and-mouth disease, the contagion of which has been spread by domestic cattle grazing in the jungles, and which kill off large numbers from time to time. The pursuit of the bison is, as a rule, associated with a great deal of hard work amid most magnificent scenery. This fact and an element of danger are sufficient to make the sport of bison shooting one of the most fascinating which can be indulged in. The best localities for bison are Travancore, the Anaimalai Hills, the Billigarangan Hills, the South Canara Hills, and the wilder parts of Godavari and Vizagapatam.

The Tiger (*Felis tigris*) is found where conditions are suitable, and is most common in the Northern Circars, Kurnool, Cuddapah, Chittoor, Coimbatore, Malabar, South Canara, the jungles at the foot

1. HILL PANTHER SHOT AT KOTAGIRI. 2. SHOT BY MR. KINMOND, VANDIPERIYAR.
3. PANTHER SHOT BY G. W. R. THOMSON. 4. FIRST SHOT!
5. RESULT OF A BEAT AT WARTYHULLY—TWO PIGS SHOT. 6. "HIS HEAD LAID LOW!"

Photo by C. Lake.

of the Nilgiri Hills, and Mysore. Perhaps nowhere in the whole of India are tigers bagged under such a variety of conditions as in the South. The usual methods are either to beat, or to sit up over a kill; but tigers may occasionally be found in the open on the grass hills of the Western Ghauts and stalked; sometimes they are pursued with dogs, while not infrequently a sportsman who has the energy to visit his ties in the early morning may find the tiger still by the kill. Elephants are seldom used for tiger shooting in the south of India, and there is little of that beating with a large number of guns which is associated with tiger shooting in Northern and Central India. Here tigers are pursued, as a rule, by a single sportsman or by parties of two or three guns, and anything like a bag of tigers is seldom heard of. Four or five tigers to a party of two or three guns in a couple of months spent in the jungle would be exceptional. In the Northern Circars the number of tigers has appreciably decreased in recent years, and this is also the case in Mysore, but elsewhere throughout the area their numbers do not appear to vary greatly if we may judge from the number of rewards claimed each year. It is interesting to note that in the districts of Ganjam, Vizagapatam, and Godavari, although tigers have undoubtedly decreased in numbers in the last twenty years, the number of human beings killed by tigers annually has largely increased There can be no doubt that one main cause, if not the sole cause, for this increase in man-eating has been the enormous decrease during the same period in those game animals which form the natural food of the tiger, and the policy which permits the indiscriminate slaughter of deer has been directly responsible for the death of many an unfortunate human being.

The Panther (*Felis pardus*) is found in almost every part of South India, and few animals have so wide a range. The panther is equally at home in the dense evergreen forests on the summits of the Western Ghauts, where he is a terrible foe to the ibex, in the lighter deciduous forests of the lower hills of both the Eastern and Western Ghauts, and in the bare, rocky hills which are found in so many of the Deccan districts and in Mysore. A very large number of panthers are shot every year, chiefly by native shikaris. In 1914 over seven hundred panthers' skins were presented for reward at the Government Treasuries. This figure, of course, excludes those shot in Mysore, Coorg, Cochin, and Travancore, so that the total number accounted for must have been close on a thousand. In spite of the large numbers killed there has been little real diminution in the numbers of these animals in recent years. The panther cares nothing for the presence of man. He will lie on a hillside overlooking a main road and in full view of the passers-by. He will stroll through a village at night, snatching a dog from the verandah of a house or boldly carrying off a goat from a pen within a few yards of the sleeping goatherds. Instances are not unknown of panthers entering a tent and carrying off a dog chained to its owner's bed. On one occasion a forest officer and his wife, sleeping in a little out-of-the-way forest bungalow, were awakened in the middle of the night to see a panther sitting on the low partition wall of the bungalow a few feet above their heads. The attraction in this case was a dog which was sleeping on the foot of the bed. Instances of the boldness of the panther might be multiplied almost indefinitely, and in attempting to bring a panther to bag the most casual methods are often the most successful. On a dark night, when sitting up over a kill, a panther may be shot by the light of an ordinary hurricane lantern suspended from a branch of the nearest tree. If missed by the first shot the panther will frequently return to the kill, sometimes within a very few minutes, and instances are known where the panther has been missed three or four times in a single night. A black variety of the panther is found in some parts of the area. It is most common in the moister jungles of the Western Ghauts, and is rarely heard of in the East and Centre.

WILD ELEPHANTS.

Photo by C. R. Valentine.

An account of the tiger and panther shooting in Southern India would be incomplete without a reference to the practice of hunting down these animals on foot with a pack of dogs. The following account is contributed by a sportsman who has had opportunities to enjoy this form of sport:—

"In the dense and extensive forests of the Western Ghauts beating is practically impossible. In fact, nothing less powerful than an elephant or a bison can force its way through the tangled undergrowth of the forest. Elephants are, however, not available. Those belonging to Government may not be used for shooting purposes, while those owned by the Indian timber merchants are valued too highly to be used for sport. Under these circumstances a pack of dogs is invaluable.

"A tiger or a panther is reported to have killed and to be lying up somewhere within the neighbourhood. The pack is sent out overnight, and at dawn is thrown into the covert to which the animal has

1. SKINS OF TIGER, PANTHER, BEAR, SPOTTED DEER, AND WILD DOG.

2. HEADS OF ANIMALS SHOT BY H. H. F. M. TYLER.

(The Jackals were accounted for by the Madras and Ootacamund Hounds.)

SAMBHUR.

ANTELOPE OR BLACK BUCK. SAMBHUR. BLACK BUCK. BLACK BUCK. SPOTTED DEER. BLACK BUCK.

PANTHER. WILD DOG. TIGER. PANTHER. PANTHER.

SPOTTED DEER. BARKING DEER. CHINKARA. SPOTTED DEER.

JACKAL. MOUSE DEER. JACKAL.

BISON. BUFFALO COW. BISON.

1. FLYING FOX. 2. MONKEY. 3. SQUIRREL. 4. BANDICOOT.

been tracked. A tiger, especially if he has just had a full meal, will seldom bolt. A panther, on being found by the dogs, invariably takes to the nearest tree. The sportsman following behind has to judge the situation by the sounds which reach him. A sudden roar followed by a yell may mean the death of the boldest hound in the pack. A sudden silence generally means that the animal has moved and that the pack is using its breath for the chase. All that the sportsman can do is to follow on, trusting either for a snap shot across a piece of open or to reach a position whence he can get in a shot while the beast's attention is distracted by the dogs. The hunt may come to a successful finish within an hour. On the other hand, if the quarry keeps perpetually changing his position, and will not stand to be bayed, the hunt may continue until the dogs are too exhausted to follow and the quarry breaks away. For sheer hard work I do not know anything to equal a hunt after an active panther in the forest. I remember a morning so spent with a well-known sportsman in Malabar. The pack, consisting of some thirty mongrels of the terrier breed, found a panther in some impenetrable lantana scrub at six o'clock in the morning. It took about one hour to shift him into the surrounding timber forest, where he took to the trees, and would have thrown off the pack had it not been for the dog-boys and ourselves, who were able to view him climbing up the trunks. On our approach he always left the tree he was on, and the pack then ran him for perhaps 200 yards, until he thought it discreet to again climb beyond their reach. As the result of about three hours' strenuous pursuit the panther was so exhausted that he lay on the bough for a moment too long, and a bullet in the neck dropped him into the middle of the baying pack below.

" The danger is not so great as might be expected, provided one has sufficient dogs of the right kind. Anything of the bulldog breed is perfectly useless. One wants a yapping terrier active enough to keep out of reach of the claws and noisy enough to distract attention. The sportsman who is referred to above had developed this form of shooting into a fine art, and so con ident was he of the ability of the dogs to keep the tiger or panther thoroughly engaged that he and his brother would crawl into the thickest thorn jungle, rifle in hand, to finish off a beast which all the efforts of the pack were unable to dislodge. Of course in cases of this kind the danger is greatly increased, and I remember being told of a case in which a panther, although gripped by some of the dogs, sprang straight at my friend's face. To protect his head he held his rifle across his face, and the panther's teeth closed on the barrels. His brother coming to his assistance fired a shot straight into the animal's chest, with the result that both he and the panther fell among the pack, and the former received a good deal of treatment which the pack intended for the latter alone.

" Taken all round, there can scarcely be any finer form of sport, and the only reason that it is not more often indulged in is the expense and difficulty of keeping up a pack of dogs in a tropical climate."

The Hunting Leopard (*Cynælurus jubatus*) is rare. It is occasionally met with in the Deccan districts and in Mysore, but few fall to the rifle of English sportsmen.

The Sloth Bear (*Melursus ursinus*) is

too well known to require description. It is most common in the north of the Presidency, being found in considerable numbers in Ganjam and parts of Vizagapatam and Godavari districts. But it is also found throughout the area in most forest-clad hill ranges, and is not uncommon in parts of Coimbatore, Mysore, the Anaimalais, and the Nallamalai Hills.

Bears are chiefly bagged by beating or prowling about in the early morning or late afternoon in the vicinity of places where they are known to lie up. Bear shooting, if pursued on foot and in moderation, is a most entertaining form of sport, and there is not infrequently a strong element of the ludicrous in the pursuit of this uncouth and somewhat stupid animal. There is quite a sufficient element of danger to make the sport exciting.

Bear cubs are frequently captured, and when taken young make most amusing and entertaining pets. A pair in the possession of the writer were great friends with a tiger cub and a greyhound, and it was most interesting to watch the four playing together. The tiger cub was the smallest of the party, and the long claws and somewhat rough methods of the bears frequently elicited from her an angry protest. The bear cubs quickly learned that the breakfast-table was a sure find for such succulent dainties as butter, sugar, and jam, and that the simplest method to attain their heart's desire was to seize a corner of the tablecloth in their mouth and pull.

On their owner proceeding on leave they were handed over to a friend residing in Madras, but here their playful ways, though entertaining to their master, were a source of embarrassment to others. On one occasion they entered a toddy shop—the owner of which of course fled—and only quitted the premises when the stock of toddy gave out. On another occasion they wandered out on to one of the main roads, and, lying in the middle of it, effectually held up a High Court Judge who was taking a Sunday afternoon drive in his carriage.

After this feat they were exiled to the nearest Zoological Gardens.

Turning now to the deer tribe, first mention must be made of the Sambhur (*Cervus unicolor*), the largest of all the Indian deer, and standing as much as 14 hands or more at the shoulder. It is found in hilly country throughout Southern India, and is most common along the great range of the Western Ghauts, in Mysore, in the Coimbatore Hills, in the Nallamalais, in the Eastern Ghauts to the north of the Palar River, and in Godavari and Vizagapatam districts. As a rule big heads are not found in the moist jungles of the west coast; the biggest horns are obtained in the Eastern Ghauts and in the Nallamalais, though fine specimens are occasionally obtained on the Nilgiri Plâteau. On the grasslands of the Western Ghauts sambhur come out to graze in the open, and may be stalked. More commonly the sambhur is found in tree forest, only coming out into the open by night, and in such conditions it requires all the sportsman's craft to fairly outwit an old sambhur stag. Sambhur are commonly beaten for, and though this is a poor form of sport when compared with stalking, it is frequently the only method of bringing them to bag.

1. VULTURES DEVOURING DEAD TIGER. 2. CAMPING IN THE NORTH OF THE PRESIDENCY.
3. BUFFALO SHOT IN VIZAGAPATAM DISTRICT BY H. H. F. M. TYLER.

SOUTHERN INDIA

The Spotted Deer (*Cervus axis*) is found chiefly in the lower jungles along the base of the hills or on the foot-hills, but occasionally ascends to a height of 3,000 or 4,000 ft. This handsome deer is intolerant of thirst, and is seldom found far from the neighbourhood of water. Its favourite haunts are among bushes and trees along the banks of nullahs and in bamboo jungle. It requires to drink regularly at least once a day, and from this fact large numbers fall victims to the native shikari, who lies in wait in the hot months, when water is scarce, near some pool to which the deer are known to resort. In the extreme south of the area spotted deer are rare. They are most numerous in the jungles at the base of the Nilgiri Hills, in the Wynaad, in the Coimbatore Hills, in parts of Mysore, in the Nallamalais, in parts of Cuddapah and Chittoor, and in the Northern Circars. The biggest heads come from the north of the Presidency, though good specimens are obtained in Coimbatore and at the foot of the Nilgiris.

The Barking Deer (*Cervulus muntjac*) is found throughout Southern India on all thickly wooded hills. It stands something less than 2 ft. in height at the shoulder, with horns which do not as a rule exceed 5 in. in length.

Other game animals which are found in the South of India are:—

PANTHER WHICH WAS ATTACKED AFTER DARK BY A PORCUPINE. OVER FIVE DOZEN QUILLS WERE FOUND.

1. The Nilgai, or Blue Bull (*Boselaphus trago camelus*).
2. The Four-horned Antelope (*Tetracerus quadricornis*).
3. The Indian Antelope (*Antilope cervicapra*).
4. The Chinkara (*Gazella bennetti*).
5. The Mouse-deer (*Tragulus meminna*), and
6. The Wild Boar (*Sus cristatus*).

PANTHER CAUGHT IN DEADFALL TRAP, COIMBATORE DISTRICT.

The Nilgai, a large animal standing 14 hands at the shoulder, with horns which average only 7 or 8 in. in length, is not much sought after by the sportsman. It is fairly common in the heavy forests of the Northern Circars, and is also found in the Nallamalais.

The Four-horn is found in the hills of the Eastern Ghauts southwards as far as the Palar River, in the Nallamalai Hills, in Mysore, Coimbatore, and the Nilgiris.

The Indian Antelope, or Black Buck, is found in open country or light jungle throughout the area from Ganjam in the north to the neighbourhood of Cape Comorin in the south, and also as far west as Mysore. It is not found on the Malabar coast. The average horn measurement in Southern India is much less than in Northern and Central India. Sixteen to 18 in. is an average head, and anything of over 20 in. is comparatively rare.

The Chinkara is found chiefly in the Deccan districts, in light scrub jungle and in waste ground where it is broken up into ravines. It is also found in parts of Mysore and in the Chittoor, Nellore, and Guntur districts.

The Mouse-deer, the smallest of Indian deer, a little animal which stands only 10 to 12 in. at the shoulder, is found along the Eastern and Western Ghauts and on outlying hill ranges, chiefly at an elevation of 2,000 ft. or under.

The Wild Boar is found throughout

1. "BAGGED!" 2. PANTHER SHOT IN VIZAGAPATAM DISTRICT.
3 AND 4. TIGERS SHOT IN VIZAGAPATAM DISTRICT. 5. A FINE TIGER.

Southern India, and is one of the commonest of wild animals. There are only one or two localities in the Ceded Districts where the sport of pig-sticking can

A MUGGUR SHOT IN THE GODAVERI RIVER.

be enjoyed, and, as a rule, wild boars are shot.

Several of the non-game animals are of interest to the sportsman, and deserve some mention:—

The Wild Dog (*Cyon dukhunensis*) is found throughout Southern India in forest country where there is sufficient game for it to live upon. The wild dog hunts in packs, lives almost entirely on game, and is a terrible foe to sambhur and spotted deer. It appears to have become more numerous in places in recent years. Fortunately its numbers are reduced by periodical epidemics of disease, possibly rabies, from which it is known to suffer. But for this epidemic there is reason to believe that their numbers would quickly increase to such an extent that game would be entirely driven out of large areas.

The Hyena (*Hyena striata*) is found throughout the jungle or in rocky hills. To the sportsman the hyena is chiefly known as a scavenger, which prowls about devouring the remains of animals that have been killed by tiger or panther, and sometimes carrying off sheep and goats from the neighbourhood of villages. The Telugu name of the hyena—"the bone-gnawer"—fitly epitomises its habits.

The Wolf (*Canis pallipes*) is found in many parts of the area in open country with rocky hills or in light jungle, preying on chinkara and antelope and killing many sheep and goats. The wolf often appears indifferent to the presence of man, but few instances are recorded of their attacking human beings.

Two species of the broad-snouted Crocodile or Muggur are found, *Crocodilus palustris* and *Crocodilus porosus*. The former is the more common, and rarely attains a greater length than 12 ft., while porosus grows to upwards of 20 ft. The distinction between the two species, however, is so slight that the average sportsman may be excused if he fails to notice any difference except in size. Muggurs are found commonly in the rivers and backwaters of the Malabar coast and in the larger rivers of the eastern part of the Presidency. They sometimes travel considerable distances overland, and are found in tanks which contain water for only a portion of the year. The muggur apparently æstivates in places, as an instance is on record of a muggur having been dug out of the mud in the bed of a tank in Kurnool district, the water of which had dried up some two months before. Muggurs are also found in isolated pools in the centre of the Nallamalais and in the Cuddupah Hills.

The Preservation of Game.

A few remarks may be added on the subject of game preservation:—

In British territory the forests may be divided into two classes, Private and State. In private forests owned by rajas and zamindars little attempt, as a rule, is made to preserve the game, though some owners prove an exception to this rule. Much of the principal forests in the north of the Presidency belong to zamindars, and over a large part of this area the Arms Act is not in force. Every village has as many guns as the inhabitants care to procure, and as no attempt is made to preserve game, wild life is being rapidly exterminated. At the present day the sportsman may tramp for miles through magnificent sal forest which could maintain a teeming head of wild life and see hardly a track. One result of this extermination of game has already been alluded to, viz. the increase in man-eating, and the majority of tigers and panthers in the area to which I am referring live almost entirely on domestic animals, causing infinitely greater loss than could possibly have been occasioned by the deer to the limited area of cultivation amid a vast extent of jungle.

As regards Government lands, generally speaking no animals except antelope and sometimes chinkara are found outside the reserved forests. Inside a reserved forest no one is allowed to shoot without a license, and game thus receives a considerable amount of protection. Where the district officer is keen on the preservation of the game of his forests the native poacher is kept more or less in hand, and no great diminution of game is to be feared. If, however, the district officer is at all slack, the guns are brought from their hiding-places, the forest subordinates are squared with a present of venison or a hide or two, and great slaughter of deer takes place.

The Nilgiri Game Association has done a great deal to preserve the head of game in this area, one of the most delightful shooting grounds in the world, where some twenty years ago fears were entertained that the hills would soon be shot out.

Of the Native States Mysore, Cochin, and Travancore all possess game laws. In Mysore it is reported that, with the exception of elephants and in parts bison, game is generally decreasing, and it is to be feared that little attempt is made to enforce the laws. In Travancore also game is said to be decreasing, partly owing to the opening up of the country and partly owing to poaching.

In the province of Coorg very little game is left. The Arms Act is not in

SPOTTED DEER SHOT IN CHITTOOR DISTRICT.

force, guns are very numerous, and wild animals are correspondingly scarce.

South India is well supplied with taxidermists. Messrs. Theobald Brothers, of

Mysore, Messrs. Van Ingen, of Mysore, and the firm of the same name at Ootacamund are first-class artists, and the sportsman may safely entrust his trophies to any of the three to be set up.

MINOR MAMMALS.

The following list, without pretending to be completely exhaustive, gives a fairly comprehensive statement of the minor mammals of Southern India:—

Bengal Monkey and Bonnet Monkey. —These are the common monkeys of the plains, respectively north and south of the Godavari River, which roughly forms the dividing line between the two species.

Lion-tailed Monkey.—Found only on the west coast and Western Ghauts.

Langur—of which four species are found.

Loris.

Wild Cat—four species, of which the most generally known is the Palm Civet, or Toddy Cat.

Mungoose—four species.

Jackal.

Indian Fox.

Indian Ratel, or Honey Badger.

Otter—three species.

Indian Marten.

Madras Tree Shrew.

South Indian Hedgehog.

Shrew—six species, of which the best known is the Musk Rat, so commonly found in Indian bungalows.

Fruit Bat, or Flying Fox.—One of the most typical of Indian animals.

Bat—some two dozen different species.

Flying Squirrel—two species.

Large Forest Squirrel—two species.

Smaller Squirrels—four species, of which the commonest is the Palm Squirrel, found in or around almost every Indian bungalow.

Rats and Mice—some thirteen species, of which perhaps the best known is the Bandicoot.

Porcupine.

Hare—two species.

Indian Pangolin, or Scaly Ant-eater.

FLYING FOXES

THE RESIDENCY, BANGALORE.

BANGALORE

BANGALORE is the chief city of the district of the same name, and it is about 216 miles distant by rail from Madras. It consists of two distinct parts, namely, the city, or *pettah*—which is the old native town—and the Civil and Military Station, often erroneously referred to as "The Cantonment." Bangalore is the seat of the Government of the State of Mysore, and it is situated in 12° 57′ N lat., and 77° 35′ E. long. It is commonly believed that the name Bangalore is a corruption of "Bengaluru," which is derived from the word "bengalu," a kind of bean, and the following legend is told in connection with the derivation: One day when King Vira Ballala was hunting he became separated from his attendants, and, losing his way, wandered about until nightfall. At last, faint and weary, he came upon a solitary hut in which an old woman lived, to whom he applied for something to eat. She had nothing better to offer him than some "bengalu"—green beans boiled in a little water—which, however, he was glad to get, and, sharing them with his horse, he passed the night in the shelter of the lowly hut. The incident speedily became known, and the village (*uru*) which sprang up took the name of Bengaluru.

The Civil and Military Station lies to the north-east of the native portion of the city, covering an area of 12½ square miles, and it is commonly referred to by the European residents as "The Station." It was established as a British military garrison in 1809, the position being assigned to the British Government for purposes of political and administrative control in 1881, the Maharaja of Mysore having renounced the exercise of jurisdiction within it, although he retained his sovereignty over the territory. The British Residency is at present (1914) occupied by the Hon. Lieut.-Colonel Sir Hugh Daly, K.C.I.E., C.S.I., I.A. He exercises the powers of a High Court, but the High Court of Judicature in Madras alone has criminal jurisdiction over British subjects in Bangalore. The Resident is, further, Judicial and Chief Commissioner of the Province of Coorg. There is a separate municipality for Bangalore city and for the Civil and Military Station. The one for the latter consists of a president, a vice-president, and of 6 official and 18 non-official members, 17 of the latter being elected by the ratepayers and one appointed by the local Trades Association. The offices of this Board are situated in the Mayo Memorial Hall, which was erected in memory of the late Lord Mayo, a former Governor-General of India. This building was transferred by the Resident to the municipal authorities with the proviso that the upper portion should at all times be available, free of charge, for all meetings of a public character.

The steady growth of the Station is attributable to various causes. Undoubtedly the healthy and invigorating climate is a prime factor in this direction, as the heat, which is usually a dry one, never exceeds from 90-95° F., while the mean temperature is 76·2°. The heaviest rains of the year fall during the months of October or November, but records show that the annual average quantity is only

BANGALORE.

1. Bishop Cotton High School. 2. Government Public Offices. 3. St. Mary's Church 4. Queen Victoria's Statue.

36 in. The season for visitors commences in the month of July, and usually continues until the end of the year. Another cause of progress is that the scholastic advantages are of so high a character that many heads of families have been induced to take up their residence there; while a third reason may be that the natural and artificial beauty of the surroundings is specially attractive. The municipal authorities have effected many improvements during the last few years, and they have been heartily supported by invividuals who in their private capacity have constructed places of business and dwelling-houses which compare favourably with those in other towns in Southern India. The provision of an excellent supply of water and the construction of a satisfactory system of drainage were among the first matters to engage the attention of the Council, who were fully alive to the fact that no town which is deficient in these respects could ever become a desirable place of residence. Water for domestic purposes is obtained from the Chamarajendra reservoir, and steps have been taken recently to ensure absolute purity by the installation of a "Jewell" filtration plant. The Health Department is a most important branch of the Council, and it controls slaughter-houses, public markets, drainage, streets, the issue of licences, and other matters. The question of sanitation is one which can never be said to be out of place on an agenda paper of a local authority, as it is only by the most scrupulous attention to this subject that epidemics of disease are averted. The staff of the Health Department consists of the health officer, 3 sanitary and 1 veterinary inspector, 16 overseers, 23 circle peons, 270 scavengers, and 300 sweepers. These officers have multitudinous duties to perform, such as the examination of animals before slaughter, the inspection of carcasses, of cowsheds, dairies, and markets, and they supervise the flushing of drains and the disinfection of stagnant pools and tanks.

The Civil and Military Station entered into a scheme with the Government of Mysore whereby the latter agreed to supply the municipality with electricity for the lighting of the streets upon payment of a certain annual sum. This arrangement came into operation on January 1, 1908, and it has worked so satisfactorily that provision has now been made for the extension of the service to private residences. Among the improvements effected by the authorities have been the reclamation of waste areas, the drainage of tanks which were the breeding grounds for the dangerous mosquito, and the demolition of insanitary hovels which passed under the name of houses. Diseases of all kinds had been rampant in the congested portions of the Station, and it was evident that drastic measures were necessary if these evils were to be removed. Squalid houses bunched together in evil-smelling courts were razed to the ground, by-lanes reeking with filth were cleaned and widened, and enlarged and improved areas were placed in the hands of contractors for the erection of dwelling-houses on sanitary principles. The inhabitants of the most thickly populated portions of the Station were induced to take up their abode in one or other of the newly-opened "lungs," and this exodus to more healthy surroundings has resulted in a very considerable amelioration of the conditions of the people.

THE MAHARAJA'S PALACE, BANGALORE.

Fraser Town is the outcome of a scheme which was proposed in the year 1906 with the view of relieving some of the thickly populated and insanitary portions of the Station. A Loans Act was passed in order to provide money at a reasonable rate of interest to such persons as were willing to erect dwelling-houses for themselves, but, as this arrangement was not sufficient to meet all demands, a number of prominent residents undertook the responsibility of providing houses which were to be let to suitable tenants at low rentals. Wide streets have been laid out and trees have been planted on either side, and electricity has been installed for lighting purposes. Among the public buildings may be mentioned the Moore Market (named after Mr. P. L. Moore, I.C.S., a former municipal president), a Receiving Post Office, dispensary, mosque, and schools for Indians. Richards Town, lying to the north of Fraser Town, is becoming an important suburb, and some very attractive residences have been built there. The railway station known as Bangalore-East serves these areas.

One of the smaller, but at the same time one of the most attractive, of the younger suburbs is Langford Town, which lies to the south-west of Richmond Town. The township is unique in character, as its residences are built very largely after the style of Swiss chalets, but a further inducement is offered by reason of its open and healthy situation. The inhabitants consist of Europeans and Anglo-Indians only. Cleveland Town and Benson Town, suburbs containing a goodly number of dwelling-houses of a superior character, lie to the north of St. John's Hill, which is noted for its comfortable cottages in a healthy locality.

The Artillery Lines are on the outskirts of the Station, and immediately to the north of them is Ulsur, which is a densely populated suburb containing a temple devoted to Subbaraya, a dispensary, and public market. The Ulsur Lake, which has an area of about 125 acres, was formerly capable of holding about 269,000,000 gallons of water, but owing

BANGALORE.

1. Cenotaph in Memory of the Storming of Bangalore. 2. Residency Road. 3. Botanical Gardens. 4. Bazaar Scene. 5. In the Bazaar.

to the accumulation of weeds of a noxious character it was drained, and the vegetable matter was burned. The municipality is now considering a scheme for the deepening and general improvement of the lake, and when the work has been accomplished satisfactorily it is hoped that a number of persons who were formerly visitors to its shores and to the Kensington Park of those days, which is situated on its north-eastern bank, will again be attracted thither. The General Parade Ground presents an animated appearance when reviews of the garrison troops are held, and the military authorities have expended a considerable sum of money in making the "Ride" round it generally attractive. Adjoining it are the barracks and lines belonging to a British and a native regiment, the Bowring Institute, the gymkhana ground, and the General Post Office. Cole's Park, in the control of the municipal authorities, is a place of resort for the inhabitants, but particularly for those of St. John's Hill, which is adjacent.

The Indian Institute of Science is situated a few miles to the north-west of the Station. It owes its origin to the generosity of the late Mr. Jamsetjee Nusserwanjee Tata, of Bombay, who in the year 1896 proposed to vest in trustees certain properties of the value of thirty lakhs of rupees for the purpose of endowing a Research Institute for India. The Government of Mysore offered 371 acres of land as a site for this building; it contributed five lakhs of rupees towards initial expenses, and agreed to make an annual contribution of fifty housand rupees. Mr. Tata unfortunately died before his scheme could be carried out, but his sons, Sir D. J. Tata and Mr. R. J. Tata, expressed their desire to give effect to the wishes of their late father. His Excellency the Viceroy appointed a provisional Committee of Management, and in the year 1908 a contract was entered into with Mr. T. C. W. Skipp, of Bangalore, for the erection of the Institute. The building is classic in design, and it is closer akin to the architecture of Southern India than is the Saracenic style of the North. The Provisional Committee provided for the establishment of six departments in pure and applied science, but only four of these were fully equipped when the first students were admitted in July 1911. A Council was appointed to take the place of the Committee, and they have caused it to be known that their object is to create a homogeneous institution in which the departments shall be at once interdependent and capable of cooperating in the solution of Indian problems, and shall be at the same time under the charge of officers, each of whom, as an expert in his own branch of learning, will be entirely responsible for the conduct of his department. Nominal fees to cover the expense of maintaining the students' quarters are charged, and the Council offer a welcome to all who are able and willing to take advantage of such facilities for study and research as they may be able to provide.

The Bowring Institute in St. Mark's Square is a handsome structure, and is one of the chief attractions of the Station. Members and their families have the use of a reading-room, billiard tables, and tennis courts, and social entertainments, including musical evenings, are frequently held. It has probably the largest library in Bangalore.

The educational advantages of the Station are of a very high standard, and mention should be made of St. Joseph's College, which was formed in the year 1857. This institution offers a splendid course of instruction to European and Anglo-Indian boys, and the results of the annual examinations show how thorough is the training of the teaching staff, of whom the Rev. S. Schmitt, M.A. (Lond.), is principal. The section for Indian pupils is in a separate wing of the extensive main building, and here, too, the same evidences of progress are observable. The European and Indian boys are about 430 and 524 in number, respectively. The Baldwin High School for boys and girls, with the names of 116 boys and about 70 girls, respectively, on the roll, belongs to the Methodist Episcopal Mission, and special educational advantages are offered for a thorough course of instruction, including preparation for Cambridge school examinations. Mention should also be made of the Bishop Cotton School with 140 scholars, in St. Mark's Road, adjoining the United Service Club, of which the Rev. J. Drury is warden; and the Bishop Cotton Girls' School, both large and flourishing establishments. St. John's Church School has an average attendance of about 135 boys and girls, St. Aloysius' School 280, the Wesleyan Missionary Secondary School an attendance of 235, and St. Andrew's School a large number of pupils.

The various hospitals in the Station are staffed by officers of undoubted ability, and modern appliances, such as the Röntgen-ray apparatus and electric light for the examination of obscure diseases, have been introduced. Special mention may be made of the Bowring Civil and Lady Curzon Hospitals in Hospital Road. Male and female patients are admitted, and about 190 beds can be made up. Out-patients, too, receive advice and medicine free of charge, and no distinction is made as to race, caste, or creed of any applicant for treatment.

The Church of England is represented by St. Mark's Church, in St. Mark's Square, opened in 1808; Holy Trinity Church, at the east end of the South Parade, consecrated in 1851; St. John's Church, on St. John's Church Road; and All Saints' Church in Ossoor Road, Richmond Town. The Roman Catholic Church has St. Patrick's Cathedral, St. Mary's, St. Francis Xavier's, and the Church of the Sacred Heart, and its missions commenced work in Mysore as early as the seventeenth century. St. Patrick's Cathedral, in Residency Road, the Mother Church of the Diocese of Mysore, is an imposing structure, having two spires and the only peal of bells in the town. St. Andrew's Church of Scotland was opened for public worship in 1866, and it contains a very fine organ and a handsome stained-glass window. The Wesleyans and Baptists have also churches in the Station.

The Bangalore Volunteer Institute and Theatre are located in exceptionally fine buildings on the Cubbon Road, opposite St. Mark's Church. The Institute is open to members of the corps, and honorary members are granted admission upon recommendation by the committee. It comprises reading and billiard-rooms, bar, and offices and stores, together with lecture hall and committee-rooms. The theatre is in constant demand for theatrical companies, dances, and other entertainments. The main hall is 111 ft. in length by 60 ft. in width, and behind the stage numerous dressing-rooms have been provided. There is ample seating accommodation for about 1,100 persons, and the whole building is lighted by electricity.

The Station public offices are situated near to the Mayo Hall, and the very handsome building was erected at a cost of Rs. 2,00,000. Accommodation is provided here for the offices and courts of the district, second, honorary, and railway magistrates, the Honourable the British Resident's Treasury, the office of the Superintendent of Excise and of the

BANGALORE.

1. A Bazaar Scene.
2. Commercial Street.
3. Washing Scene. *Photo by Wecksler.*
4. All Saints' Church.
5. Headquarters, Bangalore Rifle Volunteers

Sub-Inspector of Schools. The general market is at the junction of Broadway and Newmarket Roads, and a brisk trade is carried on daily in the sale of vegetables, fruit, fish, meat, and general stores. The building is quadrangular in shape, and the greater portion of it consists of shops and stores containing a miscellaneous collection of goods.

The industries carried on in the Station and in the district immediately surrounding it include cotton and silk milling, carriage building, tanning of hides and skins, manufacturing of tobacco and cigars, aerated waters, beer and stout, furniture, and boots and shoes; while there are many fine shops and stores in the Station occupied by carpet-makers, chemists, cigar merchants, motor dealers, electrical engineers, drapers, jewellers, engravers, and others.

The Station is the headquarters of the Bangalore Brigade, and the following troops were stationed there during the summer of 1914: The 7th (Queen's Own) Hussars; the 26th (King George's Own) Light Cavalry; the 13th Brigade R.F.A.; "S" Battery, R.H.A.; the 10th Ammunition Column, R.F.A.; the 2nd and 44th Batteries, R.F.A.; the 2nd Cameron Highlanders; the 2nd (Queen Victoria's Own) Sappers and Miners; the 61st (King George's Own) Pioneers; the 101st Grenadiers; the 108th Infantry; the 65th and 66th Half Troops A.T. Bullocks; and a detachment of the 9th Company A.B. Corps.

It is fitting that a military station should take a leading position in sports of all kinds, and these are provided for by the Bangalore Gymkhana Club, the Football Association, golf and tennis clubs, the Southern India Rifle Association, and other clubs of a similar nature. The leading social club is the United Service Club in the south-west of the Station. There is also a Departmental and Staff Club in Trinity Road.

The "Cantonment" Station of the Madras and Southern Mahratta Railway System is on the south-west side of St. John's Hill.

The population of the Station at the census of 1911 was 100,834 persons.

T. G. BAILEY & CO.
DYE-HOUSE AND FINISHING-ROOM.

T. MUNISAWMY APPA

Some of the most important engineering contracts which have been completed in the State of Mysore have fallen to the lot of Mr. T. Munisawmy Appa, who succeeded his late father in the year 1905. The latter commenced business in the city of Bangalore in 1894, and the son seized every opportunity of becoming thoroughly acquainted with the undertakings with which his father was entrusted. Among these may be mentioned: additions and alterations to the beautiful palace of the Maharaja of Mysore at Bangalore, the construction of revenue and survey offices in the same city, and the successful carrying out of a large scheme for supplying water to the Kolar gold-fields. One of the earliest trade contracts which came into the hands of Mr. Munisawmy Appa on his own account was the erection of the "Shankar Matt," a dressed-stone building of Oriental design, which is now used as a Sanskrit college. This is acknowledged to be one of the handsomest buildings in Bangalore, and the cost of it was not less than $2\frac{1}{2}$ lakhs of rupees. He subsequently constructed the new chemical laboratory at the Government Central College. This is an exceedingly fine double-storied stone building possessing an observation tower, whence an extensive view of the beautiful surrounding country is obtained. The estimated cost of this work was $1\frac{1}{2}$ lakhs of rupees. He is now (1914) engaged in throwing a bridge across the Lakshmanathirtha River on behalf of the Mysore Arsikere Railway Company, and this structure, upon which 3 lakhs of rupees are to be expended, will have a greater length and weight than any other bridge in the State of Mysore. The material is being imported from England, and it is expected that a period of about eighteen months will be required for the completion of the work. Further improvements are being made to the Maharaja's palace, and other smaller contracts are being executed with that faithful adherence to designs and with that promptitude for which Mr. Munisawmy Appa is well known.

T. G. BAILEY & CO.

The management of the cleaning and dyeing business, which had been established in the year 1880 by a Mr. Broomfield in St. John's Road, Bangalore, was placed in the hands of Mr. T. G. Bailey on his arrival in India four years later. Everything connected with the works was then in a very primitive state; but by dint of energy and perseverance great improvements were effected. Mr. Bailey became sole proprietor in 1889, and his practical experience, backed by personal supervision and prompt attention, soon obtained for him an exceedingly wide circle of patrons. The use of vegetable dyes received a severe check towards the close of the nineteenth century, when German manufacturers introduced their preparations into India, and the former have now been almost entirely superseded by the latter. The premises cover

T. MUNISAWMY APPA.

1. New Chemistry Laboratory, Central College, Bangalore. 2. Revenue and Survey Offices, Bangalore City. 3. Shankar Mutt—Front View. 4. Shankar Mutt—Side View.

nearly an acre of ground, and they comprise the owner's private residence, reception-rooms for customers, offices, separate buildings for dyeing, and wet and dry cleaning, ironing and pressing-rooms, and finishing-rooms for silks and curtains. Orders are received from all parts of India—principally from the Punjab and the Central Provinces—and from Burma and Ceylon. Mr. Bailey had the honour of doing some work for his Majesty King George V when he visited India as Prince of Wales. The supply of labour is plentiful and cheap, and about 30 hands are constantly employed, under the personal supervision of the proprietor and of members of his family. Messrs. Bailey & Co. have received thousands of unsolicited testimonials, and their pamphlets and price-lists claim that "we are the only English practical dyers of garments in India."

G. BACCALA & CO.

In the year 1900 Mr. G. Baccala commenced business at No. 26 South Parade, Bangalore, as an Italian confectioner, manufacturer of chocolates, and general caterer. He sold his interests in the concern ten years later to a Mr. J. E. Donnison, from whom Mr. J. C. Midford became the purchaser in December 1912. The latter is continuing the business under the style of G. Baccala & Co., and the premises are known as the "Prince of Wales Buildings." The firm undertake catering for dinners, banquets, weddings, garden-parties, entertainments, "At Homes," and suppers, and they are caterers by appointment to his Highness Sri Krishnaraja Wadiyar Bahadur G.C.S.I., the ruler of the State of Mysore. Chocolates and confectionery are made on the premises by Austrian and German experts, and the delicacies which are now manufactured have a great reputation throughout Southern India. This establishment is a rendezvous for all classes of men, women, and children, as there is hardly anything in the way of solid or liquid refreshments which cannot be obtained. Paterfamilias can have his steak or chop, washed down by beer, stout, or spirits, and matrons can tell each other—in strict confidence, of course —the latest scandals of the city. No one can visit this establishment without being struck with the appearance of the well-trained staff of servants who, without hurrying and scurrying, and without interminable delays, attend to their duties under the watchful eye of the proprietor.

A full-sized billiard-table, by Roberts, of Madras, invites the tired city man to while away an hour or two in an innocent pastime, and the well-furnished rooms, with their cosy nooks and corners, offer a charming retreat from the bustle of the streets. An up-to-date café-bar is on the premises, from which wholesale and retail liquors from the leading houses in England and Scotland can be supplied. A stock of the world-famous John Dewar's whiskies is kept constantly. All kinds of aerated waters are manufactured by the firm, and the ingredients are of such a quality, and the processes of boiling and sterilizing are so effectively carried out, that the utmost purity can be relied upon. It may be added that the firm obtained a gold medal for confectionery at the Bangalore Christmas Fête and Industrial Exhibition in December 1913.

G. BACCALA & CO.

1. A View of the Premises, showing Proprietor and Staff. 2. Interior.

THE BANGALORE WOOLLEN, COTTON, AND SILK MILLS COMPANY, LTD.

1. FRONT VIEW OF MILL. 2. VIEW OF MILL—SOUTH. 3. WOOL-MIXING ROOM. 4. HOSIERY PACKING ROOM. 5. HOSIERY FOLDING ROOM.

THE BANGALORE WOOLLEN, COTTON, AND SILK MILLS COMPANY, LTD.

This was originally a private manufacturing firm, who commenced business in the year 1879, and continued working until 1884, when the concern was acquired by the present company. At the time of the change in the status of the enterprise the trade was inconsiderable, but the directors realized that, with better accommodation and with improved machinery, a much larger turnover could be obtained, and results have shown that their optimism was well founded. "Quality before quantity" is the motto which was adopted by the company on its formation, and the high-class character of the output of the mills has caused a remarkably large yet steady increase in every branch of this well-known factory.

The premises have been considerably enlarged from time to time, and all of the buildings are constructed of brick and are exceedingly well lighted. Probably the main feature connected with the works is that steam-engines were abolished in 1906, and that the machinery is now driven entirely by electricity, the current being obtained from the famous Cauvery Falls, which are about 80 miles distant, near to the village of Sivasamudram.

The Cauvery River branches off into two streams, and, by a series of beautiful waterfalls, plunges 400 ft. down from the Mysore plateau to the plains of the Carnatic. The divided waters shoot with a deafening roar over the vast boulders of rock and unite again in a deep pool below. The electrical power generated here is used in the streets and buildings of Bangalore and Mysore, and it is also available for work on the Kolar goldfields, which are fully 90 miles away. The mills receive current at 2,300 volts through the Bangalore electric station, and this is equivalent to nearly 800 horse-power. The works are equipped with thoroughly up-to-date machinery, and the company is keenly alive to the importance of carefully testing any improved appliances which may be placed upon the market. Repairs are done on the premises, which have a smithy, three lathes, and punching and other machines. The cotton and woollen spindles number 23,024 and 2,340 respectively, and there are about 40 woollen looms

A special feature is made of the production of cotton yarn, which is admitted to have no superior in India, and which commands top market prices in Calcutta, while hosiery and woollen blankets are also largely manufactured. Woollen and silk hosiery is made from imported material, but all other articles are purely South Indian products. During the year 1913 about one million pounds weight of blankets alone were manufactured, and nearly the whole of this quantity was supplied under contract to the Army and Government Departments. The monthly consumption of raw material at the mills is: cotton 250,000 lb., and wool 150,000 lb. European overseers are employed in each department, and some 1,300 hands are in constant work.

Exceptionally liberal treatment is meted out to employees and their families, and every encouragement is given to them to provide for old age or infirmity by a well-managed scheme, known as the "Workpeople's Gratuity Fund." This fund is maintained at the expense of the company; 5 per cent. of the wages of a workman is placed to his credit every month; payment of the amount credited is refunded after two years' service in the case of incapacity or death; and there is no reservation whatever after service of ten years has been completed. The directors, however, go much farther than this in their generous dealings with their staff, as they grant a bonus of 5 per cent. to each individual whenever the prospects of the year enable them to declare a dividend of a certain amount. This practically means that the amount standing to the credit of an employee is increased from 5 to 10 per cent. Nor does the generosity of the directors end here, as they arrange for free medical attendance, as well as medicines, which are prepared by a fully qualified chemist in the dispensary at the mills. It only remains to be added that the workpeople reciprocate the kindly feeling which is shown to them by making it their special business to do all in their power to serve the best interests of the company. Messrs. Binny & Co., Ltd., of Armenian Street, Madras, are the managing agents, secretaries, and treasurers.

THE BANGALORE BREWERY COMPANY

There is perhaps no other country in the world where the question of "what to drink" is more important than it is in India, where serious ailments frequently result from the injudicious use of unwholesome or impure beverages. Every crank may be expected to have some particular fad, but the level-headed man-in-the-street bases his judgment upon practical experience, and he then gives his preference to such liquids as have proved to be invigorating because of their purity. For those who do not abstain from alcoholic liquors the different varieties of ale and beer afford a pleasant change from the everlasting tea or coffee, and from the fiery —sometimes criminally so—brands of spirits.

The Bangalore Brewery Company was established in 1889 by Mr. T. Leishman, whose partners at the present time are Messrs. V. Gungathara Chetty & Co. and Mr. H. T. Ivatt. The offices, stores, and other premises in Sydney Road, Bangalore, cover an area of 5 acres, and a compound, together with malthouses and sheds, occupies 12 acres in Langford Road, Richmond Town, Bangalore. A 10-quarter brewing plant has been installed, and pale ales, Pilsener, and stout are made from malt obtained from Indian barley—with a percentage of Scotch malt —and from English, American, and Bavarian imported hops. Beers are bottled on the cold storage principle, in pints and quarts, but they are also put up in casks for the convenience of those who prefer them in draught form. Officers' messes and canteens in military camps, extending as far north as Bellary, are supplied chiefly from the brewery direct, although agencies have been established in two important centres. The brewer and the chief engineer are Europeans. The office staff consists of five clerks, together with assistants; and about 100 hands are usually employed in the works.

THE MYSORE SPINNING AND MANUFACTURING COMPANY, LTD.

The cotton mills and other premises occupied by this company, which was founded in 1884, cover an area of 13 acres, and they are situated near to the railway station in the city of Bangalore. The buildings are doubled-storied, with tiled roofs, and they have been substantially constructed the lower floor of stone and the upper of brick. They include cotton-spinning and weaving factories, flour mills, offices, stores, sheds, and godowns. About 16,000 spindles and 200 looms have hitherto been running constantly, but, as further accommoda-

THE MYSORE SPINNING AND MANUFACTURING COMPANY, LTD.

1. General View of the Mills. 2. Spinning Room. 3. Pump Room.

tion has become necessary, extensions are under contemplation, which will enable the company to instal 200 additional looms. The consumption of cotton—all of which is grown in India—was 22,14,733 lb. in 1912, and the output was 10,88,101 lb. of yarn and 10,04,028 lb. of cloth. One-half of the yarn which is spun is disposed of, but the remainder is used in the mills for weaving purposes. Dyeing works have been added, and the manufacture of coloured cloths is assuming considerable proportions. Much of the company's business is done in contracting for the supply of large consignments of goods, but agents have been appointed for ordinary sales in each of the principal towns.

The flour mills are fitted with thoroughly up-to-date machinery, which was imported from Germany ; the average annual consumption of wheat is 13,40,640 lb. ; the output reaches a total of 12,97,263 lb., and the whole of this is sold in the State of Mysore.

The power for driving the machinery in the spinning, weaving, and flour factories is derived from a 500-h.p. steam-engine with four boilers, one of which is kept to meet the contingency of a breakdown.

Mr. N. S. Sirur, who has had very many years' practical experience, is the manager and engineer, while Messrs. N. Sirur & Co., whose head offices are in Bombay, are the managing agents. About 800 hands are employed regularly.

THE MYSORE TANNERY, LTD.

The chrome tanning industry in India was established immediately after the conduct of certain experiments which were made by Mr. Alfred Chatterton, C.I.E., in the Department of Industries in the Madras School of Arts, and experts who worked with him during those investigations are now associated with the Mysore Tannery, Ltd., a company which was formed in 1908, and which was the first in the field in this enterprise. The works, which cover an area of about 11 acres, are situated on the main road between Bangalore and Mysore, and about 1½ miles from the former city. All classes of hides and skins are tanned, and they are subsequently converted into the finished state for the making of harness, bags, boots, shoes, and other leather goods. The products of this factory have been brought to such a state of excellence that three gold medals were awarded to the company at the Industrial Exhibition at Mysore in the years 1910, 1911, and 1912, the judges commenting most favourably upon the quality of the entries. The machinery, which is of a modern character, is driven by a suction gas plant of 30 h.p., and the greatly increasing trade with India, Burma, and Ceylon has necessitated a considerable extension of the buildings in recent years. Boot factories have been opened in Broadway, in Madras, and at the cantonments in Bangalore, and the value of the raw material which is used at the mills during each month amounts to between Rs. 30,000 and Rs. 40,000. Agents have been appointed throughout India, and from 300 to 400 hands are regularly employed.

THE NOVELTY GOODS STORE

"Satisfaction or your money refunded" is the business motto which was adopted in 1913 by the proprietor when he opened his business in Bangalore, under the above title, at No. 5 Brigade Road. He is a wholesale and retail merchant of good standing, and a direct importer from Japan, China, Burma, Egypt, and other countries of silks, curios, lacquered metal and silver ware, rolled gold and other jewellery, carved wood furniture, real Japanese porcelain, Swiss and Japanese watches and clocks, Indian and Egyptian curios, Turkey carpets, Satsuma and Damascene ware, brasses, and other articles of fancy goods and vertu. A special feature is made of the sale of grass mats, matting, bamboo and cane baskets, bags, and furniture. General utility and piece-goods are imported regularly from England, America, and Japan. The proprietor is in direct touch with Japanese factories, and it is his intention to take up agencies for the manufactures of other countries. The assistants in the business when serving customers, either in the wholesale or retail departments, frequently say, "Compare our prices and quality with the goods of any other store; we will stand by your verdict," and the opinion in every instance has been in favour of the challengers. This fact alone will show that the proprietor gives his customers reliable quality and high-class service. Agents have been appointed at Cairo, Baghdad, Singapore, Hongkong, Canton, Shanghai, and Kobe, and the proprietor, Mr. M. H. Raza, is at the head of affairs in the Bangalore establishment.

THE NOVELTY GOODS STORE.
INTERIOR OF SHOWROOM.

H. E. ORMEROD

A very interesting motor-car trip was made early in 1914 by Mr. H. E. Ormerod and a friend, the route being from Bangalore to Bombay and back again. The car was a 10-h.p. "Calthorpe" Minor Light Car, and it was proposed that the outward journey should be accomplished in four days. The actual daily distances were as follows: Bangalore to Harihar, 174 miles; Harihar to Kolhapur, 207 miles; Kolhapur to Poona, 145 miles; and Poona to Bombay, 112 miles.

Sight-seeing in Poona and Bombay added another 130 miles, and with the return journey of 638 miles, a total of 1,406 miles was reached. Rivers had to be crossed, and some of the roads in the Mysore State were execrably bad, but no mechanical troubles of any kind were experienced during the trip, and only one puncture occurred. It must be admitted that this is an excellent reliability record for any car, and especially for a light vehicle with a chassis weight of only 6 cwt. Mr. Ormerod is sole agent in South India for these Calthorpe cars, as also for the Empire cars, and he is, further, agent for the well-known "Studebakers" and "Fords."

The subject of the note had had many years' practical experience in motor engineering before he established himself in his present premises in Bangalore in the year 1911. The buildings have an extensive frontage upon South Parade, which is the main street of the cantonments, and they comprise offices, showrooms, stores, and workshops. The latter are fitted with excellent machinery (which will shortly be driven by electricity), and the skilled mechanics employed by Mr. Ormerod are able to deal with all the repairs to any kind of motor-car or cycle. A large stock of petrol, covers, tubes, and other accessories is kept. The proprietor is an enthusiastic motorist, and he is always pleased if he can assist travellers in giving them particulars of roads, hotels, and rest-houses in the State of Mysore. Mr. Ormerod has had the honour of supplying cars for the personal use of his Highness the Maharaja of Mysore, and he was, further, called upon to furnish a considerable number of others in connection with the visit of his Excellency the Viceroy of India to that ruler.

T. C. W. SKIPP

Engineering contractors in India have a fine field for the exercise of their capabilities, as the vast size of the country, its mighty rivers, its formidable ranges of mountains, and the continual demand for the construction of, or additions to, gorgeous palaces and mammoth factories or houses of merchandise, call for the display of that skill in building operations, in the laying of railways, in putting up bridges, and in other works, which can only be exhibited by those who have a thoroughly practical as well as theoretical knowledge of the multitudinous details of important contracts. One of those whose names will for many generations be associated—not by inscriptions on foundation-stones—with feats of engineering prowess is Mr. T. C. W. Skipp, of No. 1 Cunningham Road, in the city of Bangalore. When a comparatively young man he obtained valuable experience in the undertaking which gave Bombay an unlimited supply of pure water. The "Tansa" Waterworks, as they are called, were constructed by Messrs. Thomas Glover & Co. and Messrs. Walsh, Lovett, Mitchell & Co., jointly, at a cost of 200 lakhs of rupees. When Mr. Skipp commenced business on his own account he took up the construction of railways and buildings in the Presidency of Bombay and subsequently in the Nilgiris, in the Presidency of Madras. He was afterwards employed by the Mysore Government in constructing the dams, head works, channels, and extensions to forebays, and in building a power-house in connection with the project for obtaining electric energy from the falls on the River Cauvery. Shortly after this time Mr. Skipp completed 25 miles of work on the Barsi Light Railway. This railway is the pioneer exemplar of the gradually developed system of narrow gauge light railways with heavy traffic capacity, and the attempt to achieve a much greater capacity than had been obtained previously on the 2 ft. 6 in. gauge involved many novelties and departures from usual practice. Mr. E. R. Calthrop, M.Inst.C.E., of No. 3 Crosby Square, London, E.C., was consulting engineer to the promoters.

A gigantic undertaking was entrusted to Mr. Skipp a few years ago, when a contract was signed for the construction of the Indian Institute of Science at Bangalore. The institute, as is explained in the general article at the commencement of this section, is the outcome of the genius and munificence of the late Mr. Jamsetjee Nusserwanjee Tata, who, about the year 1896, proposed to hand over to trustees properties of the capital value of 30 lakhs of rupees for the support of such a building in India. A portion of the Institute was opened in due time and the first students were admitted to the department of General Chemistry, Applied Chemistry, and Electro-Technics on July 24, 1911, and the department of Organic Chemistry threw open its doors in September of the same year. The Institute is the largest of its kind in India, and the total cost will reach about 20 lakhs of rupees. The contractor burns the lime and makes the bricks upon the site; flat roofs are covered with malthoid waterproofing; and the whole of the work has been done under the personal supervision of Mr. Skipp. Although certain portions of the building have been occupied for some time, the contract will not be actually completed until about the end of the year 1916. As many as 1,000 hands were employed in the earlier stages of construction, but this number has now been reduced to between 400 and 500 men.

H. E. ORMEROD.
AN EXTERIOR VIEW.

Mr. Skipp has received a very large number of testimonials as to the character of his work, the principal of these being from architects, civil engineers, and others who have been directly interested in his contracts.

WHITNEY-COATES & CO.

An exchange and auction mart business was established in Infantry Road, Bangalore, under the above title, in the year 1886, and after it had exchanged hands on three occasions it became the property of Mr. H. Whitney-Coates in the year 1909. The proprietor was formerly manager for Messrs. Wrenn, Bennett & Co., of Madras, and he is now trading as a general auctioneer and estate, house, and commission agent. He is a Fellow

T. C. W. SKIPP (THE INDIAN INSTITUTE OF SCIENCE, BANGALORE).

1. ELECTRICAL LABORATORY. 2. PROFESSOR'S BUNGALOW. 3. CHEMICAL AND APPLIED CHEMICAL LABORATORIES.

WHITNEY-COATES & CO.

1, 2, AND 3. EXTERIOR VIEWS.

4. THE BANGALORE MINERAL WATER FACTORY.

of the Institute of Auctioneers and Estate Agents of the United Kingdom. Regular weekly sales are held on the premises of household furniture, merchandise, and other effects, and a sound connection has been built up in the disposal of landed property. Live stock and agricultural produce is disposed of upon the instructions of clients, and several London wholesale houses are now consigning goods to the firm for sale in their mart. The firm carries a stock of boots, shoes, and leather; loans are negotiated, and all kinds of real and general property are bought or sold on commission. The firm are Government auctioneers for the Imperial Military Station at Bellary, and they are managing agents for the Bangalore Mineral Water Factory. The importation of fruit (chiefly apples) from Australia was commenced in the year 1910, and this branch of the business has proved to be a most profitable undertaking. The principal business establishment of the firm is at the corner of Infantry and New Market Roads, and they cover an area of about an acre and a half, but the firm have extensive storerooms and godowns in Hospital and Residency Roads. The proprietor gives strict personal attention to every branch of the business.

THE BANGALORE MINERAL WATER FACTORY

This factory was established in 1911 in premises on the South Parade, Bangalore, but further accommodation became necessary in the following year, and the removal of the works to No. 15 Residency Street synchronized with the appointment of Messrs. Whitney-Coates & Co. as managing agents. The very extensive buildings include a manager's bungalow, stables (with 15 stalls), and a factory which is splendidly equipped with modern machinery and plant. Electricity for motive power and for lighting purposes is obtained from the Bangalore town service. A never-failing supply of good water being absolutely essential in the making of high-class aerated waters, to prevent any possible means of contamination the processes of boiling, sterilizing, and filtering are carried out with the greatest possible care. All kinds of mineral-waters are manufactured, and nearly all of the ingredients, labels, bottles, and other requirements are imported from England. Contracts have been entered into for supplying these waters to regimental messes, clubs, hotels, and private individuals, and very large quantities are consigned by rail to all parts of the Mofussil. The daily output during the cold season is about 1,500 dozens, but at least twice that number is required for the summer months. A fully qualified European is in charge of the works, and some 50 or 60 hands are constantly employed.

THE WEST END HOTEL

Visitors who have once stayed at the West End Hotel are always anxious to return there on subsequent occasions, as it would be impossible for them to find a more comfortable, refined, and attractive residence of its kind in Southern India. It stands upon high ground between the racecourse and golf links, and the building is not only commodious, but it is sumptuously furnished and decorated in the best European style as far as is consistent with Eastern requirements. It is lighted throughout by electricity, and it has excellent accommodation for families or individual guests, while it has an unassailable reputation for the cleanliness of its 40 rooms, for its well-trained staff of attendants, and for the up-to-date lines upon which it is managed.

The owners of the hotel are Messrs. Spencer & Co., Ltd., of Madras, the well-known caterers, and it follows, therefore, that the cuisine and wines are all that can be desired. Billiards, tennis, and other games are provided within the hotel and its spacious grounds, but Bangalore is a noted sporting centre, having some half-dozen race meetings annually, together with gymkhanas, polo, golf, cricket, and other clubs.

Good stabling and garage accommodation can be had upon the premises, and cars may be obtained for parties to visit the beauty spots of the district. The manager exercises a keen supervision over the servants, and he does all in his power to secure the comfort of his guests.

1 AND 2. COFFEE BRANCHES IN FLOWER. 3. FREAK HYBRID COFFEE.
4. HYBRID COFFEE BUD IN THE PLANTAIN STAGE.

Photos by C. Lake.

THE PLANTING INDUSTRIES

By RUDOLPH D. ANSTEAD, M.A., Planting Expert, Agricultural Department, Madras; Scientific Officer to the United Planters' Association of Southern India

IN the hill tracts of Southern India, and on the alluvial flats on the west coast, tea, coffee, rubber, pepper, and cardamoms are cultivated on a large scale. Many of the coffee estates are in the hands of private owners, but the majority of the tea and rubber is controlled by companies, some of which own large tracts of country.

In each district there is a Planters' Association, and these individual associations are affiliated to a central association known as the United Planters' Association of Southern India. This body has no individual membership, but is an association of associations. Its headquarters are situated at Bangalore, where an office and library are maintained and a secretary employed. An annual meeting is held at Bangalore to discuss business relating to the planting industries, and at this meeting each District Association is represented by delegates, and has a vote in proportion to the acreage subscribing to the Central Association. The United Association is represented by a planting member, elected every three years, on the Legislative Council of Madras.

In 1909 the Government of Madras appointed Mr. R. D. Anstead, M.A., one of the officers of the Madras Agricultural Department, with the title of Planting Expert, to be scientific adviser, and give the whole of his time and services to the United Association, and a Scientific Department was formed, with an office and laboratory at Bangalore. A lot of preliminary work has been done, and it is hoped shortly to expand this Department by increasing the staff and establishing an experimental station in one of the planting districts. At present there is one Assistant Scientific Officer, with his headquarters and laboratory in the coffee districts of Mysore.

The total acreage subscribing to the United Planters' Association is about 45,000. This does not represent the whole of the planting interest, however, as a certain number of estates do not, for one reason or another, belong to the District Associations.

Coffee.

An accepted tradition has it that coffee was introduced into India about two centuries ago by a Mahommedan pilgrim named Baba Budan, who, on his return from Mecca, brought seven seeds with him

UNITED PLANTERS' ASSOCIATION OF SOUTHERN INDIA. CONFERENCE, 1914.

Photo by Felix Wecksler Bangalore

and planted them in Mysore. How true this may be it is impossible to say, but do not the Baba Budan Hills remain as a coffee-planting centre to this day? There the credible may see what are said to be the original plants grown from the seed introduced by Baba Budan, or, at any rate, direct descendants of these pioneer trees. The first systematic plantation appears to have been established in 1830 near Chickmagalur. About this time there also appears to have been coffee established in both the Wynaad and the Shevaroys. By 1846 plantations had spread to the Nilgiris. In 1910-12 the acreage under coffee in Southern India was returned as :—

	Acres.
Madras Presidency ...	51,127
Mysore State	104,652
Coorg	43,313
Cochin State	3,056
Travancore State ...	986
Total	203,134

The species of coffee chiefly cultivated is *Coffee arabica*. Several varieties of this exist under local names, but all are of the same species. In addition to this, some Marigogipe is cultivated, but it does not crop well, and *Coffee robusta* has also been tried. The latter has not proved a success in the recognized coffee districts, the elevation probably being too great.

Some work has also been done with a hybrid coffee, a cross between *Coffee liberica* and *Coffee arabica*. This produces a plant which is largely disease resistant and of increased vigour, which gives a much larger yield than the ordinary variety of coffee cultivated. The quality of the bean needs improving, as it is apt to retain too much of the harsh, bitter taste of the Liberian bean. There is, however, undoubtedly a great future for hybrid coffees in Southern India, and the Scientific Department of the United Planters' Association have established a special experimental plot for their development and study on scientific lines.

The coffee produced in India is practically all exported, the United Kingdom and France being the most important markets. In 1910 the export of coffee from British India was stated in official returns to be 34,984,000 lb. The yield cannot be calculated from these figures, however, for it fluctuated very widely with climatic conditions ruling during the year, and depends on the way in which the coffee is cultivated and manured. Probably the average native estate gives a yield of about 1 cwt. to the acre, while the European estate averages a yield of about 3 cwt. to the acre. By systematic manuring on a scientific basis, and by careful cultivation, it has been proved that an average of 5 cwt. an acre can be profitably maintained, while in favourable years the yield on limited areas may reach 10 or even 12 cwt. an acre.

UNITED PLANTERS' ASSOCIATION OF SOUTHERN INDIA. CONFERENCE, 1914, AT BANGALORE.

Photo by Felix Wecksler

Coffee needs a light soil with a free subsoil to ensure good drainage, and virgin forest land is usually chosen for planting, the jungle being felled and burned. The coffee-bushes need shelter from high wind and from the sun in the hot, dry weather, so that it is always cultivated under shade in India. Coffee will not stand frost. The districts found to be suitable for its cultivation in Southern India are the hill tracts of Mysore, Coorg, the Shevaroys, Pulnis, Anamalais, South Travancore, and Nilgiris. At one time there was a good deal of coffee in the Wynaad, but this has now been all replaced with tea. On the Pulni and Nilgiri Hills the devastations of a scale insect (*Coccus viride*) have rendered coffee cultivation almost unprofitable, and in the latter district it has been largely replaced by tea. The biggest coffee-producing districts now are Mysore, Coorg, and the Shevaroys, where it is grown at elevations of 1,500 to 3,000 ft. with a rainfall of 70 to 130 in.

The land is first cleared of all trees not required for shade and a nursery is then prepared to receive the coffee seeds. The young plants raised in these nurseries are put out into their permanent positions in the field, where pits have been made to receive them when they are one or two years old. The distance apart from the plants in the field differs very much with the variety grown, the nature of the climate and soil, the type of shade, and the size of tree to be grown. It varies from 4 to 8 ft. each way ; 7 ft. apart is a common planting distance, but the plants are also frequently put 5 ft. apart, or 1,740 trees to the acre.

The crop is always cultivated under shade in Southern India to protect it from the wind and to prevent the soil drying excessively in the dry weather. A large variety of trees are used as shade, almost each district having some tree which is considered especially good. Many of these trees are local jungle trees. Among the imported trees Silver Oak (*Grevillea robusta*) is the most widely used as a coffee shade. The tree introduced from Australia some forty or sixty years ago has rapidly become acclimatized, and has proved a useful shade tree owing to its rapidity of growth and freedom from disease. In some places no other shade is used, notably, for instance, the Ouchterlony Valley in the Nilgiris, where there may be seen from the top of the

Naduvatam ghaut a stretch of some 5,000 acres of coffee under nothing but silver oak. As a rule, however, mixed shade is used and regulated each year by careful systematic lopping and pruning. The fields are kept clear of weeds, a matter which requires little attention in old coffee, since the bushes touch one another and choke out the weeds, and the shade trees establish a thick mulch of leaves on the ground, through which weeds are unable to grow. In young clearings the soil is cultivated, but once the coffee is established and a mulch of leaves from the shade trees formed, deep cultivation is stopped.

Manures are applied each year. Indigenous manures, such as cattle manure, fish, and poonacs, are largely used, but these are supplemented with artificial fertilizers imported from Europe, such as nitrolim, nitrate of soda, basic slag, superphosphates, and sulphate of potash. Regular manuring in a systematic way, based upon the needs of the coffee and the soil, ascertained by means of soil analysis, produces a marked effect upon the crop, and where such systems are used heavy crops are obtained. South India coffee soils contain very little calcium carbonate, and are apt to become sour, so that it is necessary to apply only basic fertilizers, and an occasional dressing of lime is beneficial. Unfortunately there are no deposits of limestone rock in these districts, and most of the lime used has to be imported from the west coast, where it is produced by burning shells. This renders this work very expensive. Local deposits of limestone in the form of Kunkur are utilized in some places.

In the third year from planting the coffee-bushes begin to bear, and at five to seven years old they are in full bearing, while the age to which a coffee-bush can be profitably grown is probably in the neighbourhood of fifty years. These trees blossom from March to May, the process depending upon the district and the rain. The blossom is brought out by the early rains, usually referred to in coffee-growing districts as "blossom showers." The crop largely depends upon these showers. If they are delayed, or are not sufficiently heavy, a poor crop results ; while if heavy rain falls on the open blossom the fruit very often does not set. About a week after a good shower in March or April the coffee-blossom opens, and a coffee estate in flower is one of the most beautiful sights in the world. The fields look as if there had been a snowstorm, the bushes being masses of starry white flowers, while the syringa-like scent is almost overpowering. The blossom only lasts for three or four days, and during this time it is visited by myriads of bees and flies and honey-loving insects, which aid in its fertilization.

The crop is picked from October to January. The collecting of the crop is a very simple matter, but it necessitates a large body of labour, as it must be done fairly quickly. As soon as the berries begin to turn red, gangs of coolies are sent into the fields to pick them. The trees are gone over several times at intervals of a week or so, and the ripe berries picked off at each round, until the majority of the crop has been collected. At the last round the trees are stripped and all the remaining berries are gathered, whether ripe or not. After this it is usual, especially if the crop has been a heavy one, to glean and pick up all the berries that have been knocked off and dropped during the rush of the regular picking.

The berries are brought to the factory by the pickers, and they are measured, or weighed, and then pulped to remove the outside red jacket. This is done by a pulping-machine, which is carefully adjusted so as to take off the skin without cutting the bean. The berries are carried through this machine by a stream of water, which takes off the pulp and leaves the beans behind in a vat. The beans as they come from the pulper are coated with a slimy, sugary substance, which is difficult to remove, and can only be washed off after the sugar in it has undergone a certain amount of fermentation. This is accomplished by piling the pulped coffee into a heap and covering it over and leaving it for twelve hours or so. When the fermentation is complete the coffee is washed with water in large vats until all traces of sliminess have been removed. The water is then run off and the coffee spread out on tables, or mats, and constantly turned over in the sun until it is thoroughly and evenly dry. In this stage it is known as parchment coffee, and it is usual to send it to the coast to the coffee curers to undergo its final treatment before it is shipped. Here it is spread out in the hot sun, on large cement floors, and thoroughly dried. It is then peeled in machines which, by means of a heavy vertically revolving wheel, take off the husk, or parchment, and polish the bean inside. A bushel of parchment coffee gives about half this quantity of clean beans. The husked beans are graded into sizes by passing them through a series of revolving sieves, and finally each size or grade is "garbled"—that is, picked over by hand—having all sticks and broken beans taken out. The various grades are then bagged up and sent to the European markets.

The value of coffee depends upon many factors, such as the form of the berry, its size, colour, flavour, age, and uniformity, and one of the greatest difficulties is to devise a standard by which its merit can be definitely determined.

The prices realized for coffee during the past thirty years have undergone many fluctuations. In 1893 it fetched 105s. to 114s. per cwt. ; in 1900 it was down as low as 47s. to 50s. Since then it has steadily risen. The price is largely controlled by Brazil, with its cheap production and enormous turn-out.

Coffee is subject to the attack of about twenty different pests and diseases in India, some of which are very serious. Leaf disease, a fungus which makes yellow spots on the leaves and causes them to fall off, is said to have rendered coffee unprofitable in Ceylon, and it does a considerable amount of harm in Southern India, as does another fungus which attacks the leaves and berries during the monsoon, causing them to rot. A fungus which consumes the roots and causes the bushes to die outright also does a considerable amount of damage, but the most serious pest of coffee in South India is due to a scale insect (*Coccus viride*). This pest has rendered coffee-growing unprofitable in the Pulnis and Nilgiris to a large extent, and it has recently made its appearance in the coffee-growing centres of Coorg and Mysore. It is combated by means of sprays, and when systematically and co-operatively attacked it can be kept within bounds.

More and more attention is paid in South India each year to the scientific aspect of coffee-growing, and by the use of manures and the study of the life-histories of the various pests and diseases the industry is improving its position, and is long likely to be a profitable one in large tracts.

TEA.

The tea plant, *Camellia thea*, is indigenous in Assam, and it was discovered there about 1821. The cultivation of tea in India was recommended in 1834 by the

Governor-General, and a Commission was appointed to consider the matter. They recommended the Himalayas, Assam, and the hills of Southern India as suitable districts for its cultivation, but unfortunately overlooked the merits of the indigenous plant, and advised the importation of China tea. This resulted in failure, and this variety of tea is now never grown, but has been replaced by indigenous and hybrid teas of various kinds under a number of local names.

Tea-planting is one of the most technical of the agricultural industries, for the object is to produce a constant succession of young shoots throughout the year: only the youngest leaves on each shoot are suitable for making tea, so that the methods applied are of a special character.

Since 1853 tea cultivation has been a profitable industry in India, and the methods adopted have been continually improved, and that improvement is still going on. Pruning, plucking, cultivation, and manuring have been improved in a marked way, resulting in much larger crops of high quality tea. The manufacture of the leaf has been entirely revolutionized; hand-rolling and firing over charcoal fires have been abolished, and in the modern factory almost all the processes of tea-making are automatically carried out by machinery. The cultivation is concentrated in tracts where a heavy and well-distributed rainfall and a humid and equable climate permit of repeated flushings and plucking of the leaf. The soil must be rich and well drained, and of a light nature. In Southern India the hill tracts of the Wynaad, the Anamalais, the Nilgiris, and the elevated region over the Malabar coast, including the native State of Travancore, at elevations of 3,000 to 6,000 ft., are found suitable. About 10 per cent. of the total acreage under tea in India is situated in these districts, and a larger area is rapidly being planted up. The acreages existing in 1913 may be put at :—

	Acres.
Nilgiris	13,871
Malabar	9,774
Coimbatore	2,633
Travancore	37,430
Total	63,708

This is an increase of nearly 9 per cent. over the acreage in 1912.

The plant is grown from seed sown in nurseries in much the same way as coffee is propagated. The land to receive the plants is carefully prepared. The forest is cut down and burned, and tree stumps are removed as far as possible; drains are made at regular intervals, and pits are dug in rows about 4 ft. apart each way, and into these the young plants are put when they are six months old. The land is kept carefully clear of weeds, and frequently cultivated between the rows. When the young plants have been in the ground for six months to a year they are cut down to about 6 to 8 in. from the ground. Each plant then throws out from the stump three or four shoots, and a bush is formed. After this the bush is pruned back every two or three years. This pruning is a highly technical process, and cannot be described here. On it the success of the crop largely depends, not only as regards quantity but also quality. The bushes as they flush—that is, as the young shoots grow—are regularly plucked, and the young leaves and the tips of the young shoots taken off. The quality of the tea made depends on the number of leaves taken off with each shoot.

The leaf is immediately brought into the factory and spread out in thin layers on trays of hessian, in shady sheds at the top of the factory, warmed by hot air. Here it "withers" and becomes flaccid, and during the process an enzyme is developed, which afterwards causes fermentation. When the withering is complete, the leaf is rolled in a machine which rolls it to and fro on a table with a twisting motion. This presses out the juice on to the surface of the leaf. The rolled leaf is now allowed to ferment. It is placed for this purpose in layers, a few inches thick, in a moist, cool, darkened room. Fermentation finished, the leaf is dried, or "fired," as quickly as possible in machines which drive a current of hot air over it. After this, it is only necessary to grade it by means of sieves, and pack the tea in lead-lined wooden cases for shipment to the markets.

In the processes described briefly above, complicated chemical changes take place, and on the skill with which they are carried out depends the quality of the tea which is made. A great deal of experience and skill is needed to carry out these processes with success—especially to know when to stop the fermentation process and fire the tea.

In most of the districts in Southern India it is usual to manure the tea gardens very lightly. Oil-cakes and fish manure are largely used, and also artificial fertilizers supplying phosphorus and potash. The results of such manures have been found highly beneficial both as regards yield and quality. The yield per acre varies a good deal, not only with the methods of pruning, plucking, and cultivation employed, but also on the elevation and climate. At the highest elevations in the Nilgiris and the High Range of Travancore the frost reduces the yield, though compensation is obtained for this in respect to quality. At the lower elevations, as in the Wynaad, huge yields of lower-grade teas are aimed at and obtained. Thus in some places as much as 1,200 lb. of made tea per acre are secured, while in others the yield may be as low as 250 lb. an acre—the difference in quality between these extremes being great, with a corresponding difference in price which makes both about equally profitable concerns.

The total production of Indian tea in 1913 was 307,249,669 lb. Of this the Madras Presidency contributed 7,089,045 lb. and Cochin and Travancore 15,155,635 lb—a total for Southern India of 22,244,680 lb., or 7·2 per cent. of the production from all India. The average yields of made tea an acre in Southern India may be put at :—

	Lb.
Travancore	514
Malabar	483
Coimbatore	452
Nilgiris	393

The chief market for Indian tea is the United Kingdom, and India supplies more than half of the total quantity consumed each year in the United Kingdom. The average price per pound in London during 1913-14 of tea from the Nilgiris and Wynaad was 8·54d., and from Travancore 8·52d.

Tea in Southern India suffers from the attacks of a large number of pests and diseases, but none of them are of any very great importance or threaten its destruction, as is the case with coffee. Mosquito blight, damage done to the young leaves during the monsoon period by the puncture-like bites of a mosquito-like insect, is one of the most serious, but methods are being devised to combat this pest successfully. The facts that each year more and more land is opened up in tea in the hill districts of South India, and that it is replacing coffee in districts where that is possible, show that it is a most profitable industry.

Green Tea.

The manufacture of tea described above relates to black tea, in which the materials in the leaf are changed by fermentation, the leaf becoming brown or black, the astringency is reduced, and the aroma altered in character. In the manufacture of green tea the leaf is prepared without any alteration taking place. It is neither withered nor fermented, but as soon as it comes in from the field the leaf is steamed under pressure for a few minutes in a rotating cylinder. The moisture is then removed by a centrifugal pump, and the leaf is lightly rolled, and finally dried as rapidly as possible.

Green tea is chiefly made in China, and there it is customary, in order to obtain a good green colour in the final product, to "face" the tea by rubbing it in a hot pan with a little indigo and gypsum, some similar mixture, and in some places green soapstone is used for this purpose. The manufactured product finds a large market in America, and a few years ago it came under the operation of the United States pure food laws, and faced tea was declared adulterated. This gave an opening to Indian unfaced green teas; a cess was raised for advertizing purposes and to provide bounties, and the manufacture of green tea, which had almost died out, received a fillip. In South India a green tea factory was erected at Quilon, and when the market is favourable this kind of tea is now made. With the present high prices for black tea, the inducement to manufacture green tea is weak.

In 1912 South India produced 1,822,743 lb. of green tea, or 37 per cent. of the production from all India, and in 1913 521,399 lb., or 16 per cent. of the total production.

Hevea Rubber.

Hevea rubber was introduced into the East, through Kew, in 1876. In 1877 Colonel Beddome, Conservator of Forests, suggested that some of the plants should be put down near Nilambur. This suggestion was not carried out, but in 1879 twenty-eight plants were received from the Ceylon Royal Botanic Gardens and planted at Nilambur in June, and in 1886 three more were received from Mr. F. J. Ferguson, who was experimenting with rubber at Calicut. These trees were neglected, and many of them were allowed to die, and the experiment was considered a failure by the Forest Department until 1903, when Mr. Proudlock, the Curator of the Government Gardens and Parks on the Nilgiris, reported favourably on the west coast country as suitable for rubber planting.

The first rubber estate in South India was opened in 1902 at Thattakad, on the banks of the Periyar River in Travancore. This was followed in 1904 by estates in Mundakayam and South Travancore, and in 1905 by estates in Cochin, while since then many estates have been opened in these districts and at the foot of the Wynaad and Nilgiris, in the Nilambur Valley and its neighbourhood, which saw the first half-hearted trial of Hevea.

Hevea requires a hot, damp climate, with a heavy, well-distributed rainfall. While it is cultivated in some of the hill districts up to elevations of 1,500 ft. and more, its growth is apt to be slow. All the best localities in South India are found to be in the lower elevations along the west coast, in Malabar, Cochin, and Travancore. Here the growth is rapid, and trees can be tapped at three or four years of age. The tea districts are in the same localities, and many estates contain both tea and rubber, the latter on the lower slopes and the former at the higher elevation. In some instances a mixed cultivation of tea and rubber has been attempted, but this is not a general success.

The acreages under Hevea rubber in 1914, with the yield of rubber produced, was approximately as follows :—

	Acres.	Yield in lb.
Cochin	5,917 ...	334,000
Travancore ...	19,568 ...	1,985,462
Malabar	4,897 ...	103,404
Madras Presidency	12,381 ...	—
Coorg	1,362 ...	—
Total ...	44,125	

The land is cleared, the jungle burned, drains made, and pits prepared as in the case of tea, and the rubber seed is grown in nurseries, and either planted out in its first year or left in the nursery for eighteen months or two years, and then cut down and the stumps planted according to individual taste or variations of climate.

The trees are usually planted 20 ft. by 10 ft., but it is found that, by the time they are six or seven years old, this is too close, and alternate trees have to be removed. Whether to plant wide at the beginning or to plant closely and later on take out alternate trees is an open question, and there is much to be said for both methods. The latter is the cheaper way, as it reduces the cost of weeding, and some rubber is obtained from the alternate trees before they are removed. Clean weeding is the general rule in Southern India, or, at least, an attempt at it, and the constant scraping away of the top soil has in many places done much harm and held the trees back. In some places the use of *Crotalaria* and *Erythrina* is understood and appreciated. The *Erythrina* is grown in rows between the rubber, and when it reaches a height of 3 or 4 ft. it is topped, and the suckers are bent over until the bushes touch one another, thus forming a dense cover under which no weeds can grow. After this the suckers are cut twice or three times a year, and laid on the ground as mulch. As the rubber grows up and closes in the *Erythrina* becomes weak and straggling from want of light, and it is then pulled up.

On laterite soils deficient in humus green dressings have proved very beneficial. Manures are being increasingly applied, and are found not only to increase the rapidity of growth, but also the yield of rubber.

When the trees are three to four years old they reach a girth of 18 in., measured at 3 ft. from the base. At this stage tapping is commenced. Many systems of tapping have been, and are still, adopted, but the plan which is gradually being adopted and considered the best is as follows: The circumference of the tree is marked out into three equal areas. At a height of 12 in. from the ground a cut is made at a slope of about 20° with the horizontal, extending over one of the areas marked out—that is, one-third of the total circumference of the tree. This cut leads at the lower end into a shallow, vertical channel, down which the latex runs to a metal spout attached to the base of the tree, and so into a cup which is placed on the ground to catch it. Each day, or every other day, according to the plan adopted, a thin shaving is cut from the lower side of the sloping cut, resulting in a fresh flow of latex. When all the bark has been removed in this way from the first area, a new cut is made on the next section, at a height of 18 in. from the ground, and this section is tapped out in the same way. Finally, the third section is tapped, the initial cut being made at a height of 24 in. from the ground. When all the bark has been removed from this last section tapping is recommenced on the first section at a height of 24 in. from the ground, and so on. About eighteen cuts are made to the inch, and on this system it is about forty-two months before the first section has to be re-tapped, which gives ample time for the bark to renew. The tapping is always done near the base of the tree, as it is found that most latex is contained in this area. Great skill is needed to cut the bark so deeply that a maximum of latex is obtained and yet the tree is not wounded by damaging the cambium so that the bark heals up rapidly and smoothly. This skill the coolies employed acquire to a very high degree.

The early years of the industry saw not only many systems of tapping which have now been abandoned, some involving a large number of cuts high up the tree, but a large variety of tapping knives. Some of these were strange-looking implements, with spurs and guards devised to prevent the cut being made too deep. Most of these have now been relegated to museums, and either a double-edged chisel is used or a slight modification of the farrier's knife. With these the tappers reach a high degree of accuracy and rapidity, and are able to gauge and allow for the varying thickness in bark between individual trees.

The tapping is done in the very early morning or the late evening, when the latex flows well. In the heat of the day the latex is apt to coagulate in the cuts, and the flow soon ceases. After the allotted number of trees have been tapped, the coolies go to the first tree tapped and begin to collect the latex from the cups placed to catch it. These are emptied into enamelled buckets, in which the latex is conveyed to the factory. The cups are washed and placed upside down by the tree ready for use at the next round of tapping. Before each tree is tapped again the thin strip of rubber which has coagulated in the cut and central channel is stripped off, and this constitutes what is known as "scrap rubber," one of the lower grades.

In the collecting process, and all the processes of manufacture which follow, the utmost cleanliness is essential if a good class of rubber is to be made.

A rubber factory at which high-grade rubber is being made has many attributes of a dairy, the milk-like appearance of the latex adding to the illusion, as well as the precautions taken to ensure absolute cleanliness. One of two methods of manufacture is generally adopted. If the estate is young, and only a few trees are being tapped, and the supply of latex is consequently small, the rubber is made in the form of "biscuits" or sheets. The latex is put into shallow, round dishes, or oblong pans, and a certain quantity of acetic acid added to it. This is the coagulating agent most generally used, and after standing for some hours the rubber is found floating on the top of the dish in a white, spongy clot. This is removed and washed, and rolled by hand through a mangle, until clean. The "biscuits" are placed on racks in a warm room, or an artificial drier, and allowed to remain there until dry. The finished "biscuits" are pale amber colour, and transparent, and for this reason are popular on the market, for their purity and freedom from dirt can be judged by holding them to the light and looking through them.

On estates, however, where many trees are being tapped and a large volume of latex it being collected each day, the process of making "biscuits" occupies too much factory space and labour. Machinery must be installed to deal with large quantities of latex and wet rubber at a time. This machinery is usually driven by an oil-engine, but on estates with large supplies of timber water-gas made from charcoal is found to be a cheaper source of energy than oil, and a suction gas-engine is used. The usual process of manufacture is as follows: The latex is strained and mixed in big tanks, or baths, with the requisite amount of acetic acid, and allowed to coagulate. This coagulation is in some places hastened by means of a centrifugal machine. The coagulated rubber is rolled to squeeze the water out, and washed in rolling-machines, and then dried either by hanging up in dark lofts heated by hot air or in special drying-machines. It is then "creped"—rolled into cloth-like strips by means of heavy revolving rollers. In its final stage it is in long strips about 1 ft. or 18 in. wide, and of a light golden or pale yellow colour.

The rubber is sometimes smoked while drying. This is said to add to its strength and to enhance its value. But the methods adopted can hardly be considered satisfactory as yet. There is here a big field for experiment and research. The object is to imitate as far as possible the Para rubber as made on the Amazon, which still fetches best prices. This is coagulated in the smoke of a fire, and made in blocks, the latex being laid on in successive layers, and in all probability herein lies the secret of success, and no processes of smoking after coagulation can imitate this. There is at present a growing demand for lightly smoked ribbed sheet.

The price obtained for plantation rubber has undergone many changes during the last ten years. In 1907 the best grades fetched a maximum price of 5s. 9d. a pound, and a minimum of 3s. 8d.; in 1909 and 1910 it rushed up in a most remarkable way, creating a "boom" of unprecedented magnitude. This culminated in 1910 with plantation rubber at 12s. 8d. a pound. Since then the price has steadily fallen to a maximum of 4s. 6d. in 1913 and 3s. 1d. in 1914. At the beginning of 1915 it had reached 2s. a pound. Even at this price, however, it is a paying concern, and each year sees it put on the market at a lower and lower cost of production, which has now reached about 10d. a pound, and as the trees get older and labour and machinery is better organized, it will probably come down to 8d. At the same time, each year shows a growing demand for Para rubber, and more and more uses to which it can be put.

The yield per acre in Southern India is not so large as that obtained in the Federated Malay States, for instance, but with increased age of the trees and the growing knowledge of manurial requirements it will no doubt increase.

There are few pests of rubber to contend with, and those which do exist in South India are comparatively easy to control.

The outbreak of war in 1914 had an important effect upon the rubber industry. The first concern was, of course, the maintenance of credit—a difficult matter for plantation interests, because they had to realize their responsibility towards the native labour force. The Government and the banks took practical measures to protect labour and estates, and money difficulties were soon overcome. The moratorium, war risk insurance, declaration of rubber and tyres as absolute contraband—all these contributed to the establishment of unusual and unnatural conditions, and, coupled with the sinking of rubber at sea, the destruction of rubber factories in Europe, and the closing of Antwerp and other continental centres of supply, resulted in world-wide disorganization. The British Government prohibited the export of crude rubber from British possessions except to British ports, while consignments of rubber from Java and Sumatra to ports other than British were stopped. By these means Great Britain became the only recipient of the whole of the Middle East supply of plantation rubber, the greater part of which was wanted by the United States, Germany, France, and Russia. A decree was issued prohibiting the export of crude rubber from the United Kingdom to any port, but later permission was granted to export to the Allies.

In these circumstances supplies in London would normally have increased at a rapid rate. This was, however, prevented by the sinking at sea by the *Emden* of two large consignments, and partly by the delayed arrival of steamers and the lack of labour at the docks to unload the ships when they did arrive. The consequence was that prices were not so much affected as they might have been. In July 1914, before the war began, plantation rubber was selling at 2s. 2d. for crepe and 2s. $3\frac{1}{4}$d for smoked sheet, and at the end of December 1914 crepe was fetching 1s. $11\frac{3}{8}$d. and smoked sheet 2s. $2\frac{3}{8}$d. a pound.

Ceara Rubber.

Manihot glazovii, the Ceara rubber-tree, grows like a weed all over the East, but until recently it could not be made to give a large enough yield to be much taken up, though it will grow at higher elevations and under drier conditions than the more popular Hevea rubber. It grows well from 800 to 5,000 ft., and requires about 50 in. of rain, and it delights in four or five months of hot, dry weather. It is intolerant of heavy wind, but grows very rapidly, making shoots of 18 ft. or more from seed in a single year.

In Southern India this variety of rubber is chiefly cultivated in Coorg, the Mysore State, and the Shevaroy Hills in the Madras Presidency on a plantation scale. It was first introduced into Mysore about 1880 as a shade tree for coffee, but it proved unsuitable for this purpose, and was soon cut out. Since then, until comparatively recent years, Ceara has been regarded with a good deal of undeserved contempt as a profitable source of rubber, due to the fact that, owing to the wrong methods of manipulation, large numbers of the trees died when they were subjected to tapping. This difficulty has now been overcome, and since 1904 Ceara rubber has been extensively planted, and there now exist some 12,000 acres of it in Coorg, 300 acres in Mysore, and 200 acres in the Shevaroy Hills.

TAPPING CEARA RUBBER.

The trees can be tapped when they are three or four years old, but it is usual and better to wait until they are six years old before beginning to tap them.

In the early days of Ceara rubber great difficulty was experienced with the extraction of latex from the tree. When tapped in the same way as Hevea rubber the bark rotted, and so many of the trees died that the industry proved unprofitable. The difficulty was overcome by using a tapping system, in which a separate cut was made at each tapping occasion, a system introduced by Mr. Westland in Ceylon in 1909. This system was experimented with and elaborated on estates in Coorg during 1910, and it has proved there the best method of handling young trees. The system finally adopted after numerous experiments is to first strip the outer bark, which is tough and leathery, off that section of the tree which is to be tapped—usually one-third of the circumference—and then to cut a shallow vertical channel down the centre of this area to act as a conducting channel for the latex to the collecting-cup at the base of the tree. Having made this channel, a number of sloping cuts are made with either a Pask V. knife or a knife similar to that of a farrier's, in either case kept very sharp, on the familiar herring-bone system, arranging them in such a manner that they enter the vertical channel alternately on each side. It is important that no two cuts should meet the central channel. As a rule, six of these cuts are made, three on each side of the central channel, and making an angle of $22\frac{1}{2}^{\circ}$ with it, the cuts on each side being 1 ft. apart. At the next tapping these cuts are left alone, and in young trees no attempt is made to widen them, but six new cuts are made half-way between the original ones. If paring is attempted it usually meets with failure, as the bark in young trees is so soft that it tears and strips under the knife, and a bad wound is made which refuses to heal, and the death of the tree may result owing to rot and boring insects. On each occasion of tapping—usually in Coorg—at intervals of two to four days, six fresh cuts are put in half-way between the old ones, and the spacing can be easily arranged so that it takes at least two years to use up all the bark on the area tapped. When this is done another third section of the tree is stripped of its outer bark and tapped in the same way, so that a four-year bark renewal is obtained.

As the trees get older they can be pared in the same way to that adopted when tapping Hevea rubber. The latex is coagulated and the rubber manufactured in much the same way as is adopted with Hevea. No coagulant is necessary, however, as the latex coagulates with hot water in the dark.

As regards yield: this is much smaller

than in the case of Hevea; the tapping season, owing to the long periods of dry weather in the districts in which it is grown, being short. It approximates $\frac{1}{3}$ lb. of rubber per tree per annum for eight-year-old trees. This variety of rubber can be grown, however, where Hevea cannot, and as a subsidiary crop to coffee, has prospects in the coffee districts which

D. ELKINGTON'S TEA FACTORY, COONOOR.

are being more and more realized in Southern India.

CARDAMOMS.

The cardamom is the fruit of a perennial herb, with thick, fleshy rhizomes and erect, leafy stems, 4 to 8 ft. in height, and long, branched inflorescences which arise near the ground, which is indigenous in West and South India, in the rich, moist forests of Canara, Mysore, Coorg, Wynaad, Travancore, and Cochin. In these districts it is cultivated to a large extent by both native growers and Europeans. It is difficult to say what the total acreage under this crop is in South India, but of recent years, with an improvement in prices, large areas have been planted up, and some of the tea and rubber estates have also considerable areas under cardamoms, and there are big estates where nothing else is grown in the Anamalais and Malabar, while many of the coffee estates of Coorg and Mysore cultivate cardamoms in the gullies and ravines.

Two species are grown, the Malabar cardamom, with prostrate fruit-bearing stems and a small pod, and the Mysore cardamom, with upright fruit-bearing stems and a large pod.

The crop is grown in ravines and damp, shady places, and on the floor of the jungles after the undergrowth has been removed. Very little cultivation is done, and no manures are applied. The plants bear in their second year from planting out of the nurseries where they are raised from seed, and after a time they are thinned out and re-planted.

The cardamom flowers in April and May, and the fruits are gathered in September and October. When ripe they are broken from the scape with a stalk attached, so as not to split the pod. They are dried in the shade, graded, and sold. A few planters complete the process of drying artificially in hot-air chambers, and others bleach the pods with sulphur fumes and produce the very best varieties. This latter process, however, involves a lot of trouble, and it is usual to market them in the dry and unbleached condition.

There is a large demand for cardamoms in India as a spice, while in England and Germany they are used in the manufacture of medicines, in North Europe as a spice for flavouring cakes and in the preparation of liqueurs. The essential oil extracted from the seeds is used in perfumery in France and America. The demand, and consequently price, is variable, but of late years both have advanced considerably, and a good deal of new areas have been opened in this cultivation.

PEPPER.

Pepper was one of the most important articles of early Indo-European trade, and it has been cultivated in South India, on the west coast, from very early times —since at least the fifth century. Malabar has always been considered to produce the best pepper, though this crop is now extensively grown also in parts of the Madras Presidency and in Mysore.

In the hands of the European planter it is usually grown in conjunction with coffee, the shade trees being used as standards, up which the pepper-vines are trained. A few European-owned estates are devoted to pepper entirely. It is impossible to estimate the acreage under this crop, therefore, on account of its scattered nature. A few years ago the Wynaad was a great pepper-growing centre, but recently it has all been rooted out, and tea, which is a much more profitable crop, planted.

The vines are grown from cuttings, and the greatest care is exercised in choosing these. Some plants bear wholly male flowers, other only female flowers, while a third kind has both types of flowers. In choosing vines for propagation it is therefore necessary first of all to determine whether it has any female flowers, and also whether it has enough staminate flowers to ensure fertilization. There are three main types of good pepper, known as Balamcotta, Kallivali, and Cheriakodi, and each has particular merits making it suitable for certain localities. The price obtained for the product is very variable, and it is usually looked upon by European planters as a minor product to be grown in conjunction with coffee or some other more profitable crop.

CINCHONA.

Cinchona was introduced into India through Kew, and first planted on the Nilgiri Hills in Southern India, where Government plantations and a factory for the manufacture of quinine have been established.

The tree can be grown successfully in many of the hill districts, the Anamalais being especially suited to it. It requires an open, gravelly subsoil, a sloping exposure, with a rich loam soil. It will not stand much frost, but from 2,500 to 6,000 ft. it flourishes, and it can withstand a considerable amount of drought. Alternate periods of sunshine and rain suit it best of all. It is grown from seed or propagated from cuttings.

When the trees are fifteen to twenty-five years old the crop is harvested. This may be done in several ways. The trees may be coppiced, in which case fresh shoots spring up and are allowed to grow, and these in time are again coppiced, and

HYBRID COFFEE-TREE—CLOSE VIEW OF BERRIES.

Photo by C. Lake.

so on, or the bark may be shaved off the standing trees, as near the cambium as possible without injuring it. The bark quickly renews if this work is done carefully. Finally, the trees may be cut down and all the bark stripped from them, the stumps uprooted, and the bark stripped from the roots. Plantations treated in this way give the biggest yield of bark, and they can be re-planted.

The bark, however obtained, is dried

slowly in the sun, packed into bags, and sent to the factory or market. The history of cinchona cultivation in South India during recent years is closely bound up with the history of the Government plantations and factory in the Nilgiris.

In 1897 representations were made to the Government by the planters asking for purchase of their bark by the Government factory. In 1898 108,934 lb. of bark were so purchased at the unit rate ruling in London, based on the actual out-turn of sulphate of quinine after the bark had been worked up at the Naduvatam factory. The system of purchasing bark to supplement the yield of the Government plantations proved a success, as a considerable saving in freight and home charges was effected, and the planters benefited by this.

In the following year the Government of Madras began to increase their plantations of cinchona, the object being not to make a profit and compete with private enterprise, but to be in a position to provide the people of the country with quinine as cheaply as possible. They continued to buy considerable quantities of bark each year from the planters at market prices.

In 1908, however, the Government again proposed to extend their plantations, and this brought a protest from the planters of Southern India, who contended that the Government should buy the bark it required in the Indian market. Meanwhile prices were falling, and many planters found that it was not profitable to continue this cultivation. It was suggested that the Government should undertake to buy bark from the planters at a minimum rate of one anna per pound, and thus foster the industry. This the Government were unable to see their way to do unless the planters were willing to guarantee to maintain a certain definite acreage always under cinchona—a guarantee it was obviously impracticable to obtain. The consequence is that practically no cinchona is now being planted by private individuals, and that in existence is annually being harvested, so that year by year the acreage decreases. The acreage under cinchona in 1913 on private estates in Southern India was approximately as follows :—

PLANTAINS IN FLOWER.

	Acres.
Madras Presidency	2,486
Travancore	2,085
Coorg	176
Mysore	48
Total	4,795

MINOR CROPS.

In addition to the main crops already described, a number of minor crops are grown on a small scale in the planting districts of Southern India, some of them still being in the experimental stages.

Fruit.—The most important of these is the growing of oranges and fruit. In Coorg especially oranges are cultivated, and could be successfully grown on a large scale were means of transport to big markets like Madras and Bombay readily available. At present this is not the case, but with the coming of the proposed railway it is possible that orange-growing may become an important industry in the district.

Apples, peaches, apricots, plums, and other fruit can be grown successfully in various districts, especially in the Nilgiris and Shevaroys. Here, again, the lack of markets and transport keep this industry within small limits. In Bangalore apples, grapes, strawberries, and oranges can be grown under irrigation, and market and transport facilities are better, with the result that it is a profitable industry.

Fibres.—Sisal and other fibre plants grow readily in the planting districts. In several places sisal is to be found cultivated. In the High Range of Travancore a considerable acreage of this plant has been put down, while on the borders of Mysore and Coorg a small estate is turning out fibre with profit and success. The difficulty in the way of development of this industry is the lack of a satisfactory small machine. The only machines which are really satisfactory require an enormous acreage of sisal to feed them and keep them running at a profit.

Camphor.—In the hill tracts camphor grows readily, and it can be easily propagated by means of suckers, and it is possible that some day this industry may be developed in Southern India. In several places distillations in a small way are made, and in the High Range of Travancore there is a considerable plantation of camphor, and an experimental still has been installed which promises interesting developments.

THE LAKE, OOTACAMUND.

OOTACAMUND, THE NILGIRI HILLS, AND WYNAAD

UPON opening a map of the world one notices a triangular outline of a continent in the billowy depths of the Indian ocean ; it is coloured red to denote its connection with the " tight little island " in western seas ; it has an area of nearly 2,000,000 square miles ; and is inhabited by more than 300,000,000 persons, who represent about one-fifth of the human race. That is the Indian Empire.

No other country in the world has within its borders such a variety of physical, social, political, and religious aspects : there are the eternally snow-capped summits of the Himalayas, and the miles upon miles of low-lying, flat, and frequently swampy land in the Madras Presidency ; the turbulent hillmen of the north may be contrasted with the peace-loving *ryots* of the south ; and the hundreds of forms of caste which cause such keenly marked dividing lines between different sections of the inhabitants are as yet too firmly established to be ignored. To many people, however, this variety acts as a charm ; there is no monotony—always something to attract attention ; and as far as scenery is concerned, the district of the Nilgiris outstrips every other part of the Madras Presidency.

These hills (originally Nila-gira, meaning " The blue mountain ") consist of a great plateau formed at the junction of the eastern and western *ghauts* which run southwards through the Madras Presidency between latitude 11° 8′ and 11° 37′ north, and longitude 76° 27′ and 77° 4′ east, and are about 6,500 ft. in height. They form a district which is bounded on the north by the State of Mysore, on the south and east by the district of Coimbatore, and on the west by the district of Malabar. The extreme length from east to west is only about 38 miles, while the breadth does not exceed 25 miles. The district consists of the main plateau already referred to, and of other lands on a lower level which stretch away to the west in the direction of the Malabar coast.

Mr. W. Francis, I.C.S., in his valuable Gazetteer, says : " There are three widely different outlying tracts, namely a strip of malarious jungle skirting the northern foot of the plateau ; the Ouchterlony Valley on the west, which is a deep recess in the high wall of the plateau, named after the pioneer who opened it up ; and, still further west the country known as the South-west Wynaad (i.e. the land of swamps), a table-land of bamboo forest, paddy-flats, and bogs, lying about 3,500 ft. lower than the plateau."

In the majority of the districts of the Presidency, information as to their early

P*

OOTACAMUND.

history is obtained by tradition, or from ancient manuscripts or inscriptions on stones or in shrines, but there is a remarkable absence of such evidences in the Nilgiri district, and writers have been compelled to rely upon records of the neighbouring State of Mysore. Mr. Lewis Rice, in his "Epigraphia Carnatica," expresses the opinion that the oldest inscription belongs to the period between the years 920 and 930 A.D., and that it describes the Wynaad as being a part of the territories of the well-known Ganga Dynasty of Mysore. The Gangas appear to have been driven out by the Kadambas, whose headquarters were in the northern portion of the District of Canara, and these people were in their turn subjugated by the Hoysalas in the early part of the twelfth century. The Vizayanagar Dynasty lasted for a considerable number of years, but in 1610 the then King of Mysore became ruler of the Wynaad, and titular possessor of the Nilgiri Hills. Very little is known of the district from this time until the English Government took possession in the year 1799.

The wars in which Mysore was at this time engaged were waged on behalf of the East India Company against Hyder Ali and his son, Tipu, and it is related that in the treaty which was entered into at the conclusion of hostilities the Nilgiri plateau was ceded to the Company, but "the Wynaad, by some blunder, was granted under one name to the Company and under another designation to the young King of Mysore, whom the British had resolved to re-establish on the throne which had been seized from his family by Hyder Ali." This error was, however, subsequently rectified, and the territory was placed under the Government of Madras on June 1, 1800. In the month of October in the same year steps were taken to have a descriptive account prepared of the territories which passed to the Company under the treaty of 1799, but it was reported that "owing to the extreme inclemency of the climate, the surveyors were frightened, measured not an acre, and contented themselves with making an estimate of the quantity and quality of the land and fixing the old rates of assessment upon it." It is believed that it was not until the year 1812 that the first Englishman, an Assistant Revenue Surveyor, named Keys, reached the top of the plateau, and even then the natural attractions of the hills were not recognized. It appears to have been left to Mr. John Sullivan, Collector of the district of Coimbatore, to make it known that the scenery of the Nilgiris was of extraordinary grandeur, combining mountains, valleys, forests, and waterfalls. But there was another question under consideration, as it was evident that the cool and invigorating climate would restore invalids to health; and certain medical officers appointed by the Government entertained the idea of establishing a sanatorium at a place named Ootacamund, which was then practically unknown, but which to-day is the summer headquarters of the Government of Madras, and the favourite hill resort of the wealthy families of the Presidency.

ST. STEPHEN'S, OOTACAMUND.

THE LAKE, OOTACAMUND.

There were strong reasons for advancing the claims of the Nilgiris. Reports of the health-giving climate had already

WILD LILIES, NILGIRIS.

been circulated; the soils of the plateau and of the Wynaad were found, under proper cultivation, to be productive of good results; and the peculiarly fortunate situation of the district induced retired civil servants and others to establish their homes in such a salubrious centre. The majority of the ordinary garden vegetables of England are raised in the district, the principal being carrots, turnips, tomatoes, parsnips, cabbages, marrows, cauliflowers, peas, beans, and celery, and the towns which have come into being are well supplied with these by Badagas and immigrant Canarese. Paddy is cultivated largely, especially in the Wynaad, and other crops include wheat, barley, potatoes, ragi, and samai, although tea plantations are entitled to a place of priority. Particulars concerning many of these estates are given elsewhere in this volume, and it need only be added that the flavour of the Nilgiris tea is not excelled by that of any other kind.

Horticulturists recognize four distinct areas in connection with the flora of the district, namely, the deciduous forests of the slopes, upon which are various kinds of cedars, satinwoods, rosewoods, and teak; the moist evergreen forests of the slopes; the *sholas* or woods of the plateau; and fourthly, the grassland of the plateau. A Government plantation of Australian trees was commenced in the year 1858, and about 10,000 trees, including blue-gums, wattles, conifers, pines, and cypresses, were planted in the neighbourhood of Ootacamund.

A VIEW OF COONOOR.

The chief minerals of any real value are building stone and laterite, and in various parts of the district there are ochreous clays, iron ore, hornblendic gneisses, mica, and a small quantity of gold.

The plateau is a table-land of average uniform height, but the whole of the surface is broken by undulations which form distinct ranges of hills. One of these, running north and south from a point slightly to the east of Ootacamund, is 8,640 ft. above the level of the sea, and is known by the name of Dodabetta, or "Big Mountain." There are three other prominent peaks, namely, Snowdon, 8,299 ft.; Club Hill, 8,030 ft.; and Elk Hill, 8,090 ft. Mr. Francis, in his description of this area, says: "In the south-western corner of the district rise the Kundahs, a range of hills most prominent from Ootacamund, the chief heights in which are the precipitous Avalanche Hill, two peaks called Kudikadu and Kolari, 8,497 ft. and 8,613 ft. respectively, and the conical grass-covered Derbetta, or Bear Hill, 8,304 ft. The Kundahs Range forms a kind of rim to the side of the plateau, and is continued on the north by the great line of peaks on the south of the Ouchterlony Valley." The general appearance of the Wynaad is entirely different from the plateau, the undulations and jungle being of quite a different character. The dense forests of Benne and Mudumalai are to be seen in the north; bamboo is conspicuous around Gudalur, and coarse grass and date-palms are found in the south-west portion. The district is drained by a very large number of streams, although some of them might be more fitly described as rivers. The visitor from the land to the north of the Tweed gets the idea that he is again in Bonnie Scotland; that the rills and burns are singing to him of the moors which he knew in his boyhood, and he is almost tempted to believe that a thirty or forty pounder may rise to the fly which he has forgotten to bring with him. Nearly all of these rivers are exceedingly pretty; they meander through forest, bush, and flowering shrubs, rippling here, tumbling over precipices there, but always active in their descent to the Cauvery delta, in which they are lost. The banks of these streams are flanked with thickets of blackberry bush; wild roses are riotous in their profusion, and it would be no stretch of imagination to fancy that the country lanes of Surrey and Kent had been transferred from England to India.

Visitors to the Nilgiris in former days clambered up the steep slopes of the ranges; there were no tracks worthy of the name, and until the recuperating properties of the district became known, there was very little attempt to scale the heights. Before railways were constructed in this portion of the continent the only access to the Nilgiri Hills was by six passes, or *ghauts*, two of which terminated at Mettupalaiyam, but now the tourist can travel in the most luxurious comfort. A company was formed in February 1896 to extend the railway system into the heart of the district of the Nilgiris, and the sections which are now completed are as follows: Muttupalaiyam to Coonoor, 17 miles; Coonoor to Fernhill, 11 miles; and Fernhill to Ootacamund, about a mile and a quarter.

The Nilgiris have not yet received that credit for superiority of climate over any other hill-station in India to which they are entitled, but this is owing to the comparatively short space of time which has elapsed since it became possible to reach them with any degree of satisfaction. Each hill and valley in the district appears to have a variation in climatic conditions according to exposure to monsoons, to elevation, and other local causes; but speaking in a general way, it may be said that dry, bracing, and exhilarating are the terms which one would select in giving a description.

South Indians generally, however, will not be satisfied by merely making the hills an attraction to residents in this vast continent, but they look forward with some confidence to the time when this district of loveliness and healthfulness will be fully appreciated by the inhabitants of Great Britain. It is doubtful if there is any other area of similar size in India which offers such advantages as these hills, and it is certain that the quiet beauty of the almost English landscape and the magnificence of the tropical forests—which form such a delightful contrast—only need to be seen to be loved. A prominent Government official has written as follows: "Let a visitor take a short ride in any direction, from almost any part of the plateau, and passing along shady English-looking lanes, sheltered by thickets of blackberry and wild rose, across breezy downs, sometimes dotted with twisted crimson flowering rhododendron trees, and intersected by valleys where buffaloes wade and wallow, through dense woods carpeted with rare and beautiful flowers, gorgeous in tints, beside which the colouring of an English autumn is faint and dull, passing by native villages with their patches of cultivation and magnificent jungle trees, he will find himself on some ridge or promontory looking down from a height of from 4,000 to 6,000 ft. upon a scene which changes like the figures in a kaleidoscope." But it is not the scenery alone upon which the Nilgiris depend for their attractions; it is that health-giving climate already referred to, which restores to vigour and gives joy of living to those who are lacking in energy and vitality.

THE BEAUTIFUL DOWNS.

When English tourists, wearied by the sameness of the old continental resorts, thoroughly understand that within about fifteen days from Home they can obtain the unexampled benefits of the Nilgiris, it is practically certain that they will yield to the hills that just recognition of their unique merits which they so richly deserve.

There are three tribes of people who may be said to belong to the Nilgiris, namely, the Badagas, the Kotas, and Todas. The last-named, who are not more than about a thousand in number, are pastoralists, and are much taller and fairer than the other inhabitants of Southern India. The Badagas (cultivators) are the descendants of Canarese who migrated from the State of Mysore some time during the thirteenth century. They occupy nearly the whole of the eastern half of the plateau and have shown a keen appreciation of improved methods of cultivating their land. The Kotas have settlements at Gudalur and Kotagiri, and are usually known as "cow" men, as distinguished from Todas, who are termed "buffalo" men. Both men and women are intelligent and industrious, but they hold a very low place in the social scale on account of their propensity for eating carrion.

Native industries are practically unknown, and only those which are due to European enterprise and money have obtained any footing at all. They include breweries, tea factories, a few dairies, and printing works, but it is deplorable to have to admit that there are no working weavers on the whole of the plateau.

It will now be well to refer briefly to some of the principal towns in this highly interesting district. Ootacamund is the headquarters of the district, and the seat, during the summer months, of the Government of the Presidency of Madras. The township is situated in the centre of the Nilgiris, and although it is about 7,400 ft. above the level of the sea, it rests in a valley which is surrounded by lofty hills. Concealed in bowers of acacia, cypress, pine, and other trees, upon these heights are residences of some of the inhabitants, who, by the way, are about 18,000 in number, excepting in the season, from April to October, when visitors arrive in thousands. Owing to the elevation the climate is an unusually healthy one, and the bracing atmosphere exhilarates the spirits of the tired worker and induces him to take a considerable amount of exercise, which can be accomplished without the expenditure of much energy. The south-west monsoon commences in June and continues until the end of September, when the vegetation becomes most luxuriant, and those who are fortunate enough to be able to take up their residence there instead of in the terribly hot cities and towns in other parts of the Presidency enjoy surpassingly beautiful scenery. The north-east monsoon usually breaks in October, and is succeeded by clear skies and warm sunshine, together with cold, and even frosty, nights. The highest temperature is experienced in the months of April and May, but visitors are not inconvenienced, as it is very rarely that the thermometer rises above 75° F. Government statistics show that the number of days upon which heavy rain falls is only 19; that there are about 80 days when there are occasional showers; 28 cloudy days; and no fewer than 238 which can be described as clear and fine. The management of the town is in the hands of a municipal council, which is presided over by a salaried chairman, and questions of general improvements, sanitation, and housing accommodation are receiving the fullest consideration. As His Excellency the Governor and his Council reside in Ootacamund for about six months in the year, the Government renders financial support to the council in order that the town may be made as attractive and healthy as possible. The water supply is obtained from the Marlimund and Dodabetta reservoirs and from a considerable number of springs and wells situated on private properties.

Tea, coffee, and vegetables are cultivated largely, and one of the recognized institutions is the public market for agricultural produce which is held weekly near Hobart Park. There are several excellent shops, the majority of which are branches of large establishments in Madras, such as Spencer & Co., Ltd., Oakes & Co., Ltd., Wrenn, Bennett & Co., Ltd., and W. E. Smith & Co., Ltd.

Among the public buildings and places of interest to be seen the following may be mentioned: Stonehouse, originally belonging to Mr. John Sullivan, the founder of the town, is built on a spur of the Dodabetta Range, and is now used as Government offices. The drive to Government House is through the very beautiful Botanical Gardens, in which many varieties of English flowers are cultivated. The Governor's residence is

1. THE DROOG, FROM TIGER HILL.

2. SIM'S PARK, COONOOR.

a large and comfortable structure, without any special architectural design, but it is the centre of the gaieties to which Ootacamund is given over during the official season. The library is well supplied with standard works of every branch of literature, and provision is made for permanent or temporary subscribers to avail themselves of its privileges.

St. Stephen's Church is one of the oldest buildings on the hills, its foundation stone having been laid in 1829, while it was consecrated by the Bishop of Calcutta in December 1830. The Roman Catholics have several chapels in the district, the principal one being an imposing structure which has been built near to Government Gardens. The leading educational establishment in the Nilgiris is the Lovedale Lawrence Asylum—about 3 miles from Ootacamund—which owes its inception to Sir Henry Lawrence, who wished to have an institution for orphaned children of soldiers similar to those which had already been constructed on the Simla Hills. Branches for boys and girls have been opened, and literary education has been supplemented by training in handicrafts. A very important feature of the Asylum is the school of telegraphy, through which hundreds of boys have been able to obtain employment in Government service.

The Ootacamund Residential Club compares most favourably with those at Madras and Bangalore, and it occupies an admirable position in the heart of the European residential quarter. Very comfortable apartments are available for gentlemen who pay a visit to the town, and the many attractions of the club have been increased recently owing to the opening of a ladies' annexe, this privilege being highly appreciated by the members.

In the hill stations of India, where the inhabitants are for the most part seekers after pleasure and health, all kinds of sport are energetically supported, but Ootacamund occupies a leading position among such towns. Members of the Gymkhana Club can indulge in cricket, croquet, golf, tennis, Badminton, hockey, boating, hunting, polo, and racing. The club-house is in Hobart Park, near to the Willow Bund, and is an exceptionally attractive building. Race meetings are held in the month of May. The steeplechase fixture is held later in the year upon the Newmarket Course upon the famous downs, which, by the way, remind Britishers with considerable force of the Cotswolds in England. Polo is enjoyed by the large number of military officers who travel southwards from Secunderabad as soon as the hot weather commences. Boating is held on the lake which was formed in the basin which lies between two spurs of the Dodabetta Range.

There are several good boarding-houses and some half-dozen hotels, and it is understood that the number of the latter will be increased in a short time by the construction of a first-class building, in which the furnishing appointments will be on up-to-date lines.

The large game to be met with on the hills are elephant, bison, tiger, panther, bear, wild boar, sambur, and ibex, in addition to many kinds of wild-fowl, while excellent trout of the rainbow type may be caught in many of the rivers on the hills. The Nilgiri Game and Fish Preservation Association is doing good work in preventing the extinction of indigenous game, but it goes further than this, as it has interested itself in the introduction of animals, birds, and fish from other countries. The importations of trout ova were, however, somewhat unsatisfactory at the commencement, but there are now evidences that early difficulties have been overcome to some extent, and that future hatchings will be successful.

NILGIRI MOUNTAIN RAILWAY.

Sporting visitors to the Nilgiris should not fail to make themselves acquainted with the regulations now in force for the preservation of various species of game and fish, as drastic penalties may be imposed in case of a breach of the Game Laws.

Coonoor, the second town of importance in the Nilgiris, is situated at the head of the main *ghaut*, on what may be described as a lower ridge of the main plateau, at an elevation of about 6,000 ft. The average annual temperature is from 8 to 10° higher than at Ootacamund, and this gives a peculiarly mild climate, which is more beneficial to those in delicate health than that which obtains at its sister sanatorium already referred to. The majority of the residences of Europeans are built at an elevation of nearly 6,000 ft. above the level of the sea, while the native quarter spreads over the lower slopes of two hills, which terminate in a promontory where the united waters of three streams break over the edge of the *ghaut* and are precipitated down the gorge under the name of the Coonoor River. When the town became a municipality in the year 1866 it possessed only 42 bungalows and 263 native houses and shops, but as estates were opened up in the near neighbourhood, bringing a consequent influx of labour, and roads were constructed and the railway was completed to Ootacamund, Coonoor grew rapidly, and it is now a charming and healthy residential place of about 10,000 inhabitants. It seems to be almost superfluous to speak about open spaces or gardens in the centre of a district which—considering its size—presents such a number of magnificent vistas at every turn of its well-kept, winding roads, but a brief reference must be made to Sim's Park, which lies in a beautiful ravine on the western side of the Coonoor Peak. At the bottom of the ravine a small stream has been dammed, and a pretty artificial lake has now been formed. The park is named after Mr. J. C. Sim, I.C.S., who took the deepest interest in its formation, which commenced in the year 1874. Quite near to the park is the Pasteur Institute, which provides for Southern India similar benefits to those which are given by another establishment of the same kind at Kasauli, in the Simla Hills, for the inhabitants of the north. The building owes its existence to the generosity of Mr. Phipps, an American subject, who placed a large sum of money in the hands of Lord Curzon—who was Viceroy at that time—in aid of benevolent schemes such as agricultural schools and institutes for scientific work in the prevention or cure of diseases. The Coonoor Hospital was opened in 1855 by the Government, but the municipality subsequently undertook the control, with the proviso that State aid would be continued. Its financial position has improved since several European ladies of the district came to its rescue, and discovered ways and means of increasing annual subscriptions.

The club at Coonoor had a modest commencement with a couple of tennis courts, near to which the owner of the land, Mr. Gray, of Gray's Hotel, erected a small room for the convenience of players. The structure is still standing as a memento of early days, but portions of the present club-house were commenced in the year 1897, and by 1906 the members had a large, well-appointed home, and one which is quite able to meet the demands of the large number of visitors. A small library was erected in 1864, but the present building was completed in 1903 at a cost of Rs. 20,000. All Saints' Church, said to be one of the prettiest ecclesiastical structures in India, is very centrally situated in a charming position, and it has seating accommodation for a congregation of 225 persons. There are several schools in Coonoor, but the Roman Catholics take the lead with

1. THE RAILWAY STATION, COONOOR. 2. COONOOR MARKET. 3. GENERAL VIEW OF COONOOR.

1. TODAS. 2. A TODA CATHEDRAL. 3. A TODA FAMILY. 4. A BADAGA.

1. GOLF COURSE ON THE DOWNS, OOTACAMUND. 2. "OOTY." 3. THE RAILWAY STATION, OOTACAMUND.

St. Joseph's College, which is one of the largest educational establishments in the Nilgiris.

The Coonoor Day School has had a fairly long life, and it is highly spoken of on account of the work which has been done within its walls for the poorer sections of the European and Anglo-Indian communities.

There are good hotels and boarding-houses in the town, where visitors are entertained at charges running upwards from Rs. 5 a day.

Wellington Cantonment is about a mile and a half distant in a northerly direction from Coonoor, and is the headquarters of the officer commanding the Southern Brigade, and the principal convalescent station for British troops in Southern India. It is situated on a spur of the Dodabetta Range, and is bounded on the north by the town of Coonoor and on the west and north by portions of the Dodabetta Mountains. The first portion of the *ghaut* which runs from east to west is thickly covered with bamboo and coconut trees, but farther towards the summit (6,100 ft.) one finds a strong growth of indigenous forest trees, such as blackwood, teak, sal, wild jack, vengay, and red and white cedars. The climate of Wellington is, generally speaking, temperate and invigorating, and early European settlers were impressed with the desirability of quartering British regiments there, but especially those who had just arrived from England. This civil and military station could not by any possible means be anything but a sporting centre, and the town now possesses an energetic Gymkhana Club, in connection with which annual races are held on one of the loveliest courses in India.

Some of the Boer prisoners of war were originally detained in a camp on the racecourse, but they were subsequently transferred to the Kaity Valley, between Coonoor and Ootacamund, where the Nilgiri Cordite Factory now stands. The factory is the outcome of a determination on the part of the authorities that India shall be self-supporting, as far as possible, in the manufacture of ammunition and small arms, and when cordite super-

PASTEUR INSTITUTE.

seded gunpowder a site on the Nilgiris was deemed to be most suitable for the proposed building. The following particulars are gleaned frem Mr. Francis's Gazetteer: "The red buildings of the factory form a town by themselves, with the residences of the officers in charge perched prominently along the top of a ridge above them. Building work commenced in 1900 on a site which is 1,600 ft. above sea-level, and the main gate is on the Coonoor-Ootacamund road, about 4 miles distant from the railway station at the former place. The factory is enclosed by a high wall, and extends to an area of about 500 acres, wherein are contained nine separate branches, namely, acids, gun-cotton, nitro-glycerine, cordite, cannon cartridge, mechanical, plumbers, laboratory, and general. The staff consists of a superintendent and some 55 to 60 European chemical, mechanical, electrical, and other assistants, while the average number of native workmen is about 950."

Kotagiri is about 13 miles distant from Ootacamund, and although it is only a small station it seems to have a considerable number of regular visitors from Madras and elsewhere. It is situated about 6,500 ft. above sea-level, and its climate, though less invigorating than that of "Ooty," is colder and more bracing than Coonoor. The average temperature for the year is about 62°, which puts Kotagiri in a position of a kind of half-way house between the other two health resorts. A club has become an established fact, and golf, tennis, and other relaxations are freely indulged in.

KOTAGIRI

By C. H. BROCK

KOTAGIRI, the third hill station of the Nilgiris, is yearly becoming a more favoured place for visitors from the plains who want a quiet and restful holiday. The various buildings are scattered over a large area, and the whole station is well provided with excellent roads of an easy gradient. The station has grown in size and importance considerably during the past ten years, and it now contains two churches, two chapels, a club, hospital, two hotels, post and telegraph office, and eighty-three European bungalows, which include several boarding-houses. All these are at an elevation of between 6,250 and 6,650 ft. above sea-level, and are built round a series of knolls and valleys. The total population is now just under 6,000.

Kotagiri is situated near the eastern end of the Nilgiri Plateau, and is 21 miles distant by road to the north of Mettupalaiyam (the terminus of the broad-gauge railway), it is 18 miles east of Ootacamund, and 13 miles north-east of Coonoor. The direct *ghaut* road from Mettupalaiyam was constructed in 1872-5, is well metalled, and it has a gradient of 1 in 17. The roads in Coonoor and Ootacamund wind about over undulating country, and, with surfaces which are partly metal and partly gravel, they are very suitable for all vehicular traffic.

The name Kotagiri (formerly spelt Kotergherry) is properly "Kotarkeri," or the "Street of Kotas," and it was the chief village of Kotas in the district. Their village was situated in the middle of the station, but in 1910, for sanitary reasons, the Government gave these people a large grant of money and land to remove from the station, and the old picturesque but dirty village no longer exists.

Kotagiri was the first place on the plateau to be inhabited by Europeans, and all the earliest explorers of the hills came up through Kotagiri via Kilkotagiri, a Kota village 8 miles west of Kotagiri. The first bungalow ever erected on the hills was built by Mr. John Sullivan, Collector of

Coimbatore in May 1819, near the village of Dimhutti, just 1 mile north of Kotagiri itself, and this old house is still standing. In 1821 Lieutenant Evans Macpherson began to construct the first *ghaut* road (a bridle path) from the plains, from Sirumugai near Mettupalaiyam to Kotagiri, and he built a bungalow for himself near Jackanarai, about 1½ miles south of Kotagiri. This road was the best route to the hills from the Coimbatore side until the first Coonoor *ghaut* road was

BLUE MOUNTAIN HOTEL, KOTAGIRI.
Photo by C. Lake.

made in 1830. The opening of the latter meant that Kotagiri was neglected by incoming visitors and settlers, as it was so far from the new direct road from Mettupalaiyam to Ootacamund, and it is only of late years that the place has been attracting visitors. The oldest house in Kotagiri itself was built by Mr. R. H. Clive about 1824. By 1845 there were fifteen European bungalows in the station, and during the next fifty years practically no others were built, as during this period the only new residents of the neighbourhood were the pioneers of the planting districts, who built their bungalows on the estates which they opened up in different directions at distances varying from 2 to 10 miles from Kotagiri.

Situated higher than Coonoor and lower than Ootacamund, it is a far healthier place than either, being less relaxing than the former, and not so bleak as the latter. Kotagiri is not shut in by high hills all round, as the other hill stations are, and consequently the air is always fresh and bracing. The rainfall averages about 62 in. per annum, and it is well distributed throughout the year. The vigour of the south-west monsoon is broken by the high ranges of hills between Ootacamund and Coonoor, and is in consequence very little felt, there generally being far more wind than rain from June to August. In October and November, however, there are generally heavy showers of rain from the north-west monsoon, which fall in short and heavy bursts, chiefly at night, but the mornings are generally gloriously fresh and fine. There are occasionally slight frosts in the winter. The summer maximum temperature rarely exceeds 75°, the mean for the whole year being 61°.

From a visitor's point of view Kotagiri and its neighbourhood is full of interest. From the station itself there is on one side a grand view over the Coimbatore district, and on clear days the distant ranges of Anamalais, Shevaroys, and Palanies can be clearly seen, the latter at a distance of considerably more than 100 miles. On the other side the view of the plateau extends over numerous hills and valleys as far as Dodabetta.

The following places of interest near Kotagiri are well worth the attention of visitors: Elk Falls (5 miles). When in flood these falls are a fine sight, although they are not very high, and below them the river flows down the centre of the Orange Valley. On the road to the falls is "Sullivan's Bungalow," the first European house to be built in the Nilgiris. About 4 miles beyond the falls are the Bikkapatty Mund Reserves, where there is generally good shooting.

St. Catherine's Falls (4 miles). These falls are still finer, having a clear drop of 250 ft., although they are rather narrow except when in full flood. These are named after the wife of the pioneer planter, Mr. M. D. Cockburn.

Rungaswami's Pillar (11 miles). This is a huge detached pillar of rock, rising abruptly on all sides from the lower slopes at the edge of the plateau to a height of 400 ft. From here there is a fine view across the Moyar Valley and the Mysore Plateau beyond. These are the chief "sights," but all around the neighbourhood there are ideal places for picnics, which are in the centre of magnificent scenery and charming views.

The pioneer of coffee-planting in this part of the Nilgiri district was Mr. M. D. Cockburn, whose first estate, Kannahutty, was commenced in 1843, and some 40 acres of the original bushes are still flourishing. This small beginning has led to there now being sixty-three coffee, tea, and rubber estates, belonging principally to European private owners, and on these (approximately) 3,000 acres (about 900 acres of coffee, 1,600 acres of tea, and 500 acres of rubber) are being cultivated. In addition to these there are a very large number of small patches of coffee owned by natives. From 1875 to 1885 a lot of cinchona was planted on many estates, but the prices for the bark soon went down so much that the trees have long been uprooted to make room for the more paying product, tea, and there is now practically no cinchona growing anywhere in the neighbourhood.

The hill natives, chiefly Badagas, grow extensive crops of samai, ragi, korali, barley, peas, and potatoes, the last-named in good years being the most remunerative of all.

ACHOOR ESTATE

This estate of 4,345 acres, belonging to the East India Tea and Produce Company, Ltd., is situated about 5 miles distant from the post office at Vayitri. Mr. J. W. G. Bisset became manager in 1908, and during the six succeeding years he has opened up 330 acres, thus bringing the area under cultivation for tea to 670 acres.

The factory at Achoor is a large structure of three stories, being 180 ft. in length and 76 ft. in width, and there are two engines on the property, one of 65 h.p., driven by liquid fuel, while the other—a 40-h.p. "National"—is worked by gas. The plant consists of five rollers, two roll breakers, three down-draught siroccos, a Colombo driver, four sifters, cutting and packing machine, boiler, and

ON THE NILGIRI DOWNS.

two steamers. The average output of the factory—which, by the way, is lighted by electricity—is 500,000 lb., and the greater portion of this is sent to Calicut for shipment to London.

Mr. Bisset is assisted in the management by a European assistant, and he usually employs about 850 coolies.

Achoor is 2,500 feet above the level of the sea, and about 140 inches of rain are recorded annually. The property is 44 miles from the town and port of Calicut.

ACHOOR ESTATE.

1. Manager's Bungalow. 2. Achoor Factory. 3. View from No. 3 Field.

Two very comfortable bungalows—one of them double-storied—have been erected on the estate.

THE ANAPURA COFFEE WORKS COMPANY, LTD.

This is a coffee planters' company which was formed in the year 1891, and the directors are Messrs. J. Christie, A. G. Nicholson, J. H. Pascoe, and G. A. Marsh, while the Hon. E. F. Barber is Chairman. The managing agents are Messrs. Peirce, Leslie & Co., Ltd., of Coimbatore, and the principal business consists of the manufacture of coffee and of its disposal in the London market. At the annual auction sale in 1914 about 400 tons of coffee were sold, while the total output for the year 1913-14 was rather more than 1,000 tons. The barbaques, or drying-grounds, cover an area of about 5 acres, and about 2,000 bushels can be spread upon the floor. A steam engine is used for driving the peeling machine, and one driven by oil-power is fixed in the shed in which the beans are "sized." Between 300 and 400 women garblers are employed, whose duty it is to remove all beans of unsatisfactory quality. The manager is Mr. W. J. Campbell.

AUDA TODE ESTATE

An account of the experiences of pioneer planters in India may provide interesting reading matter for the frequenters of libraries or for the occupants of cosy drawing-rooms in Belgravia, but the recollection of those early days of struggles with difficulties is a stern fact to the men who had to face them. Mr. H. B. Winterbotham, the owner of the Auda Tode estate, arrived in India in the year 1861. The land which he selected was an almost impenetrable jungle; there were no roads worthy of the name; wild animals were numerous and enterprising; and food for master and man was extremely rough and difficult to get; and, as a matter of fact, he had been living on the property for no less than seven years before he set eyes upon a European lady.

The estate is 650 acres in extent, and the owner was engaged in the growing of coffee until 1903, when, owing to the ravages of leaf disease, the greater portion of the cultivated land was given up to tea bushes. The latter have been planted upon 130 acres, but each succeeding year witnesses a considerable extension in cultivation. The Assam hybrid variety is usually grown, and the annual yield on this property has gone up to 712 lb. of "made" tea to the acre. The dust tea, which is produced at Auda Tode, meets with a very ready sale in the district of Malabar, but the remainder of the crop is shipped at Calicut for the London market. Mr. Winterbotham has erected a comfortable residence together with a number of suitable out-buildings, which include a factory in which 600 lb. of "made" tea can be turned out daily. The estate is about 2,600 ft. above the level of the sea, and the average annual rainfall since the year 1890 (when records were commenced) has been 130 in. The post office at Perindotty is about 1 mile distant from the property.

AUDA TODE ESTATE.

1. THE BUNGALOW. 2. THE FACTORY.

Mr. Winterbotham is, further, the owner of the Muricarp estate, about

8 miles from Auda Tode, consisting of about 300 acres, one-third of which is taken up with the cultivation of pepper-trees. As many as 24 tons of dried pepper have been obtained in a season. The cost of production of pepper is not more than 2½d. lb., and the selling price in the market at the present time is about 5d.

Mr. Winterbotham manages the estates personally, and he employs about 200 hands regularly.

BARBER & PASCOE

The members of this firm are the Honourable Mr. E. F. Barber, Planting Member of the Legislative Council of Fort St. George, Madras, and Mr. J. H. Pascoe, of Nilgiri Hills, and they carry on business as agents for the sale and purchase of estate property, and act as visiting agents over a number of tea, coffee, rubber, cardamoms, and cinchona plantations. Their office is at Ootacamund, and their registered telegraphic address is "Visitates." The business was established in 1910, and each partner possesses a thoroughly practical knowledge of the management of estates, as Mr. Barber's experience extends over a period of some twenty-five years, while Mr. Pascoe has been connected with plantation work since the year 1885. The firm are visiting agent for, among others, estates owned by the COCHIN RUBBER CO., LTD., the PERIYAR RUBBER CO., LTD., the SOUTHERN INDIA RUBBER CO., LTD., the INDIAN PENINSULA RUBBER AND TEA ESTATES, LTD., the THODAPUZHA RUBBER CO., LTD., the BRITISH AND CONTINENTAL TEA PLANTATIONS TRUST, LTD., the CHERAKARA TEA ESTATES, LTD., the BOMBAY BURMA TRADING CORPORATION, LTD., the SEAFORTH PLANTATIONS, LTD., and the NILAMBUR RUBBER ESTATES, LTD. In addition, they are agents for NOBEL'S EXPLOSIVES CO., LTD., and the ROYAL EXCHANGE ASSURANCE CORPORATION.

Messrs. Barber & Pascoe are well known for their excellent judgment as to the value of estate property, and they have been employed by the Government for the valuation of land in the Madras Presidency. They are prepared to select, report upon, or purchase estates in India.

BAYLY & BROCK, LTD.

Kotagiri, where Messrs. Bayly & Brock, Ltd., have their headquarters, is a town of nearly 6,000 inhabitants, and it is situated about 18 miles distant from Ootacamund, which is the seat of the Madras Government during the summer months. The extensive business of this company as dealers in high-class coffee and tea was established by Messrs. Bayly & Brock in 1903, when a speciality was made of supplying customers with those commodities direct from the company's own estates or from those of which they are managers. Coffee is roasted at the works (the former process being carried out in a "Savage" oven), it is then ground, and when the finished sample is ready for packing it consists of one quality only—that is the highest—and it does not contain any chicory or other inferior ingredient. All chests, boxes, tins, and packets for both coffee and tea are made on the premises under the direct supervision of a responsible representative of the company. Large consignments are shipped to England, and throughout Ceylon and Burma, although nearly two-thirds of the trade is done in India by means of the prepaid parcel post. Roasted coffee intended for purchasers in India is packed in lever lid tins in parcels containing from 2 lb. to 24 lb. Raw berries—consisting of Peaberry round, extra large round, and small bean—are put up in bags of from 5 lb. to 30 lb. Orders from England are made up in 1 lb. tins or in cases of 24 lb., and the prices include all charges for postage or carriage and duty ; in other words, the packages have free delivery. Tea for local sale is put up in lead packets, in parcels of 2 lb., 4 lb., or 6 lb., or in large tins containing 5 lb. There are five grades of tea, distinguished by differently coloured wrappers, and they consist of B. and B.'s mixture, Orange Pekoe, Pekoe, Broken Pekoe, and Gunpowder. Consignments for England are sent by post or are shipped in chests which contain from 48 lb. to 70 lb., but special cases are made up when required. Messrs. Bayly & Brock's terms are "strictly cash with order or by V.P. Post," and this is the only method of conducting their business by which they are enabled to quote such low prices. An example or two may be given : 2 lb. tin of excellent coffee at Rs. 2.8, free by post ; 24 lb., with free railage to any station in India, for Rs. 26.8 ; 24 lb. in a case delivered to any railway station in England for Rs. 42 ; tea in packets of 2 lb. each from Rs. 1.14 to Rs. 3 (including postage) ; 5 lb. tins from Rs. 4.8 to Rs. 6. Chests of tea for England are quoted as follows : 50 lb. in lead packets at from 1s. 6d. to 1s. 10d. each packet. Prices, of course, vary from time to time with the market fluctations, but the above rates are the high-water mark, as the prices of Vote coffee and tea were higher in 1913 than they have been for the previous eighteen years.

There are two estates which are owned by individual members of the company. One of these is the Goonjara property of 120 acres belonging to Mr. C. H. Brock, 77 acres of which are under cultivation for coffee. This estate lies at an elevation of from 4,600 ft. to 5,200 ft., and there is an average rainfall of 67 in. The Dunhutty property, belonging to Mr. S. Bayly, and consisting of 40 acres in the Kotagiri Mettupalaiyam Ghat, is about 4,000 ft. above the level of the sea, and it enjoys an annual rainfall of 63 in. Negotiations are now in progress for the company to acquire these properties, as well as a tea estate, and when this has been effected the company will be actually growing all its own requirements for its business. The company are, further, managing agents for the following estates, namely : (1) "Kannahutty," comprising 46 acres of coffee and 15 acres of tea, with a total of 103 acres of land, belonging to Mrs. L. Hatch ; (2) "Crofton," with an area of 140 acres (60 acres of coffee) in the Kotagiri-Mettupalaiyam Ghat, the property of Mrs. H. L. Griffith ; (3) "Tuttapullum," 360 acres in extent, including 90 acres of coffee and 100 acres of tea, owned by Mr. J. T. Fellows-Wilson ; (4) "Kengarai," having a total of 206 acres, of which 70 acres are growing coffee, the proprietor being Mr. A. M. Kinloch ; and (5) "Pattikambai," 311 acres, belonging to the Scott's Family Trust Estate, containing 50 acres of coffee-plants.

In addition to the coffee and tea business the company also undertake civil engineering contracts, and they are local agents for the Atlas Insurance Company. The directors are Messrs. C. H. Brock, S. Bayly, and H. M. Hewett, the first-named being managing director, and the authorized capital is 1 lakh of rupees. A large number of hands are employed permanently, under the supervision of the managing director.

CHUNDALE

Situated about a mile and a half distant from the post office at Vayitri, in the

BAYLY AND BROCK, LTD.

1. The Factory. 2. Tin-making Room. 3. Packing-room

CHUNDALE ESTATE.

1. SUPERINTENDENT'S BUNGALOW. 2. TEA (NO. 9). 3. INTERIOR OF ROLLING-ROOM. 4. THE FACTORY.

district of Malabar, is the Chundale estate of 1,348 acres, belonging to the East India Tea and Produce Company, Ltd. Practically the whole of the 577 acres of cultivated land are planted with tea, as only a very minute portion is given up to the production of pepper.

During the year 1914 the factory—which had previously been a single-storied building for the manufacture of green tea alone—was enlarged by the construction of three upper floors, in order that additional machinery and plant for the output of black tea, as well as green, might be installed. The building, which is on the main road between Calicut and Ootacamund, is now equipped with a 40-h.p. "National" suction gas engine, a steamer for green tea, three rollers, three dryers, one sifter, cutting and packing machines, and sirocco-cased withering fans. The factory has a capacity for dealing with 400,000 lb. of "made" tea, and practically the whole of each year's crop is shipped to London.

Chundale is 2,500 ft. above the level of the sea. The superintendent—Mr. W. Morres—is assisted in the management by Mr. H. C. Davies.

CRAIGMORE ESTATES

The term Craigmore comprises a number of estates, nearly one thousand acres in extent, and the majority of them are situated within a few miles distance of Devarshola, in the district of the Nilgiris. The properties are owned by a syndicate, whose manager is Mr. K. J. Harper, who had twelve years' practical experience in planting in Ceylon prior to his taking over the control of estates in India. Indigenous seed was used in the cultivation of 250 acres of tea, and, indeed, of the 150 acres of coffee. Fully matured tea bushes have regularly given 700 lb. of produce to the acre, although one field was so grateful for its manuring that it made the heart of the manager rejoice by filling the weighing-machine until no less than 1,000 lb. had been registered. The owners are Messrs. E. A. Fulcherd and G. W. Fulcherd, and they employ 300 coolies throughout the year.

CURZON

The total area of this property is 588 acres, and it is subdivided as follows: 190 acres of tea, 68 acres of coffee, 80 acres of jungle, and 250 acres of scrub and grass. The area which is producing tea consists in almost equal proportions of high and medium to low *ghaut* lands, and the crops from these two plateaus—differing slightly in colour and flavour—form an excellent mixture when they are properly blended. The average yield of "made" tea to the acre is almost 466 lb., and fully three-fourths of this quantity is sold locally, while the remainder is consigned to London.

The factory is situated in the centre of the property, and it contains a "Davidson" turbine, a "siroccos" roller, two "Little Giant" rollers, eight down-draught and four up-draught "siroccos," and a Walker & Greig sifter. There are, further, two withering sheds, one of which is capable of dealing with 2,000 lb. of tea. The coffee-beans on this estate are above the average size, and the prices which are received are proof of the excellent quality of the prepared article. About 160 hands are constantly employed.

DAVERA SHOLA

This is one of the many beautiful estates in the renowned district of the Nilgiris, and it is held under lease from the Raja of Nilambur by Messrs. H. F. Wilbraham, H. P. Hodson, and P. Church.

Mr. J. S. Nicolls, the manager, started planting in Ceylon in 1886, and came over to India in 1904. He has been in full charge of Davera Shola since 1904. He resides in a very fine bungalow, which is situated about 38 miles distant from Ootacamund and some 7 miles from Gudalur. The property consists of 2,215 acres, of which 568 acres have been planted with tea. A special feature is made of the process of grading, and this is regarded as the secret of the absolute uniformity of the crop produced on this estate.

The factory is a fine three-storied building, 165 ft. in length and 33 ft. in width, and it contains the usual rooms for drying, sorting, grading, and packing. The machine-room is fitted with three engines—one of these is of 35-h.p., and the others are $12\frac{1}{2}$-h.p. respectively; there are, further, four rollers, a Paragon dryer, roll breakers, sifters, and other appliances. The yield for the season 1913-14 amounted to 351,000 lb., which showed an average of 659 lb. to the acre, although some of the fields returned as much as 1,090 lb. The average price of this estate's tea in the London market is just under 9d. per lb., while the cost of placing tea f.o.b. at port of shipment is about 5d. per lb. Nearly the whole of the crop is consigned to agents in London, who find purchasers from Canada and the United States of America to be among their best customers. The principal market in Southern India is at Bombay.

Mr. Nicolls has one European assistant, two overseers in the factory, and has constant employment for about 650 labourers. In addition to his responsibilities on the Davera Shola estate, Mr. Nicolls fills the post of manager of the Pullangode rubber estate, consisting of 7,000 acres, in the district of Malabar. This company was registered in London in the month of July 1910, and it has an authorized capital of £50,000. About 1,272 acres have been planted, and the yield for the period 1913-14 amounted to 20,700 lb. Mr. Nicolls is chairman of the Nilgiri Planters' Association, and he is, further, visiting agent of the Barwood estate of 248 acres of tea and coffee, and of the Periashola tea estates of 230 acres, both of which properties are situated in the Ouchterlony Valley.

DEVON ESTATE

There are many planters who were growing coffee fifteen or twenty years ago who to-day have nearly every acre of their land under cultivation for tea.

Mr. A. R. Pigott purchased the Devon estate of 600 acres in the year 1897, when he became engaged, chiefly, in the production of coffee. The average annual yield is about 12 tons, and after the crop has been cured at Calicut, it is shipped at that port for sale in London. Some years since Mr. Pigott took up tea-planting in earnest, and he now has 175 acres of healthy young trees which are full of promise. A considerable portion of the property is still covered with jungle, but this is being cleared as rapidly as possible. A residence at an altitude of 3,500 ft. commands uninterrupted views of the beautiful surrounding country, and the climate at this elevation is particularly healthy and invigorating. The nearest post and telegraph office is at Nellakota; Ootacamund is 40 miles distant, while Gudalui and Calicut are 10 and 97 miles respectively away from the estate.

Mr. Pigott is his own manager, and he usually employs 150 labourers.

DAVERA SHOLA ESTATE.

1. MANAGER'S BUNGALOW. 2. VIEW OF TEA. 3. FACTORY.

DOWNHAM

This is, primarily, a model fruit farm, and if it could be transferred bodily to become a competitor in those instructive contests among fruit farmers in the Home Counties of England which are held annually under the auspices of the Government Department of Agriculture, the owner would scorn the idea of receiving handicap points from properties which have been devoted to the cultivation of fruit for the greater part of a century. He would take his chance, and the probability is that his confidence would not be misplaced. It goes without saying that the property is most favourably situated as regards climatic conditions, but a visitor might possibly experience some surprise at the magnificent specimens of Japanese persimmons and plums, peaches, apples, oranges, strawberries, cherries, and grapes. About 50 acres of the property—which is not more that 6 miles distant from Ootacamund—have been planted with coffee, and an average amount of from six to eight tons of the harvest from this part of the estate has been disposed of annually in local markets.

EAST INDIA TEA AND PRODUCE COMPANY, LTD.

The registered offices of this company are at Nos. 1-4 Great Tower Street, London, E.C., and the agents in Southern India are Messrs. Harrisons and Crosfield, Ltd., of Quilon. The company was formed in 1907, when various estates were acquired in the Wynaad *taluq*, in the district of Malabar. The Wynaad—this being the customary designation—is, in reality, a continuation of the Great Mysore plateau, and lies above the crest of the western ghats. Each estate at the time of purchase had been partly planted with tea, coffee, or pepper, but development has been pushed forward so vigorously since the company obtained possession that the area under cultivation has been practically doubled in size. The properties originally comprised 16,637 acres, and the plantings were 2,263 acres of tea in bearing, 98 acres of young tea, 116 acres of coffee, and 193 acres of pepper, together with forest scrub and waste amounting to 13,737 acres. Further purchases brought the total up to 23,473 acres. This area now consists of tea—nearly all of which is matured—4,764 acres, coffee 452 acres, pepper 113 acres, and roads and buildings 67 acres, together with 18,076 acres of undeveloped land. There are nine properties altogether, and all are within easy access of Calicut, which is the capital town and shipping port of Malabar.

The names of the several estates and of their staffs may be noted here :—

	Superintendents.	Assistants.
Achoor ...	J. W. G. Bisset	W. G. Craig
Perrengodda	T. P. Gauld	H. C. Coverley
Chundale ...	W. Morres	H. C. Davis
Pootoomulla	A. D. McBain	—
Poonoopoya	A. E. Vernede	A. W. Mackay
Touramulla	R. Copland	J. P. Wilson
Cherambadi	P. Guard	—
Wentworth	E. R. Howlett	E. A. Cheeseman
Mayfield ...	J. E. Bisset	I. Stuart & P. Naylor

There are extremely well-equipped factories at all of the properties, excepting Poonoopoya and Cherambadi, and the green leaf from these two is manufactured at Pootoomulla and Wentworth respectively. The annual yields of the estates vary from 800 lb. to the acre down to 250 lb., but it is only fair to point out that the latter figures relate to those portions of the properties upon which there is a considerable acreage of immature tea.

The harvest for the year 1914 amounted to 2,038,250 lb. of "made" tea, and the estimate for 1915 is put down at 2,310,000 lb. The produce intended for the London market is dispatched by Messrs. Harrisons and Crosfield from the port of Calicut.

Coffee is grown at Touramulla and Mayfield to the extent of 266 and 186 acres respectively, while pepper vines on the same estates occupy 64 acres and 50 acres of land. Each estate is fully provided with permanent buildings, such as bungalows, lines for coolies, stores, and sheds. The elevation of the properties above the level of the sea varies considerably, ranging from 2,500 ft. to 3,500 ft.

The post and telegraphic facilities for the various estates are as follows : Achoor, Perrengodda, and Chundale are served by the office at Vayitri ; Pootoomulla and Poonoopoya depend upon Vellaramulla for postal business, and upon Meppadi for telegraphic conveniences ; Touramulla is near to Sultan's Battery post office, the telegraph office being "Cherambadi" ; Wentworth and Cherambadi avail themselves of the arrangements at the latter place, and Mayfield is within a reasonable distance from the Nella Cotta office.

THE GLENVANS ESTATE COMPANY, LTD.

The Glenvans property, comprising 1,212 acres, lies in the well-known Ouchterlony Valley, in the district of the Nilgiris, which is an important centre for the growing of coffee and tea.

The late Mr. James Vans Agnew, a Bengal civilian, purchased the property in 1862 from the late Mr. James Ouchterlony, and shortly afterwards sold it to his brother, the late Mr. John Vans Agnew, a Madras merchant, who named it Glenvans, and proceeded to turn a portion of it into a coffee estate, although the major part of it is still magnificent primeval forest. The present owners are the Glenvans Estate Company, Ltd., the whole of the shares being held by the children of the late Mr. John Vans Agnew, for whom one of them—Mr. A. F. Vans Agnew—is the manager.

In spite of the vicissitudes which have been experienced by growers of coffee in recent years, Glenvans still remains a very fine coffee estate, and for the season 1913-14 it gave a return of 139 tons from 410 acres of cultivation. Like all estates in the Ouchterlony Valley its coffee is sold under the name of "Naidoobatam Coffee," a brand much sought after in the London market.

After being picked, coffee is partially dried on the estate, and then sent on to Messrs. Peirce, Leslie & Co.'s works at Calicut, where it is "cured" and graded into sizes and then shipped to London for sale. Messrs. Peirce, Leslie & Co., of 14 Billiter Street, London, E.C., are the secretaries of the company, and their office is also the Registered Office of the Glenvans Estate Company, Ltd.

The property ranges from 3,200 to 4,500 ft. above sea-level, and it is situated at the western end of the Ouchterlony Valley, immediately under the Nilgiri Peak, which towers over it to a height of 4,000 ft., while on other sides the views are very fine. The distance to Gudalur, the nearest town, is 11 miles, while Ootacamund is 30 miles farther on. The road from Gudalur to the estate is suitable for motoring.

KARDOORA ESTATE

Kardoora is the name given to a group of three estates known as Nedimballe, Meppadi, and Kardoora, situated in the *taluq* of Wynaad, which belongs to the Meppadi-Wynaad Tea Company, Ltd. The total area comprises 1,832 acres, and the cultivated portion of 756 acres consists of 606 acres of tea, and 150 acres of pepper, but the owners intend to plant up a much larger acreage in due course.

GLENVANS ESTATE COMPANY, LTD.

1. Drying-ground and Coffee Store. 2. The Bungalow. 3. A General View showing Nilgiri Peak.

KODANAAD ESTATES.

1. MANAGER'S BUNGALOW. 2. INTERIOR OF FACTORY. 3. PRUNING TEA. 4. VIEW FROM ENTRANCE TO THE ESTATES. 5. FIELD OF TEA UNDER GREVILLEA SHADE.

Planting of tea bushes commenced in 1896 and continued almost uninterruptedly until 1902. The altitude of the estate ranges from 2,500 ft. to 3,000 ft., and the annual rainfall is about 100 in.

The "made" tea is sent to Calicut, where it is shipped to London. The three-storied factory on the estate is unusually well equipped with excellent plant and machinery, consisting of a 50-h.p. liquid fuel engine, a 25-h.p. oil engine, four rollers, two roll-breakers, a similar number of sifters, up-and-down draught dryers, and two withering fans, together with cutting and packing machinery.

Among other necessary buildings on the property are three bungalows of European design, one of which is used as a residence for the company's engineers.

The General Manager is Mr. T. S. Gillatt, who is assisted by Mr. D. P. O'Brien. Some 800 coolies are employed constantly.

About one-half of the village of Meppadi—in which there is a post office—is within the borders of the estate.

KODANAAD ESTATE

This estate, comprising about 950 acres, consists of three separate properties, namely: Bancadd and Warbieccan, acquired in 1867, and Kerrymanadd, obtained about a year later. The area devoted to the growing of tea is as follows: Kerrymanadd, 96 acres; Warbieccan, 112 acres; and Bancadd, 149 acres; together with an additional 10 acres of coffee-plants. Tea was first planted in the year 1870, and the greater portion of the land now under cultivation has been reclaimed from dense masses of bush and jungle. The tea which is grown upon these properties is submitted to the various processes of preparation in the factory of Bancadd. Messrs. Spencer & Co., Ltd., the well-known contractors for railway refreshment-rooms throughout Southern India, are purchasers of an enormous number of chests, but consignments are shipped direct to customers throughout the world in boxes containing 5 lb., 10 lb., or 15 lb. South America affords an excellent market, and a large quantity of specially labelled packages is sent to Bolivia. The main portion of the factory is 105 ft. in length and 22 ft. in width, but there are two wings to the building, each of which is about 15 ft. square. The machinery includes a 30-h.p. oil-engine (Blackstone), two 32-in. "Rapid" rollers, a green leaf sifter, 16 tray up-draught siroccos, together with two of size No. 1, and a desiccator (Brown). Among the excellent buildings may be mentioned a shed in which 8,000 lb. of leaf can be withered in a working day, together with a second withering store where abnormally wet leaves are dealt with. Then there are rooms where parts of boxes are fitted together, sorting, sifting, packing, and labelling-rooms, and, finally, the storing shed whence consignments are forwarded to all parts of the world. The works may be said to be complete in themselves as they not only possess an excellent plant for every stage of manufacture, but there are carpentering and repairing shops in which skilled workmen are employed.

KODANAAD

The Kodanaad estates are situated on a plateau of the Nilgiris, and the altitude ranges from 6,200 ft. to 6,600 ft. above the level of the sea. Tourists have discovered the charms of this neighbourhood, and pilgrimages are continually being made to "View Point," one of the highest ridges, from which an enchanting panorama is presented. Grim mountains are seen in the distance, looking for all the world like guardians of the dwellers in the plains which stretch as far as the eye can reach; the Moyar and other rivers sparkle in the sunlight 6,000 ft. below; an artificial lake—five acres in extent—is not the least beautiful part of the picture, and the restful shades of verdure, of forest, bush, and glen combine to form the most lovely scenery. The smaller species of game are fairly plentiful on these estates, while the larger fauna—so attractive to the true sportsman—consisting of elephant, sambur, and bison, are found in considerable numbers.

Samples of tea from these estates have been sent to various exhibitions in India and elsewhere, and the following are some of the honours which have been obtained: Gold medals at Madras in 1874, 1875, 1876, 1878, and 1879; at Melbourne in 1880; Calcutta in 1883; at Madras in 1895, 1896, 1897, 1899, and 1901; at St. Louis (U.S.A.) in 1904; at Milan in 1906; and at Bordeaux in 1907. Other awards of merit which have been received up to the present year (1915) include five first prizes, three gold medals, eight silver medals, three bronze ones, and seven diplomas, together with a number of first-class certificates. About 466 hands are employed regularly on the estates, and they are under the immediate control of the general manager, Mr. W. A. Cherry, with whom Mr. F. G. Lechler is associated as assistant manager.

There are two properties which are included in the title of the Kodanaad estates, namely, Madanaad, which belongs to the trustees of the late Mr. T. G. Hill, and Curzon, which is the property of Mrs. Elizabeth Hill and her daughters. The general management is in the hands of the late Mr. Hill's sons, who are the trustees, but Mr. Cherry is concerned in the keeping of the estate accounts.

MADANAAD

This property of 145 acres became a coffee and tea plantation in the year 1864, but it was not acquired by Mr. Hill until ten years later. The land is more than 6,000 ft. above sea-level, and this elevated situation is responsible for the large size of the coffee-bean and for the delightful aroma and flavour of the tea. The latter is grown under the shade of *grevillea*-trees, as this plan tends to increase the yield and to protect the young bushes from blight and other pests. There is a comfortable homestead on the property, and the adjoining factory is well equipped with the necessary machinery for the manufacture of both tea and coffee. The property is enclosed by a wire fence, as samburs were formerly in the habit of breaking down the growing trees. There is an excellent supply of water, the surrounding roads are good, and the nearest post and telegraph office is at Kotagiri, which is only eight miles distant. The average annual rainfall since the year 1905 is 53·76 in.

MAYFIELD

The name of Mayfield has been given to a group of four estates in the Nilgiris, belonging to the East India Tea and Produce Company, Ltd., for whom Messrs. Harrisons and Crosfield, Ltd., of Quilon, are agents. The total area is about 2,000 acres; 700 acres are planted with tea; coffee takes up 185 acres; and pepper is grown on 50 acres; but a further 500 or 600 acres will be brought under cultivation for tea at an early date. The factory is a three-storied building, containing three withering lofts, three

KODANAAD ESTATES.

1. THE FACTORY. 2. VIEW OF THE LAKE. 3. ASSISTANT'S BUNGALOW. 4. A GENERAL VIEW OF CURZON ESTATE, SHOWING BUNGALOW AND FACTORY.

MAYFIELD ESTATE.

1. Interior of Factory. 2. Pepper. 3. Coffee.

rollers, and three dryers, and the whole of the plant is worked by a "National" suction gas-engine of 40 h.p.

Coffee and pepper thrive remarkably well at Mayfield, and the produce is sent to Calicut to be cured prior to shipment to England. The greater portion of the estate is about 3,300 feet above sea-level, and the annual rainfall is about 80 in. The general manager is Mr. J. E. Bisset, who finds employment for about 1,200 labourers.

Mayfield is about 90 miles distant from Calicut, and 42 miles from Octacamund.

THE MEPPADI-WYNAAD TEA COMPANY, LTD.

The estates of Arrapetta, Kardoora, and Sentinel Rock—comprising 5,304 acres—situated in the Wynaad, were purchased in 1910, when the Meppadi-Wynaad Tea Company was formed. At that time there were 1,122 acres of matured tea bushes, 121 acres of younger ones, 125 acres of coffee, 276 acres of pepper, 57 acres of Para rubber, and 3,603 acres of reserve land. Other purchases of small properties took place, which made an aggregate of 5,304 acres, and subsequent extensions of the tea and rubber plantations increased the area of these to 1,569½ acres and 105½ acres respectively. All tea bushes, with the exception of 162 acres at Arrapetta, are fully matured.

There was a substantially-built factory on each of the estates when they were acquired by the company, but these buildings have been considerably enlarged, and important additions of modern machinery have been made. The manufactured tea is shipped by Messrs. Harrisons and Crosfield, Ltd., from Calicut to the London market.

The properties are most fortunately situated with regard to postal facilities, as the Meppadi post and telegraph office adjoin the Kardoora estate, while the Vellaramalla post office is 3½ miles distant from Sentinel Rock. The permanent buildings include bungalows, lines for coolies, stores, and sheds.

NELLIMUNDA

This estate of 781 acres is situated about 2 miles from the post and telegraph offices of Meppadi, in the district of Malabar, and 50 miles from Calicut, with which it is connected by the Government cart-road, and whence its crops of tea are shipped to England. Tea was first planted here in 1898, and nine years later Mr. C. E. Abbott became manager for the owner, Colonel F. J. Day, R.E., who resides in England.

Of the 781 acres, 376 acres have been planted with tea from jetinga seed, of which 150 acres are not yet in full bearing. The annual yield of tea is about 650 lb. per acre, and the whole crop, except dust, is consigned to London. In some of the fields the tea is grown under shade of *Albizzia Molucana*, planted years ago when coffee was grown.

The factory is being extended. The estate is in one of the best tea-growing districts in the Presidency; the climate is suitable, and the annual rainfall averages 120 in.

THE NILGIRIS BREWERY COMPANY

This brewery is the oldest in Southern India, and was purchased by Mr. Rungiah Gownden in the year 1898, although it is still conducted under the style of the Nilgiris Brewery Company. The buildings are situated near to the racecourse at Ootacamund, but a branch brewery has been established close to the cordite factory in the same town, which covers an area of about 27 acres. The plant is up-to-date in every respect, and the company have been fortunate in securing the custom of the military authorities at Madras, Trichinopoly, and other places in South India. Three types of beer, namely, English, Continental, and native, are brewed from the best hops obtainable from Kent and the United States of America, and the output is about 500 hogsheads a month. Mr. J. S. Peters, who has had several years' practical experience in the trade, is brewer and general manager.

THE NONSUCH AND UPPER DROOGE ESTATES

The estate is 7 miles distant from Coonoor, the second largest hill-station on the Nilgiris, and about 3 miles from the Karteri road-station on the Nilgiri Railway It lies at an elevation of about 6,000 ft., and has an average rainfall of 70-75 in. It consists of 451 acres, of which 250 acres are under tea, 30 acres under coffee, while 171 acres comprise forest and shola land. The bulk of the tea, with the exception of a very few acres, is all good jat, chiefly Manipuri, Jaboka, Arnakal, Singlo, and Banpara, with some 50 acres of good hybrids. Sixty acres of trees vary in age from thirty to forty years, while the remainder has been planted since the year 1904, the latest clearings having been opened out in 1910 and 1911. Given normal climatic conditions, tea in this locality is capable of yielding from 430 to 450 lb. to the acre of made tea, without manure, but with a regular manuring system, such as is in practice in Ceylon, from 550 to 600 lb. may be expected.

The crop in 1913-14 was 102,000 lb., including leaf purchased from a neighbouring estate, and the average yield per acre of "Nonsuch" tea in full bearing is 430 lb. to the acre. The trees are now being manured regularly every second year with "Complete" manures, on the system carried out for some years in Ceylon. Almost the entire crop is sold in the London market, where it has averaged during late years from 9d. to 9½d. net (after deducting cost of freight and London charges), and it has, in fact, topped the London market for complete invoices from Southern India. Some portion of the crop is sold in India, for which an average net price of 9½d. is obtained. The class of tea sold in this way is chiefly "dust," all other grades, with this exception, being, as stated, shipped to London. Teas sold in this way are put up in 1 lb. packets, or in tins containing from 5 lb. to 7 lb. according to grade, and these are forwarded by "value payable post" to the purchaser, except in the case of large orders, which are forwarded by rail. Tins containing 5 lb. of tea can also be sent to England by post (postage and duty prepaid), at a cost ranging from 8s. 10d. for the cheapest, to 12s. 8d. for the most expensive qualities. This system saves purchasers all trouble, as the tea is delivered at their addresses with all charges paid. Owing to the high prices for "bulk teas" on the London market, teas sold in this manner have not been advertised; sales, however, have steadily increased solely on the recommendations of customers, and this is chiefly due to the care that has always been taken to maintain a uniform quality. The question of "quality" is an important one for estates at a high elevation, and so long as "quality" is maintained, tea grown at high altitudes is not so subject to market fluctuations as that which is grown at lower levels, and this fact adds considerably to the value of "high elevation properties. Over a considerable area "Nonsuch" tea is grown under shade, chiefly "silver oaks" and *Albiz-*

MAYFIELD ESTATE.

1. View showing Superintendent's Bungalow. 2. Front View of Factory. 3. Six-year-old Tea.

NELLIMUNDA ESTATE.

1. Tea on Nellimunda Estate. 2. A General View. 3. The Factory, Arrapetta Estate. 4. Superintendent's Bungalow, Arrapetta Estate.

NONSUCH AND UPPER DROOG ESTATES.

1. View from Entrance. 2. Centre portion of the Estate, looking West. 3 Upper Droog Estate, looking West.

zia stipulata; the shelter acting as a protection in the dry months against drought and blights, and in the winter and in the south-west monsoon months against cold and wind. The estate is well drained and has excellent roads throughout. The factory and machinery are sufficient to deal with the crop, and there is ample withering accommodation.

The bungalow is situated close to the factory, and a very fine view of the ghat leading up from the plains and of the surrounding country is obtained. Coffee to the extent of 30 acres is also grown under shade, which, owing to the prevalence of the green bug, is kept tolerably dense. Experience has shown that this is the best and cheapest form of protection, but owing to this heavy shade the crops average only from 2 to 3 tons a year. Thirty-five acres of the opened land consist of forest, and the remainder is a good class of shola land well suited for tea.

The property belongs to Mr. L. L. Porter, of "Mostyn," Coonoor, Nilgiris, and Mr. G. A. Rutter, formerly of Ceylon and Travancore, acts as manager.

THE OUCHTERLONY VALLEY

Never in the annals of the planting world has better progress and success been manifested than in the affairs of the estate known as the "Ouchterlony Valley Estate," which claims its origin as far back as the early forties, despite the varying climatic conditions and the occasional depredations with which the management has had to contend. Many properties dating back from the opening of this vast estate have either dwindled down or have fallen into oblivion from one cause or another, but notwithstanding the adversities that this property has had to face from time to time, it stands at the present day second to none, financially and otherwise, in the vast and delightful plains of the Nilgiris. This certainly speaks volumes in favour of the timely efforts of the management and of the stability of their plans.

Before entering into details regarding the working of the estate, it may be interesting to give a brief semi-historial account of this particular part of the plains and its environs. Prominent among the structures of interest is the large Hindu Buswana Gudi Temple, on the Kelly estate, in which may be seen a large stone bull, which was found in the heart of the jungle before that estate was felled for the cultivation of coffee. In connection with this temple is held the annual festival known to the modern votary as the Maha Sivaratiri, when pilgrims from Ootacamund, Coimbatore, Mettapalayam, and the surrounding districts wend their way thither to do homage to the god to whom the temple is dedicated. Then there is the "fire-walking" temple on the Lauriston estate, in connection with which is held the annual fire-walking ceremony, performed by a sect of the Canarese coolies known as Devaraguadas. Before going through their religious performances, the men who perform this ceremony usually fast throughout the whole day. Of considerable interest, indeed, are the indigenous wild tribes of the place, including the Punniers—who are more or less slaves to a caste of people called Chetties in South-east Wynaad—the Bet Kurumbers, and the Jain (Honey) Kurumbers. The last-named are a very interesting tribe. When the late Mr. Henry Wapshare the father of the present popular and enterprising manager (Mr. J. H. Wapshare), was felling the jungle for cultivating coffee in the part of the country now known as the Balmadies estate, he suddenly came upon a gang of Jain Kurumbers frightened and huddled together. He surrounded them with the Canarese coolies who were felling the jungle at the time, and took them to his bungalow, shut them up in a godown, and fed and clothed them. When captured they were almost perfectly nude. After three or four days had elapsed he released them, by which time they had realized instinctively the nature of the late Mr. Henry Wapshare's object, and this fact, coupled with his kind and generous treatment, so impressed these men of the jungle that ever afterwards they used to flock to his bungalow with gifts of honey and other produce. This was in the early sixties. To this very day may be seen descendants of this particular tribe working industriously on the Naduvatam and Kelly estates. The late Mr. Henry Wapshare had, indeed, an exciting and laborious career, and one cannot but admire his energy when looking back to the time when he had no little amount of trouble in personally importing Canarese coolies from the Mysore country. In those days great difficulty was experienced and much expenditure incurred in obtaining labour, but the late Mr. Wapshare, who was practically the pioneer of Canarese labour in the Nilgiris, succeeded in altering matters, and this improvement, being followed up by the affable and kindly disposition of the present manager, Mr. J. H. Wapshare, labourers from the Canarese country are not only willing but anxious to obtain work under him. How the late Mr. Henry Wapshare would gather a large gang of coolies and march them along, and when in the heart of the jungle, between Bandipur and Tepikadu, the scare of robbers would cause the whole gang to beat a hasty retreat into their country, only to be re-collected with difficulty and marched back, is spoken of to this day. He was of a kind, lovable, and generous nature, and his genial disposition endeared him to the hearts of all who came in contact with him. As a mark of the great esteem and affection in which he was held, there now stands a welcome *chuttram* for coolies at Pykara, which was erected as a last tribute to his memory by his numerous friends among the planters.

The estate bears the name of the testator, the late Mr. James Ouchterlony, and had its origin in 1841, when it was first opened under a perpetual lease from the Raja of Nilambur at an annual rent of Rs. 2,020. The property is still in the possession of the Ouchterlony family, with Mr. J. H. Wapshare, a grandson, as manager for those who are interested in the Trust.

The coffee plantations are known by the following names: Barham, Forest Hill, Gudalore Mullay, Guynd, Helen, Hope, Kelly, Lauriston, Montrose, Sandy Hills, Suffolk, and Tulloos. The growing of coffee was commenced on the Lauriston property in 1842, the planter being a Mr. Wright, who came from Jamaica to be manager for Mr. Ouchterlony. The entire estate comprises about 21,000 acres, of which about 4,045 acres have been cultivated, and 3,700 acres are producing coffee. A check was given to this branch of agriculture by the ravages of the "borer" (*Xyletrecchus quadrupes*), which destroyed portions of several plantations in the early eighties. There are two species of this pest—namely, the white and the red—and they somewhat resemble an ordinary small-sized caterpillar. Their mode of destruction, however, is novel. They invariably begin gnawing from the top of the coffee-stem and gradually work their way downwards to the root, consuming the core in their progress, leaving nothing in the end but

THE OUCHTERLONY VALLEY ESTATES.

1. Pulp House, Guynd Estate. 2. Coffee Store, Guynd Estate. 3. Tea on New Hope Estate. 4 Tea Factory, New Hope Estate.

the bare wet hollow bark to rot. Their ravages were felt seveiely, and the management had to endure very anxious times. Numerous remedies were tried, but it was not until 1890 that "shade" was introduced by the late Mr. Henry Wapshare and found to be successful in helping to keep the pest under control. This "shade" was obtained by rows of silver oak-trees, interspersed with dadap (*lithosperma erythrina*), which afforded that sufficiency of shelter which is so essential to the successful growing of coffee. Each coffee-tree in the plantation receives the following dressing: 6 oz. of bones and poonac in the months of September and October, and 2 oz. of refined saltpetre in February and March, and fertility is further assisted by the application of cattle manure whenever practicable. The yield during the season 1913-14 reached a total of 850 tons of coffee, which gives an average of nearly 510 lb. to the acre. The estate has its own curing works and factory on the banks of the Beypore River in Malabar, within a few miles from the ports of Beypore and Calicut, but no less than 75 miles distant from the estate itself, and they are in charge of a European superintendent. The mode of transport is by means of carts, which occupy ten days in their journey. The works comprise very extensive barbecues or drying ground; hulling, peeling, and sizing machines, packing sheds, and three lofts for garbling, while all the machinery, which is thoroughly up to date, is run by steam-power. The process of manufacture is an interesting one; the pulp of the ripe berry, or "cherry," as it is frequently called, is first removed on each estate, and the bean, which is curiously named "parchment" coffee, is then ready to be sent in carts to the curing works for the drying process. The beans remain in the parchment state for some weeks; they are then "peeled" after exposure to the heat of the sun, and are finally "garbled" by hand. The pulping-house at Guynd is one of the largest of its kind in Southern India, and was opened in the year 1877 by Lord Lytton during his Viceroyalty in India. It bears the following inscription: "This building was opened by Lord Lytton, Viceroy of India, on the 17th September, 1877." The coffee, when fully prepared, is transferred from the curing works to Beypore for shipment to England under the brand "Naidoobatam." From time to time the manager replaces any decayed or unprofitable trees, but it is not his intention at present to increase the acreage for this produce.

The tea plantations are known as Aratapara, Hope, Naiduvatam, and New Hope. Tea was first planted in or about the year 1874, but it was nearly fifteen years later before the industry was taken up in a serious manner. This date (1889) coincided with the appearance of disease among the coffee plantations. The greater portion of the plants of the Aratapara, Hope, and New Hope estates (covering over 550 acres) are of the Assam China hybrid variety, and the average annual return is about 150,000 lb. of "made" tea. The soil around each bush is fertilized with about 4 oz. of artificial manure, which is manufactured by Messrs. T. Stanes & Co., of Coimbatore. The factory is situated on the "New Hope" property, and it consists of four rollers, two drying machines (the latter run on endless chains), one sorting machine, and an automatic packing plant and roll breaker (driven by a turbine), which is capable of dealing with 400,000 lb. of "made" tea annually. A very considerable amount of capital has been invested in the installation of machinery and appliances of an approved type, but the expenditure has been fully justified by the excellent quality of the parcels of tea which are consigned direct to London. The Naiduvatam tea estate, of about 120 acres, was opened in 1896, and the yield of green tea for last year reached the very satisfactory total of 200,000 lb. About 4,000 native labourers find constant employment. Each of the estates detailed above is represented by a superintendent and an assistant, the whole being controlled and managed by Mr. Wapshare. The Guynd estate, which is the largest, has a European superintendent in charge. There is also a European supervisor, who visits the different estates daily and submits his reports to the manager.

Contentment and happiness prevail as the order of the day throughout the vast estate—thanks to the energetic endeavours of Mr. Wapshare, who has been untiring in his efforts to bring about this gratifying state of affairs.

The surroundings are made as bright as possible, and the employees enjoy many privileges of which hundreds of thousands of their fellow-countrymen are deprived. First of all there is a well-equipped dispensary with a qualified resident medical officer in daily attendance. A hospital has been opened, and any man, woman, or child on the estate is given free advice, free hospital comforts, and free medicines. Such facilities are almost enough to tempt a man to go on the sick list; but there is no malingering at the Ouchterlony Valley, as the relationship between the manager and the work-people is not based upon a mere contract for certain services to be performed in return for a specific sum of money. Another privilege which these people enjoy is a market, where provisions, clothing, domestic appointments, and sundry goods and articles can be obtained at reasonable prices. This is considered a great boon to the employees, who formerly had to go to Gudalur, a distance of no less than 20 miles to and fro, forgoing their Sunday's rest for the purpose. This market was opened by Mr. M. Young, I.C.S., Collector of the Nilgiris, in December 1912, in honour of the Coronation of his Majesty the King-Emperor, and it is named the "King George Market."

There is a Roman Catholic Church on the Suffolk estate, and another in course of erection on the New Hope estate, which is being built by subscription, for the benefit of the increasing number of Christians. A cemetery, maintained and looked after by the proprietors, exists on the Helen estate, where members of the European community are interred.

The Ouchterlony estate was one of the first in Southern India to undergo development for coffee and tea plantations, and it has been honoured by visits on various occasions from Lord Wenlock and other Governors of the Presidency of Madras. A considerable quantity of the land lies at an elevation of about 3,000 ft., but the higher regions are fully 4,000 to 5,000 ft. above the level of the sea. There is a post office at Guynd, which is one of the group of properties included in the estate.

Herds of elephants may be seen upon the waste lands during the summer season, and every one which is shot or captured becomes the property of the Raja. Those who are fond of stalking may follow the sambur, panther, and occasionally the tiger; the jungle sheep is strongly in evidence, and wild pig may be obtained. Malabar carp were introduced by the late Mr. Henry Wapshare and the late Mr. H. Knox from the Ouchterlony Valley to the Pykara River, with the result that they have to a considerable extent driven away those

THE OUCHTERLONY VALLEY ESTATES.

1. COFFEE PLANTED IN 1842, LAURISTON ESTATE. 2. BUSWANA TEMPLE, KELLY ESTATE. 3. GARBLING. 4. COFFEE BEING MEASURED FROM THE CARTS

THE OUCHTERLONY VALLEY ESTATES.

1. Garbling Loft. 2. Sizing and Packing Store. 3. Engine-room and Peeling Shed. 4. General View of the Coffee Curing Works, Malabar

speckled beauties which are the delight of the ordinary angler.

The annual rainfall throughout the whole of the estate varies from 80 to 90 in.

The manager's office has a staff of efficient clerks for the preparation of the various estate accounts.

Except in the proportions of half of the Guynd property and half of the Lauriston (which is owned by Mr. A. C. Campbell), of one-third Hope, and one-ninth Lauriston (owned by Mrs. A. T. Ouchterlony), and one-ninth of the Suffolk estate, which is owned by the estate of the late Mrs. E. Fonseca, the remainder of the entire property and uncultivated lands, including a spacious house called "Rosemount," in Ootacamund, a small bungalow in Gundlupet, in the district of Mysore, and 40 acres of land at Bandipur, also in the Mysore district, are owned by Mr. J. H. Wapshare (son of Mrs. M. E. Wapshare, a daughter of Mr. James Ouchterlony), and by Mrs. H. H. Johnson (eldest daughter of Mr. James Ouchterlony), whose interest will revert at her death to her children, Miss E. Mabel Johnson, Miss Violet E. Johnson, Mr. Gordon McLeod Johnson, and Mrs. Helen E. Norman, and to Miss Helen M. L. Ouchterlony, Miss Ida G. Ouchterlony, Miss Harriet T. Ouchterlony, and Mr. Peyton Breay, daughters and grandson of the late Mrs. F. E. Ouchterlony (daughter-in-law of Mr. James Ouchterlony).

PANORA TEA AND PRODUCE COMPANY, LTD.

The head offices of this company are situated at 14 Billiter Street, London, E.C. The company was formed in January 1911, with the object of purchasing certain properties for the production of tea, coffee, pepper, and other produce in South Wynaad, in the Malabar district of South India. The company's estates contain 4,813 acres of land, of which 1,708 acres are cultivated on six properties, viz. Panora, 238 acres; Erramaculla, 576 acres; Poothacoolie, 222 acres; Perindotty, 439 acres; Elstone, 123 acres; and Colarie, 110 acres. Of these cultivated areas 1,466 acres are under tea, 75 acres coffee, and 167 acres pepper.

Tea is the principal product, and consists chiefly of the dark leaf Manipuri variety, which does remarkably well, the soil and climate being eminently suitable. Some of the oldest tea in the district exists on the Perindotty estate, and it was planted by the late Mr. J. R. Malcolm for Messrs. Parry & Co., of Madras, the pioneers of tea-planting in the district. The first planted tea, now some 43 years of age, is still flourishing, and yields largely, proving the productive nature of the soil. There are two well-equipped factories on the properties; one, a new one, has just been completed on Erramaculla, and the other on Perindotty is now being considerably extended.

The estates are situated on the northern slopes of the Western Ghauts and form a compact group. They have a pleasant climate, and the average annual rainfall varies from 100 to 150 in.

The management of the company in India is in the hands of Mr. B. E. Malcolm, a planter of long experience in South India, who is assisted by Mr. G. R. R. Carson-Parker and Mr. J. R. Blackham.

The nearest post office is on the Perindotty estate, and the telegraph office is at Meppadi. The properties are linked to the nearest port of Calicut by a good high road, the distance being 45 miles.

The London agents are Messrs. Peirce, Leslie & Co., and the firm's Indian office at Calicut conducts the coast agency.

From 1,500 to 1,700 hands are employed on the properties.

PERRENGODDA

The Perrengodda property is favourably situated at an altitude of some 2,500 feet above the level of the sea, and the soil consists of rich dark loam, which is easily worked. It belongs to the East India Tea and Produce Company, Ltd., and it consists of 4,851 acres of land, of which 587 acres are planted with mixed tea. Seedlings were first planted in the year 1884, and there is only one other estate in the district of Malabar which has been successfully cultivated for tea for so long a period.

Mr. T. P. Gauld, who became manager in 1913, is assisted in his duties by Mr. H. C. Coverley, and he has constant work for from 600 to 700 coolies. The factory is a fine three-storied building which has a capacity for dealing with 300,000 lb. of tea annually. The plant includes four rollers (by Jackson), four dryers (one of the Venetian type, two Davidson's down-draughts, and one Chula), three sifters, cutting and packing machines, and a steamer, boiler, and hydro for the making of green tea. All of this machinery is driven by a water turbine and a "National" 50-h.p. suction gas engine.

The whole crop is sent to Calicut, where it is shipped to England. The property has two excellent bungalows, and it is situated about 3 miles from the post and telegraph office at Vayitri.

POOTOOMULLA

Pootoomulla is the name by which two adjoining estates near Meppadi, in the district of Malabar, are usually known. About 966 acres are planted with tea, chiefly of a light, indigenous kind, but it is proposed to cultivate at least another hundred acres as soon as the manager is able to obtain an adequate supply of labourers. There is a large factory on the property, and its plant includes five rollers, two roll-breakers, three sifters, and two withering fans. The average annual yield is about 760 lb. to the acre, and the whole of the crop is forwarded direct to England for sale. The property belongs to the East India Tea and Produce Company, Ltd., and the manager, Mr. A. D. McBain, has three European assistants, and he finds employment for between 1,200 and 1,300 coolies.

RICHMOND ESTATE

The occupier of this estate—Mr. D. H. McLeod—has been engaged in growing tea since the year 1889, but it was not until 1907 that he became the tenant of Richmond, the owners of which are the heirs of Mr. James Labouchere and of Mr. J. F. Marshall, who resided in England. Between the years 1897 and 1907 a considerable amount of gold-mining took place on this property, but that which was found was so firmly embedded in pyrites that the working of a mine as a paying concern was entirely out of the question. Indigenous Assam tea-seeds were imported by Colonel Minchin in 1867, and the fruitful bushes of to-day have sprung from that stock. There are about 142 acres of full-bearing trees, and some 43 acres are now being planted.

Mr. McLeod has his own factory, in which 100,000 lb. of tea are dried in the course of a year, and it is an interesting fact that the motive-power for all the mechanical appliances in that building is obtained by working bullocks.

PANORA TEA AND PRODUCE COMPANY, LTD.

1. Factory at Erramaculla. 2. General View, Erramaculla Estate. 3. Portion of Tea on Erramaculla Estate. 4. Pluckers among the Tea at Panora. 5. Young Tea, Panora Estate.

PERRENGODDA ESTATE.

1. Manager's Bungalow. 2. View from the Office, showing Tea. 3. Perrengodda Factory

Each annual crop is sent to the port of Calicut, whence it is shipped direct to London. Richmond is about 4,000 ft. above sea-level, and it has an average rainfall of 137 in. Two hundred labourers are employed under the supervision of an overseer, but Mr. McLeod——like the majority of the planters in the Presidency — complains bitterly of the difficulty of obtaining the requisite number of hands. The nearest post office is at Pundalur, which is only half a mile distant. The nearest telegraph office is Devala, distant about 3 miles.

Mr. McLeod is interested in the management of several other estates, including one of 1,335 acres at Meppadi, 600 acres of which are planted with pepper, vines, coffee, tea, and rubber.

RIPPLE VALE AND IBEX LODGE

Ibex Lodge, the residence of Mr. D. Elkington, the owner of Ripple Vale and Ibex Lodge Hill estates, is so called from the fact that it faces the well-known Ibex Hill, on the rugged heights of which ibex are frequently seen, from the bungalow which stands some 5,700 ft. above sea-level.

The property consists of 350 acres of useful tea land, and about 176 acres and 20 acres respectively are cultivated for the growing of tea and coffee. The earliest tea plants were put down by the late Mr. William Mullaly in the year 1864, and these are still vigorous, whilst Mr. Elkington, who purchased the estates in 1912, after spending some seventeen years as a tea-planter in Ceylon, is annually adding to the acreage already under this product. The teas are packed in full and half-chests, and are sold on the Colombo market under the name of "Ibex Lodge." The factory in which they are made is a thoroughly modern structure, and it is the first three-storied building to be erected for this purpose on the Nilgiri Hills. It is equipped with a 10-h.p. liquid fuel engine (Ruston, Proctor & Co.), "Economic," "Rapid," and "Little Giant" rolling machines, two Davidson's Siroccos, and sifters. The average annual yield of dry tea is between 400 and 500 lb. to the acre, but this is likely to increase under the policy of clean cultivation and manuring which the proprietor adopts.

The cultivation of coffee in Southern India has decreased considerably in recent years owing to the prevalence of "green bug," but this pest has not been troublesome on Ibex Hill, and fair crops of exceptionally delicately flavoured high-grown Nilgiri coffee are secured, which are sold to local buyers as "parchment," though a portion is reserved which is sold as "beans" at Rs. 1 per lb., post free to inquirers.

The proprietor is ably assisted by his writer, Mr. A. Venkataswami Moodelliar, and he employs about 150 hands permanently.

Large game is to be found in the district; tigers, panthers, bears, and also small game, such as woodcock, quail, jungle, and spur fowl and hares.

The rainfall, the figures of which have been kept on the estate since 1888, averages 75 in. Ripple Vale is 7 miles distant from Coonoor post office, and is 4 miles by road from the Nilgiris railway at Kartary Road station.

ROB ROY

Frequent reference has been made in these pages to the exceedingly beautiful scenery of the Nilgiris, and a number of more than usually fine views are obtained from the bungalow on the Rob Roy estate, which is not far from the hill station of Kotagiri, where the elevation above sea-level is about 6,000 ft. Substantial buildings, including pulping-houses, factory, sheds, and stores, have been erected, and the whole of the machinery necessary for the preparation of the coffee bean for the curing process is driven by water power. A nursery for the rearing of young plants has been established, and this enables the owner (Mr. E. Sydenham Clarke) to replenish the plantation from time to time with young, healthy trees.

THE ROSE AND CROWN BREWERY COMPANY, LTD.

According to the "Madras District Gazetteer" of the Nilgiris, compiled by Mr. W. Francis, I.C.S., brewing on the hills dates back as far as the year 1826, when it would seem that the hill-grown barley was very much better than it is now. It would also appear that hop-growing was tried, but without success. Situated just off the main road from Ootacamund to Coonoor, and exactly halfway between these two places, is the Rose and Crown Brewery, which was opened in 1895. It changed hands in 1900, was subsequently attached by the Civil Courts, and was purchased by the present company in 1903. A large business is carried on with the troops at Wellington and on the west coast, and with the general public. A large supply of native beer is sent out daily to the taverns on the hills. English beers brewed for Europeans and troops is an all-malt liquor made with the finest Kent and Bohemian hops. Very special attention is also paid in regard to the system of brewing for bottling purposes. Native beer is brewed largely from jaggery, or crude cane-sugar, but in recent years rules and restrictions have been laid down which require that at least 2 bushels of malt and 2 lb. of hops must be used for each hogshead. Excellent stout is also brewed and supplied in cask or bottle. The company do all their own malting, and have lately extended their malting area by the erection of a fine building. The barley used for malting is obtained from the Punjab. Very little locally grown barley is now obtainable, and that which can be purchased has deteriorated greatly, owing, probably, to the curious methods of cultivation which are employed by local agriculturists. The malt, when kiln-dried, is brushed and cleaned by special machinery, and is then stored in sets of large bins, which are made so as to be absolutely proof against damp. Coming down from the three malting and kiln-houses one arrives at a room where the malt is ground in a special machine, which is worked by a 4½-h.p. oil-engine. Below this room are the mashing-rooms, where the first process of brewing commences. Downwards, again, one reaches two large copper vessels capable of boiling some 2,500 gallons of liquor. The next floor consists of a large room containing a hop back, as well as large open vessels for cooling and refrigerating. Below this, again, is the fermenting-room, in which are eleven huge vats, and alongside these are several large open vats where the beer is finally racked before being run down to the two cellars which are on the floor directly beneath. Adjoining the brewery is the engine-room, which contains a large vertical boiler of more than sufficient power to work all the machinery of the brewery on the lower floors. A few years back the company imported a Simon's grain-drier. The grain used in brewing is brought from the mash-tun and fed into the drier, and this drying machine is worked by a 6-h.p. Marshall's

RICHMOND ESTATE.

1. Factory. 2. Richmond Estate Bungalow (Superintendent's Residence). 3. General View, showing new Clearing.

THE ROSE AND CROWN BREWERY COMPANY, LTD.

1. General View. 2. Bungalow. 3. Bottling.

THE ROSE AND CROWN BREWERY COMPANY, LTD.

1. Copper Room. 2. Interior of Malt House. 3. Engine-room. 4. Fermenting-room.

vertical engine. The wet grain direct from the mash-tun given to milch cattle greatly increases the quantity of milk, and in the dry state it is a very highly nutritious food for horses and cattle. Near to the engine-room is a large coopering yard, where casks are made and repaired. On the lowest floor of all, below the cellars, is the bottling department, with its cleaning, filtering, pasteurizing, filling, corking, and labelling machinery. All bottle-wiring and capsuling is done by hand. A carbonating machine and a counter pressure filling machine have just been received from the continent of Europe, and these are in the course of erection. The company's offices and dispatching yard are on the brewery premises. A large acreage of land is owned by the company in the neighbourhood of the brewery, and all of it is planted with trees which will provide excellent fuel for many years to come. The general manager's (Mr. Stephen Bayly) bungalow is situated close to the brewery in delightful surroundings, and it commands a most perfect view of the hills for many miles around. The garden, with its profusion of roses and flowers of all descriptions, is a thing to be seen and envied. The elevation is 6,800 ft. above the sea-level. The climate is grand, and even in the south-west monsoon, which bursts in June and lasts until September, it is quite pleasant. The full force of the monsoon is not felt here, for as it travels inwards from the coast it gradually weakens, and every station farther east of the travelling current experiences less rainfall. The average rainfall is 50 in. per annum, and this is very evenly distributed. The average maximum temperature is 70° F., and the minimum is 44°. Frost is never experienced, and the hottest months are April and May, just before the setting in of the south-west monsoon.

SENTINEL ROCK

The Sentinel Rock estate (which overlooks the Nilambur Valley) is now owned by the Meppadi-Wynaad Tea Company, Ltd., and the whole of the plantation consists of 343 acres.

The factory contains the usual machinery and plant, such as rollers, roll-breakers, dryers, Davidson's rotary tea-sifter, and withering fans, while the motive power is derived from a 40-h.p. "National" suction gas engine.

The bulk of the crop, consisting of high-class tea, is sent to Calicut or Madras for shipment to London.

There is a pleasantly situated bungalow on the property, and lines for coolies have been constructed. The estate is about 4 miles distant from the Vellaramalla post office, and 10 miles from the post and telegraph office at Meppadi.

Mr. B. D. Darkin is manager of the place, and he employs about 350 coolies.

SUTTON AND LOUISIANA ESTATES

Every agriculturist who is worthy of the name realizes that pure seeds of the finest quality are absolutely essential to the growth of a satisfactory crop. Climatic conditions may be as favourable as possible, rain may fall in desirable quantities when and where it is most needed, and yet the produce may hardly be worth harvesting simply because the seeds were worthless. This is equally as true with regard to the tea and coffee plantations of India as it is with the magnificent wheat and barley-fields of the Western world. Hence it follows that the proprietors of these estates have set apart some five acres for the growing of seeds, and they have garnered as much as 50 maunds in a single year, although a fair average yield is about 30 maunds. When the proprietors bought the estate in the year 1909 they found the tea-seed, but it was of the best jat type and some of it was from twenty to twenty-five years old. The properties are 495 acres in extent, and they are owned by Messrs. J. Stanes, J. B. Vernede, and N. J. Stanes, the last-named being general manager. There are 230 acres of tea and 100 acres of coffee, but it is intended to cultivate a further 140 acres in the course of the next two years, leaving a small area of about 20 acres, which is not suitable for plantation purposes. Special care is bestowed upon the sowing of selected seeds in the four nurseries which have been erected, and the young trees are only transplanted when they have obtained a good start. The varieties of tea which are cultivated are about equally divided between light-leaf Assam and dark Manipuri, and all the bushes are sheltered by rows of *Grevillea robusta*, which have been planted about 48 ft. apart. The manager regards the provision of effective shade as one of the most important factors in the production of nicely coloured tea of excellent aroma.

A factory is under construction at the time of publication. The firm have their own pulping-house, in which there is an abundant supply of water for the washing of the parchment in the various processes through which it is passed, but the curing of the bean takes place at Coimbatore.

The properties are about 5,000 ft. above the level of the sea, and the rainfall averages about 60 in. per annum. Two bungalows and coolie quarters have been built, and they are about $1\frac{3}{4}$ miles distant from Kulakambie, which is the nearest post and telegraph office.

One European assistant is employed, and about 200 labourers are required constantly.

SYLK'S HOTEL, OOTACAMUND

The trying nature of the summer heat in Madras from about the 1st of April to the end of October drives quite a multitude of residents to seek the clear and bracing air of the hills, and there is no place in the Presidency which has greater attractions in the way of scenery and climate than Ootacamund, the principal town in the district of the Nilgiris.

It is situated on the summit of a plateau which is about 7,500 feet above the level of the sea, and it contains a large number of handsome private residences and public buildings. Many first-class hotels and boarding houses are open for the reception of visitors, and Sylk's Hotel is now generally recognized as the favourite in the town, familiarly known as the "Queen of Hill Stations." The premier position of Sylk's at "Ooty" is, in all probability, due to the fact that it is a branch establishment of Messrs. G. d'Angelis & Son, of Madras, whose name alone is a sufficient guarantee that the service from cellar to drawing-room will be unimpeachable.

Visitors are received from April 1st to October 31st, and there is accommodation for about 40 persons in family suites, bachelors' quarters, and detached bungalows.

Messrs. d'Angelis & Son took over the house in the year 1894, and they at once began to make additions and improvements to the building, while the whole of the interior has been entirely refurnished. The majority of the residents are pleasure-seekers and sportsmen, and the hotel is within a stone's-throw of the principal amusements. The Gymkhana Club has made provision for cricket, tennis, badminton, golf, boating, and other games; race meetings are held at frequent intervals, while meets of the famous

SENTINEL ROCK.

1. THE FACTORY AT SENTINEL ROCK.

2. SUPERINTENDENT'S BUNGALOW.

3 VIEW OF TEA.

SUTTON AND LOUISIANA ESTATES.

1. Sutton Bungalow. 2. Tea Clearing, 1911 Planting. 3. Seed-bearers, Tiamully Jat. 4. Tea Clearing, 1913 Planting

SUTTON AND LOUISIANA ESTATES.

1 AND 2. YOUNG COFFEE IN BLOSSOM. 3. AND 4. FIELDS OF OLD COFFEE IN BLOSSOM.

Ooty foxhounds are occasionally held in the grounds of the hotel.

The proprietors of Sylk's are unremitting in their personal attention to the comfort of their guests, and visitors can always rely upon cleanliness, good cooking, and civility by servants.

TAIMULLAI AND OTHER ESTATES

Taimullai is one of about seventy properties, most of which are in the State of Mysore, and in the district of the Nilgiris, all of which are owned by Messrs. A. R. Hajee Fakir Mahomed Sait & Sons, of Sultan Hall, Ootacamund. Details of only a few of these can be given here.

The Taimullai estate, in the Nilgiris, has been cultivated to the extent of about 330 acres, and the major portion of this area is devoted to the growing of coffee. The property is equipped with all necessary buildings, including a nice bungalow, store, pulping-house, and drying greens, and the coffee is forwarded to curing factories at Tellicherry, whence it is shipped to England.

There are some 204 acres under coffee and tea—principally the former—on the Sultana estate, which adjoins Taimullai, and is about 4,500 ft. above sea-level. The property comprises about 250 acres, and there is only a very small area which is unsuitable for cultivation.

The Upper Taimullai property, in the district of the Nilgiris, consists of 75 acres of land, the greater portion of which is producing coffee, together with 50 acres which are eminently suitable for the cultivation of tea.

Malaisen Gudda comprises 536 acres, with 304 acres under coffee. It is situated near to the post-office at Herebellaloo, in the district of Kadur, in the State of Mysore; Kullmudie, in the same neighbourhood, has an area of 196 acres, of which 124 are coffee land; while the Ambina Coodigay property is planted with 67 acres of coffee, 6 acres of arecanut, and an acre of cardamoms, out of a total area of 89 acres. The Halathoray property, and a large number of other estates in the same ownership, are very productive in coffee, pepper, tea, and cardamoms, and the greater portion of each year's harvest is shipped direct to London for sale. Each estate has its own pulping-house and other suitable buildings, and a separate manager is in charge of the larger holdings.

TERRAMIA

This property, consisting of 580 acres of land, was purchased by Mr. A. S. Dandison in the year 1903, when the plantations consisted of 100 acres of tea and 150 acres of coffee. Twenty acres of coffee were subsequently abandoned, and the estate now (near the close of the year 1914) shows 158 acres of tea and 130 acres of coffee. Coonoor and Ootacamund are 15 and 18 miles distant, respectively, while the nearest post office is at Kullakamby, which can be reached by a walk of about forty minutes. The property is rather more than 5,000 ft. above the level of the sea, and the records for the past thirty years of the rainfall—which is at present about 55 in. annually and well distributed—show that there has been a steady increase during late years.

It is the intention of the proprietor to develop the estate to the utmost possible extent, and as there are very few acres indeed which cannot be worked, Mr. Dandison is preparing for future planting by having a nursery in which seedlings are carefully reared. The more recently planted tea-bushes, which cover about 50 acres, belong to the Assam or Manipuri kinds, the other trees being good hybrids. Shelter from sun and wind tends to improve the yield and quality of the tea, and it is believed that it minimizes the risks of pests. Australian silver oaks (*Grevillea robusta*) have been planted, as they have proved to be most suitable for the climate.

The coffee plantation at Terramia has been established on the Brazilian system, which is that only 300 trees are planted to the acre instead of the more usual number of 1,200. This plan ensures a large yield from the trees, but it can only be adopted at high altitudes where the climate and the rainfall are suitable. The beans are pulped and dried on the estate, and the cured coffee is either sold in Coimbatore or is shipped direct to England.

The factory contains two rolling machines, an 8-h.p. (nominal) steam-engine (Marshall, Sons & Co.), a roll breaker by Walker, two Siroccos, and a pulping machine for the coffee. The premises are very conveniently arranged, and they include a box-making and packing-rooms, offices, withering-room, a coffee store, together with several lofts and other rooms.

About 20 acres of the property have been planted with blue gum-trees in order to provide fuel for factory purposes.

There are two well-built bungalows for the manager and assistant, and the policy of housing the coolies well makes the estate a favourite one with labourers. The plantations are ably managed by Mr. H. E. H. Sladen.

Terramia is a capital sporting estate, as there is no lack of tigers, sambur, panthers, jungle sheep, and bears, while smaller game, including an occasional woodcock and snipe, is very plentiful.

THIA SHOLA ESTATES COMPANY, LTD.

Very insignificant is the percentage of agriculturists or horticulturists in Southern India who realize the necessity for (1) a rotation of crops, (2) an intelligent system of manuring, and (3) the sowing of selected pure seeds; and yet satisfactory yields of cereals, roots, flowers, fruit, tea, coffee, spices, or other produce cannot be expected unless these aids to cultivation are to some extent practised. Since the beginning of the twentieth century, however, private individuals, as well as the Government, have, by instruction and example, rendered invaluable assistance to farmers and others.

The Thia Shola Estates Company, Ltd., has, since its formation in 1902, been in the van in connection with the scientific culture of land, in the cultivation and preparation of both coffee and tea, and in the manufacture of the latter. There are four separate properties, having a total of 907 acres, belonging to the company; 222 acres are planted with tea, 133 acres are under coffee, and another 150 acres of tea are to be opened up as speedily as possible. Some of the tea was planted in the early sixties, but the majority of the bushes—of the Assam hybrid variety—were put in between the years 1898 and 1913.

Acacia decurrens hedges have been grown for the purpose of sheltering and mulching the younger plants, but these are not considered necessary for the older and established bushes. The average yield to the acre from young and old bushes is at present comparatively small, but with time and careful cultivation of the land, and with proper attention to manuring and pruning, a much more satisfactory return is assured. A portion of the crop for the season 1913-14 realized an average of 10½d. lb. in London, but the bulk of the crop was sold in the Colombo market.

The factory is a substantial two-storied building, and contains the usual accom-

TERRAMIA ESTATE.

1. View of Tea from the Bungalow. 2. Tea on the Hill-side. 3. View of Coffee. 4. Coffee with Fruit. 5. Factory.

THIA SHOLA ESTATES.

1. General View from the Entrance. 2. The Factory, Thia Shola. 3. Manager's Bungalow, Thia Shola. 4. The Roll-Call

THIA SHOLA ESTATES.

1 AND 3. TEA AT CARRINGTON ESTATE. 2. NO. 7 TEA AT THIA SHOLA. 4. COFFEE AT THIA SHOLA.

modation for withering, rolling, drying, packing, and other processes. All the machinery is of a thoroughly up-to-date character, and includes a 16-h.p. liquid-fuel engine (Hornsby), two rollers ("Economic" and "Little Giant"), two dryers ("Sirocco" and a "Colombo" tea-dryer with Chula air-heater), a deflector (MacDonald), and a roll breaker, a tea sifter, and a packing machine—all Jackson's patent.

The coffee is pulped on the estate and sent down in the form of "parchment" coffee to Coimbatore, where it is cured for shipment direct to London for sale. It was first grown on these properties in 1876.

The company's estates consist of undulating hills, divided by valleys, through which flow streams reminding one of Cowper's—

. . . rills that slip
Through the cleft rock, and chiming as they fall
Upon loose pebbles, lose themselves at length
In matted grass, that with a livelier green
Betrays the secret of their silent course.

On the sides of the hills are beautiful woods known as "sholas," and farther, in the distance, are the grass-covered slopes of a higher level of the Ootacamund plateau. The altitude varies in different portions of the estate, but the average height is about 6,500 ft. above sea-level. This ensures a keen and healthy atmosphere, and no more ideal situation for a residence in the beautiful Nilgiris could be selected than that upon which the company's two bungalows have been erected.

Planters in the Nilgiris are indefatigable in their undertakings, be they connected with their daily work or with sport and amusements, and round Thia Shola they have every opportunity of bagging tiger, panther, sambur, bear, wild dog, moose deer, jungle sheep, ibex, quail, jungle and spur fowl, snipe, and hares.

The manager is Mr. G. W. Church, who employs about 200 labourers, who are principally Canarese and Badagas, with a few Tamils and Kurumbas at times. The bulk of the labour force comes from the Mysore Province. The directors of the company are the Hon. Mr. E. F. Barber, M.L.C., and Messrs. B. A. Marden and C. D. Chilcott.

The beautiful summer residential town of Ootacamund is about 22 miles distant from the estates; the nearest post office is at Kilkunda, and the nearest telegraphic office is at Kulakamby, which is some 17 miles distant.

WENTWORTH

The Wentworth estate, of 3,126 acres, is situated 1 mile distant from the post and telegraph offices at Cherambadi, in the district of the Nilgiris. It was purchased by the East India Tea and Produce Company, Ltd., and the planting of tea was commenced in the year 1897. About 450 acres have been placed under this crop up to the present time, but this area will probably be extended.

The factory at Wentworth is a fine three-storied building, 250 ft. in length by 48 ft. in width, and it has space for spreading 17,000 lb. of green leaf, and is capable of turning out 520,000 lb. of "made" tea in a twelvemonth. The manufacturing plant is up-to-date in every respect, and it consists of five rollers, four firing machines, one roll-breaker, three sifters, and a packing machine, while the engine-room contains two "National" gas engines, and one driven by oil. The whole of the produce is sent to Calicut—a distance of 63 miles—for shipment to London. About 550 coolies are employed here annually.

The Cherambadi estate adjoins Wentworth, and the crop is sent to the latter place to be manufactured.

Mr. P. Guard is superintendent on the Cherambadi estate, and Mr. E. R. Howlett, who holds a similar position at Wentworth, is assisted by Mr. E. A. Cheeseman.

WOODBRIAR

The Woodbriar tea and coffee estate belongs to a private company which is registered in Ceylon, and it is 1½ miles distant from the post office at Kallakumby and about 9 miles from the important town of Coonoor in the Nilgiris. The property is some 800 acres in extent: 300 acres are devoted to the growing of tea, and 60 acres are planted with coffee, while the remainder is being brought into cultivation at the rate of about 100 to 200 acres annually. The majority of the tea-bushes are of the Assam Hybrid variety. Some of these are twenty years of age, but very many have been growing for about ten years only. The cultivation of coffee has not been successful in the Nilgiris owing to the prevalence of disease, so it is the intention of the company to place the whole of the estate under tea.

The factory is a well-built, double-storied structure, containing withering, drying, rolling, packing, and other rooms, and the plant consists of a 24-h.p. oil-engine, two rollers, one Venetian dryer, one sifter, and a packing machine. The possibilities of the estate are being developed, and roads are being made as speedily as possible. Woodbriar is at an altitude of from 5,000 to 6,000 ft., and it has an annual rainfall of 70 in.

WOODLANDS AND OLAND

These two properties, comprising a total of 1,240 acres, are cultivated as one estate, and belong to Mr. J. H. Pascoe, who has had many years' practical experience in growing tea and coffee. The owner pays particular attention to the rearing of his young trees and bushes, which care accounts for the excellent quality and yield of his crops. All plants are grown in the nursery, and then only selected ones are bedded out. The young tea is allowed to grow up without any check for about two years; it is then pruned in order that the roots may strike to a greater depth—this being necessary as the rainfall is comparatively light. Mr. Pascoe is systematic in all that he does, and one might instance this by observing that each field is numbered, and particulars are recorded as to the number of trees, the date of planting, the amount of labour expended, and the annual yield. Shelter has been grown wherever necessary. The oldest tea was planted in 1910, with clearings annually to 1914. The crop is sold in bulk for the Colombo market.

The land upon which coffee is grown is manured annually, and although some of the trees are now fifty years of age, they are still vigorous and prolific in yield. Coffee is pulped and washed on the estate, but it is cured by the Anapura Coffee Works, Ltd.

The factory, 80 ft. in length and 40 ft. in width, has a verandah on one side, which is 17 ft. in width. The building is constructed of brick with steel frames, and the bricks and tiles, as well as the timber for the interior, have been respectively manufactured and sawn on the estate. The machinery is thoroughly up to date, and the motive-power is obtained from a suction gas-engine by Marshall, Sons & Co., of Gainsborough, England.

The acreage under cultivation is divided into two properties, as follows: Woodlands, 150 acres of coffee, 300 acres of tea; and Oland, 140 acres of coffee. The rainfall is evenly distributed; the annual average since the year 1904 being

WENTWORTH ESTATE.

1. Bungalow. 2. Gold-mining Shaft. 3. A View on the Estate.

WENTWORTH ESTATE.

1. FACTORY. 2. HOSPITAL. 3. COOLIE LINES.

WOODLANDS AND OLAND.

1. New Tea Factory. 2. The Bungalow. 3. Young Tea. 4. Field of Coffee.

about 63 in., with but 131 wet days during each twelve months. Woodlands is about 5,000 ft. above the level of the sea, while Oland is nearly 1,500 ft. lower. A considerable portion of the work of the estate is done by contract, the labour employed being obtained from various races, such as Tamils, Canarese, Telugus, and Badagas (hillmen). The proprietor has built a very pretty bungalow for his own residence, which, owing to its elevated situation, commands extensive views

WUTZLER'S GLEN VIEW HOTEL, COONOOR.

1. THE MAIN BUILDING. 2. BACK OF THE MAIN BUILDING, SHOWING TENNIS COURT.

of both mountains and plains. It, further, overlooks the Bhavani River (so famous for its mahseer fishing), and it is about 20 miles from Ootacamund and 13 miles from Coonoor. The nearest post office is at Kulukambie, only 2 miles distant, and the telegraphic address is "Twoland."

WUTZLER'S GLEN VIEW HOTEL

This is the oldest and most up-to-date hotel in the town of Coonoor, it having been established for about a hundred years. Coonoor is built round a wide and broken valley on the edge of the crest of a plateau at the head of the great ravine along which run the road and railway which connect it with Mettupalaiyam. This situation naturally gives to many of the residents a series of charming views of the beautiful scenery of the undulating plains in the valley, and the Glen View Hotel—as its name suggests—is built upon the very edge of the ravine, and it thus occupies one of the most attractive sites in the town. There are many hostelries in Southern India, away from the bustle and the other disadvantages of a large city, where one can obtain home comforts amid the pleasant surroundings, and this hotel is a notable example of "a home away from home." It is the only hotel on the Nilgiri Hills which is lighted by electricity. The property covers an area of 8 acres of ground, and it is about 1 mile distant from the railway station at Coonoor. The hotel contains 41 clean and cosy bedrooms and suites of rooms, including excellent dining and drawing-rooms, reading and writing-room, and billiard-room, together with the usual range of kitchen and domestic offices.

There is good stabling and garage accommodation, and the hotel carriages and servants meet all trains. It is quite a common thing to see advertisements of boarding-houses stating that "a good table is kept," and it is frequently found that the adjective is most inappropriate in describing the food which is placed before the poor paying guests. The case is different with "Glen View:" The genial manager—Mr. F. C. Burgess—purchases goods of the highest quality, and the visitor can rely upon dishes being served in appetizing fashion. The present *chef* of the hotel has had the honour of cooking for his late Majesty King Edward VII. Catering is undertaken for banquets, dinners, wedding parties, and picnics. Visitors can have motor trips or drives in the lovely neighbourhood; they can revel in the beautiful gardens of the hotel, or they can make use of the badminton and tennis-courts which are within the grounds.

The terms are exceedingly moderate,

running upwards according to requirements from Rs. 6 a day. The servants are about 70 in number, and they are always under the keen observation of Mr. Burgess.

The hotel is about 12 miles distant from Ootacamund.

THE WYNAAD GROUP OF ESTATES

This group consists of thirty properties in the area known as the Wynaad, in the district of the Nilgiris, and they are owned by Messrs. A. R. Haji Fakeer Mahomed Sait & Sons. As one approaches the Wynaad the impression is gained that it is a plateau of a gently undulating character, upon which a moderate amount of jungle still remains, but a closer inspection reveals heavy forests of teak and blackwood, together with small hill ranges, upon which peaks ascend to fully 4,000 or 5,000 ft. in height. The soil varies considerably, but the forest and scrub land is very suitable for the cultivation of both tea and coffee, and a sufficiency of water may always be depended upon, as there are numerous streams, originating from springs, which are known locally as *poyas*. Among plantation products of the Wynaad, coffee occupies by far the largest area, and, notwithstanding the hindrances with which planters have had to contend, the annual yield of berries has been distinctly favourable. The introduction of tea took place about the year 1835, and efforts have been made by growers from time to time to obtain seed suitable for the district, with the result that satisfactory prices are obtained on the London market.

The estates now under notice comprise 8,704 acres, which includes 1,279 acres of coffee, 1,121 acres of pepper (grown almost wholly among the coffee bushes), and 347 acres of tea, while the balance is at present in an uncultivated state. There are eight superintendents in charge of the properties, but a general manager has supreme control. The group comprises (*inter alia*) Kurrumbu, 600 acres in extent, which has 215 acres of coffee, 231 acres of pepper, and 16 acres of tea, Mr. R. Burrows being in charge; Mr. A. W. D'Souza has the oversight of ten estates, comprising 260 acres of coffee, 46 acres of pepper, and 208 acres of tea; Mr. M. Rodrigues is stationed at Motil Peak, upon which the crops are 118 acres of coffee and 3 acres of tea, together with 652 acres not yet planted; Kodalot has 70 acres of coffee, 85 acres of pepper, and 26 acres of tea; Mr. P. J. Bikram Sing supervises eight estates situated near to Gudalur town and post-office, upon which there are 463 acres of coffee, 86 acres of pepper, and 81 acres of tea.

THE LAKE AND RAILWAY TRACK, OOTACAMUND.

FRONT VIEW OF SHATIATOPE ANICUT.

IRRIGATION

By F. E. MORGAN

THE great rivers whose supplies are utilized for direct irrigation are the Godavari, Kistna, and Cauvery, all of which rise in districts where the south-west monsoon rains are heavy and practically secure. The rains of the north-east monsoon affect the minor rivers of the Presidency, from which the supplies are diverted to tanks. The majority of the rain-fed tanks receive their supplies in this monsoon.

The very heavy and almost unfailing rainfall on the west coast renders irrigation works in that locality—except in Palghat *taluq*—unnecessary, while similar works on the three large rivers make the Godavari, Kistna, and Tanjore districts secure from famine. Tinnevelly, traversed by the Tambrapani, a river which has an almost perennial flow, and the district of Vizagapatam, which has a good rainfall, are also well protected. The remaining districts are more or less liable to famine, excepting in the small areas protected by irrigation, and the most insecure are Cuddapah, Anantapur, Bellary, and Kurnool, in which the rainfall is precarious and scanty, and few important irrigation works exist or are feasible. The area upon which crops are raised in the Presidency in an ordinary year is more than 32,000,000 acres, double crops being raised on nearly one-eighth of this area, and more than 30 per cent. of the area of crops raised are dependent upon irrigation to ensure a full out-turn.

State irrigation works in the Presidency may be divided into two classes. The first comprises all the more important works which have been constructed, restored, or improved by the British Government at a capital cost of nearly 11 crores of rupees. The second class includes all the smaller tanks and river channels, many of which are of very ancient construction. Government has taken over their maintenance, and devotes considerable sums annually to their upkeep, although very few of them were originally constructed by the State or by the British Government.

There are 41 works of the first class, with a total length of main and branch canals of 4,656 miles; of this length, 1,023 miles are for irrigation and navigation combined, and distributaries of a total length of 8,903 miles, irrigate an area of nearly 3,500,000 acres, upon which 500,000 to 600,000 acres of second crop is raised in a good year. The area now irrigated is a little more than double that in the year 1875.

The main crop irrigated is paddy (rice), and of the 3,783,358 acres cropped, under the first class of works, in 1913-14, estimated to be worth $19\frac{1}{2}$ crores of rupees, no less than 93 per cent. was paddy valued at nearly 19 crores of rupees, while *ragi* was irrigated to the extent of 1·6 per cent. The average out-turn of paddy per acre was valued, in 1913-14, at from Rs. 36·5 for crops under works in the Chigleput district, to Rs. 90 to Rs. 106 for crops irrigated by the three Bhavani channels in Coimbatore—the out-turn for these channels being nearly one ton an acre. The Cauvery delta yield was valued at Rs. 46 to Rs. 49 an acre, and that of the northern deltas—Kistna and Godavari —at Rs. 59.

The second class of works, numbering more than 57,000, irrigate an area of 2,500,000 acres, and about 900,000 acres are second cropped, so that the total area under all works with which Government are connected is 6,000,000 acres, on which 1,500,000 acres of second crop are raised in a good year. Including private and zemindari works, and irrigation under wells, the total area irrigated is over 11,000,000 acres.

IRRIGATION

Of the irrigation works on the principal rivers, by far the most important are those in connection with the Cauvery, the Godavari, and the Kistna, which irrigate 2,500,000 acres in all.

The Cauvery rises in Coorg, near Mercara, and drains an area of 26,000 square miles, and on entering the delta of Tanjore, at the Grand Anicut, 8 miles east of Trichinopoly, it divides into a number of minor channels, from which irrigation has been practised from time immemorial. Tradition gives credit for the construction of the first Tanjore delta work—the Grand Anicut—to Rajah Veeranam, who came from the north of the Presidency and conquered Tanjore towards the close of the second century of our era. The work, which then was a rough stone structure of considerable depth and breadth and over 1,000 ft. long, was the greatest engineering work carried out in India prior to British rule. When Tanjore was ceded to the British in 1800, the state of affairs in the delta was critical owing to the greater portion of the supply in the river becoming diverted from the Cauvery to the Coleroon. This was remedied in 1836 by the construction of a masonry weir, the Upper Anicut (since converted into a regulator with large span lift shutters), 10 miles west of Trichinopoly, across the Coleroon, at the head of the delta, and by the reconstruction of the Grand Anicut, 18 miles below. Many other works for the improvement of the regulation were carried out, and these, with subsequent additions, and the remodelling of the old works, have resulted in increasing the irrigated area from 547,000 acres in 1801 to more than 900,000 acres at the present day (1915), 10 per cent. of which is second cropped.

The improvements effected by Government have cost 41 lakhs of rupees, from which a return of over 20 per cent. is obtained. A further 110,000 acres are irrigated in South Arcot and Tanjore districts from the Lower Anicut, which was constructed in 1837 across the Coleroon, 67 miles below the Upper Anicut. Several channels diverge from this anicut, one of which feeds the Veeranan tank in South Arcot, which is formed by an earthen embankment 12 miles in length.

The Godavari, which is one of the twelve holy rivers of India, rises some 70 miles north-east of Bombay, and falls into the Bay of Bengal, about 250 miles north of Madras, after draining 115,000 square miles. Towards the end of the first half of the nineteenth century the Godavari district, which had suffered from several famines, and the deprivation of its cloth trade, owing to the competition of Manchester, had fallen into a bad way, and Government, in considering remedial measures, deputed Sir Arthur Cotton to investigate the development of the irrigation resources of the Godavari. The result was the construction of a masonry dam or "anicut," completed in 1852, upwards of $2\frac{1}{4}$ miles in length across the Godavari, just below the village of Dowlaishweram, and 5 miles from Rajahmundry. The river at this site is over $3\frac{4}{5}$ miles in breadth, but of this more than one-third is occupied by three islands, the anicut being built in four sections. The Godavari bifurcates below the anicut, dividing the delta into three parts, which are fed by three main canals, taking off from the anicut. The total length of main and branch canals is 502 miles, and of distributaries, 2,002 miles, irrigating over 750,000 acres of first crop, and over 250,000 acres of second crop. The delta, which was in a state of extreme impoverishment before the construction of the anicut, is now one of the wealthiest in the Presidency, and where formerly means of communication was confined to rough footpaths, there are now 500 miles of navigable canals, and a similar length of roads. The expenditure on works up to date has been 1·45 crores of rupees, from which a return of over 20 per cent. is secured.

The highly successful results obtained by Sir Arthur Cotton in the Cauvery and Godavari deltas led to the construction of an anicut at Bezwada, across the Kistna River, which was completed in 1855. It consisted of a low masonry dam, nearly 4,000 ft. in length, and 16 ft. above summer water level, with the necessary regulation works at the heads of the canals which branch off on either side. These canals and their branches are 349 miles long, with distributaries totalling 2,182 miles; a length of 334 miles of the main and branch canals are navigable. This system of irrigation has cost nearly $1\frac{3}{4}$ crores of rupees, from which a return of about 18 per cent. is now obtained; the area irrigated in the Kistna and Guntur districts being over 700,000 acres. The second crop raised is negligible.

NATIVES IRRIGATING FROM A WELL.

The above three systems in 1913-14 yielded over 1,500,000 tons of paddy, valued at 13·8 crores of rupees; the areas on which this crop was raised being: Cauvery delta, 906,201 acres; Godavari delta, 882,141 acres; and Kistna delta, 701,826 acres.

The navigable canals in the northern deltas are used as feeders to the railway, and in 1913-14, 633,755 tons of goods, valued at Rs. 7·67 crores, were carried on the Godavari canals; the corresponding figures for the Kistna canals being 77,043 tons, and Rs. 59·7 lakhs. The canals in the Godavari delta are also used more for passenger traffic than in Kistna, the figures for 1913-14 being 659,493 and 64,876 respectively.

The evidence of the very large profits which would accrue to Government from the Godavari and Kistna irrigation attracted general attention to the chances that existed in Southern India of profitable water-engineering enterprise, and resulted in the formation of the Madras Irrigation Company in 1858, which was empowered to raise £2,000,000 sterling, Government guaranteeing 5 per cent. interest on £1,000,000. The only work constructed by this company was the Kurnool-Cuddapah canal from Sunkesala, on the Tungabhadra, 17 miles above Kurnool city. The canal is 191 miles in length, and it traverses the Kurnool and Cuddapah districts, crossing the River Penner, and ending in Cuddapah town. The canal is for irrigation and navigation, and was intended eventually to irrigate 500,000 acres; it was also part of an ambitious scheme to provide a waterway connecting Poona with Madras.

The largest area that has ever been irrigated is 90,285 acres, in the famine year of 1876-7, and as the canal involved a constant and increasing loss to Government owing to the necessity for improvements not carried out by the company, the latter was bought up by the State in 1882. A smaller proportion of paddy is irrigated under this system than under any other major works, and in a year of deficient rainfall a considerable area of dry crops are watered. In 1913-14 paddy was raised on 50 per cent. of the area irrigated. The prospects of this canal, which has cost 2¼ crores of rupees, are steadily improving, but the return on capital outlay is only 1 per cent.

An anicut over 2,000 ft. in length was constructed in 1862 across the Penner at Nellore. The works are on a smaller scale than those in Kistna and Godavari, but since the construction in 1886 of a similar anicut at Sangam, 20 miles west of Nellore, on the same river, more than 150,000 acres are irrigated by the two anicuts, and a return of over 8 per cent. on the capital invested is obtained. Several exceptionally large tanks are fed by the anicuts, the largest being Kanigiri reservoir, 11 miles from Nellore, to the north of the Penner, which has a capacity of 6,900,000,000 cubic feet, and a water spread of 19½ square miles.

The most important large storage works of recent construction are in connection with the Rushikuyla and Periyar systems. The Rushikuyla, in Ganjam district, is a combined system of storage and direct irrigation, and it irrigates some 100,000 acres, mainly between the town of Aska and the coast. The system is fed by two masonry anicuts across the Mahanadi and Rushikuyla Rivers, and when the supply from these rivers is insufficient, it is supplemented by water from two storage works, the Russelkonda and Surada reservoirs. Both reservoirs are formed by earth-dams of considerable size—that of Russelkonda, which is across the Boringa River, being 58 ft. in height and 4,300 ft. in length, while that of Surada, which dams the Johoro and Pathama Rivers, though of less height—44 ft.—is 3¾ miles in length.

The Periyar system, which came into operation in 1896, is the boldest scheme of irrigation which has yet been carried out in Madras, and it was designed to irrigate a large tract on the north side of the River Vaigai, in the Madura district. On the Travancore side of the *ghauts* which separate that State from the district of Madura, the rainfall is copious and unfailing, whereas that on the Madura side is sparse and precarious, giving an uncertain and poor supply to the Vaigai River. A concrete dam was therefore constructed across a gorge on the Periyar River, in the State of Travancore, and impounded water is diverted, through a tunnel 5,704 ft. long, back through the hills on the frontier, into the Suruliyar, a tributary of the Vaigai. At Peranai, 20 miles west of Madura and 86 miles from the tunnel, the supply is transferred from the Vaigai to the irrigated area, by means of a regulator, to canals and distributaries 209 miles in length. The dam is 1,241 ft. in length, and the maximum height is 173 ft., while the total amount stored in the lake formed is 16,600,000,000 cubic feet, of which 9,500,000 can be drawn off. The expenditure on the system has been a little over a crore of rupees, upon which a return of more than 4 per cent. is obtained. The irrigated area averages about 122,000 acres, with nearly 50,000 acres of second crop.

In 1908 a pumping scheme for the irrigation of 50,000 acres in Divi Island, at the mouth of the Kistna River, was brought into operation. The pumping installation consists of eight Diesel engines and centrifugal pumps capable of lifting nearly 50,000,000 cubic feet a day from the Kistna River. The irrigated area is at present 26,000 acres, but it is being developed gradually.

Anicuts (weirs or regulators) have been constructed across all the minor rivers of the Presidency, the supply in which is uncertain, and most of the anicuts therefore supply extensive storage works formed by chains of tanks.

In Ganjam district the rivers are of no great length, and in addition to those feeding the Rushikaylu system there are only two of importance for irrigation, the Langulya and the Vamsadhara; nine channels take off from these two rivers, forming the Ganjam minor rivers system, which irrigates 63,000 acres.

The chief sources of irrigation in the Vizagapatam district are the Sarada, Varaha, and Nagavalli Rivers, and two natural lakes, the Komaravolu and Kondakirla Avas, two fresh-water lakes.

On the Sarada and Varaha Rivers there are 10 anicuts, which, with some river channels, irrigate over 42,000 acres of first crop and 40,000 of second crop. A regulator of nine spans of 40 ft., across the Nagavalli River at Thotapalli, was completed in 1911, and will eventually irrigate 23,000 acres, the area at present irrigated being 17,000 acres.

In addition to the Kistna system, the only other work of any importance in the Kistna district is an anicut across the Muniyeru, a tributary of the Kistna, where it enters the British territory in the north-west of the district. At present the area irrigated is only a little more than half the 10,000 acres for which it was designed.

The Kortailiyar, in Chingleput district, feeds a number of tanks, of which the most important are the Chembrambakkam, supplied via the Cooum, and the Red Hills and Sholaveran tanks. The former, which is 14 miles from Madras, covers an area of 10 square miles, and irrigates 13,500 acres, and the other tanks, in addition to irrigating 9,000 acres, are the source of the water supply of Madras city. The Vallur anicut system, on the Kortailiyar, irrigates about 5,100 acres.

The Palar, with its tributaries, of which the Poiney is the most important, and the Cheyyar, are the chief sources of irrigation in the district of North Arcot. Large areas are irrigated by anicuts across each of these rivers. The Palar anicut was constructed in 1857, 5 miles below the town of Arcot, and supplies 270 tanks, which existed before its construction. The area irrigated, on both sides of the river,

1. WATER-LIFTING BY PICOTTAH.

2. WATER-LIFTING BY CAVALAY.

3. SIDDAPUR PROJECT.

The only good Drinking-water Well.

in a favourable year, is 81,000 acres of first crop and 30,000 of second crop.

The Poiney anicut, built in 1853, across the river on the border of the district, also supplies a system of tanks on either side of the stream, irrigating over 23,000 acres, of which in some years about 8,000 acres is second cropped.

The supply in the Cheyyar River is diverted by an anicut, which is bridged, built in 1856, at the crossing of the Arni-Wandiwash Road, supplying a large number of tanks south of the river. The area irrigated is 21,000 acres, of which two-thirds is usually second cropped.

The Poiney system returns about 15 per cent. on the capital outlay, and the two lower systems, which are subject to considerable damage from floods and cyclonic rainfall, entailing heavy maintenance charges, return about 5 per cent.

The Palar, after leaving the North Arcot district, traverses Chingleput, and is joined by the Cheyyar, both rivers irrigating a considerable area in this district. The catchment of the Palar and its tributaries being favourable for the construction of tanks, almost the whole of the drainage from an area of nearly 9,000 square miles is stored in tanks or passed into irrigation channels, and the surplus running to waste in a year of ordinary rainfall is practically nil.

The Ponniar, the Gadilam, the Vellar (with an important tributary, the Manimuktanadi), and the Coleroon Rivers irrigate a large area in South Arcot. The Coleroon irrigates in this district, from the Lower Anicut, more than 84,000 acres, which is more secure than that dependent on the other rivers, which are liable to severe floods and drought.

A large percentage of the supply in the Ponniar is utilized for irrigation, and it is first tapped in the Salem district by the Nedungal anicut, which feeds the Barur tank system. This system, which is the only one of any size in Salem, was improved as a famine work in 1877, and finally completed in 1892, has not developed to the extent anticipated. It irrigates at present about 3,500 acres.

In the South Arcot district the Ponniar irrigates 26,000 acres from the Tirukkoyilur anicut, and the Manimuktanadi has two systems of some size—the Mehamattur anicut system, 4,500 acres, and the Vriddhachalam anicut system, 8,400 acres. Three anicuts on the Gadilam irrigate an area of 10,000 acres, the largest being the Tiruvadi anicut, 7,100 acres. The area south of the Vellar, for some 50 miles from the coast, is irrigated by the Lower Anicut, and irrigation is extended to the north of the river from a regulator at Shatiatope. The system fed by this work has only two storage works of any size, the Walajah and Perumal tanks, the latter being formed by a bund 8 miles long, and the irrigation is, as is the case of the Lower Anicut system, mainly direct from the river. The area irrigated in a good season is 31,000 acres of first and 5,000 acres of second crop. Twenty miles above Shatiatope a regulator has been built across the Vellar at Pelandorai, and irrigates 12,000 acres to the south, mainly through tanks. Another regulator is under construction on this river at Thitagudi, about 20 miles above Pelandorai, to supply a reservoir, also under construction, to the north of the river of 2,407,000,000 cubic feet capacity. Channels from the reservoir will irrigate

1. PERIYAR HEADWORKS.
Regulator on right and dam on left.

2. DAM AND LAKE OF PERIYAR HEADWORKS, MADURA DISTRICT.

1. GODAVARI DELTA SYSTEM.

Head of eastern delta, Dowlaishweram lock and head-sluice; rear elevation. Completed in 1887.

2. FRONT VIEW OF GRAND ANICUT. 3. FRONT VIEW OF UPPER ANICUT SHUTTERS.

4. KURNOOL-CUDDAPAH CANAL SYSTEM.

Self-acting calingulah at 1 m. 35 chains. Front view. Approximate date of completion, 1871.

25,000 acres, and with the construction of this work the available surplus in the river in a year of average rainfall will be fully utilized.

The tributaries of the Cauvery irrigate considerable tracts in Coimbatore, Trichinopoly, and Salem districts. In Coimbatore River irrigation is all from the tributaries, the Amravati, the Noyel, and the Bhavani.

Only small areas are irrigated from anicuts on the Noyel, but 22 anicut channels on the Amravati irrigate an area of 27,000 acres, 23,000 acres of second crop being raised in Coimbatore and Trichinopoly districts. The supply in the river, in some years, is practically all used.

The main irrigation from the Bhavani is from two very old works, the Kodaveri and Kalingaroyen anicuts, two channels taking off the former anicut. The supply in this river being steady, irrigation is direct from the channels in the case of the Amravati channels, and storage-works are not required. The area irrigated by the Kodaveri anicut is over 19,000 acres, and by the Kalingaroyen anicut 11,900 acres, of which nearly 11,000 acres is second cropped.

1. GODAVARI DELTA SYSTEM.

Head of eastern delta, Dowlaishweram lock. Front elevation. Completed in 1887.

2. GODAVARI DELTA SYSTEM, WESTERN SECTION. MAIN CANAL, NIDADAVOLE WHARF.

The most important tributary of the Cauvery in Salem district is the Tirumanimuttar, which irrigates over 15,000 acres from 23 anicuts.

The Cauvery irrigates a considerable area in Salem and Trichinopoly districts by means of river channels, but none of the individual works are of importance. The only important system in Trichinopoly district is the Nandyar channel system, which irrigates 6,000 acres, one-third of which is second cropped. The only other river of importance in the south, besides the Vaigai, which has no large work except that fed by the Periyar Lake, is the Tambrapani. The river is barred by eight anicuts, watering about 80,000 acres; the upper six anicuts irrigate 37,500 acres of first crop, and 35,500 of second crop. The anicuts below these, the Marudur and Srivaikuntam, feed tank systems irrigating 17,800 and 24,700 acres, of which over 90 per cent. is second cropped.

There are no important works in Bellary district, the eight channels from the Tungabhadra only irrigating a small area.

The only rivers in the Anantapur district are the Pennar and Chitravati, the supply in which is very capricious, and there are no irrigation works of importance in connection with them.

The only work of any size in the Kurnool district yet completed, apart from the Kurnool-Cuddapah Canal, is the Cumbum tank, formed by damming the Gundlakamma River by an earthen bund, which is the highest in the Presidency (80 ft.), but is only about 100 yards in length. The tank spreads over an area of 9 square miles, and irrigates 5,700 acres, of which over 3,500 acres is second cropped in a good year.

The minor rivers in Nellore district, the Gundlakamma, the Musi, the Paleru, and the Manneru, have all very uncertain supplies, and no works of any size have yet been built on them. A reservoir of about 2,000,000,000 cubic feet capacity is under construction on the Manneru, at

1. VIEW OF HEADWORKS, PERIYAR SYSTEM, AT PERANAI, MADURA DISTRICT.

2. GODAVARI DELTA SYSTEM, EASTERN SECTION.

Dowlaishweram Anicut, with under sluices in foreground.

3. KISTNA DELTA SYSTEM.

Anicut and under sluices at Bezwada and railway bridge from lock wall.

Mopad. It will be formed by an earthern bund, 5,500 ft. in length and 70 ft. in height, damming the river. The area to be irrigated is 12,500 acres.

The minor works, those of the second class, of which there were 37,152 in 1913 maintained by Government, consisting of small tanks and spring or river channels, are of no less importance than the bigger works previously referred to, as they irrigate nearly the same total area. Of the minor tanks in the Presidency, 21,500 irrigate less than 50 acres, and only 1,600 of the minor works irrigate over 500 acres.

The low water supplies in the rivers are usually diverted to the small river channels by temporary sand or brushwood groynes, called *korambus*, extending from the head of the channel across the deep bed of the river. Spring channels are either channels fed by defined springs, or by channels tapping the storage in the sandy beds of a river. In the latter case the channel is excavated in the river bed by the cultivators concerned when the season for freshets is over.

Bellary has nearly 10,000 minor works, of which only 200 irrigate over 50 acres. Guntur has over 6,900, of which less than 300 irrigate over 50 acres.

Works irrigating over 200 acres, 3,335 in number, of which 2,776 are tanks, are in charge of the Public Works Department, and of the smaller works, 33,817, including 25,200 tanks, are in charge of the Revenue Department. The remaining works. over 20,000, consist of very small tanks, irrigating less than 10 acres, and of a large number of "spring" and river channels, also irrigating very small areas, which are maintained by the cultivators themselves. In 1883 the systematic repair of all tanks in charge of the Public Works and Revenue Departments was taken up under a Tank Restoration Scheme, which, in addition to providing for the repair of the tanks also provided for the compilation of a very complete "memoir" of each tank, giving the standard to be maintained in future. This work, which is one of considerable magnitude, is still in progress.

In addition to the Government works it has been estimated that about 2,500,000 acres are irrigated in zamindaris, chiefly from tanks, and about 71,000 acres are under private irrigation works of an insignificant nature. Irrigation from wells by means of manual labour or bullock-power, and to a small extent by oil-engines and pumps, is on the increase, and is of considerable importance, as an area of more than 1,250,000 acres is thus watered. The crops which are irrigated are usually those requiring only an occasional watering.

There are 600,000 wells in the Presidency used for irrigating purposes; of this number about three-quarters are the sole source of supply to the area irrigated, all but some 30,000, which are on the banks of rivers and streams, being sunk in dry lands. These wells are used to irrigate crops that only require an occasional watering. The remaining wells, about 150,000 in number, are used for supplementing the supply from an irrigation work whenever it fails, owing to deficient rainfall or other causes.

The total average area irrigated from wells is 1,250,000 acres of first crop, and 420,000 acres of second crop, or an average of about $2\frac{3}{4}$ acres per well, but in the Coimbatore district the average is about 4 acres. The richest districts in wells are the Coimbatore, and South and North Arcot districts. In Coimbatore there are over 75,000 wells, the area irrigated being 290,000 acres; in North Arcot there are about the same number, irrigating about 160,000 acres; and in South Arcot an area of 190,000 acres is irrigated by some 69,000 wells. Considerable areas are also irrigated under wells in an ordinary year: in Trichinopoly, 93,000 acres; Cuddapah, 84,000 acres; Madura, 74,000 acres; Salem, 63,000 acres; and Anantapur, 58,000 acres.

On the recommendation of the Indian Irrigation Commission, which sat in 1901-3, an extensive programme of investigation of possible new works was taken up, and as a result several projects have been carried out or are under construction in the districts of Vizagapatam, Kurnool, Nellore, and South Arcot.

SCENES ON THE KEMPHULLY RIVER.

Photos by C. Lake.

THE STATE OF MYSORE

MYSORE is the premier Hindu State in India, and, although its history was enshrouded in mystery for many generations, a mass of evidence has been obtained in recent years which gives accounts of its alternate prosperity and adversity from about the second and third centuries B.C. Remarkable edicts of Asoka, the third of the Mauryan kings, have been engraven on rocks and pillars, and these refer to rulers who reigned at that early period. The country was at that time torn with internal dissensions, which were succeeded by continual attacks by tribes who came from beyond the confines of the State. The Mahavalis, the Kadambas, the Rattas, the Pattavars, and the Gangas were now in possession, but the Chalukyas succeeded in wresting the greater portion of the territory from the holders between the fifth and seventh centuries. The pendulum of good and bad fortune then began to swing backwards and forwards, and the next five or six centuries witnessed the ascendancy of various races in succession. At the commencement of the eleventh century the Cholas advanced from the south, and a struggle ensued between them and the Chalukyas, but trouble speedily came from other quarters, as the Hoysalas gained very considerable power and a large area of territory, until they eventually ruled over nearly the whole of Mysore and over portions of Coimbatore, Salem, and Dharwar. Their sway received a check in the early part of the fourteenth century by reason of a Mahommedan invasion from the Deccan. A new and powerful Hindu dynasty then commenced at Vizayanagar, and the Province of Mysore was one of its earliest acquisitions. This rule continued for about 330 years, and notwithstanding a bitter hatred which existed between Vizayanagar and the Bahmani kingdom in the Deccan, a season of considerable commercial prosperity was enjoyed, but the Vizayanagar dynasty was upset in 1565 by the armies of the allied States of Bijapur, Golconda, Ahmednagar, and Bidar. A number of vassal chiefs had been granted titles to various districts in Mysore by late rulers of Vizayanagar, and one of the most important of them, the Wadiyar Raja of Mysore, asserted his independence, and became a striking power in that part of the country, laying the foundations of the present State during the year 1610. Numerous Wadiyars followed one another, and each succeeding ruler made it his business to extend the borders of his kingdom. Territories to the south, east, and north were added, and at the beginning of the eighteenth century Mysore extended from Sakkarepatna in the west to Salem in the east, and from Chiknayakanhalli in the north to Dharapuram in the south. The notorious Hyder Ali was commander of a force which the Maharaja of Mysore had placed in the field with the view of subduing Trichinopoly, and this leader deposed the Raja in 1761 and then personally assumed the government of the country, thus bringing the State under Mahommedan rule. Hyder then began to be a menace to the Carnatic possessions of the East India Company, and after many years of almost continuous warfare he died in 1782, and was succeeded by his son Tipu. The latter pursued a more vigorous policy than even his late father had done, but a number of reverses compelled him to throw himself upon the mercy of the British, when a treaty was concluded at Seringapatam in the year 1792. In 1798 he took steps to obtain assistance for the prosecution of a campaign which was to have for its object the expulsion of the British from India. Lord Wellesley endeavoured to induce this hot-headed leader to come to terms, but on the latter's refusal troops were sent against him, and the long struggle was ended on May 4, 1799, by the fall of Seringapatam and by the death of Tipu himself, which marked the close of the Mahommedan control of Mysore.

The Hindu dynasty was again set up when recognition was given to the claims of Krishna Raj Wadiyar, the three-year-old grandson of the ruler who had been deposed by Hyder about forty years previously. During his minority, however, the conduct of State matters was in the very able hands of a Brahman named Purnaiya, who continued in office until 1812, when he handed over the reins of authority to the young Maharaja. Gross mismanagement occurred between that year and 1831, and shortly after the latter date the state of affairs was so serious that the intervention of the British Government became necessary. A large body of troops was called out to quell a rebellion, and the Governor-General, Lord William Bentinck, assumed the administrative duties in 1834. The Maharaja, in the absence of issue, adopted a son in 1867, and the English Government, after refusing to reinstate the ruler, agreed that the boy should be entrusted with the government of the State on attaining his majority. In 1879—or about three years before the coming of age of the prospective ruler—certain conditions were drawn up which should govern the transfer to native rule of some 5,000,000 persons who had been subject to British control for nearly fifty years, and as this important document formed the basis of the new Constitution of the kingdom it will be advisable to reproduce extracts from it. They were as follows: (1) A clear distinction must be drawn and permanently maintained between the private fortune of the Chief and the public revenues of the State; a Civil List of fixed amount must be assigned to the Chief, and the rest of the revenues must remain available for public purposes only, through appropriation by constituted authorities. (2) There must be permanent security for the observance of established laws, rights, and usages, and the laws must only be altered by suitable legislative machinery. (3) Provision must be made for the judicial independence of the civil and criminal courts, and justice must be dispensed by regularly constituted tribunals. (4) The assessment and collection of the revenues must be made under fixed rules; all rights in the land must be defined and maintained, and no fresh taxation imposed except in accordance with law.

The administration of the country was handed over in 1881 to Chama Rajendra

1. TEMPLE AT BELUR, KADUR DISTRICT. 2. BATHING GHAT, HASSAN. 3. MAIN STREET, SAKLASPUR.

Photos by C. Lake.

1, 2, AND 3. VIEWS OF THE BABA BUDEEN HILLS. 4. MAIN ROAD, CHICKMAGALUR.

Wadiyar, who was the adopted son of the deposed Maharaja, and this ruler, with the assistance of a very capable Dewan, conducted affairs in such a manner that Mysore became an exceedingly prosperous State. He died in December 1894, and the Maharani Vani Vilasa Sunnidhana was installed as Regent during the minority of the heir. The latter, His Highness Sri Krishnaraja Wadiyar Bahadur, attained his majority in 1902, and the induction ceremonies were performed by His Excellency Lord Curzon, who was Viceroy at the time.

Lord Curzon in the course of his address stated that the Maharaja had recently attained his eighteenth birthday, and that he had passed through a minority of nearly eight years. Continuing, he said : "These have not been idle or rapid years spent in enjoyment or dissipated in idleness. They have been years of careful preparation for the duties that lay before him and of laborious training for his exalted state. He has made frequent tours among his people; he has studied their wants and needs at first hand ; and he has thereby acquired the knowledge which will enable him to understand the problems with which he will be confronted."

The Maharaja has proved to be a most capable ruler, and there has been a marked development in the industrial, social, educational, and other questions which are the basis of successful administration. His Highness is exceedingly popular, and his sympathetic attitude towards every movement calculated to improve the conditions of the people has endeared him to the hearts of his subjects. He is, moreover, a keen sportsman, and coaching, polo, tennis, and racquets find a doughty champion in the ruler of the State. He was invested with the Grand Commandership of the Star of India in 1907.

The Maharaja is head of the State, and the administration is carried on by him with the assistance of a Dewan and two Councillors. There is also a Legislative Council, which, with the Assembly of Representatives, acts as an Advisory Board.

Two years before the Maharaja attained his majority he was married to Pratapa Kumari Bai, the daughter of a Rajput chief of Kathiawar, the Rana Sahib of Vana.

The native State of Mysore lies between the 11th and 15th degrees N. lat. and the 74th and 76th degrees E. long., and it is surrounded by districts of the Presidency of Madras, with the exception of a small portion which is bounded by a portion of the smaller of the Bombay districts. Its area, including the Civil and Military Station of Bangalore, is nearly 30,000 square miles, and its inhabitants numbered about 5,750,000 at the census of 1911, three-fourths of whom are more or less directly engaged in agricultural pursuits. Ninety-two per cent. of these were Hindus; Mahommedans were represented by $5\frac{1}{4}$ per cent.; and the remainder consisted of Christians, Animists, Jains, Sikhs, Parsis, Brahmans, and Buddhists.

There are three divisions in the State, namely: (1) Ashtagram, in which are the districts of Mysore and Hassan; (2) Nagar, in which are Chitaldrug, Kadur, and Shimoga; and (3) Nandidrug, divided into the Bangalore, Kolar, and Tumkur districts. Its extreme length from north to south is about 230 miles, while it is nearly 300 miles in breadth. The State is at a high elevation between the Eastern and Western Ghauts, and it is divided naturally into two regions of distinctly different characters, the hill country lying on the west, and extensive plains and valleys in the eastern portion. One of the most conspicuous physical features consists of the *drugs*, or huge piles of rocks, which rise abruptly in many parts to a height of about 1,500 ft. above the plateau. The majority of these have been strongly fortified for many hundreds of years, and, notwithstanding their great altitude, they have an abundant supply of good water. The Eastern Ghaut Mountains separate the State from the Carnatic Provinces in the Madras Presidency, and the country rises gradually from these mountains in the direction of Bangalore, which is 3,000 ft. above the level of the sea. The highest peaks in the eastern half of Mysore are Sivaganga —about 30 miles distant from Bangalore —which reaches a height of 4,559 ft., and Nundydroog, some 36 miles from Bangalore, which is nearly 300 ft. higher. The western peaks are even more majestic. Kuduremukha, in the division of Nagar, being 6,215 ft. in height, and Mulainagiri, which is 6,317 ft. The principal rivers, which flow into the Bay of Bengal, are the Cauvery in the south, the Krishna in the north, and the North Pennar in the east, while the only one of importance which discharges its waters into the Arabian Sea is the Saraswati, which has a fall of about 960 ft. on the north-western boundary of the State.

The Malnad—or hill country—is a land of great beauty, with its forests, woods, and glades, which present such a variety of charming scenery. Plantations of areca palm and plantain may be seen on the hillsides, and here and there, nestling in the shelter of the trees, is a planter's house. The soil is very productive, and excellent yields of rice, pepper, coffee, areca-nuts, cardamoms, lemons, and oranges are obtained. The Mainad—or open country—is a very extensive one, and the black alluvial soil of the plains of the north produces heavy crops of cotton and millet. The southern and western districts are well irrigated by channels of water obtained from rivers, and here may be seen rice-fields, ragi, sugar-canes, and cocoa and areca palms, together with wide-stretching, undulating pastures, which are densely covered with coarse grass. Planters' Associations have been formed in Northern and Southern Mysore, and their members include the owners of more than one hundred plantations. The State Government is doing much to encourage the development of agriculture on a scientific basis, and there is no doubt that when farmers are able to realize the advantages of this they will readily adopt new methods of husbandry; they will secure selected seeds for sowing purposes; the value of manuring and of a rotation of crops will be recognized; and vast areas which are at present imperfectly cultivated will become sources of pleasure and profit to their owners or occupiers. The holdings of a large majority of the farmers in Southern India are very small—say from 2 to 10 or 12 acres—and the number of those who possess sufficient capital is almost infinitesimal. There is not, as a rule, money for fencing, for modern implements, or for farm buildings, and the excessive rate of interest charged for loans has prevented many a *ryot* from obtaining more than a bare existence. State help was given when some agricultural banks were opened in the year 1895, but they were not a success, and ten years later those institutions were superseded by co-operative societies, which now (1915) have branches in a large number of centres.

There has been a very marked advance in the value of manufactures during the past few years, and among the more important of these are the making of textile fabrics, ginning and pressing mills for cotton, spinning, weaving, and oil mills, sugar factories, tanneries, paper and glass-making, brick and tile works, and

1. BATHS OF THE RAJAHS, SERINGAPATAM.

2. BREACH IN THE FORT WALL, SERINGAPATAM, MADE BY THE BRITISH TROOPS IN 1799.

3. THE SALLY PORT IN THE FORT, SERINGAPATAM, WHERE TIPU SULTAN WAS SLAIN.

Photos by Nicholas & Co.

woollen mills. Glass-work is almost wholly confined to the making of bangles, and the manufacture of soap and candles is carried on in a steam factory at Bangalore; while other industries include the making of carts and implements for agricultural requirements, toy-making, and carving in sandal-wood. Sericulture, which is referred to at some length on another page, must not be overlooked, as it ranks next to agriculture in importance to the State.

A very considerable amount of money has been invested in mining in Mysore, principally for gold, manganese, and mica. The greater portion of the output of gold for the whole of India is obtained from the Mysore fields, as the following figures will show. The total quantity produced in India in 1912 was 590,554 oz., of the value of £2,271,806 sterling, and the proportion of these sums to be placed to the credit of the mines in this State is 561,065 oz. and £2,158,371 respectively. In November 1913 there were seven leading companies on the Kolar Goldfields, who were leaseholders from the Mysore Government of about 40 square miles. The Goldfields Railway connects the mines with the Madras and Southern Mahratta system at Bowringpet. That which was formerly a desolate waste is now a flourishing town, in which public buildings and literary and other institutions have been erected for the benefit of the population of about 100,000 persons. The number of employees in the mines in the year 1912 was 16,280 men who were engaged in underground work, and 9,806 hands on the surface, and the salaries and wages for that year amounted to £532,140. The authorized capital stands at £2,081,000, the amount already issued is £1,829,003, and the present market valuation in England is £5,825,265. During the year 1912 gold of a certified value of £2,158,371 was produced, and a sum of £126,654 was paid in royalties. Gold production at the commencement of operations in the year 1882 amounted to the sum of £38, and at the close of the year 1912 a total of £38,135,709 had been secured, upon which no less a sum than £1,940,373 had been paid in royalties. Other interesting figures for the same period of thirty years are as follows: Quartz crushed, 10,898,126 tons (of 2,000 lb.); bar gold obtained, 9,761,280 oz.; and the dividends paid amounted to £15,214,911. Some of the principal materials consumed or used between the end of the year 1897 and the beginning of 1912 were: Coal consumed, 2,142,557 tons; firewood, 174,280 tons; gelatine and dynamite, 10,017,333 lb.; timber, 10,264,107 cubic feet; candles, 10,919,575 lb.; mercury, 190,046 lb.; and cyanide, 7,294,605 lb. The machinery of the mines was driven by steam until the Cauvery Falls Power Works, situated at the old Indian village of Sivasamudram, were completed in 1902, when electric energy of 4,000 horse-power was transmitted to the fields.

H.H. THE MAHARAJAH OF MYSORE PERFORMING "PUJA" AT THE DASSERA FESTIVAL.

Photo by Wecksler.

The mining of manganese is of comparatively modern growth, as the metal was not discovered until about the year 1894, but the development is one of the most remarkable features of industrial progress in India. It was in 1895 that important steps were taken to extract the ore, and the Vizianagram Mining Company, Ltd., in the Madras Presidency, was the first to ascertain its commercial value. Shortly after this time valuable deposits were found in Mysore, and this gave a great impetus to mining matters in the State, so much so that the supply of land believed to be rich in metals is totally insufficient to meet the increasing demand. The ore, which is of very high quality, is exported, to be used chiefly in the manufacture of steel in the United Kingdom, in the United States of America, and in Germany. It meets with an extremely ready sale, and high prices are maintained owing to political unrest in Eastern Europe. The chief localities for obtaining this metal in Mysore are the districts of Shimoga, Chitaldrug, and Tumkur, and the returns for the State for 1912 place the output at 29,293 tons, of the value of £37,104.

Iron is found generally throughout Mysore, although the most valuable deposits have been found in the neighbourhood of the Baba Buden Hills, and it is obtained from ore and from black iron-sand. Smelting takes place in various centres in the province; there is a steam iron foundry in Bangalore, and some native foundries have been started for the repair of agricultural implements and of milling machinery.

The forests of Mysore cover an area of about 3,000 square miles, and they yield a very substantial addition to the State revenue, although it is generally believed that efficient utilization of the produce does not receive the attention from the authorities which its importance deserves. Teak is undoubtedly the principal timber in India, both as regards quality and as to the quantity exported to other countries, but sandal-wood has the pre-eminence in Mysore, as it grows in all parts of the State. It is used largely in the making of boxes, cabinets, desks, paper and book racks, and many other fancy articles, but the oil which is obtained from the roots of the tree forms the main ingredient in many of the beautiful scents for which the East has been famous for so many centuries. Wealthy Hindus show respect to deceased relatives by placing sticks of this wood on the funeral pyre. The greater portion of the wood which is sold from the forests is sent to Bombay for shipment to China, France, and Germany.

The growing of fruit on scientific principles has only recently received adequate attention, and this long period of apathy is to be deplored, as the climate appears to be eminently satisfactory for the purpose. Nearly all the indigenous Indian varieties can be produced, but several foreign kinds are now being introduced. There are many market gardens in the neighbourhood of Bangalore, and nearly all of the vegetables and fruit grown in them is sent to Madras for sale. Orchardists are now cultivating the soil thoroughly, and when the trees are properly pruned and sprayed there is no reason why this State should not take a prominent place among exporting centres.

The report on public instruction in Mysore for the period from 1912-13, submitted by the Inspector-General of Education, records appreciation of the advance which had been made in many important directions. It was shown that there were 4,568 public and private institutions, and that the names of no fewer than 129,009 boys and 27,431 girls were upon the roll. There was one school to every 6·44 square miles and to every 1,249 persons of the population. The education of Mahommedans was proceeding most satisfactorily, although the percentages of boys and girls in the schools to the male and female population was only 65·3 and 26·4 respectively. The pupils numbered 20,537, comprising 15,054 boys and 5,483 girls.

A comprehensive scheme for the development of industrial and commercial education was inaugurated during the year, and the Technical Institute at Mysore was formed by the combination of the Industrial and Engineering Schools at that place, and by the opening of a Mechanical Engineering School and of a Commercial School at Bangalore. The total number of technical schools throughout the State—according to the report—was 26, and there were 1,323 pupils. There were 7 schools for Europeans and Eurasians, and of the total of 590 pupils no fewer than 545, consisting of 290 boys and 326 girls, were children of European parents. Two first-grade colleges, namely, the Central College at Bangalore and the Maharaja's College in the town of Mysore, are affiliated with the Madras University.

There is very great wealth and variety in the fauna of Mysore, and, in fact, all the larger as well as the smaller animals and birds which are common to India may be found in the State. Some of the finest wild elephants may be met with in the jungles in the south, east, and west, but they are protected by the Government. The handsome tiger still remains an object of desire to the sportsman, and it may be found in nearly every part of the territory; other of the larger animals which are widely distributed are the panther, cheetah, bear, buffalo, bison, elk, hyæna, antelope, and wild hog, while the smaller ones include the wild cat, jackal, porcupine, and hares. Birds are very numerous, and are represented by jungle fowl, pelican, bustard, florican, wild goose, quail, partridge, pea-fowl, snipe, teal, and pigeon.

The Mysore State Railway system consists in reality of a number of branch lines radiating from Bangalore, which are connected with and are worked under contract by the Madras and Southern Mahratta Company. About 410 miles of permanent way have been laid, and in furtherance of a vigorous policy of progress the Government has decided upon other schemes of construction during the next few years.

The city of Mysore is the titular capital of the State and the place of residence of His Highness the Maharaja, but Bangalore is the administrative headquarters.

Mysore is situated at the north-western base of the Chamandi Hill, which is nearly 3,500 ft. above the level of the sea. On the summit of the latter is a very old temple, which is reached by a flight of stone steps, and when about two-thirds of the ascent have been accomplished the visitor may see a colossal figure of Nandi, the sacred bull of Siva. The city was formerly much overcrowded, and the sanitary conditions were very unsatisfactory, but the influence of the present ruler has caused the demolition of unhealthy rookeries to be followed by the laying-out of wide streets and the construction of a number of fine public buildings and private residences of a modern character. The public offices are situated in Gordon Park, on the western side of the city, and they contain a large central hall, occupied by the Mysore Representative Assembly, the District Commissioner's and Magistrate's offices, the Magistrate's Court, and the Treasury. The Victoria Jubilee Institute is used as an Oriental Library, in which special facilities are afforded for the study of Sanskrit and other manuscripts. In this neighbourhood a visit should certainly be made to the Maha-

A VIEW IN THE KADUR DISTRICT.

raja's College, the Law Courts, the Maharani's College, and the Roman Catholic Church. One of the most delightful features of the city is the Curzon Park, which was opened in 1902. The grounds are beautifully laid out with well-kept walks and secluded nooks, while the excellent shade of the trees and the fine open spaces are sufficiently inviting to induce a large number of the inhabitants to avail themselves of their attractions. The park extends along the northern and western sides of the Old Fort, and within its boundaries are the European Club, the Masonic and Town Halls, and the post and telegraph offices. Other places of interest are the Summer Palace, the Zoological Gardens, in which there is a representative collection of animals, and the Maharaja's stables, containing a considerable number of well-bred horses and a fine string of polo ponies, which give His Highness a prominent position among the sportsmen of India.

1. SERINGAPATAM. 2. BRIDGE AT SERINGAPATAM.

There are many magnificent palaces scattered throughout the East, but it is the opinion of experts as well as of private individuals that for chaste style of architecture and the lavish manner in which it has been decorated the residence of His Highness the Ruler of Mysore is not excelled by any others. Nearly the whole of the building—which is about 250 ft. in length and 155 ft. in breadth—is constructed of stone, obtained chiefly from the Chamandi Hill, but a large quantity of marble has been used for ornamental purposes. On approaching this stupendous pile of masonry one's attention is first attracted by the gilded domes in the centre and in the right and left wings, while the solidity of the structure and the beautifully carved pillars and windows cannot be overlooked. Leaving the fine open courtyard, from which access is gained to the library and armoury, one proceeds to the first floor, upon which is the Great Dasara Durbar Hall, with the throne of His Highness, in addition to music, drawing, and other splendidly furnished rooms. Some of the doors are made of rosewood, richly inlaid with ivory, while teak-wood is used for floors, ceilings, cornices, and panellings, the last-named being elaborately carved in a number of elegant designs. Private apartments and offices are situated on the second floor, and the skill of the artist is manifested as clearly here as elsewhere. Such a wealth of precious stones in the decoration of a building was, surely, never seen before: marble pillars are inlaid with jasper, cornelian, carbuncle, and other gems; red porphyry is used in the construction of the balustrades, while ironwork is covered with genuine gold-leaf. It may be added that nearly all of the skilled labourers employed on the building were obtained locally.

The exceedingly handsome structure named "The Mary Calvert Holdsworth Memorial Hospital" was completed in 1906, in memory of the wife of the Rev. W. W. Holdsworth, of the Wesleyan Mission in Mysore. The total cost of the building was more than a lakh of rupees, towards which the relatives of Mrs. Holdsworth contributed Rs. 37,500, while Her Highness the late Regent gave no less a sum than Rs. 10,000. The Government very generously presented the land to the Mission in recognition of the valuable work which it has carried on in the city for more than half a century.

The majority of the industries of the State are in evidence in the city, the principal ones being rice-milling, oil-pressing, and weaving, while the leading storekeepers include booksellers, motor and cycle repairers, furniture dealers, printers, and piece goods and other merchants. The power for lighting the streets, parks, and most of the principal buildings is obtained from the Cauvery Falls at Sivasamudram. The inhabitants of the city were estimated at the close of the year 1914 to be about 71,000 in number.

Reference may now be made to several other places, and a convenient starting-point is at the southern terminus of the Mysore State Railways at Nanjangud, where a celebrated car festival is held annually, which is attended by a large number of devotees from nearly every district in Southern India. The temple is of great antiquity, and it is particularly famous for the exquisite designs of its carvings.

Seringapatam, the former capital of the State, is 8 miles distant in a northerly direction by rail from the city of Mysore, or it can be reached by a drive of about 10 miles amid some very beautiful scenery. The town is situated on an island formed by two branches of the River Cauvery, and it is one of the most historically interesting places in the Presidency, as it was the scene of fierce conflicts between the British troops and Sultan Tipu, the son of Hyder Ali. About the middle of the eighteenth century the latter ruler had become a power to be reckoned with in Southern India, and, considering that he had a grievance against the British, he invaded the Carnatic in the year 1780 with a large force. Nothing of a decisive character had been gained when Hyder Ali died two years later, but Tipu commenced to intrigue with the French, the Mahrattas, and the Nizam of Hyderabad, and, in short, he availed himself of every opportunity of showing his hostility to the British. In

1798 he attempted to raise an army with the avowed intention of driving the English from India, and as he refused to agree to the peaceable proposals of Lord Wellesley, the famous siege was commenced which ended in the fall of Seringapatam and the death of Tipu himself on May 4, 1799. The attacking army faced an extremely heavy fire from the defenders of the fort, but it eventually succeeded in passing the breach and in overcoming the enemy. Tipu seemed to be unconscious of the danger which was threatening him, and after being abandoned by his men he was shot as he passed through one of the inner gateways. His remains were handed over to his attendants in order that the customary Mahommedan rites might be observed, and they were subsequently placed in the mausoleum which is in the Lal Bagh, or Red Garden, in the south-east portion of the island. This is also the burial-place of Hyder Ali and of his wife, Fakaruneesa Begum, and the three tombs are constructed of black hornblende, and are always covered with handsome palls. The upper portion of the mausoleum displays excellent workmanship in the carving of pillars and corridors, and the whole is surmounted by a fine dome. The subterranean dungeons—which are always shown to visitors—recall to one's mind the barbarities which were practised by Hyder Ali and by his son, more than 380 individuals, chiefly Highlanders, being found chained to the walls after the battle of Pollilore. These men were promised liberty and wealth if they would embrace the Mahommedan faith, but not a single one was found willing to purchase his life on terms such as these.

The temple of Sri Runganathaswamy, believed to have been built in the year A.D. 894, is a magnificent stone building of great dimensions, to which visitors flock in large numbers during the annual car festival in the month of January. The ruins of Tipu's palace within the walls of the fort are interesting from the fact that a considerable portion of it consisted of storehouses which were filled with gold-plate and silver, jewellery, precious stones, and costly firearms, together with an endless variety of other beautiful articles. The great mosque at the eastern end of the ruins was the favourite shrine of Hyder Ali and his son, and it is conspicuous at a distance of 20 miles, owing to the height of its minarets. Another of the sights of Seringapatam is the Daria Daulat Bagh, or "Garden of the Wealth of the Sea," which was a summer palace and a favourite resort of Tipu when the worries of rulership urged him to take physical rest. It was made particularly attractive by the gracefulness of its architecture and by the numerous paintings on the walls of incidents in the lives of nawabs and rajas of Southern India. There are several monuments which have been erected in honour of officers who fell in the final siege, and their existence cannot fail to be of interest to visitors, although the associations connected with them are of a painful character. Visitors should follow the course of the walls of the fortifications, in which they will notice that there are several picturesque gateways, the largest of these being on the eastern side of the town.

Leaving Seringapatam by rail the train branches off somewhat to the north-east, passing French Rocks, so named on account of the fierce conflicts which took place towards the close of the eighteenth century between the troops of the British and Tipu Sultan. Continuing north, the Jain village of Sravana Belagola is of special interest, containing, as it does, a colossal image of Gomatesvara, one of the most remarkable monuments in India. Passing Maddur, Channapatna, and Closepet, the city of Bangalore, the administrative capital of the State of Mysore, is reached. This is about 216 miles distant from Madras, and it is divided into two parts, one of which, namely, the Civil and Military Station, is described in notes on another page. The city, or *pettah*, which is the old native town of Bangalore proper, is 3,000 ft. above the level of the sea, and it covers an area of nearly 10 square miles, at the extreme south-west of which is the old fort. The latter is no longer used for military purposes, but it is regarded as one of the most fascinating historical relics in Southern India. Tradition has it that the fort was originally built of mud in or about the year 1535, but that it was reconstructed of stone by Mahommedans in 1761, and that when it was captured by the British in 1791 it was found to have been strongly fortified. Within the fort was the Sultan's palace, and although the walls were of mud it had been made attractive by the decorations and paintings in all the rooms. The principal Government departments were

TEMPLE GOPURAM, BELUR.

accommodated in this building until the year 1868, when new offices in Cubbon Park had been completed.

TOWN HALL, CHICKMAGALUR.

The present palace is a handsome double-storied building, which, to some extent, follows the design of Windsor

TEMPLE ELEPHANT, MYSORE.

Castle, and it is approached from the city by the Sheshadri road. It was formerly a private residence, but extensive alterations have been made, with the result that it is now one of the most attractive structures in Southern India. It is occupied by His Highness the Maharaja for three or four months in the year, but permanent quarters have been provided for Her Highness the Maharani, which are connected by a passage with the main portion of the buildinƒ The palace is situated in extensive grounds, upon which large sums of money have been expended, and a complete installation of electricity for lighting purposes has been effected.

The Government offices in Cubbon Park are built of stone in the Grecian style of architecture, and accommodation is found for council chambers, which contain a number of excellent oil paintings. The cost of the building was about four lakhs of rupees. Other fine structures within or in the neighbourhood of the park are the Sheshadri Memorial Hall, erected in honour of a former distinguished Dewan of Mysore, a statue of the late Queen Victoria at the south-east entrance of the park, and the Public Health Institute, which is the home of the vaccine, bacteriological, and toxicological departments. The Bangalore City Institute, near the south gate of the fort, is a centre of attraction for all, as its reading-room is well stocked with the principal English newspapers and magazines, and its library contains historical, fictional, and other volumes, while those who look for relaxation can find it on the tennis courts or in the billiard and card-rooms.

There are numerous parks, public gardens, and open spaces, which are conveniently situated equally as well for residents of the city as for those of the Civil and Military Station, the most important of these being the Lal Bagh, or Red Garden, which is tastefully laid out with beds of choice flowers and plants, while the grounds are intersected with well-kept drives and walks. The Cubbon Park is more than 100 acres in extent, and is greatly appreciated on account of the wealth of foliage of its trees and for the opportunities which are afforded of hearing a military band amid most beautiful surroundings.

Considerable progress has been made with several industries during recent years, and among these may be mentioned the City Brick and Tile Works, in which a special feature is made of the manufacture of fire, stable, stock, and chimney bricks, of Mangalore tiles, flower-pots, and other articles. The Mysore Spinning and Manufacturing Company, Ltd., have mills near the city station, in which about 900 individuals are employed in the working of about 220 looms and 15,500 spindles. A temporary visit to the Central Jail will be of absorbing interest both to the economist and the reformer, as primitive measures are combined with instruction in the manufacture of a host of useful personal and domestic articles.

A special feature is the making of carpets, but the output of the prison includes cloths of various kinds, towels, gunny-bags, baskets, and ropes, together with products of the carpenters' and blacksmiths' shops.

The quarters of the city in which are the native bazaars are typically Eastern in character, as there is the usual babel of tongues and the noisy competition, caused by dealers in certain commodities taking up positions in the market side by side with others in the same trade. The turnover in grain and cotton has now assumed formidable proportions, and it is anticipated that, with the advance which is being made in agricultural knowledge, the yields of cereals and fruits of the earth will be very materially increased.

TRAVELLING BY TONGA.

Photo by W. H. Reed.

The census returns of 1911 showed that there were 88,651 inhabitants, an increase of 19,204 during the previous ten years.

Travelling in an easterly direction from Bangalore the tourist arrives at Bowringpet, where passengers alight when journeying to Kolar, the chief town of the district of the same name, to which place a light railway has been opened recently. Kolar is of great antiquity, and contains a very old temple, and a number of ruins of an interesting character. Hyder Ali frequently visited there, and it is the burial-place of his father, Futtah Ali. The Kolar-Betta Hills, on the north-western side of the town, are for the most part rocky and bare of verdure, although on the summit there is a fine plateau, upon which there are several villages, whose inhabitants are engaged in cultivation of the land. The inhabitants of the town at the last census numbered about 8,200 persons. Situated about 43 miles in a north-westerly direction from Bangalore is Tumkur, the headquarters of the district of Tumkur. The town, with a population of about 6,000 inhabitants, is at the foot of the Devarayadroog Hills, which are about 3,000 ft. in height; and it is surrounded by a well-timbered and exceedingly picturesque region. It is, moreover, a most desirable place of residence during the heat of the summer months, and an additional attraction is an abundance of large and small game to be found among the hills.

Still farther to the west the train enters the district of Kadur, in which are the famous Baba Buden Hills, the loftiest range on the Mysore table-land, being about 6,000 ft. above the level of the sea. A very large number of coffee plantations may be seen here, and several planters have recently taken up the cultivation of rubber. The chief town is Chikmagalur, about 24 miles distant from the railway station at Kadur, and here are the district offices, hospital, and a club, which is exceedingly popular with the neighbouring agriculturists. Three miles to the north-west of Kadur is Birur, which is the junction for stations upon the branch line which has been opened to Shimoga. The tomb of Baba Buden, who is said to have introduced the cultivation of coffee in the State of Mysore, is shown to visitors, and as his burial-place is frequently termed the "Southern Mecca," one need not wonder that it is the scene of a very large annual pilgrimage.

Hassan, the municipal headquarters of the district of the same name, is about 27 miles south-west of Arsikere railway station, and its inhabitants were stated to number 7,461 persons at the last census. The scenery throughout this district, and particularly round about the chief town, is very attractive, and, with a mean temperature of not more than 73 degrees, the climate is specially inviting to those who have been cooped up in the cities and towns of the plains. The principal buildings are a Government Observatory and High School. Shimoga, the chief town of the district of Shimoga, is a good business place which contained 13,118 inhabitants at the census of 1911, as against 6,240 individuals in 1901. This increase of more than 100 per cent. in the short space of a decade was, undoubtedly, due to the discovery of rich deposits of manganese ore at Kempsee, which place has

P.W.D. OFFICES, MYSORE.

Photo by Wecksler.

been connected with the railway by a steam tramway. Some thousands of tons are dispatched from there, and several companies have been floated with the view of taking over the holdings of prospectors. On the northern boundary of the State is the district of Chitaldrug, which consists almost entirely of an extensive plain of more than 4,000 square miles, without any claim whatever to beauty or scenery. The chief town—Chitaldrug—is 24 miles distant from the railway station at Holalkere, and about 126 miles in a north-westerly direction from Bangalore. It is surrounded by old fortifications, which for

A MYSORE JUNGLE SCENE.

a considerable number of years were garrisoned by British troops. The chief attraction for visitors now lies in a series of subterranean chambers, in which are shrines and *lingams* of various descriptions, but the origin of the caverns is still a matter for conjecture, although the style of architecture points to a period in the early part of the fifteenth century. The census papers of 1911 showed that there were 564,243 inhabitants in the district of Chitaldrug, and that the town had 6,986 residents.

When at Shimoga the traveller will not be able to resist the temptation to visit the famous Gersoppa Falls, although a

ANGADI.

1. ANGADI BUNGALOW. 2. VIEW OF COFFEE. 3. PULPING HOUSE. 4. OFFICE AND STORES.

journey by road of some 64 miles is involved. The falls are situated on the frontier of the State of Mysore, overlooking the district of North Canara, and they are formed by the River Sharasvathi, which at this point is about 250 yards in breadth. The water plunges over a cliff (which is 830 ft. in height) in four separate falls; the first one is a sheer drop of 830 ft. into the boiling pool below; the second makes two plunges; while the third and fourth consist of a series of cascades.

In conclusion it may be added that the Maharaja and his Government are coming into closer contact daily with the actual condition of the people, and they look forward to the time when the value of a spirit of co-operation and a capacity for organization shall be recognized, and when every town and village shall be able to show some permanent improvements which have been effected by the collective work of the inhabitants. His Highness the Maharajah admirably summed up the situation in 1903 when he remarked that "it is not Governments or forms of government that have made the great industrial nations, but it is the spirit of the people and the energy of one and all working to a common end."

ANGADI

The hilly country of the district of Kadur, in Southern Mysore, in which this estate is situated, is a very favourable locality for the cultivation of coffee; the soil is suitable for the development of the trees, the altitude is not more than 3,000 ft., and the annual rainfall of 150 in. is a desirable quantity. Coffee was first planted on this property of 350 acres about the year 1884, and of the 240 acres now under that crop, a small area of the land was opened up as lately as 1913. The plants have a healthy appearance, showing signs of experienced attention, and the 205 acres in bearing yield an average annual return of 25 tons. A very good supply of water is available for all purposes from natural sources, and from the river, which forms one of the boundaries of the estate. A very pretty bungalow has an equally attractive approach by a good road, and it stands in a garden in which flowers and trees give of their best in these tropical regions. A small quantity of land is producing pepper and cardamoms, and it is proposed to extend the area under the former of these, and of coffee too.

The owner of the property is Mr. W. E. Tweedie, who is a member of the committee of the local Planters' Association, and he has had Mr. Douglas Jackson as his manager since 1912. The owner has the unusual good fortune to obtain a sufficient number of coolies, and he has constant work for 100 hands.

The majority of the districts in

ARCHULLY ESTATE.

1. THE BUNGALOW. 2. ENTRANCE TO ESTATE. 3. VIEW OF COFFEE. 4. HYBRIDS IN BLOSSOM. 5. RABBITS AT ARCHULLY.

Southern India are exceedingly rich in the diversity of their fauna, and the plumage and colouring of many of the smaller species are exquisite. Ardent naturalist as well as agriculturist, Mr. Jackson has made a special study of butterflies, and his extensive collection contains a number of gorgeous specimens.

Mudigere post office is only 10 miles distant from Angadi.

ARCHULLY

Any one who pays a visit to this estate whether he is an experienced planter or only a casual tourist—cannot fail to be impressed with the fact that it is a well-cultivated property, and that the coffee-trees are thoroughly healthy and fruitful. The area of 265 acres consists almost entirely of a life surface of land, upon which 100 acres of coffee, 20 acres of paddy, and 3 acres of cardamoms have been planted. There is no untidiness to be seen; the buildings are conspicuously neat, and the general aspect of the estate plainly demonstrates the excellent management of the owner, Mr. A. Thomson, who acquired it in the year 1899. The oldest bushes were planted in 1880, and further development was continued during the following nineteen or twenty years. Mr. Thomson is about to equip the buildings with the most approved type of machinery for the pulping and other processes through which the berries are passed.

There is a good supply of water for all purposes. The bungalow and other buildings are situated near a main road, and they are 3 miles distant from the post office at Hanbalu, and 14 miles from the telegraph office at Saklaspur. About 60 coolies are employed constantly.

Mr. Thomson is, further, the owner of the Huldi property of 69 acres, upon which there are 50 acres of coffee-bushes which are yielding an annual crop of 10 tons in weight. There is about a quarter of an acre of hybrid coffee and also about the same amount of Queensland coffee, which is not a success, as the bushes do not appear to flourish in a district where the rainfall is nearly 100 inches. The beans are cured at Mangalore and the manufactured produce is exported to European and other countries. A few pepper-vines have been planted among the coffee, and the crop—which is a very satisfactory one—is disposed of to local merchants.

Mr. Thomson personally manages the estate, and he has the continual services of about 30 hands.

BALUR

Mr. Thomas Cannon, a former part-proprietor of this estate, was the first European planter in the State of Mysore, but the property is now owned by the executors of the late Colonel George Manners Onslow and Mr. David Cannon. Coffee was first planted about the year 1841, but the whole of the cultivated area of 360 acres has been replanted, the youngest bushes having been put in during the year 1905. Steam-power is used in the pulping-house, and the manufactured coffee is consigned to Europe for sale. Balur is about 3,500 ft. above the level of the sea, and it has an excellent supply of water from natural sources, which are reinforced by an annual rainfall of 120 inches.

Mr. Ernest Lund has been manager since 1884, and he employs about 250 coolies. Postal and telegraphic facilities are within a distance of a mile and a half from the property, but a journey of about 70 miles is necessary to reach the nearest station at Kadur.

BARCHINHULLA

Southern India is essentially an agricultural country, and the greatest credit is due to pioneers who zealously continued to wage warfare against those natural forces which, unless subjugated, would deprive cultivators of the remotest chances of ultimate success. This battle against hostile natives, dense forests and jungles, or against unsuitable physical conditions, has taxed the patience and energy of even the best men in every civilized country in the world, but there is peculiar satisfaction in the reflection that human will power, human skill, and human perseverance have harnessed natural forces and have utilized them for the advancement of agricultural science.

The names of such pioneers deserve to be inscribed in prominent positions on scrolls of honour, but the most valuable testimony to their achievements is seen in the number of flourishing estates which have, to a very considerable extent, been developed by owners who have benefited by an acquaintance with the successful methods of cultivation evolved by early settlers. Mr. R. H. Elliot—the late owner of Barchinhulla—was one of those men to whom difficulties were a spur to increased determination to succeed, and the records of his work are full of interest to agriculturists generally. Mr. Elliot was not merely a practical demonstrator in scientific cultivation, but, large-hearted man that he was, he experienced great pleasure when his advice proved to be of service to others less experienced than himself. He rendered valuable help, too, in literary work, being the author (*inter alia*), of "Experiences of a Planter," and "Gold, Sport, and Planting in Mysore," and these have been of immense service to planters in Ceylon as well as in India. This gentleman died in the year 1914, and he bequeathed a life interest in the Barchinhulla property to Mr. A. R. Park, who had been manager there for a period of twenty-two years, but he stipulated that on the death of the latter the property should revert to the Elliot family. This estate was developed more than half a century ago, as coffee was planted there as early as the year 1857.

The estate comprises about 1,000 acres of land: 250 acres are producing coffee, 30 acres are cropped with cardamoms, and there are about 10 acres of Ceara rubber. There is dense original shade for the coffee-bushes, which are now in full bearing, and the average annual yield as a result of the heavy shade is comparatively high. The coffee-bean is pulped on the property, but the curing process takes place at Mangalore, where the produce is shipped to London. There is an excellent supply of water on the estate, and a large tank has been erected for its conservation for domestic purposes. The property is 3,400 ft. above the level of the sea, and an exceedingly fine panoramic view of the Ghauts, and across the plains is obtained from View Hill. A large and pretty bungalow is situated about 1½ miles from the post office at Hanbalu, and some 12 miles distant from the telegraph offices at Saklaspur.

Large game on the adjacent Ghauts is fairly plentiful, although nothing like what it used to be, and it may be mentioned that about fifty tigers have been shot from the estate during the past forty years. Mr. Park was probably the first person in India, or, in fact, anywhere, to succeed in rearing a tame Gaur (Indian bison).

BARGUAI, MUTSAUGOR, AND EACHER-YULLY ESTATES

These properties were acquired by Mr. R. A. Anderson in the year 1856, and the

BARCHINHULLA ESTATE.

1. Drying-ground. 2. Pulper. 3. Bungalow from the Drying-ground.

BARGUAI, MUTSAUGOR, AND EACHERVULLY ESTATES.

1 and 2, Coffee in Blossom. 3. Drying-ground, Cisterns, and Store. 4. View of Coffee.

work of development was commenced forthwith. High cultivation has always been practised, and a rigorous application of the principles of scientific agriculture caused the estate to become one of the most profitable in Southern India. Mr. Anderson was joined in partnership in 1868 by his cousin, Mr. Graham Anderson, C.I.E., who in 1879 and 1889 compiled two most valuable books, the titles being "Jottings on Coffee and its Culture in Mysore," and "Forest-trees in the Coffeelands of Southern Mysore." The death of the latter gentleman in the year 1914 was a serious loss to planters in India, as he had made a most exhaustive study of horticulture and forestry, and his ripe experience gained in the school of practical work caused his advice to be eagerly sought by old and young owners of estates alike.

The cousins fully grasped the important fact that when a soil has been cropped with the same genus of plant for several years in succession, certain ingredients are exhausted sooner than others, and that if this condition is not remedied disaster will inevitably follow. Rotation of crops has been instituted in order to counteract this exhaustion, but as this practice is not possible with coffee land, a change of seed, or, what is better still, a change in the variety of plant is desirable. Hence the Barguai estates have been twice planted throughout with different species of coffee, namely: the Old Munzerabad and the Coorg type, and now the Jamaica Golden-drop, which is favoured as being very consistent in yielding heavy crops of excellent quality, and it is being used for filling in supplies. The heaviest crop was gathered in 1887, when 124¾ tons were obtained, one tree alone giving as much as 11½ lb. of clean coffee. The average yield is 57 tons from about 450 acres.

The plant in the pulping-shed is driven by bullock-power, and an excellent supply of water for all purposes has been secured by the diversion of a stream which flows on one side of the estate. The beans are cured in a factory at Mangalore, and the made produce is shipped to London, where very good prices are realized in the open market. The sum of £112 a ton was received in 1912 for a quantity of pea-berry, but the highest amount ever obtained was £133.

About 36 acres of cardamoms have been planted only recently, but they are prospering well and are full of promise.

Mr. Anderson built a residence for himself on the property in 1857, but alterations and additions have been made at various times, with the result that it is now a commodious structure.

The senior partner still takes a keen interest in the management of the estate, but he has handed over a considerable portion of the responsibility to his son, Mr. R. G. T. Anderson.

Records of rainfall have been kept for fifty years, and the annual amount is shown to be about 78 in.

There are postal and telegraphic facilities at Saklaspur, which is 4½ miles distant.

BAREKODY

It has only been possible to cultivate about 120 acres in coffee and 14 acres in areca-nuts upon this estate of 410 acres, as about two-thirds of the total area consist of exceedingly poor land, which is permitted to remain as coarse grass and bush. Further than this, the management of the property was not at all satisfactory until the year 1911, when Mr. J. Ross Porter took on the control on behalf of the owner, Mr. Ross Porter. Some coffee-bushes were planted as early as the year 1868, and as the latest clearing took place in 1904 it follows that all the trees are now fully matured. After the cherries have been pulped on the premises, they are sent to Mangalore to be cured and subsequently sold. The bungalow is 3 miles distant from the post and telegraph office at Koppa, in the district of Kadur, in Mysore.

BETTAMANE

Natives planted a small part of this estate with coffee very many years ago, but when it came into the possession of Mr. M. J. Woodbridge—the present owner—a considerable amount of clearing was necessary. After this work had been accomplished, planting was again undertaken, and the latest development was effected in 1914. Bettamane, in Southern Mysore, is 170 acres in extent, and the cultivated area consists of 112 acres of Coorg jart coffee, 8 acres of cardamoms, and about 5 acres of rubber.

The bushes are fully protected by shade from trees of different varieties, and the harvest of berries is a good one, as 80 acres of mature shrubs give an average annual yield of 12 tons. The buildings in which the processes of pulping and washing of the beans take place have a very good supply of water from natural sources, and the manufactured coffee is consigned from Mangalore for sale in London. As the rubber-trees are still in their infancy the time has not arrived when they may be tapped, so that results cannot be given although there is ample ground for the expectation of a satisfactory return. The bungalow is one of those charming residences which, by reason of their situation at about 3,090 ft. above the level of the sea, and in the midst of a wealth of tropical verdure, are at once the joy of the possessor and the envy of the traveller.

The post and telegraph offices are at Mudigere, which is 9 miles distant.

OOGHULLI

Coffee-bushes were planted on this property during each year from 1901 to 1911, and the somewhat unusual plan—but effective nevertheless—of growing Para rubber-trees as shade has been adopted. There are about 15,000 of these trees in addition to a plot of 5 acres which is cultivated for rubber alone. Old and young coffee-shrubs cover an area of 155 acres. The work upon the estate—including pulping—is done by manual labour, and Mr. Woodbridge, the manager, employs about 80 hands. Rubber-trees are growing slowly at present, and it is possible that the altitude of the estate, 3,500 ft., is not particularly suitable. The owners of the property are Messrs. M. J. Woodbridge and S. H. Dennis.

OOTSEY

This and the two previously mentioned estates practically adjoin each other, and form a fine group at an elevation of over 3,000 ft. above sea-level, whence excellent views are obtained of the interesting scenery of the lower plateaus. Coffee—which is the only crop produced at Ootsey—was first planted about the year 1870, and there are 72 acres of these bushes upon the total of 111 acres.

A considerable portion of the cultivated area was replanted in 1913, and it is more than probable that the uncultivated acres will be brought into a profit-bearing state in the course of a year or two. The yield from the matured coffee-trees is a decidedly good one, as the harvest of 50 acres has given an annual average weight of 10 tons for each of the past ten years. Water for all purposes is

BETTAMANE ESTATE.

1. Ootsey Bungalow. 2. Coffee at Bettamane. 3. Drying-ground, Bettamane. 4. End of Bettamane Bungalow. 5. Orange Trees.

obtained from natural sources, and the yearly rainfall is about 95 in.

Ootsey is situated in close proximity to a Government main road, and it is one of those properties which may be expected to pay a good interest for expended capital.

Mr. Woodbridge acquired a managing partnership in 1913, and his partner is Mr. E. M. Davidson.

BICCODE

This estate of 308 acres consists of 160 acres of coffee, 108 acres of forest, 10 acres of rubber, and 30 acres which are mainly occupied by the usual plantation buildings and by the tank in which water is stored for general purposes.

The owner, Mr. C. Lake, purchased this property in 1906, and further developments, accompanied by heavy manuring, have been continued since then. The whole property consists of excellent land, situated in one of the best zones for coffee growing. There is a pulping-house with a good supply of water on the estate, and there is also ample accommodation in the shape of coolie lines. The young clearings are vigorous in their growth, and there is every prospect of their becoming as fruitful as the older ones. Some 80 coolies are employed constantly under the management of Mr. A. L. Hill.

Holalu estate, also belonging to Mr. Lake, is situated 3 miles distant from Biccode, and it is under the supervision of Mr. Hill, who has work for 80 hands throughout the year. There are 125 acres of coffee-trees growing under shade, the earliest of which were planted in 1898, and the latest in 1914. There are, in addition, 28 acres of grass land attached to the property, on which are situated the bungalow, outhouses, coolie-lines, and pulping-house. A feature of this estate is the very promising young clearing of hybrid coffee of the fifth generation—20 acres in extent—which is just coming into bearing.

Pepper-vines have been cultivated among the coffee on each estate, and they are thriving remarkably well. These two properties have proved to be a sound investment for the owner, and when all the young clearings have matured Mr. Lake will have the satisfaction of knowing that his venture has proved to be successful.

Mr. Hill resides in a nice bungalow on the Holalu property, which is a few miles distant from the post office at Bellagode, and from the telegraph office at Saklaspur. The properties consist of good flat land, well laid out with roads, and the two estates are situated near an important Government road.

Small game is plentiful, and little difficulty is experienced in getting a good bag of spotted dear, snipe, or duck.

BUPPONJI

This estate was opened up in the year 1880 by the owner, Mr. J. R. Errington, who had to encounter the usual preliminary difficulties in the way of clearing the jungle, in making roads, in planting trees for shade, and in undertaking a thorough system of cultivation of the land before he could put down any young coffee transplants. He subsequently designed and erected a very pretty bungalow, and made provision for an abundant supply of water, which is conserved in tanks for use in the outbuildings and for domestic purposes. The latest clearings for coffee were completed in 1912, and at the close of the year 1914 there were 270 acres in full profit, from which a crop of about 20 tons was gathered. Very satisfactory results are obtained from pepper vines, which are trained upon standards among the coffee-bushes, and cinchona and rubber give promise of ultimate profit. The property is about 2,800 ft. above sea-level, and it is intended to form a small tea plantation in the course of the next few years. About 100 coolies are employed on the estate, which is managed by the owner. The bungalow is 6 miles distant from the Koppa post and telegraph offices, and about 42 miles from the railway station at Tarikere.

CADAMANEY

Both climate and soil in the Native State of Mysore are supremely suitable for nearly all kinds of agricultural enterprise, hence there is no necessity for a farmer or a planter to restrict himself to the adoption of any particular branch of so important an industry as that which provides the bread, meat, spices, fruit, wool, cotton, silk, and the thousand-and-one other products of this State. There is, therefore, a large field open to the agriculturist in Southern India, and he has special advantages, as he is in comparatively close touch with the principal markets of the world.

The Cadamaney estate, which for convenience of working is divided up into five estates, is situated on the edge of the Western Ghauts on the direct route between Mysore and Mangalore. The elevation varies from 3,000 to 3,800 ft. above sea-level, and the rainfall ranges from 200 to 300 in. yearly. A portion of its 7,000 acres was originally opened up for coffee over half a century ago by Mr. J. S. Middleton, who was one of the pioneer planters in South Mysore. Owing to the system then in vogue, this coffee was grown in the open; so, although some magnificent crops were picked, the coffee was eventually wiped out by the "borer." It was then that Mr. J. S. Middleton introduced cardamoms, which have since become such an important industry in the district. The present owners of the property are Messrs. H. D. and A. Middleton.

The Cadamaney estate is now primarily cultivated for the growth of cardamoms and pepper, but there are, in addition, a fair number of cinchona and Ceara rubber-trees, and it has been proved that both tea and coffee-bushes will grow vigorously, and experiments now being undertaken with the latter are of a most promising character.

The cardamom crop-picking season extends from August to January. The crop is first washed out and then dried at a temperature of from 120° F. to 140° F.; the air in the drying-house is heated by being drawn through iron pipes (heated red hot in a furnace) by fans driven by water-power. After the shrivelled flower at the end of the berry has been removed by clipping, the cardamoms are "sulphur-bleached," and most carefully graded on the premises, and the produce is either sent to London for sale, or consigned to Calcutta for distribution to Eastern markets. The only silver medal awarded for cardamoms at the Mysore Exhibition of 1906 was secured by this estate.

Indigenous black pepper, which, by the way, is larger than the ordinary kind, is grown extensively at Cadamaney, and Messrs. Middleton have, for many years past, secured top market prices for this crop.

There is a small acreage under Ceara rubber, but it is doubtful if either this or any other variety of rubber can be regarded as a paying proposition.

Several varieties of cinchona grow freely on Cadamaney, and undoubtedly deserve greater attention. These trees are natives of South America, and are

BICCODE.

1. Woman carrying Basket of Coffee Biccode. 2. Hybrid Coffee Clearing, three and a half years old, 3. A Cardamom Ravine.

CADAMANEY.

1. General View of Cadamaney Valley. 2. Cuppeny Tullar Valley. 3. A View on the Estate.

cultivated for their bark, which yields the valuable alkaloids from which the chemist manufactures quinine, a febrifuge whose worth cannot be over-estimated. It was not until about the year 1860 that the Government of India obtained plants and seeds from South America, and experiments were forthwith made in their cultivation in the district of the Nilgiris.

The cultivation of tea is as yet in the experimental stage, but the owners are sanguine as to its ultimate results. There is a large area hitherto undeveloped that can be devoted to new products.

Bricks, lime, and timber used in the construction of the buildings were produced on the estate, and among the principal structures are four bungalows, two drying-houses, a bleaching-house, crop and grain stores.

There is a large amount of good timber on the property, which also furnishes the wood for cases used in packing the cardamom crop, each case having a capacity of about 150 lb. of bleached cardamoms. The rattan cane is common, and though Cadamaney is just outside the limits of the bamboo zone, there is a bastard variety of bamboo, known as the "Wotteh," which is extremely useful for the weaving of all kinds of basket-work, including the large hood thatched with leaves, locally called a *goraga*, worn by coolies during the monsoon, and without which it would be impossible for them to work in the heavy rains.

The opportunities for hunting big game on and in the immediate neighbourhood of the estate are exceptionally good, and the fauna includes bison, tiger, two varieties of panther, sloth-bear, sambur, barking deer, mouse deer, wild boar, and wild dog, and a considerable quantity of feathered game. Elephants are annual visitors, but are preserved by Government. Three varieties of monkey and the Malabar squirrel have to be kept down by watchmen, armed with guns, in the interests of crop protection. With an increased area under cultivation bison appear to be on the decrease, but it is interesting to note that there is a herd on the estate which can be frequently seen from the bungalows, and which quite disregards the shouts of coolies working in its vicinity. In spite of the general opinion that the ordinary cobra (*Cobra capella*) never attains a length of 6 ft., several, an inch or two over this size, have been killed on the property.

In addition to the labourers recruited in the Mysore State, Tamil coolies are imported for service, and as many as 500 hands are required during the busy season of the year, say August to March. Grain is issued weekly to these labourers. A large herd of cattle is kept for domestic purposes, and for supplying manure for the land.

Cadamaney is an exceedingly hilly property, but it is very healthy, and it has an abundant supply of good water.

The management of the property is in the hands of the partners, but they employ two European assistants, Messrs. F. Charleston and L. M. Guyver. The nearest post and telegraph offices are at Saklaspur, about 12 miles distant.

THE CAUVERY RICE MILLS

These mills—including offices, godowns, warehouses, stables, and stores—cover an area of about 5 acres, and, as they adjoin the railway station at Mysore, they have the enormous advantage of possessing a private siding; an advantage which can only be fully realized when the great saving in the cost of transport is considered. The machinery is thoroughly up to date in every respect, and it has been obtained from some of the most reliable firms in England. It has been erected upon cement foundations, and it is driven by a 25-h.p. steam-engine made by Douglas & Grant. The soil in the State of Mysore is exceedingly fertile and excellent crops of rice are obtained, principally in the districts of Mysore, Hassan, Kadur, and Shimoga, which are irrigated by channels of water drawn from several rivers. Rice is, in fact, the chief cereal grown in this State. Paddy is purchased locally, and after it has passed through various processes in the mills it is consigned to purchasers throughout the Madras Presidency. The average hourly output is about 20 cwt., and this is equivalent to 150 bags in a working day. By-products of the manufactured rice are sold locally. The proprietor, Mr. M. Siva Ram, is most assiduous in his careful supervision of every stage of the milling operations, and of the 50 hands who are regularly employed. The mills are worked both day and night during the busy season, but the proprietor, who is a confirmed believer in the necessity for a weekly cessation from work both for himself and his employees, will not, under any circumstances, permit the mills to be opened during Saturday afternoons and Sundays.

The concern is the first of its kind started in the province, where purely indigenous labour is employed and local funds are applied. Just at the commencement it had to face enormous difficulties and opposition from the public, as it was believed it would cast out of employment that section of people who entirely earned their livelihood by preparing rice by hand labour. Again, the rice-milling industry on a large scale had so far proved a miserable failure in this part of the country. The efficient management and the successful working of the company have given a fresh impetus to local talent to start similar industries. It has now the privilege to enjoy a wide reputation and the general confidence of all sections of people.

CHECKILI

This estate of 220 acres, belonging to Messrs. Binny & Co., Ltd., of Armenian Street, Madras, is situated about 12 miles distant from Chickmagalur, the chief town of the district of Kadur, in the native State of Mysore. A considerable portion of this district lies at an altitude of at least 4,000 ft. above the level of the sea, some of the loftiest ranges, indeed, running to an altitude of even 6,000 ft.; while the Checkili estate is at a height of about 3,700 ft. Cultivation of the estate, followed by the planting of coffee and a small quantity of cardamoms, commenced in the year 1894, and the final clearing took place about ten years later. Coffee-bushes cover an area of about 200 acres, and all of these are sufficiently protected by shade trees of a mixed variety, many of them of natural growth. The total crop for the first thirteen years yielded about 35 tons, but when the trees had matured the returns increased to the present figure of 40 tons.

The machinery in the pulping-house is driven by a steam-engine, and there is an abundance of water from natural sources for the washing of the berries and for household use. The bungalow is closely situated in a most attractive portion of the estate although views of the surrounding country are limited owing to the residence being almost completely shut in by hills.

Mr. W. H. F. Lincoln has been manager since 1906, and he finds constant employment for about 120 coolies. The town of Chickmagalur, with its post and telegraph offices, is 12 miles distant.

CADAMANEY.

1. Cardamoms. 2. Curing Cardamoms. 3. Some trophies shot on the Estate.

THE CAUVERY RICE MILLS.

1. Proprietor and Staff. 2 and 3. Views of the Mill. 4. Offices.

CHECKILI ESTATE.

1. Checkili Bungalow. 2. Vats and Drying-ground, Checkili. 3. General View, Chininhalli. 4. Coffee—Chininhalli Estate. 5. Cardamom Ravine.

CHETENHALLI

The climatic conditions of the native State of Mysore are such that the provision of "shade" trees for coffee-bushes appears to be an absolute necessity, and attempts which were made many years ago to cultivate coffee in the open resulted in failure. Efforts were made to reclaim portions of plantations which had been partially destroyed by the fierceness of the sun, but owners soon realized that they were expending much time and money needlessly by endeavouring to rear young plants without shade.

Mr. H. M. Northey, the managing partner (the joint-owner being Mr. E. S. Broughton) of the Chetenhalli estate, has for a considerable number of years been an earnest advocate of providing shade, and he has carried his precepts into practice, with the result that he is obtaining a most satisfactory annual yield from his trees.

The property comprises 216 acres, and this includes 200 acres of coffee and 12 acres of cardamoms. The coffee-trees, which are in full bearing, cover an area of 161 acres, and the annual crop from these has been as much as 30 tons for many years past. There is no finer sample of coffee in the State of Mysore than that which is grown at Chetenhalli, and the whole of the produce is sent to Mangalore for shipment to London. The pulping and other processes through which the bean is passed are carried out upon the premises by 150 local and west coast natives, who are under the direct control of Mr. Northey. The property lies at an elevation of 3,450 ft. above the level of the sea, and the annual rainfall is about 80 in. Chetenhalli is a remarkably healthy place, and it is conveniently situated within a distance of 2 miles from the post office at Chikanahalli, and 9 miles distant from the telegraph office at Mudigere. It has an ample supply of water for domestic and other purposes, and a very fine bungalow, whence magnificent views of the Bababudden Hills are obtained.

GOOTY KHAN

This estate, in the northern portion of the State of Mysore, was formerly known by the name of Yester, and, in fact, this designation is still its distinguishing mark in the coffee sale-rooms in London. The average elevation above sea-level may be put down at 2,300 ft. The owner, Mr. H. M. Northey, acquired the estate in the year 1907, but he has been interested in its management for upwards of a quarter of a century. It comprises some 412 acres, and the cultivation is as follows: 312 acres in coffee, cardamoms, and pepper, while the remainder consists of grass land. The planting of coffee commenced in 1877, and at the present time (1914) there is only a very small area which is not under some crop. There are 280 acres of coffee in full profit, and the annual yield has reached a total of 35 tons for several years past. As some might expect, Mr. Northey dresses his land annually with a liberal allowance of manures suitable to its requirements, and he is careful to provide a sufficiency of shade for all the bushes. There is an abundance of good water in springs and streams in all portions of the property, which is situated 1 mile distant from the post and telegraph offices at Sallebile, and 68 miles distant from Kadur, which is the nearest railway station. There is a very pretty approach to the owner's bungalow, and as the latter is built on an eminence, it commands unrivalled views of a charming country.

The cardamom-plants and pepper-vines are still young, but they give unmistakable promise of future fertility.

CHININHALLY

Contrary to the practice of the majority of coffee planters in Southern India, the proprietor of this estate—Mr. W. H. F. Lincoln—does not pulp his berries on the premises, but he has them washed and dried, after which they are sent elsewhere to undergo the other processes of manufacture. This is one of the younger plantations of the district, as the first planting of coffee only took place in the year 1906, but the trees have made such good progress that the crop for 1914 yielded about 12 tons. This represents the produce of the fully matured trees alone, but the quantity will be increased when the more recently planted growths have commenced to bear fruit. There is ample natural shade for the trees, and an abundant supply of water is available for all purposes. The buildings include a small store, sheds, quarters for coolies, and house for the writer.

Mr. Lincoln is his own manager, and he employs about 50 hands throughout the year. Chickmagalur is the nearest post office to the estate, which is situated about 3,600 ft. above sea-level.

Many plantations in the State of Mysore suffer severely from the depredations of wild animals, but Chininhally has nothing worse to fear than a few pigs.

CHUNDRAPUR

The owners of this estate of 700 acres—Messrs. J. G. and F. M. Hamilton—are recognized as leaders in plantation work in the State of Mysore, and the latter is President of the Planters' Association of South Mysore, which was founded in 1863. The surface of the land is somewhat broken in character, but about 360 acres have been cultivated, while a further area of 250 acres can be ploughed when required. Coffee-bushes have been planted under shade on 250 acres, and the well-manured soil produces a harvest of about 35 tons of produce from 200 acres of matured trees. Experiments have for some years been conducted in the growing of hybrid coffee, and such success has been obtained that this is now a regular feature of the estate. Two nicely situated bungalows and some excellent outbuildings have been erected, and they are about 5 miles distant from the post and telegraph offices at Mudigere. Samples of Ceara rubber sent from Chundrapur to London for classification were declared by experts to be equal to the best produce of Para plantations.

DOD LACKOONDA

This is an estate of 225 acres, of which 170 are planted with coffee, the remainder being grazing and paddy land. The owners of the property, which is situated in the Belur *taluq* of the district of Hassan, are Messrs. J. G. H. and J. R. Crawford. The nearest post office is at Bellagodu; the telegraph office is Saklaspur, while Banavar, the nearest railway station on the Madras and Southern Mahratta Railway, is 36 miles distant. The Government road bisects the estate and there is a good road for driving to the bungalow. The coffee is in excellent condition, and for many years the yield has been highly satisfactory, this result being due to naturally productive soil and to the liberal use of suitable fertilizers. All necessary buildings, including a bungalow, stores, and coolie lines, have been erected, and there is an abundance of local labour which is a great advantage. Mr. S. Sladden is the manager, and he employs about 100 coolies. The elevation is 3,200 ft., and the average rainfall is 70 in. per annum. Mr. J. G. H. Crawford, who is an active

CHETENHALLI.

1, THE BUNGALOW. 2. A VIEW FROM THE BUNGALOW.

member of the Planters' Association of South Mysore, is also directing agent of several coffee and other p--perties in that State, and reference to some of these will now be made.

BAITHNEY AND MOOSENKHAN

These fully developed estates consist of 285 acres of coffee, 40 acres of rubber, and some cardamoms. A perennial stream flows through the properties, but a tank has been constructed from which an ample supply of water is obtained for the pulping-house, in which the machinery is driven by bullock-power. Mr. C. K. Pittock, who has been manager since 1901, can be congratulated on a satisfactory yield from 280 acres of matured trees. Rubber was planted in 1911, and, although there is abundant promise of good results, no tapping can take place before the end of 1915, or the beginning of the following year. The estates are not more than 6 miles distant from the post and telegraph offices at Saklaspur.

CUBBONHULLY

As the planting of coffee upon this estate was only commenced in the year 1910 it follows that there are at present only a few trees from which even a small quantity of berries can be gathered, but as there is an abundance of mixed shade, a fair supply of water, and a suitable climate, it is only natural that Mr. Pittock, the manager, should look forward with some confidence to prospective harvests. About 5 acres of cardamoms have been planted, but these trees, too, have not yet reached a fruit-bearing age. As a matter of fact the estate is "in the making," and the manager and his hundred coolies are striving, by thorough cultivation, to make Cubbonhully as profitable an investment as other properties belonging to Mr. Mockett. Saklaspur post and telegraph offices are not more than 6 miles distant.

DHAITAPORE

Mr. Rutherford, who is superintendent of another group of Mr. Brooke Mockett's properties, resides on the Dhaitapore estate, consisting of 110 acres, which, with the exception of a small area devoted to cardamoms, are planted with fully grown coffee-trees. The formation of the ground is exceedingly rocky, but the elevation and climate appear to be suitable for the production of high average crops of good berries.

HERVATTI

The Hervatti estate, situated in the Belur *taluq*, is a fine property of 150 acres, owned by Captain W. L. Crawford and Mr. H. V. Crawford. The elevation is about 3,200 ft. and the annual rainfall is 60 in. The nearest post office is at Bellagode, and the telegraph office is Saklaspur, while the most convenient railway station is at Arsikere. The garden is in excellent condition and the crops are very promising.

HOSGUDDAY

Adjacent to Ubban, and controlled from that centre by Mr. Crawford, is the Hosgudday estate of 70 acres, all of which are planted with fully matured coffee-bushes, although a few cardamoms are grown in the ravines as at Ubban. The ripe berries are passed through the preliminary stages of preparation at Ubban, but curing and shipment take place at Mangalore. This estate was opened up by Mr. J. G. H. Crawford.

MULLAGAHULLY AND ARNEGALHULLY

Mr. Crawford was concerned in the early development of these estates, and after felling and clearing had been successfully accomplished, he planted 104 acres with coffee and the balance of 6 acres with cardamoms. As soon as the coffee-berries have been plucked they are carted to Ubban to be pulped, but they are cured in the factory at Mangalore. It may be mentioned that exceptionally good prices have invariably been made in the open market for the coffee which is grown upon all of the above-mentioned estates.

MUTHIGEE, IGLOOR, KITEGELALE, AND KUL TOTA

Mr. J. G. H. Crawford is managing agent for these estates belonging to Mrs. James Hunt, and the acreage of each, in the order in which they appear above, is as follows: 100, 45, 30, and 110. There is very little variation in the altitude of these properties, as all are, practically, about 3,000 ft. above the level of the sea. Coffee was planted upon the first three estates many years ago, but renewals have been necessary from time to time, as a considerable number of the original plantings were unproductive. About two-thirds of the trees are, however, now (1915) in full bearing, and the remainder are as healthy and vigorous as one could wish to see. The Kul Tota property was opened up for coffee by a Colonel Beresford, but the whole area has been replanted with the addition, lately, of cardamoms and pepper, and it is satisfactory to notice that the young trees are exceedingly promising.

OSSOOR

This estate is 470 acres in extent, and the cultivation is as follows: coffee, 400 acres; Ceara rubber, 50 acres; and cardamoms, 20 acres. The property is about 3,000 ft. above the level of the sea, and from this elevation a magnificent panorama of strikingly beautiful scenery is obtained from the verandah of the large and attractive bungalow. Other buildings include a pulping-house, fitted with a steam-engine, some sheds in which there are mills for grinding bones and crushing poonac, and a bleaching house for cardamoms. Post and telegraph offices at Saklaspur are within a distance of 3 miles. The estate is under the management of Captain W. L. Crawford, who employs large gangs of imported labour; and attached to and cultivated conjointly with Ossoor are the properties of Bellagode and Kendynmunny, comprising 65 acres and 40 acres respectively.

SOONDHULLY AND LAKOONDAH

These estates, of 105 acres and 100 acres respectively, are planted with coffee, with the exception of a small quantity of cardamoms, which are found at Lakoondah. A pulping-house at Soondhully, with machinery worked by bullock-power, does duty for the two properties, but each holding has a sufficient number of necessary buildings. The average elevation of the estates above sea-level is about 3,200 ft., and the annual rainfall is 65 in. The manager is Mr. S. Sladden.

TIPPAPUR AND APPAJIS

An area consisting of about two-thirds of these reclaimed native estates of 130 acres is occupied by matured coffee-trees, while the remainder has been planted with young bushes of first-class quality. The soil is fertile, and the excellent management, which is apparent in the cultivation of the land and in the systematic care of the plantation, is further manifested in the satisfactory yields which are from time to time obtained.

UBBAN

Coffee was grown upon this estate of 240 acres as long ago as 1854, but when it was purchased in 1876 by Mr. Brooke Mockett, it was replanted by him with trees which are now (1915) in their prime as regards fruitfulness, and which have for many years given a most satisfactory yield. Cardamoms have been planted recently, and are a valuable adjunct to coffee. There is an abundance of good mixed shade on the property, and the annual rainfall of 75 in., and the altitude above sea-level of about 3,400 ft., are, respectively, eminently suitable for the cultivation of coffee. The pulping machinery on the premises is driven by an oil-engine, but the preparing process takes place at the factory at Mangalore, where bags of the cured produce are shipped to London for sale. A very pretty bungalow is all the more desirable on account of the particularly healthy climate which is enjoyed, and other advantageous circumstances are the proximity of good roads and of post and telegraph offices at Saklaspur, which is 11 miles distant. Mr. J. G. H. Crawford is agent and general manager for Mr. Mockett, who is the owner of the 12 estates which are referred to below. Mr. E. W. Rutherford is assistant at Ubban, where some 200 coolies are employed.

HANDI

An experienced agriculturist has a dual object before him in the cultivation of his land, and each of these may be said to be dependent upon the other. He naturally selects seeds of plants which may reasonably be expected to thrive upon his estate, and at the same time he is anxious to grow such crops as will have a beneficial effect in returning to the soil those essentials to vegetable life which are continually being withdrawn.

Coffee is regarded as a "wasting" crop, as, although the skin or pulp of the berry is always returned to the land, and while leaves are constantly falling to the ground, it cannot be said that any appreciable manurial value is derived by such processes. Planters have not been slow to recognize this fact, and they have embarked upon a systematic course of sound cultivation, which includes the judicious application of suitable manures. But fertilizers cannot be effectively used unless they contain the actual substances of which the soil stands in need. A correct estimate of the capabilities of soils is therefore a *sine qua non,* and it is only when this is understood that an agriculturist can point to the sufficiency or otherwise of those organic and inorganic substances which are necessary to plant life.

Mr. H. Godwin Bower, the owner of the Handi estate, believes in careful attention being given to the provision of shade, green mulch, and bulk manures, together with as little interference as possible with the roots of the bushes. This gentleman is one of many successful planters who are firm supporters of common-sense principles of agriculture, and who do not

DOD LACKOONDA.

1. THE BUNGALOW. 2. VIEW OF COFFEE.

HANDI ESTATE.

1. Bungalow. 2. A Cardamom Ravine. 3. Two-year-old Coffee in Blossom. 4. Coffee in Blossom.

rely entirely upon science and chemistry. Coffee in the old days was grown in the open, but the ravages of leaf disease and "borer" were so terrible that many thousands of acres were completely destroyed. This led to the planting of coffee under shade, and where there is an insufficient natural supply, quickly growing trees, such as *Grevillea robusta* and *Erythrina lithosperma* are being planted. Although leaf disease and "borer" are still in evidence, their ravages are now comparatively insignificant when estates are properly cultivated and shaded. The best trees under which coffee can be grown are those which have deep roots and a heavy leaf deposit. The climate at Handi is of a particularly favourable character, extremes of either heat or cold being practically unknown. During the hottest months of the year the temperature never exceeds 90° F., and even when winter arrives, and one is wont to associate Christmastide with nipping frosts and chilling blasts, the keen and invigorating atmosphere on this property is greatly appreciated as the thermometer remains for some time at the respectable figure of 60°. The average annual rainfall is only about 77 in., but an ample supply of good water for all purposes is derived from natural streams on the estate. Cardamoms are grown upon a small portion of the property, and a few acres of paddy land are let to various tenants.

Mr. Bower entered into possession of Handi in the year 1901, and he occupies a very comfortable bungalow whence exceedingly pretty views are obtained of the beautiful scenery of the country on its northern and westc.n sides. A coffee planter, while having due regard to the claims of his estate, has always a considerable amount of spare time on his hands, and as a rule it is found that, true sportsmen as the majority are, they can have many hours of exhilarating enjoyment with both rod and gun.

HOOLI HUNDLOO.

1. The Bungalow. 2. A View from the Bungalow. 3. Cardamoms. 4. View of Coffee.

HOOLI HUNDLOO

Books have been published by the hundred in which attempts have been made to describe the transcendent beauty of scenery in Southern India, but it must be confessed that nothing short of a personal visit will enable a stranger to realize the full sublimity of the panorama, which includes rugged mountains, cultivated plateaus, forests, and rivers. It is not necessary to forsake the railway or good roads in order to witness these fine views, and in the State of Mysore, in which Hooli Hundloo is situated, there are many spots of surpassing beauty. The bungalow on this estate, for instance, is situated on an eminence which is at least 3,500 feet above the level of the sea, and the grand view from its windows extends far away to the Baba Buddan Hills.

The property, which belongs to Mr. Percy Hunt, is 250 acres in extent, and 130 acres have been planted with coffee since the year 1892. All the trees are protected by shade, and those which have come into bearing are yielding an annual crop of about 14 tons. The parchment coffee is sent to Mangalore to be cured, whence it is shipped to England for sale. A good supply of water for the early processes of manufacture is obtained from natural springs. Mr. Hunt manages the property himself, and about 80 coolies are in constant work. There are post and telegraphic facilities at Chikanhalli and Mudigere respectively.

Mr. Hunt is a member of the committee of the Mysore Planters' Association, which was founded in the year 1863.

HONEYVALE

This is a compact estate of 400 acres, and it is situated within 2 miles distance from the post and telegraphic offices at Balur, although 70 miles have to be traversed before the railway station at Kadur is reached. Messrs. Morgan Brothers acquired it more than a quarter of a century ago, and it has been their custom to clear a certain portion of the jungle annually, the latest development having taken place in 1912. The planting of coffee commenced about the year 1874, and there are now 370 acres under this crop, together with a small quantity of cardamoms, the average coffee crop being 70 tons yearly. Nearly all of the shade trees in the old coffee are of natural growth, but others have been planted to meet deficiencies. In the new clearings all the shade trees were planted at the same time as the coffee.

The final processes in the manufacture of coffee—namely, curing and shipping—take place in the factory at Mangalore (situated on the coast at a distance of 70 miles), which belongs to two of the brothers, and where hundreds of tons are carted yearly ; but the berries are pulped, washed, and dried on the estate. The machinery in the buildings is driven by an oil-engine, and the floors of the drying-grounds have been laid with Mangalore tiles. The estate is of a very hilly character, but the average elevation above sea-level is about 3,700 ft. The site upon which the bungalow has been erected for the manager, Mr. F. I. Morgan, is an excellent one, as it is very central and commands a clear view of nearly every part of the property, and this is no mean advantage where there are some 300 coolies at work.

Tigers are shot very near, one of these striped beauties having fallen to Mr. Morgan's gun in each of the past five seasons ; small game, such as Indian woodcock, snipe, hares, and partridges, are obtained in the vicinity.

GUBGULL

The opening up of this estate was taken in hand about the year 1894, and eventually the total of 210 acres had been fully cultivated, 160 acres being in coffee and 50 acres in rubber. It was subsequently discovered that trees from which rubber is derived are not a payable proposition when they are planted on land which, like Gubgull, is 2,000 ft. above the level of the sea. These trees were, therefore, cut down, and the whole area is being cropped with coffee, although some of the plants are at present only two years of age. The majority of the bushes are of the Coorg variety, but trials are being made of the two species known as "Robusta" and "Golden Drop."

The management of the estate—which is in the hands of Mr. F. I. Morgan—is practically on the same lines as at Honeyvale, and similar success has been achieved in cultivation, seeing that an average annual harvest of coffee, 30 tons in weight, is reaped from the 160 acres. A good supply of water is derived from wells which have been sunk.

The owner of the estate is Mr. H. R. Morgan.

HOSCOTTAY

Coffee-trees were first planted upon this estate, in Mysore, about the year 1869, and at the present time there are 150 acres of coffee under shade, 15 acres of Ceara rubber-trees, and 5 acres of cardamoms. The average annual yield of coffee picked from 115 acres of trees in full bearing was fully 30 tons in three successive years. The property lies at the very suitable altitude of about 3,600 ft., and the plantation has north and north-east aspects. The owners are Sir Basil Scott and Sir Lindsay Wood, and the manager is Mr. P. M. Wilkins, who has lived fourteen years upon this estate, although he has been engaged in plantation work in India for nearly a quarter of a century.

Under the same ownership and management is the Hoskerri estate, also in Mysore, which is 156 acres in extent, and within about 10 miles from the post and telegraph offices at Somwarpet. Coffee-trees of more than seven years of age occupy about 80 acres of the property, 7 acres of which were planted in 1914 ; there are four acres of cardamoms, and about 26 acres of Ceara rubber-tees. The last named have not yet been tapped, although they were planted fully seven years ago.

The Huntsey estate in the same neighbourhood is owned by Mr. T. R. Dalton, for whom Mr. Wilkins is general manager. It comprises 160 acres of coffee-trees in bearing, 40 acres of others which were planted about two years ago, and 17 acres of rubber-trees ; and of the balance of 233 acres it will be possible to cultivate nearly 100 acres. Situated upon the estate are a pulping-house, stables, a large store, and sheds, together with a small golf course. The property is some 3,200 ft. above the level of the sea, and it has an average annual rainfall of about 60 inches. About 700 camphor plants are thriving well, and they have yielded the most satisfactory return of 2 lb. from each bush. Mr. C. R. Jessop is superintendent, and he employs about 100 coolies. The Somwarpet post and telegraph offices are not more than 7 miles distant from Huntsey.

ISABEL AND NETRAKUL

This property consists of 180 acres all told, and the whole area is cultivated for coffee, which was planted periodically between the years 1888 and 1912. The estate belongs to Mr. E. C. Bolton, and is about 2,450 ft. above the level of the sea. It is situated some half a dozen miles from the post office at Koppa. A small bungalow is occupied by the proprietor's writer, and a number of outbuildings—among which is a pulping-house—have been erected. Mr. Bolton manages everything connected with the property, and he has 110 coolies on his wages sheets.

Mr. Bolton, further, manages the fully cultivated property known as Netrakul, of 170 acres, on behalf of the owners, Messrs. R. and C. S. Crawford. The plantation of coffee-bushes was started in the year 1875, and the output of the manufactured product compares very favourably in quality and quantity to the acre with the results of similar estates in Mysore, lying at an altitude of about 2,500 ft. The buildings include a very prettily situated bungalow, a pulping-house, and sheds and stores, and these have an unfailing supply of water, which is obtained from tanks on the property.

KARRADI BETTA

More than one-half of the coffee-producing area of Southern India lies within the native State of Mysore, and the district of Hassan—in which the Karradi Betta estate is situated—is noted for the number of its thriving plantations. In the first place Hassan has a remarkably

HONEYVALE COFFEE ESTATE.

1. Bungalow. 2. Coffee Wintering. 3. Drying-ground and Engine-house. 4. General View, showing Tiger Hill. 5. Coffee.

KARRADI BETTA ESTATE.

1. View from the Bungalow, Karradi Betta Estate. 2. Coffee Nurseries, Karradi Betta. 3 Artherwhully Tank.

KARRADI BETTA ESTATE.

1. Newlands Block—Young Coffee. 2. A General View, Karradi Betta 3. Caugnoor Estate. 4. Garbling Coffee.

temperate climate, the mean temperature being 73° F.; secondly, the altitude, which shows an average of about 3,500 ft., is peculiarly suitable for the coffee-growing industry; and, lastly, the soil consists of rich, deep loam, which is extremely fertile. This estate—together with others in the same neighbourhood which are referred to hereafter—belongs to Captain Edwin Hunt, a veteran planter, whose name is honoured among agriculturists throughout Southern India. Successful planters, such as this gentleman, are profoundly impressed with the necessity for ascertaining the chemical constituents of their land; they make careful observations as to texture, origin, depth of soil, and its hygrometric qualities; and they are equally insistent upon the frequent application of dressings of good manure. But the adoption of these measures alone do not ensure success: they are certainly aids to it, but there is the personal element to be reckoned with. A planter must be a man of great determination, and he should have sound practical experience, otherwise the expenditure of his force is simply energy thrown away. An inspection of the estates mentioned in these notes leads one to the conclusion that their owner commenced planting work on the right lines, and the present thriving condition of the properties proves beyond a doubt that the soundest principles of scientific agriculture have been followed during the many years of cultivation.

Karradi Betta is 550 acres in extent, and coffee monopolizes 400 acres of this total. Planting commenced in 1874, when Captain Hunt purchased the estate, and this work has been continued from time to time until there are now 300 acres in full profit. The average annual yield for the past three years has been no less than 50 tons. Some coffee plantations have too much shade, while others have too little, but the happy medium has been struck at Karradi Betta, and the high class of the manufactured product is ample testimony to the fact. Pure water, and plenty of it, is an essential upon an estate, and several tanks and wells are used for keeping a good supply for the two bungalows and for the pulping-house, where the machinery is at present driven by bullock-power; but an engine is to be installed at an early date. The district of Hassan is very beautiful, with its varied scenery of mountain, plateau, valley, river, and forest, and the views obtained from one of the bungalows especially are unusually lovely. The property is 2 miles distant from the post office at Kenchammana Hosskotie, and about 25 miles from the telegraph at Hassan. The proprietor's son, Mr. E. Vivian Hunt, is manager of the estate, and he finds regular employment for 250 hands.

Cardamoms were only planted in 1908, but the crop for the year 1914 yielded a total of a quarter of a ton.

CAUGNOOR

This property of 520 acres, belonging to Captain Hunt, and under the management of Mr. W. V. Reilly, is an old and well-known estate, as a portion of it was planted as long ago as 1855, although it was not acquired by the present owner until twenty years later. Out of a total area of 220 acres, no fewer than 200 acres are producing 30 tons of coffee annually. The bean is submitted to the pulping and other processes on the estate, and a water-turbine is to be erected to facilitate these works, but it is sent to Mangalore to be cured prior to shipment to England. A very comfortable bungalow has been erected in the midst of delightful scenery, and other buildings include pulping-house, drying and other sheds, stables, and stores. Caugnoor possesses postal and telegraphic facilities similar to those enjoyed by Karradi Betta; it has an annual rainfall of 65 in., and it is some 3,200 ft. above the level of the sea. About 150 coolies are constantly required.

Coffee-bushes were planted on the Mullapoor estate in the year 1877, when it became the property of Captain Hunt, and there are now 150 acres in full profit, the average annual yield being 20 tons. The remaining 100 acres are still covered with virgin jungle, but they will be brought into cultivation at an early date. About 120 coolies are under the ever-watchful eye of the assistant manager —Mr. W. V. Reilly—who superintends every branch of work on the estate. He selects only the best seeds for sowing in the nursery, and the utmost care is taken in the rearing of the young plants. The land has to be cleared for the reception of the seedlings; then there are the operations of lining, holing, weeding, and pruning, while it is not too much to say that on a well-managed plantation each day presents some new feature to be dealt with, calling forth the exercise of skill and determination. And then in due course comes the picking and pulping of the berries, and their ultimate consignment to Mangalore to be cured. Mullapoor practically adjoins post and telegraph offices, and has the usual range of estate buildings, such as pulping and drying-houses and other sheds and stores.

Government roads in many parts of Mysore are not models of what good highways should be, and many estates—Artherwhully by way of example—are difficult of access. This property is 18 miles distant from the town of Saklaspur, and as the Government road by which the estate is approached is, at times, too bad for words, the only plan is to saddle a horse and take a by-path, along which the journey can be completed in 8 miles. Captain Hunt purchased this property in 1888, and he at once commenced a yearly planting of coffee-bushes, and this practice has been continued up to 1912. There are now 90 acres of fully matured bushes and 85 acres of younger ones, and the latter are already showing unmistakable signs of becoming fruitful trees. Cardamoms are grown upon a further 25 acres of the property.

Estate owners in many portions of the Madras Presidency complain loudly as to the insufficiency of the supply of labour, caused in the majority of instances by recruiting agents who carry away the best of the coolies; but Captain Hunt's managers have not hitherto experienced any difficulty in obtaining as many hands as they require. Artherwhully is managed by Mr. E. Vivian Hunt, who gives employment to 150 hands.

KELGANNI

It is generally admitted that an extensive rainfall is injurious to coffee-trees, and, referring particularly to the district of Mysore, in which this estate is situated, injury is caused to the plants owing to a total absence of sun for the period from June to September. This unfavourable condition causes stagnation, checks growth, and subsequently produces a fungoid disease known as "black rot," which strips off much of the foliage as well as the unripened crop.

Light, air, a reasonable quantity of water, and certain inorganic substances are as necessary to promote healthy life in a plant as in a human being, and it is only by judicious cultivation, which seeks to retain or provide essentials and to limit the power of, or entirely remove,

KELGANNI.

1. Bungalow. 2. Young Coffee. 3. Old Coffee. 4. Seed Field. 5. Five-year-old Clearing. 6. Old Coffee.

undesirable forces, that one may expect vigorous and fruitful trees.

The Kelganni estate is visited with a very slight rainfall—less than 50 in. a year—and the excellent yields of prime coffee are attributed, principally, to this circumstance, and to the high state of cultivation in which the land is kept. The property is 155 acres in extent, and the 125 acres of coffee-plants include 40 acres of old trees, 50 acres of bushes of five years of age, and about 35 acres of others planted in 1912. The crop from the oldest trees has averaged between 5 and 6 cwt. to the acre for the past five years, while those planted in 1909 gave a similar quantity in 1913 and 1914. Naturally grown shade trees of proved varieties have been allowed to remain undisturbed, and young shade trees are planted in between. The climate in this neighbourhood is exceptionally fine, and as the altitude of the property above sea-level is about 3,600 ft., it is not surprising that the manufactured produce invariably realizes very satisfactory prices in the London market.

Seed from the estate has become very popular owing to absence of diseases and pests, and many hundreds of acres in Mysore and adjoining districts have been planted from Kelganni seed.

Charming views in every direction of the surrounding country are obtained from the fine bungalow, which is only 10 miles distant from the post and telegraph offices at Mudigere.

Although the estate is cultivated upon scientific principles, other adjuncts to successful plantation work and careful regulation of shade are not forgotten. Water, obtained from wells and tanks, is available for the various processes of manufacture of coffee and for domestic purposes.

The proprietor, Mr. L. P. Kent, employs an average number of 100 coolies.

KELAGUR, ABRAGOODIGAY, AND GOOMENKHAN

These three properties form a group under the management of Mr. C. Danvers, who took up his residence upon them in 1884. They are owned by Messrs. Binny & Co., Ltd., of Armenian Street, Madras.

The whole area extends to 535 acres, and all the land upon which cultivation is possible is now planted with coffee (344 acres), rubber (84 acres), and cardamoms. The "Chick" variety of coffee was selected when the earliest plantings took place about half a century ago, but the Coorg species was substituted in 1883 for the whole of the 344 acres. The bushes are grown under mixed shade trees, and the average weight of the annual yield for the past five years has been 60 tons.

Ceara rubber-trees were planted in 1909 and 1912, but one cannot speak of results in their case as they are not yet old enough to be tapped. Cardamoms occupy only a small portion of the properties, but the returns are sufficiently encouraging to warrant their further cultivation. Water is obtained from springs, and the supply is large enough for the washing of the berries and for household purposes. The annual rainfall is about 170 in. at Goomenkhan, and about 20 in. less at the other two places.

Balur post and telegraphic offices are 3 miles distant from Kelagur, 7 miles from Abragoodigay, and 9 miles from Goomenkhan.

Mr. Danvers employs some 250 hands throughout the year.

KESIMBURTHY

The planting of coffee of the old "Chick" variety was commenced upon this estate in or about the year 1864, but bushes of the Coorg type have been substituted on 183 acres out of 223 acres now under cultivation for this crop. The practical experience of the manager, Mr. C. Sylk, has much to do with the splendid annual yields, but contributory factors are an excellent climate and an average yearly rainfall of 84 inches. The harvest for many years past obtained from 219 acres of matured trees has been about 4½ cwts. to the acre. A sufficient supply of water, derived from natural springs, is forced through pipes to the bungalow and to the shed in which the newly plucked berries are washed. The property, which is 5 miles distant from the post office at Santaveri, in the district of Kadur, belongs to Mr. G. R. Oliver, who employs about 100 coolies.

KIRAHULLI

About 80 acres of this estate were cultivated in 1891, and the owner, Mr. H. F. Anderson, planted that area with coffee-bushes, which for some years past have been in full bearing. Younger ones are thriving upon 45 acres, paddy lands to the extent of 20 acres are let on lease to tenants, and the balance of the total of 220 acres can be brought into profitable use whenever required. Shade is obtained from several kinds of trees, naturally and artificially grown, and this provision, coupled with good farming, is conducive to the harvesting of an average annual crop of 3½ cwts. to the acre. After the berries have been passed through all necessary processes of manufacture, the product is shipped direct for sale in French markets. The secret of successful manuring lies in the knowledge as to the nature of the most desirable fertilisers and the quantity which should be used, and the general appearance of the plantation at Kirahulli is proof that the soil is receiving the exact treatment which it needs. Mr. Anderson manages the property himself, and he usually employs about 70 hands.

The post and telegraphic offices at Saklaspur are 6 miles distant.

KOTHENCOOL

The owner of this estate, Mr. H. Kerr, believes in "high" cultivation, and he has ample justification for his opinion, as the average yield of coffee for the past three years from bushes planted in the years 1901 and 1902 has been more than 4½ cwts. to the acre, and this result is undoubtedly largely attributable to the excellent manner in which the land is prepared. Various kinds of seeds have been tried with success, and a special feature is now being made of native coffee, but all plants have an abundance of shade and good water, together with the benefit of an average annual rainfall of about 125 in. A turbine is used for driving machinery for hulling coffee berries, for grinding bones, and for the crushing of corn. The property, which is 125 acres in extent, is 5 miles distant from the post office of Santaveri, and 23 miles from Birur, the nearest railway station.

KULHUTTY

Agriculturists in every country in the world have the reputation of being inveterate grumblers, and it is probable that the coffee-planters of Southern India have more legitimate ground for complaints than any other class of cultivators. They remember the time when the coffee-growing industry was in its infancy, when failures occurred owing to an absence of definite knowledge as to the most suitable type of tree to be planted, and when the

KULHUTTY ESTATE.

1. THE BUNGALOW. 2. STORES AND ENGINE-HOUSE. 3. COFFEE NURSERY. 4. COOLIE LINES. 5. COFFEE.

KUMMERGODE.

1. BUNGALOW. 2 VIEW FROM THE BUNGALOW. 3. STORES AND DRYING-GROUND. 4. YOUNG COFFEE.

questions of suitability of altitude, rainfall, and climate were not fully understood. After several estates had been fully developed there followed those terrible diseases and pests which ruined hundreds of plantations, the principal of these being commonly known as bug, borer, and leaf disease. The first to attack the coffee-tree was the black, or scaly, bug, which appeared about the year 1850. Subsequently there were the white, or mealy, bug ; the green bug, the borer, and the leaf disease which was noticed in India in 1871. Coffee planters are, therefore, engaged in a precarious occupation, and one is only too pleased to come across such a thriving estate as that of Kulhutty, near Santaveri, in the State of Mysore.

It is owned by Mrs. W. St. Claire Johnson, Mrs. S. J. Wilson, and Mr. D. H. Luxa, and it consists of 600 acres, all of which have been planted with coffee, of which only 450 acres are at present in full bearing. The oldest plants are fifty years of age, while the latest clearings took place in 1904 and 1905. The estate is unusually well supplied with excellent buildings which cover an area of about 3 acres, and these include lines for coolies, a large store, curing shed, pulping and washing houses, and hulling, winnowing, and sizing rooms.

There is one 9-h.p. oil-engine on the premises, and, in fact, the machinery includes everything which is necessary for the treatment of the berry in all the processes through which it is passed, until the "made" coffee is ready for shipment from Mangalore to London.

The Baba Booden Hills—upon which this property is situated—have for many years past been noted for the excellent quality and quantity of the crops of coffee produced there, and the average annual yield at Kulhutty for the past five years has been 90 tons.

The property lies on the slope of the Baba Booden Hills, at an altitude of about 3,500 feet, and it has an excellent supply of water from natural sources, exclusive of an annual rainfall of about 78 inches. There is a very fine bungalow which commands extensive views of mountain and valley, of forest and uncultivated land, and of an imposing waterfall. About 250 coolies are employed under the management of Mr. S. J. Wilson. The nearest post and telegraph offices are at Santaveri.

KUMMERGODE

This estate, which is 6 miles distant from the post and telegraph offices at Mudigere, in the district of Kadur, in the State of Mysore, was purchased in 1906 from Col. H. B. Sanderson, C.I.E., retired, by Messrs. St. John and Campbell Hunt, who belong to a family of planters who are exceedingly well known in Southern India. A portion of the total of 512 acres was planted originally with the old Mysore chick jart of coffee, but when this species failed the property was replanted with seed from the Province of Coorg, thus giving an area of 300 acres under coffee.

That the change was a wise one is evident from the uniformly satisfactory yields which have been reaped since then, and it may be added that the harvest from 220 acres of matured trees has given a weight of 45 tons for each of the past eight years. Those dreaded pests of the planter, the green bug (*Lecanium viride*) and the borer (*Xylotrechus quadrupes*), have not, up to the present, done any damage to this estate, but it is possible that this immunity may be due in no small measure to a high state of cultivation and to the excellent plan of having a sufficient quantity of shade trees for the protection of the bushes. A never-failing stream on the property provides an ample supply of good water, which is stored in a tank near the buildings. A moderate quantity of manure is applied annually to the whole estate, and a further area of about 120 acres will, it is expected, be placed under coffee during the next few years. A small portion of the property is depastured with cattle in order to provide a sufficient quantity of natural manure.

A very pretty bungalow, standing amid beautiful surroundings, is an altogether inadequate description of the residence of the managing partner, Mr. St. John Hunt, as it overlooks a fine stretch of park-like land, which reminds one forcibly of an English demesne.

About 150 labourers — principally coolies from the West Coast—are employed for nine months in the year.

KUTCHEN HUCKLOO

It is probable that there is no better district for sport in Southern India than the State of Mysore, as there is an abundance of game for rifle or shot-gun, in addition to a splendid variety of fish for the disciples of Izaak Walton. The sportsmen, too, are as expert as they are keen, and the worries of the day may be banished as the mist before the rising sun by the pleasurable excitement which is associated with the pursuit of animals or birds, or with the capture of fish.

The Kutchen Huckloo estate, which is situated about 5 miles distant from the post and telegraphic offices at Herebellalloo, in the district of Kadur, in the State of Mysore, is in the heart of the sportsman's paradise, which has been referred to above, but it is more than this, as it is highly cultivated on thoroughly up-to-date principles of agriculture, and it is credited with producing exceedingly heavy crops of coffee. The owners are Messrs. E. C. and L. P. Kent, and the first-named (who has been manager since the commencement of the partnership), began to plant coffee as early as the year 1893. Further development has taken place annually until 1914, when there were 265 acres of old and young trees. Bushes in full bearing now cover an area of 215 acres, and the annual yield from these for the past four years has been 46 tons in weight, although the harvest for the season 1913-14 gave a total of 62½ tons, which is an exceptionally heavy quantity.

The plantation will be enlarged at an early date, and when it is fully developed there will be 400 acres of coffee, 10 acres of rubber, and a certain quantity of cardamoms, which are expected to give an annual yield of about 25 maunds.

At an altitude of 3,350 ft. above the level of the sea is a charming bungalow with wide verandah, from which a view of four of the highest peaks of the Mysore range of hills can be seen, while the panorama in a north-easterly direction extends for a distance of more than 60 miles.

There is a good supply of water from natural sources for household purposes, and the annual rainfall is about 122 in. Some 240 coolies are employed constantly.

Bison, sambur, spotted deer, panther, jungle sheep, and wild boar can always be found on the estate lands, and tigers generally visit and levy a heavy toll on the owner's cattle three or four times a year. Small game is very plentiful, and includes hares, jungle fowl, spur fowl, mouse deer, Imperial, green and bronze wing pigeons, and, at the right time of the year, snipe and woodcock.

Very fine fishing can be had in any one of the three rivers within a distance

KUTCHEN HUCKLOO ESTATE.

1. Bungalow Toondoo Field 2. Field of Old Coffee. 3. Corkagoondie Coffee Field. 4. Kelagur Field.

of 4 miles, the heaviest *mahseer* caught by Mr. E. C. Kent being 18½ lb.

LINGAPUR

This property is situated at an elevation of 3,500 ft. in the district of Hassan, in Southern Mysore, and consists of 150 acres of land. There are 115 acres under coffee of the Coorg species, but 25 acres of this area have been planted by the owner, Mr. W. F. Scholfield. since he acquired the property in 1901. All the trees are now in profit, and the average annual yield, which has increased under the management of the proprietor, is about 3½ cwt. to the acre. Pulping is done by hand-power, and the berries are sent to Mangalore for further treatment, the produce being ultimately sold in the open market. In addition to the coffee there are five acres of cardamoms and a small area of grazing ground. The estate pay-sheets contain the names of only 60 coolies, whereas constant employment could be found for 100 hands if they could be obtained,

The owner's residence is a very pretty double-storied bungalow, from which extensive views are obtained of the interesting country which stretches far away in a southerly direction. The estate is only 12 miles distant from the post office at Saklaspur, and about 40 miles from the Banavar railway station.

MAVINKERE

The majority of the 340 acres of coffee-trees upon this estate of 400 acres were planted by Mr. W. H. Reed, who has been manager since 1897 for the owner, Mr. W. A. Lee. To him, too, must be attributed vast improvements in the general appearance of the property, such as the construction of buildings, fencing, and other matters. The stores and sheds have been designed and built with the utmost care, and the machinery —including two oil-engines in the pulping-house—is up to date in every respect. Both hybrid and Coorg varieties of coffee are being grown, but the cultivation of the former is as yet in the experimental stage. All of the bushes are in full bearing, as the oldest trees were planted in 1890, while the youngest are at least six years of age. The naturally good soil in the district of Kadur, in which this property is situated, is enriched by a course of manuring, and as the plantation is about 3,200 ft. above the level of the sea, and the bushes are well protected by shade, the conditions are so favourable that satisfactory yields are invariably obtained. In proof of this it may be said that for the past five years the annual returns have exceeded the average quantity per acre obtained from other estates in the district. All of the produce is sold in the open markets.

Very satisfactory from a financial point of view have been the receipts from cardamoms (interplanted with coffee and areca-nuts, while the paddy fields have paid handsomely for good tillage. A good supply of water is led by gravitation to the very fine bungalow, the lines for coolies, stores, and the gardens ; while the River Bhadra forms one of the boundaries of the estate.

There are few square miles of land in the State of Mysore in which there is not

LINGAPUR.

1. Bungalow, showing entrance. 2. Bagging Coffee for the West Coast. 3. Pulp House—Washing Coffee.

an abundance of game of some description, and the Mavinkere property, not to be outdone by its neighbours, is the home for spotted and moose deer, sambur, pig, and other smaller species.

Kalasa post and telegraph offices are only 2 miles distant. Some 220 coolies are employed constantly.

MOODSOOSIE

Ninety-six acres out of a total of 99 acres have been planted with coffee upon this estate, which is about 2½ miles distant from the telegraph station at Mudigere. It is owned by Mr. E. E. Broughton, and is managed by Mr. H. M. Northey, who finds regular employment for about 50 labourers. Hand pulping of the berries takes place on the property, but curing is carried out at Mangalore, where the bags of prepared coffee are shipped to London. A capital supply of water is obtained from springs and wells, and the average annual yield from the trees is about 18 tons.

MURKULL

The district of Kadur in Southern Mysore, in which this estate is situated, is of an exceedingly hilly character, but it contains rich loam soil, which is particularly suitable for the cultivation of coffee. The Murkull property, for instance, lies on the slopes of hills which rise to an altitude of about 3,200 ft. above the level of the sea, and good farming upon fertile land, a monsoon of moderate force, and a very healthy climate which is invariably experienced at this elevation, have combined in securing an annual yield of 5 cwt. of coffee to the acre for the past eight seasons.

The property, which belongs to Mr. F. Urquhart, and for whom Mr. H. G. Bonner has been manager since 1892, is 400 acres in extent, and the planting of coffee was commenced in 1885, and has been carried on regularly up to the present time. There are now (1914) 380 acres under this crop, but this area, naturally, includes a considerable number of young trees which have not yet borne fruit. An oil-engine is used for driving the machinery in the pulping, washing, and other houses, and the water required for these buildings is obtained from never-failing springs. All coffee-bushes are growing under shade, which is composed, principally, of trees which have been planted recently, as there is only a very small portion of the original jungle to be seen now.

About 85 acres of land were planted with Para rubber interplanted with coffee in 1909, but the trees have not yet been tapped. At the same time Mr. Urquhart does not look forward to any appreciable results from the rubber, as the altitude of the estate is too great. Cardamoms have been planted, and satisfactory yields have been gathered.

The sloping ground of the property faces the north-east, and from the windows of the pretty bungalow a fine view is given of Bababudeu Hills.

The post and telegraphic offices at Balur in the district of Kadur are about 4 miles distant.

MYLEMONY

This property—known sometimes as Cannon's estate—is about a mile distant from the post office at Joladalu, and some 8 miles from the telegraph buildings at Chickmagalur, in Mysore. It is somewhat of a disadvantage that there is an indifferent supply of water at Mylemony, but with the plantation at an altitude of 4,000 ft., and with thorough cultivation and a regular manuring of the soil. no fewer than 50 tons of coffee have been gathered annually for the past 26 years from 325 acres of bushes. Mr. H. Allardyce has been manager for four years, and he finds work for about 200 hands.

THE MYSORE GOVERNMENT STUD FARM

The question of a continuous supply of horses suitable for cavalry purposes in India is one which has presented immense difficulties even in the history of the present generation, and it has been "red-taped" from commanding officers to royal commissions, and from commissions to experts in breeding, and even now (1914) very little real progress seems to have been made. South Africa sent some horses of a good type between the years 1850 and 1860, and it was found that they were capable of retaining condition in hot or cold weather even when not stabled, but subsequent consignments were lacking in quality and size, owing largely to a want of knowledge of selection of parents, or, which is more probable, to the carelessness with which the growing colts and fillies were treated with regard to food and shelter.

The consequent diminution in the supply from South Africa undoubtedly led many wealthy men in India to rear as many foals as possible in the hope that this continent might not be so dependent upon foreign countries. These notes deal directly with the Mysore Government Stud Farm of his Highness the Maharajah Sir Sri Krishnaraja Wadiyar, G.C.S.I., and thanks are due to Lieut.-Colonel R. G. Jones, C.I.E., the late manager, from whose pamphlet much information has been obtained. This officer became acquainted with the farm —Kunigal by name—in 1883, and the practice at that time was to obtain stud mares from local cavalry regiments. Many of these were good types of country-bred animals standing about 14 hands 3 in. in height, with good shoulders and of great quality, and they are the ancestors of the excellent stud which is in existence to-day. Colonel Hay was appointed manager in the year 1883, and he at once realized the difficulties of the system of breeding from regimental mares, which, under the conditions then existing, had to return to camp for military duties immediately after service.

There were practically no records of any value, but Colonel Hay, a man of administrative ability, prepared registers which contained particulars of the names and addresses of the owners of the mares, the dates of service, and the results, together with descriptive features and measurements of the foals.

The stallions in those days were chiefly Arabs, although there were three or four "Walers," which were supposed to be thoroughbred. These horses were, however, almost worn out, and the manager persuaded the Durbar to grant a sum of Rs. 5,250 for the purchase of an English sire, with the result that Alvarro, a son of Pero Gomez, who won the St. Leger and Derby, was selected by General Thornhill, who was the agent in England for obtaining entire horses for India. A very fine Arab stallion (Ruby) was bought about this time from General Graves, and this horse stamped his stock with a refinement of quality which is apparent to-day in some of the best stud dams, such as Vivandiere, Opal, Garnet, Star, and others. Colonel Macintire was the next manager, and he induced the Maharajah's Government to keep a certain number of mares permanently for stud purposes, and he effected considerable improvements in the cultivation of the farm. He also

MURKULL ESTATE.

1. MURKULL ESTATE FROM TIGER HILL. 2. BUNGALOW. 3. COFFEE.

instituted a system of selling the best-looking youngsters (chiefly mares) at a low sum (Rs. 350) to induce sportsmen to take them into training, and if the animal turned out a failure as regards pace, but remained sound and fit for the ranks, he did not object to exchange the developed horse for another colt or filly. It followed, therefore, that any animals which were returned to the farm had enjoyed the advantage of good feeding and careful attention, and that although they might be unsuitable for racing, they nevertheless had gained in height and in strength, and proved to be better mothers than those which had not been galloped. In proof of this it may be mentioned that many mares, including Minelle, her daughter Vivandiere, Donna, Parvathi, Palm Clara, and others who won races, were returned to the farm and produced some excellent offspring. Colonel Macintire died in 1897, and he was succeeded as manager by Colonel Jones. The latter was confronted by difficulties from the commencement, as the then Dewan (Sir Sheshadri Iyer) insisted that the expenditure of the farm must be decreased either by a reduction in the number of animals or by the production of stock which would realize more money as remounts than had hitherto been the case. Colonel Jones instituted a searching inquiry into the matter, and he found that one of the principal causes of the heavy working cost was that a very large percentage of the mares failed to produce foals.

This led the manager to study the medical aspect of barrenness, and he discovered that the cause was due to some physical rather than to any constitutional defects. Certain steps were therefore taken, and the operations resulted in the foaling percentage being increased from about 35 to more than 80. Colonel Jones found that stock sired by Arabs, particularly coarse Arabs, was most irregular, and this was probably due to the pedigree of the stallion being somewhat mixed. For instance, the same horse will beget a monster and a pigmy, but when the mare progeny showed quality, they would, if crossed with a thoroughbred horse, throw fair-sized stock which exhibited none of the coarseness which was frequently seen in the half-bred Arabs. In fact, one must continue crossing every class of animal which is not thoroughbred with an Arab until a fairly stout mare is obtained, then the Arab short neck and shoulder must be eliminated by the infusion of thoroughbred blood. Colonel Jones continued: "Stallions should be as symmetrical as possible, with every quality of beauty and strength, but with no weak points. I consider thoroughbreds to be the most suitable (1) because they beget riding horses and not cart horses; (2) because constant elimination of bad points in the pedigree makes them less liable to get offspring of crooked shape; and (3) because they are more inbred than any other class, and therefore stamp their stock more than any stallions of mixed breed. The stallion should stand 16 hands in height, should possess great power and good clean bone, and he should be strong enough to carry at least a weight of 16 stone over a stiff country, because it must not be forgotten that a cavalryman in full marching order will scale at least 16 stone and in some cases even more than this."

There are some first-class sires now at Kunigal, and they include Courage, who is a magnificent Australian thoroughbred of the Musket, Carbine, and Yattendon strains, and who was champion of his year at the Sydney Horse Show, while another grand animal in Sugar Apple (brown) by Persimmon out of a mare by Bend Or. This sire and dam were winners of the English Derby. The Arab stallions are represented by Precious (white) and Gallant (chestnut), both of which were not very successful on the turf.

The mares on the farm are classified as follows: (1) Commoners, that is, Walers without pedigrees, Mahrattas, Kathiawars, etc.; (2) those with Arab sires; (3) those with thoroughbred sires and Arab grandsires; (4) those with two thoroughbred top crosses, that is, Arab great-grandsires; (5) those with three thoroughbred top crosses, that is, Arab great-great-grandsires; and (6) thoroughbreds. Arab stallions should be mated with commoners, but thoroughbreds should serve all the others. The system of measuring the young stock has been discontinued in favour of weighing, and this practice was highly recommended by Colonel Jones, as it enabled him to ascertain the value of the different kinds of foodstuffs according to the effect which they had upon the animals.

The duties of the veterinarian include the inspection of each animal daily, and the isolation and subsequent treatment of any which are in ill-health, and he has to regulate the food supplies and to record the weight of the stock every month. A liberal amount of exercise is essential to maintain live stock in a healthy condition, and this is given regularly under the personal supervision of the manager or the veterinarian. An enclosed racecourse—about three-quarters of a mile in length—has been made, and stretching gallops are given periodically to the majority of the animals. Foals are taken in hand when eight months old, and, with careful treatment at first, they soon begin to strive against each other out of pure love of rivalry; mares, too, are galloped until quite near to the end of their pregnancy, while the stallions, running loose, are urged round a circular "longe" by the farm rough-rider. The selection of brood mares was in the hands of Colonel Jones, and owing to his long connection with the farm, he could frequently recognize in the offspring the best points of the earlier strain, and thus choose the mares with a good chance of success. This official retired from the managership in 1912, and he was succeeded by H.H. the Yuvaraja. The latter having been appointed an extraordinary Member of Council early in 1914, the management was taken up by Lieut.-Colonel A. Jones, who is now conducting the work of the farm on the lines so successfully established by his predecessors.

The general work of the farm is carried on by coolies—under proper supervision—and this consists of the growing of grain, lucerne, and other fodder crops, and the care of buildings, fences, and paddocks, while estate books, records of breeding, correspondence, and other matters are taken in hand by clerical assistants. The veterinarian, Mr. Davidson, is an exceedingly able officer, and he has done invaluable work in connection with the artificial fertilization of barren mares, a subject, however, which is too scientific and wholly unsuitable for these pages.

Military officers as well as private individuals who have visited at Kunigal on several occasions are unanimous in their praise of the immense improvements which were effected during the fourteen or fifteen years' management by Lieut.-Colonel R. G. Jones, and they have paid a high tribute to his talent and experience, which raised the standard of the stud animals to a height which had never been attained before.

The present manager is ably maintaining the reputation of the farm, and it is not too much to say that the breeding of weedy and unsuitable animals is a thing of the past, and that the paddocks and

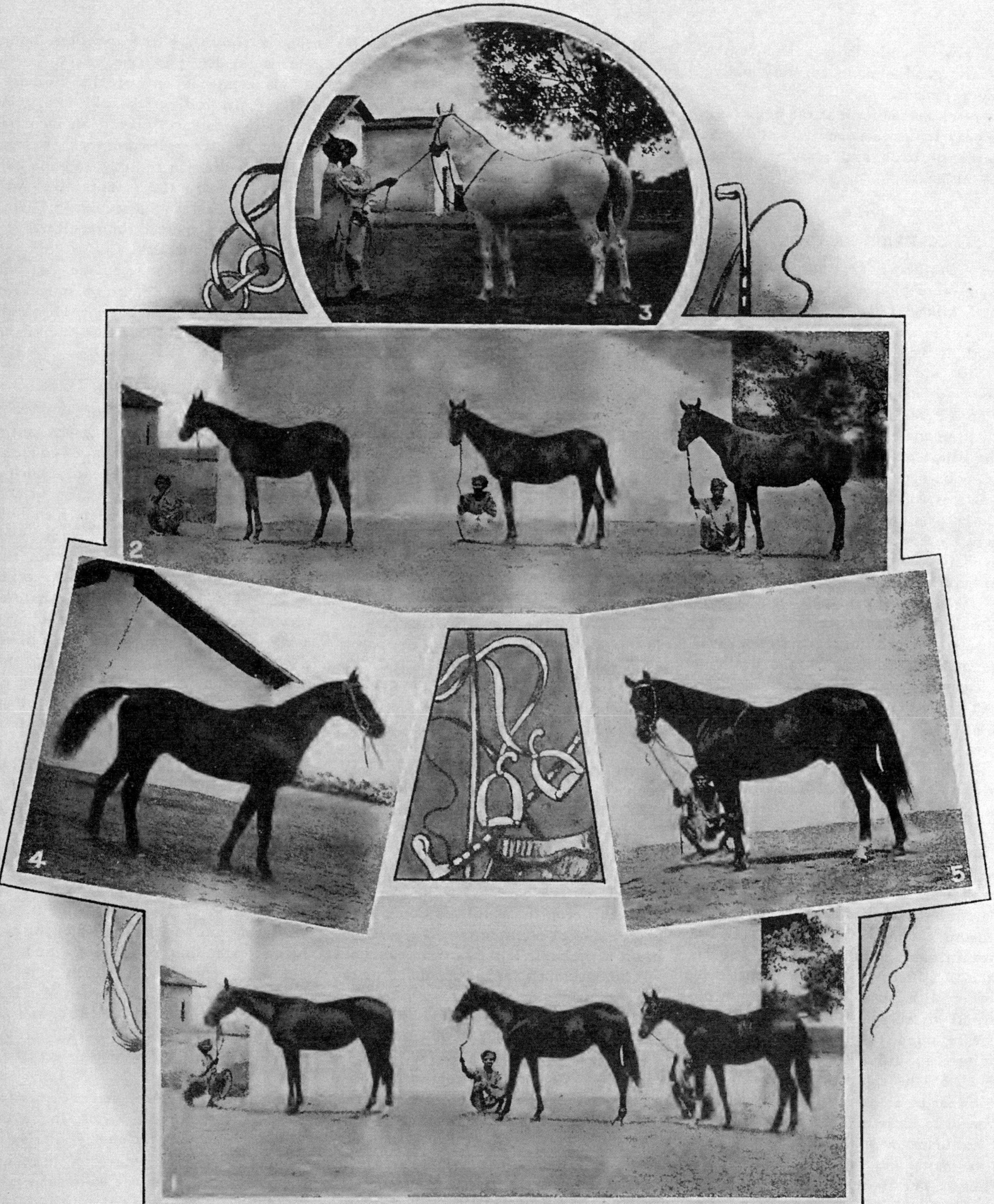

THE MYSORE GOVERNMENT STUD FARM.

1. Fillies bred on the Farm. 2. Colts bred on the Farm. 3. Precious, Grey Arab Stallion. 4. Courage, Bay Australian Stallion. 5. Sugar Apple, Brown English Stallion.

stables now contain horses and mares which are good enough for any native cavalry regiment.

The stock on the farm at the beginning of the year 1914 consisted of 10 stallions, 95 mares, 98 foals, and 4 mules, a total of 207 animals.

SAMPIGE ESTATE

The brothers Denton—John and William—were pioneer planters of coffee in the Tarikeri *taluq* of the district of Kadur, in the native State of Mysore, and although it may be safely assumed that they were not spared the extreme difficulties and dangers incidental to the opening up of virgin forest, it is some satisfaction to learn that the good work accomplished by them stands to-day as a living tribute to their persevering skill. The estates which were the first to come under cultivation by their labours were Nojay Katte, Santaweri, Kalhatti, and Kesinavarty. Another property, opened up in September 1861 and known as Sampige, belonged to Mr. John Denton, who admitted his brother-in-law, Mr. H. Courpalais, as working partner, with half share in the receipts. On the death of Mr. Denton, the whole estate was purchased from the widow by the survivi partner, and thus the latter assumed full control of the property. It was not actually a " bed of roses " to which the latter gentleman had committed himself, but he faced all obstacles with a determination to overcome them. Vexatious lawsuits are the worst of moral afflictions, and as some of these followed upon the output of capital in connection with the purchase, the new owner found that he had a by no means easy task to face. Money was scarce in many of the planting districts of the Presidency, and Mr. Courpalais, together with many others, had to put forth all his energies and take advantage of every opportunity of minimizing expenditure in order to keep the annual balance on the right side of the ledger. The owner of Sampige, however, not only managed to make a success of this estate, but he further acquired the Maskalmardi, Kurkanmatti, and the Chowdy Kan properties. The last two named estates passed out of his possession in 1891, being given by him to his brother and wife respectively. Mr. Courpalais died on June 20, 1901, and by his will he devised Sampige to Mr. Claude Courpalais, a nephew and the present owner, and Maskalmardi passed to Messrs. E. J. Courpalais and W. R. Courpalais respectively.

Sampige and Maskalmardi comprise 822 acres and 498 acres respectively, but the area cultivated with coffee is 640 and 370 acres.

The properties are situated in the Baba Budeen Hills, which is one of the best coffee-growing districts in the State.

The average annual yield of coffee upon these two estates is about 7 cwt. to the acre, and after the crop has been pulped at home it is consigned to the owners' agents in London—Messrs. T. H. Allan & Co., of 17 Gracechurch Street, E.C.—by whom it is sold.

SANTAVERI JIGNY KHAN AND BEETY KHAN

It is a prominent feature of this coffee estate that the outbuildings are more numerous than is usual on such properties, and they have been soundly constructed with the best of materials, and fitted with modern machinery and plant. The pulping-house, for instance, is roomy and airy, and the plant is driven by an oil-engine, which also provides the power for machines for crushing bones and winnowing berries. The floor of the drying-grounds has been cemented, and there are numerous stores, sheds, washing, and other rooms. The property belongs to Messrs. Porter, Hall & Co. Mr. A. C. W. Denne (who arrived in India in the year 1887), became manager six years later, and still holds this position.

One learns that the oldest coffee-bushes of the original " Chick " variety were planted in 1854, but most of the 440 acres under this crop consist of the Coorg type. The total area of the estate is 600 acres, and it is probable that a further 100 acres will be developed for the extension of the present plantation. The land is exceedingly hilly, but the elevation above the level of the sea is from 3,700 to 4,700 ft. The ranges upon which coffee-trees are cultivated slope very considerably in easterly, southerly, and northerly directions, but Mr. Denne is unable to observe that the various aspects cause any substantial difference in the quality of the produce. Coffee, which is designated "native," is sold locally, but the main portion of the crop is forwarded from the curing works at Mangalore to be disposed of in London. An abundance of indigenous and planted shade has been secured, and the beneficial effect upon the crop is shown by the excellent annual returns for the past five years.

This estate is one of the landmarks of Southern India; the old fort, which is still in existence, played an important part in the struggles between the close of the seventeenth century and the commencement of the eighteenth, when Colonel Wellesley—subsequently Duke of Wellington—dispersed the rebellious force under Sirjappa Naick.

The property is close to the post office at Santaveri, and about 17 miles from the railway station at Birur. The coolies on the estate are about 200 in number.

BEETY KHAN

One may undertake a journey of scores of miles in the State of Mysore and see an almost endless succession of coffee and other plantations. Hard roads, which are suitable for motor-cars or farm vehicles, are met with in many districts, although it is more than probable that in the experiences of every twenty-four hours there will be nothing better than an execrable track, along which progression is naturally very slow. Excepting in size, many of the estates are practically identical, although a closer inspection will reveal methods of cultivation widely differing from each other on account of the nature of soil constituents, or from varying climatic conditions. The capabilities of a manager, too, are reflected in cleanliness and tidiness, and, to a very great extent, in the fruitfulness of the trees, and the Beety Khan estate, owned by Mr. A. C. W. Denne, is comparatively small in size, but it is a good example of a well-ordered holding. It comprises 230 acres of land, situated at an elevation of 3,100 to 4,100 ft. above sea-level, and very fine views of the plains below, extending to Shimoga and Tarikere, are obtained. Fifteen acres had been planted with coffee when Mr. Denne acquired the property in 1895, and since that time he has brought the cultivated area up to 180 acres, of which 135 acres are in full bearing.

A yearly average of 60 in. of rainfall is not too much for coffee, but, in the event of there being any deficiency in this direction, a very good supply of pure water from springs and other sources is always available.

Looking back a few miles of our journey, pulping-houses with machinery driven by steam or oil-engines were noticed; in another place a pair of bullocks slowly working similar plant

SAMPIGE ESTATE.

1. BUNGALOW 2. STORES. 3. ENGINE-HOUSE. 4. COFFEE. 5. COFFEE NURSERY.

SANTAVERI JIGNY KHAN.

1. Betty Khan Bungalow. 2. Drying-grounds, Jigny Khan. 3. View of the Babu Budeen Hills, showing Crown Hill.

SIDDABILE.

1. Bungalow. 2. Waterfall 3. Coffee. General View.

were seen; while here at Beety Khan manual labour only is employed for the same process.

Some 80 coolies are employed under the supervision of Mr. H. Kerr, who resides in a very nice bungalow on the estate.

GONEKAL

This is a neat little property of 70 acres, situated about 4 miles distant from the post office at Santaveri, and the whole area is used for the cultivation of coffee-bushes, the oldest of which were planted in the year 1893. All of the trees—with the exception of 10 acres—are in bearing, and the produce is sold locally. The owner, Mr. A. C. W. Denne, manages everything, but he has installed a writer who has supervision over the coolies.

The estate is 3,300 ft. above the level of the sea, and it has an annual rainfall of 60 in.

SEAFORTH AND YELLAIMALLY

The Seaforth estate—by which name these two properties are known—formerly belonged to the Arbuthnot family of Madras, but it is now in the hands of a private company, of which Mr. J. W. H. Bradshaw is manager. It consists of 2,555 acres of land, 500 of which have been brought into cultivation. Coffee was grown at one time, but tea, chiefly of the Northern Indian variety, is now the only crop on the estate. The greater portion of the land lies at an elevation of 4,000 ft. above the level of the sea, and a most equable climate, coupled with a well-distributed rainfall of 105 in., is largely responsible for the excellent annual yield of from 600 to 650 lb. of tea to the acre. The factory, which is a double-storied building containing large withering lofts, is about 1 mile distant from the manager's bungalow, and it contains up-to-date plant which includes three rollers, two roll breakers, three dryers of different kinds, a sifter, and a packing machine which is driven by turbine water-power. Tea is put up in packets which weight 1 lb., ½ lb., and ¼ lb. respectively, and it is distributed under the brand of "Seaforth." The pick of the crop is shipped direct to London, but a large quantity is consigned to all parts of India, but principally to towns in the presidency of Madras and in the province of Mysore. Very fine panoramic views are obtained at Seaforth, the undulating plains are backed by the densest jungle, and the numerous waterfalls glisten like silver threads among the dark green of the foliage of the trees. Elephants are frequently bold enough to approach the manager's residence, and a sportsman would have bad luck if he could not, on almost any occasion during the season, bag tiger, sambur, cheetah, panther, jungle sheep, or wild pig. About 800 hands are employed on the estate. The bungalow is about 12 miles distant from Gudalur, the principal town of the *taluq* of the same name.

SIDDABILE

This estate is nearly 4,300 ft. above the level of the sea, and although the magnificent varied scenery of the State of Mysore is, at times, bewildering in its natural grandeur, visitors to Siddabile have declared that the views from the windows of the bungalow, especially in the direction of Shimoga and Birur, cannot be surpassed by any others in that portion of Southern India. There is a very fine waterfall on the property, and the indigenous forest trees and jungle, with their various shades of colouring, add a further charm to this very desirable estate. Large game is not plentiful now, but a few sambur, bear, and pig can be bagged occasionally.

The property is 600 acres in extent, and no fewer than 560 acres have been planted with coffee-trees since the year 1860, and, as the last clearing took place in 1910, it follows that practically all of the bushes are now in full bearing. About 300 acres of these trees belong to the old "Chick" variety, while the remainder are of the Coorg type. Every assistance has been given to the growth of the bushes by the planting of a large number of shade trees, and the benefits of this practice are proved by the satisfactory harvests which have been the rule for many years past. For instance, the average weight of the crop for the past ten years has been fully 98 tons. The rainfall is about 85 in., but the supply of pure water is far from being satisfactory. The ripe berries are pulped by machinery, which is driven by bullocks, but the final processes of curing and packing are carried out in the factory at Mangalore.

The owners of the Siddabile estate, Messrs. Porter, Hall & Co., have entrusted the management to Mr. A. B. Boyd, who has been there for fifteen years, and about 180 hands are in constant work.

The nearest railway station is at Birur, while the post office at Santaveri is not more than 1 mile distant.

UMBIDY

The majority of the coffee estates in the district of Kadur have a sufficient quantity of naturally grown shade, and the Umbidy property is a case in point, as the 450 acres under this crop are well protected by indigenous trees. The estate, which is 510 acres in extent, was first planted in the early fifties of the nineteenth century, and it was purchased by the father of the present owner, Mr. J. Ross Porter, in the year 1865. The surface of the land is extremely hilly with steep declivities, but there is a fair supply of water from natural sources, apart from an average annual rainfall of about 160 in.

The yearly crop of berries is about 25 tons in weight, and good prices are invariably obtained in local markets. There is a very nice bungalow on the property, and there are postal and telegraphic facilities at Koppa, a distance of about 3 miles.

WARTYHULLY

The name Wartyhully has been bestowed upon the two properties of Wartyhully and Uttallalu, and, for the purpose of management, they are regarded as one estate which belongs to Mr. Brooke Mockett, for whom Mr. C. Lake is manager. The cultivation of coffee is the principal industry, and the oldest trees were planted in the year 1887, but since Mr. Lake took charge in 1893 he has increased the planted area to 560 acres. About 60 acres of the bushes have not yet borne fruit, but the remaining 500 acres have yielded the very satisfactory return of 4 cwt. to the acre for the past ten years. The outbuildings are commodious, and the plant is replete with all modern improvements.

Parchment coffee is sent to the factory at Mangalore for final treatment, and from there is shipped to Europe. The growing of rubber bids fair to become a very important branch of work on this estate. About 50 acres have been planted with trees of the Ceara type by way of experiment, but it must be added that special attention is being given to them in order that the test may be as complete as possible. A small quantity of rubber was obtained by way of a sample from some of the trees in 1910, and the quality was so good that a silver medal was awarded at the Mysore Exhibition in that year. Cardamoms to the extent of about 25 acres have been planted among the coffee-bushes, and they have invariably returned about 1 cwt. to the acre—the crop being disposed of locally.

The site upon which the buildings have been erected, and a few acres of grazing ground, make the total area of the estate to be about 700 acres. A very fine bungalow stands in one of the prettiest parts of the property, and from an altitude of about 3,300 feet a splendid view of the surrounding country extending to the Western Ghauts and to the province of Coorg is obtained. Water, pure and plentiful, is conserved in two large tanks, and is also conveyed through pipes for use in the bungalow.

Mr. Lake has to import all his coolies owing to a shortage in the local market, and he finds constant work for 400 hands. The railway station at Banaver is 43 miles distant from the estate, and the nearest post office is at Saklaspur, about 7 miles away.

YELLIKODIGI

There are many small plantation estates in Southern India which are in appearance like well-kept gardens. Somebody always seems to be doing something ; it may be loosening the soil, or pruning, spraying, weeding, or watering ; but whatever it is, one may be sure that it is for the well-being of future crops on the property. The Yellikodigi estate of 120 acres is one of these large gardens. Planting work commenced in 1888 on the whole area, and about 15 tons of coffee have been garnered in each year for the past decade. There is a charming bungalow standing in park-like surroundings, and a most beautiful view is obtained of the distant Baba Budeen Hills. Coffee-bushes are shaded by trees of different varieties, and the major portion of the manufactured produce is sent to London, although a small quantity is disposed of locally. The estate belongs to Mr. C. H. Godfrey, for whom Mr. Arthur Durham is the capable manager.

MANGANESE MINES.

(See article on "Geology," p. 347.)

"O'ER HILL AND DALE."

GEOLOGY AND MINERALOGY

BY J. W. KIDDALL

IT is a matter for regret that until a about a couple of decades ago no serious attempt was made to obtain a concise and up-to-date geological survey of a country such as India, which, for its age, its varied formations, its mountain chains, peaks, and valleys, presents one of the most entrancing fields of research that any scientist could desire. This remark is intended to apply more particularly to South India, with which we are now directly interested.

Surveyors and engineers have at various times delved into the substratum of the continent in a number of districts in the Presidency, but it was not until the "Memoirs of the Geological Survey of India" appeared that any systematic account of researches was made. These have not, as yet, been superseded by any complete treatise on the subject, and, as a consequence, much has yet to be learned.

It is an interesting fact, proved by the presence of marine deposits south of the Himalaya Mountains and the continuity of the geological formations from North-east Africa to the west coast of India, that the whole of the Indian peninsula was at one time part of Africa, and that there was a dividing sea between the Himalayas and the present peninsula.

The two great features in the geological formation of India are the enormous area of granite and gneiss (Archæan), which really form the peninsula, and the great flow of "Deccan trap," which has largely covered the northern portion of the peninsula; and which overlies the Archæan rocks.

This trap, however, does not extend to Southern India, and it is the Archæan series of granites and gneisses with which we shall have to deal, and which will be found in nearly every district of the plains of South India.

The larger portion of the other formations met with are either composed of volcanic rocks of later date which have come up through the Archæan rocks, or are sedimentary, and formed from the disintegration either of the Archæan rocks or of the later volcanic ones.

This disintegration has been, and is, going on at a very rapid rate, and the resulting form of the surface of the country, typical of the whole of the plains of Southern India, is a comparatively flat plain, broken here and there by isolated projections, running in size from mere undulations to steep hills of 1,000 ft. in height These projections are composed of some rock which has withstood the eroding action of Indian heat and Indian monsoons better than the surrounding granite and gneiss, and they are often composed of a volcanic rock which has come up through the granite. The products of disintegration of both the Archæan and volcanic rocks have built up sedimentary formations, and the latter, in process of time, have become altered in various ways, many of them having hardened into rocks distinct from their original form.

A classification of the products of the earth, which finds general acceptance, is as follows :—

GEOLOGY AND MINERALOGY

1. Carbon and its compounds, including coal, petroleum, amber, and graphite.

2. Metalliferous minerals, including the ores of gold, silver, tin, copper, zinc, lead, antimony, iron, manganese, chromium, nickel, cobalt, and aluminium.

3. Materials for construction, including building and ornamental stone, slate, lime, cement, brick, clay, sand, and laterite.

4. Minerals used in industries as abrasive materials, mineral pigments, refractory minerals, and materials used for pottery, agriculture, and chemical industries.

5. Gem stones.

Before referring in detail to the widely differing rock and other formations of the principal districts of the Presidency, it will be advisable to take a glance in a general way at the economic side of the science of geology.

The increased production and consumption of coal in the whole of India points to an expansion of local industries, but the quantity mined in South India still remains at an extraordinarily low figure. The famous Kolar Goldfield, in the State of Mysore, is responsible for the output of nearly all of the gold which is obtained in Madras, and special notes containing the latest obtainaole figures as to the quantity and value of this mineral produced by the principal mines will be found on another page. The most abundant iron ores are the minerals magnetite and hematite, which occur in numerous places with quartz. These belong to the Archæan schist series, and are particularly abundant in the district of Salem, and in the native State of Sandur, in the district of Bellary.

It is very little more than twenty years since the manganese iron industry was commenced by quarrying in the district of Vizagapatam, and it has spread so rapidly that South India now takes second place among the many manganese-producing countries of the world. Over-production, which occurred a few years ago owing to the unprecedented demand which prevailed, naturally caused a considerable reduction in value of the ore, but after the depression of 1911 there was some shortage in the production, but values had so improved that the higher percentage in prices obtained more than counter-balanced the smaller supply.

India has for many years past been the leading country in the world in the production of mica, and about 75 per cent. of the exported mineral is consigned to the United Kingdom, which is, however, principally a centre of distribution to the United States and Germany. The largest amount of mica is obtained in the district of Nellore where mining commenced in 1892, and it belongs to the variety known as "muscovite." It is, however, believed by experts of to-day that there is a great future for this mineral in Southern India. Chromium is known to occur in the chalk hills near Salem, and near Mysore city, but the attempts made to mine it have not always been successful. Corundum may be found near Palakod and Paparapattu, in the district of Salem, and in the State of Mysore. Ochres in red, yellow, and other colours are used by natives in many parts of the Presidency in a crude form under the generic name of "geru," and a common source of supply is in the cretaceous rocks in the district of Trichinopoly.

Laterites. The rust-coloured caps which frequently cover the rocks in moist, tropical climates have for a great number of years been known as "laterites." All real laterites are "formed by a subaerial decomposition of the rocks on which they lie, and the peculiar characteristics shown by them are the result of molecular segregation among these products. For a long time laterite was regarded as merely a ferruginous clay formed by decomposition of the aluminous and ferro-magnesian silicates in the rocks which are attacked by weather, but analysis shows that much of the silica had been removed during the process of rock decomposition, and the alumina, instead of being retained as a hydrous silicate, such as in clay, is often present as a single hydrate of alumina, being stained red with the corresponding hydrates of iron, and mechanically mixed with other substances set free during the process of rock-weathering."

Building stones for construction work, and road metal, and clays are common in the southern portion of the peninsula, and various rocks of the charnockite series, found near Madras, are largely used.

It will now be necessary to refer in greater detail to many of these substances, and to state the localities in some of the chief districts of the Presidency in which they appear.

The geological formations in Coimbatore are remarkably similar throughout the district; everywhere the soil is red and largely calcareous, and the disintegrated gneiss yields lime which has been infiltrated from above. Felspar, suitable for pottery, is quite common too, and asbestos—used for medicinal purposes—is occasionally met with. The rocks are gneissic, intersected by veins of quartz, and in places covered by masses of once fluid limestone. Nodular limestone (kankar) is abundant, and the crystalline variety is found chiefly in the *taluq* of Coimbatore, near to Madukkarai and Marumadalai, which are not far from the chief town of the district. Corundrum occurs at Ganapatipalaiyam and at Padiyur in the *taluq* of Dharapuram, and at Salangaippalaiyam, both of which are in the *taluq* of Bhavani. Padiyur is noted, too, for its aqua-marina, or beryl, and the tradition that it was an article of commerce with ancient Rome is strengthened by the fact that old Roman coins have been discovered at and near to Coimbatore.

Malabar. This district consists very largely of a plateau of laterite, above which rise finely grained and generally well-laminated gneissic rocks. Quartz, hornblende, felspar, mica, garnets, magnetite, and hematite are the chief minerals found in the gneiss. The country which lies between Minangadi and Sultan's Battery on the north, and Meppadi and the head of the Choladi Pass on the south is auriferous. Pyrites is the chief source of gold, but its proportion to quartz is generally insignificant and its distribution is irregular. Reefs were worked by natives quite two centuries ago, and reports made from time to time to the Government referred to the very satisfactory prospects of the industry. The Government, however, was doubtful about the matter, and in the year 1879 appointed Mr. Brough Smith (an expert from Australia) to examine certain reefs in the Wynaad. This official was not disappointed in his examinations, but he prophesied failures at the commencement owing to speculators, who, he alleged, would form companies, pay exorbitant salaries, erect unsuitable machinery, and then the collapse would come. And so it was, as thirty-three London companies were registered in or about the year 1880 with an aggregate capital of more than £4,000,000. Sensational reports as to the discoveries of quartz and of possible yields were sent to England; shares were boomed, and as much as 50, 75, and even 100 per cent. premium was obtained on shares. Crushing began very slowly indeed; even the first results were exceedingly disappointing; a few only of the reefs were opened out, and only a small portion of the machinery was used. Within two years no fewer than fifteen companies were in the hands of liquidators, and others followed suit very quickly, bringing irreparable losses upon confiding shareholders, who had been deliberately imposed upon by those who posed as experts and who were the instigators of the fictitious reports. Nothing remains now but derelict and rusty machinery, abandoned roads, and unoccupied workings and bungalows. Gold is now being obtained in the Nilambur Valley, and a small royalty is paid for the privilege of washing for it in the upper streams of the Beyhore River. Iron ore is met with in almost inexhaustible quantities, and if coal could be mined at a cheap rate near Malabar the industry might become one of the leading industrial centres in India. The importation of iron from England, however, interfered greatly with the project, and there are now only a few forges in existence.

Apart from gold and iron, the mineral wealth of Malabar is insignificant. Mica is fairly common, and seams of coal, or carboniferous strata, occur at Beypore, Cannanore, and near Tritala, in the Ponnani *taluq*. Of building stones of an ordinary kind the district has a great supply, and grey granite of excellent quality is frequently met with. Laterite is universal, and on account of its cheapness is required largely for bridges, culverts, and buildings generally. In the mass, before exposure to atmosphere, it is soft and yielding, but under the action of the weather it hardens, and answers most purposes in place of bricks.

The Nilgiris. The hills consist of a great mass of foliated gneissose (not granite) rocks of the class now termed charnockite, together with a few later dykes of olivine-norites, and a few unimportant cases of basaltic trap on the north and on the western edge of the Undalis. The minerals of economic value on the plateau are laterite and building stone; no lime is found, and all required for building purposes must be brought from the plains. Quartz veins occur, but contain no gold or other metals in sufficient quantities to warrant extraction. Ancient gold workings may be traced along the banks of the Lovedale streams in the valley to the south of Bishopsdown at Ootacamund and at other places in the vicinity. Ochreous clays (white, yellow, and pink) found here are employed for colour-washing houses, and cups and flower vases are manufactured from them. Iron (as hematite, specular iron, and magnetite ore) occurs in small quantities on a spur of the Dodabetta Range, 3 miles east of Wellington, but it has hardly been worked at all. In some of the pegmatites in the fundamental rocks in South-east Wynaad there is a good ruby mica of fair size, and it has been mined at Cherambadi, on the western frontier of the district, by several companies and firms. A series of gold-bearing quartz reefs strikes across the Wynaad gneiss, and that it contains gold was known two centuries ago, and as far back as 1793 Malabar authorities were asked to send full information to the then Governors of Bombay and Madras. The reports were that the metal was chiefly obtained by washing the soil in beds of streams, paddy-flats, and hillsides. After this came the boom of 1880, which has been referred to above. A few natives are now doing a little washing on their own account.

South Canará, as a separate district, does not appear to have been geologically surveyed to any great extent, but records relating to the Malabar coast show that its substratum is practically identical with that of the districts of Malabar and Travancore. Laterite is undoubtedly the principal formation, although Tertiary rocks are usually found beneath it. The gneisses are not dissimilar to the rocks of the Nilgiris, although they differ in that they contain minute grains of titaniferous iron.

The district of Godavari, situated on the north-east coast of the Presidency, is marked by a definite gneissic formation of very great age, but more recent surveys have unearthed outcrops of sandstone. Gràphite, or plumbago, was formerly found in small quantities among the gneissic rocks in the north-west potion of the district, but in recent years the output has increased considerably, and very satisfactory prices have been obtained in London. Mica, too, has been found in several places, and pure rock-crystal, inferior garnets, agates, jasper, and some sapphires have been discovered in the beds of the Godavari and other rivers.

The fundamental rocks in the district of Vizagapatam are of gneissic origin. A geographical survey of India made several years ago resulted in the district being divided into four distinct zones, namely (1) the 2,000 ft. plateau in the north-west composed of the older group of Archæan gneisses; (2) the north-west portion of the 3,000 ft. plateau made up of bands of the younger Archæan sub-group of khondalite and charnockite; (3) the south-east part of the same plateau, consisting of more khondalite with local beds of iron and manganese ore and crystalline limestone; and (4) a coastward low-level zone containing minor ridges composed of khondalite, with a few bands of charnockite and gneissose granite. The most important mineral is manganese, and the mining of it was commenced in 1892 by the Vizianagram Mining Company. The two principal centres are at Kodur, where there is a pit with a floor area of nearly 90,000 square feet at a depth of more than 100 ft., and another one at Garbham, where working began in 1896. Veins of ore, visible on the surface, usually strike downwards without exhibiting any abatement in richness. Earth and ore are conveyed together to the surface of the pits, where the ore is extracted by manual labour, and it is subsequently shipped to Dunkirk, Middlesbrough (in England), and the United States of America for use in the manufacture of steel. Coarse grey steatite (potstone), found in several places, is required for the making of Hindu pots, and also for building purposes. Iron and graphite have been discovered at times, but neither mineral appears to be plentiful enough to obtain any commensurate return for working it.

Trichinopoly is an inland district in the southern part of the Presidency, and, for geographical purposes, the River Cauvery divides it into two portions, which differ considerably. The northern division consists of Archæan gneisses, granite, and sedimentary deposits, while the southern half is composed of granites, gneisses, and laterite. An important feature of the gneissic rocks is the existence of beds of magnetic iron, while other substances are quartzites and chloritic schists (containing garnet). The cretaceous rocks in this district are said to be the most interesting series of fossiliferous rocks in Southern India, as leading European palæontologists have declared that "from their peculiarly favourable position between the chalk of the Atlantic and that of the Pacific area they are eminently adapted to serve as a starting-point for observations on the zoo-geographical conditions of later cretaceous times. Their fauna combines in itself the elements both of the Western and Eastern hemispheres, and thus serves as a connecting-link between the two."

GEOLOGY AND MINERALOGY

These rocks occupy an area of nearly 400 square miles in Trichinopoly ; in the north they are hidden by the alluvium of the Villar River, while to the south they have underneath them a belt of gneiss, which separates them from the alluvium of the Cauvery. Gritty Cuddalore sandstones are found upon the cretaceous rocks in the eastern portion of Trichinopoly ; and they lie beneath sands, clays, and marine shell beds which form the coast alluvium. Valuable minerals are few in number. Several varieties of gneiss have been used in many of the temples—the huge bull of Tanjore being carved from this stone ; granite is quarried for building material, and laterite for building purposes and for the repairing of roads is obtained in several of the *taluqs*. Yellow, red, and blue ochres are found at Siruganur ; garnet quartz at Kalpatti ; and chrome ore on the banks of the Cauvery. Corundum mining is carried on in the *taluq* of Namakkal, but all other minerals are receiving less attention than they deserve.

The district of Madura is bounded on the western side by the great Western Ghauts, but it is not of great geological importance.

Certain surveys have, however, been made, and these have revealed the fact that upper and lower beds of gneissic rock, consisting of granitoid gneiss and granular quartz rocks, are found everywhere. Charnockite has been discovered in the western portion of the district, and in the same area hornblende schists are strongly in evidence. Minerals are extremely rare, but crystalline limestone has been quarried in the Tirumangalam *taluq*, and red and white fragments of transparent quartz are obtained near Srivilliputtur.

Tanjore, in the south-eastern portion of the Presidency, is affected, geologically, by the vast network of irrigation channels formed by the delta of the famous Cauvery River. The substratum of the higher levels consists of laterite rocks which are merged into the loamy alluvium of the deltaic region. Hard and heavy sandstones of the Cuddalore rock series are found near the borders of the State of Puddukkottai, these being superimposed by gritty varieties of the same rock which appears in colours of red, yellow, and purple. Minerals are deficient in quantity, and iron ore, which was formerly smelted, appears to have been entirely neglected owing to the difficulty in obtaining a sufficient quantity of fuel. What are known as "Vallam" stones appear to be peculiar to this district ; they are products of quartz, and consist of rock crystals, smoky quartz, and the amethyst. The last-mentioned are cut by lapidaries at Tanjore, and some exceedingly beautiful articles—chiefly for ornamental purposes—are the result of their work. Laterite is taken from the ground in a friable condition, and consists of a ferruginous, sandy clay, but as it is exposed for a considerable time to the action of sun and rain before it is used for building purposes, it becomes hard in substance, and is covered with an encrustation of hydrated oxide of iron. Limestone and yellow ochre are met with in only a few areas.

Bellary is the westernmost of the four ceded, or Deccan, districts of the Presidency, and by far the major portion of it consists of Archæan rocks, which are usually referred to as granitoid and gneissic. The former are said to be of very great age, and they were originally covered by the gneisses, and subsequently by the rocks of the Dharwar system. Subterranean disturbances afterwards occurred, and the gneisses and granitoids were literally intermingled for a number of years, but further erosive action took place, and the gneissic and granitoid foundations were raised to the surface and were exposed in nearly the whole of the district. Almost all of the Archæan rocks are granitic in substance, but they vary considerably in colour from light grey to blue and even pink.

DISTRIBUTING VATS, CYANIDE WORKS, MYSORE GOLD MINING COMPANY.

In the Bellary district, near Juntakal, there is a distinct volcanic neck of ultra-basic blue rock, very similar to the "blue ground" of South Africa. This carries diamonds, though they are probably not sufficiently commonly distributed in the actual "blue" to pay for working.

Like the South African "blue ground," this is very easily decomposable, and all that remains at Grurtakal of what must have been a considerable volcanic outburst, is a depression somewhat larger than the diameter of the volcanic neck and the exposed surface of the blue ground, which continues downwards. Large diamonds, however, are found in the fields round the neck, probably having been left there after the removal, by aqueous agency, of the soft and friable blue ground and small diamonds. This blue ground, now in the form of a thin band of clay, can be traced in the Kurnool series of sedimentary rocks, 40 miles away, in the direction of the then existing watershed, and this thin band of clay carries small diamonds, as will be seen under the heading of the Cuddapah and Kurnool series, together with traces of volcanic scoriæ, which undoubtedly suggest the volcanic origin of the diamonds.

The Dharwar series is the chief gold-bearing series of India. It contains among other rocks two schists, one a hornblende schist and the other a chloritic schist. Quartz veins found in either of these may be auriferous, and it is the hornblende schist which forms the "country" of the Kolar Goldfields.

The series is found scattered, somewhat in the form of "outliers," over the central portion of South India, and one long strip runs from Seringapatam nearly to Bangalore. This strip carries many auriferous quartz veins, but the proportion of payable ore in them has never been thoroughly proved.

The Dharwar rock system may be illustrated by a reference to the Kallahalligudda Hills, in the northern part of the district, and beneath these are beds of hematite quartzite, which are seen along the range which forms an imperfect semicircle. Quartz veins have been prospected for gold in several places, particularly in the village of Chitageri, where it is reported by Mr. Bruce Foote, an eminent geologist, that "short but good-looking quartz reefs are numerous in the southern and south-eastern flanks of the Jajkalgudda Hill, and they are doubtless the source of the gold which is obtained. The gold washed in my presence was sufficiently large in grain to show that some of the parent rocks most have contained distinctly visible inclusions of it." The existence of hematite in the Sandur Hills and the Copper Mountain is practically unlimited, and it is frequently found to be exceedingly rich in iron. The inhabitants smelted a considerable quantity of ore in their own primitive fashion, but these ventures have not succeeded owing to the importation of English metal, which proved to be cheaper. Manganese ore occurs on the Sandur Range, and analysis has shown that it contains fully 43 per cent. of manganese dioxide. Copper has been traced in a quartz vein near to, and also in the neighbourhood of, the town of Hospet, but little or nothing in the way of mining has taken place. Jasper is met with in the Sandur Hills, and it is presented in various tints from scarlet to pinkish white, and from grey to purple red. The attention of architects and builders has been drawn to this field, and it has been found that this stone is peculiarly suitable for ornamental work in public buildings.

The fundamental rocks of the district of Vizagapatam are "gneisses and plutonic rocks of the Archæan group. These are found in various formations according to the altitude of the surface, but they contain strata of biotite and hornblende, mixed with steatite, crystalline limestones, khondalite, and local beds of manganese and iron ore. Laterite—80 ft. in depth—is found at an elevation of about 3,500 ft. above the level of the sea, and its chief value is believed to be in the ore of aluminium, which is a component part. Graphite is used principally for giving a polish or finished surface to earthenware pots made in the district, but it has only a local reputation. Steatite, or potstone, is obtained near Jeypore, and several of the inhabitants are busily employed in quarrying it for the manufacture of images of worship.

The district of South Arcot, on the east coast of the Presidency, not far distant from the city of Madras, consists chiefly of Archæan rocks of the gneiss system, but covering these are groups of sedimentary rocks belonging to different periods. The lowest of these is the cretaceous limestone series; above this is a younger bed of Cuddalore sandstones (found at the Red Hills in the district of Pondicherry), while the topmost layer is represented by the alluvial beds of the deltas of the rivers. The oldest formation—the gneissic ones—are found chiefly in the western portion of the district, and they form the principal heights or peaks in this area. The porphyritic rock is of the kind usually found in South India, consisting of a quartz and felspar within which are imperfect crystal and hornblended rock. Next in point of age are the cretaceous limestones, which, however, are only met with in a very limited area near to the town of Parur. These are peculiarly interesting, as their existence was unknown in the Presidency until their discovery in South Arcot, and the fossils (fish and marine shells) contained in them are in many instances representatives of entirely new species. The Cuddalore sandstones are the most recent sedimentary deposit, and they are found along the banks of the Vellar River, their pink and white colour being due to the presence of ferruginous matter. About 6 miles to the west of Red Hills is a plateau upon which the sandstone formation consists chiefly of grits "much denuded and cut up into little gullies. In the beds so exposed are a number of large masses of silicified wood—trees, in fact—the only thing in fossils which occurs in any part of the Cuddalore sandstone." Some of these trees have been found to measure from 60 to 100 ft. in length, but the best of them have been broken up by natives, who have manufactured portions into brooches, seals, boxes, and other trinkets and articles. The presence of minerals is not a distinctive feature of South Arcot, but the most important are building-stones. The basic formation of the district is gneissic, and travellers—apart from geologists—have been deeply interested in observing how readily the rocks respond to fine carving, as illustrated in the new work at one of the temples at Chidambaram. One who has seen some of the chain carvings says that "they are carved from a single block of stone, and each link is separate and movable." Laterite is found in large quantities between Pondicherry and Vridhachalam, and a considerable demand exists for it for building purposes and the making of roads. According to custom which prevails in other districts, the substance is exposed to the air until it is thoroughly hard, when it is covered with an incrustation of hydrated oxide of iron, which protects it from further change.

The State of Travancore is bounded on the south by the Indian Ocean and on the east by the chain of *ghauts*, which forms a natural barrier between it and the districts of Tinnevelly, Madura, and Coimbatore. The hilly region is very extensive, and is a marked feature of the State. Without the Western Ghauts—the backbone of India—it would probably be an arid tract of land, and droughts and famines would be prevalent. Small wonder that this range is worshipped by the Travancoreans, and especially certain peaks upon which some of their favoured deities are supposed to dwell. Towards the north the mountains rise to an elevation of 8,000 ft. (with plateaus more than 7,000 ft.), Chenthavara, 7,664 ft; Kumarikal, 7,540 ft., and many others varying from 5,000 to 7,000 ft. in altitude. The State is triangular in shape, the apex being towards the south, and it owes its shape to the erosion of the old crystalline rocks which has been going on for ages in a gigantic form. The various geological formations have been arranged as follows: Recent period, comprising blown sands, tertiary sands and clays, and Azoic, gneissic series.

"The gneisses are felspathic quartzose varieties of white or grey colours, very largely charged with garnet."[1] A large portion of this series is exceedingly tough, dark grey or green felspathic rock, but hornblende is a somewhat rare component part. A feature of the Travancore gneisses is their tendency to decompose by exposure to weather into white or yellowish felspathic clayey rocks, which

[1] Dr. King's "Records of Geological Survey of India."

eventually become laterite. This weathering process of gneisses is more pronounced as one descends from the higher parts of the *ghauts*, and from an elevation of from 400 to 500 ft. it continues along the lower slopes as a sort of fringe of varying width. On approaching the level of the sea the section of laterized weather gneiss is still more defined, and it is generally covered by low, flat-topped hills. The Southern Ghauts in the State exhibit a fine appearance with their crystalline rocks, and, stretching away down to the south of the peninsula as far as the neighbourhood of Cape Comorin, the rocks are formed of massive, quartzo-felspathic, granitic gneiss, which is frequently studded with mica and garnets. The second formation of this series, that of Cuddalore sandstones, occurs between Quilon and Anjengo. The Quilon beds are seen at the base of low, laterite cliffs near the backwaters, but clear traces of them are by no means common. The beds near Anjengo, on the other hand, have been found (again quoting Dr. King) " in the cliffs edging the seashore some 12 miles south of Quilon, where they attain a thickness of about 180 ft., and have the following succession in descending order : Laterite, sandy clays, alum clays, and lignite beds." [1] These beds constitute the seaward side of the plateau country already referred to, and the terrace itself marks, like the long stretches of laterite and sandstones on the eastern side of the country, the last great or decided elevation of Southern India, prior to which, as is very probable, " the Indian land rose almost directly from the sea by its Western Ghauts, and had an eastern shore-line, which is now indicated by the inner edge of the Tanjore, South Arcot, Madras, Nellore, and Godavari belts of laterite and sandstone." It is somewhat remarkable that valuable metals and minerals are exceedingly scarce in Travancore, and may, in reality, be summed up in about five species. Gold has been traced in some places—notably in the Peermade Hills—but assays have proved that it does not exist in payable quantities. Plumbago, pure in character, is mined in three or four *taluqs* of the State, and good outputs have been obtained for several years. A royalty of four to six rupees is payable to the Government, but this sum is determined upon according to the quality of the mineral. Granite of a superior quality is found in nearly every part of Travancore, and it is used chiefly for building purposes and for the metalling of roads. It has been described as a " well-bedded, quartzo-felspathic, granite gneiss abounding in rich-coloured garnets." Mica is only sparsely distributed, but those samples which have been submitted to experts have been highly commended.

Monazite is found on the shores of the Indian Ocean, carried down by aqueous agency, and, on account of its high specific gravity, concentrated by natural methods, with other heavy minerals.

The district of Cuddapah, which lies beneath the slopes of the Eastern Ghauts and the opposing face of the plateau of Mysore, naturally forms two distinct areas of rocky formations. The lower plateaus and valleys are covered with superficial deposits of gravel, blown sands, and cotton soil. We have then (1) superficial deposits, (2) a succession of slates, quartzites, and limestones, usually known as the Cuddapah and Kurnool series, and (3) granitic gneiss. Taking the last-mentioned series into consideration first, it may be said that some of the veins are exceedingly coarse, although occasionally exhibiting traces of mica. This is soon disintegrated by exposure to weather, and as a consequence one notices in various parts of the district that smaller veined, but harder, beds are left visible while the coarser rocks have entirely disappeared. Then there are what are known as " trap-dykes," which consist of dark greenstone or diorite, and these are to be found running from east to west, sometimes for a distance of 20 miles at a stretch. The Cuddapah formations are the result of changes which have been going on for a great number of years, as what was formerly pure sandstone is now hardened quartzites ; shales and clays have become slates ; and limestones have lost much of their crystalline character. These formations occur in layers at various depths in different parts of the district, and they are frequently compact and very fine-grained. Economic geology is represented by a number of valuable minerals, among which the following may be mentioned. Diamonds have been found in the strata of the Kurnool series, in the neighbourhood of Chennoor, in the Pennair River, at Cuddapah, and in other places on this escarpment of the Cuddapah series of rocks. But they are of small size. No large ones are found, and the curious homogeneity of size suggests sedimentary deposition. The fact of volcanic scoriæ having been found in these sedimentary beds points to the probability of the diamonds having been carried from a volcanic area, such as that near Guntakal in the Bellary district, by aqueous agency, and deposited in the Kurnool beds during their formation, and before the hardening process took place. Iron ore may be found in early every portion of the district, but there are only two or three areas in which it is obtained in any quantity. Groups of villages may be seen here and there in which practically all of the inhabitants are engaged

ASSAY OFFICE, MYSORE GOLD MINING COMPANY.

[1] Dr. King's "Records of Geological Survey of India."

THE KOLAR GOLDFIELD MINING BOARD (BALAGHAT GOLD MINING COMPANY).

1. Cyanide Works and Mill. 2. Mine looking South-west. 3. Mill and Distributors. 4. Taylor's Shaft.
5. View looking North-west—Taylor's Shaft in Foreground. 6. View of Mine looking South-east.

in smelting in a somewhat primitive style, but results have recompensed them for their work, and that is, after all, the chief consideration. Lead, or sulphide of lead, is obtained principally in the Nalla Mallas, some 5 miles to the north of the road from Cuddapah to Budwail. Other workings were opened at Vanipentnah, but there is not now any traceable ore. That lead which has been mined has contained a considerable amount of silver, and some excellent specimens have been secured. Copper, too, is found, but only in small quantities, in the neighbourhood of Vanipentnah, and mining operations have never been conducted.

A very valuable asset is obtained in the remarkably good building stone which is met in nearly every part of the district. First in importance is the Nergee stone, so called from the mines at Nergee, where it is mined. It is a compact, dark grey rock which is easily split into slabs and blocks of convenient sizes. This series underlies the Cuddapah plain, and is obtained in the Nalla Mallas, and also near to Pattoor, Camalapoor, and other villages in the neighbourhood. The lower portion of the district is fairly rich in sandstones, which are exceedingly hard, and as they are not easily cut or broken up they are used chiefly for local construction work. The Cuddapah rock is known throughout the Presidency for its suitability for building purposes.

The district of North Arcot is bounded on the north by Cuddapah, on the south by South Arcot, on the east by Chingleput, and on the west by the State of Mysore and the district of Salem. This area presents many interesting geological features, and the classification of the formations may be given as follows, commencing with the topmost series: (1) Soils and deposits; (2) alluvial deposits; (3) laterite sands; (4) Cuddapah series; and (5) gneissic and granitic rocks. The gneissic series is fairly general throughout more than three-fourths of the district, and one surveyor has described it as "consisting of quartzo-felspathic gneiss, commonly syenitoid or granitoid." The eastern ridge of the Mysore plateau is granitoid gneiss, and the best presentation of it is found in the hills to the west of Ambur, in the area between Vellore and Chittoor, and in the hilly country between the Ponne River and the railway line from Madras. Magnetic ore is found in beds near to Katapadi railway station, and it is generally believed that these layers are a continuation of those which occur in the adjoining district of Salem. Lying above the gneisses is the Cuddapah series, which is almost wholly confined to the Nagari Mountains, the Tirupati Hills, and to a portion of the Vellakonda Range. These quartzites are frequently found in thick beds, and their colour varies from pale yellow to dark grey or even drab. There are strong evidences that the laterite rocks, which are only visible on the eastern border of the district, formerly extended much farther inland. The beds are very general along the eastern coastline of the Presidency, but, by a process of denudation, they terminate at a comparatively short distance from the sea. Mr. Cox, M.C.S., says: "Proofs that these laterite formations were, in part at least, formed since man's advent on earth are numerously met with in the North Arcot patches in the form of well-shaped chipped implements of palæolithic types made of quartzite." Some of these have been discovered in the debris in the surface of the gneiss near the railway station at Arkonam, at an elevation of more than 300 ft. above the level of the sea. The soil in the district is reddish in colour, sandy in texture, and is probably the result of decomposition of rocks. China clay can only be secured in tracts where there is an abundance of water, and, in the absence of a larger natural supply than that possessed by North Arcot, the construction of reservoirs appears to be an essential. This difficulty has only been partially met, and therefore the industry is not flourishing. The pottery clays which are commonly used by the people belong, principally, to the younger formations of laterite deposits, and the quality is not of a high grade.

The native State of Sandur is almost wholly surrounded by the district of Bellary, and although its area is not more than about 161 square miles in extent, its geological and mineral resources should not be overlooked. The hematites are said "to contain the richest ore in India," and specular iron, exceedingly hard, is taken from hills near its southern boundary. The smelting of softer ore is carried on in the usual native style. Deposits of manganese are rich in certain places, and as an instance of its productiveness it may be observed that quite recently "more than 83,000 tons were shipped by one firm alone."

The Government of the State of Mysore opened a geological department in the year 1894, and until a few years ago only a cursory survey has been made. Sufficient information has, however, been secured to show that rich magnetic and hematite iron ores are visible in the Baba Budeen Hills and in other places. Other minerals include manganese, copper, and lead, while corundrum may be met with in almost any portion of the country. Mica is fairly plentiful, but the quantity which has been mined has only been large enough to meet local requirements. The palace of the Maharajah at Mysore has been constructed largely of locally obtained building stones, and lime and soap-stones are thickly distributed through the State.

It cannot be said that any one of these minerals has yet been properly exploited, so that fuller particulars as to quantities and values cannot be given.

[Much information has been obtained for these notes from the District Gazetteers or Manuals of Madras, and due acknowledgment is made here as well as in other pages.]

THE KOLAR GOLDFIELD

By far the greater portion of the output of gold in India is obtained from the Kolar Goldfield, in the State of Mysore, which is one of the most important in the world; and it is said that visitors frequently lose sight of the fact that they are still in India, as an idea seems to take possession of them that they have suddenly dropped into a mining city of the West.

The field is about 55 miles distant from Bangalore, the administrative headquarters of the Government of Mysore, and it occupies a tract of land running from north to south for about 10 miles, and measuring in width from 1 to 4 miles.

Quartz veins have been worked here for gold by past generations, of whom little or nothing is known except from the traces of their attempts at mining, which, in some instances, were by no means on a small scale, as the earliest discoveries of the metal led to the sinking of shafts or pits to a depth of more than 300 ft., and many of these can be traced to-day, although the majority of them are partly filled with rubbish or are overgrown with vegetation.

Nothing of importance took place after the failure of these pits until about the year 1800, when a surveyor, named Warren, found that the natives of some of the villages were washing gold out of the soil, and after making certain investi-

THE KOLAR GOLDFIELD MINING BOARD (MYSORE GOLD MINING COMPANY, LTD.).

1. General View of Mill, Slime Plant, and Cyanide Works. 2. Edgar's Shaft. 3. Erecting Shop. 4. Picking and Sorting Floors. 5. Slime Treatment. 6 Interior of 474-H.P. Air Compressor.

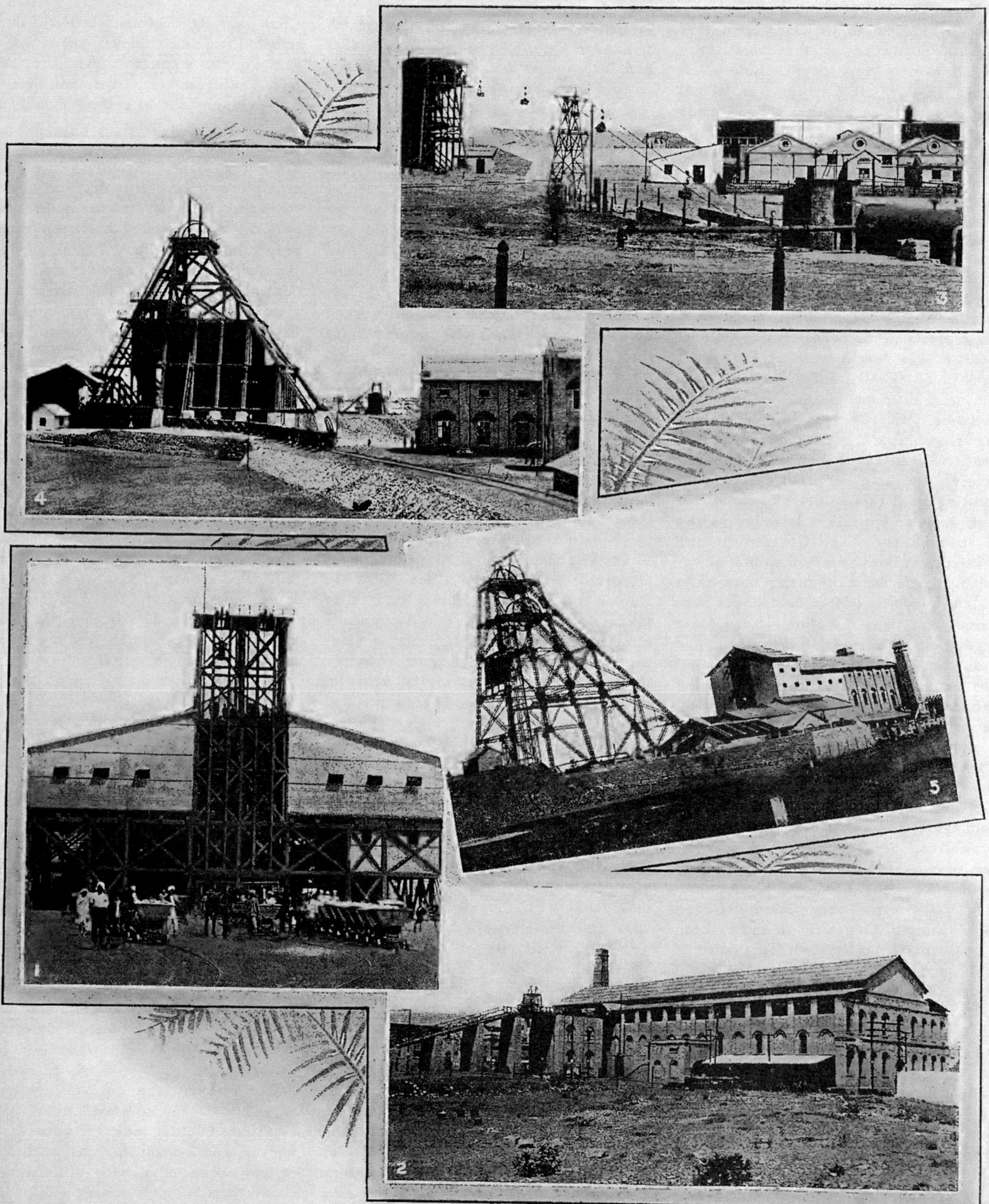

THE KOLAR GOLDFIELD MINING BOARD (THE CHAMPION REEF COMPANY).

1. Sorting Floors. 2. Mill. 3. Cyanide Works. 4. Headgear Incline Shaft. 5. Headgear Gifford Vertical Shaft.

gations he came to the conclusion that payable quantities of the metal were spread over a very considerable area. Again, however, the matter was left in abeyance until an application was made in the year 1873 by Mr. M. F. Lavelle for the exclusive right of mining in the Kolar district. Negotiations were entered into between this gentleman and the Chief Commissioners, and the request was eventually acceded to. Mr. Lavelle commenced operations in 1875, but as the undertaking was too heavy to be borne by one pair of shoulders, he, with the consent of the Government, transferred his interests in the concession to Colonel George de la Poer-Beresford, who, with a number of friends, formed a syndicate known by the name of the Kolar Concessionaires. In 1880 the latter obtained the assistance of Messrs. John Taylor and Sons, the well-known London mining engineers, and as a result of certain prospecting work carried out by that firm, a fresh impetus appears to have been given to the industry. The Government discovered that the Concessionaires were receiving large sums of money upon sales of land in which auriferous deposits were found, and they, therefore, issued fresh regulations, which, *inter alia,* made the granting of a lease of land to a new company conditional upon the latter being formed within two years with a working capital of not less than £5,000. Several companies were floated between the years 1880 and 1884, but, owing to various causes, such as the failure of lodes, or the lack of capital, many of these were compelled to cease operations.

In December 1914 the working companies were as follows: The Mysore Gold Mining Company, Ltd., with blocks totalling 2,413 acres; the Champion Reef Gold Mining Company of India, Ltd., 1,095 acres; the Nundydroog Company, Ltd., having 1,492 acres; the Gold Fields of Mysore and General Exploration Company, Ltd., with four blocks amounting to 3,575 acres; the Balaghat Gold Mining Company, Ltd., 1,328 acres; and the New Kempinkote Gold Fields, Ltd., with 1,016 acres.

The production of gold for the year ending December 1914 was certified to be of the value of £2,166,896, upon which a royalty of £126,515 was paid, while in 1893 the figures were £784,842 and £38,854 respectively.

The authorized capital of the seven above companies is £2,081,000, the amount issued is £1,893,990, and the valuation of that capital on the British market is £5,768,036; while a sum of £16,681,199 has been paid in dividends up to December 1914.

It is practically certain that there is no mining centre in the whole world where the conditions under which miners live and the treatment accorded to them are equalled by those obtaining on the Kolar Goldfield. Employment is found for about 16,000 persons underground and about 10,500 on the surface, and an annual sum of about £574,000 is distributed in salaries and wages.

The machinery in the mines was worked by steam power until the completion of the Cauvery Falls Power Works in 1902, when electric energy up to 4,000 h.p. was transmitted to the Field from Sivasamudram, which is 92 miles distant; but the success of the scheme is proved by the fact that additional plant soon became necessary owing to increased demand for power from the mines. The idea of using the falls for this purpose was conceived by Captain Lotbiniere, R.E., then Deputy Chief Engineer of the Government of Mysore, who ultimately proceeded to Europe and America to obtain tenders for the carrying out of the work. Agreements were entered into with the mining companies in 1900, and in August 1902 the power was switched on to the fields in the presence of a large number of gratified visitors. An additional supply of electricity, amounting to about 6,000 h.p.. has been installed since that date, making the total supply 10,000 h.p.

The only water supply for the inhabitants of the Kolar Goldfield was obtained originally from mine shafts and wells, but as this was insufficient and of an inferior quality, several schemes were considered with the view of remedying such an unsatisfactory state of affairs. Two large reservoirs are now in use, and they are capable of supplying a million imperial gallons of water in twenty-four hours, while the storage capacity of one of these is no less than 1,450,000,000 gallons. A deservedly high reputation has been secured by the Jewell Export Filter Company, of New York, and a contract was entered into with them in December 1902 for furnishing and fitting the plant and appliances necessary for the complete system of purification which they recommended. Each of the four circular filters has a bed 3·5 ft. in depth, and 17 ft. in diameter, and the filtered water is pumped from a reservoir through a 16-in. steel pipe to tanks near the Champion Reef Mine, whence it is distributed to the various companies, the actual quantity consumed being registered by a Venturi meter on the main pipe line. The pumping station at the Betamangalam Tank is a very handsome structure.

Mining cities in other parts of the world are said to have "sprung up in a night," so rapid was their growth; and although the Kolar Field has had many disquieting periods, the progress has been remarkably rapid. An almost barren stretch of country, desolate in appearance, and apparently unprofitable, has given way to a thriving settlement of about 50,000 inhabitants, in which have been erected stamp mills, engine houses, houses and workshops containing an excellent range of modern machinery. Attractive bungalows are seen in the residential portion of the field, but the outstanding feature of the principal buildings is their solidity. Granite of first-class quality has largely been used, and such an array of imposing structures it would be hard to find in any other mining centre. Among these may be mentioned the offices of the various mining companies, the Cauvery and Kolar Mines power stations, the club, the Church of St. Michael and All Angels, St. Mary's Roman Catholic Church, and the Government Maternity Hospital.

The companies operating on the field maintain two hospitals, where the employees and their families receive free medical aid, namely, a well-equipped general, medical, and surgical hospital of 80 beds, centrally situated at Champion Reef, dealing with sick or injured employees of all races, and a small isolation hospital recently built for European and Anglo-Indian employees suffering from infectious diseases.

The Civil Hospital at Robertsonpet has recently been erected by the Mysore Government at a considerable cost. It contains airy wards for males and females, a dispensary, an operating theatre, medical officers' quarters, and other buildings, and the whole structure is an exceedingly fine example of modern architecture.

The seekers after gold do not believe in "all work and no play," and they have established clubs for gymkhana, golf, hockey, and cricket, together with an excellent social club, with billiard tables, card-rooms, tennis-courts, and ladies rooms, and the entire front of the building is occupied by a terrace from which interesting views of the field are obtained.

The Kolar Goldfield Rifle Volunteers

THE KOLAR GOLDFIELD MINING BOARD (OOREGUM GOLD MINING COMPANY, LTD.).

1. Bullen's Shaft. 2. Kolar Goldfield Club. 3. St. Michael and All Angels Church. 4. Mill.
5. Looking South from Oakley's Shaft. 6. Oakley's Shaft and Sorting Floor.

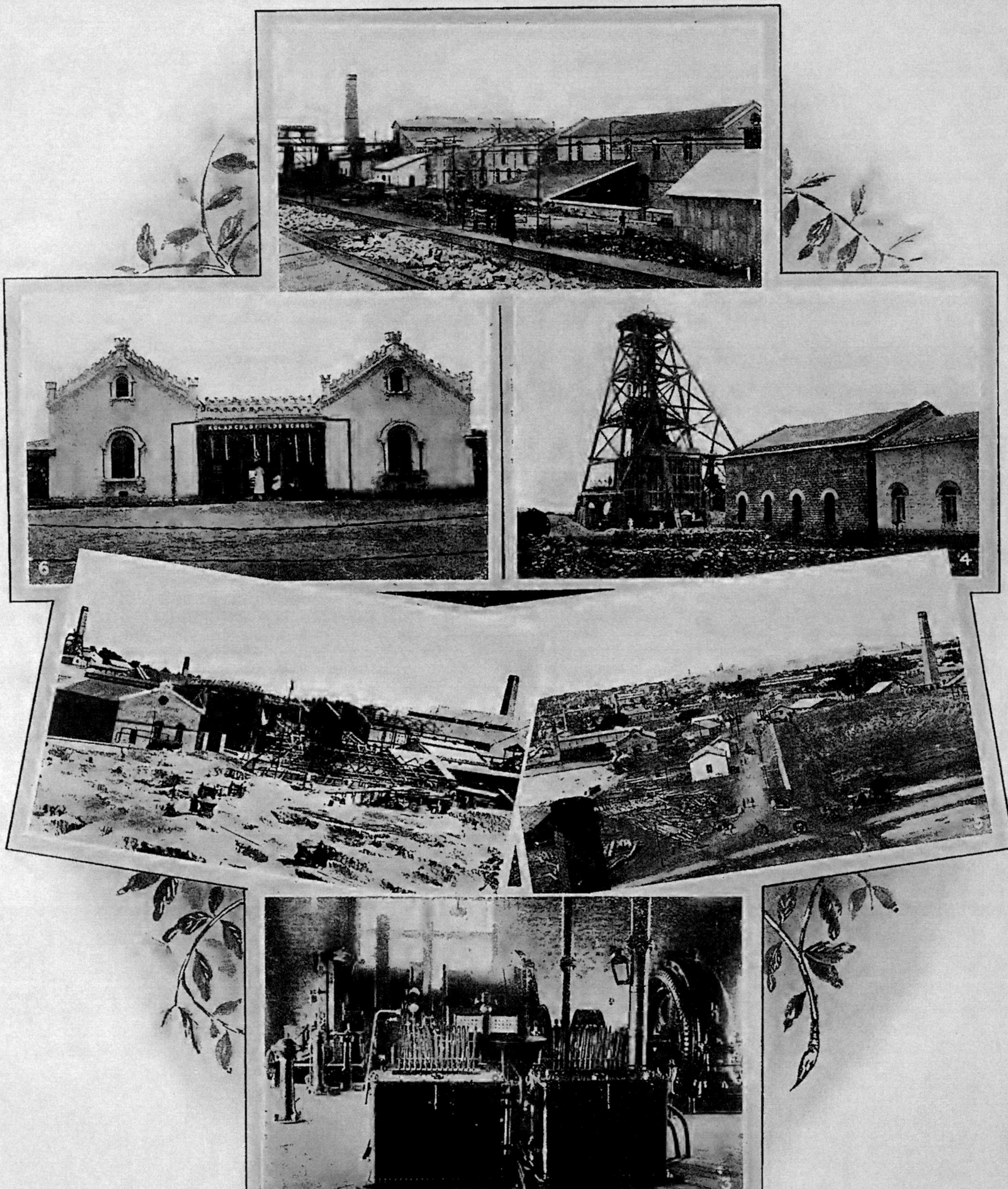

THE KOLAR GOLDFIELD MINING BOARD (NUNDYDROOG COMPANY).

1. MILL AND SLIME PLANT. 2. MILL, PERCOLATION, AND SLIME PLANTS. 3. 350-H.P. ELECTRICAL WINDING ENGINE, AT KENNEDY'S SHAFT. 4. KENNEDY'S SHAFT HEADGEAR. 5. NUNDYDROOG MINE LOOKING SOUTH. 6. THE KOLAR GOLDFIELD SCHOOL.

were attached originally to the Bangalore Rifle Volunteers, but they became a separate corps in 1903. They have a muster roll of more than 800 names, and there are mounted, cadet, cyclist, and reserve sections, in addition to eight ordinary companies.

Messrs. John Taylor and Sons, of London, are the very life and soul of the goldfields, and any scheme which has for its object the furtherance of the interests of the mines is certain to receive their fullest consideration, and support, too, if it be found practicable.

Among the public institutions should be mentioned the Mining Board, which meets every month at its offices at Oorgaum to discuss matters affecting the mines. Mr. Henry J. Gifford is chairman, Mr. C. H. Richards is vice-chairman, Mr. G. E. Payne is secretary, and Mr. H. H. Osborn is treasurer.

The Balaghat Gold Mining Company, Ltd., has its head offices at 6 Queen Street Place, London, E.C., the directors being the Right Hon. Lord Ribblesdale (chairman), the Right Hon. Lord Glenconner, Lieut.-Colonel Sir Donald Robertson, K.C.S.I., Mr. John Taylor, M.I.C.E., and Mr. Robert Taylor. The agents in India are Messrs. Gordon Woodroffe & Co., and Messrs. John Taylor and Sons are the representatives in England. The capital of the company is 212,600 ordinary shares of £1 each, and 95,400 10 per cent. non-cumulative preference shares of £1 each, all of which have been issued. The reserve fund is £13,000. The Secretary in London is Mr. W. L. Bayley, F.C.I.S., and the superintendent in India is Mr. William Pritchard.

The Champion Reef Gold Mining Company of India, Ltd., has its offices at 6 Queen Street Place, London, E.C., and the directors are Messrs. John Taylor, M.I.C.E. (chairman), the Right Hon. Lord Ribblesdale (vice-chairman), Sir John Lambert, K.C.I.E., Sir J. D. Rees, K.C.I.E., C.V.O., M.P., Mr. Edgar Taylor, and Sir John F. F. Horner, K.C.V.O. The managers are Messrs. John Taylor and Sons, and the Superintendent of the staff is Mr. Henry J. Gifford, while the agents at Madras are Messrs. Best & Co., Ltd. The capital is made up of 2,080,000 shares of 2s. 6d. each, all of which have been issued. The reserve fund is £60,000. The secretary in London is Mr. F. H. Williams, F.C.I.S.

The Mysore Gold Mining Company, Ltd., has a capital of £305,000 in 610,000 fully paid up shares of 10s.; its registered offices are at Nos. 5-6 Queen Street Place, London, E.C., and the Secretary is Mr. W. F. Garland, F.C.I.S. The chairman of the board of directors is Captain W. Bell McTaggart, D.L., J.P., while the other members are the Right Hon. Lord Glenconner, the Right Hon. Mark F. Napier, Sir J. D. Rees, K.C.I.E., C.V.O., M.P., the Right Hon. Lord Ribblesdale (vice-chairman), Mr. John Taylor, M.I.C.E., and Mr. Robert Taylor. The managers are Messrs. John Taylor and Sons, London; the agents in India are Messrs. Best & Co., Ltd., of Madras, and the superintendent is Mr. R. H. P. Bullen.

The Nundydroog Company, Ltd., own mines at Oorgaum, and they have a fully paid up capital of £283,000. The directors are Captain W. Bell McTaggart, D.L., J.P. (chairman), Mr. P. C. C. Francis, Mr. Vere H. Smith, Mr. John Taylor, and Mr. Robert Taylor. The superintendent of the mines is Mr. C. H. Richards; the agents in India are Messrs. Best & Co., Ltd., of Madras; the managers in London are Messrs. John Taylor & Sons, and the secretary is Mr. W. L. Bayley, F.C.I.S. The reserve fund has reached a total of £50,000.

The Ooregum Gold Mining Company of India, Ltd., with an authorized capital of £410,000, has registered offices at 6 Queen Street Place, London, E.C. The directors are Mr. Malcolm Low (chairman), Sir J. D. Rees, K.C.I.E., C.V.O., M.P., Lieut.-Colonel Sir Donald Robertson, K.C.S.I., Mr. John Taylor, Mr. Edgar Taylor, and Mr. C. H. Wallroth. Mr. H. M. A. Cooke is superintendent of the staff, and Messrs. John Taylor and Sons, of London, are managers. The reserve fund amounts to £75,000; the secretary in London is Mr. F. H. Williams, F.C.I.S., and the agents in Madras are Messrs. Best & Co., Ltd.

The workshops on the mines are not only exceedingly well built, but they are, further, so well fitted with modern machinery that practically anything which may be required for the mines in the way of new plant or of repairs, including castings of large size, can be turned out at the shortest possible notice. The Kolar Goldfield Railway connects the mines with the Madras and Southern Mahratta Railway at the junction of Bowringpet, 176 miles distant from Madras, and each company has a siding within its own area.

The success of the mines has led to the growth of a thriving town named Robertsonpet, situated in an eastwardly direction, in which there are aerated-water manufacturers, bakers, confectioners, contractors, cycle agents and repairers, printers, outfitters, saw-millers, and timber merchants, besides numerous residential quarters.

Educational institutions are represented by the Kolar Goldfield School for European and Anglo-Indian children, supported conjointly by the Mysore Government and the mining companies; St. Mary's Anglo-Vernacular, and numerous other Government and mission schools.

The following statement gives the output of gold and dividends paid from the commencement of operations until the 31st December, 1914:—

Mine.	Quartz crushed.	Bar Gold obtained.	Amount realized.	Dividends paid.
	Tons.	Ozs.	£	£
Mysore	4,220,871	4,142,096	16,180,456	7,765,094*
Champion Reef	3,450,471	2,964,288	11,281,540	4,183,633
Ooregum	2,557,244	1,861,072	7,006,621	2,352,591
Nundydroog	1,616,504	1,482,926	5,579,808	2,101,818†
Balaghat	668,548	420,892	1,619,190	227,800
	12,513,638	10,871,274	41,667,615	16,630,936
Other Mines	—	—	784,322	50,263
			42,451,937	16,681,199

* In addition, shares and cash realized by the sale of property to the Champion Reef Company were distributed in 1889, representing £87,500, or 50 per cent. upon the nominal capital of the Mysore Company at that time. † Further, a distribution of shares of the Jibutil Gold Mines of Anantapur, Ltd., was made in December 1911, representing £33,375, or 12½ per cent. on the present nominal capital of the Nundydroog Company.

THE WORKINGTON IRON AND STEEL COMPANY, LTD.

1. MANAGER'S BUNGALOW. 2. THE RAILWAY. 3. TIMBER TRAFFIC OF THE COMPANY.

THE WORKINGTON IRON AND STEEL COMPANY, LTD.

1. GENERAL VIEW OF THE YARD. 2. TRAIN IN THE JUNGLE. 3. 50,000 TONS OF ORE READY FOR SHIPMENT.

THE WORKINGTON IRON AND STEEL COMPANY, LTD.

1. Aerial Ropeway—Kumsi Mine. 2. Aerial Ropeway—Python Mine. 3. View of Kumsi Mine. 4. Another View of Kumsi.

THE WORKINGTON IRON AND STEEL COMPANY, LTD.

The manufacture of Bessemer steel necessitates a regular supply of good quality manganese ore, and it was this need which led the firm to invest money in the manganese deposits of Mysore. They were fortunate in obtaining the mining leases of the Kumsi areas. The Kumsi block mine was the original property, and it has yielded a matter of 400,000 tons of good mineral. Up to 1911 nothing much had been done with regard to prospecting, and more attention has been paid to extracting the maximum ore per annum. In 1911, however, prospecting parties were organized and a certain amount of systematic work was done. The results were very satisfactory, as the company added three valuable properties to their holdings. These new properties, after investigation, proved to be very rich finds, and it is only a question of constructing the necessary means of transport. The directors of the company have decided to put down an extension of 7 miles, taking off at the Sheregere station, and continuing out to the Shunkergudde property. This extension will be the same gauge as the main railway, viz. 2 ft. The prospects in this part of Mysore are really good from a manganese point of view. In fact, it is the only part of the State that is producing manganese, and, as far as can be seen from the amount of productive ore ground opened out, there is, without doubt, many more years' work to be done. This area is likely to remain an industrial centre for some considerable time, and is, therefore, a valuable contribution to the industrial development of the State of Mysore.

The properties being actually worked and in course of development by the company are : (1) Kumsi block, from which 400,000 tons have been extracted ; (2) Python Block No. 1, 5,000 tons extracted ; (3) Python No. 2, 2,000 tons ; (4) Shunkergudda No. 1, 10,000 tons ; (5) Shunkergudda Knoll, 350 tons ; (6) Shunkergudda Ridge, 100 tons. The properties numbered 2 to 6, both inclusive, are as yet in the development stage.

Kumsi Mines.—The ore body is made up of three distinct lenticular bands, striking S.W. by N.E. It is of boulder formation—the boulders being embedded in a detritus of ochre lithomarge, and what. Mr. Fermor, of the Geological Survey of India, describes as lateratoid. (There is very slight indication of what the original rocks were composed of.) The bands of ore run parallel with one another, the intervening ground being comparatively unproductive as far as the ore is concerned, and is composed of detritus, such as is described above. The ore *par excellence* is psilomelane, a heavy crystalline mineral of high manganese content. Pyrolusite and wad are met with in the workings, but only in minor quantities. The ore body exposed is 2,000 ft. in length and 400 ft. in width, and is down 80 ft. at the back wall.

Python Top Lense No. 1.—This ore body is one distinct band of ore striking E.N.E. by W.S.W., and it is also of boulder formation with an enveloping detritus composed similarly to the Kumsi one.

Python Lower Lense No. 2.—This is similar to the above in every detail.

Shunkergudda No. 1.—This body consists of two heavy well-defined bands now exposed for 1,400 ft., psilomelane being the predominant mineral. There is an overburden of 6 to 8 ft., which is absolutely unproductive, but the underlying mineral is very heavy, and, as far as can be gauged, must extend to a great depth. The strike is approximately S.E. by N.W., and the body has a distinct dip to the west.

Shunkergudda Knoll.—This body is similar in the main to Shunkergudda No. 1, with the exception that it is in close conjunction with iron ore of very good quality. It is a remarkable thing that the two minerals should have such a close contact and that the change is so sudden, as samples taken 2 ft. on either side of the dividing line gave 52·8 per cent. iron, 8·5 per cent. manganese and 51·1 per cent. manganese, and 5·1 per cent. iron—the latter resolving itself into a remarkably large and strong body of excellent mineral.

Shunkergudda Ridge.—A strong body with approximately the same strike as the other Shunkergudda bodies. The ore lies in laminated masses, and is easily worked.

The ore is transported from the mines by means of a 2 ft.-gauge railway, owned by the company, to a central depot at Shimoga. This depot is connected with the Madras and Southern Mahratta Railway Company, who transport the ore to Mormugao, whence it is conveyed by ships to the port of Barrow-in-Furness, in England, thence it is forwarded to the site of the company's works at Workington.

The company are makers of Bessemer steel rails, steel wagon and locomotive tyres, steel sleepers, fish-plates, and other requisites.

The general manager and agent for India, Mr. C. R. Valentine, arrived in the country towards the end of 1907. Mr. G. Moore is assistant-superintendent and engineer, the mines' superintendent is Mr. E. L. Duxbury, and the chief permanent-way man is Mr. J. Tomkinson. About 800 natives are employed constantly.

Very fine views are obtained from Mr. Valentine's pretty bungalow, known as "Boli," in the town of Shimoga.

The capital of the company is £2,200,000 sterling, and the directors are : Chairman, Sir John Scurrah Randles, M.P. ; managing directors, Messrs. William Burnyeat, Joseph Ellis, Herbert Edward Wilson ; other directors are : Messrs. W. J. D. Burnyeat, Richard Critchley, Wilfred Ellis, G. Geddes Glen, Major Arthur Handley (late R.A.), Franklin Mallalieu, A. H. Mallalieu, Harold Mallalieu, Herbert Valentine, and Henry Westlake ; general and commercial manager, Mr. James V. Ellis ; and secretary, Mr. James Wiley. Registered office is at Mosbay, Workington.

THE STATE OF COCHIN

THE native State of Cochin lies between $9^{\circ}\ 48'$ and $10^{\circ}\ 50'$ N. latitude and $76^{\circ}\ 5'$ and $76^{\circ}\ 58'$ E. longitude, and it has an area of about 1,420 square miles. It is divided into five *taluqs* for administrative purposes, namely, Cochin-Kanayanur, Mukundapuram, Trichur Talapilli, and Chittur, but there is, further, the small principality of Cranganur, which is under a chief, who pays tribute to Cochin. A portion of the State is bounded on the west by the Arabian Sea and British Malabar, on the north by British Malabar, on the east by British Malabar, Coimbatore, and Travancore, and on the south by Travancore, but there is a part of the Chittur *taluq* which is entirely cut off from the remainder by being encircled by British territory.

The early history of Cochin is involved in much obscurity, and the absence of reliable data may be due either to the relentless march of time or to the depredations which took place during the continual struggles which lasted until the supremacy of the British power was recognized.

The original name of the tract of country which lies between Gokarnam and Cape Comorin and between the Arabian Sea and the Western Ghauts appears to have been Chera—subsequently changed to Kerala—but this area included Salem, Coimbatore, and parts of the Nilgiris and Mysore. A tribe named the Cherumars occupied the country for a very long period, but these people were eventually displaced by the Nayars, of whose origin no record of a reliable character can be found.

It is believed that the kingdom of Chera or Kerala was in existence about 300 B.C., and a reference to ancient writers and archives makes it tolerably clear that at the beginning of the Christian era it had made considerable progress in civilization. The only information which seems to be reliable as to the early Chera kings is to be found in ancient Tamil literature, where it is stated that "Athan I, who reigned from A.D. 40 to 55, was wounded in the back while fighting at the head of his army against Karikara Chola at Vennil, and, unable to bear the disgrace of such a wound, starved himself to death." He was succeeded by Athan II, who gave place to his son Chenk-Kuddavan, who was one of the most renowned of these early rulers.

A very considerable trade sprang up between the ports of Cochin and certain cities in the Mediterranean, Phœnicians, Romans, Jews, and Egyptians dealing with the inhabitants in pepper, pearls, ivory, silk, glass, copper, brass, spices, cotton-goods, and lead.

The later kings of Kerala assumed the family name of Perumal, and one of them is reputed to have become a convert to Buddhism, and divided his kingdom among the family and some of his nobles.

The kingdom of Cochin came into existence on the division of Kerala about the sixth century, but reliable records of its early history are exceedingly sparse, and it was not until the arrival of the Portuguese in the year 1498 that a consecutive account of the struggles seems to be obtainable. It is tolerably clear, however, that several factions were formed in the subdivided areas, and that almost continual warfare was going on for many centuries. Cochin and Calicut, for instance, were ever trying to obtain the supremacy, and it is curious to note that the power of the former State was considerably weakened by the dissensions which took place in its own Royal Family. The Zamorin (king of the hills and waves) who ruled over a portion of Kerala was a chief of little importance at first, but, after the State's power was increased by the subjugation of petty rulers, he took up arms against Cochin, and for several hundred years this strife was continued. Cochin consisted of a much larger area at that tim than at present, as it covered no less than 4,000 square miles, but it was reduced from time to time by the conquests of the Zamorin in the north and the Rajah of Travancore in the south.

King Emmanuel of Portugal sent an expedition, under Vasco da Gama, in 1497, with the object of discovering an ocean route to India, and the three ships, which carried nearly two hundred men, arrived off Calicut in May 1498. Arab merchants who had firmly established business relationships in Calicut became suspicious that the advent of the Europeans would very materially handicap them in their commercial transactions, and they at once took steps to influence the Zamorin in the hope that he might discourage further visits. The Portuguese, however, returned to Europe with a valuable cargo, and this caused Emmanuel to send a fleet of thirteen ships, under the command of Pedro Alvarez Cabral, which arrived at Calicut in September 1500. When several Moorish

VIEWS OF COCHIN.

1. HILL PALACE, THE RESIDENCE OF H.H. THE RAJAH OF COCHIN. 2. ANOTHER VIEW OF THE PALACE. 3. HIGH COURT, ERNAKULAM.

vessels had been destroyed, the commander made for Cochin, and after an interchange of presents with the king, the latter offered a factory to the Portuguese in return for a promise by the commander that he would add Calicut to the Cochin territory. During these expeditions—and a further one in April 1501—the Zamorin took advantage of every opportunity of hampering the movements of the Portuguese, and these tactics led King Emmanuel to send a punitive fleet in order to crush him. This was in February 1502, and it was commanded by Vasco da Gama, and consisted of twenty well-equipped ships. Calicut was bombarded, and several Arab vessels were destroyed, and the subsequent visit to Cochin enabled Da Gama to conclude commercial treaties with the king at the latter place. Sir W. W. Hunter, in his "History of British India," says that "Da Gama's successes were stained by cruelties never to be forgotten. On capturing the Calicut fleet, he cut off the hands, ears, and noses of the crew of eight hundred men and sent them, heaped up with dry leaves, to the Rajah, to make a curry of. The teeth of the prisoners were beaten down their throats with staves. A Brahmin messenger was compelled to confess himself a spy under the torture of live coals; his lips and ears were cut off, the ears of an unclean animal—a dog—were sewn to his head, and the mutilated wretch was returned to the Zamorin." It will be readily imagined that the Zamorin and Arab merchants, smarting under the knowledge of these barbarous and revolting outrages, and, further, jealous of the friendship between their enemies and the King of Cochin, combined forces and invaded the latter State. The Zamorin's army inflicted terrible punishment upon the opposing army, and many of the noblest families in Cochin had to mourn the loss of their sons. Shortly after this it was found that the interests of the Portuguese in the East demanded that a Viceroy should reside in India, and Don Francisco D'Almeida was appointed for a term of three years. He arrived in Cochin in 1505, and, acting upon the instructions of King Emmanuel, he crowned Godha Varmah as ruler of the State.

The whole of the district originally known as Kerala now became the cockpit in which the differences between Europeans and natives themselves were fought out, and this unsettled state of affairs continued until the close of the sixteenth century.

The influence of Portugal in the East was now being weakened owing to her misrule, and the Dutch East India Company sent out a number of ships from Holland in 1595 and established themselves at several places in India, Ceylon, and in the Eastern Archipelago. The Portuguese and the Dutch now vied with each other in attempts to gain the ascendancy, and several years passed in which towns were destroyed, fortresses were taken, and the devastations of war were painfully plentiful. The first siege of Cochin took place when the Dutch fleet landed troops at Vaipin early in the year 1662, but a more decisive onslaught occurred in October of the same year, when the greater portion of the invading army landed at Pallipuram. Several positions of strategic importance were occupied, and, after a number of attacks, the Portuguese surrendered Cochin to the Dutch on February 13, 1663. The Hollanders then entered into a treaty with Veera Kerala Varmah, the King of Cochin, under which the latter agreed to deliver to the Dutch all the pepper and cinnamon produced in the State; and, on the other hand, the Hollanders undertook to protect Cochin from the assaults of her enemies. This arrangement proved to be very unsatisfactory, as the treatment meted out to the natives was exceedingly harsh, and the religious bigotry of the Europeans caused such an exodus of the inhabitants that the town was almost deserted. The Dutch soon found out their mistakes, changed their policy to some extent, and enticed the people back by milder measures, restoring to them the church at Vaipin for the services.

The power of Travancore increased very rapidly about this time, and it reached such a pitch that the safety of some of the minor States was seriously endangered. War subsequently broke out between Travancore and the Dutch, and, after a period of intermittent hostilities, negotiations were commenced for the proclamation of peace. It was, however, not until five years later (1748) that the treaty was signed and the terms of this document were "as humiliating to the Dutch as they were disastrous to some of the Malabar Powers." The Dutch remained at Cochin for about forty-seven[1] years after this date, but they never again wielded the same power as they had done previously.

[1] The Dutch surrendered Cochin in A.D. 1795.

It was not to be expected that peace could be maintained for long in a country where there were so many rulers clamouring for greater power, and where the whole of the State was literally seething with discontent. Travancore was still pushing her way towards the south of Cochin, the Zamorin was extending his borders in the north, and dangers from other sources were feared. The position of Cochin was therefore a most undesirable one, as it was next to impossible to point to the quarter from which new troubles might arise. Each succeeding ruler of Cochin found unrest throughout the country, and matters were in this slumbering, volcanic state until 1760, when a new treaty between the State and Travancore was concluded. The Zamorin realized the importance of this, and it was not long before he was engaged in a series of conflicts with the armies of the recently united people. He was eventually defeated, and agreed to pay an indemnity to Travancore, and further, to desist from hostilities against Cochin in future. Trouble arose unexpectly in 1769, when a Dutch Governor of Cochin, named Senff, who, the personification of arrogance, interfered with the Travancoreans in the building of a fort at Kuriyapilli, and a war was only averted by the friendly intervention of the Rajah of Cochin. The Sultan of Mysore had for a long time entertained a hope that he might conquer Travancore, and an opportunity for aggression occurred when the latter State successfully defeated the Sultan's proposal to purchase the fortress of Cranganur and the outpost of Azhikotta (Ayacotta) by the holding of a conference with the Dutch, which resulted in the sale being effected between the latter and Travancore herself. Tipu raised an objection to the transfer, and, as his message fell upon deaf ears, he moved his army with the view of attacking Travancore. In November of the same year (1789) he entered Cochin territory with 30,000 infantry, 5,000 cavalry, and 20 field guns, and his march through the country was attended by the perpetration of the most hideous cruelties and by wanton destruction of temples, churches, and other buildings. The Travancore lines were attacked on December 29th, and the Sultan then occupied Verapoly, Parur, and Chennamangalam, together with parts of Cranganur, Azhikotta, and Kuriyapilli, and in all of these places abominable atrocities were committed.

VIEWS OF COCHIN.

1. General Hospital, Ernakulam. 2. The Dewan's Office, Ernakulam. 3. Students' Hostel at Ernakulam.

He received a check, however, as an English force under Colonel Hartley was ordered to the front to co-operate with the Travancore forces, and the Madras army was ordered to march upon Seringapatam. This movement caused him to order the retreat of his army to his capital.

The Rajah of Cochin now entered into an alliance with Britain, and the State became a tributary to the British East India Company. Some years were spent in repairing the ravages of war, but, as the relations between the Dutch and the Rajah (which had been strained for some time) had become wellnigh intolerable, the British laid siege to the fort and put an end to the mismanagement of the Dutch in Cochin. Matters did not seem to improve as had been expected, and in 1800 Colonel Macaulay was appointed Resident in Travancore, with some supervision over Cochin. This official, who was overbearing and tactless, seemed to add fuel to the fire of discontent, and the Rajah strongly resented the attitude of the Colonel, by whom he was treated as an inferior. Macaulay had his favourites —some of whom were not renowned for probity—and they were placed in responsible positions, which they did not fail to abuse. Intrigues were the natural consequence, and a rebellion broke out at the end of the year 1808, which had for its object an attack upon British Cochin and Quilon. News of the insurrection had come to the knowledge of the authorities, and troops were immediately sent to meet the rebels, who were dispersed after the loss of several hundreds of men. Macaulay's conduct was severely condemned, and he was recalled, and the position was filled by Colonel H. M. Munro.

The country was in a most disturbed condition, and Colonel Munro's account was that "no description can produce an adequate impression of the tyranny, corruption, and abuses of the system, full of activity and energy in everything mischievous, oppressive, and infamous, but slow and dilatory to effect any purpose of humanity, mercy, and justice." The new Resident made a searching investigation into the history of the previous ten or twelve years, and when he had come to the conclusion that there was no individual in the State whom he could rely upon sufficiently to undertake the offices of Diwan, he took the duties upon his own shoulders. He set himself the task of suppressing lawlessness and of redressing grievances, and he or his assistant —Captain Blacker—made a tour of the country, when outlaws were court-martialled, and the guilty ones were summarily hanged as a salutary warning to other evildoers. The way was thus cleared for the introduction of reforms, and the following are but a sample of them. Legal courts were established, in which the procedure was simplified as far as possible, pensions were granted to retired officers, roads and bridges were constructed, and vernacular schools were opened. The Superintendent of Census Operations for the State says in his Manual of 1911: "The land revenue rose from Rs. 2,85,000 in 1811-12 to Rs. 3,27,000 in 1816-17; tobacco from Rs. 21,000 to Rs. 157,000; customs from Rs. 25,000 to Rs. 35,000; salt from Rs. 2,000 to Rs. 63,000; forest from Rs. 10,000 to Rs. 62,000; and the total revenue from Rs. 4,96,000 to Rs. 7,55,000." The Rajah wrote to the Governor-General about this date as follows: "Since Colonel Munro was appointed Resident in my country in the year 1811, that gentleman has, by his indefatigable exertions and vigilance, rescued me from an ocean of debt, in which I was unfortunately involved by the corrupt and treacherous conduct of my ministers, and has enabled myself, my family, and my subjects now to live happy and unconcerned, which favourable circumstance I cannot in justice avoid bringing to the notice of your Lordship in Council."

The time had now arrived when Colonel Munro felt that a Diwan might be appointed to carry on the progressive work which he had voluntarily undertaken, and Nanjappayya, a native of Coimbatore and an official of great experience and tact, was installed in the office in February 1818. Further reforms were inaugurated, and the seven years' work of this Diwan was greatly appreciated. The incumbent of this office in January 1840 was Sankara Warriar, who is spoken of as "the founder of modern administration," and his contemporaries described him as "a man of sturdy independence, boundless energy, untiring industry, and a glowing enthusiasm, and his long service of seventeen years was crowded with solid achievement in all departments." He had the warm support of General Cullen, who was then Resident, who described him as "the present most excellent Diwan of Cochin, by far the most independent, upright, zealous, and successful minister that the Sirkar has ever possessed." The General retired in 1860, and there was a remarkable demonstration of affection on the part of the people in all parts of the State.

A Public Works Department, with a European engineer in charge, was formed in 1868, and the progress which had been made during the previous fifteen or twenty years in the general condition of the country continued uninterruptedly.

A system of irrigation was established, canals and waterways were repaired, better roads were opened, public buildings and schools were built, and an extension of railway facilities was secured. T. Sankunni Menon, the eldest son of Diwan Sankara Warriar, was appointed Diwan in 1860. He identified himself closely with the improvements which had been effected in the government and in the general well-being of the State, and reference may be made to some of the reforms which were initiated or supported by him. He recognized the law courts (both bench and bar) by insisting that judicial appointments, and the right to practise as advocates, should only be granted to men who had qualified by examination for these positions; he instituted *Munsiffs* courts in all the *taluqs* for the disposal of petty cases; he introduced the registration of deeds and the leasing of forest lands in order to provide additional revenue; and he issued numerous regulations with the view of making the department of justice correspond as nearly as possible with that of British India. His magnificent services to the State for a period of nineteen years were recognized when he received the honour of a Companionship of the Order of the Star of India, and the Rajah reluctantly consented to his retirement, owing to failing health, on August 22, 1879. The Rajah, Sir Rama Varma, wrote a letter to the retiring Diwan, in which he said: "We shall lose in you a safe and prudent administrator, and it will be a constant regret that the conduct of affairs will no longer be guided by your wise and sagacious counsels. We fully realize that during your tenure of office the country has made vast progress in material prosperity; the resources of the land have been remarkably developed; commerce and agriculture have been widely extended; and the revenue has attained to an amount that is the highest on record. It is also due to you to state that many useful and well-considered reforms, many

VIEWS OF COCHIN.

1. INTERIOR OF CHEMICAL LABORATORY ROOM, ERNAKULAM. 2. COLLEGE, ERNAKULAM. 3. PHYSICS LABORATORY ROOM AT THE COLLEGE.

judicious acts of legislation, and many wise public measures for the improvement of the Judicial, Revenue, and Administra- Departments of the State have been initiated under your fostering care, and have produced fruit to the honour of our Government, as well as to the satisfaction and contentment of our country and people. These services have been recognized by the Paramount Power, which has conferred upon you a substantial token of its favour and appreciation. The cordial relations between our Royal House and the British Government, so happily subsisting, have been steadfastly maintained and cherished under your administration, and there is no duty of loyalty, no political obligation that has been left unfulfilled."

During the administration of his brother and successor, T. Govinda Menon, the long-standing boundary disputes between the State and Travancore were settled by an arbitrator appointed by the Madras Government, viz., Mr. J. S. Hannyngton, who, with his kind and valuable advice, guided the course of this State for a longer time than any other British repesentative except General Cullen. In his time, too, the functions of the police were separated from those of the magistracy, and the administration of Criminal Justice was placed on a sounder basis by the introduction of the Penal Code and the Criminal Procedure Code. The name of his successor, Tiruvenkita Chari, who was a Zillah judge, is associated chiefly with the spread of elementary education, started under the auspices of the experienced Educationist, Resident Mr. Grigg, as also with the reforms of the Anchal (Postal) Department.

V. Subramania Pillai, whose name is more closely connected with the Judicial Department, over which he presided for a quarter of a century, introduced the Stamp Law, and effected improvements in the administration of the Jail and Salt Departments. He opened Sanitary Boards in the important towns of the State and reorganized the Medical Department.

Mr. Rajagopalachariar initiated a spirited financial policy by utilizing the reserve funds of the State for introducing the Shoranur-Cochin Railway (Rs. 70 lakhs) and the State Forest Tramway (Rs. 20 lakhs) for tapping the virgin forests of the State, and directed a general scientific survey of the State—the first of its kind—with the view of a new settlement. He reorganized all the Departments of the State, and opened a regular account department to be worked under the Code. In 1900 the State was for the first time honoured with a visit from the Viceroy, Lord Curzon.

During his successor's (Mr. Pattabhirama Rao) time, the survey was completed and the settlement begun on a systematic and equitable basis, and the railway and tramway opened for traffic. He also effected several improvements in the excise administration of the State.

During the administration of Mr. Banerji the revenue settlement was completed; the revenue and magisterial functions separated; a Department of Public Health was brought into existence; the Devaswom Department was thoroughly reorganized and practically disestablished; the Account Department was placed on a sounder footing; an Agricultural Department was opened and the improvement of the fisheries was taken in hand; an industrial survey of the State was carried out, and schools opened for industrial and technical education. Municipal administration was introduced in four towns, Ernakulam, Mattancherri, Trichur, and Chittur-Tattamangalam. Efficient and up-to-date methods of working were introduced into all departments, and departmental procedure codified all round, with a view to ensure continuity of policy. Education made great strides in these fifteen years, and of the seventy-four regulations and proclamations now in force, as many as sixty-four were passed during this period.

His Highness the Rajah is the supreme authority in the State, and he delegates certain legislative, judicial, and executive powers to his officials. His powers are limited to the extent that he must abstain from interference in the affairs of any foreign State, and the treaty further requires him "to pay at all times the utmost attention to such advice as the British Government may offer with a view to the economy of his finances, the better collection of his revenue, the administration of justice, the extension of commerce, the encouragement of trade, agriculture, and industries, or any other objects connected with the advancement of the interests of the Rajah, the happiness of his people, and the mutual welfare of both States."

Mr. C. Achyutha Menon, in his Cochin State Manual, says: "The treaty more or less determines the matter of administration on which the advice of the Paramount Power is generally offered. They may be summarized as follows: (1) Any problem affecting seriously the finances of the State, such as the introduction of the railway and other undertakings which involve large outlay; (2) the adjustment of land revenue and other measures resulting in increased taxation; (3) measures which interfere with the existing constitution, independence, and powers of the courts of justice and the civil and criminal rights of the people; (4) fiscal or other measures, such as the imposition of export and import duties, which may seriously affect the extension and development of commerce and industry. In regard to details of internal administration, however, His Highness acts independently, consulting the Resident or not according to his discretion."

The Rajah at the present time (1914) succeeded to the *musnad* in October 1895, when he was in the forty-third year of his age. A couple of years later His Highness was created a Knight Commander of the Order of the Star of India, and in 1902 he made an extended tour in Upper India, attending the Coronation Durbar at Delhi, where he was invested with the insignia of a Knight Grand Commander of the Order of the Star of India. His Highness Sir Sri Rama Varma is now about to retire, and in vacating his office he will carry with him the deep gratitude of his people for his beneficent rule, which has ever been directed towards the welfare of his subjects.

The Diwan holds a most important position in the Government of the State, as he is responsible for the general administrative work in all departments; he is empowered to incur expenditure, up to certain amounts, for public works, and he sanctions the outlay of moneys which are provided in the annual budget after it has been approved of by the Rajah. Mr. Menon, in his Manual above referred to, says that "the Huzur Secretariat, as the Diwan's office is called, is the medium through which the latter exercises his supervision and guidance over all departments. The Secretariat consists of four chief branches, namely: (1) Revenue, which deals with land revenue, Devaswom and separate revenue (forest, anchal, and excise); (2) public works, which covers irrigation, contribution, and public works of all kinds; (3) judicial, which includes judicial, jail, and registration departments; and (4) local and legislative, in which matters relating to legislation and Sirkar Suits, medical, sanitation, education, and general correspondence are attended to."

VIEWS OF COCHIN.

1. CHINESE FISHING NETS ON THE BACKWATERS. 2. BACKWATERS. 3. WOMEN'S HOSPITAL, MATTENCHERRY, 4. ON THE BACKWATERS.

Mr. A. R. Banerji, C.I.E., of the Indian Civil Service, was appointed Diwan in May 1907, and no previous holder of the office has succeeded to the same extent in gaining the confidence of a rajah, in promoting the welfare of the State, and in securing the affection of the people. There is a universal feeling of the deepest regret throughout the State that this very able official is now retiring, and he will be remembered in Cochin for many years to come as one who laboured for the moral, intellectual, and temporal good of the whole community.

The country was hampered by heavy debt and by many difficult problems when Mr. Banerji took up the reins of office, but he has the satisfaction of knowing that the revenue of the State has greatly increased during his tenure of the Diwanship; that the various departments are in smooth working order; and that those frowning rocks of complex problems and the crippling effects of a depleted treasury have been safely passed. His successor is Mr. J. W. Bhore, of the Indian Civil Service, who has been Under-Secretary in the Revenue Department of the Madras Government.

In dealing with the physical features of Cochin, it may be observed that there are hills in the eastern portion, which are thickly studded with almost impenetrable forests of great natural beauty, where teak, ebony, and other valuable timber trees grow in rich profusion. Stretching away to the westward from the foot of the hills are undulating plains, which are well watered and highly cultivated, and these slope gradually downwards to the backwaters, which in their turn give place to a sandy seaboard, where coconut palms and rice yield abundant crops.

The most hilly portion of the State is within the borders of the Chittur Taluk, where some of the peaks attain a height of from 4,000 to 5,000 ft., but there are numbers of tablelands lying at a considerable elevation in all of the divisions.

The development of Cochin has been very materially assisted by the rivers and backwaters, which were used for transport purposes in the earliest days of its history, when roads had not been formed and when primitive kinds of boats had to be employed for the conveyance of merchandise, as even pack-bullocks only came into use in comparatively recent times. These backwaters or channels run parallel to the Arabian Sea, extending from Ponnani in the north to Trivandrum in the south, and they vary in width from less than a hundred yards up to as much as 3 or 4 miles. They have been formed by the rivers which have their sources in the hills, and which, having no other outlet than the ocean, carry to the coast a large quantity of sand and soil, and the latter coming into contact with the littoral currents are converted into beds or banks, behind which are the salt-water lagoons.

A steam launch service was inaugurated in a modest way towards the close of the nineteenth century, but in March 1913 a strong company was formed with the object of extending it from one end of the backwaters to the other. Fifteen steam and four motor launches are now employed, and arrangements have been made for the conveyance of His Majesty's mails and for the establishment of a road service in connection with the running of the boats. The principal rivers are the Alwaye or Periyar, the Chalakudi, the Karuvannur, the Ponnani, and the Chittur, but there are several small streams which are being tapped for the purposes of irrigation.

The harbours are Cochin, Malipuram, and Narakkal; Cochin is situated in British territory, but it is included in the list as nearly the whole of the seaborne trade of the State passes through this port. It has an open roadstead and an inner harbour, but the latter cannot at present offer anchorage to large ships, as the entrance is obstructed by a bar which is covered by less than 18 ft. of water. The Government of Madras recognizes the desirability of dredging and of the construction of wharves and other dock accommodation, and steps are now being taken to remove the sandbank and to provide facilities for dealing with cargoes. Narakkal and Malipuram are open roadsteads, which are frequented by ships from Cochin during the monsoon months.

The climate of Cochin is not unhealthy, although there is a heavy rainfall together with excessive humidity of the atmosphere. The soil is generally of a loamy nature, but owing to various conformations of the country its quality is not uniform, and a considerable portion of it is scarcely worth the cost of cultivation.

India is an agricultural country, and in the State of Cochin about 50·4 per cent. of the inhabitants are engaged in farming. Rice is the staple food of the people, and nearly the whole of the arable area is devoted to this crop. A considerable portion of the land is capable of producing two crops in one year, and these plots—known as "double crop niloms"—are in great demand. A very important industry is the cultivation of the coconut palm, and its products, such as oil, copra, coir yarn, matting, rope, and poonac, are the principal articles of export. The areca palm is grown extensively in the laterite regions of the State; mango, jack, Malay apple, tamarind, rose apple, citron, pomegranate, and other fruit-trees are cultivated in private gardens, while as many as eight or ten varieties of plantain are found in compounds, and more extensively in those attached to farmhouses. The cultivation of pepper has been somewhat neglected during recent years, but considerable attention is given to the growing of nutmeg, cardamom, turmeric, ginger, and betel. Coffee and tea plantations were comparatively numerous in the early eighties, but very little revenue is obtained from them at present. Rubber is receiving a good deal of attention, and the plants in the *taluqs* of Mukundapuram and Trichur thrive remarkably well. Nearly 4,000 acres have been planted, and the yield shows an average of 30 lb. to the acre. The climate and soil of Cochin are decidedly favourable for general agriculture, but the farmers are either unacquainted with modern methods of cultivation, or, on the other hand, are too poor to purchase necessary implements and machinery. The State authorities have, therefore, come to their assistance by organizing a department with a staff of inspectors who impart instruction and advice, and also distribute leaflets containing instructions and advice, and a system of loans of money upon easy terms has been arranged.

Nearly the whole of the forest area, which covers about 600 square miles, belongs to the State, and the principal trees are teak, rosewood, blackwood, ebony, irule (*X. dolobriformis*), and white and red cedar.

Cotton weaving is carried on to some extent in Chittur and Talapilli, but the progress of the industry is exceedingly slow, owing to the prejudice of the people against the use of fly-shuttle looms, which, however, is gradually dying out. Small weaving factories are coming into existence, there being one at Chittur and a more important concern at Pushpagiri, near Trichur, worked by a limited liability company. The manufacture of yarn, ropes, rugs, and matting from coconut fibre finds employment for about 8,000 men and 20,000 women, and the value of the exported produce is nearly

VIEWS OF COCHIN.

1. Looking from Kavalai Incline towards No. 2 Brake. 2. Zigzag at No. 10 Point, Kavalai. 3. Kavalai Incline. 4. Kothurnoody Bridge. 5. Komalapara Incline. 6. Engine "Lawley."

1. JEW TOWN, COCHIN.
Photo by O. M. Rocky.

2. A RAJAH'S PALACE, TRICHUR.

3. CANAL SCENE THROUGH COCHIN TOWN.
Photo by R. V Solomon.

37 lakhs of rupees. Grass mats of exquisite colouring and texture are made in the *taluqs* of Talapilli and Trichur, and coarse mats and baskets are manufactured out of bamboo and screwpine leaves. The chief exports are coconut oil, coir yarn, rope, fibre, matting, copra, oil-cake, timber, coffee, and pepper; while the imports include rice, cotton piece-goods, raw cotton, twist yarn, metals, cutlery, and general hardware.

There are nine oil mills and fifteen tile and brick factories in the State. The former are in the Cochin-Kanayanur *taluq*, and the latter are in the *taluqs* of Mukundapuram, Trichur, and Chittur.

State recognition of the necessity for a system of education took place as early as 1818, when thirty-three vernacular schools were opened for the purpose of training young men for the public service, but very little advantage was derived from these, as the curriculum was far too limited. An English school was commenced in 1818 by a missionary (the Rev. J. Dawson), but it died a natural death before three years had elapsed. District schools were subsequently opened in each *taluq*, but it was not until the year 1890 that any real progress was made, and this was effected by the organization of a Department of Vernacular Instruction. The English and the Vernacular Departments were amalgamated in 1892, when a Superintendent of Education was placed in supreme control, but in 1898 the high schools came under the direct supervision of the Diwan.

A Government Industrial and Technical School was established at Trichur in the year 1910, and instruction is given to boys in carpentry, mat-making, geometrical drawing, practical arithmetic, and other subjects; while in the female section study is devoted to domestic economy, dressmaking, needlework, and tailoring.

On February 14, 1914, a Sanskrit College was opened at Tripunithurah, where students are taught without fees and given free boarding. It is an endowed institution. A committee for the improvement of Malayalam literature has also been appointed. These are some of the Shashtipoorthi boons.

Hinduism is the religion of about 68 per cent. of the total population; Christians are returned at 25 per cent.; Mahommedans form less than 7 per cent.; and Jews, Jains, and Animists make up the remainder. There are nearly 1,900 Hindu temples and shrines in the State, in addition to 90 Mahommedan mosques and nearly 200 Christian churches and 7 Jewish synagogues.

The principal towns are Ernakulam, Trichur, Chittur, and Mattancherri. Ernakulam, the capital of the State, is the terminus of the railway line, and is picturesquely situated on the backwaters about $2\frac{1}{2}$ miles distant from Cochin. It was created a municipality in 1910, and it has a population of about 21,000 inhabitants. Many of the public buildings are exceedingly fine structures, and they include the Durbar Hall, where the British Resident pays his official visits to the Rajah; the Chief and the District Courts; the Rajah's College and the hostel attached to it; the offices of the Diwan, and many others.

NUNS FEEDING CHILDREN AT THE CONVENT, ERNAKULAM.

Trichur is said to be the oldest town on the west coast, and its foundation is attributed to Parasurama. In the centre of the town, and standing on the hillock, is the ancient temple of Wadakkunnathan and three Brahmin monasteries, and thousands of people congregate there annually for the Trichur Pooram festival. It has a population of over 23,000 persons.

Trichur is a large commercial centre, the principal articles of trade being timber, paddy, areca, and cotton fabrics, while hundreds of hands are employed in the steam saw-mills and weaving factories. The public buildings are of imposing appearance, and there is a general atmosphere of prosperity in the industrial portion of the town.

Chittur, the chief town of the *taluq* of the same name, has a population of about 8,000 persons, more than 90 per cent. of whom are Hindus. A festival called Kongapada is celebrated here in the month of March, and it is said to be held in commemoration of a notable victory gained by Cochin forces over Kongu invaders.

Mattancherri is situated on the western side of the backwater which separates it from Ernakulam, and it became a municipality in 1910. A very considerable export and import trade is carried on by Banyans and Kacchi-Memons from the Bombay Presidency. The town was once the capital of the State, and it contains an old palace which was presented to the Rajah by the Portuguese in the year 1555. It has a population of over 23,000 inhabitants.

It will be seen from these brief notes that the State has passed through most critical times, but the wise and statesmanlike policy of recent Rajahs and Diwans has placed the resources of the country on a sound commercial basis, and, what is even more important, the people have been encouraged to take a more intelligent interest in the various administrative, agricultural, and industrial problems, which will inevitably lead to an era of increased prosperity.

HIS HIGHNESS SIR RAMA VARMA, G.C.S.I., G.C.I.E. (RAJAH OF COCHIN)

THE progress of the State of Cochin during the rulership of the present Rajah Sir Rama Varma, who ascended the Musnad on September 11, 1895, has been remarkably steady, and an opportunity of recognizing this increased prosperity was embraced when the inhabitants arranged for a day of ceremonies on December 25, 1912, to celebrate the completion of the sixtieth year of age of His Highness.

The Rajah is the eldest of four brothers, one of whom died when he was Elaya Rajah, in 1899. His early years were not distinguished by any strongly marked passion for study, and it is undoubtedly true that his inherent talents were developed very largely by the sympathetic influence of a wise mother. As the years passed, however, such intellectual influences as existed at Tripunittura touched the life of the young student, and he secured high praise from the tutors who assembled there for the assiduity with which he devoted himself to self-improvement. He studied English at the same time that he was diving into the grammar, the logic, and the history of Sanskrit literature, and his books became a part of his very life, being his daily companions then as they are his cherished treasures to-day. He exhibited the greatest diligence in thoroughly mastering every subject which he took up, and his fluency of speech and his polished style of writing are the admiration of those who are brought into contact with him.

He was heir-apparent for about seven years, and this period was occupied largely in making himself acquainted with the needs of the country and with the consideration of those problems which were calculated to improve the conditions of the people. As Elaya Rajah he was called upon to assist at public durbars and other State functions, and these duties brought him into close touch with representatives of the Government of India and with the principal European residents of the State, and he won general esteem and admiration on account of his brilliant attainments as well as by his genial courtesy.

COOLIES.

The Rajah—or the Elaya Rajah, as he was then—visited different portions of the State, and he thus ascertained the actual conditions of the people over whom he would eventually reign. These tours contributed to the formation of a keen intellect, and sound judgment was brought to bear upon many questions of importance to the community which were placed before him. It should be mentioned here that neither the pursuit of studies nor the gradual unfolding of the statesman-like mind prevented the Rajah from enjoying healthy out-door recreation, and he became an expert horseman and a good shot, while the less exciting pleasures of billiards and chess found an able exponent in him.

The coronation of the Rajah in 1895 was an occasion which will live long in the memory of the people of Cochin. The speech from the Throne was marked by the enthusiasm of an optimist, it foretold the reorganization of the administrative departments of the State; and every word of the message rang in the ears of the vast concourse with a sincerity which the speaker's demeanour emphasized.

True to his promises of reform, the Rajah began his rule by "an extension of railways, by reorganizing the account system on the British Indian model, and by scientific working of the forests. These measures were followed by a survey of the State, the initiation of revenue settlement on a systematic and equitable basis, by the improvement of excise administration, by the establishment of departments of public health and agriculture, and by the provision of education in technical and other schools." Lord Curzon, a recent Viceroy, certainly cannot be accused of being lavish with his compliments upon the services of Indians, and yet he is reported to have said of the Rajah, after the latter had been reigning for about five years, that "ever since his arrival in India he had kept a careful watch on the administration of native States, and that nowhere had he seen a more enlightened administration than in Cochin, and he eloquently testified to His Highness's sterling worth, which, he was convinced, was playing the most vital part in increasing efficiency and prestige."

Towards the close of 1902 the Rajah made an extended tour in Northern India, and in the following year he attended the Coronation Durbar at Delhi, when he was invested with the insignia of a Knight Grand Commander of the Order of the Star of India. Southern India was visited in 1904; the then Prince and Princess of Wales received the Rajah in 1906, and "in December 1912 the latter attended the Grand Durbar at Delhi, when His Majesty King George V conferred upon him the insignia of the Grand Companionship of the Most Eminent Order of the Indian Empire, obtaining in the meanwhile an increase to his salute from seventeen to nineteen guns."

When the Rajah returned from Delhi, he was met by thousands of his subjects who -as has already been referred to—vied with one another in carrying out a programme of festivities on a scale of royal magnificence. Hindus, Christians, Mahommedans, Jews, Parsis, and every class and creed of people joined on this occasion in tendering their respectful congratulations to their beloved ruler. A public address was presented to the Rajah at this ceremony, and the latter replied in the most heartfelt manner. He referred to the "touching remarks about me and my administration" made in the address, and observed that the reforms "were undertaken with the view to improve the efficiency and tone of the administration, to develop the resources of the State and to increase the happiness and prosperity of the people."

It was shown that the revenues of the State increased from 19 lakhs of rupees in 1895 to 43 lakhs in 1912, and the population was about 9,00,000 in the latter year, while the figure at the commencement of the reign was 7,00,000. This material progress, however, has been accompanied by measures of true reform, by rapid strides in education, and by the development of the natural resources of the country.

His Highness has continued his studies in English as well as in Sanskrit; he is the founder of a Sanskrit school at Tripunittura; he is the author of a popular treatise on Sanskrit grammar; and he enjoys the cordial respect of a number of pupils who were taught by himself.

GEORGE BRUNTON & SON

This firm was founded by the late Mr. George Brunton, M.I.C.E., who arrived at Cochin about the year 1849, when he started saw-milling and baling coir-yarn by hydraulic presses which were made in England under his own patent. The sawing was subsequently discarded in favour of machinery to extract coconut-oil, and of general engineering works.

Mr. William Brunton joined his father in 1868, and in 1882 the firm commenced draining (by machinery) the submerged lands at Alleppey and Trichur, a distance of 40 miles to the south and north of Cochin. These lands are from 3 ft. to 6 ft. below the level of the sea, and are exceedingly fertile. It was part of the contract that the land should be drained and the machinery removed within forty days, and the work was completed in a very satisfactory manner.

Pumps of a special kind suitable for the purpose were constructed, but improvements have been effected from time to time with the result that those now in use, which are driven by steam and oil, are capable of discharging from 6,000 to 8,000 gallons every minute. These pumps belonging to the firm are still at work in the neighbourhood of Alleppey and Trichur, where the Government has permitted the reclamation of other low-lying lands, and it is distinct praise for Messrs. Brunton's machinery that other firms who have undertaken drainage work have designed similar pumps. Mr. George Brunton retired in 1891 and went to reside in England, but he paid three visits to India before his death, in 1900. Mr. William Brunton became a partner in 1885, and assumed control of the business in 1891 on the retirement of his father.

All kinds of engineering work—irrigation especially—are undertaken, under a very competent staff of European engineers, and from 100 to 115 native labourers are constantly employed.

The works are situated upon the harbour front in the centre of the business quarter of British Cochin, and cover a large acreage. They consist of double-storied buildings, which were erected in 1911; the ground floor contains heavy machinery, lathes, drills, and planing machines; in the upper portion are the pattern-making and general wood-working appliances. The motive-power is derived from steam and hydraulic engines of 30 and 40 h.p. respectively. Other buildings comprise offices and rooms for storing pressed bales of yarn. A very considerable business is done in sorting and baling loose yarn on behalf of other firms, and this work is done in a large yard and buildings which are almost adjacent to the main block. There is storage accommodation for 8,000 to 10,000 bales, and three hydraulic presses are used.

Messrs. Brunton have a large foundry at Vypeen near the mouth of Cochin harbour, and castings up to 3 tons are turned out here. Several orders have been carried out for the Government of Travancore and for many important companies in the district.

About the year 1880 the firm opened a branch at Alleppey, where the pumping plant is kept, and where a workshop is fitted up for overhauling and repairing these machines. The buildings—including offices and store-rooms—cover a large area, and the work here is under the direct supervision of Mr. Jack Brunton.

Messrs. Brunton were the first persons to introduce motor-boats into Cochin. They imported one from England in 1900, but since that date they have built some half-dozen others, and have supplied about 30 motor-engines to other firms.

THE COCHIN NATIVE MERCHANTS ASSOCIATION

The natives of India have, in recent years, developed a growing interest in the commercial welfare of their country, and they have conceived a desire to grapple with industrial problems by forming associations or chambers of commerce in order that, by a mutual exchange of ideas, they may render a service to the community at large as well as to themselves. Traders realize that it is to their common good that they should deliberate upon matters affecting their rights; they are alive to the fact that grievances are more likely to be redressed by representations which are made to Government or to other countries from a united body rather than from a single individual, and they agree that statistics showing the amount and value of exports and imports should be collected and subsequently disseminated. The Cochin Native Merchants Association has more than justified its formation, and the increasing membership is ample proof of the benefits to be derived from co-operation.

The following particulars are extracted from the annual report for the year 1912-13, which was submitted to the members on the 3rd of August, 1913. Bags of grain to the number of 1,681,733 were imported through British India steamers during the twelve months preceding the 19th of May, 1913, and 118,457 bags were received from Asiatic vessels.

The quantities of some of the goods which were exported from Cochin by steamers and native craft during the year which ended on the 30th of June, 1913, are: 456,294 bundles of coir yarn; 510,908 coils of coir rope; 163,481 bales of coir yarn; 1,122,740 *dholls* of coir; 114,468 bags of coconut poonac; and 324,275 bags of copra.

The imports during the same year included: 1,522,394 bags of paddy; 890,637 bags of rice; 1,403,281 loose coconuts; 4,289,700 gallons of kero-

GEORGE BRUNTON AND SON.

1. INTERIOR AND PORTION OF WORKSHOP. 2. MOTOR-BOAT BUILT ON THE PREMISES. 3. HYDRAULIC PRESSES FOR COIR YARN. 4. FOUNDRY.

sene oil in bulk ; 89,173 cases of kerosene, and 3,313,060 tiles.

The president of the association is Haji Abdulla Haji Adam Sait, the vice-president is Ramji Coverji (agent for Messrs. Moolji Jaitha & Co.), and the honorary secretary and treasurer is Oomer Haji Ayoob Sait.

E. AHAMED COOTTY HAJEE BROTHERS

The town of Cochin, in which this firm has carried on their business since 1877, is an important commercial seaport on the Malabar coast, as it has direct steamship communication with Europe, America, China, and Japan.

The founder of this firm, the late Mr. E. Ahamed Cootty Hajee, established his business in Cochin as a general merchant and commission agent in the earlier part of the year 1897, in the name of "E. Ahamed Cootty Hajee." In 1906 he admitted into partnership his brother, E. Cunhahamed Cootty Hajee (who had been his assistant), and his other brothers, E. Soopicutty, E. Hussain Cootty Hajee, and E. Abdirahiman Cootty, and he continued the business under the style of E. Ahamed Cootty Hajee Brothers. E. Ahamed Cootty Hajee died on the 21st day of October, 1910, and the present manager, E. Cunhahamed Cootty Hajee, then assumed control. E. Hussain Cootty Hajee, who was the branch manager of Cannanore, subsequently came down to Cochin, and he assists the present manager in the business. Employment is constantly found for 9 or 10 clerks. The firm, besides general merchants and commission agents, are also importers and exporters ot merchandise and various goods.

Between 7,000 and 8,000 tons of Indian grain are annually imported by them, and nearly the whole of this quantity is consumed by the native States of Cochin and Travancore. The chief exports, which are consigned to the principal Indian and Burmese ports only, consist of coconut oil (about 700 tons annually) and other Malabar products such as coir, pepper, ginger (nearly 1,000 tons). They have branches at Cannanore and Alleppey, and they have agents at all ports in India. Correspondence can be addressed to them in English, Tamil, Malayalam, Canarese, and Gujerathi.

They are also landed proprietors, and have lands and buildings in British Cochin and Malabar and in the native States of Cochin and Travancore.

Their place of business, in Calvethy, in British Cochin, is a well-constructed double-storied building, situated in the centre of the commercial town in front of the local branch of the National Bank of India and of the Government customhouse. It consists of warehouses, godowns with first-floor rooms inside for private use, and suitable offices. The upper story of their office-rooms is tenanted by the Madras Bank, while other premises (comprising upstair office-rooms and godowns) are occupied by Messrs. Parry & Co. The ground floor of another building is occupied by the firm of Sakkaram Bissaji, and the upper story by Messrs. Tattarou Mane and Sakkaram Bissaji Company.

E. AHAMED COOTTY HAJEE BROTHERS.

1. The Premises. 2. E. Cunhahamed Cootty Hajee. 3. E. Hussain Cootty Hajee.

K. MOIDEEN COOTTY BROTHERS

The members of this firm belong to the Kadan Kandy family, which has for several decades held a most important and honourable position in the social and commercial life of Tellicherry in North Malabar.

A general importing and exporting business was established in British Cochin in 1854 by Mr. Coonhamed, and at his death it became the property of his son, Mr. K. Moideen Cootty. The latter was succeeded by the present partners, whose names are K. Cootty Amoo Hajee and K. Coyamotty Mayancootty and Abdulla.

Extensive transactions take place in the import of grain from Rangoon, Akyab, Bassein, and other places, and for several years past the average quantity which has been purchased annually has been considerably more than 5 lakhs of bags.

The principal exports are coconut-oil, coir, and Malabar produce, and these are consigned to Indian ports.

Branches have been opened at Calicut, Tellicherry, and other Malabar ports, and many near relatives of the partners have large business interests in the State of Travancore.

The extensive premises of the firm consist of offices, warehouses, stores, and godowns, but other properties owned by them in British Cochin are occupied by a branch of the National Bank of India, Messrs. Kirkpatrick & Co., the Malabar Estate and Planting Company, Messrs. Stewart, Thompson & Co., and by Messrs. Ramchandra Mahadeva & Co.

Both partners are members of the Cochin Native Merchants' Association, while Mr. K. Cootty Amoo Hajee, who has a seat upon the Municipal Council of British Cochin, was honoured with a Coronation medal in recognition of his loyalty and of his liberality in supporting public institutions.

The late Mr. K. Moideen Cootty was granted a certificate in January 1903, in the name of the late King Edward VII, as an acknowledgment of his services as a municipal councillor, and by reason of his generous contributions in the cause of charity

RAMCHANDRA MAHADEVA & CO.

Agricultural and other products of Malabar are largely exported from Cochin, and the transactions of this well-known firm on the London market have assumed considerable proportions during the last few years.

The business was established in 1879 by Mr. Gopal Mahadeva, but, on his death in 1898, the concern was taken over by his brother, Mr. Ramchandra Mahadeva, who had Mr. A. L. Shirgavkar as a partner and manager of the firm's headquarters in British Cochin.

The principal exports are yarn, copra, and general merchandise. A speciality is made of the first named, which is prepared so carefully that the consignments of this firm are acknowledged to have no rival in the London Exchange, and they always obtain the highest prices in the sales. Hardware is a distinct feature of the import trade of the firm, and it—in addition to foreign goods—is purchased by wholesale agents in Europe, but everything is passed through the hands of the London representatives, Messrs. Gibbon & Co., of Lime Street, London.

Messrs. Ramchandra Mahadeva & Co. are agents for the following corporations, namely: The Oriental Government Security Life Assurance Company, Ltd., Bombay; the Reliance Marine Insurance Company, Ltd., Liverpool; the Continental Insurance Company, Mannheim; the

KADAN KANDY MOIDEEN COOTTY BROTHERS.

1. CERTIFICATE. 2. SAHIB BAHADUR K. KUTTIAMMOO HAJEE. 3. THE OFFICE.

RAMCHANDRA MAHADEVA & CO.

1 PASSING COIR-YARN PREPARATORY TO PACKING IN BALES. 2. RAMCHANDRA MAHADEVA (SENIOR PARTNER).

General Accident Fire and Life Assurance Corporation, Ltd., Perth, Scotland ; the Aachen and Munich Fire Insurance Company, Aachen, Germany ; and the Magdeburg Fire Insurance Company.

The banking and the insurance branch of the business contributes very considerably to the revenue of the firm, and policies have been issued in large numbers throughout British and Native Cochin.

The firm are tenants of the premises which are now occupied by them, but they intend to construct their own warehouses, godowns, stores, and offices in the near future.

Mr. Shirgavkar is chairman of the Municipal Council of British Cochin.

R. S. VASUDEVA SHENOI & BROTHER

A thriving oil factory, belonging to the firm of Messrs. R. S. Vasudeva Shenoi and Brother, is situated on the northern side of the entrance of the Cochin backwater on the island of Vypeen, belonging to the native State of Cochin. The proprietors of this firm are, by caste, Gowd Saraswat Brahmins, and their ancestors had, so far back as the sixteenth century, come down from Goa and resided in the Rajah's State to get shelter from the religious persecution of the Portuguese in that town. The gradual progress of this firm has been very marked. In 1864 one Rama Shenoi Narayana Shenoi opened business as a copra, oil and poonac (oil cake) merchant, and after having prospered well, died, leaving his affairs in the hands of his son, Rama Shenoi. In those days oil was extracted in these parts by crushing copra in wooden mills either by bullock or hand power. As soon as it was discovered that steam could also be used for driving iron mills, and that this would greatly facilitate the production of oil, these people were among the earliest in his Highness's State to obtain one of these mills and to introduce this industry on the west coast. They opened a factory with 28 mills, and soon the number was increased to 48.

Fifty tons of copra can be passed through the machine in a day of twelve hours, while the average output of oil in the same period is about 26 candies, or a little more than 6 tons in weight. This product is disposed of to European merchants in Cochin.

Specially trained experts are employed to sort the copra into three classes before it is passed into the mill, but about 100 general hands are constantly required, and these are under the direct supervision of Mr. K. Jogiah Kamath, the capable manager.

The firm own some 9,000 coconut-trees, in full bearing, which are planted at an average of from 60 to 80 to the acre, and the number of these is being increased annually.

The premises, which cover an area of 100 sq. ft. on the sea-front on Vypeen Island, consist of a very large factory, copra drying yards, offices, stores for oil and poonac, godowns, and other buildings.

The business was founded by Rama Shenoi Narayana Shenoi, and he was succeeded by his son Narayana Shenoi Rama Shenoi, who died in 1893. From 1893 to 1911 the management devolved upon Mr. A. S. Venkateswara Shenoi, the uncle of the present owners, who entered into partnership in the latter year.

The firm have been successful with their entries of oil and oil-cake at Industrial and Agricultural Exhibitions at Cochin, and several prizes and medals have been awarded to them.

R. S. VASUDEVA SHENOI & BROTHER.

1. Office and Portion of Store-room. 2. View of Oil Mill. 3. Coolies sorting Dry Copra. 4. Oil Mills.

THE MALABAR NAVIGATION AND INDUSTRIALS, LTD.

One of the primary principles of industrial economy is that a country, a town, or a village, shall have every facility for the disposal of its products at the lowest possible cost commensurate with the time which is necessary for transit. And it is this fact which has brought the great railways into existence, which has caused the substitution of steam or electricity for the primitive methods of propelling sea-going vessels, and which has opened up vast areas of fertility for the mutual benefit of producer and consumer.

In Africa, India, Australia, and other countries, the man in the "hinterland" is being brought into touch with the merchant who is prepared to buy the harvest of his fields, or the manufactured goods from his mills, and this has been accomplished by the establishment of services of coastal or canal steamers, by the making of roads, the bridging of rivers, and by the bringing of the great iron horse almost to the very gates of the farm and to the doors of the factories.

The imperfect means of communication between numerous places on the coast of Malabar in the latter part of the nineteenth century prevented the development of industrial activities, and it was not until certain private firms began to run steam launches between Cochin, Alleppey, and other centres that the foundation was laid of a number of industries which have become of considerable importance.

The Malabar Navigation and Industrials, Ltd., was formed to carry on and develop the steam and motor launch services in the backwaters of Malabar, and for this purpose the company acquired the interests of Messrs. Wallibhoy Kaderbhoy & Co., Abdulsathar Hajee Moosa, and Ahmed Hasbulla.

The proprietors of the company stated in a preliminary prospectus that they hoped to extend the services throughout from one end of the backwaters to the other, to establish road services by motor vehicles (whenever there was no unhealthy competition) for the facility of the passengers travelling by the company's launches, to arrange and enter into an agreement for the carriage of mails and parcels, and to establish and carry on certain important industrial concerns.

The boats now run from the northern extremity of the Cochin State to all the stations in the Central and South Travancore States, and they are entrusted with the conveyance of his Majesty's mails as well as those of the native States.

There are at present 23 steam and motor launches, and their names are as follows: *Alhambra, Ambala, Albania, Ambrosia, Arcadia, Auroma, Almora, Madona, Kaisar-i-Hind, Mustafa, Mecca, Vizaya, Vikrama, Vamana, Vittoba, King George, Empress Mary, Lili, Prince Victor, Nellie, Kohinoor, Medina,* and *Lady Susan.*

The places which are served by these boats are: Cochin to Kottapuram; Ernakulam to Parur; Cochin to Alleppey; Alleppey to Kottayam; Alleppey to Changanacherry; Mattancherry to Ernakulam Town; and from the Out-Agency to Ernakulam Railway Station.

Through tickets are issued to Quilon, which is the present terminus of the State of Travancore.

The company was registered on March 3, 1913, with a capital of 5 lakhs of rupees, and the shareholders have every reason to be satisfied with the working of the launches since that date.

1. A CATAMARAN. 2. OLD BOATS AT TRANQUEBAR. 3. MASULAH BOAT AND FISHERMEN.

Photo by Nicholas & Co.

MARINE FISHERIES

BY JAMES HORNELL, F.L.S., SUPERINTENDENT OF PEARL AND CHANK FISHERIES TO THE GOVERNMENT OF MADRAS.

SOUTHERN INDIA, otherwise the Madras Presidency, has by far the longest coast line of any seaboard Indian province. If the States of Travancore and Cochin are included, this sea line exceeds a total length of 1,600 geographical miles. Six different languages are spoken by the fishermen who people the Madras coasts —Tamil, Malayalam, Telugu, Uriya, Canarese, and Tulu. As will readily be inferred from this diversity and the varying character of the coast line and sea bottom in different localities, the methods of capture, the kinds of fish taken, and the practice of curing vary as immensely as if the main localities were situated on different continents.

The principal bulk of fish is captured on the west coast, off the shores of Malabar, South Canara, Travancore, and Cochin. In these districts sea-fishing attains the dignity of a national industry, employing many thousands of hands, a great fleet of boats, and a capital of no mean magnitude. Here the industry is frequently well organized by wealthy and often enterprising merchants, particularly in Mangalore, Malpe, and Cannanore, with an extensive export trade to Bombay, Ceylon, and Burmah. The bulk of this cured fish consists of salted and sun-dried mackerel, sardines, jew-fish, seer, and cat-fish.

The outstanding characteristics of this west-coast fishery is the magnitude of the sardine and mackerel industries. These, in common with the other fisheries, are carried on almost exclusively during the north-east monsoon, when this coast enjoys fine weather after the storms and floods brought by the south-west monsoon. From September to March in normal years vast multitudes of fish resort to the inshore waters to feed upon the teeming life of the shallows. Foremost among these shoals, from an economic standpoint, are sardines and mackerel, the latter a smaller species than its cousin of British waters, but which makes up for lack of individual size by the vastness of its shoals. The quantities caught vary greatly from year to year, as the shoals are extremely erratic in their seasonal abundance, due apparently to variations in the food supply in different years in the inshore waters. This phenomenon is akin to that which disturbs the prosperity of the French sardine fishery. In Malabar this uncertainty as to the annual return in abundance of the staple shoaling fishes hampers the development of the industries dependent thereon ; notably so in the case of the fish-oil and fish-guano trades, which require the provision of well-equipped up-to-date factories if they are to be carried on upon a sound commercial basis. An inquiry is at present being conducted by the Madras Fisheries Department with a view to determine the principal factors governing the seasonal movements of sardines and mackerel, and there is hope that eventually it will be possible to furnish the fish trade with reliable forecasts of the relative abundance of these fish some time in advance of the opening of the fishing season.

The nets and methods employed to catch sardines and mackerel vary greatly. In South Canara great use is made of a very large and most effective true shore-seine, called the *rampani,* or rampan net, introduced comparatively recently from Portuguese India. Farther south, in Malabar, Cochin, and Travancore, gilling nets, called *aila vala* and *chala vala,* are extensively used, as well as casting or throwing-nets. The bulk of the sardines are, however, taken in the *odam* or *peru vala,* a well-designed bag-net seine, requiring the services of two large canoes and having points of resemblance with the purse seine.

For the larger fish, comprising seer (*Cybium guttatum* and *C. commersoni*), palamin (*Chorinemus lysan*), bāmin (*Polynemus,* spp.), vala (*Chirocentrus dorab*), jew-fishes (*Sciæna,* spp.), bonito, cat-fish, and shark, drift netting is largely employed; nets of appropriate mesh being used according to the shoals that may be present. The most expert drift netters are Bombay men from the neighbourhood of Ratnagiri, who leave home for the South Canarese drift fishery under contract with fish merchants at Udipi, Mangalore, Cannamore, and other great centres. Strangely enough this object lesson has had no effect upon the local fishermen, who have so far failed to build boats of the handy and effective type worked by the Ratnagiri men; the former cling to the crank dug-out they have employed from time immemorial, and which, it has to be admitted, answers their purpose well so long as their ambition does not run to the deep-sea fishing favoured by the men from the north. A "fleet" of Vowri nets as employed by a Ratnagiri drifter is usually of excellent dimensions, running to a length of from 1 to 1¼ miles, which compares not unfavourably with European herring and mackerel drift nets as used by sailing craft.

Fixed engines are little used on the west coast, with the exception of the great estuarine harbour of Cochin, where huge "China" dip-nets line the shores, and where great prawn stake-nets are also operated largely. As already noted, the boats used, with the exception of the Rampani and Ratnagiri boats, are exclusively of the canoe type; usually they are large slab-sided dug-outs, or are built-up flat-bottomed boats modelled on the same pattern. They have no sailing qualities; a crew of eight is their usual complement—seven men at the paddles and one steering. For short distances the crews can keep up a considerable pace, which is very useful when operating the *odam,* or boat seine.

The south-west monsoon restricts fishing greatly from May to August inclusive; during this period a considerable prawn fishery is carried on at certain parts of the coast. As showing the enormous size of these prawn shoals, I may say that at one fishing village in Malabar as much as Rs. 15,000 worth of prawns have been landed in a single day by the local boats. Unfortunately the humidity of the air is so great at the time of the prawn fishery that frequently it becomes impossible to dry the catch sufficiently to enable it to be put on the market. Not infrequently much of it goes rotten, and has to be used as manure or else thrown back into the sea. Clearly this is one of many openings offered by the fishing industry to the enterprising capitalist who will adopt appropriate artificial drying methods and turn a risky and precarious industry into one where success does not depend upon the vagaries of the weather, and where profit is not a gamble on the chance of a few hours of sunshine.

On the east coast local conditions are less uniform than on the west, hence we find there far greater diversity in boats, methods, and results. According to the type of boat employed we may classify different sections of the shore-line: the northernmost is the catamaran coast, extending from Ganjam, in the north, to Point Calimere, in the south. In Palk Bay true boats prevail, capable of standing heavy seas and going long distances; this is the boat coast. Farther south, in the pearl-fishery region, of which Tuticorin is the centre, two peculiar local types have been evolved, which may be termed respectively canoe-boats and boat-catamarans. Both sail well, particularly the former, which of their kind are really admirable and able to live in a sea that no Malabar canoe would ever dream of facing.

The fishing value of the catamaran coast varies greatly. Off the mouths of the great rivers and in curves in the coast where fish food sometimes accumulates, a considerable fishing industry exists, particularly in the vicinity of large towns. The sea-fisheries of Ganjam appear to be the most backward in development, partly because of the small and miserable catamarans in use, and partly for lack of fishermen, as in the best fishing season the fisher-class are accustomed to pass over to Burmah, where they get high wages in lighterage and other harbour work. Sardines are fairly abundant in some years off the Ganjam and Vizagapatam coast, and if labour and boats were available, a large and profitable sardine fishery could be built up. Farther south sardines become scarce, their place being taken by mackerel (*Scomber microlepidotus*), whereof large quantities are taken between Madras and Cocanda. Prawn fishing, by means of great stake nets of several ingenious patterns, is practised extensively in the creeks and inlets of the Godaveri and Kistna Rivers. Southward of the Kistna, and as far as Point Calimere, a great deal of fishing—for what I can best describe as miscellaneous fish—is carried on by means of large catamarans truly so-called, consisting usually of three main logs which are temporarily tied together with the aid of special key-pieces every time they are used, and subsequently taken apart to dry and regain full buoyancy at the end of each day's work. The nets used are of two principal classes, drift-nets (*vella-valai*) and trawls (*thûri valai*). The former are usually small, owing to the limitation imposed by the poor cargo-carrying capacity of the catamaran. The manner of using the *thûri* is distinctly ingenious, and in it we see a clear anticipation of the modern otter-trawl, from which the chief difference is that two catamarans take the place of otter-boards as well as supplying the tractive power.

A peculiar fishery, pursued only on the Tanjore coast, has as its objective the shoals of flying-fish which are found in great abundance beyond the 100-fathom line off this district. Specially large catamarans have to be employed owing to the distance the men have to go and the large catches made if shoals be met with. The fact that no shelter is possible on catamarans, and that only a small quantity of food can be carried, prevents this industry developing as it otherwise would, and proper exploitation awaits the day when sea-keeping boats become available, worked in conjunction with a swift carrier. No other deep-sea fishery is prosecuted on the east coast northward of Calimere.

In Palk Strait, a remunerative fishery for the Indian salmon, or bāmin (*Polynemus*, spp.), is conducted by a fleet of heavily built boats from the villages west of Calimere. The nets used are strongly made stationary gill nets, securely anchored in position in the channels favoured by bāmin. Another fishery of considerable local value in Palk Bay is for crabs (*Neptunus pelagicus*); every night during the season many miles of wall nets are laid in the inshore waters, the crabs being entangled in the netting.

SUNRISE ON THE COOUM.

Drift-net fishing is largely prosecuted in this area, while along the southern shores of the bay and thence southwards to the Tuticorin shore, seines of large size are operated with much profit wherever the inshore waters are not obstructed by rocks.

From Pamban to Cape Comorin drift nets and *madi valai* are the chief nets employed at sea, the latter by catamarans only. The *madi* is a cross between a trawl and a boat seine, a modification of the *thûri* of the Coromandel coast.

The rocky banks of the Gulf of Mannar plateau give shelter to bottom-fish in abundance, such as are never found on the west coast, and seldom on the Coromandel coast. As a consequence lining is well established and gives employment to a considerable section of the fishing community. Trolling for the giant mackerel called seer (*Cybium*, spp.) and other large surface fish is also extensively prosecuted by swift sailing-boats hailing from villages where shelter from surf is found. Until recently numerous Sinhalese outrigger canoes came across from Ceylon specially for this fishery, which was not then carried on by local boats. A scare of cholera and the rigour of quarantine regulations have kept these men from coming for the past three years, and as a result of experiment the local men, who had never tried this fishery before, found to their astonishment that their own boats were equal to the work. By this means the local men have gained a new industry and are now prosecuting it vigorously and with profit.

A survey of the fishing industry ot the Madras Presidency would be incomplete without reference to the Laccadive Islands, where nearly every man is concerned more or less with fishing. With the exception of Minicoy no export industry exists; the islanders catch what they want for their own use and no more. Lining, spearing, and seining are the methods in general use, and the last-named is employed within the lagoons of islands and the greater reefs. At Minicoy the fishing industry is of greater importance, due to the existence there of a prolific bonito fishery. Large and swift boats are built specially for this purpose, each provided with a fish-well, wherein live bait is carried to the fishing grounds. The methods followed are almost identical with those followed by the Japanese: their main features consist in attracting the bonitos to the boat by means of live bait thrown overboard, and then of "jigging" them out of the water by a rod and line armed with a brightly tinned hook, which the bonito, in the confusion of their rushes, mistake for the silvery fish used as a lure. The fish caught are filleted, boiled, smoked, and then dried to the consistency and appearance of mahogany. The whole of the product is exported to Ceylon and Chittagong under the name of Maldive fish, and is used as a flavouring ingredient in curries.

An outstanding feature of the fishing industry in Madras is the encouragement given by Government to the efficient curing of salt fish by the provision of Government fish-curing yards, conveniently located for all important fishing centres. At these yards salt is sold to the fish-curers free of duty, a concession of great value when introduced originally on the recommendation of Dr. Day, well known for his valuable systematic works on Indian fishes. To-day, when the duty upon salt has been reduced to a very low rate, the privilege has less value, and in some places the curers are inclined to buy salt in the bazaar and do their curing on their own premises—in my opinion a retrograde step, seeing that it is difficult for the authorities to exercise supervision over the methods of private curers working on a small scale, whose methods are often anything but hygienic. If private fish-curing yards are to be the rule in future, it will then be necessary to institute a special inspecting staff to ensure the observance of sanitary methods. The improvement of curing processes is, indeed, one of the chief duties of the Fisheries Department, and much has already been done in this direction under the guidance of Sir Frederick Nicholson, the aim being to introduce methods which will ensure better keeping qualities, greater digestibility, improved flavour, and reduced cost, so that a larger amount of well-cured fish will be available for public consumption. Another aim of the Department is to increase the amount of fish taken from the sea by the introduction of more efficient methods of fishing and by the breeding and rearing of fish in fish farms, after the methods found successful in Italy and France. The most hopeful fishing device which it is hoped to introduce is that of steam trawling. Preliminary investigations have demonstrated the existence of a vast area of excellent food fish within the 100-fathom line off Cape Comorin. A rough estimate gives the area which is probably suitable for this industry as 4,000 square miles. A smaller ground of high potential value has also been discovered off Negapatam, and there is reason to believe that other good grounds are available off the deltas of the Rivers Godaveri and Kistna. Government have already decided to carry out a thorough working test under the conduct of men thoroughly conversant with British methods.

The present war has interfered with the immediate prosecution of the experiment, the men designated for the work having been drafted into the ranks of the minesweepers. Bound up with the successful prosecution of fish-trawling off the Indian coast is the problem of the preservation of fish in the fresh condition during distribution to inland consuming centres. This question is also engaging the attention of the Department, and good hopes of a successful issue are based on experiments already carried out on a small scale.

Marine industries other than the capture of food fish are not numerous in India. Reference has already been made to crab-fishing in Palk Bay, and with this exception the only ones of any importance are the pearl and chank fisheries carried on in the Gulf of Mannar and Palk Bay; a small *bêche-de-mer* fishery on the coast of the Ramnad district and in the Laccadive Islands; and the utilization of several molluscs for food, chiefly on the Malabar coast. The most important of the molluscs are mussels and clams, the former taken from rocks off the coast, usually by diving, while the latter are found in estuaries and backwaters. *Bêche-de-mer* is occasionally collected in some quantity in the neighbourhood of Pamban and the adjacent islands; it is prepared by boiling and drying for the Chinese market, being exported to Singapore.

Both the pearl and the chank fisheries are Government monopolies. The former dates back to the golden age of Tamil rule in the south; Greek and Roman writers make specific mention of towns on the Gulf of Mannar which were famous at the beginning of the Christian era as rich pearling centres, and the pearl fisheries were described as among the chief sources of revenue to the Pandiyan princes who then ruled the country. With the advent of the Portuguese these fisheries passed into the hands of the invaders, as they possessed the necessary sea power. In turn they had to yield to the Dutch, who paid great attention to the management of the pearl banks, and who profited by several good fisheries. The jealousy of the Nawab of the Carnatic in later years interfered with their profits, as the Dutch had then insufficient power to browbeat this ruler effectively, according to their custom in earlier days when they possessed greater relative power. With the passing of the Dutch and the transfer of the Carnatic to British rule at the beginning of the last century the pearl banks entered on a new era of prosperity. From 1805 to 1906 Government received from this source a net revenue amounting to Rs. 15,64,071. Since 1908 no pearl fisheries have taken place in the Gulf of Mannar, but new beds were discovered in 1914 in Palk Bay, and a net profit of Rs. 2,500 was made from the small fishery which resulted—a fishery which barely escaped utter failure owing to the disorganization consequent upon the outbreak of war with Germany three weeks before the commencement of operations. Fear of the *Emden* was the chief deterrent factor, as no pearl merchant would venture to a coast port liable to a sea-raid at any time. Apart from the small profit made at this fishery, the discovery of these Palk Bay beds is of very great importance, owing to the fact that we are now enabled to trace the origin of the swarm of pearl oyster spat which periodically repopulate the pearl banks in the Gulf of Mannar. Palk Bay is now seen to be the true home-land of the local pearl oyster.

Without the glamour that has always surrounded the pearl fishery, the chank fishery has actually more real value as a reliable revenue earner. This industry, conducted departmentally by the Madras Fisheries Department, employs a large number of divers, who are paid by returns. Two main fisheries are worked —the Tuticorin and the Ramnad. The former has been carried on departmentally by Government for over one hundred years, while the latter is a new acquisition, a fifteen years' lease having been obtained from the Rajah of Ramnad, in order to effect a consolidation of all the Madras chank fisheries under a single control. The Tuticorin fishery produces an average of 250,000 shells per annum; the Ramnad one about 150,000 at present, with prospect of considerable increase if the labour force be augmented. As showing the value of these fisheries, the total *net* revenue derived from the Tuticorin fishery alone, from 1876 to 1914 inclusive, amounts to the not inconsiderable sum of Rs. 4,73,369-10-4. The shells are almost wholly absorbed by the shell-bangle industry of Bengal, being exported in the first instance to Calcutta. An endeavour is now being made by the Fisheries Department to obtain a small power-driven shell-cutting instrument, which can be operated cheaply, in place of the present hand-saw used by

HOW THEY CATCH FISH IN COCHIN

the Bengal shell-cutters. If a power-saw suitable to the requirements of the small capitalist can be obtained, an endeavour will be made to introduce shell-cutting and bangle-making as a new industry into Madras.

FISHING

By P. B. THOMAS

THERE is first-rate fishing for the rod in many places in Southern India with three distinct classes of sporting fish found in the rivers, the estuaries, and the tanks, or lakes, respectively. In the rivers there are the mahseer, the Carnatic and Malabar carp, the black-spot, and many kinds of barils. The last three kinds chiefly frequent the rivers on the west coast and round the Nilgiri Hills, and they take the fly freely. Malabar carp are not infrequently taken up to 8 lb. in weight, and the Carnatic carp run to an extreme size of about 25 lb. The black-spot and baril are small, but they accept the fly very readily. The most sporting fish of all is the mahseer. He is found all over the south of India wherever the conditions suit him—i.e. rocky rivers at a certain elevation. The best-known localities are the Mysore, Coorg, and west coast rivers, and the Bhavani; but the Kistna and Godavari Rivers in their upper reaches, and most of their affluents, hold many fish of large size. The mahseer takes a fly indifferently, and is usually caught by spinning a dead bait or a spoon. The sport given by him is considered by many people to excel that afforded by salmon, and the first rushes of a hooked fish are so strong and quick that it is customary to spin with a salmon fly rod. With a stiff rod the breakage of any but the strongest tackle is to be feared, and as the best fishing is always in dead clear water the tackle has to be as fine as possible. The mahseer grows to a very large size. Mr. C. A. Murray-Aynsley, a well-known sportsman, has landed two fish of more than 104 lb. each, and fish of 20 lb. and upwards are common.

The rivers also hold enormous siluroids, which are not generally sought after by sportsmen, but which occasionally give good sport. One of 136 lb. has been landed on a rod with spinning tackle. Last, but not least, there is excellent trout-fishing in the streams on the Nilgiris, where the rainbow trout has been introduced with great success. The fish are plentiful and of fair size; the fishing is well looked after and is preserved, and much of it is within easy reach of Ootacamund.

The estuary fishing all round the coast of Southern India is plentiful, and the sport excellent. The best fish are the bāmin, the nair, the red and grey perch, and the megalops. The bāmin is, for his size, a more powerful fish than the salmon, and runs up many of the rivers in quantities, usually ascending and descending with each tide. Spinning a dead bait or a phantom for these fish under the arch of a bridge, or at any spot where the river is contracted and the water runs fast, gives sport of a very high order. They frequently weigh as much as 12 lb., and when there is a good run of them a rod may land half a dozen or more one after the other. They ascend nearly every river on the east and west coasts at particular seasons.

The nair fish occasionally exceeds 60 lb. in weight, and some of 20 lb. and upwards are often caught. They are to be hooked either on a spinning or a live bait, or prawn. They are a more sluggish fish than the bāmin, but as they are very powerful, strong tackle is required, with plenty of line on the reel. They are to be found in almost all the estuaries and harbours round the coast, including the Madras harbour.

The red and grey perch are rock fish, and are caught with a prawn or spinning bait. The average size of those caught in the estuaries is between 2 and 5 lb.

The megalops is a very sporting fish. They are found in the estuaries in shoals, and are to be caught on a spinning bait. They are readily acclimatized to fresh water, and afford excellent sport in several fresh-water tanks which have been stocked with them in Madras itself. Some which are caught there reach a weight of 4 lb. They take the fly well, and the hooked fish, throwing himself repeatedly out of the water when being played, will test the capability of any angler.

The tank, or lake, fish that are best known for sporting purposes are the labeo, the white carp, the murral, and the fresh-water shark. The two latter are predacious fish, usually caught on live bait, though they will take a spinning one. They are also found in the rivers. The murral runs to about 3 ft. in length, and the fresh-water shark about 5 or 6 ft., but they are usually caught from 2 to 10 lb. in weight respectively.

The labeo, the white carp, and other similar fish give very fine sport to the bait anglers. They are very cunning, and the sport equals the finest roach-fishing on a very much enlarged scale. They are to be found in most tanks which are fed by rivers, and which do not become dry in the hot weather. The labeo runs to about 3 ft., and the white carp to about 1½ ft. in length. The fish caught in a good locality should average more than 2 lb., and many will considerably exceed this. Very fine tackle, very quick striking, and some skill are required to catch these fish at all, but when the art is mastered the sport is of an excellent character.

Some of the tanks hold a small fly-taking fish called the "chilwa," which gives good sport when the tanks do not run dry.

For fishing in Southern India the sportsman should provide himself with a 14 or 16 ft. salmon rod, with an extra spinning top, and a trout rod of about 10 ft. for river-fishing. For the estuary-fishing the salmon rod with short spinning top will suffice, but a good salmon or pike spinning rod is better. For tank-fishing a roach rod is a necessity; it need not be long, but it must be very light and stiff. For all spinning, much trouble and expense is saved by using undressed or waterproofed cotton or flax lines on suitable spinning reels in preference to dressed silk lines; and the reels for the mahseer and estuary fishing should be large enough to hold 150 to 200 yards of such line of moderate thickness.

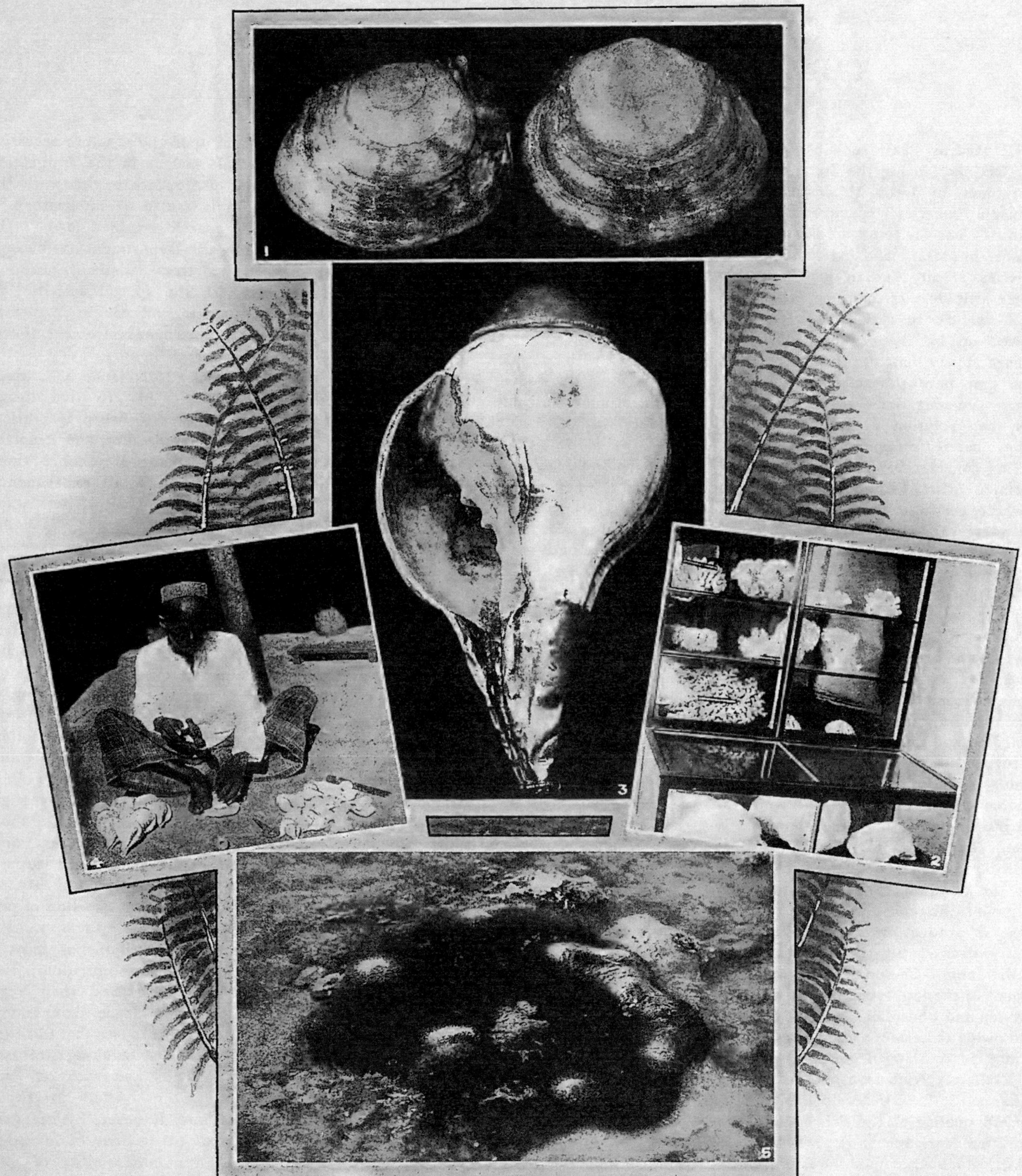

1. WINDOW-PANE OYSTERS (PLACUNA PLACENTA).
Still employed for window-glazing in Goa, Portuguese India.

2. CORALS FROM THE GULF OF MANNAR.

3. THE SACRED CONCH.
A sinistral form of *Turbinella pyrum*, used in the service of the gods in Hindu temples.

4. A MAHOMMEDAN MAKING CHILDREN'S FEEDING-SPOUTS OUT OF CHANK SHELLS (TURBINELLA PYRUM), PULICAT.
Photo by J. Hornell.

5. "DISCOSOMA," A GIANT ANEMONE.
18 inches across the disc. Photographed in water.
Photo by Vividha-kala, Mandir, Baroda.

SOUTHERN INDIA

THE MADRAS FISHERIES DEPARTMENT

BY JAMES HORNELL, F.L.S.

THE Madras Presidency has the distinction of being the first provincial Government in India to institute and organize a Fisheries Department. As the Presidency has the longest coast-line and the most important and extensive fishing industries of any Indian province, this pioneer attitude was to be expected, and has, I venture to claim, been worthily followed up by the organization which has been slowly built up during the eight years that have passed since the preliminary investigations were completed.

As the evolution of the Department has been carried on upon distinctive lines, differing considerably from those usually associated with Fisheries Departments elsewhere, the following brief outline may have interest for those who are concerned in the economic advancement of Indian industries.

The Department owes its inception to the initiative of Sir Frederick A. Nicholson, K.C.I.E., whose attention was drawn to the crying need for radical improvements in the curing of fish for human consumption, and in the preparation of oil and guano from surplus catches of sardine and mackerel. Local methods of curing were seen to be obviously capable of enormous improvement if for no other than hygienic reasons, while the preparation of fish manure not only wasted the whole of the oil present in the fish, but was conducted so crudely that the resultant product was rapidly falling into disrepute in planting circles, where a product of good quality was greatly desired by the tea-planters of South India, Ceylon, and Japan, on account of the high percentage present of nitrogen and phosphoric acid. It was indeed owing to certain agricultural investigations partly carried out in Japan that Sir Frederick Nicholson was led to take an interest in fishery development, and so the bad quality of the fish manure produced ten years ago on the Malabar coast had direct influence upon the establishment of a Fisheries Department in Madras.

The actual inception of the Department dates from July 1905, when the Government, on Sir Frederick Nicholson's proposal, instituted a Fisheries Bureau charged with a preliminary inquiry into the condition of the fisheries of the Presidency, together with an investigation of their main potentialities, and of the lines upon which improvement in methods would be most beneficial and successful. Two years were occupied by preliminary investigation, during which Sir Frederick Nicholson (now appointed Honorary Director of Fisheries Investigation) toured extensively in Madras, Europe, the United States, and Japan. His inquiries in Japan—where by a curious coincidence the present writer was also touring independently, with no idea of ever being connected with Madras Fisheries—were fruitful of many valuable results and suggestive conclusions which were embodied later in a lengthy report entitled "Fishery Inquiries in Japan."

Practical work now becoming possible and profitable, the staff was enlarged at the end of 1907, whereby Mr. H. C. Wilson, who had been engaged originally by the Nilgiri Game Association to conduct trout-breeding in the Nilgiri Hills, became an officer of the Fisheries Department as Piscicultural Expert, charged with the conduct of fresh-water investigations, while the present writer, who had been previously Marine Biologist to the Ceylon Government, was appointed in 1908 as Marine Assistant to the Director, with special charge of marine investigations other than those connected with fish preservation, whereof the Director assumed exclusive control. In the same year a small experimental station was opened at Ennore, a fishing centre 11 miles north of Madras. Here was carried on with notable success a long series of experiments in the curing of fish by smoking, salting, and other treatment. This laid the foundation of methods now fully approved, and which are in commercial operation at the large Government curing-station at Tanur, in Malabar, to which the Ennore plant was eventually transferred. It was, however, at Ennore that many of the principles governing efficient fish-curing *as applicable to tropical conditions* were worked out, and in this connection it is worthy of special note that experience showed that most of the methods successfully operated in Europe for fish-curing are not applicable without considerable modification when applied under Indian atmospheric conditions. Ignorance of this fact has been a pitfall to many who have attempted unsuccessfully to introduce European plans, and too great stress cannot be laid upon the absolute necessity for radical alterations in the application of accepted European methods if the results in India are to be satisfactory.

From the year last named (1908), the work done by the Department has become specialized in three distinct channels coinciding with the special activities of the three superior officers in charge of operations. It becomes convenient, therefore, to follow each in turn.

Sir Frederick Nicholson has given nearly the whole of his attention during the past eight years to fish preservation, oil, and guano manufacture, and from the small beginning made at Ennore there have evolved (1) a small experimental fish-canning plant at Calicut, now about to be closed in favour of (2) a canning factory at Beypore, near Calicut, capable of work on a commercial scale, and equipped with the latest patterns of machines for the making of solderless tins; while (3) at Tanur, also on the Malabar coast, a fine fish-curing yard and oil and guano factory afford ample opportunity for the testing and perfecting of methods upon sound commercial lines and under practical conditions. Both sections of the work have resulted in notable success. The utilization of sardine-oil in soap-making is another line of investigation now being taken up with much promise, Government having sanctioned the engagement of a qualified organic chemist to conduct the experiments.

To enter fully into the question of providing means for preserving fish to enable some of the inland millions of India to obtain supplies of a nutritious food hitherto practically beyond their reach would require more space than can be granted, but suffice it to say that in adapting pilchardizing and smoking processes to the Indian sardine and mackerel, great progress has been made, interrupted somewhat of late, however, by the great development of other lines of investigation, and by the impossibility of overtaking, with the present staff, all the work that presents itself. Improvement in the supply of fresh fish to inland cities and hill stations is yet another inquiry to which special attention is now being given. A special refrigerating plant, designed to treat fish by a novel and promising process recently patented in England, has already been set up, and will be at work during the coming season. Other lines of experiment are also in view, but enough has been written to show what an attractive scheme of work has been followed, and how profitable have been several of the investigations.

In the branch of Marine Investigation the problems are more elusive and less concrete than in that which treats of the commercial utilization of fishery products. In the latter the questions are largely of a mechanical and chemical nature, and may be thought out and experimented upon directly until a successful end be attained. In regard to improvements in fishery methods, to the means to be taken to increase the actual supply of fish and to the betterment of the economic and educational condition of the fishing population, deeper difficulties confront one, largely psychological in character. One has to deal with an innate conservatism which regards every plan as being unworthy of acceptance if it be contrary to preconceived beliefs and established usage. The virtual lack of any education whatever among the fishing population is perhaps the greatest source of difficulty, and a score of instances can be given where this particular shoe pinches with great effect. Hence the work hitherto done has been largely in the nature of preparation of the ground for future effort, and of scientific research whereof the fruit will not possibly be gathered for many years to come.

If, however, the lines of work intended to have immediate practical results require primary mention, the principal of these consist of (1) the organization and consolidation of the whole of the chank fisheries of the Presidency; (2) the re-organization of pearl bank inspection, and the discovery of the breeding stock whence the pearl banks in the Gulf of Mannar are replenished; (3) the working out of plans for the establishment of pearl-cultural operations; (4) the exploration of the bottom of the sea within the 100-fathom line for commercially valuable trawling grounds; (5) the rearing in confinement in coastal lagoons of prawns and food fish; (6) the establishment of a model oyster park; and (7) the planning of an up-to-date Fisheries Headquarters and Public Aquarium for Madras.

MARINE FAUNA

BY JAMES HORNELL, F.L.S., MADRAS FISHERIES DEPARTMENT

THE first impression of the zoologist who visits the Madras beach or the shores of Malabar is one of disappointment at the apparent poverty of the littoral fauna, the lack of diversity among the shells and other jetsam thrown up by the waves, the absence of a wrack-lined tide-mark, and of the rock pools abounding in life, so familiar a feature of most English shores. A longer acquaintance with what the surf flings ashore, a visit to the beach when fishing catamarans and dug-outs land their catches, or, better still, a day afloat with dredge and tow-net, or a few days among the coral islands of the Gulf of Mannar, will alter the verdict, and give glimpses of a life varied beyond belief, of animals vying with the rainbow in colouring, and putting human ingenuity to shame by the craft and skill shown in the devising of means to outwit enemies or to stalk prey.

Acquaintance with the fishes is most easily gained, for the fisherman's catches and the pretty aquarium at Madras afford ample opportunity, in the one case to note how silvery fish predominate among those of food value, while those contemned for the table are beloved of the aquarium-keeper for their gaudy colouring and uncouth shapes. Chief of these are the lovely coral fishes of the genera *Holacanthus* and *Chætodon*. In these brilliant blues, canary yellows, rich reds, and snowy whites are the predominant colours, arranged usually in stripes, sometimes vertical as in *Chætodon falcula*, horizontal as in *C. trifasciatus*, or crescentric as in *Heniochus macrolepidotus*. One of the finest, *Holacanthus imperator*, clad in blue and yellow livery, is known by Tamil fishermen as the Dhoby's wife, a sly reference to the latter's habit of borrowing the gaudy raiment of her employers. The showy scorpion fish (*Pterois russelli*), all frills and furbelows, is another conspicuously coloured common fish.

The chief food fishes having been already sufficiently referred to in the article on "Marine Fisheries," no further notice need be given here. Sharks and rays are numerous in species, the individual size frequently great. Man-eating sharks are well represented. They are seldom aggressive on these coasts, and this is probably due to the lack of deep water close inshore, a characteristic of the South Indian littoral. The hammer-head shark grows to large sizes. *Lamna spallanzani* is often taken and the fierce *Galeocerdo rayneri* is by no means uncommon in deep water. The tiger-shark, handsomest of his kind, is sometimes caught fully 14 ft. in length, while of the huge but harmless *Rhinodon typicus* a few specimens have been thrown ashore.

Of sting-rays and eagle-rays the largest is the fine horned-ray (*Dicerobatis eregoodoo*), a species which grows to the enormous width, across the disc, of 18 ft.; divers dread this more than any shark, alleging that it tries to drown men out of sheer malice, by flapping over them and so preventing their return to the surface. A large number of rays feed upon shellfish, and one in particular, the gregarious ray (*Rhinoptera javanica*), is one of the prime curses of the pearl banks, where it appears occasionally in hordes numbering several thousand individuals, and may wipe out within a few days whole beds worth lakhs of rupees. True eels (*Anguilla*) live in creeks and backwaters in fair number, but are seldom caught, as Indians are prejudiced against their use as food. The wicked-looking Murænids are often seen, usually in handsome livery: they, too, are not esteemed for food.

Of the Acanthopterygii, the sea-perches are most numerous in genera and species; they are usually taken by line fishermen on rocky grounds, such as the pearl banks of the Gulf of Mannar. Jew-fishes (*Sciænidæ*) are another numerous group, largely caught on the west coast, and esteemed both for curing and for their air-bladders ("fish-maws" or "sounds"), used in the preparation of isinglass. Cat-fish (*Siluridæ*) of certain species periodically gather upon the same coast in great shoals, and form a valuable fishery; the male has the strange habit of using his mouth as an incubatory pouch during the development of the eggs, which are the size of small marbles. The jumping gobies (*Boleophthalmus* and *Periopthalmus*) abound wherever mangrove swamps and mudflats occur. Like *Littorina* among molluscs and *Ocypods* among crabs, these fish no longer live normally in water as do their relations of ordinary habit; they pass most of their time crawling over the muddy shore and even basking in the sun on wave-washed rocks—they still require to keep their bodies damp. Pleuronectids are numerous locally. The commonest are the tongue-soles (*Cynoglossus* and *Synaptura*), which occur sometimes in great shoals off Malabar; a small but voracious turbot-like fish, *Psettodes erumei*, is fairly abundant in pairs off the same coast in deeper water. Globe-fish and file-fish are abundant, and represent the offal of the sea. The former are esteemed poisonous. The quaint coffre-fish (*Ostracion cornutus*) is not uncommon; and locally the uncouth angler-fish (*Antennarius hispidus*) is met with in numbers.

Of the primitive Chordates several species of *Amphioxus* occur; in many sands they are to be found in abundance, but distribution is distinctly local. They affect chiefly clean sands where other life is scanty. One species, *Branchiostoma pelagicum*, is pelagic, being taken only in the tow-net. The sedentary Tunicata are well represented everywhere, except on muddy bottoms. Of simple forms probably *Rhabdocynthia pallida* is most numerous; its tough, gooseberry-like bags abound on sandy ground. Molgulids are common, as are hosts of smaller forms. Colonial species are largely restricted to *Leptoclinids*; these favour specially the branched tubes of *Eunice tubifex*; Bottryllids are scarce.

Crustaceans form a very rich group in Indian seas. The crabs are particularly well represented, and diverse in form and habit. In the backwaters is found the fine *Scylla serrata*, brown, and of good flavour, having the gastronomic value held by *Cancer pagurus* in Europe. Other species of swimming crabs also abound, most notable being the blue mottled *Neptunus pelagicus*, particularly abundant in Palk Strait. The pretty yellow-tinted *Matuta lunaris* frequents the edges of estuaries; the thin and much-flattened *Graspus*, in olive-striped livery, scurries everywhere over rocks and piles at the water's edge; burrowing crabs (*Ocypoda*, spp.) dig holes on the beach and in low-lying land, sallying forth to the water's edge, veritable shadow crabs, as evening falls; often they congregate in great battalions, quartering the sands for food; they are the most alert and swift of all their kind. Mangrove swamps and mudflats give harbourage to myriads of quaint calling-crabs (*Gelasimus annulipes*), tiny fellows with one pincer absurdly large; as they hunt about for food these great pincers are every now and again stretched aloft and waved. What they mean by this absurd conduct no one knows—many guesses have been made, but none are convincing. In deep water on the pearl banks stone crabs of many kinds find homes, and, like "Brer Rabbit," a common custom is to sham death if overtaken by a possible enemy—*Calappa* is an excellent instance. This crab has a body so hollowed beneath and with such short legs that at will all these can be tucked away beneath the carapace, as a tortoise draws in head and limbs when alarmed. Indeed, we may well coin the term "tortoise-crab" for *Calappa*—so far as I know it has not been given an English name. Other death-shamming crabs are the many species of the velvet ball-crabs (*Dromia*, spp.). To still further its safety *Dromia* often seeks adventitious aid from sponges and tunicates, tearing up colonies of suitable size, which it places upon its carapace, and holds there by means of a specialized pair of claw-like legs. The living cloak—the analogue of the brushwood with which artillerymen mask their guns from the prying eyes of aviators—usually thrives in this unnatural situation, and gradually fits itself to the shape and size of the carapace. Another species I have found living in a burrow which it had excavated in the main trunk of the cauliflower-like *Spongodes*, a genus of Alcyonarians.

Commensal life appeals to many of the South Indian crustacea. Other good examples of this habit are the Galatheids; of these one species, the beautiful black and white striped *Galathea elegans*, lives on the black and white mottled feather-star (*Antedon okelli*), while another, of pink colour, lives among the branches of the same pink-coloured *Spongodes* of which the stalk is used by *Dromia* as a burrow.

Hermit-crabs are common both in the sea and in every backwater. Chief is the great hairy *Pagurus setifer*, of brilliant red colour, living in large gastroped shells. Other species often met with are *Cœnobita rugosus*, living in small shells high on the beach; *Diogenes rectimanus* on coral reefs; and *Clibanarius æquabilis* in shallow water in *Cerithium* and other small shells.

Stomatopods are well represented on the east coast, but are scarce on the west. Wherever *Zostera* or *Halophila* flats occur they abound; prawn netters catch great quantities, but, strangely enough, little or no use is made of them as food. The small *Squilla nepa* and *S. oratoria* are the species most frequently seen; the handsome black and yellow banded *Lysiosquilla maculata*, the most conspicuously coloured of the group in Indian waters, is comparatively uncommon.

No true lobsters are found in India, the animals so miscalled locally being the crawfish, *Palinurus dasypus* and *P. ornatus*. The quaint brown and broad-nosed lobster, *Scyllarus*, is not uncommon on the rocky bottom of the Gulf of Mannar and on the Coromandel coast. These also are used as food, but seldom appear in the market.

Prawns are extraordinarily abundant, particularly the Penæids. Of these *Peneus indicus* and *P. semisulcatus* are caught in enormous quantities during and immediately after the rains, both in the sea and in backwaters, and the trade in dried prawns is consequently very important where conditions are favourable. In a previous page a striking example has been given of the catches sometimes made. Generally speaking the industry is a highly promising one.

At Pamban and in the adjacent islands the sharp snapping note made by the tiny clicking-lobster, *Alpheus*, is often heard as one walks over any stretch of stones at low tide. Related species live as commensals in certain cavernous sponges and amid the branches of the alcyonarian Spongodes.

Schizopods bulk largely in the plankton under certain conditions, and form a staple food of mackerel on the Malabar coast. Copepods seldom bulk so largely as Schizopods, but they are more evenly distributed, and their species are legion instead of being few. No fewer than 283 different kinds are identified in Herdman's "Ceylon Pearl Fishery Report" (vol. i), chiefly from the Gulf of Mannar. In deep water far from land the lovely *Sapphirina* is often to be seen scintillating in iridescent colours as it darts to and fro in the transparency of the blue depths around the ship. Parasitic forms (fish-lice) are many and strangely formed—they are frequently met with, but not so

1. A LIVE-BAIT STORE BASKET USED IN THE BONITO FISHERY, MINICOY ISLAND.

A bonito boat lies at the jetty.

2. FISH-CURING IN THE HOLLOWED BUTTS OF PALM-TREES, GODAVERI DISTRICT. 3. A "CHINA" NET, COCHIN.

4. CUTTLEFISH LINES, PALK BAY.

Large shells are attached at intervals to serve as traps.

5. A BUSY SCENE. HAULING SEINES TO SHORE, UPPADA, GODAVERI DISTRICT.

Photos by J. Hornell.

commonly as a large Isopod, *Anilocra*, which sometimes affects great numbers of one of the sardines (*Clupea fimbriata*). In one case I found a shoal of these fish where eight out of fifty bore one of these parasites behind the operculum, while many more showed scars indicating the recent presence of the same parasite. *Ligia*, the large and active Isopod so often seen at home scurrying over rocks and walls at tide level, has representative species here, equally numerous and active. Many find a home on the canal boats plying in the Buckingham Canal.

Cirripedes are represented by Acorn-shells (*Balanus*) and ship-barnacles (*Lepas*), the former on rocks and stones, the latter chiefly on floating timber and fruits. Some curious genera, *Creusia*, *Pyrgoma*, and *Acasta*, live in association with corals and sea-fans, forming barnacle galls thereon, while another, *Chelonobia testudinaria*, a peculiar smooth and depressed form, lives attached to the carapace of turtles.

Mollusca are well represented in all groups, and have considerable economic importance. The principal are the pearl-oyster (*Margaritifera vulgaris*) and the chank or conch (*Turbinella pyrum*), which constitute Government monopolies, and yield substantial profits on their working; for food purposes the green mussel (*Mytilus smaragdinus*), the oyster (*Ostrea*), and several kinds of clam (*Cytherea* and *Arca*) are of much value, particularly on the Malabar coast, where present-day kitchen middens entirely composed of clam and mussel shells are common sights in the shore villages. Cuttle-fish (*Sepia* and *Loligo*) are largely caught at certain centres, particularly in Palk Strait, and used both as food and for bait. The octopus (*Polypus*) is met with often when dredging on stony bottom, but it seldom attains an arm stretch of more than 2½ ft., and never aspires to the ferocity and power of Victor Hugo's sea-terror.

Owing to the muddy character of the inshore bottom, few molluscs are found on the Malabar coast, except where rocks are found; there green mussels and rock oysters share foothold with seaweeds and barnacles. On the muddy bottom the chief conspicuous gastropods are *Murex tenuispina*, *M. haustellum*, and *Turritella*.

The coral reefs of the Gulf of Mannar and the varied bottom that extends thence seawards to the 10-fathom line constitute the favourite habitat of Indian shellfish. Sometimes vast beds are covered with a carpet of densely packed bearded mussels (*Modiola barbata*) living in a felting of byssal threads; elsewhere thousands of conchs (*Turbinella pyrum*) scour the sands for tube-worms, or pearl oysters may cover stony banks in their millions. In muddy bays, the window-pane oyster (*Placuna placenta*), still used in Goa for glazing windows, is thickly scattered, while cockles and clams often abound, especially in littoral sands and mud. These are gregarious species which have solved successfully the local problems of environment, and which claim and hold extensive territories as their own.

The coral reefs have a very diversified mollusc fauna. It is here we have to seek the beautiful harp-shell (*Harpa*), the splendid cowries (*Cypræa*), and the giant holy-water shell (*Tridacna*). Chitons live here, and *Haliotis*, never growing to a large size, may sometimes be found. In the shallows between tide-marks *Turbo*, *Trochus*, and *Nerita* are numerous under boulders.

The sandy shores of the east coast often repay a visit during the south-west monsoon. The heavy surf then casts ashore quantities of the lovely violet-tinted *Ianthina*, a pelagic snail often having its float of tiny bladders still intact. Dead shells of the pearly nautilus are by no means rare at this season, and if search be careful, sometimes pteropod shells may be found. Again, the surf sorts out and throws ashore many bivalves which we seldom find at other times—the beautiful purple-clam (*Hiatula* [*Soletellina*] *diphos*), reaching 4½ in. in length, and the pretty sunset-shell (*Cultellus radiatus*). *Dolium*, *Pyrula*, *Bulla*, and other thin-shelled gastropods are among the other jetsam to be found.

Finally, mention must not be omitted of *Cassis cornuta*, the great helmet-shell, taken usually in 11 to 14 fathoms just outside the most seaward of the pearl banks; the pretty red mottled *Cassis rufa*, used in Neapolitan cameo-work, is fairly common in the Laccadive Islands, while in the muddy sand between the 5 and 6 fathom lines in Palk Strait, the handsome melon-shell (*Cymbium indicum*) is often found together with its strange cylindrical egg-capsules wherein the young develop until they attain a length of over 1 in. before eating their way to the outside world.

The Echinoderms represented in South Indian waters are often of large size and conspicuous colouring; especially is this the case with the starfishes. On the pearl banks of the Gulf of Mannar the magnificent lake-red *Pentaceros lincki* is very common in 7 to 10 fathoms, but in shallower water the related small species *P. nodosus*, remarkable for great variability in colouring, takes the place of *P. lincki*. Off Rameswaram the fine *Anthenia pentagonula* with orange disc is frequent, and occasionally the aberrant sub-globose *Culcita schmideliana* is met with, suggestive in its form of the manner in which starfish evolved into sea-urchins. The brittle-stars are often very abundant, and some live as commensals on sea-fans and the alcyonarian *Spongodes*, or in the cavities of sponges.

Feather-stars are particularly numerous, especially a black species which is often brought ashore in seines in hundreds on the Ramnad coast, while the fine *Actinometra parvicirra* is not rare in deep water. The bleached tests of various sea-urchins are often found on the beach, including such common forms as the large thick-shelled *Cidaris*, bearing great pencil-shaped spines when alive, the delicately tinted tests of *Salmacis bicolor*, and the heart-shaped skeletons of *Lovenia elongata*. Coral reefs often harbour the dark purple *Stomopneustes variolaris* lurking in burrows, and armed with long, poisonous spines. The strangely flattened species *Echinodiscus auritus* and *Clypcaster humilis* are very abundant on sandy bottoms in some localities.

Sea-cucumbers, known in the cured condition loved by Chinamen as *bêche-de-mer*, or *trepang*, are most abundant in Palk Bay and the Gulf of Mannar, but scarce elsewhere in shallow waters. The black *Holothuria atra* is the commonest, but to the uninitiated it is difficult of recognition owing to its habit of attaching a film of sand grains over the whole surface of its body. *H. marmorata* and its near relative *H. gallensis* are both distinguished by grey bands across the body; these are often very plentiful, and where this is so the fishermen collect them for curing and export to Singapore. Most handsome of the group is *Cucumaria tricolor*, a species characterized by alternate longitudinal broad bands of canary yellow and pale purple. Of Synaptids these seas yield many, conspicuous being the great snake-like *S. beseli*, not infrequent in coral lagoons, the small purple and white striped *S. striata*, fond of living gregariously upon branched sponges, and the warted greyish-white *S. grisea*, common on the muddy bottom of Palk Strait.

MARINE FISHERIES

That heterogeneous and curious assemblage of animals lumped together under the popular term of "worms" is fully represented. Of the parasitic Cestodes, Trematodes, and Nematodes, Indian fish and molluscs have yielded great numbers, often of species and genera so far unknown elsewhere except in Ceylon, owing to the great amount of attention that has been directed to these groups locally in the endeavour to identify and work out the life histories of parasites likely to have any influence in the inducement of pearls, "fine" pearls having been shown by Professor Herdman and the writer to be due in most cases to the irritation caused by the presence of a (dead) cestode parasite in certain positions in the tissues of the pearl oyster. The parasitic worm fauna of a pearl oyster is very comprehensive ; it includes three cestodes, three trematodes, and two nematodes. The adults of most of these forms have been traced to various fish which feed upon pearl oysters, being equipped for the purpose with powerful milling teeth. Elasmobranchs, particularly the sting-rays and eagle-rays, are the principal hosts of adult cestodes ; all species of these worms show immense diversity in the forms of the suckers and hooks used to maintain a grip upon the folds of the host's intestine.

The free-living Turbellarians are frequently found under stones, but much work remains to be done in the identification of this group. Nemertines and Gephyreans too are not well known, though fairly common. The most familiar of the latter is the tiny Sipunculid (*Aspidosiphon*), which lives commensal with the small cup-corals *Heteropsammia* and *Heterocyathus*. These little corals often come up in the dredge in the Gulf of Mannar, and scarcely any are without their friend the sipunculid.

Polychæta are the true sea-worms, and space lacks even a short survey, their number being legion and their diversity protean. Polyzoa are numerous, but call for no special mention except that it is held by some observers that the crusting forms contribute in great degree to the formation of those flat calcrete slabs which constitute with dead coral much of the "rock" of the pearl banks. The massive honeycomb colonies of several species of *Lepralia* are often seen cast up on the beach, either attached to stones or to the stalks of the sea-grass (*Zostera*). Other species mantle with a limy film the surfaces of dead and living shells ; while in Palk Bay a much-branched, bushy species of *Scrupocellaria* is often found in dense tufts attached to, and concealing the valves of, pearl oysters.

Cœlenterates in their sections of corals, sea-anemones, hydroid zoophytes, medusæ, and siphonophores are perhaps the richest and most fascinating of any represented in Indian seas. The corals proper are often typical reef-builders, and form not only breakwaters to the coast-line from Pamban to Tuticorin, and the flats and reefs of the Laccadive archipelago, but they serve also as quarries to supply the coast towns with building stone and lime. Of the massive corals, *Cœloria* (brain coral), *Goniastræ* and *Favia* (star-corals), *Montipora* and *Galaxea* are the most important. A few feet below the range of the surf these corals cease to form reefs, and are met with on the pearl banks (6 to 11 fathoms) as solitary colonies scattered sparsely over the sandy bottom ; among these the most conspicuous are the great elephant-ear corals, *Turbinaria crater* and *T. cinerascens*.

Free corals are numerous, chiefly the handsome mushroom-coral, *Fungia danæ*, attaining 8 in. in diameter, and the small *Cycloseris cyclolites*, little more than an inch across ; the still smaller *Heterocyathus* and *Heteropsammia*, nearly always with a sipunculid worm as unbidden guest in the base, are sometimes quite common, forming great aggregations on gravelly bottoms. The wedge-shaped fragments of the delicate *Diaseris distorta* are occasionally locally abundant.

1. NET FISHERS ON THE BEACH. 2. FISHERMEN'S HUTS, CANNANORE.

Anemones do not bulk conspicuously in our fauna, the most noteworthy species being the giant *Discosoma*, found at low water at Pamban and the Ramnad Islands, and the strange flask-shaped *Sphenopus marsupialis* living in muddy sand in Palk Bay. The colonial Zoanthids sometimes form green carpets of great extent within the reefs, and several small anemones can be found on rocky shores if carefully searched for.

Red coral is not met with, but its near relatives, the Alcyonarians, are often very abundant. On coral reefs the leathery masses of *Scelerophytum* sometimes form grey or greenish masses several square yards in area. Cauliflower-like *Spongodes*, usually reddish in colour, are sometimes numerous on clean, sandy ground, while the long red whips of *Juncella juncea* and various Pennatulids are locally abundant in the Gulf of Mannar and off the Coromandel coast wherever conditions are favourable. The curious *Cavernularia obesa* has been taken in enormous abundance off Cochin and in smaller numbers in certain localities in the Gulf of Mannar. Sea-fans (*Gorgonids*) are very abundant on rocky bottom, especially the pretty *Leptogorgia miniacea*, so variable in colouring that I have seen on one small stone three colonies of different colours, one being yellow, another purple, and the third orange. The coarse corky *Suberogorgia suberosa* is another common species. The so-called black corals, or Antipatharia, are amongst the most striking forms brought up in the dredge on the Coromandel and Tinnevelly coasts, especially the great tree-like *Antipathes abies*, which is sometimes 6 ft. in height. Millepores are frequently found in the Laccadives.

Of Hydrozoa the most conspicuous species is perhaps *Campanularia juncea*, a species which grows in coarse, tufted colonies on stony bottom in 6 to 9 fathoms. *Halicornaria insignis* is another large species growing to 16 in. in height, and Sertularians, though common, are generally small. Large Medusæ are at times very abundant, and often accumulate in large shoals in backwaters. *Chrysaora* and *Rhizostoma* are the two best represented genera. Medusoids are not well worked out yet, and will abundantly repay study. Siphonophores are often conspicuous as the south-west monsoon brings certain pelagic species in quantity to our shores, including a small one of the Portuguese man-o'-war (*Physalia*), *Porpita*, and *Velella*, all characterized by lovely purple tints.

As to sponges, their name is legion; they are by far the commonest and most universally distributed of the sedentary organisms found in shallows and brought up by the dredge. Fortunately they have received much attention, Professor Dendy, the leading specialist on this group, having identified large collections from the Gulf of Mannar. Unfortunately they have no commercial importance, and although I recently discovered the true commercial sponge (*Euspongia officinalis*) growing in the shallows off Rameswaram, I have little hope that any industry can be established. Economically they have considerable importance, as some species (*Cliona*) do much injury by boring to shellfish of commercial value, while others occupy space which could better be utilized, and so compete with useful organisms.

Some of the most conspicuous species are the massive volcano-shaped *Petrosia testudinaria*, the orange cup-sponge *Phakellia donnani*, the scarlet ball-sponge *Aulospongus tubulatus*, the leathery umbrella-sponge *Phyllospongia holdsworthi*, the delicate black fibrous sponge *Megalopastus nigra*, and the colonies of various species of *Chalina* usually made up of a network of cylindrical branches. These are common on the pearl banks, and their bleached fibrous skeletons (*Petrosia* excepted) are often seen thrown up on the beach.

Of Protozoa, suffice it to say that the species of Radiolaria and Foraminifera in these waters are endless; away from land the Radiolarians are particularly numerous, and comprise forms of wondrous beauty. Infusoria are equally abundant in inshore water, while flagellate monads at certain seasons make patches of water along the Malabar coast foul and poisonous by the accumulation of their infinite multitudes.

In regard to biological stations it may be said that hitherto, apart from museums, India has possessed few facilities for systematic investigation of the wealth of life within her sea borders; no marine biological stations are at present existent; but before long Madras should enter the field with two, one at Madras, the other on a coral island near Pamban, at the head of the Gulf of Mannar. The former will also be the working headquarters of the Fisheries Department, and will be equipped with the necessary laboratories, an extensive aquarium open to the public, together with an economic collection of sea-products, models, and hatching apparatus and the like—everything, in fact, that is necessary to the teaching of Fishery Science. The Pamban station will be used as a feeder of the main station at Madras; it will also serve for such field work as cannot be carried on at the latter; its primary object will, however, be the investigation of pearl formation.

ON THE KEMPHULLY RIVER, THE HOME OF THE "MIGHTY MAHSEER."

Photo by C. Lake.

1. DISTRICT COURT, COIMBATORE. 2. ALL SOULS' CHURCH, COIMBATORE.

THE DISTRICT OF COIMBATORE

THE district of Coimbatore in the Presidency of Madras is bounded on the north-west by the State of Mysore, on the south by the State of Travancore and the district of Madura, on the east by the districts of Salem and Trichinopoly, and on the west by the districts of the Nilgiris and Malabar, and the State of Cochin. It has an area of 7,126 square miles, and the latest census returns showed that it then contained 2,116,564 inhabitants.

It is a matter of sincere regret that authentic records of the early history of many districts in Southern India cannot be traced ; in many instances, indeed, one must rely upon inscriptions and carvings on wood and stone ; while scraps of information may occasionally be sifted from the legends and traditions which have been faithfully treasured among the people for several generations. One of these local legends is to the effect that the district of Coimbatore formed a portion of the Cera dominions, and that the place now known as Karur, in the district of Trichinopoly, was the capital town. Further, it is related that the last Cera rajah had two sons, one of whom, Ceran by name, took over the western half of the territory (now known as Kerala), and that the brother named Kongan remained at Karur and married a Cholan princess, who, being dissatisfied with the wild nature of the country and its inhabitants—the Vedars—managed to get together a colony of Vellalars, by whom a large area of land was brought into cultivation. The contention that this district did in reality belong to the Cera kingdom receives support from the writings of Ptolemy (about A.D. 110), which refer to "Karoura, or Karur, as the capital of the Cera-putra, or son of Cera." The Kongu, or Cera dynasty, was succeeded by the rule of the Cholas in the year 878, which continued for nearly two hundred years. The territory of the Hindu kings of Vizayanagar had been extending gradually during the fourteenth and fifteenth centuries, so much so, indeed, that at one period nearly the whole of Southern India was involved, but the empire was overthrown in 1565 by the united Mussulman kings of the Deccan at the memorable battle of Talikota. In the latter part of the sixteenth century the district of Coimbatore passed from the hands of the Carnatic Viceroy, who ruled at Seringapatam, to those of the Madura Viceroy, Virappa Nayakkar. There did not appear to be any cessation of hostilities between the years 1623 and 1672, when a large portion of the district was annexed to the kingdom of Mysore. This territory (which included Coimbatore) was subsequently captured by Hyder Ali, and was afterwards taken in hand by Tipu Sultan, son of Hyder. Bloodshed and destitution followed in the wake of these two warriors, and there was no peace until Tipu was finally overthrown in 1799, and Coimbatore, as a district, came under the protection of England.

Mountain ranges include the lofty Anamalai Hills (described at length on p. 403), in the southern portion of the district, and they are connected with the Palni Hills of Madura, and the Velliyangiris, which are spurs of the Nilgiris in the north and north-west; together with the various ranges which form the whole of the northern portion of the district in the Kollyul, Satyamangalam, and Bhavani *taluqs*. The climate is not by any means unhealthy although the annual reports of Collectors prove that the seasons have been extremely variable, and that the continual complaints are of scanty and partial rainfall, especially during the months corresponding to the English April and May, also during the north-east monsoons. The mean annual temperature registered during an observation period of eighteen years was 77·6°, which is considerably lower than Madras, Madura, and other places.

The total area of the district is 5,030,420 acres, and this is represented by Government lands comprising about 4,500,000 acres; minor inam lands, nearly 300,000 acres; whole inam properties amounting to about 50,000 acres; and zemindari lands of rather more than 100,000 acres. Sir F. A. Nicholson, I.C.S., writing on this subject says: "Zemindari lands are estates on which the land tax has been fixed in perpetuity. Inam lands are those which pay either no assessment at all, or a rate lower than the full assessment. These usually consist of fields situated in ordinary *ryotwari* villages, and in that case they are called minor inams. Sometimes a whole village is held on this favourable tenure, and it is then called a whole inam, or, more commonly, a shotriem village."

The nature of soils may always be judged from the geological character of the district, and they are primarily derived from the disintegration of the gneiss, both felspathic and hornblendic, which lies beneath the surface, and is found not only in the plains but on the slopes of the hill-sides. They are, speaking generally, light and shallow, and heavy crops are the exception rather than the rule. Cholum is more extensively grown than any other product, as it is cultivated on an area which is nearly one-third of the total acreage of the district. Cumbu, ragi, horse-gram, and rice, follow in this order. Cotton is an important item too, but especially in the Erode *taluq*, while oil-seeds are sown in every part of the district. Other crops include varagu, wheat, green gram, vegetables, plantains, mangoes, coconuts, tobacco, chillies, onions, coriander seeds, sugar-cane, palmyra, gingelly, castor oils, tamarinds, and ground-nuts.

Following closely upon the great agricultural industry, upon which fully one-half of the population depend for a living, are trade concerns for the "preparation and supply of material substances," which support about one-fourth of the inhabitants. The leather industry is carried on chiefly by members of the Chakkilyan and Madiga castes, and tanneries are being worked at Coimbatore, Pallapatti, and Mettupalaiyam. Hides and skins are tanned by the use of lime, the bark of *cassia auriculata*, and myrobalans and oil, the processes commencing with liming, and followed by the removal of hair, soaking in infusions of bark and myrobalans, after which drying and oiling complete the treatment. Buckets for lifting water from the wells are manufactured out of tanned hides, each one requiring a whole hide, and as these are renewed yearly for the 85,000 or more lifts in the district, this branch industry is by no means unimportant. A very large proportion of the coffee grown upon the Shevaroy Hills and in the Nilgiris is cured at Coimbatore, where there are factories well-equipped with modern machinery. The pressing of oil from castor and gingelly seeds finds employment for about 6,000 persons, and although there is what may be termed a "country-made" mill in a large number of villages, there are three in the town of Coimbatore which have been constructed according to European plans. The manufacture of bricks and tiles and the building of carriages and carts are industries in which considerable progress has been made in recent years, and the output of to-day will compare favourably with that of any other district in the Presidency. Workers in gold, silver, brass, metals, and precious stones are about 25,000 in number, and the gongs, brass vessels, and ornaments of beautiful design and fine workmanship are true specimens of Indian art. The smelting of iron has not been prominent among industries owing to the lack of charcoal; pottery work, too, has not been prosecuted as vigorously as it might have been; while the lapidaries who work crystals for eye-glasses, together with ornaments, images, *lingams*, and other sacred symbols are very few in number. A large quantity of cotton is grown in the district, and after it has been cleaned and pressed it is forwarded to Madras or Bombay for shipment to Europe. Factories have been established at Coimbatore, Palladam, Tiruppur, and Erode, and some of these are fitted with steam-driven machinery and plant of a modern type. Sericulture and the weaving of silk were carried on at Kollyul prior to the year 1888, but this was the only part of the district where the climate was sufficiently favourable for the worm and the mulberry, which is its staple food. A very great impetus has been given to this industry throughout Southern India by the fostering care of the Government of Mysore, and by the excellent classes for teaching beginners which have been instituted by the Salvation Army at the Tata Experimental Farm, near Bangalore. The trade of the district may be summed up by a reference to the statistics of exports and imports for the past few years. The former include cotton, oil-seeds, tobacco, cereals, pulses, spices, chillies, sandal-wood, plantains, jaggery, brass and copper vessels, and leather, while among the goods introduced into the country are timber, metals and metal goods, paddy, coconut-oil, piece goods, and salt.

There was no recognized system of education in Coimbatore prior to the British occupation, as the question was left entirely in the hands of the people themselves. A report published in the year 1822 states that "schools and colleges [the word "college" was applied to small schools, probably in temples where so-called sciences were taught] appear to be supported entirely by the people; the annual payment for a scholar varied from Rs. 3 to Rs. 14; that the number of pupils in 173 'colleges' was only 724, or about 4½ to each academy." The Government showed some interest in the matter in 1826, when a Board of Instruction was formed, and collectorate and *taluq* schools were established. Progress has, however, been extremely slow, and the English language is unknown to a large proportion of the inhabitants. There are at the present time undeniable facilities for acquiring a sound education, and among the leading institutions in the town of Coimbatore are the Government Training School for Mistresses, Stanes' High School, the London Missionary Society's High School, St. Joseph's Industrial School, the Coimbatore College, and St. Michael's College, the last two taking students through all

1 BIG BAZAAR STREET, COIMBATORE. 2. THE CLUB, COIMBATORE. 3. RAJAH'S STREET, COIMBATORE.
4. VIEW FROM THE DISTRICT COURT, COIMBATORE.

courses up to degrees. The Agricultural College and Research Institute is situated about 3 miles in a westerly direction from Coimbatore, and it is a very handsome building in the Hindu-Saracenic style of architecture. His Excellency Sir Arthur Lawley, G.C.I.E., K.C.M.G., a former Governor of Madras, evinced the keenest interest in the establishment of this college, and he not only laid the foundation-stone of the building on September 24, 1906, but he formally opened the institution on July 14, 1909. The usual course for students is three years, and they are required to cultivate their own plots of wet and dry land, to engage in field farm-work, and undergo practical and theoretical training in the management of live-stock, in veterinary science, dairying, and general agriculture. There is a fine field for the Research Institute in the investigation of chemical and biological problems. The Madras Forest College, also at Coimbatore, provides practical and theoretical instruction in forestry and allied sciences to students who are desirous of entering the forest service of the Madras and Bombay Government and of native States in Southern India. The college grounds cover an area of about 167 acres, and accommodation in the building is found for about 30 resident students, in addition to quarters for professors and servants.

Reference may now be made to the physical conditions of the *taluqs* and to the principal towns and villages. Bhavani *taluq* has an area of about 715 square miles, and is situated in the north-east portion of the district. The northern and western boundaries are formed by the River Cauvery, which is spanned in the town of Bhavani by a very fine bridge of twenty-six arches. The forests are extensive, and as a consequence the various species of *feræ* are exceedingly numerous, and include the lordly elephant, the fierce bison, tigers, cheetahs, and other animals. The town of Bhavani is built at the junction of the Cauvery and Bhavani Rivers, and any importance which may attach to it arises solely from its alleged sacred position. Many pilgrims are attracted to the Sangama Iswara temple, which is worthy of a visit on account of the excellence of its sculptures. Cotton cloths and carpets are made on a small scale, but beyond these there are no industries to speak of. Kaveripuram is situated on the right bank of the Cauvery, and contains an old Sivaite temple and the ruins of a fort which occupied a most important strategical position at the mouth of one of the passes from the State of Mysore. There are about 7,000 inhabitants, six-sevenths of whom are Hindus. The Coimbatore *taluq* is the most interesting one in the whole district, not merely because it contains the chief Government offices and is the centre of the trade and commerce of the district, but because it contains some special features which will appeal to merchant and missionary, to the agriculturist and the antiquarian, and to foresters, archæologists, and sportsmen. The famous Nilgiri Hills rise almost abruptly on the northern and western boundaries of the *taluq*, while the magnificent peaks of the Anamalais form a splendid background in the south. The *taluq* is an open plateau varying in height from 1,300 ft. to 1,400 ft., and it is traversed by two rivers, the Bhavani in the north, and the Noyil in the west and south. Water is obtained for irrigation purposes by means of anicuts, by which it is diverted into channels and tanks for the subsequent enrichment of the land. The climate is, on the whole, extremely pleasant, and this is attributable mainly to the south-west monsoon, which drives a cool wind through the Palghat Gap for about three months, commencing from the last week in May. The principal crops are cholum, oil-seeds, cotton, cumbu, horse-gram, ragi, sugar-cane, coffee, and wheat, while the wet lands near to Coimbatore produce large quantities of paddy. Among the industries the following may be mentioned: tanning, the making of jaggery and arrack, oil-milling, the curing of coffee, cotton ginning, the manufacture of bricks and tiles, and spinning and weaving.

The town of Coimbatore is in the north-western portion of the *taluq*, and is about 305 miles distant from the city of Madras. Practically all of the industries which have just been mentioned as being common in the *taluq* are to be found in full work in the town. Coimbatore was formerly strongly fortified, and during the wars in which Hyder Ali and his son Tipu were engaged, the stronghold changed hands on several occasions. It was occupied by British troops in 1768; it subsequently passed to the East India Company, only to be re-taken by Tipu, from whom it was wrested in 1792; but it was not finally ceded to the British until the year 1799. It is now the headquarters of the Collector, the district judge, the Conservator of Forests, a superintendent engineer, the district surgeon, and of a number of other prominent officials. The town is about 1,350 ft. above the level of the sea, and, as it possesses good natural drainage, an excellent water supply, and a temperate climate, it is possibly more suitable as a residential place for Europeans than the majority of the towns in the Presidency. The principal buildings are the Museum, the Municipal Hospital, and the Colleges of Agriculture and Forestry, which have been mentioned above. The inhabitants are about 47,000 in number.

Mettupalaiyam is situated almost at the foot of the Madras and Southern Mahratta Railway, which has been extended to the Nilgiri Hills, and although it is a place of some importance as regards trade, its population does not exceed 800 persons. Singanallur, once a fortified town, is now a busy commercial centre with a railway-station, and a *chuttram* for the use of the large number of Brahman travellers who arrive here. Sugar-cane is grown to a very considerable extent in the neighbourhood, and local agriculturists are most progressive in their methods of cultivation. The population consists of nearly 9,000 persons, a very large proportion of whom are Brahmans. There are a few other towns and villages which are full of interest owing to the fine temples which are to be seen in them. There is Vellalur, which has nearly 6,000 inhabitants, and is situated about 4½ miles distant in an east-south-easterly direction from Coimbatore. It possesses an old Siva temple, but numismatologists will be particularly interested in learning that "in May 1842 an earthen pot was dug up at this place which contained 522 Roman silver denarii, chiefly of the time of Tiberius, Augustus, Caligula, and Claudius." At Tudiyalur and Samakkulam are ancient temples dedicated to Siva, while there are two others at Boluvampatti, the origin of which is still in doubt. The Dharapuram *taluq* in the south of the district comprises about 840 square miles, and is an undulating plateau sloping eastwards in the direction of the Cauvery River. The greater portion of the soil here is of an inferior character, and, if one may judge by the crops for, say, the past few years, its productive power is inconsiderable. The climate is, generally speaking, a pleasurable one, especially towards the end of May, when the south-west monsoon dispels the heat. Roads are fairly good in quality, and they are tolerably numerous, the principal ones being from Karur to

Mettupalaiyam, from Udamalpet to Karur, from Dharapuram to Kangayam and Tiruppur. Cholum is the principal crop, and is grown upon more than 121,000 acres; cumbu occupies 70,000 acres; oil-seeds, 37,000 acres; cotton, 25,000 acres; fodder crops, 23,000 acres; tobacco, 3,200 acres; while smaller areas are cultivated with gingelly, gram, varagu, and other produce. Industries other than agriculture are confined to the making of sugar and jaggery, and the manufacture of cloths, pots, and bricks, and the building of carts. The principal town and headquarters of the *taluq* is Dharapuram, and it is situated upon the left bank of the Amaravati River, and has a population of about 8,000 inhabitants, three-fourths of whom are Hindus. Two centuries ago the place was of some strategical importance, and history shows that it "was captured by the British in 1783; it was subsequently given up by the treaty of Mangalore, and finally yielded to General Meadows in 1790." The town is well built and contains many imposing buildings which abut upon clean and good streets. It has no industries of a special character, but a considerable trade in agricultural produce is carried on with the surrounding villages. Dharapuram is connected by road with three railway stations, namely, Tiruppur, Perundurai, and Karur.

There are not many places in Southern India which have the honour of being the home of a fine breed of cattle, as the majority of the animals one sees are of a very mediocre and nondescript type. Kangayam, a village about 20 miles to the north of Dharapuram, has this distinction, however, and the breed is called by the name of the village in which the animals are reared. Nearly a mile distant from Kangayam is a large Siva temple in which several interesting inscriptions may be seen. The inhabitants are about 7,000 in number, and comprise about 6,800 Hindus and 200 Mahommedans. Very old temples may be seen at Sivanmalai, 3 miles from Kangayam; at Vellaikkovil, 12 miles distant; at Udiyur, and at Muttur.

The *taluq* of Erode comprises about 598 square miles of land, situated on the north-eastern portion of the district, and it is virtually an undulating plateau between 500 and 600 ft. above the level of the sea. Nearly the whole of the soil consists of red sand, shallow in depth, and the crops are therefore light throughout the *taluq*, with the exception of those grown upon the wet lands near the Kalingarayan River, and in gardens near a township, where the practice of applying manure is understood. Cholum, cumbu, cotton, and other dry crops are unprofitable, as the rainfall is usually partial and variable. Nearly 130,000 acres are producing cumbu; cholum covers 39,000 acres; ragi requires 13,000 acres; rice, 17,000 acres; cotton, 68,000 acres; while areas of smaller size are devoted to oil-seeds, horse-gram, tobacco, sugar-cane, plantains, palmyra, tamarinds, and coconuts. Ordinary industries are not numerous, although a considerable number of the inhabitants are engaged in stone-quarrying, well-digging, pottery, brick-making, weaving, and working in brass, iron, and other metals. Erode, the principal town of the *taluq*, is a municipality, containing about 17,000 inhabitants, and it is the headquarters of a sub-Collector, and Assistant-Superintendent of Police, a representative of the Government Public Works Department, and other officials. It is the terminus of the Trichinopoly-Erode branch, and is the junction of the metre and broad-gauge sections of the South Indian Railway. Erode is 243 miles distant from Madras, and its railway station is provided with airy and comfortable sleeping quarters, in addition to the usual refreshment-rooms. In the time of Hyder Ali it was regarded as a flourishing town, but owing to several invasions it was subsequently almost deserted, and attractive buildings became a heap of ruins. It was finally taken over by the British in the year 1790, and when the treaty of peace was signed the former inhabitants trooped back to a place which had so many natural advantages, and in which they were determined to rebuild ruined stores and dwelling-houses. A flourishing trade is carried on in raw produce, salt, cloths, and cotton; weaving and cotton-pressing are well supported, while the chief products of the immediate neighbourhood are plantains, paddy, and betel leaves. Kodumudi, 21 miles south-east of Erode, is a prosperous wet-land village, which holds an important market for grain merchants. There are small but interesting Jain temples at the following five villages, namely, Vellodu, Tingalur (2,200 inhabitants), Vijayamangalam, Pundurai, and Konganpalaiyam, and each one has a small land endowment for the use of the priest.

The Kollyal *taluq* presents entirely different features from other divisions of the district of Coimbatore. It seems to be on a higher plane as regards elevation, climate, forests, and crops. It consists of an area of 1,076 square miles, and the general elevation of the plateau ranges from 2,500 to 3,000 ft., while here and there are ranges and peaks which are between 4,000 and 5,000 ft. above the level of the sea. The major portion of the soil belongs to the series of productive black and red loams, and as a consequence good cultivation is succeeded by satisfactory crops. The forests in this *taluq* are a most valuable asset for the Government; they cover a very extensive area, and are exceedingly dense in the southern and eastern portions, while in many parts they are entirely unexplored. Owing to the altitude of the *taluq* and to a consistently good rainfall, the yield of the various crops is fairly satisfactory, but pastoral rather than arable farming is the occupation of the majority of agriculturists, and there are several places, such as Kowdalli and Sangadi, which are well known as the home of some very fine specimens of the Alambadi breed of cattle. Dry crops include ragi, cholum, cumbu, dholl, horse-gram, pulses, and seeds, while those sown upon wet lands are paddy, sugar-cane, mulberry, and betel-vines. The township of Kollyal, the headquarters of the *taluq*, is a Union under the Local Boards Act, and has a population of about 10,000 inhabitants. A special feature is made of the manufacture of gold-coloured cloths, turbans, and handkerchiefs, and about 3,000 persons are engaged in this industry. Sivasamudram, literally sea of Siva, is an island formed by branch streams of the River Cauvery, and situated about 9 miles from Kollyal, and here are to be seen the famous Cauvery Falls, which are referred to elsewhere. Singanallur is about 7 miles distant from Kollyal, and is visited chiefly on account of the ruins of an old fort which for a time resisted the fierce attacks of the Mahrattas, but which eventually yielded to and was plundered by them. Palladam *taluq* is in the centre of the district of Coimbatore, and its area of about 740 square miles consists of flat land without the semblance of forests or hills. A portion of the Madras and Southern Mahratta Railway traverses the *taluq* from east to west, the stations being situated at Mangalam, Somanur, Sulur, and Kulipalaiyam. The average quality of the soil is distinctly superior to other portions of the district, while one may occasionally meet with tracts of rich red loam.

The principal crop, cholum, is grown upon about 150,000 acres, cumbu is cultivated on 62,000 acres, horse-gram 38,000 acres, and there are 22,000 acres of ragi and 47,000 acres of cotton. Other agricultural produce consists of onions, tobacco, paddy, sugar-cane, and turmeric. The headquarters town of the *taluq*—Palladam—has not more than about 1,200 inhabitants, but it contains the offices of the principal officials, a good hospital, police station and quarters, and a bungalow for travellers. Cotton pressing is an industry of some importance, but the majority of the people are more directly concerned in purely agricultural pursuits, which are carried on effectively upon the rich black cotton soil of the immediate neighbourhood. Káravalur contains a famous temple dedicated to Mariamman, and the greatest interest attaches to a car festival which is held annually in the presence of a large number of pilgrims. There are ancient Vishnu and Siva temples at Mondiapalaiyam, Avanasipalaiyam, and Tirumuruganpundi, the last-named being one of the seven Kongu Sivalayams. Copper, brass, and bell-metal vessels and ornaments are manufactured at Anupparpalaiyam and Angalipalaiyam.

The *taluq* of Pollachi is situated in the south-west corner of the district, and is only divided from the State of Travancore by the barrier of the Anamalai Range of hills. It is 710 square miles in extent, and travellers will at once observe beauty and variety in the scenery, superior methods of agriculture, rich soils, and remarkably good crops. The Anamalais are the subject of a special article, but it should be mentioned here that they are the source of many streams of water which are of incalculable benefit to the lower levels of this *taluq*. The full effect of the south-west monsoon is felt here, and a slightly heavier rainfall than in other *taluqs* enables *ryots* to obtain a second crop upon some of the richest lands. The acreage of the principal crops is as follows: Cholum, 104,000; cumbu, 31,000; horse-gram, 27,000; ragi, 11,200; cotton, 7,000; rice, 5,000; oil-seeds, 11,500; and tobacco, 2,000. Coffee and cardamoms are cultivated to a small extent, while chillies give exceedingly large returns annually. A small quantity of cloth is woven, and other products include horns, ivory, shellac, wax, honey, ginger, and turmeric. The town of Pollachi is the headquarters of the head Assistant-Collector; it is well built, and has an excellent local fund hospital, schools, attractive bungalows, and public offices, and it has about 6,000 inhabitants. There are strong evidences that the town was a busy commercial centre some hundreds of years ago, and it is asserted by some writers that Alexandrian merchants were in the habit of trading here. Excavations have brought to light a number of Roman silver coins, pieces of antique earthenware, images, and representations of buffaloes worked in bronze. The majority of the villages are of small size, but many of them contain ruins of exceedingly fine temples, in which interesting inscriptions may be seen. Among these are Kinattukkadavu, Kottur, and Garudankottai.

The Udamalpet *taluq* has an area of about 580 square miles, and it consists largely of an undulating plain, although there is a higher and less uneven surface in the southern and eastern portions. The

PAGODA POINT, SHEVAROY HILLS.

Photo by Nicholas & Co

THE DISTRICT OF COIMBATORE

Government Settlement Department has stated that "the soil consists of 15 per cent. of red loam, 62 per cent. of red sand, 12 per cent. of black clay, and 11 per cent. of black loam." The forests provide grazing ground for cattle when ordinary pasturage is scarce, but this is not sound practice in pastoral farming, as the losses of animals owing to wild animals must be a heavy item, there is extra expense in herding, and, what is most important, the whole of the manure which should have been adding to the fertility of the *ryot's* land is lost to him. The following crops are grown largely, and very favourable annual yields are reported: Cholum, cumbu, rice, ragi, oil-seeds, cotton, sugar-cane, and tobacco. There are no industries with the exception of the usual village type, but a brisk trade is carried on in grain, cloth, and cotton. The town of Udamalpet has a number of resident officials under the Local Boards Act; and its buildings include public offices, a high school, post and telegraph offices, and bungalows. Its inhabitants are about 10,000 in number, nearly 9,000 of whom are Hindus. Very ancient Sivaite temples are to be seen at Komaralingam, Kadattur, Gudimangalam, and Kannadipputtur. Somavarapatti, with a population of about 3,000 inhabitants, is 6 miles distant from Udamalpet, and it is noted chiefly for a car festival, which is largely attended, in honour of a goddess named Kandiamman.

The Gopichettipalaiyam *taluq* (formerly known as Satyamangalam) is enclosed by mountain ranges on the northern, western, north-western, and north-eastern sides, and the climate can hardly be said to be an enjoyable one as the hills shut out cooling breezes from the sea. Government forests cover a very large area of the *taluq*, and they abound with all kinds of game, from the elephant downwards. The cumbu crop is grown on about 110,000 acres of land, and is regarded as the principal one in the district, but as far as yield is concerned, the chief place is taken by paddy, which gives exceedingly heavy returns under irrigation from the Tadappalli and Arakkankottai channels, while cholum, ragi, cotton, coffee, and tobacco are also cultivated. A few small village manufactures are carried on, and trade consists mainly in the exportation of grain and the importation of cloths and miscellaneous merchandise. The headquarters of the tahsildar, the sub-registrar, and other officials are at Gopichettipalaiyam, a comparatively small town as regards population (2,500 inhabitants), but which is the centre of a very thriving wet-land area. Satyamangalam, the former headquarters of the *taluq*, is situated on the Bhavani River, about 40 miles in a north-north-westerly direction from Coimbatore. The inhabitants are about 3,500 in number. There is an ancient temple dedicated to Siva at Perundalaiyur, and a Vishnu temple at Kuttalattur, while at Kugalur —17 miles distant from Satyamangalam— there is another one which is said to have been built by a Cera king.

THE ANAMALAI HILLS

By C. R. T. CONGREVE

THE area known as the Anamalai Hills, in the southern portion of the district of Coimbatore, is frequently described in a general way as being divided into upper and lower ranges. The latter consist of undulating knolls with intermediate *nullahs*, which lie at an elevation of from 3,000 to 4,500 ft. above the level of the sea, while the former are noted for their magnificent scenery and for numerous rugged peaks which rise to a height of about 8,000 ft. The famous teak belt is at an altitude of from 1,500 to 3,000 ft., and a remarkable quantity of excellent timber is felled here. It is recorded that in the year 1895 a tree was cut which was 124 ft. in height, 23 ft. in girth, and which contained from 500 to 600 cubic feet of workable timber.

The greater portion of the soil is sandy loam, occasionally intermixed with gravel, and there is a gradual slope of the land in a westerly direction towards the State of Cochin. In or about the year 1865 the British Government gave an opportunity to planters to acquire estates on the eastern slopes of the hills, and, although a considerable quantity of land was taken up, there are now (January 1915) only two properties of the original holdings in existence. One of these, the Waterfall estate, belongs to the Anamalai Coffee Company, and the other, known as Waverley, is the property of the representatives of a pioneer planter of the name of Walsh. The early planters had enormous difficulties with which to contend, and not the least of these was the absence of a road of any kind whatsoever from the plains to the hills, and the only means of transport for provisions for the estates on the plateau, and of produce for the markets in the plains, was by the employment of coolie carriers. This exceedingly primitive arrangement, however, received an unexpected termination during the year 1875, when his late Majesty, King Edward VII—as Prince of Wales—visited India. The authorities had mapped out a shooting tour on the high ranges of the hills, and a bridle path had been cut through the jungle to enable His Royal Highness to make the ascent, but a serious outbreak of cholera occurred in the villages on the plains, and the proposed trip had to be abandoned. The truth of the old proverb commencing "It's an ill wind" was fully justified in this instance, however, as planters were for the first time able to employ pack-animals in place of natives for the transport of their goods. This was the "beginning of things" for planters in the district; estates were constantly being developed, and eventually there was an outcry for more land.

A considerable amount of correspondence passed between the authorities and the planters prior to October 1896, when a meeting was held at Coimbatore—the principal town in the district—at which the Collector was present on behalf of the Government, and, after much discussion, the latter agreed to throw open to planters for cultivation the whole of the western side of the watershed, comprising about 80 square miles. Applications were at once forthcoming for 17 blocks, aggregating 63,500 acres, but as the Government refused to grant more than 1,000 acres to any individual applicant, several large firms withdrew their requests. Twenty blocks, comprising 20,244 acres, were taken up subsequently, but 4,000 acres of this area were relinquished before development began.

In February 1897 Mr. G. A. Marsh

arrived at the hills with the object of superintending the opening up of an estate named Paralai, which had been purchased by a Mr. Windle, but the obstacles to be encountered were almost formidable enough to daunt the courage of any man, as the only way by which the property could be reached was along the course of a game track from the Waterfall estate, and even this had to be enlarged before coolies could proceed with their loads.

Labour troubles then commenced, as the natives refused to work for Mr. Marsh excepting at exorbitant rates, which he declined to pay. The local jungle men, who had previously made themselves scarce, subsequently began to make application for employment, and, with proper supervision, they proved to be most useful in making rough shelters and in the demarcation of the land. From 50 to 60 acres of forest were felled by Mr. Marsh that year, and they were planted with coffee obtained from the Nilgiris.

Mr. J. A. Cocker, representative of Messrs. Finlay, Muir & Co., of Calcutta, and Mr. E. J. Martin were the next arrivals, and astonishing progress was made in general development, including the completion of the path to Paralai and the extension of it to Valparai. In 1899 the Government entrusted to Mr. C. W. Wood, executive engineer in the Department of Public Works, the construction of a cart-road and of a bridge across the Ali Ai River at the foot of the hills. The making of the road was a difficult matter, as the upper section passed through dense jungle and the lower portion traversed most precipitous and dangerous ground, but engineering skill succeeded, and the results of Mr. Wood's labours are seen in the fine bridge and in the excellent cart-road which now reaches the very heart of the Anamalais.

Practically all of the estates were in the first instance devoted to the growing of coffee, but tea was started on the Monica property, and some cardamoms had been planted elsewhere.

A somewhat extraordinary incident occurred at this juncture, as the Government, acting upon a report from the Forest Department that there was a large quantity of valuable timber in the jungle, refused to continue granting more land to the planters, and thus the work of development, which had been progressing satisfactorily upon the Paralai, Valparai, Monica, Stanmore, Korangumudi, Castlecroft, Puthutotam, Iyerpadi, and other estates, was summarily checked. It was not until the year 1911 that the Government changed its policy and once more offered land to planters, when about 15,500 acres were taken up forthwith. At the present time more than 10,000 acres are under cultivation, and further development is taking place at the rate of fully 1,000 acres annually. These new estates consist almost entirely of tea. The remaining evergreen jungle is exceedingly dense, and many of the trees attain a height of 200 ft. Game, with the exception of elephants and bison, is scarce, as there is no open land upon which they can roam. Elephants visit the plantations for about six months of the hot weather, but bison are rarely seen owing to the thickness of the undergrowth.

The two principal towns are Coimbatore and Pollachi, and each of these has post and telegraphic offices.

THE SHEVAROY HILLS

By E. W. WILKINS

THE Presidency of Madras is fortunate in the possession of a group of hill sanatoria differing in their climatic and other conditions from each other, and offering a pleasant retreat to the retiring Anglo-Indian to whom a long residence in India has made his homeland unsuitable as a place wherein to spend the declining years of his life; they appeal to the jaded dweller on the plains seeking relief from the oppressive heat of the summer months (or "hot weather," as they are colloquially termed); they are invaluable to the convalescent who has tided over a serious illness and has been recommended by his medical adviser to recuperate in a cooler clime to aid in restoration to normal health; and lastly (but by no means the least), they have an attraction for the enterprising Englishman with capital to invest in a congenial and profitable enterprise. The Nilgiri and the Pulney Hills, with their charming and picturesque centres of Ootacamund, Coonoor, Kotagiri, and Kodaikanal, have their peculiar attractions for the visitor or permanent resident, but a further selection is still open to the fastidious in the Shevaroy Hills.

These hills are situated in, and form a division of, the district of Salem, and they lie between 78° 20′ east longitude and 11° 0′ 5″ north latitude, and cover an area of about 150 square miles. The highest point (Branfills Hill) is 5,400 ft. above sea-level, and Yercaud (the principal European settlement) has an elevation of 4,600 ft. The nearest railway station to Yercaud, having connection with the Presidency town of Madras on the north-east, with Tuticorn on the extreme south of the peninsula (which is now linked up with Ceylon by the recently opened route over Adam's Bridge), with Mangalore on the western coast and with Ootacamund, on the Nilgiri Hills, is Salem (or Suramungalum), which is distant about 14 miles from Yercaud, so that a traveller from Calcutta, Bombay, Madras, or Colombo, and stations connected with those towns by rail, can accomplish the whole journey to Yercaud by railway to within 14 or 20 miles. The Shevaroy plateau is approached by four passes, or *ghaut* roads or tracks, namely, two from Salem, the Kadiampatti Ghaut, 11 miles from Yercaud, from the railway station of Kadiampatti, and the Bommade Ghaut, 19 miles from the railway. The latter two are not generally, but only locally, used, and passengers visiting these hills are usually brought up (carried by coolies on hammock chairs) by the foot track leading to Salem, which is also the usual route for coolies conveying light loads and for bullocks bringing up supplies. The carriage road from Salem up the *ghaut*, which has only recently been completed, not only leads to Yercaud but also to the outlying coffee-planted districts of Nagalur and the Green Hills, and it is used by country carts bringing up heavy loads. Subsequently, when the coffee crop has been harvested—from December to May—it is available for taking down such produce. It is a Government road, kept in a good state of repair, and quite suitable for motor-cars, which are frequently used on the upward and return journeys.

The Shevaroy Hills form a *taluq*, or

subdivision of the Salem district, and Yercaud is the headquarters of the deputy tahsildar, or revenue officer, who also exercises the powers of a second-class magistrate within the limits of his subdivision. Their elevation above sea-level ranges from 2,500 ft. on the eastern side to about 5,300 ft. on the western. The greater portion of the plateau, however, is at an elevation of 4,000 to 5,000 ft. The outlying portions of these comprise Nagalur and the Green Hills, where the largest coffee estates are situated, within a radius of 10 miles of Yercaud settlement. These portions are in postal and telegraph communication with the rest of the system. The principal industry on the Shevaroy Hills is coffee growing. The coffee grown is chiefly of the Arabica varieties, and is of good quality, with a high reputation in the English market, and it commands a ready sale at average ruling prices. It is mostly exported for sale to England and France, a small proportion, however, being sold locally to dealers from the low country. This enterprise was started about seventy years ago by Europeans, and at one time it yielded very handsome returns. In 1884 crops realized £100 a ton in the market, which gave the planter a return of about 100 per cent. on his capital. Latterly, however, owing to the depreciation in prices, due to the competition of Brazil (which practically rules the market), those prosperous times are things of the past. The coffee planter has also in recent years had to contend against leaf disease and bug, but in spite of these hostile factors the industry is still a thriving one, and to those contented with a fair return on their money it is by no means to be despised. Apart from the purely commercial aspect of the matter, the planter's life is an attractive and wholesome one, and to one preferring outdoor work to more sedentary occupation it offers a very suitable outlet for one's energies. The Shevaroy plant is grown at an average elevation of 4,000 ft., and experience has shown that, other conditions being favourable, this altitude is most suitable for the cultivation of the plant. The coffee crop is harvested between the months of October and the following May, and after being pulped on the estate it is (unless sold locally) dispatched in parchment to curing works at Calicut, on the western coast, and to Coimbatore, the headquarters of the adjacent district.

It is recorded that forty years ago "the tea plant grew in great abundance on these hills," and the author of that statement saw no reason why its cultivation should not be a success, and pay even better than coffee. His expectations have not, however, been realized, and tea is now (probably because the cultivation is not scientifically developed on these hills) as extinct as the dodo.

Certain varieties of the rubber plant (Ceara and Para) thrive on these hills and grow luxuriantly, but as those varieties are not commercially of any value they are a negligible quantity. The boom in this product in the year 1910 stimulated local activity, and the systematic cultivation of the better varieties (for which sorts there is a demand) was commenced, and fairly large areas have been planted, but it is too early in the day to say how far the experiment will be a success. As all the world knows, there is at present a depression in the rubber market owing to over-production, but as

DEVIL'S BRIDGE, MOBERLY FALLS, SHEVAROY HILLS.
Photo by Nicholas & Co.

there is likely to be an ever-increasing demand for this product owing to the many uses to which it can be applied, it may be that as an industry a time will come again when prices will make the cultivation of this plant a profitable occupation.

Some twenty or twenty-five years ago there was a great "boom" in cinchona. and planters all over Southern India began to cultivate it in frenzied anticipation of the fortunes that it promised, and even the Madras Government opened up large tracts in suitable localities on the Nilgiris and in the Wynaad, and set up a laboratory for the scientific manufacture of quinine, which has been very successful. Here, again, the same story of over-production and consequent fall in prices has to be told, and for some years past cinchona cultivation on these hills has been practically abandoned. At present there seems to be a tendency towards better prices, and should this be steadily maintained and the competition by Government withdrawn (which will probably be the case if private enterprise is found to be equal to meet the demand) this industry may still revive and be worth the attention of planters. There can be little doubt that these hills are eminently suitable for cinchona cultivation, and an expert writing on this subject forty years ago says: "The sholas around the Green Hills as regards climate, elevation, soil, and moisture appear to be very suitable for the experimental culture of the cinchona. The plants have so far succeeded remarkably well." Since this was written the anticipation of the writer has been more than fulfilled.

From their geographical position and elevation the Shevaroy Hills enjoy a climate of very equable temperature. As they get the benefit of both the south-west and north-east monsoons (or the trade winds) the rainfall is considerable, 63 in. being the average amount which is registered yearly. The temperature in the shade is remarkably even throughout the year, and from observations made at Yercaud it has been ascertained that the thermometer ranges from 78° to 68° F. The hottest months are March, April, and May. In the two latter months thunderstorms, accompanied at times with heavy rain, are experienced at intervals, and the first fortnight of June generally witnesses the advent of the south-west monsoon rains, which continue until the end of August, and sometimes a little longer. The north-east monsoon (the shorter of the two but with the heavier rainfall) puts in an appearance at the beginning of October and lasts until December. Thereafter the "cold season" begins, and cloudless skies and keen and sometimes frosty weather makes the climate delightful, bracing, and invigorating in December and January. Then follows the cool but still pleasant temperature of February, and at the end of this month the cycle of the seasons again commences. It sometimes happens that one or other (and perhaps both) of the monsoons fails, and these hills, in common with the rest of India, suffer, and the gaunt spectre of famine stalks at times over large areas of the Indian plains.

The following graphic description of the scenery of these hills is taken from the official manual of the district, and it fairly paints in not too glowing colours its attractive beauty:—

"The scenery of these hills all round is beautiful; on the west the grey tints of the Shevaroyen (one of the most conspicuous peaks on the plateau from which the Shevaroys take their name) contrast well with the rich green of the foreground, while more to the north a vast gorge opens to give a glimpse of the plains. The exuberance of nature here must be seen to be believed. The dark green of the coffee with its coral gems of fruit or snowy blossoms whose jasmine fragrance hangs heavy in the air; the towering bastard Chittagong, the rippling lake, the winding and romantic paths, the nestling ferns and moss-clad boulders combine, and are inexpressibly refreshing to the sunburnt sojourner from the plains. The view of the latter from the hill-tops adds fresh zest to enjoyment, as the philosopher reflects on the sufferings of those who toil below. This is a delight from which the visitor to Ootacamund is debarred, the plains not being visible there."

There are many points of vantage (the favourite resorts of picnic parties) from which superb and extended views of the plains and of the surrounding mountain ranges can be had. On a clear day the distant Nilgiris, the Pulneys and the Anamalais (the bigger sisters, if they may be so called, of the Shevaroys), not to mention other groups of hills as picturesque but as yet unexploited by the enterprising Englishman, and the Mysore plateau can be distinctly seen, and glimpses are caught of the sacred Cauvery River as it pursues its tortuous course on its journey to the sea. To the south towers the solitary hill of Kanjamalai, almost a solid mass of magnetic iron; in the middle distance is the town of Salem; to the right the "Chalk Hills" (an outcrop of magnesite which will soon disappear from the scenery in which it was once so conspicuous an object); and nearer still the "Elephant Rock," an isolated outcrop of quartz, looking for all the world like a majestic cathedral of white marble, glistening in the sun!

The following list of the flora of the Shevaroy Hills is taken from a small volume compiled by Dr. John Shortt (a late well-known resident), called "The Hill Ranges of Southern India":—

Cultivated plants are wheat, potatoes, and sinapis, and the wild ones include *Rubus, Solanum giganteum, Sonchus Oleraceus, Berbius, Eriochlæna Hookeriana, Gnaphalium, Crotolaria, Physalis, Strobilanthes, Alsophila,* and *Aspidium.* The imported plants which thrive readily are the pear, loquat, peach, apple, guava, strawberry, plantain, citron, orange, lime, lemon, and Brazil cherry. The Australian acacias, eucalyptus, and casurina grow readily; the blue-gum (*Eucalyptus robusta* and *saligna*) have also been planted, and in recent years the silver oak (*Grevillia robusta*) has become quite common in the majority of the coffee estates as a shade plant.

The larger animals met with are the tiger (from the plains), leopard, bear, bison (rare), wild hog, jungle sheep, moose deer, hyena, jackal, hare, jungle cat, and others. Of the feathered tribe mention may be made of the jungle and spur fowl, partridge, quail, wild pigeon, woodcock, and snipe. There are no fish in the streams, but murral, which grows to a considerable size, is obtainable in the lake at Yercaud. A few snakes, mostly harmless varieties, two or three species of viper, and the cobra are met with, as well as the Russel's viper (*Daboia elegans*), the *Tumrusurius Viride, Echis Carinata,* and *Colubor Blumenbachii* (or rat snake). A large brown scorpion is common, and the black scorpion and the centipede abound in number.

The South of India is abundantly provided with mountainous tracts adapted for European settlements, and many of them are still uncolonized. The climate is, on the whole, a healthy one, although a malarial type of fever occasionally prevails. Dr. Shortt in this connection says: "Granted that once in ten years the climate for a limited period may be insalubrious, we have said all that can be adduced against it. . . . The Shevaroy fever, when it does occur, is quite as much under the control of medicine as the same form of disease elsewhere. Admitting that the hills are malarial occasionally, it is no less certain that they are free from many of these sources of diseases which abound in the plains, namely, malignant cholera and dysentery." Considering the large number of European and Anglo-Indian permanent residents (350), many of whom have lived there for several years, and considering the number of Europeans who come up during the hot weather to escape the heat of the plains, if it is an unhealthy station it might have been expected that it would long since have been abandoned as a hill resort.

A tribe of natives called *Malayalis,* the descendants of immigrants from Conjeeveram (a town near Madras—the ancient Kanchipuram), who were said to have been driven hence some centuries ago through Brahmanical persecution, are met with in numerous villages of from twenty to one hundred conically-shaped huts scattered in various parts of the plateau. They are an agricultural race, cultivating different kinds of grain and breeding cattle. They are also largely employed as labourers on coffee estates, and are a docile, quiet, if clannish and rather dirty race. They rigidly adhere to the hills, shunning the plains, which they cannot endure.

Yercaud is the oldest and largest European settlement. There are about 350 European and Anglo-Indian permanent residents on the hills, the former being in a large majority. Three-fifths of this population are settled in Yercaud, and the remainder live on the outlying coffee estates. Most of the planters live on their estates, but those having properties in the vicinity of Yercaud reside there. There are about one hundred houses in and about the station, and most of them are inhabited by their owners. The chief buildings include an Anglican church, Roman Catholic chapel and convent, French Mission and London Mission chapel and school, Leipzig Lutheran Mission chapel, post and telegraph office, public rooms and library, an English club, an hotel and boarding-houses, hospital and dispensary. During the hot months (March to July) visitors from all parts of the Presidency visit Yercaud in order to avoid the heat and to benefit by the welcome change and fresh and invigorating climate. At the club various amusements are indulged in, such as tennis, Badminton, billiards, and bridge. There are very pretty drives in and around the station, and motoring can be indulged in through charming scenery and over good roads. There are also bridle-paths leading principally to the estates, and almost any portion of the plateau can be comfortably reached on horseback. Walking and picnic parties are frequently enjoyed, and visits to the principal points of vantage to view the surrounding low country are a feature of the life of the place, especially during the summer months. Chief among the places of interest are Pagoda Point, Ladies' Seat, Arthur's Seat, Prospect Point, and Owen's Grotto, from which lovely views can be obtained. There is a weekly *shandy,* or market, on Sundays, where provisions from the low country are sold, and there are also shops for the sale of English stores and other useful and fancy articles. Many of the residents are retired officials who have settled there to pass the remainder of their days. The place is a popular hot-weather resort owing to its easy accessibility and its other attractions.

THE AGRICULTURAL COLLEGE AND RESEARCH INSTITUTE, COIMBATORE

About 2 miles to the north-west of the town of Coimbatore is the Agricultural College and Research Institute, which is the chief institution in Southern India devoted to the teaching of scientific agriculture. It is also the headquarters of nearly all the various scientific experts of the department, who, besides supervising and being responsible for the teaching imparted to the students, are also engaged in research work. Each of the different sections of chemistry, botany—divided into plant breeding and general agricultural botany—agriculture, mycology, and entomology, is under the control of an officer specially trained in his subject, and one of them also acts as principal of the college. There is, in addition, a botanical expert who is solely engaged on plant-breeding in regard to sugar-cane.

This college and institute, which is the outcome of the newer ideas and wider policy inaugurated by Lord Curzon, was opened by Sir Arthur Lawley in 1909. The land attached to the institute covers 450 acres, providing ample room for the farm, the playgrounds, and the buildings for the students and for those of the staff who reside on the estate. The colony—for such it really is—has been laid out upon an ordered plan, and it presents a very pleasing view against the wooded background of the Velliangiri Hills.

The commanding building in the colony is, of course, the college designed in the Hindo-Saracenic style by Mr. G. S. T. Harris, the late consulting architect to the Government of Madras. The brick and stone used in its construction are local productions—the granite for the fine dressed stone work being quarried in the neighbouring hills. The building is in the form of the letter "H," and it is noticeable for its spaciousness; the whole of the central portion (above which is the library) being left open below to form a magnificent hall, flanked by monolithic granite pillars. The total length of the structure is more than 300 ft., and the width of each block is 50 ft., which allows for a 25 ft. room with a 12 ft. verandah on each side. The cost, including fittings, was about Rs. 4,70,000. The museum is immediately to the left of the main entrance and contains in its handsome cases (the work of a local Industrial School), models, collections of seeds, manures, and agricultural produce of various kinds, whether raw or manufactured. The whole of the first floor of the central area is occupied by the library—the handsomest room in the building, being well fitted and well lighted, and the numerous local and foreign journals on its tables are evidence of the attempt which is being made to keep abreast of the times. The college also contains three well-equipped lecture-rooms, one of which, by an arrangement of sliding doors, can be converted into a hall 76 ft. in length, for conferences and other general meetings.

The rest of the building is occupied by the rooms allotted to the various sections. The chemistry section, for instance, includes a teaching and a research laboratory, with balance, store, and clerks' rooms; the mycological section has a large hall for its collections and for the assistants, in addition to a sterilizing, culture, store, and other rooms. A small private workroom is allotted to the head of each section. The building contains the largest and most complete herbarium in Southern India, as well as the best entomological and mycological collections. Electric light and power for driving suction and pressure plant is available in some of the rooms; water is

THE AGRICULTURAL COLLEGE AND RESEARCH INSTITUTE.

1. The Agricultural College and Research Institute. 2. View over the Tanks. 3. The Botanical Garden. 4. The Chemical Laboratory. 5. Cattle in the College Compound.

THE AGRICULTURAL COLLEGE AND RESEARCH INSTITUTE.

1. Pepper Vine, Tellicherry. 2. Cotton Carts loaded with Kappas at Koilpatti. 3. The Largest Cane on the Farm—height, 20 ft. when 11 months old. 4. Disc Plough. 5. Treading out the Corn. 6. Picking Kappas at Koilpatti.

supplied from tanks in the roof, which are filled from a well behind the college, while gas is laid on from a small Mansfield instalment.

Outside of the college premises the estate offers a good deal of interest not only to the expert but to the casual visitor. Close to the college are situated the pot-culture houses of the chemist and the mycologist, where more delicate experiments on plant nutrition and plant diseases than can be performed in the open field are in progress. Garden laboratories are also found in the insectory compound and the botanical garden, both of which are necessary adjuncts for teaching and research.

The activities of the farm centre in the yard, where are the cattle-sheds, cow-byres, store-rooms, machine shops, implement sheds, and dairy. The veterinary hospital is in charge of the veterinary assistant, who performs both executive and teaching functions. Much experimental work in the way of plant breeding and the testing of implements and manures is continually in progress, and the different conditions of the land on the farm affords peculiar facilities for these trials. Some of the soil is entirely dependent upon rain for its moisture, some is served by wells, whilst other portions are under a good source of irrigation, for which water can be obtained by direct flow.

The sugar-cane breeding station, where seedling canes for supply to the whole of India are being raised and carefully tested, is situated a short distance to the west of the college. The extraordinary variations between the different canes makes this an unfailing source of interest to student and grower alike.

Previous to the founding of this college at Coimbatore, agricultural education was given at a college at Saidapet, in the suburbs of Madras, where the opportunities for research and experimental work were not comparable with those now obtaining at Coimbatore. The course of instruction is now divided into two parts: the first, lasting for two years, is devoted almost entirely to practical agriculture, such science as it is necessary to teach being treated empirically; in the second course, extending over eighteen months, more attention is paid to the sciences and to farm management. In the first course each student has his own plot of land to attend to, and whilst he is taking part in general farm work he goes through a course of instruction in the dairy, in the care of cattle, in grafting and budding, and in the machine sheds. There is accommodation for admitting 40 students every year.

The activities of the agricultural department are now restricted to this college and research institute. District farms, of which eight at present exist, are being opened in different typical areas where the agricultural crops and problems peculiar to those tracts are under study. To each of these farms is attached a staff of peripatetic inspectors, whose duty it is to tour in the surrounding country, inculcating better principles of cultivation, distributing and establishing selected strains of seeds, giving advice on agricultural subjects. and informing the special branches at Coimbatore of the existence of insect or fungoid pests. A trained agriculturist, styled deputy-director, is in charge of the farms and of executive work in a few districts, whilst the general control is vested in a director, who is stationed at Madras, the headquarters of the Government.

The farms at present open are as follows: Koilpatti, in the Tinnevelly district, in the centre of a most important cotton tract; Manganallur, in the rich rice land of the Tanjore Delta; Taliparamba, in Malabar, among the peculiar conditions of the West Coast; while Palur, in South Arcot, is chiefly devoted to groundnut and sugar-cane. In the northern part of the Presidency there are district farms at Hagari, in Bellary, and at Nandyal, in Kurnool, the chief crop being cotton. Rice and sugar-cane are prominent features at Samalkota, in the Godavari Delta, while at Anakapalli there is varied cultivation of the Circars. Other farms will be opened for cattle, coconuts, and other live stock and produce when more trained men are recruited. The greatest progress in propagandist work has so far been made in establishing improved strains of cotton, better varieties of sugar-cane, more profitable management of rice land, and in the control of fungus disease on areca palms.

Information about the college can be obtained on application to the Principal, Agricultural College, Lawley Road, P.O. Coimbatore, and about the Department generally from the Director of Agriculture, Madras.

ARCADIA

The density of the Indian jungle in its virginal state is not calculated to inspire the heart of an agriculturist with great hope of success, and the difficulties of pioneering work have taxed to the fullest extent the courage, the patience, and the perseverance of the majority of the settlers upon the land. The Arcadia estate of 140 acres in the district of Salem became the property of Mr. C. Dickens in the year 1897. It was then in a chaotic state; it was overgrown with forest, and the only buildings could not by any stretch of the imagination be classed as anything but shanties. The clearing of the land was taken in hand immediately, the soil was ploughed, a large homestead and suitable outhouses were constructed of undressed stone which was quarried upon the property, and improvements of a general character followed one after another. The owner's residence is situated on a hill, and it commands a charming view of the plains of Salem and of the tortuous stretches of the Cauvery River. About 100 acres of the estate are devoted to the growing of coffee, which gives a return of about 4 cwt. to the acre. Coffee-plants do not, as a rule, cease bearing until they are about ninety years of age, and there are several plantations in the vicinity of Arcadia in which old stagers may be seen. The produce of the Arcadia trees is sold to Salem Chetties and to firms living in towns along the seacoast. Good coffee cannot be grown unless there is an abundance of shelter for the plants, and Mr. Dickens has provided this by having rows of silver oak, jack, dadap, albisa molicana, and other trees. Fruit of all kinds thrives remarkably well in this neighbourhood, and many planters are now obtaining young trees from Australia.

Tea-growing is not a profitable occupation in this district owing to the deficiency of the rainfall, and many persons attribute this aridity to the deforestation which has been going on for so many years. The Madras Government favours this opinion, and, owing to the strong recommendation of Mr. Cowley Brown—the Principal of the Agricultural College at Coimbatore—silver oak and fir-trees are now being planted on the tops of the hills.

Planters in the neighbourhood are seriously handicapped owing to the difficulty in obtaining labourers, as recruiting agents are enticing the men to go to the Straits Settlements, to Ceylon, and to Burma. Mr. Dickens has employment for forty hands during the season, and he personally supervises all work on the estate. He is chairman of the local Planters' Association, and this body was responsible for the construction of a good cart-road between the towns of Yercaud and Salem, and of smaller roads leading to Nagalore Green Hills, Varnia, and other places.

The nearest railway station to Arcadia is at Kadiampatty, which is about 7 miles distant, but there is a post and telegraph office at Nagalore, which is only 1½ miles from the estate.

CASTLECROFT

Tradition has it that coffee was introduced into Southern India by a Mahommedan pilgrim who, many years ago, planted a few berries in an allotment in the State of Mysore, but the earliest records of its cultivation take one back to the close of the eighteenth century, when experiments were conducted at Tiruppattur, in the district of Salem. There were, naturally, many failures at the outset, arising from unsuitability of climate, from a too-exposed position of the plantations, or from lack of knowledge of the best methods of pulping, cleaning, and curing the bean. Then, again, a succession of bad seasons commenced about the year 1865, owing to the prevalence of certain diseases, which literally devastated many plantations, and thus it followed that there were many influences at work which caused hundreds of acres of coffee to be replaced by tea.

The Castlecroft estate, however, is one which appears to be at a suitable altitude; it has a healthy climate, and it has enjoyed an immunity from the ravages of insect and other pests. The property is about 1,000 acres in extent, and it is owned by Messrs. Henry Rogers, Sons & Co., Ltd., of Wolverhampton, in England, for whom Mr. C. R. T. Congreve is resident manager. Some 616 acres are producing coffee and cardamoms, the bushes having been planted between the years 1899 and 1910. A considerable area of land is devoted to cinchona, but this is being discontinued in favour of tea. It is expected that the whole estate will be under cultivation by the end of the year 1918, and the major portion will be planted with tea. As soon as the coffee "cherry"—as the fruit is called—is quite ripe, it is picked by hand, and then taken to the pulping-house on the property. Here it is pulped by machinery, which is driven by a turbine, and, after it has been washed and dried, it is sent to the Anapura factory at Coimbatore, to be cured and prepared for sale. The average annual yield of coffee to the acre is about 3 cwt., while the cardamom crop should average about 100 lb. per acre when in full bearing. There are two bungalows on the property, and one of these—a charming residence built on the summit of a hill and commanding extensive views of delightful scenery—is occupied by Mr. Congreve himself, who has one European assistant and some 350 coolies in his employ.

The estate is about 4,000 feet above the level of the sea, and it has a yearly rainfall of 145 inches. Castlecroft is 69 miles distant from Coimbatore; it is 44 miles from the nearest telegraph office at Pollachi, and 8 miles from the post office at Valparai.

KORANGUMUDI

Situated about 5 miles from the post and telegraph offices at Valparai is the Korangumudi estate of 1,100 acres, belonging to Messrs. P. Church, H. P. Hodgson, and G. A. Marsh. This is one of the many properties in the district of Coimbatore which originally consisted of the densest forest, but some 629 acres have been cultivated and planted with cardamoms, cinchonas, and a little coffee.

The average yield per acre of cardamoms is over 100 lb., and the majority of this is sold in the country. Further development of the estate is taking place, and about 50 acres are being opened in cardamoms each year.

Mr. G. A. Marsh is the manager, and he has 250 coolies in constant work.

PERRIA KARAMALAI

The Perria Karamalai Tea & Produce Company, Ltd., the owners of this estate of more than 1,500 acres, was formed in the year 1912, with a capital of £20,000, which has been fully paid up. The head offices are at Calicut, and the directors are Messrs. J. Christie, G. A. Marsh, and C. R. T. Congreve; the managers are Messrs. Marsh and Congreve, and Mr. A. C. Cotton is superintendent. Development of the estate was commenced in 1912, and 650 acres of land have been planted with tea, which is expected to yield the first crop during 1915. A fine factory, now in course of construction, will be equipped with up-to-date machinery, and with a hydro-electric plant of 100 h.p., and residences for clerical assistants, as well as a neat bungalow and other buildings are nearing completion. A good road for all transit purposes, which extends for a distance of 2½ miles to the site of the factory, has been made by the company, and the managers are gradually making other improvements in all parts of the estate.

The major portion of Perria Karamalai is fully 4,000 feet above the level of the sea, and the rainfall, which is evenly distributed over the whole area, averages 130 inches in the course of a year.

The nearest post and telegraphic offices are at Valparai.

PUTHUTOTAM

This estate of 915 acres, situated in the centre of the hilly country of the Annamalais, in the district of Coimbatore, is owned by Messrs. G. A. Marsh and C. R. T. Congreve, and about 600 acres have been planted with coffee, cardamoms, and cinchona since the year 1900.

The property is well supplied with buildings, which include pulping-house, drying sheds, and stores, in addition to a bungalow for Mr. Marsh, who acts as manager, and for Mr. E. N. House, the superintendent.

The yield of coffee is about 3 cwt. to the acre, and after the berries have been pulped, washed, and dried, they are sent to the curing works at Coimbatore, where the process of curing is completed. Cardamoms have returned as much as 10,000 lb. in a single season. The uncultivated portion of the estate is at present covered with dense forest, but the work of clearing is being pushed forward as rapidly as possible, and it is the intention of the owners to plant the whole of the balance in the near future.

Puthutotam lies at an elevation of about 4,000 feet above sea-level, and it is situated about 5 miles from the post office at Valparai. Constant employment is found for 250 coolies.

T. STANES & CO., LTD.

The history of this company is interesting as showing how one of the most important commercial concerns in Southern India has sprung from comparatively small beginnings. Its development has been effected partly by the acquisition of various undertakings, but its growth is mainly attributable to the sterling worth of all goods which are placed upon the

PUTHUTOTAM.

1. BUNGALOW. 2. STORES. 3. CARDAMOMS. 4. NEW CLEARING. 5. FELLING TREES.

T. STANES & CO., LTD.

1. Coimbatore Coffee Works. 2. Stanes' Cotton Press and Ginning Factory. 3. Coimbatore Manure Works.
4. Coimbatore Spinning and Weaving Company, Ltd. 5. Coimbatore Mall Mills Company, Ltd.

market and to the sound experience and ceaseless energy of the partners, and, subsequently, of the directors.

It was in the year 1861 that Mr. Robert Stanes established Coffee Curing Works in connection with his family and other estates on the Nilgiris, and some twenty-five years later the private firm of Messrs. T. Stanes & Co. was formed. The annual output of coffee is about 1,000 tons, and daily employment is found for from 250 to 300 hands during the season. The next important step was the formation of the Coimbatore Spinning and Weaving Company, in conjunction with Messrs. Arbuthnot & Co., of Madras, in 1888, and upon the failure of the latter firm in 1907, Messrs. Stanes & Co. assumed entire control. These mills have about 45,000 spindles and 100 looms ; the latter are to be increased by another 200 in the near future.

The firm more recently took over management of the Coimbatore Mall Mills Company, Ltd., in which 200 looms are at work, and all the cloth which is manufactured as well as the yarn which is spun in the Spinning and Weaving Company's Mill is disposed of in India. It is a very great advantage to the company that the buildings of these mills are connected with the railway by a private siding. Steam power is used in both mills at present, but a suction gas plant has been installed in Messrs. T. Stanes & Co.'s cotton ginning factory and press in Coimbatore, where a foundry has also been started.

Another cotton ginning factory has been opened at Palladum, about 20 miles distant from Coimbatore, which is the centre of a large cotton district. There are 20 double roller gins in those premises, and they have a capacity of turning out 800 lb. of raw cotton from each machine in ten hours.

About 2,000 persons are employed in the Spinning Mills, 300 in the Mall Mills, and each of the ginning factories requires between 200 and 300 hands.

Extensive manure works have been added to the industries of the company, and about 150 labourers are engaged in making fertilizers of all descriptions. Bone meal, oil-cake meal, and other chemical and natural fertilizers are made, and about 3,000 tons of these are sold annually to planters for use on estates throughout Southern India.

European managers are in charge of the factories and other works, and this arrangement tends very considerably to the regularity and thoroughness with which every detail of work is carried out.

COLACUMBAY COFFEE ESTATE

The cultivation of this estate commenced in the year 1860, and it was purchased by Mr. T. Stanes in the year 1865. It consists of 200 acres, which are planted with coffee at an elevation of from 4,200 to 5,200 ft. Notwithstanding the ravages of leaf disease and green bug (pests which have ruined many estates), this property is in a flourishing condition owing to good husbandry, and to the care taken in combating diseases by spraying and washing the coffee-trees. In the year 1913 an excellent crop of 80 tons was yielded. The estate is now the property of the Nilgiri Plantations Company, Ltd., who own several other holdings which produce about 250 tons of coffee annually. Messrs. T. Stanes & Co., Ltd., are the sole agents of the company.

In former days nearly all of the coffee cured by Messrs. Stanes & Co. was exported to Europe, but owing to increasing local demand they have for several years directed their attention to the Indian market. Arrangements were made in the year 1906 to amalgamate their retail branch of the business with that of the United Coffee Growers Company, Ltd., and a new company was formed under the management of Messrs. T. Stanes & Co., called The United Coffee Supply Company, Ltd., which has, since July 1908, supplied large quantities of raw and roasted and ground coffee to customers in all parts of India. Their "Red Ensign" brand of ground coffee is exceedingly popular.

GLENDALE TEA ESTATES

These estates, which are owned by the Nilgiri Plantations Company, Ltd., are situated on the Nilgiris, and they comprise about 450 acres, which are planted with tea. The growing of tea on this property was commenced about the year 1860, but the system of manufacture in those distant days was very crude in comparison with that which is now in vogue. When the present manager of the company, Mr. Thomas Brown, entered upon his duties in 1881, there was hardly any machinery, and the annual output of tea, of a poor quality, was less than 10,000 lb. The appliances for drying the leaf consisted of a set of trays covered with wire mesh, and as much as 15 lb. of wood fuel was required for the drying of 1 lb. of tea.

The company own two factories, one at Glendale, Hulical, and the other at Brooklands, Coonoor.

Between the years 1881 and 1900 tea-growing did not appear to attract investors of capital in and around Coonoor ; the results were comparatively poor, the soil was neglected, and the necessary machinery had not been introduced. A great change, however, subsequently took place, and at the present time it is a most difficult matter to obtain large holdings within a reasonable distance from settlements. The majority of the plantations are at an altitude of from 4,000 to 6,000 ft., and this fact is largely responsible for the delicate aroma of the tea. Arrangements were made with the Nilgiri Plantations Company in 1911 by which the retail sales of this tea were entrusted to Messrs. Stanes & Co., and the tea is sent direct from the estates to the packing factory of this firm at Coimbatore, whence it is distributed throughout the whole of India. Under the improved conditions of cultivation, and owing to the up-to-date methods of preparation, 1 acre of land may be expected to give a return of 500 lb. of tea. Consignments can be delivered in London at 6d. per lb., and as the net selling price varies from 8d. to 9d., there is ample margin for a handsome profit.

It is probable that the greatest difficulty with which planters have to contend is the inadequate supply of labourers, which may hinder any further development of the tea-planting. One of the chief causes of this labour famine is to be found in the fact that the trade in rubber has been extending so rapidly that the tempting wages which have been offered have proved to be too attractive, and they have drawn away labour from tea and coffee estates.

STANMORE (ANAMALAI) ESTATES, LTD.

Two Ceylon planters, Messrs. E. J. Martin and O. A. Bannatine, were the pioneers in the growing of tea on the Anamallay Hills, and the property belonging to the Stanmore (Anamalai) Estates, Ltd., was one of the first to be cultivated there. The total area is about 5,000 acres ; the felling of forest trees and the removal of jungle com-

T. STANES & CO., LTD.

1. The Colacumbay Office and the Staff at Roll-call. 2. The Falls adjoining the Estate. 3. Pulp House, Colacumbay. 4. A Portion of Coffee Plantation, No. 28. 5. Glendale Tea Factory.

STANMORE (ANAMALAI) ESTATES, LTD.

1. BUNGALOW. 2. VIEW OF TEA. 3. TEA FACTORY. 4. INTERIOR OF FACTORY. 5. PACKING-ROOM. 6. THE NADUA RIVER AT STANMORE.

menced in 1898; planting was taken in hand in the following year, and the present cultivated area consists of 1,548 acres of tea, 300 acres of coffee, and 392 acres of cardamoms. The remaining portion of the estate is being developed gradually, and it will probably be devoted entirely to the production of tea. The average annual yield of pruned and matured bushes is about 700 lb. to 800 lb. to the acre, although two fields gave a return of 1,200 lb. in four seasons, without manure, from 1911-14. Messrs. T. Stanes & Co., Ltd., of Coimbatore, are retail agents for the sale of some of the produce, but by far the greater portion is exported to England.

There are two factories on the estate, one of these, 225 ft. in length and 100 ft. in breadth, is probably the largest in Southern India. It contains three engines, namely, one of 88 h.p. (by Hornsby), whose motive power is suction gas; a second one (by Crossley), of 40 h.p., driven by liquid fuel; while the third is a Cundall engine of 16 h.p., which is worked by kerosene oil. The plant is up-to-date in every respect, and it includes six rollers, two roll-breakers, one "Paragon" dryer, three siroccos, two Colombo dryers, two leaf-cutting machines, three sifters, two sets of withering fans, and a packing machine. The second factory is on another portion of the property, and it, too, is well equipped with machinery and plant.

Coffee is pulped and dried on the premises, and it is usually sold in local markets. The yield in 1913 was the satisfactory one of 7 cwt. to the acre. Cardamoms are dried and cured in separate buildings, and a portion of the crop is consigned to England for sale.

Three bungalows for Europeans have been constructed, principally of red and white cedar grown upon the property, and one of them is very prettily situated in a charming garden whence excellent views can be had of the Anamudi mountain range — the highest mountain in India south of the Himalayas, and of the elevated lands and rich plateaus of the district of Travancore. There is an abundance of large and small game on the estate, such as bison, ibex, black panther, and pig, but the most destructive to crops is the elephant, to shoot which special permission has been granted by the Madras Government.

Mr. E. W. Simcock, the manager, has had nearly twenty years' experience in planting, and his keen interest in the objects of the Anamallais Planters' Association (of which he is a member of committee) caused him to be appointed a delegate to the meeting of the United Planters' Association of Southern India, Ltd., held at Bangalore in 1914. He has four European assistants, and he employs about 2,000 hands.

The altitude of the estate varies from 3,500 ft. to 4,000 ft., and the average annual rainfall is 120 in.

The post office at Valparai is 2½ miles distant; the nearest telegraphic office is at Pollachi, and the most convenient railway station is at Coimbatore.

In addition to the above property, Mr. Simcock is manager of two other estates in the Anamallais. They are the Kallar property 2,500 acres, under tea, of which the owners are Messrs. Bannatine, Martin, and Simcock; and the Injapara estate, consisting of 420 acres, producing coffee and cardamoms, the proprietors being Messrs. Simcock, Maclure, and Martin.

VALALKADAI PEAK

The owners of estates in the neighbourhood of the Shevaroy Hills in the district of Salem can congratulate themselves upon having soil of great fertility; they enjoy a genial climate, and the average rainfall reaches the moderate figures of from 50 to 60 in. Further than this, however, there is an advantage in that the land lies at an elevation of about 4,000 ft. above the level of the sea, and this is the altitude at which the most successful cultivation of coffee is attained. The Valalkadai property, consisting of 160 acres, was purchased by Mr. S. M. Hight in the year 1893, but, with the exception of 10 acres which had been planted with coffee, the area consisted of dense jungle and scrub, and the only buildings in existence were of an exceedingly primitive character. The outlook for the owner was not an attractive one by any means, but he vigorously attacked the forest and undergrowth, with the result that there are now 150 acres of highly productive land together with 10 acres which have only recently been planted. The "Arabica" variety of coffee holds pride of place on this estate, and it shows an average yield of 4 cwt. to the acre. An abundance of shade, which is essential for coffee-plants, is obtained from rows of silver oak-trees, and these are carefully trimmed from time to time in order that they may not interfere with the maturing crop. Coffee-plants which are topped regularly give more uniform results than those which are allowed to grow naturally. The crop is picked by hand, pulped and dried on the estate, and it is then sent in parchment to be cured at Coimbatore, where consignments are shipped to London bearing the brand of "Hight's, Valalkadai, Salem." The samples from this property compare very favourably with others of Southern India, and they invariably reach a good price in the English and Continental markets.

A small plot of land was planted with Para rubber-trees in the year 1908, but there is hardly sufficient time as yet to estimate the value of the experiment.

The most convenient railway station is at Salem; it is about 28 miles distant, but there is a good road for carts from start to finish. Nagalur, which is the nearest post and telegraph office, is about 2 miles from the estate, while Yercaud—9 miles away—is the nearest town of any importance. The old ramshackle buildings have given place to some well-equipped structures, which include a homestead, a pulping-house (in which an oil-engine is used), servants' and coolies' quarters, together with sheds and drying yards.

Mr. Hight is, further, the owner of the Moganaad Peak estate, of 600 acres, which has been obtained by the purchase of several blocks of land at certain intervals since the year 1883. There are 300 acres under coffee, but about one-third of this area has been inter-planted with Para rubber-trees. The coffee crop is dealt with in the same manner as at Valkalkadai, with the exception that pulping is done by hand pending the installation of an oil-engine. The Para rubber-trees were planted in 1906 and 1912, but as the variety is proverbially slow in growth at a high elevation, it has not yet been possible to tap them. Another 300 acres were devoted to the cultivation of Ceara rubber, about the year 1911, and the plants, which are about 7 ft. apart, will be thinned as occasion may require until one acre of land will carry about 200 matured trees. This species of rubber can be tapped when the trees have reached the age of about five years.

The inadequate supply of labour has now become a serious problem for planters in this neighbourhood, and their worst fears for the future appear to be well grounded, seeing that recruiting officers are permitted free access to the country districts, where they obtain men

VALALKADAI PEAK.

1. Bungalow. 2. Moganaad Peak Coffee interplanted with Rubber. 3. Ceara Rubber, Moganaad Peak. 4. Coffee, Valalkadai Peak. 5. Pulp-house, Drying-tables, and Stores, Valalkadai Peak.

for shipment to the Straits Settlements, Ceylon, and other countries. Mr. Hight is firmly convinced that some concerted plan of action with Government support must be adopted forthwith, otherwise he sees very little hope that owners of estates will be able to obtain any returns whatever for their capital. To illustrate the difficulties which are being experienced already, it may be mentioned that about 100 acres of the Moganaad Peak estate Ceara rubber are now partially abandoned owing to the scarcity of competent hands.

One coolie to the acre is necessary on the average coffee estate, although one might manage with two coolies to 3 acres in plantations where there is an abundance of good shade.

Mr. Hight undertakes the general management of the properties, and he is ably assisted by his two sons.

THE VALPARAI ESTATES

These estates are the property of the Anglo-American Direct Tea Trading Company, Ltd., and the Amalgamated Tea Estates Company, Ltd., and they are under the management of Mr. J. Hatton Robinson, who resides at Valparai, in the Anamalais, in the district of Coimbatore.

The whole area is about 6,500 acres in extent, and 2,250 acres are cultivated with tea, coffee, cardamoms, and rubber, on behalf of the first-named company, while the clearing of 3,000 acres, to be planted in 1915 with tea for the other company, was commenced early in the year 1914. The planted portion comprises 840 acres of tea; cardamoms, 620 acres; coffee, 480 acres; and 260 acres of rubber. Tea-growing is the staple industry on the estates, and all the uncultivated land will be put under this crop in due course. A factory is being erected for the manufacture of rubber, and this building, as well as those for making tea, will be fitted with plant and machinery of a modern type. The head agents of the companies are Messrs. Finlay, Muir & Co., of Calcutta.

CRICKET IN MADRAS.

SPORT

By A. H. STEELE

RACING in Southern India cannot be said to thrive in the same way as it does in the Northern and Western Presidencies. Meetings, however, are held at Bangalore, Mysore, Madras, Secunderabad, Ootacamund, and Wellington. Of these the Bangalore and Mysore meetings are the largest, and they attract some fairly useful horses. Bangalore is the summer quarters for many of the largest Calcutta trainers, who take their various strings there during the hot months in Calcutta, and invariably give some of them a run at Mysore and Bangalore during June and July before taking them on to the famous Calcutta meeting. The late Sir A. A. Apcar's well-known string for many years always summered at Bangalore. At Kunigal, a few miles from Bangalore, His Highness the Maharaja of Mysore has a large stud farm, where he breeds some very useful horses for racing purposes. This class of horse usually has special races allotted to them, and of late years many of them have shown to considerable advantage on the turf, even when racing against the English or Australian bred animal. In this respect, however, it should be noted that the English or Australian horse—unless he be a very indifferent one—always has to give a lot of weight away to the country-bred. Up to the present the locally bred animals cannot race with the best English or Australian imported to this country, but there is no doubt they have improved out of all knowledge during the past few years, and there is every reason to believe that His Highness will continue his endeavours in the direction of improving his blood stock.

Up to about fifteen to twenty years ago racing in Madras always took place in the morning, commencing at about six o'clock, and it says much for the energy of the public that the meetings were well attended and the racing and fields were good, when it is considered that a 6 to 7 miles drive was necessary to get to the course and most enthusiasts had to return to their offices by 10 a.m. to do a day's work—and this, too, before the days of motor-cars. It is regrettable that racing has now fallen to a low ebb in the Presidency town, but it is hoped that it may yet show signs of more vigorous life.

The chief difficulty to contend with is the weather, as in the majority of months in the year it is too hot to attract outside owners, and in the few months which are available racing is always taking place in other large Presidency towns. The gate-money as a source of income to the Madras Race Club is also very indifferent, as the European population and the Indians who are keen on racing are too small in number to benefit the receipts to any extent. Coimbatore and Trichinopoly hold small meetings annually, but at these fixtures the actual racehorse is barred, and although racing is confined to hack and hunter classes, some good sport is nevertheless always assured, and the social side of these weeks is truly hospitable.

Rugby and Association football are favoured forms of amusement, the various regiments providing the nucleus for this sport. It is worthy of note that the Madras Gymkhana Club has been able to put a fairly strong Rugby fifteen into the field during recent years, and the Club's

SPORT

representatives have travelled to Calcutta and Bombay on several occasions. In 1912 they won the Bombay Cup, beating all comers, including the then undefeated fifteen from the West Riding Regiment. This regiment has a very fine Rugby record, having played in tournaments all over India for many years, and their only defeat is the one recorded above. In Calcutta the Madras team has got into the finals more than once, but it has never been able to win the cup.

1. ASSEMBLY-ROOMS OF THE MADRAS HUNT CLUB, 1812.
(From an old print.)

2. MADRAS HUNT CLUB MEET, 1865.
(From an old print.)

Polo is, of course, played in every station in Southern India but the play varies according to the regiment that is in the station. The game generally is not so strong as it is in the north, a circumstance due to the older regiments usually getting the northern stations, where they are always able to get more play against one another. Madras boasts of the finest polo-ground in India, in the grounds of Government House, Guindy.

Lawn-tennis, golf, hockey, and other outdoor games are indulged in with considerable enthusiasm. The first-named is played entirely on hard mud courts, climatic conditions being the bar against the more beautiful and preferable grass venues. Except in a few stations, "browns," made of the same material as the tennis-courts, have to be used in the place of greens for golf.

HUNTING

Hunting in Madras is a sport of some antiquity. No detailed records of the Madras Hunt exist prior to 1868, but the hunting of the jackal has apparently been carried on from a very remote date, the earliest record available being a letter dated 1776 from a gentleman then resident in Madras to his relatives at home on behalf of the then so-called "Madras Hunting Society," asking them to try and arrange for a yearly draft of twenty couples of hounds to keep up the local pack. It may be presumed that the Madras Hunt is entitled to the distinction of being the first hunt established in India. Hounds are out two days a week, and the jackal is the quarry hunted. The small Indian silver fox is occasionally found, but it usually affords little sport, as he leaves very little scent. Jackals are plentiful, and there is seldom much difficulty in finding at once, a point of some importance, as hounds throw off at daylight, about six o'clock, and hunting-men have to be at their offices four hours later. This does not leave much time, so that a quick find is indispensable.

The country hunted is not an ideal one, as it lies to the south and west of the city of Madras, and is very soft and often very false at the commencement of the season when the north-east monsoon is prevalent. The paddy fields, which are flooded with water, are deep in mire, and treacherous ground causes a lot of unseating of riders. The ground gradually dries up, until about the end of the season, February or March, it is nearly as hard as the high road, and dust is flying. It, however, usually carries a good scent, but its greatest drawback is the prickly pear, which is found nearly everywhere, and is very sore on hounds and horses. There is practically no fencing beyond an occasional "double bund." The coverts are large and very strong; almost everything that grows has thorns on it; and it is a tribute to the dash of the foxhound that he will face it

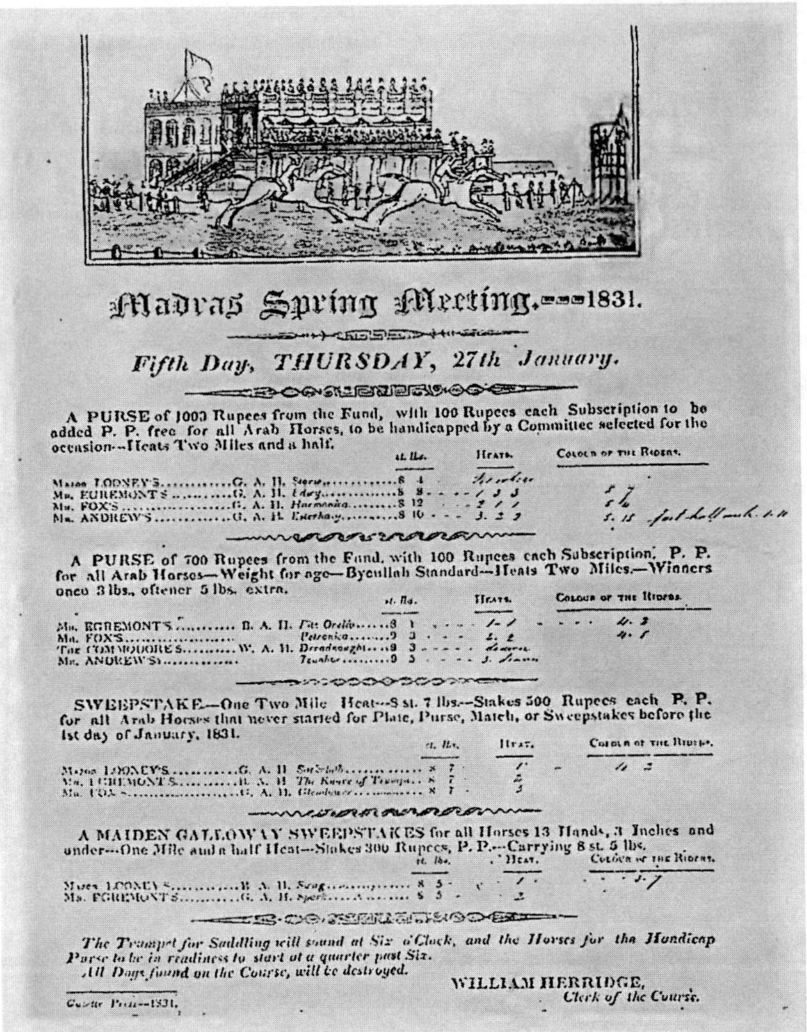
Madras Spring Meeting.—1831.

Fifth Day, THURSDAY, 27th January.

A PURSE of 1000 Rupees from the Fund, with 100 Rupees each Subscription to be added P. P. free for all Arab Horses, to be handicapped by a Committee selected for the occasion—Heats Two Miles and a half.

	st. lbs.	Heats.	Colour of the Riders.
Major LOONEY'S............G. A. H. [illegible]	8 4		
Mr. EGREMONT'S............G. A. H. [illegible]	8 8		
Mr. FOX'S............G. A. H. Harmonica	8 12		
Mr. ANDREW'S............G. A. H. Esterhazy	8 10		

A PURSE of 700 Rupees from the Fund, with 100 Rupees each Subscription. P. P. for all Arab Horses—Weight for age—Byculla Standard—Heats Two Miles.—Winners once 3 lbs., oftener 5 lbs. extra.

	st. lbs.	Heats.	Colour of the Riders.
Mr. EGREMONT'S............B. A. H. Fitz Orelio	8 1		
Mr. FOX'S............ Petrenko	9 3		
The COMMODORE'S............W. A. H. Dreadnought	9 3		
Mr. ANDREW'S............ [illegible]	9 3		

SWEEPSTAKE.—One Two Mile Heat—8 st. 7 lbs.—Stakes 500 Rupees each P. P. for all Arab Horses that never started for Plate, Purse, Match, or Sweepstakes before the 1st day of January, 1831.

	st. lbs.	Heat.	Colour of the Riders.
Major LOONEY'S............G. A. H. [illegible]	8 7		
Mr. EGREMONT'S............B. A. H. The Knave of Trumps	8 7		
Mr. FOX'S............G. A. H. [illegible]	8 7		

A MAIDEN GALLOWAY SWEEPSTAKES for all Horses 13 Hands, 3 Inches and under—One Mile and a half Heat—Stakes 300 Rupees, P. P.—Carrying 8 st. 5 lbs.

	st. lbs.	Heat.	Colour of the Riders.
Major LOONEY'S............B. A. H. [illegible]	8 5		
Mr. EGREMONT'S............G. A. H. [illegible]	8 5		

The Trumpet for Saddling will sound at Six o'Clock, and the Horses for the Handicap Purse to be in readiness to start at a quarter past Six.

All Dogs found on the Course, will be destroyed.

WILLIAM HERRIDGE,
Clerk of the Course.

Gazette Press—1831.

PROGRAMME, MADRAS SPRING MEETING, 1831.

at all. The wild "jack" as hunted in Madras is, contrary to usual conviction, by no means an unworthy substitute for the fox, and he usually takes a lot of bringing to hand.

Owing to the impossibility of keeping hounds through the hot weather, they are always disposed of at the end of the season, and a fresh pack of twenty to fifty couples is got out from home. They arrive early in October, and hunting generally commences about the first week of the following month. Hounds are unfortunately exotics on the plains of India, and even in the cold weather they are subject to all sorts of ills to which an English huntsman is a stranger. The first of these is *piroplamosis*, or tick disease, which is caused by the bite of a certain kind of infected tick, much in the same way that malaria in a human being is caused by the bite of an infected *anopheles* mosquito. The disease only made its appearance within the last twenty years, and for a long time it was an enigma, but its cause was diagnosed about seven or eight years ago, and after many experiments a cure has at last been found in "neo-salvarsan," which is injected intravenously. Before this discovery practically all hounds which got the disease never recovered.

The present kennels at the Adyar—about 5 miles distant from Madras—erected in 1908, are specially designed to exclude ticks, as no woodwork enters into their construction. No benches or straw are used, as both of these were found to harbour ticks, and hounds are bedded on a stone slab floor strewn with coir fibre, which give rise to no ill-effects, and kennel lameness is unknown.

Though the maintenance of the pack and the condition under which it is hunted are full of difficulties, the results nevertheless fully justify the trouble, as good "jacks" are plentiful, and hounds with nothing in the way of fences to stop them can, with a servicable scent, fairly race. Though hounds are seldom out for more than three hours, they, horses, and riders, have usually had, in a climate like that of Madras, quite enough by the time they get back to their van, which takes them to and from their fixtures, the farthest being about 10 miles distant from kennels.

THE OOTACAMUND HOUNDS

There seems to be no chance of finding out with any certainty when hunting first started on the Nilgiri Hills. In Sir Frederick Price's book, "The History of Ootacamund," there are a few pages on the subject, and he says that "a form of hunting jackals with long dogs was practised as far back as 1829," but the first pack of foxhounds was not taken there until 1844, by Sir Thomas Peyton. He hunted the country for a couple of years. but the pack was sold in 1846, as, in the opinion of Mr. Mostyn Owen, "a particularly bold and accomplished horseman," the country was entirely unsuitable for riding over, on account of the steepness of the hills and the danger of getting bogged. After a lapse of nearly ten years the 74th Highlanders, who were stationed at Wellington, 10 miles from "Ooty," brought a few foxhounds, and were in the habit of bringing them out on Saturdays for a day on the downs. It was entirely a regimental affair, as the "Ooty" people do not appear to have been out with the pack. A few years later—1859—the 60th Rifles attempted hunting, with a "Bobbery" pack, but they made no scientific efforts, for if the pack failed to find a drag was laid. These are all the notes that one can find about hunting in the early days.

In 1864 Mr. Dalziell's pack of foxhounds was sent up from Madras, and it was hunted by Colonel Primrose. For three successive seasons these hounds spent the hot weather season on the hills, and were hunted over the downs. The first attempt at a subscription pack was started in 1867 by Captain Fitzgerald, of the 16th Lancers, but owing to lack of funds the pack was sold off, and a Mr. Minchin hunted a mixed draft for a year or two. Mr. Breeks, a Collector of the Nilgiris, revived the waning interest in hunting in 1869, but the fortunes of the young hunt were very fluctuating until 1874, when Major Bob Jago, who is considered the father of the Oootacamund Hunt, set to work to put things on a business footing. The Government, however, seems to have thought that he spent too much time with the hounds, and he had accordingly to resign the Mastership. In 1877 Major Elmhirst, who was aide-de-camp to Lord Roberts, hunted the pack, but there were many difficulties to be met, no one in "Ooty" caring about hunting, and subscriptions being very small. The pack was almost an unmanageable one, as it had come from nearly every kennel in England, so at the end of 1877 it was sold. In 1878 another one was brought out from home, and there was a lot of unpleasantness, as a Mr. Ouchterlony, who had advanced the money for the purchase of the draft, insisted on being considered a joint-Master with Major E. C. P. Pigott. The hunt apparently struggled on with varying fortunes, but there is no record which can be found of what the sport was like. Before 1889 hounds were benched in various places, but in the year mentioned the existing kennels were built at a cost of about Rs. 4,000, so one can gather that a more general interest was taken, and that subscriptions were better than during the first few years.

The particulars already given are exceedingly meagre, and there is hardly any idea to be gathered as to whether sport was good or not. Major Elmhirst, better known as "Brooksby," is the only one who gives a glimpse of what sport the mid-Victorians enjoyed on the grassy downs of "Ooty," and he waxes eloquent about the country. There is somewhere a long account of the two years when he acted as Master, but he was not considered a good huntsman, and though he admits that the hounds were an unmanageable lot, it may have been that he was denied the gift—for it is a gift, and a rare one at that—of hunting them. Here is his description of the country: "The jackal is here in wondrous stoutness and abundance, and merrily and happily do the hill-sides ring in his honour; (believe me, my friends of High Leicestershire and Owston Wood never had a stouter varmint than we have on the Nilgiris). . . . The meet is not a lengthy proceeding. . . . We move on to draw, not a sign of blackthorn or privet, nothing but the bare hill-sides. This is how we find our jack; at least this is how we get our runs, for if we can thus hit on one, we start close upon our game, and he will make straight as an arrow, and well-nigh as swift, to his point. You may draw the *sholas*, as the thickly timbered glens that nestle on the mountain-sides are termed, but they are very dense, and once in them hounds are likely to remain until it is time to go home again." In parenthesis one may remark that it has of late years been much more the custom to draw these *sholas*, and a great many of them—briers, for instance—are not nearly so dense as they used to be. There are still some woods that are rightly dreaded. Cairn Hill is a notable example, and if a jack makes that his point, good-bye to all further sport for two, three, or even four hours. Once in them it is a herculean task to get hounds together again, for the woods abound in every sort of illicit game. But to continue "Brooksby's" description: "A find in this open country is necessarily a view. 'There he goes! there he goes!' It is no slight luck that hounds dash across the line at once, catch it up with a swing, and are off with a noise and sparkle that do them credit. Each member of the pack is straining on a scent which they must be able to see, for there is no stopping to smell. . . . Hounds breast the hill with the jack not fifty yards before them; but don't imagine that he is beaten, or even slow; it is merely a nonchalant way of his: he can make that fifty or hundred yards at any moment he chooses, and to toy with his annoyers appears to be but a pleasant pastime to this sinewy traveller. Now is the time for riding to catch 'em; and catch 'em you can't; for the hounds can stream up a hill much quicker than you can mount it, although you use your spurs so wisely and well. If you can keep the leading hounds in sight you must be riding a well-bred one, so struggle on as best you can; hustle up each brow of the hill and down each declivity, and skirt the bogs, and mark carefully the crossings. We have been running half an hour, but there is no slackening of speed, when the jack enters a *shola*. . . . 'Hark! Holloa! there he is; a hundred yards ahead!' A hound tears along at his brush; but he is absolutely too tired to seize it, and the jack pops into a welcome earth under his very nose. . . . This is a wild, sporting country, where the foxhound is not wasted, where game is plentiful, and the problem of scent is (locally) solved. To gallop over this virgin turf is a delight, and the sport is genuine and constant."

It was during the five years of Colonel Lawley's (now Lord Wenlock) Mastership—1891-5—that the Ootacamund Hunt began to be famous, and though it again suffered partial eclipses until 1902, owing to a rapid change of Masterships, it never again was the struggling affair it has been, and it seems unthinkable that hunting should ever come to an end. In 1900 the downs were made into a huge forest preserve, and named the "Wenlock

SNIPE SHOOTING.

1 AND 2. POLO AT BANGALORE. 3. HURDLE RACING, BANGALORE. 4. CAVALRY POLO GROUND, BANGALORE.

Photos by F. Wecksler.

Downs"; this area is more than 40 square miles in extent, and it constitutes the extent of the hunting-ground. In the words of Sir Frederick Price, the life of the jack within this space is "as that of the Grand Lama, except for the high privilege of dying in the course of nature or by the jaws of a pack of fox-hounds."

Captain Fife, who hunted the hounds from 1902 to 1905, was the first Master to meet more than twice a week, and he frequently had a bye-day. This was the thin end of the wedge, and when he was succeeded by Captain Heseltine (1906-9) it became the rule to meet four days in the week. This custom was kept up until 1914, when Captain Bailward (since killed in action) was at the head of affairs, and it was decided to reduce the number to three. Captain Fife was the first Master to consider seriously the question of breeding hounds in "Ooty." It has been attempted once or twice before without much success; puppies never having been put out to walk. His efforts met with such remarkable success that at the pesent time (1915) there are almost twenty couples of country-bred hounds in the kennels. Captain Heseltine, who was the best Master we have ever had, says this about country-breds: "The best and quickest wear-and-tear hounds we have are the country-breds. They go with less exertion up hill, and suffer little harm coming down." As to their speed, they are, if anything, a little too fast, and even sometimes have to be drafted for this reason. They are staunch, and have undoubtedly as good noses as the best imported hounds.

BANGALORE RACECOURSE.

Photo by F. Wecksler.

This is the only hunt that can boast of a woman kennel-superintendent. Mrs. Leech was given the post in 1909, and a more devoted and careful official could not be found anywhere. Having served under such undoubtedly good huntsmen as Captains Heseltine, Palmer, and Meyrick, she has acquired a great knowledge of hounds, and in all cases of sickness or accidents she nurses them with unfailing devotion.

There are at present forty couples in kennels composed of the best blood from the Belvoir, Bicester, Duke of Buccleuch's, Vale of White Horse, and Lord Leconfield's pack, together with twenty couples of country-breds.

YACHTING IN MALABAR

Yachting has always flourished to some extent on the beautiful Malabar coast, its chief centre being at Cochin, which, with its fine natural harbour and estuary, offers peculiar facilities for this sport. Cruising has never much been indulged in, and the chief interest centres in the racing of small craft, though His Highness the Rajah of Cochin has always been keenly interested in sailing for its own sake, and is now having a new cruiser built.

In Cochin there has been a certain amount of racing for very many years, but the boats were of all sorts and sizes. In 1896 the sport received a much-needed fillip by the construction of a modern boat, *Primrose*, by Mr. A. S. Napier, which beat the hitherto undefeated Rajah's boat, and aroused great interest in the sport, as was proved by the appearance of several new boats and owners.

The fleet, however, continued to be of a very heterogeneous character, and the boats, which ranged from three-tonners down to C.B. dinghies of the "Water-wag" type, raced under the prescribed 1888 length and sail area rate, and the fact that they still do so in the mixed class race speaks volumes for the wonderful merit of that now obselete system of measurement. In 1908 another chance came, and two new boats made their appearance. One was designed by Mr. Wiston Hope (*Ruby*) for Mr. Davey, of Alleppey, a great supporter of sailing, and the other was a Yankee creation of about the same size (half rating), built and owned by Mr. P. B. Thomas; and at Calicut, farther to the north, on the Malabar coast, this boat (*Gwen*) easily defeated the whole fleet.

The Cup course at Cochin is triangular, one of the marks being a buoy in the middle of the gut, or entrance, to the estuary. There is nearly always a considerable "chop" there, and when the wind meets the tide there is quite a nasty sea. Farther up the estuary the tide runs strongly, and with the prevailing high winds in March, when the principal regatta is usually held, there is often a good deal of rough water. These circumstances have led to the general adoption of a type of boat more suitable for

BOATING ON THE ADYAR.

exposed waters, and *Ruby* was of this class. *Gwen* was a lightly built C.B. craft of the extreme skimming-dish type, and her success revolutionized racing. The following year a beautiful boat, *Kalyani I*, designed by Mr. Linton Hope, and built in England for His Highness the Rajah, led the fleet. She was defeated in the following year by a boat (*Fiona*) of very similar lines, built by Messrs. J. T. Lewis and Colin White at Mandapam, in the extreme south of the Madras Presidency. She was, in turn, beaten in the following year by a wonderful boat, *Kathleen*, designed by Mr. Lewis and owned by Mr. White, which for three years proved more than a match for every opponent, including a new boat, *Kalyani II*, specially constructed for this race by Mr. Linton Hope, and built in England by Turk.

The success of these boats has led to the adoption of a very smart one-design class of a somewhat similar type, but drier and more capable, and interest is now chiefly centred in them.

Racing, which was for many years managed in rather a haphazard way, is now in the hands of the Malabar Sailing Club, and is very well looked after.

At Alleppey, some 30 miles south of Cochin, there is an annual regatta, which is usually attended by most of the Cochin boats, which cruise down the backwaters there, in company with the regatta at Cochin. At Alleppey an enormous land-locked breakwater, with no bad current or tides, gives a triangular course of more than 20 miles, and racing conditions for the prevailing type of boats are as near perfection as possible. Elsewhere there is sailing at Mangalore, Quilon, and other places on the coast, and interest in the sport is increasing.

THE MADRAS SAILING CLUB

This Club fleet consists of eight "Waterwags" similar to the Dublin Kingstown Bay wag class, and they have an overall length of 25 ft., a beam of 5 ft., and carry 117 square feet of canvas, and two Tom-tit class boats. Under construction are four boats of the Bembridge type. Racing is very keen, and is carried on from January to October. The races are sailed partly inside and partly outside the harbour, and His Excellency Lord Pentland, who is very keen on the sport, is the present Commodore of the Club.

1. OOTACAMUND GYMKHANA CLUB.

2. OOTACAMUND HUNT CLUB MEET.

Photos by Willie Burke.

3. GOLF LINKS ON THE "OOTY" DOWNS.

1. THE CHURCH, POLLIBETTA. 2. THE CHURCH, POLLIBETTA (INTERIOR).

THE PROVINCE OF COORG

THERE does not appear to be in existence any really authentic history of the Province of Coorg of any earlier date than the beginning of the seventeenth century, although traditions, based largely upon inscriptions found upon stones, give an insight into the troublous times which had fallen upon the province and upon the adjoining native State of Mysore during the six or seven centuries prior to that time. Mysore, for instance, had been subdued by the powerful Gangas as early as the second or third century of the Christian era, and it seems tolerably certain that Coorg was subject to the same authority between—approximately—the years 840 and 950. It was not long after this time that the Gangas were overthrown by the Cholas, who, in turn, were defeated by the Hoysalas, and the last-named tribe, after waging numerous wars (in most of which they were successful), became merged in the Vizayanagar empire. This rule was not destined to continue for long, as the Rajah of Mysore asserted his claims, and made Seringapatam his capital, leaving the Province of Coorg to be occupied by some prominent prince of the Changalvas, who had been the principal opponents of the Hoysalas. This took place about the year 1610, and the individual who caused himself to be installed as rajah was a prince of the Bedanurs, who had taken up their abode in the neighbourhood of Mercara. Events passed with tranquillity until Hyder Ali became a power in Mysore, and, further, claimed authority over Coorg. His claims were resisted by the rajahs of the latter province, who retained their independence until a dispute occurred in 1770 as to the right of succession. This was the commencement of a series of troubles, and the province, sometimes in the hands of the Coorg rajahs themselves, or again dominated by the rule of Hyder Ali or his son Tipu, became the scene of such unexampled sensuality and tyranny that the English Government intervened about the year 1830, with the result that the Coorg people expressed a wish to be placed under British rule. The Government of India thereupon accepted direct control in 1834, and a Commissioner and Superintendent were appointed forthwith.

After this brief reference to the historical associations of the province, it will be well to notice the geographical and natural features of the country. It is but a speck on the map of India, the total area not exceeding 1,582 square miles. The land is of a very undulating character, with an average altitude of about 3,000 ft. above the level of the sea, and it is enclosed by ranges of hills which reach a height of some 5,800 ft. It is bounded on the western side by the Western Ghauts, which separate it from the districts of South Canara and Malabar, while it abuts upon the State of Mysore upon the northern and eastern sides. Some thousands of acres of dense jungle were cleared many years ago in order that coffee might be cultivated, but the fertility of the soil is so great that scarcely any impression seems to have been made upon the forest. The largest river is the Cauvery, which is renowned for its sanctity and its picturesque scenery, and, together with its numerous tributaries, it drains a very large tract of land in Mysore as well as in Coorg. The climate is marked by considerable humidity, especially in the valleys, where mists and fogs prevail at times, while the average annual rainfall varies from 42 in. at Fraserpet to 209 in. at Bhagamandala. The temperature is moderate throughout the Province, the average thermometer at Mercara, by way of example, registering 73° F. in May, 67° in July, and 65° in December.

From a consideration of the soil, climate, and rainfall of a country it is a natural transition to refer to its agricultural products and general merchandise; and trade statistics, when correctly compiled, are an unerring guide to the progress or retrogression of a country. It may at once be admitted frankly that the establishment of any definite systems of commerce was an absolute impossibility during the long period of unsettlement under the rajahs when there was almost continuous warfare with Hyder Ali, Tipu, and other leaders, and when the people themselves were subjected to all kinds of tyranny, persecution, and misery at the hands of their rulers.

Rice was the principal product of the country at the commencement of the nineteenth century, although some attention was paid to the growing of cardamoms, pepper, and other crops. The whole of the revenue of Coorg—including 600 square miles of the Sulya and Puttur *taluqs* subsequently merged in South Canara—in the year 1817 amounted to Rs. 6,21,600, derived principally from land and house taxes, excise, cardamoms (then a State monopoly), and rice.

The advent of British rule in 1834 completely altered the state of affairs in the province; confidence took the place of distrust, peace reigned instead of war, and the people were encouraged to cultivate the land for their own benefit.

THE CLUB, MERCARA.

Coffee had been grown upon small plots of land for a number of years; in fact, during the rule of the rajahs it was not unknown, although those individuals who had a few plants lived in continual dread of those disasters which had befallen the plants in other districts. The time had arrived, however, when Europeans were determined to throw their energies into the production of this crop, and the first estate was opened near Mercara in the year 1854. It was evident that this question was being taken up seriously, as, within a few years, no fewer than 70,000 acres of land had been planted with coffee. The rapid expansion of the coffee industry is illustrated by the fact that whereas only 579 tons were exported in 1857, the amount had risen to 3,000 tons in 1867, and only nine years later the total had reached 4,880 tons. This prosperity was not, however, allowed to continue without a check, as disease appeared upon many estates in 1870 and 1871, and scores of plantations which had hitherto been yielding handsome returns were now literally ruined. These enemies, consisting of the "borer" and one or more of the half-dozen species of bug, brought dismay to the hearts of many planters, but so dauntless was their courage that statistics published in 1877 showed that "the total holdings and area planted were respectively 84,344 and 44,150 acres against 77,390 and 32,361 acres in 1870." The quinquennial period from 1878 to 1883 will be remembered in Coorg for the very flourishing state of the coffee industry, and for the most satisfactory prices which planters were obtaining. The high-water mark of prosperity seems to have been reached, as the year 1884 ushered in a remarkably sudden depression in the market. The price of manufactured Coorg coffee fell fully 40 per cent., owing to over-production and to the competition of the Brazilian crop. Native planters were the first to feel the effects, as their capital consisted almost entirely of money borrowed from *sowcars* at a ruinous rate of interest, which they were unable to pay; but by the year 1889 several estates belonging to European planters were either wholly or partially abandoned. A shortage of the supply from Brazil in 1890 was accompanied by a disposition on the part of capitalists to speculate in coffee, and these facts caused an improvement in prices, consignments changing hands in London at about ninety shillings a hundredweight. The appearance of insect pests in the plantations of Ceylon assisted in maintaining high values for Coorg coffee up to the year 1893, but a constant glut in the market —especially owing to parcels from Brazil —caused a gradual downward movement in price until 1900, when Indian coffee only returned about forty-seven shillings a hundredweight. Disease and insect pests were not at this juncture either so numerous or destructive as formerly, and notwithstanding the decline in value the annual exports began to increase. Statistics show that for five years ending in 1903 the average annual value of coffee sent out of Coorg was Rs. 20,98,440, and that the amount for the next quinquennial period was Rs. 23,02,200. The coffee in-

1. IN THE FORT, MERCARA. 2, 3, AND 4. VIEWS OF MERCARA.

dustry still survives in Coorg, and there are about eighty estates whose owners or agents are connected with the Coorg Planters' Association, of which the president is Mr. C. E. Murray-Aynsley. Scientific methods of cultivation have been adopted, and a systematic course of manuring with suitable fertilizers is followed by almost every individual planter.

The principal exports—exclusive of coffee—are rice, cardamoms, oranges, sandal-wood, timber, hides, and horns. When the coffee industry was in a prosperous state it was observable that a large number of rice-fields remained uncultivated, as coolies had been tempted by the prospect of gaining more money by work in the plantations; and when coffee was declining in quantity and value, statistics showed that the area under rice increased from 73,015 acres to 77,589 acres, and that the average acreage for five years ending in 1908 was as much as 80,034. Five varieties of paddy are grown in Coorg, the most common, especially in South Coorg, being the *biliana*, or *dodda batta*, which produces white rice; while the *sanna batta*—a table rice—is grown in small quantities by well-to-do people. The Revenue and Land Record Department of Coorg have, in recent years, conducted a number of experiments in the cultivation of paddy, and their reports are to the effect that the cost of production varies very considerably owing to the nature of the land and to the amount of water obtained either by rainfall or irrigation. It is, however, stated that the expenses of manuring, ploughing, rearing, and transplanting seedlings, weeding and harvesting, amount, on an average, to Rs. 25 an acre, and that a good crop may be expected to produce about 1,620 seers (a seer is about 2 lb. weight) to the acre, while a specially good harvest may return rather more than 2,000 seers.

THE CLUB, POLLIBETTA.

Oranges are usually grown from seed, and the young plants are not put out in the fields until they are three years of age, when they are placed in pits containing good soil, and even then a period of eight or ten years must elapse before any fruit can be gathered. The growing of oranges—and, indeed, of all kinds of perishable fruits—is most seriously handicapped in Coorg owing to the absence of facilities for quick transport, the nearest railway station from any point on the borders of the province being fully 60 miles distant. It is true that a very small percentage is sold in some of the local weekly markets, but nearly the entire crop is disposed of at wholesale rates in Bangalore or Mysore. Agricultural economists in Europe and elsewhere have for a number of years been preaching the doctrine of co-operation, under which, it is urged, the highest prices of the best markets would, with a comparatively insignificant deduction for expenses, reach the hands of the actual producers. The value of exported fruits has been increasing gradually, and an average for five recent years works out at more than Rs. 16,000 annually.

Cardamoms and spices are grown in evergreen forests of the Western Ghauts (in areas specially granted for such purpose), or on lands formerly acquired for coffee cultivation, but which were never planted on account of the failure of that crop on similar lands in this part of Coorg. Cultivators now complain that the expenses of rearing, harvesting, and transport are so heavy that it is extremely unlikely that the acreage will be increased. Between the years 1904 and 1905 the value of the exported consignments was Rs. 41,500, but the average for the five years ending with the season 1908-9 was only Rs. 27,240. The produce is generally purchased by local merchants. Sandal-wood to the value of Rs. 1,17,980; timber of various kinds worth Rs. 97,940; and grain and pulse averaging Rs. 2,76,000, are among the remaining exports.

A very great change came over the province after British control was established, and one of the most important signs of progress was the construction of hard roads suitable for any vehicular traffic, and this was a particularly welcome boon to the inhabitants, as it seemed to have been part of the settled policy of each of the rajahs to keep the province in as inaccessible a state as possible.

The principal trade centres are Mercara and Virajpet, to which municipal government has been granted. Important markets are held at these places, and smaller ones at Sidapur, Suntikoppa, Gonikoppal, Somwarpet, and Sanivarasante.

With the exception of the manufacture of a small quantity of coarse cloth, there are practically no industries in Coorg, as nearly 80 per cent. of the population are concerned in agricultural pursuits. In addition to general labourers and coolies on coffee estates, there are a few dealers and workers in gold, and about two hundred persons are employed as makers and traders in baskets, mats, fans, screens, and brooms. Educational advantages were available at an early date, an Anglo-vernacular school having been opened in Mercara in 1834. Since that time, chiefly through the initiative of British authorities, other schools have been commenced in the principal villages, and they have been well supported by the people.

These notes would be incomplete without a short reference to places of interest in this beautiful little province. In Mercara, which is admittedly surrounded by most picturesque scenery, the palace in the former fort—now used as public offices and the residential quarters of the Commissioner—and the mausoleums of the old rajahs are the only places of historical interest. Another former palace of the old rajahs, which resembles a large farmhouse (now used for circuit purposes), is situated in the Nalknad, about 24 miles from Mercara. The temples are of ordinary structure, and of no special architectural interest. Coorg, however, can claim a unique position in India in possessing the so-called "Royal Ditches," locally known as the *Aramanekadangas*, which, as a matter of fact, are trenches, often 30 ft. or more in depth, but averaging about 15 ft., and extending for hundreds of miles throughout the province. They pass over the highest mountains and through densest forest (whether the ground is rocky or soft), and diverge in all directions, with no fewer than four of these occasionally meeting at one place. There is no historical record about their origin or purpose, though it is surmised that they were intended as works of defence, and even Time has left little impression on this gigantic work. Of not less interest are the "dolmen" (cromlechs) of the neolithic age, which are similar to those in other parts of India, and resembling those in France and Wales.

The province is rich as regards fauna, and it is often visited by *shikars* from distant places for elephants, tigers, and bison. Birds are met with everywhere, especially parrots, of which there are five species. The flora is most luxurious, and it supplies the Forest Department with valuable timber trees of all kinds, of which sandal-wood, a Government monopoly, yields the largest part of the revenue.

ATTUR ESTATE.

1. Bungalow. 2. A View from the Bungalow. 3. View of Coffee.

ABIAL

The claim that this is one of the oldest coffee estates in South India receives some confirmation from the fact that a portion of it was planted as long ago as 1867. One of the partners, Mr. G. K. Martin, arrived in India in the year 1869, and he made yearly additions to the area under cultivation, with the result that there are now 230 acres under coffee, only 30 acres of which are nonproductive. The other partner, Mr. W. E. Tweedie, is a member of the Committee of the Coorg Planters' Association, and he has now full control of the property, as Mr. Martin has retired from any active part in the management. A dressing of manure is applied annually, and the yield of coffee has been nearly doubled since that practice came into operation. Fully matured trees on 200 acres of land have returned 60 tons a year for the past five years. Two lines for coolies have been erected, together with numerous other buildings, and employment is found for about 150 hands.

ATTUR

The coffee plantation on the Attur estate, in the province of Coorg, is an exceedingly productive one, the average annual yield for the five years from 1910-14 being the eminently satisfactory one of

5 cwt. to the acre. The property is 300 acres in extent, and it has been managed by Mr. C. G. Maclean for the past sixteen years. The trees in full bearing cover an area of 200 acres—some of these having been planted in the year 1884—while there are 50 acres of young bushes from which a crop has not yet been obtained. The pulping-machine is worked by bullocks, but a sufficiency of water-power can be obtained whenever required.

The owner—Mr. A. H. Wood—has a very pretty bungalow, and the property is about 3,300 ft. above the level of the sea.

Mercara and Suntikoppa are the nearest post and telegraph offices respectively.

BAJEECOLLIE ESTATE.

1. THE BUNGALOW. 2. PULPING-HOUSE. 3. PADDY LANDS AND THRESHING FLOOR.

BAJEECOLLIE

The practice of intensive cultivation has a very staunch supporter in Lieut.-Colonel John Logan, V.D., the owner of Bajeecollie and other estates in the Yedenalknad *taluq* in the southern portion of the province of Coorg. This gentleman has held Bajeecollie since 1879, and he has opened up and developed his properties in such a practical manner that his reputation as an agriculturist has spread throughout the whole of Southern India. This estate—which includes Wodderhulli—is 500 acres in extent, and the principal crops are coffee (300 acres), paddy (40 acres), rubber, and cinchonas. The planting of coffee, which was commenced in 1880, formed a portion of each year's work until 1914, and all of the bushes have the advantage of plenty of mixed shade. Protection is thus afforded to the growing trees, and it is generally believed that the latter are, under these circumstances, far less liable to be attacked by insect pests.

Bushes of fair average quality yield from 2 cwt. to 4 cwt. of berries to the acre in each year; a few others have given about 5 cwt., but during recent harvests an average weight of 5 cwt. has been reached, while as great a quantity as 6 cwt. has been obtained. Driving power for the machinery in the pulping-house is obtained from the use of a water-wheel, and an excellent supply of water for washing the berries and for general purposes is stored in tanks. The manufactured coffee is sold in London, and the very satisfactory quality of the consignments ensures high prices.

The cultivation of paddy has had close attention paid to it, and the yield has been considerably increased of late years.

Pepper-vines have been inter-planted with coffee, and about 4½ tons of produce are gathered annually. The rubber-trees are not always successfully grown at so high an elevation as 3,000 ft., but Colonel Logan hopes to have some fair average yields. Cultivation of the sugar-cane has been tried, and experiments are now being conducted with ginger, arrowroot, and tapioca with fair results.

Colonel Logan is a firm believer in high cultivation of his land, and during an experience extending over many years he has proved that money spent in this way and in the application of suitable manures is a splendid investment. He is the owner, too, of the Sampajiecollie estate of 250 acres, of which 140 acres have been planted with coffee-trees. This property is marked by the same superior methods of cultivation as are seen at Bajeecollie, and similar results are obtained from the annual harvests.

The entire management of the estate is undertaken by Colonel Logan, and he employs about 250 coolies. Writers are not kept on the permanent staff, as Mysore "maistries" are found to be far more satisfactory.

There is a nice bungalow on each estate, and the post and telegraph offices at Sidapur are about 4 miles distant from each property.

It would be a marked omission to close these notes without reference being made to the most important services which have been rendered by Colonel Logan to the Volunteer movement in Mysore. A meeting was held at this gentleman's residence on the Pollibetta estate, in the province of Coorg, in the year 1878, to discuss the advisability of raising a corps of volunteers, and although application was made to the Government for assistance, the matter had to be left in abeyance. The spirit of enthusiasm which had been aroused was not, however, permitted to lie dormant ; in fact, it was spreading silently but surely, and in August 1851, at the meeting which took place in South Coorg, the name of John Logan was the first to be enrolled. He had the honour of being appointed captain of "B" company on the 3rd of that month. (The enrolment of "A" company had taken place the day previously at Mercara.) Those who had at this time joined the movement were affiliated with the Bangalore Rifle Volunteers, but certain changes were made, and the "Coorg and Mysore Rifles" became the title of the new company. Captain Logan was appointed Commandant, with rank of Major, on the 1st June 1891, and a notice, published in the *Gazette* of India on the 10th June 1905, stated that "Major Logan's resignation of his commission had been accepted, and he was granted the honorary rank of Lieut.-Colonel with permission to wear the uniform of the Coorg and Mysore Rifles."

It may be added that the same businesslike characteristics and sound, practical common sense which were exhibited by the Colonel in his agricultural pursuits were manifested with the same force in the Volunteer cause, and he endeared himself to all in his command, retiring amid the most profound expressions of regret.

BELLARIMOTTI

Some 50 coolies are constantly at work upon this estate of 230 acres, which was purchased by Mr. T. J. K. Hext in the year 1911. About 120 acres of coffee have been planted under natural and artificially grown shade, and the crop for the season 1913-14 yielded no less than 20 tons. The property is situated at an elevation of some 3,500 ft , and it enjoys an average annual rainfall of nearly 120 in. The important town of Mercara is only 15 miles distant.

BILIKERI

This property is about 3.700 ft. above the level of the sea, and is situated about half a dozen miles from the post and telegraph offices at Somwarpet, in the northern portion of Coorg. About 130 acres were planted with coffee between the years 1893 and 1912, and the average amount of the crop has been about 3c tons during those years. The owner, Mr. H. C. Wood, took over the property in 1896, and he gives personal attention to the management of the farm, and he controls every detail of work connected with the plantation, from the rearing of the young trees to the time when the leaves are sent to Tellicherry to be cured.

D. CHENNABASAPPA

Somwarpet, an important township in the northern portion of the province of Coorg, was a mere hamlet at the beginning of the nineteenth century, when certain members of the Chennabasappa family migrated there from the State of Mysore. The great-grandfather of Mr. D. Chennabasappa commenced business in early life, and so assiduous was he that he soon became the owner of a considerable quantity of land. On his death the property was divided among his children, and the share which fell to the lot of the late father of Mr. D. Chennabasappa consisted of two estates with an aggregate of 550 acres.

The father purchased other properties

D. CHENNABASAPPA.
1. Bungalow. 2 View of Coffee.

in various parts of the district, and there are now 1,500 acres (planted with coffee-bushes), and between 200 and 300 acres of jungle. The estate is, in reality, a group of eight separate holdings, all of which are situated on a main Government road between Mercara and Somwarpet. The whole of the land is well manured each year, and the average annual crop of berries is about 560 lb. to the acre, which is equivalent to 100 tons of "parchment" coffee from all the trees. There is pulping machinery (worked by hand) on each of the three principal properties, namely, Boothencadu, Kusbur, and Sunticoppa, and the coffee grown upon the remaining five properties is brought to these three places. The drying process is carried out on the estate, and the parchment coffee is sent to coastal factories to be cured. The fluctuations of the market are such that the owner is occasionally able to secure better prices for the manufactured produce in India than in England, but in the majority of instances the bulk is consigned direct to London for sale. About 1,000 coolies are employed annually, but this number is considerably augmented during busy seasons. A superintendent is resident upon each of the eight properties, but the general management of the whole estate devolves upon the owner himself. Mr. Chennabasappa has built a very nice bungalow at Somwarpet, where he resides, and he has, further, constructed another dwelling-house on the Kusbur property.

This gentleman holds the position of *patel*, or headman of the town of Somwarpet, where he has acquired a considerable number of private houses. He is owner, too, of paddy fields, and of a strip of land upon which the experiments are being conducted in the cultivation of cardamoms.

Three generations of the Chennabasappa family have identified themselves very closely with the progress of Somwarpet, and it is not too much to say that they have been largely instrumental in securing very great improvements in the town. During the long period of their residence there they have been foremost in the establishment and support of many charities, but particular reference may be made to the construction of a modern primary school for boys and of the building of a large tank for the storage of water for the townspeople, both of which works have to be credited to the generosity of the subject of these notes.

CLOSEBURN

This estate is situated about 7 miles distant from the town of Mercara, in the province of Coorg, where there are post and telegraph offices. Practically all of the estates in this province consist of rich, loamy soils, which are very suitable for the growth of coffee and tea, and the Closeburn property is no exception to the rule. It is 250 acres in extent, and 150 acres of this area are planted with fully matured coffee-bushes, some of which are now forty years of age. There is an abundance of water for all purposes, and shelter trees have been provided in all parts of the estate. An average harvest yields 20 tons of coffee, and the beans are pulped, washed, dried, and hulled in the home buildings, the excellent plant being driven by an oil-engine.

It is intended to plant cardamoms, but this is only a side-line to the coffee industry.

The owner of the estate is Mr. W. M. Ball, the energetic honorary secretary of the Coorg Planters' Association, and he employs some 100 coolies.

A golf course has been opened on the estate, and the links are a distinct attraction for planters of the neighbourhood.

COORG COFFEE ESTATES COMPANY, LTD.

The headquarters of this company are at Pollibetta, in the province of Coorg, and Mr. E. L. Mahon, the general manager, has been thirty-four years as the representative in India of Messrs. Matheson & Co., Ltd., of 3 Lombard Street, London, E.C., who are the secretaries of the company. Coffee is cured and tinned on the estates—a small proportion only being roasted—and it is shipped direct to London for sale. The utmost care is taken to ensure absolute purity combined with first-class quality, and it is obvious that these objects have been attained, as several gold medals have been awarded to the company at shows in various parts of India. The company are, further, owners of sawmills and motor and joinery works, timber being purchased from the Government according to requirements.

COTA CADOO

Half a century has passed since coffee was first planted on this estate of 480 acres, which belongs to Messrs. A. C. and A. D. Campbell, for whom Mr. C. G. Maclean is manager. This gentleman has had more than thirty-five years' practical experience as a planter in the province of Coorg, and he has been most successful with coffee on this estate and upon others in which he is interested, either as owner or manager. Some 330 acres are producing coffee, and a small area is cropped with pepper in the coffee, while experiments have been made in the cultivation of rubber, sisal, and tea, but the results from these have not been sufficiently satisfactory to justify their continuance. An excellent supply of water, obtained from natural springs, is conserved in tanks, although the rainfall gives an annual amount of 75 in. All the coffee-bushes are protected by shelter trees from sun and storm, and the annual yield for the past four seasons has been about 70 tons. The machinery is up to date in every respect, and the plant in the two pulping-houses, and in the drying, hulling, and other chambers, is driven by a Hornsby steam-engine. The secret of successful planting operations is good cultivation of the land, and this includes the destruction of noxious weeds, the regulation of the amount of moisture in the soil, and the application of suitable manures Mr. Maclean pays very considerable attention to the selection of fertilizers, and the annual expenditure of fully Rs. 20 to the acre is money well spent.

The manager's exceedingly pretty bungalow is situated in a charming position, and it is only 7 miles distant from the important town of Mercara. Other buildings include stables, sheds, and stores, together with comfortable quarters for 400 coolies, although the usual number of hands employed is only about 300.

The breeding of cattle is not practised to any great extent in the Madras Presidency, but a few Nellore cows are kept at Cota Cadoo, and the strain is being improved by the use of a pure-bred Jersey bull.

COWRIEBETTA

This property of 294 acres formerly belonged jointly to Messrs. Matheson & Co., of 3 Lombard Street, London, E.C., and Mr. H. G. Grant, but a company—the Cowriebetta Estates, Ltd. — was formed in the year 1913, with Mr. Grant as general manager. The head offices are at Lombard Street, London, and the directors are John M. Macdonald and N. M. Macdonald.

This is one of the oldest coffee estates in the province of Coorg, planting having been commenced as long ago as 1876. The manager has always been a firm believer in high cultivation, but intensive agriculture is not of itself sufficient to secure a continuity of payable crops. A prime factor is the need of a good rich dark soil, which must be preserved in a clean state, and assisted from time to time by the application of suitable fertilizers. Efficiency and economy in management count for much, but even when all these aids to success are forthcoming, the planter still has to be on

COTA CADOO ESTATE.

1. Nellore Cows. 2, Bull. 3. Young Coffee. 4. Bungalow, 5. Drying-ground.

the watch for the appearance of any vegetable or insect pests which might ruin every one of his trees. That the Cowriebetta property is in able hands is evident from its generally prosperous appearance, as well as from the fact that for several years the annual harvest has brought in an average of 5½ cwt. of beans to the acre. There are 225 acres of coffee-bushes in full bearing, and the whole of this area is amply provided with trees for shelter purposes.

A few pepper-vines are grown between the coffee rows, and there are, in addition, some 30 acres of land set apart entirely for this crop. The young trees are very promising, while the older ones are doing remarkably well, adding very considerably to the revenue of the estate. A small rubber plantation—about 1½ acres in extent—has been opened.

The bungalow is commodious, and the very pretty exterior is greatly improved by the beauty of the foliage of the indigenous trees among which it stands. The estate is 3,500 ft. above the level of the sea, and it is only about 3 miles distant from the post and telegraphic offices at Pollibetta and Sidapur.

COWCOODY

This estate of 400 acres was purchased by Mr. L. Newcome in the year 1909, but it had been developed and had 40 acres of coffee-bushes upon it as long ago as 1874. At the present time there are 250 acres under coffee, of which 110 acres are fully matured trees; about 100 acres of forest have recently been felled and cleared, and subsequently planted, while of the remaining portion of the property 20 acres have been planted with cardamoms and 20 with paddy. Mr. Newcome has given much thought and attention to the question of planting, and he is strongly of opinion that bushes are in many cases placed too closely together and that space for proper development is thus denied them. He has therefore adopted a standard measurement of 8 ft. in any direction between the trees in his new clearings, experimentally.

Not a whit less important in the opinion of the owner is the necessity for shelter, and the whole of the plantation is now provided with ample shade. The ripe beans, or "cherries," as they are usually termed, have hitherto been pulped on the property by manual labour, but this practice is to be discontinued in favour of what is known as the "native" system, which is that only the stripping and drying processes will be carried out on the estate, and that the produce will be sent to a coastal factory to be peeled and cured prior to shipment to Havre or England. The average returns for the past three years have reached a total weight of 34 tons. Cardamoms have done well on the property, but the quantity of suitable land is very limited.

The outbuildings are of an extensive and durable character, having been constructed upon a foundation of stone. A small herd of about 30 cattle is kept for work on the estate.

Cowcoody is 3 miles distant from Hontsey, 34 miles from Mercara, and 7 miles from the post and telegraph offices at Somwarpet. About 200 hands are employed constantly.

CHOWHULLY

This compact little estate of 300 acres was acquired by Mr. Newcome in the year 1911, and it comprises 70 acres of coffee in full bearing, 30 acres of clearings, and about 10 acres of cardamoms. A novice would not fail to notice that the principal clause in the owner's agricultural creed is "Good cultivation," and there is abundant evidence that Mr. Newcome and Mr. G. M. Beville, the superintendent-in-charge, have, further, a thoroughly practical acquaintance with the management of plants from the nursery, through the various stages of transplanting, manuring, pruning, and picking. A sufficient amount of shelter has been provided for the protection of the bushes, and a total of 15 tons of coffee is gathered in each season. There is a very pretty bungalow on the property, and there are postal and telegraphic facilities similar to those enjoyed by the Cowcoody estate. Employment is given to some 100 coolies.

CULLALY

is another of Mr. Newcome's trim little properties, and its 90 acres of old coffee-bushes give an annual return of 20 tons. The whole estate is only 200 acres in extent, but there are 50 acres of clearings for coffee, and 3 acres of cardamoms planted in 1914, while the remaining portion is composed of grass land. About 80 hands are employed constantly. Mr. C. L. Comyns is superintendent here.

Exceedingly fine views of mountain and valley are obtained at this elevation of 3,200 ft., and the pretty bungalow is pleasantly situated in one of the most charming parts of the estate. The rainfall is regular, and does not exceed 70 in. in the course of the year.

IGOOR

This property was the seat of the old Igoor Polygar who offered considerable resistance to the forces of Colonel Wellesley (afterwards Duke of Wellington), after the defeat by the English of Tippoo Sultan, and remains of the old fortifications can be seen there to-day. Another interesting historical fact is that there are probably few other coffee estates in the State of Mysore which can show from records that planting was commenced so long ago as the year 1850. It comprises 750 acres; 100 acres are under coffee-trees in full bearing; there are 50 acres of cardamoms; while about 300 acres of the remainder consist of good jungle land, which will be cleared and developed in due course. Coffee gives an annual yield of 15 tons. The crop of cardamoms reaped in 1913-14 reached a total of 5,600 lb., and it realized 5s. a pound when sold in England.

The buildings include a comfortable bungalow, stores, and sheds, and a drying-house for cardamoms. Mr. Newcome purchased the estate in 1910, and he has the assistance of a European superintendent—Mr. R. P. M. Tipping. About 100 coolies are regularly employed.

The annual rainfall is about 140 in.

DEVERAH CADOO

The word "devara" (or devarha), meaning "holy," is applied alike to individuals or temples, or to places which are in some way associated with religious rites. It doubtless became a part of the name of this estate, as there are two temples in an adjacent piece of jungle. Deverah Cadoo formerly belonged to Messrs. Matheson & Co., of 3 Lombard Street, London, E.C., who sold it in 1881, and it was purchased in 1914 by Mr. Noel M. Scholfield, who was manager for several years.

This property has been well cultivated since its development thirty-five years ago, and its situation at an altitude of 3,100 ft. above sea-level, coupled with an annual rainfall of about 70 in., renders it exceedingly suitable for the growing of coffee of good flavour. There are 195 acres altogether, and a portion of the 153 acres now in

COWRIEBETTA ESTATES, LTD.

1. Pulping Vats and Drying-ground. 2. View of Coffee. 3. A View from the Estate. 4. The Bungalow.

COWCOODY.

1. Bungalow Grounds. 2. Bungalow. 3. Cardamoms. 4. Coffee.

DEVERAH CADOO.

1. Road leading to the Bungalow. 2. Bungalow. 3. Pulp-house and Drying Tables.

full bearing consists of trees which were planted prior to the year 1880. Mr. Scholfield appreciates the importance of having sufficient shade for his trees, which are maintained in a vigorous and profitable condition by the annual application in moderation of carefully selected manures. A fair average yield has been consistently obtained for a number of years, the estate records showing that not less than 4 cwt. of coffee-beans to the acre have been picked during each harvest for the past thirteen years.

Cattle are still used for providing the motor-power for the plant in the pulping and other processes carried out upon the estate, but the curing of the "parchment" takes place in the factory at Tellicherry. When the "made" coffee is not disposed of under the terms c.i.f. (which is very frequently the case), it is shipped to London for sale, where the consignments attract considerable attention and obtain excellent prices. Pepper was cultivated at one time at Deverah Cadoo, but the practice has now been discontinued. There is no fallow land on the estate, as every acre which can be cultivated has been given up to the extension of the coffee plantation.

Two bungalows have been erected on the property, which is 6 miles distant from the post and telegraphic offices at Polibetta, in the province of Coorg. Several species of native fauna—spotted deer predominating—are found on the estate.

ELIZA

The owner of this estate is Mr. H. R. Craig, but the management has, for a period of twenty-six years, been in the hands of Mr. H. T. Shaw, who has been in India since the year 1877. The successful working of the property is undoubtedly due to good cultivation and manuring of the land, backed up by close supervision on the part of the manager. Lime, potash, and soda are very desirable ingredients in a soil, and poonac mixed with wood-ash and bone-dust acts like a tonic when applied to coffee-plants, but experience has shown that a dressing of bones, poonac, and potash is peculiarly suitable for providing plant-food for the crops on the Eliza estate.

The property consists of 523 acres, of which 250 acres are planted with coffee, and some 50 acres with Ceara and Para rubber. The remaining portion of the estate was cultivated for coffee many years ago, but it was subsequently abandoned. By dint of hard work, however, much of this land has been reclaimed, and re-planting has taken place year by year up to 1896. Some trees in the plantation are more than fifty years of age, but they still contribute their full share to the annual harvest of beans. The yearly crop for the past decade has been about 4 cwt. to the acre, although fully 8 cwt. was obtained from some of the fields in the season 1913-14. All of the produce is sent via Tellicherry, for sale in London.

The buildings on the property consist of a pulping-house, sheds, and stores, and the motive-power for driving the machinery is obtained by the use of bullocks. There are two bungalows; one of them named "Tilly" was built in the early sixties; while the other, known as "Eliza," was constructed on a site near to the main road in the year 1882. The latter is more than usually attractive in character, and the beautifully carved jack-wood ceilings in several of the rooms are a unique feature in connection with it.

A small quantity of pepper is grown among the coffee-trees, and excellent results have been obtained. The rainfall is sufficient for all purposes, as from 60 in. to 65 in. have been recorded annually for many years past.

The coolies for whom constant employment is found are about 200 in number.

The Eliza estate is about 1 mile distant from the post and telegraphic offices at Pollibetta, in South Coorg.

THE ELK HILL COFFEE ESTATES, LTD.

This fine group of estates, situated on the north-eastern slopes of the Kodingi-Betta range of mountains, in the south-east portion of the province of Coorg, was, until May 1914, the sole property of Mr. James Chisholm, of Boroughfield, Edinburgh, Scotland, since which date the ownership has been transferred to the above company.

The first clearings on the land date back to the early sixties, when these dense forests were infested with elephants, tigers, panthers, and other wild animals, which included numerous sambur or elk, whence the property derives its name. The parts of the property next to the Government reserve forests are still occasionally visited by elephants, felines, and deer. The native name Kodagu Siriningipatna denotes a fortified position, and to this day the remains of *kadangas* (huge trenches), all converging on a common centre, where large ponds (called "tanks") existed, are to be seen, and at various times in the past buried temples and some treasure-trove have been unearthed.

In spite of the ups-and-downs to which all agricultural ventures are subject, the property grew and prospered until it reached the present area of some 1,300 odd acres, of which 1,000 acres are under coffee. There is still a little standing jungle, and the balance is under cultivation with rice, rubber, pepper, oranges, limes, plantains, guinea-grass, and fibres of almost every variety—truly a wonderfully fertile soil. Coffee, however, is the staple crop, the others being regarded as by-products, which, though they do not receive quite the same care as the coffee, still flourish.

The property is divided into two charges, which are respectively under the management of Messrs. J. Hume and P. G. Tipping, with assistants. There are no less than four fine bungalows, all situated on the side of this range, and at an elevation of some 3,500 ft., and commanding extensive and magnificent views to the north, east, and south, extending away into the Mysore State in the north, and to the Nilgiri ranges—some 90 miles distant—in the south.

The factories and buildings have been constantly kept up to date, and they are fitted with the latest machinery and lighted by electricity, which is generated on the spot.

On an average there are some 600 or more hands employed daily throughout the year. Amongst the natives the property is noted for the purity of the water, which springs from the hillsides and is conveyed through pipes to the lines, and to a fine swimming bath

FRASERPET FIBRE PLANTATION

This is one of the few estates in the province of Coorg devoted to the growing of sisal-trees of the highest quality, and it might be added that it was almost one of the first to be cultivated for this purpose About 140 acres had been planted prior to the year 1914, when arrangements were made for the immediate planting of a further area of 300 acres. Leaves which have already been plucked have measured fully 5 ft. across, and the average weight of each one has been about 1½ lb., this giving 5 per cent.

ELIZA AND PALETHODU ESTATES.

1 Bungalow, Eliza Estate. 2. View from the Bungalow. 3. Coffee.

ELIZA AND PALETHODU ESTATES.

1. Bungalow, Palethodu Estate. 2. Pulp-house and Barbeques. 3. View from Bungalow, Palethodu.

THE ELK HILL COFFEE ESTATES, LTD.

1, Elk Hill Bungalow, 2. Stores and Barbeques. 3. View from the Bungalow. 4. Fairlands Bungalow, of clean fibre. The leaves are sent to Calicut to be pressed, and the fibre is subsequently shipped to England. The manager is Mr. C. Elsee, who is assisted by Mr. J. B. Houchen.

HANCHI BETTA AND COWRI KADU

These two properties, comprising a total of about 300 acres, and usually referred to as the Hanchi Betta estates, are situated about 3 miles distant from the post and telegraph offices at Pollibetta, in the Yedenalknad taluq, in the south-eastern portion of the province of Coorg. They were purchased in the year 1881 by the father of the present owners —Messrs. G. C. Garrett and P. C. Garrett —and the greater portion had already been planted with coffee-trees. There are now 260 acres of fully matured trees, and about 40 acres of younger ones which are not yet in bearing, and all of these are protected by naturally grown or other shade trees. The annual crop from the estates averages about 40-50 tons, or nearly 4 cwt. to the acre, and this is passed through a pulper, the machinery of which is driven by bullock-power. The coffee is cured by Mr. L. King Church, Pullicoon Works, at Tellicherry, from where the finished product is shipped to London and other markets. A small quantity of pepper is also grown.

There is a general appearance of neatness and cleanliness about the estate, and this is noticeable in the buildings as on the land. There is no accumulation of rubbish; weeds are eradicated; the sheds, stores, and drying-grounds are kept in good order; and the steady manner in which the coolies discharge their duties is evidence of the close supervision and of the practical experience of the manager, Mr. G. C. Garrett.

The use of fertilizers is regarded as an essential to good crops, and every year's work includes the manuring of practically the whole of the estate.

There are two very pretty bungalows on the estate, and as they are situated amidst charming surroundings at an elevation of 3,400 ft. above the level of the sea, some exceedingly fine views are afforded. The average annual rainfall is about 65-75 in., and there is an abundant natural supply of exceptionally good water, which is a great factor with regard to a good class of labour.

HOPE

When the books of an estate show that 72 acres of coffee-trees returned no less than 49 tons of produce in a single season, one may be quite sure that the soil is rich, that it is in a high state of cultivation, and that the manager possesses an excellent practical knowledge of the detail work of planting. And yet these are the figures given for the year 1878-79 for the produce of the Hope estate, which is 2¼ miles distant from the post and telegraphic offices at Pollibetta, in the district of Coorg. It is probable that an expert agriculturist would describe an ideal soil for a coffee plantation as consisting of rich dark loam, together with silicious particles of disintegrated rocks, containing the chemical elements of plant food necessary for promoting a healthy and vigorous growth in the trees. This is a fair description of the characteristics of the soil on the Hope estate, which

HOPE ESTATE.

1. Bungalow—Front View. 2. Bungalow—Back View.

HANCHI BETTA.

1. THE BUNGALOW. 2. VIEW OF COFFEE. 3. PULP-HOUSE. 4. STORES AND DRYING TABLES.

belongs to Mrs. B. Billings, Mr. M. B. Pollard-Urquhart, and Mr. F. Macrae.

It is 287 acres in extent, and there are 100 acres of coffee under indigenous shelter trees, 50 acres of pepper, and 8 acres of vanilla, while the remainder is jungle land of good quality, which can be cultivated as required. Planting was commenced on the property by Mr. Pollard-Urquhart's father in 1873, and as the youngest trees are quite twenty years of age, the whole of the coffee area is in full profit, the produce being consigned to Tellicherry for shipment to London Pepper was first planted in 1902, and vanilla was started ten years later, while the annual returns for the past five years have been nearly 6 tons of the former crop, and 1 cwt. of the latter. A few Ceara rubber-trees are being grown as an experiment, but they are not yet old enough to be tapped.

Very fine views are obtained from the bungalow, which has been built at an elevation of nearly 3,000 ft. above sea-level.

Mr. Pollard-Urquhart is manager, and he employs about 75 coolies.

HOROOR

It is a gratifying feature in the practice of agriculture in Southern India that landowners are becoming more and more impressed with the fact that a wastage of certain constituents in the soil is continually proceeding, and, further, that unless this loss is replaced by natural or artificial means their crops will be very materially reduced in quantity as well as quality. Hence it follows that there must be intensive cultivation of the land, weeds must be eradicated, there must be scientific knowledge of the peculiar characteristics of the soil of each field, and, finally, a judicious application of the right kind of manure is essential.

One of the most enthusiastic exponents of advanced farming—and particularly of the necessity for the use of fertilizers—is Mr. W. R. Wright, who manages the Horoor estate, on behalf of three sisters and a brother. This gentleman's experience as a planter extends over a period of twenty-three years, and his keen oversight of every branch of work contributes largely to the productiveness of the estate. The property comprises 199 acres, and the 165 acres of coffee-bushes (some of which are forty years of age), and a few acres of paddy, are so well cultivated that extraordinarily good yields of produce are harvested. It must be borne in mind that coffee is one of those crops which exhaust the soil without making any equivalent return in the shape of manure, as neither the plant nor its produce is suitable for this purpose. Mr. Wright, however, meets the deficiency by allowing the estate a very liberal dressing of those fertilizers which contain the particular chemical properties necessary for the restoration of the soil to its normal condition of fertility. The average annual yield of coffee during the five years 1910-14 gave the splendid total of 40 tons, or, in other words, no less a quantity than 6 cwt. to the acre was gathered. The shade afforded by naturally-grown trees has been augmented by artificial plantings, and an excellent supply of water for the pulping-house and other buildings has been provided in three large tanks which are filled from springs on the estate. The pulping-house is situated in a most central position on the property, and after the cherries have been passed through this process they are dried, in the first place, on tables, and subsequently in the drying-grounds, which are fitted with flooring tiles. The final stage of preparation is that of curing, which takes place in a factory at Tellicherry. The finished, or manufactured, produce is now ready to be packed, or put in sacks, for shipment to England, whence it is distributed to the breakfast tables of Europe.

The buildings include a nice bungalow, a house for the writer, coolies' quarters, and a number of stores and sheds, and the estate is situated about 8 miles from the post office in the town of Mercara, while the nearest telegraph office is at Suntikoppa, a distance of 3 miles. Records of rainfall kept for the past thirty-three years show the annual quantity to have been $73\frac{3}{4}$ in. Horoor, once an area of jungle in which all the larger specimens of game abounded, is now a highly cultivated and delightful residential estate of considerable value, but this transformation is the result of a constant application of time and money on the part of the owners.

Mr. Wright employs about 150 coolies.

JUMBUR

There are some exceedingly pretty, and at the same time prosperous, estates in the district of Coorg, and this is especially the case in the northern portion in the neighbourhood of Mercara, where the altitude is about 3,700 ft. above the level of the sea. The Jumbur estate is situated about 2 miles distant from the important town of Mercara. It comprises 750 acres, of which 676 acres are planted with coffee, 41 acres with rubber, and one acre which is set apart for a nursery in which young plants are raised in order that decayed trees or those affected by disease may at once be replaced. The land is cultivated in a most thorough manner; manure is applied nearly every year, and regular spraying is carried on for the prevention of the ravages of insect pests. Coffee yields are remarkably good, as 560 acres of trees in bearing returned 150 tons annually between 1907 and 1914. The estate is well provided with suitable buildings, and those which are used in connection with the preparation of the bean are equipped with suitable machinery and plant. The owners are Captain Norman Franks, C.I.E., and Messrs. J. W. Irwin and W. E. Dickinson, the two last named gentlemen acting as managers. The labour market is well supplied with coolies, and about 500 hands are required constantly.

KANA KADU

These estates, comprising about 900 acres, are within a very short distance from the post and telegraph offices at Mercara. Planting was commenced in the sixties of last century by Mr. J. P. Hunt, who was one of the pioneers in the cultivation of coffee in that portion of the Madras Presidency. There are now about 550 acres of coffee-trees in full bearing, and the average yield per acre for the years 1909-14 varied from 4 cwt. to 5 cwt. This excellent result is due, primarily, to good cultivation of the land (which includes a systematic course of manuring), to the provision of indigenous shade for the plants, and to the careful measures which are adopted to prevent ravages by green bug, borer, or other insect pests. Pepper vines are growing between some of the rows of coffee, and no fewer than 10 tons have been sold recently in local markets, chiefly for export to North India. Cinchonas occupy about 50 acres of the estates, and a large quantity of the produce is sent to England annually. The proprietors of the estates are the executors of the late Mr. D. Rashbotham, and Mr. H. M. Mann is general manager.

HOROOR STATE.

1. Bungalow. 2. View of Coffee. 3. Coolies picking Coffee. 4. Pulp-house.

THE KARI KOLLI COFFEE ESTATE COMPANY, LTD.

A striking illustration of the development of an estate by careful supervision, clean cultivation, manuring, and by replacing bored, overborne, or unthrifty trees with healthy young ones is afforded by the coffee plantation near Mercara, in the province of Coorg. The planting of coffee commenced in 1874, and was continued during each year until 1889, when there were 200 acres of coffee, together with a small quantity of pepper. When the property was taken over in 1895 by Mr. A. J. Wright—who is now managing director of the company—the total average yearly yield of coffee was 7½ tons, or 1 cwt. to the acre, whereas in 1914 the produce averaged no less than 45 tons, or 4½ cwt. to the acre, and as much as 75 tons have been gathered.

Mr. Wright has the entire management in his own hands, but his supervision of the work on the estate is rendered doubly difficult owing to the insecurity of the labour supply. Coolies come and go, being tempted away by recruiting touts, and thus, continuity of service—which is so urgently desired by all employers—is interfered with, and some loss of time and money is naturally occasioned. About 100 hands are required throughout the year, and 150 or so during the three months of crop.

The property consists of 505 acres altogether, and it is proposed that the standing jungle or forest of about 300 acres shall be cleared and then planted with coffee as soon as a sufficiency of permanent labourers can be obtained. Land is very grateful for good treatment, and in this respect it is a fine example for thousands of human beings. It gives a generous return for every ton of fertilizers judiciously bestowed upon it, and the effect of a wise system of manuring is strongly in evidence upon this company's estate. Concentrated artificial manures are almost wholly used, as the cost of transporting a quantity in bulk from Mysore, the nearest railway station, a distance of 68 miles, would be far too costly a proceeding. The welfare of an estate—be it coffee or tea—is dependent in no small measure upon a nursery for the rearing of young plants. In former years planters were content to make use of "jungle" plants for renewals, but this practice resulted in failure, and the new system of raising seedlings either in baskets or nurseries has been almost universally adopted. Mr. Wright obtains selected seeds from other districts, as a change of soil and climate invariably produces a stronger and more fruitful tree than would be obtained from seed sown upon land which had given it birth. There are always vacant spaces to be filled along the rows of trees; some are found to bear but little fruit, and others die through overcropping, while the dreaded "borer" (*Xylotrechus quadrupes*) is continually making his ravages. The value of shade for the bushes is fully appreciated on the Kari Kolli estate, and, apart from the natural advantages of shelter, it has been found that the eggs of the borer are less likely to be hatched in those plantations which are provided with a fair amount of shade. In fact, coffee cannot be grown in the "open" in the province of Coorg.

The preparation of coffee commences in the pulping-house, which, on this estate, has machinery worked by bullock-power, and as many as 60 to 70 boxes of berries can be dealt with in an hour. Good water is conserved in three tanks, although one of these would be more correctly described as a very pretty, though small, lake. After the coffee has been cured in the factory at Tellicherry it is shipped to England for sale. The climatic conditions are very favourable for agriculture on this estate; the temperature does not run to extremes, and the records of rainfall for the past twenty years show the extremely moderate figures of 69·34 in. during each twelve months.

There is an excellent bungalow on the estate, but a special feature of the buildings is the remarkably fine lines which have been provided for the coolies. The property is about 10 miles distant from the post and telegraph offices at Saklaspur.

The nominal capital of the company is Rs. 50,000, but only Rs. 24,000 have been called up, and the annual dividend for the past five years has been declared at the rate of 20 per cent. This would be a good opportunity for any one wishing to invest in coffee. Some shares of Rs. 100 each have recently been sold for Rs. 480.

KIBRIBETTA

This estate of 245 acres, which is fully cultivated, is situated in the Nanjarapatna *taluq* in the province of Coorg, and the unusually heavy yield of about 120 tons of coffee in the 1913-14 season is undoubtedly due in a large measure to the very favourable position and elevation of the property. Planting commenced in the year 1876 with 17 acres; this was followed by 20 acres in 1879; and the remainder has been brought into cultivation more recently. The buildings on the property include two very pretty brick bungalows, a pulping-house, lines for coolies, and stores and sheds. Some 150 coolies are employed constantly on the estate, which is owned by Mr. W. S. Sullivan, for whom Mr. J. J. Mackenzie is temporarily acting as manager.

KITHERHALLI

The area of the province of Coorg does not exceed 1,600 square miles, but it might with considerable justification be termed one huge plantation of coffee, tea, and rubber. Kitherhalli is only about 220 acres in extent, but it consists of 150 acres of coffee and 20 acres of Ceara rubber. Coffee thrives remarkably well, and pays for good cultivation, as the average annual yield for some years has been not less than 6 cwt. to the acre. Rubber has only been planted recently, and experiments are being made in the production of camphor. Mr. E. P. Playford is manager for the owner, Mr. Thompson.

KOORG HULLY

This is purely a coffee-growing estate of about 280 acres, and as it is one in which old or decayed bushes are continually being replaced by young ones, it follows that there is always a fair proportion of immature trees which cause the average annual yields to vary from season to season. The weight of the crop from 1913-14 was no less than 127 tons, and all the produce is sent by ox-cart to Mangalore, whence it is shipped to the owners' brokers in London. The property is situated in a very healthy position, being about 3,200 ft. above the level of the sea, and the buildings include a very pretty bungalow, stables, pulping-house, lines for coolies, and stores. The managing proprietor, Mr. Talbot Cox, arrived in India in the year 1890, and he states that he has no difficulty in obtaining the requisite number of coolies, but he complains that those who are now available are unskilled, and that considerable time is occupied in giving them instruction.

KARI KOLLI COFFEE ESTATES, LTD.

1. A View on the Estate. 2. Bungalow. 3. Barbeque and Pulp-house. 4. Tank.

KEDUKAL

The owners of this estate are Messrs. E. L. Mahon and C. G. Maclean, and the latter undertakes the sole management, employing about 100 hands. A considerable portion of the property—which is 170 acres in extent—was cleared of jungle and planted with coffee in the year 1900, but further development of the plantation has taken place during each succeeding year, the result being that there are now (1914) 136 acres of trees. Some of these are, as yet, too young to yield a crop, but the matured bushes gave a return of 27 tons in the season 1913-14. The ripe "cherry" is pulped by hand-power on the estate, but it is intended that a system of water-power shall be installed in the near future. The parchment coffee, as the beans are called, after being pulped, is sent to Tellicherry to be cured, and the prepared product is then shipped to England for sale. The property is about 3,400 ft. above the level of the sea, and the average annual rainfall is about 80 in.

The town of Mercara — where the nearest post office is situated—is about 6 miles distant from Kedukal, while the telegraph office at Suntikoppa is not more than 3 miles away.

Pepper-vines have been planted throughout the estate. It is unfortunate that experiments made in the cultivation of sugar have not met with success. The plants grew well and gave abundant promise of becoming a profitable industry, but wild pigs and rats took a fancy to the canes, and completely consumed or destroyed them.

KEDUKAL.

1. PULPER, KEDUKAL. 2. WRITER'S HOUSE.

MANGLES BROTHERS

The association of this firm with the coffee-growing industry in Southern India dates from the year 1863, when Mr. F. Mangles began to plant coffee near Mercara in the district of Coorg. The estates consist of 2,450 acres of land, and comprise the following areas planted with coffee: Coovercolly, 930 acres; Hallery, 400 acres; Allicutty, 230 acres; and Santigherry, 225 acres. Experiments have been made in the cultivation of Ceara rubber, pepper, cotton, and cinchonas, but the results have not been sufficiently satisfactory to warrant their continuance. These properties have an average elevation above sea-level of about 3,500 ft., and it is the general experience of planters that this is the most favourable altitude. There are six pulping-houses on the four properties, and the machinery is driven by two water-wheels and four oil-engines. Records of planting and harvesting have been kept very carefully since the year 1873, and these figures show that for the past ten years the crop has yielded 5 cwt. to the acre, although in the season 1913-14 the returns amounted to 695 tons, this being at the rate of 8½ cwt. to the acre. The "parchment" coffee is cured at the factories of Mr. L. King Church, of Tellicherry, and of Messrs. Saldanha & Sons, of Mangalore, and the product is consigned for sale direct to the firm's agents in London. There are bungalows on each estate, and they are occupied by Mr. J. A. Graham—the managing partner in India—and by the other superintendents. From 1,000 to 2,000 coolies are employed constantly.

All of the properties are in most favourable positions as regards postal and telegraphic facilities, as Hallery is only 6 miles distant from Mercara, Coovercolly and Allicutty are 4 miles from Somwarpet, while Santagherry is within 1 mile of the office at Suntikoppa. The towns of Tellicherry and Mangalore are 85 miles and 95 miles distant respectively from the estate.

RAO BAHADUR C. M. NANJAPPAH

Mr. Koravanda Muttanna Nanjappah, popularly known as C. M. Nanjappah, comes of a well-known Takka (Social Head) Coorg family, having its ancestral house 4 miles distant from Mercara. His grandfather, named Muttanna, was the Sir Karekar (Commander-in-Chief) of the last Coorg Raja. Mr. Nanjappah's early education in English was acquired in the Mercara High School and in the Mangalore Provincial College, where he passed with credit the U.C.S. examination in 1876, and Matriculation in 1877. From Mangalore he went to Bangalore, where he secured very high positions in the Munsiff and Second Grade Pleader's Examination and in the Higher Grade special tests. In 1881 he was enrolled as a First Grade Pleader of Coorg Courts, and two or three years later rose to the position of an Advocate. His abilities and suavity of manners enabled him to become a leader at the Bar in a very short time, and in 1882 he was appointed Public Prosecutor of Coorg. The Government Pleadership, created in 1889, was also conferred upon him. He retired from the offices of Public Prosecutor and Government Pleader in 1905, when the Government placed on record its appreciation of his long and able services.

As a public man Mr. Nanjappah has equally distinguished himself. There is hardly any movement, institution, or society worthy of the name with which he was, or is not, in some way actively connected. He was the only non-official vice-president of the local municipality in its palmy days, and the only native elected as an honorary member of that body. He was a very active member of the Coorg Temple Committee, and he continues to be a member of the Planters' Association, which consists chiefly of Europeans. The District Board of Coorg has also had the advantage of his advice and services. His benefactions have been of such a nature as to be appreciated by the general public. Setting his face against charity, which, he considers, has the tendency to encourage indolence, he has built and handed over to the Government a school for the use of boys in his native village. In 1909 he, by a liberal grant of 5,000 rupees, founded, in the name of his wife, scholarships and stipendiaries for the benefit of girls attending the Mercara Girls' School. Plague having broken out in Mercara in 1911, and the congested portion of the town known as Laskar Bazaar being insanitary and therefore a hotbed of contagious diseases, it was resolved by the local Coronation committe to acquire that area for the purpose of levelling it to the ground and creating a park there. Mr. Nanjappah gave a munificent donation of Rs. 5,000 towards the attainment of this object.

The Emperor's Coronation Garden has been opened in the above park, and Mr. Nanjappah has erected at his own cost iron gates and stone pillars with the following inscription thereon: "This site was acquired and presented to the public of Coorg mainly through the generosity of Rao Bahadur C. M. Nanjappah, retired Government Pleader and Public Prosecutor of Coorg, and partly by public subscription, in honour of the visit of H.M. the King-Emperor to India in December 1911."

The success of the waterworks in Mercara is, to a large extent, due to him. By his influence he secured large donations, and he, personally, subscribed a handsome sum towards the cost of the work.

Despite extensive professional duties he, being naturally industrious, found time to attend to the cultivation of coffee on a very large scale, and the success which attended him in schools and at the Bar followed him in the new venture, as he soon attained the position of a prosperous planter. His coffee estate, known as Korthicad, has a cultivated area of 200 acres, and it is situated about 4,000 feet above the level of the sea. His Krishna coffee estate is in the Sunticoppa district. The nearest post and telegraph office is at Mercara.

Mr. Nanjappah resides at "Coravanda," which is a very attractive bungalow of his own in the town of Mercara.

RAO BAHADUR C. M. NANJAPPAH.

1. Rao Bahadur C. M. Nanjappah. 2. The Rao Bahadur and Family.

MYLATPUR

The owner of this estate—Mr. F. W. Gerrard—is an active member of the committee of the Coorg Planters' Association, and his experience at Mylatur extends over a period of more than twenty years. The property, consisting of 370 acres, was covered with the densest jungle when Mr. Gerrard purchased it in the year 1891, but this was a recommendation rather than otherwise, as no better coffee land can be obtained than that which has produced the most luxuriant undergrowth. The first processes of felling and clearing the forest were taken in hand energetically, and the planting of coffee-trees was commenced in 1892, thus following closely upon the heels of the work of development. Some twenty years later an area of 210 acres had been planted, and all of the bushes are in full profit with the exception of 8 acres of *Coffea Robusta* seedlings of the year 1912.

Rubber-trees occupy some forty acres of ground, and pepper is grown among the coffee bushes, while the remaining 120 acres, consisting of undulating bushland of superior quality, will be brought into cultivation by degrees, a few acres being broken up every year. Coffee-planters throughout the district of Coorg are practically unanimous as to the necessity of having shade for their crops, and since quick-growing trees have been planted, there has been a correspondingly healthier appearance of the bushes; and, further, there has been far less danger of losses from the ravages of the "borer" and other insect pests. The plant in the pulping house is driven by an oil-engine, and when the cherries have passed through the intermediate stages of preparation they are consigned to Tellicherry to be cured and subsequently shipped to London for sale.

The estate is well managed by Mr. Gerrard personally, and he exercises the closest supervision over about 100 coolies. Rubber-trees are growing well, and there is every reason to expect that a good average yield may be obtained as soon as they are old enough to be tapped.

The pretty bungalow is 3,300 ft. above sea-level, and it is about 3½ miles distant from the post and telegraph offices at Sidapur.

PALETHODU

The name Palethodu has been bestowed upon the three estates of Faith, Watekudu, and Gunikadu, which consist of 930 acres of land in the Kiggatnad *taluq*, on the southern border of the province of Coorg. The owners are Messrs. H. R. Craig and G. A. Tippetts-Aylmer, and the superintendents are Messrs. T. Aylmer and M. E. M. Blackburn, while Mr. H. T. Shaw, the manager of the Eliza estate (described elsewhere), holds a power-of-attorney for the owners, and is, further, visiting agent.

Pioneer work in clearing and developing these properties was controlled by the late Mr. J. Aylmer Hubbard, and intense cultivation was always regarded by him as an absolute essential. This means that the land is properly cultivated at the outset, and that great attention is paid to shade and manure. About 500 acres were planted with coffee between the years 1894 and 1905, and the average annual yield of produce is not less than 3 cwt. to the acre. There is one pulping-house for the three properties, and the machinery in it is driven by an oil-engine.

The cultivation of pepper has been most profitable in many parts of Southern India, and several plantation owners have produced excellent crops by utilizing the ground between the rows of coffee-trees. This method has been adopted at the Palethodus, and as an instance of the profitable nature of the plant on this property, it may be said that the crop for the season 1913-14 was sold, to be removed by the purchaser from the trees, for the sum of Rs. 10,000, while the previous year's harvest realized the high price of Rs. 16,000. A few years ago a mysterious fungoid disease attacked several pepper gardens in the Madras Presidency, but as the Palethodu estate has hitherto escaped to a great extent its ravages the proprietors intend to develop the cultivation of this plant up to about 300 acres.

A very fine bungalow has been erected upon the Faith property, and another is now being constructed at Watekudu. The estate is practically surrounded by jungle, but the Kutta post office is conveniently situated within its boundaries. Commucation by made roads is not good at the best of times, but during the wet season they are wellnigh impassable, especially between Ponampet and the boundary of the Wynaad, but they are now being taken in hand by the Government. The estate is some 3,000 ft. above the level of the sea, and it has an average annual rainfall of 80 in.

The supply of labour is fairly satisfactory, and some 400 coolies, consisting of Kanaras, Kurumbans, and Yerimbas, are employed constantly.

PEREMBOOCOLLY

The province of Coorg being situated so near to the Western Ghauts has a very equable rainfall, although subject to slight variations, and planters of coffee in earlier days found to their cost that the absence of trees for shade purposes was fatal to the well-being of their plants. The increased fertility of the bushes which followed upon the provision of suitable shelter by several planters in Mysore and Coorg has led to a general adoption of this practice, and the result has been that heavier yields of berries and of a better quality have been obtained.

Peremboocolly estate is the property of Mr. J. S. Trelawny, and it consists of 163 acres, 158 of which are cultivated with coffee. The opening of the estate was begun in 1895 with 78 acres, and since then various portions of land, some already planted with coffee, have been bought and added to the property, bringing the total to 158 cultivated acres.

The pulping-house is situated in a most central position, and has excellent drying-grounds, and there is also an engine for working the pulper and huller. The estate is well shaded with planted and natural trees, and the splendid condition of the estate shows what can be done by keen supervision and good management.

The benefits to be derived from a systematic course of manuring are well illustrated at Peremboocolly. During the past five years Mr. Trelawny has applied about 5 cwt. to the acre of fertilizers of a phosphatic, potassic, and nitrogenous nature, and the annual yield of coffee during that period has reached an average of from 30 to 35 tons, while the harvest of 1914 produced no less than the extraordinary total of 60 tons.

A very fine bungalow is situated on a hill, and commands grand views of the Western Ghauts on the south-western side; of the northern taluq of Coorg on the north, and of the Mysore plateau on the east. The estate is situated about 12 miles distant from Mercara, and 6½ miles from Sidapur, which is the post and telegraph office. The rainfall is about 75 in., and the locality is considered to be very healthy. 150 coolies are employed during the busy season.

THE PORTLAND RUBBER COMPANY, LTD.

The directors of this company are Messrs. J. and N. Macdonald, while Mr. Mahon is managing director in India for the secretaries, Messrs. Matheson & Co., of London. About 1,300 acres have been planted with Para rubber, and although a portion only of the trees came into bearing in 1914, the results obtained were such as to inspire the owners with the utmost confidence in regard to future tappings. Thorough cultivation of the land is carried out on up-to-date lines, the manager being fully alive to the importance of intensive farming. The property is near to the post office at Virajendrapett, in the province of Coorg.

MYLATPUR.

1. Rubber Estate. 2. Bungalow. 3. Coffee. 4. Pulp-house.

PEREMBOOCOLLY.

1. View leading to Bungalow. 2. View of Coffee. 3. Drying-ground.

SANDALWOOD

The owner of this estate—Mr. C. E. Murray-Aynsley—is one of the best-known agriculturists and all-round sportsmen in the Madras Presidency. He was for about ten years the master of the Murray-Aynsley hounds, and his prowess with the rod and line has been acclaimed far and wide, as he holds the record for the largest fish ever hooked on rod and line in the rivers of India. This was a mahseer, which drew the scale at 104 lb., although another one captured by the same gentleman weighed no less than 103 lb.

Mr. Murray-Aynsley is now President of the Coorg Planters' Association, and his zeal in the interests of planting generally is greatly appreciated by the members.

Sandalwood is 200 acres in extent, and it comprises 180 acres of coffee—some of which is thirty years of age—and two ravines of about 5 acres of rubber. The majority of the plantations in Coorg are situated about 3,500 ft. above the level of the sea, and this altitude is particularly favourable for the growth of vigorous coffee-trees of a very fruitful character. Owners who reside on their estate at this elevation enjoy a beautiful climate, and the surroundings of their pretty bungalows are in many instances extremely beautiful.

Other buildings on the property include a pulping-house, hulling, and a number of other stores and sheds, and the machinery is driven by a Hornsby oil-engine of 6 h.p. Sandalwood is a very fertile estate, the returns for the past four seasons showing that an average of 41 tons of coffee per annum have been gathered.

Mr. Murray-Aynsley manages the property personally, and he employs about 200 coolies.

SANDALWOOD.

1. PULP-HOUSE. 2. BUNGALOW.

SIDAPUR

The question of the best method of maintaining the productiveness of soils where cereals, root crops, or plantation trees, such as coffee, tea, or cardamoms are grown, is one of such importance that it is attracting the attention of agricultural scientists throughout the civilized world. It is unquestionable that the most successful cultivator will be the one who by scientific measures continues to produce maximum yields, at the lowest possible cost, with the least deterioration of his land. The fertility of the soil depends upon a whole series of factors, such as water, air, food substances, and the absence of injurious diseases or pests. High cultivation of land—such as in the case of the Sidapur estates—is of no avail unless the conditions just referred to are thoroughly understood, and a practical knowledge of the nature of the soil and of the constituents of plant food which may be lacking are indisputable preliminaries. When the farmer has once grasped these matters he can proceed with his tillage with a remarkable chance of success.

The manager of the Sidapur estates—Mr. W. A. F. Bracken—has achieved excellent results on this property, and he is not slow to avail himself of those aids to scientific cultivation which experience and study have brought within his reach. He is very liberal in his application of manures, but this practice is carried out in a most systematic manner,

SUNTIKOPPA.

1. Bungalow. 2. Drying-ground. 3. Pulp-house.

and with due regard to the necessities of each field upon the estates.

Sidapur estates, which are in the Yedenalknad *taluq* in the southern portion of the province of Coorg, consist of 660 acres; 556 acres have been planted with coffee-trees since the year 1870, and with the exception of 2 acres of two-year-old bushes, all of these are bearing fruit annually. From 60 to 70 tons of beans is the annual yield from 335 acres of old bushes. There are three pulping-houses on the property, one of which has an 8-h.p. oil-engine for the driving of its machinery, while the plant of the other two is dependent upon motive-power derived from the use of cattle and hand. All green coffee is peeled on the premises, but the beans are subsequently sent to Tellicherry to be cured. The manager does not supply local markets with the finished product, as the whole of the crop is consigned to London and to the continent of Europe.

Mr. Bracken evidently believes that it is not wise to have all one's eggs in one basket, as he has 80 acres of very fertile pepper-vines planted between the rows of coffee.

Messrs. Binny & Co., Ltd., of Armenian Street, Madras, are owners of the estates, which vary from 3,000 to 3,700 ft. above the level of the sea, and it may be added that this is considered to be an ideal altitude for growing coffee. An excellent supply of water is obtained from several sources, while the average annual rainfall for the past sixteen years has been 58 in.

Four bungalows have been erected, and the one occupied by Mr. Bracken occupies such a unique position that delightful views are obtained of the town of Sidapur and of the splendid country which stretches away for a distance of 40 or 50 miles.

Labourers are fairly plentiful, and about 350 are usually employed. The nearest post and telegraph offices are at Sidapur, which is within half an hour's walk.

SUNTIKOPPA

About 9 miles distant from Mercara, the chief town and seat of administration of the province of Coorg, are four coffee estates which will compare most favourably with any other plantations of a similar kind in Southern India for the clean and systematic manner in which they are cultivated, for the fruitful character of the bushes, and for the skill in management which is in evidence from the rearing of the tiny seedlings to the preparation of the "cherry" for the curing process in the factories at Mungalore and Tellicherry. The properties adjoin one another, and they comprise Suntikoppa, consisting of 500 acres, Balakadu, of 300 acres, Yemagundi, of 160 acres, and Netley, of 160 acres. The first-named property is owned jointly by Mr. Ivor MacPherson, Colonel MacPherson, and Mr. C. E. Murray-Aynsley, while the three others belong to Mr. MacPherson alone. This gentleman undertakes the sole management of the estates, and he, in common with many other agriculturists in Southern India, has to tell of the very serious problem caused by the insufficiency of the supply in the labour market. This dearth of satisfactory labourers has prevented the further development of scores of estates, but it is hoped that the action which has been taken by planters' associations with the view of checking the

SIDAPUR.

1. STORES AND DRYING-GROUND. 2. PULP-HOUSE. 3. BUNGALOW. 4. A GENERAL VIEW FROM THE BUNGALOW.

recruiting by labour agents may be crowned with success.

The Suntikoppa property formerly belonged to Mr. MacPherson's father, who commenced to plant coffee in the year 1860, and there are now some 480 acres under this crop. The trees are well protected from wind and sun, and, as a consequence, they are vigorous, healthy, and very prolific in yield, the harvest of the season 1913-14 producing as much as 120 tons. The pulping process is carried out by means of a water-power wheel and an oil-engine. Mr. MacPherson can always find employment here for about 400 coolies, but he cannot rely upon having this number continually.

The Balakadu property was first planted with coffee in 1866, but each succeeding year has witnessed the growth of the plantation by at least a few acres. Special attention is directed towards the removal of all decayed or worn-out trees, and the addition of healthy transplants keeps the estate in a remarkably level condition. The rainfall on this property is not too heavy, as the records for many years past show that the quantity has been from 75 in. to 80 in. About 250 hands are required constantly.

The Yemagundi and Netley estates may be considered together as the annual produce of each property is dealt with in the pulping-house at Netley, the machinery of which is driven by water-wheel power. The number of acres planted at each place respectively is about 160, and the harvest of 1913-14 gave a return of about 80 tons.

There is not much difference in the altitude of the several properties, but the average height above sea-level may be taken to be about 3,400 ft.

WHADDON

Oranges and pepper are grown to a small extent upon this estate of 240 acres, but the principal produce is coffee, which is cultivated upon 160 acres, situated near to the post and telegraph offices at Pollibetta in Southern Coorg. The coffee leaves are pulped by machinery driven by bullock-power, and practically the whole of the crop—which, by the way, averages about 4 cwt. to the acre—is consigned to Europe, but chiefly to London, for sale. The property belongs to the representative of the late Mr. Arthur Lambert, and the management is in the capable hands of Mr. G. C. Garrett. About 100 coolies are in constant work on the estate.

WOOLIGOOLY

The cultivation of 293 acres out of a total of 300 acres is a sufficient indication of the nature of this estate, which is situated within the post office delivery radius from Mercara, in the province of Coorg. Coffee and pepper are the principal crops, although a few rubber-trees have been planted. No fewer than 127 tons of coffee were reaped during the harvest of 1913-14. The owner, Mr. E. A. Fennell, has an exceedingly pretty bungalow, which stands in an equally attractive garden, and the two are surrounded by a country so park-like that imagination runs riot, and by fancy one is transported to the Old Country. The property is managed by Mr. Sinclair Grove, who has the assistance of a superintendent, Mr. J. Morgan, and the average number of hands employed is about 200.

WOSNULLAGOTTAY

Coffee plantations in the southern portion of the province of Coorg, in which this estate is situated, are sometimes injuriously affected by the borer and the green bug, but energetic steps have been taken by planters in recent years to combat these pests, and excellent results have been obtained. The property is 159 acres in extent, and about 116 acres have been planted with coffee-trees, but the returns have not been particularly gratifying until recently, when the management was placed in the hands of Messrs. Urquhart and Macrae. The owner is Mr. John J. Tweedie.

THE YEMMAGUGOODI ESTATES COMPANY, LTD.

A syndicate was formed in 1896 with registered offices at 27 Clement's Lane, London, E.C., for the acquisition of a group of estates situated near Pollibetta, in the Yedenalknad *taluq* in the province of Coorg. The directors are Messrs. P. S. M. Arbuthnot, H. Denison, and K. W. Arbuthnot, while Mr. E. M. Breithaupt is general manager for India.

VIEW OF NEGAPATAM FROM THE JETTY.

Photo by Nicholas & Co.

THE CITIES OF THE SOUTH

MANY visitors to India arrive at Bombay, whence they make hurried journeys to Calcutta, Delhi, Simla, and the other northern cities and towns, but historically interesting places with their ancient temples and shrines in the Presidency of Madras are frequently overlooked. Tourists fail to see the picturesque villages of the west coast; they miss much by not viewing the undulating plateaus—rich in verdure—of the Nilgiris, while the boldly outlined mountains, with their silvery rills and waterfalls, and the dense jungle, with its elephants, tigers, bears, panthers, bison, sambur, and other large game, are merely things of which they have read in railway and other guide-books. The South Indian Railway Company, Ltd., provides an excellent service of trains between Madras and Tuticorin, and the journey need not by any means be the dreary and monotonous affair which a trip of about 450 miles so frequently proves to be. Comfortable carriages with electric lights and fans, dining-room cars, and other conveniences enable the traveller to enjoy the many objects of interest along the route.

The handsome station at Egmore (Madras), designed and decorated in Indian style, is the starting-place of the tour. After passing through some of the suburbs of the city (which are referred to elsewhere), the first place deserving of notice is Pallavaram, which is a town of nearly 3,000 inhabitants in the Saidapet *taluq* of the district of Chingleput, and is situated about 15 miles distant from the terminus. Practically the only industries are tanning of hides and the quarrying of stone for construction work in the Madras harbour. The celebrated temple of Runganathaswamy is about 3 miles from Pallavaram, and huge crowds of people assemble there at the festival season held in the month of May. Vandalur, 22 miles from Madras, is remembered as the village where troops were entrenched during the Carnatic wars, and there is still to be seen a very substantial dwelling-house which was occupied in 1765 by General Joseph Smith, who was a prominent figure in those struggles. A reserved forest area is in close proximity, and excellent shooting of partridge, hare, and snipe can be obtained. The inhabitants are about 800 in number.

Chingleput is the chief town of the *taluq* of the same name. It is situated on the northern bank of the River Palar, and is almost surrounded by hills, which attain a height of about 500 ft. The centre of attraction is the Old Fort, which was constructed after the fall of the Vizayanagar power during the sixteenth century. In 1751 it was taken by Chunda Sahib from Mahomed Ali when the former was assisted by the French in an invasion of the Carnatic, but in the following year Lord Clive bombarded it and compelled

1. PILGRIMS IN THE MAHAMAKAM TANK, KUMBAKONAM.
2. PILGRIMS AT THE MAHAMAKAM FESTIVAL, KUMBAKONAM.

Photos by Nicholas & Co.

the French to yield. In 1887 the buildings of the fort were handed over by the Madras Government to the Educational Department to be used as a reformatory school for juvenile offenders. The inmates, besides receiving a good general education, are taught carpentry, blacksmith's work, tailoring, weaving, and other industries, and the district magistrate renders valuable assistance in finding employment for the boys when they leave the Institute. Chingleput is 38 miles distant from Madras, and it is the junction station for the branch line to Arkonam, on the Madras and Southern Mahratta Railway. The principal industry is that of brickmaking, but the inhabitants of the surrounding country are almost entirely engaged in agricultural pursuits. Two high schools in the town have an attendance of about 800 students. The inhabitants at the census of 1911 were 11,626 in number. The traveller should make a point of seeing the seven pagodas, which are magnificent specimens of the sculptor's art. These are monolithic temples of the Dravidian order, and archæologists have no hesitation in saying that the stones must have been carved prior to the seventh century B.C. The pagodas are 18 miles distant from Chingleput, where carts can always be obtained.

Twenty-two miles from Chingleput, and 35 miles from Madras, on the Arkonam branch line, is Conjeeveram, a town of very great antiquity, and alleged to be the most sacred place in Southern India. The attention of the visitor will naturally be directed to the three temples which are dedicated to Siva, Vishnu, and to the "loving-eyed" Parvati, the wife of Siva. The annual festival is held in the month of May, when pilgrims attend from all parts of the Presidency. A large proportion of the population of about 54,000 inhabitants is engaged in weaving very fine cloth.

Villupuram is an important junction where passengers change trains for Pondicherry, Cuddalore, and Tiruvannamalai. Adjoining the railway station are the locomotive workshops, in which a large number of European and Anglo-Indian workmen are employed. The town is the centre of a prosperous commercial and agricultural district, in which rice and ragi are grown extensively, and an especially large trade is done in ground-nuts with the French Settlement of Pondicherry. Villupuram and other places in the vicinity were the scenes of many encounters between the English and French troops in the middle of the eighteenth century, and it was not until the year 1760 that Villupuram was successfully defended against its invaders. A temple which was dedicated to Siva became the citadel of a small fort during these struggles, but the fortifications were demolished in 1803. The word Villupuram means "sacred milk." Good shooting of a general character can be obtained between the months of November and February, but permission must first be obtained from the local Government Forest Officer.

A branch line of railway, 23 miles in length, connects Villupuram with Pondicherry, which is the capital of the French Settlements in India, a description of

COLONNADE OF PILLARS (671 FEET IN LENGTH), RAMESWARAM.
One of the most remarkable structures of its kind in the world.
Photo by Nicholas & Co.

which appears elsewhere in this volume. The village of Veerampatnam is about 3 miles distant from Pondicherry, and here may be seen a very old temple, which is dedicated to the goddess Sangalaniammal, an Avatar of Kali.

Returning along the branch line to the junction at Villupuram the railway is laid in a south-south-easterly direction, and after a journey of 12 miles through a district almost devoid of natural scenery, but which has been made prosperous and inviting by the hand of man, the traveller reaches Panruti, the third largest town in the Cuddalore *taluq* of the district of South Arcot. The place is disappointing from a spectacular point of view, but its trade is very large. Ground-nuts are cultivated extensively for export to Marseilles and elsewhere, but the extracted oil and the resulting cake are shipped to Rangoon and to the Straits Settlements respectively. Other products are cotton, jack-fruit, rice, cereals, jaggery, and sugar. The soil in the immediate neighbourhood—and principally near the banks of the Gadilam River—consists of tenacious clay, and some of the finest bricks in Southern India are made here. There are some important public buildings, among which the Church of Scotland, the Roman Catholic Church, and an old Siva temple may be mentioned. Panruti and the neighbouring villages of Pudupet and Angisettipalaiyam are important centres for the weaving of red cotton cloths, which are generally worn by women of the surrounding districts. The number of inhabitants has fluctuated considerably, but it is now 10,697.

Fourteen miles in a south-easterly direction is Cuddalore New Town, and 2 miles farther from Madras is the Old Town of the same name, but the two places are united as far as local administration is concerned, and may therefore be regarded as one. The municipal limits of the town cover an area of about 13 square miles, and include several revenue villages, but the generally accepted division is as follows: the Old Town, the New Town, Manjakuppam, and Fort St. David, where the earliest settlement of the East India Company was situated. The Company was anxious to open a factory at Cuddalore, and negotiations were accordingly commenced with the Khan of Gingee for a suitable piece of land upon which it could be constructed. The necessary consent to the Company's proposals was subsequently obtained, and suitable buildings were erected in 1683. Trading concerns grew very rapidly, and in order to give protection to them Fort St. David was built, but the fortifications were considerably enlarged in 1702. The fort was besieged by the French on three occasions, and the attack upon it and the town in 1758 was successfully carried out. The British regained possession in 1760, only to lose it again twelve years later, but in 1785 it was finally restored to Britain under the Treaty of Versailles. Cuddalore is the headquarters of the district of South Arcot, and is a seaport town at the junction of the Gadilam and Ponniar Rivers. The district of South Arcot produces about three-fourths of the ground-nuts grown in the Presidency of Madras, and in the *taluq* of Cuddalore alone no fewer than 54,000 acres are cultivated for this crop. Other products of the neighbourhood are sugar, betel, tapioca, indigo, casurina, cashew, ragi, gingelly, horse-gram, castor, and cotton. The industries of the town are few in number, but they include the weaving, dyeing, printing, and ginning of cotton and the making of mats. Among the principal buildings are the Municipal Offices, the Town College, the Roman Catholic Church, St. Joseph's College, and Christ Church, but the ruins of the old fort should not be overlooked. The census of 1911 showed that the town contained 56,574 persons.

ARAVAN AND DURGA, DRAUPADI AMMAN TEMPLE, KUMBAKONAM.

Chidambaram, the principal town in the *taluq* of the same name in the district of South Arcot, is 154 miles distant by rail from Madras. The traveller will notice that the train passes over a comparatively level plain which slopes gradually toward the sea-coast. There are very few hilly ranges, and the absence of forests is to some extent compensated for by groves of trees which surround the villages. The majority of the towns and villages on the eastern coast of the province of Madras were subjected to armed attacks—chiefly by the French—during the eighteenth century, and Chidambaram had to bear the brunt of several severe onslaughts. The principal crops grown in the district which form the basis of many industries of the town are paddy, casurina, kambu, ragi, and varagu, although the inhabitants are engaged to a considerable extent in weaving silk and cotton fabrics. Education is on a far higher level in this town than any other in the *taluq*, and mention may be made of the District Board Sessional School and the Leipzig Lutheran Mission School, which has the names of more than two hundred boys on the roll. Chidambaram is, however, visited more particularly on account of the historic temple devoted to Siva (containing a shrine to Vishnu as well), which is one of the largest and most ancient in Southern India. The buildings cover an area of about 40 acres, and it is remarkable that some of the huge blocks of stone are no less than 30 ft. in height and 3 ft. square, though the nearest quarry is about 40 miles distant, on the far side of the Vellar River. It is almost inconceivable how these giant monoliths could have been removed at a time when there were practically no roads, and when the means of transport were of a most primitive character. No agreement has been arrived at regarding the age of the temple, but the evidence leads to the belief that its construction must have been commenced during the seventh or eighth centuries of the Christian era. The population of the town is given as 21,327 persons.

Still proceeding in a southerly direction, the traveller passes through Coleroon, Arasur, and Shiyali, crossing the Coleroon stream (a branch of the famous Cauvery River), which is the boundary between the districts of South Arcot and Tanjore. The latter river has its source in the Coorg Mountains, and it divides into two parts at a point about 9 miles to the west of Trichinopoly. The northern branch is called the Coleroon, while the southern one—retaining the name of Cauvery—branches off into numerous streams, thus forming a delta in which there is a large number of irrigation channels. Most luxurious crops are grown on the rich soil of this area, and groves of coconut and fruit trees form a pleasing contrast to the many arid plains in other portions of the eastern littoral. Some of the tributaries in the delta are the Manniyar, the Palavar, the Vettar, the Vennar, and the Koraiyar, and the towns of Tanjore, Shiyali, Mayavaram, Kumbakonam, Mannargudi, and other places are located on their banks.

The first town of importance after leaving Chidambaram is Mayavaram, which is a railway junction 177 miles distant from Madras. It became a municipality in 1866, and the councillors have effected very great improvements by the erection of a travellers' bungalow at a cost of Rs. 7,000, of a small market at an outlay of Rs. 2,500, and of high, secondary, and primary schools. The industries are few in number, such as the weaving of silk and cotton cloths, and the inhabitants are, generally speaking, in prosperous positions. Paddy, coconuts and plantains are the principal products of the surrounding country. The Siva temple is the chief feature of interest in the town, and the bathing festival, which takes place during the months of October and November in each year, attracts from 30,000 to 40,000 devotees. The word Mayavaram signifies "pea-fowl town," and there is a legend to the effect that Siva changed his wife, Parvati, into a pea-hen because of her refusal to obey his commands; but, the story proceeds, the husband relented, and restored her to her original form, when she worshipped and bathed in the original tank. There were 27,121 inhabitants at the census in 1911.

LION, NEAR PANDAVA RATHAS, MAHABALIPURAM.

The branch line from here runs in a southerly direction to Peralam, where a change of trains enables the traveller to visit Karikal, the chief town of the French province of the same name, where annual festivals are held at the Mahommedan mosque and at the Hindu temple. Tiruvallur Junction—on the same branch from Mayavaram—is 201 miles distant from Madras, and it is situated in the *taluq* of Negapatam, in the district of Tanjore. The inhabitants are nearly 12,000 in number, and they are engaged chiefly in the weaving of cloth, although there is a rice-mill in which more than 200 hands are employed. The principal building is the temple devoted to Siva, which contains an outer and an inner court, the former being 15 acres and the latter 5 acres in extent. The most ancient portion of the building is said to date from about A.D. 1000. A large festival is held annually in the months of March and April, and it is attended by pilgrims from nearly all parts of the Madras Presidency. The terminus of this branch line is at Arantangi, where a considerable quantity of cloth is weaved for export, and where cotton, silk, and laced cloths are manufactured. About 7 miles to the south of this town is the village of Avadiyarkoil, where there is an ancient temple dedicated to Authmanathaswami. Pilgrims pass through this place on their way to the famous shrine at Rameswaram. A branch line of railway, 19 miles in length, runs from Tiruvallur Junction in an eastwardly direction to Nagore, but 5 miles from this terminus is Negapatam, one of the most important ports in Southern India. The Portuguese appear to have been the earliest European settlers, and it was called by them the "city of Coromandel." The Dutch obtained possession of the town in 1660, but they were compelled to relinquish it in 1781, when a force was dispatched from Madras under Sir Hector Munro. It is situated on a level expanse of sand at the mouth of the River Kaduvaiyar, and the latest census returns show the population to be rather more than 60,000 persons. Negapatam was constituted a municipality in the year 1866, but the members of the Council have not a brilliant record of improvements effected since that date. The principal exports are rice, cattle (chiefly to Singapore and Penang), cotton and silk piece-goods, earthenware, ground-nuts, oil, coriander and castor seeds, tamarind, chillies, onions, ghee, tobacco, and cigars, while the imports include coal, railway construction materials, grain, and pulse. The South Indian Railway Company's locomotive works give employment to several thousands of hands, many of whom are Anglo-Indians. Steamers belonging to the British India Steam Navigation and the Asiatic Companies call regularly at Negapatam, and the bookings of passengers—especially to ports in the Far East—are very considerable. Many of the buildings are substantially constructed, and among those which should be seen are St. Peter's Church, the Government Offices, and the Wesleyan College and Church. St. Peter's is a quaint old structure, having been erected in 1774, and it contains a very fine piece of antique work in the pulpit and sounding-board. Negapatam stands high as an educational centre among the towns of the district of Tanjore, and the percentage of literate persons ranks next to Tanjore itself.

ELEPHANT, NEAR PANDAVA RATHAS, MAHABALIPURAM.

Harking back to the junction at Mayavaram with the view of continuing the journey to Tuticorin one passes through a pleasantly wooded district to Kumbakonam, 197 miles from Madras, a town which is held in the highest esteem by pious Hindus. Its site is a low, level tract of land between two tributaries of the Cauvery River, and it extends for a distance of about 3 miles in length from east to west. Historical records regarding the early days of Kumbakonam are unfortunately incomplete, but there is no reasonable doubt that it is one of the oldest towns in the Presidency, it having at one time been the capital of the Chula kingdom. There are twelve temples dedicated to Siva and four to Vishnu, while another occupies a unique position in that it is the only one in Southern India which has been erected in honour of Brahma. The most important of the sacred edifices is the Sarangapani Swami (Vishnu) temple, which has an imposing *gopuram* 147 ft. in height. The Kumbeswara Swami (Siva) temple is noted chiefly for the beauty and variety of its silver *vahanams,* or conveyances for the idols. The sacred Mahamakham tank covers an area of about 20 acres, and it is surrounded by a considerable number of small temples. A bathing festival is held in the month of February in each year, but the most notable one is that which occurs every twelfth year, attracting nearly half a million people. Kumbakonam is a busy industrial centre, and some thousands of the 64,647 inhabitants obtain a living by working in factories. Pure silk is woven for garments for women's wear; cotton cloths are manufactured from the finest threads, and vessels of brass, copper, lead, and bell-metal are made for domestic use and for export. The chief products are paddy, coconuts, betel-leaves, and plantains. Rice is milled, and oil is extracted from nuts, and these industries alone provide employment for a large number of persons. Considerable difficulty has been experienced in draining the town of its surface water, owing to the low level upon which it stands, and it is on this account not so healthy as many other towns on the east coast. Among the principal buildings are the Porter Town Hall (erected by public subscriptions in 1885 in memory of a former principal of the college), the Government College, which is affiliated to the University of Madras, the Town and Native High Schools, the Municipal Hospital, a very fine Protestant church erected in 1855, and the Gopal Rao Library, named after an eminent educationist. At Ayyampet, 210 miles from Madras, silk cloths are manufactured for sale at Benares, Nagpur, Kamptee, and other places. Visitors to the sacred shrines at Tiruvadi usually alight at this station, and complete their journey by means of country bullock *bandies* or on foot. Tiruvadi, 7 miles distant from Ayyampet, is situated in a most fertile district, luxurious crops of all kinds and a profusion of rich foliage being visible on every hand. The native name of the place—Tiruvaiyaru—meaning the "holy five rivers," was bestowed upon it from the fact that five branches of the Cauvery River flow within 3 or 4 miles of the town. The chief industry is cotton weaving, but great skill is exhibited by many of the inhabitants in carving images on temple cars. Tiruvadi is regarded as a most sacred place, and it is therefore largely inhabited by Brahmins, who compose fully one-third of the population of about 8,000 persons. The temple—dedicated to Siva—is, however, the chief attraction, and it is an exceedingly fine building, in which there are numerous inscriptions attributed to the Chola kings who were in power at the close of the tenth century. It is the principal centre of seven shrines, and immense crowds of pilgrims visit the town during the numerous festivals, some of which continue for thirteen days. The Kalyanamahal chattram (chattrams are charitable institutions for the accommodation of travellers) is an imposing building, and it has an income of more than Rs. 23,000.

Tanjore is the chief town of the district of Tanjore, and its name is derived from "Tanjan," a legendary giant who is said to have haunted the neighbourhood and who was killed by the god Vishnu. It is a junction station on the South India Railway, and is 221 miles distant from Madras. It does not hold a prominent position in the commercial world, but it is full of interest to the historian and the archæologist. The town is made up of the large and small forts which were respectively constructed by the last and first kings of the Nayakka dynasty. The walls of the old fort were built of thick masonry; they were 15 ft. in height, and were surrounded by a moat 15 ft. in depth, but they have now nearly disappeared. Within the enclosure of the small fort is the Sivaganga tank, and adjoining it is the Sivaganga garden, which owes its origin to the energy of the municipality, who caused it to be laid out in the year 1871. The great Brahadeshwara temple in the southern portion of this fort was built by Rajaraja I, in the early part of the eleventh century, and few travellers in Southern India miss the opportunity of inspecting it. The court is 500 ft. in length and 250 ft. in breadth. The main tower is 216 ft. in height, and there is a local tradition to the effect that twelve years were occupied in its construction. The great tower of the temple is 168 ft. in height from base to story, on the four corners of which are *nandis* (or bulls), 33 ft. from there to the top of the building, and 15 ft. thence to the top of the gilded *kalasam* (spiked ornament). This ornament stands on a single block of granite, said to weigh about 80 tons, and tradition says that "it was raised to its present position by means of an inclined plane commencing at a village called Sarapullam (scaffold hollow), about 4 miles north-east of Tanjore." Within the court of the temple is the small Subrahmanya temple, which is covered with extremely delicate figures and pillars, and it was pronounced by Fergusson to be "as exquisite a piece of decorative art as is to be found in Southern India," and, further, that it "is a perfect gem of carved stonework, the tooling of the stone in the most exquisitely delicate and elaborate patterns is as clear and sharp as the day it left the sculptor's hands."

NANDI, THE STONE BULL, TANJORE.

The famous Nandi bull stands opposite to the doorway of the main building, and this huge monolith has been carved out of a solid block of gneiss. It is more than 12 ft. in height, 19 ft. in length, and is estimated to weigh not less than 25 tons.

The Rajah's palace is situated within the great fort, and while certain portions of it are undoubtedly very ancient, additions have been made from time to time. There are two Durbar halls, and they contain pictures of Maratha kings, several statues, and an armoury of curious weapons, such as gold and silver-handled swords, rifles, pistols, gold caps for ornamenting elephants, and of dresses worked in lace for men and women. The library is particularly interesting, as the 23,000 volumes comprise 18,000 Sanskrit manuscripts, 8,000 of which are written on palm-leaves. The town of Tanjore is noted for its artistic manufactures, including the weaving of many beautiful and costly varieties of silk. Cotton carpets were at one time manufactured in considerable numbers by private individuals, but the only place in which they can now be produced at a profit is in the jail, where the prisoners have been taught the art of making them. Gold and silver ornaments set with costly precious stones are made by native jewellers; paintings of gods or heroes are executed on the walls of the temples and upon wood or cloth, and among other industries are the carving of wood, the making of ropes, and the manufacture of native scents. Tanjore became a municipality in the year 1866, and the Council has provided funds for the building of two markets in addition to undertaking the maintenance of two dispensaries and a number of primary and other educational institutions. The town is situated in the Cauvery delta, and it has a pleasant appearance, as there is an abundance of well-grown trees. The latest census returns give the number of inhabitants as 60,341.

SRI PASAPATHIESWARA TEMPLE, KARUR.

Trichinopoly is one of the most important commercial towns in Southern India, and it is 252 miles distant by rail from Madras. It is the chief town in the district of the same name, and it is built upon a sandy plain about half a mile from the southern bank of the River Cauvery. A municipality was formed on November 1, 1866, and numerous works were at once commenced, the principal being the adoption of a scheme for securing a sufficient water supply. A proposal was made by the Board of Directors of the South Indian Railway Company to the effect that the municipality should join them in the cost of the construction of works upon the Cauvery River in order that the same source might be available for the requirements of the railway locomotive department and of the town, and it was ultimately arranged that a pumping-station should be constructed in the bed of the river, and that the water should be forced into a reservoir on the top of the great rock in the north-eastern portion of the town, whence it would be distributed by means of pipes. The estimate for carrying out this project was rather more than four lakhs of rupees.

There are two recognized portions of the town, namely, the "Fort" and the "Cantonment," the latter being the principal place of residence for Europeans. Trichinopoly is the headquarters of the South Indian Railway Company, and the staff consists of about 600 clerks and some 500 artisans, who are supervised by European officials.

The building of the fort appears to have been commenced about the close of the sixteenth century, but it was enlarged by Visanatha, the first ruler of the Nayakkam dynasty, and subsequently strengthened by Chanda Sahib in the year 1740. Within the fort is the celebrated rock, which is 260 ft. higher than the main street and 503 ft. above the level of the sea. The ascent is made by a series of steps from two of the main streets; and on the summit is a small temple in which are inscriptions relating to the Pallavars of the seventh century.

Trichinopoly is well supplied with churches belonging to several denominations, and some of these have claims to architectural beauty. One of the pioneers of Protestant missions was the Rev. Mr. Schwartz, a Dane, who arrived in this town in 1761, and the church which he formed is now known as Christ Church. St. John's Church is situated near to the junction station, and it contains a fine memorial of Bishop Heber. A large majority of the inhabitants are Roman Catholics, who have several places of worship, the principal one having been built by the Jesuit Fathers near to the Fort station. The Lutheran Mission of Leipzig and the Wesleyans are also represented by their own churches and schools, while the S.P.G. and the Jesuits have colleges which are affiliated to the University of Madras. Trichinopoly is the home of the cigar-making industry in India, and although a considerable portion of this trade has in recent years been moved to Madras, there are still many factories in which some thousands of workpeople are employed. "Trichy" cigars, as they are called, are great favourites with smokers, and they are exported to almost every civilized country in the world.

1. THE PALACE, TANJORE.
2. SOUTH-EAST PORTION OF UPPER STORY OF FORT, TRANQUEBAR, TANJORE DISTRICT.
3. TANK WITH ISLAND, TIRUVALLUR, TANJORE DISTRICT.
4. THE MAIN GATEWAY, TIRUCHENKATTANGUDI, TANJORE DISTRICT. 5. CLOCK TOWER, TANJORE.

About one-fourth of the inhabitants are engaged in industrial concerns, the principal of which is the manufacture of textile goods. Several hundreds of persons are dependent for their livelihood on the weaving of cotton and silk tartans for Mahommedans and Hindus, and numbers of woollen blankets and carpets are made in the jail as well as by private individuals. Marvellously beautiful and artistic work is done in brass, silver, gold, and other metals, the products consisting of ash-trays, caskets, salt-cellars, scent-bottles, and many other ornamental articles. Connoisseurs in fine arts speak in terms of the highest praise of the work of these craftsmen, who paint the daintiest pictures on ivory and mica, some of these being far too small to be seen clearly by the naked eye. The tanning of hides has become a very important branch of commerce, and Trichinopoly leather-work, chiefly in shoes, has gained considerable popularity throughout the Presidency. The principal imports include raw hides, glass-ware, and tobacco, together with a number of oxen for agricultural purposes, while the exports consist of cotton, paddy, coconuts, plantains, cotton fabrics, baskets, paintings, silver-work, oilcake, cigars, buffaloes, sheep, and goats. The chief festival of the year is held at the Fort temple in the month of August, and the gods and goddess—Siva, Parvati, Ganesh, and Subramanya—are carried round the town.

THE STONE CAR, TIRUVALLUR.

The population has grown rapidly during the past four or five decades, and there are now (1915) about 124,000 inhabitants.

The municipal area of Srirangam (which is in reality an island formed by the Rivers Coleroon and Cauvery) is situated about 2 miles to the north of Trichinopoly, with which it is connected by a bridge of thirty-two arches, each of which has a span of about 49 ft. A Town Council was elected in 1871, and financial aid has been given towards the construction of the Coronation Hall, a hospital, vegetable markets, and a public slaughterhouse. The industries are unimportant, but a small trade is done in the making of musical instruments, baskets, and bangles. Srirangam is noted as the possessor of a very large sacred temple. This building is not a single structure of architectural beauty, as it would be more correctly described as a central shrine surrounded by a number of walls and lofty towers which have been erected by successive rulers. There are, in fact, seven enclosures, the outermost wall being 20 ft. 8 in. in height and 6 ft. in width at the top. The seventh (and the smallest enclosure) measures 240 ft. in length by 181 ft. in width, but Europeans are not permitted to enter this, nor the fifth and sixth quadrangles. The Vishnu temple is rich in its quantity of precious stones and metals, but the carving of the gems has been carried out in such an ineffective manner that their actual value is not apparent. Mr. J. D. Rees, in his "Tours in India," declares that there is a tradition that the famous Orloff diamond, which is the chief ornament in the imperial sceptre of the Czar, was formerly one of the eyes of the idol at Srirangam, and that it was stolen by a French deserter during the eighteenth century. The *Asiatic Journal* of 1839, chap. xxviii, says that the inscriptions in the building relate to the reign of the Chola king Parantaka I (906-46), while several others are of peculiar historical interest, as they belong to the Pandya, Hoysala, and Vijayanagar dynasties. An unfinished tower on the south side of the temple is, perhaps, the finest piece of work in all the buildings; it was intended that it should have risen to a height of about 300 ft., but its present elevation is not more than 200 ft. It may be mentioned that among the valuable plate of the temple is a golden salver which was presented by his late Majesty King Edward VII, on the occasion of his visit to India in 1875, when he was Prince of Wales. At the census of 1911 there were about 25,000 inhabitants. The Jambukeshwara temple—dedicated to Siva—is of considerable architectural beauty, and it is situated about half a mile from the one at Srirangam. The name is derived from "Jambu," the Sanskrit word for the naval-tree, and "Iswari," meaning "lord," and it is so called from the fact that the god of this temple is placed under a jambu-tree, which is held in veneration owing to its great age.

TEPPAKULAM TANK, MADURA.

When the traveller resumes the railway journey at Trichinopoly Junction he will find that the train travels through a flat yet interesting country, passing the small stations at Punguddi, Kolatur, Samudram, Vaiyampatti, and Ayyalur, near which place the district of Madura is reached. Dindigul, 310 miles distant from Madras, is the next town of importance on the route. This municipal borough is situated on an extensive plain in the *taluq* of Dindigul, having the Sirumalai Mountains on its southern side and the Lower Pulney Range on the west. Dindigul, or "The rock of Dindu," derives its name as well as its importance from the colossal monolith upon which a fortress of great strategical importance was constructed in or about the year 1605. The rock is 1,200 ft. in length, its breadth is 900 ft., and a considerable portion of it is about 1,223 ft. above the level of the sea. The fortifications command the mountain passes between Madura and Coimbatore, and, by reason of its almost impregnable position, the fortress has been the object of many invasions. As the town is built at an altitude of about 900 ft., a cool and invigorating climate is invariably experienced. Dindigul is a busy industrial centre, the principal exports being cotton, castor seeds, cigars, hides, skins, and bamboos, while the chief imports are tanning bark, salt, piece-goods, and sugar. A considerable trade is done in iron and bronze work, and there are also a few tanneries. The inhabitants are about 25,000 in number.

Upon leaving Dindigul it will be observed that, owing to the interposition of the Simuralai Hills, which are about 4,500 ft. above sea-level, the railway line to Madura has been constructed in the form of a semicircle. The only place which calls for notice on this section is Kodaikanal Road (Madras 323 miles), where passengers alight to proceed to the hill station and sanatorium of Kodaikanal, situated on the Pulney Hills. The township is comparatively small in size, but as it lies at an elevation of some 7,000 ft. above sea-level, it has a large number of supporters who claim that, as a health resort, it rivals Ootacamund. The shade temperature varies from a maximum of 76° F. in summer to a minimum of 42° in winter. There are several places of considerable beauty in the vicinity, which include the following: the Silver Cascade and Glen Falls, formed by the Parappar River, the Fairy Waterfalls, on the Pambar River, and the Pillar Rocks, consisting of three masses of granite about 400 ft. in height. There is an important Government Observatory here, and the principal scientific work of the Madras Presidency is prepared in it, on account of the equable nature of the climate. There is a good club in the township, and grounds and courts have been laid out for badminton, tennis, and other games. Several buildings are worthy of inspection, such as the English,

THE ROCK FORT, TRICHINOPOLY.

Photo by R. Vincent Solomon.

American, Lutheran, and Roman Catholic churches. There are about 4,500 inhabitants in the town.

The "Athens of Southern India" is the name which is frequently given to the city of Madura, on account of the classical beauty of the architecture of its numerous temples. It is situated on the south bank of the Vaigai River, and the graceful palm-trees overhanging the stream and the dimly seen blue summit of the Pulney Hills in the background with the lofty towers of the various shrines sandwiched in between combine in producing one of the most beautiful scenic effects in the Presidency. Madura is the chief town in the district of the same name, and for many centuries it was the political and religious capital of the southernmost portion of India. The early history of the district is derived principally from palæolithic inscriptions, although there is some other evidence that the Pandyas were at that time rulers of the land of the Tamils. Grecian and Roman historians wrote concerning the Pandya kingdoms two or three centuries before the Christian era, and Pliny, in or about A.D. 80, speaks of the "Mediterranean emporium of Modoura" of the Pandyan king. These and other references point clearly to the great antiquity as well as to the commercial wealth of Madura, and to-day (1915) it is a prosperous place of business containing a population of more than 134,000 persons. The Pandyans were succeeded in turn by the Pallavas, the Cholas, and the Mahommedans, and in 1752 the city was invaded by a mixed force under the commandership of Colonel Heron. The fortifications had been allowed to fall into decay, and its garrison had been removed, so that its surrender was a foregone conclusion, but the city entered upon a state of peace and security under British rule in the year 1801. The principal feature of interest in Madura is the great temple, which is situated about 1 mile to the east of the railway station. This building, or rather a series of buildings, is divided into two sections, the northern portion being dedicated to the god Siva, under the name of Sundarechwara, and the southern to his wife Minakshi, the "fish-eyed person." Mr. W. Francis, I.C.S., says: "Except the inner shrines probably no part of the temple is older than the sixteenth century. Four high stone walls enclose a nearly rectangular space measuring 830 ft. by 730 ft., within which is a labyrinth of store-houses, cloisters, mantapams, lesser shrines, and the sacred tank, and in the centre, surrounded by other walls with gateways and towers, the inner shrines of the god and goddess." As the visitor passes along the numerous corridors he will notice beautiful carvings in rich profusion on wood and stone; deities, notable personages, and events are depicted in various colours, and the magnificent temple jewels and ornaments of gold, silver, and precious stones which are kept in Siva's shrine are worthy of the closest inspection. The chief festivals are named Chittrai, Teppakulam, and Avanimulam. The first of these feasts is held in honour of the marriage of Siva and Minakshi; at the second one, celebrated in January and February, images of the god and

1. DANCING GIRLS AMONG THE CARVED FIGURES, RAMESWARAM.

Photo by Nicholas & Co.

2. MANTAPAM AT RAMESWARAM CONTAINING FOOTPRINTS OF RAMA.

goddess are floated on a raft in the Teppakulam tank ; while a number of the exploits of Siva are commemorated at the third, which falls in the month of August. The Teppakulam, or "tank of the raft," is an artificial reservoir, owing its construction to Tirumala Nayakka, and it is situated about 3 miles in an easterly direction from the railway station. It is 1,000 ft. in length and 950 ft. in width, and in the centre is a square island, among whose picturesque foliage is a lofty pagoda having chaste little shrines at each of the four corners. When the floating festival (mentioned above) takes place the buildings are illuminated by about ten thousand lights, while the idols from the temple are borne round the tank on a raft. The palace of Tirumala Nayakka is worthy of a visit, although it is now utilized chiefly as law courts and public offices. Madura was recognized as a seat of learning in very early times, and there are now several primary and secondary schools, some of which are supported by Roman Catholic and American Missions. The European Club is about half an hour's walk from the railway station, and it provides the usual social privileges, together with spacious grounds for tennis, croquet, and golf. There is a very large banyan-tree on the property of the club ; its trunk is 70 ft in circumference, and the branches cast shade for a distance of 180 ft. in any direction from the main stem. Madura is the centre of a most important agricultural district, and the quantity of merchandise and goods passing through the hands of the railway officials is greater at this station than at any other town on the South Indian system. Madura cloth for women's garments is well known throughout India for its superior quality, and the muslins and silks which are woven here are unsurpassed for the artistic manner in which they are made. Turbans with borders of gold and silver, and puggarees of every description are designed principally by the caste known as the Patnulkarans. A large steam cotton-spinning mill situated near to the railway station was opened by Messrs. Harvey Brothers in 1892, and several hundreds of workpeople find employment here. Brass utensils and ornaments are made in large numbers, also models of animals and insects which are fashioned of the same metal. Carvers of wood have attained a high reputation in Madura, some exceedingly fine examples of their work being seen over the doorways of houses and in the very handsome tables which are greatly in demand throughout India. Madura became a municipality on November 1, 1866, and its councillors adopted several important schemes for the improvement of the city, chief among which were the provision of a supply of water, and the construction of dispensaries and bridges. The city is not unhealthy, and it enjoys a somewhat even climate, as the average maximum temperature is 100·1° F. in the month of May, and the minimum is only 68·6° F. in January.

There are a few places of interest in the neighbourhood of Madura. Annuppanadi, for instance, 10 miles distant in a south-easterly direction, is noted for the discovery there of a number of pyriform earthenware tombs, and Kodimangalam, 8 miles to the north-west, has an ancient temple devoted to Siva, which is within a short distance from some remarkable caves.

STONE PILLARS, UTTARAKOSAMANGAI, RAMNAD DISTRICT.

It will now be convenient to notice the various places of interest which are served by the branch railway from Madura to Mandapam, on the north-east coast, opposite the island of Ceylon. The River Vaigai can be seen from the carriage windows during nearly the whole of its course to the point where it flows into the Gulf of Mannar near to the town of Mandapam. It has its source in the Varushanad range of hills, and some charming scenery, combining waterfalls, rivulets, caves, and beautiful foliage is obtained during the greater portion of its course. Thirty miles from Madura, and on the right bank of the Vaigai, is Manamadurai, a small town of about 5,000 inhabitants, in which there are temples dedicated to Siva and Vishnu. Fifteen miles farther along is the town of Paramakkudi, where the chief industry is the manufacture of muslins of fine texture and of gold lace. The products of the surrounding district are paddy, cholam, kumbu, gingelly, and other dry grains. The Chittrai festival—held in the month of May—attracts a very large number of persons, and an ancient temple dedicated to Siva is visited by crowds of pilgrims during the course of the year. The town has a population of about 12,200 persons.

Ramnad, standing at the base of a piece of land which projects towards the island of Pamban, in Palk Strait, is the chief town of the Ramnad zamindari. Its inhabitants are about 15,000 in number. The chief agricultural products of the neighbourhood are cholam, paddy, and rice, while many of the townspeople are engaged in the manufacture from palmyra-leaves of a large number of mats and baskets. A festival is held annually in a temple attached to the palace of the Rajah. There are two very ancient temples in the vicinity of Ramnad, namely, Tirupullani (or Therbasayanam) and Devipatanam (otherwise named Navapashanam), and they are respectively situated about 5 and 7 miles to the south and north-east of the station. The former is dedicated to Vishnu, and pilgrims who have been attending religious ceremonies at the famous shrine of Rameswaram invariably visit Tirupullani on their return, when further rites are observed for the purpose of completing their pilgrimage. There is a bathing-place at Devipatanam for devotees who are journeying towards Rameswaram.

Mandapam is increasing in popularity as an enjoyable seaside holiday resort. The railway authorities have provided a rest-house for visitors, and the natural attractions of the village, coupled with possibilities of recreation in sailing, sea-fishing, bathing, and shooting, are tempting enough to lure the seekers after change from the heat and dust of the inland towns.

The old route between Tuticorin and Ceylon has always been a most trying experience: one had to endure an hour's journey of 6 or 7 miles in a small and frequently unsteady tugboat before the steamer which awaited passengers could be reached; and then there was a sea-trip of no less than twelve hours to the harbour at Colombo. For many years past, however, negotiations have been in progress to effect a change, and plans of proposed bridges and other works having been prepared, conferences took place with a view of carrying out an engineering scheme of some magnitude. There is a distance of about 57 miles between the south-east coast of India and the north-west corner of Ceylon, and a portion of the mileage is covered, naturally, by the two islands of Rameswaram and Manaar, which, respectively, are adjacent to the Indian and Ceylon shores. A ridge of shifting sand, known as Adam's Bridge, lies between the two islands. In the first place the South Indian Railway Company constructed a metre-gauge line across the island of Rameswaram; then a steel viaduct was built between Mandapam and the island, thus enabling passengers to continue their train journey to Dhanushkodi, which is the terminus of the line. A proposal is on foot to erect bridges along the course of Adam's Bridge in order that trains may run uninterruptedly into Ceylon territory. At present, however, there is a ferry service of about 22 miles between Dhanushkodi and the island of Manaar, which has been connected with the Ceylon main system of railways. Three turbine steamers have been obtained by the South Indian Railway Company for the ferry service. These boats were built on the Clyde; they are 250 ft. in length, and are fitted with Parsons geared turbines and Yarrow water-tube boilers. They draw 6 ft. of water, and have been designed to develop a speed of 18 knots.

This new route was opened for passenger service by the Governor of Madras, Lord Pentland, on February 24, 1914.

The island of Rameswaram is about 25 miles in length, and it is some 6 miles in width in the western portion, while the remainder is merely a strip of sand stretching towards the island of Manaar. The chief town bears the same name as the island, and the houses—with the exception of those in the immediate vicinity of the temple—are of exceedingly primitive design. There is no shrine in the whole of India which is more highly venerated than the great temple at Rameswaram, and for hundreds of years pilgrims from all parts have congregated there for worship. It is generally believed that it was founded by Rama, and that it was erected by the Setupatis of Ramnad. The building stands in a

1. WATERFALL, KUTTALAM, TINNEVELLY. 2. GOPURAM OF THE TEMPLE, TINNEVELLY.

Photo by Nicholas & Co.

quadrangular enclosure which is 1,000 ft. in length and 657 ft. in breadth, and the principal gateway is no less than

STONE LAMP-POST IN THE SEA, IN FRONT OF THE SHORE TEMPLE, MAHABALIPURAM.

100 ft. in height. The massive character of the workmanship in the temple is its most pronounced feature, but the spacious corridors, with their ornamental columns and plaster ceilings, are distinctly imposing. The *lingam*—which, according to tradition, was placed in the temple by Rama himself—is washed daily in water from the sacred River Ganges, and the water is subsequently sold to faithful worshippers at very remunerative prices. A very valuable quantity of jewellery has been collected, and the annual income from offerings exceeds a lakh of rupees. The railway terminus is at Dhanushkodi, a place which is visited by many thousands of pilgrims.

It will be found that the distance from Madura to Tuticorin is rather less than 100 miles. After a ride of twenty minutes one sees the village of Tirupparankundram, where an ancient Hindu temple is built at the foot of Subrahmanya's rocky hill, which is about 1,050 ft. above the level of the sea. The stone from the rock is highly valued for building purposes, and it is believed that a large quantity of it was quarried for the construction of the great temple at Madura. Twenty miles from Madura is the township of Virudupati, where there are several cotton presses, and where bed-sheets of a coarse material, dusters, and other household requisites are manufactured. Maniyachi is only of importance as a junction station on the railway line which branches at this point to Tuticorin on the east and Tinnevelly and Quilon on the west. A large quantity of merchandise is entrained here, as the surrounding district is exceedingly favourable for the growth of cotton, kumbu, gram, and coriander seeds. The country on either side of the railway line is as flat as the proverbial pancake, but there are abundant evidences of sound agri-

ARJUNA'S RATHA, MAHABALIPURAM, CHINGLEPUT.

cultural knowledge on the part of the owners and occupiers of the cultivated lands. Tataparai, 437 miles from Madras, is the Emigration Depot of the Ceylon Government, and coolies who have been engaged for work on the tea estates of that island break their journey here before proceeding by steamer to Colombo. Not many minutes elapse before Tuticorin is sighted. This is the most important seaport on the south-eastern coast, and it is the southern terminus of the South Indian line of railways from Madras, from which city it is 447 miles distant. Good anchorage for small boats is available, but steamers even of moderate tonnage are compelled to remain 5 or 6 miles from the shore owing to the shallowness of the water. Communication between Tuticorin and Colombo is undertaken by the British India Steam Navigation Company's steamers, the passage occupying about twelve hours. Merchant vessels belonging to England, Japan, and other nations call periodically at Tuticorin, and a very considerable export and import trade is carried on. The town has several cotton presses, ginning factories, spinning and weaving mills, and a Government salt factory, about 1 mile from the station, affords employment for a large number of persons. Pearl-fishing was a profitable industry for very many years, but various causes have combined to bring about a decrease in the returns recently. Tuticorin was founded as a settlement by the Portuguese in the year 1540; it was subsequently held by the Dutch, but it was eventually (1825) handed over to the British. Training and high schools are maintained by the S.P.G., and there are two Roman Catholic and one Protestant church. In the commercial centre of the town are branches of the Bank of Madras and of the National Bank of India, Ltd., the offices of the Port Authorities, the Sub-Collector, the Assistant Commissioner of Salt and Abkari, and the Superintendent of Pearl Fisheries. There were 40,185 inhabitants at the census of 1911.

THE ROCK FORT, FROM THE BAZAAR, TRICHINOPOLY.

Photo by R. V. Solomon.

Tinnevelly Bridge (445 miles from Madras) is the largest town in the district of Tinnevelly, and it is situated on the left bank of the River Tambraparni, while Palamcottah—the administrative headquarters of the district—is on the right-hand side of the same river and less than 2 miles distant from Tinnevelly. Jaggery is cultivated extensively in this district, and the crop is used in sugar-mills in the town of Tinnevelly and at Nellikuppam. The local factories are owned by the East India Distilleries Company, Ltd., and by the Tinnevelly Sugar Mills Company, and one of these is capable of producing as much as 7 tons of refined sugar daily. Metal-work is engaged in by a considerable number of the inhabitants, and the weaving of carpets and cloth is carried on by prisoners in the jail at Palamcottah. Educational advantages are of a high order, and the colleges and schools controlled by the Church Missionary Society and the S.P.G. have a large number of pupils, the Sarah Tucker College, for example, having the names of between 400 and 500 scholars upon its books. The district of Tinnevelly has for a very long period been noted for the activity of its religious organizations,

THE GREAT TEMPLE AT TANJORE.

and there are many persons who are now connected with churches which were formed by St. Francis Xavier. It was in the early days a portion of the Pandya kingdom, and it—with its neighbour Madura—suffered severely at the hands of the Mahommedans at the beginning of the fourteenth century. The district was finally ceded to the British in 1801. The temple, which is situated in the centre of the town, is divided into two parts, which are dedicated to Siva and Parvati respectively. There are three towers with porches, and there are two main entrances on the eastern side. A visit should certainly be made to this shrine, as it contains a considerable number of very fine sculptures and carvings, while other buildings worthy of inspection are the Hindu and the Missionary Colleges.

The railway route takes a westerly direction from Tinnevelly, and after 2 miles have been covered the train reaches Pettai, a town of considerable importance, the majority of whose inhabitants are Mahommedans. Smaller towns named Melakallur, Sermadevi, Viravanallur, and Kallidaikurichi are then passed, and at a distance of 467 miles from Madras a stoppage is made at Ambasamudram, which has a population of 10,855 persons. This place is the headquarters of the Tahsildar and

1. VIEW FROM THE TANK, GREAT CONJEEVERAM.

Photo by Nicholas & Co.

2. WOOD-CARVING PANEL REPRESENTING KRISHNA AND GOPIS AT KUMBAKONAM.

3. WOOD-CARVING PANEL REPRESENTING GANGA ON A CROCODILE, KUMBAKONAM.

1. NEELAYATHAKSHI AMMAN TEMPLE, NEGAPATAM. 2. MAIN GOPURAM, THYAGARJA TEMPLE, TIRUVALUR. 3. VIEW OF VEDARANYASAVARA TEMPLE, VEDARANNYAM, TANJORE DISTRICT.

District Munsiff, and the majority of the inhabitants are engaged in the industry of weaving cloth. About 5 miles from here, in a south-westerly direction, is Papanasam, where there are beautiful waterfalls, which attain very great power during the rainy season between the months of June and November. Adjoining the falls is the factory of the Tinnevelly Spinning Mills Company. The town of Tenkasi—with its 15,000 inhabitants—situated on the northern bank of the River Chittar, is almost on the border of the district of Travancore. The chief products of the neighbourhood are paddy and coconuts, while the industries of the town include the weaving of cloth for exportation to the surrounding districts. There is an ancient Siva temple, which should be seen on account of the number of sculptured deities, but it has unfortunately lost much of its outward beauty owing to a fire which occurred about the end of the eighteenth century. A halt should be called at Tenkasi for the purpose of paying a visit to Courtallam, which is a favourite health resort for officials and others from various parts of Southern India. It occupies a most delightful situation in a mountain-girt valley, and an abundance of forest trees provides ample shelter from sun and wind. The Chittar waterfall is very beautiful as it thunders over several ledges of rock on its way to the pond below; it shimmers and sparkles in the sunlight, and the dark green leaves of the overhanging branches of trees and shrubs form a fitting contrast to the silvery appearance of the cascade. Hindus regard the water of these falls as possessing the power to cleanse them from sin, but Europeans are satisfied with the opportunity which is afforded for having a delightful bath amid the pleasantest surroundings. There is an area of considerable extent lying to the south side of Tinnevelly Bridge, which is not yet served by any railway.

TWELVE PILLARED MANTAPAM, GINGEE, SOUTH ARCOT.

SOUTHERN INDIA

PUDUKKOTTAI STATE

THERE are five Native States which have direct political relations with the Government of Madras, and Pudukkottai ranks third in importance. It is bounded on the north and west by the district of Trichinopoly, and it abuts upon the district of Tanjore and Madura on east and south respectively. It is 1,178 square miles in extent, and has a population of about 412,000 inhabitants. The State is also known as "the Tondaimans country," this description being derived from the family name of its ruling chiefs. Historical records concerning the territory prior to the seventeenth century are unfortunately unobtainable, but in the Singhalese annals of the war of the Pandya succession in the twelfth century it is said that "the Pandya king, Kulasekhara, fled into the hills of Tondamana," and this is the first reference to this part of the Presidency as a separate entity. The relations of the State with the Madras Government commenced during the Carnatic wars, when the Tondaiman assisted the English in wars against the French about the year 1752, and again at a later date in conflicts with Mysore, Tanjore, and the poligars of other districts. It should not be forgotten, too, that during the siege of Trichinopoly in 1752-3 the British forces relied very largely upon the Tondaiman for their supplies of provisions, and in 1756 this ruler sent some of his troops to assist Muhammad Yosuf, the Sepoy commandant of the East India Company, in the settlement of the district of Madura and Tinnevelly. Assistance of this nature was cordially rendered by the State to the British during a period of more than fifty years, and in 1844 it was declared by Act of Parliament to be "foreign territory." A political agent was first appointed about the year 1800, and the Rajah is now advised on important administrative matters by the Madras Government through the medium of the Collector of Trichinopoly, who holds the position of Agent. The present ruler is His Highness Sri Bridhadamba Sir Marthanda Bhairava Tondiman Bahadur. G.C.I.E., who was born in 1875, and as a minor succeeded his grandfather in 1886.

The State contains one town—Pudukkottai—and nearly four hundred villages, and the latest census returns stated that the inhabitants were 411,886 in number. Nearly the whole of the country consists of almost flat plain, but there are some hills of rock in several portions. Forest and jungle may be seen in the south and south-west of the State, but elsewhere the land is fairly well cultivated. A fully qualified engineer, who has several assistants, is in charge of the Public Works Department, and the construction and maintenance of roads and the care of the State buildings are zealously looked after by him. A hospital, which has been thoroughly equipped with modern appliances, was established at Pudukkottai in the year 1851, and there are several dispensaries in other parts of the State. The Rajah maintains a military force of nearly two hundred officers and men.

KHAN SAHIB SHAIK ISMAIL SAHIB BAHADUR.

1 KHADAR MOSQUE. 2. VETERINARY HOSPITAL. 3. KHAN SAHIB SHAIK ISMAIL SAHIB BAHADUR.

Among the principal villages are Tiruvappur, a suburb of Pudukkottai, which possesses an ancient Siva temple; Tirumayam, with a population of nearly 4,000 inhabitants, a very old township which is noted principally for some excellent ruins of an old fort; Narttamalai, nine miles north-west of Pudukkottai, containing temples with Buddhist or Jain images sculptured on the rock; and Kilanilai, in which is a fort built by the last of the Nayakkan kings of Tanjore about the year 1670.

KHAN SAHIB SHAIK ISMAIL SAHIB BAHADUR

The subject of this sketch is one of the leading residents in the important town of Trichinopoly, and he is highly respected not only on account of his sterling business qualities, but also by reason of his unswerving loyalty to H.M. the King-Emperor and to the British Government. He has always welcomed an opportunity of giving expression to this allegiance, and his bitterest enemy could not say of him that his devotion began and ended with the waving of flags and with the singing of the English National Anthem.

During the Coronation Durbar festivities at Trichinopoly, he provided a number of magnificent *pandals* at a considerable expenditure of money, and his meritorious act was recognized by a suitable reference in the Fort St. George Government *Gazette*, by the receipt of a certificate of honour, and by a personal distinction being conferred upon him by his Excellency the Viceroy. Shaik Ismail Sahib is the owner of landed property in four or five villages, and his consideration for the welfare of his tenants is one of the most pleasing traits in his character. He is a descendant of one of the families to whom pensionary contributions were granted by the Nawab of the Carnatic and his parents were in the enjoyment of the same. He is a wealthy man—his land-tax payable to the Government amounts to Rs. 2,000, and the income-tax about Rs. 400—but he regards his fortune in the light of a sacred trust to be used for the benefit of those who are in real need of assistance. His charitable gifts are distributed with great discretion, and many a man is indebted to this gentleman for timely assistance which has enabled him to recover a position of respectability and usefulness. He has contributed liberally for the benefit of Mahommedan institutions, of which he is a patron. A sum of Rs. 2,000 was expended by him in the erection of a new building for the High School Srirangam, which is under his patronage, and the High School Committee have erected a separate hall, styled the "Khan Sahib Shaik Ismail Sahib." An isolated hospital building for the treatment of animals suffering from contagious diseases has been constructed at his own cost in front of the S.P.C.A. Veterinary Hospital, Trichinopoly, and he, further, helps poor students of the Mahommedan community by giving school fees, clothing, and books to the utmost of his ability.

Shaik Ismail Sahib is, moreover, a keen business man, and his transactions in general merchandise reach a formidable total in the course of a year. He had a thorough training in contracting and in general engineering work, and he has successfully completed important schemes of construction for local firms, municipalities, and for the Department of Public Works.

D. NANNUSWAMY BHAGAVATHAR

The excellent quality of the goods, the novelty of designs, the moderateness of the price, and the prompt attention given to orders entrusted to a tradesman are the surest ways to command success, and success is nothing but the retention of customers when they have been secured. These characteristics have always been found in the business conduct of Mr. D. Nannuswamy Bhagavathar, fancy cloth merchant and manufacturer of all sorts of Indian cloths and other articles, whose premises are situated in Marret Street, in the town of Madura. Having an experience of fifteen years in cloth merchandise, he has established himself, on his own account, at the above address, where he has in hand an extensive assortment of Madura muslins, very rich silks, embroideries suitable for evening dresses, Indian wedding, and other fashionable cloths of the day to suit the different requirements of all nationalities. In addition to the continuance of the business on original lines, he is making a speciality of ladies' scarves, gowns, blouses, puggaries, table covers, window curtains, Madura-made silver articles of various patterns, and carved wooden tables supported by real elephant pads. Orders for any novelty are executed with diligence and satisfaction, and every endeavour is made to match the owner's designs in every respect. Further, he holds the premier position in the town in this particular line of trade.

D. NANNUSWAMY BHAGAVATHAR.

1. "Best House," Madura. 2. D. Nannuswamy Bhagavathar.

C. V. C. T. K. R. KARUPPAN CHETTIAR

The letters which precede the surname at the head of these notes appear to be a

S. R. M. A. R. RAMASWAMI CHETTIAR.

1. S. R. M. A. R. Ramaswami Chettiar. 2. S. R. M. A. R. Ramaswami Chettiar's Son. 3. House at Kanadukathan. 4. Bungalow at Patuketa. 5. Rice and Oil Mill at Patukota. 6. Rice Mill at Pillaivilagam.

somewhat formidable prefix, but, in reality, they are nothing more than an illustration of the principles of the law of heredity, and they are equally as forceful as those gigantic genealogical trees which are the pride of so many families of distinction in nearly every country of the world. By way of explanation it may be said that the ancestors of Mr. Karuppan Chettiar, who are represented by the letter "C," settled at Koratty in the district of Ramnad very many years ago, while the "V" generation founded a domicile at Kanadukathan in the same district, where their descendants have continued to reside to the present day. The family have always been bankers, and Mr. Karuppan Chettiar is the sole proprietor of the well-known establishment whose headquarters are at Rangoon, with branches at Danubya in Burma, and at Aruppukottai in the district of Ramnad, and he is, further, a partner in the firm of A. K. K. V. St. in Colombo.

This highly respected citizen, Mr. Karuppan Chettiar, has inherited the charitable disposition of his father, who expended 3 lakhs of rupees in the building of a temple at Arvakudy, dedicated to Vishnu, and who, further, gave about 2 lakhs of rupees for the construction of another shrine at Kodumudy, in the district of Coimbatore. He has also set apart a sum of 1½ lakhs of rupees for the Samskrita Patasala at Amman Sannady Street, Madura, where about 50 pupils receive free boarding and lodging, and are learning both Vedas and Shastras.

Mr. Karuppan Chettiar, who is a large landowner, was formerly an ordinary member of the *taluq* and district board of the Ramnad district, but he now occupies the important position of chairman of the Karakudy Union Panchayat.

C. V. C. T. K. R. KARUPPAN CHETTIAR.

S. R. M. A. R. RAMASWAMI CHETTIAR

Mr. S. R. M. A. R. Ramaswami Chettiar comes of a family which has been well known for its princely benefactions throughout Southern India. Mr. Chettiar's principal business, among others, is banking. His head office is at Rangoon, and he has established branches at Dedaye, Kyaiklat, Henzada, Kungyangon, Zalun, Bassein, and Thayetkon in British Burma, at Saigon, Cantho, and Chaudoc in French Cochin China, and at Madras and Patukottai in Southern India. He is also the owner of a rice-mill at Thillaivilagam, and of an oil-mill at Patukottai, which are together estimated to be worth a lakh of rupees. He is, like his ancestors, well know for his public spirit and munificence, but he has not allowed himself to be outdone by them in acts of public beneficence, as schools, colleges, and other benevolent institutions have received his support. His recent donation of Rs. 5,000 to the Society for the Prevention of Cruelty to Animals at Madras, and of Rs. 1,000 to the Economic Association in the same city, are proofs of his desire to make his wealth serviceable to furthering noble and deserving causes. It was in recognition of such acts that the Government of Madras honoured him with a medal and certificate of merit on the occasion of his Majesty's Coronation at Delhi. His silent acts of charity have won for him the love and respect of those who know him.

Among the benefactions for which the family has become deservedly famous, only the following need be mentioned: (1) 30 lakhs of rupees for repairing and adorning the temple at Chidambaram; (2) 1 lakh of rupees for erecting a choultry there; (3) 5 lakhs of rupees invested in immovable property for the up-keep of the choultry; and (4) Rs. 125,000 for the formation of a Provident Fund, the income from which is to be applied towards the expense of daily *pavadai*, which feeds 300 Deikshitars of the temple.

Mr. Chettiar recently purchased the Sillattur zamindari in the district of Tanjore, which yields an annual income of Rs. 40,000, while his other landed properties in two villages in the district of Ramnad bring in a yearly rental of Rs. 5,000.

His palatial residence of Kanadukathan, which has been built at a cost of more than a lakh of rupees, is magnificently furnished, and is fitted with electric light and other up-to-date conveniences. He is a director of the Indian Bank, and a member of the Cosmopolitan Club at Madras.

NANA VANA MANICKA DOSS

Few native physicians in Southern India can show an unbroken record of a family of seven generations who have resided in the same town and who have made their name famous by the generous gift to the poor of free advice and medicines ; but the subject of these notes, Dr. Nana Vana Manicka Doss, is able to look back with pride upon the benevolent work accomplished by six of his ancestors in Ramachandra Puram, in the taluq of Tirumayam, in the district of Trichinopoly. The doctor himself is a worthy successor of the noble-hearted members of his family of the past, and he is assiduously maintaining the high reputation for pure-minded charity which was established so many years ago. He receives and advises patients at his own house, he makes up his own prescriptions on the premises, and all this is done without any fees being demanded, his reward being the consciousness that he is doing something to relieve the terrible amount of sickness and sorrow with which he is brought into contact daily. The doctor commands the greatest respect from the Nattukottai Chetti community, and Brahmans, whether rich or poor, are not only given treatment and medicine, but they also receive food and clothing in necessitous cases. This gentleman's private residence (which has been valued approximately at Rs. 65,000) would be more correctly described as a palace, it is so imposing in appearance and its internal fittings and adornments are so chaste. Electric light is about to be installed.

Dr. Doss is unquestionably one of the most popular men in the district of Trichinopoly, and that he is not indifferent to the religious welfare of the neighbourhood is evident from the fact that he has made himself personally responsible for the construction of a temple in his own grounds at a cost of a lakh of rupees. A rice-mill is being erected, and this will afford employment for a considerable number of hands.

NANA VANA MANICKA DOSS.

1. Nana Vana Manicka Doss. 2. Residence. 3. Medical Hall.

THE GURU MEDICAL HALL AND LABORATORY

The sole proprietor of the Guru Medical Hall, Trichinopoly (Dr. A. Mathuram), is the son of Dr. Samuel Mathuram, who is now in medical charge of St. Luke's Hospital, Nazareth, in the district of Tinnevelly, in Southern India.

The doctor's great-grandfather, Mr. Nullamuthu Visuvasam, was selected by the S.P.G. Mission to be the physician and catechist to give both medical and spiritual services to the new converts in Tinnevelly at a time when there was no Western medical aid. He was born in 1805, and died at the age of ninety-one, in the year 1896. He was regarded as an eminent and popular Indian physician, and he learned much from Sanniasi (Ascetics), who favoured him with certain rare recipes, and taught him also practical Indian chemical science. He afterwards became a specialist in diseases of children. His rare and valuable specialities obtained from the Sanniasi Guru are now prepared solely by Dr. A. Mathuram, in his Guru Medical Laboratory, and these medicines are to-day used by many, and specially by the mission agents in different parts of Southern India.

Dr. Samuel Mathuram, the father of Dr. A. Mathuram, was selected by the Mission for admission to the Government Medical College, Madras, in order to learn the Western medical science, and he took a full course of studies from 1870 to 1874, obtaining a diploma of the grade of sub-assistant surgeon. Soon after he left the college he was sent to Irangalore, in the district of Trichinopoly, where he opened a Mission dispensary. As he was a diplomaed medical officer, the Government gave warm assistance and raised the dispensary to the status of a hospital with all equipments. He laboured there for seventeen years, and was afterwards employed in establishing a similar institution in the Nagalapuram Circle, in Northern Tinnevelly. Here he won the support of the Hindu Rajah of Ettaiyapuram, who gives even to-day £40 annually to the Mission in the name of the hospital. Afterwards the S.P.G. Mission decided that he should fill the place of Canon and Doctor Margoschis in St. Luke's Hospital, Nazareth, which is the chief S.P.G. centre in South India. He has worked for the Mission for forty years, and he is still doing active service there. His works are praised by European District-Surgeons, Bishops of South India, and by European missionaries.

Dr. A. Mathuram being the firstborn of the fourth generation, inherited the secret recipes of Guru medicines, and he then joined the Prince of Wales's Medical Institution at Tanjore, to undergo a full course of Western science. He obtained a diploma in 1900, and as a special advantage, and by merit, he was selected to take the sole charge of a hospital at Aruppu-kota, in the district of Madura. During his residence there he practised both the Ayurvedic and Western medical systems upon his hospital patients, and improved his knowledge by getting additional information from various *Sanniyasis,* whom he met as specialists. From his experience with thousands of patients he evolved a combination of medicines and found them to be highly efficacious for the present-day human needs.

Speedy and permanent cures followed his treatment, and he received correspondence from different parts of the country, and as he felt that he could not serve two masters any longer, he established a business for the supply of medicines to distant patients. He prepares and supplies on a large scale the following medicines: Guru tooth-powder, testified to be the most efficacious tooth preserver, and a cure for bad teeth; nerve and general tonics are sent on hearing the present and past history of each case; Malabar balm, a most efficacious remedy for all pains and aches of whatever origin; Malabar hair-oil, claimed to be the best for hair and cranial nerves; uterine cure and tonic; a seven-day cure for gout and rheumatism; specific for eczema and sores (one week cure); children's specific, health pills and Kastoori carminative pills; diarrhœa cure; liver corrective and tonic; three-days cure for jaundice; three days cure for malaria; Danwantri senthooram: a three-days cure for all diseases of venereal origin; for painful disorders of the intestines; and for all nerve pains and wind troubles; a chronic diarrhœa cure; the great lung specific; the popular wind troubles cure; and many others.

PREPARATIONS FROM THE GURU MEDICAL LABORATORY, TRICHINOPOLY.

Since the doctor commenced practice, many medical men (who are known to the family) began to request him to supply them with Trichinopoly cigars also, which have a deserved reputation for high-class quality. The demands became so great that a separate department has been opened in order to cope with the very large number of orders from practitioners in all parts of the country.

A. & F. HARVEY

The firm of Messrs. A. & F. Harvey, which is very largely interested in the cotton industry, was founded in 1879, purely as a cotton-exporting firm, by Andrew and Frank Harvey, at Virudupatti, where the press then acquired is still being worked. The great possibilities of the industry and its allied interests presented themselves with such force that, with the support of English friends, cotton spinning mills were established, first at Ambasamudram, and later at Tuticorin and Madura; and, as a necessary adjunct, ginning factories and presses were erected at Virudupatti, Satur, and Tuticorin. The success of these mills has been such that, in order to cope with the increased demand, it has been necessary to enlarge each to more than twice its original size.

The Tinnevelly Mills commenced working at Ambasamudram in the year 1884, the motive power being obtained from the famous Papanasam Falls, which are situated in close proximity. The erection of this mill was a work of some magnitude, as all machinery and everything connected with it had to be transported a distance of 30 miles in country bullock-carts, over very indifferent roads, and in the course of the journey two rivers had to be forded. The railway, now running direct to Quilon, in those days had

HH

A. & F. HARVEY.

1. General View, Madura New Mills. 2. Reeling-room, Madura Mill. 3. Blow-room, Madura Mill. 4. 2,500 H.P. Engine, Madura Mill. 5. Coral Mills, Tuticorin.

A. & F. HARVEY.

1 AND 2. WATER CHANNELS, TINNEVELLY MILLS. 3. NEW MILL PIPE LINE, TINNEVELLY MILLS. 4. NEW MILL TURBINE HOUSE, TINNEVELLY MILLS. 5. INTERIOR VIEW, TINNEVELLY MILLS.

only been constructed as far as Tinnevelly, 30 miles from the site of the mill. The mills were greatly enlarged in 1906, and 41,472 spindles are now running, giving regular employment to about 1,500 hands. The mills were the first in India to be driven by water-turbine.

The Coral Mills at Tuticorin were opened in 1889, and to cope with the expansion of business the premises had to be extended in 1898 to over twice their original proportions. About 1,800 hands are regularly employed in connection with the working of 43,120 spindles.

The Madura Mills are the largest in Southern India, and form one of the most important industrial concerns. The original mill, built near the railway station at Madura, started work in 1892 with 36,344 spindles. In 1913 an entirely new and separate mill was erected adjacent to the original one, with a working complement of 70,192 spindles, giving regular employment to about 3,000 hands, to which has to be added about 1,500 employed in the original building.

No expense was spared in the equipment of the premises, and the finest modern machinery has been installed. The engine of 2,500 h.p. is the product of the best workmanship, and is in itself a monument of modern-day excellence.

The capital of the various mills is as follows: The Madura Mills Company, Ltd., Rs. 20,000,000; The Coral Mills Company, Ltd., Rs. 15,000,000; and The Tinnevelly Mills Company, Ltd., Rs. 12,000,000.

The mills are dependent largely on local consumption for the disposal of their production, but considerable shipments are made to China, Rangoon, and various other markets, where their yarns are much in favour and command a ready sale.

Skilled Europeans from Lancashire are responsible for the inside management of the mills, under the supervision of the present partners, namely, Messrs. Andrew Harvey, D. Miller, A. Harvey, jun., and J. Craig Harvey.

The firm also represents several important concerns, among which may be mentioned The Clan Line of Steamers, Ltd., The Nippon Yusen Kaisha (Japan Mail Steamship Company), The Osaka Shosen Kaisha Steamship Company, The Bibby Line of Steamers, The Royal Insurance Company, Ltd., and the Kanan Devan Hills Produce Company, Ltd.

RABBI B. J. M. KULASEKHARA-RAJ

India is essentially a country of cults (or particular rituals or systems of worship), and the history of the religious faiths of to-day carries the student back to the origin of creeds. Many of these systems, such as Hinduism, Buddhism, and Jainism, are autochthonous, while others were formulated in the early days of the Christian era, with the exception of the doctrines proclaimed by the Jews who arrived in India during the sixth century B.C. One of the sects which has arisen in later days is connected with "Jehovah-Messianism," or "The Indian Church of the Only Saviour," and it was founded in the year 1857 by one Rabbi A. N. Chattampillai-Aiya (born October 24, 1823), who was a student of many European and Oriental languages and literature, residing at Prakasapuram, near Nazareth, in the district of Tinnevelly. The adherents were about 6,000 in number in the early seventies, but owing to lack of support and to incessant persecutions there are now (1915) only five churches, with a membership of about 1,000 persons. One of the principal tenets of this society is that the Christianity of the present day is not identical with the teachings of the early Apostles, but that the thousand-and-one nonconforming branches of religious activities are offshoots of a new faith, founded on the anti-Jewish or unchristian principles of Hadrian, Constantine, Justinian, and other Roman and Christian emperors in contradiction of the Holy Scriptures. Jehovah-Messianics, in their interpretation of the Divine Books, observe the seventh-day Sabbath, the festivals of the new-moon, the feasts of "Pascha" (the Passover), the "harvest" (the Pentecost), of "trumpets," of the "expiation," the "ingathering," and of "booths," offering firstfruits, incense, meat, and other sacrificial oblations in the presence of Jehovah. They submit themselves to bodily purifications, and assert that these were ordained by Jehovah to commemorate the fall and the expiation of the sins of our first parents. Such Hindu rites as are not inconsistent with Scriptural ideas are not rejected, and the text of the Hindu law with regard to marriage and inheritance is generally accepted.

The present leaders of the body are Messrs. Nabhi P. V. Pandion and B. J. M. Kulasekhara-raj, sons of the founder. The founder's two daughters remain virgins for religion's sake.

Rabbi Chattampillai-Aiyar (still alive) was an ardent collector of books from the year 1850, and he succeeded in gathering together about 10,000 volumes on various subjects, chiefly Oriental and religious, in the following languages, namely, Sanskrit, Pali, Tamil, Malayalam, Canarese, Hindustani, Arabic, Hebrew, Greek, Latin, French, English, and German. In addition to these the library contains hundreds of old Tamil palm-leaf manuscripts, and about 10,000 coins belonging to the Pandya, Chola, Chera, Telugu, Mahommedan, and other dynasties of South India and Ceylon.

Mr. B. J. M. Kulasekhara was born in the year 1873, and he is endeavouring to further the interests of the cause which was originated by his father, and to publish valuable historical and other works. To this end he is compiling a philological dictionary and a grammar of the Tamil language, having special reference to Sanskrit and other languages of India; also an early history of the Tamil country on new and original principles; he has prepared many numbers of his "Aids to the History of Dravidam" series, and "Sources of Tamil Lexicography" series, as well as an Anglo-Tamil magazine entitled *The Light of Dravidam and the Orient* (*Dravida-Purva Dipam*). He has also made literary contributions to the local Government Ethnographic, Gazetteer, and Archæological Publication Departments. His most interesting production, however, is the "Jehovah-Messianic Religion Explained," which is issued in four parts. The first part deals principally with the origin and motive of the doctrines and practices of the Bible and the history of their gradual rejection by the Christians, the object of the author being to bind together the people of the world—Jews and Gentiles alike—in the truths of that book. The second part is styled the "Tora-Bible and its Weedy Books," and it gives the accounts of the genuine, apocryphal, and pseudonymous books of the Jewish and Christian faiths. The Jehovah-Messianic religious precepts and practices are classified and explained in the third part, while the fourth, "Tora-Ethics," sets forth, in tabulated form, the various moral injunctions of the Bible. Other religious works from the pen of this author include "Incarnate Revelation," a treatise on Christology, and an edition of the Bible containing various readings and translations according to the canon of the Jehovah-Messianic Church, together with the "Light of Religion," which is to be published in magazine

KHAN BAHADUR P. R. M. KASSIM MOHAMED MARAKAYAR.

1. KHAN BAHADUR P. R. M. KASSIM MOHAMED MARAKAYAR. 2. P. R. M. ABDUL RAHIMAN MARAKAYAR. 3. THE KHAN BAHADUR'S BUNGALOW.

form. Rabbi Kulasekhara-raj is most enthusiastic in the study of religious works and in orientological researches, and he is ever ready to proceed to any part of the world where he may be able to extend his knowledge, or where his vast experience and great abilities may be of service to others.

KHAN BAHADUR P. R. M. KASSIM MOHAMED MARAKAYAR

The ancestors of Khan Bahadur P. R. M. Kassim Mohamed Marakayar have, for many generations, been residents of Mandapam, and they have been engaged in commercial enterprises of many kinds. The present proprietor has followed his predecessors in an extensive business as a general merchant and commission agent, but he is more widely known owing to the prominent position which he has taken in connection with the social advancement of the people among whom he lives. Khan Bahadur Marakayar is the owner of seven villages, namely: Karkudi, Orathur, Periya-Ithambadal, Thanichiyam, Kilambal, Kumukkotaai, and Saiyalur, and he possesses several other large landed properties in the near neighbourhood. The title of Khan Bahadur was conferred upon him by the Madras Government in recognition of his charitable gifts to public institutions, and one of these of a particularly deserving character was the bearing of the cost of the construction of a hospital at Mandapam. Another instance of his munificence occurred when he contributed most liberally to the making of a road—8 miles in length—on behalf of the pilgrims who travel from Ramnad to Devapatam. The Khan Bahadur is, further, the owner of "Hare Island"—a gift from the late Rajah of Ramnad—where he had the honour of entertaining his Excellency Lord Ampthill, Governor of Madras, who presented to his host a gold ring set with gems as a souvenir of his visit. Europeans in Mandapam have good cause for honouring the Khan Bahadur, as he has constructed a metalled road between that town and Thouithoray, and it is noteworthy that the name of "Lawley's Road" was conferred upon it by permission of H.E. Sir Arthur Lawley, then Governor of the Madras Presidency, who presided at the opening ceremony during a three days' visit to Mandapam.

The horizon of the Khan Bahadur's generosity is exceedingly wide, and with the love for dumb animals which is characteristic of a true man, he erected a water-trough at Ramnad for the use of horses and cattle. The Collector of the Ramnad district took a prominent part in the inaugural proceedings in connection with the gift, and he was supported on the occasion by the Rajah and by the leading inhabitants. Yet another example of the Khan Bahadur's munificence is the proposed construction of a building at Mandapam in which the Mohammedan community may have the opportunity of reading the Koran and other literary works. Nearly a lakh of rupees will be necessary to complete the scheme, and the Khan Bahadur intends to provide for the annual cost of the library and of feeding the poor by making a charge upon the revenue of the village of Saiyalur.

The Khan Bahadur's commercial enterprises are wide in character, but in every branch of the business there is seen the intelligent control which the proprietor exercises. The loading and unloading of cargo at Mandapam is undertaken, and a fleet of about 30 large boats is engaged in this service. About 1,000 hands are employed throughout the year. The British India Steam Navigation Company is represented at Mandapam by the Khan Bahadur.

The subject of the sketch has been a member of the Taluq and District Boards of Ramnad for a very long time (even before the bifurcation of the Ramnad district), and he has, further, had a seat on the District Board of Madura. He has taken very considerable interest in matters of local self-government, and he is deeply attached to the family of the Rajahs of Ramnad, and has rendered great services to them on various occasions and in many directions. He has built bungalows at Mandapam for accommodating European officials and travellers, and he has been of immense help to them in securing provisions and providing for their comfort.

A certificate of merit was received by him at the time of the Coronation of his Majesty King George V in recognition of his public spirit and usefulness, and he was granted a medal on the occasion of the recent famous Delhi Durbar. He has, further, afforded great help to the Madras Government in chank and pearl fishery enterprises.

RAO SAHIB DR. M. ABRAHAM PANDITHER (Avl.).

Recognition of true worth in a human being is not always forthcoming until the name of the person most concerned is nothing but a memory. Fortunate is he who during his lifetime is in a position to lessen the burdens of others more unfavourably situated than himself; or to give pleasure to thousands through the instrumentality of soul-stirring music; or to relieve the suffering from painful and obscure diseases. Every civilized country in the world has had its physicians, scientists, philanthropists, musicians, artists, statesmen, and other notabilities; some of these achieved enduring fame and lived to enjoy it; while sadly too many ended their days "unwept, unhonoured, and unsung." The people of India are anything but churlish in their acknowledgment of their fellow-men who have gained distinction for themselves by their acts of munificence or skill, and these notes are contributed to show the high esteem in which Rao Sahib M. Abraham Pandither, Avergal, of the Karunanithi Medical Hall, in Tanjore, is held.

This gentleman was born on the 31st of July, 1860, at Sambur Vadagarai, in the State of Travancore, and his ancestors trace their origin to the ancient Kun-Pandian family. He was put to school at Surandai, in the district of Tinnevelly, and in 1874 he was sent to the C.V.E.S. Normal School at Dindigul, where he became a teacher after three years' study. His grandparents on both sides were medical practitioners, and were well-versed in Tamil medical literature, so that it was no wonder that the natural proclivities of the youth inclined towards medicine. He wished to initiate himself into the order of the Yogees on the Shuruli Hills, near the sources of the Vaigai, in the district of Madura, and with this object in view he repaired to those mountains during the summer recess of 1877. Among those to whom he paid his respects was an anchorite, Karunananda Rishi, who was so well impressed with the views and high ideals of the youth to serve humanity, that he immediately selected him for the work of alleviating suffering by the administration of the now world-famed Karunananda medicines. He gave the student the necessary recipes with the list of ingredients and drugs, and the directions for preparing the medicines, and it is stated that the effect of these remedies was truly remarkable. During the Christmas of 1882 he married Gnana Vadivu Ponnammal, of Nanjankulam, and three months later the couple joined the Lady Napier Girls' School, Tanjore, as Tamil Pandit and head mis-

RAO SAHIB DR. M. ABRAHAM PANDITHER.

1. Rao Sahib Dr. M. Abraham Pandither. 2. Mrs. Abraham Ponnammal. 3. Mrs. Abraham Paukiam Ammal. 4. Miss Abraham Maragalavalli Ammal. 5. Jothimoney Selva Pandyan Abraham. 6. Varaguna Pandyan Abraham. 7. Soundra Pandyan Abraham. 8. Sundara Pandyan Abraham. 9. Dr. Pandither's Family.

stress respectively. Their success here in giving secular education, in teaching moral lessons, in shaping social conduct, and in imparting elementary principles of hygiene, was so remarkable that they won the golden opinion not only of pupils but of parents and neighbours. But that which endeared them more and more to the citizens of Tanjore was the application of their Karunananda remedies for everyday ailments, and the slow but steady popularity of these remedies induced Mr. Pandither to devote all his leisure hours to the study of the more abstruse Tamil literature bearing on medicine. He took great pains to understand the real, and often hidden, sense of the writers, and did not attempt any preparation which he did not understand thoroughly, nor would he administer anything unless he had perfect reliance on its efficacy. The confidence of his patients made his practice so extensive that in 1890 he was, with much reluctance, pressed to resign his teachership, for the more humanitarian work of alleviating pain and misery. Gradually his research work into Hindu medicine made steady progress, and the Indian world, especially the Tamil world, in South India, Ceylon, Burma, the Straits Settlements, and South Africa is to-day reaping the fruits of his patient labours.

Among the special preparations for which Mr. Pandither's name has become famous are: Sanjeevi pills, useful in cases of cold, cough, dysentery, deafness, bowel and liver affections, and other ailments. Sanjeevi thylam, or ointment, used with Sanjeevi pills for some of the complaints mentioned above, although it is recommended to be used alone for fits, convulsions, poisonous stings, skin diseases, rheumatism, and dislocation of muscles. Maha Gorosanei pills—for indigestion, whooping-cough, giddiness, excessive heat, and as a mild aperient. Samaya Sanjeevi is resorted to for diarrhœa, cholera, and kindred complaints; Aghrana Sanjeevi is prepared for affections of the eye, ear, the nostrils, and brain, while Jeevathara Sanjeevi Senthuram, and a dozen other medicines as efficacious as those specifically mentioned are prepared.

Hundreds of unsolicited testimonials referring to marvellous cures wrought by these medicines, and, further, testifying to the deep gratitude of patients have been received by Mr. Pandither. Brief extracts from a few of these may be of interest. Mr. T. Arunachalam Pillai, manager, Senior Surgeon and Sanitary Commissioner's Office, Bangalore, wrote: "I have much pleasure in testifying to the efficacy of Karunananda Sanjeevi pills and Kara mathirai (pills) in the treatment of bubonic plague cases. I have tried the above medicines in 23 cases, of which 20 proved successful. My friends call these drugs a sovereign remedy for bubonic plague." Mr. K. S. Ramachandra Iyer, chief clerk, Medical Department, P.W., Penang, said: "I have found your Sanjeevi pills an excellent remedy and infallible antidote for the venom which follows the bite of the Malay serpent in these parts." Mr. M. S. Maria Pillai (diplomaed in medicine and surgery, Madras), of Chicknayakanhalli, in the district of Tumkur, declared that a patient of his of about twenty-six years of age "was suffering from enlargement of the tonsil, had difficulty in deglutition, and had lockjaw with hurried breathing and imperceptible pulse, and that he administered Sanjeevi pills and ointment, together with Maha Gorosanei pills, and that within 48 hours the sufferer was completely cured." Rev. G. Gnanamuthu, M.A., F.M.U., Professor of English, S.P.G. College, Trichinopoly, claimed that Mr. Pandither's pills "were used with beneficial results by members of his family in cases of fever, dyspepsia, dysentery, and other ailments."

The business capacity of this enterprising gentleman was exemplified in the acquisition and improvement of the Karunanandapuram experimental farm. Not far from the railway station of Tanjore there was a dreary and apparently unattractive piece of land. With keen eyes the future agriculturist observed that there was water in the depressions even in the driest summer, and he at once concluded that there must be perennial springs underground. He accordingly purchased the property on November 16, 1899.

It was no easy task to clear the prickly-pear and bushes and to get rid of poisonous snakes and other reptiles, but Mr. Pandither was buoyed up by his determination to overcome all obstacles and to transform the existing wilderness into a literal "garden of roses." A few trees were planted for the first time on the 9th of August, 1902, on the Coronation Day of his Majesty King Edward VII, and a board was fixed on the ground in commemoration of the occasion. Varieties of grafted mangoes and jack-fruit-trees were planted next in order, and many different varieties of cocoanut plants, guavas, oranges, apples, figs, Kabul pomegranates, peaches, dates, palms, vines, plantains, cashew-nut-trees, tamarinds, bamboos, and teak have been successively cultivated from time to time in small quantities as an experiment. Water for these trees was a necessity, and the first well to be sunk was 22 feet square and 40 feet in depth. In August 1904 a 9½-h.p. Crossley oil-engine and a 4-inch centrifugal pump were installed, and the well itself was completed at great cost. In the following year a boring apparatus was hired from Pondicherry, and the bottom surface of the well was bored in four different places to the depths of 190, 108, 110, and 113 feet respectively. A Hotwell turbine Worthington centrifugal pump has been purchased to ensure a perpetual supply of water. In 1905 a windmill-pump was imported from Liverpool, and a second well was sunk 8 feet square and 75 feet in depth. The reservoir has a capacity of 23,000 gallons. A third well—a circular one—was 22 feet diameter and a depth of 50 feet, as well as three other wells to irrigate the young seedlings, were sunk subsequently.

Many kinds of sugar-cane from the Government farms at Samalkotta and Palur have been successfully cultivated at Karunanandapuram, and while experimenting with these a new sport-cane variety was discovered by Mr. Pandither, and it was taken from his estate to be tried at the Government Farm, Palur, by Mr. C. A. Barber, D.Sc., F.L.S., the Government botanist. In the agricultural exhibitions of South India the sugar-canes from Karunanandapuram have invariably been awarded first prize, and *The Agricultural Journal of India*, October 1906, says: ". . . Finally the striped cane growing in Mr. Abraham Pandither's garden at Tanjore, has given rise to a new ashy cane, which appears to be well worth a trial."

The cultivation of Australian golden maize and the Himalayan varieties has also been successful, and two new varieties have been formed by crossing the former with the country-grown type. Arrowroot, too, has been grown with profit, and roots such as King yam potatoes, and other vegetables are also experimentally cultivated to a small extent.

During the course of the last seven years the produce from this farm has been shown at various agricultural exhibitions, and 6 gold medals, 37 silver medals, 7 bronze medals, and numerous first prizes

RAO SAHIB DR. M. ABRAHAM PANDITHER.

1. Trade Mark. 2. Karunanandapuram Farm Villa—Front View. 3. Sixth Music Conference Group.
4. The Lawley Electric Printing Office. 5. Residence of Dr. Pandither. 6. Coronation Memorial Tree.

and certificates of merit have been awarded. A Government medal and a prize of Rs. 100 have also been obtained for the exhibition of the best farm-reared cattle.

Mr. Pandither has been very much encouraged in his undertaking by visits from many influential persons to the farm, among these being: Their Excellencies Sir Arthur and Lady Lawley, the Lord Bishop of Madras, the French Governor of Pondicherry; the Hon. Sivaswami Iyer (Avl.), C.I.E., C.S.I.; the Commissioner of Agriculture, the Rajah of Ramnad; Prince Sri Narayanan Thambi of Travancore; Messrs. Benson, Sampson, and Couchman, Government Agricultural Directors; Mr. N. Kunjan Pillai, M.A., Director of Agriculture, Travancore; Mr. R. Cecil Wood, Principal of the Agricultural College, Coimbatore, and others.

Their Excellencies Sir Arthur and Lady Lawley visited the farm on the 22nd of February, 1908, and after mango and jack-fruit-trees had been planted in honour of the day, his Excellency wrote in the visitors' book: "I have spent a thoroughly enjoyable morning at the farm of Abraham Pandither, who kindly invited me to see the various experiments which he is now conducting. Herein is a tale of diligence, enterprise, and skill in the field of agriculture which is unique in my Indian experience and therefore the more interesting. I carry away with me the most delightful memory of my visit, the charm of which was enhanced by the courtesy of my host and hostess, and the charming entertainment of which we were the recipients."

A mahogany-tree was planted on November 1, 1908, in commemoration of the proclamation in connection with the Jubilee of her Majesty the Queen-Empress, Victoria, when she assumed the sovereignty of India in 1858, and an inscription to that effect was erected in a prominent position, while another one was planted on the 22nd of June, 1911, in honour of the Coronation in England of his Imperial Majesty George V, Emperor of India.

The proprietor never loses sight of the fact that the farm is intended to be instructive as well as experimental, and he has accordingly issued pamphlets in English and Tamil regarding the best method of cultivating maize, sugar-cane, and the new sport-cane. His main object in doing this is to induce cultivators to realize the dignity and usefulness of tilling the soil, and to show them that, as agriculturists, they can have that independence which is rarely to be found in other occupations of life.

By gradual purchases the acreage has increased from 70 to 550, including first-class wet lands watered by the Cauvery system, and every encouragement is shown to *ryots*. The farm is managed by Mr. Pandither and members of his family, so that the latter might usefully spend their time and money for their own benefit; but they also work with the full hope that their feeble attempts may be of some use to their countrymen. The owner's efforts to improve the estate and to convert this tract of waste-land into an orchard have met with the success which they so well merited, and as a commercial venture alone the work has proved more than remunerative. Mr. Pandither is an ardent agriculturist, and he carries out important experiments in the cultivation of garden and field produce; he takes great interest in the industrial and commercial movements of the country, and by dint of his own perseverance he is to-day a wealthy man, and one of the most capable, respected, and influential landlords in Southern India.

Mr. Pandither's energies were tireless, and from 1909 a substantial building was slowly and steadily rising in the big compound to the west of his palatial residence, and when it was approaching completion in 1911 all the necessary plant for a model printing office was set up. The plant consists of a large-sized cylinder machine with self-feeding and delivery apparatus. Platen machines of different sizes powerful enough for embossing, box-making, cutting, and creasing, a Herculean proof-press, a self-clamp guillotine, an enormous hot press, a superior mill-board cutter, a wire-stitching machine, perforator, die-sinker, and combined punching and eyeletting and type-casting machines. The whole of this machinery is driven by an electric installation with a dynamo of 12-h.p. driven by a Crossley gas-engine of 16-h.p. The printing press is named "The Lawley Electric Printing Press," after Sir Arthur Lawley, G.C.I.E., K.C.M.G., a former Governor of Madras, and it is capable of meeting all the requirements of the Tamil districts.

Amidst his multifarous avocations Mr. Pandither has found time to bestow great attention and care on the education of his children, and, understanding that the importance of music could hardly be over-estimated, he gave them a sound training both in Western and Southern Indian harmony. Their proficiency is of a high order, and their voices are exquisitely sweet, melting the heart and holding the listener spellbound. Two of his daughters have obtained first-class diplomas in the London Trinity College local higher examinations in the seventh grade, while the father is a master musician of the highest order, being deeply versed in theory and practice. Untiring efforts are being made by the latter to resuscitate the Carnatic music from the low position to which it has fallen, and being convinced that this national culture must be preserved by the people if it is to be preserved at all, he established the Tanjore Sangeeta Mahajama Sangam in 1912. Regarding this Mr. V. P. Madhava Row, C.I.E., Dewan of Baroda and Chairman of the Fourth Conference, said: "His first observation was that Mr. Pandither had laid the public under great indebtedness to him by organizing that Sangam and bringing together the Pandits to lecture to them on the various aspects of Indian music. He had thereby helped the revival of that fine art, which had, for several causes, been dwindling in that city—once the home of music, and of many other arts and many an industry—and he offered substantial encouragement to those who were still devoted to it. He had, practically, created the opportunity and the means for the study and practice of the Indian system of music, which, in this country, was once the duty of kings to patronize. Such, indeed, was the work Mr. A. Pandither had imposed upon himself, and it was extremely creditable to him that the work had been financed solely by him."

Mr. Pandither's wife, Gnana Vadivu, Ponnammal, died on the 15th of December, 1911, after a short illness, and a few months later he married Bhagyammal. She manages all domestic affairs and assists Mr. Pandither in his enlightened supervision of the several branches of his business. She has displayed superior talents in music composition, and in correcting inaccuracies of some of the Ragams in vogue. Mr. Pandither's views are cosmopolitan, seeing that he has helped the various religious communities, and his consideration for the poor and afflicted is shown by his readiness to help in the cause of charity.

Of his celebration in commemoration of the Coronation of his Majesty the King-Emperor, George V, at Delhi, the Madras newspapers wrote: "The garden party by Rao Sahib Abraham Pandither at Karunanandapuram was a brilliant success. Every section of the community was fully represented, and more than 7,000 people gathered from the town to see the picturesque garden, while fully 3,000 poor people were sumptuously fed and clothed."

In recognition of his public services the title of "Rao Sahib" was conferred upon him on the 25th of June, 1909. In presenting the *sanad* of "Rao Sahib" to Mr. Pandither, Mr. J. P. Bedford, I.C.S., said that "he had much pleasure in handing to Mr. Abraham Pandither the *sanad* conferred upon him by the Government of India. He was a man of exceptional practical energy and ability, and his career had been a phenomenal success, his chief claim to distinction being his agricultural farm, which bore witness to his industry and enterprise." In recognition of his public benefactions the undermentioned certificate and Durbar medal were presented to him :—

"By command of his Excellency the Viceroy and Governor-General in Council, this certificate is presented in the name of his Most Gracious Majesty King George V, Emperor of India, on the occasion of his Majesty's Coronation Durbar at Delhi, to M.R. Ry. Rao Sahib M. Abraham Pandither, Avergal, son of Muthuswami Nadar, in recognition of his public benefactions.

(Signed) "HAROLD STUART,
"Ag. Chief Secretary to the
Government of Madras.

"MADRAS,
"*12th December*, 1911."

The *Indian Patriot* of the 19th of February, 1915, in referring to this gentleman said: "Another remarkable man of whom Young India has heard much and whose activities are well known is Abraham Pandither. We knew him as a practical agriculturist, we knew him as an excellent medical man. When we went to him in the dark hours of the evening he was poring over some proofs of a music work, to which, at great devotion of time and wealth, he has been applying himself. Proprietor of an up-to-date press, enthusiast of every kind of useful activity, a man of inexhaustible energy and confidence in himself, Abraham Pandither is an example for Young India. 'Be ever active and strive to do good' is the message of his life."

G. CHINNIAH PILLAY

This merchant, whose extensive business includes the holding of important contracts, is a good example of a comparatively insignificant person who has succeeded in life by dint of his own exertions and character. He is the owner also of many acres of land (paddy) in the district of Trichinopoly. He also owns fairly big cocoanut and mango gardens. He is mainly interested in beer, but he also deals in wine, and he holds leases of country liquor shops. The total annual rent paid by Mr. Pillai to the Government of his leased shops (beer and country liquor) in eight districts of the Madras Presidency is about Rs. 240,000.

Mr. Pillay is a very charitable man, daily feeding 40 poor and destitute persons in his house. To crown his charitable activities he is erecting a *choultry*, costing about Rs. 50,000, on the Srirangam Road at Chintamony. He has in contemplation the endowment of the choultry with a quantity of land in order that provision may be made for the continuance of this excellent work of supplying the bodily needs of the poor. He lives in East Andar Street, Trichinopoly, and the name of his fi-m is Messrs. G. Chinniah Pillay & Son.

G. CHINNIAH PILLAY.
CHOULTRY ON SRIRANGAM ROAD.

V. P. PUCKIRIESWAMY PILLAY

"Banker, merchant, and agent" are the principal words on the official letter paper of Mr. Puckiriesawmy Pillay, and, in a sense, they are fairly comprehensive terms, but they do not give an adequate idea of the extent of the business which is now being carried on. A modest beginning was made in 1891 in Burma in banking alone, but it was not long before the proprietor became a piece-goods merchant, a general commission agent, and importer of hardware goods, with corresponding agencies in London, Manchester, Glasgow, Darwen, Burnley, Leipzig, and Amsterdam. The head office in India is at Negapatam (where the registered telegraph address is "Merry"), but branches have been opened at Madras (telegraphs "Dhooti"), at Rangoon (telegraphs "Happy"), and at Kanyuitkwin, Pyu, Nyaungchidauk and Tantabin in Burma.

N. MAHOMED MEAN ROWTHER BAHADUR

The skin and hide trade has undergone a considerable change in Southern India during the last few years, and the steady improvement in values is due principally to the improved methods of treating the raw material, and in placing the industry on a sound commercial basis. One well-known merchant who has passed through this transition stage is the gentleman whose name appears at the head of these notes. He commenced business in or about the year 1883 with one factory, but he has succeeded so well that he now owns 3 tanneries at Sembattu, about 5 miles distant from Trichinopoly.

Rough goat-skins cost from 5 to 6 as. lb. in 1890, but to-day the value varies from 8 to 10 as., while the "finished" skin realizes Rs. 3 for the lb. weight, exclusive of freight, commission, and other charges. Agents of merchants in the United States of America visit the district of Trichinopoly, and their purchases tend to maintain the highest price of the raw material, but the quality of the skins which they buy is not of the same standard of quality as that which is insisted upon by the local tanneries.

There is practically no cattle-breeding industry in this neighbourhood, as nearly all the grazing land is in the hands of the Forest Department. Artificial food is, therefore, necessary for those animals which are kept, and the increased cost of feeding them naturally keeps their value at a higher level than would otherwise be the case.

Mr. Rowther has local buying agents, but large purchases of both hides and skins are made in the Bangalore, Salem, and other districts.

Fleshing machinery of a modern type, driven by a steam engine, was installed in 1910, and this process has greatly improved the quality of the skins.

The factories are now having a monthly turnover of 30,000 sheep and goat-skins, and about 5,000 hides, and consignments are sent regularly through the South Indian Export Company for sale by Messrs. DeClermont & Donner, of 27 St. Thomas's Street, London, E.C.

The tanneries are large and well-appointed buildings which cover an area of about 7 acres; the monthly establishment charges, including salaries and wages, amount to Rs. 5,000, and some 150 hands are employed.

N. MAHOMED MEAN ROWTHER BAHADUR.

1. VIEW OF THE TANNERY, SEMBATTU. 2. FLESHING AND SLAKING.

Mr. Rowther takes a deep interest in the local government of the district in which he resides, and he has been a municipal councillor for several years. His private residence is at Palakarei, near Trichinopoly.

RAO BAHADUR A. ANNASWAMY THEVAR

Ukkadai, a village in the taluq of Tanjore, in the district of Tanjore, is situated in the centre of an estate bearing the same name, which has been in the possession of a very distinguished family—named Thevar—for considerably longer than two centuries. The nearest railway station is Ammapet, on the branch line of the South Indian Railway, which runs from Tanjore to Nagore.

The first of the family to bring the estate to the notice of the public was Salya Thevar, but later, in the line of succession, there came Venkatachala, who attracted attention generally, but particularly of the East India Company. By his unstinted benevolence he saved many households in his neighbourhood from ruin by discharging liabilities and by helping young and old alike to become independent of charity. Money was scarce in those days, and *ryots* in ordinary stations of life were not able to pay their *kist* to the Government. The lands of these poor people were, in consequence, sold by auction for the recovery of arrears of assessment, but Venkatachala Thevar purchased the properties and gave them back to their respective owners free of payment. The people thus relieved revered him as their saviour, but his spirit of benevolence spread over a larger area than his immediate surroundings.

In the eighteenth century security of person and property was endangered by men of the Robin Hood type, but this enterprising benefactor assisted the East India Company to bring these notorious characters within the grip of the law. At that time there lived Ramalinga Padayachi, a notorious and desperate dacoit, who was a great menace to the safety of the public, and who, at the head of a gang of robbers as desperate as himself, openly defied the Government, and plundered the Government Treasury. The East India Company sought the aid of Venkatachala Thevar, and the latter rendered willing service to the police in arresting the outlaw and in bringing him to justice. But, by the help of his gang, this desperado made his escape from gaol, and the Government, placing its trust in the ability of Venkatachala Thevar, specially deputed him to trace and arrest the runaway. This was successfully accomplished, and the Government, recognizing the services of the captor, determined to offer him a valuable bracelet set with rubies and diamonds. His Excellency, Lord Elphinstone, the then Governor of Madras, in response to an invitation, visited the village of Ukkadai in 1840, and he not only formally presented Mr. Thevar with the bracelet from the East India Company, but on his own behalf handed to him another jewel of similar value. These two emblems of honour are still preserved in the family, and are worn on very important occasions.

RAO BAHADUR A. ANNASWAMY THEVAR.

1. FRONT VIEW OF THE BUNGALOW. 2. BUNGALOW—BACK VIEW. 3. JEWELS PRESENTED BY THE EAST INDIA COMPANY. 4. RAO BAHADUR A. ANNASWAMY THEVAR. 5. VENKATACHALA THEVAR. 6. APPAVA THEVAR.

Mr. Thevar at another time rendered assistance to the Government in surveying and assessing lands when the Hon. Rama Aiyengar was the Settlement Commissioner, and the Government, in acknowledging his services, gave him several acres of land for his *choultry* free of *kist*.

The present owner of Ukkadai is Annaswamy Thevar, who took over the property from the Court of Wards in 1893, and from the very day upon which he assumed control he devoted his entire attention to the improvement of the estate. He subsequently constructed a dispensary for out-patients at the Raja Mirasdar Hospital at Tanjore, and this was an addition which was sadly needed in so large an institution. The building was opened by H.E. Sir Arthur Elibank Havelock, G.C.M.G., G.C.I.E., the then Governor of Madras, when he visited Tanjore on the 16th of August, 1898. Mr. Thevar was awarded a Certificate of Merit at the time of the Diamond Jubilee of her late Majesty, Queen Victoria, in recognition of the assistance he had rendered to the District Board of Tanjore. In the year 1900 he began the cultivation of an agricultural farm upon his estate, not only for his own benefit, but also for the instruction of the public by demonstrations and experiments. Modern methods of husbandry are practised thoroughly, up-to-date implements are in use, and various kinds of manures are applied in the growing of sugar-cane, cotton, English vegetables, and different varieties of cereals and plants. Mr. Benson, Director of Agriculture of the Presidency of Madras, while camping at Mannargudi in 1905, proceeded to Ukkadai where Mr. Thevar was carrying on a number of experiments which the former had suggested in the previous November, and Mr. Benson was highly pleased with the results, especially with regard to various kinds of paddy and sugar-cane—the latter of which had not hitherto been grown in Tanjore.

Mr. Annaswamy Thevar subscribed Rs. 150 when the Kumbakonam Agricultural Association was formed, and he gave an undertaking to collect donations from Madathi Pathees (heads of *Muts*) in the district.

At the Tanjore Exhibition, held in 1906, a large variety of experimental crops, vegetables, and fruits, as well as articles of pith work from the Ukkadai estate, was shown, and several certificates and silver and gold medals were awarded.

On the 10th of September, 1897, Mr. Thevar received a Certificate of Merit in the name of her Majesty, the late Queen Victoria, for his many acts of benevolence and for his generous donation to the Raja Mirasdar Hospital at Tanjore. In 1903 he obtained another certificate in the name of his Majesty the late King-Emperor, Edward VII, in honour of his public gifts and his services upon the District and Taluq Boards of Tanjore. He was the only Mirasdar in Tanjore who was invited to the Delhi Durbar, held on the 12th of August, 1902, and, six years later, he had bestowed upon him the title of Rao Bahadur, the *sanad* being presented by H.E. Sir Arthur Lawley, G.C.I.E., K.C.M.G., the Governor of Madras, who, in an interesting speech, eulogized his many charitable actions and his devoted services to the public. Sir Arthur, in the course of his address, said : "From the moment that Mr. Annaswamy Thevar succeeded to his estate he has consistently and in various directions shown himself to be a man of public spirit. He came forward on more than one occasion to give generous donations for the alleviation of the sick and suffering ; he has generously provided for the feeding of the poor ; he has for a long time been a member of the District Board, where his services and advice have been most valuable, and he has shown himself to be a man of enterprise and determination in the management of his estate. I am glad to be able to congratulate him to-day on the honour which has been conferred upon him, and to tell him how highly we, as Government, appreciate his public spirit and the services which he has rendered to the District of Tanjore. May I, in offering you this *sanad*, give you my congratulations."

On the 12th of December, 1911, on the occasion of the Coronation of his Majesty King George V, Emperor of India, Mr. Thevar received, at the hands of H.E. the Viceroy, Baron Hardinge of Penshurst, in honour of his public benevolence, another Certificate of Merit, and in celebration of this memorable day he remitted some thousands of rupees to the poor *ryots* upon his estate.

IN THE PACKING DEPARTMENT OF WELSH BROTHERS CIGAR FACTORY AT TRICHINOPOLY.

In the *choultry* of Rao Bahadur Annaswamy Thevar, which is situated in the village of Ukkadai, people, irrespective of caste and creed, are daily fed, the average annual number being about 50,000 persons.

WELSH BROTHERS

Trichinopoly is the home of the cigar-making industry in India, and "Trichi smokes"—as they are familiarly called—are known almost as well in Europe as they are in Asia. The business of cigar manufacturers, which is carried on at Trichinopoly and elsewhere under the

S. RM. M. CT. PETHACHI CHETTIAR (ZEMINDAR OF ANDIPATTI).

1. The Zemindar's Family Mansion at Kanadukathan. 2. S. Rm. M. Ct, Pethadri Chettiar. 3. New Choultry at Chidambaram. 4. Temple at Chidambaram. 5. The Old Choultry.

style of Welsh Brothers, was established in the year 1881 by Mr. T. S. Subramani, and this gentleman is still proprietor and manager.

Tobacco is imported from Holland, and only the choicest leaves are used for factory purposes. It is no mean tribute to the quality of the Welsh cigars that they are in greater request than ever, although they have been on the market for more than thirty years. The "Excelsior" brand is specially registered in India, and these are noted for delicacy of flavour and pleasant aroma. They can be purchased in attractive boxes at prices which range—according to size of the cigar—from Rs. 8 for 50 to Rs. 21 for 100 delivered free of all charges to any part of the United Kingdom. Another brand is known by the remarkable name of "Mother's Milk," and any one who cannot from personal experience express an opinion as to their value must accept the evidence given in an illustrated catalogue, which says that "these cigars in taste, aroma, and fine flavour are all that can be desired by good judges." Other brands which have met with great favour are "Specials," "Prides," "Planters," "Java Rodgers," "Bouquet," "Java Whiffs" at Rs. 1.8 per 100, "Camalias" at Rs. 2, famous "Flor-de-Welsh" and "Twists," 5 in. in length, at Rs. 4 and 8, and "Gold Foils" at Rs. 60 per 1,000. This is only a sample of the good things which are manufactured by this firm, and the proprietor has every reason to be proud of the vast number of unsolicited testimonials which he has received. Specially prepared cheroots are exported to Gibraltar, Australia, Bermuda, and London, and the agents in the last-named city are Messrs. Darley and Butler. From 25 to 50 hands are employed in the factory at Trichinopoly. Branches have been opened at No. 4 Broadway, Madras, and at Tuticorin, and nearly all of the European clubs in Southern India are supplied with special cigars from these three places. The yearly output of the factory shows an average of about 15 lakhs.

THE ZEMINDAR OF ANDIPATTI

The Andipatti Zemindari, situated in the district of Trichinopoly, in the Madras Presidency, is one of the oldest pre-British Palayams, and as it was near the point where the territories of the rival Chera, Chola, and Pandya dynasties met, it really played a part in their ancient struggles. The Palayam seems to have fallen into the hands of the Chola king at the beginning of the tenth century, and for the next six hundred years shared the fortunes of the rest of the district. On the dissolution of the Vizayanagar Empire in the last half of the sixteenth century, the Palayam, along with the neighbouring famous town of Karur, fell under the Nayakans of Madura, and was frequently attacked and occupied by the Mysore armies. Finally, in the beginning of the nineteenth century, the Palayam came into the hands of one of the descendants of the ancient Polygars. His claims were duly recognized by the British Government, a *sanad* was issued, and the Peshkash was settled. The Zemindari became involved in 1880, and was taken under management by the Government, but was finally sold by them in 1897 to the famous Nattukottai Chetty, Mr. Chidambaram Chettiar, of Kanadukathan. On his demise it descended to his younger son, the present Zemindar, Mr. S. Rm. M. Ct. Pethachi Chettiar, a gentleman now rising in fame in Southern India for his benevolent charities and philanthropic attitude towards every question affecting the welfare and interests of the people of Southern India.

Born in the year 1889, he is now barely 24 years of age. Nevertheless he found opportunities within such a short time to extend the sphere of his benevolent activities throughout the southern districts of the Madras Presidency. The first incident to bring him to the front rank of the South Indian notables was the opportune and voluntary help which he extended towards the Tamil Sangam of Madura—a purely national institution of the Tamilians, resuscitated after a long interval of many ages by that patriotic nobleman of South India, Sri Pandithorai Thevar, Zemindar of Palavanatham. Standing alone in support of the institution and sustaining it singly, the President-Founder found it impossible to cope with the increasing responsibilities, and Mr. Pethachi Chettiar came forward with a handsome donation and a substantial monthly contribution, and offered his personal services to boot. His offer was accepted, and he was made the Vice-President of the Sangam, the Rajah Sethupathi of Ramnad taking the Presidentship some time after the demise of the President-Founder, Sri Pandithorai Thevar. The Tamilians know that the object of the institution is to rouse them from their lethargy of ages and bring them into one fold, as was done in the days of the Pandya and Chola kings, and they also know how to appreciate the self-sacrificing efforts of such noble souls.

The Saiva Sabah of Palamcottah is another which made his name famous. The Zemindar contributed not only large sums of money for the missionary work of the Sabah, but also made a present of a fine press to help in the dissemination of the principles of the Saiva religion by means of pamphlets and books. The press is named after him as the "Pethachi Press." The Sabah, in recognition of the princely support of the Zemindar and his services to the same, unanimously acclaimed him as a life patron at a great public meeting which was specially held for the purpose.

The Nattukottai Chetty community, consisting of the merchant princes of Southern India, have not yet realized their potentiality in the affairs of their country, and it is one of the youthful ambitions of this loyal young patriot to make his community realize it and to raise them to a position which would, in no way, be less than that which is held by statesmen-bankers of Europe and America in the politics of their continents. The ***Pax Britannica*** offers a good opportunity, and of course the Zemindar takes full advantage of it for the fulfilment of his ambitions. The spending of lakhs and lakhs of rupees year after year on the renovation of time-worn temples and in the construction of new ones, and the revival and maintenance of institutions which have had their origin in prehistoric times, have, from time immemorial, been the exclusive privilege of this community. The ancestors of the present Zemindar had the lead in such matters, and the grand edifices erected and maintained until this day at Chidambaram, Swamimalai, Karur, Thiruvanaikoil, Thiruplathurai, and some other places, for the worship of the deities, were all from funds of his family. But the present Zemindar thinks, and thinks rightly, that what has been done up to now in this direction is more than enough, and that there are other vital matters which should engage the attention of the monied aristocracy, if the condition of the people is to be ameliorated and the country made to advance side by side with the other nations in their march of progress. He closely watches the Western scientific world mastering the forces of nature one by one, and subjecting them to the use of man, and thinks of the potent possibilities of his own community in this direction, which now lie dormant in them. The Nattukottai Chetty community, as every one knows, are the Jews of Southern India in point of wealth, and the world would stand aghast if it were informed of the amount of capital which lies buried in the small money-lending shops possessed by the Chetties through the Eastern world. The present Zemindar has, with his keen intellect, realized the immense possibilities for the advantageous use of such capital, and with a view to make his community realize the same, he himself sets an example to his countrymen by his life and actions.

The institutions, whether public or private, which have not received the patronage of this philanthropic gentleman, are very few. The support of indigent families, the education of the poor youths of the country, the encouragement of arts and industries, the endowment with large sums of money of really deserving educational institutions, the resuscitation of religious, literary, and other national bodies, form the daily and hourly work of this young Zemindar. The development of the agricultural resources of his Zemindari on modern lines has been taken in hand in good earnest ; proposals for agricultural farms and model schools within the Zemindari now occupy the attention of its owner.

TUTICORIN.

Photo by Nicholas & Co.

PRESIDENCY COLLEGE, MADRAS.

EDUCATION

By H. DODWELL

EDUCATION offers perhaps more difficulties than any other subject to Indian Governments—and at least as many in Madras as elsewhere. There are, in the first place, the difficulties involved in selecting the system and methods best calculated to improve the mental and moral status of the people; and then, in the second place, the difficulties of directing education along these ideal lines in a country which is only collectively rich, and where funds are constantly lacking in comparison with the work that has still to be done. On the one side there are continual controversies as to methods; education ought to furnish this or that or the other. On the other side there are the people who constantly demand an extension of educative agencies; for example, the adoption of universal elementary education. And between the rival demands of those who say that education should be improved and those who say it should be extended, the path of educational authorities is beset with thorns.

Until the fifties of the nineteenth century education in Madras was left very much to missionary enterprise, and appears to have been in a far less advanced condition than it was in either Bengal or Bombay. The famous Halifax dispatch of 1854, which laid down principles of Government action destined to be adopted and expounded by all who came thereafter, proposed the immediate establishment of Universities in Bengal and Bombay, but observed that a similar institution in Madras should await the development of a sufficient number of colleges, or of schools which could be developed into colleges. It is only since that time that Madras has become the most highly educated province of British India. Indeed, it is a far cry from the 183 schools with their 16,000 pupils of 1857 to the thirty odd thousand institutions with their million and a quarter pupils of to-day. It is at least apparent that much has been done, although doubtless it falls short of the absolutely possible, to realize that diffusion of education among the people which the dispatch of 1854 laid down as the basis of educational policy.

In consequence of the orders contained in that dispatch, a Government Department was formed under the control of a Director of Public Instruction, and the University of Madras was established in 1857. It was modelled largely on the University of London—that is to say, it was to be mainly an examining body, with colleges affiliated to it scattered all over the Presidency. Its examinations also imitated the examinations of that University. The first two, the Matriculation and the First-in-Arts, consisted of papers in a certain number of specified subjects—for matriculation, English (four papers); a vernacular or classical language (two papers); arithmetic, geometry, and algebra; physics and chemistry; history (English and Indian) and geography. For the First-in-Arts the subjects were English (four papers); a vernacular or classical language (two papers); algebra, trigonometry and geometry, physiology or physiography, and the history of Greece and Rome. These obstacles overcome, the student proceeded to the B.A. examination. This was divided into three branches, which could be taken separately. The first was English language and literature; the second a classical or vernacular language; the third "the science branch." This last included mathematics, science, philosophy, and history, any one of which might be taken. The examination was a compromise between an honours and a pass examination, the passed students being arranged in three classes. Finally there was the M.A. examination, for which students had to write a thesis and answer papers on a specialized subject.

The purpose of these courses appears plain enough. In the first place specialization was delayed to the last possible moment. After a boy left the high school and joined the college classes he still had to pass another examination in subjects so diverse as physiology and Greek history, and the subjects were selected so as to fill up gaps in his school courses, and to secure what was believed to be a general education. Only then was anything like specialization allowed to begin. In the second place, there is to be noticed the great part occupied by English. It constituted a necessary third in all the examinations leading up to the B.A. degree, and the reason evidently is that a sound knowledge of English was (and truly) reckoned indispensable for that self-culture, that continuation of intellectual interests, that private and individual pursuit of further knowledge, which educationists have always aimed at cherishing and encouraging.

These courses have recently been profoundly altered. The Matriculation Examination is no longer the only avenue of entrance to University classes. A school-leaving certificate has been introduced, to show both the marks obtained in a public examination in certain specified subjects and the marks obtained on the regular school work in those subjects and others not presented for the public examination but taught in the schools. Moreover, a boy who has obtained poor marks in certain subjects or groups of subjects in the public examination may appear in these subjects later with a view of improving his marks. Theoretically at all events this is a great improvement on the rigid matriculation system. It affords a clue of some sort to a boy's work at school as well as to his capacity to answer question papers. The elasticity of the system also makes it popular; and the result of its introduction has been that the Matriculation Examination, though it still exists, has ceased to count. Only an insignificant number of individuals continue to take it, and admissions to colleges are made almost exclusively on the school-leaving certificates.

Again, the University curriculum has been totally changed. It was felt that there was no organic connection between the First-in-Arts Examination and the various B.A. courses. A very large number of students seemed to think that they had reached a definite stage—had, in fact, taken a degree of sorts—when they passed the First-in-Art Examination. That examination has accordingly been abolished, and a new Intermediate Examination prescribed in its place. This consists of two branches, one compulsory and the other optional. The compulsory part includes English of a more advanced nature than was required for the First-in-Arts and vernacular composition; the optional part includes a number of groups, such as mathematics, physics and chemistry, which naturally leads on to a degree in mathematics or natural science; or ancient history and logic, which naturally leads on to a degree in history and philosophy.

Having passed this examination, the student then has a choice between a pass and an honours course in the branch of study in which he elects to take his degree. The pass course lasts two years, the honours three. The first examination for the B.A. honours under these new regulations was held in 1914, when 67 candidates successfully took the honours course, as against 263 who took the new pass course.

These changes in the examination courses do not exhaust the new tendencies visible in the University. One feature of the old system was that it had proved barren of anything like research. It would appear that it had not been successful in working that intellectual curiosity which impels those possessed by it ceaselessly to inquire into the causes of things. But it is now hoped that the superior training undergone by honours students will bear fruit in research. Post-graduate studentships are now granted to promising students who desire to pursue a special line of study. This matter, too, is likely to be facilitated by the creation of University professorships, for the University has drifted some way from the original conception of a purely examining body. Appointments have already been made, including that of one distinguished scholar to the Chair of Comparative Philology, and that of another to the Chair of Economics. It would be premature to speculate whether these steps will really lead to the foundation of a school of research under the University's guidance Such a school certainly will not spring up suddenly. It will take time, and possibly involve many disappointments. But the design is worthy of all applause.

Meanwhile it must be observed that the University itself is in a state of incomplete evolution. It was established (under a vicious theory of the nature and functions of a University, such as was the natural product of the mid-Victorian age) as a territorial University. Its sole business was the examination of all the students of the colleges within its appointed area. But its recent development is inconsistent with that conception. A teaching University cannot teach students scattered over the length and breadth of Southern India. A University professor cannot lecture at once to students in Madras, in Bangalore, in Trivandrum, and in Trichinopoly; and if he confines his ministrations to the presidency town, the colleges situated elsewhere are, naturally enough, hurt at the advantages enjoyed by the Madras colleges. In the face of these and similar difficulties which are involved by recent developments of University policy, it is to be hoped that the old idea of a territorial University will die away, and that residential teaching Universities will develop wherever there are funds and students enough to support them. Such a development is evidently still remote; if there were no other reason there would still be the difficulty of funds, but in time that may disappear. Meanwhile it is worth noting that a residential teaching University is about to be established at Benares, and, at the time these words are being written, the details of its organization are being discussed in the Imperial Legislative Council. The system of territorial Universities under which India has hitherto been portioned out has therefore already been broken into.

SOUTHERN INDIA

It is scarcely too much to say that the University has progressed from the point of view from which the acquisition of knowledge as tested by examinations appears the one thing needful, to that saner and more elevated standpoint which reveals the importance of culture and the relative insignificance of the acquisition of facts. Such progress corresponds closely with the movement of English thought on the subject. In the fifties and sixties, when the Halifax dispatch was drafted and the University was organizing itself for the performance of its functions, it was a widespread belief that knowledge and culture were synonymous terms. All that was needed, men thought, to develop civilization in India was the diffusion of knowledge—sometimes it was even narrowed down to the diffusion of useful knowledge. But fortunately the theory of education has been modified and developed very considerably since those early days. We now believe that the essential part of education is the training of the mind, the strengthening of the mental faculties, the formation of the character, far more than the learning of facts, however numerous or diverse.

The University has responded to that change partly by revising its courses and partly by moving away from its original position as a merely examining body. The colleges composing it have also developed very considerably. Of these the most important is the Government College at Madras, called the Presidency College. It was founded as a high school in 1841, and was raised to the status of a college in 1853. At the present time it has in all some 200 students in the various years of the honours courses, rather more studying for the pass course of the B.A., and 220 students for the intermediate. To teach these it has 14 professors, assisted by a numerous staff of lecturers. The other large college in Madras which is affiliated in honours (for it must be noted that of the 15 first-grade colleges only 5 are at present affiliated in honours) is the Christian College, founded and maintained by the Free Church of Scotland Mission. It developed out of a school founded in 1839, and opened its college classes in 1865. This now has between 800 and 900 students altogether, but of these only 115 are taking the honours course, and the rest are pretty equally divided between those studying for the pass B.A. and those studying for the Intermediate. The other important college is the Jesuit College of St. Joseph at Trichinopoly. This developed out of a school founded at Negapatam in 1844, and removed to Trichinopoly in 1883. This is rather stronger in numbers than the Christian College, having over 950 students on its rolls; but of these nearly two-thirds are studying in the intermediate classes, under 300 in the B.A. pass class, and only 79 for honours. There are also colleges under the control of the respective native States in Mysore, Travancore, and Cochin, as well as various others managed by missionary or local bodies.

In regard to collegiate education in general there are two main defects, both of which are recognized and combated so far as circumstances permit. The problem of education in general is to produce that effect upon the mind and character which we call for shortness' sake "culture." That is not an easy thing under any circumstances, except where the student is predisposed in the desired direction—a comparatively rare thing. But the difficulties become greatly increased when the aim is not only to develop this culture of the mind, but when that has to be brought about by means of a foreign medium of instruction, English, employed to convey the conceptions and theories of a civilization differing *toto cœlo* from the Indian. If, then, the problems of education are difficult in England, what must they be in Madras? And while the difficulties are considerably greater, the instruments for achieving success are appreciably weaker. If Indian life and thought are really to be interpenetrated with Western culture, it must evidently be by means of Europeans and European-trained Indians, and these are relatively few. Suppose the case of a professor of history. His business is not only to teach facts—that is easy enough—but also to convey a strong, abiding impression of historical methods and reasoning; and unless he does so no one else either will or can. Or take a professor of chemistry. If he fails to inspire his class with a spirit of meticulous accuracy in the laboratory, how can any of them ever hope to carry out even the simplest experiment successfully? or who else is there to show them the only method of work? Yet while this is so, consider how many students any professor has to pass through his hands in an Indian college. The proportion of professors to students at the Presidency College is roughly 1 to 40, and at the other large colleges mentioned above as 1 to 60, and they can rarely meet outside the lecture-hall or library. It is clear that personal influence is considerably diffused and largely lost. However, the honours courses afford a partial remedy. It is evidently better that what personal and direct contact is possible should be contact with the best students, and by the operation of the new courses in the Madras University the best students are in the main shepherded apart, and receive something more nearly resembling personal attention and direction than is possible in other classes. In this way something, at all events, is done to minimize an inevitable evil.

The other great difficulty in the way of successful collegiate education consists in a relative absence of corporate life among the students themselves. The University is not residential; the colleges are very little so. It is true that of recent years almost every college has established one or more hostels for the residence of students, but in the first place the great majority of the students do not reside in these hostels; and in the second they are separated one from another by rigid rules of caste. One sect of Brahmans will not eat with another; no sect of Brahmans will eat with a non-Brahman, and so on. If it were confined to a mere question of eating it would not perhaps matter so much, although the common refectory is assuredly the breeding-place of sociability. But the caste question goes farther than that. It limits friendships and intimacies; it involves jealousies and dislikes; with its clean, deep cleavages it cuts straight across what should be a collegiate unity. This combined with the scattering of students among multitudinous and too often miserable lodging-houses, and perhaps also with a certain aloofness of mind, results in the absence from the Indian colleges, in the south at all events, of that tradition which forms so important and valuable an influence in English colleges. Not that the students do not have their sports and clubs and unions. They read papers before their fellows, and debate solemnly the pros and cons of the matter. But it is all not a little artificial and unreal. There is little or none of that active pressure on a student by his companions, moulding him into a more definitely social animal, which one may regard as one of the most important fruits of University training.

Perhaps also another aspect of the Madras student deserves a few words, for it has, I think unjustly, been turned into a source of accusation and criticism. It is certainly true that the student comes to the University principally for the sake of the degree he will get, and which will assist him to obtain a better post than he could otherwise have hoped for. This object certainly far outweighs any such disinterested purpose as the pursuit of knowledge for its own sake. That is very rare. But, after all, this only implies a difference in degree and not in kind between the Eastern and Western student. A degree in most places in the world is a commodity possessed of a definite value; and a University career is sought by us as well as by others chiefly because it leads up to a better career in after life than would otherwise be open. And just as the Indian student casts away his books and forgets his studies the moment he has passed his examination, so also do many of ourselves. With us the proportion of men who never lose their intellectual interests is far larger than it is among the Indian students; but that is, partly at least, accounted for by the fact that our studies are for the most part intimately associated with the origins and development of the civilization in which we live, whereas theirs are different, strange, sometimes even hostile to their inherited modes of thought and feeling.

The schools of the Madras Presidency are divided into three grades—high, middle, and elementary. The high schools form the feeders of the University, and formerly the curriculum pursued in them was dominated by the requirements of the University Matriculation Examination, which was taken by all pupils who passed through the full high school course. And as the success of schools was judged largely by the number of their passes in that examination, there was a constant temptation to cram the pupils with that minimum knowledge which would enable them to secure a pass. There can be no doubt that the teaching left much to be desired—indeed, there was little teaching in the true sense of the word. The teaching of English consisted mainly in the exposition of a reader word by word, so that the pupil was left without much more knowledge than was involved in the collection of a number of synonyms, without any idea as to the diverse use and suitability of the synonyms themselves. The teaching of history, of geography, even of science, was reduced to the learning of text-books. There was no doubt a diffusion of knowledge secured by this process, but the system hardly merited the name of education; nor were the pupils who suffered under it adequately trained either for any useful occupation or for the pursuit of further knowledge under the University. In fact, education had fallen into a vicious circle. Bad teachers sent up bad students to the University, which in its turn gave a further supply of bad teachers to the schools.

This evil tendency was naturally accentuated by another, which is so pervasive of the educational world as to constitute an almost universal misfortune. In all countries pedagogy offers a career financially inferior to that of nearly every other profession which is recruited out of the same social stratum. The result is that men take up school-teaching (with very few exceptions) as a last resort. They have to earn a living, and cannot do so in any other way. Schoolmasters are therefore mainly recruited from among the least vigorous and least effective of their class. Nor can anything else be reasonably expected until schoolmasters are better paid, i.e. until people are more fully aware of the evils of bad education and are willing to spend money to avoid them. This general evil has been prevalent in Madras also. The best graduates go into Government or other service, leaving the residuum for education.

The matter is therefore at bottom largely financial; and in touching finance we touch the crux of all education in India. The south, like the north, is collectively rich and individually poor. The revenues of the Government are great; but the functions which Government has to perform are spread over enormous areas and disproportioned populations. Education has always been short of funds, and there have been constant efforts to carry out large policies with inadequate funds and by means of underpaid agents. Here as elsewhere, however, undeniable improvement has taken place. The funds available for education arise from three main sources—public revenue of all sorts, fees paid by students and private subscriptions, missionary funds, and so on. It is not uninteresting to compare the funds provided thirty years ago with those available today under these three heads. Thirty years ago Government and local bodies provided altogether about $16\frac{1}{3}$ lakhs of rupees, fees amounted to about 10 lakhs, and subscriptions, endowments, etc., to about $8\frac{1}{4}$ lakhs. Nowadays Government funds provide about 60 lakhs, fees about 40 lakhs, and endowments about the same sum. If recent non-recurring grants made by the Government of India were taken into account the amount furnished by Government would be appreciably larger. Even as it is the amounts are considerable; the total expenditure more than quadrupled between 1882 and 1912; and as the total number of scholars of all sorts increased only about three times (from about 400,000 to about 1,200,000), it is apparent that more is now being spent on the education of the individual pupil than was formerly the case. Indeed, without this the improvements that have actually been made would have been impossible. For example, as I have already pointed out, science teaching formerly consisted in the repetition of text-books; but now the high schools have been obliged to spend considerable sums of money on laboratories and apparatus, without which the study of science is impossible. It is somewhat disheartening that this reform should have been criticized in certain quarters as designed to increase the cost of education; but, in fact, education in all times has been a thing that people have been reluctant to pay for adequately.

The most controversial question now at issue in Southern India is the question of the degree of rapidity with which elementary education should be extended. The matter was brought up prominently by the late Mr. Gokhale some years ago, and has excited attention ever since. On the one side it is urged that after two generations of educational activity the mass of the people are still untouched by education; that if any real progress is to be made in developing and improving the economic position of India the people must first be educated; and that the only way in which this can be brought about is by laying down a policy which has universal and compulsory education as its ultimate end, and which will begin by experimenting in especially favourable urban areas.

It is impossible not to sympathize with the ideal which inspires these proposals. But the weakness of the arguments in favour of immediate action is revealed by the comparison between India and England, on which most of them are based. In the first place, we find the amount of money devoted to education by the State in England compared with that which can be afforded by the Indian Governments; and then, too, we have the further comparison between the universal and compulsory system in England and the fact that only a third of the boys and not a tenth of the girls of school-going age in the Madras Presidency are being educated. But of course no argument can be drawn from such comparisons on account of the fundamental difference between the two countries. There must be a very considerable increase in the productiveness of India per head of population before educational policy can afford to emulate these wider schemes, and meanwhile all that is really practicable is to prepare the way for a possible future development. That is, in fact, what is being done in Madras, where the Government have promised to increase the annual grants for elementary education by 2 lakhs of rupees every year, provided no extraordinary financial situation should arise: in fact, the increased allotments for the last four years exceed the promised increase in that period by 8 lakhs.

It seems to the present writer, however, that one should beware a too sanguine anticipation of results from elementary education in the Presidency. The teachers are, and must necessarily be, poor material. They get about Rs. 10 to Rs. 12 a month, which in some cases is increased by their also acting as village postmaster, but even so they get little more than an ordinary domestic servant. Again, their training is negligible; and further, the inspection of elementary schools is of necessity left almost wholly to the subordinate inspecting officers. In all three aspects the great difficulty is lack of money. There are some 30,000 elementary schools. Even the smallest increase of pay to the teachers would involve a very large annual expenditure; the training of so many teachers would involve large and expensive establishments; and the provision of a more competent inspecting agency would in the same way and for the same reason be at present impossible.

But perhaps enough has been said on this subject, and in conclusion a few words on the probable future of education in Southern India may be permitted. The problem is in itself remarkable. The indigenous culture of the country, in certain directions reaching to a remarkable level of achievement, is yet characterized by an incompleteness resulting from the almost complete neglect of other aspects; and at the same time this culture is limited by caste and its results to a section of the people. Brought into contact with this by more or less successful educational methods there is the Western culture—the essentially practical thus set up against the essentially metaphysic, induction opposed to deduction, observation of the world without opposed to meditation on the world within. What are the consequences likely to be, and are they such as we should desire?

The consequences might conceivably be the complete amalgamation of the two cultures, the interpenetration of the one by the other; and if that should by chance prove to be the case, their respective qualities are so complementary that it would seem to be a fortunate mixture. One might hope to see something more or less analogous to the mediæval culture of Europe, itself the product of Romanic and Germanic influences. Such a result would afford the solution surely most to be desired.

The consequence that seems most to be feared is that the older Indian culture should be killed off by Western education. This fear is not infrequently expressed nowadays by Indians of what one may call the Neo-Hindu school. For example, it was said the other day that inspection of schools by Europeans was undesirable, because it would foster the development of European rather than of Indian ideals. But surely, unless we take a very narrow view of what culture really means, there is no possibility of Indian culture being overlaid or destroyed. Indian culture, I take it, is not and cannot be a thing existing independent of the Indian mind and ways of thought. The phrase is, in fact, merely a generalization, implying the collective qualities of the Indian mind at any given moment, and equivalent to the collective character of the peoples of India. But they are what they are by reason of a long history, by reason of conditions of race and climate and society enduring through many generations. However much the modern Indian may be imbued with Western knowledge and ideas, it is apparent that their consequences and working will not be the same in him as in, say, an Englishman. The resultant of any course of education must be profoundly affected by the inherited qualities of the individual and the race; and so with the question of the effects of European education upon the Indian, he will not and cannot be converted into a European; his distinctively Indian qualities will inevitably persist, and modify the influences of the foreign culture brought to bear upon him. Nothing like denaturalization is desirable or possible. But, on the contrary, it seems by no means impossible that the foreign culture with *its* special qualities may modify and (one may hope) strengthen weak places, neutralize defects, increase liberty and the power of action, and yet not injure the specific qualities on which Indian culture may pride itself.

1. CANNANORE

2. FORT ST. ANGELO, CANNANORE.

THE MALABAR COAST

A TRIP along the western coast of Southern India, taking *en route* the State of Travancore, and the districts of Malabar and South Canara, would in all probability provide the tourist with a greater variety of scenery than could be found within an area of similar extent in any other part of India. Far away to the west among the rollers of the Arabian Sea are the lovely coral reefs of the Laccadive Islands, rising from their bed amid the bluest of seas, flecked here and there with white foam where the turbulent waters lash themselves on rocky promontories, while on the eastern side are graceful, feathery palms, flourishing on the beach itself, and stretching away behind them are the majestic Western Ghauts, which shelter the peaceful dwellings of the inhabitants of the plains. These houses are not huddled together according to the fashion which prevails on the eastern coast of the Presidency, as nearly each one stands in the centre of its own compound, securely fenced in and protected from the power of the sun by a clump of palms, fern-trees, or giant plantains. Behind these dwellings the land rises gradually, until one reaches paddy fields and avenues of coconut-trees, and then come the spurs, jungles, and deep ravines which mark the beginning of the hills. Towering above the whole of this lower level are the famous ghauts, which maintain an average height of 5,000 ft., but which occasionally soar upwards with peaks which rise to about 8,000 ft. above the level of the sea. A word or two about these ghauts, which are so important a feature in India. From the extreme north of the district of Malabar they run southwardly in a parallel line with the coast, and about 20 miles distant from it, until they reach Vavul Mala (7,673 ft.), which is due east of Calicut. At this point they turn slightly to the east, then to the north round the Nilambur Valley, and thence in a southwardly direction until they become merged in the giant Anamalais. These ghauts are undoubtedly the source of many a river which irrigates hundreds of acres of land which would otherwise be parched and unfruitful.

But we are forgetting the promised trip, during which it is proposed to notice towns and villages of interest, commencing with Calicut, the capital of Malabar, and one of the principal seaports of the Presidency. The town is situated on the banks of the River Kallayi, and it is recorded that "the warrior, Tipu Sultan, and the Madras Railway Company tried in vain to induce the inhabitants to move 6 miles farther south to the site marked out by nature for a great city at the mouth of the Beypore River." All that can be seen from ships at anchorage are the lighthouse and pier, the whole of the remainder of the town being entirely concealed among palm-groves. The Municipal Council has only within the past two decades shown any real activity in undertaking improvements for the town, such as the provision of a better water supply, and the construction of a drainage system on modern principles of sanitary science. For its apathy and neglect it has frequently been censured by the Government, but it is pleasing to note that at a recent review of municipalities it received "honourable mention." It now maintains three hospitals, while a fourth is upheld by the Basel German Mission, which was established here in the year 1842. There are several first-class educational institutions, which include the Government School of Commerce, the Zamorin's College, two high schools, the Government Upper Secondary Training School, and St. Joseph's Boys' European High School. The offices and warehouses of the principal merchants are, practically, on the sea-coast, while the headquarters of the Collector and Superintendent of Police of the district, the Madras Bank, and the railway station are situated near the centre of the city. The Malabar Club, on the Beach Road, in Calicut, was established in 1864, and it comprises about 200 members, inclusive of married men whose wives are eligible for membership. The manufacture of tiles and weaving are the two principal industries in Calicut, while the exports are very considerable, and include timber, coir, coconut, pepper, and ginger. Steamers lie in the roadstead—about 2 miles from the shore—as there is no harbour, but nevertheless a very large quantity of merchandise passes through the port. There are several ancient temples, and more than forty mosques in the town, but very few of these have any interest from an architectural or archæological point of view. Calicut is the headquarters of the Malabar Volunteer Rifles, raised on August 14, 1885. The regiment has been recruited very largely from the populous Anglo-Indian community, and it has detachments at Cochin, Tellicherry, and Cannanore. The census of 1911 showed that there were 78,427 inhabitants.

VIEW OF TELLICHERRY.

Before proceeding to the north, it would be well to notice now a few places of interest lying to the south. Six miles from Calicut the traveller will see from the carriage windows the town and seaport of Beypore, which, prior to the opening of the railway, had flourishing shipbuilding works, ironfoundries, and a canvas factory. The exports, however, are still so considerable that the port holds the fifth place of importance in the district. The Beypore River, which draws most of its waters from the crest of the Western Ghauts, is crossed by the railway at this point, and it then discharges itself into the Arabian Sea. A few miles farther to the south one sees the Kadalundi River, which has a course of about 75 miles, and is navigable for small boats for a considerable distance at certain seasons of the year. After the train has passed the fishing villages of Tanur and Tirur, where there are several ancient temples and mosques, the railway branches inland in a south-easterly direction, passing through a fertile part of the district, which is fed by the great Ponnani River, and eventually the station of Shoranur is reached. This is the junction for the Cochin State Railway, and it is, further, the centre of a large area of land which produces very fine crops of paddy. The Ponnani River is here spanned by a splendid bridge. Still farther to the east is Olavakkot, the junction for the branch

THE CUTCHERY, TELLICHERRY.

line to Palghat, which is the receiving station for large quantities of timber. Olavakkot is a small place of about 3,000 inhabitants, but the scenery is very attractive, and from its elevation of 800 ft. above sea-level the railway descends to a plateau, prettily wooded and dotted here and there with picturesque villages. The Ammai Amman temple, which is near to the station, has many features of archæological interest, while in the vicinity there are numerous Hindu temples, the most important being one at Kalpathi, which is dedicated to Siva. Palghat, the chief town of the *taluq* of the same name, is situated on a branch of the Ponnani River, and was reported to have a population of 44,319 persons at the census of 1911.

About 2 miles distant from the railway station are the ruins of an old fort which was erected prior to the year 1767 by Hyder Ali, in order to guard his communications on the west coast during the period of hostilities between him and the Nayars. Municipal administration has been a decided success, but there are several factors which have contributed to this desirable end. First of all, the surrounding country is of an exceedingly fertile nature, and as many roads converge here, the Council has been able to raise large sums of money in the shape of tolls upon goods entering into or passing through the town. But revenue has been spent judiciously in the construction of important public buildings and in general improvements. The Victoria College—one of the finest institutions of its kind in Malabar—was originally a rate school, but in 1884 the Government transferred the management to the Municipality. The Dance Market, opened in 1897, new Council Offices, and dispensaries, are among the principal works which are due to municipal activity. The chief industries are the weaving of country cloths and the manufacture of coir mats.

ON THE RIVER, CALICUT.

A MALABAR BATHING TANK.

Returning again to our starting-point—Calicut—the visitor will be charmed by the beauty of the route upon which he is travelling towards the north. On the right-hand side are the ever-changing colours of the mighty ghauts with their lofty peaks standing as sentinels over the extremely neat villages of the plains ; vegetation abounds in rich luxuriance ; while the restless waves of the ocean on the west roll in nearly as far as the railway track. Quilandi was at one time a flourishing port, and the place of embarkation and landing of pilgrims proceeding to or arriving from Mecca. The principal feature of interest at the present time is an exceedingly fine old mosque, which was founded in the year 1779. The train runs practically on the sea-beach at this point, and, indeed, it maintains this proximity to the ocean for many miles. It runs through the pretty villages of Tikkodi and Kottakal, shortly afterwards reaching Badagara, which lies at a little distance to the north of the Kotta River. This is a thriving seaport, with a population of nearly 12,000 inhabitants, in which the principal buildings are the District Munsiff's Court, hospital, post and telegraph offices, customs and port offices, and a bungalow for travellers. Coconuts and copra are exported in large quantities, but there are no local industries of much importance. A few miles farther one notices the French settlement of Mahe (which is referred to elsewhere), and then the town of Tellicherry forms a convenient resting-place. The first thing which attracts the attention of travellers on alighting from the train is the picturesque situation of the town. It is built upon a series of thickly wooded low hills, which stretch towards the beach, while the existence of a group of rocks in the sea forms a natural breakwater. Tellicherry is the headquarters of the pepper trade in the district of Malabar, although a large number of persons are engaged in the curing of coffee and the preparation of ginger for export. The latest census returns show that the town has about 28,000 inhabitants.

Still hugging the sea-coast, the train passes Dhamadam Island, and then Kadambur appears in sight, where, owing to the physical formation of the land, the railway takes a wide sweep to the east and then suddenly to the west, when the important seaport and military station of Cannanore is seen. The town is 468 miles from the city of Madras, and has a population of about 28,000 inhabitants. It is divided into two portions, known as the Old Town and the Cantonment, and it is one of the healthiest and coolest places on the Malabar coast. It is believed that the original Fort St. Angelo was constructed between the years 1505 and 1507, but the present one belongs to a considerably later period. It is strongly built of laterite on a rocky promontory, which is washed on three sides by the sea, while on the fourth side it is supported by a dry ditch and bastions. A modern lighthouse has recently been constructed within its walls. Industries are not great in number, but they include weaving, dyeing, and the manufacture of caps of fine canvas, beautifully embroidered by Mapilla women. The exports consist chiefly of tea, coffee, pepper, cardamoms, oil, coir, copra, and ginger, but beyond sugar, raw cotton, and piece goods, little is done in importing. A very pretty semicircular bay fringed with groves of coconut-trees may be seen on the south side of the promontory, and snugly sheltered by these palms are the old palace of the Ali Rajah and a very fine mosque.

JAMALABAD ROCK FORT, SOUTH CANARA.

After leaving Cannanore the railway once again leaves the coast, and after 5 miles have been covered the train arrives at Vallarpattanam or Baliapatam, which is a thriving town on the south bank of the river of the last-mentioned name. Visitors should make a point of seeing the ruins of an old fort which may be found on a high cliff overhanging the river, while the remains of an ancient temple—within the fort—are well worthy of inspection. A ride of about 10 miles brings one to Madayi (or Pazhayangadi), a village which is crammed with specimens of ancient architecture, which will be of intense interest to archæologists. There are traces of an old fort, of a temple of the Chirakkal, or Kollatiri, family, which is allied to that of the Maharajahs of Travancore, and of a natural cave which extends for a long distance under laterite rock. Payyanur is the last railway-station in the district of Malabar before entering South Canara, in which about 640,000 persons depend chiefly on agriculture for a means of livelihood. This is about 61 per cent. of the whole population.

The first place to be noticed in this district is Nileshwar, which is 501 miles distant from Madras. Fish-curing is engaged in by a considerable number of the 10,000 individuals, and large quantities of salt fish are exported annually. This is a very fine sporting centre, and elephant, tiger, and sambur are met with in forests which almost adjoin the railway station. Hosdrug—derived from *hosa* ("new") and *drug* ("fort")—is noted for what are now the ruins of an exceedingly fine fort, which occupies a commanding position and can be seen from a very long distance. Pallikarai is another village on the sea-coast in which attention will be drawn to an ancient fort, which it is believed was destroyed by Tipu Sultan. Kasaragod, 27 miles distant from Mangalore, is the chief town of the *taluq* of the same name, and is built on the banks of the Chandragiri River. The only industries worth mentioning are the manufacturing of bricks and tiles, weaving, and fish-curing, but from an historical point of view Kasaragod is decidedly full of interest. The fort, believed to have been constructed about the middle of the sixteenth century, is on the western side of the railway station,

STREET SCENE, OLD TOWN, CANNANORE.

Photo by R. V. Solomon.

while in an easterly direction are the ruins of another fort which was built many hundreds of years ago. There are several mosques and temples, one of the latter being dedicated to Siva.

Mangalore is the terminus on the west coast of the South Indian Railway, and it is 550 miles distant from Madras. The principal charm of the towns and villages along this coast is that they are literally buried among palm groves, and as they are swept by the invigorating breezes of the Arabian Sea, the residents enjoy an elysium of cool and quiet restfulness which few places in other districts of the Presidency are able to give. There are about 48,000 inhabitants in the town, which is built upon the north bank of the Netravati River. Mangalore is the only town in the district of South Canara which has obtained local self-government in the shape of a Municipal Council, which consists of twenty members, four of whom are Europeans. The chief items of expenditure have been caused in connection with public works, public instruction, hospitals, dispensaries, water supply, and drainage, and the town can now show well-laid-out roads and attractive residences, especially in the European quarter. Chief among the educational establishments are the Government College, St. Aloysius's College, St. Ann's Convent High School, established in 1870, and the Basel Mission High School. The industries include brick and tile and coffee-curing factories, oil-pressing, pottery works, printing, weaving, coir making, and wood and metal carving; and the exports consist of coffee, spices, rice, bricks, tiles, oils, salted fish, and raw tobacco. Ocean-going steamers cannot cross the bar and enter the harbour, but Arabian *bágálas* and other small boats are employed for the transport of cargo between ship and shore. The Mangala Devi temple is an ancient structure, and is worthy of a visit, especially as it is situated at a very short distance from the railway station. There is a Siva temple at Kadiri, about 2 miles from Mangalore, and one dedicated to Krishna at Udipi, some 37 miles distant. The town appears to have been an important commercial centre early in the fourteenth century, and this possibly accounted for many of the raids to which it was subjected. The Portuguese were masters of the whole of this portion of the coast for a considerable number of years, while Mangalore itself subsequently fell into the hands of Hyder Ali, and at a later date of his son, Tipu Sultan. British forces obtained possession in 1799, and since then it has enjoyed a period of comparative tranquillity.

1. LANDING PLACE, CALICUT. 2. VICTORIA HALL AND TANK, CALICUT. 3. STREET SCENE, CALICUT.

THE LACCADIVE ISLANDS AND MINICOY

THE Laccadive Islands are of coral formation, and they lie off the coast of Malabar, between 8° and 12° N. lat., and 71° and 74° E. long. The largest of these, Androth, with a population of about 2,500 persons, is nearly 2 square miles in extent, and is about 125 miles west-south-west of Calicut. Kalpeni, to which are attached the islets of Cheriyam, Tilakam, and Pitti, is due south of Androth, and 150 miles south-west of Calicut. It is about 1 square mile in extent. Kavaratti, on the north-west of Kalpeni, is about 1¼ square miles in extent, and has about 2,000 inhabitants. Agatti, the western-most island of the group—220 miles distant from Calicut—has an area of rather more than 1 square mile, and the population at the most recent census numbered some 1,200 souls. An uninhabited islet called Kalpitti in the same lagoon, and Bingaram, Tinnakara, and Parali, enclosed in another reef 7 miles to the north, are attached to Agatti.

"Minicoy does not belong either geographically or ethnologically to the Laccadive Islands, but is the northernmost portion of the distinct archipelago known as the Maldives. It is 2 square miles in extent, and lies about 250 miles south-west of Calicut. The inhabitants are about 2,700 in number. Viringilli, or small-pox island, which is uninhabited, except in times of epidemic disease, lies in the western portion of the same lagoon."[1] There is a great similarity in the physical aspects of the islands, and it is a curious fact that not one of the two groups has land more than 12 or 15 ft. above the level of the sea. The soil is very poor, as it consists chiefly of disintegrated rock, together with a small quantity of humus. The principal crops are paddy, varagu, cholam, yams, and sweet potatoes. Coconuts are obtained on all of the islands, while bread-fruit, tamarind, banyan, lime, and areca are fairly common. The inhabitants of Androth and two or three other islands are Mapillas, while those of Minicoy are believed to have descended from the original population of Ceylon.

The principal industry is coir twisting, in which women of all grades find employment, although a large number of the islanders are engaged in tapping trees for toddy. Nearly all of the men are expert boat-builders and seamen, and many of them are found on ships trading with the Far East. Boys are exceedingly clever in making conical silk caps, which sell readily in the Maldives and Ceylon.

The early history of the islands is enveloped in mystery; some students believe that, under other names, they are spoken of by writers in the time of Pliny the Elder, but local traditions refer to Cheraman Perumal as the organizer of the earliest settlement. Al Biruni, writing in 1030 A.D., speaks of the "Dyvah Kanbar, or Coir Islands, and the Dyvah Kuzah, or the Cowrie Islands, to distinguish by these terms the Laccadives from the Maldives." The four northern islands and two open reefs are attached to the Collectorate of the district of South

1. COCONUT PALMS IN A MALABAR VILLAGE.

2. KALLAI BRIDGE, CALICUT.

[1] C. A. Innes, I.C.S.

1. PILLARS IN THE BHIRADEVI MANDAPA, CHANDRANATHA JAIN TEMPLE, SOUTH CANARA DISTRICT.
2. A JAIN PRIEST'S TOMB, MADABIDIRI, SOUTH CANARA.
3. THE MANA-STAMBHA, IN FRONT OF SANTESVARA JAIN TEMPLE, VENUR, SOUTH CANARA.
4. GUMMATEESVARA JAIN STATUE, KARAKAL, SOUTH CANARA.

Canara, while the four southern ones belong to the head of the house of Cannanore, but owing to mismanagement they have been placed under the administration of the Collector of Malabar.

Local self-government is ably conducted by the people themselves under the guidance of an Amin, who is assisted by a Council of Elders on each island. This Amin acts as judge in petty civil and criminal cases, but important ones are referred by him to the mainland for settlement.

C. AARON & SONS

The weaving of cotton and woollen goods has made less progress in the district of Malabar than in any other portion of Southern India, but pleasure may be derived from a visit to an establishment of this nature owned by Messrs. C. Aaron & Sons, of Cannanore.

The premises were established in 1892 by Mr. C. Aaron, who, with two hand-looms, began to weave cotton-goods for local purposes only. It was not long before a larger number of looms became necessary owing to the expansion of business, and it was realized, too, that such looms should be capable of producing different patterns in the manufactured articles. The next step in advance made by Mr. Aaron was the mercerization of yarn, or, in other words, the placing of a silk-like finish on cotton textures. This was followed by weaving of woollen goods. So steady and yet so rapid has been the progress made in this industry that to-day there are 150 hand-power looms which are producing cotton, mercerized yarn, woollen goods, and all descriptions and patterns suitable alike for suitings, shirtings, and other articles of clothing, Turkish and other towels, banians for football jerseys, and a number of other articles. A stock of colours was imported in 1904, and since that time the processes of blending the colours and dyeing have been carried on. The firm have travelling agents for the sale of their goods throughout India, Burma, and Ceylon, but they possess a very large number of private customers. Diplomas, certificates of merit, and cash prizes have been awarded to Messrs. Aaron at Industrial Exhibitions held at Cochin, Cannanore, Mysore, and Vizagapatam. Mr. Aaron supervises every branch of the business, and he employs an assistant, Mr. M. Krishman, and about 300 hands.

Mr. Aaron is now the owner of a tile factory, which was opened recently on the Baliapatam river, and about 4 miles distant from Cannanore, where all kinds of flooring and roofing tiles and earthenware goods of a decorative character are made by hand. The weekly output of tiles is about 15,000 in number, and each of these is stamped with the name "C. Aaron & Sons." The proprietor resides close to this factory, and he visits his weaving works on alternate days. Some 50 coolies are employed in this yard.

C. AARON & SONS.

1. THE WEAVING ESTABLISHMENT. 2. WINDING THREADS.

P. ALBUQUERQUE & SONS.

This firm was established in 1868 by the late Mr. Paschal Albuquerque (grandfather of the present proprietor), at Panimangalore, near Mangalore, in the district of South Canara. Within a year, however, the business—which was chiefly the manufacturing of tiles, bricks, and lime—had assumed such large proportions that Mr. Albuquerque found it necessary to have his factory in the heart of the town of Mangalore, in order to avail himself of shipping and other allied conveniences. The history of the firm has, since that time, been one of uninterrupted and unqualified success. On the death of the founder, his son, Mr. J. S. Albuquerque, who was then holding a high position in Government service, assumed the management, and his many-sided activities helped to further strengthen the good name which the firm had already acquired.

Mr. Albuquerque was one of the "City Fathers" of the municipality for more than twelve consecutive years, the vice-president of the Mangalore Roman Catholic Provident Fund for nearly fifteen years, an active member of the Board of Administration of the Mangalore Cathedral for nearly twenty years, a director of the Catholic Union Club for several years, and a member of the Taluq Board of Mangalore for a very considerable period. His strong personality and charm of character made him *persona grata* with whomsoever he came in contact, and his death in 1908 was most keenly felt by all classes and communities in the district of Canara. His eldest son, Mr. P. F. B. Albuquerque, now guides the destinies of the firm, and, with a thorough knowledge of every detail of the business over which he gives his personal supervision, the firm is making rapid strides in the way of continued success. He has already introduced several up-to-date innovations; modern machinery has been erected, and a coal-kiln has replaced the one for which wood fuel was required. Mr. J. W. F. Albuquerque, the younger brother in the family, is now rendering valuable assistance in the management of the business.

This was the first India tile-factory to be started in the district, and although many others have come into existence since then, this old-established house is well able to maintain its supremacy, and it is the only Indian factory whose tiles are specially recommended for Government buildings. Their tiles, flooring and ceiling bricks, and ornamental and artistic earthenware are in great demand throughout India, Burma, and Ceylon, and they are even consigned to East Africa and Australia.

The firm are also manufacturers of slaked and unslaked lime of excellent quality, and both of these are urgently required by planters and contractors for manurial and building purposes respectively. They are, further, the owners of several large and neatly laid-out casurina and coconut plantations, and these are in considerable favour as health-resorts by the *élite* of Mangalore.

The partners are not so absorbed in their business concerns as to be indifferent to the claims of their less fortunate fellow-men, for it is well known that there is, perhaps, not a single charitable institution in or near to Mangalore which has not been the recipient of the generous benefactions of the members of this firm.

P. ALBUQUERQUE & SONS.

1. J. S. Albuquerque (late proprietor). 2. A View of the Factory. 3. A View from the River.

ALVARES & CO.

A business for the manufacture of tiles was established at Mangalore, in the district of South Canara, on the west coast of the Presidency, in the year 1878, and it was subsequently purchased by Mr. Simon Alvares, of Bombay, who commenced to trade under the style of Alvares & Co.

Mr. Alvares threw heart and soul into the concern, and it was not long before largely increased accommodation and a more modern stamp of plant became necessary in order to meet the growing demands for high-class tiles from Bombay, Karachi, Jaffna, Colombo, and from the East Coast of Africa, from Zanzibar to Mozambique. The old premises and the business were therefore sold lock, stock, and barrel, and new buildings, covering from three to four acres of land, were erected on the bank of the River Netravati in the year 1907.

Clay is quarried in the Netravati and Gurpur Rivers, and is then burned in Buhrer coal-kilns. The factory is replete with up-to-date machinery, and it has a capacity for turning out from 25 to 30 lakhs of tiles annually. These are made according to what is known as the French pattern, and a special feature is made of the production of them, and of others for roofing, ceiling, and ornamental purposes, together with earthenware work of a general character. The buildings consist of three drying and one machine shed, together with three oil engines, two coal kilns, godowns, and offices, and the factory, which is managed by Mr. E. S. Alvares, a son of the proprietor, who employs about 300 hands, exclusive of the clerical staff. The machinery includes nine tile presses with dies, two large double roller pug-mills, and other necessary plant. The offices at Bombay are under the supervision of Mr. E. Alvares, while those at Colombo and Jaffna are in the hands of Mr. Joseph P. Alvares, who conducts the business in Ceylon under the name of Joseph & Co.

The firm started in 1890 at Bombay the first dairy factory to be opened in India, and it was christened at the outset the

"English Dairy Company." Mr. Simon Alvares is sole proprietor of the Bunder-Mangalore General Agency, carrying on business as a general merchant and importer of artificial manures. This gentleman is honorary magistrate of Mangalore, non-official visitor at the jail, member of the landing and shipping committee at the same port, President of the Catholic Co-operative Credit Society, Ltd., a director of the Canara Public Conveyance Company, Ltd., a leading member of the Catholic community, and one of the administrators of the Mangalore R.C. Cathedral.

ALVAREZ & CO. (THE MANGALORE TILE COMPANY).

1 THE WORKS. 2. SHIPPING TILES AND UNLOADING CLAY. 3. INTERIOR OF TILE WORKS.

S. R. BALAKRISHNA & CO.

The building contractor's business of Mr. V. V. Shanmukha Mudaliar has for many years past been one of the successful concerns in Southern India. In the year 1905, however, it became apparent to the proprietor that it would be a decided advantage to him if he could open a timber merchant's business in the district of Malabar. He therefore entered into negotiations with Mr. T. Ramiah, another successful contractor, and with Mr. V. L. Balakrishna Mudaliar, who were both admitted as partners in the new firm, which was styled S. R. Balakrishna & Co., and Mr. B. S. Tirupurantaka Mudaliar was appointed manager. The latter had considerable experience in accounts and organization, and his energy and intelligent work—under the direction of Mr. Shanmukha Mudaliar, the founder—caused such a rapid extension of trade that he was rewarded by being taken into the firm as managing partner in 1908, when Mr. T. Ramiah voluntarily retired. The firm deals in all Malabar hard and soft timbers, such as Oorooppoo, Erool, Messua Ferrea, Vellamarudu, white cedar, red cedar, Benteak, Malabar mahogany, and many others which are useful for house-building, mining, cabinet making, carriage building, and other purposes. Mr. Shanmukha Mudaliar is a man of keen discernment, grasping opportunities as they were presented to him, and it was at his instance that the firm purchased a furniture factory which had been carried on successfully for a number of years by Mr. V. Krishna Menon, B.A. Manual labour had been employed previously, but the new owners imported wood-working machinery of an up-to-date type, and they erected an oil-engine from which the motive-power was obtained. Mr. Menon became managing partner, and it is very largely due to his zeal and practical experience that the "Calicut Furniture Company"—as the venture is styled—has established an enviable reputation for its upright business methods, for the high-class quality of the manufactured articles, and for personal and prompt attention to all orders. A comparatively recent addition to the industries of the company is a saw-mill, in which timber of all descriptions can be cut into suitable sizes and lengths for the use of buildings and mines. The machinery of the mill, which includes vertical bands and circular-saws, is driven by a suction gas-engine, and as the fuel consists of sawdust, a waste product otherwise unsaleable, the cost of firing is a negligible item. Messrs. B. S. Tirupurantaka and V. L. Balakrishna have identified themselves closely with the organization of this branch of the business, and the suc-

S. R. BALAKRISHNA & CO.

1. Wood-working Machinery driven by Oil-engine. 2. In the Saw-mills 3. Vertical Band-saw.

cessful working of the mill will be largely due to their exertions. Mr. V. V. Ramalinga Mudaliar, who has been most assiduous in obtaining markets for the company's timber at the Kolar Gold Field and elsewhere, has been taken into partnership recently. The exporting of timber to European countries has not engaged the attention of merchants in India to any great extent, and it is possible that this neglect arises more particularly from a lack of knowledge of the kinds which are mostly in demand in the Western world. With the view of obtaining definite information on this all-important point, two members of the company —Messrs. V. V. Shanmukha and V. L. Balakrishna—proceeded to the Continent in the year 1912, and that tour has resulted in the making of arrangements for annual shipments of valuable timber. The head offices of Messrs. Balakrishna & Co. are at Kallai, in South Malabar, and their registered telegraphic address is "Latifolia, Calicut."

THE BASEL MISSION INDUSTRIES

It is an indisputable fact that the Basel Mission has proved to be a most important factor in the establishment and development of industries in Southern India, and although its ministerial and lay representatives have placed all possible facilities in the way of the people of the Presidency to enable them to engage in manufacturing, weaving, or in becoming skilled in handicrafts, they have never lost sight of the primary object of their mission, namely, the uplifting of those who were cradled in ignorance and superstition, and who were almost entirely without enlightenment in all matters pertaining to their social and moral welfare. It was in October 1834 that the first three workers connected with the Basel Mission College in Switzerland landed at Calicut, an historical town on the coast of Malabar, on the shores of the Arabian Sea, and it was about six years later that the first steps were taken in the organization of industries. A commencement was made with a printing press, which was set up at Mangalore—about 137 miles to the north of Calicut; this was followed by weaving establishments, tile manufactories, and mechanical departments. The most important of these industries is that of tile-making, and this will be noticed first. A tile-press, worked by hand-power, was started at Jeppoo, Mangalore, in 1866, but it was a small beginning, as only 12 hands were employed, and the daily output did not exceed 500. Bullock-power was used subsequently, and in 1881 the machinery was worked by steam. Other factories have been opened—at Calicut, in 1873, where about 220 labourers are employed in making 12,000 tiles daily; at Kudroli, a suburb of Mangalore, in 1882; at Malpe, in South Canara in 1886; at Codacal, with 290 hands; at Palghat, in Malabar; and at Ferok, about 7 miles distant from Calicut, in 1905. These seven factories are fully equipped with up-to-date machinery driven by steam-power, and they find employment for about 2,000 persons. All the goods manufactured in these yards are of superior quality, and they include flat roofing and ridge tiles, skylights, ventilators, ridge and hip terminals, finals, grooved spire tiles, hourdis, or ceiling-slabs, well and chimney bricks, salt-glazed tone and earthenware drainage pipes, terra-cotta vases, flower pots, and other sundry articles. These products are sold throughout the Indian Empire, Burma, Ceylon, British East Africa, the Straits Settlements, Sumatra, Basra, Aden, British North Borneo, and Australia.

Weaving was introduced in 1844 in accordance with the tastes and habits of the people living on the West Coast at that period, and in 1851 a trained specialist from Germany brought to India the first hand-loom with fly-shuttle. Cotton checks were woven in the early days, but after Jacquard looms had been set up the output comprised, among other things, ordinary table and household linen (such as table-cloths, towels, and serviettes), damask linen of ordinary and mercerized materials, jersey *banians*, shirts, and ladies' and children's underwear. The principal factories are at Cannanore and Calicut, and there are branch establishments at Nettur, near Tellicherry, at Chombala, in the district of Malabar, and at Codacal, near Tirur, about 36 miles distant from Calicut. Products have been exhibited at various times, and nine gold and a similar number of silver medals have been awarded to the Mission. The mechanical branch was started in 1874, when implements of a minor character were made for the tile and weaving factories. Boys have been trained in the institution, and many have become engine-drivers, firemen, and blacksmiths. More recent work has consisted of the making of water and night-soil carts, lamp-posts, iron gates, iron safes, household and office furniture and fittings, and of the construction of iron bridges for the P.W.D. in the district of South Canara.

The Basel Mission Press has developed to such an extent that about 80 hands are now employed in the shops and offices, and the machinery prints school-books, religious literature in half a dozen different languages, does colour-printing, and job-work of all kinds. The physical and social welfare of the employees is not overlooked, as there are provident institutions, savings bank and sick funds, hostels for young men and girls, and the Mission is encouraging a spirit of self-reliance among the people, and is making it possible for them to earn the "right to live."

B. M. D'SOUZA & SONS

The manufacture of tiles was commenced by Mr. B. M. D'Souza in Mangalore in the year 1887, and it was not long before the enterprising habits of the proprietor caused such a remarkable expansion of the industry that additional accommodation became an absolute necessity. As it was found impossible to extend the then existing premises, a site on the banks of the Netravati River was obtained, and an entirely new factory was erected. Coal kilns were built, and improved machinery was installed, including a clay crusher, pugmills, and presses, which are driven by a 12-h.p. steam-engine, and a 14-h.p. boiler, both by Holdsworth & Sons. The annual output of the works is from 15 to 20 lakhs of tiles, and each one of these is stamped with the name of the firm over an anchor, or with the words "Emanuel & Sons" over a crown. Clay is quarried some 12 miles from the factory, and it is brought in carts to the river, where it is transferred to boats for direct conveyance to the works. The majority of the tiles are exported to most of the ports and stations of the Madras and Bombay Presidencies, and also to Zanzibar, Mombasa, Dar-es-Salaam, for public and private buildings, and also to the municipal, railway, and Government departments. Tiles of numerous kinds and designs are manufactured, but a speciality is made of those required for roofing purposes. Several Native States have also become purchasers of a large quantity of these particular goods, and many are also being sent to the new capital city of

S. R. BALAKRISHNA & CO.

1. B. S. Tripurantaka Mudaliar. 2. V. Krishna Menon. 3. V. L. Balakrishna Mudaliar. 4. V. V. Shanmukha Mudaliar. 5. V. V. Ramalinga Mudaliar. 6. V. L. Dhanaram Mudaliar.

Delhi. About 200 hands are constantly under the supervision of the proprietor.

Mr. D'Souza is also a merchant and general commission agent, and he has opened offices on the Bunder in Mangalore, where he handles coffee, cardamoms, spices, pepper, copra, cocoanuts, forest produce, and areca-nuts. A managing partner, Mr. Bhanu Shanker, has been taken in to conduct the Bunder business, which is carried on under the name of Bhanu Shanker & D'Souza & Co.

Mr. D'Souza is a prominent member of the community in Mangalore, and holds some honourable positions among local societies. He is, further, a Municipal Councillor and also director of the Mangalore Roman Catholic Provident Fund.

He carries on the business on his own account in the name of B. M. D'Souza & Sons, and the tile-works are situated at Mangalore, in the district of South Canara. The telegraphic address is "Highland, Mangalore."

B. M. D'SOUZA & SONS (HIGHLAND TILE WORKS).

1. TILE PRESS. 2. A PORTION OF THE FACTORY. 3. MODELS.

KERKIE COONDAH

The approach to the principal bungalow on this estate gives the visitor a very good idea of the hilly nature of Kerkie Coondah itself and of the district of Kadur in which the property is situated. Rugged yet very beautiful scenery is presented on every hand, and on arrival at the residence, which is built on an eminence, one is immediately attracted by the charming gardens and lawns by which it is surrounded.

The estate is owned by Major F. Clifford and Mr. C. H. Browne, and the latter, who is manager, employs about 250 hands. Although the surface of the property is of a very undulating character, its average height above the level of the sea may be said to be about 3,000 ft., which, as far as the State of Mysore is concerned, is an exceedingly appropriate altitude for plantations, and particularly those devoted to coffee. The property consists of 800 acres, and comprises 300 acres of coffee (planted almost yearly from 1879 to 1914), a considerable quantity of cardamoms, pepper, areca nuts, and 25 acres of Para rubber.

After the coffee beans have been pulped by steam-driven machinery on the estate, a portion of the "parchment" and "native" produce is sold locally, but by far the largest quantity is sent to Mangalore, whence it is placed in the manufactured state on the open market, or is consigned under special orders to ports in Australia. Notwithstanding the fact that a very large number of the plants are too young to bear fruit, the yearly harvest of the matured bushes reaches as much as 45 tons in weight. The rubber-trees appear to thrive well, and the smaller plants, including the cardamoms, pepper, and areca nuts, are very productive.

Four miles distant from the estate are the post and telegraph offices at Sallebile.

BALEHONNUR

The question whether rubber-trees growing over coffee were injurious—if not fatal—to the latter, has created a considerable difference of opinion, but if the Balehonnur estate is to be taken as a guide, it would seem that no danger what-

THE KERALA RUBBER COMPANY, LTD., AND CALICUT ESTATE.

1. Manager's Bungalow, Kerala Estate. 2. The Factory, Kerala Estate. 3. General View, facing West, Kerala. 4. Tea Clearing, Kerala Estate. 5. Tea planted in 1911, Kerala Estate.

ever is to be feared. Here is a property of 700 acres, and the cultivation is as follows: Coffee, 205 acres; Para rubber, 190 acres; and 30 acres of Ceara rubber. Some of the coffee-bushes were planted as early as 1884, but the average annual yield of trees in full bearing is now about 25 tons in weight. Para rubber grows very slowly at an elevation of 2,300 feet (which is the altitude of Balehonnur), but the trees are to be tapped in 1915.

The Ceara-trees—which were planted in 1906—have made rapid progress, and when they were tapped recently the quality of the rubber was pronounced to be excellent. The average annual rainfall is about 80 inches.

Pepper-vines have been planted among the coffee-bushes, and very satisfactory returns of a profitable nature have been obtained. A pretty bungalow is so situated that extensive views are presented of the interesting country beyond the Bhadra River, which is one of the boundaries of the estate. The Balehonnur post and telegraph offices are not more than a mile distant from the property.

The owner of the estate is Major Clifford, the manager is Mr. F. W. Hight, and Mr. C. H. Browne is visiting agent.

THE CALICUT ESTATES SYNDICATE, LTD.

The property of this company, consisting of 1,850 acres, is admirably situated from a commercial point of view, and it is bounded on one side by the Beypore River, which is navigable for small craft from the town of the same name, at its mouth, as far as the company's headquarters. The company propose having their own launch to convey agricultural and other produce to and from Beypore, about 6 miles from the important seaport of Calicut. The fully developed area comprises 704 acres, consisting of 634 acres of rubber-trees and 70 acres of tea, but planting was only commenced in the year 1912.

The surface is of a generally undulating character at an elevation of about 100 feet above sea-level, and a consistent annual rainfall of 120 inches is experienced. It is too early to give any report as to yields, but everything points to successful results.

Mr. C. H. Browne is managing director of the company, and his son, Mr. H. Browne, is manager. Constant employment is found for 500 hands.

GUDIE TOTA

This is another well-known coffee estate in the neighbourhood of the post town of Sallebile, and it is one of a group of similar properties which are under the able control of Mr. C. H. Browne. There are 205 acres of coffee planted here, and a considerable portion of that area was developed in the late seventies, just after the period in which the "borer," then the fungoid leaf disease, and other insect pests, had almost crushed the very souls of the most ardent planters by the devastation which they caused. Gudie Tota, however, appears to have escaped the troubles, and, indeed, it seems to have gone ahead from the very start. It is true that some of the bushes were planted as recently as the year 1913, and these are, therefore, in the miniature stage. About 160 acres are in full profit, and the annual crop shows an average of 40 tons weight, although the heaviest quantity which has been reaped was 62¼ tons in 1904. The whole estate is 250 acres in extent. Quite a number of compact little estates of a few hundred acres lie side by side throughout the whole of this portion of the State of Mysore, and they seem to vie one with another in the presentation of scenery which is unsurpassed in South India. Here, at Gudie Tota, there are silvery streams winding tortuous courses through the ravines of the estate in which the cardamoms have been planted. At an elevation of 3,300 feet is the small but pretty bungalow, whence charming views are obtained.

The owner is Mr. Henry Hart, and he —through his manager—employs 150 hands constantly.

THE KERALA RUBBER COMPANY, LTD.

The estate of 3,600 acres of the Kerala Rubber Company, Ltd., is situated in the Manjeri taluq of South Malabar, and it promises to be one of the most productive rubber plantations in Southern India. The property was purchased from a private syndicate in 1910, and the company was then formed with a capital of £50,000. Mr. C. H. Browne is managing director for India, Mr. Campbell Hunt is general manager, and the London agents are Messrs. T. H. Allan & Co.

The estate is exceedingly hilly in character, but one does not notice any fatigue in walking over its uneven surface when the attention is held by the majestic Nilgiri Hills, which rise precipitously to a height of 8,500 feet. There are 1,700 acres of Para rubber-trees (*Hevea Brasiliensis*), which were planted between the years 1907 and 1914. The soil hereabouts is rich in all those constituents which are necessary for vigorous and healthy plant life, and no better proof of this can be given than by referring to the following figures which have been culled from the estate books. The first tapping of the trees—which took place in 1912—was estimated to produce 5,000 lb. of dry rubber, but this amount was easily surpassed. The estimate for the following year was 30,000 lb., and this was exceeded by 6,000 lb., and the estimate for 1914 was 82,000 lb., and was exceeded by 8,000 lb. A fine large factory, having a capacity of 500,000 lb., has been erected, and very superior smoked sheet rubber is manufactured annually. The produce is shipped at Calicut for the London market, where excellent prices have hitherto been gained. An experiment has been made in the cultivation of tea, and the venture has proved to be so satisfactory that about 1,000 acres are about to be planted. The annual rainfall of 140 inches is distributed evenly over the whole of the estate, but there is, in addition, an ample supply of water from natural sources for general use on the property.

The manager and four European assistants reside on the estate, and about 1,500 coolies are employed. Several excellent roads have been constructed, the principal one affording good communication with the town of Calicut, which is 52 miles distant.

THE WANDOOR ESTATES SYNDICATE, LTD.

The business of this syndicate consists solely of the cultivation of rubber, and 150 acres were planted in the year 1911, followed by about 70 acres in 1913.

There is an excellent supply of water for all purposes, and the necessary buildings and machinery for manufacturing the rubber will be erected this year. A cursory glance at the plantation enables one to declare that the prospects of future harvests are distinctly encouraging, and as the necessary labourers can be engaged locally there is no reason to expect other than satisfactory financial results. The estate is only some 300 feet above the level of the sea, and the annual rainfall is about 120 inches. Postal business is transacted at the office on the Kerala

THE KERALA RUBBER COMPANY, LTD., AND CALICUT ESTATE.

1. 1911 Rubber—Wandoor Estate. 2. General View, Calicut Estate. 3. River Scene, Komapara. 4. Superintendent's Bungalow, Calicut Estate.

Rubber Company's estate, and the port of Calicut is 48 miles distant.

Mr. C. H. Browne is managing director of the syndicate, and Mr. Campbell Hunt is manager.

YELLIEMUDLOO

This estate of 300 acres, situated about 3 miles from Sallebile, is the property of Messrs. C. H. Browne and F. Rodewald. Out of a total of 340 acres no fewer than 225 acres were planted with coffee-bushes between the years 1891 and 1909, and all of these are now (1914) in full bearing. Shade trees, of course, play an important part in the successful growth of coffee in the State of Mysore—in fact, it is generally recognized now that such provision is an essential, but good cultivation and skilful manuring are necessary adjuncts. The annual harvest of berries now shows an average yield of not less than 40 tons.

The estate is well supplied with excellent out-buildings, and a constant supply of water of the purest quality is obtained from springs for private use and for the processes of pulping or washing the berries. Cardamoms have been planted among coffee-bushes in the ravines of the property, and their cultivation has proved to be most remunerative. The estate is an admirable habitat for various species of fauna; it is hilly, and yet there are numerous ravines; and an abundance of drinking water for the animals is assured by a number of springs and by a river which flows through the property. The sport afforded on the estate is remarkably good, tiger, panther, bison, and sambur abounding. Mr. Browne is manager, and he employs about 180 coolies.

O. MAMI KUNHI HAJI.

1. Office. 2. Office and Workshop. 3. O Mami Kunhi Haji, Sahib Bahadur.

O. MAMI KUNHI HAJI

"During the three years 1907-10 in which I held charge of the Cannanore subdivision of the Madras Public Works Department, Mr. O. M. K. Haji carried out a very large number of works, perhaps two or three hundred of all sorts, and varying in amount from Rs. 5 to Rs. 50,000. I found that whether the works were very small or very large they were carefully supervised and every effort was made to secure uniform quality, and that the highest. I have never known a better all-round contractor." Such is an extract from a letter addressed to Mr. O. Mami Kunhi Haji by Mr. P. H. England, A.M.I.E.E., on the 24th May 1911, and a better testimony could not be given to any man.

Mr. Haji's late uncle, O. Oomer Kutty, founded the business of a timber merchant and public works contractor in the year 1865, and he succeeded, by industrious habits and by strict personal attention, in building up a very sound connection. This gentleman died in 1908, and in the same year Mr. Mami Kunhi Haji (who had been manager for a quarter of a century) became sole proprietor. He conducts large wholesale and retail transactions in all kinds of Malabar timber, the receiving depôt for which is on the Baliapatam river, 5 miles distant from Cannanore, and a quarter of a mile from the railway station at Azikal. Heavy logs are sawn here when required, but the lighter ones are cut up on the home premises, and a large stock of thoroughly seasoned wood is stored at each place. Many of the leading merchants of Bombay, Karachi, Bhavnagar, and other places pay periodical visits to Mr. Haji's yards and stores for the purpose of purchasing timber, and the large quantities which they buy are shipped on their own sailing-boats to various ports in Southern India. A very large quantity of timber is taken annually to the Kolar Gold Fields in Mysore.

Mr. Mami Kunhi Haji is a recognized contractor in Cannanore to the Public Works Department of the Madras Government ; he is further entrusted with large orders from the military authorities in the district, and many of the principal works in the area between Calicut and Mangalore have been carried out by him. The premises in Cannanore, which are about 2 acres in extent, comprise godowns, sheds, stores, and blacksmith's, furniture-making, and paint shops. Various kinds of work are undertaken in the smithy, and at the present time new iron doors are being constructed for the local jail. Mr. Mami Kunhi Haji claims that his success in business is entirely due to his own personal supervision. It is a fixed rule with him that not a single consignment of large or small goods is despatched until he has satisfied himself that the purchaser's wishes have been complied with. He has recently erected, opposite his present stores, a fine double-storied building constructed of laterite and supported by iron columns and girders. A ferro-concrete floor has been put in between the upper and lower stories, and the woodwork throughout is of unexceptionable quality and finish. There is a large yard behind the building, and it is intended to erect new workshops in which it is proposed to install modern machinery, which will be driven by a steam-engine.

Mr. Haji is the owner of several very nice bungalows in and around Cannanore, and H.E. the Governor—Lord Pentland—occupied one of them during a recent visit to that town.

THE MALABAR WEAVING COMPANY

It is an undoubted fact that India is not at the present making the most of her possibilities in the matter of the supply of the world's markets with cotton. This is made clear by a reference to Government statistics, which show that the United States of America supply more than 50 per cent. of the total amount required for consumption, while India does not contribute more than 16 per cent. Another unsatisfactory feature is that the American cotton is far superior to the other in quality, and this fact accounts for the very serious diminution in the number of orders from English manufacturers. It is, however, some consolation to learn that agriculturists in India are endeavouring to remedy this most unsatisfactory state of affairs. Cotton is one of the indigenous products of India, and it has been cultivated there for a very great number of years. Improved methods of weaving have been introduced, and credit is due to those who are trying to grow better-class raw material and to those who—like the Malabar Weaving Company—are anxious to offer to the public manufactured articles of the highest quality.

This company was formed in 1901 by Mr. T. Christian, who for thirty-five years previously had been connected with the well-known Basel Mission Industries at Mangalore and Cannanore. Unpretentious premises were opened at Cannanore in which there were 10 looms employed in the manufacture of cotton trouserings and coatings, but an extraordinary demand for these articles sprang up, and extension followed hard upon extension, until there were—in November 1914—45 hand-looms turning out cotton checks, imitation tweeds, towels, mercerized suitings, ginghams, tweeds, and sundry other articles of standard quality. The "counts" of yarn which are used range from 30's to 80's, and these are imported direct from Manchester, while the fittings for the looms are made in Germany.

The company has a very large annual turnover, obtained principally through travelling agents in India, Burma, and Ceylon.

Dyeing of cotton yarn is carried out on the premises when practicable, but in some instances dyed yarn is imported from England and Germany. Specimens of manufactured articles from the company's factory have been accorded high praise at industrial exhibitions, and gold, silver, and bronze medals have been gained at Cannanore, Ettaiyapuram, Nagpur, Calcutta, Madras, Vizagapatam, and Mysore. The staff of employees has grown from 10 weavers and 5 women in 1901 to more than 100 skilled workmen and women in 1914. A few months after Mr. Christian commenced business he admitted two gentlemen into partnership, but they retired very shortly afterwards, leaving Mr. Christian in full ownership. Messrs. A. T. Christian and J. W. Christian—sons of the proprietor—are now assisting in the management of the business.

PREMISES OF THE MALABAR WEAVING COMPANY.

The premises cover more than an acre of ground in the European portion of Cannanore, near to the military barracks. Further, they adjoin the compound of a well-known hostelry, and Mr. Christian is always pleased to receive visits from the hotel residents, and he is happy when he can conduct them over the works and explain to them the interesting processes of manufacture.

R. MANACKJEE

For several years after the middle of the nineteenth century the forest trees of the district of Malabar were—through ignorance of their qualities—known under the generic term of " jungle-wood " ; and it was largely due to the efforts of Mr. A. Brown, of Calicut, that the value of Malabar timber was brought into prominence. This gentleman was the founder (about the year 1880) of the business now conducted at Kallai, near Calicut, by Mr. R. Manackjee, and he erected two large and thoroughly up-to-date saw-mills, which are to-day known as The New Malabar Timber Yards and Sawmills, Ltd. The present proprietor was associated with Mr. Brown from the commencement, but the latter has now practically retired.

The area of about five acres upon which the premises stand formerly consisted of the densest jungle, but the entire vicinity is now a veritable hive of commercial industry. The yards and buildings have an excellent frontage on the left bank of the Kallai River, thus affording excellent facilities for transport by water as well as by road, and there is, further, a private railway-siding from Kallai, which is only about 200 yards distant. Mr. Manackjee holds a standing contract with the Kolar Gold Fields Company for the supply of 24 different classes of timber, all of which were specially introduced by him to the notice of the company. Prominent among other leading purchasers are the Ceylon Government and the Public Works Department of the Government of Madras. An export trade, direct to Europe, is carried on with consignments of rosewood, ebony, and red cedar, which are shipped at Calicut. A very good connection has been established with Hamburg, Antwerp, Havre, and London, but temporary suspension of this has become necessary owing to European troubles. Large stocks of all kinds of log and sawn timber are kept on hand in order that purchasers —who range from important Government departments to builders and merchants —may always obtain exactly what they require at the shortest possible notice.

Purchasing agents travel through the Mysore, Cochin, and Travancore forests, and all logs, excepting those from Mysore, which reach Kallai by rail, are floated on rivers to such places as may be desired. Mr. Manackjee supervises every branch of the business, and he usually employs about 100 sawyers and coolies.

R. MANACKJEE.

1. Office at Kallai. 2. Timber Truck with Logs for the Gold-fields. 3. Log-sawyers.

MORGAN & SON

The town of Mangalore, a seaport of considerable importance in the district of South Canara, is the centre of the coffee-curing industry in the Presidency of Madras, and several hundreds of hands are employed in the factories there during the busy season, which continues from the 1st December to the end of April. One of these curing works was started by the late Mr. Henry Mann in the year 1862 for the purpose of curing the coffee grown on his own estates on the Sampagi and Mercara Ghats, in the Province of Coorg. He was joined in partnership in the following year by the late Mr. James Hungerford Morgan, the style of the new firm being H. Mann & Co. The business which had been so successfully

MORGAN & SON.

1. Coffee Works. 2. Manure Works. 3 and 4. Tile Works.

launched by Mr. Mann had expanded so rapidly owing to the sound economic principles upon which it was based, that when the two partners threw their united energies into the concern they soon made the discovery that a considerable enlargement of the factory had become a necessity. They therefore caused the premises to be increased to a size which would enable them to turn out fully 1,000 tons of "cured" coffee every year, and at the same time they made it known that they were prepared to cure consignments of the raw article on behalf of neighbouring planters. Mr. Mann's share of the business was, on his death in 1880, purchased by Mr. H. R. Morgan, son of the surviving partner, and the firm has since then been known by the name of Morgan & Son, although there have been some changes of a private nature with regard to vested interests. The works were again extended, new and more modern machinery was added, until they are now (1915) extensive enough to deal with as large an annual quantity as 2,000 tons.

The firm are owners of some valuable coffee estates in the Native State of Mysore, which have given remarkably good results. Owing to the difficulties experienced in crossing the River Netravati, which lies between the Coorg estates and Mangalore, a considerable portion of the produce from the Coorg districts has lately been diverted to Tellicherry—a port about 100 miles in a southerly direction—but upon the completion of a bridge across the river which is now being constructed, such produce will again be cured and shipped at Mangalore.

About the year 1895 Messrs. Morgan & Son began the manufacture of artificial manures for use on their own estates, but, as in the case of the curing of coffee, this branch has now been extended in order that the requirements of other planters may be met.

Tile works were started at Mangalore by the partners of H. Mann & Co. in the year 1873. A peculiar kind of clay found in the Netravati River was used, and it has proved to be so superior for manufacturing purposes that "Mangalore" tiles have gained a unique reputation throughout India. The above works were taken over by Mr. J. H. Morgan on the death of Mr. Mann, and they have subsequently been managed by Mr. C. H. Morgan on behalf of those who are personally concerned in them.

As instancing the growth of this trade it may be said that the annual output of roofing tiles has risen from 300,000 to 2,500,000, and still the demand is exceedingly keen, owing to the expressed judgment of purchasers that as regards quality and style of workmanship these tiles are second to none in India.

Messrs. Morgan & Son use the prefix "Jeppo" in connection with the names of their undertakings, and thus it is that the Jeppo Coffee & Manure Works and the Jeppo Tile Works are known throughout the length and breadth of the continent.

The telegraphic address of the firm is "Morgan, Mangalore."

JAVARAJ OTHAMCHAND & CO.

The business of a timber merchant, general contractor, and commission agent is carried on under the above name by Mr. Javaraj Othamchand, whose ancestors were engaged in commerce in the district

JAVARAJ OTHAMCHAND & CO.

1. Javaraj Hurukhchand. 2. The Office.

of Malabar some 200 years ago. The owner's great-grandfather, Ramchand Khinji, established himself at Porbundar, in the district of Kathiawar, a village which has since become recognized as the ancestral home of the family. The grandfather transferred the business to Calicut, and the present owner and his late father, Hurkhchand, were born in that town. The latter greatly enlarged the scope of the business by dealing in grain, coir, and other Malabar produce, and he subsequently began to trade in all kinds of timber indigenous to that district. Mr. Javaraj Huruckchand took over the concern in the year 1891, and he has made a special feature of the timber branch, and particularly of matchwood, which is sent to Karachi and other ports for exportation to match factories in Europe. Other kinds of timber for which there is a considerable demand, both locally and on the Continent of Europe and in Bombay, are rosewood, erool, pilamorudoo, benteak, jungle-wood, etc. In order to maintain a stock of timber sufficient to meet all inquiries, Mr. Javaraj employs a staff of touring agents who purchase logs and then cause them to be brought down through various rivers to seaport towns.

The proprietor does a very extensive trade in supplying—under contract—all kinds of wood goods to merchants in the mofussil, and he has just entered into a contract for the delivery of 50,000 sleepers to the South Indian Railway Company.

Purchasers of timbers can have logs sawn to any measurements that may be required, and no fewer than 150 labourers are kept on the premises for this work alone. Mr. Javaraj retains the management of the business in his own hands, and he is the sole proprietor of the above firm, and his strict personal attention to every branch of work enables him to maintain the worthy reputation which was gained by his ancestors.

A. B. PINTO & SONS.

1. Tile Factory and New Construction. 2. A. B. Pinto (Proprietor).

A. B. PINTO & SONS

The manufacture of bricks, tiles, and pottery in the district of South Canara, on the west coast of the Presidency, is a flourishing industry giving employment to a large number of its inhabitants, and it is, moreover, one which has become increasingly valuable as an asset by reason of the greatly improved character of the outfit owing to the introduction of up-to-date machinery. The extensive business now carried on by Messrs. A. B. Pinto & Sons at the Oriental Tile Works, in the town of Mangalore, was founded in the year 1885 by Messrs. Coelho Bros., and after it had, at a later date, passed through the hands of Messrs. B. S. & P. F. X. Saldanha, it was purchased by the present owners in 1911. Mr. A. B. Pinto, the senior partner, entered the firm with sound practical experience which had been gained during the previous fifteen years, and it was not long before the knowledge acquired by him was manifested in the general improvements which he initiated, not the least of which was the substitution of coal kilns for those which had hitherto depended upon wood for fuel. The works are now (March 1915) capable of turning out about 20 lakhs of tiles every year, but when certain extensions and alterations, now in hand, have been completed, the number will, it is expected, exceed 30 lakhs. The machinery for crushing, pugging, and moulding the clay is driven by a 16-h.p. engine and a 20-h.p. boiler, but "pressing" of tiles is still done by hand. Messrs. Pinto & Sons have a very wide circle of customers in Australia, British East Africa, and Zanzibar, while the railway and other Government departments have entrusted them with important contracts. Credit is undoubtedly due to them for the very great care which is exercised in packing consignments for shipment, railage, or, occasionally, cartage, to coffee plantations in Mysore, and this work is so skilfully performed that an allowance of 2 per cent. for breakages leaves an ample margin for losses.

The works are situated on the bank of the Netravati River, and one's attention is immediately drawn to the manufacturing and drying-sheds, to the machinery, godowns, offices, and a private bungalow. Additional godowns are being erected for the safe storage and protection of tiles during the months of June, July, August, and September, when the severity of the monsoon renders shipping of consignments an impossibility.

Mr. A. B. Pinto personally supervises every branch of the business, and he employs 6 assistants and about 150 labourers.

PEIRCE, LESLIE & CO., LTD.

The business which is now carried on by this company was established in a comparatively small way by a private firm in the year 1859, and its growth has corresponded with the steadily increasing commercial prosperity of the Malabar coast. The private firm was converted into a limited liability company in 1901, and its registered offices are at 14 Billiter Street, London, E.C. The headquarters of the company in India are at Calicut, with branches in Cochin, Tellicherry, Mangalore, and Coimbatore. The company's business as merchants covers all branches of imports and exports. Their factories include hydraulic baling presses at Calicut and Cochin, and a manure and a matting factory at Calicut; they also have works at Calicut for the preparation of ginger and cardamoms. As steamer agents and charterers they are largely interested in the shipping business of the Malabar coast, and they hold a number of agencies for important steam shipping companies. They are managing agents of the Malabar Coast Chartering Coalition, and are Lloyds' agents in Cochin and Mangalore. One of the most important branches of the company's business is the preparation and shipment of plantation coffee. They are agents for a large number of estates, and have coffee curing works at Calicut, Tellicherry, and Mangalore; and they are also managing agents of the Anupura Coffee Curing Works at Coimbatore. The shipment of tea and rubber also forms a prominent part of the company's business. They are secretaries and agents for the Panora Tea and Produce Company, Ltd., the Periakaramalai Tea and Produce Company, Ltd., the Eddivanna Rubber and Tea Company, Ltd., and the Pudukad Rubber Company, Ltd.

Other agencies include the following: The Clan Line, Nederland, Rotterdam Lloyd, Hamburg-Amerika, East Asiatic Company, and Northern Steamship Companies, the Hansa Line, Asiatic Steam Navigation Company, Ltd., Standard Oil Company, of New York, German Potash Syndicate, Nitrogen Fertilizers, Ltd., Commercial Union Assurance Company, Ltd., Union Insurance Society of Canton, Ltd., Thames and Mersey Marine Insurance Company, Ltd., London Assurance Corporation, Standard Life Assurance Company, South British Fire and Marine Insurance Company of New Zealand, and the Sea Insurance Company, Ltd.

D. J. REGO & SONS.

1. Factory Wharf. 2. A Portion of the Factory.

D. J. REGO & SONS

The tile and brick-manufacturing business carried on by Messrs. D. J. Rego & Sons, at Mangalore, was founded in the year 1865 by the late Mr. P. P. Lobo (uncle of the present proprietors), who traded under the name of Lobo & Sons, and it was taken over by Mr. D. J. Rego in 1900.

This is the oldest factory of its kind in Mangalore, and as it had been in the family for so many years, Mr. Rego was possessed by a very natural desire to perpetuate the connection. Alterations and improvements were effected to such an extent that few traces of the old establishment are now visible.

Coal kilns, for example, have superseded the old-fashioned kilns which consumed wood only, and modern machinery has replaced that which had become obsolete. A special feature is made of roofing and flooring tiles of a standard pattern, although the partners are always prepared to adopt any designs which may be submitted by their patrons. The pugmill and the crushing machine are driven by a 12-h.p. steam engine by Marshall & Sons, of Gainsborough, England, but the plant for pressing tiles is worked by hand.

The majority of the tiles are sent to the firm's depôt at Mazagon, in Bombay, whence they are consigned to places in all parts of Northern and Central India, in addition to Mombasa, Zanzibar, and Madagascar, although large quantities are exported to Goa and Cochin.

Messrs. Rego & Sons purchase a considerable number of tiles from smaller factories in Mangalore, and these are sold to customers in the countries above mentioned.

The factory premises cover an area of about 3 acres, and they comprise godowns, sheds, and offices. The eldest son, Mr. J. P. Rego, is sole manager, and he usually employs about 80 labourers.

N. SAMY & CO.

It is a very satisfactory criterion of the manner in which a business is carried on when customers return again and again to place orders with the proprietor. It shows that the goods sold were equal to what they were represented to be; it proves that straightforward business methods were employed, and it is evidence that strenuous efforts have always been made to give entire satisfaction to purchasers.

This firm of timber merchants was founded by the late Mr. N. Samy in the year 1882, and it is unfortunate that, at the time of his death in 1906, his sons were juniors, and were therefore unable

PEIRCE, LESLIE & CO., LTD.

1. PORTION OF THE PREMISES AT COCHIN, SHOWING CASKS CONTAINING COCONUT OIL. 2. COPRA CUTTING.

3. COIR-YARN BEING PRESSED INTO BALES FOR SHIPMENT.

to continue the business until working partners had been admitted. The firm carry on an extensive trade in all kinds of indigenous timber from the States of Cochin, Mysore, and Travancore, and the district of Malabar. The various classes of produce of these forests are exported to centres in India, and to European, African, and American ports. The consignments to Europe consist chiefly of ebony and rosewood; America takes ebony and red cedar, and the last-named wood is supplied to Australia in considerable quantities.

The firm have held contracts for the delivery of certain classes of timber to the South Indian Railway Company, to the Department of Public Works, and to many of the principal public buildings in Calicut. Their yards, workshop, and premises cover an area of about 6 acres, and they have an extensive frontage on the Kallai river, which affords excellent facilities for transport. The firm are owners of several godowns, where a large stock is kept of timber which is sawn to standard lengths.

N. SAMY & CO.

1. Office. 2. Naracasherry Samy (Avl).

BASIN BRIDGE JUNCTION, MADRAS.

RAILWAYS IN SOUTHERN INDIA

IT would hardly be possible to overestimate the extent of the influence of railways upon the trade and industries of the world, as there are now very few agricultural and commercial centres which are not linked together by the iron horse. Civilization has, by the same means, been widely extended, races of human beings have been brought into contact with and have influenced each other, and the economic development of the past fifty or sixty years has totally eclipsed the progress made during several previous centuries. What could be more astounding than the difference between the engine constructed by George Stephenson in 1814—which, by the way, travelled at the rate of 6 miles an hour—and the powerful locomotives of the present day!

The first railway to be completed for passenger service in England was opened between Stockton and Darlington in 1825, and one would like,. just by comparison, to place the vehicles of those early trains side by side with the luxuriously appointed coaches with their electric lighting and bath and dining-rooms, which the ordinary traveller has now come to expect. Specially designed carriages provided with all the comforts which an ingenious mind can conceive are absolutely essential in a country such as India, where journeys are long and frequently tedious owing to the peculiar physical features of the continent, the insufferable heat, and the concomitant trying conditions which one is called upon to endure in the tropics.

It was a considerable time atter the establishment of railways in England that the question of their construction in India was even mooted, and then it was deemed advisable to conduct practical tests as to their suitability for the special requirements of the East. Records show that the building of three experimental lines was authorized in the year 1845, but the work of general construction was not taken in hand until after the promulgation of a Minute of the Marquis of Dalhousie, K.T., in 1853, wherein the Viceroy, "after dwelling upon the great social, political, and commercial advantages of connecting the chief cities by rail, suggested a great scheme of trunk lines, linking the Presidencies with each other, and the inland regions with the principal ports. This reasoning commended itself to the Directors of the East India Company, but as there was no private capital in India available for railway construction, English companies, the interest on whose capital was guaranteed by the State, were formed for the purpose. By the end of 1859 contracts had been entered into with eight companies for the construction of 5,000 miles of lines, involving a guaranteed capital of £52,000,000."

THE SOUTH INDIAN RAILWAY COMPANY, LTD.

THE lines formerly owned and worked by the Great Southern Railway of India and the Carnatic Railway Companies were amalgamated on July 1, 1874, under the title of the South Indian Railway Company, which, on January 1, 1891, was purchased by the State, and handed over, together with the Villapuram-Guntakal State section and the Shoranur-Cochin Native State line, to be worked as one undertaking by the present South Indian Railway Company.

This company was registered in the year 1890, with its head offices at 91 York Street, Westminster, London, S.W. The chairman is Sir Henry Kimber, Bart., the managing director is Mr. N. G. Priestley, and the other directors are Sir Douglas Fox, M.I.C.E., Mr. W. H. Notman, Sir J. D. Rees, K.C.I.E.. M.V.O., M.P., and Mr. A. J. Yorke. The Hon. A. Muirhead, C.I.E., is agent for the railway company in India, Mr. T. J. McCloughin is general traffic manager, and Mr. T. H. le Mesurier is secretary.

The railway system traverses the most picturesque and the most historically interesting portion of the continent, from Mangalore on the west coast to Madras on the east, and there are endless attractions for tourists in the ancient temples and shrines at Madura, Trichinopoly, Tanjore, Chidambaram, and a host of other places.

On March 31, 1914, the open lines reached a total of 1,753 miles, and about 94 miles were under construction, or sanction had been given for the work, thus making a total of 1,847 miles. Particulars of the main and branch lines are as follows : (*a*) The South Indian Railway (5 ft. 6 in. gauge section) extends from Jalarpet—132 miles distant from Madras —to Mangalore, a port on the west coast, in the district of South Canara. The train travels from Jalarpet in a southerly direction for about 5 miles to Tiruppattur, the centre of a district which produces fairly large quantities of paddy, grain, and castor and gingelly seeds. Seventy miles to the south-west is Salem, celebrated for its iron and steel foundries, and for weaving, dyeing, and the manufacture of bamboo mats. Erode, 243 miles from Madras, is a very important municipality in the district of Coimbatore, and it is a junction station where large quantities of paddy, saffron, plantains, cotton, and chillies are received for transport by rail. It contains two ancient temples, dedicated respectively to Siva and Vishnu. Numerous Hindu temples may be seen in and around Olavakkot, the principal ones being the Ammai Amman building, near to the station, and the Siva shrine at Kalpathi. This is an exceedingly picturesque district ; the numerous villages are clean and neat in appearance, and they are surrounded by a profusion of beautiful trees. Shoranur is the junction for the Cochin State Railway, and is 360 miles from Madras. The main line now runs in a north-westerly direction to Calicut, a busy seaport, where a large quantity of pepper, ginger, timber, coir, and coconuts is shipped for export. The train arrives at the French settlement of Mahé, at the 450th milestone from Madras, and about 20 miles farther to the north is Cannanore, an old-fashioned town which was visited by Vasco da Gama in the year 1498. Copra, coir, and pepper are exported. The terminus of this line is at Mangalore, where large quantities of coffee, rice, and tobacco are exported by railway and sea.

The Nilgiri branch commences on the main line at Podanur Junction, and 306 miles distant from Madras is Coimbatore. a pleasant town at an altitude of 1,350 ft., where there are spinning and weaving mills, coffee-curing works, and cotton-ginning factories. The terminus of the broad-gauge system is at Mettupalaiyam, which is situated at the foot of the Nilgiri Hills.

The gross earnings of this portion of the South Indian Railway for the year ending on March 31, 1914, were Rs. 7,01,73,755, the net amount was Rs. 79,54,816, and the proportion of expenses to earnings was 62·39.

(*b*) The South Indian Railway (3 ft. $3\frac{3}{8}$ in. gauge section) includes the main lines from the Beach Station in Madras to Tuticorin in Southern India, and from Villapuram to Katpadi, together with the following branches, namely, the Arkonam, Pondicherry, Nagore, Pulliarpati Quarry, Erode, Pamban, Tinnevelly, Wharf. Capper Quarry, and Salt.

The Beach Station is the junction in the city of Madras of the Madras and Southern Mahratta Railway, and it is most conveniently situated, as the warehouses and godowns of the leading mercantile firms are within a distance of a few hundred yards. Further than that, it has sidings which connect it with the extensive wharfage accommodation constructed by the Port Trust authorities at the Madras Harbour. The train passes through the very fine station at Egmore (Madras) and other places until Chingleput is reached. This place has a very interesting old fort, which was erected about the close of the sixteenth century, but probably a still greater attraction to tourists is the Seven Pagodas and the Siva temple of Tirukalukundram, which are in the vicinity. Villupuram, 102 miles from Madras, in the district of South Arcot, is an important junction and receiving station for large quantities of rice, *ragi*, ground-nuts, and indigo. The old and new towns of Cuddalore claim attention next, as, independently of the large railway traffic which is noticeable here, the port is one of the most eligible on the east coast. Weaving and dyeing are the principal industries, and the chief products are paddy and sugar cane. Passengers for Tanjore, Negapatam, and other places change at Mayavaram Junction. The distance from Mayavaram to Kumbakonam is about 20 miles, the latter place being famous for sixteen temples devoted to Vishnu and Siva. The chief source of interest, however, is the annual bathing festival held in the Mahamakhan tank, at which it is estimated that nearly half a million persons are present. Tanjore is the principal town in the district of the same name, in which paddy is grown in very large quantities. About 252 miles from Madras is Trichinopoly, the headquarters of the South Indian Railway Company, Ltd., and a municipal town which attracts large numbers of visitors on account of its antiquity and of its fort, which played an important part in the wars of the seventeenth and eighteenth centuries. The principal products of the district are paddy, plantains, coconuts, and mangoes. Proceeding in a north-westerly direction, the train passes the quaint old town of Dindigul, the centre of a district in which there are several thriving industries connected with agricultural pursuits, and a few miles farther Kodaikanal Road is reached, where motor-cars or other means of conveyance can be secured for the travellers' ride to Kodaikanal, the famous hill station on the upper ranges of the Pulney Hills, in the district of Madura. This sanatorium is about 7,000 ft. above the level of the sea, and

1. A CABIN AT BASIN BRIDGE.

2 AND 3. VIEWS AT BASIN BRIDGE JUNCTION.

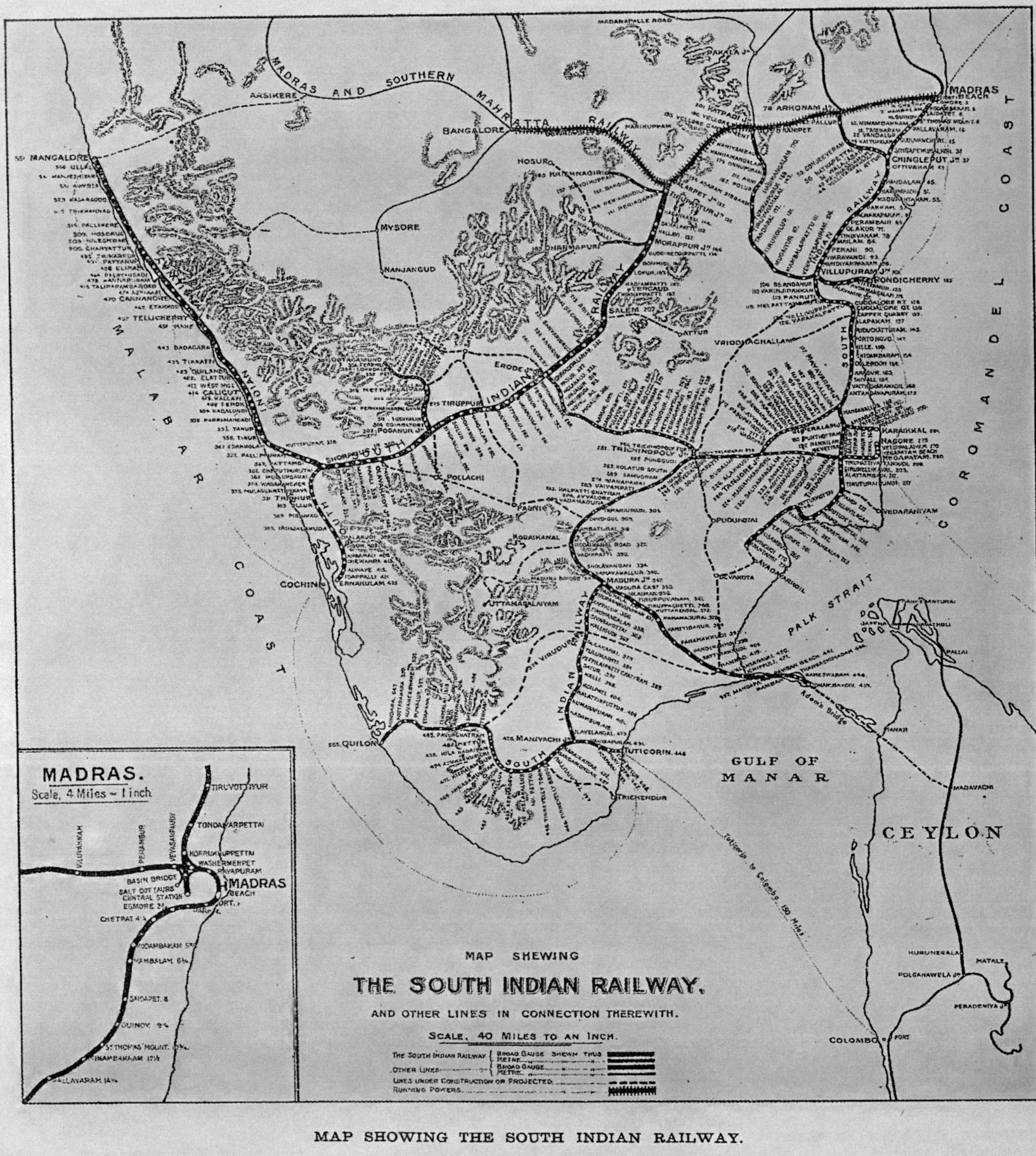

MAP SHOWING THE SOUTH INDIAN RAILWAY.

it is blessed with a remarkably cool and bracing climate. The district of Madura is noted for its manufactures rather than for agricultural produce, although a considerable quantity of paddy and plantains is grown. The district traffic superintendent and the district and assistant engineers of the South Indian Railway system reside at Madura. Maniyachi, a junction whence the line deviates to the east to Tuticorin and to Quilon on the west, is 425 miles distant from Madras, and 19 miles farther is Tuticorin, the terminus of the main line. There is naturally a considerable amount of traffic here, as it is the chief port of the district, and all kinds of merchandise are received from Ceylon and elsewhere to be forwarded upon the railways of Southern India.

The Arkonam branch is 39 miles in length, and the principal town on this section is Conjeeveram, where the number of passengers who entrain for Madras and other centres is very large, and during festivals thousands of visitors arrive by train from all parts of India. Arkonam is an important junction with the Madras and Southern Mahratta Railway, where passengers change for that company's north-west and south-west lines.

The principal station on the branch from Villupuram to Pondicherry is Chinnabasamudram, which is on the frontier of the French settlement, of which the town of Pondicherry is the headquarters. This settlement is fully described elsewhere in this volume. The Nagore branch is 53 miles in length from Tanjore, and throughout the whole of this distance there are numerous temples where large festivals are held, which are attended by crowds of worshippers, who travel many miles to be present. Nearly the whole of the 87 miles of branch line between Trichinopoly and Erode are in the district of Trichinopoly, from which a very considerable tonnage of agricultural produce is forwarded by goods trains.

One of the most important branches of the South Indian Railway is that which extends from Madura to Mandapam, Rameswaram, and Dhanushkodi, where the newly-established ferry service conveys passengers by steamer to Talaimannar, in Ceylon. This route between Colombo and Southern India is much shorter and infinitely preferable to the Tuticorin journey, which involved an hour in an uncomfortable tug and twelve hours on a steamer. The South Indian Railway Company have constructed three turbine vessels, and they have been specially designed for this service, which was opened to the public on February 24, 1914. Other small branches make a total of 881 miles.

As the statistics of working upon this section for the year 1913-14 include the Nilgiri, the Morappur-Dharmapuri, and the Tiruppattur - Krishnagiri Railways, some reference to them must be made here. The original Nilgiri Railway Com-

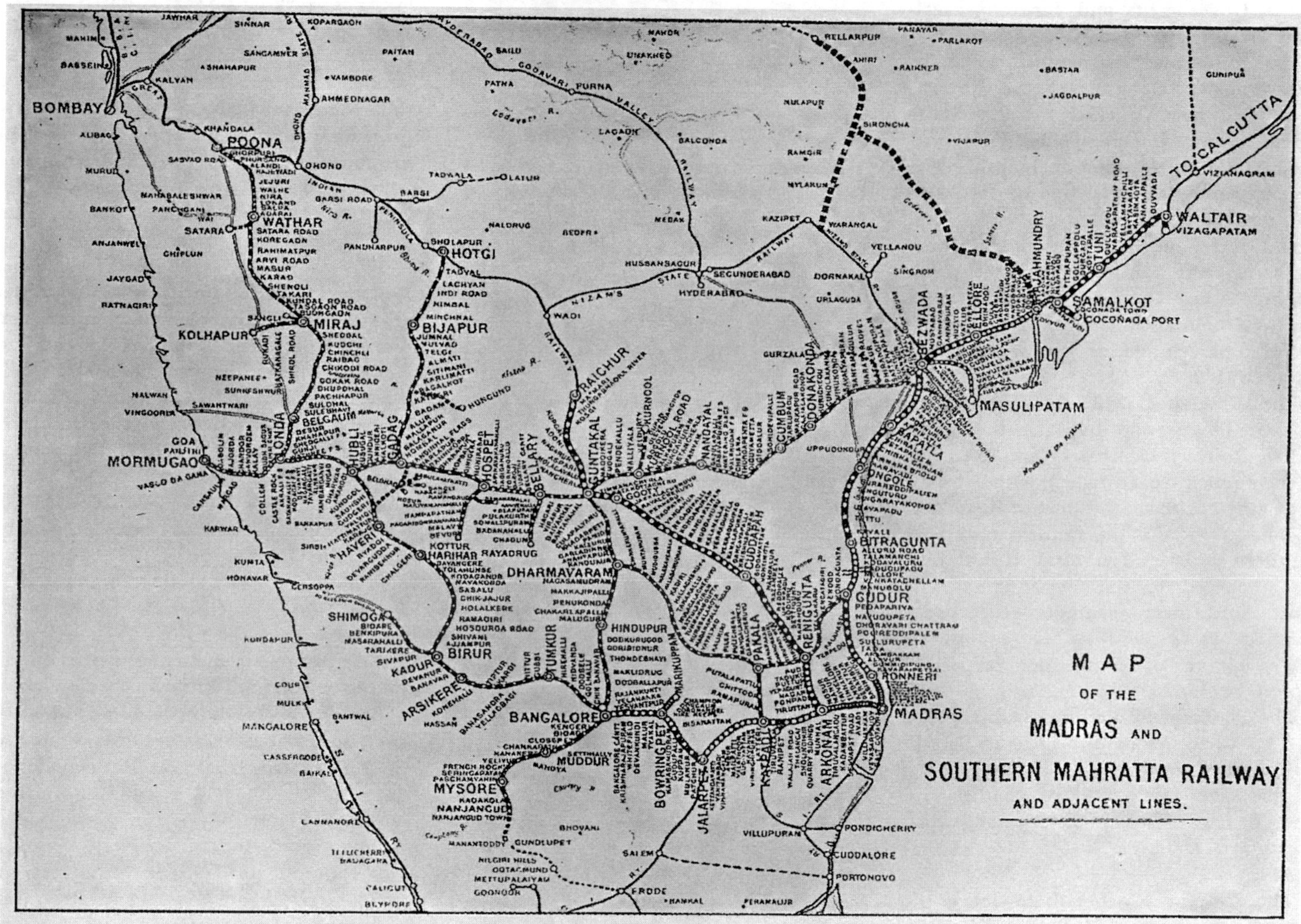

MAP OF THE MADRAS AND SOUTHERN MAHRATTA RAILWAYS.

pany was registered on September 30, 1885, with a nominal capital of 25 lakhs of rupees, and a contract was entered into between the Secretary of State and that company in February 1886. Eventually the line from Mettupalaiyam to Coonoor was purchased by the Government, who extended it to Ootacamund, which is more than 7,000 ft. above the level of the sea, and is the favourite hill resort in the summer months for the members of the Government and for other residents of the Presidency.

The Morappur-Dharmapuri, of 2 ft. 6 in. gauge, belonging to the Government, has been worked by the South Indian Railway Company since January 1, 1908, and it is 73 miles in length. The Tiruppattur-Krishnagiri line of the same gauge is 25 miles in length. The total capital outlay on these sections on March 31, 1914, was Rs. 26,41,473, the gross earnings were Rs. 2,80,70,002, the net earnings amounted to Rs. 1,17,27,495, and the percentage of net earnings on outlay was 6·42.

The Peralam-Karaikkal Railway, 15 miles in length, was built by the South Indian Railway Company (and paid for by the French Government), with the view of placing the town and port of Karaikkal in connection with the railway system of Southern India. The total capital outlay amounted to Rs. 7,23,786, and the gross and net earnings respectively were Rs. 65,513 and Rs. 21,393, giving a percentage of 2·96 upon expended capital.

The Pondicherry Railway, with a gauge of 3 ft. 3⅜ in., is about 8 miles in length, and extends from the east bank of the Gingee River to the town of Pondicherry. The net earnings were Rs. 63,016, which shows a percentage of 11·08 on capital outlay.

The Shoranar-Cochin State line is the property of the Cochin Durbar, and was worked by the former Madras Company until January 1, 1908, when it was taken in hand by the South Indian Railway Company. It is 65 miles in length, and the train proceeds along the west coast of the Presidency from Shoranar Junction to Trichur, the old capital of Cochin, where thousands of people assemble at the annual festival of Puram. Forty-five miles to the south is Ernakulam, the terminus, which is an important town of about 22,000 inhabitants, a large number of whom are interested in the production of paddy, betel, and coco and areca-nuts. After payment of expenses of maintenance and working, the net proceeds were Rs. 2,79,356, this being 4 per cent. on the outlay.

MORMUGAO HARBOUR.

The Tanjore District Board Railway extends from Mayavaram to Quarry, a distance of 103 miles, but branches from Indamangal to Mannargudi and from Tiruturaipundi to Vedaraniem were sanctioned on October 15, 1912. The contract between the Secretary of State and the South Indian Railway Company relating to working powers is dated July 22, 1897. The net earnings of the 103 miles was Rs. 3,49,568, being 6·71 on expended capital. The principal towns on the route are Mutupet, a centre for growing coconuts, Patukkottai, whence ground-nuts are exported, and Arantangi, which produces large quantities of paddy, Kumbu, ragi, cholam, tobacco, and ground-nuts.

The Tinnevelly-Quilon (Travancore) Railway is divided into British and Native sections. The first-named comprises the district between Tinnevelly and the British frontier near to Shencottah, with a permanent way of 50 miles, while the latter runs from Quilon to the frontier of the Travancore State, near Shencottah, and covers a distance of 97 miles, although a portion between Quilon and Trivandrum (39 miles) was only sanctioned in October 1913. The net earnings on the whole line amounted to Rs. 3,55,800, representing 2·18 on the total cost.

The commencement of work on the Podanur-Pollachi Railway (3 ft. 3⅜ in. gauge), from funds provided by the District Board of Coimbatore, was authorized in a telegram from the Railway Board dated November 18, 1913, and the total length is 25 miles.

The South Indian Railway Company has running powers for passenger and goods trains from Madras to Bangalore, a distance of 219 miles.

In December 1912 there were 25 engines belonging to the "M" class, which are used for drawing mail and passenger trains over portions of the metre-gauge line, and about 49 of the "B" class, which are required almost wholly for goods service. Other engines, somewhat older, are required for branches of this line. All of these were built by the North British Locomotive Company, Ltd., of Glasgow, the Vulcan Foundry, or by Messrs. Kerr, Stuart & Co. The carriages are principally of the vestibule corridor type, and the accommodation for first and second-class passengers is fitted with elec-

1. CASTLE ROCK TUNNEL, M. & S.M. RAILWAY GHAUTS, NEAR GOA FRONTIER.
2. DUDH SAGUR STATION, W.I.P.R. GHAUTS. 3. ESCARPMENT VIADUCT, W.I.P.R. GHAUTS.
4. CATCH SIDING, GUROLI STATION, POONA GHAUTS (M. & S.M. RAILWAY).

tric lights and fans. The goods wagons are chiefly of the bogie type, and have a carrying capacity of about 20 tons, with tare of 10 tons.

Returns show that there are altogether, on the metre-gauge section, 276 engines, 604 bogie coaches and 603 four-wheeled vehicles, 597 bogie wagons, and 3,302 four-wheeled wagons. The 2 ft. 6 in. gauge system has 6 engines, 21 bogie carriages, and 48 bogie goods wagons.

Nearly the whole of the country through which the South Indian Railway trains pass is so flat in character that there is not a single tunnel, excepting in the Nilgiris and over the *ghauts* in the State of Travancore.

The completion of the ferry route between India and Ceylon has already caused an appreciable increase in the number of travellers between the two countries, and, but for the troublous times in Europe, the number of tourists anxious to view the interesting temples in Southern India would be very much greater. Messrs. Spencer & Co., Ltd., the well-known caterers of Madras, hold the contract for supplying refreshments at all of the principal stations, and also in the vestibule dining cars on the metre-gauge main-line trains.

The principal workshops at Negapatam were built in the year 1866, but additions have been made to the original structures on several occasions. There are facilities for the repair of engines and vehicles of the metre-gauge type only, and for the construction of a certain class of rolling stock. The shops are well fitted with modern machinery and plant obtained from leading manufacturers in Great Britain. Broad-gauge rolling stock is sent to shops at Podanur, and, in order to obviate the inconvenience which arises from having two separate centres for repairs, a proposal is under consideration to remove all works to Trichinopoly, where rolling-stock of both gauges could be accommodated.

An excellent guide is published every two or three months, which contains up-to-date time-tables, fares between South Indian stations, rates for live stock, luggage, and special articles, a list of fairs and festivals, and descriptive notes on places of interest served by the South Indian system.

THE MADRAS AND SOUTHERN MAHRATTA RAILWAY COMPANY, LTD.

THE Madras and Southern Mahratta Railway Company, Ltd., was originally known as the Madras Railway Company, and on the expiration of the contract on December 31, 1907, the lines owned by that company were purchased by the Secretary of State. On January 1, 1908, the then existing Madras Railway (with some slight alterations in certain sections), was made over to the Southern Mahratta Railway Company, to be worked by them, the new designation being the Madras and Southern Mahratta Railway Company, Ltd.

The headquarters of the company are situated at 91 York Street, Westminster, London, S.W., and the sixty-first report of the directors and a statement of accounts for the year ending on March 31, 1914, were presented to the stockholders at an ordinary general meeting held at the company's offices on December 16, 1914.

The length of lines open for traffic was shown to be 3,132·83 miles, divided as follows: (*a*) Company's and State lines, 1,520·80 miles (metre gauge), and (*b*) 1,031·73 (broad gauge); (*c*) the Mysore State lines, 411·23 miles; and (*d*) other worked lines, 169·07 miles; detailed particulars of which are: (*a*) The metre-gauge lines, 3 ft. 3⅜ in. in width, extending from the coast on the Arabian Sea on the west to Bezwada, in the district of Kistna, in the eastern portion of the Madras Presidency, passing through such important centres as Dharwar, Hospet, Bellary, Guntakal, Nandyal, and Cumbum; and they also include the following branches: Hubli to Harihar, Londa to Poona, Guntakal to the frontier of Mysore, Bellary to Rayadrug, Hospet to Kanivihalli, Katpadi to Dharmavaram, and Pakala to Gudur. This system is connected with the South Indian Railway at Arkonam and Katpadi, thus forming direct through communication with all stations in the southern portion of the continent. (*b*) The broad-gauge section, 5 ft. 6 in., connects the principal places in the Presidency with each other, and, by making use of other railways, travellers can obtain main through routes without break of gauge between Madras, Calcutta, Bombay, and Upper India. The route from Madras to Calcutta is along the eastern coast of the Presidency to Waltair, which is the junction with the Bengal-Nagpur Railway, and the headquarters of the district of Vizagapatam. For Bombay the line runs from Madras to Raichur, in the dominions of the Nizam of Hyderabad, which is the junction of the Great Indian Peninsula Railway The principal stations *en route* to Raichur are Arkonam, a connecting link with the South Indian Railway, Renigunta, Cuddapah, Gooty, where there is an almost impregnable fortress, and Guntakal. The main line in the south-west covers 132 miles between Madras and Jalarpet, while the connecting branches are from the Beach Station to Veyasarpandy, Walajah Road to Ranipet, and from the junction at Jalarpet to the cantonment and city of Bangalore, the seat of Government of the State of Mysore. (*c*) The Mysore railways—which are the absolute property of the Government of that State—were constructed and equipped with rolling stock and all other appliances, but they are maintained and worked by the Madras and Southern Mahratta Railway Company. Included therein are the following sections: Mysore, the Mysore-Nanjangud line, the Hindupur branch, and the Birur-Shimoga and Kolar Gold-fields Railways. (*d*) Other lines which are worked by the company are the West of India Portuguese, the Kolhapur State, the Sangli State, the Bezwada-Masulipatam, and the Dhone-Kurnool (State) Railways.

Taking the revenue transactions of the whole system for the year 1913-14, the earnings have amounted to Rs. 4,27,55,468, as compared with Rs. 4,13,00,387, showing an increase over 1912-13 of Rs. 14,55,081, or 3·52 per cent.; the expenses amounted to Rs. 2,39,03,958, or 55·91 per cent. of earnings as compared with Rs. 2,21,88,532, or 53·72 per cent., showing an increase over the previous year of Rs. 17,15,426, or 7·73 per cent.; the result being a decrease in the net earnings of Rs. 2,60,345, or 1·36 per cent.

The share of the net earnings of the

1. DORABHAIR VIADUCT, CHELAMA GHAUTS, BELLARY-KRISHNA RAILWAY.
2. VIADUCTS ON CHELAMA GHAUTS, BELLARY-KRISHNA RAILWAY. 3 AND 4. TUNNEL, POONA GHAUTS.

company's and State lines for the year 1913-14 amounted to Rs. 1,64,35,233, as against Rs. 1,67,32,310 in 1912-13, showing a decrease of Rs. 2,97,077, or 1·78 per cent.

The Madras and Southern Mahratta Railway is worked under an agreement with the Secretary of State for India, under which the Government guarantees interest in sterling on the nominal amount of the capital of the company at 3½ per cent. per annum, any surplus profits earned being divisible between the Government and the company in proportion to their respective shares in the total capital. The capital of the Secretary of State was stated in the above agreement to be £11,250,000, and that of the company to be £5,000,000, which, with debentures issued prior to January 1, 1908, brought the grand total to £17,615,000. The construction account showed that £19,546,682 had been expended; new capital, raised by debentures and stock (after providing for certain outlays), amounted to £1,937,489 15s. 10d.; thus leaving a balance for further expenditure of £1,504,084 1s. 7d.

A meeting of stock-holders was held on June 17, 1914, when, in anticipation of detailed accounts, a final dividend for the financial year of 1913-14 was authorized. With the *interim* dividend of 15s. per cent. paid on January 1, 1914, and the dividend of 15s. and the bonus of 10s. per cent. paid on July 1, 1914 (in addition to the guaranteed interest of 3½ per cent.), the total distribution for the year amounted to 5½ per cent., and the balance of the surplus profits and interest on investments, approximately £26,000, was added to the reserve fund.

The directors referred in their report to the serious disturbance of Indian trade caused by the depredations of the German cruiser *Emden* on British shipping in Eastern waters, and stated that while they did not think it possible to expect the immediate resumption of normal conditions, they trusted that, with favourable rains followed by good crops, the revenues might at no distant date take an upward course.

A reference to the published statement, however, shows that during the second half of the year 1912-13 the commodities carried upon the whole system weighed 2,046,839 tons, and that in the corresponding portion of the succeeding year the quantity amounted to 2,155,288 tons. There was an increase in consignments of raw and manufactured cotton, fruits and vegetables, oil-seeds, sugar, and wood, while decreases were noticeable in grain and pulse, manganese ore, and provisions. The number of passengers carried during the periods above mentioned was 13,219,403 and 14,437,321 respectively, while the gross earnings of the coaching traffic were Rs. 60,92,945 and Rs. 64,20,810.

The principal terminus of the system is at the Central Station, Madras, which is situated opposite the General Hospital, and within a few hundred yards of the municipal offices in the newly-constructed Ripon Buildings. It is a handsome stone and red brick structure, having four covered - in platforms, together with spacious waiting and refreshment-rooms, and it is surmounted by an artistically-designed clock-tower, which rises to a height of about 136 ft. The station-master's, clerks', parcels rooms, and ticket offices are on the ground floor of the building, while the upper story is occupied by the general traffic manager and his staff.

About a mile to the north of the Madras (Beach) Station, which is the city junction of the Madras and Southern Mahratta and South Indian Railway systems, is Royapuram, where the majority of the offices of the first-named company are at present situated, and where, in bygone days, the construction workshops were located. Between the years 1858 and 1860 steps were taken with the view of establishing works of a more permanent character at Perambur, about 4 miles distant from Madras, and towards the close of the year 1863 a portion of the engine erecting and other machine shops were built, but the accommodation was limited to twelve engines and six boilers and a proportionate number of carriages and wagons, the number of engines then on the line being about seventy.

Extensions of the shops were carried out in 1870, 1877, and 1881, but in the year 1900 a very comprehensive scheme was prepared by the then deputy locomotive superintendent, Mr. A. Pilkington, under the orders of Mr. C. E. Phipps, locomotive superintendent at that time. Building operations were commenced in 1901, but a delay of several years occurred, owing to a lack of necessary funds. The works and grounds now cover an area of about 66 acres and about 5,500 hands are employed, 500 of whom are Europeans and Anglo-Indians.

Perambur is well worthy of a visit, as there is much of a very interesting character in seeing "the beginning of things," when the component parts of the powerful engine or the luxurious saloon carriage are being placed together.

First of all one reaches the foundry, in which are steam and electric cranes, grinding machines, and cast-iron cupolas (with melting capacity of 5 tons). In the wheel and tyre shop one sees about twenty lathes for engine and wagon wheels, hydraulic wheel-press, drilling machines, and an electric overhead crane with a lifting power of 5 tons. In the nut and bolt shop are bolt, nut, finning, and swedging machines, grinding-stones, saws, and furnaces. The millwright's shop contains drilling, milling, planing, screwing, and other machines, screw-cutting lathes, circular and other saws, electric motor of 35 h.p., a surfacing lathe with 36-in. centres, testing machines, and an electric overhead travelling crane of 15 tons capacity. The machine shop is a large building, and is fitted with, *inter alia*, machines of various sizes for turning, screw-cutting, boring, planing, slotting, lapping, and drilling, together with an extensive assortment of appliances of a similar character. The brass-finishing shed has screw-cutting gap lathes, turret lathes of different sizes, milling and other machines. From here we pass to the erecting shop, in which there are four 45-ton electrically-driven travelling cranes, more than thirty jib cranes (25 cwt.), and about twenty-five portable pneumatic drills and riveters. The coppersmith's department is fitted with tube-grinding, cutting, and testing machinery, and an electric motor. Turning to the smith's shop, one sees about a dozen large and small steam hammers, about 130 round and square forges, furnaces, hot-iron saw, and two jib cranes. The spring and fitting shops contain drilling, buffing, punching, shearing, and spring-testing machines. The boiler shop is crammed with a general assortment of plant and appliances, including machines for plate edge planing, punching, plate bending, radial arm drilling, flanging, and straightening, pneumatic portable drills, hydraulic accumulator, three hydraulic jib cranes (25 cwt.), two electric cranes (25 tons), two others (5 tons), pneumatic hammer, iron band-saw, and pneumatic plant and piping. The saw-mill is situated in close proximity to those departments which require cut timber, and it is fitted with eight electric motors of 35 h.p., six of 25 h.p., and eleven of 15 h.p., nearly thirty circular saws, vary-

KISTNA BRIDGE, M. & S.M. RAILWAY.

ing in diameter from 18 to 42 in., planing, tongueing, grooving, tenoning, mortising, and grinding machines, lathes, and band and cross-cut saws. The greater portion of the contents of the workshops was obtained from the leading manufacturers in Great Britain.

The electric power-house must be noticed, as it contains one of the most up-to-date systems in India. Some particulars relating to it are extracted from the *Railway Gazette* of November 12, 1913:—

"The building is constructed with bricks, and its dimensions are 130 ft. in length and 48 ft. in width. The installation is made up of six units—two steam and four Diesel sets. The steam plant consists of two Beliss & Morcom triple-expansion non-condensing steam engines, coupled to generators made by the Electric Construction Company, of Wolverhampton, and the boiler-house contains five hand-fired, dish-ended Lancashire boilers, 30 ft. by 9 ft., fitted with superheaters made by John Thompson, of Wolverhampton. The oil plant consists of four 300-h.p. single-acting Diesel engines by Carels Freres, of Ghent, and lowering the temperature of the water is carried out by the use of a hot-well wooden cooling tower and an elevated cold-water tank. Centrifugal pumps are employed to raise the water from the hot well to the cooling tower, and from the base of the latter to the cold-water tank The crude oil storage tanks have a capacity of 50,000 gallons. The main switchboard is of white marble, and consists of six generator and seven distributing panels, and there is also a small auxiliary switchboard which controls the various motors in the building. The system of distribution is a two-wire one with a pressure of 500 volts, the supply to each shop being conveyed by means of bare overhead lines to the entrance, and thence by cable to the distributing switchboard. The basement of the building is used for storing purposes."

On the metre-gauge section at Hubli well-equipped shops were erected in 1882 for the maintenance of locomotive, carriage, and wagon stock, and other works have been constructed at Bangalore for the upkeep of the vehicles of the Mysore railways.

A matter of very great importance to Indian railways generally, and one which has lately been engaging the serious attention of the authorities, is the supply of sleepers, and owing to the diminishing

THE GODAVERI BRIDGE, M. & S.M. RAILWAY.

quantity of suitable timber there has been an increase in the cost of sleepers during the past few years. Proposals were made to substitute steel, cast iron, and reinforced concrete, and tests made with these in various parts of the continent have been eminently successful.

This railway system—with its branch lines—taps the richest agricultural area of the Madras Presidency; it passes through some of the finest scenery in India; and it is connected with some of the most important commercial centres in Southern India. A brief reference to some of these centres may be given.

Arkonam—43 miles distant from Madras—is the junction of this system with the South Indian Railway, and it has good accommodation for travellers, together with refreshment-rooms for Europeans and Indians. Jalarpet—in the district of North Arcot—is the headquarters of a district traffic superintendent of the Madras and Southern Mahratta Railway. After passing this station there is a gradual ascent until the plateau of Mysore is reached, which is more than 3,000 ft. above the level of the sea. The cities of Bangalore and Mysore are referred to at length on another page. The wealthy Kolar Gold-fields are only a few miles distant from Bowringpet, which is a populous and thriving commercial centre, and in a north-westerly direction are the growing towns of Tumkur, Kadur, Arsikere, and Shimoga. Still farther to the north are Hubli, a centre of the cotton trade, having a number of ginning and pressing factories; Belgaum, a cantonment station of some importance; Mormugao, a busy port with a fine harbour on the Arabian Sea; and Poona, the junction with the Great Indian Peninsula Railway, which is a city of about

ON THE NILGIRI RAILWAY.

100,000 inhabitants. This place is the headquarters of the Bombay Army, but it has several thriving industries, such as the manufacture of clay figures, metalwares, silk cloth, and brocades.

The towns on the broad-gauge line from Arkonam to Raichur include Cuddapah, which contains some interesting specimens of Indian architecture; Guntakal, the junction of the broad and metre-gauge lines of the system; and Raichur, in the Nizam's dominions, where constant struggles took place between Hindus and Mahommedans some centuries ago. Travellers leaving Madras on the north-eastern section pass through Gudur, the centre of a large rice-growing district; Ongole, noted for its excellent breed of cattle; Bezwada, a place of the deepest interest to archæologists, with its rock-cut temples of the Buddhist period; Rajahmundry, which commands the canal system of the delta of the Godaveri River, and carries on a large trade in rice; Samalkot, the junction for the Cocanada branch; and Waltair, one of the most desirable health resorts on the east coast. Vizagapatam is reached by a branch line from Waltair, and it has a considerable export trade in jute, manganese, and jaggery. The town is historically interesting, and it contains a population of about 40,000 inhabitants.

Refreshment-rooms for Europeans and Indians are provided at the principal stations, but special dining-cars are attached to the mail trains to the north. Messrs. Spencer & Co., Ltd., of Madras, are contractors for this service, in connection with which they employ a large staff of well-trained servants.

The Board of Directors consists of Colonel Sir Wm. S. S. Bissett, R.E., K.C.I.E. (chairman), Sir Trevredyn R. Wynne, K.C.S.I., K.C.I.E. (Government director), and Messrs. John O'Connell, L. R. Windham-Forrest, Colonel W. V. Constable, R.E., Colonel Sir Donald Robertson, K.C.S.I., and Mr. E. E. Sawyer, M.I.C.E.

1. WARKALAY TUNNEL, TRAVANCORE.
Photo by J. B. D'Cruz.

2. WADA CHANNEL, CHOREKOTTA BRIDGE, ALLEPPEY.

THE STATE OF TRAVANCORE

THERE are five native States in the Presidency of Madras, and Travancore, which is the largest of them, is one of those ancient Hindu dynasties which at one time exercised sovereignty in Southern India. It is bounded on the north by the British district of Coimbatore and the native State of Cochin; the Indian Ocean washes its western and southern shores; and the British districts of Madura and Tinnevelly lie on the eastern side. It has an area of 7,129 square miles; its population numbers about 3,500,000 persons, and its revenue is approximately 128 lakhs of rupees. The distance from the extreme north to Cape Comorin in the south is nearly 200 miles, and the greatest width of the State is 75 miles.

There is a considerable amount of uncertainty about the early history of Travancore, but there is direct evidence that about the commencement of the eighteenth century the State was continually at war: at one time the quarrel was with the Dutch; on another occasion the State of Cochin was the enemy; and then again the latter State made common cause with Travancore against the Hollanders. The Government had at that time become enfeebled by the rule of a succession of weak princes, but when the famous king Martanda Vama succeeded his uncle Rama Varma in 1729 he at once commenced a thorough inquiry into the un desirable condition of the country. He was only twenty-three years of age at the time of his accession, but his business acumen was such that he realized that there were no properly organized departments for the transaction of the business of the State; that the finances were in an extremely unsatisfactory condition; and that the country contained a number of petty chieftains who, surrounded by followers of the most unprincipled type, had frustrated attempts to establish a settled form of government. Martanda Varma succeeded in demonstrating that he was king, and that he would brook no interference with his sovereign power; he instituted economic reforms, and placed at the head of the departments men of undoubted integrity; he secured discipline, and finally raised an army which during subsequent years showed a true allegiance to its chief. His reign of twenty-nine years was, however, marked by a series of wars, but the net result was the retaking of portions of the State which during previous reigns had been lost to the kingdom. This south-western part of the Presidency now became a hotbed of intrigues, nawabs, zamorins, and maharajahs associating themselves with the heads of petty principalities whose sole aim was the subjugation of legitimate rulers of recognized States. The Dutch and French made several attempts to secure a footing, but there were other forces to be contended with, as the East India Company had already become a semi-political power in the Presidency, and Hyder Ali, the "Lion of Mysore," was continually demonstrating the strength of his adherents. Martanda Varma died in 1758, and was succeeded by his nephew Rama Varma, whose rule was characterized by wisdom, justice, and humanity, which endeared him to his subjects. He was rightly adored as the "Dharma Rajah" (the good and just king), a title of honour which has remained with the Travancore maharajahs ever since, and Englishmen called him the father of his people. Serious conflicts subsequently occurred between the Travancoreans and Hyder Ali, and later with his son, the famous Tipu, but the latter was eventually defeated by British troops in 1792. In the year 1795 a treaty of perpetual alliance was concluded between the East India Company and the Rajah of Travancore, in which the Company undertook, *inter alia*, to "defend and protect the country dependent on the Rajah of Travancore against unprovoked attacks." Sir T. Madhava Row, K.C.S.I., in reviewing the reign of the illustrious Rama Varma, says: "It was during this reign that the countries conquered by Travancore were fully and satisfactorily settled; peace and order were completely established; deposed chiefs acquiesced quietly in honourable retirement, and new subjects found themselves in the enjoyment of blessings to which they had long been strangers."

The next ruler, Bala Rama Varma, was of a weak and vacillating disposition, and his reign, from 1798 to 1810, was marked by his truckling to an unscrupulous set of favourites whose sole aim appeared to be to instal themselves in positions of influence which had for many years been occupied by men of integrity and ability. This was the commencement of another period of misrule; revenues were not properly collected, owing to the jealousy existing between the newly created officials; and as a result the treasury was soon empty. During the short period of four years the Rani Gouri Lakshmi Bayi introduced many reforms, and brighter days for the State followed rapidly. She lived and worked for the amelioration of the condition of the people, and it was with a genuine outburst of regret that her death was announced in 1814. The regency of Parvathi Bayi continued from this date to the year 1829.

Rama Varma (Swati Tirumal) succeeded to the throne in 1829, at the early age of sixteen years, and his scholastic attainments were of a high order, he being a fluent speaker and writer in English, Sanskrit, Persian, Hindustani, and Telugu, and was the author of several important works. The first gubernatorial visit to Travancore took place in 1830, when Mr. Lushington left Madras for the purpose of inspecting the country and of discussing its affairs with the reigning prince, and it is recorded that very great improvements in administration followed this visit. Among these may be mentioned the opening of munsiff's courts, the establishment of a code of civil and criminal laws based upon English enactments, the opening of an English school and an observatory at Trivandrum, and the introduction of the art of European engineering. Martanda Varma was thirty-two years of age when he succeeded his late brother in 1847, and he was a born ruler, high-minded and sympathetic, but resolute in his sense of justice towards his subjects. He contributed specimens of carvings to the London Exhibition of 1851, but the one which attracted most attention was an ivory chair, or throne, which had been specially designed for his own use. A total failure of crops, caused by floods, occurred in 1852, and this had the effect of seriously affecting the revenues of the State, an embarrassment which was felt for a considerable time. This taxed to the utmost the administrative capabilities of the Maharajah and his advisers, but they succeeded in again placing the Treasury in a sound position. Rama Varma, one of the most successful sovereigns of Travancore, ascended the *musnud* on September 7, 1860, and it was his misfortune that, during his first year of office, his country suffered excessively from the failure of periodical rains, and from the ravages of a black caterpillar which destroyed all standing crops. The Government did its utmost to alleviate the consequent distress, but thousands of the poorer classes died of hunger. This, however, did not prevent the Maharajah from inaugurating reforms, chief among which were the arrangements made for the conveyance of private letters at rates framed upon the British Indian model. The cause of education was advanced by the equipment of an Arts College at Trivandrum, and the opening of scores of English and vernacular schools throughout the State. On the death of this able and wise Maharajah on May 31, 1880, the following notification appeared in the *Fort St. George Gazette*: "His Highness ascended the *musnud* on October 19, 1860, and his reign has been marked by the development of enlightened principles of administration, which have placed Travancore in the first rank of native States." His Highness Rama Varma (Visakham Tirumal) began to reign on June 17, 1880, and he was indefatigable in applying himself to the minutest detail of administrative work, while at the same time he zealously encouraged the study of literature, music, and art. He was elected a Fellow of the Linnean Society, a Fellow of the Royal Geographical Society, and a Fellow of the Statistical Society of London, and was the author of many important works. He unfortunately died in 1885, and to quote Mr. Nagam Aiya, "he endeavoured to squeeze into five short years of his reign the work of a whole lifetime, for he believed in the poet's ideal, 'one crowded hour of glorious life is worth an age without a name.'"

The present Maharajah, His Highness Sir Rama Varma, G.C.S.I., G.C.I.E., was born in September 1857, under the star "*mulam*," hence his local name of Mulam Tirumal. Among the reforms which have been inaugurated by His Highness, the first place must be given to the establishment, in the year 1888, of the Travancore Legislative Council, which is composed of eight members, five official and three non-official, with the Dewan as *ex-officio* President. Improvements were subsequently effected in the administration of the Education Department, and a secretary to Government was appointed to check the work of the inspectors. An English normal school was opened at Trivandrum, the capital of the State, for the training of teachers, and a reformatory school was established for the benefit of juvenile offenders. The starting of an agricultural demonstration farm and school was another proof of the progressive character of His Highness's training, and this was followed by a scheme for the development of agricultural education among the cultivating and landowning classes.

There were widespread rejoicings in 1905, when the Maharajah had completed twenty years of his reign, and it was recognized generally that in no other similar period of the history of Travancore have so many improvements and reforms been quietly effected. The Madras Government sent their congratulations "on the continued prosperity of the State, and the steady efforts made

1. WAR DANCE DURING A FESTIVAL AT TRIVANDRUM. 2. MARRIAGE PROCESSION, TRIVANDRUM.
3. STREET SCENE DURING A FESTIVAL, TRIVANDRUM.

Photos by J. B. D'Cruz.

by His Highness to maintain an efficient administration," and added that the Maharajah's rule had been marked "by wise guidance, sound judgment, and great solicitude for the public good."

Travancore is one of the most picturesque portions of Southern India, as there is a wonderful variation of mountain, forest, and plain. Lieutenants Ward and Conner, after their survey of the country, said: "The face of the country presents considerable diversity, although its general character, except in the southern parts, is extremely abrupt and mountainous The coast is generally flat; retreating from it, the surface immediately becomes uneven, roughening into slopes which gradually combine and swell into the mountainous amphitheatre which bounds it on the east. The area along the coast, for its whole length, presents a fertility so near to the sea that it imparts a peculiar character to the landscape. This rich and variegated tract is flanked by a mountainous barrier, and is finally contrasted with the sombre magnificence and desolate solitude of those wilds of which the elephant seems to be the natural master; and though the landscape may be too much made up of this wild scenery, it boasts many striking localities and peculiar beauties, if not of the sublime, at least of romantic and picturesque kinds." Sir J. D. Rees, M.P., a former British Resident in Travancore, writes: "Words fail me to describe the lovely scenery. Tall, upright standards of huge timber trees, palms of every kind, including the exquisitely graceful areca, tree ferns, creepers, ferns, and flowers, all spring from a tangled undergrowth of iral reed. The pepper-vine clings to the large timber trees, and ropes of rattan and giant branches, hidden in creepers, combine to construct an ever-varying but unending bower. Roads lie by the side of deep and fearful ravines, thickly overgrown with moss and shrub, and through a continuous belt of tall and stately forest tenanted by the majestic elephant and the royal tiger." The chain of *ghauts*, which forms the backbone of India, forms a distinct boundary-line on the east, and it would hardly be possible to over-estimate the value to the State of this range. But for it the country would be arid and unfruitful, and droughts and famines would be constant owing to the probable absence of rains and rivers. In the northern portion of the State the mountains rise to a height of about 8,000 ft. above the level of the sea, while adjoining plateaus are not less than 7,000 ft. The group of hills known as the Anamalais is the most important one, its highest peak, Anamudy, being 8,840 ft. in height. There are from twelve to fifteen recognized passes, which are used principally by merchants and others when paying business visits to towns and villages in surrounding districts.

ON THE BACKWATERS, ALLEPPEY.

Travancore is particularly fortunate with regard to the number of its rivers, and as the rainfall is regular and abundant, there is always an ample supply of good water. The Periyar is the largest and by far the most important river. Its total length is 142 miles, and it is navigable for 60 miles from its mouth. Other rivers are the Minachil, which rises on the Peermade plateau at an elevation of 3,500 ft.; the Ranni (or Pamba), which is 90 miles in length; the Kallada, the third as regards length in Travancore; the Kolhayar, which rises at an altitude of 4,500 ft., and after shooting over falls descends to the plains, where it leisurely wends its way to the sea.

One of the most important features in the State of Travancore is its extensive backwater system, which adds very materially to the prosperity of the country, owing to the facilities which are given for the transport of merchandise, and especially so during the monsoon seasons, when the sea is naturally rough, and when the shipping or landing of cargo is rendered difficult, if not impossible. These backwaters are really inlets from the sea, and they are connected with each other by navigable channels.

A system of education may be said to have been commenced in the State in the year 1834, when an English school was established, and it should be added that the Travancoreans are filled with pride when they reflect that this was the first English school to be opened in Southern India. It is somewhat strange that instruction in the vernacular was not taken in hand seriously until 1867. It was not, however, until 1894 that any real reforms were inaugurated by the Government, and that year witnessed the adoption of a sound scheme of administration, inspection, and State aid. This was a step in the right direction, and it soon became evident that, as a result of this forward policy, the school had increased very rapidly in efficiency. A distinct advance was again made in 1902, when schools were classified as High, Middle, Upper Primary, and Lower Primary. The progress which has been made has been remarkably rapid, and Travancore now occupies a foremost position in India in educational matters, even when compared with other native States or with British provinces.

This State is interested, primarily, in agriculture, as nearly 50 per cent. of the three million inhabitants are dependent upon it in some shape or form for a means of livelihood. The principal crops are cereals, pulses, spices, condiments, garden products, roots, and oil, while the hill country is devoted to tea, coffee, rubber, and cinchona. Cotton of the Caravonica type has been introduced, and good results are anticipated. There is little doubt that hundreds of years before the Christian era the products of the districts in the south-western portion of India were sent to the leading markets of the ancient world. Mr. Nagam Aiya says: "Though it may be a bold conjecture to postulate that the cinnamon and cassia, which played an important part in the religious services of the ancient Jews, had been supplied from Malabar, it may be taken as an undoubted historical fact that the adventurous sailors of King Solomon had found their way to these ancient shores and returned to Syria with their tiny crafts laden with silver, ivory, apes, and peacocks."

The principal exports are copra—the dried kernel of the coconut—coconut-oil, coir (shipped chiefly as coir yarn and matting), areca-nut, coffee, and tea, consigned to British India, England, and France; jaggery and molasses, sent to British India and Cochin; ginger, to British India, Ceylon, Muscat, Pondicherry, London, France, and New York; and salt fish and hides, the trade in which is increasing rapidly. The imports consist chiefly of piece goods; cotton from British India; thread; wine, and sugar.

It was not until the sixties of last century that the making of roads was undertaken seriously, but since that time some hundreds of miles of foot-tracks have been made available for cart traffic. The most important ones are the Main Southern Road, from Trivandrum to Aramboly, 54 miles in length; and one from Trivandrum to Courtallam, via Shencottah, 67 miles; while others are from Trivandrum to Quilon, Quilon to Shencottah, Trivandrum to the northern frontier, via Kottayam, 155 miles, and Kottayam to Gudalur, via Peermade, about 70 miles in length. Particulars regarding the extension of the South Indian railway system from Tinnevelly to Quilon are given in a separate article, and it only remains to be added that it is exceedingly probable that other lines which have been suggested will, ere long, become an established fact.

Architecture and sculpture are twin arts, and the most chaste designs in each branch are observable in the temples and shrines of the State. Mr. Nagam Aiya observes: "In the temple of Sri Padmanabhaswami at Trivandrum there is abundant evidence of excellent sculpturing. In the fine broad open corridor, in the form of an oblong supported by 324 stone pillars, and covered with a terraced roof, and known as the Seevali Mantapam, the two rows of granite pillars and the stone ceiling above have been made the objects of the talent of the sculptor." Carving in wood, ivory, and stone has reached a remarkable height of efficiency in Travancore, and many of the choicest specimens have been exported to London. Among other prosperous industries may be mentioned weaving, the manufacture of lace, oil-pressing, metal-work, carpentry, the mining of plumbago and mica, and the manufacture of salt.

The mountains and forests of Travancore abound with large and small game of all kinds, and the keenest sportsman could not fail to be satisfied with the large numbers of elephant, tiger, leopard (including the black variety), bears, bison, sambur, and various kinds of deer and wild-fowl.

Trivandrum, the capital of the State, is the administrative headquarters, and contains the residence of His Highness the Maharajah, the Government Offices, and a large number of imposing public and private buildings. The fort is built in the form of a square; its four sides measure 11,320 ft., of which 5,796 ft. are constructed of granite, 2,445 ft. of laterite, and 2,919 ft. of mud, and within the square are a large pagoda and many streets of houses occupied by Brahmins. Many residences—chiefly tenanted by Europeans—are situated at a considerable altitude, and they command an extensive range of beautiful scenery. The temple is held in very high esteem by the people, who congregate in large numbers at two important annual festivals. Old commercial enterprises have gained new life, and new ventures have sprung into existence since the extension of the railway to Quilon opened up an important section of the country. The number of inhabitants at the census of 1911 was 57,882.

JUNGLE SCENE, TRAVANCORE.

Alleppey, in the Ampalapuzha *taluq* of the district of Quilon, is the principal seaport in Travancore, and its harbour affords safe anchorage for all steamers during the greater portion of the year. The town, which contains about 25,000 inhabitants, is the centre of very great commercial and industrial activities, and among these may be mentioned tile factories, oil-pressing, and the manufacture of coir mats.

Cape Comorin is the southernmost point of India, and it is frequented by a large number of visitors who regard it as a particularly healthy place of residence, although the majority of its temporary residents are attracted on account of pilgrimages which are celebrated there.

Colachel is one of the oldest seaports of the State, and vessels call here for coffee, salt, and other commodities for coast ports and Ceylon. It formerly belonged to the Dutch, but the latter were driven out in the year 1751.

Kottayam, with a population of about 18,000 souls, is charmingly situated among the loveliest scenery on the banks of the River Minachil. A very considerable trade is carried on here, and its position on the main road to Peermade enables its merchants to deal promptly and effectively with consignments intended for shipment.

Nagercoil was at one time the seat of the Travancore Government, and is still the second town in the State in point of number of inhabitants. Missions have flourished here, especially the London Missionary Society, which controls a second-grade college and a printing press. The temple is held in great veneration, and the pagoda is dedicated to the serpent god. Exceedingly fine lace-work is made by Mission converts.

Parur is a town of great antiquity, with a population of about 13,000 inhabitants. The Rajahs of Parur made it their capital many years ago, but its decline came about during the period when Tipu's power was at its zenith, and it was eventually partially destroyed by that warrior.

Peermade is much favoured by Europeans in search of health, as it is situated far above the plateaus, and is consequently regarded as one of the principal sanatoria in the State. It is said to have been the residence of a Mahommedan saint named Peer Mahomed, hence its name.

Quilon is credited with having a population of nearly 20,000 inhabitants, and it is the western terminus of the Travancore branch of the South Indian Railway. It is one of the seaport towns of the State, but it has a very considerable trade in local manufactures and industries. Chief among these are fish-curing, the making of coir ropes, cotton weaving, and brick and tile making, while more artistic work is represented by the engraving of silver plates and silver ornaments, comprising insects, dishes, tumblers, brooches, and other articles of vertu. The products of the immediate neighbourhood include cereals, coconuts, areca-nuts, and pepper. There are a few large factories in the town where the curing of coffee, the manufacture of ornamental tiles, and the sawing of timber are carried on. The principal exports are coir yarn, copra, pepper, nuts, and timber, while grain, tobacco, cloth, and spirits are imported.

Shencottah, at the foot of the *ghauts* on the main road from Tinnevelly to Quilon, is an important trade centre, whence coconuts, iron plates, spoons, and plantains are exported. A large number of persons are engaged in weaving and in the manufacture of bricks and pottery. The town contains two temples, dedicated to Siva and Vishnu, while another one is to be seen at Tirumalai, about 3 miles distant. The inhabitants were about 10,000 in number at the census of 1911.

NAIR CHILDREN, TRAVANCORE.

ARNAKAL

This estate of 1,425 acres was purchased in 1880 by Mr. G. L. Ackworth, who now resides at Hill Ash, Dymock, in Gloucestershire, England, and for whom Mr. D. McArthur, of Mungamullay, near Periyar, in the native State of Travancore, is managing agent. It was originally planted with coffee and cinchona, and at the time of sale only about 60 acres had been cultivated. This small area was subsequently planted with tea, and at the present time (1914), there are 725 acres of tea-bushes (625 acres of which are in full bearing), and about 100 acres of others which are nearly two years of age. All of this consists of tea of the indigenous kind, with the exception of the original 60 acres. A limited amount of cattle manure is applied annually, and the average yield is about 750 lb. to the acre. A capital range of the usual estate buildings has been erected, but the principal structure is a very fine factory which is equipped with up-to-date machinery and plant. A 36-h.p. Hornsby oil-engine provides the necessary motive-power, but a 24-h.p. Cundall oil-engine is held in reserve in case of accident. The tea is carefully packed in chests branded with the estate mark, and it is consigned direct to London for sale by the owner's agents, Messrs. Alston, Arbuthnot & Co., of Crutched Friars, E.C.

A European superintendent resides upon the property, and about 650 coolies are employed constantly. The soil at Arnakal is of a very fertile character, and the elevation above sea-level of about 3,000 ft.—coupled with an excellent climate and an annual rainfall of 120 in.—is mainly responsible for the excellent quality of the crop.

The post office at Vandiperiyar is distant about 3 miles.

CARADY COODY

The native State of Travancore, which is situated in the extreme south-west portion of India, is a very picturesque district, and owing to fertility of soil on the undulating plateaus and a generally salubrious climate, it produces excellent crops of tea, coffee, and rice.

The Carady Coody estate is 4½ miles distant from the post and telegraph office of Vandiperiyar in this State, and it contains 1,104 acres, of which 522 acres are planted with tea, while the remainder consists of white grass land and jungle.

The owner, Mr. R. H. Goldie, was the pioneer of grassland tea-planting in the neighbourhood of the Peermade Hills, and his action has been followed by the opening up of a large number of similar plantations. Many years ago Mr. Goldie obtained a free Government grant of 300 acres of so-called waste land, which was covered with elephant grass some 12 to 14 ft. in height, and it was understood that this gentleman was to undertake the experiment of clearing the dense undergrowth and of cultivating the soil for the planting of tea. It appears that the first bushes which were put in were of the hybrid jat type, but it was found that this kind was not suitable for the district, and

ARNAKAL ESTATE.

1. Pluckers in a Field. 2. A View of the Estate. 3. Factory. 4. Manager's Bungalow.

CARADY COODY ESTATE.

1. Factory. 2. Tea-field yielding 1,330 lb. Tea per Acre. 3. Writer's House and Coolie Lines. 4. Bungalow. 5. Interior of Factory.

that it would not be likely to yield a really payable crop. A change was therefore necessary, and seed of superior indigenous stock was purchased from Northern India, with the result that this estate is now producing a tea of exceptional quality. The original hybrid jat-bushes have not been uprooted, and if they are not so profitable as those of more recent growth, they have, at any rate, proved to be extremely hardy. The average annual yield of good black tea is 750 lb. to the acre, although one field of 26 acres has given a return of more than 1,000 lb. during each of the last six years, while one crop exceeded 1,200 lb. The factory is fitted with two Hornsby oil-engines of 32-h.p. and 45-h.p. respectively, and the other machinery includes four rollers, two roll breakers, two sifters, one packer, one auto-expresser, and four dryers, together with two hot-air fans in the lofts of the main building. The tea made in the factory is, as a rule, shipped direct to London under the estate brand, although a portion is occasionally consigned to Cochin via Kottayam, which is 56 miles distant by road from the property. An exception to this procedure was made some years ago, when for two successive seasons the entire crops were sold under contract to a purchaser in Toronto, Canada.

A considerable portion of the estate is about 3,750 ft. above the level of the sea, and there is an average annual rainfall of 127 in. The property is ably managed by Mr. W. H. G. Leahy, and he usually employs about 400 coolies, although he requires an additional 150 hands during the busy season.

THE CENTRAL TRAVANCORE RUBBER COMPANY, LTD.

The pioneer work of cutting out boundaries and felling the trees upon an area of rather more than 2,000 acres of land when the above company was opened was not carried out without encountering many dangers owing to the attacks of wild animals, especially elephants and pigs, and after development of the work had been commenced a very considerable amount of damage was done by these marauders. The property is situated in the southern valley of the district of Mundakayam, in the State of Travancore, and it is connected with the Kottayam-Kumalimain road by a private cart-road 7 miles in length. The land was acquired in 1905 and 1906 by Mr. Horace Drummond Deane-Drummond, partly from the Government of Travancore and partly from his Highness the Vanjipuza chief, Chengnoor, who is the owner of many thousands of acres of very valuable jungle. There are now (1915) 1,401 acres of Para rubber; 196 acres have been planted with tea; and there are still about 469 acres of forest land awaiting development. The estate was taken over by the Central Travancore Rubber Co., Ltd., on its formation in the year 1906. Shortly after the company obtained possession of the property an exceedingly severe epidemic of cholera and smallpox swept through the valley, resulting in complete disorganization of the labour force of the estate, as in addition to those who succumbed to disease a large number of coolies fled from the affected district.

About 22 acres of land on the hills were planted with tea as an experiment in 1911, and as the results were so satisfactory, the area under this crop has been increased to nearly 200 acres. Tapping of rubber-trees was commenced in a small way in 1911—the crop for that year producing about 10,000 lb. In the following year it was found necessary to build and equip a rubber factory, and a corrugated iron structure was accordingly erected and subsequently equipped with machinery, including a 36-h.p. National suction-gas engine, and a complete battery of Shaw's heavy rollers. Gas is extracted from charcoal, which is burned on the estate at a cost of about Rs. 12 a ton. The rubber is dried by hot air being forced by a fan, or *chula*, into the upstairs loft, when it is distributed through corrugated iron pipes in which holes are drilled in order that the heat may be regulated. The latex is first rolled into very thick strips, or lace, which can be dried in about three days, and it is subsequently rolled again in order to form thicker lengths, or *crepe*. The process of manufacture occupies six or seven days, and the product is then transported by bullock-carts to the Government cart road, whence it is conveyed by motor-lorries to Cochin, for shipment to England. The factory is lighted by electricity, which is supplied by a dynamo attached to the machinery, and it is connected by telephone with the principal bungalows of the company's European staff.

A feature of interest on the estate to archæologists and others is the ruin of a very ancient Hindu temple, wherein sacrifices of goats and animals take place at certain annual festivals.

The directors of the company are Messrs. W. B. Rankin (chairman), R. P. Macfarlane, J. Durie Pattullo, Tom B. Jones, and K. E. Nicoll.

CHISHOLM, EWART & CO.

This firm was established in the year 1890 by Mr. D. G. Cameron and Mr. E. C. Chisholm, who commenced business in partnership at the important industrial centre and seaport of Quilon as general merchants and agents, and as proprietors of sawmills and of brick and tile and joinery works. Mr. Cameron sold his interest in the firm in 1900, and Mr. E. M. Ewart joined Mr. Chisholm, when they began to trade under the name of Chisholm, Ewart & Co.

Quantities of timber—teak, hopea, and other hardwoods—are obtained from the Government forests in Travancore. Wood is seasoned before it is manufactured into roof timbers and joinery of all sorts, and doors and windows; and all soft-wood timber is made into various sizes of packing boxes. Machinery of a modern type has been installed in the factory, and the plant is driven by a 70-h.p. Crossley suction gas-engine. The works are most conveniently situated on 10 acres of land adjoining a canal, which is the main artery of the extensive area lying between Trivandrum and Ernakulam.

The brick and tile works are some 10 acres in extent, and about half a mile distant from the sawmills. A special feature is made of the production of roofing and flooring tiles of plain and ornamental designs, but the firm is prepared to execute orders for any kind of earthenware or terra-cotta goods. The average monthly output is from 7 to 9 lakhs, and although the local demand is exceptionally good, large consignments are shipped to all parts of Southern India and to Burma and Ceylon. Great care has been taken in the selection of modern machinery, and the partners are always ready to make a thorough trial of any plant of an improved character which may be placed upon the market, and no expense is spared in procuring such as may commend itself to their judgment. The present machinery is driven by two suction gas-engines of 200 h.p., and by one steam-engine of 80 h.p.

There is a branch at Colachel, about 80 miles from Quilon. Here a considerable trade is carried on in the exportation of country produce, but the principal industry is the preparation of fibre for shipment to London to be made into brushes. The number of employees varies from time to time, but about 700 hands are usually required. The partners personally supervise every detail of the business, and their agents in London are Messrs. Vavasseur & Co., Ltd.

DARRAGH, SMAIL & CO.

The town of Alleppey owes much to the late Mr. Darragh, the founder of this firm, who was the pioneer in the yarn industry on the west coast. He was an Irishman by birth and a weaver by trade, and, like thousands of other sons of Erin, he went to the United States of America, where he became a naturalized American subject. When he arrived at Calcutta about the year 1855 he found that coir yarn was brought there from the west coast and shipped in small quantities by sailing ships from Calcutta to the States, and as it was his intention to develop this export trade, he established himself at Alleppey, and it may be remarked that he was the first European to do so. His business was commenced in a very small way, but it stands to his credit that he was the first man to teach the natives of the district to spin yarn by wheel instead of by hand. Success attended his efforts simply because he threw the weight of his practical experience and energy into every detail of work, and he gradually developed the scope of his industries until he became general merchant and banker in a large way of business. He began to charter sailing vessels on his own account; he inaugurated the planting of tea in the hill districts of Travancore; he introduced paraffin oil and lamps among the natives in and around Alleppey; and he was the first trader to make direct shipments of copra from Alleppey to Marseilles.

Mr. Darragh became owner of several large tea and coffee estates in the hill districts, and he also erected cotton-spinning mills at Quilon which were fitted with English-made machinery.

Mr. Henry Smail, who came to India in 1881, was admitted as a partner in 1885, and the New York business in Water Street, New York, was thereafter conducted by him under the name of Darragh & Smail, while in 1898 London offices were taken at No. 5 Fenchurch Street, E.C., under the title of Henry Smail & Co. Both of these establishments are still in existence.

Mr. G. H. Davey, who joined the firm at Alleppey as manager in 1885, was admitted as partner in the Indian business in 1898.

Practically all of the industries which were originally taken up have been continued up to the present time, although the export trade has been largely increased, and shipments are now made of copra, pepper, ginger, turmeric, nux vomica, and all kinds of raw and manufactured coir yarn.

The coir yarn and mat factory at Alleppey is equipped with imported machinery of a modern character, and over half a million square yards of matting and a quarter of a million door-mats can be turned out in a season.

The buildings, which are constructed of laterite and tiles, cover an area of about 9 acres, and they include factories, godowns, stores, warehouses, and very good offices.

The firm are agents for various inland estates of rubber, coffee, tea, and cardamoms, and they have branch agencies throughout the State of Travancore.

Large premises situated at the Beach are used by the firm in connection with the preparation and shipment of produce to other countries.

About 1,500 hands are generally employed.

DYMOCK

The history of the cultivation of tea in Southern India is not an unbroken record of unfailing successes, as planters, in common with agriculturists in all parts of the world, have had to contend with many difficulties which have, in numerous instances, been simply another name for financial loss. It was not merely that the major portion of the most desirable land was covered with almost impenetrable jungle which called for the exercise of undaunted courage, untiring patience, and of no small amount of hard work, together with the expenditure of a considerable amount of money before it could be brought into a fit state for cultivation, but unfavourable seasons and depressed markets have levied their toll upon annual revenue. For instance, during the quinquennial period between the years 1903-4 and 1907-8 there was a marked diminution in the quantity of tea exported to the United Kingdom, and this adverse condition was even more noticeable about the close of the year 1912. The next year was heralded by a most gratifying increase in the demand in London, but perhaps the principal feature of interest was a distinct advance in the trade with China and Asiatic Turkey.

The Dymock Estate, near Periyar, in the State of Travancore, comprising 632 acres, offers a good illustration of what can be accomplished by skilful management backed up by indomitable perseverance. It was virgin forest-land when it was purchased by Mr. J. D. Deane Drummond from the Government of Travancore in 1909, but 312 acres have already been planted with Assam tea, while further development will be continued until the whole of the estate is cultivated. The bushes came into bearing at two years of age, when they yielded about 300 lb. to the acre; the fourth year's produce was 600 lb.; and it is estimated that when they are in full bearing—say the seventh or eighth year—they will give as much as 1,000 lb. to the acre. The factory is equipped with modern machinery, which includes a National 30-h.p. suction-gas plant. The manufactured tea is packed in chests which are marked with the word "Dymock," and it is sent in bullock-carts to Kodaikanal Road railway-station, a distance of 90 miles, whence it is conveyed to the port of Tuticorin, there to be shipped for London or Colombo.

The property adjoins the group of estates belonging to the Wallardie Tea Estates, Ltd., of which Mr. Drummond is manager, and it is only 5 miles distant from the post and telegraph offices at Vandiperiyar. Some 300 coolies are employed constantly under the supervision of a European superintendent, who resides in a nicely appointed bungalow on the estate.

EBRAHIM THAMBY ADIMA & SONS

The manufacture of coir matting and mats affords occupation for a large number of individuals—especially women—in Southern India, and the industry has developed to such an extent that consignments are now exported to the continent of Europe and other parts of the world. A business of this character was established at Alleppey in the fifties of last century by Ebrahim Thamby Adima. It was a very humble beginning, but the proprietor soon found that his goods were gaining in favour, that his annual output was increasing, and that a greater demand for first-class mats was noticeable. The

DARRAGH, SMAIL & CO.

1. General View of the Factory. 2. Yarn Selecting Sheds. 3. Office.

DYMOCK ESTATE.

1. View in front of Bungalow. 2. View looking towards Bungalow. 3. View of Estate from the West. 4. Factory. 5. View from Factory to Bungalow.

founder lived to see his venture on a sound commercial basis, and his eldest son, Adima Abdolkader Bava, is now the sole proprietor.

Only the best stocks of the raw material, or "yarn" (usually called Anjango), are purchased for manufacturing purposes, and the weaving process is carried on by hand-looms, 80 in number, for matting, and about 120 for mats. The standard sizes of the latter range from 24 in. in length by 14 in. in width to 48 in. and 30 in. respectively.

Matting is woven into lengths of 50 yards, with a width of from 18 in. to 72 in. These are the customary sizes, but orders for any other measurements or for special styles or designs are carefully executed.

Made-up stock is not kept on hand, but a large quantity of raw material is stored in order that there may be no delay in meeting orders. Mats and matting are exported to Europe and Australia, and the value of the annual shipments is about Rs. 8,00,000.

The proprietor manages the business himself, and he is assisted by his brother, Adima Ebrahim (who is yard superintendent), and by his brother-in-law (Sulaiman), superintendent of works. Some 275 hands are employed in the factory. The telegraphic address of the firm is Ebramtamby, Alleppey.

FAIRFIELD

This estate of 633 acres is in the native State of Travancore, and it is one of the oldest in the Peermade district. The first tea on this property was planted about the year 1882, and that was of a hybrid character. Previously to this coffee and cinchona had been cultivated. The area under tea was subsequently increased to about 180 acres. There was no factory at that time, and the tea was therefore manufactured by manual labour in a shed. The estate was then gradually opened up with indigenous tea, and a factory was built, which was enlarged in the year 1898. This factory was burned down in 1908, and a new one, erected in 1909 to replace this, has been fitted entirely with new machinery of a modern character, with the exception of a small 10-h.p. Dudbridge engine which was saved from the old building. During the year 1913 an additional engine was put in, and this is one of 40-h.p. (Brunton) driven by oil. During the time that the new factory was being erected the leaf from this estate was manufactured upon a neighbouring property.

At the present time there are 439 acres under tea, and this will probably be increased to 500 acres. The yield is between 400 and 500 lb. of made tea to the acre, but with cultivation, which is now being carefully done, this yield will be much increased. One field of 27 acres has given as much as 1,100 lb. of made tea an acre without the land having been manured. There is an ideal rainfall of 180 in. a year. All the made tea is sent to the London market, only a very little being sold locally. The reserve land consists chiefly of thick jungle containing some very good timber, so the estate is amply supplied with wood fuel for many years to come, which is a great consideration.

All requisite buildings have been solidly constructed, and the manager's bungalow, erected at an elevation of 3,700 ft., commands a fine view of nearly the whole of the property, while the mountains known as the Kanan Devan Hills may be seen in the far distance. A portion of Fairfield is nearly 4,000 ft. above sea-level, and the whole area is plentifully supplied with water for manufacturing and household purposes.

The owners of the estate are Lady Bertha Dawkins, Lady Maud Wilbraham, and Mr. R. P. Roissier; and the latter, who is the manager, employs about 400 coolies.

The nearest post and telegraph offices are at Aruday, Peermade, a distance of some 8 miles.

HARRISONS AND CROSFIELD, LTD.

A branch of the well-known commercial house of Messrs. Harrisons and Crosfield, Ltd., of Nos. 1-4, Great Tower Street, London, E.C., was opened at Quilon, in the native State of Travancore, in January 1911. Prior to this date all South Indian business was conducted through their branch office at Colombo. The firm's interests have increased very rapidly since 1911—especially with regard to estate agency, which is made a prominent feature—and they now represent the following among other companies: The Malayalam Rubber and Produce Company, Ltd., The East India Tea and Produce Company, Ltd., The Meppadi-Wynaad Tea Company, Ltd., The Wallardie Tea Estates Company, Ltd., and the Rubber Plantations Investment Trust, Ltd. In addition the firm are shipping and forwarding agents for numerous other estates in Southern India, and, in order to cope with the great influx of business which has taken place, they have opened other

EBRAHIM THAMBY ADIMA & SONS.
1. MACHINE ROOM. 2. THE YARD.

FAIRFIELD ESTATE.

1. Fairfield Factory. 2. 27-Acre Field. 3. A View on the Estate. 4. Pluckers at Work. 5. Bungalow.

HARRISONS AND CROSFIELD, LTD.

1. The Quilon Office, 2. Engineering Works. 3. The Moulding Shop. 4. The Machine Shop.

branches at Calicut, in the district of Malabar, and at Alleppey, Kottayam, and Trivandrum, in Travancore.

In May 1911 the firm purchased, as a going concern, the extensive tile works and saw-mills at Quilon belonging to Messrs. Cameron & Co., and these have been very considerably developed. Tiles and earthenware goods are manufactured to any design, and consignments are forwarded to all parts of Southern India, while a considerable quantity are exported to Ceylon. The saw-mills and factory are employed in the manufacture of tea-chests from cotton-wood, and of furniture from teakwood and Indian rosewood; and the stores contain a very large stock of estate tools and requisites.

In 1912 the firm opened engineering works at Quilon, but these have been extended so greatly that they have now become one of the largest of their kind in Southern India. This department is under the charge of four fully qualified engineers who have made a special study of machinery required in the manufacture of tea and rubber. Any orders connected with engineering can be executed here; repairs of all kinds are undertaken, and estimates, plans, and specifications are furnished.

The firm are sole agents in Southern India for the following: Messrs. Davidson & Co., makers of "sirocco" tea machinery and ventilating fans; the new Brown's patent triple-action tea-roller; Robinson's rubber-washing mills, made in all sizes and driven by hand or power; Ruston, Proctor & Co., Ltd., Lincoln, England, makers of successful suction-gas and oil-engines, and suppliers of "Ruston" gas and producer plants; the "Passburg" vacuum drier, which is suitable for drying rubber, cocoa, aniline dyes, pastes, glues, vegetables, and fruits; the Colombo Commercial Company's crepe rubber driers; Messrs. Allan Whyte & Co., manufacturers of the highest class of iron and steel wire ropes for tea shoots, hoists, and elevators; the British Kromhout marine oil-engines, varying from 8 h.p. to 90 h.p.; Messrs. Lee, Howl & Co., makers of hand and power pumps of every description; "Argyll" motor-cars. and for "Raleigh" and other well-known cycles.

Agencies are held for the British India Steam Navigation Company, Ltd., and the Asiatic Steam Navigation Company, Ltd., whose steamers run between Quilon and Bombay, Colombo, Madras, Calcutta, and other intermediate ports. The firm undertake shipments of produce and arrange sales in London and Continental markets, and they, further, book cargo to London, New York, and European ports generally. Insurances are effected against marine, fire, and life risks, and loss of profits, and the principal offices represented are the Atlas Assurance Company, Ltd., the Standard Life Office, and the London and Lancashire Fire Insurance Company.

The directors of the company are Messrs. C. Heath Clark (chairman), C. Arthur Lampard, George Croll, H. Eric Miller, John H. Schmidt, Gerald S. Townend, and Hugh T. Crosfield, and the registered offices are at Nos. 1-4 Great Tower Street, London, E.C. In addition to their interests in South India, the firm have establishments at Batavia, Calcutta, Kuala Lumpur, Medan, Montreal, Melbourne, New York, and Tangier, and they have agencies for estates in Java, Sumatra, the Federated Malay States, and Ceylon. The branch at Quilon is under the management of Mr. J. Mackie, who is assisted by a staff of twelve Europeans. The telegraphic address of the firm is "Crosfield."

P. JOHN & SONS.
OIL MILL AT ALLEPPEY.

P. JOHN & SONS

The firm of P. John & Sons consists of six members of a wealthy Syrian Christian family who have been honourably associated with the commercial life of Alleppey, in the State of Travancore, for a considerable number of years. The business was established in 1895 by the present partners, who are owners of two oil-mills in the town, one being situated on the southern bank of the Commercial Canal, while the other—a smaller one—has been erected near to the same waterway in that portion of Alleppey known as Chungam.

About 3,000 tons of copra, most of which is purchased locally, are dealt with annually in the large mill, and the oil is shipped to New York, London, and Hamburg, while poonac (which is a by-product) is disposed of principally in the last-named city. The modern machinery in the factory is driven by an 85-h.p. steam-engine, for which wood and coconut-shells are used as fuel. Employment is found for about 100 hands. About 1,800 tons of copra are passed through the smaller mill in the course of a year, and the produce is disposed of in a similar manner to that which obtains in the other factory. Two kinds of oil are made: the superior quality, known as Cochin oil, is exported to European countries, and nearly all of the inferior sort is sold in Calcutta, Rangoon, and Bombay.

The partners, who are natives of Kottayam, own a fine family ancestral property

HARRISONS AND CROSFIELD, LTD.

1 AND 2. SAW-MILLS. 3. MANAGER'S BUNGALOW, KONEY ESTATE. 4. RUBBER CLEARING, KONEY ESTATE.

in that village, consisting of 700 acres of coconut-trees in full bearing. Another of their estates comprises 600 acres of tea-bushes at Karinkulam in the district of Peermade, and this property is fully equipped with factory, lines for coolies, and other necessary buildings.

Cardamoms are grown upon 500 acres of land on high ranges of hills in the Thodupuza district, and the produce is sold by auction annually at good prices. The firm formerly owned 1,200 acres of Para rubber-trees in the same district, and when this property was sold in 1910 to the Malayalam Rubber Company, the partners retained a three-fourths share in it. The firm are managers of the Malankara Para rubber estate of 1,700 acres in the district of Thodupuza, but as the trees have only been planted recently, tapping of the bark had not been commenced at the time of the preparation of this account.

The telegraphic address of the firm is Johnsons, Alleppey.

The managing proprietor of the firm is Mr. P. John Mathew.

THE KANAN DEVAN HILLS PRODUCE COMPANY, LTD.

This company was formed in the year 1895 for the purchase and development of certain estates situated on one of the highest ranges in the northern portion of the State of Travancore. The capital was fixed at the sum of £1,000,000, but as the whole of this was sunk in the acquisition and opening up of the properties, further shares were subsequently issued, increasing the amount by £500,000. The estates —26 in number—comprise an area of 137,431 acres, and, twenty years ago, they consisted almost entirely of jungle and grasslands, without so much as a single road. The company had to face the difficulties and dangers which are inevitably the lot of all pioneers, but so much has been accomplished that at the close of the year 1914, about 17,300 acres had been cultivated with tea, 525 acres were devoted to cinchonas, 850 acres to Para rubber, 379 acres to sisal, and 130 acres to camphor. Each estate is under the management of a European, who, on the larger properties (which vary in size from 1,300 acres to 300 acres), has the help of a European assistant.

There are 16 fully equipped tea factories on the estates, and two others are in course of construction. In every instance the appliances are of a modern character; some are driven by water, others by oil or steam, while nine have their motive power in electricity, which is obtained from the company's central station. The largest of these buildings has a capacity for making 1,000,000 lb. of tea annually, and even the smallest one can deal with a quarter of a million pounds. The average annual yield of "made" tea is between 600 lb. and 700 lb. to the acre, although some fields have produced 800 lb., while individual plots have given as much as 1,200 lb. It is anticipated that the returns for the current year (1914) will exceed eight and a quarter million pounds, but it is tolerably certain that this figure will be exceeded when further development has taken place. Planting is still being carried on at the rate of about 500 acres a year.

The cultivation of sisal is still in its infancy, but the oldest trees—planted in 1909—offer remarkably good prospects, and younger ones, which are being put into the ground each year, are equally vigorous and healthy. A small factory for extracting fibre has been erected, and all the latest improvements in machinery and plant are in evidence.

About 200 acres of rubber were planted in 1906, and this was followed by a similar quantity in the following year; 178 acres in 1908; 100 acres in 1911; another 100 acres in 1912; and 70 acres in 1914. Tapping has only been started recently, the company being convinced that the trees should be fully matured before that operation takes place. It is expected that at least 10,000 lb. of manufactured rubber will be obtained during the present year. The factory is a temporary structure, but a model building, fitted up with up-to-date appliances, is nearing completion.

Cinchona - trees, planted by early settlers some years before the company's purchase of the estate, appear to have thriven well, and it was expected that by the end of the year 1914 no fewer than 146 tons of dry bark would be exported to London for the manufacture of quinine.

Camphor is as yet in the experimental stage, while the cultivation of coffee has proved to be so unprofitable that nearly all of the trees have been cut out to make room for tea.

The staff consists of 67 Europeans, including estate managers and assistants, engineers, a resident medical officer, a transport manager, and some 18,000 coolies, exclusive, however, of those in the native office and the servants in bungalows, whose inclusion will make an additional 500 persons.

The company formerly had a private organization for the supply of labour, which was under the management of Mr. A. F. Martin, who is now director of the U.P.A.S.I. This branch was carried on at an annual average cost to the company of Rs. 56,000. The account for rice supplied to the coolies on the properties appears to be enormous, as it formerly ran to about Rs. 12,000 every week, but in order to be in a better position to deal with this question, the company now own a rice mill at Trichinopoly, which is kept running throughout the year in milling paddy, which is bought in the surrounding neighbourhood. The machinery includes a 23-h.p. steam engine, and a husk-burning furnace, together with two shelling and four hulling machines.

When the company acquired the property there were only a few bridle-paths, and the question of transport was naturally one which had to be taken in hand at once. The first development in this direction was the opening of a road from Munnar (in the centre of the district), through the entire estates to the head of the *ghat*, a distance of 21 miles, with a rise of 1,500 ft. The next step was the construction of an aerial ropeway from the head of the *ghat* to the plains below, and these schemes very greatly facilitated the conveyance of goods and produce to and from the estates. A monorail tramway line was laid along the road in 1899, the trucks being hauled by bullocks, and this service sufficed until the year 1908, when the greatly enlarged output of the estates necessitated the installation of more speedy transport. For this purpose a 2-ft. gauge steam tramway was completed in 1909, and the company have now organized a regular passenger and goods service in addition to their being entrusted with the conveyance of his Majesty's mails. Three locomotives are in constant use; one is of 80 h.p., and the other two are 40 h.p. respectively, but the company are expecting another from England which is rated at 100 h.p.

The building of this tramway cost about Rs. 301,702, and this sum also covers rolling-stock consisting of nine wagons, two first-class passenger cars, and two second and third-class composite carriages.

The cultivated portions of the estate are at an altitude varying from 4,500 ft. to 6,500 ft., but the highest points of the property are the grass hills which terminate in the Aneimudi Hill (8,827 ft.), which is the highest peak south of the Himalayas in India.

As one might expect, there is an abundance of game of all kinds, and rich as the State of Travancore is in the species of its fauna, the area covered by these estates is perhaps the richest of all. A sportsman has opportunities of bagging elephant, tiger, bison, panther, ibex, sambur, and wild pig, in addition to an assorted variety of the feathered tribes, and if he be a follower of Izaak Walton he will be able to whip all the perennial streams which have been stocked with fine specimens of brown trout. It is only recently that one of the managers on the property landed a very nice four-pounder.

A European medical practitioner has quarters attached to a hospital, which has been erected near to Munnar, and this officer has full control over dispensaries on each of the properties. This is a boon which is greatly appreciated by the large number of labourers, and especially those who have families and to whom prompt advice is more than usually acceptable.

The produce of each property bears a special distinctive mark, and it is further branded with the name of the company, who forward it by bullock-cart from the station on the plains to Kodaikanal Road, whence it is conveyed by rail to Tuticorin, for direct shipment to Colombo and London.

Munnar is a small township which has sprung up side by side with the development of the estates, and it comprises post and telegraph offices, co-operative stores, a church, clubhouse, and a native bazaar, all of which has been built at the expense of the company. The Government has erected a rest-house and bungalows for two engineers, while about 5 miles distant from the township is the British Residency, which is occupied for about two months in the year. The co-operative stores have become the property of a limited liability company, which was formed by the European employees on the estates, who hold all the shares, and in accordance with real business principles all kinds of groceries and provisions are purchasable at Madras prices.

The ropeway is carried from the foot of the *ghat* to the station at the eastern end of the estates, and extends for a distance of $2\frac{1}{4}$ miles, with a rise of 4,000 ft. It consists of two continuous steel wire ropes, $\frac{7}{8}$-in. diameter, the bottom and upper sections being 16,000 ft. and 12,800 ft. respectively in length. The motor power is derived from electricity generated by water, two Pelton wheels, each of 40 h.p., being used for driving two electric generators of 30 kilowatts.

The Munnar Valley Electric Works were started by the company with the idea of supplying several neighbouring factories with driving power, and they now have four Pelton wheels (one of 200 h.p. and three of 100 h.p.), which work four dynamos, having a total capacity of 375 kilowatts. This power is transmitted to nine different factories lying within a radius of six miles, and several bungalows on the same estates receive their electricity for lighting purposes from the same source. These works were the second of their kind to be established in India, and the first to be utilized in connection with machinery for manufacturing tea.

Each estate is fully equipped with bungalows, permanent buildings, quarters for coolies, and other necessary stores and sheds.

The general manager, who resides on one of the estates, is Mr. H. L. Pinches; the managing agents for India are Messrs. James Finlay & Co., of 1 Clive Street, Calcutta, and the head offices are at 22 West Nile Street, Glasgow.

The foregoing notes were obtained on the spot from the Manager, Mr. H. L. Pinches, but owing to his absence later in England, we were unable to have them revised and corrected, as usual; while the managing agents in Calcutta informed us of their inability to undertake the responsibility.

KUTIKUL

This estate belongs to the Mundakayam Valley Rubber Company, Ltd., which was formed in 1906, and whose offices are at 199 High Holborn, London, W.C. The managing director is Mr. O. A. Bannatine, and the other members of the Board are Messrs. Walter G. Kent (chairman), Robert W. Hammond, and Reginald Boulton.

Remarkable progress has been made in the development of this property, as it was purchased about the time of the formation of the company, and there are now (1914) no fewer than 1,166 acres planted with Para rubber-trees out of a total area of 1,396 acres. This is an achievement with which the shareholders have every reason to be satisfied, especially when it is remembered that the estate was originally a mass of dense jungle.

MUNDAKAYAM VALLEY RUBBER CO., LTD.
1. FACTORY, KUTIKUL ESTATE. 2. NO. 3 DIVISION.

Some 460 acres of land were cleared and planted in 1906; 176 acres were similarly treated in the following year; 154 acres in 1908; 117 acres in 1909; and 230 acres in 1910; while the work was completed between 1911 and 1913. The oldest trees, tapped in 1910, gave a return of 1,500 lb. of rubber, and to show the virility of the trees it is interesting to note that two fields which produced a crop of 22,000 lb. in 1911, yielded no less than 64,000 lb. in the following year, which was followed by a crop in 1913 of

127,500 lb., averaging 200 lb. of rubber per acre, the highest yield per acre over a large area in South India in that year. It is estimated that the harvest of 1914 will be as much as 160,000 lb. The latex is manufactured on the premises by modern machinery, which is driven by a 36-h.p. Hornsby-Ackroyd oil-engine. The buildings include a factory, three bungalows, lines for coolies, sheds, and stores. The manager, Mr. J. R. Vincent, is assisted by four Europeans, and he employs some 650 coolies. The property is 6 miles distant from the post office at Mundakayam, in the State of Travancore.

The Vailamallay estate of 2,000 acres, situated in the southern portion of Travancore, is also owned by the company. About 369 acres were planted with Para and Ceara rubber during the years 1907 and 1908, and it is believed that the first tapping, which will take place during the present year, will yield 10,000 lb. of latex. Nearly all the buildings are of a temporary character, as the directors prefer to adopt a safe policy of postponing the erection of permanent structures until the estate has had time to become self-supporting. It should be added that this course of action was endorsed by the shareholders at the annual meeting held in London on June 30, 1914.

The rainfall in this neighbourhood is much smaller than in many parts of Southern India—the average for several years being only 70 in.—and this accounts for the fact that the growth of Para-trees is much slower than that of Ceara.

The manager—Mr. Charles Hunnybun—employs about 150 coolies constantly.

P. LAKSHMAN RAJU

A considerable proportion of the architectural work in Southern India at the present time is based very largely upon Western ideas and conceptions, and although there are in a vast number of the older buildings very beautiful results of the work of draughtsmen and contractors, it is equally true that improved methods of construction have been adopted to a very large extent. This is the case more particularly in those districts in which the influence of the Public Works Department has been specially exerted.

One of the leading contractors in Southern India, who has constructed some remarkably fine buildings which will remain for generations as tributes to his skill, is Mr. P. Lakshman Raju, of Trivandrum, the chief town in the State of Travancore, and a brief description of two or three of these structures may be given here. First of all there is the Girls' College building, which includes a fine library and music hall. The foundation of the former of these two was commenced with a layer of cement, followed by rubble, while the superstructure consists of bricks, pointed with cement over face bricks for the exterior portion. On three sides of the building are two verandahs, one of which has segmental arches "turned" with reinforced cement concrete, while the upper one has ornamental wooden brackets between pillars of masonry. The upper floor is made of paving tiles placed upon concrete slabs, which are laid on beams of the same material. Very satisfactory arrangements for the students to enter or leave the building in absolute comfort and safety have been made by providing a fine main wooden staircase near the front verandah, and by the construction of a spiral one—made of cement—which is fixed inside the library room. Excellent workmanship is manifested in the plain roof and in the portico in front of the building, which has been constructed with masonry piers and segmental arches. The railings in the upper veranda between the portico parapet walls are made of expanded metal sheets fitted to square iron uprights. The music hall is a fine building to the south of the library, and it consists of one long room having upper lights and wooden sunshades over doors and windows. There is further a corridor connecting the library with this hall, the floor of which is made of reinforced cement concrete slab, placed over masonry piers and concrete cantilever beams.

The out-patient buildings in the General Hospital at Trivandrum comprise two separate blocks ; one of these, called the middle one, is the dispensing and drug room, which has a corridor at each end, these leading respectively to the dispensaries for men and women, while the second block is reserved entirely for females. The foundations and basements are built of rubble over a layer of concrete ; the superstructure is constructed with bricks, and the floors are cemented concrete. Between the ornamental pillars round the verandah and corridors are tastefully designed wooden brackets of fretwork. The middle block has separate roofs for the main building and the verandah, and Malabar gables have been provided for the corridors.

The Law College, also at Trivandrum, is still under construction, although considerable progress has been made. The basement and superstructure of the lower story of this building consist of rubble, the exterior of which is to be pointed with cement, while the interior will be plastered. Wire-cut bricks have been used in the construction of the upper story, and they will be coated with rough-cast plaster, while the floor consists of reinforced cement concrete slabs placed over concrete beams. All sills and lintels of doors and windows are to be in blocks of the same material as the floor, and the sunshades in the front curved bays and the columns in the upper verandah and in the lecture-hall will be of similar kind of work. The building has a fine roof curved at each end, and it is fitted with large Malabar gables with elaborate carvings in wood. It has, further, a picturesque portico with fluted brick columns, over which are beams of reinforced cement concrete. It is not possible to refer to the elegant interior constructive and decorative work, but that it will be completed in a thoroughly satisfactory manner goes without saying when it is remembered that the contract is in the capable hands of Mr. P. Lakshman Raju.

THE MALABAR COMMERCIAL CORPORATION, LTD.

Facilities for the transport of human beings as well as merchandise have been very greatly augmented since the introduction of motor-cars, and towns and villages which were formerly, as far as means of communication are concerned, about as far apart as the poles, are now linked together by a regular service. Cars and cycles of every description are running on good and bad roads in every country in the world ; they are met with in the arid deserts of Africa ; the trackless plateaus of India are traversed by them, and even in the ice-bound fields of the arctic regions the familiar hooter is heard. The immense saving of time owing to speedy locomotion is an incalculable asset to private individuals and business men alike, and in those lands where the intense heat has an injurious effect upon horses, the advent of the car must be hailed with supreme satisfaction.

The Malabar Commercial Corporation, Ltd., was formed in March 1911, and to it belongs the honour of being the pioneers of petrol motor service in the State of Travancore. Business was commenced with a "Renard" car, built by the

P. LAKSHMAN RAJU.

1. Girls' College, Trivandrum. 2. Front View, Out-patients' Dispensary Buildings, General Hospital, Trivandrum. 3. Back View of Out-patients' Dispensary. 4. Law College Building (under construction).

THE MALABAR COMMERCIAL CORPORATION, LTD.

TYPES OF VEHICLES OWNED AND RUN BY THE MALABAR COMMERCIAL CORPORATION, LTD.

Daimler Company, of Coventry, which conveyed passengers, agricultural produce, machinery, and general goods between Kottayam and Mundakayam.

Mr. R. M. Saywell, the present manager of the company, arrived in India from England in June 1911, bringing with him two motor buses and two open char-à-bancs, made by Messrs. J. E. Hall, Ltd., of Dartford. These vehicles were the first of their kind to be utilized in the service of the public in Travancore, and they were placed on the road between Trivandrum and the towns of Quilon and Nagercoil. These cars became so popular that other companies speedily followed the lead of the Malabar Corporation. It is only recently that a contract was secured by this company for the conveyance of the mails between Trivandrum, Quilon, and Nagercoil, and five "Girling" parcel cars have been specially imported for this purpose.

The premises in Trivandrum include a large garage, in addition to workshops in which motor repairs of all kinds are executed by a staff of competent workmen. These shops are equipped with lathes, drilling and grinding machines, and a hydraulic tyre-press, which was the first to be introduced into Southern India. The machinery is driven by a 7½-h.p. oil-engine. Motor-cars are let out on hire, and any kind of vehicle or any appliances for car or cycle are imported as required.

The Corporation consists of Indian gentlemen only, and no European capital has been subscribed. The registered offices are at Alleppey.

THE MALANKARA RUBBER AND PRODUCE COMPANY, LTD.

This is one of the largest joint stock companies in Southern India founded and managed entirely by Indian gentlemen. The company—whose headquarters are at Kottayam, in the State of Travancore—was registered in the year 1910 with a capital of Rs. 450,000, in shares of Rs. 30, and Mr. P. John John is managing director. The property belonging to the company comprises nearly 1,700 acres of land situated on each bank of the Thodupazha River, in Travancore, and it is split up into five divisions, each of which is in charge of an assistant-superintendent.

About 1,180 acres of the estate were planted with Para rubber-trees between the years 1909 and 1912, and there are, further, 120 acres of coconuts. It is estimated that the cost of planting, rearing, and maintaining rubber-trees to the time of maturity is about £25 per acre. The company anticipates being able, in 1915, to tap some 600 acres of trees, which will then have reached four or five years of age.

The estate is fully equipped with commodious bungalows, a hospital for the employees with excellent "lines" for coolies, of whom there is an abundant supply locally, and it is admirably situated as regards communication with towns and districts in the Madras Presidency, as there are ample facilities by road, railway, and waterway. The nearest railway station is at Alwaye, 36 miles distant, on the Ernakulam-Shoranur branch, and there are good cart roads connecting it with the property, while the Thodupazha River is navigable for a considerable distance. The post office at Thodupazha is not more than 3 miles away.

A singularly even distribution of rainfall is experienced, about 120 inches being registered annually.

THE MALANKARA RUBBER AND PRODUCE COMPANY, LTD.
1911 RUBBER, NO. 1 DIVISION.

THE MALAYALAM RUBBER AND PRODUCE COMPANY, LTD.

This company, formed in the year 1909, has its registered offices at Nos. 1-4 Great Tower Street, London, E.C. The directors are Messrs. Charles A. Lampard (chairman), George Croll, Edward L. Hamilton, H. M. Knight, George N. Thomson, and Frederick Walker, J.P., and Messrs. Harrisons and Crosfield, Ltd., are secretaries. The company are owners of very large holdings in the State of Travancore, comprising 20,658½ acres, which are made up as follows: tea, 3,485½ acres; rubber, 8,789 acres; cardamoms, 587 acres; roads and buildings, 168 acres; and uncultivated land, 7,629 acres.

The "Venture" group, belonging to the company, consists of seven estates in the Kalthuritty Valley, on both sides of the Quilon line of railway, there being three stations within easy access, the principal one of which is Temalai, which is 42 miles distant from Quilon. The seven properties are Venture, Nagamally, Ambanaad, Isfield, Koravanatavalam, Florence, and Swarnagiri. They are 8,700 acres in extent, and are cultivated as to 3,639 acres with Para rubber, and as to 1,387 acres with Assam indigenous tea. Rubber is grown at an altitude ranging from 500 ft. to 1,500 ft., and tea at an elevation of 1,000 ft. to 2,200 ft. The three estates, Koravanatavalam, Florence, and Swarnagiri, are entirely devoted to rubber production, but when they were acquired by the company only about 400 acres had been planted out of a total of some 2,000 acres. The other four estates are producing both tea and rubber, but only 1,500 acres of rubber and

THE MALAYALAM RUBBER AND PRODUCE COMPANY, LTD.

1. Manager's Bungalow. 2. Nagamallay Rubber Field, 10 Years Old. 3. Ambanaad Tea Clearing. 4. Tea Clearing with Pluckers, Venture Estate.

THE MALAYALAM RUBBER AND PRODUCE COMPANY, LTD.

1. Tea Factory, Venture Estate. 2 and 3. Exterior and Interior Nagamallay Rubber Factory. 4. Tea Factory, Ambanaad.

200 acres of tea had been planted at the time of purchase. Each holding is under European management, and has a complete set of necessary outbuildings. Rubber factories are conveniently situated on the Florence and Nagamally properties, and another is in course of erection in Koravanatavalam, and their position is such that they can be conveniently used in the manufacture of the raw material produced by the whole group. There are tea factories on the Venture and Ambanaad properties, and they are fully equipped with up-to-date machinery. The produce is shipped direct to London. The seven estates were acquired by the company in 1909 by obtaining a concession of 10 square miles of land from the Travancore Government, and by the purchase of two other properties.

The general management is in the hands of Mr. John Stewart, but there are superintendents at each separate estate. The superintendent at Venture is Mr. A. W. Leslie, assisted by Mr. W. Vass McMurtie; Nagamally, Mr. A. W. White; Ambanaad, Mr. L. G. Knight, with Mr. C. E. L. Lister as assistant; Isfield, Mr. T. L. Jackson and Mr. W. G. Thom; Koravanatavalam, Mr. J. H. Parkinson, with Messrs. A. Mackie and R. N. W. Jodrell; Florence, Mr. R. Branson and Mr. Parsons; and Swarnagiri, with Mr. Upcher as superintendent.

The high range group consists of two estates, Surianalle and Lockhart, having a total area of 3,137 acres, of which 2,100 acres are planted with tea, although 1,100 acres are not yet in bearing. These properties are about nine miles apart, and they are situated in the Travancore High Range at an altitude which varies from 4,500 ft. to 6,200 ft. above sea-level. The uncultivated portion of the properties will be opened up in course of time.

Permanent buildings, such as bungalows, lines for coolies, stores, and sheds, have been erected, while the factories are fully installed with up-to-date machinery. The buildings on each estate are equipped with telephone, electric light, and a number of wire shoots. Chests of "made" tea are brought down from Surianalle by small pack-ponies—each animal carrying from 60 lb. to 100 lb.—to the foot of the ghaut, whence they are conveyed by bullock-cart to Kodaikanal Road railway station, to be forwarded to Tuticorin, where they are shipped direct to London. The packages from Lockhart are first carted to Munaar; they are then conveyed for 20 miles over the Kanan Devan Hills Produce Company's light railway to the top station, whence they travel by aerial ropeway to the foot of the ghaut, where they are transferred to bullock-carts for removal to Kodaikanal Road station.

Mr. C. Fraser is manager of the estates, and his assistants at Surianalle are Messrs. W. Wise, A. B. Byres, and P. G. Fraser; while at Lockhart Mr. W. Fraser is superintendent. Lockhart is two miles distant from the post office at Devicolam, and there are both post and telegraph offices on the Surianalle estate.

Some 12 miles distant from Surianalle, on the Cardamom Hills, is the Gudampara estate, which is managed by Mr. C. Fraser, who has Mr. R. F. Vinen as resident superintendent. The area comprises 665 acres, and 587 acres have been planted with cardamoms. The permanent buildings on the estate include bungalows, lines for coolies, stores, sheds, and a curing-house, and all of these are fitted with the needful appliances. The produce is forwarded to Tuticorin, whence it is shipped to England.

Another estate belonging to the company which is of considerable importance in the production of rubber is the Lahai property of 2,277 acres, but it is only partially developed, and planting did not commence until the year 1908. Some 1,480 acres have, however, been opened up, and further cultivation is being proceeded with as circumstances permit.

Smoked rubber is being manufactured, and all the produce goes via Tuticorin to London. The estate is situated in the Rani Valley, about 40 miles distant from the railway station at Punalur, and about 68 miles distant from Quilon. Telephonic communication has been established between the bungalows and the factory. The property is managed by Mr. J. A. Anderson, and he is assisted by Messrs. J. Hall and M. J. O'Brien.

The Kaliyar estate is situated in the northern portion of the State of Travancore, about 20 miles distant from Alwaye, on the Ernakulam-Shoranur railway line, and some 30 miles from Cochin, which is the nearest town of any importance. It comprises 1,518 acres, and the plantings of rubber have been as follows: 124 acres in 1907, 410 acres in 1908, 106 acres in 1909, 40 acres in 1910, 297 acres in 1911, 123 acres in 1912, and 56 acres in 1913, making a total of 1,156 acres. Those trees which were planted in 1907-8-9 have been tapped, and the produce is shipped to London. Modern machinery has been installed in the factory, and the numerous buildings have been well constructed and fitted with all necessary appliances. The property is managed by Mr. A. C. Morrell, who is assisted by Messrs. H. R. Parker and Dunning.

The Mundakayam group consists of three estates—Mundakayam and Boyce, which practically adjoin each other, and Cheruvalley, about 5 miles distant. They comprise an area of 4,361 acres, 2,513 acres of which have been planted with rubber, and the balance will be opened up in the course of time. The Cheruvalley estate has been planted with 1,000 acres of rubber-trees, but none of these are yet in bearing. There is a fully-equipped factory on the Boyce property, in which the rubber produced there and upon the Mundakayam estate is manufactured. The superintendent at Mundakayam is Mr. W. Hendry, whose assistant is Mr. P. Napier. Mr. S. P. Eaton is in charge of the Boyce property, with Mr. C. P. Hendry as assistant, and at Cheruvalley Mr. E. Hall is superintendent, with Mr. Macpherson as assistant. The company's eastern agents are Messrs. Harrisons and Crosfield, Ltd., Quilon, who also attend to the shipping of the produce.

MERCHISTON

This estate, one of the few remaining private properties of the kind in the district, was among the first to be opened in South Travancore. In the early 'seventies 700 acres were purchased from the Government of the State by Messrs. C. & E. Young, in conjunction with Messrs. T. R. & William Marshall. Half the property was opened in coffee, under the management of the latter, and when leaf disease devastated coffee, and caused the abandonment of its cultivation, Mr. William Marshall bought out his brother's interest in half the property and began tea planting.

The estate possesses a good factory, equipped with up-to-date machinery and all necessary buildings. The coolie lines are permanent buildings, the accommodation being ample for the necessary labour force, and an excellent supply of running water, which never fails, makes the place a healthy one for the workers. A private road connects the factory with the Government road to Trivandrum, 34 miles distant, whence all tea is conveyed on its way to the London market.

MERCHISTON ESTATE.

1. Tea Field. 2. General View. 3. Tea Factory, 4. The Bungalow.

Situated on the western slope of hills, which rise to an altitude of 4,000 feet, the fields at Merchiston are very steep and very stony, but tea flourishes, and gives an average yield of over 550 lb. of "made" tea to the acre. The application of manure has been recently tried, and excellent results have followed—certain fields producing more than 1,000 lb. to the acre.

The bungalow, built in 1876 by the late Mr. W. Marshall, stands at an elevation of 2,296 feet, and commands an extensive and beautiful outlook over the country to Trivandrum and the distant ocean, upon which steamers and native craft can be seen by the naked eye.

This charming residence is still occupied by Mrs. Marshall, who is assisted in the management of the estate by her nephew, Mr. R. J. A. Moore. The casurina-trees which encircle the bungalow were planted nearly forty years ago; and in the pretty garden roses, violets, honeysuckle, and maiden-hair ferns grow most luxuriantly. About half an acre of coffee around the bungalôw is the only survival of the original plantation.

During the "coffee days" a planter's life was less strenuous than that of a tea-grower, as the annual crop afforded more opportunity for sport and holiday-making than the continuous round of "plucking" and the manufacture of tea. In the eighties a yearly race meeting was held in Trivandrum by the coffee planters, and at these the owner of Merchiston, who was a keen all-round sportsman, raced his own ponies.

An interest in Invercauld estate (582 acres) has been recently purchased by Mrs. Marshall, and this neighbouring property is being developed and worked in conjunction with Merchiston. But the completion of a factory, which is now being built, will shortly render it self-contained.

It should be mentioned that in the neighbourhood of these two estates the cost of labour has more than doubled during the last quarter of a century. A load of 60 lb. was formerly carried 12 miles to the nearest cart road at a cost of 4 chuckrams, or less than $2\frac{1}{2}$d. This equalled a day's wage, whereas similar work now costs 6 annas (6d.).

S. P. MEL & CO.

The head offices of this firm are at Colombo, where premises were opened in the year 1895, but the establishments in Southern India are at Trivandrum and Mundakayam, both in the native State of Travancore. The partners of the Trivandrum branch are Messrs. S. P. Mel and T. N. Motha, the latter being general manager.

On entering the fine buildings, which cover half an acre of ground in the main street of Trivandrum, a visitor's attention is attracted by the magnitude of the miscellaneous assortment of imported and Indian goods, and the impression is given him that nearly every article in a catalogue of merchandise can be obtained here. The firm very appropriately describe themselves as general merchants, and their store-rooms, shelves, and show-cases are well stocked with all kinds of liquors, provisions, hardware, crockery, drapery, millinery, gentlemen's outfitting, patent medicines, and a host of other trade and household requisites. Agencies are held for "His Master's Voice" gramophones, Humber and other cycles

S. P. MEL & CO.

1. Exterior View. 2. Portion of the Showroom.

and motor appliances, and the firm are also agents for the National Mutual Life Association of Australasia, Ltd. Imported goods are obtained through the firm's agents, Messrs. John Shaw & Sons, of Wolverhampton, England.

The Trivandrum establishment was not opened until the year 1906, but among the principal customers are the British Resident, European Club, and the leading English and Indian residents of the town. Contracts are held with the Excise, Police, Public Works, and other departments of the Travancore Government.

The branch at Mundakayam, opened in 1912, is conducted on the same lines as at Trivandrum, and business operations are prospering at a rapid rate.

PEVARANTHANAM

The transformation which has taken place upon this estate during the short period of eight years has been nothing short of marvellous. The jungle had grown with such luxuriance that an almost impenetrable mass covered the whole of the property, and it required the exercise of indomitable energy and perseverance to bring the land into a fit state for cultivation. Pevaranthanam was purchased in October, 1906, by Mr. H. B. Kirk (who is now associated in partnership with Mr. Henry Ward), and it speaks volumes for the management that in November of the same year no less than 10 acres of forest had been cleared and planted with Para rubber-trees. The whole of the estate, consisting of 763 acres, has now been opened up, but there is still a small area which will be planted in the course of a year or two.

This is, primarily, a rubber estate, and although the 630 acres of trees cannot be said to be fully matured, the plantation has already given abundant promise of satisfactory yields of latex. The first tapping took place in 1910, when about 40 lb. of rubber to the acre were obtained from 10 acres of trees, and the same trees gave as much as 262 lb. only four years later. About 10 per cent. of the rubber planted in the year 1910—covering an area of 253 acres—is now (1914) only being lightly tapped, as Mr. Kirk holds pronounced views upon the advisability of postponing incisions in the bark until the girth of the trees is at least 18 in.

About 133 acres of indigenous Assam tea-bushes were planted during the years 1910 and 1911, and the first plucking (which occurred in 1912) yielded 12 lb. to the acre; about 148 lb. were obtained in the following year, and the estimate for the same field for the season of 1914-15 is 350 lb. with pruning. The tea-seed was originally obtained from Ceylon. It should be mentioned that Mr. Kirk is a strong advocate of the annual application of suitable manures, and the satisfactory returns of both rubber and tea are largely due to this practice.

Up-to-date plant for the manufacture of both rubber and tea is contained in one factory, and it has been decided that, during the year 1915, a 35-h.p. liquid-fuel engine shall replace the one of 15 h.p. which is at present being used.

The proposed Peermade-Mundikaya ropeway will traverse the property from the western to its eastern boundary, and as the angle-station (or turning-point) will be within 500 yards' distance of the factory, it will be possible for the manager

PEVARANTHANAM ESTATE.

1. Bungalow and 1910 Tea. 2. 1906 Rubber. 3. Factory.

to avail himself of mechanical means of transport and thus obviate the use of cattle, which are so liable to the much-dreaded plague known as foot-and-mouth disease.

An abundant supply of water is obtainable from the Kokayaar river, which flows through the estate and discharges itself into the backwaters at Sittar. The lowest portion of the estate—which by the way is in the State of Travancore—is 500 ft. above the level of the sea, but the land slopes upwards in northerly and southerly directions until it attains an altitude of 1,400 ft. Mr. Kirk is sole manager, and he resides in a pretty bungalow which has been erected on the highest part of the property. A sufficient number of coolies can be engaged locally, and this is a distinct advantage as it means a large reduction in advances, the amount owing per capitum being only Rs. 8, which sum is recoverable in one month if necessary. This arrangement compares most favourably with other countries which employ Indian labour. Mr. Kirk has the assistance of two European assistants, and he employs 550 hands.

Pevaranthanam is 2½ miles distant from Mundakayam, where there are post and telegraph offices and a motor transport depôt.

THE POONMUDI TEA AND RUBBER COMPANY, LTD.

This company was formed in the year 1900 with a capital of £53,000, and it was reconstituted nine years later with a nominal capital of £60,000, of which the sum of £53,307 has been called up. The property consists of three estates, named Poonmudi, Bon-Accord, and Braemore, all of which are situated in the district of Poonmudi, in the native State of Travancore. The estates comprise an area of 3,276 acres; the cultivated portion runs to 1,710 acres of tea and rubber; while forest and other lands make up the remaining 1,566 acres. Mr. J. S. Valentine—who is managing director—arrived in India in 1875, and at that time the properties were planted with coffee. All the coffee succumbed to disease in the early 'eighties, and only cinchona—which had been interplanted with the coffee—escaped destruction. Tea of hybrid jat and high-class indigenous types was planted on Poonmudi in 1884, and in portions of the other properties, the seed being obtained from Hukinguri in Assam, and Manipuri. An excellent climate is experienced throughout the year in the neighbourhood of these estates, and a liberal rainfall of about 160 inches is registered annually, the heaviest downpour occurring in the months of June, July, August, October, and November.

THE POONMUDI TEA AND RUBBER COMPANY, LTD.
1. THE FACTORY. 2. BUNGALOW. 3. GENERAL VIEW.

The Poonmudi plantation has, for the past seven years, given an annual return of 611 lb. of tea to the acre, although some of the best fields have yielded from 1,000 lb. to 1,200 lb.; Bon-Accord shows an average of 565 lb. up to 800 lb. to the acre; and Braemore returns about 541 lb. up to 800 lb. to the acre. A very good demand exists for the seed throughout Travancore and the Island of Ceylon. There are now (January 1915) 1,510 acres of tea and about 200 acres of rubber on the three estates.

A very substantial three-storied factory has been erected at Poonmudi—the two lower floors being of solid stone, while the top one is constructed of wood and iron. The building is 120 feet in length by 36 feet in width, and it is fitted with modern machinery and with duplicate power steam and oil-engines. There is a similar factory at Bon-Accord, while the one at Braemore is equipped with plant for the manufacture of both tea and rubber. All the produce is shipped under the company's brand via Cochin or Tuticorin for sale in London.

The crop of rubber for the year 1914 realized 42,200 lb., and was of excellent quality, while the harvest of tea pomo-natured fields and from young clearings amounted to 781,000 lb.

Each estate is provided with bungalows, lines for coolies, and other buildings, while there are dispensaries at Bon-Accord and Poonmudi—the one at the latter place being in charge of a fully qualified apothecary. There is an ample supply of labourers, and the 2,000 coolies on the three estates are obtained in equal proportions from the districts of Tinnevelly, Malabar, and South Travancore.

Mr. Valentine resides at and is in charge of Poonmudi. Mr. R. Ross, with Mr. David Welsh, assistant, is in charge of Bon-Accord, and Mr. I. R. N. Pryde acts in a similar capacity at Braemore. The directors of the company—whose registered offices are at 4 Lloyd's Avenue, London, E.C.—are Messrs. J. R. Hugh Pinckney (chairman), Guy Owen, Erlysman C. Pinckney, and James Smith Valentine, who resides on the estates in India.

The most conveniently situated post office for all three estates is at Kallar, near Trivandrum. Mr. Valentine has made special provision for the maintenance of good health among the coolies; they are provided with medical attendance and medicines from the dispensaries, and cases of disease are treated on the estates. Religious services are held in a Roman Catholic chapel at Poonmudi, periodical visits being made by a parish priest of Trivandrum.

RIPLEY & MACKAY

This business was founded in 1904 by Mr. W. St. B. Sydenham, a partner in the firm of Messrs. Ripley & Co., of Bimlipatam and Cocanada, who took Mr. I. F. Mackay into partnership with him. Mr. Sydenham's share was purchased four years later, and Messrs. I. F. and F. F. Mackay became sole proprietors. The premises in Alleppey in which the business is carried on were owned originally by Messrs. Arnold Cheney & Co., of New York, who were importers of kerosene oil and exporters of oil; coir, and other coconut products; but Messrs. Ripley & Mackay bought them out lock, stock, and barrel, and the latter are now engaged as manufacturers of coir yarn and fibre, and they export large quantities of those materials, and of copra, pepper, ginger, and other Malabar produce to Europe and the Colonies, where representatives have been appointed. The works, stores, and offices now cover an area of nearly 4 acres, and about 450 hands are constantly employed under the direct supervision of the partners. Branches, which are maintained principally for the purchase of produce, have been opened at Cochin and at Calicut.

The firm are agents for the Commercial Union Insurance Company of London, the Sea Insurance Company of Liverpool, and the British Dominions General Insurance Company.

Their shipments bear the well-known brand of R. & Co., enclosed in a diamond-shaped mark.

THE RUBBER PLANTATIONS INVESTMENT TRUST, LTD.

The property belonging to this company is 2,615 acres in extent, and it was acquired by the Rubber Plantations Investment Trust, Ltd., in the year 1910. The work of opening up the estate was proceeded with on completion of the purchase, and in the same year about 99 acres of Para rubber-trees were planted. Tea bushes from selected seed obtained from Northern India were subsequently put in, and towards the close of the year 1914 the plantings were 600 acres of rubber and 588 acres of first-class tea.

The estate is situated on the borders of dense jungle, and it is therefore subject to the unwelcome attentions of large and small game, but especially of elephant, sambur, bison, and pig. Separate factories for the manufacture of rubber and tea are in course of construction, and each of these buildings will be installed with machinery and plant of the most approved designs. The prospects of the company are distinctly encouraging, and although the property—known as Koney—is the only estate owned by them in Southern India, they hold large interests in several properties in South India, Ceylon, Sumatra, Java, and the Straits Settlements.

Bungalows, lines for coolies, and a number of stores and sheds have already been erected, and work now in hand is progressing so satisfactorily that everything will doubtless be in readiness for the first harvest of tea, which will commence before the end of the year 1915. The rubber-trees are growing at an altitude of about 300 ft.; tea bushes are thriving at an elevation of 600 ft., and the whole estate enjoys an average rainfall of 125 in.

The property is managed by Mr. Charles Hall, who employs some 500 coolies. The registered offices of the company are at Nos. 1-4 Great Tower Street, London, E.C., and Messrs. Harrisons and Crosfield, Ltd., are agents in India.

SHALIACARY

It is probable that a return of 200 lb. of rubber to the acre credited to a plantation in South Travancore in the year 1913 was a record yield for Southern India up to that time; but priority of place, it would appear, must now be given to the Shaliacary property, near Punalur, in the same State, as it produced 250 lb. to the acre during the season of 1914, and the estimate for 1915 is put down at 300 lb.

The estate was purchased by the Rani-Travancore Rubber Company, Ltd., in 1905, and the total area of 785 acres has been planted with rubber-trees which are now in full bearing. All the produce is manufactured on the premises, and it is subsequently exported to London, via Tuticorin and Colombo, the packages being marked with the usual brands of the company and of the estate.

Modern machinery has been imported at considerable cost, and the factory is now fully equipped with excellent plant which is driven by a 60-h.p. Tangye gas-engine, although a 36-h.p. Hornsby oil-engine is held in reserve. The crop for 1915 will be smoked sheet rubber, and the latest and most approved types of smoking-house and appliances are being erected. The buildings, in addition to the factory, include two bungalows, stores, sheds, and coolies' lines, which have tiled roofs and contain 120 rooms.

The mountains and forests of Travancore afford some of the best sport to be had anywhere in India, especially in the shape of large game, and the Shaliacary estate in particular is recognized as an ideal spot for a hunter, as the "bill of fare" ranges from the modest junglefowl to the lordly elephant.

SHALIACARY ESTATE.

1. View on the Estate. 2. Factory. 3. Rubber. 4. Bungalow.

SITTAR ESTATE.

1, River Scene, 2. Factory. 3. Manager's Bungalow. 4 A General View.

Mr. T. P. M. Alexander is manager, and he and one European assistant control the work of a native staff of 300 hands.

There are post and telegraph offices and a railway-station at Punalur, which is 5 miles distant. The headquarters of the company are at Thames House, Queen Street Place, London, E.C.; the forwarding agents are the Colombo Commercial Company, Ltd., of Ceylon, and the visiting agent is Mr. W. Coombe.

SITTAR

The native State of Travancore in which this estate is situated is one of the most picturesque portions of Southern India; the surface is undulating with fertile hills and valleys alternating, and, with the exception of the mountainous wilds in the interior, the soil is rich enough for every branch of agriculture to be carried on with prospects of success. The Sittar property, by way of example, is well known as one of the most valuable, and at the same time one of the oldest, Para rubber estates in Southern India, and its management is in the able hands of Mr. H. S. K. Morrell, who is assisted by Mr. H. C. Seymour. It comprises 1,004 acres of land, and the owners are the Rani-Travancore Rubber Company, Ltd.

Dense virgin forest covered the whole area in the year 1903, when the work of clearing was commenced, and it was about a year later when planting was taken in hand. The records of the development of the estate give the following figures: 136 acres were planted in 1904; 518 acres in 1905: 53 acres in 1907; 13 acres in 1909, 130 acres in 1911, and 37 acres in 1913, making a total of 887 cultivated acres. The average annual yield to the acre has hitherto been about 260 lb., but the year 1915 is expected to give a return of 300 lb., as many of the younger trees in the plantation will be ready to be tapped. The property is well provided with all necessary buildings, such as three bungalows for Europeans, and quarters for office staff and coolies, fitted with the most modern machinery, including a 56-h.p. Tangye suction-gas plant and an emergency steam engine of 49 h.p. Manufactured rubber is shipped under the estate brand to London, through the agency of the Commercial Company, Ltd., of Colombo. The property has an abundant supply of water from the Sittar river and its tributaries, by which it is bisected, and these streams have an additional value as they are stocked with indigenous fish of the salmon or trout or other fighting type so dear to the heart of the keen sportsman. All species of game common to India are to be found on this estate and in the immediate neighbourhood, but the damage caused by elephants—and in a somewhat lesser degree—sambur and wild pig, is a very serious matter to the owners.

Sittar is "far from the madding crowd," as the nearest railway-station and telegraph office are at Punalur, which is 43 miles distant, while the post office at Vadasirikara is 12 miles away.

Employment is found for from 400 to 500 coolies.

ROWE, WHITE & CO.

A very large number of tea, coffee, and rubber estates in Southern India are in the hands of companies which were formed in London with a large proportion of the capital subscribed by British shareholders, and in the majority of such instances the properties are controlled by a prominent English firm who have agencies in various parts of India. These firms are frequently secretaries of such companies, but in other cases they merely exercise a kind of supreme managership on behalf of the capitalists. A firm with extensive connections throughout Southern India is that of Messrs. Rowe, White & Co., of 4 Lloyd's Avenue, London, E.C. Their principal agencies in Southern India at the present time are: the Stagbrook Rubber & Tea Estates, Ltd., holding 2,473 acres; the Southern India Tea Estates, Ltd., having 2,990 acres; and the Twyford & Ashley Tea Estates Co., Ltd., with an area of 1,999 acres, making a grand total of 7,462 acres. Of this aggregate, some 3,767 acres have been planted with tea, and 1,023 acres are producing rubber; while the balance, which is being held in reserve, will be opened up in due course. Messrs. Rowe, White & Co. have the control of many other large interests in Southern India, Ceylon, the Straits Settlements, and Sumatra, and their representative in India as regards the above-mentioned companies is Mr. J. A. Richardson, of Ashley, near Peermade, in the State of Travancore.

THE STAGBROOK RUBBER AND TEA ESTATES COMPANY, LTD.

This company was formed in 1908, and the estate known as Stagbrook consists of three properties, namely, Stagbrook, Hope, and Maimallai (near Peermade, in the State of Travancore), purchased from Mr. H. Drummond Deane.

A considerable number of acres were planted with inferior jât tea when the estate was purchased, but all additions since that time have been of an indigenous character reared from seed obtained in Northern India. The total area of the estate is 921 acres, and the plantation consists of 834 acres. The average annual yield from all tea of whatever quality is 650 lb. to the acre, although individual fields have returned 1,200 lb., while no fewer than 517,000 lb. have been gathered during the season of 1914. One might refer here to the plucking capabilities of coolies. Naturally they vary very considerably, according to the grit in the labourer, but 120 lb. of green leaf are frequently put to the credit of one coolie for a day's work during the busy portion of the year. One "boy" distinguished himself in April 1914 by accounting for 1,567 lb. of green leaf during the working days of that month. It is interesting to visit the factory to watch the various processes by which the green leaf is converted into the dried black tea which finds its way to the markets of the world. Let attention be paid to the wonderful machinery which works with all the precision of a fully tested chronometer; notice how the "withered" leaf is carefully rolled, the contrivances by which fermentation is controlled, or the means by which firing is effected, and at a later stage how the "sifting" is carried out, and how the different grades of "made" tea are packed in lead-lined chests. In a word, it may be said that all possible requisites for an up-to-date factory are in evidence on the Stagbrook estate.

The motive power is obtained during the wet season by the use of a 40-h.p. turbine, while during the dry weather a Cundall 16-h.p. oil-engine, and a Dudbridge 25-h.p. oil-engine are called into service. The chests of manufactured tea are branded with the name of the estate, and are subsequently shipped to London for sale. The estate is 3 miles distant from the post office at Peermade, and the average elevation above the level of the sea is 3,500 feet. A somewhat heavy rainfall is experienced, as the register shows an annual amount of 200 inches. About 600 coolies are employed constantly.

The registered offices of the company

THE STAGBROOK RUBBER AND TEA ESTATES COMPANY, LTD.

1. Stagbrook Factory. 2. Stagbrook Division. 3. Hope Division. 4. Eldorado Factory. 5, View of Rubber. 6. Rubber with Tappers.

are at 4 Lloyd's Avenue, London, E.C., the secretaries being Messrs. Rowe, White & Co., at the same address; the general manager in India is Mr. J. A. Richardson; while the superintendent at Stagbrook is Mr. H. C. Westaway.

The Stagbrook company are owners, too, of the Eldorado group, and this name has been conferred upon two estates, namely, Eldorado and Kokayar, which are situated along the banks of the Eldorado river, near Mundakayam, in the State of Travancore. The properties were purchased from Messrs. Drummond, Deane, & Owen & Pinckney. Para rubber-trees have been planted as follows: 45 acres in 1904, 160 acres in 1905, 345 acres in 1906, 108 acres in 1907, 254 acres in 1908, 34 acres in 1909, and 77 acres in 1911. Between 170 and 200 trees were planted to the acre originally; subsequent plantings were at the rate of 150 trees, but as this number has been found to be too great, thinning out is taking place, with the result that in future an acre will not be occupied by more than 120 trees. Those trees which have been cut out are being burned for the production of charcoal. The annual yield of latex has been progressing steadily, as the following figures will show: 10,000 lb. in 1910, 30,000 lb. in 1911, 58,000 lb. in 1912, and 94,000 lb. in 1913, while for the season of 1914 the crop obtained was 139,000 lb. The group is well provided with bungalows, permanent buildings, lines for coolies, and a factory which is connected by a good cart road with the Kottayam-Peermade main road. This building is fully equipped in every respect, the machinery and plant are of modern design, and an excellent 60-h.p. Crossley suction-gas plant has been installed. All manufactured rubber is conveyed by motor service to Kottayam, and it is then transferred over the backwaters to Cochin, where it is shipped direct to London. The rainfall is comparatively heavy, about 180 inches being recorded annually. The superintendent, Mr. Danvers Davy, is assisted by two Europeans, and some 800 coolies are employed.

THE SOUTHERN INDIA TEA ESTATES COMPANY, LTD.

Four estates, adjoining each other, near Peermade, in Travancore, named Glenmary, Kuduakarnam, Woodlands, and Ladrum, and having an area of 1,721 acres, together with a reserve of 1,269 acres, are owned by the Southern India Tea Estates Co., Ltd. A portion of the three properties (Glenmary, Kuduakarnam, and Woodlands) was originally planted with coffee, but when the crisis occurred which resulted in the destruction of so many plantations, this area was uprooted, and the vacant land was planted with tea.

It was a misfortune that these early plantings of tea were of the inferior jât, but that error in judgment has, to some extent, been rectified by raising subsequent transplants from seed of indigenous Assam or some other reliable variety. Rapid strides have been taken during the past twelve years in further development, and the Glenmary property in particular has produced some very fine seed-bearing trees which have contributed largely to the planting of an extensive area in the neighbourhood of Peermade. Intelligent observers have been impressed with the fact that there is a deeply rooted conservatism among agriculturists in India, and that innovations are invariably looked upon with distrust, if not with suspicion. Practice, however, is a fine teacher, and a strict adherence to antiquated methods of cultivation is being superseded by a keen desire to adopt systems of tillage which have given results which were previously unheard of. It is only during the past two or three years that the soil on these estates has had the benefit of manure, but a new era has dawned in which thorough cultivation—which naturally includes the use of suitable fertilizers—will be systematically carried out. Hitherto the annual crop of "made" tea has reached a total of from 600 lb. to 700 lb. to the acre, but it is practically certain that this quantity will be increased very considerably in the near future. The f.o.b. cost per 1 lb. of tea from these estates for the year 1913-14 was 25·03 cents, exclusive of capital expenditure. The tea grown upon these properties—and in the immediate neighbourhood—has not been confined to jungle soil, as considerable tracts of grass and park lands have been experimented with, and they have proved to be so satisfactory that similar areas on other estates are now being opened up. The Glenmary property has its own factory, which is capable of dealing with 500,000 lb. of tea annually, and its thoroughly modern machinery is driven by a 50-h.p. Hornsby suction-gas engine. There is another factory at Kuduakarnam, but since the purchase of the Ladrum estate in 1912, it has been deemed advisable, from an economical point of view, to enlarge the building on the former place in order that it may suffice for the two properties. The machinery at present includes two 37-h.p. Hornsby suction-gas engines. The Woodlands factory is a very fine building, in which there are a 40-h.p. turbine worked from a dam on the Maimallai estate for eight or nine months of the year, together with an auxiliary plant of an 18-h.p. oil-engine. The factories are lighted by electricity, which is generated from the machinery in the several buildings. The general manager is Mr. J. S. Wilkie, who resides at Glenmary, and there is a European superintendent in charge of each estate. The total number of coolies employed is about 1,700.

The company was formed in 1895, and the successful working of the estates is shown by the fact that a dividend of 17½ per cent. was declared during the last financial year. The directors are Messrs. T. C. Owen, A. Valentine Holland, Buxton Laurie, and Walter Graham, and the registered offices of the company are situated at 4, Lloyd's Avenue, London, E.C.

THE TWYFORD AND ASHLEY TEA ESTATES COMPANY, LTD.

Four well-known estates, situated near Peermade, in the State of Travancore, named Twyford, Vembanard, Ashley, and Bison Valley, are historically interesting as they belong to the oldest plantations in Southern India. The first two of these properties were originally obtained by the Rev. Mr. Baker, who arrived in Travancore in 1819, and they have remained in the possession of the Baker family up to the present time. Another family is deserving of mention, however, in connection with these estates, as the Ashley and Bison Valley properties were opened up by the late Mr. J. D. Munro, who was a contemporary of Mr. Baker, and it is interesting to note that descendants of these pioneers are signatories to the document of the formation of the Twyford & Ashley Tea Estates Co., Ltd., which is now (1915) in course of formation, and is taking over the above-mentioned estates. The company is, in reality, a private family affair designed with the object of securing economical management. The present owners of the four estates are Miss Baker, Mrs. J. A. Richardson, Mrs. J. S. Wilkie, and Miss Munro, while the general manager, Mr. J. A. Richardson, resides on the Ashley property.

THE SOUTHERN INDIA TEA ESTATES COMPANY, LTD.

1. MANAGER'S BUNGALOW. 2. GLENMARY ESTATE. 3. KUDUAKARNUM FACTORY. 4. KUDUAKARNUM TEA. 5. LADRUM ESTATE. 6. WOODLANDS DAM.

The growing of coffee was in its ascendancy at the time of the opening up of the estates, but the trees which were planted failed there, as they did in hundreds of other instances, and the owners, anxious to save the situation, commenced to plant tea. Subsequent experience proved that the selected variety was anything but satisfactory, and nearly the whole of the cultivated portion of the estates has now been planted as follows: The Twyford and Vembanard properties have 773 acres of tea with 624 acres of reserve land, and Ashley and Bison Valley have 410 acres of tea, together with 192 acres of reserves. The large majority of these bushes have been reared from seed of a high-class indigenous character which was secured in Northern India. The uncultivated land is being opened up gradually, and nothing less than seed of first-class quality is being obtained. A prominent feature of these estates is the particularly fine new factories on the Vembanard and Ashley properties, which are equipped with modern machinery and plant, and which are fitted throughout with electric light. The Vembanard factory is considered to be one of the finest in the district, and it contains two Hornsby oil-engines of 30 h.p. and 20 h.p. respectively. It is capable of dealing with from 600,000 lb. to 700,000 lb. of "made" tea annually. The factory on the Ashley property, too, has an installation of up-to-date plant, which includes a 20-h.p. oil-engine. Some 300,000 lb. of tea are manufactured here in the course of a year. The other buildings on the properties are substantially built, and no detail has been overlooked in making their fittings as near perfection as possible. Constant work is found for about 900 coolies.

THE TRAVANCORE RUBBER COMPANY, LTD.

This company is the outcome of an amalgamation of the Travancore Rubber Company, the Paloor (Travancore) Rubber Co., Ltd., and the Orkaden River (Travancore) Rubber Co., Ltd., and the arrangement was carried through in the early days of the year 1914. There are 2,986 acres of land, and 2,164 acres have been planted with Para rubber, but the whole area has been subdivided into four separate properties, adjoining each other, namely, Kadamankulam, Manikal, Aneikulam, and Paloor. The first planting took place in 1905, when 85 acres were opened up at Kadamankulam, which, in those days, belonged to a private syndicate who sold the estate to the original Travancore Company in January 1907. The Orkaden River Co. was a subsidiary to the Travancore Rubber Co., and was formed in 1909, while the Paloor Co. was the private property of Messrs. J. A. Richardson and Gordon. The amalgamated estate stretches for a distance of 6 miles on both banks of the Orkaden river, commencing at the 35th mile on the Kottayam-Kumaly Government cart road and extending as far as the lands owned by the Central Travancore Rubber Co., Ltd.

There are now 1,325 acres of trees in full bearing, and the estimated crop for the 1915-16 season is 291,675 lb., while the previous year's returns were 218,374 lb. Between 1905 and 1906 some 218 trees were planted to the acre; this number was subsequently reduced to 150, and during the present year (1915) the clearings are being brought down to 110 trees to the acre. A very large factory, having a 62-h.p. Crossley suction-gas plant, has been erected on the Manikal estate (which is the nearest to the Government cart-road), and there are convenient gathering sheds in which the latex is reduced to "sponge" before being sent to the factory. The Peermade-Kottayam Transport Company's motor-lorries' terminus is on the Travancore Company's estate, and this service is utilized in the conveyance of all manufactured rubber to Kottayam to be put on boats in the backwaters for transfer to Cochin, whence it is shipped on steamers bound for London, where it is sold through the company's agents, Messrs. Dickson & Co. The company's estates are held on renewable lease from the independent Vanjipuzha chief, who holds land from the Government of Travancore free of all cess, in return for assistance rendered by his family to the Government during the Tippoo wars. The original lease was for a period of twelve years, but it is renewable at the expiration of every twelfth year on payment of a fee of 2 annas an acre. The company's taxes were originally 2 annas to the acre, but they have increased to a rupee, which has been fixed as the standard amount to be paid in future. The 822 acres of unplanted land on the Company's properties consist of jungle land, which is at present a reserve for the supply of fuel, but when they have been cleared they will make an admirable site for tea, as the soil is exceedingly fertile, and the elevation above sea-level varies from 500 feet to 1,000 feet. All charcoal used by the suction-gas plant at the factory is made on the property by burning rubber-trees which are being cut out in the process of thinning. Each estate is fully equipped with excellent outbuildings, lines for coolies, and bungalows, and the latter are connected by a private telephone wire with the factory, which is lighted by electricity, generated from a dynamo driven from the main shafting. The State of Travancore is noted for the variety as well as the number of its species of large and small game, and an intrepid sportsman may generally rely upon meeting with elephant, sambur, pig, panther, and tiger, in addition to any quantity of smaller animals and birds.

The secretaries of the company are Messrs. J. K. and W. P. Lindsay, of 16, Queen Street, Edinburgh; Mr. J. A. Richardson is managing director and visiting agent in India, and the managing superintendent is Mr. R. Harley. The latter has 5 European assistants, and from 1,500 to 2,000 coolies, including Moplahs from the coast of Malabar, Tamil, and other labourers. Fully one-half of the employees are obtained without advances being granted, but where payment is made the amount averages about Rs. 10 a man.

The post office at Mundakayam is on the estate, the building being rented by the postal authorities from the company. The estate varies in altitude from 350 feet to 500 feet, and the average annual rainfall is about 170 inches.

THE MUNDAKAYAM-PEERMADE MOTOR TRANSPORT AND AERIAL ROPEWAY COMPANY, LTD.

There are many exceedingly rich agricultural districts in Southern India which, owing to their almost inaccessible position in mountainous regions, are not giving returns which are in any way commensurate with their possibilities. Bullock-carts are proverbially slow and often unreliable, and it is very frequently the case that produce garnered from fertile acres cannot be disposed of to the best advantage. The problem of overcoming the obstacles of difficult and expensive transport led Mr. J. A. Richardson, of Ashley, near Peermade, to give the question most serious consideration, and, as he represented a number of estates which were severely handicapped owing to their situation, he, on behalf of three companies under his management, brought

THE TWYFORD AND ASHLEY TEA ESTATES COMPANY, LTD.

1. Twyford Bungalow. 2. Factory, Yembanard. 3. Tea at Twyford. 4. Ashley Bungalow. 5. Factory at Ashley. 6. View of Ashley Estate.

THE TRAVANCORE RUBBER COMPANY, LTD.

1, Interior of Factory. 2. The Factory. 3. Tapping Rubber. 4. Aneikulam Bridge. 5. Coolies bringing Latex to Coagulating Shed.

THE MUNDAKAYAM-PEERMADE MOTOR TRANSPORT AND AERIAL ROPEWAY COMPANY, LTD.

1. Motor Lorries, Mundakayam. 2. Motor Garage, Mundakayam. 3. The Staff. 4. A few of the Company's Vehicles at Kottoyam Garage. 5. Manager's Bungalow.

from England in 1912 two Halley motor-lorries, each capable of carrying three tons. A syndicate was formed among a number of owners of Peermade and Mundakayam estates on the 1st of December, 1912, and a service was forthwith inaugurated for the carriage of estate produce, general goods, and supplies, as well as passengers, between Kottayam and Mundakayam, covering a distance of 35 miles. The venture was so successful that two other lorries of a similar make, but with a carrying capacity of four tons, were ordered from England, and on their arrival one of the three-ton vehicles was converted into a *char-à-banc* for passenger service only. A report was placed before the syndicate after 13 months' working, and it showed that, notwithstanding the difficulties attendant upon new schemes, and the payment of all preliminary expenses, together with a deduction on account of depreciation, a dividend of 8·69 per cent. for the year could be declared. These disbursements would, under ordinary circumstances, have been spread over a number of years, but the syndicate had agreed to sell the goodwill of their business and the rolling-stock to a number of gentlemen. The sale was completed on the 1st of January, 1914, and a newly formed company, styled the Mundakayam-Peermade Motor Transport & Aerial Ropeway Co., Ltd., forthwith arranged to continue the motor service which had been commenced by the syndicate. The idea of the new company was to get into business relationship with the owners of estates on the Peermade plateau, but it was found that the ascent was too formidable, and that a motor-lorry could not climb the ghaut farther than Mundakayam. A possible solution of the difficulty was put forward by Mr. J. A. Richardson (Chairman of the Transport Company since its inception), who ordered a survey to be made for the construction of an aerial ropeway from the plateau to the motor transport terminus at the 35th milestone on the Peermade-Kottayam main road. This survey was entrusted to Mr. Ledger, F.R.G.S.; two schemes were submitted, namely, (1) a three-section ropeway, and (2) a fixed rope system with endless haulage rope taking loads right through without handling at the angle station. The matter received careful consideration, and it was eventually decided to adopt the fixed rope system, which, Mr. Richardson said, would be more expensive in the initial outlay, but it presented greater advantages both in cost of working and upkeep. The conveyance of goods and produce between Mundakayam and Peermade had hitherto been effected by bullock-carts by the ghaut road—14 miles in length—but this means of transport was virtually unobtainable during the hot months owing to lack of water and pasture on the ghaut. In order to overcome these difficulties the proposed ropeway would connect Mundakayam with the top of the ghaut, and produce would be conveyed up and down at a great saving of time, labour, and expense. It is confidently believed that this easier method will lead to the cultivation of a considerable area of land in Peermade which has not yet been developed. The order for the ropeway and machinery and engines, together with all requisite material, has been placed with Messrs. Bullivants & Co., of London, but the construction has been entrusted to Messrs. Harrisons & Crosfield, Ltd., of Quilon, who will be guided by an expert from the supplying firm in London. The ropeway will be 5½ miles in length; the height from base to summit will be 3,000 feet, it will convey 4 tons an hour in carriers having a capacity of 920 lb., and the velocity will be at the rate of 450 feet a minute. The power is to be supplied by crude-oil engines, which will be fixed at the terminus on the plateau. Fitting shops will be erected at this spot, with the view of dealing with all repairs to the roadway and lorries of the company, and, further, to meet the requirements of various factories in the neighbourhood. Hopes are entertained of extending the motor service to Vandiperiyar, thus securing the carriage of merchandise in that district, and diverting it via Kottayam and Cochin instead of through Kodaikanal Road and Tuticorin, which necessitates a long and expensive railway journey, in addition to a tedious time by bullock-cart from the estates to the railway. It is expected that the ropeway will be in full working order before the close of the year 1915. The motor-lorry section has already proved to be a financial success, and the Peermade traffic, with the ropeway, will be a most valuable addition. Mr. J. A. Richardson has been the moving spirit in this enterprise, and to him and to his colleague, Mr. J. R. Vincent, the greatest credit is due.

The company was registered under Travancore Regulation I of 1863, on the 11th day of August, 1914, with an authorized capital of Rs. 6,00,000 (divided into 12,000 shares of Rs. 50), but the present issue is Rs. 3,30,000. The directors are Messrs. J. A. Richardson, J. R. Vincent, and J. Dell, and the registered offices are at Kottayam.

THE PEERMADE TEA COMPANY, LTD.

A syndicate of planters in the neighbourhood of Peermade, in the native State of Travancore, acquired the Cheenthalaar estate of 2,250 acres in 1911, and they developed and planted 750 acres with tea-bushes in the following year. The property, together with its then existing crops, was sold in 1914 to the Peermade Tea Co., Ltd., whose registered offices are at Cochin. The directors are Messrs. J. A. Richardson, J. S. Wilkie, J. Graeme Sinclair, and T. C. Forbes, and the agents in India are Messrs. Peirce, Leslie & Co., Ltd. The manager, Mr. W. E. Forbes, is assisted by Mr. T. S. Conner, and about 600 coolies are employed throughout the year. It is intended to open up the property to the fullest possible extent, and it is confidently expected that 2,000 acres will eventually be planted with dark-leaved North Indian indigenous tea, an acre of ground being occupied by about 2,600 trees. It may be mentioned that the cost of clearing and cultivating, and of the construction of a factory (which is nearing completion), will not be less than £25 an acre. The directors are much impressed with the possibilities of this estate, and a glance at what has already been done shows that the work of development is being taken in hand in a thoroughly practical manner. For instance, the most important subject of drainage was one of the first aids to successful agriculture to be undertaken; it being realized that a superfluity of moisture prevents the air from entering the soil and thus destroying all chances of decomposition. Draining of the subsoil is as necessary as digging is for the surface, and no practical cultivator can afford to ignore either of these essentials. The Cheenthalaar property is being drained in a systematic manner, but this is only one of the many improvements which are being effected. Weeds are not allowed to attain vigorous growth, decayed or unhealthy bushes are replaced by sound transplants, and the application of suitable manures will have an incalculable effect upon those trees which will come into bearing in 1915, as well as upon those of a younger age. The buildings

THE PEERMADE TEA COMPANY, LTD.

1. Pruning Two-year-old Tea. 2. Two-year-old Tea before Pruning. 3. View of the Valley. 4. Bungalow. 5. Nurseries. 6. View from the Bungalow.

comprise bungalows and lines for coolies, together with sheds and stores of various sizes. The factory is being built upon modern plans, and the machinery will be of the most approved and up-to-date character. Teak and blackwood—grown upon the estate—have been used in the construction of all the buildings. The property is of a very undulating nature, and, although it lies at an elevation of from 2,500 ft. to 2,800 ft., it has an excellent supply of water for general and domestic purposes. The average annual rainfall is about 160 in.

Much of the future welfare of an estate depends on having a nursery from which a supply of healthy plants may be drawn, and the manager of Cheenthalaar has set apart an area of about 20 acres upon which transplants will be reared. One might be asked to define the first essential in obtaining seed of undoubted quality, and the answer would be "selection." "And the second one?" says the questioner: the reply is still "selection", while a possible third inquirer would have the word "selection" hurled at him with all the force of conviction.

The means of communication between farms, or between estates and the nearest railway station, are frequently very inadequate, but good roads have been constructed in all parts of this property, and excellent facilities for transport to Kottayam and other places have thus been opened. There is a considerable quantity of heavy jungle here, and its thickness forms the lair of tiger, bear, elephant, bison, and sambur. Eleven miles from Cheenthalaar are the post and telegraph offices at Peermade.

THE TRAVANCORE TEA ESTATES COMPANY, LTD.

This company was formed in 1896 by Mr. H. M. Knight, a well-known planter in Southern India, for the purpose of acquiring land for the establishment of tea plantations in the native State of Travancore. The managing director to-day (1914) is Mr. H. K. Rutherford, and the general manager in India is Mr. D. McArthur, who resides at Tungamullay, near Vandiperiyar, in the above-named State. There are eleven different properties belonging to the company, and a separate account of the work carried on at each place is necessary in order to appreciate the magnitude of the interests which are controlled by Mr. McArthur and his assistants. It must be borne in mind that practically the whole of the land consisted originally of dense virgin jungle, and that there had not previously been the slightest attempt at cultivation. It was, therefore, a task of no ordinary character with which the original manager, Mr. H. M. Knight, was confronted, but his ripe experience, coupled with an unconquerable determination to succeed, has placed the company in a foremost position among the tea-growers of Southern India. The initial expenses were heavy indeed, as the task of clearing the land, of equipping the several properties with bungalows, quarters for coolies, factories and machinery, and of general development, including the making of roads, was completed at a cost of not less than £25 an acre.

The Bonami estate, of 819 acres, was opened up about the year 1880, and some 300 acres were planted with coffee and cinchona, but since it came into the hands of the company in 1896 those crops were discontinued, and 796 acres have been cultivated for the growing of hybrid and indigenous teas. The yield has been steadily increasing year by year (due largely to a liberal application of basic slag), and some of the fields are now returning from 900 lb. to 1,000 lb to the acre. A factory, 140 ft. in length, fitted with modern machinery for making the tea, has been erected, and the plant includes a 42-h.p. Hornsby oil-engine, together with another by Dudbridge of 25-h.p., which is kept in reserve to meet any emergency. The greater portion of the crop is shipped from Cochin to London for sale. About 300 head of cattle are kept for transport service and for domestic use. A European manager resides on the property, and about 800 coolies—chiefly Tamils—are employed constantly. Bonami is 9 miles distant from the post and telegraphic office at Peermade; it is 53 miles from Kottayam; it lies 3,600 ft. above the level of the sea, and it has an annual rainfall of about 153 in.

Koliekanum, comprising 1,195 acres, was a wilderness of the densest jungle when the company acquired it in 1896, and during the course of the next three years about 676 acres were thoroughly cleared and cultivated for the reception of seeds or transplants. Ninety-four acres and 17 acres were respectively planted with Pará and Ceara rubber, and the remainder was prepared for indigenous tea. The soil in this plantation has not yet been manured, but the average annual yield is not less than 650 lb. to the acre. A large three-storied factory has been constructed, and manufactured tea is consigned to London through the port of Cochin. The machinery is of the most approved type, and the motive-power is derived from Hornsby and Dudbridge oil-engines of 42-h.p. and 26-h.p. respectively. Ceara rubber-trees have been discarded owing to unsuitability of local conditions, but Para ones were planted 18 ft. apart in each direction, and although they have not yet been tapped, they are exceedingly well grown. The elevation—which varies from 2,600 ft. to 3,600 ft.—is suitable for them, and it has been proved that, while a high altitude is not conducive to early maturity, the bark of the trees is much thicker than it is upon those at a lower level. A European manager resides on the estate, and about 700 coolies are employed constantly. Koliekanum is 10 miles distant from Peermade post and telegraph office.

The growing of coffee in India received a decided check a few years ago when the disastrous ravages of the leaf-bug cleared off many of the most promising plantations, and it is only in certain districts and at an altitude of from 3,500 to 4,500 ft. that the risk of planting bushes is now undertaken. The Pambanar estate, of 1,148 acres, was planted with 140 acres of coffee and about 60 acres of tea when it was acquired by the company, but the coffee was uprooted and the cultivated portion of the property now consists of 621 acres of tea in full bearing, and of 38 acres of immature trees. All tea is of the indigenous kind with the exception of the original 60 acres of the hybrid type. The remaining 489 acres will be cleared and cultivated for a similar crop as soon as circumstances permit. A yield of 650 lb. is generally secured, and the tea, which is prepared on the property, is shipped to London through the ports of Cochin and Tuticorin. The fine factory —140 ft. in length—has been fitted with up-to-date plant, which is driven during the eight rainy months of the year by a turbine fixed on a dam built across the River Pambanar, while a 32-h.p. Crossley oil-engine is used during the remaining four months. A European manager is resident on the property, and about 750 coolies are regularly employed. Pambanar is 2 miles distant from the post and telegraphic offices at Peermade; it lies at an elevation of 3,400 ft., and it has an annual rainfall of 130 in.

There were about 90 acres of hybrid

THE TRAVANCORE TEA ESTATES COMPANY, LTD.

1. General View, Mount Estate. 2. Factory from 54¾-Acre Field, Koliekanum. 3. 21¾-Acre Field, Koliekanum Estate
4. General View of Tangakal Estate. 5. A Vibw of Vandiperiyar.

tea-bushes on the Granby estate of 298 acres when it was acquired by the company, but the whole of the remaining ground has since then been sown with seed of the indigenous kind. Numerous buildings have been erected on the property, and the factory contains all the necessary plant for the process of manufacture, including an 18-h.p. oil-engine by Crossley. Cases of made tea are marked with the estate brand, and are shipped direct to London via Tuticorin. The excellent average yield of 650 lb. to the acre is undoubtedly due very largely to the systematic manner in which the soil is periodically manured. Coolies to the number of 250 are required constantly, and their work is under the careful observation of a resident European manager. Granby is 5 miles distant from the post and telegraphic office at Vandiperiyar.

The Mount and Savirimully estates adjoin, and they are being worked separately under one management until certain projected developments on the latter have taken place. When the company became possessed of these properties the Mount had upon it a mixed crop of some 80 acres of tea and coffee, and it now has 523 acres of indigenous tea in full profit, giving an average annual return of 650 lb. to the acre. Savirimully comprises some 194 acres, and 111 acres were originally planted with hybrid tea and cinchona, while it now has 146 acres of mature trees and 40 acres of younger ones, all of which are of the hybrid type with the exception of those recently planted. About 550 lb. of tea to the acre is harvested annually in this plantation, and the whole of the produce from the two properties is sent to Tuticorin for shipment to London under the Mount estate brand. A European manager is resident at Mount, and he is in charge of some 650 coolies. These estates are between 2,600 and 3,400 ft. above the level of the sea, and about 125 in. of rain are recorded annually.

The Munjamullay property of 1,024 acres is part of an estate of 2,340 acres which was purchased in 1896, and then divided into four portions, the remaining three, named Injikadu, Nellikai, and Pasumallay, being described separately hereafter. This group is situated in the Periyar Valley, through which flows the river of the same name, and as all the land was heavily timbered with virgin forest at the time of purchase a heavy expenditure was necessary before actual cultivation could be commenced. Portions of the properties were planted in 1898, but no further development was possible between 1899 and 1906 owing to the prevalence of malaria. Manjamullay had 299 acres of indigenous tea-bushes in 1898, and when Mr. McArthur assumed control in 1906 he planted 84 acres of rubber in order to obtain a suitable encampment for his coolies. These trees have flourished remarkably well, and although they grow more slowly at an altitude of nearly 3,000 ft. than those on a lower level, an extra year in arriving at maturity is compensated for by an increase in thickness of bark. Some isolated trees were planted in 1899 by way of experiment, and these were tapped with most satisfactory results in 1909. The trunks of a few of these are 68 in. in circumference. There are, further, on this property 309 acres of tea-bushes in full bearing, in addition to 204 acres of younger ones. Although manure has not yet been applied, the average yield of tea is about 800 lb. to the acre, while some of the fields have given a return of 1,400 lb. Modern plant has been obtained for the factory, and the machinery includes a 32-h.p. Crossley oil-engine, while a 10-h.p. National oil-engine is in reserve for cases of emergency. A European manager resides on the estate, and he has the services of an assistant and about 550 coolies. Munjamullay is 83 miles distant from Kodaikanal Road railway station, and the Vandiperiyar post office is situated on the property.

The Injikadu plantation, which is worked in conjunction with the Munjamullay estate, is 252 acres in extent, and it is situated about half a mile from the post office at Vandiperiyar. About 53 acres were planted with tea in 1898, a further area of 187 acres was opened up in 1906, and application is now being made to the Government for an additional 260 acres in order that the property may be large enough to be cultivated separately. The young plants are only now approaching maturity, but the older trees give an average annual yield of 750 lb. to the acre. A factory will be erected on the property when the grant of further land has been obtained. There is a very comfortable bungalow for the resident superintendent, and suitable accommodation has been provided for the 200 coolies who are employed.

Nellikai, a property of 523 acres, had 52 acres of indigenous tea-bushes planted in 1898, and a further area of 392 acres has been developed since that date. The yield is about 550 lb. to the acre, and the crop is sent to the factory on the Munjamullay estate to be manufactured. It is proposed to erect a factory during the year 1915, when the chests of "made" tea will be consigned to Tuticorin for shipment to London. The buildings now on the property include a bungalow for the assistant manager, and suitable lines for about 350 coolies. Nellikai is situated on a main road about 1 mile from Vandiperiyar; it is at an altitude of 2,600 ft., and it has an annual rainfall of 85 in.

Pasumallay comprises 541 acres. When Mr. McArthur became manager of the company, he planted 140 acres of this property with rubber, but two years later a herd of elephants made its appearance and raided the plantation with such effect that only about 35 trees were left out of a total of 27,000. The land which was thus cleared was forthwith put down to tea, and the estate now consists of 35 acres planted in 1898, and of 338 acres which have been grown since that date. The oldest bushes return about 800 lb. to the acre, although some of the fields have yielded as much as 1,400 lb. An excellent factory—built in 1913—has been fitted with approved machinery and plant of a thoroughly modern character, and the motive-power is obtained from a 20-h.p. Crossley oil-engine. The chests of made tea are marked with the station brand, and are then shipped to London at the port of Tuticorin. Mr. McArthur has established a nursery—20 acres in extent—at Pasumallay, where tea-plants required for the plantations on all of the estates are reared. This land is irrigated by water which is pumped by machinery from the Periyar river. An assistant-superintendent, who resides in a neat bungalow on the property, has charge of about 350 coolies.

There are a number of stones in the Thengakal river, near Vandiperiyar, in the district of Travancore, which greatly resemble coconuts, and thus it came about that the name Thengakal was bestowed upon the estate which will be noticed next. Coffee was planted here in the early seventies, and this property and the adjoining one of Thathekanum are said to hold the record for the heaviest yields in Southern India, the crop being no less than 2 tons of dry coffee to the acre in a single season. These two properties—upon which 94 acres of indigenous tea had been planted—were pur-

THE TRAVANCORE TEA ESTATE COMPANY, LTD.

1. 38-Acre Field, Mount Estate. 2. Bungalow, Pambanar. 3. Factory, Pambanar Estate. 4. Periyar (Sinclair's) Bridge.

THE WALLARDIE TEA ESTATES, LTD.

1. THE FACTORY. 2. VIEW FROM BUNGALOW. 3. PART OF THE ESTATE. 4. ANOTHER VIEW.

chased by the company in 1896, and since that time they have been cultivated under one management and under the name of Thengakal alone. A very serious epidemic of malaria caused the company to abandon the estate in the year 1900, and it was not until 1911 that possession was retaken. About 330 acres are now producing indigenous tea of first-class quality; in fact, the Assam jât in the 94 acres originally sown is said to be equal, if not superior, to any other jât in Southern India. The factory is fully equipped with machinery, which includes a 20-h.p. Crossley oil-engine. The superintendent in charge resides on the property, and he employs some 400 coolies. Thengakal has not, hitherto, been in a desirable position with regards to its means of communication, as the best available route has been along a bullock track, but a road has now been constructed between the estate and the village of Vandiperiyar—a distance of 7½ miles—and the cost of this work, and of a bridge of three spans over the Letchimi river, is being borne by the company. The estate is from 2,500 to 3,300 ft. above the level of the sea, and it has a well-distributed rainfall of 125 in.

The various estates owned by the company are 6,999 acres in extent, and application has been made to the Government for a further 815 acres. About 5,219 acres have been opened up to the present time, and 3,613 acres are occupied by trees in full profit. More than 200 acres of the total have been developed since 1906, but the greatest portion of this work has been done since 1909.

The company has had its full share of difficulties, but there has been efficient management on the part of Mr. McArthur and his assistants, and the days of storm and stress have been succeeded by an era of marked prosperity.

THE WALLARDIE TEA ESTATES, LTD.

The head offices of this company are situated at Nos. 1 and 4 Great Tower Street, London, E.C., and the agents in India are Messrs. Harrisons & Crosfield, Ltd., of Quilon, in the native State of Travancore. The properties of the company are about 8,000 acres in extent; 1,130 acres of this total—comprising Wallardie, 261 acres, Plakkad, 372 acres, and Chenkara, 497 acres—were purchased from Jesuit priests whose headquarters were at St. Joseph's College, Trichinopoly, and the balance, consisting of virgin forest land, was bought from the Travancore Government. Some 184 acres of tea had been planted on the three above-mentioned estates prior to their sale to the company, and the timber on a further area of 230 acres had been felled, but circumstances arose which caused the latter to be temporarily abandoned. This portion was afterwards reclaimed, and developments which have since taken place bring the total area of cultivated land up to 1,350 acres. Progress in opening up the estate is made at the rate of about 600 acres a year, and it is proposed that each block of land of this measurement shall be worked as a separate unit, having its own superintendent, its books of accounts, its factory, bungalow, and other necessary buildings. The majority of the old tea-bushes are of the Assam variety, and this kind has proved to be so suitable for the district that it is being continued in every subsequent planting. The soil upon these estates is of exceptionally good quality, being a very deep rich brown loam, and agricultural experts have expressed the opinion that more productive land cannot be found in Southern India. Some of the plantations have been yielding crops of 800 lb. of tea to the acre for a number of years, but it is anticipated that there will be a return of 1,000 lb. when the younger trees come into full profit. Each of the Wallardie and Chenkara properties has been provided with a factory which is equipped with modern machinery and plant, including oil and suction-gas engines by Ruston, Proctor & Co., of Lincoln, England. The chests in which the manufactured tea is packed are marked with the name of the particular estate upon which the crop has been grown, and the whole of the yield is shipped at the port of Tuticorin for the London market, where satisfactory prices are invariably obtained. The majority of the plantations are not more than about 2,800 ft. above the level of the sea, but the richness of the soil and the well-distributed annual rainfall of about 95 in. (which includes the south-west and north-east monsoons) contribute largely to the excellent annual output and to the high-class quality of the tea. A nursery—60 acres in extent, and probably the largest in Southern India—has been established for the rearing of seedlings, and a sufficient supply of young plants can always be depended upon, notwithstanding the rate at which the estates are being developed. This plot is irrigated with water which is pumped from a tributary of the Periyar river.

The general management of the whole group of properties is in the safe hands of Mr. J. D. Deane Drummond, who is assisted by four European superintendents, and about 2,000 coolies are employed regularly. The nearest post office is at Vandiperiyar.

N. P. NARIELWALLA & SONS.

1 AND 3. COCO-MATTING, "VICTOR" PATTERN (REVERSIBLE).

2. ALLEPPEY CARPET (MADE FROM BEST SPECIAL TWIST YARN). 4. "KHORASHANI" FIBRE MAT.

THE TRADE OF MADRAS

BY T. E. WELBY

THE trade of the Madras Presidency is conditioned by certain facts which should be mentioned at the outset of any examination of the subject of this article. The first and most important of them is that the Presidency lacks coal and any large amount of readily exploitable mineral wealth. The second is that in its 1,200 miles of coast-line there is no good natural harbour, that of the capital being the result of elaborate and prolonged engineering effort applied to an open roadstead. The third is that, unlike Bombay, its chief city is not on the shortest main route between India and Europe. The fourth is that, except in regard to banking and money-lending, it does not contain any non-European class comparable for enterprise in business to the Parsis of Bombay.

There are no great indigenous industries, though weaving is fairly important. Factories are not numerous, the bulk of the more noteworthy being concerned with cotton. Nevertheless, the trade of the Madras Presidency attains substantial dimensions, the exports being worth Rs. 26,88,37,000, exclusive of Government stores and treasure, and the imports, with similar deductions, being worth Rs. 16,53,68,000. Comparison with the average figures for the previous quinquennium shows an upward tendency. The excess of exports over imports has been fairly steady for some years, amounting to about Rs. 10,00,00,000.

Imports.—The chief items under this head in their order of importance are (1) cotton manufactures (Rs. 4,68,58,000); (2) metals and ores (Rs. 1,93,26,000); (3) cotton twist and yarn (Rs. 1,22,49,000); (4) railway plant and stock (Rs. 1,20,00,000); and (5) machinery and mill fittings (Rs. 71,90,000). Other articles of some importance are, again in order of importance, sugar, spices, oils, hardware, wearing apparel, provisions and oilman's stores, paper and pasteboard, motor-cars and cycles, liquors, glass. Certain of these articles call for some remark. Of those imports which come under the head of articles of food and drink, some growth is noteworthy in malt liquors and port wine, and in patent foods and condensed milk; but the case of sugar is more remarkable, for there is growing appreciation of molasses as a substitution for and improvement on palm and date jaggery as an article used in the making of spirits. As for oils, kerosene represents about 75 per cent. of the total imports. Foreign petrol has no opening in Southern India, the increasing requirements being met from Burma. Figures under the head of manufactured articles are likely to alter a good deal in the near future, owing to the elimination of German and Austrian enterprises, especially in regard to glassware, about half of which used to come from Austria alone. As for machinery, the items in order of value are prime movers other than electrical, electrical machinery and textile machinery, mining machinery. Sewing and knitting machinery is quite considerable in importance. Agricultural machinery has been a very minor item, but this is now mounting up. Cotton goods, as we have seen, are of much importance, representing as they do nearly 30 per cent. of all foreign imports in value. In 1913-14 the quantity of twist and yarn imported was over 12,000,000 lb., of which nearly 11,500,000 lb. came from Great Britain. Piece goods were imported in the same year to the extent of Rs. 229 lakhs (grey), Rs. 114 lakhs (white), and Rs. 116 lakhs (coloured). This trade is a British monopoly, the foreign share in it being quite insignificant. Of minor imports, matches may be mentioned; of these Norway and Sweden supply nearly 90 per cent.

Exports.—The chief exports, in order of value, are seeds (Rs. 5,32,89,000); leather (Rs. 3,47,20,000); raw cotton (Rs. 3,08,96,000); grain and pulse (Rs. 2,45,91,000); coffee (Rs. 1,52,40,000); tea (Rs. 1,46,16,000). Other exports of interest are cotton manufactures, jute, spices, rubber, oil-cakes, oils, hides, and skins.

Among the articles of food and drink, grain and pulse obtain first notice. Of rice in the husk the export is annually variable; the figures for 1912-13 were over 400,000 cwts., worth Rs. 14,55,000. Of rice not in the husk, much the more important export, the amount sent out, chiefly to Ceylon, in the year 1913-14, was 3,098,000 cwts. Spices are of considerable importance, the pepper exported being worth about Rs. 36,92,000. Tea in 1913-14 was exported to the extent of nearly 12,000,000 lb., worth Rs. 86,71,000 for the United Kingdom, 5,287,000 lb. for Canada, 3,871,000 lb. for Ceylon, and 344,000 lb. for other countries. The average value of South Indian tea over a period of years has been slightly above 10 annas 6 pies (10½d.) a lb. Of coffee the United Kingdom in 1913-14 took 92,317 cwts., worth Rs. 55,32,000, France took 97,507 cwts., Austria-Hungary took 12,133 cwts., and other countries were Germany, Belgium, and Ceylon. The average price per cwt. in 1905-6 to 1910-11 was Rs. 46 7 annas, but for 1913-14 the price worked out to Rs. 59 3 annas.

The commercial interests of Madras are watched over by a Chamber of Commerce, representing the European mercantile firms, and having a nominee on the Madras Legislative Council, and by a similar Indian body. At various times the Madras Chamber of Commerce has done valuable work, and it has had some conspicuously able Presidents. It must, however, be added that, speaking broadly, and allowing for numerous individual exceptions, the European commercial community of Madras is not disposed to force on the development of trade along lines which are novel or experimental. There might, indeed, be a good deal of excuse found for a critic who accused some sections of it of excessive conservatism. It has, however, had one great shock in recent times—the collapse of the historic and highly influential firm of Arbuthnot & Co., in 1906. This firm had the most elaborate and extensive business relations. It was, in fact, interested in almost every variety of enterprise in Southern India, and in respect of several it was dominant. Its failure, and the arrest, trial, and conviction of its head, were events which shook the whole fabric of commerce in Madras, and though matters have since been righted, the effects are here and there still visible.

Within the limits indicated in the earlier part of this article, Madras has great possibilities. Their realization is, however, not likely until communications have been further developed by the construction of branch railways by District Boards, a subject to which of late much attention has been given. These bodies are entitled to levy a special cess for the purpose, and working terms are governed by a definite Government scale which is fairly liberal to both the District Board and the main railway companies, while it provides adequate security for payment of interest. Certain tendencies in the Indian, as distinguished from the European, business world of Madras also deserve mention here. The older type of Indian business man is often very astute, but his methods are not of the best. The new type is usually not a man of affairs at all, but rather an academic person who happens to be an enthusiast for the development of indigenous enterprise and the defeat of what he considers "the exploitation of India." It is not necessary to dwell on the resultant evils. They are but what might be expected in a period of economic transition, and should be removed in course of time. Madras undoubtedly has a commercial future of importance as well as a curiously interesting past.

1. TEMPLE DE SIROUCAMISPARAR, VILLENOUR. 2. TOUR DE SIROUCAMISPARAR, VILLENOUR.

FRENCH SETTLEMENTS

PONDICHERRY

Of the five French settlements in India, four are situated within the Madras Presidency, and the most important of these is Pondicherry, which covers an area of 115 square miles, in the district of South Arcot. It extends for a distance of 5 miles along the coast of the Bay of Bengal, and the most curious feature of its physical formation is the exceedingly irregular outline of its northern, western, and southern boundaries. A considerable portion of its surface consists of an alluvial deposit formed in the delta of the River Ponnaiyáz, and in those places where boring for artesian wells has taken place it has been shown that the substratum is made up entirely of sand, clay, and gravel.

French settlers were met with in the Presidency of Bombay in the early part of the seventeenth century, and they subsequently occupied Trincomalee, on the eastern coast of Ceylon, but in 1672, on being driven from the island by the Dutch, they established themselves at San Thome, near Madras. Their residence at the place only lasted for a couple of years, however, and one of their leaders, François Martin, then induced about sixty of his fellow-countrymen to accompany him to an insignificant hamlet (now the town of Pondicherry), containing a few fishermen's cottages, and steps were taken to form a settlement and to protect themselves by means of fortifications. Very little progress seems to have been made during the first fourteen or fifteen years, and when a war broke out between Holland and France in 1693 the forts were compelled to yield to the heavy artillery of the Dutch. Restoration took place under the Treaty of Ryswick in the year 1699, and then followed a period of fifty years' rest from strife, during the earlier portion of which M. Martin displayed remarkable energy in the conversion of a malarial swamp into a healthy settlement which gave abundant promise of agricultural possibilities.

Five years were occupied, from 1701 to 1706, in the construction of a new fort, subsequently known as Fort Louis, and when it was completed in August 1706 it was consecrated with great ceremony and pomp. This auspicious event was commemorated by M. Martin being made first Governor of the settlement. It was unfortunate that this distinguished man did not live long to enjoy his well-merited honour, as he died on December 30, 1706, and was buried on the following day in the chapel within the fort which he had built.

The British forces under Sir Eyre Coote captured the settlement in 1761, but restored it in 1763, and from this time forward to the year 1816—when it was finally handed over to the French—it had been captured and returned on two different occasions. M. Dumas, who was appointed Governor in 1735, was an able and popular official, but the one who did more for the development of Pondicherry than any other individual was the famous Joseph Dupleix, who had previously served as Governor of the settlement at Chandernagore, in the delta of the River Hooghly, near Calcutta. He was the hero of the successful resistance of a siege of fifty-four days' duration instituted by Admiral Boscawen in July 1748, but in the days of peace which followed he was instrumental in causing vast improvements to be made in the town and its immediate surroundings. It should be mentioned here that when Sir Eyre Coote took possession of the capital in January 1761, practically all the buildings within the fortifications were levelled to the ground, and some years elapsed before much had been done in rebuilding.

Pondicherry is to-day (1915) a remarkably clean and well-built town; its streets are wide, and have been constructed at right angles, and it consists of two distinct portions, namely, White and Black Town, within which Europeans and natives are domiciled strictly within their own areas. An esplanade extends along the sea-front for a distance of about a mile and a half, and near the centre of it is the entrance to a fine pier, 332 metres in length, which is connected by a branch line with the town railway station. Ocean-going ships are compelled by reason of the shallowness of the water to anchor in the open roadstead, and all merchandise—whether imports or exports—is transferred to them from the end of the pier by means of native *masulah* boats. Railway wagons can be loaded or unloaded on the pier or the foreshore, and communication with inland towns is obtained through the junction at Villapuram, which is situated on the main line between Madras and Tuticorin, about 23 miles distant from Pondicherry.

The Muttrapoliem waterworks scheme ensures an unlimited supply of good water for drinking purposes, and the construction of the electric motor station has enabled the municipality to cater for the comfort of the inhabitants by providing electricity for the lighting of the streets and private residences. There are four spinning and weaving mills in which some 7,600 hands are employed throughout the year in working 71,213 spindles and 1,622 looms, and there are also two well-equipped ironworks and foundries, a bone-mill, and an ice factory.

The very rapid expansion of the ground-nut trade in the Presidency has resulted in large shipments being consigned from Pondicherry, although the greater portion of the nuts are grown in British territory. Bags of unshelled nuts, owing to the bulky nature, are charged almost twice the amount of freight paid on kernels alone; but notwithstanding this disadvantage the proportion of unshelled to shelled nuts shipped from this port has considerably increased during the past three years as the number of decorticating machines has not kept pace with the extension of the area under cultivation. To illustrate the growth of the shipping trade in nuts at Pondicherry it may be observed that in the year 1880 only 238,780 bags were exported, whereas in 1913 the quantity had risen to 1,242,946 bags.

SON EXCELLENCE MONS. ALFRED MARTINEAU, GOUVERNEUR DES ETABLISSEMENTS FRANCAIS DANS L'INDE.

Other exports include cotton cloth (chiefly blue dyed material for the Straits Settlements and Indian ports), oilcake, areca-nut, castor-oil, coconut-oil, chillies, coffee, hides, indigo, rice, coriander, gingelly, tamarind, and dried fish. The principal imported goods are cotton, gunny bags, paper, sugar, and wines and spirits.

BRITISH CONSULATE, PONDICHERRY.

Special importance is attached to Pondicherry with regard to its trade in wines and spirituous liquors, which are admitted free of duty, and passenger steamers are in the habit of replenishing their stocks there at much lower prices than are charged at ordinary cities and towns within the Presidency. Merchants usually keep large stocks of brandy, gin, whisky, champagne, rum, beer, and vermouth.

Steamers belonging to the British India Steam Navigation Company, trading between Rangoon and Negapatam, call at Pondicherry every week; other vessels in the same ownership put into port once a fortnight in the service between Madras and Singapore, and ships of the Messageries-Maritimes, Clan, Hall, and the Asiatic Steam Navigation Company's lines touch there at frequent intervals.

The first feature of interest to be noticed on leaving the pier is the Place Dupleix, in the centre of which is a bronze statue which has been erected to the memory of Joseph Dupleix in recognition of his invaluable services to his native country as well as to the land of his adoption. Near to this is the Place du Gouvernement, in which is Government House (which is an exceedingly handsome structure), together with a number of other imposing public and private buildings. There are three hotels, and a fully furnished bungalow, where travellers may reside three days free of charge, has been erected near to the station. Visitors should not omit seeing the High Court, the Public Library, and the Cathedral of Nôtre Dame des Anges, which was built in the modern Italian style between the years 1851 and 1855. Pondicherry is the seat of a Roman Catholic Archbishop, the suffragans of the diocese being the Bishops of Mysore, Coimbatore, Kumbakonam, and Malacca; and it is the headquarters of the French Roman Catholic Missions in India.

CHURCH OF ENGLAND, PONDICHERRY.

The town is divided into eight municipalities, or *communes*, as they are termed locally, and its population at the census of 1911 numbered about 185,000 persons.

Tourists should certainly pay a visit to the villages of Veerampatnam and Aryankuppam, which are respectively 3 and 4 miles distant from Pondicherry, as at the former place there is a most interesting old temple erected in honour of the goddess Sangalaniammal (an Avatar of Kali), while at the latter place archæologists will be amply repaid for their journey when they see the very fine old Roman Catholic church.

Other villages in the settlement include Villanur, where there is a temple in which are inscriptions relating to the Vizayanagar dynasty, and Bahur, which is famous for an ancient shrine.

The supreme head of the administration of the settlement is His Excellency the Governor, and there is a General Council consisting of twenty-eight members, of whom twelve are elected to represent Pondicherry, eight for Karikal, four for Chandernagore, and two each for Mahé and Yanaon.

KARIKAL

There is some doubt as to the exact date when the French settled at Karikal, in the district of Tanjore, but it is more than probable that it was between the years 1739 and 1741, when they lent assistance to Chanda Saib, Rajah of Trichinopoly, in his attempt to conquer the district of Tanjore during a dispute which had arisen between two cousins as to the right of succession. They had previously occupied the town of Karikal and some ten neighbouring villages, but about eight years later a formal concession was made by the Rajah of Tanjore of an additional 81 villages. This number was increased to 113 in 1760, and at the commencement of the year 1915 the figure stood at 110 villages, the whole covering an area of 33,787 acres.

The settlement is divided into three *communes*, each of which is governed by a mayor and a number of elected councillors, but it is provided that one-half of the number of seats in the Karikal municipality shall be occupied by Europeans. The Civil Administrator—who holds the highest official position—is subordinate to the Governor of Pondicherry. Karikal is situated within the delta of the majestic Cauvery River, and the soil is exceptionally fertile, as it is irrigated by the following tributaries, namely, the Nandalar, Nattar, Arasalar, Tirumalarajanar, Mudikondanar, Vanjiar, and Nular. Practically the whole of the land is devoted to the cultivation of paddy, and a very considerable trade in rice is carried on with Ceylon and other merchants. The town is the terminus of the Peralam-Karikal branch line of the South Indian Railway Company, Ltd., and it is 198 miles distant from Madras. It possesses some very fine buildings, including Government offices, the residence of the Administrator, the Church of Nôtre Dame des Anges, and a number of State-controlled schools.

The port has excellent accommodation for dealing with sea-borne trade, and large consignments of rice, bricks, pottery, betel-nuts, sandal-wood, spices, and other goods are exported annually, while the chief imports consist of wines, spirits, and petroleum. It may be observed that during the year 1912 no fewer than 102 ships, with cargoes of the value of 2,250,000 francs, entered the port, and that in 1913 the vessels numbered 107, while the value of the shipments exceeded 3,250,000 francs. Steamers belonging to the British India Steam Navigation and other shipping companies call regularly in connection with an important passenger service with Penang, Singapore, and other Eastern cities. A little native cloth is woven by hand, but the inhabitants may be said to be dependent for their livelihood upon the cultivation of the land.

MAHÉ

Mahé is a small settlement with an area of about 5 square miles, and it is situated on the southern bank of the Mahé River in the district of Malabar, on the west coast of the Presidency. Early in the eighteenth century the French had obtained some recognition as traders in the northernmost portions of Malabar, but in 1725 a few ships under the command of M. de Pardaillan were ordered by the Governor of Pondicherry to proceed to a place named Mayyazhi, a few miles distant from Tellicherry, and to demand its surrender. The town appeared to the French commander to be well-nigh impregnable, owing to the natural strength of its position, and the proposed attack upon it was postponed. One of the officers of the squadron, Mons. Bertrand François Mahé de Labourdonnais, devised a plan by which he was able to land a sufficient number of soldiers to force capitulation. The scheme was cleverly conceived and as cleverly executed, and the town was renamed Mahé, as a compliment to the leader of the attack. The town is pleasantly situated on rising ground, and although it is small in size, its trade, especially in agricultural produce, is of considerable dimensions. A fine building, which is worthy of inspection, is the Roman Catholic church, to which large numbers of people are attracted by the festival of Corpus Christi. The popu-

STATUE OF DUPLEIX, PONDICHERRY.

lation of the settlement in 1911 was found to be about 11,000 persons.

YANAON

It is generally believed that this settlement was formed by the French in or about the year 1750, when they established certain industries there, and history seems to confirm this view, as records show that a territory of about 3½ square miles was granted to the settlers in 1752. Like other French possessions in Southern India, however, Yanaon was the scene of many fierce conflicts until treaties, agreed to in 1815, finally restored the settlement to the French. The Administrator is chairman of an elected Council of six members, but supreme control of affairs rests with the Governor of Pondicherry. The town is situated about 10 miles from the mouth of the Godaveri River, and it extends for a distance of 7 miles along the banks of that stream and of its tributary, the Coringa.

There were about 5,000 inhabitants in the year 1911, and these may be said to obtain a livelihood from the cultivation of the land as there are no industries worth mentioning at the present time. Some of the buildings are really fine in appearance, and the majority of the structures show that Western ideas have prevailed in the style of architecture. Purely local affairs are managed by a Municipal Council of twelve members, who have succeeded admirably in their endeavours to make the town as clean and healthy as possible. Educational advantages for boys and girls have been provided for by the opening of two schools, which are under municipal control.

THE GROUND-NUT TRADE

THE present commercial importance of Pondicherry is based almost entirely upon the ground-nut industry, in which a very large export business, chiefly to Marseilles, has been developed within recent years. These nuts closely resemble in appearance, and slightly in taste, the American "pea-nuts," and they are at present used chiefly in the manufacture of soap at Marseilles. It is further stated that the oil extracted from the nuts is often used as a substitute for pure olive oil. The nuts are known in Pondicherry as *arachidès*, and the major portion of the crop is exported as *arachides decortiquees* (shelled groundnuts), while the remainder is consigned as *arachides en cosses* (ground-nuts in the husk). The export of shelled groundnuts from Pondicherry in 1912 amounted to 1,062,203 bags of about 166 lb., and to show how rapidly this business has developed it may be mentioned that in 1911 1,041,696 bags were shipped, while in 1880 the number was only 238,780 bags. Ground-nuts sent in the husk amounted to 164,414 bags in 1912, while two years previously they were just about half the quantity, or 82,680 bags.

This industry is now making rapid headway throughout British India, but it seems to have owed its origin to this French colony, which apparently began the cultivation on a large commercial scale at the suggestion of soap manufacturers in Marseilles. Pondicherry was the only port in India which exported ground-nuts, but there is now considerable rivalry with Madras, Bombay, Cuddalore, Porto Novo, and Negapatam. Very much of the product now shipped from Pondicherry is grown outside of the French territorial jurisdiction, and altogether it is estimated that the Pondicherry-Madras area devoted

MAHÉ (FRENCH MALABAR).
Photo by R. V. Solomon.

to these covers about 500,000 acres, while that of Bombay is about 94,000 acres. The city of Madras exports about one-third of the quantity sent from Pondicherry, but the port of Cuddalore is now a keen competitor.

Out of the total exports of shelled ground-nuts from Pondicherry in 1912, amounting to 1,062,203 bags, the city of Marseilles received 861,330 bags; Trieste, 73,727 bags; Antwerp, 43,847 bags; while nearly all of the remainder went to Dunkirk and Hamburg. Mills have been opened recently in Calcutta and elsewhere in Bengal for the manufacture of ground-nut oil and soap by French methods, and this may cause some diversion of the export trade toward that portion of India. The nuts produced in the neighbourhood of Pondicherry contain from 40 to 45 per cent. of oil in the kernels.

The growing of nuts appears to be quite a profitable industry. A circular of the local Chamber of Commerce at Pondicherry, issued in April 1913, quoted shelled nuts at about £2 16s. a French candy (one candy is equivalent to three bags of 166 lb. each). On well-managed land in the Pondicherry district a crop of 3,200 to 3,500 lb. of unhusked nuts to the acre may be raised.

The prices for ground-nuts are naturally higher when exported in the shelled state, not only because of the waste thus eliminated, and in the saving of freight, but also because it has been found that the nut meets with less deterioration from moisture and heat if its husk is removed before being baled. This higher relative local value for the shelled nuts is causing most of the export to take this form, and the use of shelling or husking machines has become a necessity. A large number of the machines in the Pondicherry district are of Indian make, and are rather crude in construction, although they seem to answer the purpose fairly well. The cost of these machines is about £24. Several of the leading export firms in Pondicherry who buy nuts in the husk are now shelling them with their own machinery, which are of French types, and which do the work in a thoroughly efficient manner. It would seem as if American nut-shelling machines might be introduced with advantage in connection with this industry, but up to the present none of these machines seems to have been heard

THE ANGLO-FRENCH TEXTILE COMPANY, LTD.

1. General View. 2. Engine-room. 3. Blow-room.

of in the district. The ordinary type of machine in use at Pondicherry is capable of shelling about 48 bags a day. The refuse husks are sold locally for fertilizers at about 2d. a bag.

THE ANGLO-FRENCH TEXTILE COMPANY, LTD.

This limited liability company was formed in the year 1898 at Pondicherry, the chief city of the French settlement on the Coromandel coast, about 105 miles distant by road from Madras. It is employed in the spinning and manufacturing of blue guinees, blue Bafts, and Selampoor and superior grey sheetings. The registered offices of the company are at No. 41 Eastcheap, London, E.C., and the managing agents in India are Messrs. Best & Co., Ltd., of Madras.

THE ANGLO-FRENCH TEXTILE COMPANY, LTD.
OFFICES.

S. COOPPOOSAWMY IYER & CO.

It is an incontrovertible economic principle that the export by a country of its raw materials is radically unsound. The whole, or at least part, should be turned into manufactured goods, as this course would not only provide employment for a large number of hands, but the products, which under ordinary circumstances would be purchased as imported articles, will have been produced in the country, and the cost of them will not have been sent abroad. Considerable satisfaction has been experienced in industrial circles in Southern India in recent years by reason of the fact that fully-equipped mills have been erected for dealing with nuts and oil-seeds and other important industries which are associated therewith—such as soap and candle making, which are already being actively supported.

In spite of the extensive production of ground-nut kernels in the Presidency of Madras, the oil industry is confined to the country presses. There are very few well-equipped oil-mills, but it only requires the expenditure of some capital and the display of activity on the part of landholders in order to place this industry on a sound commercial basis.

Messrs. S. Cooppoosawmy Iyer & Co. commenced business at Pondicherry about the year 1884, dealing in ground-nut kernels, oil cakes, coprah, indigo, and other products. They obtain nuts from all parts of India, and the process of removing the shells is expeditiously and satisfactorily carried out in their own mills, which have been fitted with thoroughly up-to-date machinery. The kernels are of the finest quality, and they stand high in the estimation of purchasers at Marseilles, Hamburg, Genoa, Trieste, and other European ports. The seeds are called "machine decorticated clean ground nut kernels." The firm are large exporters of the ordinary kernels, which are shelled by processes which are common in the country districts. Coprah is purchased chiefly in towns in the eastern portion of the presidency—along the coast-line of Madras—and oil cakes, manufactured by the firm, are forwarded to Java, Hamburg, and other places. Branches have been opened at Negapatam and Cuddalore, but Mr. Cooppoosawmy Iyer manages the whole

THE ANGLO-FRENCH TEXTILE COMPANY, LTD.

1 and 2. Weaving-sheds, 3 and 4. Spinning-rooms.

of the business from his headquarters at Pondicherry.

The proprietor is a French citizen ; a member of the Chamber of Commerce at Pondicherry, and he is local agent for the British Dominions Insurance Company.

Certificates were obtained for entries of coprah and oil-cake at the Industrial Exhibition at Pondicherry in 1899.

S. COOPPOOSAWMY IYER & CO.

1. S. COOPPOOSAWMY IYER. 2. OFFICE AND STAFF.

The banking business of the firm is entrusted to the Banque de l'Indo-Chine at Pondicherry.

FILATURES AND TISSAGES GAEBELE

The two spinning and weaving mills belonging to this firm are situated in the communes of Modeliarpeth and Cossapalioum in the French Settlement of Pondicherry on the Coromandel coast. The mills, which are constructed of brick and iron, are fully equipped with improved machinery which has been imported from England, and the buildings are lighted throughout by electricity. It may be said that no expense has been spared in making every working part of the factories as thoroughly modern in character as possible. The volume of trade which passes through the firm's hands in a year is sufficient proof of the excellence of the manufactures. One large building has been set apart for waste spinning. The mills have no fewer than 10,000 spindles and 260 looms. The principal motive-power is steam, which is obtained from two boilers, but there is, also, a patent Campbell suction-gas engine of 240 h.p.

Cotton is purchased in large quantities at several places on the west coast and at Cocanada, on the east coast, to the north of Madras. An abundant supply of water is obtained from artesian sources, and steam coal, which is delivered in the yards at 21s. a ton, is bought from Calcutta.

A special feature of the manufactures of these mills is the production of cloth which is dyed an indigo blue colour, and the system under which this is done is one which has been known to the French for considerably more than one hundred years. The greater portion of the whole output of the factories is exported to Morocco, Cochin-China, Senegal, and to London. Complaints are numerous among shippers that they are continually being hampered in their trade on account of the insufficiency of the number of steamers which put in at Pondicherry.

The firm have their own workshops in which skilled artisans effect repairs which are necessary for any part of the plant, and the offices are situated in a building which practically adjoins the mills.

The first spinning mill in India was erected in Pondicherry by Mons. Blin, an ancestor of Mons. Gaebele, who is the present manager of the firm.

The wages of the employees (who number about 550) have increased 40 per cent. during the past six years. Gold and silver medals have been awarded for exhibits at Lyons, Bordeaux, and Marseilles.

The three brothers Henry, Albert, and Fritz Gaebele take general management in the works ; their telegraphic address is " Gaebele," Pondicherry.

FILATURES AND TISSAGES GAEBELE.

1. A Partial View. 2. Weaving Department. 3. Blue Cloth ready for Packing. 4. General View, Industries Renmies Mills. 5. The Cossapalioum Mills.

RENF GAUDART.

1. General View of Workshop. 2 and 3. Fitting Shop. 4. Portable Ground-nut Decorticator.

RENE GAUDART

An inventor may be described as an individual who contrives and produces something which did not previously exist ; he is a man who possesses the power of imaginative conception, and who has, further, the faculty of giving form or oeing to that which has been formulated in his brain. These men of genius occupy an honourable position on the scroll of the world's benefactors, and the only regret is that the reward due to many of these worthies is not reaped by them during their lifetime. Inventions have revolutionized the commerce of the world ; they have solved the problem of aerial flight; they have connected continents, and have revolutionized our methods of life.

Mons. Rene Gaudart, a fully qualified engineer, with offices and workshops in the Boulevard du Sud, in Pondicherry, is an inventor whose whole soul is wrapped up in the patenting of improved machinery, but principally of that kind which is required in the agricultural world. He has already obtained patents for plant for rice milling and for distilling, but he has numerous other projects which are, as yet, in the embryotic stage. For instance, he is experimenting in his private laboratory with a machine which is designed to produce coconut grease from the oil of the kernel, while another machine is being made which, it is claimed, will remove the cotton from seed for the manufacture of gunpowder without any damage being done to the seed itself.

Mons. Gaudart's workshops, therefore, are a "means to an end," and they have been constructed and equipped with the sole object of rendering him assistance in the carrying out of those important designs which his fertile imagination is continually evolving. The dimensions of the premises are 200 ft. by 250 ft. ; the machinery in the four small foundries consists of four drilling, one shaping, and other machines ; a large lathe, and an extraordinarily complete set of tools and accessories of a general character. A 15-h.p. oil-engine is used in dealing with all heavy work. Between 60 to 70 hands are constantly employed in the workshops, and M. Gaudart, who is his own manager, gives personal supervision to every branch.

The engineering business was only commenced in October 1913, but since that date M. Gaudart has done a considerable amount of building and contracting for the English and French Governments, and one eminently satisfactory piece of work has been the construction of a small bridge at Bangarvaikal.

SIALLY SRIRAMOULOO CHETTY.

SIALLY SRIRAMOULOO CHETTY

It is nearly two hundred years since the ancestors of Mons. Sially Sriramouloo Chetty established themselves in Pondicherry, and the earliest of these pioneers were engaged in weaving yarn and in dyeing cloth.

The third generation abandoned the dyeing business, but they retained the yarn industry and commenced dealing in ground nuts and sugar. The last-named is imported in large quantities from Java, Mauritius, and Europe, while nuts are exported to France. Solidified molasses are obtained from Java, on behalf of the Pondicherry Government distillery, and no fewer than 5,000 tons were imported during the year 1913.

Mr. Chetty is assisted by his uncle in the management of the business, and he is, further, a landowner, possessing some 120 acres, which are under cultivation.

The principal business address is Komiti Street, Pondicherry, but a branch establishment has been opened at 50 Govindappa Naick Street, Madras.

SERICULTURE

NOTES SUPPLIED BY THE SUPERINTENDENT OF THE TATA SILK FARM, BANGALORE CITY.

THE industries which are indirectly connected with the cultivation of the land are exceedingly numerous, but comparatively few agriculturists appear to realize how exceedingly helpful to the annual balance-sheet these aids may become. It is only within the past twenty or thirty years, for example, that dairying has—in some countries—been recognized as one of the most profitable adjuncts of the farm ; sericulture is now strongly recommended by experts who have shown payable results ; and more recently it has been demonstrated that a considerable income may be made annually by cultivating the mulberry-bush and rearing the silkworm. It is true that silk was manufactured in India some hundreds of years ago, but it cannot be said that a thriving industry has been maintained. The Government of India has on two or three occasions given assistance in the matter, but, whether it was owing to a lack of interest on the part of the people, or to want of experience or energy on the part of the official demonstrators, the venture was not attended with success. The Government of the native State of Mysore, in the Madras Presidency, however, undismayed by failures of the past, is encouraging the silk industry, and it has recently appointed an expert, who is endeavouring to induce landholders to plant mulberry-trees on a much larger scale, and is giving advice and assistance in the rearing of silkworms and in the treatment of cocoons. An experimental farm, too, has been opened at Chinnapatna, and provision is being made for the training of students who will eventually be employed in the management of model rearing-houses for the worms. Sericulture, when thoroughly understood, is undoubtedly a profitable undertaking, and it has been proved that there are several villages in Mysore in which seven or eight individuals have been able, collectively, to produce cocoons to the value of from Rs. 1,500 to Rs. 2,000 as the result of a single year's work. There are several species of French and other European worms which can be reared safely in Southern India, but the "Mulberry" and "Eri" types are greatly in the majority. The selection of suitable land for the growing of mulberry and castor-trees, which respectively provide food for the two species of silkworms referred to, is an all-important question, but a thorough ploughing and manuring of the soil, and careful attention to the rearing of young plants are not to be overlooked. Too much attention cannot be given to the young worms in the first few days of their existence, and the operations of feeding, cleaning, and moulting must be carefully watched. Eri worms are more easily reared than Mulberry ones, as they are stronger and are not so liable to diseases which affect the latter, and another difference between the two kinds is that Eri silk must be spun on a spinning-machine, as it cannot be reeled. Mulberry cocoons are steamed and then dried in the sun, reeling usually taking place after an interval of two or three days.

It is gratifying to notice that the Salvation Army authorities have been most successful in their efforts to show what can be done in sericulture, and they have accomplished marvellous results since the year 1910, when they took over the control of the Tata Experimental Silk Farm, about 2 miles distant from the city of Bangalore.

Commissioner Booth-Tucker, Head of the Salvation Army in India, paid a visit to the farm recently, and said that "phenomenal progress had been made," that "silk-throwing, warping, twisting, and weaving had been added to the branches," and that "instead of turning out students who are looking for highly-paid Government appointments, we are training numbers of workers who can go back to their villages and duplicate what they have seen here." Students are now flocking to the farm to undergo a course of instruction, and the practical experience which they gain cannot fail to be of incalculable benefit to the country at large. Passing reference may be made to the syllabus of a six or twelve months' course of study, published by the manager of the farm and school. The subjects cover an exceedingly wide field,

1. GROUP OF STUDENTS AT WORK. 2. SPINNING AND RULING MACHINES.
3. A HARVEST OF MYSORE COCOONS. 4. SILKWORMS. 5. A SMALL HAND LOOM.

and they include ploughing and preparing the land, planting mulberry and castor-trees by cuttings or from seed, manuring, pruning, diseases in plants, the rearing of worms, carding and disinfecting eggs, feeding worms, diseases of worms, steaming and drying cocoons, making twists and knots, packing silk (with press) for Europe, weaving on three different kinds of looms, bleaching, winding bobbins, and throwing, doubling and twisting, making warps, and dressing for finishing silks after weaving.

The greatest credit is due to Mr. Edward Jackson, the painstaking expert manager of the farm, who has been good enough to supply many of the particulars given in these notes. This gentleman says that if Indian silk is well reeled it is as good as, if not better than, any other. In order to emphasize the importance of this process, the manager states that he recently saw five bundles of raw silk waiting at a railway station for dispatch, and that, after he had ascertained the weight of the parcels, he found that if the silk had been treated in the manner adopted at the farm it would have realized a further sum of Rs. 500. Mr. Jackson adds that South Indian sericulturists cannot compete with European or Japanese silk markets.

A bale of silk from the farm was shown by Messrs. Durant, Bevan & Co. at the London Silk Exhibition in 1912, and it attracted great attention from the visitors, who included their Majesties the King and Queen and other members of the Royal Family. Ten gold medals, eight silver medals, five of bronze, and many certificates have been awarded to the Tata Farm exhibits for specimens of worms reared there, for reeling silk, and for weaving silk cloths. The Army officials are nothing if not thorough, and they are not only teachers of sericulture but they are prepared to supply reeling and re-reeling machinery, glass guides, pulleys, spinning-machines, mulberry cuttings and seeds, Eri, Mysore, and French eggs, trays, and other appliances. It is now confidently believed that sericulture is being taken up in earnest in Southern India, and there is every prospect of a valuable industry being permanently established.

1, 2, AND 3. VIEWS OF ST. ALOYSIUS' HIGH SCHOOL, VIZAGAPATAM.
4. SHRINE OF OUR LADY OF THE SACRED HEART, VIZAGAPATAM.

MADRAS TO VIZAGAPATAM

THE economic development of a country is almost entirely dependent upon its means of communication by road or rail between the several areas of production and the principal commercial towns and seaports. The southern portion of India—taking Madras as a starting-point—is well provided with sections of main and branch lines; it has a north-eastern system leading to Waltair, the junction with the Bengal-Nagpur Railway for Calcutta; it is connected with the Native State of Mysore and Bangalore in the central portion of the province; travellers for the north and north-west can reach such important places as Bellary, Mormugao, Bijapur, Raichur, Poona, and Bombay; while a train journey of about 550 miles enables the visitor to see Trichinopoly, Erode, Madura, Tinnevelly, and Quilon, which is on the north-west coast in the State of Travancore.

As the train emerges from the Central Station of the Madras and Southern Mahratta Railway at Madras, a view is obtained on the immediate left-hand side of the Moore Market, the Victoria Hall, the Ripon Municipal Buildings, and the People's Park; on the right are the lighthouse on the High Court structure, the busy bazaars of Georgetown and other districts of the city; while farther to the east is the azure blue water of the Bay of Bengal. As soon as the open country is reached one notices thousands of graceful palms, which contrast delightfully with the rich dark-green verdure of the banyan and other fully-grown trees. At the time of writing (September 1914) the south-west monsoon has enabled agriculturists to cultivate and clean their lands, and healthy-looking crops are evidence of the thorough manner in which that work has been performed.

The train crosses numerous channels of water, which are of incalculable value for irrigating purposes or for the drainage of those areas which occasionally suffer from having too much moisture. Shortly after the tenth mile post has been passed the visitor arrives at Ennore, which can also be reached by road through Tondiarpet, or by one of the boats which ply on the Buckingham Canal from Madras. This village is an ideal place for a picnic, there being plenty of open spaces for games, an abundance of shelter afforded by clumps and avenues of trees, and an unbroken sheet of water which is gracefully fringed with palms and bamboos. Ennore was formerly a fashionable week-end resort for the residents of Madras, and even now there are many exceedingly comfortable bungalows which may be obtained for short or long visits. This is the Government headquarters of the Salt Department of the district of Chingleput, and a very large quantity of salt is obtained from numerous pans and shipped annually to Calcutta and other ports. One of the chief attractions of the present day is the large salt-water lake, in which visitors may bathe and fish with the keenest appreciation of the beautiful surroundings.

THE SEA CUSTOMS, COCONADA.

Before continuing the journey to the north a visit should certainly be made to Pulicat, the trip being accomplished by boat in from five to six hours. The village is an old Dutch settlement, which was founded in the year 1609, and it is to be regretted that there are now (1914) hardly any traces of a fine old fort which was constructed by the Hollanders. Pulicat Lake is a fine sheet of water about 37 miles in length, and from 3 to 10 miles in breadth. The train continues to travel in a parallel line with the Coromandel coast, and at some stations the sea is not more than a few miles distant. About 86 miles from Madras is Gudur, which is the junction between the broad and metre-gauge sections on that portion of the Madras and Southern Mahratta Railway which opens up the very heart of the Presidency as far as Mormugao, on the west coast, and which has important stations at Renigunta, Pakala, Tumkur, Shimoga, Dharmavaram, and other places. Gudur is the principal town of the *taluq* of the same name, and is the centre of a district which produces exceedingly large quantities of rice. The next place of importance is Nellore, the administrative headquarters of the district of Nellore, and a town of considerable antiquity and of historical interest. This district, together with others on the east coast, was dominated successively by Mahommedan, Dutch, French, and English, and it finally came under British rule in the year 1801. The River Penner, whose source is in the Nilgiris, has a course of more than 70 miles in the district of Nellore, and although for nearly nine months in the year its bed is rocky and almost dry, yet when the stream is in flood—usually for about sixty days—it is fully 500 yards in width and 30 ft. in depth. A considerable quantity of land, both to the north and south of Nellore, is irrigated by an anicut, from which numerous channels are diverted, and this fact accounts for the very satisfactory crops of paddy which are harvested here. The municipality had a population of 33,246 persons at the census of 1911.

Bitragunta, in the district of Nellore and 131 miles distant from Madras, has a fine temple dedicated to Vishnu, to whom a large number of pilgrims pay homage at each annual festival. This village has achieved a notoriety which has not been attained by any other town or hamlet in Southern India. Just as in days gone by love-sick couples fleeing from inconsiderate parents or unreasonable guardians in England were wont to make their way with all haste to the village blacksmith at Gretna Green, in Scotland, before whose anvil, which served as altar, they plighted their troth, so, in like manner, Indian youths and maidens, unable to meet the expenses which a rigid caste imposes upon marriage ceremonies among their own relations, flock to Bitragunta from all parts of the Presidency for the purpose of qualifying for the sometimes dubious pleasures of married life. The Eastern Ghauts, which run from north to south for nearly the entire length of the province, may be seen at intervals on the western side of the train, and the Mannaru and other small rivers which drain, rather than irrigate, the land, are crossed between Bitragunta and Singarayakonda, where there are temples in honour of Narsimhaswamy and Varahaswamy. Ongole (182 miles distant from the terminus), with a population of 13,286 persons, is the chief town of the *taluq* of the same name in the district of Guntur. The Ongole breed of cattle is considered to be one of the best in India, and large numbers are exported annually to Australia, Java, South America, and other places. Vishnu and Siva temples, which are worthy of inspection, are to be seen here. Tenali, a thriving municipality on the banks of the Nizampatam Canal, in the district of Guntur, is an important centre from which the produce of the rich fields of the delta formed by the tributaries of the Kistna River is exported. The town is connected by a good metalled road with Guntur, the chief town of the district, and it contains some 18,000 inhabitants.

Bezwada is the headquarters of the Chief Assistant Collector of the district of Kistna, and is 268 miles distant from Madras. The town is undoubtedly an ancient one, and archæologists will revel in an inspection of temples of the Buddhist period which have been cut out of the solid rock, and, further, of some very old Hindu pagodas. The broad-gauge eastern coast line of the Madras and Southern Mahratta Railway is connected at Bezwada with the metre-gauge system to the shores of the Arabian Sea on the western side of the Presidency, and it is, further, a junction with the State Guaranteed Railways of the Nizam of Hyderabad. In addition to the importance of the town as regards railway traffic, it comes into prominence as the centre of the canal system of the Kistna delta, and it is connected by good waterways with Rajahmundry, Coconada,

Masulipatam, Ellore, and the city of Madras. The Municipal Council is actively engaged in promoting measures for general improvements in the borough, and its buildings include the offices of the tahsildar, the assistant collector, and the superintendent and assistant engineers of the Public Works Department, together with munsiff's court, public dispensary, and jail. Local industries are not numerous, but the principal ones are ginning and rice factories, in which many hands are employed. The inhabitants are about 33,000 in number.

Before continuing the journey from Bezwada to Calcutta and the north, it would be well to travel in an easterly and then in a southerly direction by the branch line (52 miles in length) to Masulipatam, the administrative headquarters of the district of Kistna. The town is 318 miles distant from Madras, and its inhabitants were 42,123 in number at the last census. Masulipatam is a seaport of some importance, as its railway facilities for the reception and forwarding of merchandise from and to the vast inland territory practically adjoin the harbour, and thus the more costly and tedious transport by road is avoided. A couple of centuries ago the town was occupied by Portuguese, Dutch, and French in succession, but it fell into the hands of the English in the year 1759. Tourists will be interested in some remarkably quaint old tombstones in a disused cemetery, while there are several temples which contain a large number of inscriptions. The only industries worthy of mention are the manufacture of carpets for export to England, and of "Palampore" cloths which are consigned to Bombay and Persia. A fine monument has been erected in memory of more than 30,000 of the inhabitants who were swept away by a tidal wave in 1864. Ellore, 305 miles from Madras, was formerly the capital town of the Northern Circars, which included the districts of Ganjam, Vizagapatam, Godaveri, Kistna, and part of Nellore. The weaving of carpets is carried on to a considerable extent, but trading in agricultural produce—of which paddy is by far the most important item—is the staple industry. At a distance of about 55 miles from Ellore the train arrives at Godaveri, which is in the centre of the town of Rajahmundry, and is a station for passenger use only. This point marks the beginning of the fine bridge which crosses the huge River Godaveri. This river flows from almost one side of the peninsula to the other; its length is about 900 miles, and it receives the drainage from 115,000 square miles, an area larger than that of England and Scotland combined. "Rising near the village of Trimbak, in the Bombay Presidency, and about 50 miles from the Arabian Sea, it flows in a south-easterly direction, passing through the Deccan and the Nizam's dominions. Its course for 500 miles is through a country that has been little explored, and part of which is covered with primeval jungle. About 30 miles above the point at which it is crossed by the railway the channel, which has varied from 1 to 2 miles in width, begins to contract, the hills close in on either side, and the water finally rushes through a gorge barely 200 yards in width. The river widens again on reaching the alluvial plain of the delta, and at the anicut, 3 miles below the bridge, is $3\frac{1}{2}$ miles from bank to bank, including the space occupied by islands."[1] The railway bridge at Godaveri consists of 56 spans, each of 160 ft. between centres of piers, or a total length of 8,960 ft. About 5 miles to the south of Rajahmundry, at Dowlaishwaram, the river is nearly 4 miles in breadth, although some islands take up about one-third of this distance. An anicut has been thrown across the river at this place, from which a huge system of channels and tanks is available for the distribution of the waters of the Godaveri over an immense area.

The town of Rajahmundry is the headquarters of the *taluq* of the same name in the district of Godaveri; it is 361 miles distant from Madras, and it has a population of about 48,500 persons. Probably the earliest reference to Rajahmundry in available records occurs in a Telugu translation which appeared in the reign of Rajaraja, between the years 1022 and 1062, in which the town is described as "Rajamahendrapattanam," or the city of Rajamahendra. The town became an important strategical place during the extension of the Eastern Chalukya dominions, but the Mahommedan forces entered the town after they had overthrown the Kakatya dynasty. This was in or about the year 1323. Troublous times followed for a period of about two centuries, until it became the frontier town of the Orissa community in 1543. Rajahmundry was selected by the French general, Bussy, as his headquarters when the area known as the Northern Circars was ceded to France in 1753, and it remained in that position until the English invasion of 1758. Occupation by the French, and subsequently by the Nizam, took place, but Lieutenant (afterwards Sir Henry) Cosby finally obtained possession on behalf of the British. The head assistant collector, the sessions judge, and the district superintendent of police have offices here, and the town contains, fur-

GROUP OF "DAGOBAS," SANKARAM, VIZAGAPATAM DISTRICT.

1 "Madras and Southern Mahratta Railway Guide."

ther, travellers' bungalows, *chuttrams*, and municipal council buildings. The district of Godaveri was one of the first in the Presidency to take up the question of provision of educational establishments, as in the year 1826 the then Collector, under instructions from the Government, opened schools at Rajahmundry and Coconada. The Rajahmundry College and the Government Training College are the two principal institutions at the present time, although excellent facilities for acquiring a thorough training are provided by a number of high, secondary, and primary schools. A considerable trade is carried on at Rajahmundry in timber and in minor forest produce, such as tamarinds, nux vomica, honey, wax, and gall-nuts, the greater portion of which is shipped to Europe and Ceylon. Among other industries the following may be mentioned: Silk and cotton weaving; the manufacture of brass, copper, lead, and bell-metal vessels and ornaments; fresco work, wood-carving of excellent quality (very largely used for platforms upon which gods are carried); the making of large quantities of gingelly, castor, and coconut oils; tanning of skins and hides and the manufacture of boots and shoes; printing, at about half a dozen offices; and rice-husking in mills. A Municipal Council was formed in 1866, and it now consists of eighteen members. Neither improvements nor public works of any magnitude have been executed, but three markets have been opened, a rest-house for poor persons has been erected, and support is given to the hospital and to two or three choultries. About 31 miles in a north-easterly direction from Rajahmundry is Samalkot, which is the junction of the branch line to the town of Coconada, the chief town of the district of Godaveri. Samalkot enjoys excellent railway facilities with the north, south, and western portions of the Presidency. and it has, further, the inestimable advantage of being connected by canal with Coconada and Rajamundry. Plain and fancy cotton cloths are woven, and chintz is stamped and dyed by many inhabitants, but the principal industry is that of the refining and distilling of sugar by the Deccan Sugar and Akbari Company, Ltd., for whom Messrs. Parry & Co., of Madras, are managers. The cultivation of sugar-cane was attended with considerable loss owing to the ravages of the moth-borer and of the fungus known as *Iraria barberi*, and the Government, in its praiseworthy endeavours to make investigations into the cause and possible prevention of these pests, opened an experimental farm, and deputed Mr. C. A. Barber, then Government botanist, to conduct the inquiries. Very satisfactory results have been obtained, and the scope of the inquiry has now been very materially enlarged.

Coconada is one of the busiest seaports of the Presidency. There are offices here for the Collector of the district, the District Forest Officer, Engineer of the Public Works Department, and medical, sanitary, and port officials. Educational establishments have been well supported by the inhabitants, and they now include the Pithapuram Rajah's College, which was founded in the year 1852 as a general English and vernacular school, an English lower secondary school for boys, and two English and four vernacular lower and secondary schools for girls. The population of the town numbered 54,110 inhabitants at the census of 1911, and a municipality was formed in 1866. Very important improvements have been effected by the councillors, the principal one being the Victoria Waterworks, which were completed in 1903. Water is obtained from the Samalkot Canal, and it is passed from a storage reservoir through filter-beds into a second reservoir, whence it is distributed throughout the town. The industries include weaving, the manufacture of copper, brass, and bell-metal vessels and ornaments, wood-carving, boot and shoe-making, printing, and rice-milling, but special attention is given to the manufacture of gingelly, coconut, and castor oils. The port lies in the south-west portion of Coringa Bay, and a large quantity of shipping is carried on with the principal towns of India and the Far East. Large vessels are compelled to find anchorage about 5 miles from the shore, but there is sufficient depth of water to enable vessels of 100 tons to convey produce to and from the harbour. Many of the leading commercial houses in the Presidency have agents in the town, and important shipping companies are represented by the following steamers, and the British Indian Steam Navigation Company, the Clan Line of steamers, and the British Indian Steam Navigation Company, Ltd. The chief exports are cotton, rice, paddy, oil seeds and cake, food grains, fibre, and castor oil.

Upon leaving Coconada an endeavour should be made to pay a visit to Coringa, which is about 10 miles distant in a southwardly direction. It was formerly one of the busiest seaports and shipbuilding centres on the east coast, but owing to the silting up of the harbour it is now several miles inland. Proceeding again by train the traveller arrives at Tuni, which is 426 miles from Madras. Many of its inhabitants—who are about 9,000 in number—are engaged in dyeing, the stamping of chintz, and in brass and other metal-work, but a large business is carried on in the manufacture of gingelly and castor oil.

Waltair, 485 miles distant from Madras, is the headquarters of the district of Vizagapatam, and the official residence of the Collector, the District Judge, the Deputy Commissioner of Forests, the District Forest Officer, and other Government servants. It is, further, the junction station of the Bengal-Nagpur Railway Company. Waltair is noted for the remarkable uniformity of its temperature, as it rarely varies more than two degrees in twenty-four hours, and it is consequently becoming a very popular health resort, and especially as it is situated in the midst of delightful scenery. A branch line, 2 miles in length, runs in a southerly direction to Vizagapatam, which is a fine old seaport with a considerable amount of interesting history attached to it. Mr. W. Francis, I.C.S., says: "The antiquity of this principality (district of Vizagapatam) is amply established. It is referred to in Brahmanical and Buddhist literature assigned by Professors Macdonnel and Rhys Davids to the fifth and sixth centuries respectively before the Christian era; by the Sanskrit grammarians Katyayana and Panini, who flourished in the fourth century B.C.; and, further, in the Ramayana and Mahabharata." The next reliable reference to the country is that it was conquered in 260 B.C. by Asoka, the great emperor of the Buddhist Mauryan realms. A series of invasions followed, commencing with a conquest by the Chalukyas of Bombay in the sixth century A.D. The Cholas were in power between the years 999-1000, but they were ousted by the Gangas, who, in turn, were defeated by the Cholas during the eleventh century, and it may be added here that inscriptions of the Chola king, Kulottunga I (1098-9), may be seen in the very ancient and beautiful temple dedicated to Narasimha, "The man-lion incarnation of Vishnu," and known as Simhachalam, or "lion hill," which occupies a commanding position near Vizagapatam, at an altitude of about 800 ft. above the level of the sea. The Mahommedan period commenced in 1568, but the rulers were weak, and revolts and disturbances were continually taking place. The English settled in the town of Vizagapatam, and the Dutch commenced trading in Bimlipatam, but these occurrences were not of sufficient importance to influence political events of the day. The French came upon the scene shortly after this, and serious disturbances took place, sometimes between Europeans and Indian rulers, and occasionally among the Europeans themselves. In 1758 Vizagapatam was taken from the French by the Rajah of Vizianagram, and the district was ceded to the English in 1765, but internal troubles appeared to be as frequent as in former years, owing chiefly to the maladministration of the Rajah. Zemindars, too, were subsequently in a continual state of discontent, and special powers, conferred upon the Government by Act of Parliament in the year 1839, became necessary in order that the disaffection might be crushed. Individual outbreaks have frequently occurred since that period, but little difficulty has been experienced in quelling them. Such, in brief, is an outline of the early history of a municipality and seaport which now has a population of more than 43,000 inhabitants. A large amount of merchandise passes through the port, its exports consisting mainly of jute, manganese, indigo, all kinds of grain, gingelly seed, oils, hides, skins, and jaggery; while imports include piece goods, cotton twist, yarn, and glass-ware. There are several local industries, among which may be mentioned the weaving of cotton into rugs and carpets and into articles of clothing for men and women, and the turning of wood and lacquering. Very beautiful work is executed by a few firms who manufacture fancy goods, such as chess-boards, trinket-boxes, and card-cases from tortoiseshell, ivory, and horns. The various processes sometimes include the preparation of sandal-wood as a foundation, the polishing of horns and shells, and the carving of ivory according to the most ornate designs representing gods and flowers. There was a tremendous amount of "spade-work" in this district before any advance at all could be made with regard to educational matters, and things were so bad even a few years ago that the dwellers in the *taluqs* of the plains were said to be more illiterate than the people of any other district in the Presidency. The Government now maintains training schools in addition to other establishments, at which technical education classes are in evidence. The list includes, further, the Mrs. A. V. Narasinga Rao College, St. Aloysius' High School, together with several primary and secondary institutions. Vizagapatam became a municipality in 1858, and the Council has, from its birth, shown an admirable spirit of progress and reform. To its efforts are due the building of a commodious municipal hall, with library, reading-room, and young men's institute; two profitable sewage farms were started by it; swamp land has been reclaimed; and roads and bridges have been constructed with the view of making the town easier of access.

THE MAIN CANAL, GODAVERI.

Photo by Nicholas & Co.

The coast line near Vizagapatam is broken by a bluff headland known as Dolphin's Nose, which is 1,174 ft. above the level of the sea, while immediately to the north of the town is Simhachalam (the lion hill), which has just been referred to. Returning to the junction at Waltair, travellers for Calcutta and other places to the north will be taken in hand by the officials of the Bengal-Nagpur Railway, and the first station of importance is Vizianagram, which is the second largest town in the district of Vizagapatam. It is 38 miles distant from Waltair and 523 miles from Madras, and its inhabitants were about 38,000 at the close of the year 1911. It consists of two parts, which are separated by the Peddacheruvu, or large tank, which is utilized for the irrigation of a large tract of land. One of these, consisting of the civil station and deserted cantonment, contains a large number of comfortable bungalows, surrounded by well-shaded compounds, and the roads—which run at right angles—are kept in a very clean condition. A distinct contrast is presented by the other division, the native part of the town, as it is a real hive of hard-working traders, many of whom have become exceedingly wealthy. Local government by a Municipal Council was granted in the year 1866, but it must be confessed that the bulk of the improvements in the town have been carried out chiefly by the Rajah of Vizianagram and his ancestors, and that the sixteen representatives of the people have been quite content to enjoy the honours of office without bearing a due share of responsibilities. The town is indebted to the Rajah and his family for a college, a Sanskrit school, hospitals, and the Prince of Wales' Market, while the councillors claim credit for a clock-tower in Santapeta Street, at a cost of about Rs. 5,000, and for their municipal offices, upon which the sum of Rs. 7,500 was spent. Another important municipality in the district of Vizagapatam is Anakapelle, which is situated about 21 miles to the west of the town of Vizagapatam, and has a population of about 20,000 inhabitants. It has a well-earned reputation for its industries in brass and iron vessels, cotton cloths, sheetings, woven jute, jaggery, glass bangles, and brass and metal work, and in its large markets, held on Sundays, purchases may be made of most of these articles. Bimlipatam, the fourth municipality as regards size in the district, is very picturesquely situated at the mouth of the Chittavalasa River, and statistics show that it is the busiest seaport in the district. There is a very considerable export trade in manganese, jute, cotton fabrics, jaggery, tobacco, and surplus stocks of agricultural produce, while the chief imports consist of piece goods, sugar, iron, and other metals. It is reported that in the seventeenth century the Dutch constructed a fort here, which measured 135 yards from east to west, and 145 yards from north to south, but there is very little to be seen at the present day beyond a flagstaff bastion.

APPANA VENKATA KRISHNAYYA.

1. Appana Venkata Krishnayya. 2. Office Premises. 3. Cotton Ginning and Rice Factory.

When the 566th milestone from Madras is reached the train enters the district of Ganjam, which is bounded on the north by Puri, in Orissa, and on the east by the Bay of Bengal. The district proper contains a population of about 1,870,800 individuals, but the inhabitants of the Agency—about 350,000 in number—must also be taken into consideration.

Mr. Francis, in his explanation of the teım "Agency," says that it consists of "certain areas which are inhabited by backward people to whom it is considered inexpedient to apply the whole of the ordinary law of the land. They are accordingly administered under a special enactment by the Collector in his special capacity of 'Agent to the Governor' for these tracts; the ordinary courts of justice have no jurisdiction within the agencies, and the Agent is endowed with unusual powers, he being the chief civil and criminal tribunal."

The only three municipalities in the district are Berhampore, with a population of 31,000 inhabitants, Parlakimedi, having 18,300 residents, and Chicacole, numbering about 17,500 persons.

APPANA VENKATA KRISHNAYYA

The town of Bezwada, in the district of Kistna, has every reason to be proud of one of her inhabitants, not merely for his successful business career, but on account of his wise philanthropy in the distribution of the wealth which he has acquired. That individual, the subject of these notes, having separated from his brother in the year 1890, established himself independently as a merchant, dealing principally in rice, cotton, gunny-bags, kerosene oil, and other goods. Business capabilities thrown into the right groove, and upright methods in the conduct of trading, told their tale in this instance, as they have done in thousands of others.

Venkata Krishnayya Garu became an exporter of grain to all parts of India, and he also started banking operations, through which he was able to render valuable assistance to his customers, while at the same time he was advancing his own interests. In the year 1900 he acquired a mill of a dual character, where cotton is ginned and rice is ground, during their respective seasons, by the same machinery. About 400 bags of paddy can now be dealt with daily, and the product is consigned to the chief towns in India. Cotton to the weight of about 60 candies (one candy = 500 lb.) can be ginned in a day, and the greater portion of the manufactured article is disposed of to European firms in India.

It was at the instigation of Venkata Krishnayya Garu that Sri Tripura Sundari Cotton Press Co., Ltd. (of which he is the secretary and treasurer), was formed in 1904. Modern machinery, including a 40-h.p. steam-engine, was imported from England, and some 200 bales of cotton are passed through the plant in a single day. Venkata Krishnayya Garu is a busy man, controlling every branch of his business and supervising the work of a large number of mill-hands and clerical assistants. He has also unselfishly devoted a considerable portion of his time to the welfare of the public by serving as an honorary magistrate for fifteen years. He is a prominent member of the "Vaisya" community, and is secretary of the charities instituted by them, which are known as Sri Kanyaka Parameswari charities. Under their auspices Sri Kanyaka Parameswari Hindu High School—of which he is the secretary—is maintained at Bezwada, where nearly 700 boys are educated. He has, further, at his own cost, constructed at Bezwada a fine temple and a commodious choultry, which are being maintained from his private funds.

B. CHANNAYYA BROTHERS.

BALABADRUNI CHANNAYYA AND SON.

B. CHANNAYYA BROTHERS

The partners in this firm belong to one of the oldest and most respected families in the district of Vizagapatam, and they have either inherited or acquired about 400 acres of land in addition to a quantity of household property in Bimlipatam, the headquarters of the taluq of the same name. It is, however, the commercial enterprises of Messrs. Channayya Brothers with which we are now more particularly concerned. A general commission agency business was commenced in or about the year 1880 by Mr. Grandhy Gurayya, the maternal grandfather of the present owners, and, notwithstanding the unpretentious character of the venture, the founder's energy and obliging habits succeeded in building up a sound trading concern, to which banking was added in 1900. Mr. Gurayya died four years later, and Mr. Channayya and two brothers became proprietors.

The firm have discontinued buying on commission, and now purchase large quantities of various kinds of oil-seeds, jute, hemp, jaggery, and other produce which are sold to European firms who export direct to other countries. Some idea of the extent to which this business has grown may be gathered from the fact that during the year 1914 no less than 80,000 candies (480 lb.) of jute and nearly 2 lakhs of bags of oil-seeds passed through the hands of the partners, and these are only two items which have been culled from the firm's books. It may here be remarked that this huge concern is the natural outcome of the remarkable business capacity and sterling qualities of Mr. B. Channayya.

The banking business is run upon strictly economic principles, and it is conducted entirely for the convenience of customers from whom produce is bought.

Godowns, which are capable of holding 10,000 bags of produce, are situated on a bank of backwater of the River Gosthani, and merchandise is conveyed by surf-boats to steamers which lie about a mile from the shore of Bimlipatam port.

The 400 acres of land belonging to the partners consist of 100 acres on the banks of the Kistna River, near Bezwada, which are irrigated from adjoining canals; a further 200 acres on the Navagal River, and balance of 100 acres in the neighbourhood of Bimlipatam.

Mr. B. Channayya is a member of the Municipal Council of Bimlipatam, and President of the Saraswati Samaj Association. He is also director of the Bimlipatam and Calingpatam Jute Baling Company, Ltd.

THE ELLORE RICE MILLS

Real progress has been made in recent years in local government matters and in the social conditions of the inhabitants of the district of Kistna, and it is generally admitted that much of the credit for these developments is due to the ceaseless energy and the wise counsel of Mr. Mothay Gangu Raju of Ellore. This gentleman was one of the promoters of the Kistna Jute & Cotton Mills Co., Ltd., at Ellore, and he was the constructor and is now manager of the rice mills at the same place, which belong to his joint family.

Building operations were commenced in the year 1900, and before the close of the year the necessary quantity of machinery had been imported from England through the agency of Messrs. Ralph Douse & Co., of Bombay. The premises were of comparatively small dimensions, and after the lapse of five years it was found that the business had grown to such an extent that additional space and machinery had become necessary. A suitable piece of land adjoining the Kistna Mills was secured for the new structure, and an installation of new plant, together with the best part of the old, was carried out at the earliest possible moment. The new arrangements enabled the owner to increase his turnover to a very considerable extent, and the mills are now capable of dealing daily with 1,000 bags of paddy, each one weighing 166 lb. Machinery is driven by steam obtained from three engines, namely, a 20-h.p. "Atlas," and two others of 14-h.p. respectively. Two of these drive the plant for the production of boiled rice, while the third is used for the hulling and other processes through which the paddy is passed. Boiling takes place during each night, with steam derived from two boilers, each of which has a pressure of 125 lb. Paddy, purchased locally, is conveyed to the mills by bullock-cart, railway, and canal—chiefly the last-named, and the prepared rice is sent by train to Coconada, where it is shipped to Ceylon and Mauritius.

All the buildings are very substantially built of brick, stone, and wood, but special mention should be made of the offices, manager's bungalow, and godowns, which are capable of holding 50,000 bags of paddy and 10,000 bags of rice. The mills have a floor area of 38,063 square feet.

Mr. Atchayya is, further, a general merchant and banker, advancing money to clients—including Zemindars and other notable persons—on security of landed property, and the family to which he belongs are owners of the Zemindary of Vissannapett, about 35 miles distant from Ellore, and of considerable property in the Kistna and adjoining districts. The greater portion of these lands are situated on the banks of canals, and are, in consequence, easily navigated by the *ryots* to whom they are leased for growing paddy. There are, however, about 1,000 acres adjoining the Kollar Lake, and about 6 miles distant from Ellore, which cannot be irrigated from canals, and to meet this difficulty a pumping system has been installed by which water is raised from the lake and subsequently deposited on the fields. The pumping is done by two Ruston & Proctor oil-engines of 60-h.p. and 20-h.p. respectively. About 200 hands are employed constantly.

Reference has already been made to the personality of Mr. Mothay Ganga Raju, but a word or two must be added as to the lavish scale upon which he distributes his wealth. Acts of benevolence, unrecorded perhaps in any list of donations, are a matter of daily occurrence, but there are those lasting memorials of brick and stone which are permanent reminders of that deeply-rooted sympathy for his fellow-beings which is one of Mr. Ganga Raju's strongest characteristics. One of his benefactions is a choultry at Ellore, built in memory of his father, Mr. Mothay Venkataswamy. At this institution arrangements have been made for the daily feeding of any number of poor people of any creed or caste, and funds to the extent of Rs. 30,000 have been provided for the maintenance of the building and for the continuation of this truly magnificent work.

THE INDIAN LEAF TOBACCO DEVELOPMENT COMPANY, LTD.

This company was formed with the definite object of growing, curing, purchasing, and manufacturing Indian tobacco, but operations have recently been confined to growing and purchasing the leaf. Cultivation is now restricted exclusively to the northern fields of the continent, while grading and other processes of the enormous quantity which is bought annually are carried on at Guntur, the administrative capital of the district of the same name, which is situated on the east of the Presidency.

The company are said to be the largest individual buyers of tobacco in South India. All purchased tobacco is graded by expert Europeans, who have had a long practical acquaintanceship in growing and curing.

The methods of curing adopted by *ryots* were exceedingly crude until the establishment of this company, when these agriculturists profited by instruction and practical demonstrations given to them.

Trade returns show that fully 75 per cent. of South Indian tobacco is sent to Burma for the manufacture of cheroots.

INNES & CO.

Coconada, now one of the busiest seaport towns in the Presidency of Madras, had not reached a position of importance in the early forties of the nineteenth century, when Messrs. E. de Lenares & Co. established themselves there as general exporting and importing merchants. The expansion of business, however, was contemporaneous with the growth of the town, and in 1873 the *personnel* of the firm was entirely changed and the name was altered from Lenares & Co. to Innes &

THE ELLORE RICE MILLS.

1. FRONT VIEW OF THE MILLS. 2. BACK VIEW. 3. HULLING MACHINES AND RICE STORAGE ROOM. 4. PADDY DRYING PLATFORMS. 5. PROPRIETOR AND STAFF.

Co., the partners at that date being Messrs. J. L. Innes, G. Innes, and K. Narsinga Row. Upon the death of Mr. G. Innes, the two remaining partners continued trading until 1895, when Mr. K. N. Row was succeeded by his son, Mr. K. Suryanarayanamurty Naidu, who has been sole proprietor since 1908, when Mr. J. L. Innes retired.

The firm are exporters of all kinds of local produce, including seeds of all descriptions, jute, hemp, coir yarn, rice, ground-nuts, cane jaggery, and rice-meal, to all parts of the world. Agents have been appointed at all coast ports from Calcutta to Madras, while the firm's European correspondents are Messrs. Forbes, Forbes, Campbell & Co., in London, Messrs. Erhardt & Co., Ltd., of Hamburg, and Messrs. H. Beau & Co., at Marseilles.

The business premises, which abut upon bank and post office roads, form a compact square block, and they include offices, godowns, stores, and a building which is leased to the Government postal authorities. The whole of the property is almost on the bank of the mighty River Godaveri, which ranks next in importance in India to the Ganges and Indus, being about 900 miles in length, and receiving the drainage from 115,000 square miles. All goods intended for export are loaded upon lighters in the river, and are subsequently transferred to ocean-going steamers, which are compelled to anchor about 7 miles from the town owing to shallow water in Coringa Bay. Messrs. Innes & Co. are owners of three sailing vessels which ply between Coconada and Rangoon, Moulmein, Cochin, Colombo, and other ports; their canal boats are used for conveying paddy to the Coringa Company's factory (this factory is referred to below), and their lighters are capable of accommodating from 250 to 800 bags of produce. The firm's salt (credit) branch has grown extensively and the annual turnover is now between 2½ and 3 lakhs of rupees. Several islands in the Godaveri River have been leased from the Government with the view of growing tobacco, and of demonstrating what can be accomplished by properly directed irrigation. Four Hornsby oil-engines of 24 h.p., 16 h.p., 12½ h.p., and 7 h.p. respectively drive centrifugal pumps which raise water from the river and from wells, but there are, in addition, a few hand pumps for irrigating seed-beds upon which a comparatively small quantity of moisture is required. Pumps and other plant were ordered according to suggestions made by Government officials who are engaged in making experiments with tobacco, cholam, jute, sugar-cane, chillies, and plantains, but the first two of these are regarded as being the most important.

Mr. Naidu has always been a public-spirited man, and the Government, in recognition of his many acts of generosity, and in honour of his work upon the Municipal Council, of which he is the present chairman, conferred upon him the title of Rao Bahadur in 1911. One particularly worthy instance of Mr. Naidu's benevolence was the gift of land for a dispensary at Coconada, which is controlled by the municipality chiefly for the benefit of indigent persons. Mr. Naidu has been for several years a member of the taluq and district Boards; he has a seat upon the Port Conservancy Board, and he is one of the managing committee of Pittapur Raja's College. He is, further, the owner of a considerable quantity of land and household property in Coconada and in surrounding districts. Mr. G. M. Lake is manager of the business; the clerical staff numbers from 60 to 80 hands, and the coolies vary from 50 to 200 according to the time of year.

The firm are agents for the Ellerman Steamship Lines (City & Hall), the Société de Navigation a Vapore de Veneiza, the New Zealand Insurance Company, the Commercial Union Fire Assurance Company, and the Gokak Water Power and Manufacturing Company of Bombay.

THE CORINGA COMPANY, LTD.

The business of rice-milling carried on by this company was established in 1834 by Mr. E. D. Lenares, who continued it in his own name until the year 1872, when he retired into private life upon the formation of the Coringa Company, Ltd. All the shares were taken up in Coconada, and nearly three-fourths of them were obtained by Mr. K. S. Naidu. The property of the company is situated upon one of the banks of the Godaveri River at Nellapally, about 14 miles distant from Coconada, and it includes two rice-mills, factory, godowns, offices, and other buildings. A private canal which connects the river with the factory compound greatly facilitates the movement of produce, as paddy can be taken by boats direct to the mills, while the cleaned rice can be conveniently handled when it is ready for export. The machinery has been replaced by thoroughly up-to-date plant driven by steam, and each mill has a capacity for dealing with 1,000 bags of rice in a working day of 12 hours. The output of the mills comprises boiled and raw rice, and consignments are shipped to Java, Singapore, Japan, Ceylon, Mauritius, and practically all South Indian ports.

A European manager is in charge of each mill, and about 200 coolies are employed regularly.

THE KRISHNA JUTE AND COTTON MILLS COMPANY, LTD.

When this company was formed in July 1904, Messrs. Mothay Ganga Raju and Mothay Subbarrow were desirous that the whole of the shares to be issued should be taken up by residents in the town or neighbourhood of Ellore, in the district of Kistna, and they were not disappointed in this respect, as, with a nominal capital of 5 lakhs of rupees, the sum of Rs. 4,48,500 was subscribed locally. It was originally proposed to erect buildings for the milling of jute and cotton, and although a factory was constructed, and necessary shafting was installed in connection with the latter commodity, no further steps have been taken with regard to that portion of the proposal. The jute mill, which was completed in 1907, is a substantial brick and stone building, with structural ironwork, and it comprises a main hall, godowns for jute and sundry tools, workshops, stores, boiler and other tools, offices, and manager's bungalow.

The directors were determined to have the best machinery procurable, and they obtained through the well-known firm of Messrs. Marshall Sons & Co., Ltd., of Gainsborough, England, and of Bombay, one steam engine of 750 i.h.p., and two boilers, while an emergency boiler was purchased from Messrs. Spurr, Inman & Co., Ltd. The most modern description of plant has been secured from leading makers, and it includes machinery for the following purposes: Jute softening, breaker cards, finisher cards, first drawing, second drawing, roving, 1908 spindles, warp and weft, winding, beaming, 85 looms, measuring, damping, calendering, cutting, and baling press. There is, further, a cleaning and teasing machine which is used for the second handling of wastage from the first process, the resulting product being available for making ropes for tying bales. Three-ply and

INNES & CO. (THE CORINGA COMPANY).

1. The Office. 2 The Staff. 3. Coringa Company, Ltd. (Rice Mills). 4. Paddy Landing-place.

THE KRISHNA JUTE AND COTTON MILLS COMPANY, LTD.

1. General View. 2. Spinning, Winding, and Roving Department. 3. Looms, Calendering and Measuring Machines. 4. Main Engine-room, 5. Secretary, Manager, and Clerical Staff.

five-ply twists are made for stitching and darning bags, as well as for sale.

About 8,000 gunny-bags are made in the mill every day, and this, as a rule, involves the consumption of from 25 to 30 candies of jute, although the actual output depends largely upon the quality of the raw material. The standard sizes of bags are 40 in. by 29 in., 40 in. by 28 in., 44 in. by 28 in., 34 in. by 28 in., and 40 in. by 24 in., the last of which is made of striped material. About 7,000 candies (500 lb. each) of jute are required annually, but an ample supply is procurable in the Kistna and adjoining districts, the best samples being obtained in the neighbourhood of Vizianagram.

There is always an exceedingly good demand for gunny-bags throughout Southern India, but the supply is invariably insufficient during the harvest season, from November to March. Sewing of the bags by hand is considered to be far more satisfactory than work done by machinery, and women stitchers, who are paid at the rate of 2 annas for 25 bags, can earn from 6 to 8 annas daily. Cloth, 30 inches in width, is woven under contract, and a weaver can usually make from 12 annas to 1 rupee daily.

A good supply of water is secured for the mill by gravitation through pipes from a canal which is fed by the River Kistna, and there is, in addition, a storage tank in the compound which is capable of holding a sufficient quantity for nearly five months. The workshops are fitted with lathes, circular saws, machines for drilling, wood turning, and planing, and all ordinary repairs for the company's mill and for others in the vicinity are carried out by skilled mechanics. There is also a foundry.

The premises are about a mile and a half distant from the railway station at Ellore, and they cover an area of about 8 acres. The workpeople include men, women, and children (all of whom are obtained locally), and constant work is found for from 650 to 700 persons.

Mr. Mothay Ganga Raju is secretary and treasurer, and Mr. C. F. W. O'Brian is manager and engineer.

MOOTHA MANIKYAM

A banking, exporting, and commission agency business, founded at Coconada in 1860 by the late Mr. Mootha Ramannah Garu, was, on the death of the proprietor, taken over as a family concern by the elder son. The latter was anxious to retire into private life in 1910, and he and his brother, Mr. Mootha Manikyam, agreed upon a division of the estate, the younger son becoming sole owner of the original business. The system of banking is thoroughly up-to-date in all its branches, and the clients are not only numerous but they include some of the most influential Zemindars and notabilities of the Godaveri and other districts. Money is advanced to regular customers on security of land, crops, and occasionally jewellery.

The quantity and value of exported goods have increased very considerably in recent years, and consignments now include cane jaggery, castor, cotton, and gingelly seeds; ground nuts; *nux vomica*; myrobolans, rice meal; fibre, hemp, jute, cotton; various kinds of oil, and rice, paddy, grams, and grains. The greater portion of the exports are sent to London, but a market for paddy and rice is found in Ceylon. Produce of all descriptions is purchased on commission, and Mr. Manikyam is prepared to transact business in any part of the world and to

MOOTHA MANIKYAM.

1. MOOTHA MANIKYAM. 2. OFFICE.

undertake the importing of goods under the commission system.

This gentleman is the owner of a considerable quantity of landed property in the district of Godaveri, and of bungalows and commodious residences in the town of Coconada. As an instance of the profitable nature of the undertakings, and of the large-hearted generosity of Mr. Manikyam and his brother, it may be mentioned that, when the partition of the estate was effected in 1910, they allotted a sum of Rs. 75,000 (Rs. 50,000 in cash, and the balance in landed property) for the purpose of building a choultry at Coconada, and of providing food for travellers, and for Sanskrit and Vedic students. Rs. 5,000 were given to Coconada Annadana Samajam (a refreshment house for the poor), which is a public institution supported entirely by voluntary contributions. A sum of Rs. 1,500 was presented by Mr. Mootha Manikyam alone to the fund for securing educational facilities for Vysia students.

This busy banker merchant is also a partner in the firm of Messrs. Roberts & Co., cigar manufacturers, of Coconada ; he is a member of the local literary association or native club, and he is a director of the Coconada Trading Co., Ltd.

MAJETY SRISAILAM PANAKALU & CO

The four partners in this firm are members of the Majeta family, who have been established in the village of Kantam Raju Kondur for several generations. Their ancestors were distinguished as men of sterling conduct and as generous helpers of religious movements, and these characteristics are strongly exemplified in the descendants of to-day. In or about the year 1900 three brothers, including two members of the present firm, built a Siva temple at Bathapudi, near Mangalagiri, and the donors not only support this building at their own expense, but they bear the entire cost of an annual festival there.

The business now carried on by the firm was established at Guntur about the year 1884 by M. Veerayah (a brother of one of the present proprietors), who traded in salt and other commodities. The original name of the firm was M. Muthiyaloo and Sree Saylam, but it was changed to Majety Srisailam Panakalu three years later, when the partners were Sree Salem Majety and M. Panakalu. These two have now (1914) been joined in partnership by M. Subbarayadu and Mr. Guravayah, and the four relatives have now established an extensive connection in Southern India as commission agents for the sale of all kinds of grain, rice, dhall, chillies, tobacco, and coriander and other seeds. The firm buy and sell on commission, but they have standing orders with merchants in a large way of business for supplying them at current market rates with various sorts of merchandise and of agricultural and general produce. A special feature is made of dealing in chillies, and very large quantities of these pods and of rice and grain are consigned to Madras city.

The telegraphic address of the firm is "Srisailam, Guntur."

RIPLEY & CO.

An Indian merchant's business, consisting largely of commission agencies and exporting, was founded by the late Mr. George Ripley at Bimlipatam, in the district of Vizagapatam, about 1854, and the enterprise has grown with the years to such an extent that the annual shipments of locally-grown produce by the above firm amount to about 25,000 tons. Branches have been opened at Coconada, Vizagapatam, Colingapatam, and Baruna, while an office was opened in 1904 at No. 6-8, Crutched Friars, London, under the style of Messrs. Sydenham & Plund.

All kinds of produce are consigned to Europe and the United States of America, while the imports include bar-iron and cement. The firm are agents for the following companies : The British India Steam Navigation Company, the Clan Line of Steamers, the Commercial Union Insurance Company, and the British Dominions General Insurance Company, and they are managing agents for the Bimlipatam and Colingapatam Jute Baling Co., Ltd. The last-named company was formed in 1905 with a capital of $1\frac{1}{2}$ lakhs of rupees, and its four hydraulic presses are turning out some 700 bales daily during the season (bales of 400 lb.), although each machine is capable of pressing 225 bales in eleven hours.

The premises at Bimlipatam are situated on the sea front, and comprise offices, godowns, stores, and sheds. The branch businesses at Colingapatam and Coconada are managed by Europeans.

Y. VUPPANAH BROTHERS.
1. Office Premises. 2. Godowns.

Y. VUPPANAH BROTHERS

Competition in all branches of commercial life has become so keen that business men who lack enterprise and energy soon find that they are being left behind in the race for success, and their experiences resolve themselves into a mere struggle for existence. It is a pleasure, therefore, to visit an establishment such as that of Messrs. Y. Vuppanah Brothers, who have made remarkable progress since the year 1912, whe. ey commenced trading as general me iants at Coconada.

There is an all-pervading atmosphere of what the Americans call "hustling," and the spirit of determination is stamped on the faces of the brothers. Large transactions take place in rice, paddy, and general produce, and some of the best customers of the firm are resident in Mauritius and Ceylon. A small rice mill at Coconada is employed almost wholly in connection with the firm's own produce, although milling is done for a few regular customers. Produce is conveyed by native sailing craft from Coconada to steamers which are anchored about 7 miles distant from land. Messrs. Y. Vuppanah Brothers are owners of a few paddy fields, but as the yield is altogether insufficient for their requirements, large quantities of grain are purchased from local growers. Between 4 and 5 lakhs of bags of rice are already being handled in the course of a year, but this number will, doubtless, be greatly exceeded when the business-like qualifications of the partners are more widely known.

Godowns, which are capable of holding 10,000 bags of rice, have been secured, and as they are situated on the banks of the Godaveri Canal, they afford peculiar facilities for the transport of produce. A factory has recently been opened where a staff of skilled workmen is employed in turning out all kinds of carriages which are completed with thoroughly up-to-date fittings. A speciality is made of the painting of motor and other cars, and of repairs to every kind of vehicle. Although this branch of business has only just been commenced, the brothers have met with most encouraging support from important local personages for whom orders have been executed.

The brothers have appointed agents at Tenali, Bezwada, Ellore, Rajahmundry, Salur, Parvatipur, and Berhampore, in order to meet the requirements of their customers, but all correspondence is passed through the head office at Coconada.

Messrs. Vuppanah Brothers personally undertake the management of the business, but they have admitted two working men as silent partners.

About 100 coolies are employed in addition to the factory artisans.

GRINDING RICE FLOUR.

Photo by J. B. D'Cruz.

TWISTING FIBRE COCHIN STATE.

INDUSTRIES

By K. TRESSLER, Director of Industries

INDIA, a country which possesses one of the oldest civilizations, can claim also to have one of the most ancient industrial systems. There are frequent references in the Rig Veda (1500 B.C.), indicating that many arts had at a remote period been carried to a high state of excellence, and in the Yajur Veda mention is made of gold-cloth, or brocade. In the Institutes of Manu (prior to A.D. 200) also many passages occur bearing on industrial occupations, as, for instance (chapter xiii., 130): "Let a weaver who has received ten palas of cotton thread give them back increased to eleven by the rice-water and like used in weaving. He who does otherwise shall pay a fine of twelve panas."

During the Middle Ages Indian productions, more particularly textiles, were highly prized in Europe, and were largely exported. Indeed, it may be said that until the beginning of the new industrial era, which dates back to the discovery of the steam-engine (1784), industries in India were at least as important and highly developed as those of any other country. Many kinds of cloth, for instance, owe their name to their Indian place of origin, e.g. calicoes (Calicut), muslins (Masulipatam), and Salampore to the town of that name. During the last century and a quarter, however, European countries generally have modified their method of production in accordance with modern industrial principles; whereas in India the more primitive system of industry, which may be termed the "cottage system," still prevails. Indeed, until about ten years ago, it might be said that, with the exception of a certain number of spinning-mills in Bombay and Calcutta, industries of the modern factory type was non-existent in India.

About that time a wave of patriotic enthusiasm, which revealed itself in one way by a series of political crimes, and in another by an attempt to displace foreign imports by indigenous goods, passed over India. A very considerable amount of money was sunk in various enterprises, but the individuals who started them, though in some cases actuated by excellent motives, were usually nothing more than amateurs, and, to any one not blinded by patriotic zeal, it was clear from the first that, in competition with European manufactures representing the result of at least a century of evolution, these attempts were doomed to failure.

The position was at once pathetic and ridiculous. The childlike confidence in human honesty that prompted one sugar-company to hand a large part of their capital over to a "Mr. Jones, of Glasgow," on his promise to purchase machinery, and the bewilderment of the company when repeated telegrams to "Jones, of Glasgow," failed to elicit a

1. A POTTERY BAZAAR. 2. BANGLE BAZAAR. 3. TODDY-TAPPER CLIMBING COCONUT TREE.

Photos by Nicholas & Co.

4. TWISTING COIR, COCHIN. 5. KNIFE-GRINDER.

Photo by Nicholas & Co.

response, together with the failure of another company for the reason that the secretary had spent all the capital for immoral purposes, are facts which throw a certain amount of light on the character of Swadesi enterprise ten years ago. The fact of the matter was that none of these *entrepreneurs* had even the haziest notion as to what industry really meant. As scheme after scheme failed, they began to see that something was wrong; but even then they did not properly realize where the fault existed. The root of the trouble lies in the Indian social system—the caste system. For a primitive civilization. the division of labour into water-tight compartments, so to speak, has much in its favour, but it precludes any form of co-operation (which is the essence of modern industry), and it stifles progress. It discourages independent thought, and leads to the acceptance of authority rather than reason. Thus it came about in the course of time that the work of the hereditary labouring classes degenerated into the slavish reproduction of the methods of their primitive ancestors, while the intellect of the country devoted itself to speculation in intellectual philosophy. The spread of education has scarcely influenced the working classes at all, and so far as the intellectual individuals are concerned it has only slightly diverted their course of thought from the purely metaphysical to the scarcely less abstract and impractical mazes of legal thought. What the nineteenth century produced was a philosophically minded class, with a fine contempt for all kinds of manual labour, and completely dissociated from intelligent working men. This is not a promising basis upon which to build up industries.

The failure of the first Swadesi movement led to a reaction, and for the next few years capitalists were chary of investing capital. With a view of encouraging commercial enterprises a special "Department of Industries" was created in Madras. As a result of this step, and possibly for other reasons also, popular notions regarding industry have become a good deal healthier during the last decade, but even so, the time when South India will be in a position to undertake manufacturing on modern lines is still remote. The educated Indian is fond of committing his thoughts to paper, and he invariably writes a great deal of arrant rubbish on this subject. Occasionally sensible views are expressed, but views by themselves are of little use, and the translation of theory into practice still presents difficulties which, if not exactly insuperable, are very great. Although considerable progress has been made, the Indian has not yet accepted the fact that modern industry is an essentially Western conception, and one therefore that must be approached from the Western, or practical, point of view. He still has a feeling that the things to which he attaches value—knowledge of his classics and University degrees—must be regarded as industrial assets, and, possessing qualifications of this kind, he is unwilling to undergo that lengthy practical apprenticeship which is the essential condition for success.

Accordingly, we find a youth with a B.A. degree and a few months' technical study posing as a technical expert, and questions such as costs, round which modern manufacture turns, are ignored because there are no University classes in such subjects. For the same reason, initiative and originality are not adequately developed.

Whether these defects can be overcome by technical education is too large a question to discuss here, but it is evident that until a good deal more progress has been made the chances of industry on a modern manufacturing basis in India are in the hazy future.

This fact has been recognized by Government, and the policy of the Department of Industries is in the first instance to develop technical education. At the same time it is felt that industry itself should not be entirely ignored, and although manufacture, as carried on in Europe, is at present out of the question, steps are being taken to pave the way for such an ultimate development by encouraging small industrial units in which individuals can obtain some elementary idea without the risk attaching to production upon up-to-date methods.

The following table indicates more or less the present industrial position :—

Description of Occupation.	Males.	Females.	Total.	Large Factories.		Small Factories.		Cottage Industry.	Miscellaneous.
				No.	No. of Workers.	No.	No. of Workers.	No. of Workers.	No. of Workers.
Planting, etc.	19,645	15,795	35,440	106	30,045	97	5,395	—	—
Mining	4,886	3,446	8,332	21	7,015	27	1,317	—	—
Salt	769	282	1,051	—	—	—	—	—	—
Textiles	452,081	288,372	740,453	30	24,047	79	3,889	712,517	—
Hide and skins	49,632	6,914	56,546	10	1,620	60	2,955	51,971	—
Wood	198,036	82,480	280,516	5	1,044	16	724	278,748	—
Metals	73,987	7,102	81,089	15	3,880	19	4,690	72,519	—
Ceramics	85,147	47,799	132,946	16	3,858	34	1,395	127,693	—
Chemical products, etc.	20,614	8,189	28,803	11	4,048	45	1,944	—	—
Food industries	37,186	134,221	171,407	26	6,131	123	5,560	—	159,716
Industries of dress and toilet	134,185	30,457	164,642	5	1,189	12	523	162,930	—
Furniture industries	1,654	241	1,895	1	134	3	185	1,576	—
Building industries	199,883	83,988	283,871	2	524	3	98	—	283,249
Construction of means of transport ...	19,999	6,581	26,580	21	14,673	19	923	10,984	—
Production and transformation of physical forces	419	13	432	1	207	3	176	—	—
Industries of luxury, printing, book-binding, etc.	121,916	8,568	130,484	20	5,652	35	1,604	123,228	—
Totals	1 420,039	724 448	2,144,487	290	104,067	575	31,378	1,542,166	442,965

It will be observed that there are more than 2,000,000 individuals, or about 5 per cent. of the population, engaged in industry of one kind or another. Of the total number of industrial workers, rather more than 70,000 are employed in what are classed as large factories.

1. SORTING TANNED SKINS. 2. SORTING RAW SKINS. 3. PRESSING BALES OF SKINS. 4. KNIFE-WORK BARK PROCESS.

But this number includes 30,000 under the head of "Planting," the majority of whom are engaged in tea-picking, and it also includes 10,000 workers in factories which are classed as "large" (because a considerable number of individuals are employed), but which in reality provide only unskilled employment, as, for instance, fish-curing, oil-installations, and others. If allowances are made for work of this kind, the total number of individuals who can really be regarded as industrial workers in large factories falls to about 60,000, and 24,000 of these are operatives in cotton-mills and 15,000 workers in railway or dockyard workshops. Apart from "Planting" factories (most of which are managed if not owned by Europeans), there are 180 large factories in the Madras Presidency, of which nearly half are under European control and management, and provide employment for rather more than 50,000 operatives and workmen. Indian industrial enterprise is therefore limited in South India to rather less that 100 factories, wherein considerably less than 10,000 workmen are found.

It has already been observed that the Government of Madras were the pioneers of the policy of State aid for industry in India, but, broadly speaking, their policy has hitherto been the development of small industrial units rather than the inauguration of large factories. The undertakings falling under the "large factory" class therefore may be regarded generally as the results of private European enterprise, while industries of the "small factory" class, on the other hand, mostly owe their inception to State aid of one kind or another. In 1914 there were about 500 small industrial undertakings, and 500 power-pumping plants in existence in South India. During the year 1913-14 the amount of private money handled by the Department was about five lakhs of rupees, which sum may be taken as a rough measure of the extent of the annual development of industry attributable to State aid. In addition to the development of technical education and of industrial undertakings, the Department of Industries also investigates new processes, makes practical demonstrations of improved methods, and serves as a Bureau of Information. Madras is at present the only Presidency where these practical facilities are afforded.

It has been observed that there are about 500 power-pumping plants now at work, and if "lift" irrigation can be termed an industry, it is the one which is most largely practised in the Presidency of Madras. Next to it come rice-hulling, cotton-ginning, the decortication of seed, and oil-pressing.

The number of individuals employed in small factories is about 30,000, and in small and large factories together about 135,000. As the total number of industrial workers exceeds 2,000,000, it is evident that the great majority of them are not factory workers. The building trade provides employment for about 300,000 people, and the food industry (mainly the pounding of rice and the drawing of toddy) engaged the services of 160,000 persons. The remaining industries are mostly of the "cottage" type, and the total number of these workers is about 1,500,000, or 75 per cent. of the total number of individuals registered as "industrial."

The majority of the industrial workers in South India are therefore of the "cottage" class, and their distribution is given below :—

Cotton weavers	578,000
Carpenters	146,000
Basket-makers	135,000
Boot-makers and leather workers	123,000
Potters	119,000
Workers in precious stones and metals	115,000
Blacksmiths	58,000
Rope-makers	53,000
Tailors	37,000
Silk weavers	36,000
Wool weavers	23,000
Other metal workers ...	20,000
Other Industries... ...	57,000
Total	1,500,000

Coming now to industries in detail we find that planting is very largely carried on in the Western Ghauts. The area under tea is about 63,708 acres ; coffee, 203,134 acres ; and rubber, 44,125 acres ; and the total export of these commodities in 1913-14 aggregated nearly £2,500,000 in value.

A large amount of capital is invested in mining operations in the Presidency, and reference should be made first of all to the important Kolar Gold-fields in the State of Mysore, where a considerable number of profitable mines are being worked, the chief of which is that of Oregaum. Gold is also mined in the district of Bellary. The total production of gold in the Kolar fields and in the Madras Presidency averaged during the past five years about 252,960 oz., valued at £323,450. In the northern part of Mysore there are considerable deposits of manganese ore, and in the neighbourhood of Salem iron in a very pure form (magnetic iron ore) occurs. From the Salem iron ore excellent Indian iron and steel was formerly prepared, and ancient weapons of this material are of extremely good quality. Owing, however, to the lack of fuel the ore cannot be worked in competition with imported pig or finished sections. On the coast of Travancore deposits of monazite are also worked. Deposits of very pure magnesite are found near Salem, but mining has now been discontinued. On the east coast there are considerable deposits of mica of a profitable character. The metal is obtained by surface workings, and the total exports during the year 1913-14 amounted to about 500 tons of a value of £60,000.

Coal has only been found in the district of Kistna (Singarene), but the beds are comparatively small and the output is limited. Graphite occurs on the east coast and in Tinnevelly, and ochre-earths are found in the south of the Peninsula. The name Golconda (near Bezwada) is associated with diamonds, but there are at present no workings. Copper is said to exist in Kistna, and probably there are other mineral deposits, but the resources of the Presidency have not been surveyed.

Considering the area of the Madras Presidency, mining must be regarded as being in a backward condition, excepting in connection with the two minerals of gold and mica. Private capitalists have been somewhat slow in coming forward, and it cannot be denied that they do not receive any encouragement in this direction, or otherwise they are under some restriction which makes it a very unproductive sphere for possible investors.

Although the timber reserves of Southern India are large, yet in the aggregate they are small from the industrial point of view, and owing to this shortage of fuel material expansion of industries connected with mining is not to be expected. In the Kolar Gold-fields the motive power is electricity, which is obtained from Sivasamudram, in Mysore. There are several places in the Presidency where water power is available, but hitherto no attempt has been made to utilize this source of energy, although schemes of one kind or another have been under contemplation for some time.

Salt is a State monopoly, and is obtained chiefly by the evaporation of salt water. Some pans are worked by Government, but the majority are in the hands of lessees whose output is checked by Government inspectors. The salt industry is an important one, for although the price has been materially reduced by the Government during the last few years, the total value of the prepared article during the year 1913-14 amounted to Rs. 17 lakhs.

There are several large spinning and weaving mills in the Presidency, the majority of which deal with cotton, and there is one large woollen mill in Bangalore. Twelve factories employ nearly 20,000 operatives, and the cotton-spinning and weaving industry represents by far the largest "factory" trade in the Presidency. There are also a number of cotton-ginning mills, of which, however, only four employ more than 50 workmen. Included under the heading of textile are four jute presses and two jute mills (the latter employing about 1,800 hands), besides which there are also one or two other mills of this kind started by Swadesi enterprise which are now idle.

A certain amount of industrial work is done in connection with the manufacture of coir matting, and there is one large factory for this purpose on the west coast, in addition to numerous small ones. Textiles also include palmyra-fibre, which, however, is only cleaned, and not worked up.

The remaining industries are mainly traditional cottage ones, and as these represent the most characteristic feature of Indian village life at the present moment, they may be dealt with at somewhat greater length.

As will be observed, the majority of individuals engaged in textile industries are "cottage" hand-loom workers. This industry, though very extensive, is still, so far as appliances are concerned, in a comparatively backward condition, and it is a matter of surprise that, with the equipment available, such excellent work as that which secured for India a reputation in textiles should have been turned out. The pit loom has been used until quite recently—fly-shuttles being almost unknown. The Jacquard mechanism was not employed, although complicated substitutes were in evidence. The Madura loom is a marvel of intricacy.

When the Department of Industries was first established, Mr. Chatterton, the Director, took up the hand-loom weaving question, and for the past ten years attempts have been made to popularize improved appliances throughout the Presidency. At the present moment two peripatetic weaving parties are demonstrating the advantages of fly-shuttle looms, of Jacquard attachments, and other modern appliances, and it is estimated that already more than 25,000 looms have been introduced in this manner. It is interesting also to note that in the course of the past fifteen years the number of hand-looms has increased very largely. This is a vital question to a large section of the industrial population of South India, but it is much too wide to discuss in a brief review. It is usually believed that the advent of the power-loom must necessarily lead to the abolition of hand weaving, but this presumption does not

1. REMOVING HUSK FROM COCONUT. *Photo by J. B. D'Cruz.* 2. POUNDING RICE, ALLEPPEY 3. BASKET AND MAT BAZAAR. *Photo by Nicholas & Co.*

appear to be altogether justified. It is tolerably certain that there is a permanent field for hand-loom products, in which, at any rate at present, the power-loom does not compete too severely. More especially is this the case with finer kinds of cloth, as, for instance, *angavasthrams*, with pattern borders made in Salem and Madura, women's cloths of finer quality and design as made in Tanjore, Kumbakonam, and Conjeeveram, and *gulpada* and sulseed made in Trichinopoly for the use of rich Mahommedans. The preparation of solid bordered cloths (which are in great demand) also represents a line in which power competition is not to be feared. There is also a considerable trade done in the so-called Madras handkerchiefs, which are largely sent to East Africa, and *lungis*, which are shipped in large quantities to the Straits Settlements.

Unlike other parts of India, the export of raw hides and skins is not of great importance, being much overshadowed by that of tanned goods, while in the case of hides many more are imported than are exported. During the last few years the export of raw hides has never reached 1¼ lakhs, and has on one occasion been well below Rs. 10,000. Skins to the amount of almost 43 lakhs have been exported, about 40 per cent. of these going to the United States, 20 to France, 15 to Germany, and 10 to England. These exports are, however, largely exceeded by the imports, chiefly from other parts of India by rail, which are valued at almost one crore of rupees per annum. In tanned skins the export trade is very large, aggregating during the past five years about 2¼ crores, and almost the whole of this is sent to the United Kingdom, but a very large proportion finds its way from there either to the continent of Europe or America. Except for the United Kingdom, the only country buying any quantity direct is the United States of America, which takes goods to an annual value of about Rs. 25 lakhs. Nearly all of the tanned hides are consigned to, and are used in, the United Kingdom, the quantity going elsewhere being almost negligible. The average quantity exported for the last five years has been about Rs. 1¼ crores per annum.

The process of tanning in the Madras Presidency varies little, and it consists of soaking and washing the hide or skin to free it from dirt and salt, and to soften it in the dried state. After this the hide or skin is soaked in a milk of lime until the hair becomes loose, when the latter is scraped off by means of a concave knife, the pelt being suspended on a palmyra-palm beam during the operation. The flesh is removed in a similar manner, and then the hide or skin is washed in several changes of water and worked over the beam a number of times to free it from lime. It is then put into tubs containing a certain amount of avaram (*Cassia auriculata*) bark, and handled each day for about one week, when the procedure is repeated twice or thrice if necessary. When the final dressing with bark has taken place the hide or skin is again worked on the beam, and subsequently placed in a strong infusion of myrabolans, where it is left for a few days. It is once more worked over the beam, is slightly oiled and hung up to drain, after which it is set out on a table and then dried. Finally the skins are softened and trimmed.

Many tanneries are situated in the immediate vicinity of Madras, and there are several near Trichinopoly, Dindigul, and Coimbatore, while single tanneries are found all over the Presidency, varying in size from those having only half-a-dozen workmen to some with more than a hundred. The tanneries are, as a rule, owned by Mahommedans, chiefly Labbais, but the processes are usually supervised by Pariah *maistries*, who are in many cases quite clever at their work. There is one tannery near Madras, working on modern lines, which makes several classes of finished leathers for local uses, but elsewhere nearly all of the work is done for export.

WOODWORK.

According to the census of 1911, about 6½ lakhs of the population of this Presidency were depending for their support on industries connected with wood and timber. Of these the actual workers amounted to 282,401 in number. (See Table I.)

The principal sources of supply of timber for manufacture are the forests of the Presidency, but a considerable quantity is imported from Burma, Siam, Java, and Ceylon. Teak is the wood which is most largely used, while others, such as rosewood, ebony, venteak, maruthin, and sandal are employed in conformity with the needs of the work. There is large export trade in wood and timber with foreign countries, as evidenced by the figures in Table II.

TABLE I.

	1901.			1911.		
	Males.	Females.	Total.	Males.	Females.	Total.
Sawyers, carpenters, turners, etc.	127,136	4,108	131,244	139,068	7,515	146,583
Basket-making and other industries of woody material	61,354	81,480	142,834	58,968	74,965	133,933
Cabinet-making, carriage painting, etc.	762	43	805	1,644	241	1,885
Totals	189,252	85,631	274,883	199,680	82,721	282,401

TABLE II.

	1909–10.	1913–14.
	Rs.	Rs.
Teakwood	98,000	2,47,000
Other kinds of timber	3,61,000	3,81,000
Ebony	14,000	10,000
Sandal-wood—		
Exported to United Kingdom	84,000	3,22,000
,, Germany	1,78,000	8,38,000
,, United States	2,00,000	3,00,000
,, France	78,000	1,45,000
,, other countries	14,000	78,000
Total Sandal-wood	5,54,000	16,83,000

Sandal-wood is grown chiefly in the plateau of Mysore. The best heart wood is used for carving, and the root, with the chips and shavings, is exported through the three principal seaports on the west coast. These are used for the extraction of sandal oil, and for the manufacture of scents in France and Germany. Owing to the great demand for teak for constructional purposes, railway wagons, and furniture, its price during the last decade has risen considerably, and Australian timbers, such as jarrah, have been introduced into the market in recent years. The trees are felled by Moplah merchants on payment to the owner of a *kuttikanam*, or stump fee, and after being roughly squared the logs are dragged by elephants to the depôt on the coast, or are railed by means of forest tramways, as in the Cochin State. Sawing is mostly done by hand, and gives occupation to a large number of workmen in Malabar. There are about half-a-dozen small saw-mills in the Presidency which are driven by steam, oil, or electricity, the largest of which is in Calicut.

In the section in the last census report dealing with industries the following observation occurs: "Compared with most countries of the world, in India timber is very expensive, owing not so much to the shortage of supply as to the inferior quality of the wood yielded by the timber trees of the forests. The chief defects are their great weight, extreme hardness, and rough fibrous structure."

Woodwork in Southern India has existed from ancient times as a cottage industry, while the artisan formed an important unit of the village organization in his various capacities as *thachan* (carpenter), *kollan* (blacksmith), *kannan* (brass-smith), *thattan* (goldsmith), and *kalthachan* (stonemason). To the *thachan*, or carpenter, was allotted the duty of supplying woodwork for the construction of houses, the manufacture or repair of agricultural implements and carts for *ryots*, wooden seats, benches, cots, swings, children's cradles, and other needs of the inhabitants of the village, but he was occasionally called on to make sugar and oil-crushing mills during the season.

Artisans belong to the caste called "Kammalans" in Tamil and Malayalam, "Kamasalas" in the Telugu districts, and "Panchalas" in the Bellay and Canarese tracts. In the census of 1911 they numbered eight lakhs of males and females. They trace their descent from Viswakarma, the son of Brahma, and artificer of the gods, and they dispute the superiority of the Brahman caste. Those on the east coast wear the sacred thread, just like the Brahmans, but they do not engage the service of Brahmans in their religious observances like other castes. They have *purohits* of their own, who recite the Vedic Mantras and conduct all their ceremonies similar to the Brahman, and they have their own religious head. Many of them are vegetarians; some of them, as at Perambalur, in the Trichinopoly district, even abstaining from taking ghee and milk, and use vegetable oil, asserting that the former are of fleshy origin. Though conservative in their methods of work, they are not lacking in intelligence, while many of them have taken advantage of modern education, and are employed in Government service or are practising as Vakils. The Kammalans of Malabar, on the other hand, do not claim to be equal to the Brahmans, nor do they wear the sacred thread. They accept the position of a polluting caste, and are not allowed in the temples or into Brahman houses. The highest subdivision is the Asaris, who are carpenters. These wear the sacred thread at certain ceremonies connected with house-building.

As already observed, the methods of working are those of the old world, based on the rules and principles laid down for their benefit in the Shilpa Sastra and its Agamums by their originator, Viswakarma. The tools used by the Asaris are of a most primitive type, and are wasteful of both time and energy, yet notwithstanding this the caste-men have exhibited very great skill in their work. In order to train these people in the use of modern labour-saving devices, and in the value of time as an economic factor in industry, many schools have been started by the Government and by missionary bodies. Artisan pupils, however, did not give the time necessary for proper instruction, and parents withdrew their children very frequently in the middle of their studies to help them at home, and this was before they had derived any real benefit from the classes.

The ordinary Hindu does not require and does not possess much in the way of furniture, his wants being met by a cheap wooden bedstead, a chair, a table, chest of drawers, an easy chair, one or two benches for visitors, a stool, a cashbox, and a wooden box in which he keeps costly clothes and vessels, although a sofa is sometimes used by those inclined to luxury.

It is a peculiarity of Hindus that, unlike Europeans, they manage most of their avocations in life sitting on the floor with their legs crossed, and this may account for the small quantity of furniture in their dwellings as compared with residents in the West. Articles of good workmanship and taste were manufactured in Madras twenty years ago by Messrs. Deschamps & Co., but the works have since been closed and their place taken by innumerable small shops which manufacture furniture of inferior workmanship and of little artistic merit. Latterly, however, larger firms have taken up the industry, and there are now four joinery concerns in Madras worked by power, together with seventeen others in the district worked either by power or hand. In addition to Indian manufactures a large quantity of furniture is imported, and in 1913-14 this amounted to 2¼ lakhs of rupees, consisting of—

	Rs.
Bedsteads (iron)	63,500
Other furniture of wood ...	1,31,500
Furniture of other materials...	31,000
Total	2,26,000

There is a very small export trade in goods manufactured of wood (exclusive of furniture), and it is declining rapidly, as may be seen from the following figures:—

	Manufactures in wood other than furniture.	Furniture and cabinet ware.	Total.
	Rs.	Rs.	Rs.
1909-10	80,137	16,872	97,059
1910-11	1,14,444	39,636	1,54,100
1911-12	31,611	22,616	54,227
1912-13	21,208	31,753	52,967
1913-14	13,526	32,605	46,131

WOODCARVING.

Colonel Baden Powell, R.E., writing about the carving industry of Mysore, observes: "In India, as elsewhere, the art instinct of the people first found expression in the decoration of its temples, and when the instinct grew into the desire for the decoration of dwellings or of articles in ordinary use, the figures, columns, and carvings of the temples were naturally adopted for purposes altogether outside of religion. So we find, from the beginning, that the sandal-wood carvers followed the models before them on the walls of their shrines. Unfortunately, after the architects and sculptors who elaborated the walls of Belgavi and Halabid had disappeared, a period of distinct art decadence appears to have set in, and has lasted down to the present day. No original artist arose to treat the subjects of the Hindu pantheon with entire originality or to effect modern improvements on the designs of his predecessors, and the woodcarvers have slavishly adhered to the same original models, with the result of establishing in their work a purely conventional style. In every article that we have seen, unless in the few cases where the copy of a European picture or print has been attempted, there is to be found the same ever-recurring type of Hindu god or demon, of flower, foliage, of tracery and border. There may be diversity in the arrangement or juxtaposition of each conventional part, but the art impression conveyed to the mind by one carved article, whatever it be, is exactly that conveyed by another." This description is true of the state of art in the whole of Southern India. Carving in wood was carried on to a high pitch of development in this Presidency: then there was a pause. Afterwards the same models were copied, and in many places decided decadence —even in this stagnant stage—set in, owing to lack of encouragement on behalf of the moneyed classes, and owing to the alteration of the old designs to suit the taste of the European tourists. At present in Mysore, Madura, and Travancore good, genuine specimens of the old kind of work are still produced.

Mysore is the centre of sandal-wood carving; combs, toilet and jewel boxes, small images, toys, chessmen, fans, and walking-sticks are being made. The articles turned out for Europeans are card and pencil-cases, watchstands, mirror and photograph frames, envelope boxes, album covers, inkstands, paper-cutters, pen and book-racks, and walking-sticks. Elaborately worked address-caskets, cabinets, and jewel-boxes for presentation purposes are made to order.

At Tirupathi, in the district of North Arcot, and in the adjacent villages, mythological figures are carved in red sanders-wood or white wood, and though rough in finish they are bold in style. The domestic utensils in the shape of *chembus*, cups, and plates are turned out on the lathe. These vessels are not infrequently made of Achamaram (*Hardwickia binata*), which resembles red sanders-wood, but is more liable to crack.

In Travancore very spirited and well-executed designs are carved on coconut shells; and at Karkala, in South Canara, young coconuts are in like manner neatly carved with conventional and mythological designs. This industry is carried on in the Cannanore Jail, principally by the Moplahs of Malabar.

There is a Government institution in Madras—the School of Arts—where instruction in woodcarving and other art industries is given to artisan pupils of the Presidency. The following is extracted from the account given in the monograph on woodcarving in Southern India: "This institution owes its origin to the disinterested efforts of the late Dr. Alexander Hunter, M.D., who in 1850 established at his own expense a school for the promotion and encouragement of industrial arts in the Presidency. The object was to arrest the decay of indigenous arts, and to introduce new industries where the need for such was keenly felt. After a short time the school was taken over by the Government, and during the fifty years of its existence it has done much to achieve the objects for which it was originally founded."

Woodcarving was first started in 1877 in a desultory kind of way, and later on Mr. E. B. Havell, when superintendent of the school, established a regular class with the help of one Meenakshi Asari, of Ramnad, whose services he secured during his tours. This man was succeeded by his son, R. Kalimuthu Asari, who was a student of the school for some time, and who is still in charge of the carving classes. Carving is done on teak, rosewood, and ebony.

Madura is an important centre of indigenous art handicraft. It was the capital of the Pandya kingdom, whose rajahs patronized the fine arts, and so attracted craftsmen from far and near to their courts. Domestic shrines, carved *mantapams*, sideboards, small tables, and teapoys were made until recently in the Madura Technical Institute, but this class has now been closed. A number of private dealers, however, still manufacture similar articles to order.

The Victoria Technical Institute in Madras was founded with the object of assisting industrial arts in a practical manner. It undertakes orders from Europeans, and entrusts the execution of them to really competent workmen, who work under its supervision.

With regard to the decline of woodcarving in Southern India the following note by the late Pandit Natesa Sastri, M.F.L.S., is interesting. He says: "This art had once attained higher perfection in India than in any other country, European or Asiatic. The woodwork of Gujerat in Western India, of Kashmir Lahore, and Benares in Northern India, and of Mysore and Travancore in the South, were once the best specimens of their kind in the whole world, but they have now perished with their patrons, the old kings. And the common fashion of the day is plainness, or European plainness, as some would call it, denying to those intelligent nations all love of art. There are certain things in which art would be unnecessary, and in certain others in which the want of art is felt. The Hindu always requires carvings in his doorways; his shrines where the household god is placed and worshipped are generally excellent specimens of woodwork inlaid with ivory, and the fan with which the god is fanned on the *Pujah* occasion is always a good specimen of workmanship. Now, except in the remnants of these arts which have been handed to us from old days, these works have been fast disappearing from our country, and in place of these vanishing relics a European workmanship, or an imitation of it, is adopted. I have now to remind our countrymen that what we have until now been copying as European art are only the worst specimens of it, as the best are never seen here. Between the years 1855-8, when our artists began to copy European methods a great deal, two or three Western artists, who had with them several bad specimens of their work for which they did not find any ready sale in their own country, travelled to India and sold them in the territories of Maisur and Travancore. The workmen in these places copied them and transmitted their productions to their fellow-workmen in different parts. The whole of the artists in Southern India have been copying these inferior patterns, and thus filling our country with very unsatisfactory work. Art is seldom found among the carpenters of to-day, and if we find anything at all it is a poor imitation of an old unscientific European model. The little woodwork South India can boast of is now carried on in the Ramnad and Sivaganga zemindaries of the Madura district and in Tinnevelly. The houses of the southern enterprisers, the Nattukottai-Chetties in Devakottai, and of a few other villages near Sivaganga, contain some fine carvings in wood, as also do the palaces of Sivaganga and Ramnad and the cars of Madura and Tinnevelly."

METAL-WORK.

Metallic utensils have been in use in India from very ancient time. In the Code of Manu instructions are given for cleaning copper, iron, bell-metal, and lead pots, and the followers of Islam are forbidden by their Dhuri Muktar to eat out of gold and silver plates, but to use earthen, copper, or brass ones. The latter are manufactured mostly by Kammalans and Kamasalas, of whom a brief description has been given in the section relating to woodwork. There were on March 31, 1911, about two lakhs of people dependent on metal industries for their livelihood, and 81,000 of them were actual workers, as will be seen from the following statement:—

TABLE III.

	1901.			1911.		
	Males.	Females.	Total.	Males.	Females.	Total.
1. Forging and rolling of iron and other metals	266	—	266	845	3	848
2. Ploughs and other agricultural implements	951	39	990	551	137	688
3. Makers of arms, guns, etc....	1,080	22	1,102	212	5	217
4. Other workers in iron and makers of tools	51,840	3,972	55,812	52,882	5,555	58,437
5. Workers in brass, copper, and bell-metal	14,248	826	15,074	14,672	1,095	15,767
6. Workers in other metal, tin, zinc, lead, etc.	4,237	267	4,404	4,783	307	5,090
7. Workers in mints, die-sinkers, etc.	190	—	190	42	—	42
Totals	72,812	5,126	77,838	73,987	7,102	81,089

As late as 1861 the magnetic iron ores at Kanjamali, in the district of Salem, were worked for the Porto Novo Iron Company, but the venture was given up owing to the prohibitive cost of collecting the ore and charcoal. At present all the more valuable metals required are imported in the form of sheets, ingots, or slabs. In Table IV the average imports for the five years ending 1913-14 are shown.

Iron and steel are mostly imported from the United Kingdom, Belgium, and Sweden; tin from the Straits Settlements and zinc from Belgium; while copper, German silver, and lead are obtained chiefly from Great Britain. Brass and yellow metal is sent in large quantities from the United Kingdom and Germany, and in 1913-14 more than 3,000 tons were imported, 21 lakhs of rupees in value coming from the former as against 13 lakhs from the latter country. Aluminium is supplied from the United Kingdom and the United States. The various metallic wares in use may be classified as follows: Pots for drawing, storing, and drinking water, such as *kudams, tondis, ghungalams, chembus,* and *lotahs*; cooking and eating utensils, which include *tavalais, andais, degasis,* plates, and other articles; sacrificial vessels used in divine service both in houses and temples; and other goods, such as lamps, betel, or *pan-supari* trays, boxes, spittoons, *chunam* receptacles, and locks.

Cooking and eating utensils are fashioned mostly out of bell-metal and brass, as copper is not used by Hindus for this purpose, though Mahommedans prefer to cook their food only in tinned copper vessels. Tin is not used for large waterpots on account of its heaviness and cost, and silver and bell-metal were at one time almost universally used for plates for food, but aluminium, on account of its comparative cheapness and lightness, has now begun to supersede these metals.

The processes of manufacture are hammering, beating, and casting, the last-named being done by the copper or wax process, and not by piece moulding. Sheet brass and sheet copper are never cast, but are beaten into shape, and when the article has to be fashioned out of several pieces each part is beaten to the required shape and then the whole is soldered together. Riveting is only employed with aluminium and iron. Tin vessels play an important part in the households of Hindus for minor cooking operations. The metal is received in blocks or bars, and these are melted and beaten out into various shapes. Kumbakonam is specially noted for the manufacture of such utensils. Such of these as are subjected to constant use and frequent scrubbing and washing are made in a perfectly plain form, and do not bear any ornamentation. Spinning is unknown to the majority of the Indian workmen, though it has been introduced in the aluminium industry.

The following are the remarks of Mr. W. S. Hadaway, the present superintendent of the School of Arts, on the methods of metal working: "We may find occasionally slight differences of manipulation, but in methods, and even in the tools used, the essential points are identical. A somewhat curious point is in the working up of a sheet metal which is being

TABLE IV.

Metal.	Tons.	Value in lakhs of rupees
Copper...	657	8·04
Yellow metal	3,025	28·61
German silver	113	1·63
Lead	634	1·83
Tin	150	4·09
Zinc	360	1·73
Brass	58	0·70
Aluminium	—[1]	5·39
Quicksilver	6	0·21
Iron.		
Pig and old iron	1,151	0·66
Manufacture of iron and steel, used as raw materials	43,847	67·31
Manufacture of steel	7,987	9·34
Totals	57,988	129·74

[1] Figures for 1909–10 to 1911–12 not available.

hammered into, say, a *chembu*, or some form in which there is a decided drawing in, or narrowing, of a neck or other part."

The Indian workman holds and hammers his metal in a manner which, to the European, seems back-handed; that is, the part of the object nearest him would be the part held away by the European workman, and the strokes of his hammer would be towards him instead of away from him, but the result produced is the same, while the Indian gains in one way over the European, for he invariably uses his feet to help him to steady the metal. He can thereby bring his sheet into the required form in a fewer number of "courses" than the Westerner; and were he capable, physically, of working for as many hours in the day, he would prove to be more efficient at hammered work, as he undoubtedly is already with metal which is cast.

Lathes are used to a great extent in *finishing* hammered work in India, but beyond some few large manufacturing concerns conducted more or less on European lines, they are not commonly employed by native artisans for spinning That this state of affairs may continue is a thing very much to be desired, for there is probably no mechanical metal-working process which has so little in its favour (excepting the questionable one of output) as that of spinning.

Stamping has its uses, artistic as well as otherwise; but as commonly employed in Europe it turns out the flimsiest and most tawdry examples of the metal-worker's art. The hateful "Swami" work of Tanjore, a modern phase of a once beautiful art, is an instance of the uninteresting product obtained by this questionable process, even though, in this case, the rough details from the dies are finished afterwards by hand labour. This case is, however, fortunately exceptional.

PLAIN WARES.

In almost all important towns throughout the Presidency common domestic utensils are manufactured, copper, silver, tin, aluminium, brass, bell-metal, and German silver being the metal most generally used. Enamelled ironware and tinned iron sheet are imported largely, the latter being employed for a variety of articles. Special value is attached to the waterpots made at Tanjore and Kumbakonam, the brass travelling sets and betel-boxes of Tinnevelly, the brass locks and lamps of Dindigul, the bell-metal gongs of Coimbatore, and to the brass *bohinis* of Mysore. In Malabar the braziers, known as *chembotis*, are exceptionally skilful in casting all kinds of lamps and vessels called *urulis*, these sometimes attaining 5 or 6 ft. in diameter. The bell-metal alloy used by them is specially valued, as curd is supposed to turn green less rapidly in them than in similar vessels made elsewhere. German silver was once much favoured for *lotahs*, rose-water sprinklers, sandalpelas, trays, and anklets; but it has lost its attraction as it tarnishes in time after exposure, and very rapidly if it comes in contact with brackish water. Electro-plated copper-ware is now used in its place, and enamelled iron coffee kettles, trays, tiffin carriers, ladles for serving soup, and tumblers are in extensive demand. Aluminium, although an altogether novel and recent introduction, has to a large extent supplanted German silver or enamelled iron.

MAKING PALM-LEAF MATS, COCHIN.

The aluminium industry was first started in India by the Madras Government in 1898, and was developed under the management of Mr. Alfred Chatterton. Considerable initial difficulties had to be overcome, the principal among which were the novelty of the metal to the native worker and the conservatism of the Indian population. These were patiently but slowly mastered, and in September 1903 the business was transferred to the Indian Aluminium Company, which has been carrying on the concern ever since. Gradually the metal, on account of its comparative lightness and reasonable cost, established itself in popular favour, and many private workshops subsequently took up the industry. At present the output is very considerable, and vendors in aluminium may be seen even in villages far removed from the railway, and as evidence of its increasing popularity it may be mentioned that imports of the metal have more than quadrupled during the last decade.

In decorative metal-work there has been a considerable decline (as in similar art industries), principally due to want of encouragement, but the descendants of the old artisans, known as *stapathis* and *shilpis*, who built and embellished the temples and palaces of the rajahs in ancient times, are still to be found here and there, and through the efforts of the Victoria Technical Institute they are provided with a certain amount of work. Genuine specimens of the ancient metal-work for which Southern India was once famous may be obtained from the Institute.

All processes of decoration employed in Europe for metal-work, such as inlaying or encrusting, chasing and repoussé, engraving and casting, are well known to the Indian worker, but enamelling is not now practised in the south.

The chief centres of the decorative industry are Tanjore, Tirupati, Vellore,

Travancore, Sivaganga, and Belagunta, in Ganjam, while Tanjore is noted for trays of "Swami pattern," produced for the Anglo-Indian market. The base is brass or copper; the inlay is first stamped in a mould and then chased and finished, and this is subsequently attached to the base by an under-cut outline, which is hammered over the edge of the inlay. In old specimens of this work the applied metal inlay did not bear embossed ornamentation, the decorative design being simply incised. Specimens of bowls, *chembus, pachapatrams,* spoons, caskets, and candle-stands of "Swami" ware may be seen at the Victoria Technical Institute, in Madras. Very similar work to that described is also done at Tirupati, but the inlay bears neither repoussé nor incised ornamentation, and here also small images of gods, cast in two metals, one over the other, are produced.

At Vellore brass trays with representations of mythological figures of gods, goddesses, and animals are produced. The design is sketched on the trays by incising the details, and portions of the background are pierced, but repoussé ornamentation is not resorted to.

Travancore is famous for "Koft" work, this process consisting of "silver applied either as wire or thin sheets on blackened iron. The surface of the iron is crossed by slanting strokes of a sharp chisel, which produce a roughened surface not unlike that of a file. There are sharp points to catch and hold silver sheet or wire when this is hammered on to the iron, and this beating produces a smooth, finished surface." *Hukkas,* trays, spittoons, and water vessels with spouts are made by this process. This method is distinct from "Damascening."

At Kurumbalur, in Trichinopoly, metal-work of a unique character was produced for the European market, *chembus* and other articles being cast in zinc or brass, which by juxtaposition formed different designs. Only one family is engaged in this industry, and owing to the lamentable decease of some of its members the goods manufactured are much as they were some twenty years ago, although endeavours are being made to revive the industry. A good specimen of a hand-bell made at Vizagapatam is on view at the Victoria Technical Institute; it is cast in bell-metal, and the handle is moulded in a separate piece in brass, representing the boy Krishna dancing on the Kalindi serpent, the two being soldered together.

Various kinds of toys of sheet copper, brass, and of the several kinds of alloys are also manufactured, these usually including figures of gods, men, animals, and dolls' houses. These are presented specially to infant brides at the time of marriage. A new and curious kind of flexible fish, called *Shokala Matcha* in Uriya, is made of brass or silver at Bellagunta, near Russelkonda, in the Ganjam district, but only two families are engaged in its manufacture. Other models of fishes and serpents are also made to order, and there is a good demand for these, as the workmanship is really excellent.

Inferior imitations in bronze of toads, lizards, snakes, and other animals are produced at Sivaganga and Madura, and in South Canara toys of the legendary *bhoothams,* or devils, are cast in brass and sold in large numbers.

Wherever metal-work is carried on numerous other articles are also made, such as ornamental figures, door-handles, brass fittings for carriages, seals, badges,

1. CARTING BRICKS.

2. CLEANING COCONUT FIBRE.

and inkpots. Copper and brass ornaments are very rarely worn by higher-class Hindu ladies, who prefer silver or gold; but such ornaments are very popular among the poorer class, and some of the specimens, such as those worn by the Khonds and other aboriginal ladies, are of very good design.

It will thus be observed that the requirements of the Presidency are met locally—manufactured metal utensils being imported only in small quantities, the trade has not been much influenced by modern machinery, and there are practically no exports of this class of goods.

CERAMICS.

The manufacture of earthenware appears to have been practised in India from very ancient times, and it is said that when the gods churned the ocean for nectar the necessity for something to hold the liquid was felt, and Viswakarma made the first waterpot for the purpose, Another account attributes the creation of potters to the god Siva. According to this version, it so chanced that on the occasion of the marriage of Siva with Parvati no pot could be found for the ceremonies, and Siva thereupon created a man and a woman out of the beads from his necklace, and bade them manufacture vessels for the benefit of the world.

The potters in this Presidency, called *kusavars* in Malabar, believe that they are descended from a Brahman father and a Sudra mother. They are generally of the Saivite sect, and observe all the usual Hindu festivals and ceremonies. They appear in some parts of the west coast to have acted as priests in temples before the advent of Brahmans, and they once exercised kingly sway over South India. The era current in this Presidency is named after Salivahana, the potter king. This regal race of potters has now, however, become extinct, and the potters of to-day, except in a very few instances, are poor. They are orderly and inoffensive, and not as a rule overburdened with intelligence.

Though the manufacture of domestic earthenware was practised from the remotest antiquity, the industry never got beyond the rude stage in which it exists at present almost everywhere in India. The abundance of raw material, and the ease with which it can be manipulated into vessels, have rendered it of so little value that even the poorest can afford to throw it away from time to time and replace it with new. The chief impediment to further development of the manufacture is the religious prejudice of the Hindus to the use of these vessels for any length of time. According to the Shastras an earthen vessel once touched by food is defiled, and it can only be purified by being baked again in the fire; and on the occasion of an eclipse, be it of the sun or moon, or on the occurrence of a death, either in the house or of that of a relative of the household, all the pots are thrown away. The potter has, therefore, to confine his attention to the production of cheap articles in order to meet the current demand. Indeed, no ornamentation on earthenware has ever been attempted excepting for pots used for holding the sacred fire on marriage occasions. These vessels, painted with various floral and other designs, are sent to the bridegroom's house with the bride. Thus the chief demand is for inexpensive unglazed pottery for domestic use, which includes water vessels, cooking-pots, eating and drinking vessels, oil-pots, *chatties* for storing and churning milk, smoking bowls, *hukka* bases, lamps, lampstands, ovens, and big jars for holding toddy. Various other kinds of goods are also produced, such as drums, drainage and rain-water pipes, rings for wells, shells for fireworks, grain jars (sometimes 6 or 8 ft. in height), and tiles.

The principal tools are the wheel, the turning stick, a convex stone, a wire to cut off the goods from the wheel, a series of mallets for beating out the vessels, a pot to hold water, and a scraper. The ordinary materials are the dark grey clay found in the bed of every village tank, earth from building sites, cow-dung, sand, and ashes, while clay of superior quality is also used. The method of fashioning and baking the articles resembles those adopted in other districts. The defects of this process are thus summarized by Mr. E. Holder, a former superintendent of the Madras School of Arts: Firstly, the size of the potter's wheel, which requires the potter to stoop over it in an uneasy attitude; secondly, the irregularity of its speed and a tendency to come to a standstill or to swerve in its motion; and thirdly, the time and labour expended in spinning the wheel afresh whenever its speed begins to slacken. The mode of firing is also defective, as the heat given out is not fully utilized. Big circular vessels which cannot be shaped on the wheel and other forms of ware are made by being pressed in moulds and finished off afterwards, and in this manner many of those huge earthen images of warriors, elephants, and other quaint figures which adorn the temples of local village deities are made.

In the School of Arts at Trivandrum modern methods of pottery manufacture are taught; but notwithstanding the occurrence of a variety of fine clays (including white kaolin), the industry has not attained any considerable success owing to the disinclination of the local population to use higher class goods. The small number of Europeans in Travancore can alone be depended upon to purchase the articles made in this school.

In the districts of Malabar and South Canara modern methods, such as those adopted by the Basel Mission Establishment, are followed in the manufacture of bricks and tiles, and the industry has developed to a considerable extent, as may be seen from the following figures for coastal trade:—

		Export 1903-4.	Export 1913-14.
Mangalore	...	3,91,822	7,83,338
Cochin	...	nil	1,62,432
Calicut	...	nil	52,818

From the foregoing remarks it will be observed that South India cannot be regarded as an industrial country, and that local conditions are unfavourable to industrial development as this term is understood in Europe. The requirements of the population are on the whole simple, and as such can usually be met by the village workers just as well as by organized factories.

In large cities there is no doubt an increasing appreciation of cheap luxuries, that is, of goods which can only come within the reach of the average person by being manufactured on a large scale. But the up-country districts are as yet untainted by this desire, and as long as they remain so the market for machine-made goods is likely to remain small.

There is another side of the question to be considered, namely, the scarcity of fuel and minerals, which militates against the establishment of industries on a large scale. From the industrial point of view the most important raw materials produced are cotton and oil seeds. As has already been explained, a certain number of cotton and weaving-mills have been started, but until a few years ago they were not capable of producing anything finer than 30's, and even now the bulk of the cotton is exported to Europe, where

THE CARPET-MAKING INDUSTRY.

1. Spinning and Teasing the Wool. 2. Preparing the Warps. 3. Weavers at the Loom. 4. Preparing the Dye-stuffs. 5. Indigo Vat.

it can be more advantageously handled. Large quantities of oil seeds are also produced, but these are almost entirely exported in the form of seed, partly on account of transport difficulties connected with the export of oil, and partly on account of the opportunities for adulteration which this form of export affords. A further drawback is that the residual oilcake is not generally used in India for manuring and feeding purposes. Thus the pressing of oil in the country, having usually been regarded as necessitating the subsequent export of both products, i.e. oil and cake, has not been considered as a commercial proposition, although there is a distinct future for this industry.

Another industry which offers scope for development is the manufacture of chemical or mechanical pulp from the large forest reserves of the Presidency, and at the present moment experiments are being made in the Department of Industries. The manufacture of matches and pencils is also being investigated, but such undertakings are not likely to assume large dimensions. Experiments are being conducted in the making of glassware, and proposals for the distillation of wood have been under consideration for some time. But, speaking generally, private enterprise is shy of embarking in industrial work, and it seems unlikely that Government pioneering, unless substantially backed by public opinion and public money, will achieve very much. Further, it seems questionable if it is even reasonable to try and develop the industry beyond a certain point. Agriculture is, and must remain, the staple industry of Southern India.

A certain degree of industrial development is absolutely essential to the welfare of the country for one very weighty reason, namely, that rainfall in India is of a precarious character. Absolute dependence on agriculture is liable to lead to fluctuations of income, resulting in extreme cases of famine, but by opening out sources of wealth independently of rainfall there is a possibility of lessening the danger of semi-starvation. As a protective measure, therefore, there is everything to be said in favour of industrial development, but when it advances beyond the point where it ceases to be protective and becomes merely productive, it is doubtful whether it can be regarded—in Southern India at least—as beneficial.

A. K. VENKATARAMA AIYER AND A. K. RANGANATHA AIYER.
POLICE LINES, TRIPLICANE.

A. K. VENKATARAMA AIYER AND A. K. RANGANATHA AIYER

These two traders entered into partnership in the year 1911, when they opened a timber-yard and warehouse at No. 65 Wallajah Road, Madras, and all kinds of sawn and seasoned wood are kept in stock for the manufacture of household furniture. Fittings have been supplied for the Government Banqueting Hall and to various public institutions, while a considerable quantity is made up for sale to local firms. Ornamental furnishings were prepared for the Government Medical College, and this order was executed with such great care that the principals of the institution are placing other orders in the hands of the firm. The designing and upholstering are planned by an expert, and the ordinary cabinet-work is attended to by thoroughly efficient men, who are under the direct supervision of the proprietors.

In October 1913 the partners determined that, in order to compete successfully with other firms, it was absolutely necessary that they should undertake engineering work, and the success which has attended the union of the two branches in so short a time is truly remarkable. Before the end of 1913 they had been entrusted with contracts in connection with the laying of the foundation-stone of the University Library, the construction of a large amphitheatre, and of two canopies for the visit of the Viceregal party to Madras in December of that year. These were followed by orders for new buildings for the police in the Ice House Road, Triplicane, at an estimated cost of Rs. 40,000; but this contract and some others have not yet been completed. An efficient manager has been appointed, and from 100 to 150 hands are employed, according to the nature and extent of the works.

The private residence of the partners is at Raganatha Villas, Mylapore.

O. M. SUNDAREM AIYANGAR

One of the pioneer importers of teak logs and scantlings into Madras from Rangoon was the late Mr. P. Narayana Aiyangar, who commenced business as a wholesale and retail timber merchant in the year 1878. When he died, in 1902, he was succeeded by his son, O. M. Sundarem Aiyangar, who continued to trade on the lines laid down by his father; but he increased the scope of the business by adding the allied branches of engineering and contracting. Father and son have made a special feature of dealing in teakwood, and the present proprietor has a very large number of regular customers throughout the Madras Presidency, in the Mofussil, and in the native States. Jarrah has recently been imported from Australia, and as this hard wood is

O. M. SUNDAREM AIYANGAR.

1. O. M. Sudarsanam Iyengar. 2. O. M. Sundaram Iyengar. 3. Office Group. 4. Timber Yard. 5. O. M. Narayana Iyengar. 6. O. M. Krishnasawmy Iyengar.

being more extensively used for railway sleepers, for ships' plankings, and similar purposes, arrangements have been made for periodical shipments. Between the years 1895 and 1909 this merchant supplied timber—principally in the way of sleepers—teak keys, building materials, and manufacturing timber over a distance of 4,000 miles to the old Madras Railway Company; the Madras and Southern Mahratta Company then took over the Madras system and continued purchasing from Mr. Sundarem Aiyangar; but since that date all supplies have been obtained under public tender. Contractors engaged in the construction of large public and private buildings meet with every consideration when making extensive purchases of timber, and this fact, coupled with the practice of cutting scantlings to any lengths which may be required, has materially contributed to the development of the business. The principal place of storage of timber is in the yards in Sydenham's Road, Madras, which are about 10,000 sq. ft. in extent, but a considerable quantity is placed on the beach in close proximity to the city.

Mr. Sundarem Aiyangar is personally responsible for the management of the business, and he employs three or four clerks in his offices, together with about eight regular labourer, although occasions arise when this number has to be doubled, or even trebled.

S. AMBROSE

An Indian Christian overseer, builder, and cabinet-maker, who holds an excellent record for the construction of public and private buildings, is Mr. S. Ambrose, of Milan House, Royapettah, in the city of Madras. Mr. Ambrose commenced his business career in 1891 as a clerk in one of the sub-divisions of the then consulting architectural division in the Department of Public Works; but he was at the same time receiving private tuition from one of the instructors of the Civil Engineering College, Madras, the subjects studied being surveying, the drawing of plans, the preparation of estimates, and engineering. In 1894 he joined the class for artisans and sub-overseers of the Civil Engineering College, Madras, obtaining a certificate of merit; and he subsequently served in the Departments of Public Works in Madras and at Travancore. He had qualified as a first-grade sub-overseer when he resigned his appointment at the former place.

The following ten years were spent by him as an assistant in the service of Mr. W. N. Pogson, F.R.I.B.A., of Madras, and he gained invaluable experience in connection with the construction of several buildings of importance in Southern India. It must be conceded that the training received by Mr. Ambrose during these years pre-eminently fitted him for the successful conduct of the business which he established on his own account in 1908. A preliminary circular stated that he undertook (1) to prepare designs and estimates for buildings of every description, and, further, to enter into contracts for the execution of the works; (2) to attend to repairs and improvements of existing buildings; (3) to supply furniture for schools, offices, and bungalows; and (4) to inspect sites for building purposes and to value properties of every description for sale and purchase. Although orders for work of a general character began to flow in from all quarters, it soon became apparent that clergymen, missionaries, and managers of educational and charitable institutions were to be the principal supporters of Mr. Ambrose, and from that time forth he seemed to be recognized as the Southern India contractor for churches and school buildings. Reduced charges are still made to missionaries of all denominations as follows: for the preparation of plans and estimates for (1) mission buildings erected entirely at the cost of mission funds a commission of 1½ per cent. of the cost, and (2) for mission buildings constructed with grants from the Educational Department a commission of 2 per cent. of the cost.

Some of the principal contracts which have been executed to the entire satisfaction of engineers, architects, and missionaries relate to: the British Resident's office and other works at Trivandrum at a cost of Rs. 26,000; the Church of the Good Shepherd, S.P.G., Sullivan's Gardens, Royapettah, Madras, costing Rs. 15,500; Wren, Bennett & Co.'s new furniture showroom, Madras, Rs. 20,000; the Thomas Memorial Chapel, S.P.G., Ramnad, Rs. 12,000; St. Ebba's High School for Girls, Royapettah, Rs. 31,000; Church of the Holy Cross, S.P.G., Nandyal, Rs. 17,000; additions and improvements to the Oriental Assurance Buildings, Georgetown, Madras, Rs. 40,000; the S.P.G. Mission Buildings, Nandyal, Rs. 33,000; other buildings for the same mission, including choultry and dispensary, Rs 12,646; and a Hostel for Indian Girls, St. Thomas's Convent, St. Thome, Madras, Rs. 17,000.

Although incomplete as a record of Mr. Ambrose's engagements, this list is sufficiently comprehensive to show that the contractor enjoys the confidence of a wide circle of influential patrons. The Rev. A. F. R. Bird, M.A. (Oxon), Principal and Manager of the S.P.G. High School and Training College at Nandyal, stated in a letter that he is glad to bear testimony to the admirable manner in which the important construction works at that place had been carried out. Mr. F. Inigo Thomas, F.R.I.B.A. (London), certified that Mr. Ambrose built the Thomas Memorial Chapel at Ramnad, and that he carried out the designs in a creditable manner. Mr. J. M. Lewis, architect, Madras, says that the additions to the College House at Kilpauk were well done under his supervision. Mr. A. R. Subramani Aiyar, Sub-divisional Officer, Public Works Department, wrote as follows: "Mr. S. Ambrose has executed two important grant-in-aid buildings for the S.P.G. Mission at Nandyal, costing more than Rs. 27,000, within a period of 20 months. Considering the difficulty of obtaining labour and cost of materials, I consider that the time taken to complete these buildings is very satisfactory."

Dr. C. Frimodt Moller, M.B., B.C.H., Medical Missionary Danish Mission, Timksilur, South India, wrote as follows: "I have received the plans and estimates sent by you, and find them very satisfactory. I am enclosing cheque for Rs. 138 in full payment according to your bill."

Many persons who have been brought into contact with Mr. Ambrose in business matters speak in high praise of the conscientious manner in which he carries out his duties, while others refer to his obliging manner, his courtesy and anxiety to please his employers, and his careful supervision of the smallest details.

THE ANANDA PRESS

The printing and the stationery business which is carried on under the name of R. Venkateshwar & Co. belongs to Mr. V. Ranganatham Chetty, who commenced business in 1891. In his early

S. AMBROSE.

1. S. Ambrose 2. Mission Bungalow, S.P.G., Giddalore. 3. Elementary Training School, S.P.G., Nandyal. 4. High School Extensions, S.P.G., Nandyal. 5. Church of the Holy Cross, S.P.G., Nandyal. 6. Thomas Memorial Chapel, S.P.G., Ramnad. 7. Church of the Good Shepherd, Royapettah, Madras.

THE ANANDA PRESS.

1. A VIEW OF THE WORKS. 2. COMPOSING HALL. 3. MACHINE-ROOM 4. BINDING AND RULING-ROOM

days he had a thoroughly practical training in the compositors'-room, as well as in the retail shop, and it is this experience which enables him to control the mass of detail work which is a portion of each day's programme. The concern has grown from a modest beginning to one of the leading establishments of its kind in the city, and the proprietor now finds employment for about 220 assistants. The buildings are in two blocks; the retail department, in Popham's Broadway, known as the Madras Stationery Mart, which is in charge of Mr. Ranganatham Chetty's nephew, Mr. V. S. Ramachandra Chetty, contains a well-selected assortment of commercial and fancy writing-papers, account-books, pencils, pens, mathematical instruments, cyclostyle duplicating apparatus, cabinets, bags, and a general stock of sundries; while the printing works, known as the "Ananda Press" and supervised by another nephew, Mr. V. A. Keshub Chandra, are situated in a very fine three-storied structure in Loane Square, which is right in the heart of the busiest portion of the principal banking, Government, municipal, and mercantile offices of the city. The plant in the works consists of a number of large modern machines, six of which are for general printing, five for jobbing orders, and five for type-casting. Busy hands may be seen manufacturing and binding books, stereotyping, die-sinking, copper-plate printing, machine-ruling, and preparing rubber stamps. The proprietor does a considerable portion of the printing for the Madras and Southern Mahratta Railway, and he is always prepared to enter into contracts for general or artistic work. The show-cases in the Broadway shop contain a grand selection of books, which are published in nearly all of the Indian languages as well as in English, and these comprise historical and geographical volumes for students, in addition to literature of a higher kind for the general reader.

One of the secrets of the success of the Ananda Press is that only expert workmen are employed, and as every process is subject to the keen and practical supervision of the owner, it will be understood that customers can always rely upon efficiency, combined with the highest quality of workmanship.

THE ANDHRA PATRIKA PRESS

Important printing works were established under the above name at Bombay in the year 1908, but they were transferred to a large double-storied building on the Second Line Beach in Madras in December 1913. The sole proprietor is Mr. K. Nageswara Rao, who is, further, the owner and editor of the newspaper called the *Andhra Patrika*. The machinery comprises one double royal, one double demy, one single demy supreme delivery, and one hand press, and these are exclusive of treadle plant of crown folio size, cutting-machine, and other necessary accessories. Commercial, artistic, and general printing is undertaken, and as only fully competent workmen are employed, it is not surprising that the public of Madras have already recognized the efficiency with which all orders are executed. The *Andhra Patrika* newspaper is published daily and weekly in the Telugu language, and it

THE "ANDHRA PATRIKA" PRESS.

1. A General View of the Andhra Patrika Office. 2. The Machine-room. 3. The Paper.

APPAH & CO.

1. VIEW OF THE PREMISES. 2. K. T. BHASHYAM NAIDU (SENIOR PROPRIETOR). 3. THE STAFF.

has a very wide circulation throughout Southern India. It has more than 6,000 regular subscribers for its weekly edition, some of whom reside in distant parts of the world.

An annual number, containing about 300 pages of demy quarto size, is issued, and this production is full of real, live reading matter, and its pages are profusely and handsomely illustrated. Mr. Rao personally supervises everything in the editorial, the machine, and other rooms, and he finds constant employment for about 50 hands.

Mr. Rao is the discoverer of the famous balm known as Amrutanjan, and this preparation is declared to be a universal remedy for all the aches and pains to which mortal flesh is heir, and commands a large sale throughout India. The main office for the supply of this preparation is at 109 Frere Road, Bombay, but selling agents have been appointed in the principal towns of the Presidency.

APPAH & CO.

It is an unsatisfactory feature of the commercial life of to-day that there are many firms who have gained leading positions in prominent business centres by methods which are open to the greatest censure from all right-minded persons. Deception has been cloaked by the thin veil of plausibility, and the honest sample sent on trial is followed by a consignment of distinctly inferior goods. The days are not past when sand increases the weight of a pound of sugar, or when a layer of brown paper takes the place of sound leather in the sole of a shoe, or when an alleged woollen garment contains from 30 to 40 per cent. of shoddy. The business life of to-day teems with examples of lightly veiled frauds, and the straightforward merchant or trader frequently has to battle against unscrupulousness, as well as to meet the ordinary competition which results from varying prices in buying and selling markets.

The predominant policy of this firm of Appah & Co., since its establishment in 1894, has been "Honesty is the best policy." All that is summed up in this time-honoured aphorism has characterized each transaction; and the truth of the adage is exemplified by the unbounded confidence that customers have always reposed in this firm.

The partners in the firm, Ketty-Timappa Bhashyam Naidu and Ketty-Narayanappa Naidu, belong to a distinguished and respectable family whose ancestors, Bin-Timappa Naidu and his grandson, Ketty-Narayanappa Naidu, were of great service to the Honourable East India Company in the seventeenth century. When the Company's agents were obliged to remove their factory from Armagaon they sought the assistance of Bin-Timappa, an inhabitant of Palacole (a Dutch factory near Maddepollam), in using his influence with native princes on the Coromandel coast to establish a factory there. He accordingly came to Madras and procured permission from one Damarla Venkatappa Naick for the building of a factory in that city, and he also assisted in the construction of a town on the north side of the factory. He subsequently invited people from different parts of the country (by the aid of a cowle from the Company's agents) to settle there by allotting separate lands for both right and left-hand castes. He further caused two pagodas (one of Vishnu and another of Siva) to be built there, calling the former Chennakesavaperumall and the latter Chennamalleswaram, both of which designations are derived from the same root-word. To this day his descendants (the proprietors of Messrs. Appah & Co.'s business) receive honours from those temples. To Ketty-Narayanappa Naidu (his grandson), Thomas Pitt, Esq., Governor of Fort St. George and Counsel for Affairs of the Right Honourable East Indian Company, was pleased to grant exemption from all manner of customs other than the 5 per cent. duty, a concession already made to the Portuguese and Armenians. His son Timappa also received the same privilege. The cowle under which the above-mentioned concession was made was dated July 12, 1700.

Messrs. Appah & Co. are commission agents and merchants, dealing chiefly in chillies, coriander-seeds, grain, and turmeric. They do not export on their own account, but other commission agents purchase goods from them in large quantities for shipment to Colombo, Galle, Penang, Singapore, Rangoon, and occasionally to London and other European markets. Consignments of produce are received by the firm from the districts of Guntur and Nellore, from the taluk of Ongole, and from other important centres in the Presidency. Their extensive stores are situated at No. 2 Chinnathumbi Modali Street, Georgetown, Madras.

ASVIN & CO.

The partners of this firm of wholesale and retail chemists and druggists and dealers in all goods connected with medicine and pharmacy are Mr. L. Sankaranarayana Chetti and Mr. Vasa Varadiah Chetti, and they are direct importers of patent medicines, surgical appliances, high-class drugs, perfumery, soaps, and a thousand and one other requisites for every phase of domestic life. The business was established in 1902, and large stocks of drugs, chemicals, and other goods are obtained at regular intervals direct from England, France, Japan, America, and Germany, but the majority of the patent medicines are purchased through accredited agents. The reputation of the firm for dealing in drugs and other articles of the highest quality has secured patronage from several of the native States, from the South Indian Railway authorities, from Co-operative Stores in various districts in the Presidency, and from mission hospital stations throughout the Mofussil.

It would be impossible to refer to a tithe of the valuable drugs and patent and proprietary medicines which are constantly stocked, but mention may be made of some of the more important items. The firm are wholesale agents for the Presidency of Madras for Odol, the well-known dentrifice; they are sole agents for Nyal's famous preparations; and they stock the well-known specialities of Messrs. Burroughs, Wellcome & Co., of Messrs. Oppenheimer, of Messrs. Frederick Stearns & Co., of Messrs. Parke, Davis & Co., of Messrs. Burgoyne, Burbidges & Co., and of Messrs. C. J. Hewlett & Son, whose laboratories in London have been established for more than 100 years.

The spacious two-storied premises at No. 6 Bunder Street, Georgetown, Madras, are the head office, where the wholesale orders from the Mofussil are attended to, while those on the Broadway are used as a branch office, where retail dispensing business is conducted. The prescriptions of physicians are made up with the greatest care, and hospital authorities and others can rely upon having sound drugs and upon a splendid selection of surgical instruments.

The very complete and well-got-up catalogue which has been issued is a valuable aid to the conduct of business between the headquarters staff at Madras and the very large number of customers who have to rely upon the services of the railway or the post office for the delivery of their orders. The partners supervise every branch of their extensive business, and they employ four fully qualified assistants.

Mr. Vasi Varadiah Chetti occupies separate offices, in which he conducts a sound banking concern, which was founded by his father, Vasa Baliah Chetti, about the year 1892, and every possible consideration is given to financial transactions with clients.

Mr. L. Sankaranarayana Chetti, the senior partner, is a member of the Southern India Chamber of Commerce.

N. R. BAGDY & CO.

There is no scarcity of chemists and druggists in Madras, and perhaps it is as well that this should be so in view of the fact that there are many diseases affecting humanity in this part of the world which require immediate drastic treatment, and it is an inestimable boon that preparations of proved worth are now so easily obtainable. The extensive business carried on by Messrs. N. R. Bagdy & Co. as wholesale and retail

ASVIN & CO.

1. L. Sankaranarayana Chetti. 2. Vasa Varadiah Chetti. 3. C. N. Krishnaswami Chetti (Chief Manager).

N. R. BAGDY & CO.

1. A portion of the Showroom. 2. The Staff.

chemists and druggists was established in the year 1904 by Mr. Sreekishen Peety and Mr. Ramgopal Bagdy, who entered into partnership in a spacious and costly building at No. 439 Mint Street, which is an exceedingly busy portion of Madras. The internal fittings of these premises, including electric lights and fans, were put in at very considerable cost ; but it soon became apparent to the partners that it was necessary, owing to the great expansion of business, to open another establishment, and the customers of the firm were so insistent in their demands, that a branch office and dispensary were opened at No. 178 China Bazaar Road:

The firm deal largely in high-class drugs, patent medicines, surgical instruments, optical goods, and other requisites for the hospital and nursery, or for ordinary domestic purposes ; and in order that the whole stock may be thoroughly up to date and quite fresh, consignments are received every fortnight from the principal manufacturers in England, the Continent of Europe, and America.

Practically all of the well-known medicine preparations can be supplied by this firm, but their own specialities, which are exceedingly popular, include specifics for coughs, ague, dysentery, and diarrhœa ; citrate of magnesia, toothache drops, laxative pills, pain balm, indigestion mixture, tooth-powder, compound syrup of sarsaparilla, genuine seidlitz powders, iron and quinine tonic, ringworm ointment, Snanaranjani bathing-oil, marking-ink, and mixtures for the alleviation of neuralgia and other troublesome ailments.

The confidence of the public has been gained with regard to the dispensing of prescriptions, as their branch contains drugs of first-class quality only, which are made up by qualified practitioners—in fact, every department of the two establishments is under the management of able experts, and yet, with all these safeguards, the partners are dominated by one supreme idea, and that is to supply goods of unquestionable quality at the lowest possible prices consistent with current market rates.

The optical department of this firm is well stocked with every description of lenses, gold, solid nickel, and other spectacles, neutral-tinted eye-preservers, artificial human eyes, glare-protectors, and a host of other high-class English sundries for this important branch of the business. To postpone the time for procuring spectacles when the eyes feel tired after reading or when letters blur and run into each other is one of the most serious mistakes that can be made, and there is no excuse for a person who continues to suffer pain or inconvenience when such firms as Bagdy & Co. have up-to-date instruments for testing the sight and when properly adjusted glasses can be supplied. The firm have gone to very considerable expense in procuring these scientific appliances, and it only remains to be added that this very delicate work of examination is in the safe hands of fully qualified opticians.

THE BALA NARASU FOUNDRY AND RICE MILLS.
INTERIOR VIEW OF THE WORKS

BALA NARASU FOUNDRY AND RICE MILLS

These premises occupy an area of about nine acres of land in Wall Tax Road, in the city of Madras, and the business was established in 1900.

Every kind of engineering is executed in the foundry and workshop, which are fitted throughout with the most modern plant for the production of any class of structural and mechanical works. Rice, flour, seeds, crushing and other machinery is continually being constructed, and renewals or repairs receive careful attention at the hands of competent workmen. A considerable amount of work has been undertaken for the Government, the Port Trust, and municipalities, and the latter has been supplied with a large quantity of sanitary requisites. Designs and estimates are furnished promptly, and every crate of plant or machinery is inspected by the superintendent before it is permitted to leave the works. The rice mills are run upon a system which prevails at Rangoon, and the firm has a branch at Nellore. The firm buy and crush rice on their own account only. Between 150 and 200 hands are constantly employed.

T. BATCHACHARRY

It is a sufficient guarantee of the practical acquaintance of a tradesman with the details of his business when it is known that he has worked his way from apprentice to journeyman, from journeyman to manager, and from manager to master ; and it usually happens that these are the men who attain the highest positions of honour and responsibility in the commercial world. Mr. T. Batchacharry was thoroughly in earnest when, as a boy, he began to learn the rudiments of carpentering ; he watched the workmen as they used the plane, the chisel, the saw, and other tools ; and he carefully followed the process of development which took place between the plain log of wood and the artistic piece of furniture. He commenced business on his own account about the year 1894 by manufacturing all kinds of household appointments to the order of customers, but about five years later he began to contract for engineering work, in order that he might be in a better position to compete with other tradesmen. One of his early successes was in connection with the extension of the photographic studio on the second floor of the Government Revenue Board Office. This was followed by the construction of a bungalow at Chetput for Messrs. W. E. Smith & Co., Ltd., at an estimated cost of Rs. 13,000; then came the erection of a bungalow for Mr. James Short, solicitor, of Numgambakam, which cost about Rs. 20,000.

P. M. A. MUTHIAH CHETTIAR.

Afterwards the firm was occupied for 24 months in making extensions to the Christian College, which cost about Rs. 1,70,000. In connection with this undertaking it should be mentioned that the whole of the fittings of the science laboratory, the library, and the balcony were made in the contractor's workshop.

In December 1911 a certificate of merit was awarded to Mr. T. Batchacharry for the excellent manner in which this work was carried out, and the following is a copy of the document in question: "T. Batchacharry has been the contractor both for the buildings and for the furniture in connection with the extension of the Madras Christian College. All his work has been pronounced to be good by competent judges and his carpentry work specially so. The furniture for the physics and chemistry laboratories is well and neatly done. (Signed) J. M. RUSSELL, Bursar."

Special praise was bestowed upon him for the beautiful woodwork and ornamental fixtures on the staircase and for the dadoes fixed upon the walls and in the secretariat office and library in the old Council-room of Fort St. George. Contracts were completed more recently for a school for European girls at Royapettah (Rs. 13,000) and for the Roman Catholic Church of St. Joseph, in the High Road, Vepery. Mr. T. Batchacharry is his own manager, and he frequently employs as many as 100 trained carpenters, in addition to other labourers. His business address is No. 1 18 Chengalvaraya Modaly Street, Triplicane.

P. M. A. MUTHIAH CHETTIAR

This general merchant and banker was born at Kottaiyur, in the district of Ramnad, in the Presidency of Madras, and in the year 1900 he succeeded his late father, P. M. A. Ramasammy Chettiar, who founded the business in the early sixties in Coral Merchant Street. Merchandise of a general character is imported from England, but a speciality is made of Manchester piece goods and of sundries, which are imported in fairly large quantities. Banking was commenced for the benefit principally of the customers of the firm, but it is now conducted upon a large scale with private individuals as well. Money up to any amount is advanced on deeds, notes, policies, or other satisfactory securities, and the whole of the business is conducted on thoroughly up-to-date lines. Branches have been opened in Burma and Ceylon, but those offices are controlled by the headquarters in Madras and Kottaiyur. About 200 hands are employed in the two enterprises.

Mr. Muthiah Chettiar is highly respected in business and in private circles, and, busy man though he is, he devotes a considerable portion of his time to assisting in the management of local affairs. He is a member of the Southern India Chamber of Commerce, of the Mahajanasabha, and of several other public bodies; and he is a director of the Indian Bank, Ltd., and of many other commercial and financial companies. Mr. Muthiah Chettiar looks back with profound pleasure upon a trip which he made to England at the time of the coronation of H.M. King George V. It should be added that he has brought to a satisfactory and impressive conclusion the ornamental and original works of the celebrated temple of Tiruvalangadu, in the district of Chittur, at a cost of about four lakhs of rupees.

P. A. CHOCKALINGA CHETTY

The registered telegraphic address of this well-known timber merchant at Madras is "Teakwood," and this word has been most happily chosen, as Mr. Chockalinga Chetty specializes in the importation of teak from Burma and Siam. He commenced business in Wall Tax Road about the year 1902, and for three generations his ancestors were, and now he is, connected with the commercial life (dealing in timber) of the Presidency, and of its chief city in particular.

Teak scantlings are imported in standard length and thicknesses, in addition to logs of suitable sizes for

T. BATCHACHARRY.

1. BUNGALOW OF JAMES SHORT, ESQ., AT NUNGAMBAKAM. 2. ST. JOSEPH'S CHURCH, VEPERY—FRONT VIEW. 3. T. BATCHACHARRY, CONTRACTOR. 4. THE NEW BUILDING AT CHRISTIAN COLLEGE.

P. A. CHOCKALINGA CHETTY.

1. P. A. Chockalinga Chetty. 2. Proprietor and Staff. 3 and 4. In the Timber Yard.

being sawn to given dimensions. There is a wholesale as well as a retail branch of his business, and among his numerous customers are Government and private contractors in Madras, the Mofussil, in the dominions of the Nizam of Hyderabad, and in the State of Mysore. Imports of timber take place almost weekly, and with the exception of heavy logs, which are floated ashore, all the consignments are landed by boats.

The timber-yards in Wall Tax Road, which cover an area of about 200,000 sq. ft., belong to Mr. Chockalinga Chetty, but a portion of the property is sub-let to other merchants for storage and sale of their stock. The proprietor retains full control over the business, and he employs about 20 regular hands, besides many more who are engaged during any extra pressure of work.

THE CITY STABLES.

1. EXTERIOR. 2. INTERIOR. 3. WORKSHOP.

THE CITY STABLES

The jingling of bits and curbs and the ring of iron-shod hoofs are still pleasant sounds to be heard in stable and stall, and it is some satisfaction to realize that the motor—valuable as it undoubtedly is in many respects—cannot entirely supersede the friendly horse.

At the same time, "facts are stubborn things," and the wise man is he who is prepared to accept the changed condition of affairs. Cabs and carriages drawn by horses are fast disappearing from the public streets, but hack and hunter and pony are still necessary for the enjoyment of man. The City Stables were opened in 1892 by Mr. Ghansham Singh, but the latter was succeeded in 1913 by his nephew, the present proprietor, Mr. T. Jaswant Singh. This gentleman is the son of Rao Bahadur T. Jaysingh, the veteran Indian police officer, and he is the great grandson of Kaiser Singh—or Kizza Singh—the hero of the battle of Plassey, which laid the foundation of the British Empire in India, serving under Lord Clive in 1757. Mr. Ghansham Singh was a zealous business man, and he won the esteem of his friends and admirers by his benevolent spirit and love for the poor and needy. The extensive premises opposite Government House, in Wallajah Road, in Madras, have accommodation for 80 animals, and the proprietor enters into arrangements for stabling his clients' horses by the day, week, or month. A fully qualified veterinary surgeon attends to the treatment of accidents or sickness among the animals, and young horses are thoroughly broken to harness or saddle.

All sorts of carriages are built, and prizes have been awarded at several exhibitions. Horses are imported from Australia and New Zealand, and a large commission agency is carried on. Mr. Singh, however, understands that he must not be left behind while others are motoring ahead. He is therefore about to open motor works on a large scale. He will build the bodies of new cars, all kinds of repairs will be undertaken by experienced men, and, in short, it is the owner's intention to make a special feature of this branch of the business.

Weekly sales by auction of horses, carriages, landed properties, household furniture, and other goods are held; and Mr. Jaswant Singh is auctioneer by appointment to the following departments, namely: (1) in military services

—to the Station Supply Office Madras Brigade, the Divisional Stores Office, the Army Clothing Department, and the Madras Volunteer Guards Office ; (2) in civil departments—to the High Court, the Stationery Office, the Stamp Office, the General Post Office, the Telegraph Stores, the Superintendent of Prisons, the Presidency College, and to the Corporation of Madras.

It will be readily understood from the foregoing that Mr. Singh has a large and important clientéle, and that he has secured the confidence and respect of all who have had business dealings with him. He employs a capable manager, together with five clerks and a small army of workmen and stable assistants.

V. COORATHALWAR CHETTY

This engineering contractor commenced business in Madras in 1892, and he has gained the highest praise from architects and engineers for good workmanship, promptitude, ability to control a large number of men, and for his invariable courtesy to his employers. Military works were taken in hand first, then followed contracts with the Government Salt Department, and with the Madras-Bezwada State railway authorities for the construction of all works, including bridges, one of the latter being thrown across the Arni River ; and earthwork and bridges in four miles of construction were subsequently taken in hand for the South Indian Railway Company on its Travancore branch.

For about five years prior to August 1906 Mr. Chetty was employed by the engineer of the Basin Bridge Junction Works of the Madras Railway Company, and a certificate was given that his duties had been most satisfactorily performed. Two years later Mr. Duncan, district engineer, wrote that "Contractor V. Coorathalwar Chetty has carried out work for me in connection with the provision of new quarters for Eurasian and native staffs at Bitragunta, including a school and institute, to the value of Rs. 1,11,000. He performed his work to my satisfaction, and I never had any trouble with him as to delay in progress or in settling accounts. He is one of the best contractors I have worked with." The Perambur extension works were the next to be contracted for, and Mr. Chetty built a new paint-shop and stores, a power-house, a new erecting shop, a carriage-lift shop, a main drain and pipe tracks, and Mr. Williamson, A.M.I.C.E., said that "He is a specially good brickwork contractor, and he has turned out first-class work ; he is prompt in carrying out all orders, and he is never behind with his work ; during the four years he has been with me he has given complete satisfaction." The Swarnamukhi and Pennar Rivers (extension works) on the north-east line of the Madras and Southern Mahratta Railway were next bridged with structures of laterite and granite respectively, and the materials for the latter were quarried about 180 miles distant from the river. Another bridge on the north-west line of the same company has been built recently over the Uttukur tank in the Cuddapah district.

Mr. H. Lingard, engineer in charge of bridge works, said that "the work turned out by Mr. Chetty is first class, and is expeditiously done. He has a large command of labour and capital, and has always carried out his work to my entire satisfaction. I can strongly recommend him as a contractor." Mr. Chetty is now engaged in work of general character in four sections, extending over 140 miles in length, on the north-east line of the Madras and Southern Mahratta Railway.

All contracts are carried out under the direct supervision of Mr. Chetty or of his partners, Messrs. S. Kuppiah Raju and C. Krishnasawmy Chetty, who have been associated with him since the business was established.

A very complete contractor's plant is kept, and about 2,000 hands are generally employed.

T. NAMBERUMAL CHETTY

One may travel through the countries of the world and view with admiration historic mansions whose gilded salons have not lost their pristine glory, of castles whose ivy-clad turrets were the scenes of blood-curdling deeds, or of abbeys and cathedrals within whose sacred precincts men of hallowed memory were wont to rebuke the unlicensed liberties of libertines, but the occasions are very rare when a passing thought is given to the man whose intellect designed them, or of him whose skill was exercised in their construction. And yet these structures have remained as monuments to their memory for centuries after the bones of architect and builder have crumbled to dust. What is true of yesterday is true of to-day, and the many palatial modern edifices which are to be seen throughout India and admired by the passer-by, will also live when the "man on the works" has passed into oblivion.

There are some magnificent buildings in the Madras Presidency, and many of them stand to the credit of Mr. T. Namberumal Chetty, who—since the year 1880—has carried on business in Madras and elsewhere as a contractor, engineer, and builder. He can look with a paternal affection upon some of the finest buildings in Madras, such as the Technical Institute, the Y.M.C.A. buildings, the Law College, the Connemara Library, the Bank of Madras, the Victoria Memorial, the new National Bank of India, Ltd., and many others.

Sir Arthur Havelock, Governor of Madras, at the opening of the Victoria Students' Hostel Buildings on January 29, 1900, said : "Mr. Namberumal Chetty will have his name recorded in Madras in connection with many large and beautiful buildings in stone, brick, and mortar. It should be a proud remembrance for him and his descendants that he has had so much to do with the beautifying of the city."

Mr. Namberumal Chetty's dwelling-houses, of which he owns a number, are well known for their improved standard as compared with those ordinarily available in Madras. He is a tramway concessionaire, and owns a small line—a feeder to the Madras and Southern Mahratta Railway—at the Trivellore railway-station.

In November 1901 the Government bestowed upon him the title of "Rao Sahib" in recognition of his enterprising spirit.

He is also a very large timber merchant, and he imports large quantities of timber from Rangoon and Moulmein, while a wholesale trade is carried on with local dealers under the management of Mr. C. T. Alwar Chetty, B.A., who is a partner in this branch.

Mr. Namberumal Chetty is managing director and lessee of the Trichur Timber and Saw Mills, which is considered to be one of the best, if not the best, in India. It is a thoroughly equipped and up-to-date mill, and it has a capacity of converting logs to the extent of 100 candies a day. Timber is consigned to London, Liverpool, Germany, New York, and South Africa, as well as to Colombo, Bombay, and Calcutta. Some 200 hands are employed here.

This successful contractor is deservedly

V. COORATHALWAR CHETTY.

1, Opening of the Swarnamukhi Bridge Extension. 2, Basin Bridge Junction Station. 3, Power House, Perambur Workshops. 4, Railway School at Bitragunta. 5, Proprietors and Assistants.

T. NAMBERUMAL CHETTY.

1. THE CONNEMARA LIBRARY AND TECHNICAL INSTITUTE, MADRAS. 2. THE Y.M.C.A. BUILDINGS, MADRAS. 3. THE LAW COLLEGE, MADRAS.
4. THE VICTORIA MEMORIAL HALL, MADRAS.

Photos by M. Doss & Sons.

T. NAMBERUMAL CHETTY (THE TRICHUR TIMBER AND SAW-MILLS).

1. Goliath Crane for Loading and Unloading. 2. The Log Bandsaw Machine. 3. Front View of the Mill.

popular with all classes of people, and his kindliness of manner is exemplified in the innumerable generous actions which have been performed by him.

Seven cupolas, together with a bust of H.M. King George V, were presented by him to the district of Chingleput on the occasion of the Coronation in 1911, and a life-size statue of his Majesty was erected by him in Saidapet, near Government House, Guindy.

M. V. CUNNIAH CHETTY & CO.

"Esplanada Hall," being No. 189 China Bazaar Road, Madras, is a most imposing commercial house in one of the principal business centres in the city, and a very extensive trade is carried on by Messrs. M. V. Cunniah Chetty & Co., who started in the year 1896 as general merchants, outfitters, tailors, and shirt-makers. The managing partners are Messrs. P. Bhashicarloo Chetty and P. Rajamannar Chetty, who belong to a very respectable and influential family, and the steady progress which has been made by the firm under its ablest members is proof of the integrity which has been displayed throughout in all their transactions. The business is conducted under their direct management, assisted by an efficient and well-trained staff. A huge stock is kept of piece goods of every description, of cotton, wool, silk, linen, trunks, bags, and other travelling requisites, all of which are of the best British and Continental manufacture. A marked advance has taken place in the department of shirt-making and tailoring, and this branch is under the control of capable cutters who have had a long and varied experience. There is a choice and exclusive selection of designs in cloth in the tailoring department, and the shelves are stocked with a large quantity of famous Calicut checks, tweeds, linens, and cotton goods which are unsurpassed for their hard-wearing qualities. "Swadeshi" goods of purely Indian manufacture obtained from all the principal manufacturing centres are exhibited for sale and there is a considerable demand for these articles throughout the Presidency. The premises in which the business is carried on are very extensive, and the magnificent showrooms, in which the stock is shown to the best advantage, are fitted with electric lights and fans. Shopping under such conditions affords pleasure to visitors, and the place itself with its magnificent showrooms is well worth a visit at any hour of the day.

The firm have regular importations of goods from the principal markets in Europe and elsewhere.

P. RUNGIAH CHETTY & SONS

The managing partners in the above-named firm of Messrs. M. V. Cunniah Chetty & Co. are proprietors, along with Mr. P. Ramaswamy Chetty, of this large wholesale and retail business which was established in or about the year 1879. They deal largely in wines, ales, spirits, oilman's stores, patent medicines, tea, perfumery, stationery, soaps, and other goods. The liquors are of the purest quality obtainable; all kinds of brands are obtainable to satisfy the tastes of the most exacting connoisseur, and the general mercantile stores and goods are unquestionably of the best manufacture. The warehouses and showrooms are situated at No. 190 China Bazaar Road, Madras, and are practically next door to the outfitting establishment mentioned above.

The firm have an extensive and high-class clientèle throughout India and the Far East, and they are direct importers of wines and spirits from the best distilleries and vineyards of Europe, including the United Kingdom. Other articles are constantly obtained from the leading manufacturing centres.

The registered telegraphic address is "Bashraj."

PERUMALL CHETTY & SONS

"The largest and cheapest house in Southern India" is the description given by Messrs. Chetty & Sons in an advertisement which appeared in a local directory, and a recent visit to their warehouse gives one the impression that this description is by no means exaggerated. Started by V. Perumall Chetty in 1840 on a humble scale, the firm has gradually developed itself into the foremost wholesale and retail stationers in the Madras Presidency. The founder's three sons and a grandson constitute its present partners, each being in sole charge of a department.

The premises in Stringer's Street, Madras, are very extensive, and a hive of bees in summer could not present a better illustration of activity. The ground floor is divided into a number of rooms in which one sees shelves and cabinets with writing and printing paper, notepaper and envelopes in all sizes and shapes, fancy stationery, pencils and pens, writing and printing inks, wedding, visiting, and other cards, stylo and fountain pens, mathematical instruments, artists' colours, toilet requisites, travellers' cases, fancy goods, copying presses, typewriters, duplicating apparatus, leather bags, account and memorandum books, office, cash, and dispatch boxes, Gladstone bags, steel trunks, stationers' sundries, and numerous other goods.

Messrs. Chetty & Sons are also the proprietors of the "Premier Press," Madras, carried on under the name and style of "Hoe & Co.," at 5 Stringer's Street, Georgetown, Madras. In this branch their leading lines of business are letter-press printing, bookbinding, account-book manufacturing, copper-plate printing, die-sinking, relief stamping, illuminating, rubber stamp making, engraving, machine ruling, and the printing and publication of diaries. Colour printing is their speciality. The firm are the recognized contractors for printing to the South India Railway as well as to almost all the municipalities, and local fund district boards of the Madras Presidency. They are printers by appointment to his Excellency the Governor of Madras, besides being printers to private companies and the public in general.

Their printing machinery is thoroughly up to date, the motor power being obtained from electricity. About 500 hands are employed in the Madras warehouse and two retail shops. There is a branch office at Trichinopoly to meet the urgent demands of the S.I. Railway General Offices.

Messrs Chetty & Sons do not issue elaborate catalogues and price-lists wherein goods are advertised which are never kept in stock, but they rely upon giving the utmost satisfaction to their numerous customers by selling only the best articles at the lowest possible prices. Inquiries made personally or by letter are promptly attended to in a courteous manner, and great care is taken in packing and dispatching consignments.

The firm have a very wide and important connection with railway companies, local fund boards and municipalities, native States, mining companies and municipal corporations, in addition to the leading banking and other institutions in Southern India.

Many gold and silver medals as well as certificates have been awarded to

M. V. CUNNIAH CHETTY & CO. AND P. RUNGIAH CHETTY & SONS.

1. Exterior M. V. Cunniah Chetty & Co. 2. The Showroom at M. V. Cunniah Chetty & Co. 3. Exterior P. Rungiah Chetty & Sons. 4 One of the Departments at P. Rungiah Chetty & Sons. 5. P. Rajamannar Chetty. 6. P. Bhashicarloo Chetty.

PERUMALL CHETTY & SONS (HOE & CO.).

1. View of the Premises. 2. Composing-room. 3. Ruling-room. 4. Binding-room.

Messrs. Chetty & Sons for the excellence of the exhibits displayed by them at various exhibitions.

Messrs. Hoe & Co.'s pocket and colonial diaries are well known for the useful information they give, and they are the most popular companions for business men throughout Southern India.

The partners are: Mr. V. Ramanjum Chetty, Mr. V. Alwar Chetty, Mr. V. Ethirajulu Chetty, and Mr. V. Thiruvengadathan Chetty.

E. VENCATAKISTNAMAH CHETTY & SON

In or about the year 1884 a very modest little business was commenced by Mr. E. Vencatakistnamah Chetty, who became a general merchant, importer, and commission agent at No. 27 Vencatachella Iyer Street, Madras, and who was the grandfather of the present proprietor. Some ten years later a factory was opened in Mint Street for the making of chutney, curry, spices, and preserved fruits and jellies, and this branch has now become the most important feature of the concern.

The choicest ingredients have always been used, and this fact has caused the sales of the condiments to increase to such an extent that it has been necessary to enlarge the works very considerably, and further, to instal new and improved machinery. Curry is sent out in tins which range in weight from $\frac{1}{4}$ lb. up to 28 lb.; chutney is put up in casks and bottles; preserved fruits, jellies, spices, and pepper are sold in tins, bottles, and jars; and all of these are placed upon the market under the trade-mark of the "Temple" brand. Consignments are exported to the United Kingdom, to Australia, and New Zealand, while sales in India are effected in all portions of the continent. The sole distributing agents in England are Messrs. A. Murcott & Co., of Birmingham; Messrs. Bume & Reif are representatives in Hamburg; and several leading firms act in a similar capacity in the principal cities and towns in Australia. It should be mentioned that all of these condiments are manufactured from Indian products with the exception of the fine salt, which is procured from England. The proprietor exercises general supervision over every branch of the business, and he employs four clerks in his offices and about 100 employees in the factory. Many gold and silver medals have been awarded to these condiments at exhibitions in London, Lyons, Brisbane, Christchurch, and Madras, and the steadily increasing demand for these goods is abundant evidence of their popularity.

The firm, acting on behalf of Madras merchants, import large quantities of hardware, stationery, and general merchandise from the United Kingdom, the continent of Europe, and from America, and they are sole agents in Southern India for Messrs. Edward Lloyd & Co., paper manufactures of London.

An electrical branch has been opened recently at Sunkuraman Street under the name of the South Indian Electric Stores, and a large stock of lights, lamps, and accessories is kept there. Contracts are entered into for installations or repairs, and a fully qualified engineer and a number of expert workmen are employed.

E. VENCATAKISTNAMAH CHETTY & SON.

1. SHOWCASE OF CONDIMENTS. 2. C. MANAVALA CHETTY. 3. TRADE-MARK, "TEMPLE" BRAND.

The cable address of the firm is "Temple," Madras.

CHATHOORBHOOJA DOSS KHUSAL DOSS & SONS

There is no more honoured name than Khusal Doss in the whole of Southern India, and there are few charitable institutions which have not benefited very considerably by the unostentatious generosity of this firm, the junior partner of which now occupies the honourable position of Sheriff of Madras.

Before referring specially to the life and character of Dewan Bahadur Govind Doss Chathoorbhooja Doss, it may be well to observe that the business of the firm as bankers and yarn and general merchants was established in the year 1828, and that during a period of nearly a century the various partners have acted up to a very high standard of commercial honour. The grandfather and father of the present proprietors carried on an extensive trade in silk, musk, and spices, but other industries have been added from time to time. Large transactions now take place in cotton yarn, and in Benares and South Indian cloth, and an embroidery factory, the first of its kind in this part of the country, giving employment to a large number of hands and turning out brocades of exquisite workmanship, has been erected recently. Messrs. Chathoorbhooja Doss Khusal Doss and Sons are agents for the Burma Oil Company, and, with numerous subagents in most of the principal places in the Presidency, carry on an extensive business in the sale of oil under the name and style of Messrs. Baniams & Co. The banking business is a valuable adjunct, and the facilities which are afforded to customers are undoubtedly very largely responsible for the extent of the financial transactions, which are considerable.

There are only two brothers in the partnership now, Mr. Girdher Doss Chathoorbhooja Doss and Govind Doss Chathoorbhooja Doss. The former attends to the twist and yarn business, while the latter, with an all-round ability, is managing the entire business of the concern, and has considerably added in recent years to the large partnership estate, notwithstanding the varied and princely gifts of munificence by which the family has become famous in Southern India. Dewan Bahadur Govind Doss Chathoorbhooja Doss was born in 1878, and although still a young man of five-and-thirty years, he has crammed into his life a long and honourable record of philanthropy of which older men might be justly proud. He inherited with his large fortune sound commercial principles, and while he has greatly added to his knowledge of business, he has always maintained strict integrity in his dealings, and this has endeared him to all who meet him in public life.

Wealth is unfortunately in many instances possessed by persons who are lacking in true sympathy, and when such individuals are constrained to part with subscriptions, the act is so devoid of the essence of charity that the giver knows nothing of that pleasure which comes to one who renders assistance out of a large and generous heart. Dewan Bahadur

CHATHOORBHOOJA DOSS KHUSAL DOSS & SONS.

1. Dewan Bahadur Govindoss Chathoorbhooja Doss, Sheriff of Madras.

2. *Standing:* D. K. Asher, G. Kishandoss, G. Laldoss, V. Jamnadoss; *Seated:* Dewan Bahadur Govindoss Chathoorbhooja Doss, G. Haridoss, C. G. Narayanadoss

Govind Doss is the exact opposite of the misanthrope. He gives liberally because he loves to do good ; it is a deep sorrow to him to see others in suffering or distress, and he unostentatiously distributes his wealth and takes a pride in doing it. His energies are bent on strengthening the tie which binds India to England, and he regards the connection as part of a distinct plan of Providence.

Mr. Govind Doss Chathoorbhooja Doss has been the recipient of the titles of Rao Bahadur and Dewan Bahadur at the hands of the Government, and any one who is acquainted with his record must admit that the honours are justly deserved. To the memorial of the loyal Indian subjects for his late Majesty King Edward he subscribed the sum of Rs. 10,000. Of his Majesty King George he offered to erect a statue in coronation robes in memory of the Delhi celebrations of 1912. The statue, which will be in bronze, is in the course of preparation by an eminent artist in England, under the supervision of Sir Arthur Lawley, who was formerly Governor of Madras, and in whose tenure of office the idea was mooted and encouraged. The statue has not been finally cast, but his Majesty has already displayed a keen interest in the work and is reported to have graciously accorded more than one sitting to the artist. It is expected to be an ornament to the city when it arrives, and it is estimated to cost about Rs. 45,000. Dewan Bahadur Govind Doss Chathoorbhooja Doss was one of the presentees at the King's levee at Calcutta.

Mr. Chathoorbhooja Doss has given liberally to various other objects. The Anjuman-i-Mufad-i-Islam was the recipient of a princely gift of Rs. 10,000 when its resources had dwindled to almost nothing consequent on the failure of the late firm of Arbuthnot & Co. He supplemented the gift subsequently with a further sum of Rs. 10,000 for the Lawley Hall in the Anjuman buildings. His love of dumb creatures, and a desire to mitigate the sufferings to which they are continually subjected, induced him to present a site of land to the Madras Panjrapole—an asylum for sick, infirm, and abandoned animals—worth Rs. 25,000. He takes a deep interest in the working of this institution, and he gave a further handsome subscription of Rs. 6,000. Among his other charitable and philanthropic acts may be mentioned the erection of Dharamsalas or Choultries at Raichur and Manmad, the latter costing over a lakh of rupees. Manmad is a railway junction of great importance in Central India, where numerous passengers experience great difficulty for want of a rest-house and for good arrangements. Dewan Bahadur Govind Doss is a much-travelled man, and, with an eye to the convenience of travellers, has started this Dharamsala, which is nearing completion. With certain railway facilities for which he is negotiating with the G.I.P. Railway Company, the Dharamsala is bound to prove most valuable to railway travellers from east to west and from the north to the south of the continent. The Dharamsala at Raichur is also supplying a great want brought to his notice, he is ever ready with his help. To the South African Relief Fund he readily gave Rs. 1,500, and in the Victoria Caste and Gosha Hospital he endowed a bed the other day at a cost of Rs. 2,100.

Dewan Bahadur Govind Doss Chathoorbhooja Doss has a charming personality and a striking address and bearing. He is a young man in the bloom of youth and health ; a man of high integrity and lovable character—in fact, an ornament to Madras society. He is loved throughout Southern India, and it is the earnest prayer of all who know, or who have heard of him, that he may long be spared to continue his good and honourable work in the service of the State, of the public, and of humanity at large.

STAFF OF MURLI DOSS RAM DOSS & CO

To the widows of the Carnatic family he gave Rs. 1,500, to a science hall and laboratory at the Srirangam High School, named after his Excellency Lord Pentland, he gave Rs. 3,000, and this list might almost be indefinitely prolonged if a tithe of the Dewan Bahadur's charitable actions were set forth.

The subject of this sketch is a man of deep religious convictions, and his intense devotion to his *Gurus* is the inspiration of his higher life. There is not a soul who is aware of the extent of his benefactions, but it may be sufficient to show that he is a man who places a greater value upon the consciousness of well-doing than he does upon the mere titles which have been conferred upon him. His sympathies are cosmopolitan, and when instances of destitution or suffering are

MURLI DOSS RAM DOSS & CO.

The head of this firm deals very largely in yarn, but he also indents upon European wholesale houses for both hard and soft goods—sugar is imported from Java, metals come from various towns in England, soft piece-goods are from Manchester, and general sundries for domestic and personal use are purchased in the majority of the countries of Europe. Mr. Doss is not an exporter, nor does he keep goods in stock, but the orders which are obtained by his travellers in Southern India are executed entirely under the indent

GOCOOLA DOSS JUMNA DOSS & CO.

1. A View of the Shop. 2. Purushothama Doss Gocooladoss. 3. Dwarkadoss-Govardandoss. 4. Gocoola Doss Jumna Doss & Co.

method. Banking is carried on in connection with the mercantile business, and money is advanced on property, shares, and other securities. The yarn and banking branches are conducted at No. 73 Mint Street, Madras, under the style of Murli Doss Ram Doss & Co., but the remaining industries are worked under the name of "The Madras Import Company." The business was established about the year, 1873 by the father and uncle of the present owner, who has Mr. Gokal Doss as manager over about 25 clerks. Mr. Doss owns a considerable quantity of land and property in the city of Madras, and he resides at 73 Mint Street.

N. RAM DOSS.

1. N. Ram Doss. 2. Close of a large Diamond Deal.

GOCOOLA DOSS JUMNA DOSS & CO.

There is a vast amount of conservatism in the characters of many of the old-established merchants in India, and there are hundreds of commercial houses in which partnership has been strictly limited to members of the same family. The business carried on by Gocoola Doss Jumna Doss & Co., at No. 201 China Bazaar Street, Madras, is a good illustration of this statement. It was founded in 1883 by Gocoola Doss, who died in 1897, and it then passed into the hands of the present owners, who are brothers, namely Dwarka Doss Govardan Doss, who is a director of the Buckingham and Carnatic Mills, and Purushothama Doss Gocoola Doss. The title of the firm has been retained in the same form as that which was adopted by representatives of the Doss family when they entered into the commercial life of the Presidency at the beginning of the nineteenth century.

The business is now a very extensive one, the partners dealing in silk cloths, embroidery, yarn, and other goods, and a very considerable commission agency has been built up. Money is lent on property and jewellery, and rents are derived from 20 or more houses in Madras alone. The firm are agents for colour merchants in Bombay, who supply powders and paste for dyeing purposes. Mr. Dwarka Doss Govardan Doss has managed the business since the year 1888, and he resides in the house No. 95 Narayana Mudali Street, Madras, in which his great-grandfather lived nearly one hundred years ago.

The brothers manage certain charities in the sacred place of Conjeevaram, 40 miles distant from Madras. In these charities five houses are allotted to Brahmans, who are required to keep them neat and to reside in them, and each householder is paid Rs. 3.8 a month for its upkeep. A yearly festival in the temple on the Thasaraday is celebrated out of the funds derived from these charities, and the latter are at present looked after by the junior member of the family, Purushothumadoss Gocoola Doss. He also is the honorary secretary of the Mandiram belonging to Sri Madana Mohunjee, one of the richest spiritual heads of the Guzaratee community.

N. RAM DOSS

One of the most notable instances of personal grit and of determination to succeed in scaling the ladder from the lowest rung to the top is that which is presented by the life history of Mr. Ram Doss, who is a diamond merchant,

PARAMANANDA DOSS AND CHOTA DOSS.

1. A View of the Shop. 2. The Proprietors. 3. Gumastas Group. 4. Residence.

jeweller, and precious stones dealer, carrying on business at 2-64 Mint Street, Sowcarpet, Madras. He was born at Seringapatam in 1859, and ten years later he arrived in Madras, and with a boy's pluck, yet with a man's head on the shoulders of a mere child, he started out to retail matches at the princely salary of Rs. 1.8 a month. Hadji Kasim Salay Mahomed & Co., piece-goods merchants, of Mysore, employed him from 1876 to 1887 at a remuneration which commenced at Rs. 5 and eventually reached Rs. 20; the next ten years were occupied as working partner in the firm of Chater Bhudoss Chashaldoss & Sons, who were direct importers of goods from England and Germany, and at the close of this decade his share of the net profit amounted to no less than Rs. 30,000.

Mr. Doss was a broker in precious stones from 1897 to 1901, when he became a fully fledged merchant. He now has important business transactions with Mr. A. D. Adler, of Belgium, Mr. Simon Misrali, and Messrs. Ravashanker Jagijivan & Co., both of Bombay, Mr. Jack Freedman (diamond-cutter), A. Salt et Fils, Leon Yakar and Eli Esquiange, of Antwerp, Messrs. Leon Menasthe & Co., of Bombay, Messrs. J. Stiller & Sons, of Paris, and many others.

Mr. Doss has inherited the valuable gift of being an exceptionally fine judge of all kinds of precious stones, and his services are frequently requisitioned in making valuations of collections of gems.

Very large stocks of emeralds, pearls, and rubies are kept, but the principal feature of his business is dealing in diamonds, which he purchases in the rough state in parcels, which sometimes cost as much as Rs. 5,000. Stones are set to any designs which may be required, and 10 or 12 competent workmen are employed, under his personal supervision.

Agents have been appointed in Bombay, Delhi, Calcutta, Benares, Jodhpur, Mysore, Hamburg, and in London, and his own travellers make periodical visits to all of these places.

Justice cannot be done in these brief notes to this collection of stones, as it is of such magnificence that it simply beggars description; but really good judges who have inspected the gems declare them to be the finest in Southern India. The telegraphic address of Mr. Doss is "Tiger," Madras.

PARAMANANDA DOSS AND CHOTA DOSS

This firm of Benares cloth merchants was established in Madras in 1888, and it is the oldest of its kind in Southern India. Among the special features of the stock which are set forth in printed catalogues are Cashmere shawls with lace or silk embroidery, Calcutta linen cloths, China white silk pieces, Benaresi-wares khilat and kincob pieces, "dawanies" ravikas, Pitham baram cloths, Salem and white "dovaty angavastrums," white and coloured turbans, "conjeevaram," Madura white upper cloths with fancy laced borders, Bombay silk-figured scarves and Poona "saries," Assam silks and velvets of different patterns, and a number of other artistic materials and garments. Large stocks of goods are kept, and special manufacturers have been appointed in various places to prepare new designs, according to the firm's instructions, in order to meet the public demand, which is ever changing owing to the vagaries of the female mind. Large quantities of khilat pieces are stored, and these are sold principally to persons who are desirous of making presents to Rajahs and Zamindars in connection with wedding ceremonies. The partners claim that their goods cannot be excelled in quality, and that their prices are exceedingly low in comparison with those charged by other firms.

Gold medals and first-class certificates of merit were awarded to Messrs. Paramananda Doss and Chota Doss for their exhibits at the Industrial and Art Exhibitions, Madras, in 1903, at the Industrial and Agricultural Exhibition at Bombay in 1904, and at the Agricultural Exhibition of the I.N. Congress at Benares in 1905. Maharajas, Rajas, Zamindars, and others of the higher classes in Southern India are regular patrons of this firm, and a very large connection has been established with persons who reside at a distance and who send their orders by post.

The business is carried on under the personal supervision of the partners at No. 16 Luckmoo Doss Street, Parktown, Madras, and the telegraphic address is "Silken," Madras. The partners are Lall Doss, Krishna Doss, and Baboo Doss, and all are sons of Chota Doss.

SALAY MAHOMED HAJI EBRAHIM & CO.

1. FRONT VIEW OF SHOP. 2. SALAY MAHOMED HAJI EBRAHIM SAIB.

SALAY MD. HAJI EBRAHIM & CO.

The trade-mark of this firm, which is the figure of a lion carrying an open umbrella over his head, is sufficiently unique in character to attract attention, but its claim to recognition throughout Southern India rests rather upon its reputation for the supply of high-class goods. The firm are wholesale dealers in umbrellas, hosiery, cutlery, fancy goods, felt and Turkish caps, towels, and other articles at No. 229 Esplanade Row, in Madras; but there is an adjoining retail branch store (named "The Madras Umbrella Mart") for the sale of umbrellas, parasols, and walking-sticks. The importations of the firm—either direct or through agents—include hats from the world-famed Christy and from Italy, umbrellas from several of the leading makers in England; cutlery, fancy goods, and towels are obtained from Germany, while Japan is the principal source of the hosiery supply. Large stocks of these goods are kept in hand, and travelling sale agents visit the chief towns and villages in Southern India, although the greater portion of the business is done in the mofussil, where a considerable wholesale trade is carried on with merchants.

The ancestors of the proprietor arrived in Madras from Bombay about the year 1884, but the present business was established in 1909. There are a couple of godowns quite near to the stores, while there is another one in an adjoining street. The owner is personally responsible for the management of the business, and he usually employs about 15 hands.

THE ENGLISH CYCLE IMPORTING COMPANY

There are, in all probability, twenty or more manufacturers of motor-cars, motor-cycles, and cycles who may be considered to be in the van in this line of business, and the principal difficulty with which a prospective purchaser is confronted is to know which particular type will be the most suitable for his requirements. Without a word of disparagement of other makers, the English Cycle Importing Company claim that the machines for which they are agents are superior to others in elegance of design, in soundness of construction, in wearing capability, and, what is of considerable importance, in giving good value for money. The company started as wholesale importers at Coconada about the year 1900, but owing to the rapid development of the business the headquarters were removed to 23 Broadway, Madras, the premises at the former place being retained as a branch establishment. Another branch—dealing chiefly with motor-cars, motor-cycles, and their accessories, and known as the Motor Trading Company—has been opened at Kardyl Buildings, Mount Road, Madras. A very good selection of motor and ordinary cycles is kept in stock, and agencies are held for the following: the Rover, the Sun, and New Hudson motor-cycles; and the Rover, Raleigh, Rudge-Whitworth, Centaur, Royal Enfield, Barton Humber, Singer, Rolfe, Sun, and other popular high-grade pedal cycles. The company imports large quantities of "Primus" stoves, "Hill" mantles, incandescent gas-lights, American gold-medal camp cots, tricycles, perambulators, and footballs, while a special feature is made of fountain pens of the very best quality. Several thousand cycles and a large quantity of accessories, including cycle and motor goods, are disposed of annually, and as the company is in direct communication with manufacturers it follows that the profits of "middlemen" are avoided, and that the most favourable terms can be offered to customers. The increasing popularity and reputation enjoyed by the firm as one of the largest and most reliable wholesale importers in Madras is well known throughout India, Burma, and Ceylon.

THE ENGLISH CYCLE IMPORTING COMPANY.
A PORTION OF THE SHOWROOM.

THE "GUARDIAN PRESS"

The business firm known as the "Guardian Press" was established in 1850, in a comparatively small way, for the purpose of carrying out the special work of publishing "Ramayana" in the Tamil language. The present proprietors, Messrs. G. C. Loganadham Mudaliar and G. C. Nataraja Mudalair, are relatives of the principals in the firm of Messrs. Thompson & Co., who hold a foremost position among the printers of Madras. The two brothers had an excellent training in the printing, binding, publishing, and stationery trades, and their enterprising methods have been rewarded with much success. The business, which is now carried on at 20 Second Line Beach, in Madras, came into their hands in the year 1907, and it expanded so rapidly that it became necessary to open other departments with a capital of nearly one lakh of rupees for up-to-date machinery, plant, and appliances. Although a speciality is made of printing and binding, the firm are extensively engaged in the manufacture of type and rubber stamps. Illustrated catalogues, posters, labels, visiting and other cards, and artistic printing of every kind has been produced in such style that the "Guardian Press" has obtained an excellent reputation for good workmanship. The "Guardian Diary"—an everyday *vade mecum* for the man in the street or office—has been published since 1910, and nearly 20,000 of these useful books are sold annually in Southern India. It was in 1910, too, that the partners were appointed by the Government of Madras as agents for the sale of their publications; they subsequently became printers to Messrs. Longmans, Green & Co., to the Corporation of Madras, to the Indian Industrial Conference, and to a number of the leading companies and firms in the Presidency.

The English composing department is equipped with 70 stands, each of which has four sets of different type cases, and it is furnished with a large number of frames, tables, galleys, and racks. The jobbing branch has 350 sorts of heading types for various works, together with 50 kinds of wooden types for posters. The machine-room is very complete in its arrangements, and it contains modern plant by the best English makers. All the motive power is derived from electricity, which is supplied by the Madras Electric Supply Corporation. The book-binding-room is fitted with plant and appliances for every kind of work, such as ledgers, cash and day books, and law and other volumes. Modern type-casting machinery has been installed, and 15 founts of English-made matrixes are now producing 3,000 lb. of type every month.

Nearly 200 hands are employed, under the personal supervision of the proprietors, and the latter are now reaping the reward which is invariably associated with strict attention to the wishes of customers and with a rigid adherence to punctuality in the execution of orders.

THE "GUARDIAN PRESS."

1. Workmen. 2. Composing-room. 3. Printing-room. 4. Binding-room.

HARRISON & CO.

It would be impossible to describe in detail the varied and choice stock kept in this establishment, but a visit to the showrooms will convince the most exacting person that the wants of everybody can be met, no matter what his or her particular choice or taste may be. All the latest novelties that are manufactured in England and on the Continent in the confectionery line are represented, and, apart from their own manufactures, are the purest, finest, and best obtainable in the East, and include such comestibles as chocolates in plain and fancy boxes, crystalized fruits and creams, caramels, Turkish delights, almond-pasted fancies made in exact imitations of flowers, fruits, and vegetables, and, during festive seasons, such delicacies as are manufactured for the occasion. The firm make a speciality of bride-cakes, and they are able to claim that their productions in this line have figured prominently in most of the important and fashionable weddings for very many years. The quality of the cake itself is of the richest possible make, while the decorations are most artistic, and the mode of packing them is such that they guarantee a cake to arrive safely at any destination in the world. As caterers they are in a position to undertake functions of any description and magnitude either locally or in the mofussil, and they will be pleased to send estimates and specimen menus for banquets, ball suppers, dinners, receptions, picnics, shooting-parties, tournaments, and sports at inclusive rates for servants and all necessaries.

In recent years the firm have been entrusted with the catering for the most important functions in the Presidency, all of which commissions they have carried out punctually and satisfactorily. They have provided the Caledonian Society's annual dinner for several years in succession, and all guests have always expressed entire satisfaction at the manner in which the banquet was served, at the high-class quality of the table requisites, and at the excellent quality of the dishes. In wines they hold a large, varied, and choice stock of selected vintages and choice reserves, such as Amontillado, Oloroso, and Vino Secco.

There is a well-appointed restaurant on the first floor of the premises at No. 168 Popham's Broadway, Madras, where meals are served at short notice, and light refreshments and ices are obtainable from 8 a.m. to 11 p.m. daily, Sundays included, while a string band is in attendance every Wednesday and Saturday evening until 11 o'clock. There is also a separate department for hire goods, such as crockery, cutlery, glass and electro-plated ware, table linen, dining and drawing-room furniture, and carpets.

The factories and warehouses occupy very large premises on the Broadway and in adjacent streets, and the business is conducted on strictly scientific and hygienic principles. Warrants of appointment as confectioners and caterers to his Excellency the Governor of Madras and to his Highness the Rajah of Cochin's Durbar have been granted to this firm, which was established in 1891. The proprietor devotes personal attention to all orders, and his long, practical experience enables him to give the utmost satisfaction.

THE INDIA PRINTING WORKS

These general and extensive printing works are situated in Armenian Street, Madras, facing the High Court, and near to the Law College, the First Grade Educational Colleges (such as the Christian College and the Pachiappas), and to all the leading commercial and trading firms. It is owned by Mr. S. Subramaniam, who spares no pains to meet, and who is scrupulously solicitous of, the requirements, and at times the idiosyncrasies of his large and representative clientèle. Between 80 and 90 hands are constantly employed, and all kinds of printing work, high-class magazine and bookwork, commercial illustrated catalogues, pictorial covers, and job posters and leaflets are executed with artistic nicety, neatness, and elegance. A few minutes' interview with the manager, Mr. N. S. Balakrishnan, reveals the business capacity of the controlling force of this large establishment, and customers are generally satisfied with the promptness with which work is executed and with the manner in which it is carried out.

The printing plant is thoroughly up to date in every respect. It is driven by electricity, and it includes one double crown machine (by Elliot), one double royal of German make, Phoenix and Prouty treadle, gilding and cutting machines, hot and double royal presses, and one galley press. The composing-hall is divided into four sections: (*a*) jobbing, (*b*) general work, (*c*) Tamil, (*d*) Telugu and Sanskrit. The sections are carried on independently of each other; each one has its own imposing-stone, and there are departments for binding, ruling, and gilding ledger and other books of account. Printing is done for the Bank of Madras and for several other important companies and firms, and artistic sale catalogues are a distinctive feature of these works. An extensive connection has been established in the mofussil and in the southern portion of the Presidency generally.

The proprietor of the Press also owns the copyright in a fortnightly legal periodical, entitled the *Indian Law Journal*, which is edited by a High Court lawyer of over twenty years' standing in the profession. The journal has a large circulation in all parts of India and the protected native States. It is the only journal in India which gives the current decisions in full of the Privy Council, the Chartered High Courts, and the non-Chartered Superior Courts in India and Burma, and the Statutes, Rules, and Orders promulgated from time to time by the Government of India, the various provincial Governments, and the chief Controlling Revenue and Judicial Authorities. Each number of the journal contains a valuable selection of cases decided by the House of Lords, the Privy Council (on appeal from the Colonies), the High Court of Justice in England, in the King's Bench, Chancery, and Probate Divisions, and in the Court of Appeal, such as are useful in the construction of Indian Statutes *in pari materia* or whose principles are applicable to the uncodified law of India. A general legal miscellany, covering between 30 and 40 pages, precedes each number of the reports, and this chronicles interesting legal incidents, reminiscences, and amenities of Bench and Bar, anecdotal legal notes of a humorous character, notes of interesting American and colonial decisions, and a brief résumé of contemporary legal literature. Each number contains an intelligible syllabus index, and the latter is followed up by periodical cumulative indexes consolidating the previous ones. The subscription is very moderately fixed at Rs. 1 for each number, inclusive of all expenses. It is very popular in India with the legal profession and judiciary, and it should prove useful to law students prosecuting their studies in the English Inns of Court, as well as to counsel engaged in Indian Appeals before the Judicial Committee of the Privy Council.

M. DORAISAMY IYENGAR AND BROTHERS

Mr. M. Doraisamy Iyengar commenced business as a timber merchant, with Mr. T. Seshadry Iyengar as co-partner, in 1894, under the name and style of "M. Doraisamy Iyengar and T. Seshadry Iyengar." On the dissolution of the partnership in 1906, the present firm of M. Doraisamy Iyengar and Brothers was established, and it is practically commanding the Madras timber market, owing to the skill and wide experience of the senior partner (which extend over nearly a quarter of a century), coupled with the hearty co-operation of his three brothers, who are University men possessing high educational and commercial attainments. The firm formerly acted as agents to Messrs. Shaw, Wallace & Co., of Madras, for N.I.H.M. Java teak.

The firm are large importers of timber of several varieties from Rangoon, Moul-

HARRISON & CO.

1. Exterior View. 2. Wedding Cake.

THE "INDIAN LAW JOURNAL" AND INDIA PRINTING WORKS.

1. EXTERIOR OF INDIA PRINTING WORKS. 2. THE STAFF. 3. COMPOSING-ROOM. 4. MACHINE-ROOM.

M. DORAISAMY IYENGAR AND BROTHERS.

1. Front View of the Office. 2. Side and Front View of the Office. 3. M. Doraisamy Iyengar. 4. M. Chakravarthy Iyengar. 5. M. Seshadry Iyengar. 6. M. Sudarsanam Iyengar.

mein, Bangkok, Mandalay, Java, Singapore, and the Andaman Islands, and these imports include square and round logs, battens, scantlings, planks, posts, boards, sleepers, and flitches.

A very wide connection has been established throughout Southern India, both on the sea coasts and inland, and large quantities of all kinds of timber are supplied to merchants, both in the interior and in the out-ports against contracts fixed either annually or from time to time. Assorted stocks of teak-wood, steam-sawn scantlings of all sizes and lengths, suitable for floors, joists, rafters, posts, doors, windows, office partitions, high-class polished furniture, and framework, are kept at Madras, and fresh consignments of timber are received weekly from Burma and other countries. It has been alleged that contractors and builders have not always been able to procure on a given date all sizes to their requirements in mill-sawn timber, but Doraisamy Iyengar and Brothers hold such an immense stock that they are readily able to meet all orders with that promptitude for which the firm is justly famous. Among the numerous important customers of the firm are the Government of Madras, the railway authorities, municipalities, Taluq Boards, and unions. Well-seasoned timber of special sizes and lengths and of superior quality is essential for the making of sound furniture, and it is by using these specially cut sizes that the consumption of wood is minimized and the charges for the made-up goods are kept at the lowest possible prices. This firm keeps a good stock in hand to meet the heavy and constant demand of a large number of the leading cabinet-makers and upholsterers of the Presidency, who are counted among its best customers.

It has ever been the policy of the firm to supply the right goods at the right time ; they always guarantee entire satisfaction, as all orders are attended to by the proprietors themselves ; and it is their straightforward dealing in business which has won for them the high position and esteem which they now command.

G. VENKATRAMA IYER.

RESIDENCE OF THE DISTRICT ENGINEER (S.I. RAILWAY COMPANY) AT TANJORE, ERECTED BY G. VENKATRAMA IYER.

T. SASHADRI IYENGAR

The largest timber merchant's business in Madras is that which is owned by Mr. T. Sashadri Iyengar, of Sydenham's Road, near Salt Cottaurs, and he has had sole control since 1906, when the partnership which had subsisted for about fifteen years between himself and Mr. Doraiswamy Iyengar was dissolved by mutual consent. From 1913 the business has been managed by his two able sons, Mr. T. Rangaswami Aiengar and Mr. T. Srinivasa Chariar, B.A., their father having retired owing to increasing age. Six clerks are kept in the office, and about ten labourers are constantly employed, although extra hands are engaged when necessary.

The timber-yard in Sydenham's Road covers an area about 12,000 sq. ft., and a very large and varied stock is kept here, as well as on an extensive storage-ground on the sea beach. A special feature is made of the importation of teak from Rangoon and Moulmein, but logs and scantlings cut from different kinds of trees are obtained from Palghat, Mysore, Burma, Siam, and other places. Sawn timber is imported periodically from Rangoon, and all cargoes, with the exception of bulky logs, are landed by boats, floating by water not being viewed with favour.

Much of this is imported to the principal ports in India, and a very large trade is done with the Government and with Government and railway contractors in the Madras Presidency. Contracts are entered into for supplying wholesale merchants throughout the mofussil, and the latter frequently avail themselves of the very liberal terms—namely, a credit for two months—which Mr. Sashadri Iyengar is able to offer them.

The majority of the large buildings which have been constructed recently in Madras have been fitted with timber from these yards, and it is no small satisfaction to this contractor and supplier that a very large proportion of his customers consist of companies and firms who have been dealing with him for a number of years and have thus shown their confidence in him.

There is also a sawing department attached to the timber-yards, where scantlings and planks are neatly cut, according to orders, and these are delivered with that promptitude which is a *sine qua non* with every successful business man.

G. VENKATRAMA IYER, B.A.

It has frequently been observed that persons who have received higher University education are apt to look upon business careers with disfavour. They generally prefer to enter Government service or to join the overstocked professions of law and medicine, with very doubtful prospects of success. Considerable difficulty was until very recently experienced in the carrying out of contracts for Government and private works for want of educated, intelligent, and properly trained contractors. Fortunately the prejudice against business careers shown by educated people is being overcome ; still, it was courageous on the part of Mr. G. Venkatrama Iyer, a graduate of about fifteen years' standing, to have sought a future outside Government service, espe-

T. SASHADRI IYENGAR.

1. THE TIMBER YARD. 2. OFFICE. 3. T. RANGASAMI IYENGAR. 4. T. SRINIVASCHARI

cially as he comes from a family connected for longer than a generation with the higher ranks of Government service. After a course of apprenticeship and thorough business training he established himself in business about the year 1906, in Mount Road, Madras, as a contractor, builder, furnisher, and general mercantile agent. His firm has executed building and other works for Government departments, the Bank of Madras, the National Bank of India, and other important companies. Contracts for buildings and their requirements, articles of furniture, and all manner of wood and iron work, uniform clothing, and its requisites are executed by his firm, and manufacturers have shown the greatest confidence in him by seeking his advice and co-operation for the disposal of their goods. He has recently erected for the South Indian Railway Company, Ltd., a very pretty dwelling-house at Tanjore, in which reinforced concrete has been largely used in construction, an illustration of which is given herewith.

V. KALYANARAM IYER & CO.

Scholarly men and women who have made their names famous in the world of literature are deserving of the highest praise not only from the student of history, of political economy, of the sciencies, of theology, the drama, or of fiction, but from the young who are taking their first steps in learning. The publisher, too, is a benefactor, as he sends his books to every corner of the globe for the enlightenment or the amusement of young and old alike. The inhabitants of Madras certainly cannot complain that the facilities for the purchase of books are few in number, as there are numerous establishments where thoroughly up-to-date stocks are kept. One of the best known of these in Madras is this firm, which carries on its business at No. 190 The Esplanade, one of the principal thoroughfares in the city. It was founded in May 1884 by Mr. V. Kalyanaram Iyer, who was sole proprietor until 1900, when he took in a partner, who retired from the partnership in 1904. Then Mr. K. Ramaratnam Aiyer, B.A., the present proprietor, joined the firm as an assistant and manager, and subsequently bought out the original owner and became sole proprietor, keeping the title of the firm unchanged.

The firm are general booksellers and publishers, and they are agents for the sale of Government publications. All kinds of books—from a penny reader to an encyclopædia — are kept, and all of them, with the exception of those in Tamil, are imported from England and America. Books to the value of about Rs. 40,000 are purchased annually, and these consist very largely of college and school books, of legal works, fiction, novels, and general literature. The firm have direct relations with several colleges and schools, which they regularly supply with text-books for educational purposes in addition to literature of a varied character for the libraries of the institutions. It may be added that the firm are the publishers of the special Indian editions of Dr. Marden's world-famous inspirational books. The proprietor personally manages every department with his principal assistant, Mr. K. Mahadevan. The telegraphic address is "Kalyanaram."

V. KALYANARAM IYER & CO.
SHOWROOM.

V. R. KAMATH & CO.

Thousands of persons put new furniture into houses annually, but probably 75 per cent. of those individuals do not "furnish" their dwellings, for the simple reason that they are lacking in artistic taste, and are consequently unable to make such a combination of domestic articles as will produce a perfectly harmonious effect. It is fortunate for such people that they can call to their aid firms who make a speciality of giving advice and assistance, and who go farther, indeed, by supplying all household requsites from a wooden spoon to an elaborate drawing or bedroom suite.

The partners of Messrs. V. R. Kamath & Co. are Messrs. U. Vittal Rao and P. W. Kamath, and both of them had considerable practical training in cabinet-making and in decorative furnishing before they established themselves in business in 1907. Indigenous wood, seasoned on the premises and purchased in the Madras Presidency, is used for manufacturing purposes generally, but a quantity of teak is obtained from Burma. Furniture has been supplied by this firm to Government House, Madras, to the Governments of Cochin and Travancore, to the Prime Minister of Hyderabad, and to the nobility throughout Southern India. The stand for the Presidency casket which was presented to H.M. King George V on his recent visit to India was made by Messrs. Kamath & Co., and it was greatly admired by all who saw it. The premises are situated in Mount Road, which is the leading thoroughfare in Madras, but greater accommodation has become a necessity owing to the rapid growth of the firm's business.

Persons who scan the daily newspapers will see that Messrs. Kamath & Co. are great believers in the value of advertising, as there is scarcely a literary sheet of importance in the Presidency which does not set forth the advantages to be obtained by dealing with them.

The carving of wood is undertaken by experts, but every order which is received is personally attended to by one of the partners.

Between 150 and 200 hands are constantly employed.

NAGRAJ KAUNMULL

True art is the ability to appreciate the beautiful in painting, sculpture, literature, or science, or to conceive in the mind and to transfer to canvas, marble, metal, tapestry, or other substance impressions which have been received either from a study of scenery, or of a figure which passes before the eye, or has been produced by the imagination of the brain. Every age has had its artists, and even the crude specimens of painting and sculpture which have been unearthed after centuries of burial bear unmistakable signs of the artistic temperament which, under other circumstances and at other times would have been considerably developed.

V. R. KAMATH & CO.

ENTRANCE TO THE FURNITURE SHOWROOMS AND FACTORY.

India, with her philosophy and traditions, has had her sculptors and painters, and in the latter school one might refer to typical examples of early art which appeared in paintings which were produced between the first century before Christ and the sixth or seventh centuries of the Christian era. The greater portion of these have perished, but it was in the reign of the Emperor Jehangir (1605-28) that painting in India reached its highest point of excellence.

In passing, one might observe that the period between the years 1600 and 1800 produced some very noted masters in all branches of literature, science, and art. There were Shakespeare, Milton, Goethe, and Scott, those giants in poetry, drama, and novel; we had Rubens and Rembrandt among painters; and Galileo, Harvey, and Newton were prominent among the brilliant scientists of that period. The work which was done by Indian painters of that age was excellent in artistic taste; real life seems to have been infused into their portrait miniatures, and the greatest accuracy marked the carrying out of their designs.

It was doubtless one of these talented men who illustrated a very rare manuscript which was written in Hindi about the year 1600, and which has been in the possession of the Kaunmull family for many generations. It is called Panchathanthra, and while it savours somewhat of the fables of Æsop, it differs from that well-known work in that it has a strong leaning towards the dramatic. It presents a faithful portraiture of Hindu life at the commencement of the seventeenth century, and the characters of the narrative are represented by human beings, animals, and birds. The illustrations, which number about 360, and are beautifully painted by hand in choicest colours, are so exquisitely done that they convey a world of meaning to the reader. Special interest attaches to these paintings, as the artist has not merely faithfully depicted his animals and birds in lifelike form, but he has invested their faces with living beauty. On one page there are animals apparently talking, discussing, or quarrelling; another picture shows us birds fluttering from tree to tree and carolling their sweetest songs just through sheer happiness and joy of freedom;

NAGRAJ KAUNMULL.

The Remarkable Book and some of its Illustrations.

another set of paintings finely illustrates the palaces of kings and courtiers of these days, while others depict battles between the dependents of two love-lorn grandees, all for the love of a lady. A highly interesting and clever drama has been added, and this is enriched by illustrations depicting love, hate, passion, court life, and other striking episodes which are presented on the theatrical stage.

"A thing of beauty is a joy for ever," and the volume in question is, without doubt, one of the unique antiquities of the choicest handiwork rarely to be met with in any country. It is believed that the work was prepared in obedience to the order of one of the early native princes of Rajputana.

Rajputana is rich in historical romance and chivalry, and the Rajputs are the aristocracy of India, being in possession of very large areas of land either as owners or receivers of rents. The Kaunmulls of to-day are direct descendants of the Rajput nobles, and they can trace their ancestry for an almost indefinite period. The present head of the house has a number of title-deeds of his properties in Rajputana, and he possesses some of them more than 150 years old, and a magnificent collection of art treasures. Mention may be made of the Old and New Testaments contained in three volumes, which were printed in the Dutch language at Amsterdam by Pieter Mortier in the year 1700. These books contain a very large number of excellently wrought steel engravings, and they are in a perfect state of preservation.

Mr. Nagraj Kaunmull is, further, a wholesale and retail dealer in precious stones (principally diamonds), and his services as a valuer of these are frequently requisitioned.

Mr. Nagraj Kaunmull, a son of the above-named, is in partnership with Mr. C. Sundara Ramanjulu Naidu, B.A., carrying on business as Italian marble merchants at No. 50 Broadway, Madras, under the style of Somasundara & Co. They have regular importations of stone from Carrara, and this is worked up for columns and steps in buildings, for tables, and, occasionally, for tombstones. The business was not established until the year 1912, but the firm employs about twenty hands constantly.

KING & CO.

A business which has stood the test of three decades of commercial prosperity and depression is one which may be rightly looked upon as one of the sound industrial establishments of a city, and the firm of King & Co. of Madras is a case in point. The partners are the brothers Rao Saib C. Cunnan Chetty and Mr. C. Ramanujam Chetty, but the grandfather and father of the present owners established themselves about the year 1880. The business subsequently passed into the hands of an uncle in conjunction with the brothers, but the latter have been sole proprietors since 1912. The firm have large transactions throughout India in timber, sugar, and spirituous liquors, and they also hold sales by auction at regular intervals of imported piece goods. Timber is imported from Rangoon, Moulmein, Bangkok, and Java; sugar is indented from Java, and the agency of the Nellikuppam sugar factories is held by the firm. Messrs. Chetty own extensive godowns and offices at No. 4 First Line Beach, and they employ about 30 hands constantly. When his Excellency the Viceroy, Lord Hardinge, visited Madras towards the close of the year 1913, a magnificent arch was constructed by the firm in his honour.

KING & CO.
VIEW OF THE PREMISES.

R. KASIVISVANATHA MUDALIAR

My Lady Nicotine has many votaries, and diverse are the forms in which homage is paid to her in different parts of the world. In England the old habit of snuff-taking has gone out of fashion, but it prevails in India in undiminished popularity.

"Shunmugan" snuff! What a charm of consolation, comfort, joy, and gladness these two words mean to an Indian! Famous ever since its introduction in 1839, Shunmugam snuff rules the market, and it commands the largest sale throughout India, Burma, Ceylon, the Straits Settlements, and South Africa. It is the acme of quality and genuineness, and in its manufacture no trouble and expense are spared. Tobaccos are purchased from the original places of growth, and the greatest care is taken in the blending of high-class varieties which are known only to the manufacturer by reason of his long experience in this line of business, and this has been the secret of success for more than seventy years. Almost every post brings letters of praise

PREMISES OF R. KASIVISVANATHA MUDALIAR.

for the snuff, and countless are the tributes from customers from every quarter. Since the reader may rightly desire to participate in such universal appreciation of this remarkable product, he is directed to R. Kasivisvanatha Mudaliar, Post Box 140, Madras.

RAJVAIDYA NARAYANJI KESHAVJI

Rajvaidya Narayanji Keshavji, the proprietor of the world-renowned pharmacy, Ayurvedodaya Aushadhalaya Jamnagar of Kathiawar, sprung from a distinguished family of physicians who were successively Rajvaidyas to their Highnesses the Jamsahibs of Jamnagar during the past two hundred years. The Ayurvedic medicines which were manufactured by the doctor's predecessors were so efficacious that they afforded prompt and certain relief in cases where the disease was obstinate, chronic, or even deemed incurable.

In the year 1896 the proprietor founded the Ayurvedodaya Pharmacy, and, at the urgent request of a large number of friends, he issued advertisements in the leading newspapers and periodicals in India setting forth the benefits to be derived from the use of the various preparations. This naturally caused a considerable increase in business, but there was a sad side to the picture, as every post brought heart-rending letters from suffering patients, and the proprietor, who is possessed of a deeply sympathetic nature, was induced to publish, in the Gujarati language, a pamphlet entitled " Vaidya Vidya," which claims to be an infallible guide to those who desire to remain absolutely free from the ravages of disease.

This pamphlet was then issued in the following languages, namely: Telugu, Canarese, Tamil, Bengali, English, Hindi, Marathi, and Urdu, while translations in the Malayalam, Burmese, and Sinhalese tongues are now in the press. The earlier printed editions were distributed gratuitously far and wide, and orders for medicines began to pour in from all parts of India. Rajvaidya then saw the necessity for having branches in the chief cities, and he forthwith opened establishments in Bombay, Calcutta, and Madras, in order that patients might be supplied quickly with any preparation which might be required. Residents in Burma and Ceylon then asked for facilities for obtaining these miraculous preparations, and agents were accordingly appointed in Rangoon and Colombo, but the steadily increasing sales point to the fact that still further agencies will have to be opened.

Thousands of unsolicited testimonials have been received from Maharajas, Shethias, and others, while a medal and a certificate of merit were awarded at the Benares Industrial Exhibition.

SUBRAI KOTTADIA V.

This precious stones merchant obtains his supply of diamonds direct from continental markets, and his is a noted house at Madras for moderate prices and for the highest quality of the gems. With an up-to-date business system Mr. Subrai Kottadia V. deals largely with retail and wholesale customers, and he is in close commercial touch with princes and other leading men in Southern India. Jewellery is also manufactured from other precious stones to suit the fancies of customers, and all work is done by thorough experts. Mr. Subrai Kottadia's premises are at 85 Nyniappa Naick Street, Sowcarpet, Madras, and his telegraphic address is " Precious."

RAJVAIDYA NARAYANJ KESHAVJI.

N. M. S. SADASIVIER KRISHNIER & CO.

A trader commenced business about the year 1870 in Madras in a very humble manner as a dealer in gold thread and twist, and to him belongs the honour of being the first man to engage in the industry in the city. This was Sundararamier, and he, by his energy and foresight, built up a large and lucrative business. He was regarded as a prince among the merchants of Southern India, and there are many of his relatives and friends living to-day who have reason to remember with gratitude the very practical manner in which they were assisted by him, as he never refused help in any case of real need. Numbers of instances, too, could be quoted where prosperous merchants of to-day owe their position to the helping hand which he put forth when they were starting upon their commercial careers. After his death in 1911 his sons, N. M. Sadasivier and Krishnier, continued the well-established business, on the sound practical lines laid down by the founder.

Gold thread is imported in large quantities direct from Lyons in France; twist, or cotton yarn, is obtained under indent from Manchester and from the firms at Madras, and the greater portion of these goods is disposed of in the mofussil. Several travelling agents are employed regularly, but each of the partners undertakes three or four business tours each year in order to keep in touch with their customers. The brothers are natives of Madura, where a branch business has been carried on at No. 1137 East Marret Street, and they are owners of these premises as well as of a considerable quantity of land in the neighbourhood of that town.

The elder brother, Sadasivier, is manager at Madura, while the younger has the supervision of the head office at Madras. About 34 hands are constantly employed at the two establishments. The telegraphic address is "Pervading."

THE LAW PRINTING HOUSE

An eminent lawyer once said: "Reports are the means by which judicial determinations are disseminated, or, rather, they constitute the very disseminations itself." The law is in a continual state of growth by the accretions of judicial decisions, and the importance which courts attach to judicial precedents renders their publications an absolute necessity. Books of reference, well written or compiled, are of incalculable value to the Bench as well as to the Bar, and works—such as those which are prepared by the Lawyer's Companion Office, started by the late lamented Mr. T. V. Sanjiva Row and published by the Law Printing House, in Madras—are repositories of a wealth of legal information. Mr. T. V. Sanjiva Row, who was a first-grade pleader at Trichinopoly, first started his law publications in the year 1885, and he issued a monthly digest of case-law from the reported High Court judgments. One of his chief ambitions was to bring out "a serial publication containing, *in extenso*, all the decisions of the highest judicial tribunals of the land in such a manner as would meet the requirements of the ordinary practitioner, and priced sufficiently low so as to be within reach of every one." His efforts in this direction were continued until the year 1900, when his practice at the Bar had grown to such an extent that his literary work had to be discontinued for

SUBRAI KOTTADIA V.
DIAMOND MERCHANT.

a time. During the following year, however, Mr. Row decided to relinquish a considerable number of his court engagements in order that he might devote more of his time to authorship. In 1903 he published the second edition of his famous "Digest of Privy Council Rulings," a work which received cordial support from the Government of Madras, from the United and Central Provinces, and from the legal professions especially, This treatise was so well received that ence and in constant practical use, with all the case-law noted in their appropriate places, thus aiding the busy practitioner in understanding the real object and scope of the several sections of each of such enactments." The "Current Index of Indian Cases" is in the tenth year of issue; it is published monthly, and is a digest of cases reported in all the law journals in India, both official and non-official, and it is consolidated once in every six months. "The Lawyer's veritable storehouses of most useful and up-to-date information." "The All-India Digest," published in two sections, Criminal and Civil, is another most useful work. The criminal section covers two volumes, while the civil section runs to more than ten volumes, of about 1,000 pages each. Every case reported in all the law reports published in this country from 1811 up to date is digested, classified, and logically arranged under appropriate headings and sub-headings, with

N. M. S. SADASIVIER KRISHNIER & CO.

1. N. M. SUNDARARAMIER (FATHER). 2. N. M. S. SADASIVIER (ELDEST SON), AND N. M. S. KRISHNIER (YOUNGEST SON). 3. THE PREMISES IN MADRAS.

Mr. Row became more and more impressed with the need of systematic law publishing in India, and during the latter part of the year 1903 the "Lawyer's Companion" Office was established in Trichinopoly, where he secured the cooperation of a number of *vakils* to assist him in the work of writing various works on law, which were then, and for some time afterwards, continued to be printed at private presses in that town and in Madras. Among such publications may be mentioned the "Lawyer's Companion," which contains commentaries on almost all the "important acts of everyday reference" (Civil and Criminal) is a most valuable production, and the *Madras Mail*, in a review in its issue of December 6, 1910, says: "These volumes give an historical survey of the case-law contained in the Indian Law Reports, official and private. Unlike several other similar books of reference, they show at a glance the several points of law dealt with in each case, and, what is more, they give all the subsequent cases found in the numerous legal periodicals in the country bearing upon every such point. No member of the legal profession can afford to be without these volumes, as they are numerous cross-references, with foot-notes of cases subsequently decided, and with historical memoirs. This work is a gigantic and monumental one, being in every respect better than its rivals in the field."

The work of writing and compilation is done at Trichinopoly, Madras, and to some limited extent in Calcutta, but up to this time the printing of the books had been entrusted to local firms. Early in 1909 Mr. Sanjiva Row became convinced that it would be more satisfactory if he had a printing press of his own, under his personal supervision, and he

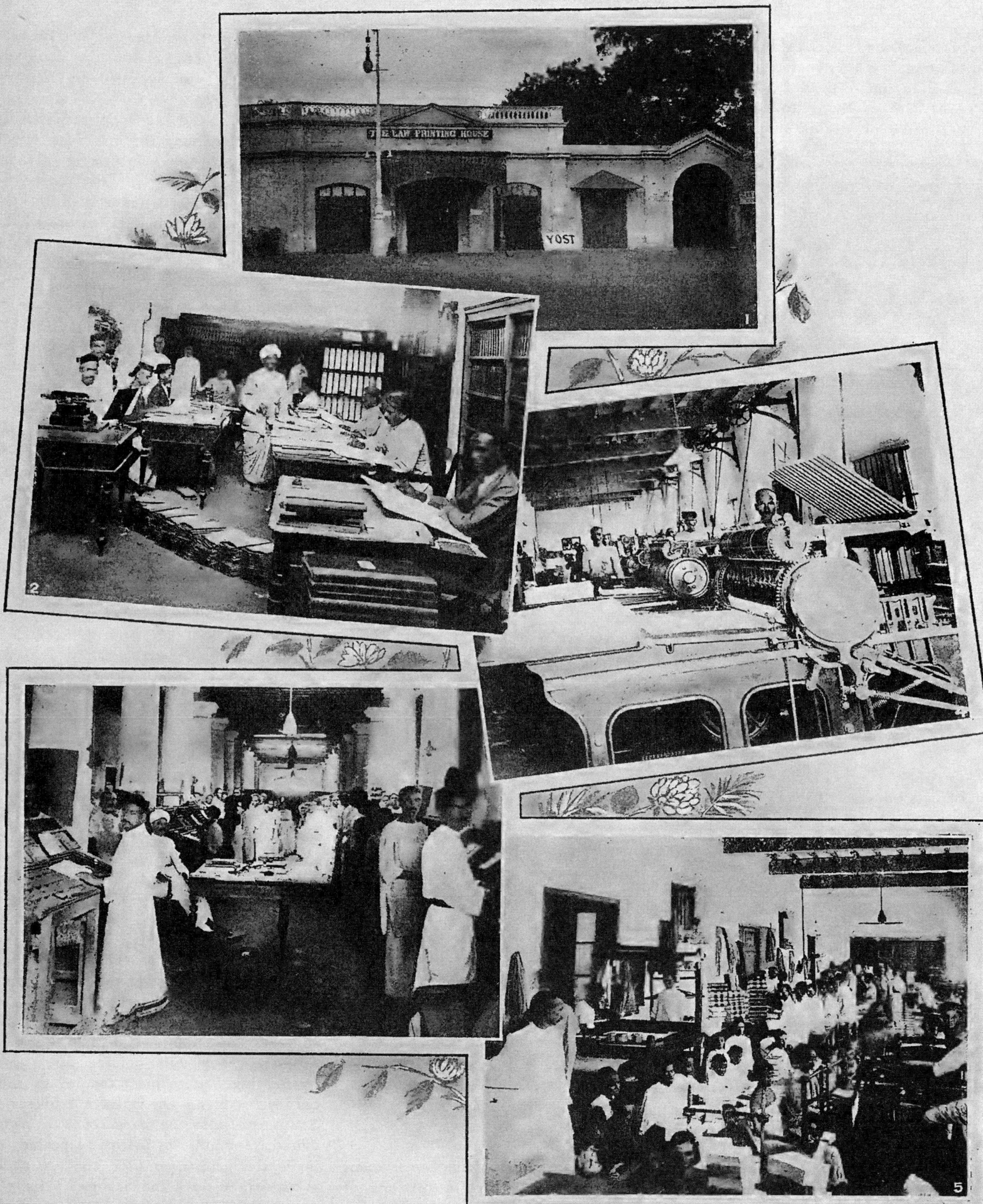

THE LAW PRINTING HOUSE.

1. EXTERIOR. 2. THE OFFICE. 3. COMPOSING HALL. 4. MACHINE-ROOM. 5. BINDING DEPARTMENT.

accordingly established the Law Printing House in Madras.

Mr. Row, unfortunately, died in September 1910, without living to see the gradual realization of all his ambitions. Messrs. T. A. Venkaswamy Row and T. S. Krishnasawmy Row, his nephew and his son, sole proprietors of the Law Printing House, have succeeded him, and in their press they find regular employment for about 450 hands. The work of authorship and compilation is still done by the professional gentlemen who were assisting the late Mr. T. V. Sanjiva Row. The year 1913 marked an epoch in the history of the Law Printing House, as in April of that year permission was obtained from the Government of India to make verbatim reprints of the Indian Law Reports from the year 1876 to 1900, and this work is now being done under the style of the "Indian Decisions, New Series."

SOHUNMULL CHORDIA SAH AGURCHUND MANMULL.
BANKER.

Thoroughly modern machinery has been obtained from Messrs. W. Dawson & Son, Ltd., of London; a complete stock of type was supplied by Messrs. Stephenson, Blake & Co., and two oil-engines of 8 and 12 h.p. respectively are used for driving the machines, which are able to turn out 4,000 pages of royal octavo every month.

General printing is undertaken, but the proprietors make a special feature of the publication of legal volumes, while the plant in the binding department is up to date in every respect. The publishers have gained the confidence of the general public by reason of the excellent workmanship displayed and by the steadiness with which it is being carried on.

Leading members of the Bench and Bar have given their warm patronage to this establishment, and many are the letters of commendation which have been received from judges and practitioners.

It is hoped that the "Lawyer's Companion" Office and the Law Printing House, which came into existence under such favourable auspices, will continue to do the useful work they are now turning out, and flourish as permanent institutions of the country.

SAH AGURCHUND MANMULL

There is no truer barometer of prosperity or depression in the trade of the world than the information which is given in the balance-sheets of its banking institutions. The money market is controlled by financial experts, and the stability of a country or a firm may be gauged by the nature of the terms upon which a loan can be secured. Bankers, therefore, hold a most responsible position, and they can, to a very great extent, make or mar a country by granting or refusing financial assistance. Bankers ought to be the best friends of commercial firms; they are the custodians of accumulated capital; they are discounters of bills; and in times of necessity they will bolster up a man by helping him to meet temporary difficulties. Among the private bankers of Southern India the name of Sah Agurchund Manmull is justly respected, as he is the proprietor of a concern which is conducted on sound business principles and which is staffed by assistants who vie with their chief in their courteous behaviour to the bank's customers.

The institution was founded in 1847 by Agurchund Sowcar, grandfather of the present proprietor, Sohunmull Chordia, and on the death of the former, in 1891, the business was transferred to his son, Sah Manmull Chordia, who was a magistrate in the district of Jodhpur for a period of three years. After his death, in 1895, the widow of Sah Manmull adopted the present proprietor, Sohunmull Chordia, who is still carrying on the business under the same style or firm of Sah Agurchund Manmull. The operations of the bank were comparatively small at first, but they have now attained very large proportions, owing to the strictly honourable and up-to-date methods which have been a feature of the management.

The greater portion of the bank's business consists in the collection of salaries, pensions, dividends, legacies, and other moneys on behalf of regimental officers and Government officials; but the professional and commercial section of the clients is now exceedingly large.

The late Agurchund Sowcar bequeathed one lakh of rupees for charitable purposes, and the interest from this sum (which is invested in Government securities) is still being distributed to necessitous institutions and persons by the present proprietor. Mr. Sohunmull, the sub-proprietor of the aforesaid firm of Sah Agurchund Manmull, gives personal supervision to the affairs of the bank, but his sterling character has earned for him the position of Jaghirdar of the villages of Kuppam Badur and Chinna Paramala, in the district of North Arcot. His private acts of charity are known to be very numerous, although the particulars relating to them are a "sealed book"; but his latest public benefactions include a donation of about Rs. 2,500 to the Madras S.P.C.A., together with a sum of Rs. 3,000 to the Panjrapole, in the same city.

This gentleman occupies an honourable position among his Jain co-religionists, and, owing to ill-health, he was reluctantly compelled to decline the presidency of the annual Congress which was held at Secunderabad in 1913. Mr. Sohunmull is the owner of a quantity of immovable property in Madras, as well as in Jodhpur, Kucheruj, and Marwar, in the Western Rajputana States Agency.

Each of the two previous proprietors of the bank made provision in his will for the expenditure of a sum of Rs. 20,000 for the feeding of a number of poor people during the period of the funeral ceremonies, and special permission had to be obtained from the Maharajah of Jodhpur before so large a sum of money could be spent, as it is the practice of the authorities in that State to satisfy themselves that a prospective donor of charity is able to bear the necessary cost.

T. B. MEHTA & SONS

No more choice collection of diamonds, emeralds, rubies, and pearls can be seen in the city of Madras than that which is carried by this firm in their establishment at No. 453 Mint Street; and it may be added that the business is one of the oldest of its kind in Southern India, as it was founded early in the nineteenth century. The founder was T. Balakrishmehta, the father of the present proprietor, and on his death the two sons, T. Subraya Mehta and T. Nilakanta Mehta, jointly continued the business, under the name of T. B. Mehta & Sons. T. Nilakanta Mehta has since died, and Subraya Mehta is now sole owner.

Diamonds, which are cut in continental markets, are imported continually, although some old Indian stones are occasionally obtained. A very large stock of gems and made-up jewellery is kept on hand, but a speciality is made of the setting of stones, according to designs submitted by his customers. Many Rajahs and important personages have been supplied with jewellery by this firm, and the business, which was commenced in a small way with a limited amount of stock, has now grown to very considerable dimensions. This success has only been achieved by the strict personal attention and the indomitable energy of the proprietor, who is now assisted in the management by his sons.

T. B. MEHTA & SONS.
T. SUBRAYA MEHTA, T. RAMANATHA MEHTA, AND T. RANGANATHA MEHTA.

P. LOGANATHA MUDALIAR

Much of the architecture in India has undergone a considerable change since the commencement of the twentieth century, due to the partial acceptance of certain Western ideas by Oriental designers, and it must be admitted that the results have not always been satisfactory. No complaint of this nature can, however, be made against some of the principal buildings which have been erected by Mr. Loganatha Mudaliar, of Vaihyanatha Mudali Street, Madras, as they are striking witnesses of sound work which has been carried out on truly artistic lines. The proprietor had obtained a thoroughly practical knowledge of engineering and contracting before he commenced business on his own account in 1902. The first important building to be constructed was St. Mark's Church at Bangalore, which cost Rs. 50,000 ; this was followed by the Medical Students' Hostel at Royapuram, for which the estimate was Rs. 35,000 ; and then came the Government of Madras Central Record Buildings, which are opposite the railway-station at Egmore, and which were to cost one lakh of rupees.

It is only in recent times that reinforced concrete has been used in foundation work in Southern India ; but its immense advantages in a low-lying country, such as that near the city of Madras, for instance, cannot be overestimated. No fewer than 450 wells were sunk and subsequently filled with this substance prior to the erection of the power-house for supplying electricity to the corporation for lighting purposes, and two lakhs of rupees were expended upon this contract.

The latter portion of the year 1909 witnessed a memorable event in the annals of the Madras Corporation, as on December 11th his Excellency the Earl of Minto, Viceroy of India, laid the foundation-stone of new municipal offices. The work of construction was entrusted to Mr. Loganatha Mudaliar, and the ceremony of opening the new building was performed on November 26, 1913, by the present Viceroy, H.E. Lord Hardinge of Penshurst. The magnificent edifice is known as "Ripon Buildings" (being named after a former popular Viceroy), and it is situated at the south-west corner of the People's Park and within a few hundred yards of the Central Station and the General Hospital. It is 252 ft. in length and 126 ft. in width ; it has three stories, and the tower, which is 132 ft. from the level of the ground, contains a clock with four dials, each of which is 8 ft. in diameter. The ground floor, which is occupied by the Revenue Department, contains 16 rooms, having a superficial area of about 25,000 ft. ; the first floor has 22 rooms, which are for the use of the President of the Corporation and of the General and Health Departments ; and the second floor, with 20 rooms, provides accommodation for the Council Chamber and for the officers of the Works Department. The contractor bestowed exceptional care over the foundations, and the building rests upon 750 wells, of a diameter of 5 ft., sunk to about 17 ft. below the level of the ground, and each of these was filled with reinforced concrete. The total cost has exceeded $7\frac{1}{2}$ lakhs of rupees, of which no less than $5\frac{1}{2}$ lakhs were paid to Mr. Loganatha Mudaliar for his share of the work. About 3,000 of the élite of Madras and the neighbourhood were present at the opening ceremony, and they were unanimous in their praise of the excellent appearance of the noble pile of buildings, and the skill of the contractor was warmly eulogized.

Mr. Loganatha Mudaliar is, further, the proprietor of a general store at No. 10 Davidson Street, Georgetown, Madras, and here he carries on an extensive business as a direct importer of hardware and other goods from England and from the Continent of Europe. These include superior English and continental cements ; polished and unpolished marble slabs of all sizes are obtained from Italy and Belgium ; while rolled cathedral glass of all colours, paints, rough-cast plates of all sizes, English polished plate-glass, iron safes, wire netting, and iron, steel, and galvanized roofing and fencing materials are amongst the general merchandise that can be supplied. It will be seen that this list—incomplete though it may be—is a very comprehensive one, and every requisite for the construction of buildings and for other works can be obtained here. Among the firm's clients are the Government of Madras, several municipalities, railway companies, architects, engineers, and other contractors. The proprietor undertakes contracts of all kinds, and he gives the most careful personal attention to every detail of work. It only remains to be added that Mr. Loganatha Mudaliar has the pigeon-holes of his writing-desk crammed with complimentary letters from municipalities, engineers, and others, all of which refer to his practical knowledge, his skill as a builder, and to his courteous and honourable conduct towards employers and employees alike. Space must, however, be found for the following two letters, which are addressed to Mr. Loganatha Mudaliar in connection with the construction of the Ripon Buildings.

Writing on March 30, 1914, Mr. James R. Coats, B.Sc., Assoc.M.Inst. C.E., engineer to the Corporation of Madras (Works Department), says :—

"Mr. P. Loganatha Mudaliar was the contractor for Ripon Buildings, the cost of which was over $5\frac{1}{2}$ lakhs of rupees, not including electric, sanitary, and other fittings. He completed the work satisfactorily and in time. He can read plans and understands details of building work. He has a good command of labour, including labour for special kinds of work. I consider him a reliable and intelligent contractor, capable of doing good work and in quick time."

Mr. P. L. Moore, C.I.E., I.C.S., President of the Corporation of Madras, wrote on April 30, 1914, confirming the opinion of Mr. Coats in every respect.

N. MOONOOSAWMY MUDALIAR

The subject of these notes held the important position of licensed plumber to the Corporation of Madras between the years 1891 and 1894, but he then commenced business as an engineering contractor, giving his special attention to operations connected with waterworks. Sound practical experience was the foundation of the success which has attended Mr. Moonoosawmy Mudaliar's efforts, and he has earned very high praise indeed from professional men under whom he has worked. In November 1895 Mr. P. B. Mahony, Assistant Engineer, P.W.D., Madras, wrote that "he completed the whole of the waterworks scheme at Government House, Guindy, which has been working very satisfactorily ever since." Other contracts included the laying and joining of pipes at the Adoni and Tanjore Waterworks, at Conjeeveram, in connection with which he constructed infiltration works, engine and boiler-house, laying and joining pipes, and building a large service reservoir. This work was followed by the laying of an infiltration-pipe and the sinking of 15-ft. diameter wells in the bed of the River Cauvery for the Trichinopoly Waterworks, and by the construction of the whole of the new waterworks at Guntur, costing about two lakhs. Mr. J. A. Jones, Sanitary Engineer to the Government of Madras, issued a certicate on October 30, 1903, wherein he stated that "the above works were carried out in a substantial manner and exactly according to the terms of the contract." "I have always felt satis-

P. LOGANATHA MUDALIAR.

1. Central Record Buildings, Madras. 2. P. Loganatha Mudaliar. 3. Medical Students' Hotel, Madras, 4. Madras Electric Supply Corporation,

fied," Mr. Jones added, "when I was able to allot a contract to Moonoosawmy Mudaliar." Many other contracts with the Government and with private individuals in the city of Madras were carried out successfully, and at the present time (April 1914) for the Corporation of Madras a 30-in. main five miles long and distributing mains and branches of water-pipes are being laid in the principal streets of Madras. Main work is nearing completion, and the branches will take one or two years to complete. About 200 hands are now being employed, but the owner gives the closest personal attention to the detail work of every contract.

Mr. Moonoosawmy Mudaliar takes the deepest interest in the social and moral welfare of his co-religionists, and the temple, which adjoins his residence and is known as the "Vinayagar Shrine," has recently been enlarged and subsequently renewed with granite, and nearly the whole of the cost has been borne by this gentleman. In 1902 he established a school at Pursewalkam, which was named "The Hindu Girls' Religious Charity," and he meets all expenses, with the exception of a small grant in aid which has been made by the Government. About 200 girls attend this school, where they receive instruction in local dialects, in religious and general subjects, including history, geography, arithmetic, needlework, and cooking. A printing press is an adjunct to the school, and arrangements have been made for the printing of religious books for use by the scholars and for sale to the public generally.

Mr. Moonoosawmy Mudaliar, resides and carries on business at Ganesa Villas, Vepery.

N. MOONOOSAWMY MUDALIAR.

1. N. Moonoosawmy Mudaliar. 2. Vembady-Venayager Temple, Vepery. 3. The Hindu Religious Charity Girls' School, Pursewaukam. 4. Residence of N. Moonoosawmy Mudaliar.

C. MUNISAWMY MUDALIAR

The timber business carried on by this merchant at Wall Tax Road, Madras, was established by the proprietor in 1900, and it has grown to its present large dimensions as a result of the sound practical experience of the owner and by reason of the employment of up-to-date methods in supplying good materials with characteristic promptitude. Scantlings of a standard size and teak wood are imported weekly in large quantities from Rangoon, and a special feature is made of the hand-sawing of scantlings from squares to any size that may be required.

Large contracts have recently been completed for the supply of railway-sleepers to the value of $1\frac{1}{4}$ lakhs of rupees, and several other agreements of a similar character are still on hand. A very large quantity of teak is always in stock on the owner's premises and on the beach, while not less than 10,000 sq. ft. of land is maintained for the storage of the scantlings which are kept in hand in the Wall Tax Road yard. This provision is necessary, as the majority of the leading contractors in the neighbourhood obtain their supplies of teak, scantlings, and planks from this depot. Timber has been purchased from these stores for most of the important buildings which have been erected or altered in recent years, and among them may be mentioned the Egmore Railway Station,

C. MUNISAWMY MUDALIAR.

1. TIMBER YARD. 2. SAWING YARD. 3. C. MUNISAWMY MUDALIAR. 4. C. KUMARASAWMY MUDALIAR. 5. V. KUPPURAMA MUDALIAR.

the Maternity Hospital, Government Houses in Madras, and Southern Mahratta Railway. Planks of timber are kept under cover, but scantlings are exposed to all weathers in order that they may be seasoned thoroughly. The sawing-yards adjoin the workshops and offices, and the whole of the extensive business is under the supervision of the owner, who is assisted by his son, Mr. C. Kumarasawmy Mudaliar, and by his son-in-law, Mr. V. Kuppuram Mudaliar. About 25 hands are constantly employed, but this number is increased considerably when occasion demands.

A. SAMINATHA MUDALIAR & SONS

The founder of this firm—Mr. A. Saminatha Mudaliar—was born at Bangalore in April 1868, and after receiving secondary educational privileges in the London Mission High School at that place, he was taken in hand by an uncle, who imparted to him a sound commercial training. When the time arrived for his commencing business on his own account he became contractor for general supplies to the messes and canteens of the Queen's Own Sappers and Miners, and subsequently of the 2nd Yorkshire and other regiments. Shortly after this he held a permanent licence for the sale of beer in tavern No. 6 in Bangalore, and, when the system of selling by auction the right to hold these licences came into force, he entered into competition with other merchants, with the result that at the present day (1914) he is the proprietor of a considerable number of tavern shops in that city. Mr. Saminatha then turned his attention to the manufacture of aerated waters, and in 1880 he entered into partnership with Mr. A. Bavadeen Sahib, the style of the firm being A. Bavadeen & Co. This business increased very rapidly indeed, and after twelve years' trading about twenty branches had been opened in the Presidency, and the head offices were removed to Madras. The partnership was dissolved in the year 1900, and Mr. Saminatha continued the working of the factory in his own name. Several other mineral water works came into existence about this time, but they were imperfectly equipped with machinery, as they only possessed Sirdar Club three-bottle hand machines. Mr. Saminatha's foresight and keen business acumen enabled him to perceive that the proprietors of these works had insufficient capital to obtain the necessary plant and materials, and he began to import them and then to supply them on most advantageous terms, the purchase price being repayable by easy instalments. He has, by these means, been concerned in the establishment of more than 500 factories in the Madras Presidency alone, and he is still prepared to render financial assistance for the opening of others. Messrs. A. Saminatha Mudaliar & Sons are the largest importers of and dealers in aerated water trade requisites in Southern India, and they are able to supply any quantity on demand. The firm are representatives of Messrs. A. Boake Roberts & Co., Messrs. Stevenson & Howell, Ltd., Messrs. W. J. Bush & Co., of London, and Messrs. Duckworth & Co., of Manchester, for the sale of essences and oils, and they are agents for Codd's patent soda-water bottles, for Messrs. William Barnard & Sons, Messrs. E. Bercfitt & Co., and Messrs. A. Alexander & Co., of London; and, until 1909, they were agents of Sirdar Carbonic Gas Company, Bombay. They are, further, sole representatives for the sale in the Presidency of liquid carbonic acid gas, manufactured by the East India Distilleries and Sugar Factories, Ltd., for whom Messrs. Parry & Co., of Madras, are managing agents.

The firm are carrying on a large business as dealers in cycles, pneumatic tyres, photo materials, Java and beetroot sugars, pig lead, and yellow, brass, and copper sheets. The capital of the firm is about 3 lakhs of rupees. Mr. Saminatha Mudaliar is assisted in the management of the business by his eldest son, Mr. A. S. Natesa Mudaliar. The registered telegraphic address is "Gas," Madras.

P. L. PADMANABAM NAIDU

Notwithstanding the fact that India has thousands upon thousands of acres of dense forests, a large quantity of timber is imported annually from other countries. Mr. Padmanabam Naidu, who is a contractor at Royapuram, a suburb of Madras, is one of such importers. He obtains teak logs and scantlings from Rangoon, and jarrah wood from Australia; and large quantities of these are supplied under contract to the railway authorities, to the Public Works Department, to the workshops of the Civil Engineering College, and to merchants and builders throughout the Madras Presidency. Household furniture is made on the premises from rosewood and from white and red cedar, and every article which is issued from the workshops is guaranteed to be of the finest quality. Mr. Padmanabam Naidu has had about twenty-five years' practical business experience, and this is of immense value to him in connection with the preparation of estimates for the construction of buildings. A landing and shipping agency has been added to contracting work, and important firms, such as Messrs. Binny & Co., have accorded their support to the project. There are three places of business altogether: one is opposite the police-station at Royapuram, another adjoins the Royapuram saw-mills, and the third is on the Basin Bridge Road. Competent labour is plentiful, and about 50 hands—exclusive of 7 clerks in the offices—are constantly employed.

M. P. NARASIMACHARI

The words "small profits and quick returns" are printed on letter-heads and in advertisements of thousands of business concerns in all parts of the world, and it is admitted that the principle contained in them has formed the foundation of most of the important industrial enterprises of the century. Mr. Narasimachari believes in selling his goods at moderate profits, and he is satisfied that this practice has been largely responsible for the rapid expansion of his business as a timber merchant and contractor, which has been established for a number of years at Surianarayana Chetty Street, Royapuram, in the north-eastern portion of the city of Madras.

A special feature is made of the importation of first-class Burma teak logs, but consignments of similar timber are obtained from Moulmein, Tavoy, and Penang, while all other kinds of wood can be supplied at short notice, as a large general stock is invariably kept on hand. Adjoining the timber-yard is a saw-mill in which all sizes of rafters, beams, joists, scantlings, and planks are cut and supplied promptly. Doors and windows of any pattern are made to order, and the proprietor has the sole right of supplying teak to the agents of the Madras and Southern Mahratta Railway and South Indian Railway systems, the wood being required for railway and bridge-sleepers, and for crossings. Purchasers of many years' standing of timber from this yard have found that they can always rely upon obtaining sound and well-seasoned wood, and every possible assistance is rendered to customers in order that they may buy

A. SAMINATHA MUDALIAR & SONS.

1. Proprietor in his Car. 2. Some of the Staff 3. Kamakoti Buildings.

exactly what they require, both in quality and size. All goods for sale can be inspected at the depôt or elsewhere; accurate measurements can be taken and then embodied in a statement to be handed to the purchaser; and as soon as these preliminaries have been disposed of, delivery to railway trucks in Madras can take place.

Mr. Narasimachari is confident that his stock is of a consistently superior quality, and that his prices are so reasonable that he is always prepared to welcome a visit from executive engineers, departmental public works overseers, contractors, and others in order that they may make a personal inspection of the timber and compare quotations with others in the market before they place their orders elsewhere.

The proprietor is personally responsible for the supervision of every department in his business, and he is particularly careful to give prompt delivery in all instances. His telegraphic address is "Burmateak—Madras."

OSMAN, HASSAN & CO.

The business of dealing in hides and skins, along with many other industries, has undergone a rapid development in recent years owing to the introduction of up-to-date machinery for dealing with the raw material. Those who a few years ago bought and sold wet skins now have conveniences for salting, drying, dressing, and tanning. Two of the members of this firm, Messrs. V. H. Osman Saib and Said Hassan Saib, commenced business at Borgampad Rajahmundry about the year 1894 as purchasers of wet skins and, as a side line, as dealers in local timbers. They held contracts with the Forest Department, and had an extensive business, a large quantity of logs, deals, and planks being sold to customers in Rajahmundry, Bezwada, and other places. The partners then opened tanneries at Rajahmundry, Ambur, and Ellore, but the turnover of this branch was very small at that time, although it gave good promise of ultimate improvement.

The firm was reconstructed in 1913, when Madras was made the headquarters of the prosperous foreign trade which has been carefully built up. Under the new regime the above-named partners are associated with Messrs. Abdul Karim Saib and H. Abdul Jabbar Saib. Purchasing agents collect skins and hides at various places throughout India, and these are subsequently tanned and then exported to the United Kingdom, the United States of America, and to Australia and Japan. Grading, sorting, and baling is carried out at the Madras premises, which are at No. 91 Thambu Chetty Street. The firm have agents in London, Liverpool, Boston, Tokio, Yokohama, and Kobe, who cable their requirements as occasion requires.

Some idea of the extent of the operations of Messrs. Osman Hassan & Co. may be gathered from the fact that they employ a daily average of 2,000 hands at their various depots, and this is exclusive of the office staff at headquarters.

Mr. M. Abdul Karim Saib is the general manager of the foreign branch of the business.

M. P. NARASIMACHARI.

1. M. P. NARASIMACHARI. 2. PROPRIETOR AND STAFF.

OSMAN, HASSAN & CO.

1. In the Madras Stores. 2. The Tannery, Ellore. 3. Polishing Leather, Rajahmundry Works.

R. PATEL & CO.

There is no industry which has progressed so rapidly during the twentieth century as the manufacture of motor-cars and cycles, and one of the oldest firms in the trade in Southern India is that of Messrs. R. Patel & Co., of the Madras Cycle Mart, which is opposite the High Court of Justice in China Bazaar Road, Madras. Mr. Patel, who established the firm in 1903, recently disposed of the business, and the present proprietors are Messrs. S. D. Grant, F. Bryamshaw, and A. F. Khabardar.

A special feature has been made of the agency for the Abingdon-King Dick motor-cycles, which are renowned for their strength and reliability. These machines are constructed with all the latest improvements, and the most recent models embody all the salient points which on other similar single-cylinder makes have proved to be necessary, and they possess many details which stamp them with individuality. Among the ordinary cycles which are sold by the firm are the following: The "Triumph," the "Fleet," and the "Minoru" (of which the last is specially built for them in Coventry), and these vary in price from Rs. 85 to Rs. 250.

The buildings occupied by the firm include an excellent sale store, four go-downs, and workshops in which repairs of all kinds are executed by fully competent men. All kinds of machines are kept in stock, and appliances are imported for

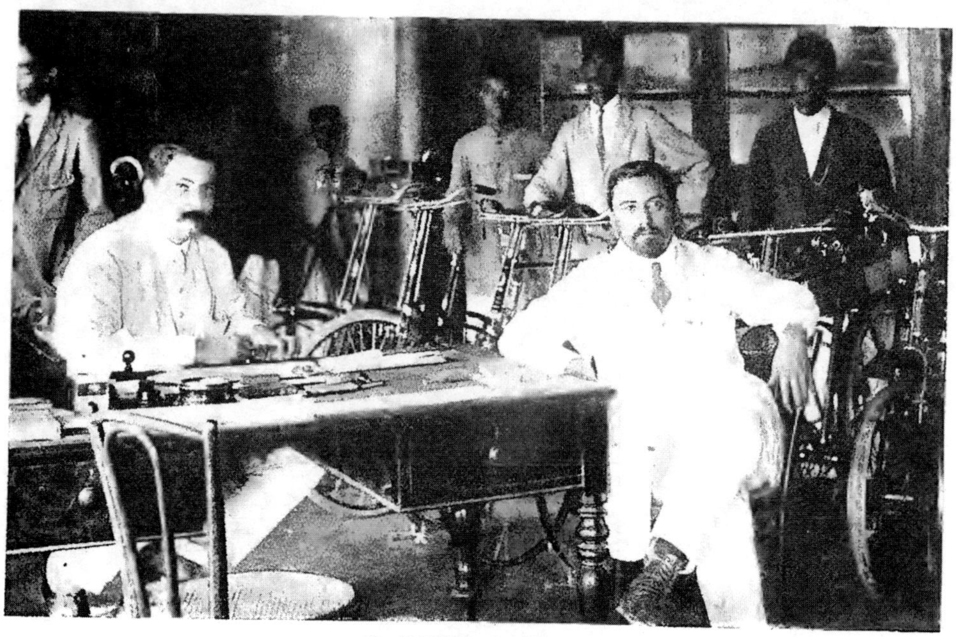

R. PATEL & CO.

A Portion of the Showroom.

the benefit of local private customers and for sale to trade merchants throughout Southern India. The firm's travellers visit the principal towns in the Presidency, and the general management is in the hands of Mr. A. F. Khabardar, who has held this position since the year 1908. Messrs. Patel & Co. are sole agents for Components, Ltd., and the Peter Union Tyre Company, and they specially import calcium carbide and other accessories in very large consignments.

PAYNE & CO.

The proprietors of this firm's business are Messrs. Soorampally Chinapapiah Chetty & Sons, who are well known in commercial circles in Madras, and as general and fine art colour printers, machine rulers, account-book makers, engravers, die-stampers, rubber-stamp makers, and paper merchants. Papiah Chetty commenced business in or about the year 1869, but he did not take over the printing and other works at No. 14 Francis Joseph Street until 1904. Immense improvements have been made with regard to the machinery since that date, and the composing and other rooms are now replete with thoroughly modern plant. Electricity has been installed for the motive power and for lighting purposes. Messrs. Payne & Co. are printers to many leading commercial firms and insurance and other corporations and companies, and they pride themselves upon the fact that they retain old customers owing to the neat and expeditious manner in which they execute all orders entrusted to them. Their special features are fine art and job, book, and catalogue printing, the manufacture of account-books, the making of rubber-stamps, and engraving and ruling. The firm have a very large connection throughout the whole of the mofussil, and they are justly entitled to the high reputation which they have acquired in the printing world of Southern India.

PAYNE & CO.

1. Front View. 2. Machine-room. 3. Composing-room. 4. S. C. Papiah Chetty (Proprietor).

JAL PHIROJ & CO.

The sole proprietor of this firm is Mr. Phiroj M. Clubwala, who is a general merchant and importer at No. 169 Devarja Modelly Street, Park Town, Madras, and at Palace Road, Madura. He has been successful in business, and he has, further, been closely identified with many religious and social movements. There are two buildings in the city with which the name of Mr. Clubwala will ever be associated, as he caused them to be erected in memory of his late son Master Jal, who died at Madras on February 9, 1906. One of these is a Parsi Fire Temple—the first of the kind in the Presidency of Madras—which was constructed at Royapuram in August 1910. The fire which was lighted at the opening of the place of worship is kept burning continually, and sandalwood is the chief fuel. The other gift was a "daramsala," which is situated near to the temple, and this is the only rest-house for Parsis in the city of Madras. Mr. Clubwala's private residence is at No. 35 Main Road, Royapuram, and it is in the vicinity of the temple.

JAL PHIROJ & CO.

1. THE JAL PHIROJ MEMORIAL HALL—TO BE USED AS A REST-HOUSE FOR PARSIS. 2. JAL PHIROJ FIRE TEMPLE, ROYAPURAM. 3. THE LATE MASTER JAL PHIROJ.

P. S. PONNOOSAWMY PILLAY.

1. FRONT VIEW OF PREMISES. 2. PROPRIETOR AND STAFF.

P. S. PONNOOSAWMY PILLAY & SON

The proprietor of this establishment assumed control in 1894 of the cabinet-making and upholstering business which was founded by his late father in the year 1854.

The stores and offices are at Nos. 40, 41, and 42 Rattan Bazaar Row, Madras, and between 200 and 300 men are constantly employed in them and in the numerous factories. Furniture is made for prince or peasant, for palace or a two-roomed flat, but a special feature is made of high-class work such as has been carried out for Government offices, schools, mission houses, clubs, railway stores, military mess-rooms, and for many of the leading Rajahs, Nawabs, and Zamindars. The principal hotels in Madras have been furnished from these works, and many important orders have been executed for European residents.

Upholstering in silk, leather, or cotton is done by hand by experienced persons. Messrs. Pillay & Son have more than 20 factories in various parts of the Presidency, but they, further, import a considerable quantity of furniture from Messrs. Fitter Brothers, of Birmingham, and from Mr. Leonard Tauber, of London. The goods obtained from the latter are of Austrian manufacture, and although the firm have a preference for English makes, they are compelled to purchase on the Continent in order to compete favourably with other firms.

T. SAMYNADA PILLAY

One of the leading engineers and contractors of the Madras Presidency is Mr. T. Samynada Pillay, formerly of Bangalore, but now of Madras, who commenced business in the year 1879 after having acquired a sound practical knowledge of every detail of work in these important branches. Many large contracts were obtained by him, and these involved the investment of a large amount of capital and the employment of a considerable number of men. A few of the principal works which were carried out may be referred to. The Bangalore pure-water reservoir—capable of holding sufficient to supply the whole town for five days—was built of cement and granite stone slabs at a cost of 1 lakh of rupees, and it was completed in the short time of ten months. The executive engineer of the Mysore D.P.W. gave a certificate in January 1896 that the work had been carried out in a very satisfactory manner. About a couple of years later new lines for the Imperial service troops were erected at Bangalore. These included quarters for officers and men, stables, mess-rooms, armoury, magazines, and other stores; and this huge undertaking, which extended over a period of three years, cost more than 8 lakhs of rupees. Here, again, the principal engineer wrote that the work had been done with care and diligence and to his entire satisfaction, both as to the quality of the work and its progress. Following upon this came the construction of transport lines near to the Maharajah's palace at Bangalore, together with the levelling of his Highness's polo ground. Subsequently Mr. T. Samynada Pillay completed motor and power-houses at the Cauvery Falls, in addition to power-houses at the Bangalore city cantonments and at the Kolar goldfields. The building of the "Sashadri Iyer" Memorial Hall in Cubbon Park, Bangalore, was followed by the extension of general offices at Trichinopoly for the South Indian Railway, but the construction of the buildings in the Madura railway colony, which was just then taken in hand, was a very comprehensive scheme. Quarters were erected for station-masters, drivers, guards, firemen, porters, schoolmasters and mistresses, for hospital attendants, and locomotive firemen, together with a church, hospital, and recreation and other rooms. These works cost about 8 lakhs of rupees. The handsome railway-station at Egmore, Madras, is another tribute to Mr. Samynada Pillay's skill. It has exceedingly large and well-ventilated waiting, refreshment and cloak-rooms, in addition to the usual offices for the stationmaster and his army of assistants, and the cost of this work exceeded 17 lakhs of rupees. A contract of far greater magnitude, however, is now being carried out in Madras. It is for the construction of new offices for the Madras and Southern Mahratta Railway on a site which is immediately opposite the General Hospital; and the foundations of the building are unique, as they are the first to be laid in India of reinforced concrete. The estimated cost is rather more than 20 lakhs of rupees.

The contractor has, further, to supply the railway authorities with teakwood sleepers, and during the year 1913 the quantity delivered was worth about 2 lakhs. Mr. Saminatha Pillay has his own brick-kilns on the Poonamallee High Road, and burning is done by a special process in which steam coal-dust is used. Contracts have been entered into for supplying the Madras Municipality, while other builders have their requirements met from these kilns. The output shows an average of 10 lakhs a month from two kilns. The brick and pottery work produced in three years is of excellent quality. Specimens of wood-carving which were shown at the Delhi Exhibition of Indian art manufacturers were awarded a bronze medal together with a certificate of merit. Mr. Saminath Pillay gives personal attention to every branch of work, and he is ably assiste by his brother, Mr. T. Chinnasawmy Pillay. About 560 workmen are now employed.

It will be seen from the earlier portion of these notes that this contractor has received the highest praise from engineers for the skill with which he has carried out most important works, and it is a source of satisfaction to him to know that his straightforward conduct h earned for him an honoured na throughout Southern India. Some of the testimonials, which have been given voluntarily, contain such sentences as these: "He is one of the best contractors in the Bangalore division." "I can confiden recommend him to any one requiring a good and reliable contractor." "He is an exceptionally good contractor, in fact, the best I have come across in Southern India." "He is a man who can be depended upon for carrying out special large works with integrity and according to the very letter of the specifications." "He is one of the best contractors down my way."

RAMASAWMY & CO.

The partners of this firm are A. L. A. R. Arunchellam Chettiar, Zemindar, Devakota, O. R. M. O. M. Subramaniam Chettiar, of Devokata, and P. L. N. K. Menachi Sundrum Chettiar, of Devakota, and it is mainly due to the integrity and business qualifications of the last-named, who is managing director, that the business has grown so rapidly. The firm was established in premises on the Second Line Beach in Madras in February 1907, but as improved and more extensive accommodation is now necessary, possession will be taken almost immediately (April 1914) of a fine building, at No. 100 Armenian Street, which contains excellent offices with showrooms and ample space for storage purposes.

T. SAMYNADA PILLAY.

1. T. Samynada Pillay. 2. Group at Egmore Station. 3. Group at Bungalow.

T. SAMYNADA PILLAY.

1. Madura Railway Colony. 2. Egmore Station, Madras. 3. South Indian Railway Offices, Trichinopoly. 4. Brickfield, Amanjikera.

RAMASAWMY & CO.

1. A Portion of the Office. 2. Office Staff. 3. P. L. N. K. Mee Natchi Sundram Chettyar.

K. SAMBASIVA RAO & CO.

1. A Portion of the Showroom. 2. K. Sambasiva Rao.

The managing director has been connected with the wholesale and retail piece goods trade ever since he began his commercial life, and his early experience was obtained in various parts of the Madras Presidency and in the district of Tanjore. The reputation of the firm has become established so firmly that orders are received regularly from customers in the Mofussil and elsewhere without the intervention of travelling agents.

White, grey, and coloured goods and yarn—with grey shirtings and jaconets as special features—are imported from Manchester, while towels and woollen and cotton shawls are obtained from Germany. The partners of the above firm hold the sole agency for the Presidency for White Mulls of Messrs. J. and A. Leigh & Co., of Preston, England; their Manchester agents are Messrs. Galbraith & Co., Messrs. Robert Barber Brothers, Ltd., and Messrs. G. F. Manley & Co., the latter for the supply of yarns only, while the agents in Germany are Messrs. Farkel Werner & Co., of Hamburg.

K. SAMBASIVA RAO & CO.

This business was only established in the early part of the year 1914, but the proprietor, who has had many years' practical experience, hopes that, by keeping good materials and by devoting careful personal attention to detail work, he may be able to build up a sound, profitable trade. A large stock is kept of all kinds of paints and materials which are required by contractors, builders, and decorators, and these are imported from England, principally through agents. The stock includes Carson's and Hubbuck's paints, oils, varnishes, turpentine, dry colours, coal-tar, asphalt, pitch, whiting, chalk, resin, distempers, water-colours, and paint, drawing, and white-washing brushes. Contracts are entered into for the supply of these materials in connection with the construction of important buildings, and at the present time orders are being executed for Admiralty House, Madras, which belongs to H.H. the Raja of Vizianagram.

The prospects of the firm are distinctly encouraging, and Mr. Sambasiva Rao's faith in the expansion of trade will be demonstrated in the course of a few days (April 1914), when a further large importation of paints and other goods will be received. It is intended to keep a considerable quantity of building cement as soon as arrangements have been completed for the purchase of godowns for storage purposes, and negotiations are now in progress for obtaining the sole agency of some of the leading brands of paints, varnish, and cement.

The business premises of the firm are at No. 23 Venkatachella Mudelly Street, Madras, and they cover an area of 1,200 sq. ft.

Ordinary labourers are obtained when required, but Mr. Sambasiva Rao employs four clerks in his office, he retaining full management of indoor as well as outdoor work in his own hands.

THE RIPON PHARMACY.

1. The Ripon Pharmacy. 2. Dr. N. Venkataswami Chetty.

RIPON PHARMACY

This pharmacy, situated at Nos. 19 and 21 Sydenham's Road, Periamet, Madras, was primarily opened in 1913 by Dr. N. Venkataswami Chetty, M.B. & C.M., of the University of Madras, its proprietor, for the careful and accurate compounding of his own prescriptions. To that end the pharmacy has been placed under the management of qualified and competent men. It is stocked with fresh drugs and chemicals, and with very carefully-selected patent medicines necessary for his patients. Its situation at Periamet may be said to be right in the very heart of the city. Owing to the great extension of the operations of the pharmacy it has become necessary to devote the whole ground floor of the buildings to the show-rooms and the compounding department and stores. The first floor of the premises contains consulting-rooms with apartments specially set apart for surgical purposes, for which provision has been made according to the latest scientific principles. For specialized work and for work in the department of bacteriology, Dr. N. Venkataswami Chetty has collaborateurs in Dr. S. R. Rao, M.B. and Ch.B. (Edin.), and Dr. B. Rajagopal, L.R.C.P. and S. (Edin.), D.P.H. respectively.

H. MOHAMED BADSHA SAHIB & CO.

The founder of this firm—H. Mohamed Badsha Sahib—was born in the year 1795, and he commenced business in the High Road, Triplicane, Madras, in 1812, dealing principally in crockery and glassware. These commodities were subsequently withdrawn from sale in favour of small piece goods, which the proprietor then imported. With a view to the extension of his business relationships, and in order to become acquainted with the imports and exports of various countries, Badsha Sahib paid a visit in 1866 to Arabia, Egypt, and other countries, and on his return to India he commenced dealing in indigo with Cairo, Asia Minor, and Bagdad, with the result that a very comfortable fortune was made. The work attendant upon the great expansion of trade which followed upon that voyage proved to be a severe strain upon the proprietor, and, in order to be relieved of a portion of his responsibilities, he admitted into partnership in 1873 his second and third sons, H. Mahomed Abdulla Badsha Sahib and H. Mahomed Abdul Shukur Badsha Sahib. This arrangement was continued until June 4, 1881, when the father retired into private life, transferring his share, right, title, interest, and his share in the goodwill to two other sons—namely, H. Mahomed Abdul Aziz Badsha Sahib and H. Mahomed Abdul Salam Badsha Sahib.

The newly constituted firm were designated merchants and commission agents in indigo, piece goods, Madras handkerchiefs, skins, hides, and tamarinds. The senior partners, H. Mahomed Abdulla Badsha Sahib, and H. Mahomed Abdul Shukur Badsha Sahib, respectively, died on June 13, 1891, and September 5, 1892, leaving the other two brothers in sole possession. During the year 1892 H. Mahomed Abdul Salam Badsha Sahib, proceeded to Cairo, Mecca, and other places with the view of recruiting his health, and in the meantime his place in the firm was temporarily filled by another brother, H. Mahomed Kuddus Badsha Sahib. The latter has been in business on his own account as a merchant and commission agent since 1883, but in January 1890 he was joined in partnership by a younger brother, H. Mahomed Abdul Hadi Badshi Sahib, and they established a lucrative connection as dealers in indigo, tamarind, coffee, pepper, piece goods, mica, and other produce, in addition to holding agencies for general insurance companies. This firm, who had a European manager, was well known throughout the United Kingdom, Europe, America, Egypt, Arabia, and Japan. A very serious calamity occurred in 1894, when H. Mahomed Abdul Salam Badsha Sahib, a partner in the original firm—who had been in search of health for the two preceding years—succumbed to his physical weakness, and this misfortune occurred at a time when the two businesses had assumed vast proportions and could ill spare the services of any one of the partners. An arrangement was then entered into by which the members of the two firms joined forces, under the title of H. Mahomed Badsha Sahib & Co.; but on the death of Khan Bahadur H. Mahomed Abdul Hadi Badsha Sahib the partnership was dissolved as a preparatory step to further reconstitution. The two surviving brothers, Khan Bahadur H. Mahomed Abdul Aziz Badsha Sahib and Khan Bahadur Mahomed Abdul Kuddus Badsha Sahib, thereupon formed a new partnership, under the original name of H. Mahomed Badsha Sahib & Co., and traded as general

HAJEE MAHOMED BADSHA SAHIB & CO.

1. The Office. 2. Khan Bahadur Hajee Md. Abdul Azeez Badsha Sahib. 3. Khan Bahadur M. A. Kuddus Badsha Sahib.

merchants, commission agents, and as miners of diamonds, mica, and manganese. They are large exporters of mica, mica splittings, indigo, tamarinds, Madras handkerchiefs, carpets, rugs, ground nuts, and other produce, and they import all kinds of piece and woollen goods, steel, iron, hardware, sugar, cotton threads, paints, cement, stationery, glassware, crockery, and other sundry articles. The firms are agents for the Central Agency of Glasgow, for Messrs. Blundell, Spence & Co., and for the following insurance companies: the Nord Deutsche Insurance Company, of Hamburg (Marine), the British Dominions General Insurance Co., Ltd., of London (Fire and Marine), the Western Assurance Company, of Toronto and London (Fire and Marine), and the Phoenix Life Assurance Co., Ltd., of London.

The place of business of the firm is at 22 Errabalu Chetty Street, Madras. The following particulars relating to the personal characteristics of the two partners will be read with interest:—

Khan Bahadur Haji Mohamed Abdul Aziz Badsha Sahib, the Turkish Consul at Madras and a prominent leader of the Mahomedan community in Southern India, was born in the year 1858, and is a son of the late Haji Mohamed Badsha Sahib, the founder of the well-known firm of Messrs. H. Md. Badsha Sahib & Co., of Madras. The Khan Bahadur received his early education chiefly at home, and he was well grounded in the Persian and Arabic languages before he was barely sixteen years old. Although of a studious and retiring habit, he was compelled by his father to put his books aside in order to take a share in the management of a concern which was then daily growing in extent and importance. His early training under his father has, however, been of immense service, and he is now widely known as one of the most successful men in the commercial world of Southern India. The firm of Messrs. Haji Md. Badsha Sahib & Co., of which he is at present the senior partner, has, under his management, taken the foremost place among the native commercial houses in the Presidency of Madras.

In the year 1885 he started on a pilgrimage, and after visiting Mecca, Medina, Jerusalem, and several sacred places in Arabia, he made an extended tour throughout the greater part of Egypt. After an absence of about a year from the Presidency, he returned in perfect health and quietly resumed his old commercial life with freshened energy and enthusiasm. In the year 1892 the post of Turkish Consul at Madras, which was held by one of his brothers, became vacant, and he was thereupon appointed Consul by his Majesty the Sultan. Ever since the creation of the Consulate one of the members of the Badsha family has had the honour of holding that office, and though the trade relations which exist between Turkey and Madras are not of a very important character, the holder of the office has ever enjoyed a commanding position among the Mahomedan community, especially of that section which recognizes the Sultan as its religious head.

Extremely pious and of a truly charitable disposition, the Khan Bahadur has always been a friend of the poor and the needy, particularly of his own community, and he is for this reason very much beloved and respected by all classes of his countrymen. His Majesty the Sultan has conferred upon him the Order of Osmanieh, third class, and for his exertions in collecting money from India for the Hamede-Hedjaz Railway project he received a gold medal from the same source. The Government of India have also honoured him with the title of Khan Bahadur in recognition of his many public services, but the simplicity of his life and habits is such as would lead all who are unacquainted with him to suppose that he is rich neither in this world's goods nor in any of its honours. Reserved in manners, kindly and sympathetic in disposition, Khan Bahadur Haji Mohamed Abdul Aziz Badsha Sahib leads a retired and unostentatious life.

Khan Bahadur Mahomed Abdul Kuddus Badsha Sahib has been recognized as one of the prominent and leading members of the Mahomedan community, and he belongs to the well-known and distinguished "Badsha" family. He is the seventh son of the late venerable and respected Haji Mahomed Badsha Sahib, who was one of the most industrious and successful merchants of his day in Southern India, and who was the founder of Messrs. H. Mahomed Badsha Sahib & Co., a leading Indian firm of the Madras Presidency, of about ninety-five years' standing. His late father received the Hamidea Decoration, No. 2, from the Sultan of Turkey on account of his benevolence and his magnificent contributions in connection with the Turko-Russian War, and he was also granted the title of "Effendi."

Khan Bahadur M. A. Kuddus Badsha Sahib was born on February 14, 1865, and, in addition to his private tuition at home, he was educated at the Government Madrassa-Azam, where he obtained a fair knowledge of the English, Arabic, Persian, Hindustani, Tamil, and Telugu languages. From his boyhood Khan Bahadur Kuddus Badsha Sahib evinced a great desire to become a merchant, the natural instincts and aptitude for which he possessed, and his subsequent career has shown that he entered upon an occupation for which he is eminently fitted.

The business of his late father, Haji Mahomed Badsha Sahib, was at that time one of the leading indigo and piece-goods merchants, not only in India but in Egypt, Arabia, the United Kingdom, the United States of America, Turkey, and Persia, and he was widely known as "Malikuttujar"—the head of the merchants.

Khan Bahadur Kuddus Badsha Sahib started his own business in 1883, but he joined the firm of Messrs. H. Mohamed Badsha Sahib & Co. as a partner in 1894, since which time the business has been considerably extended, owing to the amalgamation of his own establishment with that of the firm. Several new departments were opened by him. Although he was fully engaged in business, the circumstance did not prevent him from taking an active part as a citizen in the cause of the welfare and advancement of the Moslem community, nor from participating in all movements of public interest. Though an extremely busy man, he has never refused to render assistance or to give his advice whenever it has been required by his numerous friends and well-wishers. He is a favourite in social circles, as he possesses a very genial, kind, and sympathetic disposition, and he treats those who call on him with great courtesy. Those who know the Badsha family assert that among the sons Khan Bahadur Kuddus Badsha Sahib in many respects not only resembles his father in personal appearance, but he has apparently inherited his charitable and pious disposition and his keen business instincts.

Khan Bahadur Kuddus Badsha Sahib is the second partner of the firm of Messrs. H. Mohamed Badsha Sahib & Co.; he is the Turkish Vice-consul at Madras, Trustee of the Madras Port Trust, Vice-president of the Southern

India Chamber of Commerce, Vice-president of the South India Athletic Association, Ltd., Commissioner of the Corporation of Madras, and a member of the Standing Committee of the Council. Two Sayeedea Zenana girls' schools in Madras, designed chiefly for the benefit of the girls of his community at Georgetown and Triplicane; two Mahomedan boys' day schools and two Mahomedan boys' night schools for religious instruction are solely maintained by him. These are the only institutions of their kind in Southern India where free education is imparted. He takes a keen interest in the education of girls. He is a member of the Anjuman-i-Mufid-Ahla-Islam Madras, Vice-president of the Madras Presidency Moslem League, of the Mahomedan Educational Association of Southern India, of the Anjumanai - Himayathai - Ahla - Islam, a Governor of the Victoria Caste and Gosha Hospital, a member of the Cosmopolitan Club, Treasurer of the Young Men's Indian Association, an executive member of the Society for the Prevention of Cruelty to Animals and of the Society for the Prevention of Cruelty to Children, a member of the Executive Committee of the Mahajana Sahab, Treasurer of the Indian National Congress, Trustee of the Victoria Public Hall, Manager and Muthawalle of the Badsha Mosque and of the "Kuddusia" Mosque at Triplicane, the latter having been built at his own personal cost.

Khan Badahur Kuddus Badsha Sahib has started the Unani and Ayurvedic Medical School, Hospital, Dispensary, and Library, and these two systems of treatment have been of immense benefit to people throughout India. He has also held the following appointments, namely: elected additional member of the Madras Legislative Council from December 1909 to December 1912 on behalf of the Mohamedan community of the northern group of the Madras Presidency, official visitor of the Reformatory School at Chingleput, Honorary Magistrate of Madras, Chairman and Director of the Indian Aluminium Co., Ltd., for more than twelve years a member of the Trivellore and Saidapet Taluq Board, Treasurer of the Anjuman-i-Mufid-Ahla-Islam, a member of the Agri-Horticultural Society of Madras, and Treasurer of the Central Executive Committee appointed in connection with the presentation of the Madras Presidential Address to his Majesty the King-Emperor of India at the Durbar at Delhi. He was, further, Sheriff of Madras during the year 1913, and Treasurer of the Lord Hardinge's Children's Treat Fund and of the 1st Royal Dublin Fusiliers' Reception Fund, in addition to being a member of the New General Hospital Committee. There is scarcely any post of public importance which he has not held at one time or other. He possesses several Jaghirs, Zemindaries, Shrotriems, and a diamond-mine, and he is the pioneer of the mica industry in the Madras Presidency. He has invented and manufactured mica wares, for which he has been awarded medals at various exhibitions. The village of Kuddusabad, in the district of Nellore, where some of the mica-mines are situated, has been named after him. He received a gold medal from the Sultan of Turkey in connection with the construction of the Hamidea Hedjaz Railway, and three of his elder brothers, who have been Turkish Consul at Madras, received the title of "Khan Bahadur" from the British Government. The Khan Bahadur has a large family, five of whom are very promising boys, and they appear to take after the father, as they are very persevering in their efforts to acquire knowledge and business experience. He is invariably invited to co-operate in all functions and movements of public interest at Madras, and he has always rendered cheerful and willing service. The Khan Bahadur is extremely plain and simple in his dress and habits, and he strictly adheres to his national costume.

Khan Bahadur Kuddus Badsha Sahib has always set his face against anything which savours of disloyalty and disrespect; he is very keen in supporting the tradition of his ancestors, and, like his late father and brothers, he is a loyal and devoted subject of the British Empire. He is a peaceful, law-abiding citizen, and possesses a truly charitable spirit. Zealous in good works, pious, sober, even-tempered, a courteous gentleman, and a friend of the poor and destitute of all castes and creeds, he commands the respect and esteem of a large circle of friends. The subject of the note has great faith in total abstinence, and he never scruples to express his abhorrence of falsehoods, immorality, gambling, and other kindred vices. The Khan Bahadur was invited by the Government of Madras to attend the Imperial Durbar at Delhi on December 12, 1911, where he was the guest of the Government. At the Durbar he paid his homage to his Majesty the King-Emperor on behalf of the Mohamedan community who are British subjects of the Madras Presidency. The title of "Khan Bahadur" was conferred upon him in connection with the Coronation honours, and he was granted a Coronation medal by the Government of India at Delhi, and was presented to his Imperial Majesty at the levee held at Calcutta on January 2, 1912. He has also received the "Khan Bahadur Medal."

A. S. HAKIM MOHAMED SHAMSODIEN SAHIB

The subject of these notes belongs to a family which for several generations has enjoyed a great reputation for skill in scientific practice and for ministering to the general welfare of the community. Mr. A. S. Hakim Mohamed Shamsodien Sahib was born in the year 1874 in the village of Govindagudi, in the taluq of Kumbakonam, in the district of Tanjore, and he received the customary primary secular and religious instruction in his native place until 1889, when, owing to the sudden death of his father, other arrangements for his further education became necessary. He was sent to Madras, where he studied medicine for a period of eleven years under the capable tuition of his uncle, Mr. Hakim Mohamed Nizam-ud-din Sahib, who is one of the leading physicians in that city. The painstaking scholar developed into the skilled practitioner, and, acting on the advice of his uncle and other friends, he established himself at No. 106 Sowcarpet, Madras, by opening the Unani Medical Hall. The doctor threw his heart and soul into his professional work, and even at this early period in his career his energies were specially directed towards the discovery of some new medicinal preparation which might become popular on account of its efficacy in the treatment of some peculiarly distressing ailment

With unflagging zeal he persevered in his experiments, until he eventually fixed upon the idea of preparing a medicated snuff which would be a safe remedy for headaches, neuralgia, diseases of the eyes and nose, and for scrofula. It is claimed that this fragrant preparation (which is registered as "A.S.") is an efficient substitute for the ordinary tobacco powder which has been in use for so long a time, and several persons who were suffering from one or other of the diseases named

A. S. MOHAMMED SHAMSUDDEEN SAIB.

1. A. S. Sugantha Mookkuthool Villa. 2. A. S. Mohammed Shamsuddeen Saib. 3. Snuff Factory. 4 Medicated Preparation and Packing Department. 5. Group of the Staff 6 and 7. Certificates.

gave the new discovery a thorough trial, and they were unanimous in testifying to its excellent curative properties. Sample bottles were then sent to Zemindars, landlords, merchants, Government officials, and others, and the majority of these persons voluntarily sent testimonials in which the wonderful effects of the snuff were described. The majority of the remedies for diseases or ailments are distinctly unpalatable and objectionable, but the medicated snuff is not only soothing, but it gives a pleasing sensation when it is applied. It has a sale of Rs. 500 a day, and it is sent to France, Germany, the United States of America, South Africa, Arabia, Egypt, Afghanistan, and Ceylon, and in India, where it is more widely known, it is most highly appreciated, as it is priced so low that it is within the reach of every one.

The doctor has a large establishment, consisting of three departments, namely (1) the manufacturing, (2) the packing and labelling, and (3) the correspondence, and each of these is under the supervision of a separate head. His brother, Hakim Shaik Dawood Sahib, a great Tamil scholar, is the supervisor of the packing and labelling-room. His Tamil works are (1) "Vaidhya-amirtha Bhodini," a book of medicine; (2) "Navanitha Niyanan Nayana Sundari or Nobulnanak Nanaksunder Charitaram"; (3) "Amir Hawza," in five volumes; and (4) "Mahijabin Charitaram." Another brother, A. Zyualabdin Sahib, is in charge of the manufacturing department.

All the brothers have acquired an extensive and varied knowledge of wild herbs and drugs, and this was one of the characteristics of their ancestors, who were the physicians of the Tanjore Royal Family, which, in return for their services, conferred upon them large jaghirs and valuable gifts. Many of their patients bear testimony to the fact that a simple touch of one of these skilled practitioners gives relief from many troublesome ailments. Several gold and silver medals, in addition to certificates of merit, have been awarded to the snuff at various exhibitions.

M. A. HYATH BATCHA SAIB & CO.

The business in which this firm is interested was commenced by Mr. Hyath Batcha Saib at Bangalore in 1872, when it consisted of tanning and dealing in green skins and hides. A transfer of the concern to Madras took place in 1887, and about ten years later Messrs. P. N. Muthuswami Naidu, B.A., and Mr. R. Thirumalaiswami Naidu brought in their piece-goods and yarn business, along with the British Agency, which the former held, and became partners with the proprietor. The new firm then commenced a large piece-goods trade, which has developed to a remarkable extent, and they also import sundry merchandise from Europe, and export mainly wool and tanned hides and skins direct to England. A very considerable stock is kept, but the principal method of transacting business is by indenting from the leading houses at Home. The tannery is only a side line now, but all skins which are handled by the firm are tanned before shipment. The premises on the Second Line Beach in Madras consist of fine, roomy stores and comfortable offices, in which about 25 assistants and clerks are employed, while the tannery finds work for 500 or 600 hands. Messrs. M. A. Hyath Batcha Saib & Co. have corresponding agents in London, Glasgow,

M. A. HYATH BATCHA SAIB & CO.
FRONT VIEW OF OFFICE.

BANGY HYATH BADCHA SAHIB & CO.

1. Proprietor and Bungalow. 2. First Process of Tanning. 3. Final Process. 4. The Palar River adjoining the Tannery.

Manchester, Liverpool, New York, Paris, Hamburg, Milan, Hongkong, Tokio, Bombay, Calcutta, Karachi, Rangoon, and other centres of trade, and they are local representatives of the Norwich Union Mutual Life Insurance Society.

BANGHI HYATH BADSHA SAHIB & CO.

This firm of hide and skin merchants was established in 1874 by Banghi Khader Badsha Sahib, uncle of the present proprietor, who assumed entire control on the death of the founder in 1908, he having purchased the shares of all the other partners.

The offices in Madras are at No. 232 Angappa Naick Street, but the real headquarters and the principal tannery are at Ambur, which is a town on the Madras and Southern Mahratta Railway, about 113 miles distant from the chief city of the Presidency. Hides and skins are tanned with bark obtained from Mysore and other forests, and they are subsequently sorted and classified, and the majority of them are exported through Madras firms to England. There is another factory at Belgaum, which is a British cantonment in the Bombay Presidency, and at these two tanneries about 100,000 sheep and goat skins and from 3,000 to 5,000 hides are dealt with every month. The firm have established a regular system of buying agencies throughout India, and all hides and skins are consigned direct to the factories. These are situated at Bijapur, at Ilkal, Muddsbihal, Talikoti, and Guledgudi, all in the district of Bijapur; at Dharwar, Belgaum, Bailhongal, Ambur, Gundlpet, Bagalkot, Gadag, Satara City, Kolhapur City, and at Shoraput, near Gadgeri. Agents buying on commission only have been appointed at Bezwada and in the State of Mysore.

At a recent exhibition held at Arni, in the district of North Arcot, under the auspices of the district Conference, which is a branch of the Indian National Congress, tanned skins were exhibited with very great success, and it should be added that this was the only firm to be requested by the Conference to forward exhibits.

A leading feature of the firm's productions is the manufacture—by a special process—of leather for boot soles. This is known as the "Banghi" sole, and it has attained a great reputation for durability, especially in Rangoon and in Northern India.

The works at Ambur cover about 20 acres of ground, and they are complete with capital quarters for 300 employees. The water required for the tannery is pumped by a 12-h.p. steam-engine from wells which are filled by percolation from the River Palar, which is quite near to one of the boundaries of the property. It is an undoubted fact that the excellent tanning work which is done at this place is due almost entirely to the splendid water which is used.

The Belgaum tannery is also well provided with machinery and plant, and quarters have been provided for 100 workmen.

The firm are, further, owners of about 30 acres of coconut plantations and gardens, and this area also is irrigated from the Palar River.

The proprietor has a comfortable residence in close proximity to the Ambur tannery.

FRONT VIEW OF PREMISES OF K. HAJEE ABDUL KHADER SAIB LAULBATCHA SAIB.

K. HAJEE ABDUL KHADER SAIB LAULBATCHA SAIB & CO.

The partners in this firm are known throughout the Presidency as dealers in raw skins and hides, as tanners and exporters of tanned goat and sheep skins, and raw, dry, and wet salted skins to Europe and America. The business was established in the year 1900, and tanneries were opened at Aludu Halli, near Bellary, and at Thongal, near Madras. The firm's purchasing agents buy raw goat and sheep skins from Tanjore, Trichinopoly, Cuddalore, Dindigul, Madura, Tuticorin, Pondicherry, and from many other important towns in Southern India, but the greater portion of the raw hides are obtained from the district of Bellary and from the important skin-trade centres in the States of Mysore and Hyderabad and in the Mahratta country. Great attention is paid to skin-tanning, including sorting, grading, and baling for foreign markets, and this care is largely responsible for the satisfactory prices which are obtained in the London market, continental and American buyers being eager for those bales which are branded with the company's trade-mark, K.A.L., enclosed in a diamond mark.

All consignments are sent through the agency of the South Indian Export Company, of Madras, whose London agents are Messrs. de Clermont and Donner. About 200 hands are employed at each of their tanneries daily, and these are exclusive of the business assistants, partners, and clerical establishment at the headquarters at Periamet, Madras, and at the branch office at Bellary. The general management of the business is in the hands of Mr. K. Hajee Abdul Khader Saib.

T. A. SANKARANARAYANAN, M.B. & C.M.

The ranks of the medical and surgical profession are filled with men of the highest intellectual attainments, and it is remarkable to notice the progress which has been made in recent years in the discovery of improved methods of treatment of diseases and in an advanced knowledge of the curative properties of the various products of the mineral and vegetable kingdoms. The days of the "general" practitioner seem to be passing away, and the graduates of to-day make a point of specializing in some particular branch of medicine or surgery.

Dr. Sankaranarayanan passed through the University of Madras with great distinction, and he began to practice in the city in the year 1904, making the treatment of the ears, nose, and throat a distinctive part of his studies. The consequence of this is that he has become so widely known and his reputation has grown to such an extent that he has been compelled to erect a private hospital for the greater comfort of his numerous patients. This building is admirably situated at the junction of four streets in Broadway, and it is fully equipped with every scientific contrivance for the most up-to-date treatment of the cases with which the doctor has to deal. There are 24 beds in the building, and those who have been inmates speak in no uncertain manner of the skill and the kindly consideration of the doctor and of his capable staff of assistants and nurses. There is no other institution of a similar kind in Madras, and evidence of the popularity not only of the building itself but also of the proprietor was given, when more than 2,000 persons assembled at the opening ceremony in April 1914. Dr. Sankaranarayanan is entitled to the thanks of the whole community for having—at a cost to himself of more than Rs. 50,000—placed such a means of help within the reach of the humblest citizen. The doctor's father is highly respected in the district of Tinnevelly, where he is Zemindar of Kulatur.

DR. T. A. SANKARANARAYANAN.

Photo by M. Doss.

1. DR. SANKARANARAYANAN, M.B. AND C.M. 2 AND 3. VIEWS OF THE PRIVATE HOSPITAL.

V. RAMASAWMY SASTRULU & SONS

This is the foremost Telugu printing and publishing firm in the Presidency of Madras. It was established by the father of the present proprietor, V. Venkateswara Sastrulu, in the year 1863. At that period there were very few printing presses in Madras, and the Government entrusted this firm with their Telugu bookwork. The late V. Ramasawmy Sastrulu transferred the business to Mysore, as the Maharajah promised to patronize him. As the population consisted mostly of Canarese people the proprietor did not receive the encouragement he deserved, and the concern had to depend entirely on the bounty of the late Maharajah. As a consequence of this, the business was then removed to Madras. The prospects of the concern now improved, and the firm, through its connections, was able to accomplish a lot of useful work. The late V. Ramasawmy Sastrulu for nearly forty years published almost all the existing Telugu and Sanskrit works (in Telugu character), together with commentaries on numerous Telugu classics, and the masterly way in which he edited and published very many rare books, which were hitherto unknown to the world at large, made him popular among all classes of people in the Telugu country. The late Maharajahs of Vizianagram and

V. RAMASAWMY SASTRULU.

FOUNDER OF THE FIRM OF V. RAMASAWMY SASTRULU & SONS.

Venkatagiri handsomely supported his labours in the cause of Telugu literature, and, at their suggestion, he undertook the gigantic work of writing and publishing the Ramayana, with elaborate Telugu commentaries. This publication is a monumental work of 15 volumes (royal octavo), one which is a lasting memorial to its able projector.

The name of V. Ramasawmy Sastrulu is a household word in the Telugu country. Formerly, there was only one body of type, called "Great Primer," in the Telugu language, but Mr. Sastrulu invented a new class of type, which goes by the name of "English Body," and the printers of to-day realize how useful this new type is. He died in 1901, leaving the business in the hands of two trustees as his son was young. The latter had an English education and is a clever business man, with an admirable training for the career before him. He assumed charge of the works in 1909.

The printing press is properly equipped with all modern appliances, and there is a large stock of Telugu books very neatly printed and bound. Owing to the excellent work which is done, and to the high-class character of the literary stock-in-trade, the firm has a prosperous career before it.

It may be added that the firm undertakes printing in English and Tamil in addition to Telugu, and that its business establishments in Madras are as follows: The book department is at 192 Esplanade Row; the printing press at 69 Malia Perumal Street, Georgetown. The proprietor's residence is at 323 Trivathyur High Road, Tondiarpet.

S. M. SHAMSUDDIN

It was in the year 1912 that Mr. S. M. Shamsuddin commenced business on his own account as a dealer in hides and skins, but as he had a quarter of a century's practical experience at his back, he began with the best stock-in-trade that any man can possibly have. And he has turned that experience to good account, as he is now a buyer of large quantities of tanned skins, which are sorted, classed, baled, and marked under his personal supervision prior to their being shipped to America, in which country there are firms who place regular orders with him. Skins to the number of between five and six lakhs are handled annually, but the business, although still in its infancy, has already given unmistakable evidence of a growth which is likely to surpass even the sanguine expectations of the proprietor himself. The sorting and baling godown, which is in Moor Street, Madras,

S. M. SHAMSUDDIN.

1. S. M. SHAMSUDDIN. 2. FATHER AND SON.

has a floor space of about 4,800 sq. ft., and the offices are situated at No. 53 Perianna Maistry Street. The owner is prepared to execute orders to any extent, and he has genuine openings for marketable goods in several countries of the world. Labourers are engaged as required, but an unlimited supply can always be depended upon.

K. S. SHIVJI

The Madras establishment of the merchant's business carried on for many years at Bombay by Mr. K. S. Shivji was opened in 1903, and the very extensive trade which is now carried on throughout the mofussil abundantly justified the optimism of the proprietor. He is a wholesale and retail hardware merchant, and occupies a large shop and other premises at No 8 Broadway, Madras, while his storage godowns are situated within a short distance from the main building.

Consignments of all kinds of goods are imported periodically from England, Austria, the United States of America, and Germany, and Mr. Shivji's best customers include the railway companies, the municipalities of the Madras Presidency, and several of the Government institutions and departments.

There is an excellent assortment of stock always on hand, and it includes glass, enamel, and plated ware ; cutlery ; Indian and French harmoniums ; American organs ; Austrian thief and fireproof safes ; Primus, Optimus, Jewel, and other cooking and heating stoves ; Hink's, Dittmar's, and other hanging, table, and wall lamps ; hurricane lanterns ; tea, breakfast, and dinner services ; fancy painted, gilt, and cut-glass presentation articles, and chandeliers and fittings ; gold medal camp furniture ; steel cash-boxes ; glass chimneys and tumblers : carriage lamps and bells ; Washington and Kitson lights and light accessories ; and upright and inverted single and double mantles.

Orders from towns away from Madras receive the most careful attention, and only fully experienced packers are employed in the delivery branch.

About ten assistants are employed regularly under the immediate oversight of the owner. The Bombay business is managed by the proprietor's brothers.

THE SOUTHERN INDIA CHAMBER OF COMMERCE

Chambers of Commerce are organizations which are thoroughly representative of the best elements in the business activities of a country or district, and the necessity for their formation for the protection and assistance of trade must be apparent to all who are desirous of promoting natural interests. The principle of co-operation which was manifested by the establishment of the Southern India Chamber of Commerce in October 1909 has permeated every branch of mercantile and industrial life, and had a wide-reaching influence on the general community. The Chamber seeks to encourage new industries, to hold conferences upon questions affecting the rights of the public, to render aid in the removal of grievances by constitutional methods, to assist in the registration of trade-marks, to collect and distribute statistics relating to international and local trade, to form refer-

K. S. SHIVJI.

1. Showroom. 2. Exterior

ence libraries of books containing concise information on general matters of business, and to establish museums of commercial products or to organize exhibitions, either on behalf of the Chamber or in co-operation with others.

Such, in brief, are the objects of the Southern India Chamber of Commerce, whose Memorandum of Association provides for the admission as permanent and honorary members of merchants, bankers, shipowners, tradesmen, representatives of commercial, railway, and insurance companies, brokers, persons and firms engaged in commerce or trade, agriculture, mining, manufacture, and joint-stock companies, who are eligible for election. Honorary membership is offered to officials and others indirectly connected with trade, commerce, or manufactures in the Madras Presidency, or to those who may have rendered distinguished service to the interests represented by the Chamber. The subscription of permanent members carrying on business in Madras is Rs. 24 per annum, while those who reside outside of the city are required to pay a yearly sum of Rs. 10.

The Executive Committee consists of 27 leading business men, and the following is the list of office-bearers for the year 1914: President, Rao Bahadur P. Theagaroya Chetty; vice-presidents, Khan Bahadur M. A. Kuddus Badsha Sahib and Dewan Bahadur Govindoss Chathoorbhujadoss; honorary secretaries, Messrs. Moulana Abdus Subban Sahib and V. Arunagiri Naidu; members of the committee, the Secretary, Indian Bank, Ltd., Messrs. P. N. Muthuswami Naidu, C. T. Alwar Chetty, B. Chitti-Babu Naidu, Rao Sahib T. Namberumal Chetty, C. Ramanujam Chetty, N. Rajagopalan, P. Aiyanna Chetty, C. Gopal Menon, T. Seetharam Chetty, Khan Bahadur Waljee Laljee Sait, Mahomed Musa Sait, Yakub Hassan Sait, Hajee Mahomed Haneef Saib, Hajee H. Mahomed Abdul Azeez Sahib, C. Srinivasa Chariar, M. Venugopal Naidu, S. V. Ramaswami Mudelliar, Dewan Bahadur K. Krishnaswami Rao, C.I.E., Jamal Mahomed Saib, D. V. Hanumantha Rao, Meer Abdur Rahiman Saib, and C. Duraiswami Aiyengar, assistant secretary.

THE "SWADESAMITRAN"

This is the first and only daily newspaper which is published in Tamil—the chief language of South India—and it has the largest and most widespread circulation of any Tamil publication of this Presidency, circulating not only in South India, but also in Upper and Lower Burma, Ceylon, Penang, Singapore, the Federated Malay States, Sumatra, Borneo, Cochin China, and South and East class newspaper, its general policy being a progressive one upon Western lines, and it is devoted to the creation of a strong and loyal public opinion among the educated masses, and represents almost the entire Tamil reading public.

THE SOUTHERN INDIA CHAMBER OF COMMERCE.
THE MADRAS OFFICES.

Africa. It penetrates into the interior parts of South India, being read in the villages and in the cities by landlords, merchants, officials, and students, who never see—even if they are able to understand—an English paper. It is a high-

It stands to the credit of the *Swadesamitran* that its editor was the only representative of a vernacular publication in this Presidency to receive an invitation to attend the Imperial Durbar held at Delhi by their Imperial Majesties King

George and Queen Mary in 1911. The newspaper was founded in 1882, and is being conducted by Mr. G. Subramania Iyer, the veteran journalist of South India, who was formerly editor and proprietor of a leading English daily, and he is ably assisted by his son, Mr. T. S. Visvanathan. As a medium for advertisement it has few equals, and it is resorted to by all the largest advertisers in England and America.

A general printing business is also conducted upon a small scale in Madras, and the plant includes four Wharfedale machines, which are driven by electric motor-power. Employment is found for about 80 hands.

THE "SWADESAMITRAN."

1. FRONT AND SIDE VIEW OF THE "SWADESAMITRAN" BUILDING. 2. THE "SWADESAMITRAN."

T. AMBASANKER TAWKER

One is forcibly reminded of the old proverb, "*Poeta nascitur non fit*," when reflecting upon the curious fact that the ability to judge diamonds and other precious stones is hereditary, and that no amount of training will enable a man to become an expert in detecting flaws or in assessing values unless he has derived from an ancestor the primary principles of discernment between real and spurious gems. Mr. Tawker, who resides at 85 Mint Street, Madras, is a wholesale and retail diamond and precious stones merchant, and he has no difficulty in tracing the ownership of his business from father to son during the last two hundred years at least. Gems are purchased at Antwerp and in other continental cities, and the owner has a very considerable sale for them throughout the whole of the Presidency. A large stock of made-up jewellery is kept on hand, but Mr. Tawker, with his long experience, is prepared to execute special orders to meet the particular requirements of his customers.

Prospective purchasers, on visiting this establishment, will be shown a magnificent collection of stones of dazzling brilliancy which vary so much in size and shape that the expensive taste of Rajas can be met equally with the more modest requirements of the ordinary work-a-day maiden or youth. Traders, as well as private individuals, have such unbounded confidence in Mr. Tawker's judgment that they frequently employ him to give expert opinion as to the quality and value of all kinds of stones. The proprietor manages the business personally, but he has the able assistance of his son, Mr. A. Bala Krishna Tawker.

THOMPSON & CO.

The general printing, publishing, and stationery business, which was established by Mr. O. Candasawmy Mudaliar in 1879, is being continued by his wife under the name of Thompson & Co., and is one of the best known commercial houses in Popham's Broadway, Madras. The printing machines, which are driven by an 8-h.p. motor-engine, are six in number, and these are exclusive of treadle and other machinery for general work. A very large stock of high-class stationery, suitable alike for business and private purposes, is kept, and the diaries and calendars which are published every year by the firm are neat in appearance and of convenient size. It may be observed that a special feature is made of artistic printing, and very chaste designs are issued from this press. A visitor to the premises will observe fully 200 employees busily engaged in the various departments. At one point a number of workmen are making account and other books; in another part of the large building are engravers, die-sinkers, copper-plate printers, rubber-stamp makers, bookbinders, and type founders; while the general staff includes store-room keepers, packers, and dispatches, the daily round of labour proceeding with regularity under the vigilant eye of Mr. T. K. Swaminathan, the general manager.

Messrs. Thompson's travellers visit all the towns throughout the Madras Presidency, but the business connections of the firm extend from one end of Southern India to the other. The bookselling department is supplied by frequent importations from England and the continent of Europe. The stock kept is a comprehensive one, all classes being catered for—from the statesman to the schoolboy. The firm are agents for all the leading London publications, and they hold the copyright of "Shepherds' Manual of English," a book which has a very large sale in India, Burma, and Ceylon.

S. VAIDYA & CO.

The proprietor of this patent-medicine business—Mr. P. S. Sethurama Iyer—spent many years of his earlier life in the Government service in various parts of the Presidency, but he gave up these routine duties in 1908 with the object of assisting in the development of Indian industries and of benefiting the community by placing upon the market reliable remedies at reasonable prices. The headquarters are at Park Town, Madras, and branches have been opened at Esplanade, in the same city, and at China Bazaar

T. AMBASANKER TAWKER.

1. T. Ambasanker Tawker. 2. A. Bala Krishna Tawker. 3. Sorting and Appraising.

S. VAIDYA & CO.

1. OFFICE AND TRAVELLING STAFFS. 2. STALL IN THE PARK FAIR AND INDUSTRIAL EXHIBITION, MADRAS. 3. "JINTAN."

Street, Trichinopoly, while travelling agents visit the chief towns and villages throughout Southern India, including the native States. Messrs. S. Vaidya & Co. are sole representatives in Southern India for (1) the Alembic Chemical Works Co., Ltd., Bombay and Baroda; (2) Professor T. K. Gajjar's rational preparations, Girgam, Bombay; (3) Jintan (Japanese) pills; (4) C. K. Sen & Co., Calcutta; and other well-known firms.

The Alembic Company are manufacturers of chemical, pharmaceutical, and toilet requisites, and they are distillers of rectified spirits, essential oils, and attars. Professor Gajjar's remedies are for such diseases as typhus, typhoid, and malarial fevers, plague, and cholera, and good results have been obtained in cases of pneumonia, phthisis, and consumption. Several gold and silver medals have been awarded to the proprietors for many of his specialities, and Messrs. S. Vaidya & Co. obtained first prizes for the best decorated stalls at the exhibition promoted by the South Indian Athletic Association held in the People's Park, Madras, in December 1913, and at the Industrial Exhibition held in the same city about the same date. Mr. Iyer has succeeded in extending his business beyond his most sanguine expectations, and it is his intention to establish permanent agencies in every portion of the Presidency. He recently received a pleasurable recognition from Messrs. H. Morishita & Co., Japanese manufacturers, for the great assistance given by him to Messrs. Iwahashi & Yamakiwa of that firm when they visited India in order to extend their commercial relationship with that country.

A small factory has recently been opened for the manufacture of brass candlesticks of various designs, and in material, workmanship, and finish these articles have been so favourably received that the demand for them is steadily on the increase, necessitating a further extension of this line in the near future. Of late, Mr. Iyer has, with his usual zeal and earnestness, taken up the cause of encouraging vernacular publications. He has published vernacular translations of the sacred books of the Hindus, the Upanishads, and others. He is also publishing a vernacular medical journal called *Vaidya Mitran* to popularize both the Western and Eastern treatments of suffering humanity. It goes without saying that such publications, which reach the millions, will be the best medium for the advertisements of all nations and trades.

Mr. Iyer is a highly respected man of business, and his reputation for medicines and brass candlesticks is so great that he is continually being approached by firms who are anxious to become selling agents for him.

P. VENCATACHELLUM SUBRAMANIAM PILLAI

Indian condiments manufactured by Mr. P. Vencatachellum, of Nos. 1, 2, and 3 Popham's Broadway, Madras, have a world-wide reputation, as they are made of the finest ingredients and are flavoured with the choicest aromatic spices, while his equally famous jams and jellies are most carefully prepared from selected fruits.

The proprietor's late father, Mr. P. Vencatachellum, senior, commenced business in quite a small way in 1860 in the same premises which are used to-day by the eldest son as offices and showrooms. A condiment factory, in which manual labour was employed, was started in Umpherson's Street, behind Popham's Broadway, but the demand for these articles increased so rapidly that a larger building has been erected and equipped with modern machinery from England.

Mr. P. Vencatachellum, junior (or Subramaniam Pillai), began to assist in his father's business in the year 1870, and for five years he combined this work with his school studies. In 1875 he became formally connected with the establishment, and although only twenty-two years of age at the time, he was considered to be competent to undertake the management. He was the right-hand supporter of his father until the latter's death in 1887, and strong evidence was then forthcoming of the appreciation of his work, as he received a special bequest for his able assistance and business-like qualities. Mr. Vencatachellum Subramaniam Pillai then became sole proprietor, and his faithful adherence to his determination to produce condiments of first-class quality has placed him head and shoulders above any other maker of similar goods, and the result is that there is a constant increase in the number of orders from England, Australasia, and elsewhere. The first direct overseas shipment took place in 1871, when a consignment was sent to London as an experiment through Messrs. Gordon, Woodroffe & Co.

Since the Vencatachellum brand became known in the market, however, large quantities have been continually supplied to several firms in Great Britain. These consignments have been sent through Messrs. J. A. Sharwood & Co., Ltd., since 1893, when they were appointed sole agents in London. Although the trade with Australia was started in a similar manner by forwarding sample shipments through the late firm of Messrs. Maxwell & Co., of Madras, products of the factory had been previously taken to that country by private persons, who introduced them in Melbourne and Sydney, and large quantities are now sent to the principal cities in Australia, New Zealand, and Tasmania. Some of the specialities shipped to the above countries are as follows: Madras curry-powder and paste, chutney, pickles, chillies, sauces, jams, and jellies. Many firms have in the past acted individually as agents for the sale of these articles throughout Australia, but Mr. Vencatachellum has now appointed Messrs. A. E. Fisher & Sons, Proprietory, Ltd., of Flinders Lane, Melbourne, as sole representatives, and regular monthly consignments are sent to them for all Australasia.

In 1889 Mr. Vencatachellum Subramaniam Pillai purchased as a going concern the South India Ice Factory, which has been worked on behalf of Madras shareholders for about three years. When in 1891 he found that the machinery was out of date, and that the concern, as it then stood, was not likely to pay, the old building was pulled down and the machinery was scrapped, and a modern plant was imported from England to be ready for the new factory. The works are fitted with duplicate machines of the British Linde-Compression system, each of which is capable of making 5 tons of ice in a day of 24 hours. A storeroom, capable of holding 200 blocks of ice, each of 400 lb. is attached to the factory, and a separate plant for refrigerating purposes has been provided. About 200 hands are employed in the two factories. Ice is supplied to Government House, the Madras Club, and other clubs and hotels, officers' mess-quarters, and other important public and private institutions and residences, while a considerable quantity is forwarded daily by rail to various towns. It is a curious fact that though only a few years ago Indians had a strong prejudice against the use of ice, they are now remarkably good customers. When the new factory had been completed, Mr. Vencatachellum Subramaniam Pillai, with the generosity for which he is so well known, supplied 200 or 250 lb. of ice every day to the hospitals in Madras at his own expense; but the Boards of Management subsequently expressed a wish to pay at the usual rates, and they are now supplied with several thousands of pounds in weight. A fully qualified engineer is in charge of the works.

As a business man he has been eminently successful, and no fewer than 31 gold and silver medals and certificates have been awarded for Mr. Vencatachellum's manufactures from the year 1873.

Reference may now be made to matters which are more immediately connected with the private life of Mr. Vencatachellum. The late Mr. Justice Boddam remarked as follows in reference to the will of his late father:

"It seems to me fairly clear that what the testator meant was that his son Subramaniam, whom he obviously looked upon as a capable and trustworthy person, should be the man in whose hands his shop and trade would be safe, and that it should be carried on, and that he was a person whose capacity and honesty was such as would justify the testator in leaving in his hands the conduct of the shop and business."

Mr. Vencatachellum Subramaniam Pillai is a large landholder, having about 75 private houses and lands in Madras, a dozen of which are large residences situated in the most fashionable suburbs of the city, like the Adyar and Nungambakam. Mention may be made of one of them, called "Brodie Castle," which is occupied by the Hon. Mr. W. O. Horne, C.S.I., I.C.S. Another in the same suburb, called "The Grange," is tenanted by the Hon. Sir Harold Stuart. The property known as "Somerford" is occupied by Mr. Justice Miller, while that known as "Morison Gardens" is let to Mr. W. Ross Munro, of the National Bank. "Graemes Gardens" is occupied by Mr. Simpson, of the South India Export Company, and the property known as "Bishop's Gardens" is let to Mr. Allan, of the Presidency College.

Throughout the whole of his life Mr. Vencatachellum Subramaniam Pillai has been a quiet but generous subscriber to some of the Madras charities, schools, and friend-in-need societies, while one school is solely maintained by him. It is called "P. Vencatachellum Poor School," where 150 boys and girls are taught free, and it is recognized by the Government. One temple has been founded and is maintained by him, and in his case it can be truly said that his wealth is not being hoarded in a miserly way, but is being devoted to the alleviation of suffering and to helping those who are making a brave stand against unfavourable odds in the battle of life.

The following certificate was received from the Government of India:

"By command of his Excellency the Viceroy and Governor-General in Council this certificate is presented in the name of her Most Gracious Majesty Queen Victoria, Empress of India, to M. R. Ry. P. V. Subramaniam Pillai, Averga, merchant, son of P. Vencatachellum, in recognition of his charities to the depressed classes. (Signed) J. Frederick Price, Chief Secretary to the Government of Madras, Ootacamund, 10th September, 1897."

Mr. Vencatachellum Subramaniam Pillai is one of the most loyal subjects in the whole of the British Empire, and on several occasions has shown his devotion to the throne. Notably was this the case on the occasion of the Diamond Jubilee of the late Queen Victoria in 1897, when he was the genial host at one of the most lavish entertainments that has ever been given in Madras. It is not generally known that Mr. Vencatachellum Subramaniam Pillai was the provider of the banquet, as his natural modesty made him send out the invitations (under the nom-de-plume of a "Loyal Subject") through a committee constituted by himself. More than 300 of the leading European ladies and gentlemen of Madras and a similar number of Indian gentlemen were entertained at a sumptuous banquet in the Victoria Public Hall, and the supper, concert, and the theatrical performance which followed received the warmest praise from the delighted guests. Three European bands of music were engaged on the occasion. A unique feature of the concert was that a number of Indian Christian ladies sang songs in chorus, and this was only the second occasion on which a public appearance of this character ever took place, the first being at the reception given by the same host to Bishop Thoburn of the Methodist Episcopal Mission. Several young European ladies, who had been especially selected on account of their excellent voices, contributed largely to the enjoyment of the evening.

The following extracts from the *Madras Mail* refer to this subject and to other entertainments previously given by Mr. Vencatachellum Subramaniam Pillai on Jubilee Day:

"Reference, too, must be made to the illuminations, the bulk of which, north of the Mount Road, were so generously provided by Mr. P. Vencatachellum." (It should be noted that the Press and the public in general call Mr. P. Vencatachellum Subramaniam Pillai simply Mr. P. Vencatachellum, which is the title of his business.) "Apart from the contributions to the general fund, there have been several special contributions for special objects. For instance, 'A Loyal Subject' has undertaken to feed 220 adults in the Friend-in-need Society's Home, 110 children in Mrs. Firth's three schools, 170 children in the Pudupet Methodist Mission School, 145 in Mrs. Lazarus's Poor School, 1,000 poor in Dakshinamurthi Muttam, Washermanpet, and 1,100 poor near St. Lazarus's Church, St. Thomé."

"'A Loyal Subject'—whose name it is hoped will leak out later on, for he deserves that he should be widely known—has also given Rs. 500 towards the casket in addition to undertaking some very expensive arrangements for the fitting celebration of the commemoration. . . . With regard to illuminations 'Loyal Subject' has undertaken to light up two miles of roadway from Washermanpet down Popham's Broadway past the Fort Glacis, round by the Medical College and Central Station, and along the Poonamallee Road as far as the Friend-in-need Society's Home. He will also erect four beacons on the Island. A pyrotechnic display—provided by the ever-generous 'Loyal Subject'—will conclude the programme to be observed on the Island."

"The Poonamallee Road from the Friend-in-need Society's Home to the Victoria Hall was illuminated, the portions in front of the hall being brilliant with the very thorough arrangements which 'Loyal Subject' had made to make the entertainment a success. A huge illuminated arch surmounted by a beacon spanned one of the gateways, while the central gateway was filled in with an illuminated device in white and ruby glow-lights, bearing the words 'The Diamond Jubilee' and 'God bless the Queen Empress, 1837 to 1897, V.I.,' and finally the initials 'P.V.,' which ought to have been a sufficient indication of 'Loyal Subject's' identity. Victoria Hall was crowded with the guests bidden to the entertainment, who were received at

P. VENCATACHELLUM.

BUNGALOWS OWNED BY P. VENCATACHELLUM.

the side entrance under a *shamiana*, by the reception committee, from which Col. Moore was unfortunately absent owing to an accident. Surgeon-Lieut.-Col. H. D. Cook, however, took his place, and was assisted by M. Viraraghava Chariar. A very elaborate musical programme (both vocal and instrumental) of 21 items, European and native, was gone through, at the end of which 'The Parsi Theatrical Company' gave a performance of the Hindustani opera, 'Bihari Parastan.' A most *recherché* supper was laid for the European guests in the large lower hall of the building, while the native guests had their comforts attended to in one of the upper verandas. The whole building was most elaborately and beautifully decorated, and it speaks volumes for the energy, expedition, and resources of 'Loyal Subject' that he was able to do this in the few hours at his disposal, the hall being only handed over to him that morning. The weather, contrary to expectation, did not much mar the success of the beautiful illuminations, though the high land-wind prevailing prevented their being maintained as long as they might otherwise have been. Of the decorations in Georgetown, those in Popham's Broadway were of a very artistic and beautiful character. Messrs. P. Vencatachellum & Co. (who have done so much to make the Jubilee celebration in Madras a success), besides dressing their premises, put up an archway across the road with suitable inscriptions."

The following extracts from *The Hindu*, relate to what Mr. Vencatachellum Subramaniam Pillai did on the occasion of the same Jubilee:

"It is no longer necessary to retain the pseudonym behind which 'A Loyal Subject' was screening himself all along. If he had assumed it in meekness and shyness it does not justify us to adopt it in our appreciation and gratitude for him. His identity was at one time a curiosity when his very handsome offers were being announced, but it has become revealed now when his liberality and hospitality have been established, demonstrated as they were so grandly on such a loyal and joyous occasion as the Queen's Jubilee. The co-operation of Mr. Vencatachellum with the committee, his handsome subscriptions, which with a few others, rendered possible the feeding of the poor, the elegant arrangements he had made to observe the day on his own account, the decorations and the illuminations he carried out at his own expense, the magnificent entertainment he gave last night to the various communities of Madras on a princely style of hospitality—these have helped to swell the beauty and the impressiveness of the demonstrations, besides enlarging and emphasizing the essentially popular character thereof. Mr. P. Vencatachellum, who has acquired fame in his business, first came forward as a public man in connection with the movement for the elevation of the Panchama community, for whose benefit he, as a distinguished member of it, opened and endowed schools, whose maintenance is a charge on his liberality, whose improvement is a source of anxiety for his mind. His next appearance before the public is in connection with the Jubilee of yesterday, and it goes without saying how eminently successful has been his attempt. He had been aided in his arrangements by the co-operation and advice of a number of his friends, and by the working members of the Jubilee Committee—Sir George Moore and Mr. B. H. Chester in particular. The eighteen beacons put up on the Mount Road, on the Island, on the Esplanade, and elsewhere, the whole of the illuminations on the Island, most of those on Popham's Broadway, the decking and lighting up of the premises and the surroundings of the Town Hall were all his undertakings. On the public road, opposite to the Town Hall, there was a blaze of illumination produced by the burning beacons and the glittering lamps. An arch of fire semicircled the entrance, with the welcomes, rejoicings, and blessings to the Queen inscribed thereon, shining in their variegated colours. The grounds of the compound were baized or carpeted, while over the doorway a canopy of silk canvas had been erected. Mr. Vencatachellum played the host with pleasant address and courtesy, warmly receiving the guests on alighting, and subsequently conducting them upstairs. He had requested a number of representative gentlemen among the various communities to assist him in the matter of issuing invitations and in receiving guests. The entertainment took place in the upper hall, where a highly interesting programme had been selected, suited to the tastes of the different sections of the audience. The celebration of the Jubilee by Mr. Vencatachellum may be said to be the crown of the whole proceedings, and the Madras programme minus his contribution would have been a very poor, scanty one."

All temples situated on the roads between Mr. Vencatachellum's own temple for the public at Washermanpet and the ice factory on the Poonamallee Road had special ceremonies at his cost. No fewer than 2,000 Hindus of all sections congregate every week in this gentleman's own temple.

The coronation of the late King Edward VII provided Mr. Vencatachellum Subramaniam Pillai with another opportunity of showing his loyalty, and receptions and entertainments were again the order of the day. The Hindu idea of kingship is that the ruler on the throne is the representative upon earth of the Supreme Being, and the festivities and ceremonies of the day were carried out in accordance with that view. In the first place there was a huge gathering of Christian missionaries and many Indian Christians of all denominations in the Memorial Hall, where addresses were given and refreshments partaken of, and these were followed by amusements. A special festival was celebrated in Mr. Vencatachellum's own temple—Dakshinamurthi—and another was held at Pachaiyappa's Hall, which included a musical entertainment concerning the King-Emperor's Coronation by the late renowned Kristna Bagavather, who was assisted by Panchapakasa Sastry, and to each of these celebrities a gold medal was presented by the host. A similar meeting was held at the Thondamandalam Thuluva Vellalers' High School, where a Kalakshepam relating to the Coronation was performed. The evening of that day will never be forgotten by the thousands who witnessed the magnificent illuminations of Popham's Broadway and Poonamallee Road, and of some public buildings like Pachaiyappa's Hall and the Memorial Hall, which were carried out at Mr. Vencatachellum Subramaniam Pillai's expense.

In December 1896 Mr. Vencatachellum Subramaniam Pillai gave a public reception to Bishop Thoburn of the Methodist Episcopal Mission, about which the good Bishop wrote to the *Indian Witness* as follows:

"At Madras, however, a reception had been prepared of a character so unique that I was not only surprised but also deeply gratified both by the spirit with which it was proposed, and the very generous manner in which it was carried out. A Hindu gentleman—Mr. P. Vencatachellum—had secured a large hall, fitted it up in the most sumptuous manner, and invited the Conference to accept a public reception in his name."

P. VENCATACHELLUM.

CERTIFICATES AWARDED FOR INDIAN CONDIMENTS.

The *Bombay Guardian* of January 2, 1897, has the following remarks about the same reception:

"About 200 guests were entertained with beautiful music, and after the banquet an address of welcome to the Bishop and the Conference was given by Rev. J. Lazarus, and that was replied to by the Bishop in his usual happy way." It may be added that this was the first occasion in which many Indian Christians sat at dinner with European gentlemen, and some Indian ladies were persuaded to shake off their shyness and come forward to play on the piano and to sing in public.

In the "Triumphs on the Cross" by Miss Grace Stephens the following remarks were made about Mr. P. Vencatachellum Subramaniam Pillai's liberality on the occasion of laying the corner-stone of the Harriet Bond Skidmore Memorial by Bishop Foss, in December 1897, at Vepery:

"Through the kindness of Mr. P. Vencatachellum, who undertook all the expenses of the occasion, a large pavilion was erected to accommodate 2,000 people. The beacon lights that towered 60 ft. in height were typical of the true Light of the World that will shine with His own radiant brightness into the hearts of the people. The principal streets leading to the grounds were illuminated. Refreshments, flowers, garlands, and rose-water of the very best were in abundance, and the scene of that evening will always remain with us as a thing apart, unique in its grandeur and splendour."

It will be seen from the above sketch that the subject of it is worthy of the profound respect in which he is held by the public of Madras, and not the least praiseworthy traits in the character of this loyal benefactor is that he bestows his gifts in such an unobtrusive manner that their value is greatly enhanced.

SRI VIJAYA & CO.

1. Showroom. 2. Proprietor and Staff. 3. A. Nammalwar Chetty.

SRI VIJAYA & CO.

The present proprietor of the extensive business carried on under the above name at Nos. 1 to 3/194 Esplanade, Madras, is A. Nammalvar Chetty, and although he has been engaged in commercial life since the year 1894 he did not open this establishment until June 1910. He is a direct importer of stationery, fancy goods, millinery, hosiery, perfumes, musical instruments, and sundry other articles from England, Germany, France, Italy, and Japan, and he also makes extensive purchases in Bombay and Calcutta. A special feature is made of the sale of steel-trunks and dispatch-boxes, of leather goods, of black lead-pencils made for the firm by A. W. Faber and Johan Faber, of Bavaria, of the "Vijaya" fountain-pen, which is made in London, together with Waterman's and Swan fountain-pens. The firm have a very choice selection of 18-carat rolled gold chains, pendants, and brooches, and their stock of fancy buttons for vests is composed of every variety of the most ornate character.

The stationery department has a splendid assortment of writing and other papers, and the other sections are well stocked.

Mr. Chetty gives personal attention to the business and he has a capable staff of assistants.

THE FORESTS OF MADRAS

BY S. COX, CONSERVATOR OF FORESTRY

THE area of forests under the administration of the Madras Forest Department is roughly about 20,000 square miles scattered throughout the twenty-three districts into which the Madras Presidency is divided. In addition to this area there is also a considerable acreage of forest belonging to the feudatory States, Travancore, Cochin, and others; or within the large zemindaries, Jeypore and Venkatagiri by way of example, most of which is now managed on definite sylvicultural lines by officers trained at one or other of the Government Forest Colleges.

In prehistoric days nearly the whole of the Madras Presidency must have been a forest-clad country, with cultivation confined to a narrow strip along the coasts and to the sides of the greater rivers. Even in later days the proportion of forest to cultivated land was probably higher than in most parts of the peninsula. Madras escaped the invasion of the nomadic tribes whose flocks and herds destroyed such vast areas of forest in Upper India, and, owing to the mountainous and unhealthy character of so large a portion of it, the forests were left unpopulated to comparatively recent times.

During the early years of British occupation the Government, following the practice of native rulers, encouraged by every means in its power the increase of cultivation at the expense of the forests, with the result that the boundaries of the latter were gradually pushed back towards the hills and mountains, to which they are now almost entirely confined.

The hills themselves had already been invaded by the aboriginal or semi-original tribes retreating under the pressure of competition with the more civilized people of the plains, and large areas of forest were devoted to a form of shifting cultivation, the principal feature of which is the felling and burning of the forest for the sake of a temporary crop on the otherwise uncultivable hill-slopes.

Such was the gradually increasing destruction of the forests that in the early part of the nineteenth century the British Government became seriously concerned as to the lack of timber, especially teak, for shipbuilding and construction; and various spasmodic attempts were made by aboriculturists of questionable experience to conserve the more valuable timber forests. Planting even was started, and in 1884 the first of the great Nilambur teak plantations was formed.

But it was not until a good many years later that the importance of forests from the general economic point of view began to be realized, nor until the deputation of Sir Dietrich Brandis, the then Inspector-General of Forests to the Government of India, to report upon the subject, that any definite forest policy was established. Dr. Brandis, at the request of the Madras Government visited the Presidency in 1883, and as the result of his detailed inspection of the forests, certain broad lines of treatment were recommended, and have been since carried out, subject to such modifications as experience has shown to be necessary.

The action of forests in raising the subsoil water level, in preventing floods, and the scouring of soil from the hill-sides, and in mitigating the effects of intense heat, is now generally admitted; while their value as a permanent source of timber, fuel, and grazing to an agricultural population, becomes every year more evident. The policy of Government is therefore to conserve and improve the forests, especially on mountain and hill-slopes where forest growth can exert the greatest influence on the local economic conditions, and where its existence does not conflict with the claims of agriculture.

It was necessary at the start to introduce an Act under which the selection and settlement of the very large area of forest required to carry out this policy could be given a legal status. It was also necessary to introduce a larger service of officers trained in European forestry to manage the "settled" area on sylvicultural lines. Dr. Brandis's recommendations on these points were accepted, and the introduction of the present Madras Forest Service and of the technical management of the State forests may be said to date from the year 1884.

Up to the end of last century almost the whole energies of the forest service were confined to the selection, survey, settlement, and demarcation of the reserved forests, and as a consequence progress in actual conservancy and improvement of the forests was small. With the completion of settlement the Department was left with immense property, the management of which was, and still is, faced with difficulties of many kinds. In the first place, Government has had to meet the general scepticism with regard to the value of forests, a scepticism by no means confined to India, and it has been compelled to face the almost universal feeling, due to centuries of uninterrupted enjoyment, that the forests belong to and should be freely used by the people.

JACK FRUIT TREE.

Secondly, it has to contend with practices, centuries old and harmless enough when the greater part of the country was under forest, which are now a cause of great injury to the country, such, for instance, as burning the forest to produce an early growth of grass, lopping of forest growth for the feed of cattle, shifting cultivation involving the cutting and burning of the growth, and other methods destructive of forest on a large scale.

Thirdly, there are special difficulties due to the rapid increase of population and wealth throughout the country, such as the ever-increasing number of cattle dependent on the forests for grazing, the enormous herds of goats kept by skin dealers, whose trade in skins with America and Europe is, or was, one of the most lucrative in the Presidency; and the ever-increasing pressure on the State forests for timber and fuel due to the cultivation of large areas of forest land left as such for the enjoyment of the villagers themselves. Lastly, there is the financial difficulty connected with the management of an estate largely unproductive of revenue, and in many cases in a very degraded condition. Such undeveloped forests as still exist can only be exploited after heavy expenditure on oads and buildings, and it may be added that nowhere within the Madras Presidency are there such large areas of valuable timber forest as exist in Burma.

These difficulties are now being dealt with. The goat has been driven out of the State forests; shifting cultivation within the limits of the latter has also been stopped; attempts are being made to confine the forest-grazing cattle to the more valuable breeds, and especially to those required for agriculture; and means for the protection of forests from fire have been introduced throughout the Presidency on a fairly large scale. In addition to these somewhat restrictive and unpopular measures, Government is also engaged in the education of the agricultural population towards a knowledge of the practical benefits of forest conservancy by handing over to the management of the village communities the forests which are in the immediate neighbourhood. It is hoped that the practical results and benefits to be derived by personal management will do more to teach the *ryot* than any other form of education.

The State timber and fuel forests are at the same time being opened up with communications in order to make fuller use of the existing resources, and to meet the ever-increasing demand for timber and fuel. With so many difficult problems to solve, and with so large an area to deal with, the Forest Department is expanding year by year in the number and in the training of its officers.

It has been subject to constant reorganization during the last thirty years, and being admittedly insufficient to carry out its work, it is on the verge of fresh changes. The organization of the Department is on the same lines as that of other Indian provinces; but there are one or two points connected with it which are worthy of mention. Nowhere in India is the forest officer brought into more intimate relations with the agriculturist than in Madras. By far the greater proportion of the Presidency forests are of the type which provides the *ryot* with the small timber, fuel, and grazing with which his agricultural profession is ultimately concerned, and in no other province are the forests more intermingled with, or adjacent to, the crop-bearing area. The forest officer has therefore to work hand-in-hand with the revenue officer, and the Collector of the district is by his position *ex-officio* head of the forest department in his district. Similarly, in place of the Chief Conservator of such Governments as that of Burma, or the Central Provinces, the head of the Forest Department in Madras is one of the civilian members of the Board of Land Revenue.

With the gradual increase in the intensive management of the forests and the greater professional ability of the staff due to the provision of special education, this close control by non-professional officers will probably cease; but it has been of great service during the early

1. TODDY-DRAWERS ON COCONUTS. 2. "ARENGA SACCHARIFERA" (SAGO PALM) IN FRUIT. 3. TALIPOT PALM ("CORYPHA UMBRACULIFERA"). 4. MELANOXYLON AT OOTACAMUND. 5. THE NEEM ("MELIA AZADIRACHTA"). 6. PALMYRA PALMS IN FRUIT, AND A DATE PALM. 7. THE TAMARIND "TAMARINDUS INDICA"). 8. DATE ("PHŒNIX SYLVESTRIS").

Photos by P. F. F.

stages of administration, not only in overcoming the prejudices which are caused by all new measures of forest conservancy, but by directly interesting a large body of able civilian officers in the difficult problems of forestry.

With regard to forest education, two recent reforms in Madras call for some notice. Up to within a few years ago the Rangers, the executive officers of the Forest Department, were trained at the Imperial Forest College at Dehra Dun. The number which could be annually admitted there was strictly limited, and therefore insufficient to provide for the needs of the Madras service. This fact, together with the certainty that the *cadre* of Rangers required a great increase, prompted the Madras Government to institute a Forest College at Coimbatore for the training of its own men.

The second reform was the institution of vernacular schools for the training of foresters and forest guards, who form the protective establishment of the forest service. Four schools are annually held in selected districts, in which a six months' course of practical work is given under the general superintendence of the local district forest officer.

It is too early to experience the benefit of these institutions, but no doubt has ever existed of the necessity of special education in all branches of the department, and there is every reason to hope for remarkable results, especially as the improvement in the education is being connected with a simultaneous improvement in the pay and prospects of the staff.

The Madras Forest Department consists at the present moment of the following administrative grades of the Imperial Forest Service: 4 Conservators, 22 Deputy Conservators, and 5 Assistant Conservators; while those of the Provincial Service include 8 Extra Deputy Conservators, and 23 Extra Assistant Conservators. The executive grades consist of 172 Rangers and 219 Deputy Rangers, and the protective grades have employment for 292 Foresters and 1,487 Forest Guards.

ELEPHANT PULLING LOGS OF TIMBER.

The Imperial service officers are recruited from England, and have to spend two years in special forest training, partly on the continent of Europe, after having taken a science degree at one of the major Universities. The provincial forest service is obtained locally from among the more highly educated classes, and its members are trained at the expense of Government in the Dehra Dun Forest College, except in such cases as they are directly promoted from the class of Ranger.

For forest administrative purposes the Madras Presidency is divided into four "Circles," to each of which a Conservator is attached. He is the head of the Forest Department within his circle, and adviser to the Government on all forest matters within it. Under him are the divisional forest officers, who are either Deputy and Assistant Conservators, or senior members of the provincial forest service, and have charge of the whole or part of the forests of a revenue district. The forest area is divided into "ranges," in executive charge of Rangers, while the ranges are subdivided into "beats," in charge of Foresters and Forest Guards, who are responsible for their protection.

In addition to the above permanent and pensionable grades of forest service there is, of course, a considerable permanent clerical staff attached to the service, as well as a large body of elephant-men, cattle-men, *tannadars*, *peons*, plantation and forest watchers, gardeners, and so forth, on the temporary and non-pensionable scale.

One of the most urgent reforms now under consideration is the substitution of permanent pensionable officers for the numerous members of the temporary establishments who are in receipt of small wages, and who are, as a rule, untrustworthy.

The forests of the Madras Presidency may be divided roughly into three classes, namely, (*a*) the forests covering the main hill and mountain ranges; (*b*) the smaller scattered forests adjoining the villages; and (*c*) the plantations. In the first class are found some very extensive forests, such as the Nallamalais in the Kurnool district, with an area of about 2,000 square miles, and the forests along the Eastern and Western Ghauts; but it would be a mistake to imagine that even in the largest of these areas there is anything approaching to "virgin forest," except in situations which are almost inaccessible to the human being.

By far the greater portion of the forest has suffered from excessive felling, grazing, and from forest fires, with the result that the Forest Department is more concerned with the restoration of despoiled forests than with the exploitation and sale of timber on a large scale. The smaller forests in the vicinity of villages are still worse, and the shortage of small timber and fuel is already severely felt in localities where thirty years ago such experience was extremely unlikely. The various measures of restoration now being undertaken vary widely according to place and circumstance, but generally speaking they follow the lines of opening up the larger forests with a system of roads and buildings; of systematic protection by the use of many miles of fire lines, and of the employment of special patrols; of limiting all felling to definite areas where it is carried out on sylvicultural lines for the improvement of the forest crop; and of regulating the grazing to prevent the destruction of young growth which will form the future crop.

In the smaller forests, from which the daily requirements of village fuel have to be met, the present practice is to cut back the existing degraded forest and to restore the growth again from the old stumps under the protection of fences and

"SIDEROXYLON TOMENTOSUM" AND "CINNAMONUM WIGHTII" ON THE NILGIRI DOWNS.

Photo by P. F. F.

stone walls. Luckily the power to form coppices is a characteristic of most Indian trees.

With regard to plantations, experience has shown that the time and money spent on them would have been better spent on the improvement and protection of the natural forest. Planting is a very expensive undertaking, and it is not a practical means of forest restoration on a large scale, although years ago it was the only measure to which thought was ever given. At the same time the plantations which the Department possesses have served an excellent purpose. If it had not been for Government enterprise in planting casuarina along the east coast the scarcity of fuel in the coast towns would have reached famine point. Similarly the introduction of the eucalyptus on the Nilgiri Hills is due to Government action, and it has had the result of saving the natural evergreen forests and of providing very cheap fuel, without which the ordinary Indian could hardly exist at that elevation.

The most remarkable plantation owned by Government is, however, the teak plantation of Nilambur, in the Malabar district. This plantation was commenced in 1844, and has been extended year by year until it now covers an area of several thousand acres, and is valued at about 80 lakhs of rupees. As a commercial speculation it has been a great success, the thinnings from the forest having already more than paid for the cost of formation and tending; but even in this case it is scarcely disputed that the money would have been spent to more general advantage had it been devoted to the development of the natural teak forests on the Western Ghauts.

Among the various types of forest in Madras the following may be mentioned:—

The Sal Forests.—The district of Ganjam and the northern half of Vizagapatam fall within the zone of the sal (*Shorea robusta*), which extends to the foot of the Himalayas. The sal is particularly valuable timber owing to its toughness and durability, and is in great demand for large beams and for railway sleepers. It

TEAK IN FLOWER.

Photo by P. F. F.

has the characteristic, uncommon among Indian timber trees, of growing gregariously and forming what are technically known as "pure" forests. There are large areas of Government sal forest in the Gumsur *taluq* of Ganjam, which are of great future value. They have suffered, like most other Indian forest, from reckless exploitation and from fire, but they are rapidly recovering under the treatment which they now receive. The Jeypore zemindari is also rich in sal forest, which is now being managed on sylvicultural principles.

The Teak Forests of the Dry Zone.—Farther to the south, along the banks of the Godavari, in the southern parts of Jeypore zemindari, and in the Nallamalai forests of Kurnool, the dry zone of teak (*Tectona grandis*), which covers a considerable area of Central India, is entered. Teak here grows to a comparatively small size compared with that in the teak forests of Burma or of the west coast, but the timber is exceptionally hard and good. In the Nallamalais the tree has been largely cut out by timber merchants previous to the advent of forest conservancy, and in the Eastern Ghauts large tracts

HANGING ROOTS OF THE BANYAN ("FICUS BENGALENSIS") FORMING PILLARS.

Photo by P. F. F.

of teak forest have been destroyed by hillmen in the process of their shifting cultivation, although a considerable quantity still remains and will rapidly improve with protection and sylvicultural treatment.

The Hardwickia Binata Forests.—Farther to the south again, in the Cuddapah, Nellore, and Ceded Districts, and in the valleys of the Cauvery and Bhavani Rivers, the *Hardwickia binata* is found. The Hardwickia forests are characteristic of the dry, central area of the Presidency, and are seen at their best on the low, rocky hills of the Deccan, where the rainfall is about 30 in. The tree is a very handsome one, with graceful foliage, and it is valued for its hard, heavy timber, and for the fibre from the bark. It grows gregariously in patches of greater or less extent. Unfortunately, occurring as it does in some of the most arid, stony country in the Presidency, it has been exposed to much damage by graziers, who lop the leaves and branches for fodder, and there are at present no large areas of forest fit for timber operations on a large scale.

The Red-sanders Forest.—The red-sanders is a tree of considerable interest. It has, like its brother species, the padouk (*Pterocarpus dalbergeoirdes*), of the Andaman Islands, a very local distribution, and is almost confined to the small hill ranges of the Velligondas, Lankamalais, and Sechachellam Hills of the Cuddapah and Nellore districts. The tree was formerly greatly valued for the dye

TRUNK OF A TREE SHOWING THE BUTTRESSES.

extracted from its timber and roots, and "red-wood" billets have been a form of exported trade to Europe for at least two hundred years. The natural dye has now been supplanted by the artificial one, and the foreign demand for the wood, which has led to wholesale destruction of the red-sanders forests, is now limited to local requirements.

The latter are, however, very large and in excess of the supply. The timber is used for posts, carving, and boxes, and there is a large trade in carved idols made of this wood, which are sold at the Tirupati and other temple festivals. If sufficient timber were available it would be used for house-building, carts, and agricultural implements; but the area of red-sanders forests is so limited, and the forests have been so cut about during the last two centuries, that only small timber is available in limited quantities.

The red-sanders tree is a very handsome one, especially during the hot season when it puts out its new canopy of vivid emerald green. Like the Hardwickia, with which it is associated, it prefers the dry, rocky hill-slopes of small hill ranges with a rainfall seldom exceeding 40 in.

Sandal-wood Forests.—The sandal-wood (*Santalum album*) is found sporadically throughout Mysore, Coorg, the Ceded Districts, and the Carnatic, but it does not anywhere form a considerable portion of the forest in which it occurs. In fact, it is commonly found in very open forests, in hedgerows, and along the borders of cultivation.

Research in recent years has proved the tree to be—in the later stages of its growth—a parasite on the roots of other trees; a fact which accounts to some extent for its sporadic appearance, for the failure of all attempts to form sandal plantations, and for very considerable variations in the value of the wood. There is still much to learn on the subject of the growth of sandal-wood, especially with regard to the origin and spread of a curious disease known as "spike," to which it is very susceptible.

A full-grown sandal-wood-tree is probably the most valuable tree in the world, although it seldom reaches a height of 40 ft. Its value lies in the essential scented oil which is found in the heart-wood and roots. For this oil there is an enormous European and a considerable local demand. Most of the timber is sent to Europe, where the oil is extracted, and some idea of the value of scented wood is obtained from the fact that during the year 1914 the sales of sandal-wood in Madras realized an average of about Rs. 1,000 per ton of roughly prepared billets. The oil is used for scents and medicine, and in India the wood is to some extent used for making small carved boxes and for inlaid work.

The main supplies of sandal-wood come from Mysore, where the exploitation brings to the State an annual profit which may amount to as much in a favourable year as 20 lakhs of rupees. In Madras the total annual output is only about 250 tons, but this will be gradually augmented as the special measures for the protection of the forests in which sandal-wood occurs begin to take effect.

The Deciduous Forests of the Western Ghauts.—These valuable forests are found along the west coast of the peninsula, between the Western Ghauts and the sea, and on the foot-hills and lower slopes and plateaus of the mountains, up to about 4,000 ft., where they gradually merge into the pure evergreen type of forest. They contain a great variety of valuable timber trees, such as the teak, the rosewood, the ironwood, Pterocarpus, Lagerstroemia, Terminalias, and others, which under the influence of a heavy rainfall and a forcing climate grow to a great size.

Much of this type of forest has disappeared owing to the increasing demand for timber, and to the facilities for transport afforded by the west coast rivers, but valuable teak and rosewood forests still exist in Cochin, the lower Anamalais, the Wynaad, and in parts of Mysore and Coorg. Teak reaches its maximum size in these forests, which are very similar in constitution to those of Lower Burma and Siam.

The Evergreen Forests of the Western Ghauts.—The evergreen forest zone occupies the slopes of the great mountain ranges in Canara, Coorg, Malabar, the Nilgiris, Coimbatore, Cochin, and Travancore. In these forests the trees grow to an immense size, the largest being, perhaps, Tetrameles, Dipterocarpus, and Canarium. At altitudes of about 5,000 ft. *Mesua ferrea* and *Hydnocarpus Wightiana*, both very valuable trees, are found, as

IN WESTERN MYSORE.

well as *Cedrela toona*, the red cedar, so largely used for the manufacture of tea-boxes.

At still higher altitudes trees of more temperate zones appear, such as the ilex, eugenias, and others, and on the summit of the hills rhododendrons are characteristic of the forest growth, which is low and stunted.

THE FINANCING OF DISTRICT RAILWAYS

By Sir FRANCIS J. E. SPRING, K.C.I.E., M.I.C.E., M.I.M.E.

IN its arrangements for the financing of short lines of railway of local interest, to be constructed and worked for the most part by the main lines to which they will serve as feeders, the Madras Presidency for many years past has set a bright example to the rest of India—an example so far but scantily followed. Of the twenty-five districts which go to form the Presidency of Madras, seventeen have, by the middle of the year 1915, imposed taxation on themselves for the special purpose of financing short branch lines of railways of local interest within their borders. And here, for the benefit of readers unfamiliar with the mechanism of Indian government, it had better at once be explained that a "district" in India is an administrative area corresponding more or less with a county in England or with a department in France. The average population of a district is more or less, throughout India, a million persons, though some have double and some half this population. Under the provincial or local government concerned the district is ruled by a civil service official, over the greater part of India known as a "Collector," whose functions differ little from those of the *prefét* in France or the *prefetto* in Italy. The administrative committee, known in England as the County Council, is represented in the Madras Presidency, as well as in other parts of India where local self-government is in a forward state, by the "District Board," within whose area of control are *taluq* and village boards, corresponding more or less with the parish councils in England—at least nearly enough so to satisfy the thirst for information of potential readers of this chapter. Throughout India, excluding the Native States, the Government of India is overlord of all land in a sense less obscured than in England the King is. The land revenue forms one of the chief items of the public revenue, and is collected in each district by the Collector, or chief State official. The Collector in all cases is president of the District Board, but to many of the more advanced Taluq Boards power to elect their own non-official president has nowadays been delegated by Government. Under an Act of the Legislature *ad hoc* —in Madras called the "Madras Local Boards Act V of 1884"—these boards impose and spend local taxation; that is, what in England is termed "rates" as distinguished from excise and the other items of the general taxation of the country. The objects on which the locally levied "rates" may be expended are, of course, strictly defined by law, and consist chiefly of roads, hospitals, schools, sanitation, and so on. Ordinarily —one or two districts only forming exceptions—the rates or cess leviable by a District Board for the purpose of Madras Act V of 1884 may not exceed the limit of one anna (1d.) for every rupee (1s. 4d.) of the revenue levied by Government, as overlord, on all occupied land in the district. In other words, whatever the Government "land assessment" may be, the local authority has power, for its local purposes under its Act, to collect one-sixteenth part of such assessment.

Ordinarily the local needs of a Madras district, other than its railway needs, are barely met from the sixteenth part of the State land assessment leviable for local purposes. But so long ago as 1878 one of the districts, that of Tanjore, finding that with one-fourth of this levy unexpended it could provide for its local needs very amply, conceived the idea of applying the unexpended fourth to the making of cheap light railways within its borders. The Tanjore Board was partly led to adopt this policy because of the scarcity and cost of good road-making material within its boundaries as well as by the consideration that railways may be relied upon, to a greater extent than roads, to give some return on the capital expended on them as well as to pay for the cost of their maintenance. Correspondence then ensued between the Provincial and Imperial Governments and the Secretary of State for India on the subject of the permissibility of the proposed policy in view of Imperial financial responsibilities. So protracted were the negotiations that it was not until sixteen years after their commencement that the first piece of railway locally financed in the district of Tanjore was got into running order. This was the 54-mile railway from Mayavaram to Mutupet, which cost about 25 lakhs of rupees, or £167,000, of which half had been contributed by Government and the other half by the district, out of savings, as already explained, from the local taxation—one-sixteenth part of the Government land cess—which the law enabled it, in common with all other districts, to levy. It may be mentioned here that, in the year 1900, the Tanjore Board bought up the Government half-share of the Mayavaram-Mutupet Railway. And here also, before turning to the case of other districts, it may be stated that by the year 1915 Tanjore had increased the mileage of her district railways from 54 to 112, and had secured sanction for another 20 miles, which are now under construction. So far all Tanjore's lines have averaged about Rs. 48,000, or £3,200 per mile, land being free, and rolling stock, in return for a rent for its use, being provided by the South India main line of railway, by which the local branches are worked. It may here be added that the railway policy of the Tanjore District Board has been a conspicuous success financially, with the result that many more boards have hoped, and some so far with success, as shall be shown, to follow her example.

So far, amongst Madras districts, Tanjore is unique in finding itself able to finance its local railways out of the margin left over from its legally leviable taxation, after providing fully for all other needs. All the other districts, so far, have found no such margin. Therefore when, in the year 1900, it became necessary, in view of other desired changes, to amend the Madras Act V of 1884, the opportunity was taken to insert a new clause giving Madras District Boards power to increase their legally leviable cess by one-fourth—that is, by one sixty-fourth, or 0·0156 per cent., of the amount of the annual land assessment levied by Government on all occupied land. In amending the Act the proviso was made that this additional cess (three pies, or one farthing, per rupee of the land assessment) was not to be levied until such levy should have been determined on by a resolution of a District Board supported by not less than three-fourths of the members of the board present at the meeting, such resolution being confirmed six months later by a like majority. When, in 1900, the Act was amended, it was estimated that the annual sum which, under the new powers so conferred on them, the Madras districts might levy amounted to about Rs. 12,68,000, or £85,000 per annum—a sum sufficient, at $4\frac{1}{2}$ per cent. interest, to warrant the raising of enough money for the building of about 600 miles of railway at about the cost per mile of the Tanjore lines.

A judgment whether the District Boards of Madras Presidency other than Tanjore have been fast or slow in availing themselves of the powers vesting in them under the amended Local Boards Act must depend on their critics' conception of speed or its opposite in such matters, but the facts are as follows. By the end of the year 1910-11 nine out of the 25 boards had imposed the new taxation on themselves to the amount of about Rs. 6,13,000 per annum, or nearly half of the levy contemplated as possible for all the 25 districts. The accumulation of the extra cess lying unexpended in the hands of these nine districts had amounted on the same date to about Rs. 44,21,000. Then there occurred a fresh exhibition of interest in the matter, due perhaps to the action of certain would-be promoters as well as to offers of aid by the Bank of Madras, and the removal of limitations to be referred to later. The result was that by the middle of 1915 17 out of the 25 districts had imposed the new taxation upon themselves. Of these 17 boards 13 had by the date named actually taxed themselves to the extent of Rs. 8,15,000 per annum, and had accumulated, unexpended, about Rs. 100,00,000, or £667,000—a by no means inconsiderable sum under the circumstances. As regards progress in the preparation of railway projects, to be undertaken as funds become available and as working agreements are made, the following facts may be of interest, though the figures are not a true measure of the lines likely to be taken in hand, for some of the projects are for alternative gauges and routes. The boards had prepared projects as follows:—

Gauge 5 ft. 6 in., 119 miles, at an average cost of Rs. 66,000.

Gauge 3 ft. $3\frac{3}{8}$ in., 540 miles, at an average cost of Rs. 45,000.

That something better than good intentions and the collection of certain moneys had grown out of the extra-cess policy may be judged of by the following facts. As already fully explained, Tanjore within its ordinary cess and without the aid of the special cess has secured the construction and running of 112 miles of railway, all paying well, while 20 more miles are under construction. The district of Kistna succeeded some years ago in getting 52 miles of railway made from Bezwada to Masulipatam, at a cost of Rs. 22,00,000, lent to it by Government on the security of the special cess. These 52 miles are now paying about 7 per cent., thus setting the cess free for the guaranteeing of further loans, and also contributing a by no means negligible sum to the general assets of the district. The district of Guntur has secured the construction from its special cess, at a cost of about Rs. 13,70,000, of the 5 ft. 6 in. gauge Tenali-Repalle Railway, 21 miles in length, to be made and worked by the Madras and Southern Mahratta main line of railway of that gauge, and it is to be opened in January 1916. The district of Coimbatore has secured the construction and working by the South Indian main line of railway of its 25-mile Podanur-Pollachi branch (which is expected to be open in August 1915), on the metre gauge at a cost of Rs. 10,85,000. Thus certain of the District Boards in the Presidency have already secured, from their own resources some 200 miles of railway, of which more or less than half has had to depend on the special three-pie cess. They have in hand actual funds to the extent of about Rs. 100,00,000, or sufficient for the construction of, more or less, another 230 miles; and they have taxed themselves on a scale adequate for the guarantee of interest on the cost of about another 300 miles. This may be accepted as a fine record of the results of a self-governing policy—a record which, undoubtedly will go on improving with the passage of years, and as the payment of good dividends by existing lines sets the cess free, as in the case of Kistna, further extension of the network of minor branch lines of local interest is fast coming into existence as the result of the policy. For the lines so financed the boards concerned would, in all probability, have had to wait indefinitely if it had been necessary that the lines in question should struggle for a place in the "All India Railway Programme."

This reference to the All India Railway Programme makes some explanation necessary for readers who happen not to be financial and railway experts. It is obvious that in borrowing money, as it does every year in the London money market for the requirement of India's development in railway and other directions, the Government of India is obliged to watch very carefully the fluctuation of the money market, and to offer its loans to the investing public in such a manner as not to upset the market so far as to make the loans too expensive. Thus a loan at, say, $3\frac{1}{2}$ per cent. may be deemed to be a more or less relatively expensive loan if for every, say, Rs. 95 raised from the public Government binds itself to pay, at some future time, Rs. 100. From this it follows that if in any given year the country's demands for railways and the like declare themselves as being so far in excess of those of previous years that, if they are to be met, an abnormal amount of money must be borrowed—so much so indeed as to make the loan a dear one—compliance with the demands in question must be curtailed with a strong hand should it become clear that the effect of such compliance will be a general lowering of the price of Indian securities. In order to meet this difficulty the Government of India decides from time to time how many millions sterling, eight, nine, twelve, etc., may be spent in a year, or annually for a brief series of years; and it is within the limits of these millions that the promoters of railway projects ordinarily—that is, if they feel it necessary to rely on any form of State guarantee—must struggle for a place. From this it follows that if some system of outside guarantee can be devised which shall not necessitate the inclusion of any given railway project in the trammels of the All India Railway Programme, the chances of projects so excluded will at least be uncomplicated by the broad financial considerations which have made it necessary to devise the Programme policy. Thus, for example, a railway project so obviously good in itself that capital may be counted on to flow to it without any sort of a hint of guarantee, would of course be outside the Programme. Similarly projects are now ruled to be outside the Programme if they are financed by means of District Board cesses, whether this capital is derived from the accumulated cess or from loans raised by such boards on the security of their cess, or is offered by private capitalists or firms of promoters on the security of the cess. There are other ways also of securing the exclusion of railway projects from the stifling bonds of the Programme, e.g. the "branch-line terms" arrangement, under which a main line cedes certain advantages to branch promoters out of its own surplus earnings. But this being a treatise on Madras District Board railway development and not on the general railway finances of India, it may suffice here merely to mention branch-line terms as one device for their exclusion.

From the above it will be clear that freedom from the squeeze and struggle for a place in the Programme, and, as a result of that freedom, the earlier construction of the lines in which districts are interested, may be secured by those boards who find themselves able either (*a*) to offer the guarantee of their cess collections to railway promoters, (*b*) to go on the market themselves and raise loans on the security of the cess, or (*c*) to build up capital by accumulating their cess collections. Progress in either or all of these directions has, necessarily, up to the present been slow. The business is new to the boards; official chairmen have much else to attend to; unofficial vice-chairmen, mostly lawyers, and the majority of the members of the boards, also mostly lawyers, are devoid of the necessary experience, and moreover, as a race, are profoundly suspicious and distrustful of anything novel or unfamiliar. Now, however, with the great success of the Kistna District Railway before their eyes as an object-lesson, they are tumbling over each other to take a share in the new policy. Seventeen out of twenty-five of the districts by the middle of 1915 had, as already stated, self-imposed the cess that will enable them to make the offer to the investing public which will secure them the lines that interest them, and most of them are already prepared with more or less fully matured schemes either sanctioned by competent authority or nearly ready for submission for sanction.

Few of the boards have in their services professional engineers with sufficient railway experience to be trusted to prepare reliable schemes and estimates and to give effect to them when sanctioned. And even when a district line is proposed to be carried out by a company of promoters, a board is unlikely to give the desired guarantee in the absence of expert advice as to the character and adequacy of the project and of its estimate. Hence there has arisen the satisfactory and very suitable arrangement whereby the main line of railway that will work the branch line when built prepares its project and its estimate. The main lines have an ample supply of skilled professional talent, and if they have a fault it is in proposing to equip the little branch lines on somewhat too high a standard—a fault on the right side if there is no doubt about the potential paying character of the traffic. Moreover, the main-line companies build these lines at cost price—an arrangement very advantageous to the District Boards.

Many of the boards show a strong tendency to keep out the projector, and so to maintain the lines as their own property, whether by the accumulation of the cess or by a direct loan, or by both. They are apt to fail to see the limitations of the market for such securities as they have to offer, the distrust of investors, and especially of trustee investors, in the novel form of security, and the better access of some projectors to larger and more enterprising money markets than the boards themselves have easy access to. Moreover they are tempted very strongly by the hope that by retaining all the profit in their own hands they may secure some relief of their general taxation. In adopting this attitude towards promoters the boards seem to lose sight of the consideration that it is of far higher importance to a district that it should get its railway anyhow, and get it quickly, rather than that, after delay in getting it, there should be some small alleviation of taxation. If a board can raise the money at once, well and good. But in a restricted market it may easily happen that a private promoter may, under the board's guarantee, succeed in getting the line into running order years before the board itself, on its own initiative, could have raised the money and made the line. What is wanted all the time, in the interests of the million or so of inhabitants, mostly ignorant cultivators of which the board is more or less the articulate agency, is that the infructuous cost of transport between field and port of the produce of the fields and of the foreign produce which returns in exchange for it, should be reduced to the lowest possible figure. The railway, as soon as open, effects this to so considerable an extent that the increased prosperity of the cultivators in the neighbourhood of railways is matter of common knowledge all over the Indian peninsula. From these considerations it follows that District Boards will be wise to welcome the advent of competent promoters of railways relying on the board's guarantee from the cess, if by such advent the railways can only be got running a year or two sooner than would otherwise be possible. If in such a case a board has accumulations of the cess it can employ them no better than by taking shares in the promoter's enterprise, thereby to some extent securing the advantages which, by themselves making the railway, they might look forward to.

Securities created on the guarantees of District Boards laboured for some years under two serious disadvantages: firstly, they were not trustee securities; and secondly, the Presidency banks might not touch them. The latter disability has now been removed by the amendment in 1907 of the Presidency Banks Act of 1876, section 36 (*a*) of which empowers such banks to invest in District Board debentures. The former disability has been held by competent authority to disappear whenever a High Court—or presumably a Chief Court—shall have declared that within the area of its jurisdiction such securities shall be trustee securities. A declaration to this effect has already been made by the Madras High Court, from which it follows that trustees in the Madras Presidency may handle these securities as freely as a Presidency bank may now deal with them. Efforts are in progress to induce the other High Courts in India, or some of them, to make a similar declaration, in which case the market for raising money on the security of Madras District Boards' resources will be greatly extended.

There are obvious advantages in the use of a uniform model arrangement for the working of all branch railways, financed as described by the main lines of railway to which they will serve as feeders. Therefore the Madras Government, under the advice of the Indian Railway Board, has been at great pains to devise such an agreement. The model in question has already middle of 1915—been accepted by all of the districts interested. In view of the fact that the main line working company have, ordinarily, no property in the State-owned line which is leased to them, the agreement is made, not between the company and the District Board, but between the latter and the Secretary of State for India; and, at the same time, a secondary agreement as between the Secretary of State and the main-line working company secures the fit and proper working of the branch by this company.

Once a District Board shall have, by two successive resolutions as laid down in the Act, decided to levy the special railway cess, it has no power to cease to levy the cess without sanction of Government. And from this it follows that the security offered, whether to shareholders in branch-line companies or to holders of debentures under the board's guarantee, is as good as a State security based on similar conditions. That is while it cannot be contended that the security is as good as if it were based on the whole of the net revenues of India or even on those of a province, yet although based only on certain taxation levied within the limits of a comparatively small area, viz. a district, it is quite as reliable for the purpose in view as if it had a larger basis. Needless to say, Government may always be trusted to see that no larger a guarantee is given than is warranted by the extent of the cess. But it seems necessary to make it clear that the security for the debentures is not merely the net earnings of the railways themselves and the income derived from the special cess, but the whole of the resources of the District Board concerned.

Madras may well claim to have set a fine example in this matter to the rest of India, and there is every reason to expect, now that certain initial difficulties have been removed, that there will, in the near future, be an important development of short branch railways of local interest financed on the basis of local taxation *ad hoc*, and worked by the main line of railway, of which the branches in question will be valuable feeders. In view, moreover, of the excellence of the security, there seems to be every reason for the hope that later, when the investment is better understood by the public, as much money as is wanted may be forthcoming at 4 instead of at $4\frac{1}{2}$ per cent.

THE LITERATURE RELATING TO SOUTHERN INDIA

By EVANS LEWIN, F.R.Hist.S., F.L.A., Librarian of the Royal Colonial Institute

ABOUT no part of the overseas British Empire has a more extensive literature been written than about India. Without taking into account the enormous native literature—written in any of the thirteen distinct languages that form the fundamental bases of the numerous Indian dialects, ranging from the sacred books of the Buddhists and Hindus to the latest productions of the native press—there is an almost overwhelming mass of books written in European languages. So extensive is this literature, sociological, historical, and purely descriptive, that it would be almost impossible for the student to master the contents of even a tithe of the books relating to India. The country is, in fact, a continent of differing languages, civilizations, religions, and customs; compact as a geographical unit but multipartite in its political or ethnological character. Of the 13 principal languages 8 are connected with Sanskrit, whilst 4 which are not related to Sanskrit—Telugu, spoken by 21,000,000; Tamil, spoken by 17,000,000; Kanarese, the language of 11,000,000; and Malayalim, spoken by 7,000,000—are peculiar to Southern India. No attempt will be made in the present article to deal with the literature in any of these languages, nor will any attention be devoted to the ever-increasing output of books written by Indians in the English language, which is used freely by over one million Hindus and by large numbers of the Mahommedan community.

But in dealing with the literature relating to Southern India one great difficulty is apparent. Although the Madras Presidency and the Native States attached to it form a fairly distinct unit in India, it is not possible to confine a survey of the literature of the southern portion of the peninsula entirely to works relating specifically to Madras, because for a proper understanding of the subject books of a general character, containing large sections devoted to Southern India, are also essential.

Probably no Government has been more generous in its attitude towards historical, archæological, ethnographical, and literary work than that of India. The enormous and continuous output of official reports, many of which, written by experts in their own particular subjects, are of great value, shows no sign of abatement. On the contrary, from all parts of India comes a continuous flow of official publications, almost appalling in its magnitude, certainly calculated to impress one with the industry and ability of Anglo-Indian officialdom. But so far as the ordinary student of India is concerned, he may confine his attention to six sets of publications issued under the auspices of the Indian Government. The first of these, the excellent gazetteers, now published for almost every district in India, and containing a mass of descriptive, statistical, historical, and ethnographical information, have been issued for many years, and form an invaluable survey of India as it exists at the present time. They contain a complete picture of Indian life, religions, manners, and customs, and number some hundreds of volumes and parts. To these may be added the "Imperial Gazetteer of India," by that prince of Indian statisticians, the late Sir William Hunter, a truly monumental work, first issued in nine volumes in 1881, and subsequently enlarged into the twenty-six volumes of the latest (1907-8) edition. The third of these publications, the remarkable series of volumes dealing with the Census of India, a work ever increasing in size and value, contains a mass of information useful to the student of Indian affairs; whilst the fourth, the volumes issued by the Archæological Survey, are remarkable for their critical and historical estimate of the remains of Indian civilizations scattered so profusely throughout India, and for the lavish use of illustration in elucidation of the text. The Archæological Survey, with its various branches in the different Provinces and States, has performed a notable service in making available for the student the wonders of Indian art and architecture. The fifth of these publications is the Ethnographic Survey, whilst the sixth is the publications relating to agriculture and botany issued by the various Agricultural Experiment Stations and Botanical Gardens. With these volumes at his command the student of India has a large and diverse library to help him in his studies.

Of the works dealing with India generally which should be read before attention is devoted to Southern India, two books by Sir William Hunter, "History of British India" (1899-1900) and "The Indian Empire: its Peoples, History, and Products" (1893), H. G. Keene's "History of India" (1906), and James Mill's "History of India" (6 vols., 1830), give a good general idea of Indian history; whilst Vincent A. Smith's "Early History of India," which has special reference to Southern India, is the best and most recent account of Indian history prior to the advent of Europeans. With respect to the fascinating history of the East India Company, Beckles Willson's "Ledger and Sword" (2 vols., 1903), and W. H. Carey's "Good Old Days of Honourable John Company," are popular works likely to be of interest to the general reader, whilst "The English Factories in India," a series of volumes edited by William Foster, the Registrar and Superintendent of Records at the India Office, and the "Calendar of the Court Minutes of the East India Company" (12 vols.), are suitable for the more advanced reader, desirous of studying the original documents of the period. Of special value in connection with the history of Southern India is S. Krishnaswami Aiyangar's "Ancient India." The author, who is Examiner in History at Madras University, has here developed a series of essays showing a deep acquaintance with the comparatively neglected study of the ancient dynasties of the South, particularly the Chola dynasty, which makes his work of more than ordinary value. Of other books dealing with India generally, the following are the principal recent works which should be consulted. M. Joseph Chailley, well known as a prominent member of the French colonial school and an impartial writer on British administration in the East, has written a comprehensive survey of British policy under the title of "Administrative Problems of British India" (1910). This work is notable because it gives the foreign point of view, and is, moreover, a careful and accurate survey of our administrative policy. From the British standpoint Sir John Strachey's "India: its Administration and Progress" (1911), gives the clearest and most concise view of the progress and administration of the Indian Empire, and should be studied in conjunction with Sir William Lee-Warner's admirable book on "The Native States of India" (1910). From the Indian point of view S. M. Mitra's "Indian Problems" (1910), an excellent and temperate survey of the conditions confronting the Anglo-Indian administration, is of special value; whilst on the subject of the political and social unrest, symptomatic of the progress of India and its changing social and economic conditions, Sir Valentine Chirol's book, "Indian Unrest" (1910), is of more than ordinary value. With this hasty introduction we may now proceed to a survey of the literature relating more especially to the southern portion of the Peninsula.

The literature descriptive of this part of India may be said to have commenced with the European travellers who in the fifteenth and sixteenth centuries found their way through Persia or across the Indian Ocean to the shores of India. The chief source of many of these highly entertaining but often exceedingly valuable accounts, some of which seem like fairy tales, whilst others are but plain matter-of-fact narratives, is the various collections of voyages made during the Elizabethan age by the industrious collectors of travellers' tales. To the industry of men like Ramusio, a Venetian who published a collection of voyages entitled "Delle Navigationi e Viaggi" (1583-1613); Richard Hakluyt, whose "Principal Navigations, Voyages, and Discoveries of the English Nation" (1598-1600), is a remarkable thesaurus of travel and adventure; and Samuel Purchas, whose great works, "Purchas, his Pilgrimage, or Relations of the World in all Ages" (1613-26), and "Hakluytus Posthumus, or Purchas his Pilgrimes," based on the papers left by Hakluyt, are classics of the geographical world, is due a deep debt of gratitude. Not only did they preserve many narratives that would otherwise, in all probability, have perished, but they helped to focus attention upon the wonderful maritime activity of the sixteenth century. To these three great collections must be added the volumes by the Hakluyt Society, which contain all that is best and rarest in geographical literature. So far as Southern India is concerned the student may commence his investigations with the narrative written by Nicolo de' Conti, a Venetian, who, accompanied by his wife, left Damascus in the year 1419 and wandered in the East for nearly a quarter of a century, visiting India and journeying to Meliapur, where was the reputed tomb of St. Thomas, the Apostle of the Indies, and then, as now, a place of pilgrimage, and thence to Ceylon. Conti was a shrewd and careful observer, and when he finally returned to Europe an account of his journeys was written at the command of the Pope (Eugene IV) by his secretary, Poggio Bracchiolini. This is one of the earliest narratives of travel in Southern India, and English translations are contained in Purchas and in vol. xxii. of the publications of the Hakluyt Society. This volume, entitled "India in the Fifteenth Century," and edited by R. H. Major, contains several important narratives of Indian travel. Two other voyages contained in this valuable collection are those of the Russian traveller Athanasius Nikitin and of Hieronimo di Santo Stephano, a Genoese who travelled down the Malabar coast to Ceylon and thence along the Coromandel coast. Both the narratives of Conti and Nikitin contain valuable particulars about the kingdom of Vijayanagar, then dominating the greater part of Southern India, and stretching from the Krishna (Kistna) River to Cape Comorin. One of the best accounts of this ancient dominion is contained in Robert Sewell's "A Forgotten Empire" (1900), but the historical works of Vincent Smith should also be consulted with respect to the ancient history of Southern India.

It is highly probable that many of the narratives of early travellers in India were either never written, or if written were lost or never published. Some may still be found in the archives of the Vatican or in the monastic libraries of Spain and Portugal. Although India was practically an unknown country until Vasco da Gama burst into the Indian Ocean, it had been visited by Europeans from time to time long before the Portuguese established their empire in Asia. Thus, for instance, our own King Alfred sent an embassy to India, which carried presents to the Nestorian Christians at Meliapur. But such intercourse was so rare that when Vasco da Gama first arrived at Calicut after his memorable voyage round the Cape of Storms (Cape of Good Hope), he was astonished to find himself addressed in the Castilian tongue by two Moorish traders from Tunis. "May the devil take thee! What brought thee hither?" they cried. The incident shows that, as is well known, there was considerable intercourse between India and the West through the medium of the Arabs and Moors. Full details of Vasco da Gama's voyage may be read in the *Roteiro*, an anonymous journal published by the Hakluyt Society; in the "Lendas da India," by Gaspar Correa, also published by the Hakluyt Society; in Ramusio's collection; and, for those who are poetically inclined, in the "Lusiad" of the Portuguese poet, Camoens, who himself travelled in the East Indies during the years 1553-69. With the arrival of Vasco da Gama and the establishment of the Portuguese in Asia, the literature relating to Southern India, as distinct from the rest of the country, may be said to commence. Both Calicut—the seaport at which the Portuguese first arrived—and Goa, which speedily became the capital of their Asiatic empire, are in Southern India, and round these two cities the chief activities of the Portuguese were centred.

The best account of the Portuguese in India has been written by Frederick C. Danvers, and was published in 1894, but there have been many other books on the subject, such as the Rev. J. D. D'Orsey's "Portuguese Discoveries, Dependencies, and Missions in Asia and Africa," and R. S. Whiteway's "Rise of Portuguese Power in India" (1899), which are worth consulting. Of Portuguese historical narratives the "Commentaries" of Alfonso d'Albuquerque, the great Viceroy of the Indies (written by his natural son, Braz d'Albuquerque, and translated by Birch for the Hakluyt Society, in four volumes. published in 1875-84), and the collection of narratives made by the historian João de Barros, many of which are moving and fascinating stories, should of course be consulted; whilst of other original sources the narrative of travel written by Mendez Pinto, who has been called Mendex by those who have regarded him as a notorious liar, is in reality a valuable and fairly reliable account. The story of his twenty-one years in South-east India, entitled "Peregrinacam" (1614), has been translated into English, and an account of Pinto has been edited by the well-known traveller Arminius Vambery, under the title "Voyage and Adventures of Fernão Mendez Pinto," and published in the Adventure Series.

Passing from the Portuguese, another early traveller in Southern India was Ludovico di Varthema, a native of Bologna, who made his way to Calicut, and journeyed down the coast to Ceylon. His narrative is of great value, and has been republished by the Hakluyt Society. Another traveller—if, indeed, he were a traveller and not a compiler—is Duarte Barbosa, whose "Description of the Coasts of East Africa and Malabar" has been edited for the Hakluyt Society by Lord Stanley of Adderley. His account also is of much value, but has not the same personal interest as the narrative left by Varthema. There is considerable doubt as to the authorship, for it has also been attributed to the great discoverer Magellan. Cesar de Federici, or Caesar Frederick as he is called by the industrious Purchas—an Italian who travelled in the East between the years 1563-81—also describes Southern India. His account is of special value because he visited the ruined city of Vijayanagar, the downfall of which had only occurred a few years previously (1565). He gives an interesting account of this city which had so long fought against the Mahommedan power, and certainly saved Southern India for Hinduism.

There are several narratives of English travel in Southern India. In 1583 "Master Ralph Fitch, Merchant of London," in conjunction with two companions, Newbery and Leedes, travelled to India by way of the Euphrates and visited Goa, and made his way across the country to Bengal. But he, in common with most other travellers in India at this period, was attracted rather to the Court of the Great Mogul than to the southern portions of the country. William Methold, however, who was in India at the beginning of the seventeenth century, travelled in Southern India and visited Golconda, which, on the disappearance of Vizayanagar, had been left the strongest power in the southern portion of India. His account, contained in Purchas's collection, and entitled "Relation of the Kingdom of Golconda," is of value because there is very little from European writers relating to this part of India at that period. William Bruton, in company with Ralph Cartwright, also journeyed in South India, and travelled along the Coromandel coast on his way to Bengal. His "News from the East Indies, or a Voyage to Bengalla," contained in Hakluyt's collection, is a journal of great interest.

Of early Dutch travellers the well-known Jan Huyghen van Linschoten alone need be mentioned. In 1583 he arrived at Goa, where he witnessed the arrest of Ralph Fitch and his companions, and where he remained for five years, finally sailing for Cochin in 1589. The account of his travels, of which the Dutch original was published in 1596 and the English translation five years later, is chiefly valuable for its exposure of the decay of the Portuguese Empire in the East and the author's observations concerning the Malabar coast. In addition to these accounts there are several French narratives and one Italian that must be mentioned. Four names are famous in the history of French travel in India: Bernier, Tavernier, Thevenot, and Chardin. The first, Francois Bernier, a physician, spent several years at the splendid court of Aurangzebe, of which he wrote a fascinating and accurate account, but he has little to say of Southern India. The second, Jean Baptiste Tavernier, a dealer in precious stones, visited Golconda, Goa, and other portions of South India. His famous "Six Voyages" was first published in 1676, and was long one of the most popular narratives of travel. It has been translated into most European languages, and several editions in English have been published, the best of the latter being the translation by Dr. V. Ball, published in 1890. The third of the French travellers, Jean de Thevenot (not to be confused with Melchisedech Thevenot, the collector of travels), wandered throughout India, and visited Golconda and Masulipatam. His "Travels into the Levant" was published in 1687. The fourth, Jean Chardin, also a dealer in precious stones, after spending some years in Persia, visited India, but has little to say about the southern parts of the country. These, with the "Storia do Mogor" of Niccalao Manucci, complete the list of more important works containing references to Southern India. Manucci, a Venetian physician, journeyed in different parts of India, and, after an eventful life, left behind him a narrative of his wanderings which has been called "one of the most extraordinary documents bearing on Indian history that we possess." It remained in manuscript, and was never published until it was re-discovered at Berlin and issued in the Indian Text Series under the editorship of Mr. Irvine in 1907. An abridged edition of this invaluable narrative has since been issued.

It is only possible to indicate briefly some of the more important of recent works dealing with the history of Southern India. The rise and decline of the French is admirably told by Colonel

G. B. Malleson, who, in addition to his "History of the French in India" (1893), has written several other historical books. The Madras Government has performed a useful work in issuing a series of "Selections from the Records of the Madras Government," whilst the story of Madras itself is excellently told by Mrs. Frank Penny in her "Fort St. George" (1900), in Foster's "The Founding of Fort St. George" (1902), and in David Leighton's "Vicissitudes of Fort St. George," published at Madras in 1902. The best book dealing with the history of Madras is Lieut.-Colonel Henry Davison Love's "Vestiges of Old Madras" (1640-1800), published in four volumes in the Indian Records Series in 1913. This work, popular in style, but based upon a close study of documentary evidence, contains many curious particulars concerning the early history of Madras, and should be read in conjunction with J. Talboys Wheeler's "Madras in the Olden Time," published in three volumes at Madras in 1861. The author of the latter was editor of *The Madras Spectator* and professor in the Madras Presidency College. A book by another journalist, Sir Charles Lawson, who was editor of *The Madras Mail*, entitled "Memories of Madras" (1905), contains historical and biographical accounts of famous Madras characters, such as "Diamond Pitt," Governor of Fort St. George and founder of the Pitt family, Macartney, Cornwallis, and the Arbuthnots. The life of another celebrated character long connected with Madras, Streynsham Master, is excellently told by Sir Richard Carnac Temple in two volumes issued in 1911 under the title of "The Diaries of Streynsham Master." This book contains a fascinating account of the life of an official in Madras at the end of the seventeenth century, and is a quaint and amusing narrative. "The Pirates of Malabar and an Englishwoman in India Two Hundred Years Ago" (1907) is also worth reading for its account of contemporary manners on the Malabar coast, whilst Lieut.-Colonel W. J. Wilson's "History of the Madras Army," Colonel H. M. Vibart's "Military History of the Madras Engineers and Pioneers" (2 vols., 1881-83) and J. R. Coombes' "History of the Madras Volunteer Guards" (1907) should be consulted by those who wish to know how great a part the Madras regiments played in the pacification of India.

In addition to these historical works there are others dealing with the history of Christianity in Southern India. When it is remembered that Christianity was introduced into India by St. Thomas, whose shrine is venerated at Meliapur (Mylapore), and that the Church of the Nestorian Christians was never entirely destroyed even when the Portuguese commenced their missionary labours, it will be seen how rich a field for historical research there is in this one subject alone. The best accounts of St. Thomas and the early Christians are contained in Bishop A. F. Medlycott's "India and the Apostle Thomas" and A. Little's "India in Primitive Christianity" (2 vols., 1909), whilst the part taken by the Portuguese missions in their active endeavours to Christianize India can be studied in Mr. D'Orsey's book, already mentioned, and in many other works. Original sources of information are, of course, the celebrated "Lettres Edifiantes," written by the Jesuits and forwarded to their Superior at Rome. The operations of the Church of England in Madras are described with considerable humour by the Rev. Frank Penny in his two admirable volumes entitled "The Church in Madras" (1904-12), and J. A. Sharrock's "South Indian Missions" (1910) gives a good and concise account of missions at the present day.

Of descriptive works dealing with Southern India there is a plentiful supply. Edgar Thurstan's "The Madras Presidency, with Mysore, Coorg, and the Associated States" (1913), is an excellent and concise account, written by one who was Superintendent of the Madras Museum for a quarter of a century, and also Chief of the Ethnographic Survey. Other descriptive books are F. E. Penny's "On the Coromandel Coast" (1908); Lady Lawley's "Southern India," recently published; H. Aynsley's "On Tour in Southern India" (1883); H. Drury's "Life and Sport in Southern India" (1890); Sir J. D. Rees' descriptive account of the tour of the Duke of Clarence in Southern India (1891); M. M. Shoemaker's "Quaint Corners of Ancient Empires: Southern India" (1899); and Sir M. E. Duff's discursive and interesting "Notes from a Diary kept chiefly in Southern India" (2 vols., 1899).

The important subject of ethnology is comprehensively dealt with in the learned survey written by Mr. Thurstan and published by the Indian Government under the title of "Castes and Tribes of Southern India" (7 vols., 1909)—a truly monumental work of great value to the student. Mr. Thurstan's "Ethnographic Notes in Southern India," Kanakasabhai Pillai's "The Tamils Eighteen Hundred Years Ago" (1904), P. S. P. Rice's "Occasional Essays on Native Indian Life" (1901), I. F. Hewitt's "Ruling Races of Prehistoric Times in India" (1894), Dr. W. H. R. Rivers' able book on "The Todas" (1906), and the excellent Bulletins issued by the Madras Government Museum since the year 1894 should also be consulted. In connection with the great Native States attached to the Madras Presidency the monumental work written by Francis Buchanan, who was sent by Lord Wellesley on a journey to report upon the resources of this portion of India, should be read. It was first published in the year 1807 under the title of "A Journey from Madras through the Countries of Mysore, Canara, and Malabar," and so great is its value that it was re-published in 1870. Two excellent, though popular, books on Mysore are Robert H. Elliot's "The Experiences of a Planter" (2 vols., 1871) and his "Sport and Coffee-planting in Mysore" (1894), whilst James Salmond's "A Review of the Decisive War with the late Tippoo Sultaun" (1800) is still valuable as a record of those turbulent times. The great State of Travancore is dealt with in the comprehensive historical and descriptive "Travancore State Manual" (3 vols., 1906) by V. Nagam Aiya, and in Henry Bruce's "Letters from Malabar and on the Way," which contains a description of both Travancore and Cochin. B. L. Rice's "Mysore and Coorg from the Inscriptions" (1909) is entirely historical and archæological. Ootacamund, the chief town in the Nilgiri Hills and the principal sanatorium for the Madras Presidency, is excellently described by Sir Frederick Price in a fine volume issued at Madras in 1908, whilst Sir Richard Burton, the celebrated traveller, wrote about this district in his "Goa and the Blue Mountains" (1851), a book which, like all Burton's works, is well worth reading.

In imaginative literature very little has has been produced by Anglo-Indians resident in Southern India. The great Anglo-Indian writers of the present generation, such as Rudyard Kipling and Mrs. Steele, have generally been connected with Central and Northern India, which appear to have exercised a greater fascination than any portion of the southern country. Nevertheless there was considerable literary activity in a small way in Madras in the early years of the last century. A press had been established there at the end of the eighteenth century when both *The Madras Courier* and *The Madras Gazette* started publication, the former in 1790 and the latter five years later. In addition *The Madras Journal of Literature and Science* and *The Oriental Magazine and Indian Hurkuru* (1819) catered for those of literary tastes, whilst more recently *The Madras Quarterly* and *The Indian Review* have appealed to a wide circle of readers not only in India, but in the United Kingdom and America.

THE PRESS IN SOUTHERN INDIA

THE art of printing was introduced into India by the Goa Jesuits about the middle of the sixteenth century, but for a considerable length of time they used only Roman characters in their publications. There is reason to believe that they occasionally issued sheets containing news, but, unfortunately, there are at the present time only fragmentary specimens of their work in existence. The Province of Bengal may be credited with taking the first steps towards the real establishment of the newspaper press in India, as it was only about seven years after the administration of that portion of the continent had been taken in hand by the British Government (i.e. in 1780) that the first paper—*The Bengal Gazette*—was issued by an Englishman in Calcutta. Bombay was practically its own master soon after the year 1665, but it was not until 1789 that this province launched forth into the frequently stormy waters of journalism, when *The Bombay Herald* appeared. Editors in the Madras Presidency entered the arena at a much later date, but before referring specifically to some of the more prominent papers now in existence, brief notice may be taken of the difficulties under which the publication of news suffered. *The Bengal Gazette* assumed great latitude of expression, and it soon managed to draw down upon itself the anger of the authorities owing to the scandalous nature of its paragraphs, and newspaper and editor went into oblivion in the year 1782. The control and censorship of the Government of the day was undoubtedly irritating, and particularly with regard to any criticism levelled against its servants, and while there certainly was no "freedom of the press," it must be admitted that the sheets of news then distributed to the public contained grossly irregular items. Before the commencement of the year 1800 several editors had been "sent to Coventry," while a number of others had been "placed on the carpet," and were compelled to apologize in an ample manner. When the Marquis of Wellesley was Governor-General in 1798 the Government promulgated stringent regulations, which included the submission of all news to a censor before publication, and such a considerable amount of ill-feeling was engendered by these measures that not a few editors were deported, this being the penalty for a breach of the rules. It is not surprising that this rigid surveillance should almost strangle a newly-born profession, and as a consequence editorial chairs began to be occupied by an inferior class of men. Some relaxation of the burdensome provisions, however, took place about the year 1818, when the censorship was withdrawn by the direction of the Marquis of Hastings, G.C.B., and his liberal policy was continued by his successors, Lord William Bentinck and the Earl of Amherst. Scrutiny of news was re-established over the vernacular press in 1878, and by an Act of Parliament framed in the same year. Provincial Governments were empowered to take repressive measures against such of those journals which might transgress certain very wide canons of loyal conduct and of political criticism, but a proviso was inserted to the effect that no action should be taken against offenders without the previous sanction of the Supreme Government in each case. This statute was repealed by another one in 1910, in which powers were granted (*inter alia*) for the suppression of books, newspapers, or pamphlets containing anything of a seditious character calculated to throw contempt upon His Majesty the King-Emperor or his Government, or which reflected in any improper manner upon civil servants or upon any loyal subjects of the Crown. Publishers of newspapers were brought under the control of the authorities, and severe penalties were fixed for the issue of any matter of an objectionable character. These safeguards were deemed necessary in view of the fact that outrages, which were continually occurring throughout India, were invariably traceable to some article or item of news which had appeared in certain journals.

Government reports show that when the whole of India came under British rule in 1858 there were not more than 20 Anglo-Indian and about 24 Indian newspapers in the country. At the present time there are considerably more than 100 published in the Madras Presidency alone, and the printing offices of this province send forth nearly 1,200 periodicals, while the total number for the whole of India is only a few more than 1,900.

The first Bengali newspaper in British India was printed and published by the Serampore missionaries on May 28, 1818; it was called *Samachar Darpan*, or *The Mirror of News*, but it ceased to exist in the year 1841. The Marquis of Hastings wrote to the editor expressing approval, and he avowed that "it was salutary for the supreme authority to look to the control of public scrutiny."

The following particulars have been obtained respecting some of the best-known publications in the Madras Presidency:—

The Madras Times was established in the year 1860, and it pursues a policy of an independent character at its centrally situated offices in Mount Road in the city of Madras. It is published every morning in the English language, and its columns contain news from all parts of the world and comments on current topics, together with special notes on Church matters, proceedings in the High Court, music, sport, education, and on questions which are usually discussed at public meetings of Indians. An excellent supply of cable news is given, and its leading articles are up to date in every respect. The company has a capital of Rs.200,000, and Mr. Glyn Barlow, M.A., is the editor. The *Times* circulates throughout the Madras Presidency, the States of Mysore, Hyderabad, Cochin, Travancore, and Púdukkottai, in nearly every other part of India, and in Great Britain.

The Madras Mail is owned privately,

and the editor is Mr. Arthur E. Lawson, C.I.E. The circulation of this daily (evening) paper has progressed steadily since its birth in the year 1868, and it is now read throughout the Madras Presidency, the States of Mysore, Cochin, and Travancore, as well as in Hyderabad, the Central Provinces, and Burma. This was the first evening paper to be issued in India, and it is a favourable medium for all kinds of advertisements. The offices are at 6 North Beach Road, Madras.

The Cochin Argus is the oldest newspaper on the coast of Malabar, having been commenced in the year 1869. It contains news of general interest in political, religious, social, mercantile, agricultural, and industrial matters, and it is well known in Burma, Ceylon, the Straits Settlements, Europe, the United States, and throughout India, but principally in the district of Malabar, in Cochin and Travancore, and in other parts of the Madras Presidency.

The first English newspaper to be published in the State of Travancore was *The Travancore Times,* whose editor has always endeavoured to disseminate information which would assist in the important work of the elevation of the backward communities in that State, although its political and social columns are much appreciated. Its subscribers and readers are found in Ceylon, Cochin, the Straits Settlements, Bombay, Calcutta, and throughout Travancore and the remainder of the Madras Presidency. The proprietress is Mrs. P. C. Joseph, and Mr. D. C. Joseph, of Sahaya Street, Nagercoil, is the editor of the paper, which was started in the year 1875.

The establishment of the Government Agricultural College and Research Institute and of the Madras Forest College at Coimbatore has tended to intensify local interest in matters pertaining to the scientific cultivation of the land, and the proprietor and editor of *The Coimbatore Crescent*—Mr. S. P. Navasimmala—naturally makes a special feature of interesting articles on this subject. The first issue of the paper was on October 15, 1881, and the journal is sent to all parts of Southern India, Burma, Penang, Singapore, and to Durban, in South Africa. Its general news includes notes on political, social, and religious subjects.

The Kolar Gold-fields News, which was established in 1896, is an independent weekly journal, designed principally to safeguard mining interests generally, but it contains interesting news of all kinds for European and Indian readers alike. The paper is, naturally, greatly appreciated by the residents on the fields, but it is well known throughout the Madras Presidency and in Bengal, Burma, and England. The editor is Mr. A. Cornelius, of Bowringpet, in the district of Kolar, in the State of Mysore.

The newspaper called *United India and Native States* is owned and edited by the Rev. K. S. Krishnaswami, of Jones Lane, Georgetown, Madras, and it has been in existence since 1899. It is described as being "radical in social reform, broad in religion, and moderate in politics," while one of its main features is a review of the latest English and Indian publications. Poetry and the drama receive considerable attention, and the paper is a strong advocate of the interests of minority communities. It circulates throughout India—chiefly among intellectual readers—and in all the Native States.

Mr. K. N. Sivarajan, B.A., is the proprietor and editor of *The Malabar Quarterly Review,* which was started in 1901. It is devoted to the discussion of scientific, philosophic, historic, and literary questions, and it circulates in nearly every part of India.

The Wednesday Review, published at Teppakulam, in the district of Trichinopoly, has all the features of an English weekly newspaper, and it aims at enabling the people of India to realize more and more the advantages of British supremacy and to promote a better understanding between rulers and the ruled. It was first published in January 1905, and its patrons are found in all the Presidencies and States in India. The sole proprietor and editor is Mr. S. M. Raja Ram Rao.

The Madras Law Times is a weekly journal of notes and reports of the Madras High Court and of the Judicial Committee of the Privy Council. It also contains articles on interesting questions of law, short notes on English cases, reviews and cuttings from English and foreign legal publications, and various other matters. The journal has been in existence since 1906, and the editor is Mr. T. Prakasam, Barrister-at-Law, of 5 Kondi Chetty Street, Georgetown, Madras.

An up-to-date weekly newspaper published on Saturdays at Trivandrum, in the State of Travancore, is *The People's Weekly,* which is devoted to social and political reform on radical lines. It has an interesting budget of general news, and racily written character sketches are a new and acceptable feature. The *Weekly* has a wide circulation in Southern India—especially on the west coast—and in Burma and Ceylon. It is about four years of age, and the owner and editor is Mr. K. N. Sivarajan, B.A., of Trivandrum.

The Presidency of Madras is lamentably deficient in illustrated journals, and therefore the publication of *Sama's Portfolio of Drawings* in January 1912 was especially welcome. It is designed to enlighten and interest the people by means of artistic pictures, and it is greatly appreciated not only in Madras but also in Calcutta, Bombay, and other centres. The publisher is Mr. M. S. Sama, of Venkatachala Street, Triplicane, Madras.

The Bangalore Daily Post Company, Ltd., has a nominal capital of Rs. 50,000, and its registered offices are at 7 St. Mark's Road, Bangalore. The editress is Miss A. E. Dawson, who is also sole secretary and manageress. Among other publications issued from this office is *The Planter's Chronicle,* a monthly journal containing items of news, market reports, and instructive articles upon matters of special importance to the large number of planters in Southern India.

The Indian Patriot is published daily and tri-weekly in the English language, and the editor is Mr. C. Karunakara Menon, B.A., of 23 Errabalu Chetty Street, Georgetown, Madras.

Ootacamund, situated in the district of the Nilgiris, the summer quarters of His Excellency the Governor of Madras and of the Members of the Council of Fort St. George, has a weekly English newspaper called *The South of India Observer,* which contains items of general news, but owing to the large number of planters in the neighbourhood and of sportsmen who reside in the town for several months in the year, prominence is given to matters connected with hunting, polo, tennis, golf, cricket, and other favourite games.

The Tanjore and South Indian Times is published weekly in English, although extra copies are printed in the Tamil language. It is well supplied with interesting news of a general character, but it makes a special effort to develop the interest of its readers in educational matters.

Trichinopoly is the place of publication of *The Ambrosia,* a high-class monthly English journal which is issued for the express purpose of giving information to the people regarding the maintenance of public health, and the efforts of the editor in this direction are fully appreciated.

THE LITERATURE RELATING TO SOUTHERN INDIA

The East Coast News is printed at Vizagapatam, in the north-eastern portion of the Presidency, and, while it is a favourite medium for advertising, it always publishes an interesting budget of local news.

New India is one of the oldest newspapers in the Presidency, but its name has been altered on several occasions. For some years prior to 1914 it was known as *The Madras Standard*, but when it was purchased by Mrs. Annie Besant the title of *New India* was adopted. It is published daily in English, its leading articles are bright and crisp, and its readers are greatly increasing in number.

The Adyar Bulletin is published on the fifteenth of each month at Adyar, near Madras, by Mrs. Besant. It contains articles from eminent theosophical authors, short stories, and articles of general interest and instruction. The same publishing house also issues *The Commonweal*, a weekly journal of reform, dealing with live topics of international concern. The cardinal principles shaping the policy of this newspaper are altruistic, recognizing the existence of a real connection between the various movements in vogue. Political, social, religious, artistic, economic, scientific, and philosophical developments are also recorded, and current events and questions of public interest throughout the world are discussed.

The Indian Review is a monthly periodical, published in English at Madras by Messrs. G. A. Natesan & Co., and edited by Mr. G. A. Natesan. The title-page states that it is "devoted to the discussion of all topics of interest," and certainly a glance at the table of contents shows that a wide range of subjects is dealt with. A copy promiscuously taken from the shelves includes articles and notes on "Colour Prejudice in the Colonies," "The Problems of Indian Currency," "The Economic Mineralogy of Ancient India," "Maurice Maeterlinck," "Indian Banking Enterprise," and "Industrialism and its *Ana*," together with literary reviews, agricultural and commercial section, illustrations and portraits, current events, and other questions of importance having relation to the interests of India.

THE FOREIGN AND COLONIAL COMPILING AND PUBLISHING COMPANY

THE main purpose of these volumes is to arouse in the English-speaking peoples an intelligent and enduring interest in the King's Dominions and Colonies beyond the seas, and at the same time to give such an accurate picture of each section of the Empire as shall make them standard works of reference for all who desire a fuller knowledge of the enormous resources and commercial possibilities of each Colony. To this end the compilers and editors have kept in view the Rt. Hon. Joseph Chamberlain's words, spoken when he held office as Secretary of State for the Colonies, and after he had returned from his colonial tour. "Books," said Mr. Chamberlain, "were required on the Colonies both for use within themselves and at home and abroad; books giving the history, commerce, industries, and resources of each country; to prove what industrial enterprise could attain under new and sometimes hard conditions."

Mr. Somerset Playne, F.R.G.S., founder of the Foreign and Colonial Compiling and Publishing Company, who is the compiler of these volumes, has now been associated with this class of publication for several years. The books themselves are compiled from information gathered by personal calls on farmers, merchants, and industrial concerns, the country journeys involving many thousands of miles of travel and the expenditure of a large amount of money, and the information thus gained together with any opinions expressed by the person interviewed, for the improvement of his district or town, or the industry generally in which he is engaged, is entered in the work under that person's name. It is confidently believed that the first-hand information thus carefully collected, and presented in sumptuous and attractive form, with all the aid that lavish and artistic photographic illustration can give, will not only place the country before the world in a clearer and more favourable light, and in truer perspective than ever before, by fully revealing the general grandeur of its scenery and the magnificence of its resources, but will *ipso facto* render most material aid in its social and industrial progress and development.

Volumes have been graciously accepted by His late Majesty King Edward VII, His Majesty King George V, and H.R.H. the Duke of Connaught; while the Colonial and Foreign Offices, as well as the Governments of the various Colonies and Possessions, have invariably taken a keen interest in these books, having assisted by granting free railway passes and by the purchase of numerous copies of the works for libraries and general distribution.

The Foreign and Colonial Compiling and Publishing Company was started by Mr. Playne in 1908 for the purpose of compiling a standard work of reference on British East Africa. This volume was practically "off his own bat," but with the very able assistance of Mr. F. Holderness Gale, who has collaborated as Editor since that date, and to whom credit is due for the historical records in each subsequent volume until his death in 1914, when the services of Mr. Arnold Wright, our present Editor and Historian, were obtained. "East Africa," which received the highest encomiums from the London and Colonial Press, was followed in 1910 by "Cape Colony," which is a volume of some 800 pages, illustrated with upwards of 2,000 photographs. At this period Mr. J. W. Bond joined the staff as a compiler, and Mr. R. Vincent Solomon was appointed to the post of chief clerk and secretary, while later the literary department was strengthened by the addition of Mr. J. W. Kiddall. The services of Capt. H. H. F. Stockley, F.R.G.S., were then secured as another compiler for the "Orange Free State" volume, and as soon as this was completed the whole staff sailed for New Zealand, via Australia.

A few words regarding the mode of travelling in the various countries which were visited may be of interest. As far as the volume on East Africa was concerned, the whole of the work of compilation was done by Mr. Playne, not in a luxurious saloon railway car, nor even a comfortable motor-car, but upon the back of a mediocre mule. The photographers, too, had to rely on this not too comfortable beast of burden, or, in the alternative, they had to make use of the ordinary "push-bike." Many adventures with lions and rhinos were recorded, and long journeys over native tracks through the bush frequently involved a night in the open without food, and also with grave doubts as to one's whereabouts.

Numerous hardships were experienced by the staff in Cape Colony and in the Orange Free State; nights had to be spent on the bleak hills, in unsavoury sheep sheds, or under the Cape cart (which, however, is the most satisfactory method of transit in those parts); and one photographer was snowed up for a week on the mountains above Cathcart, without any means of communication. Several narrow escapes from the treacherous *drifts* across rivers were met with, and on more than one occasion it was a case of stripping off one's clothing and of taking to the water in order to turn the frightened horses and bring the outfit safely to the opposite bank. Many breakdowns, and in fact complete wrecks occurred to the Cape carts and horses, owing mainly to the abominable state of the mountain roads; but when it is realized that members of the staff covered some 15,000 miles, it is singularly fortunate that mishaps were unattended by any serious results. Southern India was the next field of operations, and here a tour of over 7,000 miles was done in a motor-car by Mr. Somerset Playne throughout the Anamalais, Nilgiris, Wynaad, and the West Coast, Coorg, and Mysore; while Mr. J. W. Bond and other members of the staff motor-cycled throughout Cochin, Travancore, and most parts of the Madras Presidency.

SOMERSET PLAYNE, F.R.G.S.

COMPILER OF "EAST AFRICA," "CAPE COLONY," "NEW ZEALAND," "SOUTHERN INDIA," ETC.

The life of the compilers, and to a certain extent that of the photographers, is one of constant change and excitement. Many a bad spill, resulting in a long walk, has occurred; many a tyre has had to be repaired in pelting rain or in excessive heat; and it will be admitted that motoring on unknown, and frequently bad, roads at night when flocks of sheep or herds of cattle are lying about, must occasionally be attended by disaster. To suddenly round a corner and your head-lights to show a wild elephant evidently contemplating whether to take your car as a personal insult, or to retire into the jungle, is far from being a pleasant experience; and yet this happened on more than one occasion, but luckily the jungle was in each case favoured. But, after all, these misfortunes, though distressing at the time, are usually a source of amusement subsequently.

SOMERSET PLAYNE, F.R.G.S.

The compiler of works of the magnitude of "East Africa," "Cape Colony," "Orange Free State," "New Zealand," and "Southern India," their "People, Commerce, Industries, and Resources," must of necessity have had considerable experience of the world, and Mr. Somerset Playne has had a more varied career, and can boast of a wider acquaintance with the Britains beyond the Seas than most men. He was educated at Clifton College, and at St. Edward's School, Oxford. At the age of nineteen he paid his first visit to the United States, spending most of his time in the West, and indulging for some months in the joys of ranching and cow-boy life. He was called home to England, but the spirit of adventure quickly reasserted itself, and Mr. Playne sailed for South Africa, where he spent some time on Angora goat and ostrich farms. The Matabele Rebellion was then a very recent memory, and Francis Town was still the terminus of the railway, but Mr. Playne went up-country to the then new Rhodesia, and at Inyati took a hand in big-game shooting, store-keeping, and trading.

THE LITERATURE RELATING TO SOUTHERN INDIA

After having travelled in every part of Africa south of the Zambesi, Mr. Playne took part in 1899 in an expedition into German East Africa, and on his return from this trip he made the acquaintance for the first time of British East Africa, travelling over the Uganda Railway from Mombasa to Voi, which was then the terminus of the line.

Another visit to the Old Country followed, and then Mr. Playne tempted fortune for the second time in South Africa, meeting with experiences not infrequently the lot of those who venture in "new" countries. Later he joined a firm which was engaged on the compilation of an encyclopædic work on Natal, and on the completion of the task in that colony he returned to England to superintend the passing of the volume through the press.

For the same firm Mr. Playne later supervised the compilation of books on Ceylon, the Federated Malay States, Hong Kong and Shanghai, and visited Java, Labuan, Borneo, and Formosa. Then, having meanwhile severed his connection with the business which had carried him to the Far East, he travelled through India, and sailing from Bombay, arrived in British East Africa in November 1908, on which country he then compiled his now well-known standard work.

Another trip to Europe, via Cairo, followed; thence he sailed to Cape Colony, where he arrived in March 1910. Returning to England in 1911, the "Cape Colony" work was subsequently passed through the press. Having previously started on the "Orange Free State" volume, which had been carried on during his absence, another journey to South Africa was necessary, and after a stay of a few months he sailed, in 1912, for Australia, and later to New Zealand, from whence he proceeded in September 1913 to the scene of his recent labours in Southern India.

Mr. Somerset Playne is a Fellow of the Royal Geographical Society, a Freemason, and a member of the Royal Societies and Sports Clubs.

THE FORT, VELLORE.

Photo by Nicholas & Co.

CUDDAPAH, BELLARY, AND VELLORE

THE northern districts of the central portion of the Presidency are liberally provided with railway and road facilities, and a journey from Madras across the country which lies between the Bombay Presidency on the north and the State of Mysore on the south is full of interest, owing chiefly to the variety and splendour of the scenery. Forty-three miles distant from Madras is the important junction of Arkonam, which may conveniently be made the starting-point for the proposed trip. From this station there are in reality three different sections of the Madras and Southern Mahratta Railway, all of which converge at Guntakal, in the district of Anantapur. The northernmost of these three sections may be taken into consideration first of all. Eight miles distant from Arkonam and about 51 miles from Madras is Tiruttani, which should be visited on account of the very sacred temple of Coomaraswamy which is situated on a hill not more than a mile from the railway station. Hindus congregate in large numbers at the monthly feasts which are held, and an immense concourse of pilgrims attends two grand annual festivals called Audi Kirthicai and Tai Kirthicai. Not far from here is a very high rocky peak named Narayanavanam, upon which lights were formerly burned in order to guide ships into Madras Harbour. The distance between here and the coast is about 64 miles. Renigunta is 41 miles due north of Arkonam, and it is a junction for three branch lines; one proceeds in a north-easterly direction to Gudur, a large rice-producing centre near to the east coast; another branch extends to the north-west to Cuddapah, Gooty, and Guntakal, thence to Raichur, Hotgi, Poona, and Bombay; while the third commences in a westerly direction as far as Pakala, where there is a deviation to the north towards Dharmavaram and on to Guntakal. Within about 14 miles distance of Renigunta is the Rajah Mahal, which was built by the Telugu kings of Chandragiri several centuries ago. The peculiarity of the structure is that no wood has been employed in the building; it is all granite, and the style of architecture is unique. There is, too, an ancient temple, dedicated to Sri Vencatasa Perumal, on Tirupati Hill, 7 miles from the station.

Taking train from Renigunta on that section which leads to Bombay, one passes through an undulating area of rich quality, while on either hand the charm of the picturesque and ever-varying scenery is not soon forgotten. After crossing the fine River Penner the train enters the district of Cuddapah, and attention is then directed to a small place called Vontimitta, where there is a large and beautiful temple dedicated to Vishnu, and built by Vontadoo and Mittadoo. It has been erected on the *bund* of a tank, and it is noted for the excellent sculptural work with which it has been enriched. Cuddapah, the headquarters of the district of the same name, is reached at the hundred and sixty-second milestone from Madras. With the exception of certain Government officials there are not many European residents, although the Hindu community is remarkably strong in numbers. The Government offices were formerly occupied by the Nawab of Cuddapah, and lovers of a beautiful style of Indian architecture will revel in the opportunities afforded them by numerous buildings in the district surrounding the town. The River Penner and the railway line have for several miles been running parallel with each other, and near to the station at Kondapuram the train crosses the Chitravati River a few miles above its junction with the Penner. The two rivers, in their united force, rush through the narrow Gundikotta gorge, upon whose cliffs are exceedingly fine ruins of an old fortress, which was regarded as being almost impregnable. The next place where a halt should be called is Tadpatri, in the district of Anantapur, which is situated on the banks of the River Penner, about 2½ miles distant from its railway station, and 228 miles from Madras. Tradition says that the town was founded about four hundred years ago by a descendant of one of the Vizayanagar kings, who is further believed to have been the instigator of the building of the temples of Rama, Iswara, and Chintaraya. The sculpturing—which is splendidly executed—represents the adventures of Rama, Krishna, and other mythological persons. A large trade is carried on in cotton goods and cloth, and there are two cotton-presses and a large distillery. The inhabitants are about 9,000 in number. Thirty miles from Tadpatri is Gooty, which possesses a fortress of immense strength, which was once a Mahratta stronghold. It has been constructed on the Gooty Rock, which overshadows the town, and a description of it given by Colonel Wilks, a well-known writer of Indian history, may be given here. He says: "The fort is composed of a number of strong works, occupying the summits of a circular cluster of rocky hills connected with each other, and enclosing a level space which forms the site of the town. An immense smooth rock, rising from the northern limit of the circle, and fortified by gradations surmounted by fourteen gateways, overlooks and commands the whole of the outer work and forms a citadel which famine or treachery alone can reduce." The rock is about 2,170 ft. above the level of the sea, and upon its summit are a number of buildings in which State prisoners were formerly confined. Guntakal is a junction station between broad and metre gauges of the Madras and Southern Mahratta Railway, and we may notice a few places which lie somewhat to the north of the main line.

Shortly after leaving Guntakal the district of Bellary is entered, and the principal town of this northerly route (which leads to Raichur, Poona, and Bombay), is Adoni, the headquarters of the *taluq* of Adoni, and a commercial centre of considerable importance. It is situated at the foot of a cluster of steep and rugged hills about 2,000 ft. in height—upon which are the ruins of an ancient fortress, in addition to several houses, temples, and mosques. The district of Bellary—and

ONE OF THE TOMBS OF TIPPU SULTAN'S FAMILY, VELLORE.

Photo by Nicholas & Co.

1. RAMA TEMPLE, TADPATRI, ANANTAPUR. 2. JAIN TEMPLE, RATNAGIRI, ANANTAPUR.
3. PILLAR OF LAKSHMI SHRINE, TADPATRI, ANANTAPUR.

Adoni in particular—is no exception to the prevailing custom in the Presidency, that about three-fourths of the inhabitants obtain their livelihood by agricultural pursuits. The chief industry is the weaving of coarse white cloths for men, of carpets, and of coloured silks for women. The Adoni rugs or carpets are manufactured principally by Mahommedans, and their fame has reached most of the important towns of the Presidency, in addition to Bombay, Calcutta, and London, to which places they are exported in considerable numbers. Cloths are occasionally woven with narrow silk borders, or by having the warp or woof made of silk, but fault has been found as to their durability. A number of Madras merchants have established agencies at Adoni, and they have found employment for a large number of the inhabitants by the opening of several cotton-presses, which are worked by steam. The inhabitants of Adoni voluntarily applied that municipal self-government should be granted to them, and the Act conferring the necessary powers was introduced in May 1865. The principal undertakings promoted by the Council have been the construction of excellent offices for themselves, and of a Jubilee Market for the town, which was erected at a cost of Rs. 10,000. The census of 1911 showed that the population consisted of nearly 32,000 persons. Still travelling in a northerly direction, the train passes through Kupgal, a small town of no particular importance, and it subsequently reaches the Tungabhadra River station, which is the last stopping place of the Madras and Southern Mahratta Railway upon this section within the borders of the Presidency. The village is a small one, but it is filled to overflowing at certain periods of the year, when pilgrims arrive to bathe in the waters of the river, which is held to be sacred. The river is an important one, as it practically forms the boundary of the district of Bellary on its northern and western borders, and it eventually discharges its waters into the Kistna, in the district of Kurnool. The girder bridge, which is on the frontier of the Bombay Presidency, consists of fifty-eight spans, each of which is 64 ft. in length.

Some 43 miles in an easterly direction from Guntakal is Dronachellum Junction, from which there is a branch line, 32 miles in length, to Kurnool, the chief town of the district of the same name. The principal Government officials are here, including the Collector, the District Judge, and the Executive Engineer, and it has a population of about 26,000 inhabitants. A fine fort was formerly in existence, but it appears to have been dismantled about the year 1865, although some of the members of the family of a former Nawab resided in the palace—within the enclosure of the fort—for some years later. The chief buildings consist of Municipal Offices, a hospital, and court-houses, while there are fine open spaces for the benefit of the people at Queen's Park, the Maidan, and the Esplanade. Nandyal, the only other municipal town in the district of Kurnool, is 38 miles distant by rail in an easterly direction from Dronachellum. A considerable amount of wheat is grown in the neighbourhood, and a busy trade is carried on in cotton, indigo, and jaggery. It contains Local Fund, Elementary, and

1. SCULPTURE SHOWING SIVA, WITH FOUR HANDS, DANCING, PUSHPAGIRI, CUDDAPAH.
2. SCULPTURE OF ARJUNA, PUSHPAGIRI, CUDDAPAH. 3. RANGANATHA TEMPLE, GANDIKOTA, CUDDAPAH.
4. MAIN "GOPURAM," KOTHANDARAMA TEMPLE, VONTIMITTA, CUDDAPAH.

Normal Schools, and a special feature is the existence of nine Sivaite pagodas. The inhabitants are about 16,000 in number.

Returning to the junction at Guntakal the journey towards the west coast may be undertaken. The early stages of the route are not marked by any noticeable features of mountain range or wooded scenery, but interest is aroused when the train arrives at Hagari, where the large river of the same name is crossed by a bridge of thirty-four spans, 64 ft. in length. Nine miles to the west of the bridge is Bellary, the capital of the district and the headquarters of the Collector, Judge, and other prominent officials. The district has the appearance of an extensive plateau supported, as it were, by the Eastern and Western Ghauts, but showing a considerable difference in the altitude of various portions. The bed of the Tungabhadra River in the north is about 1,000 ft. above the level of the sea; in the centre of the district the elevation is about 1,500 ft.; and on the Mysore frontier in the south the tableland is fully 2,200 ft. in height. Afforestation has been carried on with vigour during recent years, and a well-wooded area is now superseding what could only formerly be described as a treeless plain. The town of Bellary has avenues of trees in its streets, and this is calculated to temper the oppressive heat which is experienced from February to the end of May. Bellary is divided into two parts, namely, the city proper and the cantonment, in each of which there is a railway station. Places of business, public buildings, and private residences are constructed on the plateau round two rocky hills, one known as Fort Hill, and the other as Face Hill, or Face Rock. The sides of these hills are covered with huge boulders, which have, through the action of the weather, become detached, and this has caused the place to be graphically described by Tommy Atkins, in his vernacular, as "two bloomin' heaps of road metal." There are upper and lower forts; the former is on the summit of Fort Hill, which is 1,976 ft. above the level of the sea, and about 480 ft. above the town; while the lower one, near to the cantonment railway station, is protected by a solid wall and ditch. There are a number of public buildings within the latter fort, and they include magazines, supply and transport stores, an arsenal, headquarters of engineers and other officials, the main guard, school, and churches. Among the industries (excluding agriculture, which takes first place), are the weaving of cotton cloths, cotton ginning and spinning mills, woodcarving, and the making of mats and tatties. The trade of Bellary is very extensive with the surrounding villages, but it is noted in statistics that even a greater amount of commercial enterprises is conducted with important towns in the Bombay Presidency. The town is tolerably well supplied with educational establishments, which include the Wardlaw College, founded in 1846 by the Rev J. S. Wardlaw, D.D., of the London Missionary Society, Government Training Schools, St. Joseph's European School, St. John's Secondary School, St. Philomena's High School for European girls, and other primary and secondary institutions. The inhabitants were about 35,000 in number according to the latest census returns.

QUEEN'S PALACE, CHANDRAGIRI.

The last station on this section of the Madras and Southern Mahratta Railway before entering the Nizam's territory is Hospet, with a population of nearly 20,000 inhabitants. For several miles before arriving here the traveller will have noticed that the train was proceeding along a valley between the extensive and picturesque range of the Sandur and Daroji Hills, and the colours of the trees varying between dark purples and browns formed a fine contrast to the lighter shades of the vegetation on the lower lands. Records show that the town was built in or about the year 1515, and that it was at one time "a strong city fortified with walls and towers," but very little of its pristine glory remains at the present day. Industries and arts, however, still find employment for a considerable portion of the residents, and the principal of these are the weaving of cotton cloths for women, the making of jaggery, tanning of skins and hides, and the manufacture by Jains of brasswork cattle bells, rings, and horns. Hospet is now visited principally on account of its proximity (7 miles distant) to the ruins of the old city of Vizayanagar, but now called Hampi. The early part of the fourteenth century marked the advance of the Mahommedans from the north, who overran the whole of the Deccan with an immense force, and anarchy and strife reigned supreme until the famous Hindu empire of Vizayanagar was formed at Hampi, when the tide of the invasion from the north was effectively checked for a period of rather more than two hundred years, when Vizayanagar, as a city, was practically obliterated. The city was about 10 square miles in extent, and the ruins speak volumes for the magnificence and wealth of temples, palaces, and other buildings. Visitors should not fail to see the Ramachandraswami temple, built for the private worship of the king, Krishna Deva, of the remains of his royal palace, the throne-room, pavilion, the elephant stables, and the queen's bath, in which the reservoir still remains. Day after day could be spent with the greatest delight among the ruins, and visitors might picture for themselves the departed glories of a magnificent city.

Returning to the junction at Guntakal reference may be made to a section of railway which serves several important towns in south and south-easterly directions to Dharmavaram, through Pakala, and thence to Arkonam, our original starting-point. The distance from Guntakal to Anantapur is about 43 miles. The latter town was originally known by the name of Anantasagaram, and local history gives colour to the tradition that it was built in the year 1364 by Chikkappa Wadiyar, Dewan to the Rajah of Vijayanagar, and that it was seized by Hyder Ali in 1775. It subsequently became the residence of Sir Thomas Munro, Bart., a former Governor of Fort St. George, and it is now the capital and the only municipal town in the district of Anantapur. The number of its inhabitants has increased at a fairly rapid rate, and the population at the census of 1911 was given as 8,457 persons. Among the principal buildings are the magisterial and police offices, court-house, a dispensary, and post and telegraph offices. Industries are of a minor character, and such as are commonly engaged in by village communities, but a considerable local trade is carried on in rice, cotton, gram, and other cereal and vegetable produce. Educational facilities are provided by the Municipal High School and the Government Training and Girls' Schools. Twenty miles farther to the south is Dharmavaram, which is a small township of some 6,000 inhabitants, chiefly Hindus, the majority of whom are employed in manufacturing silk and cotton cloths and rough blankets. From this point the line diverges in two directions, namely, to the south-east to Katpadi and to the south to Hindupur and Bangalore, and thence to the east to Katpadi. Taking the southern route under notice first, the traveller should endeavour to make a short stay at Penukonda, which was the place of residence of some of the Vizayanagar kings, but which is exceedingly full of interest in these times by reason of the large number of ancient ruins of structures which exhibit absolute contrasts in style of architecture, owing to the town having been occupied successively by Mahommedans and Hindus. Archæologists, however, will not quarrel with other visitors, who will find great enjoyment in viewing Penukonda's well-cultivated vineyards and its gardens, in which pomegranates and guavas have been grown with considerable profit. After passing the small town of Hindupur, the railway enters the Kolar district at Goribidnur, and passes into the State of Mysore, on its way to Bangalore, which is 219 miles distant from Madras. The Kolar district and gold-fields, and Bangalore, are referred to on another page in this volume. The route from Bangalore is in an easterly direction through a very picturesque country in which the peaks of the ghauts and the undulating valleys of the plateaus are the most prominent features, and in which the varying tints in dark greens and browns of the dense vegetation present such a wealth of beauty that one would fain linger for ever among this delightful scenery. Bowringpet, 43 miles distant from Bangalore, is the junction for the Kolar Gold-field Railway branch system, and it is one of those towns which have progressed rapidly from a comparatively unpretentious place to a populous and thriving commercial centre. It will be noticed that the train is ascending a steep gradient, and 15 miles farther, when crossing the ghaut at Mulanur station, the permanent way is laid at an altitude of 2,000 ft. above the level of the sea. The next station is Patchur, and immediately upon leaving this place the train ascends the Kuppam ghauts, with gradients of one in sixty-eight. The grandeur of the scenery is perfect, and one experiences increasing regret as the milestones are left behind. Jalarpet is the connecting junction with the South Indian railway, but it has no commercial industries. Ambur, 113 miles distant from Madras, is situated on the banks of the Palar River, and a very large trade is carried on in coconuts, betel, and oranges, while the tanning of leather is a thriving industry. There are two temples in the vicinity, dedicated respectively to Nageswara and Samudrammah, which attract thousands of pilgrims annually. The Palar River flows near to the railway line for a considerable distance from this point, and the next place of interest is Gudiyatham, in which the chief industry is weaving, while Lubbias, Vanias, and Canarese merchants carry on a brisk trade in jaggery, hides, tamarinds, tobacco, and ghee. The annual festival, known as Gangammal Jathrai, is attended by thousands of pilgrims, while a large temple at Palliconda—2 miles distant—should not be missed. The latest census returns showed the number of inhabitants to be more than 24,000. Katpadi, 81 miles distant from Madras, is another junction with the South Indian Railway, and 2 miles from the station the Palar River is crossed by a masonry bridge about half a mile in length. Four miles in a southwardly direction is Vellore the most important place in the district of North Arcot.

RAMZAN MASJID, ADONI BELLARY.

Vellore is situated on the banks of the Palar River, and is a thriving centre of an enormous trade in grain. The town is a municipality of about 50,000 inhabitants, and is the headquarters of the sub-Collector and the Medical Officer of the district, Forest Officer, Engineer, and sub-Magistrate. It was formerly a stronghold of the Vizaynagar kingdom, but it was subsequently captured by the Mohammedans, and in the eighteenth century it was closely identified with the struggles for supremacy of several nations of South India. The chief object of interest is the old fort, within whose walls is a temple containing excellent specimens of stone carving in the Dravidian style. A most interesting description of the fort

TOMB OF ABDUL WAHAB KHAN, KURNOOL.

is given by Mr. A. F. Cox, M.C.S., in the North Arcot volume of the Madras District Annuals, and he says: "It is one of the most perfect specimens of military architecture to be found in South India. It is traced on an irregular four-sided figure. The fortifications consist of a main rampart, broken at intervals by round towers and rectangular projections. There is a solid masonry counterscarp and a covered way round three sides. The main walls are built of massive granite, admirably cut to point and fitted together without mortar, while the upper parapets are built of, or lined with, brick-work, in which the embrasures are cut. On the south face there is a raised bastion on which the flagstaff stands, and there are two small round towers, raised above the main works, at the south-east and north-east angles. The old entrance was by a winding roadway with massive gates protected by a drawbridge; but during recent years a straight road has been cut through the rampart. On the south side there is also a footway which crosses a ditch on a stone causeway, and there is no other means of admission." At the entrance to the temple is a very fine *gopuram*, with massive gates and fine carvings. The finest sculpture in the temple is to be found in the *kallianamantapam*, or hall, in which the idol was placed when his marriage was celebrated annually. Monolithic sculptures and pillars representing mounted figures are among the most beautiful of the many chaste decorations, and special notice should be taken of the fact that each pillar is carved out of a single stone.

The next station to Katpadi is Tiruvalam, where there is an ancient and very sacred Hindu temple, which should be visited if possible, and about 2 miles farther to the east the train crosses the Ponne River by a very substantial masonry bridge. Walajah Road, 65 miles distant from Madras, is a municipality, and the headquarters of the Tahsildar, the sub-Magistrate, and other officials, and it has about 10,000 inhabitants. The town presents a neat and clean appearance; its streets are broad and well drained, and its buildings are characterized by a uniformity of construction which is not inconsistent with an objectional similarity. A hundred years or more ago the town was one of the busiest commercial centres in Southern India, but although it has declined in popularity a fair amount of trade is carried on in the weaving of silk and cotton, dyeing, the making of carpets, and the manufacture of oils. There is no other place of any particular interest until the train reaches Arkonam, our starting-point; but there is a section of about 142 miles between Dharmavaram and Pakala, lying between the routes taken on our forward and return journeys, which must be referred to, although there are very few places at which the trip need be delayed.

About 42 miles distant from Dharmavaram is Kadiri, where a brief stoppage should be made in order that a visit may be paid to the Vishnu temple of Narasimmahswami, which is the centre of attraction for thousands of pilgrims at the annual festival held in the month of February. The chief products of the neighbourhood are wheat, gram, cholam, cumbu, castor seeds, tamarinds, and tanning bark. The last two stations before reaching the junction at Renigunta are Tirupati West and Tirupati East, but they represent the town at the foot of the famous hill, known as Lower Tirupati, and the temple on the hill, known as Upper Tirupati. The chief occupations of the inhabitants are carving in redwood and sandal-wood, and the making of images and ornaments of brass and other metals. The temple is exceedingly rich, and the chief deity is Sri Vencataswara Perumal. About a mile from the town is the "Kapila Tirtam," in which all pilgrims bathe before ascending the sacred hill.

The last halt may be made at Mulacalacheruvu, where there is an ancient temple named Chenragavari Thevallam, situated near to the railway station, and another one called Konsi Kondarayadoo Thevalam, which is frequented by large numbers of Hindus.

The junction of Arkonam is soon reached after passing Renigunta, and tourists may begin to "pack up their traps" ere they again enter the Central Station at Madras.

1. DETAILS OF PARAPET WALL, HAMPI, BELLARY. 2. KING'S BALANCE, NEAR VITTALARAYA TEMPLE, HAMPI.
3. DETAILS OF THE AMMAN SHRINE, HAZARI RAMA TEMPLE, HAMPI.
4. JAIN TEMPLE AT HEMAKUTAM, HAMPI, BELLARY. 5. GROUP OF JAIN TEMPLES, HAMPI.

THE NATIVE STATE OF SANDUR

THE Native State of Sandur is situated almost in the centre of the district of Bellary, and it is bounded on the north, east, and west sides by the Hospet *taluq*, and on the south by the Kudligi *taluq*, with the exception of a strip of about 4 miles, which abuts upon the State of Mysore. It is only 24 miles in length, and its greatest width is not more than 12 or 13 miles, while its inhabitants are about 13,517 in number. The history of Sandur really commences at the time of the overthrow of the empire of Vizayanagar by the Mahommedan kings in 1565, when a number of semi-independent chiefs set themselves up as rulers of various portions of the dismembered empire. One of these, the poligar of Jaramali, eventually constituted himself master of Sandur, but he was deposed by a Maratha named Siddoji Rao, of the Ghorpade race, who was the ancestor of the present Rajah. One member after another of this family held peaceful sway over the territory for a number of years, but between the years 1775 and 1776 Hyder Ali, in the course of his raids, took possession of the State after he had acquired Bellary, Gooty, and other places. Peace was made with Tipu Sultan—Hyder's son—in 1792, and the Ghorpades were permitted to retain Sandur as their inheritance, but it is recorded that none of them ventured to reside there until after Tipu's death.. In or about the year 1800 some friction occurred in the family, chiefly on the question of succession, and Siva Rao, who was the nominal head of the State, expressed himself as being willing to exchange his territory for a *jaghir* of the value of Rs. 8,000 in the estates belonging to the East India Company. Sandur therefore came under British rule, but owing to further troubles Sir Thomas Munro, then Governor of Madras, recommended that Siva Rao should be reinstated. This proposal was sanctioned by the Governor in the year 1818. Mr. J. G. Firth, a retired tahsildar of the district of Bellary, became agent to the Rajah, and he was the first to receive the title of Dewan. The present head of the State, Rajah Venkata Rao Rao Sahib Hindu Rao Ghorpade Senapati Mamalikat Madar, was born in July 1892, and was recognized as ruler in 1893. Mr. W. Francis, I.C.S., says: "The administration is now in the hands of the Dewan subject to the general authority of the Collector of Bellary, who is, ex officio, political Agent for the State. No legislation is undertaken in Sandur, but such of the Acts of the Legislative Councils of the Governments of India and Madras as appear to be suitable are brought into force by publicly notifying their adoption.

Physically, the State is a long, narrow valley enclosed by two parallel walls of hills whose peaks vary in height from 3,000 to nearly 4,000 ft. above the level of the sea. These ranges are rich in minerals, as they present excellent specimens of hematites, manganese ore, and jasper rocks. Entrance to the valley is practically limited to two beautiful gorges which pierce the hills from the east and west, and this naturally-formed protection of the State has been of invaluable service to the inhabitants. The principal crops are cholam, korra, sajja, pulses, betel, and tobacco, while the industries are confined to the weaving of cloth.

Sandur, the chief town, is situated on the road which connects the two gorges, and it is separated from Chikka, or "little Sandur," by the River Narihalla. The Rajah's palace is in the centre of the town, and the Dewan's quarters immediately adjoin it. The shrine in the Vithova temple contains a number of finely carved stone pillars, but an exquisite ceiling is the architectural attraction.

Ramandrug is a sanatorium on a plateau of about a mile in length, and its buildings include barracks, a hospital, and a number of private bungalows. The Trigonometrical station is about 3,256 ft. above the level of the sea, that is, some 1,400 feet higher than the one at Sandur, which is constructed in the valley.

THE NATIVE STATE OF BANGANAPOLLE

THIS is a small State in the district of Kurnool, having an area of only about 255 square miles, and possessing a population of less than 40,000 inhabitants. The principal town, Banganapolle, has had a considerable amount of money expended upon it in the construction of improved buildings and in the opening up of wide and pleasant thoroughfares, and a large amount of trade is carried on in general merchandise, although the principal transactions are connected with wheat, rice, and cholam, which are the chief crops of the surrounding country.

During the eighteenth century the State was transferred by the Nizam of Hyderabad to the Sultan of Mysore, but it was subsequently restored to the Nizam, who in the year 1800 handed over full control to the Government of Madras. Maladministration tended to check all attempts at progress, and matters went from bad to worse until it became necessary to remove the Nawab Fateh Ali Khan in 1905. The present ruler is Nawab Sayid Gulam Ali Khan, who was formally installed by His Excellency Sir Arthur Lawley, G.C.I.E., K.C.M.G., on December 19, 1908, and he is assisted by the Dewan, Khaja Akbar Hussain. Since that time many improvements have been effected, and Banganapolle can now offer inducements, not only to visitors but to permanent residents.

1. NELLORE BULLOCK. 2. "LOADED UP." 3. NATIVE BULLOCK TRANSIT.

AGRICULTURAL PROGRESS

BY D. T. CHADWICK, M.A., I.C.S., DIRECTOR OF AGRICULTURE, MADRAS

THE southern section of India, which comprises the Madras Presidency and the Native States of Mysore, Travancore, and Cochin, is situated entirely in the tropics, but owing to physical configuration of the land, the diversities of soil and the climatic differences therein, the methods of agriculture followed are very varied. This region includes the luxuriant vegetation of the western littoral as well as dry, arid plains, where famine is always a possibility, in the portion adjoining Hyderabad and Bombay. Near the east coast stretches of indifferent soil with uncertain rainfall are interspersed with rich tracts thoroughly protected by large irrigation works and free from all danger of drought.

ECONOMIC CONDITIONS

The land is, generally speaking, divided among a very large number of small cultivators, the vast majority of whom, whether they be actual owners or only tenants, possess occupancy right in the soil, and consequently cannot be disturbed in possession so long as they pay the Government revenue or certain rent, each of which can only be revised at long periods and within certain limits in accordance with variations in the price of produce. A certain number of those who possess many lands lease them to tenants, who frequently hold only an annual—or short term—lease. This system especially prevails in the rich rice deltas of Tanjore, Kistna, and Godaveri, and wherever there are sure and constant facilities for irrigation, and also on the west coast in Malabar. Rents for rice land most frequently take the form of a share of the produce, the landlord taking as his rent either half, one-third, or sometimes three-fourths of the gross grain yield, but the straw is left with the tenant. On lands depending for their water entirely on rain, rents much more frequently consist of money payments.

Under customary Hindu law male members of a family are entitled to a definite share of the family property, and as land is the chief and favourite form of investment, it very frequently happens that on a partition of the family property each member gets as his share fields which are scattered in different parts of the village, and occasionally it happens that very many of the fields are actually divided into the necessary number of subdivisions, of which each member takes one. The result is that it is very rare to find the whole of a man's holding in a compact block. His fields are situated in different parts of the village, and are of varying size. This has a very profound bearing upon the agricultural economy of Southern India, because it means that implements have frequently to be carried or moved to small and distant fields, and therefore it is essential that they should be light and portable. It renders supervision over hired labour more difficult, and it makes it almost impossible for a farmer to fence a considerable portion of his land for the pasturage and care of cattle. The country is thus practically in the condition which some two or three centuries ago in England was known as "open field," and there are very few fences, hedges, or ditches to prevent any one from going straight across country. The cattle of the village are usually grazed together on the stubbles or other waste land, which increases the difficulty of any farmer who attempts to take special care with his breeding stock, or who endeavours to cultivate a different system of crops from his neighbours.

IMPLEMENTS

Compared with the results of the application of machinery to agriculture in younger countries, South Indian implements at first sight appear to be very crude, very fragile, and very inefficient, but a close examination reveals in many cases a great ingenuity in making workable practical implements out of the simplest material.

The Plough

There are several kinds of indigenous ploughs of different weight but of one general pattern. They consist of a roughly shaped block of wood, shod with an iron point. They have only one handle, and scratch the surface soil rather than invert it. In fertile lands with the more profitable crops fields are ploughed both lengthwise and crosswise in order to get the whole of the soil moved. For such lands the demand for small cheap mould board ploughs is coming into existence, but for the reason already given, and because the local farmer has not yet become accustomed to pay much money for agricultural implements, these must not cost more than a pound each delivered in the village if any considerable sale for them is to be expected. Deeper ploughing is obtained by the use of a heavier block of wood in the main body of the plough, on which heavy stones are sometimes also heaped. In many parts of the country a very cheap and simple seed-drill is used, which practically consists of three, four, or five light ploughs, behind the point of each of which a small hole is bored ; pieces of bamboo or tin tubes connect these holes with a wooden cup near to the driving handle, and as the man drives the drill forward a woman or another man walks beside him, keeping the cup full of seed, which trickles down the tubes into the furrow left by the plough. The seed is then covered by driving over the ground a large, light instrument, of which the base is a band of iron. Where the seed-drill is used the farmer uses a harrow, consisting of a number of hoes with iron plates of a size to fit in between the rows of seed. These are used for inter-cultivating as the crop grows, and do their work very cheaply and efficiently. Where seed has been sown "broadcast," weeding, of course, has to be done by hand. Hitherto the supply of labour has been plentiful and cheap, but wages are rising, and there are indications of a more extended use of cheap labour-saving implements. Harvesting is done almost entirely by the sickle. With some crops merely the heads are removed, and the straw is taken from the field; but the rice crop is cut close to the ground by means of a sickle in the first instance. Owing to the lack of roads and scattered holdings crops are carried to the threshing-floor on coolies' heads. Almost the only implement used for threshing cereals is found in the Ceded Districts, where it is required for cholam or sorghum—one of the large millets. It consists of a heavy stone roller, which is dragged backwards and forwards over the heaped heads of grain.

GRAFTED MANGO PLANTS, THREE YEARS OLD.

Practically all winnowing is done by hand. Grain is taken up in small quantities on a tray made from palm leaves and gently shaken from a height of about 6 ft., so that the corn, chaff, and dust fall slowly to the ground. A day of steady, gentle breeze is chosen, so that as the heavier grain falls direct the chaff and dust will be blown to one side. In regard to the commercial crops, such as cotton, ground-nut, coconut, and oil-seeds, more machinery is required. They will be described under the heading of each crop.

CATTLE

All draught is supplied by bullocks, which are almost invariably driven in pairs. The bulk of the people of the country are vegetarians, and as the cow is a sacred animal to a vast majority of the people the flesh is very rarely eaten, the cattle being kept primarily for purposes of work. Buttermilk and ghee (clarified butter) enter very largely into the food of all classes, but more attention has in the past been paid to rearing strong and useful bullocks than to evolving heavy milking breeds. Much of the buttermilk and ghee is obtained from buffalo milk, which is exceedingly rich in butter fat. Many of the cows which are kept in the country are either maintained for the manure which they give or for the bullocks to which they may give birth, and in this last case the calves get practically all the milk. Even of those cows which are classed as milkers the annual yields of milk are probably only from 1,000 to 2,000 lb. in weight, though there are several which could be ranked higher. Thus the foundation for starting dairies such as are understood in the West hardly exists. Except in one or two special areas no care is taken to ensure cows being covered by selected bulls, and thus there is no pedigree stock in the country. All the village cattle herd together, they mate indiscriminately, and cows are not infrequently barren for one or two or more years. In spite of all these drawbacks, however, there are a few places in which very pure and well-bred animals are reared. Chief attention is paid to the young male stock, and bullocks which are obtained are excellently fitted for the work they have to do. The young stock is not castrated, but the testes are destroyed by mulling (squeezing between clamps) when the animals are about three years of age. This operation is not, however, always effectually performed, and this increases the difficulty of retaining a pure breed. Foot-and-mouth disease, rinderpest, black

1. WEEDING THE PADDY. 2. HARROWING. 3. A CONSIGNMENT OF FODDER.

Photos 1 and 2 by Nicholas & Co.

quarter, and other diseases occur generally, but Indian cattle possess great natural immunity from the first-named, and this greatly increases their value for export to other tropical countries.

There are three main breeds, two of which enjoy more than a local reputation. The first is the Nellore, or Ongole, which comes chiefly from the Guntur district, on the east coast. The bullocks are usually white, occasionally having some iron-grey marking; they are very powerful and strong in the bone, docile, and well suited for heavy draught work on roads or for heavy agricultural work on heavy soils. Great attention is given to rearing the calves, and large numbers have been bought at high prices for Java, Brazil, and the Philippines. Many of the cows are also very fair milkers. The next is the Kangayam breed, which is chiefly reared in a dry district to the east of Coimbatore. The bullocks are smaller than the Nellore ones, but are quicker, more handy, and possessed of harder feet. They are consequently well fitted for light draught work on the roads and on the lighter gravelly red soils which are found in the south of the Presidency. The other chief breed—the Alambadi—comes from near Mysore. It is as a rule intermediate in size between the last two, and although it does not last as long as either of the others it is in great favour for road work, especially in hilly districts. In the tract in which it is largely reared—South Mysore—and the adjoining portions of the Madras Presidency, it finds most of its grazing in the forests. When fodder is scarce the farmer gives most attention to the bullocks, which, whilst they are in work, usually get some concentrated food in the shape of corn seed. Bulky fodder consists of rice, and cholam or sorghum straw, and the working bullocks get the pick of these. The rest of the animals have to depend as a rule upon what little grazing they can find, though in the hot weather it is the custom in many places, as, for instance, in Kistna and Godaveri, to remove them to the forests. Much of the manure is patted out into thin cakes, dried, and used as fuel, and what is left over is usually thrown into a manure-pit, to be applied later to the more valuable fields. Practically no attempt is made to utilize the urine for manurial purposes.

OTHER LIVE STOCK

Tending and care of sheep is the occupation of one particular caste, which also deals in goats. There appear to be four varieties of sheep in Southern India, although most flocks are now more or less mixed. They range in colour from a dark red or black, on which hair is more prominent than wool, and from white with black marks to pure white. The wool is so short that it is rarely possible to remove the fleece as a whole, and the average annual clip is only about 1 lb. weight to a sheep. Flocks are usually let out for manuring the land, on which they are penned for one or more nights. Running with the sheep are frequently many goats, which the shepherds find to be profitable to keep because they are more prolific, and a very considerable trade is carried on in skins. Little or no trouble, however, is taken as to their breeding.

In the towns along the main roads many small ponies are in use, which possess extraordinary powers of endurance. They are bred locally, but the industry is not a large one, as they are practically never used for any agricultural purpose. Pigs are thoroughly unclean animals, and only the lowest classes have any interest whatever in them.

Considerable quantities of poultry are to be found in most parts of the country, and the Indian game bird is well known for its fighting propensities. The eggs as a rule are very small, and here, again, little or no attention is paid to breeding and rearing. In some villages more care is given to ducks, which are driven over the rice lands shortly after the crops are harvested. Excepting for the one or two breeds of bullocks which have been mentioned, and which are rightly and justly famous for their working capabilities, their general utility, and their hardness, the South Indian farmer is not, as a rule, a rearer of live stock. In arable farming, on the other hand, he is in many ways very skilled.

IRRIGATION

In this tropical country the scheme of crops which a farmer raises depends in the first place on what facilities he has for getting water. Most of the rivers have been dammed in several places in their courses, and from each of them channels have been dug for many miles, making it possible to irrigate, by direct flow, large tracts of country. In the Godaveri and Kistna deltas, for instance, there are between 1,500,000 and 2,000,000 acres watered in this manner. The extent of irrigation in the Cauvery channels in Trichinopoly and Tanjore are comparable with either of these; whilst water is diverted to land from smaller rivers and streams and from the very large number of tanks. A tank is a reservoir of water, which may cover only a small extent or extend to many square miles, but it is always formed by building a large *bund* across some valley or natural depression. In the Madras Presidency alone there are more than 11,333,000 acres irrigated every year from channels, tanks, or wells, of which about 10,000,000 acres are under the first two. There is another very important class of land which gains its value and distinction from the method by which water is applied to it, and that is the so-called garden land. This area is from 1,500,000 to 2,000,000 acres in extent, to all of which the water is raised from wells, which number over 600,000. They are to be found in all districts, but are especially common in the centre and the south of the Presidency, as, for instance, in the North and South Arcot, Salem, Coimbatore, Trichinopoly, Madura, and Tinnevelly districts. The presence of a well almost always connotes intensive cultivation. The water is usually lifted in very large iron or leather buckets by bullocks, which, as they walk down a ramp, drag up from the well the bucket full of water; they are then unyoked and walk again to the top of the ramp, or are backed up the ramp without unyoking as the bucket descends. Many of the larger wells in the south which possess a copious supply of water have recently been provided with oil-engines, and where the flow of water is sufficient the work is more economically and quickly done. There are more than four hundred of these engines now at work, but whether the water is raised by bullock power or by oil-engines the cost is very considerable, and the land under the well receives as a rule most careful attention. Two or three crops a year are grown, of which one at least is a very payable vegetable crop; or ragi; or perhaps a crop of considerable commercial value, such as Cambodia cotton, ground-nut, or sugar-cane. These lands are usually kept very clear of weeds, and receive most of the manure that the farmer can spare. For a few years previous to the outbreak of war the very high prices which were being obtained for most agricultural produce were reflected in the farming economy by a considerable increase in the number of wells. On the edge of the well a few fruit-trees, such as coconuts or other useful agricultural trees, are usually found, which yield profit to the owner and afford shade to the bullocks and their driver. In Coimbatore wells are exceptionally deep and large, and either bullocks or oil-engines are used. In other parts of the country where the water is nearer to the surface it is frequently raised by means of the *picotta*, which is essentially a simple lever. The bucket is attached at one end of this lever, and it is raised by two or three men walking along a crossbeam, which is fixed at such a distance above the ground as to bring the bucket easily to the surface as the beam dips under the weight of the men.

CROPS

More important crops will be described briefly in the order of cereals, pulses, commercial crops, and plantations.

CEREALS—*Rice*

This is the most important food crop in Southern India, and the area under rice in this Presidency is usually two and a half times larger than that under any other single crop. It is grown to a greater or less extent in all districts, and under very diverse conditions. Starting from the north the chief areas of the east coast are found in Ganjam, in the deltas of the Godaveri and Kistna, around the Penniar in Nellore, in Chingleput and South Arcot, throughout the lower Cauvery in Trichinopoly and Tanjore, around the Periyar in Madura, and on the sides of the Tampraparni in Tinnevelly. On the west coast also, in Malabar and South Canara, it is the prevailing crop. In the central districts of the Presidency wherever it has been possible to throw a dam across the river or to make a tank, rice is to be found. On the west coast, which receives an annual rainfall of more than 100 in. in the monsoon, rice is grown entirely by the rainwater, and practically without any artificial aids. In a part of Ganjam where the rainfall is about 55 in. a year a somewhat similar method is attempted, but with very varying success. Even so about 7,000,000 out of the 10,000,000 acres annually under rice are cultivated under irrigation works made by man. All the fields on which rice is grown under any system are carefully bunded and levelled so that water can be let in to a uniform depth and later drained gently away. The average size of a rice-field is only about one to two-thirds of an acre. With the advent of the first rains these, fields are carefully ploughed, and water is let in to thoroughly moisten the soil until, if transplantation is intended, it stands to a depth of 2 or 3 in. The land has been thoroughly baked in the hot, dry weather, and if the soil is at all a heavy one it will have cracked deeply. It thus requires a vast quantity of water to be reduced to a fine puddle. Ploughing, levelling, and natural manuring is continued until the whole becomes fine mud.

There are two distinct methods of sowing, depending chiefly upon the certainty of the supply of water throughout the whole of the growing season, and where this can be depended upon it is customary to transplant the rice seedling and not sow the fields broadcast. In this system a small area of seed bed, about one-seventh of the extent to be transplanted, is very carefully prepared as early as possible. Its soil is first reduced to a very fine tilth, and well manured with thoroughly rotted farmyard manure. The seedlings are transplanted when from 21 to 40 days old, according to the variety, and are often put in such thick bunches that more than 100 lb. of seed per acre is used, but if care be taken in transplantation equally good results can be obtained by using about 25 lb. of seed to the acre. In most places seedlings are pushed into the soil in bunches of 5, 10, 15, or even 20, a practice which results in great waste, as most of them fail to mature. If the seed has been sown in the seed-beds and strong seedlings are obtained, equal yields are got by transplanting singly. After transplantation the field is left for a day to allow the seedlings to become established, and then water is again let in. Nothing then remains to be done except to keep the field flooded, changing the water as convenient. About ten days before the crop is ripe for harvest all the water is drained off and the field allowed to dry, when the crop rapidly ripens. It is then cut by sickles and carried to the threshing-floor.

GRAFTED MANGO PLANTS, THREE YEARS OLD

This paddy, as the unhusked rice is named, can be easily kept without much loss for a year or more in large earthen jars, securely covered by baked mud. In the north of the Presidency another method is followed. Large hollow balls of dry straw are filled with grain and built into a stack, the whole being covered thickly with straw, and the stack is then placed on a platform raised some 3 or 4 ft. above the level of the ground. The crop is usually threshed directly after harvest, and in only a few places is it stacked.

Other Methods of Cultivation

In many parts the seed is sown directly in the field, and while the initial cost may be less, subsequent weeding charges are increased, and the yield is not so uniformly good as from transplanted paddy. The seed is either sown broadcast or in lines by means of the seed-drill. In Kurnool it is usual to drill the paddy direct into the field and not let any irrigational water upon it until the crop is about one-half to two-thirds grown. Elsewhere the field is kept moist, and when once the plants have established themselves it is irrigated very similarly to transplanted paddy.

Second Crop

Under most of the large irrigation works, such as those on the Godaveri, the Cauvery, the Tampraparni, and the Periar, as well as under tanks, two crops of rice are frequently taken off the same land in one year. The same practice obtains on the low-lying lands on the west coast. In a few places farmers will even get three crops a year. Where two are taken one is, as a rule, a long-period rice, requiring from five to six months to mature, whilst the other one requires only three months. In the south and on the west coast one crop follows the other immediately, and, in fact, the seedlings of the second crop are often ready for transplantation before the first crop has been harvested. In Godaveri, however, where the first crop is harvested at the end of November or December, it is not possible to introduce a second crop to grow immediately, as the nights at that time of the year are very cold. Thus, although there is a plentiful supply of water, the second-crop sowing is deferred until February.

Manures

As rice is grown under swamp conditions, and each man has a right to the drainage water from the fields of his neighbour, nitrates do not form a suitable and practicable form of manuring for rice land. The constant passage of water through the fields gradually alters the relative mechanical distribution of the soil particles, tending steadily to accumulation of the finer ones, and it is above all things essential to maintain the natural texture and drainage of the soil. For this purpose the addition of bulky organic manures, resulting from green crops grown on the land and ploughed in in the form of leaves and twigs, is the most desirable. A very heavy toll is levied on the natural vegetation of the forest and on wasted dry lands, but the practice of growing a leguminous crop during the off-season and then ploughing it into the soil is slowly and steadily gaining ground. Cattle manure is also used, and, in fact, most organic manures, such as fish or guanos, are suitable. Chiefly in South Arcot, but also in other districts, an application of oil-cakes, such as margosa, castor, pungam, and to a lesser degree ground-nut cake, as a top dressing during the growth of the crop is given, although in many parts it has been shown that a small addition of phosphates is preferable.

There is practically no rotation of crops on the rice-fields, and as there are lands which must have yielded two crops of rice only for at least one hundred years, it is very fortunate that no serious mycological disease has so far appeared. The crop, too, as a whole is surprisingly free from insect pests, but there is a small caterpillar which bores into the stem and pupates there, causing the paddy to turn white and die.

On the hill-slopes of the west coast, where the rainfall is plentiful, the jungle is often cut down, the land ploughed, and a crop of inferior paddy, known as "hill paddy," is frequently sown. No attempt is made either to manure the land or to *bund* it in order to regulate the application and drainage for water. The method of cultivation is wasteful, the quality of the rice obtained is poor, and the yield is comparatively small. Somewhat similar conditions prevail in the interior parts of Godaveri and the Circars, where rice is at times grown purely as a dry crop.

Yields

The average yield of rice per acre in the Presidency is from 1,700 to 2,000 lb. although on many of the better tracts yields of about 3,500 lb. are regularly obtained. As the water supply of the land is derived from irrigation works which have never failed, the certainty of the yield combined with the simple nature of the cultivation required make rice lands an attractive investment to the Indian who has saved money but is not a farmer by instinct, or who has not the time to spare for managing his lands. In parts of the Tampraparni Valley, in Tinnevelly, rice lands realize from £150 to £200 an acre, and rentals run up to £5, £6, or even £7 per acre, while the landlord provides no permanent building in the form of granaries or barns. These lands probably form some of the most highly-rented areas in the world for purely arable farming. The whole of the cultivation expenses are borne by the tenant, though occasionally, in order to ensure the maintenance or the fertility of the land, some more careful landowners will bear a portion of the cost of manuring.

Food Grains on Dry Lands

The area is slightly greater than that under rice: thus in the Madras Presidency about 11,500,000 to 12,000,000 acres are under cereals which are grown on dry land and do not require so much water for irrigation as rice. Ninety per cent. of this crop is under one or other of the following three crops: Cholam (sorghum), a large millet, spiked millet (*Pennisetum typhiodium*), and ragi (*Elusine coracana*), of which the first equals the other two together in importance. Several varieties of cholam are cultivated, and, with cotton, it forms part of the regular rotation on the black soil of the Ceded Districts, and of Guntur. In the south one kind is very frequently grown on red soils under irrigation from wells, and it gives very high yields of grain. Further, it is at times sown thickly so that the grain does not mature, and the crop is then cut entirely for fodder. Yields are very variable according to the season and locality, and may normally range from 300 lb. of grain to something over 1,000 lb. to the acre.

Spiked millet is chiefly found in the southern portions of the districts of Salem, Coimbatore, and Trichinopoly, and in the last-named division it takes the place of cholam in rotation in black soils with cotton, but in the other districts it is more generally found on the red soils watered by wells. It is shorter in the straw and generally inferior to cholam both for fodder and grain, although the yields are very similar in quantity.

The two above-mentioned crops are grown during the monsoon periods on ordinary dry land. The soil is ploughed after the early rains, and the seed is either broadcasted or sown by means of the drill. The use of the seed-drill for cumbu is extending steadily in the southern districts, whilst in the north of the Presidency its use is common for both cholam and cumbu. In both cases at harvest-time the heads only of crops are cut, and the bulk of the straw is removed from the land at a later date.

Ragi is the last standard cereal crop of Southern India. It is intermediate between cumbu and cholam on the one side and paddy or rice on the other. It is therefore sown on ordinary dry lands in hilly tracts, or at the foot of hills where rainfall is fairly plentiful, or in the drier districts on those wet lands which possess only a precarious supply of water, or on garden lands to which water has to be lifted from wells. There are several varieties of ragi, and little or no care is taken to keep them distinct. The land must be very well prepared, and the seedlings are frequently raised in seed-beds and subsequently transplanted. The yields of grain are proportionately heavy, as more than 2,000 to 3,000 lb. to the acre are obtained from garden lands, while about half this quantity is obtained from dry lands. The straw also may weigh up to 6,000 and 8,000 lb. With ragi and practically most other crops grown under garden conditions the custom is not to sow the seed on the ridges with intervening furrows, as would be done in the west, but to make small rectangular shallow beds in which seedlings are reared, and to which water can be diverted in turn.

The other important cereal crops consist chiefly of a variety of millets, especially Italian millet (*Setaria Italica*) and samai (*Panicum miliare*).

The pulse family is very well represented in Southern India, the chief of which are horse-gram (*Dolichos bificorus*) —more than 2,000,000 acres are sown annually in the Madras Presidency alone

—red gram (*Cajanus Indicus*), green and black gram (*Phaseolus Mungo*), field bean (*Dolichos lablab*), and Bengal gram (*Cicer arietinum*). One or other of these leguminous crops is usually found in the rotations practised upon dry lands. The majority of them are sown as mixtures with other crops, although on the poor and thinner soils horse-gram is very frequently sown by itself. The yields are exceedingly variable, but in the case of red gram considerably more than 1,000 lb. an acre are at times obtained. Market gardening as understood in Western countries is hardly practised at all, but most houses have a small plot of land where a large variety of vegetables is grown.

Commercial Crops

The commercial crops fall practically under two heads, fibres and oil seeds, both of about equal importance, and in the Madras Presidency alone, excluding the area under coconuts, there are some 3,000,000 acres every year under each of these. A long way behind these two in importance come sugar-cane and dyes.

Fibres

Far and away the most important fibre is cotton, with its 2,660,000 acres, and an annual output in the neigh-400 lb. each. There are four chief cotton tracts, the produce of each having a distinctive position in the world's market. The first of these is in the neighbourhood around Guntur, which produces Coconada cottons and short, white, harsh fibre. That from the Ceded Districts of Kurnool, Bellary, Cuddapah, and Anantapur is known as Northerns and Westerns, and is similar to that produced in the adjoining portions of Bombay and Hyderabad. It is also a short fibre, from $\frac{2}{3}$ to $\frac{3}{4}$ in. in length, very strong and variable in colour, although some varieties are exceedingly white. In the centre of the Presidency, around Salem, another short staple cotton is found, slightly longer than the Northerns and Westerns, but otherwise very similar to them. In the extreme south of Tinnevelly there may be seen one of the few indigenous Indian cottons, whose fibres are fine, slightly over 1 in. in length, and generally of a creamy appearance. All these kinds of cotton are associated with black soil areas, and are grown under rain without further irrigation. They are sown after the worst of the monsoon has passed, and they ripen as the hot weather begins to approach, excepting in the central districts and in parts of the extreme south. The seed is sown by means of the drill, and the crop is gathered by women, who are paid in kind. Until within the last ten years ginning was very largely done by small wooden machines worked in the houses by hand labour, but these have now been almost entirely replaced by power machinery. In the north of the Presidency a very large number of such small ginning factories have been established; whilst in the south a small number of large and thoroughly equipped factories serve the needs of the various districts.

GRAFTED MANGO PLANT, ONE YEAR OLD.

Considerable improvement in Tinnevellies and in the Northerns and Westerns have been achieved in recent years by a system of selection and distribution of pure seed of superior strains. Many trials have been made to introduce some of the upland varieties of American cotton, and also to grow Egyptian kinds under irrigation. For nearly a hundred years such efforts have been made, but as far as the American and Egyptian cottons are concerned all ended in failure. Within recent years, however, a variety suited for irrigation on garden lands has been successfully introduced. It is about $1\frac{1}{2}$ in. in length, of very good colour, and with fairly good ginning percentage, and, above all, it is a very heavy yielder. It was introduced through Pondicherry, and is known as Cambodia cotton, but much work has still to be done on this crop to obtain uniformity and evenness. The practice of watering the cotton preparatory to ginning hardly exists at all, but there is a considerable amount of intentional or unintentional mixing of varieties.

In the extreme north-east of the Presidency, around Vizagapatam, a fibre which is frequently called Bimlipatam jute is grown, and it is largely used for very coarse bags. It is a monsoon crop, giving heavy yields. All attempts to introduce Bengal jute have failed.

Oil Seeds

Originally the chief oil seeds cultivated in Southern India were gingelly and castor. Linseed is hardly found at all, but latterly pride of place has undoubtedly been taken by groundnut, the cultivation of which during the last six years has spread amazingly. In the Madras Presidency alone the extent under this one oil seed is annually about 1,500,000 acres, and it is challenging cotton as the most widely spread of the commercial crops of Southern India.

It was at first grown largely around South Arcot, but it is now spread throughout the whole of the centre and north-west of the Presidency. It does well on those light red soils which receive a fair rainfall or a little irrigation. The chief expense is in regard to the matter of harvesting, when all the field has to be dug over by hand, and in normal seasons yields range from $\frac{1}{2}$ to 1 ton per acre of nut. The produce is mostly exported to Marseilles, either shelled or unshelled, but chiefly as kernels. In order to remove the husk, which forms about 20 to 25 per cent. of the total weight, the nuts are beaten and shaken in machines driven by oil-engines, or they are placed in heaps, slightly moistened, and then threshed with sticks by coolies. In the former case some of the kernels become broken, but they are all dry. On the market they command a higher price than those prepared in the second manner, some of which are damp, and are thereby liable to ferment. In well cultivated nuts the oil content is about 40 per cent. of the kernel. On account of the high prices latterly obtainable many *ryots* have sown this crop repeatedly on the same land, leading necessarily to a slight deterioration both in weight of nut and oil. There are two seasons for this crop, one on the dry lands when such is sown in June and July, and the other on the garden lands, which are usually prepared in February and March. The nut is most widely cultivated, and is one of the Mozambique varieties.

Other important oil seeds are gingelly

and castor. The cultivation of gingelly is generally somewhat of a gamble. It may be found somewhere at any time of the year, and on favourable conditions the yields are very good, but frequently little or nothing is obtained. The oil is extracted locally in presses worked by bullock power, and it is largely used for domestic and household purposes.

Castor is chiefly found in Chittoor and North Arcot, in the Circars, and in the extreme south of Ramnad and North Tinnevelly. It is also grown widely in small scattered portions, either on garden or on good dry lands. The cake obtained after extraction of the oil is greatly valued for manurial purposes for sugar-cane and for rice.

Sugar-cane

The area under sugar-cane has fluctuated greatly in recent years, and is now in the Madras Presidency a little under 100,000 acres, yielding about 175,00 tons of unrefined sugar. In these tropical countries the cane stands on the ground for a whole year, most of which time it requires water to a greater or less extent. About a quarter of the total area is found in the Vizagapatam district, but other important centres are Bellary, South Arcot, Coimbatore, and Ganjam. It is generally cultivated on the low-lying rice lands, where, as a matter of fact, it is liable to suffer from an excess of water, but there is a growing tendency at present to plant it on rich garden lands to which water can be lifted. Of the local indigenous canes the white variety from Coimbatore is about the best. In many parts of the other districts the local canes have been entirely superseded by thick rich canes introduced from other tropical countries. Of these red Mauritius, on account of its general hardiness, is most in favour, but other importations have been made also from Java and Mauritius. In many places canes grow to very considerable heights, but the average weight per acre is not very great, being about 25 tons. Looked at purely from the point of view of cultivation the country is very well suited for a large extension of this crop, although other factors militate against it very strongly, the chief of which is the scattered nature of the holdings. As a crop it requires much labour, but it is exceedingly profitable. The chief local demand in India is for *gul*, or jaggery (unrefined sugar) and not for the white sugar familiar in other countries. The local practice is to crush the cane (immediately it is cut) in three-roller iron mills worked by bullock power, and the juice thus extracted is boiled in large open pans until it is of sufficient consistency to set in a solid mass on cooling. When this point is reached it is either made up into balls or run into moulds and allowed to set. According to the quantity of juice which has been strained, to the scum which forms during the boiling process, and to the amount of lime mixed with the juice during boiling, the colour of the jaggery varies from bright rich gold to dark, dull brown. By this system of manufacture the glucose is not separated from the sucrose, and thus a larger quantity of sweet matter is obtained from the juice than if refined sugar were made, but it does not keep so well. Each grower deals personally with the small quantity of canes which he has grown, though in a few cases there are professional boilers who tour the villages and convert the juice into jaggery. Unless sugar-cane is handled as soon as it is cut the juice rapidly deteriorates in value, and consequently if a central sugar factory equipped with modern machinery is to be run at a profit, the factory must be able to control the supplies of cane from its immediate neighbourhood. This accounts for the fact that in most other countries land fit for cane is either owned by, or is attached to, the factory. In Southern India, on the other hand, most of the land suitable for sugar-cane cultivation is already in private occupation and commands very high prices in the open market, and as these lands are divided into small portions among a very large number of owners it is practically impossible for a factory to acquire rights over a large and compact block. Cane is planted everywhere before the commencement of the hot weather, and it is harvested after the monsoon rains are over. In the south the setts are usually planted in rows, but in Godaveri they are frequently simply pressed into the moist ground. Later the soil is banked up, and manures—especially organic ones—are worked in, and water is let into the ditches between the ridges. Another sort of sugar almost as important as that of sugar-canes is obtained from the juice of the palmyra palm. This will be described in the section under plantations. In the last two years an agricultural station has been opened near Coimbatore at which canes are being raised from seedlings and carefully tested in the hope of finding some richer kinds to replace existing varieties.

Dyes

The chief cultivated dye in Southern India is undoubtedly indigo, but the acreage has steadily declined owing to the competition of synthetic products. The plant is grown either on light red soils in tracts which receive an ample rainfall or on somewhat richer soils which obtain water from wells. It is also found as a "catch" crop on rice lands after the rice harvest is over. When dye is extracted the plant is often cut twice—the first cutting being about 1½ ft. above ground—after which the crop sprouts again and is subsequently removed. The plant is taken the same day and tightly packed in a large cistern into which water is run, and boards are then placed over the top of the vat and are kept in position by heavy crossbeams. The plant is allowed to soak for ten or twelve hours, during which time a heavy fermentation takes place. The liquid is then drained off into another vat, after which coolies beat and stir the matter thoroughly with flails until the dye begins to emerge. The whole is then allowed to settle ; the clear natant liquid is drained off, and the residue is taken to copper vessels in which it is boiled. It is then pressed into hard cakes, which readily find a market after having been kept some time. The refuse of the stalks and leaves after fermentation forms an excellent manure. Indigo itself, if ploughed into the land in a green state, has beneficial effects on the following rice crop, and concurrently with the fall in price of the dye the practice of using indigo solely for manurial purposes has increased.

Tobacco

Tobacco is another very profitable crop, and it is now cultivated more widely than indigo. It is chiefly found in Guntur, Vizagapatam, Godaveri, Madura, and Kistna. In the south it appears it is a garden crop, irrigated from wells, on richly manured fields. The fertile alluvial islands in the Godaveri river are also well suited for tobacco, and the varieties grown are, as a rule, somewhat coarse in texture but of strong flavour. The ordinary methods of curing are very crude. The leaf, and even at times the whole plant, is cut and hung from coir ropes in open sheds to ferment. No attempt is made to control the moisture and temperature, with the consequence that uniformity of colour is rarely obtained. Most of it is used as "fillers" for cigars or for the small local cheroots, or the leaf is soaked wholesale in molasses, in which form it is used for chewing. It is generally taken as a sort of savoury after chewing areca nuts and betel leaves.

Another exceedingly profitable crop on the wet lands is the betel vine. It is trained upon trees of the Sesbania family. The crop stands on the land for a year or eighteen months, during the greater part of which time the larger leaves can be plucked. They are sent daily by express trains to all parts of India, and are eaten or chewed with areca nuts to make the famous *pansupari* of India.

Another crop grown under very similar conditions to betel leaves is plantains, the commonest and most general fruit of Southern India. There are very many varieties, ranging in sizes from 8 or 10 in. to 1½ to 2 in. The skin varies in thickness from the finest shred to a thickness of about a quarter of an inch, whilst in flavour the fruits vary from a decided mealiness to the soft, sweet, rich flavour more usually associated with ripe fruit. In colour they may be red, green, or any shade of yellow. They are formed in large bunches, which are usually cut before they are completely ripe and hung for a short time until they have matured. The crop stands on the ground for about two years, during which time it requires constant watering and careful tillage. Attempts have been made many times to utilize economically the fibre of the stalk, but they have not met with great success. The large, wide, clean green leaves form the usual plates for domestic use, and are thrown away after each meal. This crop ranks with sugar-cane and betel leaves for profit and cultivation.

Among the spices, turmeric is cultivated everywhere, whilst ginger is found in North and South Malabar.

Plantations.

Palm-trees of one variety or another form the most useful orchard trees of Southern India, but the coconut is the best known. The annual crop of nuts in the Madras Presidency is in the neighbourhood of a thousand millions. They are found in their greatest luxuriance on the Malabar coast and in the Amalpur *taluq* of the Godaveri district, while they form the only agricultural product of the Laccadives and Aminidivi Islands off the west coast.

The best gardens are found in the rich soils adjoining the backwaters stretching from Travancore to South Canara, and also along the sandy seacoast. But each year the cultivation of this palm is extending in the valleys and along the hill-slopes inland. Thus experience in Southern India shows that the old saying "a coconut should be within sight of sea" is entirely false. To obtain a full yield from a garden the trees require constant manuring, and the soil around them should be thoroughly cultivated. The appearance of the west coast is entirely different from that on the east. In the former there are comparatively few villages; and most of the houses away from the larger towns are found nestling in tidy coconut gardens, the country possessing the appearance of a continued series of neat and well-kept homesteads. The number of trees to an acre is usually taken to be from sixty to seventy, whilst the number of nuts from each tree varies very greatly, according to the attention which the garden has received. The seedlings are planted at the bottom of pits about 2½ ft. in depth, and the tree usually begins to bear fruit in about ten years' time and continues to bear for another sixty years or more. The Malabar copra, or, as it is better known commercially, Cochin copra, commands the highest price on the world's market on account of its good quality. It is all sun-dried; the husks are soaked in water, preferably in pits adjoining alluvial flats, until they rot, when the fibrous portion is easily removed by beating the husks with small wooden mallets. The value of this fibre depends very largely on its colour, that which is of a rich golden brown commanding the highest price, coir rope and mats being made from it. Much of the copra is exported, but a large quantity is crushed in the local presses for the extraction of the coconut oil, which is very largely used for domestic purposes throughout the Presidency. The leaves of the palm are used for thatching and *thatties*, and for making mats and trays, but the trunk is not of much value for timber. Gross returns from coconut are frequently very high, and the gardens are often let on leases of twelve years' duration.

The other great palm of the east coast is the palmyra, which is found at its best in South Tinnevelly and in the Kistna districts. One caste of Indians gain their livelihood by climbing this tree and extracting the juice, which, if it be allowed to ferment, becomes "toddy," the ordinary intoxicating drink of the country, or if the fermentation be checked by the addition of lime, the juice is boiled down, and jaggery or unrefined sugar is obtained. In Tinnevelly, the Palghat *taluq* of Malabar, around Erode in Coimbatore, and in the upland portions of Kistna, the quantity of sugar thus obtained is very considerable, and as another source of sugar the palmyra palm is probably equal in its total yield to the sugar-cane. As with the coconut, the leaves are put to a great variety of uses, and in the olden days, when they were dried, they formed a substitute for paper for documents. The timber of the tree when fully grown is exceedingly hard and impervious to white ants, and there is a Tamil proverb to the effect that the palmyra is useful for a hundred years whilst it is alive, and for another hundred years after death. It is found to perfection in dry, sandy tracts. The wild date is not economically of much importance, although in parts of the country it is tapped for its juice, but very little success has hitherto been obtained with fruit-forming trees. The last of the very valuable palms is the areca, which is found in its perfection in the southern portion of Malabar adjoining Cochin State. The areca garden should be planted exceedingly closely, and it will yield nuts for about forty years. It is chiefly found on the lower slopes leading down to the most fertile valleys, and it thrives in rich soil possessing plenty of organic matter. It requires watering throughout the year.

Fruit-trees.

Contrary to the widely received opinion, South India is not well furnished with fruit-trees. The most famous is the mango, of which there are a very large number of varieties, and grafted mangoes are rightly numbered among the best of fruits of the world, but the season for them is short, and the trees are very uncertain yielders. The best varieties are found in Salem and Chittoor districts. They come into fruit during hot weather.

Another fruit very largely eaten is the big, strong-smelling jack, which can either be eaten or cooked as a vegetable. It is chiefly found on the west coast.

Oranges are grown extensively on the hills, although some varieties with very thick skins are found in the plains. They are to be obtained on any day of the year in the towns, Bangalore being a great collecting centre for them. Lime-trees are also very widely distributed, and yield freely. In North Malabar and South Canara cashew nuts are frequently found in many gardens and on waste lands. The nuts are very largely consumed locally, but a considerable quantity is exported to Europe. In the inland portions of North Malabar, pepper forms one of the chief crops. The vines, propagated from runners, are trained on quick, straight-growing trees, and they require an abundance of shade during the hot weather, the yield of a garden depending largely on the manner in which the shade is received. The flowers are formed after the outburst of the monsoon in July, and the berries are harvested about December or January. The most useful manure consists of leaf in some form or other. A pepper garden is always somewhat of a gamble, partly because the price is apt to fluctuate so largely, and also because the continuance of cloudy weather encourages the attacks of insects which may cause much loss. The actual trade is largely in the hands of Mahommedans, who have advanced money to the cultivators of the gardens.

Besides these crops there is a very large number of minor ones, which, owing to lack of space, cannot be specially referred to.

The area under all crops in the Madras Presidency alone is nearly 14,000,000 acres in extent; and the manures used are chiefly leaves cut from waste, or forests, or leguminous crops grown specially for such purpose and ploughed in; also cattle manure, sheep dung, and the poonacs made from the various oil seeds. In a year when a successful catch of sardines on the west coast has happened, fish manure is largely used and much prized, and there is an increased scope for its use and also for phosphates in some of their many forms. Unfortunately most of the bones collected in the country are now exported, as their value does not appear to be fully appreciated locally. When under crop large tracts of the country present a rich appearance, a visible testimony to the inherited agricultural skill of many generations of farmers. It is the sight of the communal and waste lands, and also of the ordinary village cattle, which mars the results of this ceaseless industry.

KARUNANANDAPURAM TANK.

CONCLUDING NOTE

BEFORE taking final leave of this volume, the compiler feels it to be his duty to make special acknowledgment of the services of those who contributed so markedly to the successful outcome of the enterprise. To some extent a stranger in a strange land, he had no claim, other than his record of work done in other spheres, to any special consideration when he commenced his labours. But nothing could have been happier than the conditions under which he actually prosecuted his enterprise in the Madras Presidency. A kindly disposition to lighten the work of himself and his representatives went hand in hand with the most charming hospitality and a *camaraderie* which never failed under the most exacting conditions. But bright as the compiler's memories are of his South Indian experiences, he would be conveying a wrong impression if he allowed it to be understood that the work was all plain sailing. In the midst of the work of compilation, news of the terrible European war was received, and all business seemed likely to be at a standstill: then came the reaction, and "Business as usual" was the order of the day. Still, serious delays were inevitable, and during the meanderings of the now famous *Emden* we were somewhat doubtful about dispatching our valuable letterpress and photographs to England. Later, thanks to the gallant British Navy, which still continues to rule the seas, every mail has since carried parts of our volume, up to the last chapter.

The general members of the staff actively engaged in Southern India rendered efficient and loyal service throughout the period in which the book was in process of production. Special thanks are due to Mr. J. W. Bond and Mr. H. H. F. Stockley, compilers. The latter was only with us during the opening stages of the work, and has since then, I regret to say, been severely wounded while upholding British traditions in the Dardanelles; to Mr. R. Vintcent Solomon, who superintended the Madras office, and through whose hands all letterpress and photographs passed; and to Mr. J. W. Kiddall, to whose pen is due the various descriptive articles of the towns and districts, together with the article on "Geology."

The compiler was especially fortunate in securing from expert authorities in the Presidency valuable monographs on the subjects with which they are acquainted. In this connection thanks are due and are tendered to His Excellency the Right Hon. Lord Pentland, P.C., G.C.I.E., Governor of Madras; the Hon. Sir Harold Stuart, K.C.V.O., K.C.S.I., I.C.S., the Hon. Mr. A. G. Cardew, C.S.I., I.C.S., the Hon. Mr. P. S. A. Sivaswami Ayyar, C.S.I., C.I.E., the Hon. Mr. Alan Butterworth, I.C.S., Chief Secretary to Government, and Mr. J. W. Bhore, I.C.S., Dewan of Cochin, for their advice and kindly co-operation; to Sir Francis J. E. Spring, K.C.I.E., Chairman of the Madras Port Trust, for his article on "The Financing of District Board Railways," and for other help. Grateful acknowledgments are also due to the following gentlemen for the articles against their names: To Mr. W. B. Hunter, of the Bank of Madras (Finance); Mr. J. Hornell, F.L.S., Superintendent of the Pearl and Chank Fisheries (Marine Fisheries and Fauna); Mr. Rudolph D. Anstead, M.A. (Planting); Mr. K. Tressler, Director of Industries (Industries); Mr. D. T. Chadwick, M.A., I.C.S., Director of Agriculture (Agriculture); Professor P. F. Fyson, B.A., F.L.S. (Flora); Mr. F. E. Morgan (Irrigation); Mr. W. S. Hadaway, Superintendent of the Government School of Arts (Arts and Crafts); Mr. H. Dodwell, of the Government Record Department (Education); Mr. C. Hayavadana Rao (Native Races); Mr. Evans Lewin, Librarian of the Royal Colonial Institute (Literature); Mr. S. Cox, Conservator of Forests (Forestry); Mr. A. H. Steel (Sport); Mr. P. B. Thomas (River Fishing); Mr. H. H. F. M. Tyler (Fauna); and Mr. T. E. Welby, of *The Madras Mail* (Commerce); and also to Messrs. C. H. Brock, C. R. T. Congreve, E. W. Wilkins, and the Superintendent of the Tata Silk Farm, Bangalore, for other contributions. Thanks, too, must be given to Dr. J. R. Henderson, Curator of the Madras Museum; Mr. A. B. Strange and Mr. W. W. Bissett, of the Madras and Southern Mahratta Railways; and to the Hon. A. Muirhead and Mr. T. le Mesurier, of the South Indian Railway system.

During a visit to England in March 1914 I was lucky to secure the valuable services, as Editor-in-Chief and Historian, of Mr. Arnold Wright, the well-known author.

Thanks are also due to Messrs. J. F. Peters, W. van der Lowen, and M. Wecksler, of the general staff, for photographic assistance; and to the following firms for permission to reproduce the various illustrative photographs: Messrs. Weile & Klein, Nicholas & Co., and Mr. Willie Burke, all of Madras; the Madras Archæological Department, for a number of exceedingly interesting photographs; Messrs. W. S. Hadaway and J. B. D'Cruz; also to the following amateur photographers: Mrs. A. Moore, and Messrs. H. H. F. M. Tyler, C. Lake, Professor P. F. Fyson, W. H. Reed, J. Hornell, J. S. Hawkins, and O. M. Rocky. My sincere thanks are also tendered to Messrs. Unwin Brothers, Ltd., Printers, of Pilgrim Street, London, E.C., for the care and attention devoted to the preparation of the work for publication.

The Foreign and Colonial Compiling and Publishing Company.

INDEX

The black figures indicate the principal notices in this work.

INDEX

C

INDEX

INDEX

F

G

INDEX

INDEX

INDEX

INDEX

INDEX

INDEX